Juvenile JUSTICE

DATE DUE

FEB 2 3 2010	
MAR 1 0 2010	
MAR 2 8 2010	
NOV 0 7 2011	
DEC 0 2 2012	
APR 0 1 2013	

*I dedicate this book to the late Richard Moreno, who introduced
me to the world of juvenile justice; to my friends and fellow POs who have committed
themselves to justice for juveniles; to my professors, who helped me link practice, theory,
and research; and to Dorothy, for her unconditional love and support.*

—Richard Lawrence

*I dedicate this book, all the books in this series, and everything of
value that I have ever done to my father, George Hemmens, who showed me the way;
James Marquart and Rolando del Carmen, who taught me how; and Mary and Emily,
for giving me something I love even more than my work.*

—Craig Hemmens

Juvenile JUSTICE

A Text/Reader

Richard Lawrence
St. Cloud State University

Craig Hemmens
Boise State University

Los Angeles • London • New Delhi • Singapore

For information:

SAGE Publications, Inc.
2455 Teller Road
Thousand Oaks, California 91320
E-mail: order@sagepub.com

SAGE Publications Ltd.
1 Oliver's Yard
55 City Road
London EC1Y 1SP
United Kingdom

SAGE Publications India Pvt. Ltd.
B 1/I 1 Mohan Cooperative Industrial Area
Mathura Road, New Delhi 110 044
India

SAGE Publications Asia-Pacific Pte. Ltd.
33 Pekin Street #02-01
Far East Square
Singapore 048763

Printed in the United States of America

Library of Congress Cataloging-in-Publication Data

Juvenile justice: A text/reader / Richard Lawrence, Craig Hemmens.
　　p. cm.
Includes bibliographical references and index.
ISBN 978-1-4129-5036-7 (pbk. : acid-free paper)
　　1. Juvenile justice, Administration of—United States. 2. Juvenile delinquency—United States.
3. Juvenile courts—United States. 4. Juvenile corrections—United States.
I. Lawrence, Richard. II. Hemmens, Craig.

HV9104.J8655 2008
364.360973—dc22　　　　　　　　　　　　　　　　　2008003523

Printed on acid-free paper

08　09　10　11　12　11　10　9　8　7　6　5　4　3　2　1

Acquiring Editor:	Jerry Westby
Associate Editor:	Elise Smith
Editorial Assistant:	Eve Oettinger
Production Editor:	Diane Foster
Copy Editor:	Kristin Bergstad
Typesetter:	C&M Digitals (P) Ltd.
Proofreader:	Jenifer Kooiman
Indexer:	Jeanne Busemeyer
Cover Designer:	Edgar Abarca
Marketing Manager:	Jennifer Reed Banando

Contents

READINGS

READINGS

READINGS

READINGS

READINGS

READINGS

Other Titles of Interest

Foreword

You hold in your hands a book that we think is something new. It is billed as a "text/reader." What that means is we have attempted to take the two most commonly used types of books, the textbook and the reader, and blend the two in a way that will appeal to both students and faculty.

Our experience as teachers and scholars has been that textbooks for the core classes in criminal justice (or any other social science discipline) leave many students and professors cold. The textbooks are huge, crammed with photographs, charts, highlighted material, and all sorts of pedagogical devices intended to increase student interest. Too often, though, these books end up creating a sort of sensory overload for students and suffer from a focus on "bells and whistles" such as fancy graphics at the expense of coverage of the most current research on the subject matter.

Readers, on the other hand, are typically comprised of recent and classic research articles on the subject matter. They generally suffer, however, from an absence of meaningful explanatory material. Articles are simply lined up and presented to the students, with little or no context or explanation. Students, particularly undergraduate students, are often confused and overwhelmed.

This text/reader represents our attempt to take the best of both the textbook and reader approaches. This book comprises research articles on juvenile justice. This text/reader is intended to serve either as a supplement to a core textbook, or as a stand-alone text. The book includes a combination of previously published articles and textual material introducing these articles and providing some structure and context for the selected readings. The book is broken up into a number of sections. The sections of the book track the typical content and structure of a textbook on the subject. Each section of the book has an introductory chapter that serves to introduce, explain, and provide context for the readings that follow. The readings are a selection of the best recent research that has appeared in academic journals, as well as some classic readings. The articles are edited as necessary to make them accessible to students. This variety of research and perspectives will provide the student with a grasp of the development of research, as well as an understanding of the current status of research in the subject area. This approach gives the student the opportunity to learn the basics (in the text portion of each section) and to read some of the most interesting research on the subject.

There is also an introductory chapter explaining the organization and content of the book and providing context for the articles that follow. This introductory chapter provides a framework for the text and articles that follow, as well as introducing relevant themes, issues, and concepts. This will assist the student in understanding the articles.

Each section will include a summary of the material covered. There will also be a selection of discussion questions. These summaries and discussion questions should facilitate student thought and class discussion of the material.

It is our belief that this method of presenting the material will be more interesting for both students and faculty. We acknowledge that this approach may be viewed by some as more challenging than the traditional textbook. To that we say Yes! It is! But we believe that if we raise the bar, our students will rise to the challenge. Research shows that students and faculty often find textbooks boring to read. It is our belief that many criminal justice instructors would welcome the opportunity to teach without having to rely on a "standard" textbook that covers only the most basic information and that lacks both depth of coverage and an attention to current research. This book provides an alternative for instructors who want to get more out of the basic criminal justice courses/curriculum than one can get from a basic textbook that is aimed at the lowest common denominator and filled with flashy but often useless features that merely serve to drive up its cost. This book is intended for instructors who want to go beyond the ordinary, basic coverage provided in textbooks.

We also believe students will find this approach more interesting. They are given the opportunity to read current, cutting-edge research on the subject, while also being provided with background and context for this research.

We hope that this unconventional approach will be more interesting, and thus make learning and teaching more fun. Criminal justice is a fascinating subject, and the topic deserves to be presented in an interesting manner. We hope you will agree.

—Craig Hemmens, J.D., Ph.D.
Department of Criminal Justice
Boise State University

Preface

This book is a combined text and reader that examines the juvenile justice system. The book focuses on the law enforcement, judicial, and correctional responses to juvenile offending. We discuss the legal and administrative procedures to prevent and control juvenile delinquency, and the most recent research on the juvenile justice system. The focus of the book is on juvenile justice rather than juvenile delinquency, but we have provided a brief overview of the major theories and explanations of the causes of juvenile delinquency. This book is different from most juvenile justice textbooks and readers. It is not a standard textbook with a summary of current research and no original material, nor is it simply a reader with a collection of articles on different topics. It combines the features of a textbook with original research articles carefully selected from some of the best academic journals and written by experts in juvenile justice. The introduction to each reading has been adapted from the authors' abstract and expanded somewhat to give readers an overview of the purpose, main points, and conclusions of each article. We have retained nearly the entire contents of the original articles, but we have edited the readings in the interests of reduced length and readability. We have omitted tables of complex statistical analyses, but have retained the more basic statistics tables. We have retained the authors' discussions of statistical findings and conclusions based on those findings. The editing process is *not* consistent across all readings, as some articles contain more complex statistical analyses. We have included the complete reference citation of the articles for readers who wish to review the original unedited articles. The text and readings include summaries and discussion questions to guide readers, and we have included a list of Web Resources at the end of each section. Sage Publications will maintain a Web site that will have additional readings available online that we were not able to include in the book.

Our goal in writing this book is to provide readers with an overview and discussion of the developments and major issues in juvenile justice. We believe that this unique approach of combining a text and a reader will provide students with an understanding of the juvenile justice system and an introduction to some of the best original research articles by experts in the field. There is an abundance of excellent literature on juvenile justice that summarizes findings of qualitative and quantitative research, using a variety of methodological approaches, including legal, historical, criminological, and related behavioral and social science perspectives. We invite you to join us in examining the juvenile justice system and reading some of the best original research articles on the law enforcement, judicial, and correctional responses to juvenile delinquency.

⌘ Ancillaries

To enhance the use of this text/reader and to assist those using this book as a core text, we have developed high-quality ancillaries for instructors and students.

Instructor's Resource CD. A variety of instructor's materials are available. For each section, this includes PowerPoint slides, Web resources, a complete set of test questions, and other helpful resources.

Student Study Site. This comprehensive student study site features chapter outlines students can print for class, flashcards, interactive quizzes, Web exercises, and more.

⌘ Acknowledgments

We would like to extend our heartfelt thanks and appreciation to several persons who helped in the completion of this book. We are grateful to Jerry Westby, Executive Editor of Sage Publications, developmental editors Denise Simon and Elise Smith, and the other editorial and production assistants who helped bring this work to print. This book would not have been possible without their support and expert guidance throughout the project. We are also grateful to Erin Conley for providing the draft manuscript for How to Read a Research Article. Howard Snyder, Melissa Sickmund, and Ann Stahl of the National Center for Juvenile Justice offered invaluable assistance in making available the latest statistics on juvenile arrests, court cases, and juvenile corrections populations. We offer special thanks and condolences to the family of Dr. Tory Caeti who as coeditor of *Youth Violence and Juvenile Justice* provided several articles for review before his recent untimely death. We want to acknowledge the excellent work of the authors of the articles included in the readings sections of the book. We express our appreciation to them, and ask their indulgence in our editing decisions that resulted in modified reprints of their original work.

Several persons reviewed original manuscripts for the book. Their comments and suggestions were helpful in organizing the material, clarifying some points, and adding material that had been overlooked. We are thankful to:

James David Ballard
California State University, Northridge

Peter J. Benekos
Mercyhurst College

Jeb A. Booth
Salem State College

Christina Caifano
California State University, Bakersfield

Camille Gibson
Prairie View A & M University

William Kelley
Auburn University

Megan Kurlychek
University of South Carolina

Jodi Lane
University of Florida

Daniel Richard Lee
Indiana University of Pennsylvania

Alfredo Montalvo
Emporia State University

David L. Myers
Indiana University of Pennsylvania

Frances P. Reddington
Central Missouri State University

Nancy Rodriguez
Arizona State University

Michael T. Stevenson
The University of Toledo

Joseph B. Sanborn, Jr.
University of Central Florida

Kimberly Tobin
Westfield State College

Jennifer L. Schulenberg
Sam Houston State University

Sharon Tracy
Georgia Southern University

Clete Snell
University of Houston Downtown

Michael G. Turner
University of North Carolina, Charlotte

We appreciate the support of administrators and our colleagues at St. Cloud State University and Boise State University, who helped to create a collegial working environment where academic research and writing are valued and supported. Finally, we want to thank Dorothy and Mary, who supported us in this work and tolerated the time away from them as we completed this project.

—Richard Lawrence
St. Cloud, Minnesota

—Craig Hemmens
Boise, Idaho

About the Authors

Richard Lawrence is Professor of Criminal Justice at St. Cloud State University in Minnesota. He earned a Ph.D. in Criminal Justice at Sam Houston State University; an M.A. in Psychology at St. Mary's University, San Antonio, Texas; and a B.A. in Psychology at Bethel University, St. Paul, Minnesota. He has published 2 books on school crime and juvenile justice and is the author of more than 40 articles and chapters published in academic journals and books.

Craig Hemmens holds a J.D. from North Carolina Central University School of Law and a Ph.D. in Criminal Justice from Sam Houston State University. He is the Director of the Honors College and a Professor in the Department of Criminal Justice at Boise State University, where he has taught since 1996. He has previously served as Academic Director of the Paralegal Studies Program and Chair of the Department of Criminal Justice. Professor Hemmens has published 10 books and more than 100 articles on a variety of criminal justice–related topics. His primary research interests are criminal law and procedure and corrections. He has served as the editor of the *Journal of Criminal Justice Education*. His publications have appeared in *Justice Quarterly*, the *Journal of Criminal Justice*, *Crime and Delinquency*, the *Criminal Law Bulletin*, and the *Prison Journal*.

INTRODUCTION

Juvenile crime is a serious problem in the United States and most other nations. A majority of young people admit to engaging in some types of delinquent behavior, though only a small number of youth are ever apprehended by police officers, and even fewer are ever referred to a juvenile court. The majority of crimes committed by juveniles are offenses such as theft and shoplifting, vandalism, drug and alcohol use, disorderly conduct, and simple assaults that include hitting, kicking, and fights that do not result in serious injury. Many youth engage in behavior such as curfew violations, running away, disobeying parents, school truancy, and alcohol violations, referred to as "status offenses" because they apply only to juvenile-age youth and children, and are not punishable under a state penal code.

Most serious property and personal violent crimes are committed by adult offenders over the age of 18, but a great deal of attention is directed at delinquent behavior and juvenile offenses. Criminologists, social scientists, lawmakers, and policy makers have focused their efforts on examining the causes of juvenile crime, and on developing programs and public policies to prevent delinquency and correct juvenile offenders.

The *purpose of this book* is to introduce readers to the history and development of juvenile justice; the roles of police, detention and intake, judicial professionals, probation and corrections officers; and to discuss the future trends and directions of juvenile justice. These topics will be covered through introductory and overview essays, followed by reprints of original essays and research studies that have been published in academic research journals.

The Extent and Seriousness of Juvenile Delinquency and Victimization

Children and youth are victims of theft and violent crimes. Some juveniles are victims of abuse and neglect at the hands of their parents or other caregivers. Child victimization has been linked to problem behaviors, delinquency, and criminal behavior later in life. An understanding of victimization and juvenile delinquency is therefore important for a better understanding of the most appropriate juvenile justice system responses to these problems. Some highlights from *Juvenile Offenders and Victims: 2006 National Report* (Snyder & Sickmund, 2006) indicate the seriousness and extent of juvenile victimization in the United States:

- On average, between 1980 and 2002, about 2,000 juveniles were murdered annually in the United States.
- In 2002, on average, four juveniles were murdered daily in the United States.
- Children under 6 years of age who were victims of murder were most often killed by a parent.
- Nearly 1 million (906,000) children were victims of abuse or neglect in 2003, a rate of 12 victims per 1,000 children ages 0–17.
- As juveniles age, they are less likely to be victims of a violent crime by a family member.
- About two thirds of violent crimes with juvenile victims occur in a residence.
- Youth between ages 7 to 17 are about as likely to be victims of suicide as they are to be victims of homicide.
- About half of all violent crimes experienced by male and female students occurred in school or on the way to and from school.
- Many youth are subjected to inappropriate and potentially dangerous experiences on the Internet. (Snyder & Sickmund, 2006, pp. 19–52)

Juvenile offending is often perceived to be extensive and serious, despite the fact that most serious property and violent crimes are committed by offenders over 18 years of age. Violent crimes committed by juveniles under 18 years of age have actually declined in the past several years. Crimes committed by youth are newsworthy events that get a lot of attention from the news media. Violent crimes naturally are reported more often, and get a disproportionate amount of news coverage, so the public often gets a distorted view of the true extent of juvenile crime. Television, radio, and newspapers play an important role in society, informing the public about important events. Citizens depend on the media as sources of information. Most Americans' knowledge and opinions of crime and justice are based on what they see on television and read in the newspapers (Warr, 2000). Research studies have shown that television and the news media present a distorted and exaggerated view of the extent and seriousness of crime, and tend to portray racial minorities as responsible for the majority of crime (Dorfman & Schiraldi, 2001;

Surette, 1998). The extensive national television and news media reporting of school shooting incidents presented the false impression that most schools are unsafe and violent places, and that children and youth are more at risk of victimization in schools than elsewhere (Lawrence & Mueller, 2003). In fact, only a small percentage of violent victimization and homicides involving juvenile victims occurs in schools. Children and youth are at greater risk of victimization in their own homes and in other parts of their communities. Understanding the true extent and source of juvenile crime and victimization is the first step to effectively responding to the problem.

Homicide tends to receive the most attention in government and news media reports of deaths of children and youth. Death by homicide, however, is *not* the most common causes of death of children and young people. According to the Centers for Disease Control and Prevention, the leading cause of death for children and youth is accidents and unintentional injury; homicide ranks fourth for children ages 5–9, fifth for youth ages 10–14, and second for youth and young adults ages 15–19. More youth aged 10–14 were victims of suicide (244) than homicide (202) in the United States in 2003 (Heron & Smith, 2007). The rank and frequency of leading causes of death for young people are reported in Table I-1. Other reports have confirmed that suicide is a leading cause of death of young people. Snyder and Sickmund (2006) reported that suicide was more prevalent than homicide among white juveniles between 1990 and 2001 (p. 25). The statistical reports from the Centers for Disease Control and Prevention remind us that homicide is not the leading cause of death, and many deaths can be prevented through better education and supervision to prevent accidental deaths and through more comprehensive provision of mental health services for young people. Law enforcement and juvenile justice officials are focusing efforts on reducing the number of homicides and nonfatal victimization of juveniles.

Table I-1	Ten Leading Causes of Death, United States, 2003: All Races, Both Sexes		
	Age Groups		
Rank	5–9	10–14	15–19
1	Unintentional injury 1,096	Unintentional injury 1,522	Unintentional injury 6,755
2	Malignant neoplasms 516	Malignant neoplasms 560	Homicide 1,938
3	Congenital anomalies 180	Suicide 244	Suicide 1,487
4	Homicide 122	Congenital anomalies 206	Malignant neoplasms 690
5	Heart disease 104	Homicide 202	Heart disease 393

SOURCE: Heron, M. P., & Smith, B. L. (2007). Deaths: Leading causes for 2003. *National Vital Statistics Reports, 44*(10), 17.

⬚ Measures of Juvenile Offending

The primary measures of juvenile crime are official measures by police, courts, and corrections; self-report measures; and victimization surveys. *Official crime statistics* are often considered the most accurate measures of crime and are the ones most often reported in the news media and by justice agencies. They are not a precise measure of the true extent of crime, however, because many crimes are not reported to police or other criminal justice agencies. The problem of unreported crime led criminologists to devise other "unofficial" methods of measuring crime. *Self-report measures* are confidential questionnaires administered to samples of youth who voluntarily report on their own involvement in delinquent activities, whether or not they were ever caught. Self-reports provide a more complete picture of juvenile delinquency, but are not completely error free since they depend on subjects' honesty and reliability of memory. *Victimization surveys* are a third measure of crime designed to supplement official statistics and self-report measures. The National Crime Victimization Survey (NCVS) has been administered regularly to a representative sample of the U.S. population, asking respondents whether and how often they have been victims of crime and asking about the perpetrators and circumstances of the crime. The NCVS is limited to juvenile victims aged 12–17, so younger victims are not included. Victimization surveys are not as reliable and accurate for measuring juvenile offending as are official measures and self-reports. Victims may not be able to identify their perpetrator; and even if they can, they may not know if the perpetrator is a juvenile or a young adult offender. Victimization surveys of crime are not highly reliable and error-free measures, nor are they intended to replace official police statistics. The School Crime Supplement (SCS) to the NCVS is a more accurate measure of juvenile victimization, but it is limited to crimes that occur in and around schools (see Lawrence, 2007).

In summary, self-report and to a lesser extent victim surveys are valuable supplements to official statistics and provide information about crime that is not available from police and court statistics. Each of the crime measures has strengths and weaknesses, but together they provide the best available measures of juvenile crime. Readers desiring to know more about the extent and seriousness of juvenile victimization and offending are encouraged to see *Juvenile Offenders and Victims: 2006 National Report* (Snyder & Sickmund, 2006).

Official Statistics on Juvenile Offending

Official measures of juvenile offending include statistics compiled by police, courts, and corrections. Many juvenile offenders who are arrested by police, however, are not referred to a juvenile court or correctional agency, so the latter two statistical reports do not include many offenders who are known to police. Local, county, and state police reports are compiled by the Federal Bureau of Investigation (FBI) and published in an annual report on *Crime in the United States,* more commonly known as the Uniform Crime Report (UCR) (Federal Bureau of Investigation, 2006). While the UCR is considered the "official" report on crime in the United States, it is at best an estimate, since many crimes are not reported to police. Crimes are more likely to be reported if they involve a serious injury or large economic loss, and if the victim wants law enforcement involved. Changes in crimes reported therefore represent more than changes in the number of crimes committed. They may also reflect changes in victims' willingness to report crimes. UCR statistics report the number of arrests made, not the number of persons arrested. A person can be arrested more than once in a year. Furthermore, one arrest can represent more than one crime, and UCR data report only the most serious offense for which a person was arrested. Those interested in more details on the method and accuracy of the FBI's UCR data should turn to Snyder and Sickmund (2006) and the FBI's report on *Crime in the United States* (Federal Bureau of Investigation, 2006). The number and percentage of arrests of persons under age 18 are reported in Table I-2.

| **Table I-2** | Juvenile Arrests in 2005 | | | | |

Most Serious Offense	2005 Juvenile Arrest Estimates	Percentage of Juvenile Arrests		Percentage Change	
		Female	Under Age 15	1996– 2005	2001– 2005
Total	2,143,700	29%	30%	−25%	−6%
Violent Crime Index	95,300	18%	31%	−25%	0%
Murder, manslaughter	1,260	10%	10%	−47%	16%
Forcible rape	3,940	2%	37%	−25%	−15%
Robbery	28,910	9%	23%	−34%	13%
Aggravated assault	61,200	24%	34%	−20%	−5%
Property Crime Index	418,500	34%	34%	−44%	−15%
Burglary	78,000	12%	33%	−44%	−13%
Larceny-theft	294,900	42%	35%	−43%	−15%
Motor vehicle theft	37,700	17%	23%	−54%	−24%
Arson	7,900	14%	59%	−24%	−12%
Non-Index Offenses					
Other assaults	247,900	33%	41%	4%	9%
Forgery, counterfeiting	4,200	31%	12%	−52%	−31%
Fraud	8,200	35%	18%	−31%	−13%
Embezzlement	1,200	44%	6%	−15%	−40%
Stolen property (buying, receiving, possessing)	22,300	17%	25%	−48%	−16%
Vandalism	104,100	14%	42%	−28%	−3%
Weapons (carry, possess)	44,800	11%	34%	−14%	24%
Drug abuse violations	191,800	17%	16%	−10%	−7%
Driving under influence	17,800	22%	2%	−4%	−13%
Liquor law violations	126,400	36%	9%	−20%	−13%
Drunkenness	15,900	24%	12%	−39%	−21%
Disorderly conduct	201,400	32%	40%	3%	14%
Curfew and loitering	140,800	30%	28%	−27%	0%
Runaways	109,000	58%	35%	−44%	−16%

SOURCE: Adapted from Snyder, 2007, p. 3.

Law enforcement agencies arrested an estimated 2.1 million juveniles in 2005. Juveniles (under 18 years of age) accounted for 12% of all violent crime arrests in 2005, including 5% of murders, 11% of forcible rapes, 15% of robberies, and 12% of aggravated assaults, and 26% of all property crime arrests in 2005 (Snyder, 2007, p. 1). The number of arrests of juveniles for murder has been declining since the peak year of 1993 when there were 3,790 juvenile arrests for murder; in 2005 there were 1,260 juvenile arrests for murder, about one third of the number in 1993. Of the estimated 1,650 juveniles murdered in 2005, 36% were under 5 years of age, 71% were male, 50% were white, and 50% were killed with a firearm (Snyder, 2007, p. 1). There was a slight increase (2%) in juvenile arrests for murder from 2004 (1,110) to 1,260 in 2005. The juvenile arrest rate for simple assault increased slightly, and females accounted for 33% of those arrests (Snyder, 2007).

Juvenile arrests disproportionately involved minorities. The racial composition of the juvenile population in 2005 was 78% white, 17% black, 4% Asian/Pacific Islander, and 1% American Indian. Most Hispanics (an ethnic group, not a race) were classified as white. Of the juvenile arrests for violent crimes in 2005, 48% were white youth, 50% were black youth, and Asian youth and American Indian youth each made up 1%. For property crime arrests, the proportions were 67% white youth, 30% black youth, 2% Asian youth, and 1% American Indian youth. Black youth were overrepresented in juvenile arrests (Snyder, 2007, p. 9).

◪ Self-Report Measures

Criminologists have used self-report studies such as the National Youth Survey to get a more accurate measure of the true extent of delinquency (Elliott, Huizinga, & Ageton, 1985). Self-report surveys provide a more comprehensive measure of delinquency than police reports, but they also have weaknesses. The samples used are relatively small and may not be representative of the population of juvenile offenders, so the results may underreport juvenile crime. Self-report studies are also vulnerable to response errors, as youth may overstate or underreport their offending behavior. Self-report measures do, however, offer an important supplement to official measures of delinquency and provide a more complete picture of the true extent of juvenile crime. Results of self-report measures show that delinquent behavior is spread more equally among youth of all social classes, and in fact white middle-class youth report involvement in offenses such as drug violations to a greater extent than lower-class and minority youths (Elliott et al., 1985). Self-report measures are very important for their contribution to providing a more complete picture of delinquent behavior. Findings that some delinquent behavior is nearly universal among all youth regardless of social class or ethnic and racial group led to the development of additional research and theories to explain delinquent involvement of middle-class youth and females. Elliott (1994) has emphasized the importance of using and integrating both self-reports and official statistics to gain a more complete understanding of the extent and seriousness of juvenile delinquency. Self-reports are regularly used to supplement official records, especially for the kinds of delinquent activities that are less likely to be reported by police. The "Monitoring the Future" surveys administered regularly to high school students are a good example of the value of self-reports for assessing the extent of young peoples' drug and alcohol abuse and other delinquent behavior (Johnston, O'Malley, Bachman, & Schulenberg, 2004).

▲ **Photo I-1**   Juvenile males are at risk of engaging in deviant and delinquent behavior.

Source: Getty Images.

⊠ Delinquency Causation: An Overview

Juvenile delinquency may be caused by a multitude of factors. Some explanations focus on the individual and include biological, psychological, and rational choice theories. Social explanations place the causes of delinquency in the structure of society, cultural differences, and social processes. Still other theories explain delinquency as a function of societal reactions to deviance, or conflict between the dominant and less powerful groups in society. Most of us have an opinion about what causes delinquency. Popular opinions include poverty, unemployment, poor parenting, peer pressure, gangs, and drugs. Criminologists and social scientists have sought for years to better understand and explain the complex origins and etiology of crime and delinquency. Criminological theories are constantly being developed, tested, and revised based on research studies that support or question their accuracy. The criteria for theories that best explain delinquency causation among youth from a variety of backgrounds and social settings are that the theories be (1) clear and simple, (2) testable, (3) based on observations and research data, and (4) logically consistent.

The number and complexity of theories explaining delinquency can be overwhelming, as criminologists seem to be competing with each other for the most correct and comprehensive theoretical perspective. In reality, however, the number and variety of delinquency theories attests to the complexity of the problem; its variation among subcultures and social classes; and across gender, ethnic, and racial lines. No single theory can adequately explain all the reasons behind deviant behavior and delinquency of youth, but the predominant theories, when considered together, are able to explain most delinquent behavior. Several criminologists have developed integrated theories of crime that combine the best features of several theories.

Why study theories of crime and delinquency? Crime is a problem that affects society and the quality of life for every citizen. Thousands of persons are victimized each year, and many more who have not suffered actual victimization have a fear of crime; crime thus affects the everyday behavior of most citizens. In addition to the effects on individuals, crime costs local, state, and federal governments billions of dollars each year. A problem of this magnitude demands our utmost attempts to understand its origins and causes. Social scientists have spent years studying the varieties of criminal behavior and the factors that seem to underlie the problem. The study of crime theories is not simply an academic or intellectual exercise. Understanding the causes of crime is essential in order to make rational, informed responses to the problem of crime. Laws, policies, and delinquency prevention programs are based on beliefs about what causes the problem. Those who argue in favor of passing tougher laws to combat crime assume that offenders are acting rationally and may be deterred by tougher laws and harsh punishment. Those who, on the other hand, argue for more rehabilitation and treatment programs assume that underlying psychological problems, alcohol, or substance abuse have led to juvenile offending. Still others, who believe that unemployment, poverty, and related social problems are responsible for delinquency, would direct resources and remedial programs in that direction. Most of the explanations and responses are valid and appropriate for certain at-risk and delinquent youth, under given circumstances and conditions. To assume, however, that one crime prevention strategy will work effectively for all offenders under all circumstances is naive and doomed to fail. As with any problem facing society, it is necessary to understand the origins and causes of delinquency in order to make policy decisions that are more realistically in line with the true nature of the problem. Of course, no single explanation can account for the variety of delinquent behaviors of youth, and most of the major theories of causation do offer sound explanations for delinquency that are based on empirical research. The best theories also offer recommendations to policy makers for the most appropriate programs and strategies for delinquency prevention.

Types of Delinquency Theories

Explanations of delinquency fall into one of two broad categories, the first being the *classical, or choice, theory*. Classical theory is based on the early writings of Cesare Beccaria (1738–1794) and Jeremy Bentham (1748–1832). According to classicism, persons have free will and commit crime based on a voluntary, rational choice. It was assumed that since crime was a rational choice, criminal offenders could be deterred by punishment. Classical theory has thus been referred to as a utilitarian approach to crime. Rational explanations of crime currently receive wide support among those who believe that crime occurs when an offender decides that the probable gain from illegal behavior outweighs the possible costs of getting caught, convicted, and punished. *Routine activity theory* (Cohen & Felson, 1979), for example, holds that crime and delinquency occur when there is a suitable target, an absence of capable guardians, and the presence of a motivated offender.

Rational choice theory maintains that the logical response to crime is punishment as a deterrent. *General deterrence* discourages individuals from delinquency by threats and the punishment of offenders as examples. *Specific deterrence* discourages offenders from repeating their crimes by showing that crime does not pay and by threatening to punish them more harshly the next time. Punishment and deterrence may work to reduce delinquency only if juvenile offenders believe they are likely to be caught and punished. Tougher laws are effective, therefore, only when they are accompanied by additional expenditures for law enforcement, courts, and corrections.

Positivist theories are the second type of explanation. Positivists hold that behavior is determined or caused by factors over which individuals have little or no control. Positivist explanations originated with the 19th-century criminologist Cesare Lombroso, the first person credited with using the scientific method to study crime. Lombroso identified distinguishing physical characteristics of criminals in prison, and believed they were "born criminals." His early theory was discredited for failure to include a control group for comparison, but his work influenced others who studied the relationship between body types, deviance, and crime. Current positivist explanations hold that delinquency is based on genetic factors, IQ, learning disabilities, and psychological characteristics. Because delinquency is not a freewill, rational choice, but is determined by characteristics outside the person's control, the appropriate responses are treatment or change strategies rather than punishment.

Biosocial Explanations of Delinquency. Genetic, biochemical, and neurological factors influence behavior. *Genetic-inheritance* studies indicate that behavioral tendencies may be passed on from parents in the same way as physical features. The explanation is supported by studies of twins reared together and apart (by adoptive parents), with identical twins behaving similarly even when reared in a different environment. *Biochemical* explanations note that chemical imbalances in the body influence behavior, hyperactivity, deviance, and sometimes delinquency. The connection between nutrition and delinquent behavior has received considerable attention in the juvenile justice system (Schauss, 1981). *Neurological* explanations describe brain impairments, including learning disabilities (LDs) such as attention-deficit/hyperactivity disorder (ADHD) that are related to antisocial behavior. A higher proportion of learning-disabled children are arrested and incarcerated. An estimated 10% of children in the general population have learning disorders, but an estimated 26% to 73% of adjudicated delinquents have a learning disability (Zimmerman, Rich, Keilitz, & Broder, 1981). Research conclusions are mixed as to whether LDs actually cause delinquency, or whether youth with LDs are simply more likely to be arrested and adjudicated than other youth (Malmgren, Abbott, & Hawkins, 1999). Neurological disorders and learning disabilities may be genetic, inherited factors; they may be caused by severe head trauma, an accidental fall, or physical abuse; and there is evidence that exposure to toxic substances such as lead interferes with brain functioning and affects behavior. Children with lead contamination are more at risk of having a reading disability, lower class standing in high school, and increased absenteeism, and are more likely to have dropped out of high school (Needleman, Schell, Bellenger, Leviton, & Allred, 1990); and there is a relationship between lead poisoning and delinquency (Needleman, Riess, Tobin, Biesecker, & Greenhouse, 1996). See Table I-3 for a summary of biosocial explanations.

Psychological Explanations. Psychologists study development of the personality from childhood, through inherited and unconscious influences; mental illness and psychopathology; intelligence and reasoning ability; social learning theory and behavior; and the role of learning and moral development. Psychoanalytic theorists attempted to explain individual personality based on early life experiences and unconscious desires and drives. Juvenile delinquency, according to this explanation, is thought to be a result of a weak ego and superego.

Intelligence and Delinquency. Psychologists developed measures of intelligence or IQ, and noted a relationship between reasoning ability and susceptibility to deviant and delinquent

Table I-3	Biosocial Explanations of Delinquency	
	Explanation	*Strength*
Genetic	Delinquent traits and predispositions are inherited; deviance, criminality of parents may predict children's deviance.	Explains why only a small percentage of youth in high-crime areas become delinquent; and why some youth in low-crime areas do become delinquent.
Biochemical	Delinquency is a function of diet, vitamin intake, hormonal imbalance, food allergies, or toxic chemicals.	Shows how chemicals and the environment interact with personal traits to influence behavior.
Neurological	Delinquents often have brain impairments; learning disabilities, attention-deficit/hyperactivity disorder, and brain dysfunctions are related to deviance.	Explains irrational violent behavior and delinquency; shows how personal traits interact with the environment to influence behavior.

behavior. Criminologists have concluded that IQ is more important than race or social class for predicting delinquency (Hirschi & Hindelang, 1977), and that low IQ is related to delinquent involvement independently of the effects of socioeconomic status (Moffitt, Gabrielli, Mednick, & Schulsinger, 1981, p. 155). Anthony Walsh (1987) analyzed IQ and offense data from the files of male delinquents and concluded that those with lower IQs commit impulsive and spontaneous crimes that offer instant gratification, while more intelligent offenders are more "future oriented" and tend to commit crimes that require planning and offer deferred gratification, but that also lead to more valuable payoffs (pp. 288–289). Other research findings suggest that children with lower IQs who are identified as disruptive and having behavior problems at an early age may be helped to avoid further delinquent behavior in adolescence if they receive early intervention from school counselors and family therapists (see Gordon, 1987).

Behaviorist psychology has demonstrated that both animal and human behavior can be explained by stimulus-responses in which rewarded behavior tends to be repeated and behavior that is not rewarded may be extinguished. Most juvenile correctional facilities and residential placements apply this principle through a "token economy" or step system that rewards residents for good behavior. *Social learning theory* explains behavior as a result of persons observing and imitating other persons (see Bandura, 1977). Social learning theory is able to explain delinquent behavior across racial, cultural, and social class lines. Juveniles from high-crime neighborhoods who have good parenting and positive role models do not become delinquent. Other youth from good families of financial means in good schools and neighborhoods do engage in delinquent behavior. The difference may be explained by disengaged parents, influence from antisocial peers, popular culture, or violent media. *Moral development theories* (see Kohlberg, 1969; Piaget, 1932) focus on how children learn social rules and make judgments on the basis of those rules. In terms of Kohlberg's theory, delinquents are at a lower level of moral development than nondelinquents. They are more likely to define right and wrong in absolute terms, they focus more on external consequences, act to avoid punishment, and show little concern for the feelings of others. See Table I-4 for a summary of psychological explanations of delinquency.

Table I-4	Psychological Explanations of Delinquency	
	Major Premise	*Strengths*
Psychodynamic	Development of unconscious personality; early childhood influences, weak egos, damaged personality cause delinquency.	Explains onset of deviance and delinquency, across class lines and regardless of social problems or peer influence.
Behaviorism	Stimulus-response, conditioning; behavior is modeled after others, is reinforced by rewards, and is extinguished by punishment.	Explains the role of parents and peers; the role of family; media and popular culture influence delinquency.
Cognitive	Intelligence (IQ); reasoning processes, perception of environment influences behavior and moral development.	Shows how delinquent behavior patterns change over time; persons mature and develop moral reasoning.

Sociological Explanations of Delinquency

Sociological explanations emphasize social influences on individuals caused by the structure of society, social disorganization caused by societal change, subcultural differences, and social processes that influence behavior. *Social structure theorists* claim that such forces as social disorganization, status frustration, and cultural deviance lead lower-class youths to become involved in delinquent behavior. *Social disorganization theory* was developed by Shaw and McKay (1942) at the University of Chicago. They noted that urban growth produced a condition of social disorganization characterized by urban density, overcrowding, substandard housing, low income, unemployment, poor schools, and family problems. The increase in crime that occurred with urban growth was due not so much to immoral, crime-prone immigrants but to social disorganization and conditions over which individuals have little control. *Strain theory* explained delinquency as caused by the "strain" or frustration of not having an equal ability or means to achieve commonly shared goals such as economic or social success. The "opportunity-structure" theories (Cloward & Ohlin, 1960) prompted government-funded policies such as "Head Start" and jobs programs for lower-class youths, to enhance educational and employment opportunities and reduce delinquency. Robert Agnew (1992) extended Merton's (1957) theory of strain and anomie to better explain varieties of delinquent behavior through a *general strain theory*. *Cultural deviance* (or subcultural) theorists emphasize the difference in values and attitudes of lower-class and middle-class youth. Youth from socially disorganized neighborhoods marked by unemployment, poverty, and social problems develop values and attitudes of that subculture. Cultural deviance theory suggests that youth violate the law because they follow the values of their lower-class community. Walter Miller (1958) described a number of "focal concerns" that dominate lower-class cultures and often run counter to lawful, middle-class behavior.

In summary, social structure, strain, and cultural deviance explanations claim that delinquent acts are often expressions of frustration because of limited educational and employment opportunities, particularly of lower-income and disadvantaged youth. Delinquent acts are viewed as reactions to the frustration caused by blocked opportunity. Social structure and strain theories are supported by considerable research evidence in explaining a great deal of delinquent behavior.

▲ **Photo I-2**   Juveniles vandalizing an abandoned inner-city building illustrates the social disorganization explanation of delinquency.

SOURCE: Getty Images.

Social process explanations focus not on societal structures, but on social interactions between individuals and environmental influences that may lead to juvenile offending. *Differential association theory* was developed by Edwin Sutherland, who believed that delinquency is learned behavior as youths interact with each other. Sutherland's differential association theory remains an important explanation for juvenile delinquency, that delinquency is learned like other behaviors (Sutherland & Cressey, 1970). This explanation also has a positive appeal as it holds that youth are changeable and can be taught prosocial behavior. *Social control theory* begins with the premise that the way to understand delinquency is to know the characteristics of persons who are *not* delinquent. Travis Hirschi (1969) identified four elements of the social bond that help youth avoid delinquency: *attachment* (affection and respect for parents); *commitment* (to socially acceptable activities and values); *involvement* (in conventional activities); *beliefs* (respect for the law and societal norms). Hirschi's control theory has generated a considerable amount of research and has contributed to understanding the relationship between delinquency and the family, peers, and the school.

Developmental and Life-Course Theories. Sampson and Laub (1993) point to evidence that delinquency varies by age: Though delinquency tends to peak in the teenage years, there is an early onset of delinquency, as well as continuity of criminal behavior over the life course. Moffitt (1993) has studied the psychological development of children and youth and offers evidence that most adolescents who engage in delinquency do not persist into adult crime. Developmental or life-course explanations attempt to account for differences among offenders who begin offending at an early age and continue offending, and those who begin in adolescence and seem to grow out of it.

General and Integrated Theories. Criminologists have taken the best parts of different theories and combined them in a single general or integrated theory. Gottfredson and Hirschi (1990) combined the strong points of the classical traditional (otherwise referred to as the "rational-choice" model) and positivist theories that crime is caused by biological, psychological, or socioeconomic factors. In an extension of Hirschi's (1969) control theory, they describe the offender as an individual who lacks self-control and tends to be impulsive, insensitive, physical (more than mental), a risk-taker, short-sighted, and nonverbal. The *general theory of crime* aptly describes juvenile delinquents whose lack of self-control draws them to criminal acts that offer excitement, risk, deception, and power; and criminal or antisocial adults whose lack of self-control results in unstable marriages, friendships, and jobs (Gottfredson & Hirschi, 1990, p. 89).

Social Reaction Theories: Labeling and Conflict

Social reaction theories focus on how society, social institutions, and government officials react to crime and delinquency. They are different from psychological or sociological explanations in that they explain crime as being caused by how laws are written and enforced, and how social institutions and justice agencies react to crime and criminals. *Labeling theory* begins with the assumption that most youth engage in some deviant acts, based on findings from self-report studies. The labeling perspective contends that repeated delinquent behavior is caused by society's reaction to minor deviant behavior. Becker (1963) proposed that those in society who make and enforce the rules "create" deviants by labeling persons, who in turn act out the deviant behaviors consistent with their new identity. Labeling theory provides an explanation for why many youths involved in minor deviant acts often escalate to more serious delinquent acts following police contact and juvenile justice processing. Juvenile diversion policies were developed in response to labeling theory, to keep minor offenders from associating with serious offenders in the court and corrections system, and to reduce the possibility of their escalating to more serious criminal involvement.

Conflict theory emphasizes the role of social and political institutions as causes of crime, rather than individual characteristics and criminal tendencies of offenders. Conflict

Table I-5	Sociological Explanations of Delinquency	
	Major Premise	*Strengths*
Social Disorganization	Social changes cause breakdown of formal and informal controls, increase in crime.	Explains urban crime rates, increase in crime with change and growth in cities.
Strain	Persons who lack the means to attain goals legitimately do so illegally; lower-class persons feel strain or frustration trying to meet middle-class goals.	Explains crime among the lower class, and among those who lack equal education and employment opportunities.
Cultural Deviance	Persons from groups having different life patterns or "focal concerns" are judged by the dominant culture.	Explains why lower-class and minority groups are overrepresented in the justice system.
Social Process	Persons learn delinquent behavior from others; the presence of social bonds helps reduce the probability of delinquent involvement.	Explains why delinquency occurs among middle- and lower-class youth; shows the importance of parents, positive peers, and school.

theorists note the presence of conflict and competition among social classes and groups in society (Quinney, 1974). Conflict results when social class groups in power implement laws and policies that support their own views and practices. Conflict theory offers an explanation for why certain deviant and illegal behaviors are enforced and punished more severely than others. Certain laws "criminalize" behavior that was previously not a crime, while other harmful actions are exempt from criminal laws and punishments. Reiman (1990) applies conflict theory to explain why "the rich get richer and the poor get prison." Inconsistencies in drug enforcement policies in the United States are an example. Criminal laws and their enforcement tend to focus more on crimes committed by the lower class, while many white-collar crimes are ignored or punished lightly. Critical or conflict theorists contend that laws written by those in power are done so in order to serve their own interest, and to keep the lower class in its place. Labeling and conflict theories challenge our thinking on current societal reactions to delinquency and crime, and they remind us that some changes in laws and policies may be a necessary part of delinquency prevention and crime reduction.

A comprehensive discussion of theories and research on the causes of delinquency is beyond the scope of this book. We have provided only a brief overview of the more prominent theories and explanations. The best criminological theories of delinquency have been tested repeatedly, and include policy implications that inform juvenile justice practitioners and lawmakers on the most effective programs and strategies to prevent delinquency. Interested readers are encouraged to refer to Tibbetts and Hemmens (in press) and other excellent texts that discuss more fully the theories of criminology and causes of juvenile delinquency.

☒ The Organization and Contents of the Book

The book is divided into seven sections, with each section dealing with a specific part of juvenile justice and related issues. Each section begins with an introductory essay, followed by selected readings that represent some of the best research and writing on juvenile justice. The research-based articles provide the reader with an understanding of the development and current status of research on juvenile justice. The seven sections include the following:

- History and development of the juvenile court and justice process
- Police and juvenile offenders
- Juvenile detention and court intake
- Transfer to adult criminal court
- The juvenile court process
- Juvenile corrections
- The future of juvenile justice

The first section provides a *history and development of the juvenile court* and justice process, from the "child-saving" movement to the first juvenile court, and the recent trends to adopt more features common to the adult criminal court and to hold juvenile offenders more accountable for crimes. The introductory essay concludes with a discussion of the federal and state legislative changes to juvenile statutes and the juvenile court process. The readings in the first section include an article by Alexander Pisciotta on the "child savers" and the promise and practice of the doctrine of *parens patriae;* a reading by Ted Ferdinand on the history of juvenile justice; and a reading by Barry Krisberg in which he traces the development of juvenile justice in America and the attempts of the system to serve marginalized and wayward youth.

The second section, on *police and juvenile offenders,* provides a summary of police roles and responsibilities with juvenile offenders. Here we focus on police–juvenile relations; police roles and discretion; race as a factor in juvenile arrests; alternatives to police arrest and custody; and special police roles with juveniles. We conclude Section II with readings by Dennis Rosenbaum and his associates on the police D.A.R.E. program; Susan Guarino-Ghezzi on "reintegrative police surveillance of juvenile offenders"; Gordon Bazemore and Scott Senjo on police encounters with juveniles under a community policing model; Craig Hemmens and Katherine Bennett on the enforcement of juvenile curfews; Eric Fritsch, Tory Caeti, and Robert Taylor on a police antigang initiative that involved aggressive curfew and truancy enforcement; and finally an article by Anthony Braga and his associates on the Boston police department's "Operation Ceasefire" initiative that used problem-oriented policing to reduce youth gun violence.

The third section, *juvenile detention and court intake,* provides an overview of the postarrest process for juvenile offenders. We discuss the juvenile court intake process; the detention decision for youth who pose a risk to the community; the conditions and consequences of being detained; the issue of preventive detention and predicting dangerousness; assessment of juvenile risks and needs; diversion and alternatives to juvenile court referral; and the prosecutorial decision-making process that may result in a petition alleging delinquency, a waiver to criminal court, or other nonadjudicatory alternatives. The readings in the third section include an article by Michael Lieber and Kristan Fox on the impact of race and detention on juvenile justice decision making; Daniel Mears and William Kelly on assessments and intake processes in juvenile justice processing; and a research report by Douglas Young and his coauthors on new assessment technologies in a juvenile justice agency.

The fourth section deals with the increasing trend toward *transfer of juvenile offenders to adult criminal court.* The juvenile court has traditionally had sole jurisdiction over all crimes involving juvenile-age offenders. All juvenile cases initially have been filed in the juvenile court, which had the authority to waive jurisdiction and transfer the case to criminal court. The purpose of this section is to provide an overview of waiver and transfer; examine judicial and legislative developments in juvenile transfer; examine alternatives to juvenile transfer, including "blended sentencing"; discuss the law, science, and juvenile transfer; present research on the effects of juvenile transfer; and discuss the future trends in juvenile transfer. The readings in Section IV include a research report on recidivism of juveniles transferred to criminal court by Lawrence Winner and his associates; an article on the impact of laws for transferring juveniles to criminal court by Daniel Mears; an article by David Myers on punishing violent youth in adult court; and Joe Sanborn's article on developing policy for excluding youth from juvenile court.

The fifth section provides an overview of *the juvenile court process* and the changes and developments over the past 100 years since the origin of the first juvenile court. The juvenile court was originally developed as an informal quasi-judicial process that incorporated more civil procedures than criminal court procedures. The judge was viewed as a "father figure" who presumably acted in "the best interest of the child." A number of U.S. Supreme Court decisions in the 1960s suggested that juveniles received the "worst of both worlds": neither the treatment promised them, nor the due process procedures common to adult criminal court. After presenting the number of juvenile court cases and growth trends each year, this section examines the roles and responsibilities of juvenile court officials; the juvenile court process; and juvenile court trends and reforms. The readings in Section V include an article by Robert Mennel on the origins of the juvenile court and juveniles' legal rights; an article by Barry Feld in which he notes the examples of injustice inherent in the juvenile court, and recommends the adoption of due process procedures similar to the criminal court; an article by Joe Sanborn on factors that seem to affect juvenile court dispositions; and an article by Lori Guevara, Cassia Spohn, and Denise Herz on the issue of race and legal representation in juvenile court.

In Section VI we discuss the developments in *juvenile corrections* and the issues involved in changing juvenile offenders. Correctional programs and facilities for juvenile offenders have historically emphasized a treatment objective rather than a goal of punishment that is common for adult corrections. Juvenile facilities, however, have often resembled adult prisons with few rehabilitative features. This section examines the history and developments of institutional and community corrections programs for juveniles; juvenile probation; the development and effectiveness of intermediate sanctions; research on effectiveness of juvenile corrections programs; and current issues and future trends in juvenile corrections. The readings in Section VI include an essay on reexamining community corrections models by Richard Lawrence; an article on the impact of boot camps and traditional institutions on juvenile residents by Doris MacKenzie and her associates; an article by Jodi Lane and associates that reports on incarcerated juveniles' views and perceptions of adult versus juvenile sanctions; and an article by David Altschuler and Rachel Brash on confronting the challenges and opportunities of reentry.

The seventh and final section of the book addresses *the future of juvenile justice.* Juvenile justice has changed dramatically over the past century, from a child-saving movement, to a treatment-oriented system, and more recently to a "get-tough" movement focused on holding juvenile offenders more accountable, like adult criminals. In this concluding section of the book we summarize those developments and changes in juvenile justice; discuss a number of factors that will affect the future of juvenile justice; discuss some important policy issues and questions that must be faced in the future; and we conclude with a discussion of future trends for juvenile justice in the 21st century, including a public health approach and a comprehensive strategy for delinquency prevention. The readings in the final section include an article by Brandon Welsh on the public health approach for preventing juvenile violence; an article by Jeffrey Butts and Daniel P. Mears on the prospects of reviving some of the original juvenile justice perspectives in a get-tough era; an article by Alida Merlo and Peter Benekos on defining juvenile justice in the 21st century; and a reading on the comprehensive strategy framework by James Howell.

It is our intention and hope that this book will provide readers with an excellent understanding of the developments and major issues in juvenile justice. This book takes the unique approach of providing an introduction and discussion of the major developments and topics in juvenile justice, along with our review of some of the major studies, research reports, and literature on juvenile justice; and then combines our presentation with many of the best essays and research reports that have been previously published in academic journals. We believe that this unique approach is superior to most other books on juvenile justice. We invite you to explore with us the dramatic developments and changes in juvenile justice. The means by which communities, social institutions, and justice agencies respond to juvenile crime and violence is vitally important for the entire criminal justice system and public safety. As you will discover, there are many points of view and very little consensus as to the most effective means for preventing juvenile crime and responding to juvenile offenders.

WEB RESOURCES

Juvenile Offenders and Victims: 2006 National Report: http://ojjdp.ncjrs.gov/ojstatbb/nr2006/downloads/NR2006.pdf

For the latest juvenile justice statistics, visit OJJDP's *Statistical Briefing Book*: http://ojjdp.ncjrs.gov/ojstatbb/index.html

FBI Uniform Crime Report (UCR): http://www.fbi.gov/ucr/ucr.htm

The National Crime Victimization Survey (NCVS): http://www.ojp.usdoj.gov/bjs/pub/pdf/cnh05.pdf

Monitoring the Future self-report survey data: http://www.monitoringthefuture.org/

The *Sourcebook of Criminal Justice Statistics:* http://www.albany.edu/sourcebook/

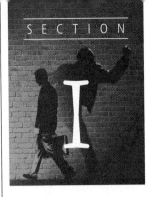

HISTORY AND DEVELOPMENT OF THE JUVENILE COURT AND JUSTICE PROCESS

SECTION HIGHLIGHTS

- Historical Overview of Juvenile Justice
- The Origins of American Juvenile Justice
- Houses of Refuge and Legal Doctrines
- The "Child-Saving" Movement
- The First Juvenile Court
- The U.S. Supreme Court on Juvenile Justice
- Juvenile Versus Criminal Court: Legal and Procedural Distinctions
- Federal and State Legislative Changes

The American juvenile justice system has developed over the past century with a number of differences that distinguish it from the adult criminal justice process. Juvenile justice advocates supported the differences on diminished youthful offender accountability and legal understanding, and youths' greater amenability to treatment. The first juvenile court was established in Chicago, Illinois, in 1899; yet a century later there is still considerable debate over the goals and the legal procedures for dealing with juvenile offenders. The question of whether juvenile offenders should be tried and sentenced differently than adult offenders elicits strongly held opinions from citizens, policy makers, and professionals. The juvenile justice system was established on the principle of individualized justice and focused on rehabilitation of youthful offenders. While due process protections were considered important, they were considered secondary in importance given the court's emphasis on care, treatment, and rehabilitation for juveniles. It was believed that youths could be held responsible for their unlawful behavior and society could be protected through an informal justice system that focused on treatment and "the best interests of the child." This approach is still appropriate and effective for the majority of juvenile offenders whose crimes range from status offenses, to property offenses, to drug offenses. The juvenile justice system has come under increasing scrutiny, however, as a growing number of juveniles are involved in violent crimes, especially school violence, gang-related violence, and assaults with weapons resulting in fatalities and serious injuries. Despite the fact that juveniles are involved in a proportionately small number of murders each year, violent crime committed by juveniles elicits widespread media coverage. The public and political/legislative response to juvenile violence has been to demand more accountability and punishment, resembling that of the criminal justice system. One century after the development of the first juvenile court, the system faces a multitude of challenges and questions.

⊠ Historical Overview of Juvenile Justice

Laws and legal procedures relating to juvenile offenders have a long history, dating back thousands of years. The Code of Hammurabi some 4,000 years ago (2270 B.C.) included reference to runaways, children who disobeyed their parents, and sons who cursed their fathers. Roman civil law and canon (church) law 2,000 years ago distinguished between juveniles and adults based upon the idea of "age of responsibility." In early Jewish law, the Talmud set forth conditions under which immaturity was to be considered in imposing punishment. Moslem law also called for leniency in punishing youthful offenders, and children under the age of 17 were to be exempt from the death penalty (Bernard, 1992). Under fifth-century Roman law, children under the age of 7 were classified as infants and not held criminally responsible. Youth approaching the age of puberty who knew the difference between right and wrong were held accountable. The legal age of puberty (age 14 for boys and 12 for girls) was the age at which youth were assumed to know the difference between right and wrong and were held criminally accountable.

Anglo-Saxon common law that dates back to the 11th and 12th centuries in England was influenced by Roman civil law and canon law. This has particular significance for American juvenile justice because it has its roots in English common law. The Chancery courts in 15th-century England were created to consider petitions of those in need of aid or intervention, generally women and children who were in need of assistance because of abandonment, divorce, or death of a spouse. Through these courts the king could exercise the right of *parens patriae* ("parent of the country"), and the courts acted *in loco parentis* ("in place of the parents") to provide services in assistance to needy women and children. The principle of *parens patriae* later became a basis for the juvenile court in America. The doctrine gives the court authority over juveniles in need of guidance and protection, and the state may then act *in loco parentis* (in place of the parents) to provide guidance and make decisions concerning the best interests of the child.

⊠ The Origins of American Juvenile Justice

The separate system of justice for juveniles has developed just over the past 100 years. Following the tradition of English law, children who broke the law in 18th-century America were treated much the same as adult criminals. Parents were responsible for controlling their children, and parental discipline was very strict and punishments were harsh. Youth who committed crimes were treated much the same as adult criminal offenders. The law made no distinction based on the age of the offender, and there was no legal term of *delinquent*. The American judicial procedures in the 19th century continued to follow those of England, subjecting children to the same punishments as adult criminals. Some punishments were very severe. Youth who committed serious offenses could be subjected to prison sentences, whipping, and even the death penalty. During the 19th century, criminal codes applied to all persons, adults and children alike. No provisions were made to account for the age of offenders. Originally there were no separate laws or courts, and no special facilities for the care of children who were in trouble with the law.

A number of developments during the 19th century paved the way for a separate system of justice for juveniles. An increase in the birthrate and the influx of immigrants to America brought a new wave of growth to American cities. With this growth came an increase in the numbers of dependent and destitute children. Urban youth and children of immigrants were thought to be more prone to deviant and immoral behavior than other youth. Early reformers who were members of the Society for the Prevention of Pauperism expressed dissatisfaction with the practice of placing children in adult jails and workhouses. They called for institutions that would instruct delinquent youth in proper discipline and moral behavior (Mennel, 1973).

⊠ Houses of Refuge and Legal Doctrines

The doctrine of *parens patriae* provided the basis for official intervention in the lives of wayward youth. Parents were expected to supervise and control their children, but when it became apparent that parents were not properly controlling and disciplining their children, the State was given the authority to take over that responsibility. The Society for the Reformation of Juvenile Delinquents in New York advocated for the separation of juvenile and adult offenders (Krisberg, 2005, p. 27), and in 1825 the New York House of Refuge was established to take in dependent, neglected, and delinquent youths. Other houses of refuge in Boston and Philadelphia were soon established, and these were followed shortly thereafter by reform schools for vagrant and delinquent juveniles. State reform schools opened in Massachusetts in 1847, in New York in 1853, in Ohio in 1857; and the first State Industrial School for Girls was opened in Massachusetts in 1856 (Law Enforcement Assistance Administration, 1976, p. 65).

▲ **Photo I-1**   Police officers take a young boy into custody in the late 19th century. (© Bettmann/CORBIS)

The doctrine of *parens patriae* was first tested in the Pennsylvania Supreme Court case of *Ex parte Crouse* in 1838. The father of Mary Ann Crouse argued that his daughter was illegally incarcerated without a trial. The Court denied his claim, stating that the Bill of Rights did not apply to juveniles. The Court stated that when parents are found to be "incompetent" in their parental duties, the state has the right to intervene and provide their child with guidance and supervision. The *Crouse* ruling was based on what the Court believed was the best interests of the child and the entire community, with the assumed intentions that the state could provide the proper education and training for the child. As states intervened in more juvenile cases, especially ones involving minor misbehavior, the concept of *parens patriae* would later meet more legal challenges.

The early juvenile reform schools were intended for education and treatment, not for punishment, but hard work, strict regimentation, and whippings were common. Discriminatory treatment against African Americans, Mexican Americans, American Indians, and poor whites remained a problem in the schools. Sexual abuse and physical attacks by peers (and sometimes staff members) also were problems. Institutional abuses against incarcerated juveniles came under increasing criticism by the last half of the 1800s. The practice of taking custody of troubled youths under the concept of *parens patriae* led many by the mid-1800s to question whether most youths benefited from the practice. There is evidence that the State is not in fact an effective or benevolent parent, and that there was a significant disparity between the promise and the practice of *parens patriae*. The author of the first reading in this section (Pisciotta, 1982) reviewed the *Ex parte Crouse* ruling and noted that subsequent legal decisions revealed that judges in the 19th century were committing minors to reformatories for noncriminal acts on the premise that the juvenile institutions would have a beneficial effect. In theory, reformatories were "schools" that provided parental discipline, education, religious instruction, and meaningful work for incarcerated youth. Pisciotta (1982) examined the records, annual reports, and daily journals of superintendents, and found a significant disparity between the theory and practice of juvenile incarceration. He noted that discipline in the juvenile reform schools was more brutal than parental, and inmate workers were exploited under an indenture or contract labor system. The schools were marked by institutional environments that had a corrupting influence on the residents, as evidenced by assaults, homosexual relations, and frequent escapes.

Critics of this extensive State intervention argued against intervention on behalf of youth over minor, noncriminal behavior, and claimed that reformatories were not providing the kind of parental care, education, or training that was promised under the *parens patriae* doctrine. In a legal challenge, the Illinois Supreme Court ruled that "we should not forget the rights which inhere both in parents and children. . . . The parent has the right to the care, custody, and assistance of his child" (*People v. Turner*, 55 Ill.280 [1870]). The Court ruled that the state should intervene only after violations of criminal law and only after following due process guidelines. The ruling actually did little to change the prevailing practices in most other states, however. It would take later court decisions to clearly define the rights of children and their parents in State intervention.

⊠ The "Child-Saving" Movement

The failure of the houses of refuge and early reform schools brought more interest in the welfare of troubled youth who were abandoned, orphaned, or forced to work under intolerable conditions. In the latter half of the 19th century, following the Civil War period, humanitarian concerns were directed toward troubled children and their treatment. A pivotal point in the development of the juvenile justice system in America was what became known as the "child-saving movement" (see Faust & Brantingham, 1979; Law Enforcement Assistance Administration, 1976). The child savers were a group of reformers that included philanthropists, professionals, and middle-class citizens who expressed concerns about the welfare of children. They pushed for state intervention to save at-risk children through shelter care and educational programs. The result of this child-saving movement was to extend government intervention over youth behaviors that had previously been the responsibility of parents and families. The leading advocates in the child-saving movement believed that such youth problems as idleness, drinking, vagrancy, and delinquent behaviors threatened the moral fabric of society and must be controlled. If parents could not or would not control and properly supervise their own children, then the government should intervene. They pushed for legislation that would give courts jurisdiction over children who were incorrigible, runaways, and those who committed crimes.

⊠ The First Juvenile Court

The latter part of the 19th century, following the Civil War, was marked by a reform movement that led to the development of a separate court for juveniles. Some states, including Massachusetts in 1874 and New York in 1892, had passed laws providing for separate trials for juveniles. The first juvenile court was established in Cook County (Chicago), Illinois, in 1899. The *parens patriae* doctrine was the legal basis for court jurisdiction over juveniles and was central to the juvenile court philosophy, because children who violated laws were not to be treated as criminals. Children were considered less mature and less aware of the consequences of their actions, so they were not to be held legally accountable for their behavior in the same manner as adults. Under the juvenile justice philosophy, youthful offenders were designated as delinquent rather than as criminal, and the primary purpose of the juvenile justice system was not punishment but rehabilitation (see Mennel, 1972).

The juvenile courts sought to turn juvenile delinquents into productive citizens by focusing on treatment rather than punishment. The laws that established the juvenile courts clearly distinguished their purpose as different from the adult penal codes. A ruling by the Pennsylvania Supreme Court in the case of *Commonwealth v. Fisher* in 1905 supported the juvenile court's purpose, and illustrates how the court's role in training delinquent children superseded the rights of children and their parents.

> The design is not punishment, nor the restraint imprisonment, any more than is the wholesome restraint which a parent exercises over his child. . . . Every statute which is designed to give protection, care, and training to children, as a parental duty, is but a recognition of the duty of the state, as the legitimate guardian and protector of children where other guardianship fails. No constitutional right is violated. (*Commonwealth v. Fisher*, 213 Pa. 48 [1905])

The Pennsylvania Supreme Court thus supported the juvenile court's treatment objectives over the rights of the juvenile or the parents. For the next 50 years juvenile courts continued the practice of legal interventions over a broad range of juvenile cases, from status offenses to criminal code violations. The focus on offenders' needs for supervision and rehabilitation more than on offenses committed had an impact on judicial procedures and decisions. Decisions of what cases would go to court were made by a juvenile court intake division, unlike criminal court where district attorneys made the decisions. Juvenile court intake considered extralegal as well as legal factors in deciding how to handle cases, and had discretion to handle cases informally, diverting cases from court action.

Because the purpose of the juvenile court was for the protection and treatment of the child and not for punishment, the juvenile proceeding was more civil than criminal. The juvenile legal process was purportedly "in the best interests of the child," so the hearing was more informal, unlike the more formal, adversarial criminal court process. Advocates believed that children did not need the formal procedural rights common in criminal court, so they were denied many of the legal rights of adults, such as formal notice of the charges and the right to legal counsel. The juvenile reform efforts were also based on the growing optimism that application of the social sciences was more appropriate for handling juvenile offenders than the law. Delinquency was viewed more as a social problem and a breakdown of the family than a criminal problem. Thus, social workers, probation officers, and psychologists took the place of lawyers and prosecutors.

▲ **Photo I-2**   A juvenile court proceeding in 1910. Judges often conducted hearings informally and privately in their chambers in the first juvenile courts. (© CORBIS)

They examined the background and social history of the child and the family environment to assess the child's needs, and then developed a treatment plan that was intended to change delinquent juveniles. The author of our second reading in this section (Ferdinand, 1991) notes that the juvenile court judge was expected to be more like a father figure than a legal jurist. The focus was on offenders and not offenses, on rehabilitation and not punishment, and this was to be accomplished through individualized justice for juvenile offenders.

The development of the first juvenile court in Chicago was followed shortly by one in Denver, and by 1945 all states had juvenile courts (see Ferdinand, 1991). For the first half of a century after it was first developed, the juvenile court system went largely unchallenged in the manner in which juvenile cases were processed. Despite some differences among states and jurisdictions, there was general agreement on the goals and objectives of juvenile justice, and how it should be similar to, and distinct from, the criminal justice system. The author of our second reading (Ferdinand, 1991) summarizes the criticisms of the juvenile court, particularly the failure of treatment programs, and offers a proposal to counter those criticisms.

⊠ The U.S. Supreme Court on Juvenile Justice

The policies and practices of the juvenile court went unchallenged for the first 60 years following its origin and development. The stated purpose of the juvenile court was for treatment rather than punishment, it resembled an informal civil proceeding more than a criminal trial, and the most severe sanctions for adjudicated delinquents were less than 1 year in a residential facility. Despite the fact that juveniles did not receive the same due process protections in court as those accorded adult offenders in criminal court, the attorneys who provided legal counsel for juveniles saw little reason to question the juvenile court process or dispositions. This began to change in the 1960s, however, as it became apparent in a number of court cases that juveniles were being sentenced to institutions resembling adult prisons or transferred to criminal court, but without due process protections common to criminal court. Criticisms of some of the long-standing practices of the juvenile court were highlighted in a number of U.S. Supreme Court cases beginning in the 1960s.

Kent v. United States

Morris Kent, age 16, was on probation when, in 1961, he was charged with rape and robbery. He confessed to the offense, and his attorney filed a motion requesting a hearing on the issue of jurisdiction because he assumed that the District of Columbia juvenile court would consider waiving jurisdiction to criminal court. The judge did not rule on the motion for a hearing, but waived jurisdiction after making a "full investigation," without describing the investigation or the grounds for the waiver. Kent was found guilty in criminal court and sentenced to 30 to 90 years in prison. Appeals by Kent's attorney were rejected by the Appellate courts. The U.S. Supreme Court ruled that the waiver without a hearing was invalid, and that Kent's attorney should have had access to all records involved in the waiver, along with a written statement of the reasons for the waiver. *Kent* is significant because it was the first Supreme Court case to modify the long-standing belief that juveniles did not require the same due process protections as adults, because the intent of the juvenile court was treatment, not punishment. The majority statement of the justices noted that juveniles may receive the "worst of both worlds"—"neither the protection accorded to adults nor the solicitous care and regenerative treatment postulated for children" (383 U.S. 541, 86 S.Ct. 1045 [1966]).

In re Gault

Gerald Gault, age 15, was on probation for a minor property offense when he and a friend made what was described as obscene comments in a telephone call to a neighbor woman. Gerald was picked up by police and held in a detention facility until his parents were notified the next day. Gerald was not represented by counsel at his court hearing. The victim was not present and no evidence was presented regarding the charge, but Gerald was adjudicated delinquent and committed to a training school. (The maximum sentence for an adult making an obscene phone call would have been a $50 fine or 2 months in jail.) An attorney obtained later by the Gaults filed a writ of habeas corpus that was rejected by the Arizona Supreme Court and the Appellate Court, but was eventually heard by the U.S. Supreme Court. The Court found that Gerald's constitutional due process rights had been violated; it ruled that in hearings that could result in commitment to an institution, juveniles have the right to notice and counsel, to question witnesses, and to protection against self-incrimination (387 U.S. 1, S.Ct. 1428 [1967]).

In re Winship

Samuel Winship, age 12, was accused of stealing money from a woman's purse in a store. A store employee stated that Samuel was seen running from the store just before the money was reported missing, but others in the store disputed that account, noting that the employee was not in a position to see the money actually being taken. At the juvenile court hearing, the judge agreed with Winship's attorney that there was some "reasonable doubt" of Samuel's guilt, but New York juvenile courts (like those in most states) operated under the civil law standard of "preponderance of evidence." Winship was adjudicated delinquent and committed to a New York training school. Winship's attorney appealed the case on the issue of the standard of evidence required in juvenile court. The U.S. Supreme Court ruled that the standard of evidence for adjudication of delinquency should be "proof beyond reasonable doubt" (387 U.S. 358, 90 S.Ct. 1068 [1970]).

McKeiver v. Pennsylvania

Joseph McKeiver, age 16, was charged with robbery and larceny when he and a large group of other juveniles took 25 cents from three youths. At the hearing, the judge denied his attorney's request for a jury trial, and McKeiver was adjudicated and placed on probation. McKeiver's attorney appealed the case to the state Supreme Court, which affirmed the lower court. The case was then appealed to the U.S. Supreme Court, which upheld the lower court rulings. The Court argued that juries would not enhance the accuracy of the adjudication process, and could adversely affect the informal atmosphere of the nonadversarial juvenile court hearing process (403 U.S. 528, 91 S.Ct. 1976 [1971]). The significance of *McKeiver* is that it is the only one of these first five cases in which the U.S. Supreme Court did *not* rule that juveniles must receive all the same due process rights as adults in criminal court.

Breed v. Jones

Gary Jones, age 17, was charged with armed robbery and appeared in Los Angeles juvenile court, where he was adjudicated delinquent. At the disposition hearing, the judge waived jurisdiction and transferred the case to criminal court. Jones's attorney then filed a writ of habeas corpus, arguing that the waiver to criminal court after adjudication in juvenile court violated the double jeopardy clause of the Fifth Amendment. The court denied the petition on the basis that juvenile adjudication is not a "trial." The case was appealed to the U.S. Supreme Court where the Justices ruled that adjudication is equivalent to a trial, because a juvenile is found to have violated a criminal statute. Jones's double jeopardy rights had therefore been violated, and the Court ruled that double jeopardy applies at the adjudication hearing as soon as any evidence is presented. A juvenile court waiver hearing must therefore take place before or in place of an adjudication hearing (421 U.S. 519, 95 S.Ct. 1779 [1975]).

These U.S. Supreme Court cases profoundly affected the legal process and procedures in juvenile courts throughout the United States. Additional procedures and legal forms were instituted, from the county or state's attorney prosecuting the cases down to the intake probation officer working with juveniles referred from police departments for delinquent behavior. The overall purposes of the juvenile court remained the same, but court personnel were now required to inform the youth and their parents of due process rights. State legislation quickly followed to amend juvenile court procedures in accordance with the Supreme Court rulings.

⊠ Juvenile Versus Criminal Court: Legal and Procedural Distinctions

Distinctions between juvenile and adult offenders are based on English common law, which formed the basis for a separate juvenile justice system. At the core of this distinction is the question of what age and under what circumstances children are capable of forming *criminal intent*. More than 1,000 murders are committed by juveniles every year. Many citizens and policy makers react to what is perceived as a growing trend toward more juvenile violence with demands to punish violent juvenile offenders like adult criminals. Under law, however, two elements are necessary in order to find a person guilty of a crime. Most attention is focused on the first element, the criminal act itself. The second element, criminal intent, is equally important, though often overlooked. In weighing evidence against a suspect, a court must determine that there is sufficient evidence for both a criminal act and criminal intent, known as *mens rea* or "guilty mind." The critical question is: At what age is a child capable of understanding the differences between right and wrong and of comprehending the consequences of a criminal act before it occurs? The answer to the first question appears clear to most persons, who would argue that even very young children know that killing a person is wrong. It is less clear whether children charged with violent crimes have carefully weighed the consequences of their actions, however, or whether they have formed criminal intent comparable to that of an adult. Laws and policies that place limitations on youths' drinking, driving, and marrying and entering into other contracts illustrate our belief that they are not equally prepared as adults to engage responsibly in these activities. Based on the belief that youth do not have equal capacity for careful thinking and awareness of the consequences of their behavior, young people are treated differently and allowed limited responsibility under the law for most other critical decisions while they are minors. Judicial experts generally agree that legal sanctions for criminal behavior should be consistent with laws limiting juveniles' legal rights in other areas. Distinctions between legal procedures for juveniles and adults therefore stem from the differences in juveniles' maturity, limited knowledge of the law and its consequences, limited legal responsibility, and the belief that youth should be processed separately from adults throughout the judicial system.

Distinctions Between Juvenile and Criminal Procedures

Juvenile justice grew out of the criminal justice system, so they share common ground. The main features that have distinguished juvenile court proceedings from criminal court proceedings may be summarized as follows:

- *Absence of legal guilt.* Because juveniles are generally less mature and often unaware of the consequences of their actions, they are not held legally responsible for their actions to the same extent as adults. Legally, juveniles are not found guilty of crimes, but are "found to be delinquent." Juvenile status, generally being under 18 years of age, is a defense against criminal responsibility, much like the insanity defense. Exceptions are made in cases of more mature juveniles who have committed serious offenses. The juvenile court may then waive jurisdiction and transfer the case to criminal court.

- *Treatment rather than punishment.* The stated purpose of the juvenile court is treatment of the child and community protection, not punishment as for adult felony offenders in criminal court.

- *Informal, private court proceedings.* Juvenile court hearings are more informal and in many states they are not open to the public, with usually only the child, parents, attorneys, and probation officer present. Hearings have often been held in the judge's chamber. The majority of hearings are informal, noncontested, nonadversarial proceedings that take less than 10 minutes. This practice is rooted in the original child-saving philosophy that the purpose of the court was for treatment, not punishment. Proceedings for more serious juvenile offenders are now often open to the public.

- *Separateness from adult offenders.* Juvenile offenders are kept separate from adult offenders at every stage of the juvenile process, from arrest (or "taking into custody") to detention; pretrial and court proceedings; to probation supervision and institutional corrections. All juvenile records are also maintained separately from adult criminal records, including in computerized information systems.

- *Focus on a juvenile's background and social history.* A juvenile's background and the need for and amenability to treatment are considered of equal importance with the offense committed when making decisions on handling each case. This is consistent with the stated purpose of treatment rather than punishment. The assumption that court officers can assess and treat juveniles' needs is open to question. Basing the length of "treatment" on the child's needs as well as the offense has come under criticism. Children committing relatively minor crimes but with "greater needs for treatment" are often supervised for longer periods of time than more serious offenders who have been determined to be less "in need of treatment."

- *Shorter terms of supervision and incarceration.* The terms of probation supervision, confinement in a detention center, or commitment to a correctional facility are usually shorter in duration than for adult offenders—generally not much longer than 1 to 2 years, on average. In recent years many states have revised their juvenile statutes, extending jurisdiction and length of incarceration over violent juvenile offenders.

- *Distinctive terminology.* Consistent with the need to treat juveniles differently from adults because of their immaturity and limited legal accountability, different terms are used when handling juveniles at each stage of the process. Juveniles are "taken into custody," not arrested; transported to a detention center, not booked into jail; a petition for delinquency is filed with the court, not a criminal indictment; the result is an adjudication of delinquency rather than conviction of a felony or misdemeanor crime.

Purpose Clauses for Juvenile Courts

The distinctions noted above indicate that the primary purpose of the original juvenile courts was prevention and treatment, more than punishment. There is variation among states in how they describe the purposes of the juvenile court, and many states' juvenile codes have been amended in recent years. The purpose clause of several states is based on the Standard Juvenile Court Act that was originally issued in 1925. The 1959 revision used by some states declares that a child who comes within the jurisdiction of the juvenile court shall receive care, guidance, and control appropriate for the child's welfare; and when removed from parental custody the court shall provide care equivalent to what the parents should have provided (Snyder & Sickmund, 2006, p. 98). Other states have drawn from the *Legislative Guide for Drafting Family and Juvenile Court Acts.* This publication from the late 1960s lists four purposes for the juvenile court: (1) to provide for the care, protection, and wholesome mental and physical development of children involved with the juvenile court; (2) to remove from children committing delinquent acts the consequences of criminal behavior and offer a program of supervision, care, and rehabilitation; (3) to remove a child from the home only when necessary for his or her welfare or in the interests of public safety; and (4) to ensure their constitutional and other legal rights (Snyder & Sickmund, 2006, p. 99). The most common purpose clauses among states today have components of Balanced and Restorative Justice that give equal attention to three concerns: (1) public safety, (2) individual accountability to victims and the community, and (3) the development of skills to help offenders live law-abiding and productive lives.

In summary, jurisdictions vary in the extent of their distinctions between juvenile and criminal justice. Some of the distinctions are less visible today as states modify the purpose clauses of their juvenile laws, and place more emphasis on public safety and individual accountability that are common in criminal codes applicable to adult offenders. As many of the traditional distinctions between juvenile and adult laws have begun to fade, there has been considerable discussion recently about the possibility of merging the juvenile and criminal justice systems. These changes are based upon beliefs and assumptions about juvenile crime, its causes, and whether juvenile offenders are amenable to treatment or should be held accountable and punished similar to adult offenders. Laws and policy decisions should ideally be based upon an understanding of delinquency and what research findings have indicated as the most effective sanctions and responses for preventing juvenile crime and changing young offenders.

⊠ Federal and State Legislative Changes

During the first 100 years of history and development, juvenile justice practices were a function of state and local jurisdictions. Local city and county juvenile courts processed juvenile cases, and referred youth to probation supervision or to public or private residential programs. The federal government's role in juvenile justice was virtually nonexistent for the first 60 years of development. Concurrent with U.S. Supreme Court decisions requiring certain due process rights for juveniles in court, a special Presidential Commission and the American Bar Association in separate actions were also critically examining juvenile delinquency and the juvenile justice process. The President's Commission on Law Enforcement and Administration of Justice (1967b) recommended narrowing the range of offenses going before the juvenile court; and groups such as the American Bar Association–Institute of Judicial Administration (1982) called for an end to adjudicating and incarcerating status offenders in juvenile institutions. The U.S. Congress in the Juvenile Delinquency Prevention and Control Act of 1968 recommended that children charged with noncriminal or status offenses be removed from formal adjudication and commitment to detention centers and juvenile institutions. Juvenile lockups and training schools housed many youths whose only "crime" was disobeying their parents, running away, or school truancy. Advocates of such practices argued that involvement in status offenses was the first step toward more serious delinquency and that early intervention might prevent serious delinquency. Opponents noted the unfairness of punishing youths for minor deviant behavior, and voiced concerns about the adverse effects on status offenders being housed with older, hard-core juvenile offenders. Congress passed the Juvenile Justice and Delinquency Prevention Act of 1974 that required as a condition for receiving formula grants the deinstitutionalization of status offenders and non-offenders, as well as the separation of juvenile delinquents from adult offenders. In the 1980 amendments

Table I-1	Core Requirements of the Juvenile Justice and Delinquency Prevention Act of 2002
Year[a]	*Major Requirements of the Juvenile Justice and Delinquency Prevention Act*
1974	The deinstitutionalization of status offenders and non-offenders requirement specifies that juveniles not charged with acts that would be crimes for adults "shall not be placed in secure detention facilities or secure correctional facilities."
1974	The sight and sound separation requirement specifies that "juveniles alleged to be or found to be delinquent and [status offenders and non-offenders] shall not be detained or confined in any institution in which they have contact with adult persons incarcerated because they have been convicted of a crime or are awaiting trial on criminal charges." This means that juvenile and adult inmates cannot see each other and no conversation between them is possible.
1980	The jail and lockup removal requirement states that juveniles shall not be detained or confined in adult jails or lockups. Exceptions: juveniles being tried as a criminal for a felony or who have been convicted as a criminal felon; 6-hour grace period to temporarily hold juveniles until other arrangements can be made; jails in rural areas may hold delinquents up to 24 hours.
1992	The disproportionate confinement of minority youth requirement specifies that states determine the existence and extent of the problem in their state and demonstrate efforts to reduce it where it exists.
1996	Regulations modify the Act's requirements: (1) In nonresidential areas in jails, brief, accidental contact is not a reportable violation; (2) permit time-phased use of nonresidential areas for both juveniles and adults in collocated facilities; (3) expand the 6-hour grace period to include 6 hours both before and after court appearances; (4) allow adjudicated delinquents to be transferred to adult institutions once they have reached the state's age of full criminal responsibility, if such transfer is expressly authorized by state law.

Source: Adapted from Snyder & Sickmund, 2006, p. 97.

[a]The years the requirement was first included in legislation.

to the 1974 Act, Congress added a requirement that juveniles be removed from adult jail and detention facilities. The reforms that began in the 1960s continued into the 1970s as community-based programs, diversion, and deinstitutionalization became the highlights of juvenile justice policy changes (Snyder & Sickmund, 2006). The major provisions of the Juvenile Justice and Delinquency Prevention Act are summarized in Table I-1.

▨ Changes and Trends in Juvenile Justice

The history and development of the juvenile court and a separate system of justice for juveniles has presented a picture of a benevolent, caring system that has promoted the "best interests of the child." Children and youth were separated from adult offenders in a legal process that combined both civil and criminal law. Juvenile court dispositions consisted mainly of a year or less of probation supervision or short-term treatment in "houses of refuge" or "reform schools." The early juvenile court clearly distinguished its goals and purposes as different from the goals of punishment and deterrence for adult offenders. Overall, the juvenile court process was promoted as progressive, humanitarian, and an improvement on the older practice that failed to differentiate offenders by age.

Questioning the Child Savers

The view of the juvenile court as a benevolent, humanitarian development that promoted the "best interests of the child" has not been shared by everyone. Anthony Platt (1977) has portrayed the child-saving movement as simply a part of a larger social movement in the 19th century. The "child savers," according to Platt, were a group of middle- and upper-class Americans who were concerned about the growth of a lower-class population of immigrants and unruly children who were not properly supervised and disciplined by their parents. The child savers' primary concern was to discipline and train these youth to enter the labor force and support the growth of corporate capitalism in America. Others have joined Platt in questioning the benevolent and humanitarian motives of the juvenile court. Pisciotta (1982) noted that there was a significant disparity between the care promised to minors by juvenile court judges and the actual training and care provided for them in houses of refuge, reform schools, and through the system of contract labor. The care provided was often more abusive than parental and the contract labor system was more exploitation than training, leading Pisciotta to conclude that the state was not an effective parent under the doctrine of *parens patriae.* Krisberg (2005), the author of the third reading in this section, noted that the child savers viewed the lower-class urban families as a potentially dangerous class that could threaten order and progress in America. He has questioned the benevolent image of the child-saving practices, noting that lower-class youth were "placed out" with rural families and required to do long hours of hard labor. Black youth were leased out to railroad, mining, and manufacturing companies with little regard for their age, similar to the convict lease system common in adult prison programs. The exploitation of labor and inhumane living conditions raises questions about the benevolent and humanitarian goals of the early juvenile court.

Cycles of Juvenile Justice

Every generation has had the opinion that many if not most young people are behaving badly, and are much worse than the previous generation (Hamparian, Schuster, Dinitz, & Conrad, 1978). Bernard (1992) noted that every generation for the past 200 years or more has held the belief that the current cohort of juvenile delinquents is the worst ever and commits more crime than other groups. Bernard referred to a "cycle of juvenile justice" as tougher laws were passed in response to the "juvenile crime wave" and the mistaken assumption that juveniles commit more crime because the laws are too lenient. The assumption that lenient juvenile justice policies encourage juveniles to "laugh at" the system and commit more crimes leads the public and lawmakers to demand more punitive policies, less leniency, and harsher punishments for juveniles. DiIulio perpetuated this belief that juvenile crime was getting worse when he predicted a juvenile crime wave based on projections of the Philadelphia Birth Cohort Study and the growth of the juvenile population (Bennett, DiIulio, & Walters, 1996). Assuming that the Philadelphia cohort from the 1960s was applicable to the nation in the 1990s, DiIulio and his associates predicted that a large group of what he called juvenile "super-predators" would dramatically drive up the violent crime rate. Juvenile crime experts including Snyder and Sickmund (1999) and Howell (2003) have noted the methodological and statistical errors that incorrectly led to the super-predator myth. In short, it is a mistake to use aggregate or group data to predict individual behavior and trends, and it is a mistake to assume that crime rates from one decade will remain constant through following decades. Juvenile violence in fact has been decreasing each year since the peak year of 1994 (Snyder & Sickmund, 2006). Despite the annual decrease in juvenile crime over the years, perceptions of a juvenile "crime wave" and lenient laws prompted a number of changes away from the original juvenile justice philosophy of treatment toward more severe sanctions and a punitive philosophy.

Legislative Changes and "Getting Tough"

Following the federal statutory guidelines and the U.S. Supreme Court decisions that occurred in the 1960s and 1970s, the pendulum began to swing toward law and order in the 1980s. In response to public perceptions that serious juvenile crime was increasing and that the system was too lenient with offenders, many state legislators responded by passing more punitive laws. Some laws removed juvenile offenders charged with violent crimes from the juvenile system; other laws required the juvenile justice system to be more like the criminal justice system, and to treat more serious juvenile offenders as criminals but in the juvenile court. The result has been to exclude offenders charged with certain offenses from juvenile court jurisdiction, or to have them face mandatory or automatic waiver to criminal court. In some states, concurrent jurisdiction provisions give prosecutors the discretion to file certain juvenile cases directly in criminal court rather than in juvenile court (Snyder & Sickmund, 2006).

The trend continued through the 1990s as state legislatures continued to pass more punitive laws in an effort to deal more harshly with juvenile crime. Five areas of change have emerged as states passed laws to crack down on juvenile crime. Most of the statutory changes involved expanding eligibility for criminal court processing, sentencing juvenile offenders to adult correctional supervision, and reducing confidentiality protections that have been customary for juvenile offenders. Between 1992 and 1997, all but three states changed laws in one or more of the following areas:

- Transfer provisions: Laws in 45 states made it easier to transfer juvenile offenders from the juvenile to the criminal justice system.
- Sentencing authority: Laws in 31 states gave criminal and juvenile courts expanded sentencing options.
- Confidentiality: Laws in 47 states modified or removed traditional juvenile court confidentiality provisions by making records and proceedings more open.
- Victims' rights: Laws in 22 states increased the role of victims of juvenile crime in the juvenile justice process.
- Correctional programming: As a result of new transfer and sentencing laws, adult and juvenile correctional administrators developed new programs (Snyder & Sickmund, 2006, pp. 96–97).

The changes in juvenile justice laws reflect the belief that leniency in juvenile court processing accounted for what many perceived to be dramatic increases in juvenile crime. The tougher laws are based on the assumption that juveniles who commit "adult-like" crimes are equally culpable as adult offenders. Lawmakers pushing for "get-tough" legislation used phrases such as "adult crime, adult time" to win approval for statutory changes to existing juvenile laws. Juveniles who commit crimes that would be punished as felony convictions if committed by adults, the belief was, should be prosecuted and punished like adult offenders. The tougher laws also were intended to send the message to serious or chronic juvenile offenders that they will be held more accountable. The movement away from rehabilitation and treatment and toward retribution and "just deserts" has occurred simultaneously in both the criminal and the juvenile justice systems. Garland (2001) has documented political and social changes over the past 30 years that have led to demands for more formal social controls of juvenile and adult offenders. The changes that led to more formal controls have been the rising crime rates, challenges to the welfare system, a growing concern for victims, a more diversified population, and a perceived inability of families and other social institutions to control their deviant members. Until the 1980s, criminal justice practitioners generally recognized what criminologists had identified as the causes of deviant behavior, including inequities in society and the social influences on the offender. Under the practice of indeterminate sentencing, the courts took into account the individual and social problems that likely influenced the offender's criminal behavior, and individualized sentences were based on the crime as well as the offender's treatment needs. That practice has given way to determinate sentencing and the belief that individuals of all ages choose to commit crimes and need to be held accountable for their actions. Despite the movement to "get tough" with juvenile offenders, there is evidence that the public has not entirely given up on the possibility of saving children. The authors of our last reading (Moon, Sundt, Cullen, & Wright, 2000) show that there is still public support for juvenile rehabilitation.

Juvenile justice experts have differing opinions on the results and consequences of the statutory changes in juvenile justice. Research evidence is mixed as to whether tougher laws are likely to have much effect on reducing juvenile crime. The laws have clearly resulted in more juvenile offenders being waived to criminal court prosecution and sentencing and more juvenile offenders serving time in adult correctional facilities. What is not clear is whether the tougher laws have any significant deterrent effect on juvenile offenders. We will discuss more of the changes and reforms in the juvenile court and changes in correctional processing in later sections of the book.

The End of the Death Penalty for Juveniles

The death penalty for juveniles convicted of murder has been a controversial issue. The United States has until recently been one of the few nations in the world, and the only democratic, industrialized nation, to allow the execution of juveniles convicted of murder (Cothern, 2000; Streib, 2005). From 1973 through 2004, a total of 228 juvenile death sentences were imposed; 22 (14%) resulted in execution and 134 (86%) were reversed or commuted (Streib, 2005). The majority of those executions (13, or 59%) occurred in Texas. Juvenile death sentences have accounted for less than 3% of the nearly 7,000 total U.S. death sentences since 1973, and two thirds of those were imposed on 17-year-olds, while about one third were imposed on 15- and 16-year-old juveniles (Cothern, 2000). As of the end of the year 2005, a total of 20 states authorized the execution of juveniles (under 18 years): 9 states specified the minimum age at 16 or less, 5 states specified the minimum age at 17, and 6 states did not specify a minimum age (Snell, 2006). The number of states that allow the death penalty for juveniles under 18 has been declining for years, and most states with statutes authorizing the juvenile death penalty have neither imposed nor carried out the death sentence on a person convicted of murder as a juvenile (Death Penalty Information Center, 2007).

On March 1, 2005, the United States Supreme Court ruled in *Roper v. Simmons* (U.S. 125 S.Ct. 1183) that imposition of the death penalty on persons who were under age 18 at the time of their crimes was cruel and unusual punishment and therefore a violation of the Eighth and Fourteenth Amendments. The *Roper* decision is the third and final ruling on juveniles and the death penalty in the past 20 years. In 1988 the U.S. Supreme Court in *Thompson v. Oklahoma* (487 U.S. 815) held that execution of juvenile offenders under age 16 violated the Eighth Amendment against cruel and unusual punishment. The next year (1989) the Court held in *Stanford v. Kentucky* (492 U.S. 361) that the execution of juvenile offenders 16 and 17 years of age was *not* unconstitutional. Fifteen more years passed before the Supreme Court in *Roper* put an end to the execution of all juvenile offenders under 18 years of age. In a close 5–4 majority opinion, the Court drew upon an earlier decision in *Atkins v. Virginia* (536 U.S. 304) forbidding execution of the mentally retarded. In *Roper* the Court held that

> capital punishment must be limited to those offenders who commit "a narrow category of the most serious crimes" and whose extreme culpability makes them "the most deserving of execution." (*Atkins v. Virginia,* 536 U.S. at 319; and *Roper v. Simmons,* 125 S.Ct. at 1186)

The decision was based in part on the earlier *Thompson* decision and rested on what the Court recognized as three general differences between juveniles under 18 and adults, and why juvenile offenders cannot be classified among the "worst offenders." First, because juveniles are susceptible to immature and irresponsible behavior it means that "their irresponsible conduct is not as morally reprehensible as that of an adult" (*Roper v. Simmons,* 125 S.Ct. at 1186; *Thompson v. Oklahoma,* 487 U.S. 815 at 835). Second, the Court reasoned that because juveniles still struggle to define their own identity, "it is less supportable to conclude that even a heinous crime committed by a juvenile is evidence of irretrievably depraved character" (125 S.Ct. at 1186). Third, because the Court recognized juveniles' diminished culpability compared with adults over 18, then (similar to the mentally retarded, in *Atkins*) "neither of the two penological justifications for the death penalty—retribution and deterrence of capital crimes by prospective offenders . . . provides adequate justification for imposing that penalty on juveniles" (125 S.Ct. at 1186). In ruling against the death penalty for juvenile murderers, the Justices acknowledged that they could not deny or overlook the brutal crimes that too many juvenile offenders have committed. While the State may no longer execute those juveniles under 18 for murder, the Court added a reminder that "the State can exact forfeiture of some of the most basic liberties" (125 S.Ct. at 1197); that is, a life sentence in prison. The *Roper* decision will have an impact on 20 states, 9 of which had specified the minimum age for the death penalty at 16, 5 states at 17 years, and 6 states with no minimum age established. Of the 38 states that authorize capital punishment, 18 of the states and the federal judicial system had already specified 18 as the minimum age for execution (Snell, 2006).

The close 5–4 decision of the Supreme Court was not without controversy. In the majority opinion, Justice Kennedy noted the trend in the United States of moving consistently away from executing juveniles, and he noted the overwhelming international sentiment against executing persons under 18. In a dissenting opinion, Justice Sandra Day O'Connor protested that the majority had not demonstrated that there existed a sufficient national consensus against executing juveniles to conclude that the practice violated the Eighth Amendment, and she argued that the sentence should be available for imposing the death sentence on juveniles who commit the most heinous murders. In an opinion of the other three dissenters, Justice Scalia (who has expressed opposition to allowing international laws and legal decisions to influence

American case law) objected to the majority's reliance on national consensus and trends in other states, arguing that is more within legislative policymaking. Justice Scalia also argued that the majority opinion was based on a selective, incomplete reading of social scientists' conclusions regarding juveniles and the death penalty.

The substitute for the death penalty that the majority opinion suggested for juveniles who murder is also not without question and controversy. Life in prison without parole (LWOP) has been raised as an issue now that thousands of juveniles have been sentenced to life in prison, and the American Civil Liberties Union (ACLU) has recommended that the maximum prison sentence for juveniles should be 25 years (Benekos & Merlo, 2005). The practice of LWOP for juveniles in the United States also constitutes a violation of Article 37(a) of the United Nations Convention on the Rights of the Child, which holds that

> no child shall be subjected to torture or other cruel, inhuman or degrading treatment or punishment. Neither capital punishment nor life imprisonment without possibility of release shall be imposed for offences committed by persons below eighteen years of age. (Office of the High Commissioner for Human Rights, 1989)

The meaning of "cruel and unusual" has changed considerably over the past years, and not too long ago (1989) the U.S. Supreme Court in *Stanford v. Kentucky* held that executing juveniles did not violate this standard. Considering the "evolving standards of decency," Benekos and Merlo (2005) suggest that life imprisonment for juveniles may well be the next issue to be confronted by the Court.

SUMMARY

The history and development of the juvenile court and justice process are highlighted by a number of points:

- Laws and legal procedures relating to juvenile offenders have a long history, dating back thousands of years.
- American juvenile justice was based on English common law that dates back to the 11th and 12th centuries.
- The legal doctrines of *parens patriae* and *in loco parentis* enable the State to take custody of a child and to exercise parental authority, and to provide guidance, protection, and needed services to needy children.
- Before the development of the juvenile justice system in America, parents were expected to control and discipline their children; juveniles who committed crimes were treated the same as adults.
- Houses of refuge were developed in New York, Boston, and Philadelphia in the 1800s, and were the first step toward development of reform schools.
- The "child-saving movement" was begun by a group of concerned child reform advocates who pushed for State intervention to save at-risk children through shelter care and educational programs.
- The first juvenile court was established in Chicago (Cook County), Illinois, in 1899, to provide for separate trials for juveniles.

- Juvenile court procedures went unchallenged for 60 years, until some of the long-standing practices of the juvenile court were overturned in a number of U.S. Supreme Court cases beginning in the 1960s.
- Juvenile justice procedures have traditionally been distinguished from criminal justice procedures for adults, by different terms and emphases.
- The Juvenile Delinquency Prevention and Control Act of 1968 recommended that children charged with noncriminal (status) offenses be handled outside the court system.
- State and federal legislation has altered many of the original treatment goals, instituted more punitive measures, and excluded many serious or chronic youthful offenders from juvenile jurisdiction.
- The U.S. Supreme Court in *Roper v. Simmons* (125 S.Ct. 1183 [2005]) held that the death penalty for juveniles was unconstitutional.

KEY TERMS

Breed v. Jones

"Child savers"

Criminal intent/*mens rea*

Houses of refuge

In loco parentis

In re Gault

In re Winship

Juvenile Justice & Delinquency Prevention Act

Kent v. United States

McKeiver v. Pennsylvania

Parens patriae

Purpose clauses

Reform schools

Roper v. Simmons

Stanford v. Kentucky

Thompson v. Oklahoma

DISCUSSION QUESTIONS

1. Based on your understanding of the earliest laws relating to juvenile offenders (Code of Hammurabi, Roman civil and canon law, Jewish and Moslem laws), discuss whether they are significantly different from today's or are quite similar.

2. Do you believe the power and authority of a state under the doctrines of *parens patriae* and *in loco parentis* are too severe or are appropriate under most circumstances?

3. Give an example of how some laws and policies governing youthful offenders are, in the opinion of some persons, too invasive and punitive. Offer support for how the laws and policies are for the best interests of children and youth.

4. Do any of the provisions of the Juvenile Justice and Delinquency Prevention Act reflect the movement to "get tough" on juvenile offenders? What provisions seem to emphasize some of the original goals of juvenile justice?

5. Present an argument for the following positions: Federal and state legislative changes to juvenile justice are (1) based on the latest research findings on deterrence and effective correctional approaches, or (2) are based more on perceptions of increases in juvenile crime and public and political demands for more punitive sanctions.

6. Summarize arguments for and against the death penalty for juveniles. Based on readings in this text and supporting documents, what do you believe are the strongest arguments for each position?

WEB RESOURCES

The following Web sites provide information and discussion on the history and development of the juvenile justice system:

American Bar Association Juvenile Justice Center, on the juvenile death penalty: http://www.abanet.org/crimjust/juvjus/EvolvingStandards.pdf

Juvenile Offenders and Victims: 2006 National Report: http://ojjdp.ncjrs.gov/ojstatbb/nr2006/downloads/NR2006.pdf

Youth Law Center, on juvenile justice: http://www.buildingblocksforyouth.org/issues/

Death Penalty Information Center: http://www.deathpenaltyinfo.org/

Bureau of Justice Statistics, on capital punishment: http://www.ojp.usdoj.gov/bjs/pub/pdf/cp05.pdf

Juvenile Death Penalty Facts and Figures: http://www.abanet.org/crimjust/juvjus/dparticles/factsheetfactsfigures.pdf

Convention on the Rights of the Child (United Nations): http://www.unhchr.ch/html/menu3/b/k2crc.htm

How to Read a Research Article

As you travel through your criminal justice/criminology studies, you will soon learn that some of the best known and/or emerging explanations of crime and criminal behavior come from research articles in academic journals. This book has research articles throughout the book, but you may be asking yourself, "How do I read a research article?" It is my hope to answer this question with a quick summary of the key elements of any research article, followed by the questions you should be answering as you read through the assigned sections.

Every research article published in a social science journal will have the following elements: (1) introduction, (2) literature review, (3) methodology, (4) results, and (5) discussion/conclusion.

In the introduction, you will find an overview of the purpose of the research. Within the introduction, you will also find the hypothesis or hypotheses. A hypothesis is most easily defined as an educated statement or guess. In most hypotheses, you will find that the format usually followed is: If X, Y will occur. For example, a simple hypothesis may be: "If the price of gas increases, more people will ride bikes." This is a testable statement that the researcher wants to address in his or her study. Usually, authors will state the hypothesis directly, but not always. Therefore, you must be aware of what the author is actually testing in the research project. If you are unable to find the hypothesis, ask yourself what is being tested and/or manipulated, and what are the expected results?

The next section of the research article is the literature review. At times the literature review will be separated from the text in its own section, and at other times it will be found within the introduction. In any case, the literature review is an examination of what other researchers have already produced in terms of the research question or hypothesis. For example, returning to my hypothesis on the relationship between gas prices and bike riding, we may find that five researchers have previously conducted studies on the increase of gas prices. In the literature review, I will discuss their findings, and then discuss what my study will add to the existing research. The literature review may also be used as a platform of support for my hypothesis. For example, one researcher may have already determined that an increase in gas causes more people to roller skate to work. I can use this study as evidence to support my hypothesis that increased gas prices will lead to more bike riding.

The methods used in the research design are found in the next section of the research article. In the methodology section you will find the following: who/what was studied, how many subjects were studied, the research tool (e.g., interview, survey, observation . . .), how long the subjects were studied, and how the data that were collected were processed. The methods section is usually very concise, with every step of the research project recorded. This is important because a major goal of the researcher is "reliability," or, if the research is done over again the same way, will the results be the same?

The results section is an analysis of the researcher's findings. If the researcher conducted a quantitative study (using numbers or statistics to explain the research), you will find statistical tables and analyses that explain whether or not the researcher's hypothesis is supported.

If the researcher conducted a qualitative study (nonnumerical research for the purpose of theory construction), the results will usually be displayed as a theoretical analysis or interpretation of the research question.

Finally, the research article will conclude with a discussion and summary of the study. In the discussion, you will find that the hypothesis is usually restated, and perhaps a small discussion of why this is the hypothesis. You will also find a brief overview of the methodology and results. Finally, the discussion section will end with a discussion of the implications of the research, and what future research is still needed.

Now that you know the key elements of a research article, let us examine a sample article from your text.

Saving the Children: The Promise and Practice of Parens Patriae, 1838–1998

Alexander W. Pisciotta

Crime & Delinquency, Vol. 28, pp. 410–425, 1982

1. What is the thesis or main idea from this article?

◆ The thesis or main idea is found at the end of the introduction of this article. Pisciotta directly states on page 412, ". . . it is the purpose of this study to assess the validity of the assumptions underlying the doctrine of *parens patriae* as it was applied before the founding of the juvenile court in 1899."

2. What is the hypothesis?

◆ The hypothesis is also found in the introduction of this article. Following the stated purpose of the research, Pisciotta concludes the introduction with his research statement regarding *parens patriae,* which is stated as: "Justices across the country, throughout the 19th century, invoked *parens patriae* on premises which were, at best, questionable" (p. 413). In other words, Pisciotta is interested in the validity of the rehabilitation process of wayward juveniles.

3. Is there any prior literature related to the hypothesis?

◆ As you may have noticed, this article does not have a separate section for a literature review. However, you will see that Pisciotta devotes a section related to the literature in the introduction. Here, Pisciotta spends a considerable amount of time discussing court rulings based on the rehabilitative principles delineated in *Ex parte Crouse*. This is to lead the reader into understanding the effect of the precedent established in *Ex Parte Crouse* and how, in support of Pisciotta's hypothesis, the invoking of *parens patriae* was based on an unfounded premise due to the lack of internal research in juvenile institutions.

4. What methods are used to support the hypothesis?

◆ Pisciotta's methodology is known as a historical analysis. In other words, rather than conducting his own experiment, Pisciotta is using evidence from history to support his hypothesis regarding the questionability of invoking *parens patriae* in the 19th century. When conducting a historical analysis, most researchers use archival material from books, newspapers, journals, and so on. Pisciotta makes mention that he is using the records of a number of juvenile institutions, as well as investigative reports.

5. Is this a qualitative study or quantitative study?

   ◆ To determine whether or not a study is qualitative or quantitative, you must look at the results. Is Pisciotta using numbers to support his hypothesis (quantitative) or is he developing a nonnumerical theoretical argument (qualitative)? Because Pisciotta does not utilize statistics to support his overall conclusion in this study, we can safely conclude that this is a qualitative study.

6. What are the results and how does the author present the results?

   ◆ Because this is a qualitative study, as we earlier determined, Pisciotta offers the results as a discussion of his findings from the historical analysis. The results may be found in the conclusion of this article. Here Pisciotta states that "the available investigations and records of the nineteenth century juvenile institutions offer compelling evidence that the state was not a benevolent parent. In short, there was significant disparity between the promise and practice of *parens patriae*" (p. 425).

7. Do you believe that the author/s provided a persuasive argument? Why or why not?

   ◆ This answer is ultimately up to the reader, but looking at this article, I believe that it is safe to assume that the readers will agree that Pisciotta offered a persuasive argument. Let us return to his major premise: Justices throughout the country, throughout the 19th century, invoked *parens patriae* on premises that were, at best, questionable. Pisciotta supports this proposition with a historical analysis of investigative reports that shed light on the abuse, slavery, religious conflict, and violence that existed within the juvenile institutions. This evidence compels the reader to agree with Pisciotta that there was a disparity between the promise of a benevolent parent invoking a solid system of rehabilitation, and the actual practice of the juvenile institutions.

8. Who is the intended audience of this article?

   ◆ A final question that will be useful for the reader deals with the intended audience. As you read the article, ask yourself, to whom is the author wanting to speak? After you read this article, you will see that Pisciotta is writing for not only students, but also professors, criminologists, historians, and/or criminal justice personnel. The target audience may most easily be identified if you ask yourself, "Who will benefit from reading this article?"

9. What does the article add to your knowledge of the subject?

   ◆ This answer is ultimately up to the reader, so ask yourself, "What do I know now that I did not know before reading this article?" You may find yourself answering that you did not know about the abuse that took place within the juvenile institutions. Perhaps you did not know this history of *parens patriae* and how invoking *parens patriae* not only was based on questionable premises, but also affected the juvenile courts of the 20th century. All in all, as you finish reading the article, you should be able to add something new to your knowledge of the subject. This is the beauty of research.

10. What are the implications for criminal justice policy that can be derived from this article?

◆ Pisciotta offers implications for criminal justice policy at the end of this article. In the concluding paragraph he states: "If there is any practical lesson to be learned from evaluating the historical record of *parens patriae,* it is, perhaps, that contemporary child savers would be well advised to assess objectively, rather than assume, the 'benevolent' effects of their rehabilitative efforts" (p. 425). In other words, any policy must be thoroughly investigated before assumptions about its validity may be made.

Now that we have gone through the elements of a research article, it is your turn to continue through your text, reading the various articles and answering the same questions. You may find that some articles are easier to follow than others, but do not be dissuaded. Remember that each article will follow the same format: introduction, literature review, methods, results, and discussion. If you have any problems, refer to this introduction for guidance.

READING

Saving the Children

The Promise and Practice of Parens Patriae, 1838–1898

Alexander W. Pisciotta (1982)

⊠ Parens Patriae: The Promise of Salvation

The landmark decision incorporating *parens patriae* into the American legal structure was ruled upon by the supreme court justices of the state of Pennsylvania in 1838. In this case, the Pennsylvania court was presented with an appeal on a writ of habeas corpus submitted by the father of one of the inmates immured in the Philadelphia House of Refuge—Mary Ann Crouse. Mr. Crouse maintained that his daughter (who had been committed by his wife, without his knowledge, as "incorrigible") was illegally detained because she had not been granted the benefit of a trial on account of her age. Unfortunately for Mary Ann and her father, the justices of the Pennsylvania court rejected this interpretation of the law and rendered a unanimous decision which concluded that the Bill of Rights (in this case the sixth and ninth sections) did not apply to minors. The justices based their opinion on the doctrine of parens patriae, which, heretofore, had been an English jurisprudential innovation. "May not the natural parents, when unequal to the task of education, or unworthy of it," asked the judges, "be superseded by the *parens patriae* or common guardian of the community?"[1]

The justices' *per curiam* opinion clearly indicates that they based their ruling on the assumption that the Philadelphia House of Refuge had a beneficial influence on its charges: "The House of Refuge is not a prison, but a school where reformation and not punishment is the end." The justices also clearly specified their reasons for assuming that the Philadelphia institution was a "school" and not a prison: "The object of charity is reformation, by training . . . inmates to industry; by imbuing their minds with the principles of morality and religion; by furnishing them with means to earn a living; and, above all, by separating them from the corrupting influence of improper associates."[2]

Although parens patriae was not directly employed as a rationale for the founding of houses of refuge—four were already in operation by 1838—the administrators of juvenile reformatories across the country were eager to proclaim, after 1838, that their institutions were organized and operated upon the rehabilitative principles delineated in *Ex parte Crouse*. "The language employed by the Supreme Court of Pennsylvania," declared the managers of the New York House of Refuge in 1862, "expresses the idea which the managers desire to bring to the public, in regard to the character and object of the House of Refuge of this City."[3] The keepers of the

Source: *Crime & Delinquency, 28*(3), 410–425, July 1982. Downloaded from http://cad.sagepub.com at SAGE Publications on November 19, 2007.

Baltimore House of Refuge echoed the optimism of their New York counterparts when they concluded that they had "done good work for man, and for the city and commonwealth—for the cause of humanity and God."[4]

Based upon assurances received from the keepers of juvenile institutions that they were, indeed, providing education, religious instruction, parental discipline, and training for future employment, magistrates across the country did not, for the rest of the century, hesitate to follow the precedent established in *Ex parte Crouse* and reject writs of habeas corpus which challenged the powers afforded to the state under parens patriae.[5] In a representative case, when the parents of Francis Degnen challenged the right of the managers of the New York House of Refuge to hold their son on a charge of petty theft until he reached the age of majority—an offense for which an adult could be incarcerated for only six months—the justices of the New York State Supreme Court issued a unanimous ruling in favor of the keepers of the refuge which resounded the rationale employed by the Pennsylvania justices thirty-one years earlier:

> Even if there is any ambiguity in the language, it should be construed liberally, for the authority given to the institution is beneficial in its effect on the individual prisoner and on society; in relation to the former, the exercise of the authority amounts to a commutation of ordinary punishment. Strictly speaking, confinement in the House of Refuge does not partake of the degradation or physical suffering to which persons are subject. Its discipline is reformatory, with the view of saving persons, during the susceptibility of tender years, from total profligacy, and restoring them to society in a condition no longer dangerous to it.[6]

There was, however, a significant flaw in the logic of the courts: Their knowledge about the internal operations and "benevolent effect" of reformatories was derived almost solely from information imparted by the managers of these institutions.[7] The justices ruling in the case of Mary Ann Crouse assumed that the Philadelphia House of Refuge had a beneficial effect on the children because the prominent members of the board of managers assured the court that their charges were receiving moral, religious, and educational instruction at the same time that they were learning a trade. Judges in other states blindly followed the precedent established by the Pennsylvania court and repeated its error by not closely investigating the internal affairs of these institutions in order to make certain that they were, indeed, "great charities." The result, as might be expected, was that the opinions rendered by the courts in juvenile cases throughout the century were "distressingly similar."[8]

In response to this oversight by the courts, it is the purpose of this study to assess the validity of the assumptions underlying the doctrine of parens patriae as it was applied before the founding of the juvenile court in 1899. Were inmates in reformatories provided with parental discipline, meaningful labor, religion, and education? Were they "separated from the corrupting influence of improper associates" in institutions that were truly reformatory in nature? An examination of the records of a number of juvenile institutions, as well as investigative reports, strongly suggests that there was a significant disparity between the theory and practice of these reformatories. In short, justices across the country, throughout the nineteenth century, invoked parens patriae on premises which were, at best, questionable.

The State as Disciplinarian: Parental or Abusive?

One of the conditions under which the courts reserved the right to invoke parens patriae and separate children from their natural parents occurred when the parents physically abused their offspring. Judges justified this intervention by promising to place the children under the care of reformatory school administrators who were humane and compassionate; and the managers of the "benevolent institutions" reinforced this belief by describing their methods of discipline in terms that were almost identical to those employed by the keepers of the Western House of Refuge in 1851: "The discipline of the institution is intended to be mild, conciliatory and parental but firm."[9] There was, however, often a considerable difference between the rhetoric of the keepers and the reality confronting the inmates; even for an age in which stern corporal punishment was expected of parents,[10] the techniques of subjection applied in many reformatories could not, by any reasonable standard, be described as "parental" in nature.

An investigation into the internal affairs of the Providence Reform School in 1868, for example, revealed that inmates were punished with rattans and a "cat" with six twelve-inch leather thongs attached to a wooden handle—for recalcitrant children, the wooden handle was used as a whipping surface. Eban J. Bean was one of a number of former employees who described Superintendent James Talcott's method of discipline:

Bean: He was stripped naked in the room, his fingers put on the wall as high as he could reach, and he was licked with what I should call a cat o'nine tails. . . . He was licked 'til the blood ran down his back.

Alderman: How long did the punishment last?

Bean: I should say about five or ten minutes. He boxed the boy first, he boxed his face, and slapped his face. He bloodied the floor considerably. He first talked, and then the boy stripped for him.[11]

The testimony of the inmates supported the allegations of cruelty raised by the former employees. William DeMars provided a graphic description of one of his encounters with the institution's official disciplinarian, Mr. Rockwell:

DeMars: Mr. Rockwell has knocked me around and punched me in the guts, knocked me down and knocked me out of breath; he struck me in the head and knocked me senseless, so that I lay on the ground before I could get my breath; I was senseless.

Alderman: When he struck you in the guts, did he knock all your senses out?

DeMars: No, sir; he struck me in the head and knocked all my senses out.[12]

Female inmates were treated with almost as much severity. The testimony revealed that it was a common practice to have their "dresses taken down, so as to expose the upper part of their back and shoulders, and punishment by the strap." In defense of this mode of discipline, the superintendent pointed out that a female officer was "usually present" to supervise the whipping.[13] The girls were also subjected to the punishment of being tied and "ducked" under water in a large tub. Mary Symonds's experience with the superintendent was similar to other reported cases:

Alderman: Did he put you in all over?

Symonds: He put my head where my feet ought to go in the bath tub, and held me under the water for a few minutes.

Alderman: Did he keep you there till you strangled?

Symonds: He just held me and then took me out; I halooed, and said something to him that I ought not to say, and then he put me back again; I swore at him, and he ducked me a second time.

Alderman: What did he do then?

Symonds: He slapped me on the side of the face, and I halooed murder.[14]

An investigation of the State Reform School at Westborough, Massachusetts, in 1877 revealed an even more elaborate system of punishments. Flogging with the "cat" was, once again, the primary method of maintaining order, and each of the officers was permitted to administer corporal punishments at his own discretion. The experience related by seventeen-year-old Cornelius Callahan is disturbingly similar to the stories told by the inmates of the Providence Reform School eight years earlier[15]:

> Mr. Phillips punished me. He made me take off my jacket and pants. He wanted me to bend over. I did not. He strapped me for a long time while standing up; then I went on my knees. He put his hand on my throat. I could not speak, but made a motion for him to take his hand off my throat. He whipped me until the blood ran down my legs.[16]

The keepers of the Westborough Reform School also placed their more obstreperous children in a "sweatbox," which was ten inches deep and fourteen inches wide with three one-inch slits in the front for air holes; one boy testified that he was locked in the "sweatbox" for seven days from half past five in the morning until a quarter past six at night with his hands strapped behind him. The straightjacket was also commonly used; and, for those children who would not submit to any of these forms of punishment, the keepers applied a steady stream of ice cold water from a hose until the recalcitrant child repented.[17]

The methods for securing the subjection of the inmates in the country's first juvenile reformatory—the New York House of Refuge—were equally severe. An 1872 investigation revealed that in addition to whipping the inmates, the superintendent hung boys by their thumbs for serious infractions of the rules.[18] In 1879, representatives from the State Board of Charities found marks on the boys indicating that they had received a "severe flogging." The inmates were punished with a variety of instruments, including a nineteen-inch leather strap.[19] The investigators of the New York House of Refuge might well have been describing the modes of discipline applied in nineteenth century reformatories across the country when they concluded that, in contrast to the assumptions of committing judges, "corporal punishment is, and always has been, a conspicuous feature of the discipline of the House; and it is manifest that a main reliance is placed upon it for the accomplishment of the reformatory work proposed."[20]

⬚ Contract Labor: Training or Exploitation?

Throughout most of the nineteenth century, reformatory managers used a system of contract labor in order to fulfill the mandate of the *Crouse* decision of "training its inmates to industry" and "furnishing them with a means to earn a living."[21] Although there were a number of variations, the programs of labor were essentially similar. Private businessmen supplied machinery, material, and overseers; the inmates supplied their labor; and the managers of the institution were paid on a per diem or piece-price basis. The inmates received either a menial sum or, as was more generally the case, no remuneration at all. The items produced in the New York House of Refuge in 1857 were almost identical to the goods produced in other institutions. The boys worked under contract for five to seven hours each day making shoes, clothes, wire, sofa springs, and cane chairs, while the girls were responsible for the institution's domestic chores. "Every child from the oldest to the youngest has a daily task wisely adapted to its age and ability," explained the chaplain of the New York House of Refuge. "A trade in most instances is thus secured."[22] The managers of the Cincinnati House of Refuge expressed the optimism of managers across the country when they proclaimed that "the contracting system is decidedly the most advantageous in all respects."[23]

In practice, however, the system of contract labor did not fulfill the expectations of judges who believed that they were sentencing minors to a term of vocational education. An investigation of the system of contract labor in fourteen institutions in New York State in 1870 by the noted penologist, Enoch C. Wines, is most enlightening. The unequivocal conclusion of Wines's committee was that "[t]he contract system is bad and should be abolished,"[24] a finding certainly not consistent with the exhortatory evaluations of the managers. The investigators were most critical of the system of contract labor in operation at the New York House of Refuge, which was viewed, ironically, as a model program of labor at this time.

The testimony of five former employees of the shops of the New York House of Refuge revealed a number of serious abuses. The overseers bribed the boys with tobacco and "sandwiches, sausages, and pie" in exchange for increased production, and reported good workers on fabricated charges so that they would not secure early release dates; "small boys were required to do as much as a man outside."[25] The most serious finding, however, was that the boys were severely whipped when they did not fulfill their production quotas. One former employee who had worked in the shops for eight years testified that he had "seen boys punished for not completing their tasks, so that the blood ran down their boots."[26] Another witness described the disciplinary ritual in practice during the three years in which he was employed:

> The Superintendent or his Assistant used to come around daily, at about ten o'clock, to receive complaints; if he thought a boy ought to be whipped, he sent him down to the closet; when the boys came back, I have seen stripes on their back through holes in their shirts, and it was a common saying among the boys, "You'll get the stars and stripes."[27]

The primary beneficiary of the contract labor system was not the inmates; rather, it was the contractor, George Whitehouse. After hearing the contractor's former bookkeeper, George Coffin, testify that shoes produced in the open market for $.50 could be made by the boys for $.15, Wines's committee investigated the financial status of Mr. Whitehouse. Their findings were not at all consistent with the presumed rehabilitative effects of contract labor. In 1869 the contractor realized a profit of $183,875 from the labor of the 575 boys in the institution. "We put it to all fair-minded men, we put it to the managers themselves," asked the commissioners in disbelief, "whether the contractor on Randall's Island pays a fair price for the labor he obtains there? . . . In the thirteen years during which he has held the shoe contract on Randall's Island, the contractor has built up a large fortune for himself."[28] The effects of working for Mr. Whitehouse, and of being in the refuge were, perhaps, most aptly stated by book-keeper Coffin. "I have known boys sent there for some trivial offence [sic] who were not bad boys at bottom when they first went there, but who became, in a short time, as thoroughly hardened as in any institution." In contrast with the assurances of the managers that their institution was a "school," Coffin concluded that "it is generally understood up there that the boys are not reformed."[29]

◧ Religion: Salvation or Proselytization?

Nineteenth century judges and reformers who cited the doctrine of parens patriae also did so on the grounds that by placing wayward children in reformatories they were saving them from a godless existence by "imbuing their minds with the principles of morality and religion."[30] Almost without exception, religious instruction consisted of nonsectarian chapel services on Sunday mornings followed by Sunday school classes in the afternoon, as well as daily prayer. The managers of reformatories, once again, did not hesitate to reassure the courts that they were fulfilling the principles of *Ex parte Crouse*. "The Chaplain's Department," concluded the keepers of the State Reform School at Westborough, "is one of vast importance to the highest welfare of the boys, involving worth of the spiritual as well as the temporal well being of those under its charge."[31] The managers of the New York House of Refuge supported their claims of salvation in the same year by noting that although 66 percent of the children had never learned any verses of Scripture at the time of entering the refuge, 53,166 verses had been committed to memory and recited by the end of the year.[32]

In reality, however, control over the religious instruction of children in reformatories was a symbolic source of dispute between the Protestant managers, who maintained that they were saving the children of foreign-born Catholics from lives of depravity and crime by exposing them to nonsectarian services, and Catholic clergymen and parents, who felt that their sons and daughters were being stolen from them and molded into heretics.[33] In essence, the confrontation over the proselytization of the children mirrored the tensions and hostilities that characterized the relations between native Protestants and foreign-born Catholics outside the walls of juvenile institutions, as native Protestants attempted to maintain their control over the political, economic, cultural, and religious structures of society. The Catholic view of the New York House of Refuge in the nineteenth century, as one instance, was succinctly stated in 1879 by Father Ignatius Renauld:

> . . . they [the Catholic church] consider that everything in the House, so far as religious ministration is concerned—whether by the Chaplain or by the institution or otherwise—is Protestant; the Bible used is the Protestant Bible; the Prayer, as used, has the Protestant conclusion which Catholics do not have in the Lord's Prayer; while the order of the service carried on is considered as Protestant by the Catholics at large.[34]

An unusually sympathetic chief justice of the supreme court of Illinois, Isaac Redfield, expressed a similar concern about the purpose of the Chicago Reform School in 1870 when he observed that a Catholic child "cannot be torn from home and immured in a Protestant prison, for ten or more years, and trained in . . . a heretical and deadly faith, to the destruction of his own soul."[35]

The perceptions of Father Renauld, Justice Redfield, and others who questioned the intentions of the keepers of juvenile institutions were generally well-founded. From the opening of the New York House of Refuge in 1825, as one example, the managers vehemently opposed all attempts by Catholic clergymen to hear confessions or hold mass on Sundays. Even after the Western House of Refuge—a model of the New York City institution which was opened in Rochester, New York, in 1849—incorporated without incident separate Catholic services into its regimen of reform, the keepers of the city institution remained adamant in their resistance, and warned that allowing priests to attend their flock "would be at once a breaking down of the discipline, and lead to disorganization."[36] When Catholic clergymen and laymen finally appealed to the state legislature to force the keepers of the refuge to permit secular services, the Protestant managers offered extraordinary resistance, and even sent members of their "law committee" to Albany armed with briefs which charged that the passage of such a law would be illegal. Although the Protestant managers succeeded in quashing several bills presented in the legislature, the growing political influence of Catholics finally resulted in the passage of a law ordering the keepers to allow mass on Sundays in 1892.[37] In essence, the managers of the New York House of Refuge, Chicago Reform School, and other institutions were not incorrect in proclaiming that they were "imbuing their [charges'] minds with the principles of morality and religion," in accordance with *Ex parte Crouse;* they merely neglected to note that the indoctrination was restricted to the Protestant faith.

◼ Apprenticeships: A Home in the Country?

The ultimate test of the success of juvenile institutions in transforming neglected, dependent, and delinquent minors into God-fearing, law-abiding, and hard-working citizens, in accordance with the principles of parens patriae, was, in the view of the keepers, reflected in the successful reintegration of the youths into the community through apprenticeships. The system instituted at the New York House of Refuge in 1825, once again, served as a model throughout the nineteenth century. Once the inmates had resided in the New York institution for a sufficient amount of time, and had participated in the regimen of reform with a significant degree of compliance, they appeared before the institution's "indenture committee," which was composed of several members of the board of managers. At the discretion of the board, the children—who were always committed for indeterminate terms which could not extend beyond the age of majority— could be returned to their parents or discharged to a master who was required to sign a contract wherein he agreed to provide the apprentice with food, clothes, shelter, religious instruction, and a nominal payment when the apprentice reached the age of majority. Boys were generally apprenticed to farmers in the country, and girls were exclusively placed as domestics.[38] In essence, the apprentice system transferred the responsibility of parens patriae from the state to the master.

As evidence of the success of the apprentice system, the managers of the New York institution included "representative letters" from the masters in their annual reports. The report from the master of J. H. was standard:

> In answer to your circular in regard to J. H., I inform you that he learns pretty well, and will, I think, make a bright man. I feel so much interest in him that I intend to see that he has a good trade. He often speaks of you in the highest terms. His morals are good, and I intend doing all I can for him.[39]

Letters from the apprentices were also offered as testimony to the successful adjustment of the apprentices. "The place that I now live is one of the most beautiful I was ever in," wrote one boy, "and Mr. B. and his lady, with whom I live, treat me kindly as their son."[40] Based upon reports of this nature, it is understandable that

the managers concluded that "it is ground of congratulations that so many have been provided with homes in the country amid the peaceful occupation of farm life."[41]

In contrast with the exhortations of the keepers, the terms of the indenture contract were generally not fulfilled. A random sample of 210 case histories selected between 1857 and 1862 from the records of the New York House of Refuge reveals that 72 percent of the inmates either ran away, voluntarily returned to the refuge because they were not pleased with their placement, were returned to the refuge by their master, or committed an offense and were incarcerated in another institution.[42] Entries in the superintendent's daily journal indicate that the relationship between master and apprentice was generally not as congenial as the administrators suggested in the "representative letters" cited in their annual reports. For instance, Margaret Shaw voluntarily returned to the refuge complaining that she "has had bad treatment, that Mrs. Pitcher is intemperate and that she has not been in Sunday school or church since she left the house."[43] Thomas Collier was forced to run away because he was "badly clothed and stated that he ran away because he [his master] abused him, and had tied and whipped him."[44] A number of female apprentices faced a different type of problem. When Mary Gash returned to the superintendent and informed him that she was pregnant by Mr. Rue, her master, the superintendent, perhaps naively, "advised her to return to Mr. Rue and inform Mrs. Rue of her condition . . . and ask for care and protection."[45]

The experiences of the apprentices from the Western House of Refuge were often as unpleasant. Thomas Dorney voluntarily returned to the Rochester institution in 1856 complaining that he was "not properly treated," and the superintendent also noted that "his feet were frosted and appeared half frozen."[46] Charles Darby returned in 1858 complaining that his master had "whipped and abused him."[47] That the primary interest of many of the masters was not the reformation of the children, but profit, also seems evident. One Mr. Fletcher returned his apprentice, and the superintendent noted his explanation: "He [the apprentice] was a great eater, that he [Mr. Fletcher] took two bushels of wheat to the mill the day after he got the boy and it did not last at all, he also noted that their groceries went much faster, had to go to the grocery quite often."[48]

The discrepancy between the promise and the practice of the indenture system was not, however, solely a result of the cruelty and greed of the masters, for it was not unusual for apprentices to escape as soon as they got their first chance. The note received by the superintendent of the New York House of Refuge from the master of James Wells stating that the boy "left him before he got out of the city"[49] was not exceptional. Other well-intentioned masters actually demonstrated exceptional forbearance. John Cooper was returned to the refuge by his master when, after being pardoned three times, "he began his old capers last night, for the fourth time entered Mr. Grove's bedroom with the evident intention of stealing his pocket book."[50] Another master whose apprentice stole $50 and ran away was undoubtedly speaking for Mr. Grove, and a number of other masters, when he wrote to the superintendent of the New York institution in 1862 denouncing him for "bringing such boys out to this country and palm[ing] them off as good, honest, industrious boys when they know there is no honesty, industry or any good trait of character about them."[51] It seems, then, that the failure of the apprentice system was not only a result of the cruelty and greed of some masters, but also a result of the unwillingness on the part of a significant number of children to give their parental substitutes a chance to teach them a trade and provide them with a home in the country.

⬚ The State: An Effective Parent?

Perhaps the most significant commentary on the ability of the state to act in *loco parentis* is reflected in the behavior of the inmates toward their parental substitutes. An examination of the extant records of juvenile reformatories reveals that, behind the imposing walls of these institutions, hidden from the purview of the judiciary and the public, the children often did not interact with their keepers in a manner that would suggest that they perceived the state as a benevolent parent. The frequency of attempted escapes, assaults upon guards and fellow inmates, attempted arson, and homosexual relations indicates that the inmates were not "separated from the influence of improper associates," as suggested in *Ex parte Crouse*. Instead, based on the fact that most of the inmates were incarcerated for what would today be termed status offenses, it is more likely that the inmates were introduced to new forms of vice.

Although an official of the New York House of Refuge proclaimed that inmates "will never run away, whatever may be their opportunities . . . if placed on [their] honor,"[52] the frequent reference made to attempted and successful escapes in the superintendent's daily journal indicates that the inmates did not share this opinion. In fact, between 1825 and 1875, 184 prisoners succeeded in escaping, while hundreds of others were thwarted in their attempts.[53] Escapes were also a major problem in other institutions. The determination and imagination demonstrated by the inmates of the Western House of Refuge were not unusual. John Hicks, for instance, eluded the officer who was taking him to the Rochester institution by jumping off of a train while it was traveling at forty miles per hour.[54] In the same year, 100 boys took advantage of an open gate and fled.[55]

Inmates who were not astute enough to secure their freedom by outwitting their keepers sometimes resorted to violence. At least three guards were murdered by inmates in attempts to escape from the New York House of Refuge, and dozens of others were fortunate to survive assaults made with knives, bats, blackjacks, bricks, and pipes.[56] Officer J. H. Tower provided a graphic description of an attack by the boys which says as much about their determination to gain freedom as it does about their feelings toward their keepers:

About five o'clock in the morning of March 16th I was lying on the platform in the hall reading. The boy Schaffer hit me on the head with a blackjack. . . . When I came to three boys were on top of me. The boy Schaffer was choking me. The boy Mellori was tying my legs. When I went to rise up the boy Rawls struck at me with a knife.[57]

The inmates did not, however, direct all of their frustrations against the officers: Deadly weapons were also used by the inmates against their peers. Much of the violence, throughout the nineteenth and into the twentieth century, was attributable to disputes over money and tobacco between gangs that were divided on ethnic lines. "A few fellows call themselves 'Ups,'" explained one gang member. "They call themselves 'Ups' and get some other fellows and get money from people, and another gang would try to get the money from them, and they would fight and stab each other."[58] This inmate's description was not at all inaccurate. In 1900, only one year after the doctrine of parens patriae was used as the underlying rationale for the founding of the juvenile court in Chicago, one boy was stabbed in the back, another in the head, and two in the neck.[59]

The danger of fire was also a pervasive threat in nineteenth century reformatories. The concern of managers across the nation was expressed by Superintendent Samuel Wood of the Western House of Refuge when he observed that "there is no safety for us, but in the most constant vigilance."[60] Although Superintendent Wood enforced the standard rule of reformatories, which prohibited any employee or visitor from bringing matches into the institution, fires were still started, including endeavors that resulted in $60,000 dollars in damage to a shop in 1864 and the complete destruction of the department for females in 1887. The inmates of the New York House of Refuge vented their hostilities in a similar manner: One shop alone was burned to the ground in 1861, 1884, and 1899. The manager's concern with the threat of arson is reflected in the maintenance of fifty-two separate insurance policies in 1867 valued at over $364,000.[61]

Homosexual relations were also a disturbingly common practice among the inmates. In the Western House of Refuge the problem became so pervasive that the superintendent warned that "unless the problem is dealt with more vigorously, more severely, the time is near at hand when it will be of infinite damage for any boy committed to the institution whom, at the time of his commitment, is not already a sexual pervert."[62] Nor was the problem restricted to the boys. The matron of the Western House of Refuge denounced the open dormitory system in 1887 as the "most diabolical system yet devised for the demoralization of the girls!" She went on to explain that "in spite of the constant vigilance of a watch-woman who gives her whole attention to one dormitory, the black and the white girls elude her and get together in bed."[63]

◪ Conclusion

It would certainly be an oversimplification and distortion of history to suggest that all reformatory managers were cruel xenophobics whose primary concern was the proselytization of innocent Catholic children, that inmates never benefited from their incarceration, or that reformatories were complete failures in achieving their objectives (whatever those were). However, the available investigations and records of nineteenth century juvenile institutions offer compelling evidence that the state was not a benevolent parent. In short, there was significant disparity between the promise and practice of parens patriae. Discipline was seldom "parental" in nature, inmate workers were exploited under the contract labor system, religious instruction was often disguised proselytization, and the indenture system generally failed to provide inmates with a home in the country. The frequency of escapes, assaults, incendiary incidents, and homosexual relations suggests that the children were not, as the Pennsylvania court presumed in 1838, "separated from the corrupting influence of improper associates."

Based on the historical record of parens patriae, one must wonder how the doctrine could have been extended and employed as the legal and moral foundation of the juvenile court in 1899. Even more perplexing, perhaps, is the fact that the juvenile court and parens patriae were hailed as humanitarian innovations well into the 1960s. It was not until 1966, when the United States Supreme Court issued its opinion in *Kent* v. *United States,* that the legal and moral foundation of the juvenile justice system was called into question. In his widely cited opinion, Justice Fortas warned that while the state promised minors "parental" treatment under parens patriae,

There is evidence, in fact, that there may be grounds for concern that the child receives the worst of both worlds: that he gets neither the protections accorded to adults nor the solicitous care and regenerative treatment postulated for children.[64]

If there is any practical lesson to be learned from evaluating the historical record of parens patriae, it is, perhaps, that contemporary child savers would be well advised to assess objectively, rather than assume, the "benevolent" effects of their rehabilitative efforts. It is certainly ironic, and perhaps even tragic, that the humanitarian imagery projected by supporters of the juvenile justice system has, for decades, buried the "evidence" that the child "receives the worst of both worlds." It may seem paradoxical to contemporary child savers that the initial step toward developing a truly humane juvenile justice system requires the abandonment of unfounded humanitarian rhetoric, but the historical inconsistency between the promise and practice of parens patriae seems to leave few alternatives.

✂ Notes

1. Ex parte Crouse, 4 Wharton (Pa.) 9 (1838).

2. Ibid.

3. Society for the Reformation of Juvenile Delinquents, *Thirty-Seventh Annual Report* (New York: Wynkoop, Hallenbeck and Thomas, 1862), p. 14.

4. Managers of the Baltimore House of Refuge, *Sixth Annual Report* (Baltimore: James Lucas and Sons, 1857), p. 7.

5. For two exceptions to this generalization, see The People v. Turner, 55 Illinois 280 (1870); and Ex parte Becknell, 51 Pacific Reporter (Ca.) 692 (1897). Both of these rulings were quickly overturned in ensuing appellate decisions, so that their effect was minimal.

6. The People v. Degnen, 54 Barbour's Supreme Court Reports 165 (1869).

7. Sanford J. Fox, "Juvenile Justice Reform: An Historical Perspective," *Stanford Law Review,* June 1970, pp. 1204, 1206; Steven L. Schlossman, *Love and the American Delinquent: The Theory and Practice of "Progressive" Juvenile Justice, 1825–1920* (Chicago: University of Chicago Press, 1977), p. 14.

8. Douglas R. Rendleman, "Parens Patriae: From Chancery to the Juvenile Court," in *Juvenile Justice Philosophy: Readings, Cases and Comments,* 2d ed., Frederic L. Faust and Paul J. Brantingham, eds. (St. Paul, Minn.: West, 1979), p. 82.

9. Western House of Refuge, *Second Annual Report* (Albany, N.Y.: Charles Van Benthuysen, 1851), p. 5.

10. Robert Bremner et al., eds., *Children and Youth in America,* vol. 2 (Cambridge, Mass.: Harvard University Press, 1971), pp. 117–18.

11. *Investigation into the Management of the Providence Reform School, Made by the Board of Aldermen, under the Direction of the City of Providence* (Providence, R.I.: Hammond, Angell and Co., 1869), p. 218.

12. Ibid., p. 591.

13. Ibid., p. 389.

14. Ibid., p. 628.

15. The similarity in the testimony of inmates who experienced, and former employees who witnessed, the administration of punishments in nineteenth century reformatories precludes any possibility that their accounts were contrived. The witnesses were generally questioned individually, and there is also a similarity between the testimony heard before different investigative committees.

16. *Extracts from Testimony Taken before the Committee on Public Charitable Institutions on the Management of the State Reform School at Westborough* (n.p., 1877), p. 17.

17. Ibid., pp. 4–6.

18. New York State Commissioner of Public Charities, *Record of the Proceedings and Testimony*

before a Committee of State Commissioners of Public Charities at the House of Refuge in New York (New York: Thitchener and Glastacter, 1872), pp. 91, 106–07.

19. New York State Board of Charities, Report of the Committee of the State Board of Charities Appointed to Investigate the Charges against the Society for the Reformation of Juvenile Delinquents (Albany, N.Y.: Weed, Parsons, 1881), pp. 27–28.

20. Ibid.

21. Ex parte Crouse.

22. Bradford K. Peirce, A Half Century with Juvenile Delinquents: The New York House of Refuge and Its Times (1868; rep. ed. Montclair, N.J.: Patterson Smith, 1969), p. 84.

23. Board of Directors of the Cincinnati House of Refuge, Seventh Annual Report (St. Louis: Missouri Democrat Book and Job Office, 1857), p. 6.

24. New York State, Report of the State Commission on Prison Labor Together with the Proceedings of the Commission (Albany, N.Y.: Argus Company, 1871), p. xi.

25. Ibid., pp. 141, 146, 163, 164, 169.

26. Ibid., pp. 181–82.

27. Ibid., pp. 163–64.

28. Ibid., p. xxiv.

29. Ibid., p. 169.

30. Ex parte Crouse.

31. State Reform School at Westborough, Eleventh Annual Report (Boston: William White, 1857), p. 6.

32. Society for the Reformation of Juvenile Delinquents, Thirty-Second Annual Report (New York: Wynkoop and Hallenbeck, 1857), p. 27.

33. For support for this theme, see Robert S. Pickett, House of Refuge: Origins of Juvenile Reform in New York State, 1815–1857 (Syracuse, N.Y.: Syracuse University Press, 1969), p. 15; Anthony M. Platt, The Child Savers: The Invention of Delinquency (Chicago: University of Chicago Press, 1969), p. 74; Fox, "Juvenile Justice Reform," p. 1195; Rendleman, "Parens Patriae," p. 79; David J. Rothman, The Discovery of the Asylum; Social Order and Disorder in the New Republic (Boston: Little, Brown, 1971), p. 207; Robert M. Mennel, Thorns and Thistles: Juvenile Delinquents in the United States, 1825–1940 (Hanover, N.H.: University Press of New England, 1973), pp. 5–8, 15–16; Alexander Liazos, "Class Oppression: The Functions of Juvenile Justice," The Insurgent Sociologist, Fall 1974, p. 8; Harold Finestone, Victims of Change: Juvenile Delinquents in American Society (Westport,

Conn.: Greenwood Press, 1976), p. 18; Schlossman, Love and the American Delinquent, pp. 19–20, 35; Alexander W. Pisciotta, "The Theory and Practice of the New York House of Refuge, 1857–1935" (Ph.D. Diss. Florida State University, Tallahassee, 1979), pp. 18–22.

34. New York State Commissioner of Public Charities, Record of the Proceedings and Testimony before a Committee of State Commissioners of Public Charities at the House of Refuge in New York, p. 172.

35. Quoted in Rendleman, "Parens Patriae," p. 93.

36. New York Commissioner of Public Charities, Record of the Proceedings and Testimony before a Committee at the House of Refuge in New York, p. 134.

37. Pisciotta, "Theory and Practice of the New York House of Refuge, 1857–1935," pp. 119–21.

38. Ibid., pp. 72–74.

39. Society for the Reformation of Juvenile Delinquents, Thirty-Third Annual Report (New York: Wynkoop, Hallenbeck and Thomas, 1858), p. 45.

40. Ibid., pp. 52–53.

41. Ibid.

42. Pisciotta, "Theory and Practice of the New York House of Refuge, 1857–1935," p. 132.

43. Superintendent's Daily Journal, Apr. 18, 1866. Documents of the New York House of Refuge, Record Group 518, New York State Archives, Albany, N.Y. (Hereafter, all documents in the New York House of Refuge Collection will be cited as DNYHR.)

44. Minutes of the Indenture Committee, Apr. 17, 1887, DNYHR.

45. Superintendent's Daily Journal, July 25, 1872, DNYHR.

46. Superintendent's Daily Journal, Feb. 15, 1856, Documents of the Western House of Refuge, Record Group 519, New York State Archives, Albany, N.Y. (Hereafter, all documents in the Western House of Refuge Collection will be cited as DWHR.) At the request of the New York State Archives, the names of inmates taken from the DNYHR and DWHR have been changed to protect anonymity.

47. Ibid., Jan. 23, 1858.

48. Ibid., June 18, 1874.

49. Case History No. 7329, DNYHR.

50. Superintendent's Daily Journal, Oct. 30, 1886, DNYHR.

51. Minutes of the Indenture Committee, Sept. 25, 1862, DNYHR.

52. Society for the Reformation of Juvenile Delinquents, *Forty-Sixth Annual Report* (New York: Joseph Longking, 1871), p. 38.

53. Society for the Reformation of Juvenile Delinquents, *Fifty-First Annual Report* (New York: National Printing Co., 1876), p. 79.

54. Superintendent's Daily Journal, June 3, 1860, DWHR.

55. Ibid., July 24, 1860.

56. Pisciotta, "Theory and Practice of the New York House of Refuge, 1857–1935," p. 229.

57. Minutes of the Acting Committee, Mar. 22, 1901, DNYHR.

58. Special Hearings on the House of Refuge, 1909, DNYHR, p. 114.

59. Pisciotta, "Theory and Practice of the New York House of Refuge, 1857–1935," p. 231. In the annual reports of the New York House of Refuge, the physician noted that he had treated eight "puncture wounds" in 1908, eleven in 1909, nine in 1913, and twelve in 1917. The euphemism "puncture wounds" was substituted for stabbing by order of the Board of Managers after the state legislature began to raise questions about violence in the institution.

60. Superintendent's Daily Journal, Mar. 29, 1850, DWHR.

61. Pisciotta, "Theory and Practice of the New York House of Refuge, 1857–1935," p. 233.

62. Letter from Superintendent Franklin Biggs, 1902, DWHR.

63. Matron's Daily Journal, Apr. 6, 1887, DWHR.

64. Kent v. United States, 383 U.S. 541 (1966).

DISCUSSION QUESTIONS

1. What legal claim was made by the father of Mary Ann Crouse? What was the decision of the Pennsylvania Court?

2. Can you offer examples where the "rhetoric" and the "reality" of *parens patriae* were different in actual practice, according to this case?

3. What was the role of religion in early "child-saving" practices and juvenile reformatories?

4. What was the role of "apprenticeships" in child-saving and juvenile institutions? Were these beneficial to children? Why or why not?

5. According to evidence offered by Pisciotta, was the State an effective parent? Why, or why not?

READING

Many of the problems in juvenile justice can be traced to the 19th century when *parens patriae* programs were established with little attention to their influence upon one another. As newer programs for status offenders were begun, older centers received mainly hardened delinquents, and their policies became more punitive. In the absence of clear communication, cooperation, guidance, or understanding of administrators and policy makers, more of the entire system became more punitive. Theodore Ferdinand believes that a solution to this criminalizing of juvenile justice might entail a state-level department devoted to the treatment of delinquents in the community or in custodial facilities, and small facilities that are limited to 15–20 beds each, focusing on narrow segments of the delinquent population. In this article he provides an overview of the history and development of the juvenile court, the failure of treatment, and why many failed, and he concludes with a proposal for more effective treatment programs in juvenile justice.

History Overtakes the Juvenile Justice System

Theodore N. Ferdinand (1991)

Justice systems have a way of shaping their parts to the needs of the whole, and the juvenile justice system is no exception. Many of the juvenile court's problems can be understood in terms of how the court adjusted over the years to the custodial institutions, clientele, and treatment facilities it served. Its deficiencies today stem largely from its roots in the civil courts and the difficulties it encountered in fulfilling *parens patriae* in a system of juvenile institutions already dominated by a custodial if not a punitive viewpoint. The juvenile justice system has acted very much as a loose but dynamic system over the last 165 years, and to understand its difficulties we need to look to the historical contradictions that were built into the juvenile justice system during its early years.

Of particular interest are several questions that have been raised repeatedly over the years. First, what purposes did the juvenile justice system serve when it was introduced in eastern cities during the early 19th century, and what role did the juvenile court play in that system when it was introduced in the early part of the 20th century? Second, why has treatment been such an uneven enterprise in juvenile justice? Is the process of treating delinquents fraught with such obstacles that consistent successes are impossible, or are less formidable reasons responsible for this inconsistency? Finally, why has juvenile justice been unable to maintain a parens patriae focus within its custodial institutions? Is there an inherent flaw in such institutions that ultimately vetoes any long term effort to improve juveniles in institutions?

Many have addressed these and similar questions, and along these lines Cohen (1985) has identified four distinct approaches to the problems of the justice system. The "conventional" view asserts that flaws in the justice system derive basically from the limitations of its pioneers. If their vision is partly cloudy, or their commitment falters, their reforms ultimately founder on inertia and indifference. But different leaders inject new enthusiasms, and the overall result is gradual progress in the justice system through the cumulated efforts of its visionaries over generations.

The second approach, "we blew it," as represented by David Rothman (1980) in his work, *Conscience and Convenience,* is less optimistic. It sees the sources of ineffectiveness in the justice system in the inevitable triumph of mindless routine and parochial interest over moral purpose. The possibility of lasting progress in the justice system is compromised by custodial inertia and trivial, convenient routine.

Cohen (1985) describes in addition two other approaches: "It's all a con" and, most recently, "destructuring." Foucault (1979) represents the first with his suggestion in *Discipline and Punish* that the justice system before all else buttresses order in civil society by its threat of punishment, however ineffective it may be in rehabilitating offenders. It is indispensable as a reinforcement of responsibility, no matter how dismal its treatment record or brutish its methods. We must forgive its ineffectiveness for the sake of its crucial symbolic value. The "destructuralists," today's visionaries, are less programmatic and

SOURCE: *Crime & Delinquency (37)*2, 204–224, April 1991. © 1991 Sage Publications, Inc.

more idealistic. They claim that order overwhelms and stultifies humanity, and to reawaken moral ideals in society, order must be sacrificed.

My approach to this issue concedes the importance of juvenile justice as a symbol of responsibility, but I locate the failures of juvenile justice not simply in compromise with routine, nor in the fallibilities of its pioneers, but in the conflicts that different approaches have built into juvenile justice over the years. We must probe the sources of juvenile justice's ailments in the 19th century, if we ever hope to understand their essential nature and correct them.

✉ The 19th Century Origins of Juvenile Justice

During the Jacksonian era industrialization took firm root in several American cities. As trade with Europe, the Caribbean, and other American cities flourished, as new factories for spinning yarn and weaving cloth were built, and as new schools opened, employment grew more plentiful. The slow drift of population to centers of commerce and industry grew very quickly to sizable proportions in the northeast, and several American cities began to encounter adolescent misbehavior and waywardness in a variety of forms (see, for example, Ferdinand 1989, pp. 94–97). Not only were wayward children nuisances on the city's streets, but when convicted of crimes in the criminal courts, they were sometimes sent to adult prisons where they mixed with hardened convicts and became career criminals.

But unless wayward children were criminals, the criminal courts had no jurisdiction over them. A convenient doctrine—parens patriae—however, enabled the civil courts to step in and take custody of these wayward or dependent children. The criminal law served for those children who had violated the criminal code, but for those who were merely beyond control, or whose parents were negligent, parens patriae sufficed. The child's first responsibility was to obey his or her parents, and the nascent juvenile justice system awaited those few who steadfastly rejected parental authority.

Furthermore, in many eastern cities bold plans for compulsory education were underway (see Schultz 1973). On the eve of the industrial revolution in 1789 Boston authorities established a system of free grammar schools, and in 1821 the city opened its first public high school, Boston English High. By 1826 Boston's school system enrolled a majority of its school-aged children (Kaestle and Vinovskis 1980).

These new schools represented a second arena wherein many children were held accountable. Just as children who were beyond parental control and roamed the city at night could not be ignored, so too children who disrupted school or truanted needed to be held in check. Parens patriae was applicable here as well, because the children were in school for their own well being. The schools' problem children became a second concern for the nascent juvenile justice system.

In short, as compulsory education and industrialization swept America's cities in the 19th century, they produced a growing troop of wayward, incorrigible children who resisted in one fashion or another the efforts of society to shape them for adulthood. Something like a juvenile justice system was needed to bolster the authority of the family and the school in industrializing America so that both could be more effective in socializing young people. The juvenile justice system, as it emerged, represented the community's attempt to come to grips with a new social status: the juvenile.

At first the effort was limited to the major cities where education and economic development were centered, but soon it spread to entire states as whole regions were developed. The juvenile was expected to be obedient to both parents and teachers, and if he refused, he was held liable by the courts. The juvenile justice system was basically a sociolegal institution for holding juveniles accountable and for strengthening both the family and the school as they adapted to the changing social order.[1]

Recently John Sutton (1988) uncovered evidence that strongly confirms this view of the relationship between emerging school systems and juvenile justice. He investigated the impact of growing school enrollments on the introduction of juvenile reformatories in the latter half of the 19th century and found it more powerful than either industrialization or the growth of government. According to Sutton (1988, p. 114), "from 1850 to 1880, a 1 percent increase in school attendance is associated with a 13 percent increase in adoption rates (of juvenile reformatories)."

As a concept of the juvenile emerged, the juveniles' parents and teachers were responsible for them, and they were expected to obey both. Parens patriae was the relevant legal doctrine, because it allowed the state to intervene when either the family or the school was deficient. Because parens patriae was available only in the civil courts, juvenile delinquency was lodged in that jurisdiction. It covered all but the major criminal offenses by juveniles, which were still handled in the criminal courts.

Under parens patriae the civil courts acted in behalf of the child against ineffective parents or the child himself and provided dispositions that a responsible parent would. If the parents could control the child, the courts accepted them as the proper guardian. For the most part, state appellate courts endorsed this mission for the court, (see, for example, *Ex parte Crouse* 1838; *In re Ferrier* 1882; *Commonwealth v. Fisher* 1905; Garlock 1979, p. 399).

The civil courts still could not deal with juveniles who violated the criminal law, and many communities continued to send serious juvenile offenders to the criminal courts. Although most were sent to juvenile facilities upon conviction, some were still sent to adult institutions (see Garlock 1979, Appendix).

Several facts stand out regarding the juvenile justice system up to 1899. First, it consisted of a very diverse collection of private and public institutions and community programs including probation for minor delinquents and status offenders, all served by the civil court and its doctrine of parens patriae. A survey (see Mennel 1973, p. 49) of 30 juvenile reform schools conducted in 1880, for example, found an extraordinary heterogeneity.

Six accepted children convicted of crimes punishable by imprisonment, and 14 took children who had committed minor offenses. Thirteen schools specialized in children rebelling against parental authority; seven accepted mainly neglected or deserted children; and five dealt with children committed by their parents for various reasons.[2] Coordination among such a diverse group of custodial institutions and the civil courts must have been difficult, indeed.

Second, the civil court with its doctrine of parens patriae provided moral leadership within the system. But its authority was at best exhortatory and informal. It had little control over the staffing, budgets, practices, or objectives of the far flung juvenile programs it served.

Third, this system was kept largely separate from the criminal justice system. Juvenile miscreants who warranted a criminal court hearing by virtue of serious offending were handled as adults. The rest were handled by the civil court and sent to juvenile facilities. In the 19th century a bifurcated justice system handled a bifurcated population of juvenile offenders. The early juvenile justice system neatly avoided today's complexity in which serious offenders are handled along with minor offenders in a single, parens patriae system.

This system was the result of separate initiatives at several different levels of government over the better part of a century. Even though most juvenile facilities were guided at first by a parens patriae philosophy, the system had no central authority that could impose a focus or common mission on the whole. Without a central organizing authority, however, the system was left to respond as local conditions dictated. And it continues today to embrace a growing variety of public and private facilities (Sutton 1990, pp. 1369–70).

Moreover, as the 19th century drew to a close, it was becoming clear that the civil courts could not handle the sheer volume of juvenile cases coming into the system. As early as the Civil War, for example, the mass of juveniles arrested in Boston was already large, and the same was true of other eastern cities as well.

During the 1820s and early 1830s very few juveniles were charged with serious offenses in Boston's felony court—the municipal court. But by 1850 indictments had grown in the municipal court to 220 per 10,000 juveniles (Ferdinand 1989, Figure 2) and were the fastest growing component in Boston's crime problem. Furthermore, between 1849 to 1850 and 1861 to 1862 the arrest rate for juveniles rose 479% from 506 to 2,932 per 10,000 juveniles (Ferdinand 1989, Figure 3).[3] After the Civil War, juvenile arrests in Boston receded somewhat from the high rates of the Civil War period (Ferdinand 1989, Figure 3). Still, from 1870 to 1900 they ranged between 7,900 and 11,200 arrests annually.

This sizable flow of juvenile cases no doubt strengthened the argument that juveniles needed a specialized court—a court that was attuned to their special needs. First, they needed a judge who was familiar with the social psychological nuances of family conflict as well as the legal complexities of family/child problems. They needed a legal doctrine that took into account their social deficits as well as their misbehavior. Juveniles also needed a court whose officers were closely familiar with the range of facilities available for troubled children and could assign each to a program that was geared to his or her own needs.

The older civil court served the legal needs of juveniles, but it was devoted foremost to other issues. It dealt with divorces, torts, contracts, and wills—all adult issues. The civil law was narrow and intricate, and few probate judges or lawyers had a strong interest in the psychology of juveniles or their facilities and potential. They were largely amateurs in those areas most relevant to juveniles and their problems.

Frederick Wines, a noted criminologist, commented in Chicago in 1898 that "an entirely separate system of courts [was needed] for children . . . who commit offenses which would be criminal in adults. We ought to have a 'children's court' in Chicago, and we ought to have a 'children's judge,' who should attend to no other business" (quoted in Mennel 1973, p. 131).

⬡ The New Juvenile Court

In 1899 the Illinois legislature enacted the first juvenile code and established, in Chicago, the first juvenile court. Its jurisdiction extended to virtually all juveniles—serious criminal offenders, status offenders, and neglected and dependent children. It embraced a much wider jurisdiction than the 19th century juvenile justice system ever had. Nevertheless, its mandate was to deal with all of them by means of parens patriae.

Several contemporary observers commented on the new court's usefulness. The new court gave custodial institutions "the legal status and powers that they have most stood in need of and "in large cities juvenile courts are little more than clearing houses to get together the boy or girl that needs help and the agencies that will do the most good" (Sutton 1988, p. 143). It gave authority to social services, it provided intelligent assessments of juveniles, and it assigned them to programs that were closely related to their needs. It offered a specialized knowledge of and commitment to juveniles and their needs that the old civil courts could never provide.

In their enthusiasm, however, the reformers failed to ask whether serious offenders with criminal intent were appropriate subjects for a parens patriae court.[4] Furthermore, the new court did little to unify the juvenile justice system. It was still a very loose collection of programs and facilities with no central direction.

Despite these defects the remaining states quickly followed Illinois' example, and 30 states had established juvenile courts by 1920. By 1945 all had. The juvenile justice system was separate from the adult system. Parens patriae was the philosophic foundation of the court, and many if not most of its facilities and programs subscribed to that perspective.

These programs, as we have seen, had emerged in haphazard fashion during the preceding 80 years and most were organized by state or city governments. Because the juvenile court was generally lodged at the county level, juvenile programs both public and private were still largely free to follow their own mandate.

The new court was hailed as a visionary institution that would bring clarity, order, and humanity to the emerging juvenile justice system. In addition the new court provided a podium for the parens patriae approach in the justice system, and its early judges were outspoken in advocating treatment and humane care for offenders.

Judge Benjamin Lindsey of Denver, for example, was one of the first to argue in behalf of juveniles, and in 1904 he wrote, "The Juvenile Court rests upon the principle of love. Of course there is firmness and justice, for without this [sic] there would be danger in leniency. But there is no justice without love" (quoted in Mennel 1973, p. 138). Many of the early judges felt the same way, although many were critical of Lindsey's flamboyance.

The juvenile court maintained an informal atmosphere and gave the judges ample room to carry out their rehabilitative philosophy. The early courts were fortunate in that many judges showed a deep sympathy for young delinquents. Judge Richard Tuthill, the first judge of Chicago's juvenile court, proclaimed, "I talk with the boy, give him a good talk, just as I would my own boy, and find myself as much interested in these boys as I would if they were my own" (quoted in Mennel 1973, p. 135). Judge George W. Stubbs of Indianapolis said, "It is the personal touch that does it. I have often observed that if . . . I could get close enough to [the boy] to put my hand on his head or shoulder, or my arm around him, in nearly every such case I could get his confidence" (quoted in Mennel 1973, p. 135). With the appearance of the juvenile court in many communities, vigorous and often eloquent spokesmen for a parens patriae handling of juveniles got, and kept, the public's attention.

As the juvenile court spread through the states during the first 2 decades of the 20th century, however, commitments to juvenile institutions went down (Sutton 1990, p. 1392). A growing number of judges were becoming uncomfortable with custodial institutions for children.

Parens Patriae and Fairness

Shortly after World War II the critique of the juvenile court got underway with Paul Tappan's (1946) keen analysis of the court's due process failures. Tappan, a legally trained criminologist, pointed out that many constitutional rights of juveniles were ignored in the parens patriae juvenile court.

Others took up the same complaint (see Allen 1964 and Caldwell 1961). They noted that the court's therapeutic measures, even when sincerely applied, often turned out to be worse than routine punishments. It was not unusual in the 1960s to find that status offenders were punished more severely than all but the most serious delinquents (see Creekmore 1976; Cohn 1963; and Terry 1967), and racial discrimination in the juvenile court, though not found in some courts, was all too common (see Thornberry 1973; and Fagan, Slaughter, and Hartstone 1987; but see also Rubin 1985, pp. 203–5; Cohen 1976, pp. 51–54; and Dungworth 1977).[5] Such flagrant violations of equal protection under the law were intolerable especially in the charged atmosphere of the 1960s and 1970s.

A Growing Demand for Reform

In addition to Tappan's early criticism of the court's due process lapses and the discovery of racial and gender biases, steady reports of scandalous conditions in state training schools began to surface (see Rothman 1980, pp. 268–86 and Deutsch 1950). The need for reform in juvenile justice was inescapable, and the response took several forms.

First, the states attempted to cope with difficulties inherent in combining serious and minor offenders in the same system by separating status offenders from delinquents in confinement and later, by removing most of them (status offenders) from the juvenile court's jurisdiction. California differentiated delinquents and status offenders in its original juvenile statute, and in 1962 New York passed a Family Court Act, which among other things distinguished status offenders (renamed PINS) from delinquents. In 1973 the New York Court of Appeals ruled in *In re* Ellery (1973) that the policy of confining PINS with delinquents in an institution was unconstitutional, although in 1974 in *In re* Lavette (1974) the same court ruled that PINS could be confined in facilities organized for PINS.

In the decades that followed many states enacted similar statutes, separating status offenders and delinquents both in definition and treatment, and by the late 1970s many had gone even further by making court-ordered treatment plans for status offenders voluntary. Such children had committed no criminal offense and legally did not deserve custodial confinement.

Juvenile justice in the United States seemed to be following a path charted in Scandinavia in which problem juveniles under 22 years of age are treated voluntarily in social agencies, and serious offenders after 15 years of age are handled in the criminal courts (see Sarnecki 1988). Such a plan often fails, however, in that it permits status offenders to respond with either a "political" compliance to treatment suggestions or an impulsive rejection of them.

The Failures of Treatment

At the same time ambiguities surrounding the rehabilitative approach spurred the federal government to sponsor a host of delinquency prevention projects. In the mid-1960s under the impetus of President Lyndon Johnson's War on Poverty, a major effort to prevent delinquency and rehabilitate delinquents was undertaken by the Office of Economic Opportunity. As a centerpiece the War on Poverty mounted a massive preventive program on the Lower East Side of Manhattan—Mobilization for Youth. It was modeled after the Chicago Area Projects and addressed the problems of preschool children, juveniles, gangs, schools, and community adults. But it was too broad and complex to evaluate, and we will never know as with the Chicago Area Projects whether this community approach to delinquency prevention was effective.[6]

More specialized programs dealing with distinctive facets of delinquency were also fielded in Boston, Chicago, and elsewhere. Studies of innovative juvenile programs were funded in Michigan, Massachusetts, and Utah, and community-based treatment programs in California were generously supported. The federal government in conjunction with the Ford Foundation and other private groups sought to determine whether juvenile justice could remedy its ills.

Sentiment for reform of the juvenile justice system was strong, but the direction of reform was still hotly debated. Should it focus on pre-delinquents with the idea of keeping them out of the juvenile justice system, should it reform the court itself, or should it concentrate on juvenile institutions? Much hinged on the outcome of the War on Poverty programs, and millions of dollars were spent to insure that sound methods and skilled researchers were used. But to nearly everyone's dismay, few if any initiatives were effective. In the 1960s the detached worker program investigated by Walter Miller (1962) in Boston and later in Los Angeles by Malcolm Klein (1971) were worse than ineffective. Klein found that in Los Angeles detached workers actually made delinquency worse. Gerald Robin (1969) evaluated the Neighborhood Youth Corps and its attempts to provide counseling, remedial education, and supervised work for juveniles in both Cincinnati and Detroit. He found no positive effect in either program.

In Provo, Utah, Empey and Erickson (1972) designed a community program for delinquents in which they participated in group therapy sessions for 5 or 6 months. Empey and Erickson compared the delinquents with a comparison group of boys who had simply been placed on community probation and a second comparison group that had been sent to the state training school. Although the boys in the community treatment program averaged about half as many arrests as the boys who were sent to a training school, the difference between them and the boys placed on probation was small. Moreover, when a similar program was repeated at Silverlake in Los Angeles, boys in the community treatment program showed only slightly lower delinquency rates than boys who were sent to an open institution for delinquents (Empey and Lubeck 1971). In effect the failure of these several delinquency treatment programs discredited treatment as a method for reforming delinquents or predelinquents.

To be sure successes were also found among the treatment projects. Probation, for example, has been thoroughly studied in terms of the degree of supervision afforded juveniles and its success rate (see Diana 1955; Scarpitti and Stephenson 1968). The results indicate that despite haphazard supervisory practices a large majority of juveniles complete probation without further incident and go on to crime-free adult lives as well.

Further, Warren (1976) and Palmer (1974) reported strong results in treating specific types of delinquents in the community when compared with similar youngsters sent to custodial institutions in California. In addition the studies of Street, Vinter, and Perrow (1966) in Michigan discovered that benign institutions with supportive staffs were much more effective in molding positive attitudes in children than custodial institutions and punitive staff. The former were especially successful in instilling a prosocial climate among the bulk of their children. Finally, Kobrin and Klein (1983, chapters 5, 6) found that the level of coordination of diversion programs with established juvenile justice agencies strongly influenced their success. Where diversion programs were implemented in close cooperation with existing agencies, they were usually effective, but where the two worked at cross-purposes, diversion was ineffective.

Nearly all of these studies have been rigorously scrutinized, and serious reservations have been lodged against several (see, for example, Lerman 1975). However, the critics have not been able to defeat the obvious conclusion that significant numbers of juveniles respond to sound treatment programs, especially when these juveniles are assigned to program and treatment staff according to their need (see Lipsey 1991 and Andrews et al. 1990). Despite these results, the view took hold that treatment, whether in an institution or in the community, is ineffective in reducing delinquency (Martinson 1974)

⊠ The Crisis in Juvenile Justice

The conclusion that treatment does not work seemed to strike a chord in the nation at large, and the advantage swung quickly to those who favored a retributive approach to delinquency. Criminologists had been arguing for decades as to the causes of delinquency and the best methods of treatment. This quarrel was more basic and more serious.

The evidence was by no means unequivocal, but the fact that a retributive response was so widely endorsed suggests that something much deeper was responsible. No doubt a general disillusionment with professionalism and government was a factor as well as the conservative views of the Nixon and Reagan administrations.

If the juvenile court could not provide wholesome treatment for juveniles under its care, it seemed to imply that the parens patriae court was discredited. Parens patriae was a noble idea, but if the juvenile court could not act effectively as a parent, the least it could do was act effectively as a court by finding guilt justly and by administering punishments fairly. In effect the juvenile court and parens patriae were held hostage to the ineffectiveness of community and institutional treatment programs in rehabilitating delinquents!

Why Do Treatment Programs Fail?

As we have seen, the juvenile court has never had much influence over treatment programs, whether in custodial institutions or in the community, because both were almost always organized by independent agencies. The one program the court did control, probation, has been effective in helping delinquents regain their social composure. In effect the juvenile court and parens patriae have been evaluated not only in terms of their relevance to the needs of juveniles, but also in terms of their ability to guide the rest of the juvenile justice system along the path of treatment.

The critics of the parens patriae court expected it to impose its rehabilitative mission on the rest of juvenile justice despite its very limited ability to shape therapeutic programs whether in the community or in custodial institutions. It was doomed from the start by the contradiction between its mission and its limited authority.

The parens patriae court did not fail. The state failed, because it enacted a parens patriae court without providing solid support for community and institutional treatment programs. True, state programs, first as individual juvenile institutions and then more recently as systems of state juvenile facilities, have been established, some even predating the juvenile court. But these programs had as their first objective the confinement of juveniles in large institutions where custodial policies and attitudes soon dominated (see Schlossman 1977; Brenzel 1983; Pisciotta 1985). Rehabilitation, though used effectively as a public relations device, was almost always a secondary consideration with these state-based programs. Rarely has a state agency had any responsibility for funding and directing treatment programs in the community for delinquents.

Many treatment institutions and community programs were established over the years with the help of private philanthropy, religious groups, social welfare agencies, and even the federal government. But these were either underfunded or short term, or both. These nonstate programs were hobbled by uncertainty. Because state correctional agencies were committed basically to providing secure facilities and nonstate rehabilitative programs were uncertain both as to funding and to endurance, inevitably the parens patriae effort fell short.

No state agency had primary responsibility for the treatment of delinquents, and no state agency developed the necessary skills in creating and administering programs for delinquents. However, without cumulative experience in staffing and administering treatment programs, no one gained the necessary skills to guide such programs. Ironically, in most states the only state agency serving delinquent youth was the department handling juvenile corrections. States became skilled in developing custodial facilities for juveniles, but no state agency had lengthy experience in providing effective treatment programs for juvenile delinquents.

A Proposal

It would seem that the solution to the problem of effective treatment programs is straightforward. A continuing public authority is needed with responsibility for treatment programs both in the community and in juvenile institutions.[7] Where it should be situated in the hierarchy of state services to juveniles, or the scope and details of its responsibilities to delinquents need not concern us here. Whether it should be an independent department, part of the Department of Social Services, or the Department of Juvenile Corrections and Parole is not at issue at this point. Its mission should be treatment, and it should be in effect the court's rehabilitative arm, just as juvenile corrections is the court's custodial arm.[8]

Treatment programs for juveniles with psychological or social needs are as essential in civil society as unemployment insurance is for adults. Many juveniles need wise, skilled help in making a sound adjustment in adolescence, but unfortunately many cannot get such help from their families or anyone else, and to deny them by abandoning treatment programs is in effect cruel and socially destructive.

Treatment has worked only haphazardly because it has not been championed consistently by experienced agencies with roots in local communities. Where such agencies have emerged, as in Massachusetts during 1972 in the Department of Youth Services and in Utah during 1981 in the Division of Youth Corrections, the results have been generally humane and effective.[9]

Massachusetts under the Department of Youth Services has been using a system of community-based treatment programs for its delinquents since 1972 with solid results (see Loughran 1987). On any given day its youthful clients number about 1,700. Some 1,000 youths live at home and participate in a wide variety of treatment and educational community programs. The remaining children, 700, are divided between foster homes (30), nonsecure residential programs (500), and secure facilities (170). Serious offenders are dealt with via careful screening for violent tendencies, emotional stability, threat to the community, and social needs and are given programming specially designed for their situation.

The results in Massachusetts have been noteworthy (Miller and Ohlin 1985; Krisberg, Austin, and Steele 1989). In the beginning budgetary costs of caring for children via a system of community-based treatment programs were slightly more than for the old network of custodial institutions (Coates, Miller and Ohlin 1976, chapters 7, 8). However, the two systems were compared as of 1974, after only 2 years experience under the new system. More recently the system has become more effective, and today the annual cost per child in the Department of Youth Services (DYS) is about $23,000 compared with $35,000–40,000 reported by many other states (Krisberg, Austin, and Steele, 1989, pp. 32–37).

Since 1974 DYS has strengthened its program, and by 1986 delinquency arraignments in Massachusetts had dropped by 24% from their 1980 level (Massachusetts Department of Youth Services 1987, p. 10).[10] Further, delinquency arraignments for all released offenders compared with their level before admission to DYS is about one half, and arraignments for chronic or violent offenders decreased by slightly more than half (Krisberg, Austin, and Steele 1989, p. 19). In addition, the number of adult inmates in Massachusetts who had also been clients of the juvenile justice system in that state dropped from 35% in 1972 to 15% in 1985 (Loughran 1987). Since 1974 recidivism rates measured in terms of delinquency arraignments among DYS youth have dropped sharply, from 74% in 1974 (see Coates, Miller, and Ohlin 1976) to about 51% in 1985 (Krisberg, Austin, and Steele 1989, pp. 24–25). In comparison with other states where recidivism has been measured comparably, DYS dischargees have equaled or bettered the recidivism rates of all other state systems (Krisberg, Austin, and Steele 1989, pp. 26–32). These results suggest that many serious juvenile offenders within the Department of Youth Services have been helped by their experiences in the system.

In Utah, a new Division of Youth Corrections modeled after the Massachusetts Department of Youth Services was inaugurated in 1981 with full responsibility for secure and community-based treatment programs for delinquents in the state. Although the system is still too new to offer firm evidence of its effectiveness, its architects are delighted with results so far.

First, the shift to community-based programming required a budget $250,000 less than the old custodial-oriented system (Simon and Fagan 1987). The number of beds in secure facilities in Utah dropped from 450 in 1976 to 70 in 1986, while beds in community facilities increased from under 50 to 157 during the same period. Children in jails dropped from more than 700 in 1976 to 26 in 1986, and status offenders in detention declined from 3,324 to only 162 between 1976 and 1986. The shift was on to nonsecure facilities in Utah under the new treatment-oriented system.

Proof of its results is in the system's effects on delinquents. Preliminary data indicate that, as in Massachusetts, the community-based system is probably less criminogenic than the custodial system it replaced. A study by the Utah Division of Youth Corrections (1986) found that 73% of the youths who had received community placements remained free of criminal convictions for 12 months following their release, although fully 76% of the youths confined in secure facilities were reconvicted during their first year after release. Even here their offenses were much less serious. Before commitment these youths had averaged 24 convictions, including many serious violent and property offenses. After their term in Youth Corrections they were convicted primarily of minor offenses.

The twin goals of rehabilitation and justice can be blended effectively in the juvenile justice system. If dependable diagnostic and treatment programs can be made available to juvenile judges via a state treatment authority, justice in adjudication can be balanced with humane, effective treatment in dispositions.

Bifurcation: A Stumbling Block?

A difficult problem still remains. The history of juvenile justice confirms that secure facilities tend to become more punitive with age. Since the time of the houses of refuge, custodial institutions have shown a clear custodial drift with time (Ferdinand 1989, pp. 87–93).

According to Cohen (1985, pp. 218–35) institutions tend to differentiate themselves into custodial, punitive, exclusionary programs and rehabilitative, community-based, inclusionary programs. Cohen saw this bifurcation as paralleling a bifurcation of the system's clientele. On one hand, we have a small stream of stigmatized, antisocial offenders committed to a criminal way of life. On the other, we have a large stream of tractable but problem-bound offenders who want to become contributing citizens. Punitive, exclusionary programs serve the former and transform them into hardened, predatory criminals who are feared and shunned by the community. Inclusionary programs serve constructive offenders who are still looking for a rewarding life in mainstream society. Many of them, however, become agency-dependent and socially peripheral (see Ferdinand 1989).

According to Cohen (1985, chapter 7) inclusionary programs themselves become punitive and stigmatizing and are transformed thereby into exclusionary programs by virtue of the fact that newly established programs draw off the best clientele from older programs, leaving them to deal mainly with intractable inmates. As older programs adapt to a deteriorating population mix, they change slowly into punitive centers. Inclusionary programs gradually become exclusionary programs, and a long term pattern of institutional decay is established as the system repeatedly attempts to reform itself by reaching out to more responsive populations and relegating the rest to older, established programs.

Although Cohen was interested primarily in the adult system, he describes almost exactly the century-long development of juvenile justice in the United States (Ferdinand 1989). The houses of refuge were greeted enthusiastically by reform-minded progressives, only to see them transformed into punitive, stigmatizing institutions over the years (Brenzel 1983; Pisciotta 1982). The same was true of the state juvenile reformatories established in the last half of the 19th century (Rothman 1980; Schlossman 1977).

Ultimately, the juvenile correctional system in many states came to resemble a hierarchical system (see Steele and Jacobs 1975, 1977) of punitive, exclusionary institutions at the deep end (the maximum-security level) serving predatory, antisocial inmates, coupled with inclusionary, community-based programs at the shallow end serving a social tractable clientele with more focused problems. As each new program came on stream, it attracted the most promising clientele and the most progressive staff, and the rest were forced to adapt as best they could in the ensuing realignment.

An answer to this repetitive pattern of reform and decay, however, is not difficult to imagine. New programs need not focus on just the more tractable, responsive clientele. They could focus also on the other end—on the more serious, predatory offenders. After all, these are the offenders that spell the most trouble for society in the long run, and any advances in dealing with their problems would certainly be helpful. In this case the older programs would be asked to give up some of their *least* responsive inmates; their inmate mix would improve with each reform at the deep end; and one source of custodial drift, at least, would be arrested.

Such a policy would avoid drawing off the more promising clientele from the older, more experienced centers, but it would also foster small, specialized treatment settings—exactly the kind of centers that foster personal relationships among staff and children and thereby offer a chance for the staff to influence youth in positive ways (Street, Vinter, and Perrow 1966). Such centers are also easier to manage and supervise, with the result that treatment policies can be implemented more consistently over the long term.

This policy has been followed by Massachusetts since 1972—small, treatment oriented centers for virtually all juveniles in the Department of Youth Services (the largest is only 36 beds)—and no doubt some of the success of the DYS can be attributed to the positive attitudinal climate that small centers usually generate (see Krisberg, Austin, and Steele 1989, p. 4). But if this analysis is correct, this policy will also help to inhibit the souring of the custodial centers as their programs become routine.

A system of small treatment facilities must still be closely monitored lest some of them stray from their assigned mission. There is always the possibility that a center will develop punitive policies for other reasons. To avoid such missteps it is essential that each center be held closely accountable to clear standards of performance. Each center should be required to justify its policies with verifiable research.

⊠ Conclusion

Few maintain that juvenile justice has lived up to its promise in the United States, and many assert that its future lies basically with a due process/just deserts orientation. If treatment and rehabilitation are abandoned, however, in favor of a just deserts policy whereby serious delinquents are punished in large, custodial institutions, several untoward consequences would probably result.

First, delinquency would deepen in seriousness and expand its sway, laying the foundation for a worsening problem among adult predatory criminals in the years ahead. Second, an important voice for humane programs in the justice system would be stilled with the result that a monolithic retributive system and its programs would prevail not only in delinquency but in criminal justice as a whole.

The difficulties of treating juveniles in residential centers are, however, soluble. Differentiated systems of small, community based treatment facilities in both Massachusetts and Utah have shown themselves as more humane; comparable in cost; and more effective than the traditional network of juvenile custodial institutions. A permanent state agency committed to delinquency treatment programs would be a more responsible manager over the long term than the haphazard collection of private philanthropy, correctional departments, and federal agencies that have spearheaded most treatment reforms in the states up to now.

State departments of treatment services for delinquents also need research arms that can evaluate their programs with an eye to weeding out those programs that are ineffective. They need detailed information on their programs to represent the rehabilitation philosophy to state government and the mass media. The people of a state must ultimately choose the direction that is best for them, but they must be fully informed of the alternatives.

If such departments were available at the state level, it would give an immense lift to the juvenile court. This court has long pursued parens patriae in the community but with uncertain success and lately with waning confidence. A department of treatment services could provide both the variety in community programming and political support that the court needs to carry out its mission effectively.

The juvenile court cannot be both classification agent and programs agent for the rehabilitative process. It was never given a mandate to sponsor community-based treatment programs. The court is reasonably effective as a juvenile classification and assignment agency, but it needs an effective right arm to create and evaluate treatment programs throughout the state geared to local needs. Local juvenile courts working hand in glove with a state department of treatment services could finally realize the full potential of parens patriae.

To improve the juvenile court it is important to strengthen its links with the rest of the system, especially with those agencies that sponsor treatment programs. Up to now responsibility for these programs has been left mainly to custodial or private initiatives. Without a concept of the system as a whole, reform of the court inevitably focuses on inappropriate remedies, and the situation of delinquents only deteriorates. If the failure to rehabilitate juveniles lies with juvenile custodial facilities, reform should focus there and not solely on the parens patriae mandate of the court. Historical analysis can pinpoint the sources of the court's difficulties and thereby suggest appropriate lines of reform. Without such analyses our efforts will remain limited by ideological blinders and our reforms will decay as usual into tomorrow's problems.

⬛ Notes

1. It is interesting that as the juvenile court's jurisdiction over status offending has eroded in the last 30 years, runaways and school misbehavior have grown dramatically (see Gough 1977, pp. 283–87; Shane 1989). Although other factors have been active in this arena, the court's abandonment of status offenders may have contributed to the reemergence of these problems in the modern era.

2. Overlap among these schools accounts for the fact that their sum is much more than 30.

3. These figures were computed from statistics issued by the Boston Police Department and the U.S. Bureau of the Census. The population data for 1860 were gathered during an especially turbulent period, and may have missed a substantial portion of the transient population including juveniles. Thus delinquency arrest rates for that period may be overestimated.

4. In this sense the new court was a step back from the old civil court, because it handled both the most hardened, serious offenders in the same way as minor status offenders.

5. There is no room in juvenile justice for racial or gender bias, but most studies of bias have ignored an important fact that throws new light on the problem. Because the community (parents, school officials,

and neighbors) enjoys wide discretion in defining juvenile offending, an officer's decision to make an arrest, or a court's decision to detain a juvenile depends heavily on the biases of the complainant (see Hazard 1976; and Black and Reiss 1970). Where a biased victim demands action against a minority juvenile, chances are good that the police or the court will comply. A dismissal is difficult, if a complainant seeking punishment is close at hand. Thomas and Cage (1977) found in a study of more than 1,500 juveniles that their sanctioning in court was more severe if someone close to the case was pushing it.

6. Earlier the renowned Chicago Area Projects initiated by Henry Shaw and Clifford McKay in the 1930s probably had been successful, even though a failure to use an experimental design rendered a definitive statement as to their success impossible (see also Schlossman and Sedlak 1983).

7. We might call this authority the Department of Youth Services. Many states have a Department of Family Services that serves nondelinquent children, and the Department of Youth Services would offer many of the same programs for delinquents and children at risk of delinquency. It would coordinate its efforts with the juvenile courts, just as juvenile corrections does. Three state agencies, therefore, would provide social services to adolescents: Juvenile Corrections, which manages custodial institutions for juveniles; the Department of Youth Services, which manages the treatment effort for juvenile delinquents; and the Department of Family Services, which manages the treatment function for nondelinquent youth. Further consolidation of these three agencies need not be ruled out.

8. Some will say, "The state has already proven its ineptness in programs for youth. It does not deserve a second chance." My response is, if that is true, then the *only* alternative is the status quo, that is, a due process court and punitive juvenile institutions. Rehabilitating delinquents is too important to abandon simply because the state has stumbled in its efforts to fulfill parens patriae. If we can understand some of the reasons behind the state's ineptness, for example, a primary commitment to security in facilities, we can correct them.

9. Youth Services Bureaus, an offspring of Lyndon Johnson's 1960s campaign against delinquency,

represented a similar effort to bring treatment programs together under a single community agency. They were locally financed and suffered budget problems in many small cities, and they often differed with judges as to what delinquents needed.

10.   Certainly, other factors, for example, the downside of the baby boom and the cooling of the drugs epidemic among high schoolers, have contributed to this decline. But the size of the decline—24%—is consistent with a positive effect from juvenile justice.

✄ References

Allen, Francis A. 1964. *The Borderland of Criminal Justice.* Chicago: University of Chicago Press.

Andrews, D. A., Ivan Zinger, Robert D. Hodge, James Bonta, Paul Gendreau, and Francis T. Cullen. 1990. "Does Correctional Treatment Work? A Clinically Relevant and Psychologically Informed Meta-Analysis." *Criminology* 28:369–404.

Black, Donald J. and Albert J. Reiss, Jr. 1970. "Police Control of Juveniles." *American Sociological Review* 15(February):63–77.

Brenzel, Barbara M. 1983. *Daughters of the State.* Cambridge: MIT Press.

Caldwell, R. G. 1961. "The Juvenile Court: Its Development and Some Major Problems." *Journal of Criminal Law, Criminology, and Police Science* 51:493–511.

Coates, Robert B., Alden D. Miller, and Lloyd E. Ohlin. 1976. *Diversity in a Youth Correctional System.* Cambridge: Ballinger.

Cohen, Lawrence E. 1976. *Delinquency Dispositions: An Empirical Analysis of Processing Decisions in Three Juvenile Courts.* National Criminal Justice Information and Statistics Service, Law Enforcement Assistance Administration. Washington, DC: U.S. Government Printing Office.

Cohen, Stanley. 1985. *Visions of Social Control.* Cambridge: Polity Press.

Cohn, Yona. 1963. "Criteria for Probation Officers' Recommendations to the Juvenile Court." *Crime & Delinquency* 1:267–75.

Commonwealth v. Fisher 213 Pa. 48, 1905.

Creekmore, Mark. 1976. "Case Processing: Intake, Adjudication, and Disposition." Pp. 119–51 in *Brought to Justice? Juveniles, the Courts, and the Law,* edited by Rosemary Sarri and Yeheskel Hasenfeld. Ann Arbor: University of Michigan.

Deutsch, Albert. 1950. *Our Rejected Children.* Boston: Little, Brown.

Diana, Lewis. 1955. "Is Casework in Probation Necessary?" *Focus* 34(January):l–8.

Dungworth, Terrence. 1977. "Discretion in the Juvenile Justice System: The Impact of Case Characteristics on Prehearing Detention." Pp. 19–43 in *Little Brother Grows Up,* edited by Theodore N. Ferdinand. Beverly Hills, CA: Sage.

Empey, Lamar and Steven G. Lubeck. 1971. *Silverlake Experiment: Testing Delinquency Theory and Community Intervention.* Chicago: Aldine Press.

Empey, Lamar and Maynard Erickson. 1972. *The Provo Experiment: Evaluating Community Control of Delinquency.* Lexington, MA: Lexington Books.

Ex parte Crouse, 4 Whart. 9, Pa. 1838.

Fagan, Jeffery, Ellen Slaughter, and Eliot Hartstone. 1987. "Blind Justice? The Impact of Race on the Juvenile Justice Process." *Crime & Delinquency* 33:224–58.

Ferdinand, Theodore N. 1989. "Juvenile Delinquency or Juvenile Justice: Which Came First?" *Criminology* 27:79–106.

Foucault, Michel, 1979. *Discipline and Punish.* New York: Vintage Books.

Garlock, Peter D. 1979. "'Wayward' Children and the Law, 1820–1900: The Genesis of the Status Offense Jurisdiction of the Juvenile Court." *Georgia Law Review* 13:341–448.

Gough, Aidan R. 1977. "Beyond Control Youth in the Juvenile Court—the Climate for Change." Pp. 271–96 in *Beyond Control: Status Offenders in the Juvenile Court,* edited by Lee E. Teitelbaum and Aidan R. Gough. Cambridge, MA: Ballinger.

Hazard, Geoffrey C., Jr. 1976. "The Jurisprudence of Juvenile Deviance." Pp. 3–19 *in Pursuing Justice for the Child,* edited by Margaret K. Rosenheim. Chicago: University of Chicago Press.

In re Ellery C., 347 N.Y. 2d 51 1973.

In re Ferrier, 103 111. 367, 1882.

In re Lavette M., 359 N.Y. 2d 201, 1974.

Kaestle, Carl F. and Maris A. Vinovskis. 1980. *Education and Change.* London: Cambridge University Press.

Klein, Malcolm. 1971. *Street Gangs and Street Workers.* Englewood Cliffs, NJ: Prentice Hall.

Kobrin, Solomon and Malcolm Klein. 1983. *Community Treatment of Juvenile Offenders.* Beverly Hills, CA: Sage.

Krisberg, Barry, James Austin, and Patricia A. Steele. 1989. *Unlocking Juvenile Corrections: Evaluating the Massachusetts Department of Youth Services.* San Francisco: National Council on Crime and Delinquency.

Lerman, Paul. 1975. *Community Treatment and Control.* Chicago: University of Chicago Press.

Lipsey, Mark W. 1991. "Juvenile Delinquency Treatment: A Meta-Analytic Inquiry into the Variability of Effects." *Meta-Analysis for Explanation: A Casebook.* New York: Russell Sage Foundation.

Loughran, Edward J. 1987. "Juvenile Corrections: The Massachusetts Experience." Pp. 7–18 in *Reinvesting in Youth Corrections Resources: A Tale of Three States,* edited by Lee Eddison. Ann Arbor: School of Social Work, University of Michigan.

Martinson, Robert. 1974. "What Works—Questions and Answers About Prison Reform." *Public Interest* 32: 22–54.

Massachusetts Department of Youth Services. 1987. "Annual Report 1986," pp. 1–16. Boston: Author.

Mennel, Robert M. 1973. *Thorns & Thistles.* Hanover, NH: University Press of New England.

Miller, Alden D. and Lloyd E. Ohlin. 1985. *Delinquency and Community.* Beverly Hills, CA: Sage.

Miller, Walter. 1962. "The Impact of a 'Total-Community' Delinquency Control Project." *Social Problems* 10:168–91.

Palmer, Ted. 1974. "The Youth Authority Community Treatment Project." *Federal Probation* 38: 3–14.

Pisciotta, Alexander W. 1982. "Saving the Children: The Promise and Practice of Parens Patriae, 1838–1898." *Crime & Delinquency* 28: 410–25.

———. 1985. "Treatment on Trial: The Rhetoric and Reality of the New York House of Refuge, 1857–1935." *American Journal of Legal History* 29: 151–81.

Robin, Gerald N. 1969. "Anti-Poverty Programs and Delinquency." *Journal of Criminal Law, Criminology, and Police Science* 60: 327

Rothman, David J. 1980. *Conscience and Convenience.* Boston: Little, Brown.

Rubin, H. Ted. 1985. *Juvenile Justice,* 2nd ed. New York: Random House.

Sarnecki, Jerzy. 1988. *Juvenile Delinquency in Sweden.* Stockholm: National Council for Crime Prevention, Information Division.

Scarpitti, Frank R. and Richard M. Stephenson. 1968. "A Study of Probation Effectiveness." *Journal of Criminal Law, Criminology, and Police Science* 3: 361–69.

Schlossman, Steven L. 1977. *Love and the American Delinquent.* Chicago: University of Chicago Press.

Schlossman, Steven L. and Michael Sedlak. 1983. "The Chicago Area Project Revisited." *Crime & Delinquency* 29:398–462.

Schultz, Stanley K. 1973. *The Culture Factory Boston Public Schools, 1789–1860.* New York: Oxford University Press.

Shane, Paul G. 1989. "Changing Patterns of Homelessness and Runaway Youth." *American Journal of Orthopsychiatry* 59:208–14.

Simon, Cindy and Julie Fagan. 1987. "Youth Corrections in Utah: Remaking a System." *National Conference of State Legislatures* 12:1–12.

Steele, Eric H. and James B. Jacobs. 1975. "A Theory of Prison Systems." *Crime & Delinquency* 21: 149–62.

———. 1977. "Untangling Minimum Security: Concepts, Realities, and Implications for Correctional Systems." *Journal of Research in Crime and Delinquency* 14:68–83.

Street, David, Robert D. Vinter, and Charles Perrow. 1966. *Organization for Treatment.* New York: Free Press.

Sutton, John R. 1988. *Stubborn Children.* Berkeley: University of California Press.

———. 1990. "Bureaucrats and Entrepreneurs: Institutional Responses to Deviant Children, 1890–1920s." *American Journal of Sociology* 95: 1367–1400.

Tappan, Paul. 1946. "Treatment Without Trial?" *Social Problems* 24:306–11.

Terry, Robert. 1967. "Discrimination in the Police Handling of Juvenile Offenders by Social Control Agencies." *Journal of Research in Crime and Delinquency* 4: 212–20.

Thomas, Charles W. and Robin J. Cage. 1977. "The Effects of Social Characteristics on Juvenile Court Dispositions." *Sociological Quarterly* 18: 237–52.

Thornberry, Terence P. 1973. "Race, Socioeconomic Status and Sentencing in the Juvenile Justice

System." *Journal of Criminal Law and Criminology* 64:90–98.

Utah State Division of Youth Corrections. 1986. "Planning Task Force Final Report." Salt Lake City, December.

Warren, Marguerite. 1976. "Intervention with Juvenile Delinquents." Pp. 176–204 in *Pursuing Justice for the Child,* edited by Margaret K. Rosenheim. Chicago: University of Chicago Press.

DISCUSSION QUESTIONS

1. How did compulsory education and problem schoolchildren affect the early juvenile justice system?

2. What were the criticisms directed at the juvenile justice system after World War II?

3. Ferdinand disputes the belief that juvenile treatment programs were a failure. What are some examples of effective juvenile treatment programs?

4. What is Ferdinand's proposal for treatment in juvenile community and institutional programs?

READING

Barry Krisberg traces the development of juvenile justice in America and how it was patterned after the British and European justice systems. He discusses the failures of the early U.S. juvenile justice system to adequately serve marginalized youth, and the role of houses of refuge and child savers in the history of juvenile justice. The Progressive Era of American juvenile justice is highlighted with a discussion of the Child Guidance Clinic Movement, the Chicago Area Project, the Mobilization for Youth, and changes in institutional and community-based corrections and the juvenile law.

The Historical Legacy of Juvenile Justice

Barry Krisberg

The first institution for the control of juvenile delinquency in the United States was the New York House of Refuge, founded in 1825, but specialized treatment of wayward youth has a much longer history—one tied to changes in the social structure of medieval Europe. These same changes prompted the colonization of the New World and led to attempts to control and exploit the labor of African, European, and Native American children.

Virtually all aspects of life were in a state of flux for the people of Europe in the later Middle Ages (16th and 17th centuries). The economy was being transformed from a feudal system based on sustenance agriculture to a capitalistic, trade-oriented system focusing on cash crops and the consolidation of large tracts of land. In religious matters, the turmoil could be amply witnessed in the intense struggles of the Reformation.

SOURCE: B. Krisberg. *Juvenile Justice: Redeeming Our Children* (2005).

Politically, power was increasingly concentrated in the hands of a few monarchs, who were fashioning strong centralized states. The growth of trade and exploration exposed Europeans to a variety of world cultures and peoples.

For the lower classes of European society, these were "the worst of times." The rising population density as well as primitive agricultural methods led to a virtual exhaustion of the land. Increasing urban populations created new demands for cheap grain, and landlords responded by increasing the fees paid by peasants who worked the land. Large numbers of peasants were displaced from the land to permit the growth of a capitalist pasturage system. The standard of living of the European peasantry dropped sharply, and this new, displaced class streamed into the cities and towns in search of means of survival. The workers and artisans of the cities were deeply threatened by the prospect that this pauper class would drive down the general wage level. Most European towns experienced sharp rises in crime, rioting, and public disorder.

To control and defuse the threat of this new "dangerous class," the leaders of the towns enacted laws and other restrictions to discourage immigration and contain the movement of the impoverished peasantry. "Poor laws" were passed, preventing the new migrants from obtaining citizenship, restricting their membership in guilds, and often closing the city gates to them. Vagrancy laws were instituted to control and punish those who seemed a threat to the social order. Certain legislation, such as the Elizabethan Statute of Artificers (1562), restricted access into certain trades, forcing the rural young to remain in the countryside.

Urban migration continued despite most attempts to curtail it. The collective units of urban life, the guild and the family, began to weaken under the pressure of social change. Children often were abandoned or released from traditional community restraints. Countless observers from the period tell of bands of youths roaming the cities at night, engaging in thievery, begging, and other forms of misbehavior (Sanders, 1970).

At this time family control of children was the dominant model for disciplining wayward youth. The model of family government, with the father in the role of sovereign, was extended to those without families through a system of *binding out* the young to other families. Poor children, or those beyond parental control, were apprenticed to householders for a specified period of time. Unlike the apprenticeship system for the privileged classes, the binding-out system did not oblige the master to teach his ward a trade. Boys generally were assigned to farming tasks and girls were brought into domestic service.

As the problem of urban poverty increased, the traditional modes of dealing with delinquent or destitute children became strained. Some localities constructed institutions to control wayward youth. The Bridewell (1555) in London is generally considered the first institution specifically designed to control youthful beggars and vagrants. In 1576 the English Parliament passed a law establishing a similar institution in every English county. The most celebrated of these early institutions was the Amsterdam House of Corrections (1595), which was viewed as an innovative solution to the crime problem of the day.[1] The houses of correction combined the principles of the poorhouse, the workhouse, and the penal institution. The youthful inmates were forced to work within the institution and thus develop habits of industriousness. Upon release they were expected to enter the labor force, so house of correction inmates often were hired out to private contractors. Males rasped hardwoods used in the dyeing industry, and when textile manufacturing was introduced to the houses of correction, this became the special task of young woman inmates.

The early houses of correction, or so-called "Bridewells," accepted all types of children including the destitute, the infirm, and the needy. In some cases, parents placed their children in these institutions because they believed the regimen of work would have a reformative effect. Although it is debatable whether the houses of correction were economically efficient, the founders of such institutions dearly hoped to provide a cheap source of labor to local industries. The French institutions, called *hospitaux generaux,* experimented with technological improvements and different labor arrangements. This often brought charges of unfair competition from guilds, who feared the demise of their monopoly on labor, and businessmen, who felt threatened by price competition at the marketplace. Some authors stress the economic motive of these early penal institutions: "The institution of the houses of correction in such a society was not the result of brotherly love or of an official sense of obligation to the distressed. It was part of the development of capitalism" (Rusche & Kirchheimer, 1939, p. 50).

The enormous social, political, and economic dislocations taking place in Europe provided a major push toward colonization of the Americas. People emigrated for many reasons— some to get rich, some to escape political or religious oppression, and some because they simply had nothing to lose. Settlement patterns and the resulting forms of community life varied considerably. In the Massachusetts Bay Colony, for example, the Puritans attempted to establish a deeply religious community to serve God's will in the New World. The Puritans brought families with them and from the outset made provisions for the care and control of youths.

In contrast, the settlement of Virginia was more directly tied to economic considerations. There were persistent labor shortages, and the need for labor prompted orders for young people to be sent over from Europe. Some youths were sent over by "spirits," who were agents of merchants or ship owners. The spirits attempted to persuade young people to immigrate to America. They often promised that the New World would bring tremendous wealth and happiness to the youthful immigrants. The children typically agreed to work a specific term (usually 4 years) in compensation for passage across the Atlantic and for services rendered during the trip. These agreements of service were then sold to inhabitants of the new colonies, particularly in the South. One can imagine that this labor source must have been quite profitable for the plantations of the New World. Spirits were often accused of kidnapping, contractual fraud, and deception of a generally illiterate, destitute, and young clientele.

Other children coming to the New World were even more clearly coerced. For example, it became an integral part of penal practice in the early part of the 18th century to transport prisoners to colonial areas. Children held in the overcrowded Bridewells and poorhouses of England were brought to the Americas as indentured servants. After working a specified number of years as servants or laborers, the children were able to win their freedom. In 1619 the colony of Virginia regularized an agreement for the shipment of orphans and destitute children from England.

That same year, Africans, another group of coerced immigrants, made their first appearance in the Virginia Colony. The importation of African slaves eventually displaced the labor of youthful poor because of greater economic feasibility. The black chattels were physically able to perform strenuous labor under extreme weather conditions without adequate nutrition. These abilities would finally be used to describe them as beasts. Also, the high death rates experienced under these conditions did not have to be accounted for. The bondage of Africans was soon converted into lifetime enslavement, which passed on through generations. The southern plantation system, dependent on the labor of African slaves, produced tremendous wealth, further entrenching this inhuman system (Stamp, 1956; Yetman, 1970). Racism, deeply lodged in the English psyche, provided the rationale and excuse for daily atrocities and cruelties.[2]

Studies of slavery often overlook the fact that most slaves were children. Slave traders thought children would bring higher prices. Accounts of the slave trade emphasize the economic utility of small children, who could be jammed into the limited cargo space available on slave ships. Children were always a high proportion of the total slave population, because slave owners encouraged the birth of children to increase their capital. Little regard was paid by slave owners to keeping families together. African babies were a commodity to be exploited just as one might exploit the land or the natural resources of a plantation, and young slave women often were used strictly for breeding. A complete understanding of the social control of children must include a comparison of the institution of slavery to the conditions faced by children in other sections of the country.[3]

Another group of children who often are ignored in discussions of the history of treatment of youth in North America are Native Americans. In 1609 officials of the Virginia Company were authorized to kidnap Native American children and raise them as Christians. The stolen youths were to be trained in the religion, language, and customs of the colonists. The early European colonists spread the word of the Gospel to help rationalize their conquests of lands and peoples. But an equally important motivation was their interest in recruiting a group of friendly natives to assist in trade negotiations and pacification programs among the native peoples. The early Indian schools resembled penal institutions, with heavy emphasis on useful work, Bible study and religious worship. Although a substantial amount of effort and money was invested in Indian schools, the results were considerably less than had been originally hoped:

> Missionaries could rarely bridge the chasm of mistrust and hostility that resulted from wars, massacres and broken promises. With so many colonists regarding the Indian as the chief threat to their security and the Indians looking upon the colonists as hypocrites, it is little wonder that attempts to win converts and to educate should fail. (Bremner, Barnard, Hareven, & Mennel, 1970, p. 72)

Unlike attempts to enslave children of African descent, early efforts with Native Americans were not successful. Relations between European colonists and Native Americans during this period centered around trading and the securing of land rights. These contrasting economic relationships resulted in divergent practices in areas such as education. Although there was general support for bringing "the blessings of Christian education" to the Native American children, there was intense disagreement about the merits of educating African slaves. Whereas some groups, such as the Society for the Propagation of the Gospel, argued that all "heathens" should be educated and converted, others feared that slaves who were baptized would claim the status of freemen. There was concern among whites that education of slaves would lead to insurrection and revolt. As a result, South Carolina and several other colonies proclaimed that conversion to Christianity would not affect the status of slaves (Bremner et al., 1970). Many southern colonies made it a crime to teach reading and writing to slaves. A middle-ground position evolved, calling for religious indoctrination without the more dangerous education in literacy (Bremner et al., 1970; Gossett, 1963).

In the early years of colonization, the family was the fundamental mode of juvenile social control, as well as the central unit of economic production. Even in situations where children were apprenticed or indentured, the family still served as the model for discipline and order. Several of the early colonies passed laws requiring single persons to live with families. The dominant form of poor relief at this time was placing the needy with other families in the community (Rothman, 1971). A tradition of family government evolved in which the father was empowered with absolute authority over all affairs of the family. Wives and children were expected to give complete and utter obedience to the father's wishes. This model complemented practices in political life, where absolute authority was thought to be crucial to the preservation of civilization.

Colonial laws supported and defended the primacy of family government. The earliest laws concerning youthful misbehavior prescribed the death penalty for children who disobeyed their parents. For example, part of the 1641 Massachusetts *Body of Liberties* reads as follows:

If any child, or children, above sixteen years of age, and of sufficient understanding, shall CURSE or SMITE their natural FATHER or MOTHER, he or they shall be putt to death, unless it can be sufficiently testified that the Parents have been very unchristianly negligent in the education of such children: so provoked them by extreme and cruel correction, that they have been forced thereunto, to preserve themselves from death or maiming: *Exod* 21:17, *Lev* 20:9, *Exod* 21:15. (Hawes, 1971, p. 13)

Although there is little evidence that children were actually put to death for disobeying their parents, this same legal principle was used to justify the punishment of rebellious slave children in the southern colonies. Family discipline typically was maintained by corporal punishment. Not only were parents held legally responsible for providing moral education for their children, but a Massachusetts law of 1642 also mandated that parents should teach their children reading and writing. Later, in 1670, public officials called tithing men were assigned to assist the selectmen (town councilmen) and constables in supervising family government. The tithing men visited families who allegedly were ignoring the education and socialization of their children. Although there are records of parents brought to trial due to their neglect of parental duties, this manner of supervising family government was not very successful.

The family was the central economic unit of colonial North America. Home-based industry, in which labor took place on the family farm or in a home workshop, continued until the end of the 18th century. Children were an important component of family production, and their labor was considered valuable and desirable. A major determinant of a child's future during this time was the father's choice of apprenticeship for his child. Ideally the apprenticeship system was to be the stepping stone into a skilled craft, but this happy result was certain only for children of the privileged classes. As a consequence, children of poor families might actually be *bound out* as indentured servants. The term of apprenticeship was generally seven years, and the child was expected to regard his master with the same obedience due natural parents. The master was responsible for the education and training of the young apprentice and he acted *in loco parentis,* assuming complete responsibility for the child's material and spiritual welfare. Although apprenticeships were voluntary for the wealthier citizens, for the wayward or destitute child they were unavoidable. The use of compulsory apprenticeships was an important form of social control exercised by town and religious officials upon youths perceived as troublesome (Bremner et al., 1970).

The industrial revolution in North America, beginning at the end of the 18th century, brought about the gradual transformation of the labor system of youth. The family-based productive unit gave way to an early factory system. Child labor in industrial settings supplanted the apprenticeship system. As early as the 1760s there were signs that the cotton industry in New England would transform the system of production, and by 1791 all stages in the manufacture of raw cotton into cloth were performed by factory machinery. The Samuel Slater factory in Providence, Rhode Island, employed 100 children aged 4–10 years in cotton manufacture. Here is a description of the workplace environment:

They worked in one room where all the machinery was concentrated under the supervision of a foreman, spreading the cleaned cotton on the carding machine to be combed and passing it though the roving machine, which turned the cotton into loose rolls ready to be spun. Some of the children tended the spindles, removing and attaching bobbins. Small, quick fingers were admirably suited for picking up and knotting broken threads. To the delight of Tench Coxe, a champion of American industry, the children became "the little fingers . . . of the gigantic automatons of labor-saving machinery." (Bremner et al., 1970, p. 146)

During the next two decades, the use of children in New England industrial factories increased, and children composed 47%–55% of the labor force in the cotton mills. The proliferation of the factory system transformed the lives of many Americans. On one hand, enormous wealth began to accumulate in the hands of a few individuals. At the same time, the switch from a family-based economy to a factory system where workers sold their labor meant that many families were displaced from the land. A large class of permanently impoverished Americans evolved. The use of child labor permitted early industrialists to depress the general wage level. Moreover, companies provided temporary housing and supplies to workers at high prices, so that workers often incurred substantial debts rather than financial rewards.

Increased child labor also contributed to the weakening of family ties, because work days were long and often competed with family chores. Children were now responsible to two masters—their fathers and their factory supervisors. Work instruction became distinct from general education and spiritual guidance as the family ceased to be an independent economic unit. Conditions of poverty continued to spread, and the social control system predicated upon strong family government began to deteriorate. During the first decades of the 19th century, one could begin to observe a flow of Americans from rural areas to the urban centers. As increasing economic misery combined with a decline in traditional forms of social control, an ominous stage was being set. Some Americans began to fear deeply the growth of a "dangerous class" and attempted to develop new measures to control the wayward youth who epitomized this threat to social stability.

The Houses of Refuge (1825–1860)[4]

Severe economic downturns in the first two decades of the 19th century forced many Americans out of work. At the same time, increasing numbers of Irish immigrants arrived in the United States. These changes in the social structure, combined with the growth of the factory system, contributed to the founding of specialized institutions for the control and prevention of juvenile delinquency in the United States (Hawes, 1971; Mennel, 1973; Pickett, 1969).

As early as 1817, the more privileged Americans became concerned about the apparent connection between increased pauperism and the rise of delinquency. The Society for the Prevention of Pauperism was an early attempt to evaluate contemporary methods of dealing with the poor and to suggest policy changes. This group also led campaigns against taverns and theaters, which they felt contributed to the problem of poverty. The efforts of several members of this group led to the founding in New York City of the first House of Refuge in 1825. The group conducted investigations, drew up plans and legislation, and lobbied actively to gain acceptance of their ideas. In other Northeastern cities, such as Boston and Philadelphia, similar efforts were under way.

A number of historians have described these early 19th-century philanthropists as "conservative reformers" (Coben & Ratner, 1970; Mennel, 1973). These men were primarily from wealthy, established families and often were prosperous merchants or professionals. Ideologically, they were close to the thinking of the colonial elite and, later, to the Federalists. Popular democracy was anathema to them because they viewed themselves as God's elect and felt bound to accomplish His charitable objectives in the secular world. Leaders of the movement to establish the houses of refuge, such as John Griscom, Thomas Eddy, and John Pintard, viewed themselves as responsible for the moral health of the community, and they intended to regulate community morality through the example of their own proper behavior as well as through benevolent activities. The poor and the deviant were the objects of their concern and their moral stewardship.

Although early 19th-century philanthropists relied on religion to justify their good works, their primary motivation was the protection of their class privileges. Fear of social unrest and chaos dominated their thinking (Mennel, 1973). The rapid growth of a visible impoverished class, coupled with apparent increases in crime, disease, and immorality, worried those in power. The bitter class struggles of the French Revolution and periodic riots in urban areas of the United States signaled danger to the status quo. The philanthropy of this group was aimed at reestablishing social order, while preserving the existing property and status relationships. They were responsible for founding such organizations as the American Sunday School Union, the American Bible Society, the African Free School Society, and the Society for Alleviating the Miseries of Public Prisons. They often were appointed to positions on boards of managers for lunatic asylums, public hospitals, workhouses for the poor, and prisons.

The idea for houses of refuge was part of a series of reform concepts designed to reduce juvenile delinquency. Members of the Society for the Prevention of Pauperism were dissatisfied with the prevailing practice of placing children in adult jails and workhouses. Some reformers felt that exposing children to more seasoned offenders would increase the chances of such children becoming adult criminals. Another issue was the terrible condition of local jails. Others worried that, due to these abominable conditions, judges and juries would lean toward acquittal of youthful criminals to avoid sending them to such places. Reformers also objected that the punitive character of available penal institutions would not solve the basic problem of pauperism. The reformers envisioned an institution with educational facilities, set in the context of a prison. John Griscom called for "the erection of new prisons for juvenile offenders" (Mennel, 1973). A report of the Society for the Prevention of Pauperism suggested the following principles for such new prisons:

These prisons should be rather schools for instruction, than places of punishment, like our present state prisons where the young and the old are confined indiscriminately. The youth confined there should be placed under a course of discipline, severe and unchanging, but alike calculated to subdue and conciliate. A system should be adopted that would provide a mental and moral regimen. (Mennel, 1973, p. 11)

By 1824 the society had adopted a state charter in New York under the name of the Society for the Reformation of Juvenile Delinquents and had begun a search for a location for the House of Refuge.

On New Year's Day, 1825, the New York House of Refuge opened with solemn pomp and circumstance. A year later the Boston House of Reformation was started, and in 1828 the Philadelphia House of Refuge began to admit wayward youth. These new institutions accepted both children convicted of crimes and destitute children. Because they were founded as preventive institutions, the early houses of refuge could accept children who "live an idle or dissolute life, whose parents are dead or if living, from drunkenness, or other vices, neglect to provide any suitable employment or exercise any salutary control over said children" (Bremner et al., 1970, p. 681). Thus, from the outset, the first special institutions for juveniles housed together delinquent, dependent, and neglected children—a practice still observed in most juvenile detention facilities today.[5]

The development of this new institution of social control necessitated changes in legal doctrines to justify the exercise of power by refuge officials. In Commonwealth v. M'Keagy (1831), the Pennsylvania courts had to rule on the legality of a proceeding whereby a child was committed to the Philadelphia House of Refuge on the weight of his father's evidence that the child was "an idle and disorderly person." The court affirmed the right of the state to take a child away from a parent in cases of vagrancy or crime, but because this child was not a vagrant, and the father was not poor, the court ruled that the child should not be committed. Judicial officials did not wish to confuse protection of children with punishment, because this might engender constitutional questions as to whether children committed to houses of refuge had received the protection of due process of law.

The related question of whether parental rights were violated by involuntary refuge commitments was put to a legal test in *Ex parte Crouse* (1838). The father of a child committed to the Philadelphia House of Refuge attempted to obtain her release through a writ of habeas corpus. The state supreme court denied the motion, holding that the right of parental control is a natural but not inalienable right:

> The object of the charity is reformation, by training the inmates to industry; by imbuing their minds with principles of morality and religion; by furnishing them with means to earn a living; and, above all, by separating them from the corrupting influence of improper associates. To this end, may not the natural parents, when unequal to the task of education, or unworthy of it, be superseded by the *parens patriae,* or common guardian of the community? The infant has been snatched from a course which must have ended in confirmed depravity; and, not only is the restraint of her person lawful, but it would have been an act of extreme cruelty to release her from it. (*Ex parte Crouse,* 1838)

The elaboration of the doctrine of *parens patriae* in the Crouse case was an important legal principle used to support the expanded legal powers of the juvenile court. It is important to recognize the significance of both social class and hostility toward Irish immigrants in the legal determination of the Crouse case.[6] Because Irish immigrants were viewed at this time as corrupt and unsuitable as parents, it is easy to see how anti-immigrant feelings could color judgments about the suitability of parental control. As a result, children of immigrants made up the majority of inmates of the houses of refuge.

The early houses of refuge either excluded blacks or housed them in segregated facilities. In 1849 the city of Philadelphia opened the House of Refuge for Colored Juvenile Delinquents. Racially segregated refuges were maintained in New York City and Boston only through the limited funds donated by antislavery societies. Because refuge managers viewed all young woman delinquents as sexually promiscuous with little hope for eventual reform, young women also received discriminatory treatment.[7]

The managers of houses of refuge concentrated on perfecting institutional regimens that would result in reformation of juveniles. Descriptions of daily activities stress regimentation, absolute subordination to authority, and monotonous repetition:

> At sunrise, the children are warned, by the ringing of a bell, to rise from their beds. Each child makes his own bed, and steps forth, on a signal, into the Hall. They then proceed, in perfect order, to the Wash Room. Thence they are marched to parade in the yard, and undergo an examination as to their dress and cleanliness; after which they attend morning prayer. The morning school then commences, where they are occupied in summer, until 7 o'clock. A short intermission is allowed, when the bell rings for breakfast; after which, they proceed to their respective workshops, where they labor until 12 o'clock, when they are called from work, and one hour allowed them for washing and eating their dinner. At one, they again commence work, and continue at it until five in the afternoon, when the labors of the day terminate. Half an hour is allowed for washing and eating their supper, and at half-past five, they are conducted to the school room, where they continue at their studies until 8 o'clock. Evening Prayer is performed by the Superintendent; after

which, the children are conducted to their dormitories, which they enter, and are locked up for the night, when perfect silence reigns throughout the establishment. The foregoing is the history of a single day, and will answer for every day in the year, except Sundays, with slight variations during stormy weather, and the short days in winter. (Bremner et al., 1970, p. 688)[8]

Routines were enforced by corporal punishment as well as other forms of control. Houses of refuge experimented with primitive systems of classification based on the behavior of inmates. The Boston House of Reformation experimented with inmate self-government as a control technique. But, despite public declarations to the contrary, there is ample evidence of the use of solitary confinement, whipping, and other physical punishments.

Inmates of the houses of refuge labored in large workshops manufacturing shoes, producing brass nails, or caning chairs. Young woman delinquents often were put to work spinning cotton and doing laundry. It is estimated that income generated from labor sold to outside contractors supplied up to 40% of the operating expenses of the houses of refuge. The chief problem for refuge managers was that economic depressions could dry up the demand for labor, and there was not always sufficient work to keep the inmates occupied. Not only were there complaints that contractors abused children, but also that such employment prepared youngsters for only the most menial work.

Youths were committed to the houses of refuge for indeterminate periods of time until the legal age of majority. Release was generally obtained through an apprenticeship by the youths to some form of service. The system was akin to the binding-out practices of earlier times. Males typically were apprenticed on farms, on whaling boats, or in the merchant marine. Young women usually were placed into domestic service. Only rarely was a house-of-refuge child placed in a skilled trade. Apprenticeship decisions often were made to ensure that the child would not be reunited with his or her family, because this was presumed to be the root cause of the child's problems. As a result, there are many accounts of siblings and parents vainly attempting to locate their lost relatives.

The founders of the houses of refuge were quick to declare their own efforts successful. Prominent visitors to the institutions, such as Alexis de Tocqueville and Dorothea Dix, echoed the praise of the founders. Managers of the refuges produced glowing reports attesting to the positive results of the houses. Sharp disagreements over the severity of discipline required led to the replacement of directors who were perceived as too permissive. Elijah Devoe (1848), a house of refuge assistant superintendent, wrote poignantly of the cruelties and injustices in these institutions. There are accounts of violence within the institutions as well. Robert Mennel (1973) estimates that approximately 40% of the children escaped either from the institutions or from their apprenticeship placements. The problems that plagued the houses of refuge did not dampen the enthusiasm of the philanthropists, who assumed that the reformation process was a difficult and tenuous business at best.

Public relations efforts proclaiming the success of the houses of refuge helped lead to a rapid proliferation of similar institutions (Rothman, 1971). While special institutions for delinquent and destitute youth increased in numbers, the public perceived that delinquency was continuing to rise and become more serious. The founders of the houses of refuge argued that the solution to the delinquency problem lay in the perfection of better methods to deal with incarcerated children. Most of the literature of this period assumes the necessity of institutionalized treatment for children. The debates centered around whether to implement changes in architecture or in the institutional routines. Advocates of institutionalized care of delinquent and dependent youths continued to play the dominant role in formulating social policy for the next century.

The Growth of Institutionalization and the Child Savers (1850–1890)

In the second half of the 19th century, a group of reformers known as the Child Savers instituted new measures to prevent juvenile delinquency (Hawes, 1971; Mennel, 1973; Platt, 1968). Reformers including Lewis Pease, Samuel Gridley Howe, and Charles Loring Brace founded societies to save children from depraved and criminal lives. They created the Five Points Mission (1850), the Children's Aid Society (1853), and the New York Juvenile Asylum (1851). The ideology of this group of reformers differed from that of the founders of the houses of refuge only in that this group was more optimistic about the possibilities of reforming youths. Centers were established in urban areas to distribute food and clothing, provide temporary shelter for homeless youth, and introduce contract systems of shirt manufacture to destitute youth.

The Child Savers criticized the established churches for not doing more about the urban poor. They favored an activist clergy that would attempt to reach the children of the streets. Although this view was somewhat unorthodox, they viewed the urban masses as a potentially dangerous class that could rise up if misery and impoverishment were not alleviated. Charles Loring Brace observed, "Talk of heathen! All the pagans of Golconda would not hold a light to the ragged, cunning, forsaken, godless, keen devilish boys of Leonard Street and the Five Points . . . Our future voters, and President-makers, and citizens! Good Lord deliver us, and help them!" (quoted in Mennel, 1973, p. 34). Brace and his associates knew from firsthand experience in the city missions that the problems of poverty were widespread and growing more serious. Their chief objection to the houses of refuge was that long-term institutionalized care did not reach enough children. Moreover, the

Child Savers held the traditional view that family life is superior to institutional routines for generating moral reform.

Brace and his Children's Aid Society believed that delinquency could be solved if vagrant and poor children were gathered up and "placed out" with farm families on the western frontier. Placing out as a delinquency-prevention practice was based on the idealized notion of the U.S. farm family. Such families were supposed to be centers of warmth, compassion, and morality; they were "God's reformatories" for wayward youth. Members of the Children's Aid Society provided food, clothing, and sometimes shelter to street waifs and preached to them about the opportunities awaiting them if they migrated westward. Agents of the Children's Aid Society vigorously urged poor urban youngsters to allow themselves to be placed out with farm families. Many believed that western families provided both a practical and economical resource for reducing juvenile delinquency. The following passage from a Michigan newspaper gives a vivid picture of the placing out process:

Our village has been astir for a few days. Saturday afternoon, Mr. C. C. Tracy arrived with a party of children from the Children's Aid Society in New York . . .

Sabbath day Mr. Tracy spoke day and evening, three times, in different church edifices to crowded and interested audiences. In the evening, the children were present in a body, and sang their "Westward Ho" song. Notice was given that applicants would find unappropriated children at the store of Carder and Ryder, at nine o'clock Monday morning. Before the hour arrived a great crowd assembled, and in two hours *every child was disposed of,* and more were wanted.

We *Wolverines* will never forget Mr. Tracy's visit. It cost us some tears of sympathy, some dollars, and some smiles. We wish him a safe return to Gotham, a speedy one to us with the new company of destitute children, for whom good homes are even now prepared. (Mennel, 1973, p. 39)

Contrary to the benevolent image projected by this news story, there is ample evidence that the children were obliged to work hard for their keep and were rarely accepted as members of the family. The Boston Children's Aid Society purchased a home in 1864, which was used to help adjust street youth to their new life in the West. The children were introduced to farming skills and taught manners that might be expected of them in their new homes.

Another prevention experiment during the middle part of the 19th century was the result of the work of a Boston shoemaker, John Augustus. In 1841, Augustus began to put up bail for men charged with drunkenness, although he had no official connection with the court. Soon after, he extended his services to young people. Augustus supervised the youngsters while they were out on bail, provided clothing and shelter, was sometimes able to find them jobs, and often paid court costs to keep them out of jail. This early probation system was later instituted by local child-saving groups, who would find placements for the children. By 1869 Massachusetts had a system by which agents of the Board of State Charities took charge of delinquents before they appeared in court. The youths often were released on probation, subject to good behavior in the future.

These noninstitutional prevention methods were challenged by those who felt an initial period of confinement was important before children were placed out. Critics also argued that the Children's Aid Societies neither followed up on their clients nor administered more stringent discipline to those who needed it. One critic phrased it this way:

The "vagabond boy" is like a blade of corn, coming up side by side with a thistle. You may transplant both together in fertile soil, but you will have the thistle still. . . . I would have you pluck out the vagabond first, and then let the boy be thus provided with "a home," and not before. (Mennel, 1973, p. 46)

Many Midwesterners were unsettled by the stream of "criminal children" flowing into their midst. Brace and his colleagues were accused of poisoning the West with the dregs of urban life. To combat charges that urban youths were responsible for the rising crime in the West, Brace conducted a survey of western prisons and almshouses to show that few of his children had gotten into further trouble in the West.

Resistance continued to grow against the efforts of the Children's Aid Societies. Brace, holding that asylum interests were behind the opposition, maintained that the longer a child remains in an asylum, the less likely he will reform. (The debate over the advantages and disadvantages of institutionalized care of delinquent youth continues to the present day.) Brace continued to be an active proponent of the placing out system. He appeared before early conventions of reform school managers to present his views and debate the opposition. As the struggle continued over an ideology to guide prevention efforts, the problem of delinquency continued to grow. During the 19th century, poverty, industrialization, and immigration, as well as the Civil War, helped swell the ranks of the "dangerous classes."[9]

Midway through the 19th century, state and municipal governments began taking over the administration of institutions for juvenile delinquents. Early efforts had been supported by private philanthropic groups with some state support. But the growing fear of class strife, coupled with increasing delinquency, demanded a more centralized administration. Many of the newer institutions were termed *reform schools* to imply a strong emphasis on formal schooling. In 1876, of the 51 refuges or reform schools in the United States, nearly three quarters were operated by state or local governments. By 1890, almost every state outside the South had a reform school, and many jurisdictions had separate facilities for male and female delinquents. These institutions varied considerably in their admissions criteria, their sources of referral, and the character of their inmates. Most of the children were sentenced to remain in reform schools until they reached the age of majority (18 years for girls and 21 for boys) or until they were reformed. The length of confinement, as well as the decision to transfer unmanageable youths to adult penitentiaries, was left to the discretion of reform school officials.

Partially in response to attacks by Brace and his followers, many institutions implemented a cottage or family system between 1857 and 1860. The cottage system involved dividing the youths into units of 40 or fewer, each with its own cottage and schedule. Although work was sometimes performed within the cottages, the use of large congregate workshops continued. The model for the system was derived from the practice of European correctional officials. There is evidence from this period of the development of a self-conscious attempt to refine techniques to mold, reshape, and reform wayward youth (Hawes, 1971).

During this period, a movement was initiated to locate institutions in rural areas, because it was felt that agricultural labor would facilitate reformative efforts. As a result, several urban houses of refuge were relocated in rural settings. Many rural institutions used the cottage system, as it was well suited to agricultural production. In addition, the cottage system gave managers the opportunity to segregate children according to age, sex, race, school achievement, or "hardness." Critics of the institutions, such as Mary Carpenter, pointed out that most of the presumed benefits of rural settings were artificial and that the vast majority of youths who spent time in these reform schools ultimately returned to crowded urban areas.

The Civil War deeply affected institutions for delinquent youth. Whereas prisons and county jails witnessed declines in population, the war brought even more youths into reform schools. Institutions were strained well beyond their capacities. Some historians believe that the participation of youths in the draft riots in northern cities produced an increase in incarcerated

youths. Reform schools often released older youngsters to military service to make room for additional children. Due to the high inflation rates of the war, the amount of state funds available for institutional upkeep steadily declined. Many institutions were forced to resort to the contract labor system to increase reform school revenues to meet operating expenses during the war and in the postwar period.

Voices were raised in protest over the expansion of contract labor in juvenile institutions. Some charged that harnessing the labor of inmates, rather than the reformation of youthful delinquents, had become the raison d'être of these institutions. There were growing rumors of cruel and vicious exploitation of youth by work supervisors. An 1871 New York Commission on Prison Labor, headed by Enoch Wines, found that refuge boys were paid 30 cents per day for labor that would receive 4 dollars a day on the outside. In the Philadelphia House of Refuge, boys were paid 25 cents a day and were sent elsewhere if they failed to meet production quotas. Economic depressions throughout the 1870s increased pressure to end the contract system. Workingmen's associations protested against the contract system, because prison and reform school laborers created unfair competition. Organized workers claimed that refuge managers were making huge profits from the labor of their wards:

> From the institutional point of view, protests of workingmen had the more serious result of demythologizing the workshop routine. No longer was it believable for reform school officials to portray the ritual as primarily a beneficial aid in inculcating industrious habits or shaping youth for "usefulness." The violence and exploitation characteristic of reform school workshops gave the lie to this allegation. The havoc may have been no greater than that which occasionally wracked the early houses of refuge, but the association of conflict and the contract system in the minds of victims and outside labor interests made it now seem intolerable. (Mennel, 1973, p. 61)

The public became aware of stabbings, fighting, arson, and attacks upon staff of these institutions.

All signs pointed toward a decline of authority within the institutions. The economic troubles of the reform schools continued to worsen. Additional controversy was generated by organized Catholic groups, who objected to Protestant control of juvenile institutions housing a majority of Catholics. This crisis in the juvenile institutions led to a series of investigations into reform school operations.[10] The authors of these reports proposed reforms to maximize efficiency of operation and increase government control over the functioning of institutions in their jurisdictions. One major result of these investigative efforts was the formation of Boards of State Charity. Members of these boards were appointed to inspect reform schools and make recommendations for improvements but were to avoid the evils of the patronage system. Board members, who were described as "gentlemen of public spirit and sufficient leisure," uncovered horrid institutional conditions and made efforts to transfer youngsters to more decent facilities. Men such as Frederick Wines, Franklin Sanborn, Hastings Hart, and William Pryor Letchworth were among the pioneers of this reform effort. (Mennel, 1973, p. 61)

Although it was hoped that the newly formed boards would find ways to reduce the proliferation of juvenile institutions, such facilities continued to grow, as did the number of wayward youths. These late-19th-century reformers looked toward the emerging scientific disciplines for solutions to the problems of delinquency and poverty. They also developed a system to discriminate among delinquents, so that "hardened offenders" would be sent to special institutions such as the Elmira Reformatory. It was generally recognized that new methods would have to be developed to restore order within the reform schools and to make some impact upon delinquency.

Juvenile institutions in the South and the far West developed much later than those in the North or the East, but did so essentially along the same lines. One reason for this was that delinquency was primarily a city problem, and the South and far West were less urbanized. Another reason was that in the South, black youths received radically different treatment from whites. Whereas there was toleration for the misdeeds of white youth, black children were controlled under the disciplinary systems of slavery. Even after Emancipation, the racism of southern whites prevented them from treating black children as fully human and worth reforming. The Civil War destroyed the prison system of the South. After the war, southern whites used the notorious Black Codes and often trumped up criminal charges to arrest thousands of impoverished former slaves, placing them into a legally justified forced labor system. Blacks were leased out on contract to railroad companies, mining interests, and manufacturers. Although many of these convicts were children, no special provisions were made because of age. Conditions under the southern convict lease system were miserable and rivaled the worst cruelties of slavery. Little in the way of specialized care for delinquent youth was accomplished in the South until well into the 20th century. The convict lease system was eventually replaced by county road gangs and prison farms, characterized by grossly inhumane conditions of confinement. These were systems of vicious exploitation of labor and savage racism (McKelvey, 1972).

Juvenile Delinquency and the Progressive Era

The period from 1880 to 1920, often referred to by historians as the Progressive Era, was a time of major social structural change in the United States. The nation was in the process of becoming increasingly urbanized, and unprecedented numbers of European immigrants were migrating to cities in the Northeast. The United States was becoming an imperialist power and was establishing worldwide military and economic relationships. Wealth was becoming concentrated in the hands of a few individuals who sought to dominate U.S. economic life. Labor violence was on the rise, and the country was in the grip of a racial hysteria affecting all peoples of color. The tremendous technological developments of the time reduced the need for labor (Weinstein, 1968; Williams, 1973).

During the Progressive Era, those in positions of economic power feared that the urban masses would destroy the world they had built. Internal struggles developing among the wealthy heightened the tension. From all sectors came demands that new action be taken to preserve social order and to protect private property and racial privilege (Gossett, 1963). Up to this time, those in positions of authority had assumed a laissez-faire stance, fearing that government intervention might extend to economic matters. Although there was general agreement on the need for law enforcement to maintain social order, there was profound skepticism about attempts to alleviate miserable social conditions or reform deviant individuals. Some suggested that if society consisted of a natural selection process in which the fittest would survive, then efforts to extend the life chances of the poor or "racially inferior" ran counter to the logic of nature.

Others during this era doubted the wisdom of a laissez-faire policy and stressed that the threat of revolution and social disorder demanded scientific and rational methods to restore social order. The times demanded reform, and before the Progressive Era ended, much of the modern welfare state and the criminal justice system were constructed. Out of the turmoil of this age came such innovations as widespread use of the indeterminate sentence, the public defender movement, the beginning of efforts to professionalize the police, extensive use of parole, the rise of mental and IQ testing, scientific study of crime, and ultimately the juvenile court.

Within correctional institutions at this time, there was optimism that more effective methods would be found to rehabilitate offenders. One innovation was to institute physical exercise training, along with special massage and nutritional regimens. Some believed that neglect of the body had a connection with delinquency and crime. Those who emphasized the importance of discipline in reform efforts pressed for the introduction of military drill within reform schools. There is no evidence that either of these treatment efforts had a reformative effect upon inmates, but it is easy to understand why programs designed to keep inmates busy and under strict discipline would be popular at a time of violence and disorder within prisons and reform schools. As institutions faced continual financial difficulties, the contract labor system came under increasing attack. Criticism of reform schools resulted in laws in some states to exclude children under the age of 12 from admission to reform schools. Several states abolished the contract labor system, and efforts were made to guarantee freedom of worship among inmates of institutions. Once again, pleas were made for community efforts to reduce delinquency, rather than society relying solely upon reform schools as a prevention strategy. The arguments put forth were reminiscent of those of Charles Loring Brace and the Child Savers. For example, Homer Folks, president of the Children's Aid Society of Pennsylvania, articulated these five major problems of reform schools in 1891:

1. The temptation it offers to parents and guardians to throw off their most sacred responsibilities . . .

2. The contaminating influence of association . . .

3. The enduring stigma . . . of having been committed . . .

4. . . . renders impossible the study and treatment of each child as an individual.

5. The great dissimilarity between life in an institution and life outside. (Mennel, 1973, p. 111)

One response was to promote the model of inmate self-government within the institution's walls. One such institution, the George Junior Republic, developed an elaborate system of inmate government in 1893, in which the institution became a microcosm of the outside world. Self-government was viewed as an effective control technique, because youths became enmeshed in the development and enforcement of rules, while guidelines for proper behavior continued to be set by the institutional staff. The inmates were free to construct a democracy, so long as it conformed to the wishes of the oligarchic staff (Hawes, 1971).

The populist governments of several southern states built reform schools, partly due to their opposition to the convict lease system. But, these institutions too were infused with the ethos of the Jim Crow laws, which attempted to permanently legislate an inferior role for black Americans in southern society. One observer described the reform school of Arkansas as a place "where White boys might be taught some useful occupation and the negro boys compelled to work and support the institution while it is being done" (Mennel, 1973, p. 12). Black citizens, obviously displeased with discrimination within southern reform schools, proposed that separate institutions for black children should be administered by the black community. A few such institutions were established, but the majority of black children continued to be sent to jail or to be the victims of lynch mobs.

Growing doubt about the success of reform schools in reducing delinquency led some to question the wisdom of applying an unlimited *parens patriae* doctrine to youth. In legal cases, such as *The People v. Turner* (1870), *State v. Kay* (1886), and *Ex parte Becknell* (1897), judges questioned the quasi-penal character of juvenile institutions and wondered whether there ought not to be some procedural safeguards for children entering court on delinquency charges.

The state of Illinois, which eventually became the first state to establish a juvenile court law, had almost no institutions for the care of juveniles. Most early institutions in Illinois had been destroyed in fires, and those that remained were regarded as essentially prisons for children. Illinois attempted a privately financed system of institutional care, but this also failed. As a result, progressive reformers in Chicago complained of large numbers of children languishing in the county jail and pointed out that children sometimes received undue leniency due to a lack of adequate facilities.

A new wave of Child Savers emerged, attempting to provide Chicago and the state of Illinois with a functioning system for handling wayward youth.[11] These reformers, members of the more wealthy and influential Chicago families, were spiritual heirs of Charles Loring Brace, in that they, too, feared that social unrest could destroy their authority. But through their approach, they hoped to alleviate some of the suffering of the impoverished and ultimately win the loyalty of the poor. Reformers such as Julia Lathrop, Jane Addams, and Lucy Flower mobilized the Chicago Women's Club on behalf of juvenile justice reform. Other philanthropic groups, aligning with the powerful Chicago Bar Association, helped promote a campaign leading to the eventual drafting of the first juvenile court law in the United States. Although previous efforts had been made in Massachusetts and Pennsylvania to initiate separate trials for juveniles, the Illinois law is generally regarded as the first comprehensive child welfare legislation in this country.

The Illinois law, passed in 1899, established a children's court that would hear cases of delinquent, dependent, and neglected children. The *parens patriae* philosophy, which had imbued the reform schools, now extended to the entire court process. The definition of delinquency was broad, so that a child would be adjudged delinquent if he or she violated any state law or any city or village ordinance. In addition, the court was given jurisdiction in cases of incorrigibility, truancy, and lack of proper parental supervision. The court had authority to institutionalize children, send them to orphanages or foster homes, or place them on probation. The law provided for unpaid probation officers, who would assist the judges and supervise youngsters. In addition, the law placed the institutions for dependent youth under the authority of the State Board of Charities and regulated the activities of agencies sending delinquent youth from the East into Illinois.

The juvenile court idea spread so rapidly that within 10 years of the passage of the Illinois law, 10 states had established children's courts. By 1912, 22 states had juvenile court laws, and by 1925 all but two states had established specialized courts for children. Progressive reformers proclaimed the establishment of the juvenile court as the most significant reform of this period. The reformers celebrated what they believed to be a new age in the treatment of destitute and delinquent children. In *Commonwealth v. Fisher* (1905), the Pennsylvania Supreme Court defended the juvenile court ideal in terms reminiscent of the court opinion in the Crouse case of 1838:

> To save a child from becoming a criminal, or continuing in a career of crime, to end in maturer years in public punishment and disgrace, the legislatures surely may provide for the salvation of such a child, if its parents or guardians be unwilling or unable to do so, by bringing it into one of the courts of the state without any process at all, for the purpose of subjecting it to the state's guardianship and protection.

Critics, pointing to the large number of children who remained in jails and detention homes for long periods, expressed doubt that the court would achieve its goal. Some judges, including the famous Judge Ben Lindsey of Denver, decried the seemingly unlimited discretion of the court. With so much diversity among jurisdictions in the United States, it is difficult to describe the functioning of a typical court. As the volume of cases in the urban areas soon overwhelmed existing court resources, judges became unable to give the close personal attention to each case advocated by the reformers. As little as 10 minutes was devoted to each case as court calendars became increasingly crowded. Similarly, as caseloads soared, the quality of probationary supervision deteriorated and became perfunctory.

It is important to view the emergence of the juvenile court in the context of changes taking place in U.S. society at that time. Juvenile court drew support from a combination of optimistic social theorists, sincere social reformers, and the wealthy, who felt a need for social control. The juvenile court movement has been viewed as an attempt to stifle legal rights of children by creating a new adjudicatory process based on principles of equity law. This view misses the experimental spirit of the Progressive Era by assuming a purely conservative motivation on the part of the reformers.

Although most reformers of the period understood the relationship between poverty and delinquency, they responded with vastly different solutions. Some reformers supported large-scale experimentation with new social arrangements, such as the Cincinnati Social Unit Experiment, an early forerunner of the community organization strategy of the war on poverty of the 1960s (Shaffer, 1971). Other reformers looked to the emerging social science disciplines to provide a rational basis for managing social order. During the Progressive Era, there was growth in the profession of social work, whose members dealt directly with the poor.[12] Progressive reformers conducted social surveys to measure the amount of poverty, crime, and juvenile dependency in their communities. They supported social experiments to develop new behavior patterns among the lower classes to help them adjust to the emerging corporate economy. The development of mental testing became crucial in defining access to the channels of social mobility and for demonstrating, to the satisfaction of the white ruling class, their own racial superiority. Moreover, biological explanations of individual and social pathology rationalized the rise in crime and social disorder without questioning the justice or rationality of existing social arrangements.

The thrust of Progressive Era reforms was to found a more perfect control system to restore social stability while guaranteeing the continued hegemony of those with wealth and privilege. Reforms such as the juvenile court are ideologically significant because they preserved the notion that social problems (in this case, delinquency, dependency, and neglect) could be dealt with on a case-by-case basis, rather than through broad-based efforts to redistribute wealth and power throughout society. The chief dilemma for advocates of the juvenile court was to develop an apparently apolitical or neutral system while preserving differential treatment for various groups of children. The juvenile court at first lacked a core of functionaries who could supply the rationale for individualized care for wayward youth, but soon these needs were answered by the emergence of psychiatry, psychology, and criminology, as well as by the expanding profession of social work.

✎ The Child Guidance Clinic Movement

In 1907, Illinois modified its juvenile court law to provide for paid probation officers, and the Chicago Juvenile Court moved into new facilities with expanded detention space. The Juvenile Protective League, founded by women active in establishing the first juvenile court law, was intended to stimulate the study of the conditions leading to delinquency. The members of the Juvenile Protective League were especially troubled that large numbers of wayward youth repeatedly returned to juvenile court. Jane Addams, a major figure in U.S. philanthropy and social thought, observed, "At last it was apparent that many of the children were psychopathic cases and they and other borderline cases needed more skilled care than the most devoted probation officer could give them" (Hawes, 1971, p. 244).

But the new court facilities did provide an opportunity to examine and study all children coming into the court. The Juvenile Protective League promised to oversee this study of delinquency, and Ellen Sturges Dummer donated the necessary money to support the effort. Julia Lathrop was chosen to select a qualified psychologist to head the project. After consulting with William James, she selected one of his former students, William A. Healy. Healy proposed a 4- to 5-year study to compare some 500 juvenile court clients with patients in private practice. The investigation, according to Healy, "would have to involve all possible facts about heredity, environment, antenatal and postnatal history, etc." (Hawes, 1971, p. 250).

In 1909, the Juvenile Protective League established the Juvenile Psychopathic Institute, with Healy as its first director and Julia Lathrop, Jane Addams, and Judge Julian W. Mack on the executive committee.[13] The group, in its opening statement, expressed its plans

to undertake . . . an inquiry into the health of delinquent children in order to ascertain as far as possible in what degrees delinquency is caused or influenced by mental or physical defect or abnormality and with the purpose of suggesting and applying remedies in individual cases whenever practicable as a concurrent part of the inquiry. (Hawes, 1971, pp. 250–251)

Jane Addams added her concern that the study investigate the conditions in which the children lived, as well as the mental and physical history of their ancestors.

Healy held an MD degree from the University of Chicago and had served as a physician at the Wisconsin State Hospital. He had taught university classes in neurology, mental illness, and gynecology; had studied at the great scientific centers of Europe; and was familiar with the work of Sigmund Freud and his disciples. The major tenet of Healy's scientific credo was that the individual was the most important unit for study. Healy argued that the individualization of treatment depended upon scientific study of individual delinquents.

Healy and his associates published *The Individual Delinquent: A Textbook of Diagnosis and Prognosis for All Concerned in Understanding Offenders* in 1915. This book, based on a study of 1,000 cases of repeat juvenile offenders, was intended as a practical handbook. The methodology involved a study of each offender from social, medical, and psychological viewpoints. Healy even did anthropometric measurements, suggested by Cesare Lombroso and his followers, although Healy doubted that delinquents formed a distinctive physical type.[14] However, Healy never was able to locate a limited set of causes for delinquency through empirical observation He stressed the wide range of potential causes of delinquency, including the influence of bad companions, the love of adventure, early sexual experiences, and mental conflicts. At this stage, Healy adopted an eclectic explanation of delinquency: "Our main conclusion is that every case will always need study by itself. When it comes to arraying data for the purpose of generalization about relative values of causative factors, we experience difficulty" (Mennel, 1973, p. 165). Despite exhaustive research, Healy and his associates could not find distinctive mental or physical traits to delineate delinquents from nondelinquents.

Later, in 1917, Healy advanced his theory of delinquency in *Mental Conflicts and Misconduct.* In this work, Healy stressed that although individuals may experience internal motivation toward misbehavior, this usually results in their merely feeling some anxiety. When mental conflict becomes more acute, the child may respond by engaging in misconduct. These ideas were heavily influenced by the work of Adolf Meyer, whose interpretation of Freud had a major influence on U.S. psychiatry. Healy agreed with Meyer that the family was a crucial factor in delinquency: "The basis for much prevention of mental conflict is to be found in close comfortable

relations between parents and children" (Hawes, 1971, p. 255). Healy's emphasis on the family was well received by those in the delinquency prevention field who had traditionally viewed the family as God's reformatory.

The significance of Healy's work cannot be overemphasized, as it provided an ideological rationale to defend the juvenile court. Healy's work gave legitimacy to the flexible and discretionary operations of the court. Although some used Healy's emphasis on the individual to minimize the importance of social and economic injustice, there is evidence that Healy understood that delinquency was rooted in the nature of the social structure:

> If the roots of crime lie far back in the foundations of our social order, it may be that only a radical change can bring any large measure of cure. Less unjust social and economic conditions may be the only way out, and until a better social order exists, crime will probably continue to flourish and society continue to pay the price. (Healy, Bronner, & Shimberg, 1935, p. 211)

Healy's work also gave support to the concept of professionalism in delinquency prevention. Because juvenile delinquency was viewed as a complex problem with many possible causes, this rationale was used to explain the increased reliance on experts. In the process, the juvenile court became insulated from critical scrutiny by its clients and the community. If actions taken by the court did not appear valid to the layman, this was because of a higher logic, known only to the experts, which explained that course of action. Moreover, the failure of a specific treatment program often was attributed to the limits of scientific knowledge or to the failure of the court to follow scientific principles in its dispositions.

After his work in Chicago, Healy went to the Judge Harvey Baker Foundation in Boston to continue his research, where he began actual treatment of youths. Healy became a proselytizer for the child guidance clinic idea. Working with the Commonwealth Fund and the National Committee for Mental Hygiene, Healy aided the development of child guidance clinics across the nation. These efforts were so successful that by 1931, 232 such clinics were in operation. There is even a report of a traveling child guidance clinic that visited rural communities in the West to examine children. The child guidance clinic movement became an important part of a broader campaign to provide mental hygiene services to all young people. The clinics initially were set up in connection with local juvenile courts, but later some of them became affiliated with hospitals and other community agencies.

In Sheldon and Eleanor Glueck's classic delinquency research, they evaluated the success of Healy's Boston clinic. In *One Thousand Juvenile Delinquents: Their Treatment by Court and Clinic* (1934), the Gluecks found high rates of recidivism among children treated at the clinic. Healy, though deeply disappointed by the results, continued his efforts. The Gluecks continued, in a series of longitudinal studies, to search for the causes of delinquency and crime.[15] Like Healy, they maintained a focus on the individual, and they increased efforts to discover the factors behind repeated delinquency. The work of the Gluecks reflected a less optimistic attitude about the potential for treatment and rehabilitation than that found in Healy's work. They emphasized the importance of the family, often ignoring the impact of broader social and economic factors. It is ironic that the thrust of delinquency theories in the 1930s should be toward individual and family conflicts. As 20% of the American people were unemployed, the effects of the depression of the 1930s must have been apparent to the delinquents and their families, if not to the good doctors who studied them with such scientific rigor.

⊠ The Chicago Area Project

The Chicago Area Project of the early 1930s is generally considered the progenitor of large-scale, planned, community-based efforts with delinquent youth. The project differed from the dominant approaches of the time, which relied on institutional care and psychological explanations for delinquent behavior. The Chicago Area Project, conceived by University of Chicago sociologist Clifford Shaw, was an attempt to implement a sociological theory of delinquency in the delivery of preventive services. The theoretical heritage of the project is found in such works as *The Jack-Roller* (1930), *Brothers in Crime* (1938), and *Juvenile Delinquency and Urban Areas* (1942), all written by Shaw and his associates. They attributed variations in delinquency rates to demographic or socioeconomic conditions in different areas of cities. This environmental approach assumed that delinquency was symptomatic of social disorganization. The adjustment problems of recent immigrants, together with other problems of urban life, strained the influence on adolescents of traditional social control agencies such as family, church, and community. Delinquency was viewed as a problem of the modern city, which was characterized by the breakdown of spontaneous or natural forces of social control. Shaw contended that the rapid social change that migrant rural youths are subjected to when entering the city promotes alienation from accepted modes of behavior: "When growing boys are alienated from institutions of their parents and are confronted with a vital tradition of delinquency among their peers, they engage in delinquent activity as part of their groping for a place in the only social groups available to them" (Kobrin, 1970, p. 579). The Chicago Area Project thus viewed delinquency as "a reversible accident of the person's social experience" (Kobrin, 1970).

The project employed several basic operating assumptions. The first was that the delinquent is involved in a web of daily relationships. As a result, the project staff attempted to mobilize adults in the community, hoping to foster indigenous neighborhood leadership to carry out the programs with delinquent youth. The second assumption was that people participate only if they have meaningful roles; therefore, the staff attempted to share decision making with neighborhood residents. To maximize community participation, staff members had to resist the urge to direct the programs themselves. The final premise of the Area Project was that within a given community there are people who, when given proper training and guidance, can organize and administer local welfare programs. A worker from within the community, who has knowledge of local customs and can communicate easily with local residents, is more effective in dealing with delinquency problems. The project staff believed that placing community residents in responsible positions would demonstrate the staff's confidence in the ability of residents to solve their own problems.

The Area Project was overseen by a board of directors responsible for raising and distributing funds for research and community programs. In several years, 12 community committees developed in Chicago as "independent, self-governing, citizens' groups, operating under their own names and charters" (Sorrento, quoted in Sechrest, 1970, p. 6). The neighborhood groups were aided by the board in obtaining grants to match local funds. Personnel from the Institute for Juvenile Research at the University of Chicago served as consultants to local groups. The various autonomous groups pursued such activities as the creation of recreation programs or community-improvement campaigns for schools, traffic safety, sanitation, and law enforcement. There were also programs aimed directly at delinquent youth, such as visitation privileges for incarcerated children, work with delinquent gangs, and volunteer assistance in parole and probation.

Most observers have concluded that the Chicago Area Project succeeded in fostering local community organizations to attack problems related to delinquency (Kobrin, 1970; Shaw & McKay, 1942). Evidence also shows that delinquency rates decreased slightly in areas affected by the project, but these results are not conclusive.

Shaw explained the difficulty of measuring the impact of the project as follows:

> Conclusive statistical proof to sustain any conclusion regarding the effectiveness of this work in reducing the volume of delinquency is difficult to secure for many reasons. Trends in rates for delinquents for small areas are affected by variations in the definition of what constitutes delinquent behavior, changes in the composition of the population, and changes in the administrative procedures of law enforcement agencies. (Witmer & Tufts, 1954, p. 16)

The Illinois State Division of Youth Services took over all 35 staff positions of the Area Project in 1957. It appears that this vibrant and successful program was quickly transformed into "a rather staid, bureaucratic organization seeking to accommodate itself to the larger social structure, that is, to work on behalf of agencies who came into the community rather than for itself or for community residents" (Sechrest, 1970, p. 15).

The Chicago Area Project, with its grounding in sociological theory and its focus on citizen involvement, contrasts sharply with other delinquency prevention efforts of the 1930s. Its focus on prevention in the community raised questions about the continued expansion of institutions for delinquent youth. Although some attributed support of the project to the personal dynamism of Clifford Shaw, this ignores the basic material and ideological motivation behind it. It would be equally shortsighted to conclude that child saving would not have occurred without Charles Loring Brace or that the child guidance clinic movement resulted solely from the labors of William Healy. Certainly Shaw was an important advocate of the Chicago Area Project approach, and his books influenced professionals in the field, but the growth of the project was also a product of the times.

Because no detailed history exists of the founding and operation of the project, we can only speculate about the forces that shaped its development. We do know that Chicago at that time was caught in the most serious economic depression in the nation's history. Tens of thousands of people were unemployed, especially immigrants and blacks. During this period, a growing radicalization among impoverished groups resulted in urban riots (Cloward & Piven, 1971). The primary response by those in positions of power was to expand and centralize charity and welfare systems. In addition, there was considerable experimentation with new methods of delivering relief services to the needy. No doubt, Chicago's wealthy looked favorably upon programs such as the Area Project, which promised to alleviate some of the problems of the poor without requiring a redistribution of wealth or power. Both the prestige of the University of Chicago and the close supervision promised by Shaw and his associates helped assuage the wealthy and the powerful. Shaw and his associates did not advocate fundamental social change, and project personnel were advised to avoid leading communities toward changes perceived as too radical (Alinsky, 1946). Communities were encouraged to work within the system and to organize around issues at a neighborhood level. Project participants rarely questioned the relationship of urban conditions to the political and economic superstructure of the city.

Later interpreters of the Chicago Area Project did not seem to recognize the potentially radical strategy of community organization within poor neighborhoods. Its immediate legacy was twofold—the use of detached workers, who dealt with gangs outside the agency office, and the idea of using indigenous workers in social control efforts. Although detached workers became a significant part of the delinquency prevention strategy of the next three decades, the use of indigenous personnel received little more than lip service, because welfare and juvenile justice agencies hired few urban poor.

The success of the Chicago Area Project depended upon relatively stable and well-organized neighborhoods with committed local leaders. Changes in the urban structure that developed over the next two decades did not fit the Chicago Area Project model. The collapse of southern agriculture and mass migration by rural blacks into the cities of the North and West produced major social structural changes. This movement to the North and West began in the 1920s, decreased somewhat during the depression years, and later accelerated due to the attraction provided by the war industry jobs. During this same period, large numbers of Puerto Ricans settled in New York City and other eastern cities. Although economic opportunity attracted new migrants to the urban centers, there was little satisfaction for their collective dreams. Blacks who left the South to escape the Jim Crow laws soon were confronted by de facto segregation in schools, in the workplace, and in housing. Job prospects were slim for blacks and Puerto Ricans, and both groups were most vulnerable to being fired at the whims of employers. In many respects, racism in the North rivaled that of the South. The new migrants had the added difficulty of adapting their primarily rural experiences to life in large urban centers (Coles, 1967; Handlin, 1959).

Racial ghettos became places of poverty, disease, and crime. For the more privileged classes, the situation paralleled that of 16th-century European city dwellers who feared the displaced peasantry or that of Americans at the beginning of the 19th century who feared the Irish immigrants. During this period, riots erupted in East St. Louis, Detroit, Harlem, and Los Angeles. To upper-class observers, these new communities of poor black and brown peoples were disorganized collections of criminals and deviants. Racism prevented white observers from recognizing the vital community traditions or the family stability that persisted despite desperate economic conditions. Moreover, the label *disorganized communities* could be used ideologically to mask the involvement of wealthy whites in the creation of racial ghettos (Ryan, 1971). A liberal social theory was developing that, though benign on the surface, actually blamed the victims for the conditions in which they were caught. Attention was focused upon deviant aspects of community life, ascribing a culture of poverty and violence to inner-city residents and advocating remedial work with individuals and groups to solve so-called problems of adjustment. The following quote from the National Commission on the Causes and Prevention of Violence (1969) is illustrative of this posture:

> The cultural experience which Negroes brought with them from segregation and discrimination in the rural South was of less utility in the process of adaptation to urban life than was the cultural experience of many European immigrants. The net effect of these differences is that urban slums have tended to become ghetto slums from which escape has been increasingly difficult. (p. 30)

Delinquency theorists suggested that lower-class communities were becoming more disorganized, because they were not characterized by the stronger ties of older ethnic communities:

> Slum neighborhoods appear to us to be undergoing progressive disintegration. The old structures, which provided social control and avenues of social ascent, are breaking down. Legitimate but functional substitutes for these traditional structures must be developed if we are to stem the trend towards violence and retreatism among adolescents in urban slums. (Cloward & Piven, 1971, p. 211)

Irving Spergel, leading authority on juvenile gangs, suggests that social work agencies made little use of indigenous workers after World War II because delinquency had become more aggressive and violent. Welfare and criminal justice officials argued that only agencies with sound funding and strong leadership could mobilize the necessary resources to deal with the increased incidence and severity of youth crime.

The movement toward more agency involvement brought with it a distinctly privileged-class orientation toward delinquency prevention. Social service agencies were preeminently the instruments of those with sufficient wealth and power to enforce their beliefs. The agencies were equipped to redirect, rehabilitate, and, in some cases, control those who seemed most threatening to the status quo. Workers for these agencies helped to perpetuate a conception of proper behavior for the poor consistent with their expected social role. For example, the poor were told to defer gratification and save for the future, but the rich often were conspicuous consumers. Whereas poor women were expected to stay at home and raise their families, the same conduct was not uniformly applied to wealthy women. The well-to-do provided substantial funding for private social service agencies and often became members of the boards that defined policies for agencies in inner-city neighborhoods. The criteria for staffing these agencies during the two decades following World War II included academic degrees and special training that were not made available to the poor or to people of color.

Social agencies, ideologically rooted and controlled outside poor urban neighborhoods, were often pressured to respond to "serious" delinquency problems. During this period, the fighting gang, which symbolized organized urban violence, received the major share of delinquency prevention efforts. Most agencies, emphasizing psychoanalytic or group dynamic approaches to delinquency, located the origin of social disruption in the psychopathology of individuals and small groups. The consequence of this orientation was that special youth workers were assigned to troublesome gangs in an attempt to redirect the members toward more conventional conduct. Little effort was made to develop local leadership or to confront the issues of racism and poverty.

Detached worker programs emphasized treatment by individual workers freed from the agency office base and operating in neighborhood settings. These programs, with several variations, followed a basic therapeutic model. Workers initially entered gang territories, taking pains to make their entrance as inconspicuous as possible. The first contacts were made at natural meeting places in the community such as pool rooms, candy stores, or street corners:

> Accordingly the popular image of the detached worker is a young man in informal clothing, standing on a street corner near a food stand, chatting with a half dozen rough, ill-groomed, slouching teenagers. His posture is relaxed, his countenance earnest, and he is listening to the boys through a haze of cigarette smoke. (Klein, 1969, p. 143)

The worker gradually introduced himself to the gang members. He made attempts to get jobs for them or arranged recreational activities, while at the same time persuading the members to give up their illegal activities. Manuals for detached workers explained that the approach would work because gang members had never before encountered sympathetic, nonpunitive adults who were not trying to manipulate them for dishonest purposes. A typical report states, "Their world (as they saw it) did not contain any giving, accepting people—only authorities, suckers and hoodlums like themselves" (Crawford, Malamud, & Dumpson, 1970, p. 630). This particular account even suggests that some boys were willing to accept the worker as an "idealized father." The worker was expected to influence the overall direction of the gang, but if that effort failed, he was to foment trouble among members and incite disputes over leadership. Information that the workers gathered under promises of confidentiality was often shared with police gang-control officers. Thus, despite their surface benevolence, these workers were little more than undercover agents whose ultimate charge was to break up or disrupt groups that were feared by the establishment. These techniques, which focused on black and Latino youth gangs in the 1950s, were similar to those later used with civil rights groups and organizations protesting the Vietnam War.

There were many critics of the detached worker programs. Some argued that the workers actually lent status to fighting gangs and thus created more violence. Other critics claimed that the workers often developed emotional attachments to youthful gang members and were manipulated by them (Mattick & Caplan, 1967). Community residents often objected to the presence of detached workers, because it was feared they would provide information to downtown social welfare agencies. Although studies of the detached worker programs did not yield positive results, virtually all major delinquency programs from the late 1940s to the 1960s used detached workers in an attempt to reach the fighting gang.

⬙ The Mobilization for Youth

During the late 1950s, economic and social conditions were becoming more acute in the urban centers of the United States. The economy was becoming sluggish, and unemployment began to rise. Black teenagers experienced especially high unemployment rates, and the discrepancy between white and black income and material conditions grew each year. Technological changes in the economy continually drove more unskilled laborers out of the labor force. Social scientists such as Daniel Moynihan (1969) and Sidney Wilhelm (1970) view this period as the time in which a substantial number of blacks became permanently unemployed. Social control specialists for the privileged class surveyed the problem and sought ways to defuse the social danger of a surplus labor population.

The Ford Foundation was influential during this period in stimulating conservative local officials to adopt more enlightened strategies in dealing with the poor (Marris & Rein, 1967; Moynihan, 1969). Once again an ideological dash occurred between those favoring scientific and rational government programs and those who feared the growth of the state, demanded balanced government budgets, and opposed liberal programs to improve the quality of life of the poor. The Ford Foundation, through its Grey Area projects, spent large amounts of money in several U.S. cities to foster research and planning of new programs to deal with delinquency and poverty.

The most significant program to develop out of the Grey Area projects was the Mobilization for Youth (MFY), which began in New York City in 1962 after 5 years of planning. It aimed to service a population of 107,000 (approximately one-third black and Puerto Rican), living in 67 blocks of New York City's Lower East Side. The unemployment rate of the area was twice that of the city overall, and the delinquency rate was also high. The theoretical perspective of the project was drawn from the work of Richard Cloward and Lloyd Ohlin:

"A unifying principle of expanding opportunities has worked out as the direct basis for action." This principle was drawn from the concepts outlined by the sociologists Richard Cloward and Lloyd Ohlin in their book *Delinquency and Opportunity*. Drs. Cloward and Ohlin regarded delinquency as the result of the disparity perceived by low-income youths between their legitimate aspirations and the opportunities—social, economic, political, education—made available to them by society. If the gap between opportunity and aspiration could be bridged, they believed delinquency could be reduced; that would be the agency's goal. (Weissman, 1969, p. 19)

The MFY project involved five areas—work training, education, group work and community organization, services to individuals and families, and training and personnel—but the core of the mobilization was to organize area residents to realize "the power resources of the community by creating channels through which consumers of social welfare services can define their problems and goals and negotiate on their own behalf" (Brager & Purcell 1967, p. 247). Local public and private bureaucracies became the targets of mass protests by agency workers and residents. The strategy of MFY assumed that social conflict was necessary in the alleviation of the causes of delinquency. Shortly after MFY became directly involved with struggles over the redistribution of power and resources, New York City officials charged that the organization was "riot-producing, Communist-oriented, left-wing and corrupt" (Weissman, 1969, pp. 25–28).

In the ensuing months, the director resigned, funds were limited, and virtually all programs were stopped until after the 1964 presidential election. After January 1965, MFY moved away from issues and protests toward more traditional approaches to social programming, such as detached-gang work, job training, and counseling.

Another project, Harlem Youth Opportunities Unlimited (Haryou-Act), which developed in the black community of Harlem in New York City, experienced a similar pattern of development and struggle. The Harlem program was supported by the theory and prestige of psychologist Kenneth Clark, who suggested in *Dark Ghetto* (1965) that delinquency is rooted in feelings of alienation and powerlessness among ghetto residents. The solution, according to Clark, was to engage in community organizing to gain power for the poor. Haryou-Act met sharp resistance from city officials, who labeled the staff as corrupt and infiltrated by Communists.

Both MFY and Haryou-Act received massive operating funds. Mobilization for Youth received approximately $2 million a year, Haryou-Act received about $1 million a year, and 14 similar projects received more than $7 million from the federal Office of Juvenile Delinquency.[16] It was significant that, for the first time, the federal government was pumping large amounts of money into the delinquency prevention effort. Despite intense resistance to these efforts in most cities because local public officials felt threatened, the basic model of Mobilization for Youth was incorporated into the community-action component of the War on Poverty.

In 1967, when social scientists and practitioners developed theories of delinquency prevention for President Lyndon Johnson's Crime Commission, MFY was still basic to their thinking (President's Commission on Law Enforcement and the Administration of Justice, 1967). Their problem was to retain a focus upon delivery of remedial services in education, welfare, and job training to the urban poor without creating the intense political conflict engendered by the community action approach. The issue was complicated because leaders such as Malcolm X and Cesar Chavez and groups such as the Black Muslims and the Black Panther Party articulated positions of self-determination and community control. These proponents of ethnic pride and "power to the people" argued that welfare efforts controlled from outside were subtle forms of domestic colonialism. The riots of the mid-1960s dramatized the growing gap between people of color in the United States and their more affluent "benefactors."

It is against this backdrop of urban violence, a growing distrust of outsiders, and increased community-generated self-help efforts that delinquency prevention efforts of the late 1960s and early 1970s developed. A number of projects during this period attempted to reach the urban poor who had been actively involved in ghetto riots during the 1960s. In Philadelphia, members of a teenage gang were given funds to make a film and start their own businesses. Chicago youth gangs such as Black P. Stone Nation and the Vice Lords were subsidized by federal funding, the YMCA, and the Sears Foundation, In New York City, a Puerto Rican youth group, the Young Lords, received funds to engage in self-help activities. In communities across the nation there was a rapid development of summer projects in recreation, employment, and sanitation to help carry an anxious white America through each potentially long, hot summer. Youth patrols were even organized by police departments to employ ghetto youths to "cool out" trouble that might lead to riots. Few of the programs produced the desired results and often resulted in accusations of improperly used funds by the communities. Often financial audits and investigations were conducted to discredit community organizers

and accuse them of encouraging political conflicts with local officials.

One proposed solution that offered more possibility of controlled social action to benefit the young was the Youth Service Bureau (YSB; Norman, 1972). The first YSBs were composed of people from the communities and representatives of public agencies who would hire professionals to deliver a broad range of services to young people. The central idea was to promote cooperation between justice and welfare agencies and the local communities. Agency representatives were expected to contribute partial operating expenses for the programs and, together with neighborhood representatives, decide on program content. Proponents of the YSB approach stressed the need for diverting youthful offenders from the criminal justice system and for delivering necessary social services to deserving children and their families. Ideally YSBs were designed to increase public awareness of the need for more youth services.

The YSBs generally met with poor results. Intense conflict often arose between community residents and agency personnel over the nature of program goals, and YSBs were criticized for not being attuned to community needs (Duxbury, 1972; U.S. Department of Health, Education, and Welfare, 1973). Funds for these efforts were severely limited in relation to the social problems they sought to rectify. In some jurisdictions YSBs were controlled by police or probation departments, with no direct community input. These agency-run programs temporarily diverted youths from entering the criminal justice process by focusing on services such as counseling.

The most important aspect of the YSBs was their attempts to operationalize the diversion of youth from the juvenile justice process, although the effort's success seems highly questionable. Some argue that diversion programs violate the legal rights of youths, as they imply a guilty plea. Others warn that diversion programs expand the welfare bureaucracy, because youths who once would have simply been admonished and sent home by police are now channeled into therapeutic programs. Still others believe that diversion without social services does not prevent delinquency. In any case, a major shift has occurred from the community participation focus of the Mobilization for Youth to a system in which community inputs are limited and carefully controlled. This change in operational philosophy often is justified by the need to secure continued funding, as well as by claims of increasing violence by delinquents. It is important to remember, however, that these same rationales were used to justify a move away from the community organizing model of the Chicago Area Projects of the 1930s. Whenever residents become involved in decision making, there are inevitably increased demands for control of social institutions affecting the community. Such demands for local autonomy question the existing distributions of money and power and thus challenge the authority of social control agencies.

◩ Institutional Change and Community-Based Corrections

Correctional institutions for juvenile delinquents were subject to many of the same social, structural pressures as community prevention efforts. For instance, there was a disproportionate increase in the number of youths in correctional facilities as blacks migrated to the North and the West. In addition, criticism of the use of juvenile inmate labor, especially by organized labor, disrupted institutional routines. But, throughout the late 1930s and the 1940s, increasing numbers of youths were committed to institutions. Later on, the emergence of ethnic pride and calls for black and brown power would cause dissension within the institutions.

The creation of the California Youth Authority just prior to World War II centralized the previously disjointed California correctional institutions.[17] During the 1940s and 1950s, California, Wisconsin, and Minnesota developed separate versions of the Youth Authority concept. Under the Youth Authority model, criminal courts committed youthful offenders from 16 to

21 years old to an administrative authority that determined the proper correctional disposition.[18] The CYA was responsible for all juvenile correctional facilities, including the determination of placements, and parole. Rather than reducing the powers of the juvenile court judge, the Youth Authority streamlined the dispositional process to add administrative flexibility. The Youth Authority was introduced into California at a time when detention facilities were overcrowded, institutional commitment rates were rising, and the correctional system was fragmented and compartmentalized.

The Youth Authority model was developed by the American Law Institute, which drew up model legislation and lobbied for its adoption in state legislatures. The American Law Institute is a nonprofit organization that seeks to influence the development of law and criminal justice. The institution is oriented toward efficiency, rationality, and effectiveness in legal administration.

The treatment philosophy of the first Youth Authorities was similar to the approach of William Healy and the child guidance clinic. John Ellingston, formerly chief legislative lobbyist for the American Law Institute in California, related a debate between Healy and Clifford Shaw over the theoretical direction the new Youth Authority should follow. The legislators, persuaded by Healy's focus on diagnosis of individual delinquents, ensured that the clinic model became the dominant approach in California institutions.

Sociologist Edwin Lemert attributed the emergence of the CYA to the growth of an "administrative state" in the United States. In support of this assertion, Lemert noted the trend toward more centralized delivery of welfare services and increased government regulation of the economy, together with the "militarization" of U.S. society produced by war. Lemert, however, did not discuss whether the purpose of this administrative state was to preserve the existing structure of privilege. The first stated purpose of the CYA was "to protect society by substituting training and treatment for retributive punishment of young persons found guilty of public offenses" (Lemert & Rosenberg, 1948, pp. 49–50).

The centralization of youth correction agencies enabled them to claim the scarce state delinquency prevention funds. In-house research units publicized the latest treatment approaches. In the 1950s and the 1960s, psychologically oriented treatment approaches, including guided-group interaction and group therapy, were introduced in juvenile institutions. During this period of optimism and discovery, many new diagnostic and treatment approaches were evaluated. Correctional administrators and social scientists hoped for a significant breakthrough in treatment, but it never came. Although some questionable evaluation studies claimed successes, there is no evidence that the new therapies had a major impact on recidivism. In fact, some people began to question the concept of enforced therapy and argued that treatment-oriented prisons might be more oppressive than more traditional institutional routines (Mathieson, 1965). Intense objections have been raised particularly against drug therapies and behavior modification programs. Takagi views this as the period when brainwashing techniques were first used on juvenile and adult offenders.[19]

Another major innovation of the 1960s was the introduction of community-based correctional facilities. The central idea was that rehabilitation could be accomplished more effectively outside conventional correctional facilities. This led to a series of treatment measures such as group homes, partial release programs, halfway houses, and attempts to decrease commitment rates to juvenile institutions. California was particularly active in developing community-based correctional programming. The Community Treatment Project, designed by Marguerite Warren in California, was an attempt to replace institutional treatment with intensive parole supervision and psychologically oriented therapy. Probation subsidy involved a bold campaign by CYA staff to convince the state legislature to give cash subsidies to local counties to encourage them to treat juvenile offenders in local programs. Probation subsidy programs were especially oriented toward strengthening the capacity of county probation departments to supervise youthful offenders.[20]

Proponents of the various community-based programs argued that correctional costs could be reduced and rehabilitation results improved in a community context. Reducing state expenditures became more attractive as state governments experienced the fiscal crunch of the late 1960s and the 1970s.[21] It also was thought that reducing institutional populations would alleviate tension and violence within the institutions, but it appears that these community alternatives have created a situation in which youngsters who are sent to institutions are perceived as more dangerous and, as a result, are kept in custody for longer periods of time.

The ultimate logic of the community-based corrections model was followed by the Department of Youth Services in Massachusetts, which closed all of its training schools for delinquents. Youngsters were transferred to group home facilities, and services were offered to individual children on a community basis (Bakal, 1973). The Massachusetts strategy met intense public criticism by juvenile court judges, correctional administrators, and police officials. Some recent attempts have been made to discredit this policy and to justify continued operation of correction facilities, but the Massachusetts strategy has influenced a move to deinstitutionalize children convicted of status offenses—offenses that are considered crimes only if committed by children, such as truancy, running away, or incorrigibility. In 1975, the federal government made $15 million available to local governments that developed plans to deinstitutionalize juvenile status offenders.

At the moment, the forces opposing institutionalized care are making ideological headway due to past failures of institutional methods in controlling delinquency. However, previous experience suggests that the pendulum is likely to swing back in favor of the institutional approaches. Already there is increased talk about the violent delinquent and the alleged increases in violent youth crime; these words have always signaled the beginning of an ideological campaign to promote more stringent control measures and extended incarceration or detention. It is also significant that most states are not firmly committed to community-based treatment. Most jurisdictions still rely on placement in institutions, with conditions reminiscent of the reform schools of 100 years ago. Children continue to be warehoused in large correctional facilities, receiving little care or attention. Eventually they are returned to substandard social conditions to survive as best they can.

Changes in Juvenile Court Law

In the late 1960s the growing awareness of the limitations of the juvenile justice system resulted in a series of court decisions that altered the character of the juvenile court. In *Kent v. United States* (1966) the Supreme Court warned juvenile courts against "procedural arbitrariness," and in *In re Gault* (1967) the Court recognized the rights of juveniles in such matters as notification of charges, protection against self-incrimination, the right to confront witnesses, and the right to have a written transcript of the proceedings. Justice Abe Fortas wrote, "Under our Constitution the condition of being a boy does not justify a kangaroo court" (*In re Gault,* 1967). The newly established rights of juveniles were not welcomed by most juvenile court personnel, who claimed that the informal humanitarian court process would be replaced by a junior criminal court. Communities struggled with methods of providing legal counsel to indigent youth and with restructuring court procedures to conform to constitutional requirements.

The principles set forth in Kent, and later in the Gault decision, offer only limited procedural safeguards to delinquent youth (Kittrie, 1971). Many judicial officers believe the remedy to juvenile court problems is not more formality in proceedings, but more treatment resources. In *McKiever v. Pennsylvania* (1971), the Supreme Court denied that jury trials were a constitutional requirement for the juvenile court. Many legal scholars believe the current Supreme Court has a solid majority opposing extension of procedural rights to alleged delinquents. The dominant view is close to the opinion expressed by Chief Justice Warren Burger in the Winship case:

> What the juvenile court systems need is less not more of the trappings of legal procedure and judicial formalism; the juvenile court system requires breathing room and flexibility in order to survive the repeated assaults on this court. The real problem was not the deprivation of constitutional rights but inadequate juvenile court staffs and facilities. (*In re Winship,* 1970)

The Supreme Court's decision in *Schall v. Martin* (1984) signaled a much more conservative judicial response to children's rights. Plaintiffs in *Schall v. Martin* challenged the constitutionality of New York's Family Court Act as it pertained to the preventive detention of juveniles. It was alleged that the law was too vague and that juveniles were denied due process. A federal district court struck down the statute and its decision was affirmed by the U.S. Court of Appeals. However, the U.S. Supreme Court reversed the lower courts, holding that the preventive detention of juveniles to protect against future crimes was a legitimate state action.

The Emergence of a Conservative Agenda for Juvenile Justice

From the late 1970s and into the 1980s, a conservative reform agenda dominated the national debates over juvenile justice. This new perspective emphasized deterrence and punishment as the major goals of the juvenile court. Conservatives called for the vigorous prosecution of serious and violent youthful offenders. They alleged that the juvenile court was overly lenient with dangerous juveniles.

Conservatives also questioned the wisdom of diverting status offenders from secure custody. The Reagan administration introduced new programs in the areas of missing children and child pornography, which were problems allegedly created by the liberal response to status offenders. Substantial amounts of federal funds were spent on police intelligence programs and enhanced prosecution of juvenile offenders.

Changes in federal policy were also reflected in the actions of many state legislatures. Beginning in 1976, more than half the states made it easier to transfer youths to adult courts. Other states stiffened penalties for juvenile offenders via mandatory minimum sentencing guidelines.

The most obvious impact of the conservative reform movement was a significant increase in the number of youths in juvenile correctional facilities. In addition, from 1979 to 1984, the number of juveniles sent to adult prisons rose by 48%. By 1985 the Bureau of Justice Statistics reported that two-thirds of the nation's training schools were chronically overcrowded.

Another ominous sign was the growing proportion of minority youth in public correctional facilities. In 1982 more than one half of those in public facilities were minority youths, whereas two thirds of those in private juvenile facilities were white. Between 1979 and 1982, when the number of incarcerated youth grew by 6,178, minority youth accounted for 93% of the increase. The sharp rise in incarceration occurred even though the number of arrests of minority youth declined.

⬕ Summary

We have traced the history of the juvenile justice system in the United States in relation to significant population migrations/rapid urbanization, race conflicts, and transformation in the economy. These factors continue to influence the treatment of children. The juvenile justice system traditionally has focused on the alleged pathological nature of delinquents, ignoring how the problems of youths

relate to larger political and economic issues. Both institutional and community-based efforts to rehabilitate delinquents have been largely unsuccessful. Those with authority for reforming the juvenile justice system have traditionally supported and defended the values and interests of the well-to-do. Not surprisingly, juvenile justice reforms have inexorably increased state control over the lives of the poor and their children. The central implication of this historical analysis is that the future of delinquency prevention and control will be determined largely by ways in which the social structure evolves.[22] It is possible that this future belongs to those who wish to advance social justice on behalf of young people rather than to accommodate the class interests that have dominated this history (Krisberg, 1975; Liazos, 1974). However, one must be cautious about drawing direct inferences for specific social reforms from this historical summary. William Appleman Williams (1973) reminds us, "History offers no answers per se, it only offers a way of encouraging people to use their own minds to make their own history."

⬕ Notes

1. Thorsten Sellin, *Pioneering in Penology,* provides an excellent description of the Amsterdam House of Corrections.

2. This issue is well treated by Winthrop Jordan in *The White Man's Burden.*

3. Sources of primary material are N. R. Yetman, *Voices from Slavery,* and Gerda Lerner, *Black Women in White America.* Another fascinating source of data is Margaret Walker's historical novel, *Jubilee.*

4. Historical data on the 19th century rely on the scholarship of Robert Mennel, *Thorns and Thistles;* Anthony Platt, *The Child Savers: The Invention of Delinquency;* Joseph Hawes, *Children in Urban Society: Juvenile Delinquency in Nineteenth Century America;* and the document collection of Robert Bremner et al. in *Children and Youth in America: A Documentary History.*

5. *Delinquent children* are those in violation of criminal codes, statutes, and ordinances. *Dependent*

children are those in need of proper and effective parental care or control but having no parent or guardian to provide such care. *Neglected children* are destitute, are unable to secure the basic necessities of life, or have unfit homes due to neglect or cruelty.

6. A good description of anti-Irish feeling during this time is provided by John Higham, *Strangers in the Land.*

7. The preoccupation with the sexuality of female delinquents continues today. See Meda Chesney-Lind, "Juvenile Delinquency: The Sexualization of Female Crime."

8. This routine is reminiscent of the style of 18th-century American Indian schools. It represents an attempt to re-create the ideal of colonial family life, which was being replaced by living patterns accommodated to industrial growth and development.

9. The term *dangerous classes* was coined by Charles Loring Brace in his widely read *The Dangerous Classes of New York and Twenty Years Among Them.*

10. The classic of these studies is that of E. C. Wines, *The State of Prisons and Child-Saving Institutions in the Civilized World,* first printed in 1880.

11. Platt, *The Child Savers: The Invention of Delinquency,* pp. 101–136, and Hawes, *Children in Urban Society: Juvenile Delinquency in Nineteenth Century America,* pp. 158–190, provide the most thorough discussions of the origins of the first juvenile court law.

12. Roy Lubove, *The Professional Altruist,* is a good discussion of the rise of social work as a career.

13. A few earlier clinics specialized in care of juveniles, but these mostly dealt with feeble-minded youngsters.

14. Anthropometric measurements assess human body measurements on a comparative basis. A popular theory of the day was that criminals have distinctive physical traits that can be scientifically measured.

15. Longitudinal studies analyze a group of subjects over time.

16. By comparison, the Chicago Area Project operated on about $283,000 a year.

17. John Ellingston, *Protecting Our Children from Criminal Careers,* provides an extensive discussion of the development of the California Youth Authority.

18. California originally set the maximum jurisdictional age at 23 years, but later reduced it to 21. Some states used an age limit of 18 years, so that they dealt strictly with juveniles. In California, both juveniles and adults were included in the Youth Authority model.

19. Paul Takagi, in "The Correctional System," cites Edgar Schein, "Man Against Man: Brainwashing," and James McConnell, "Criminals Can Be Brainwashed—Now," for candid discussions of this direction in correctional policy.

20. Paul Lerman, *Community Treatment and Social Control,* is a provocative evaluation of the Community Treatment Project and Probation Subsidy.

21. See James O'Connor, *The Fiscal Crisis of the State,* for a discussion of the causes of this fiscal crunch.

22. This perspective is similar to that of Rusche and Kirchheimer in their criminological classic, *Punishment and Social Structure.*

⊠ References

Alinsky, S. (1946). *Reveille for radicals.* Chicago: University of Chicago Press.

Bakal, Y. (1973). *Closing correctional institutions.* Lexington, MA: Lexington Books.

Brager, G., & Purcell, F. (1967). *Community action against poverty.* New Haven, CT: College and University Press.

Bremner, R., Barnard, J., Hareven, T. K., & Mennel, R. M. (1970). *Children and youth in America: A documentary history* (Vol. 1). Cambridge, MA: Harvard University Press.

Cloward, R., & Piven, F. (1971). *Regulating the poor.* New York: Pantheon.

Coben, S., & Ratner, L. (Eds.). (1970). *The development of an American culture.* Englewood Cliffs, NJ: Prentice Hall.

Coles, R. (1967). *Children of crisis: A study of courage and fear.* Boston: Little, Brown.

Crawford, R., Malamud, D., & Dumpson, J. R. (1970). Working with teenage gangs. In N. Johnson (Ed.), *The sociology of crime and delinquency.* New York: John Wiley.

Duxbury, E. (1972). *Youth bureaus in California: Progress report #3.* Sacramento: California Youth Authority.

Glueck, S., & Glueck, E. T. (1934). *One thousand juvenile delinquents: Their treatment by court and clinic.* Cambridge, MA: Harvard University Press.

Gossett, T. (1963). *Race: The history of an idea in America. Dallas,* TX: Southern Methodist University Press.

Handlin, O. (1959). *The newcomers.* New York: Doubleday.

Hawes, J. (1971). *Children in urban society: Juvenile delinquency in nineteenth century America.* New York: Oxford University Press.

Healy, W., Bronner, A., & Shimberg, M. (1935). The close of another chapter in criminology. *Mental Hygiene, 19,* 208–222.

Kittrie, N. (1971). *The right to be different: Deviance and enforced therapy.* Baltimore: Johns Hopkins Press.

Klein, M. (1969, July). Gang cohesiveness, delinquency, and a street-work program. *Journal of Research on Crime and Delinquency, 143.*

Kobrin, S. (1970). The Chicago area project: A twenty-five year assessment. In N. Johnson (Ed.), *The sociology of crime and delinquency.* New York: Wiley.

Krisberg, B. (1975). *Crime and privilege.* Englewood Cliffs, NJ: Prentice Hall.

Lemert, E. M., & Rosenberg, J. (1948). *The administration of justice to minority groups in Los Angeles County.* Berkeley: University of California Press.

Liazos, A. (1974). Class oppression and the juvenile justice system. *Insurgent Sociologist, 1,* 2–22.

Marris, P., & Rein, M. (1967). *Dilemmas of social reform: Poverty and community action in the United States.* New York: Atherton.

Mathieson, T. (1965). *The defences of the weak.* London: Travistock.

Mattick, H. & Caplan, W. S. (1967). Stake animals, loud-talking and leadership in do-nothing and do-something situations. In M. Klein (Ed.), *Juvenile gangs in context* (pp. 121–125). Englewood Cliffs, NJ: Prentice Hall.

McKelvey, B. (1972). *American prisons.* Montclair, NJ: Patterson Smith.

Mennel, R. (1973). *Thorns and thistles.* Hanover: The University of New Hampshire Press.

Moynihan, D. (1969). *Maximum feasible misunderstanding.* New York: Free Press.

National Commission on the Causes and Prevention of Violence. (1969). *To establish justice, to ensure domestic tranquility.* Washington, DC: Government Printing Office.

Norman, S., (1972). *The youth service bureau: A key to delinquency prevention.* Hackensack, NJ: National Council on Crime and Delinquency.

Pickett, R. (1969). *House of refuge: Origins of juvenile justice reform in New York, 1815 – 1857.* Syracuse, NY: Syracuse University Press.

Platt, A. (1968). *The child savers: The invention of delinquency.* Chicago: Chicago University Press.

President's Commission on Law Enforcement and the Administration of Justice. (1967*). The challenge of crime in a free society.* Washington, DC: Government Publishing Office.

Rothman, D. (1971). *The discovery of the asylum.* Boston: Little Brown.

Rusche, G., & Kirchheimer, O. (1939). *Punishment and social structure.* New York: Columbia University Press.

Ryan. W. (1971). *Blaming the victim.* New York: Random House.

Sanders, W. B. (1970). *Juvenile offenders for a thousand years.* Chapel Hill: University of North Carolina.

Sechrest, D. (1970). *The community approach.* Berkeley: University of California, School of Criminology.

Shaffer. A. (1971). The Cincinnati social unity experiment. *Social Service Review,* 45, 159–171.

Shaw, R., & McKay, L. (Eds.). (1942). *Juvenile delinquency and urban areas.* Chicago: University of Chicago Press.

Stamp, K. M. (1956). *The peculiar institution.* New York: Random House.

Weinstein, J. (1968). *The corporate ideal in the liberal state.* Boston: Beacon Press.

Weissman, J. (1969). *Community development in the mobilization for youth.* New York: Association Press.

Williams, W. A. (1973). *The contours of American history.* New York: New Viewpoints.

Witmer, J., & Tufts, E. (1954). *The effectiveness of delinquency prevention programs.* Washington, DC: Government Printing Office.

Yetman, N. R. (1970). *Voices from slavery.* New York: Holt, Rinehart and Winston.

DISCUSSION QUESTIONS

1. What groups of youth were ignored or treated poorly by the early juvenile justice system?

2. What were some of the types of behavior that were punished in the colonial juvenile justice system, and what types of punishment were proposed?

3. What were the Houses of Refuge and what was their purpose?

4. Who were the "child savers" and what did they propose for dealing with delinquent youth?

5. What was the Progressive Era and what were some developments in juvenile justice during that period?

6. What were the changes in juvenile justice that began in the 1970s and 1980s?

READING

Juvenile rehabilitation has been criticized in recent years, and some have questioned whether the public continues to support the correctional policy of saving youthful offenders. The authors of this article administered a statewide survey to Tennessee residents to assess the degree of public support for juvenile rehabilitation. Results showed that survey respondents indicated that rehabilitation should be an integral goal of the juvenile correctional system. They also support a range of community-based treatment interventions and favor early intervention programs over imprisonment as a response to crime. The findings of the survey revealed that the public's belief in "child saving" remains firm, and indicated that citizens do not support an exclusively punitive response to juvenile offenders.

Is Child Saving Dead?

Public Support for Juvenile Rehabilitation

Melissa M. Moon, Jody L. Sundt, Francis T. Cullen, John Paul Wright

At the close of the nineteenth century, the United States witnessed an unprecedented movement to save its children from physical and moral harm. The "child savers," as champions of this movement have come to be known, sought wide-reaching reforms and advocated for such diverse policies as child labor laws, compulsory schooling, the establishment of kindergartens and play grounds, and the development of bureaus of child health and hygiene (Platt 1969; Rothman 1980). Among the

*[Originally published in 2000 in *Crime & Delinquency,* 46(1), 38–60.]

SOURCE: *Crime & Delinquency, (46)*1, 38–60, January 2000. © 2000 Sage Publications, Inc.

most ambitious reforms that the progressive child savers supported, however, was the establishment of a system of juvenile justice. Now, a century after its creation, the juvenile court has experienced a period of sustained criticism. In this context, the question emerges as to whether the public continues to endorse the rehabilitation of juvenile offenders. The current study thus investigated whether child saving has indeed lost the public's faith or remains a policy that citizens believe should be an integral feature of the state's correctional response to juvenile offenders.

✖ Attacking Juvenile Rehabilitation

The juvenile court was based on the novel idea that a separate system of justice should be established for delinquent youths. The progressives argued that the punishment of juveniles in the adult criminal justice system was damaging and inappropriate. Compared with adult criminals, wayward youngsters were believed to be less responsible for their actions, less likely to benefit from punishment, and more amenable to change. Moreover, the progressives maintained that because delinquents were vulnerable, the state, acting as a kindly parent (*parens patriae*), should be given wide discretion to ensure the best interests of the youths under their supervision. Thus, the child savers proposed a system that would accomplish the dual goals of protecting the child and the community. The foundation of this system of justice was an overriding belief that juvenile delinquents could be saved; that is, it was thought that youthful offenders could be rehabilitated and brought back into the folds of society (Rothman 1980).

Beginning in the late 1960s, however, faith in the progressive system of juvenile justice began to erode, and the system, along with the rehabilitative ideal, was attacked on numerous grounds. The promise of rehabilitation had gone largely unrealized. The benevolent principles on which the system was based stood in stark and ironic contrast to the punitive reality of the juvenile justice system (Feld 1993). Among liberals, the juvenile justice system was looked on as a coercive instrument of social control and was attacked on the basis that the rehabilitative ideal, with its emphasis on individualized treatment, had resulted in the abuse of discretion and in the arbitrary, differential treatment of delinquent youths; conservatives agreed that the juvenile justice system was flawed but viewed the system in a vastly different light: Child saving, it was argued, had led to the lenient treatment of dangerous youths and to the victimization of the public (Cullen, Golden, and Cullen 1983).

In the 100-year anniversary of the juvenile court, serious concerns remain about the viability of this system. Under scrutiny from a diverse group of critics, the juvenile justice system has undergone several significant changes in the past 30 years. For instance, in Illinois (the home of the first juvenile court) the juvenile system has been altered to reflect a balanced and restorative model of justice. This model purports to give equal attention to the rights and needs of the juvenile, to the rights and needs of the victim, and to the protection of the community (see, e.g., Bazemore and Day 1996). Consistent with this shift in philosophy, Illinois has enacted legislation that increases the length of time that juveniles may be held in custody and detention, has provided for more extensive fingerprinting of youths, has created a statewide database to track young offenders, has placed limits on the number of station adjustments allowed for delinquents who are not officially cited by the police, and has removed special protective language from the juvenile court process (e.g., an "adjudicatory hearing" will now be referred to as a trial) (Dighton 1999).

The changes initiated in Illinois are not unique or isolated. At the end of 1997, 17 states had redefined their juvenile court purpose clauses to emphasize public safety, certain sanctions, and/or offender accountability (Torbet and Szymanski 1998). Furthermore, between 1992 and 1995, 40 states modified their traditional juvenile court confidentiality provisions to open juvenile court records and to make proceedings more public (Sickmund, Snyder, and Poe-Yamagata 1997). Similarly, during this same time period, 40 states and the District of Columbia passed laws making it easier to transfer juveniles to adult court by lowering the minimum age at which a youth may be waived and by expanding the number of offenses that qualify for transfer (Torbet and Szymanski 1998). As a result, the United States experienced a 33 percent increase in the total number of juvenile cases waived to adult criminal courts between 1986 and 1995. During this same time period, waivers for personal crimes and drug offense cases increased 100 percent and 180 percent, respectively (Sickmund, Stahl, Finnegan, Snyder, Poole, and Butts 1998). Correctional programs for juveniles also are becoming more punitive in nature, focusing on public safety and offender accountability (Torbet and Szymanski 1998).

It is frequently suggested that the changes in the juvenile court have been precipitated by two factors: high rates of serious juvenile crime and a shift in public attitudes toward youthful offenders. Between 1988 and 1994, for example, the United States experienced more than a 100 percent increase in the number of murders committed by juveniles (Snyder 1998a). This trend, coupled with the commission of a number of disturbing and highly publicized crimes involving youths, seemed to signal that a new generation of highly violent, young "super-predators" was lurking in our future (see, e.g., DiIulio 1995; cf. Snyder 1998b).

Although juveniles accounted for only 12 percent of the total arrests for violent crimes in 1997, and although juvenile arrests for murder have declined by 39 percent since 1993 (Snyder 1998a), juvenile crime continues to evoke fear and concern among the public. For example, a 1998 survey found that Texans were nearly unanimous in the belief that juvenile crime is a serious problem today (Gonzalez 1998). Similar results have been obtained in national surveys. A 1996 poll found that more than 80 percent of the public felt that "teenage violence is a big problem" in most of the country, although only 33 percent believed that teen violence was a "big problem" in their own communities (*The Public Perspective* 1997).

Contemporary discussions about youthful offenders also have taken on a decidedly punitive flavor in the past 10 years. Public reaction to the caning of teenager Michael Faye stands out as a stark example of the public's recent punitiveness toward young offenders. After being found guilty of vandalism in Singapore, Faye was punished by caning. Rather than being outraged, however, the majority of the American public expressed support for the sanction, even when they were informed that the beating was likely to physically scar the youth for life (Pettinico 1994).

There also is evidence that the public supports getting tough with youthful offenders in this country (*The Public Perspective* 1997). A 1994 poll found, for example, that 52 percent of the public thought that society should deal with juvenile crime by giving juveniles the same punishment as adults. In contrast, only 31 percent supported placing less emphasis on punishment and more emphasis on trying to rehabilitate youths. In a comparable survey, more than 70 percent of a national sample reported that "toughening penalties for juvenile offenders so young people know there are severe consequences to crime" would make a major difference in the reduction of violent crime (only 6 percent of the sample felt that such a policy would make no difference). High levels of public support for the death penalty for juveniles are also regularly reported. A 1994 Gallup poll found, for example, that 72 percent of the public favored the death penalty for "a teenager who commits a murder and is found guilty by a jury" (Moore 1994).

Although it is apparent that the public is worried about juvenile crime and holds punitive attitudes toward youths, most discussions about reforming the juvenile justice system have failed to consider whether the public continues to view the rehabilitation of young offenders as a legitimate correctional goal. As is frequently the case in general discussions about public attitudes toward crime, it is assumed that increased support for punishing juveniles has also signaled a commensurate decline in support for treatment, but this may not be the case. Indeed, despite sweeping reforms aimed at altering the juvenile court to reflect retributive and punitive goals, it is uncertain that the public wants a juvenile justice system based exclusively, or even primarily, on punishment. This oversight is particularly notable given the centrality of the goal of rehabilitation to the traditional juvenile justice system. Again, the objective of our research was to explore these issues and to assess whether the public continues to support the rehabilitation of juveniles.

⊠ Support for Juvenile Rehabilitation

As previously discussed, recent public opinion polls suggest that the public supports getting tough with youthful offenders (see also Roberts and Stalans 1997; Triplett 1996). A handful of polls and research findings, however, challenge the idea that citizens have relinquished their faith in child saving. Indeed, survey research suggests three conclusions. First, findings reveal that the public continues to believe that rehabilitation is a core goal of juvenile corrections. Second, existing research indicates that the public not only embraces the rehabilitation of juveniles, but also that it is more supportive of treating juveniles than adults. Third, juveniles are generally thought to be more amenable to change than are adults; and similarly, the public believes that the rehabilitation of juveniles is effective.

Two recent studies have specifically questioned the public about their views on the main purpose of the juvenile court. When respondents in a national survey were asked whether the main purpose of the juvenile court should be to "treat and rehabilitate" or "punish" young offenders, Schwartz, Kerbs, Hogston, and Guillean (1992) found that more than three out of four citizens— 78.4 percent—said that the juvenile court should treat and rehabilitate juveniles, whereas fewer than 12 percent said punish; 10 percent reported that both goals should be pursued equally. Likewise, in a 1995 national poll, survey participants were asked "which goals should be the most important in sentencing juveniles." Half of the respondents answered rehabilitation,

31 percent selected retribution, 15 percent favored deterrence, and 4 percent supported incapacitation (Gerber and Engelhardt-Greer 1996). Thus, in both studies rehabilitation was the preferred goal of the juvenile court by a substantial margin.

Survey research also indicates that the public is more supportive of treating youthful offenders than they are of treating adults. A 1994 poll of Texans found, for instance, that although only 39 percent of the respondents endorsed trying to rehabilitate adult criminals, 70 percent favored rehabilitation for juveniles. Furthermore, nearly two-thirds of the respondents in this poll were willing to pay for juvenile programs to keep kids out of trouble, and 81 percent strongly or "mostly" agreed that removing children from bad environments and teaching them moral values and skills could help them become law-abiding (Makeig 1994). Likewise, more Oregon residents in a 1995 poll reported that they preferred that money be spent to rehabilitate juvenile offenders (92 percent) than to rehabilitate adult offenders (73 percent) and to punish juvenile offenders (77 percent) (Doble Research Associates 1995). Applegate, Cullen, and Fisher (1997) report similar findings. In their 1996 survey of Ohio residents, more than 95 percent of survey participants agreed that it is important to try to rehabilitate juveniles who have committed crimes and are now in the correctional system; for adult offenders, close to 86 percent agreed with a comparable question. Finally, 79 percent of San Francisco residents reported that they preferred that a 16-year-old boy convicted of selling crack cocaine, with a prior record, an abusive mother, and an absentee father, be placed in a residential treatment facility rather than be detained at the California Youth Authority (Moore 1996).

The public also believes that juveniles are promising candidates for treatment. A 1994 poll of Texas residents found that 76 percent of survey participants strongly or mostly agreed that juveniles have a better chance of being rehabilitated than adults (Makeig 1994). In a related line of inquiry, research has found that the public believes in the efficacy of juvenile treatment. Cullen et al. (1983) found, for instance, that although 20 percent of a sample from an Illinois community agreed that the rehabilitation of adults just does not work, only 10 percent felt that the treatment of juveniles is ineffective. A 1988 poll also found that more than two out of three Californians disagreed that youth who commit serious crime cannot be rehabilitated and should be locked up without any attempt at rehabilitation for as long as the law allows (Steinhart 1988). Similarly, a 1985 survey of Cincinnati and Columbus, Ohio, residents found that three of four respondents believed that rehabilitation programs were very helpful or helpful for juveniles. The comparable figure for adults was about 6 of 10. A replication of this research conducted in 1995 found that 8 of 10 Cincinnati residents believed that juvenile rehabilitation was very helpful or helpful; in contrast, for adults the figure was again 6 of 10 respondents (Sundt, Cullen, Applegate, and Turner 1998).

Together these findings indicate that the public continues to support the correctional treatment of juveniles. It should be noted, however, that the public is less willing to support rehabilitation when this option is portrayed as a lenient response to crime or when it is suggested that an emphasis on rehabilitation will lessen the punishment given to youths (see, e.g., *The Public Perspective* 1997). Finally, support for rehabilitation declines when questions ask about treating chronic or violent offenders and when questions specifically use the word rehabilitation (Gerber and Engelhardt-Greer 1996).

Although illuminating, the existing research is limited in an important way. Most of the polls and studies reviewed above have asked respondents only one or two questions about the issue of juvenile rehabilitation. Accordingly, they stop short of providing a systematic investigation of whether the public continues to believe in the rehabilitative ideal. In contrast, in the present study, we advanced our understanding of the public's attitudes toward the treatment of youthful offenders by having assessed a broad range of attitudes toward juvenile rehabilitation.

 Method

Sample

The data for this article were drawn from a larger survey conducted in 1998, which examined citizens' attitudes on various juvenile justice policy issues. Using a statewide database of residents' addresses, a questionnaire was mailed to a random sample of 1,500 people living in Tennessee. After the initial mailing, 217 surveys were returned as undeliverable. Subsequently, a replacement sample of 217 randomly selected residents were mailed a copy of the questionnaire.[1] Using an amended version of Dillman's (1978) Total Design Method, both groups were sent a reminder postcard, and two additional copies of the questionnaire were sent to increase the response rate.[2] A total of 539 usable surveys were returned, or a 40 percent response rate.

The modest response rate raises questions about the generalizability of the results. There are two reasons, however, why the findings reported here are unlikely to be affected by sample bias. First, to check for potential biases, a sample of 50 nonrespondents was contacted by telephone and asked a subsample of the questions from the survey. Their responses were then compared with those of sample participants to determine if any differences existed between these groups. Statistical analyses revealed no significant differences in the answers provided by the survey respondents as opposed to those provided by the nonrespondents polled by telephone. Accordingly, there was no evidence that respondents and nonrespondents varied in their attitudes toward juvenile justice policy issues.

Second, a major finding of this study was the public's consistent support for rehabilitation. This finding is unlikely to be an artifact of the sample's demographic composition because the study was conducted in a southern state and the respondents were primarily White and tended to be politically conservative. To the extent that these characteristics affect correctional attitudes, they should presumably increase expressions of punitiveness and decrease protreatment sentiments (see, e.g., Applegate 1997). Thus, if anything, the composition of our sample would likely slant the opinion data we report against finding support for rehabilitation.

The sample consisted of 272 (51.4 percent) males and 257 females (48.6 percent). The respondents were predominately White (91.8 percent) and their average age was 53. Of the sample, 50 percent had postsecondary education, whereas more than one-third had received a high school diploma or GED. Only 10 percent of the sample did not have a high school education. The respondents were asked to rank their general political views and how religious they would describe themselves using a Likert-type scale of 1 to 6, where 1 was *very liberal* (or *not very religious*) and 6 was *very conservative* (*or very religious*). The respondents' mean response for political views was 4.24, indicating a more

conservative sample. With a mean of 4.73, the respondents also professed to be religious. The respondents were fairly evenly distributed over the income categories, although almost 30 percent reported an income above $50,000.

Measures

This survey contained a number of measures that assessed the public's views on the goals of juvenile institutions, the justifications for intervening with juveniles, and what community-based treatment options should be available for juveniles. Following each question, respondents were provided either with a closed-ended set of choices or with a Likert-type scale that was used to express their level of agreement.

Previous research on correctional attitudes has most often focused on the goals of corrections

Table 1	Respondents' Views on What Is and What Should Be the Main Emphasis in Juvenile Prisons and the Amount of Importance Placed on Each (in percentages)

A. Main Emphasis of Juvenile Prisons

Goals of Imprisonment	Is	Should Be
Rehabilitation: Do you think the main emphasis in juvenile prison is [should be] to try and rehabilitate the adolescent so that he [sic] might return to society as a productive citizen?	29.4	63.3
Punishment: Do you think the main emphasis in juvenile prison is [should be] to punish the adolescent convicted of a crime?	16.8	18.7
Protection: Do you think the main emphasis in juvenile prison is [should be] to protect society from future crime he might commit?	17.6	11.2
Not sure	36.1	6.7

B. Importance of Goals of Juvenile Institutions

Goals of Imprisonment	Very Important	Important	A Little Important	Not Very Important
Rehabilitation	64.5	30.0	4.3	1.1
Punishment	42.5	52.1	4.3	1.1
Protection	43.2	47.0	8.4	1.3

(Cullen, Clark, and Wosniak 1985; Cullen, Skovron, Scott, and Burton 1990; Gottfredson and Taylor 1984; Gottfredson, Warner, and Taylor 1988; Harris 1968; Schwartz et al. 1992). Thus, for the first set of questions, we used the global questions posed by Harris (1968). The respondents were first asked what they thought was the main emphasis in juvenile prisons. This question was then repeated, except that the respondents were asked what should be the main emphasis of juvenile prisons. They were instructed to choose only one of the following four options: punish, rehabilitate, protect society, and not sure (see Table 1 for the wording of these choices). These questions were employed to determine the level of consistency between what citizens thought should be the main emphasis in juvenile prisons as opposed to and what goal they believed was actually being pursued by these institutions.

Using the same three goals—rehabilitation, punishment, and protection of society—the respondents were next asked to rank the level of importance of each of these goals of juvenile prisons (Applegate 1997). A Likert-type scale was provided where 1 = *not important,* 2 = *a little important,* 3 = *important,* and 4 = *very important.* In the previous questions, the respondents were only asked to choose one option; in this question, however, they were instructed to rate the level of importance they placed on each of the goals presented.

Second, to investigate further the public's support for various justifications for intervening with juvenile offenders, we relied largely on a set of 10 items used previously by Applegate et al. (1997) and Cullen et al. (1985). These statements asked the sample members what they thought should be done with juvenile offenders. The respondents were provided with a Likert-type scale where 1 = *strongly disagree,* 2 = *disagree,* 3 = *slightly disagree,* 4 = *slightly agree,* 5 = *agree,* and 6 = *agree strongly.* The responses to these items allowed us to assess the support given to rehabilitation as opposed to retribution, deterrence, and incapacitation. The actual statements for each of these categories are listed in Table 2.

Third, to explore what citizens believe is the most successful type of rehabilitation efforts the

respondents were asked to reply to three statements about what they thought was the best way to rehabilitate juvenile offenders. These measures were slightly modified from those used by Applegate et al. (1997). Using the 6-point, agree-disagree Likert-type scale previously discussed, the respondents were asked to report their level of agreement or disagreement with each of the following statements:

The best way to rehabilitate juvenile offenders is: (1) to teach them a skill that they can use to get a job when they are released from prison, (2) to try to help these offenders change their values and to help them with the emotional problems that caused them to break the law, and (3) to give them good education.

Fourth, because many juvenile offenders are given sentences that include supervision by the courts in the community and that require participation in treatment programs, we wanted to determine which community-based options were most and least likely to be supported by the public. The sample members were asked to indicate whether they do not support at all, slightly support, moderately support, or fully support a variety of local programs and supervision options. These options fell into one of six main categories: counseling, drug/alcohol, education/vocational, restorative, "tough love," and monitor. To ensure that each program or supervision option was fully understood, a definition was provided for each option. The correctional options, including their definitions, are presented in Table 3.

Finally, we included two questions used previously in a telephone survey conducted by Fairbank, Maslin, Maullin, & Associates (1998). First, we asked respondents to indicate which of the following two statements was closest to their opinion. (1) "Our main priority should be to build more prisons and youth facilities to lock-up as many juvenile offenders as possible," or (2) "our main priority should be to invest in ways to prevent kids from committing crimes and ending up in gangs or prison."[3] These responses were employed to determine whether citizens believe that youths should be saved or that society should give up on youths and build more prisons where they can be locked away.

The second question asked was whether "there is an age at which [they] believe it is too late to help a young person." A simple dichotomy of either yes or no was provided. If the respondent answered yes, he or she was asked to write down the specific age at which he or she estimated that youths could no longer be helped. Once again this question attempted to measure whether citizens believe that youths can be changed and at what age rehabilitative efforts will no longer be beneficial to these youths.

Results

The Goals of Corrections

In public opinion research, one of the most common ways of exploring correctional ideology is to ask what citizens endorse as the goal of imprisonment. Consistent with this literature, Panel A in Table 2 presents the respondents' views on what is and should be the main emphasis in most juvenile prisons. When asked what the purpose of imprisoning wayward youths is, more than one-third of the sample was not sure. Among the remaining goals, rehabilitation had the most support, with almost one in three citizens choosing this option. Taken together, the punish- and protect-society options were only slightly more often selected than offender treatment (34.4 percent to 29.4 percent).

The data on what should be the goal of juvenile incarceration is even more salient because they revealed the respondents' correctional preferences. Recall that this was a forced-choice question, and thus it measured which goal the citizens most strongly endorsed. It is noteworthy, therefore, that nearly two-thirds of Tennessee residents embraced rehabilitation as their preferred correctional goal. The support for treatment was 33.4 percentage points higher than for the protect society and punish responses combined. These findings suggest

that the public wishes rehabilitation to remain an integral purpose of the juvenile justice system.

This conclusion received additional credence from the data presented in Panel B of Table 1. Consistent with previous research, the respondents believed that juvenile prisons should serve multiple correctional goals. Thus, more than 9 in 10 sample members stated that it was important or very important to use imprisonment to rehabilitate, punish, and incapacitate youthful offenders. Note, however, that in the "very important" category, the percentage of the sample selecting rehabilitation (64.5 percent) was more than 20 points higher than the comparable percentage for the punish and protect society options.

We also explored public support for the various goals of corrections through 10 statements that the respondents rated, using a 6-point, agree-disagree Likert-type scale. Table 2 presents these data, combining the agree responses (*strongly agree, agree, agree a little*) and the disagree responses (*strongly disagree, disagree, disagree a little*). Again, we see that the respondents endorsed multiple correctional goals but were especially supportive of juvenile treatment.

As seen in Table 2, almost 95 percent of the respondents agreed that it is important to rehabilitate juvenile offenders who have committed crimes and are now in the correctional system. Items 2 and 3 revealed that Tennessee citizens also supported rehabilitation both in the community and in prisons. Finally, three-fourths of the sample favored treating even juveniles who have been involved in a lot of crime in their lives (see Item 4).

Table 2 also shows that support for retribution or just deserts were strong; more than 9 in 10 respondents agreed that young offenders deserve to be punished because they have harmed society. A clear majority—nearly two-thirds—supported punishing juveniles as a specific deterrent (Item 6). Note, however, that 40.4 percent of respondents believed that prisons might increase crime because prisons are schools of crime, and 57.6 percent agreed that sending young offenders to jail will not stop them from committing crimes (Items 7 and 8). The sample's ambivalence about the utility of incarcerating youthful offenders was

Table 2	Respondents' Level of Agreement for Various Goals of Imprisonment (in percentages)		
Correctional Goal		Agree[a]	Disagree[b]
Rehabilitation			
1. It is a good idea to provide treatment for juvenile offenders who are supervised by the courts and live in the community.		89.0	11.0
2. It is a good idea to provide treatment for juvenile offenders who are in prison.		94.8	5.4
3. It is important to try to rehabilitate juvenile offenders who have committed crimes and are now in the correctional system.		94.6	5.4
4. Rehabilitation programs should be available even for juvenile offenders who have been involved in a lot of crime in their lives.		76.4	23.6
Retribution			
5. Young offenders deserve to be punished because they have harmed society.		91.5	8.5
Deterrence			
6. Punishing juvenile offenders is the only way to stop them from engaging in more crimes in the future.		63.3	36.7
7. Putting young people in prison does not make much sense because it will only increase crime because prisons are schools of crime.		40.4	59.6
8. Sending young offenders to jail will not stop them from committing crimes.		57.6	42.4
Incapacitation			
9. We should put juvenile offenders in jail so that innocent citizens will be protected from people who victimize them—rob or hurt them—if given the chance.		13.7	86.3
10. Since most juvenile offenders will commit crimes over and over again, the only way to protect society is to put the offenders in jail when they are young and throw away the key.		20.8	79.2

a. Agree combines the responses of those who said they strongly agreed, agreed, and slightly agreed.

b. Disagree includes those who strongly disagreed, disagreed, and slightly disagreed.

even more pronounced in the responses to Items 9 and 10 in Table 2. About 8 in 10 sample members disagreed that incapacitating juvenile delinquents— "throwing away the keys"—was a prudent correctional policy.

Support for Types of Correctional Intervention

The respondents were also asked how they wished juvenile lawbreakers to be dealt with when they are not sent to prison, but instead are placed back into the community under the supervision of the court. Table 4 presents the extent to which the sample supported various correctional options. Again, the Tennessee public appeared to endorse multiple approaches to intervening with youths under court supervision. Of the 14 options presented, 9 were fully supported by a majority of the sample, and all 14 were fully or moderately supported. Even so, some variations in responses warrant attention.

Table 3	Respondents' Levels of Support for Various Community Corrections Options (in percentages)			
Correctional Option	Fully Support	Moderately Support	Slightly Support	Do Not Support
1. Counseling				
Individual: Having the youth meet with a counselor who would try to solve the emotional problems that caused the youth to get into trouble in the first place.	55.4	26.4	14.3	13.9
Family: Having a counselor meet with the entire family and the juvenile to attempt to uncover any issues within the family itself that could be affecting why the juvenile is committing crimes.	61.3	25.9	10.1	2.7
Group: Having a counselor meet with a group of delinquent youths to try to solve the emotional problems that caused them to get into trouble in the first place.	43.8	29.7	18.4	8.1
Anger management: A program designed to teach youths how to recognize and control their anger.	49.7	30.0	15.4	4.9
2. Drug/alcohol				
Drug/alcohol treatment: Having youths enter a program to eliminate their addiction to drugs and or alcohol.	67.6	21.3	8.9	2.1
Drug testing: Having youths give a urine sample to test if they are using alcohol and drugs.	80.3	11.8	5.4	2.5
3. Educational/vocational				
Educational programs: Having youths participate in a program to get their high school diploma if they have not finished high school.	71.9	18.4	7.0	2.7
Vocational programs: Teaching youths a skill (such as plumbing, air conditioning repair, or secretarial skills) so they can get a job.	64.9	23.5	9.2	2.3
4. Restorative				
Victim restitution. Having the youth work in order to pay back the victim for any damages that the youth caused.	82.9	12.6	3.3	1.2
Community service: Having the youth work in the community (without pay) on such projects as restoring or painting old houses, cleaning up trash on highways, or planting trees in public parks.	77.9	14.7	5.2	2.1
5. Tough love				
Boot camp: Having youths go through a program that is similar to basic training in the military	54.8	24.1	14.5	6.6
Scared straight: Having youths visit an adult prison where inmates yell, insult, and scare youths to deter them from committing any future crimes.	41.5	20.3	23.1	15.1

(Continued)

Table 3 (Continued)				
Correctional Option	Fully Support	Moderately Support	Slightly Support	Do Not Support
6. Monitor				
Electronic monitoring: Requires that the juvenile wear a bracelet that tells the probation officer whether he or she is at home.	48.2	24.3	17.5	10.0
Home incarceration: Having youths stay in their homes rather than staying in prison. Youths on home incarceration would only be allowed to leave their houses for certain reasons, such as meeting with their probation officer, attending a treatment program, or going to the doctor.	22.7	23.2	31.1	23.0

First, although the respondents supported all forms of counseling, the level of support was most pronounced for counseling that involved the entire family. Second, the sample endorsed drug treatment, but they especially favored drug testing. Third, both victim restitution and community service were highly embraced. This finding is noteworthy because these correctional interventions are integral to the emerging movement of restorative justice. Fourth, the approach of tough love—using boot camps and, particularly, "scared straight" programs to build character—were supported, although this support was lower than that given to most other correctional interventions. Fifth and relatedly, the approach of home incarceration was the least supported option. In fact, a majority of the sample either did not support or only slightly supported this option.

Taken together, these results suggest that the respondents did not believe that there is an inherent conflict between interventions that emphasize treatment and those that emphasize control. They did not see such approaches as incompatible but as complementary. Thus, Tennessee residents believed that youthful offenders should be monitored, drug tested, compelled to repair the harm they caused, and even subjected to some tough love—programs that used intrusive, if not harsh, measures to instill character. At the same time, the public was committed to exposing wayward youths to a range of traditional treatment interventions, including counseling, education, vocational training, and drug/alcohol treatment.

The survey also contained three items, rated with an agree-disagree Likert-type scale that asked the respondents what would be the best way to rehabilitate juvenile offenders: a good education, teaching them a skill, and helping these offenders change their values and helping them with the emotional problems that caused them to break the law. A high percentage of the sample agreed with each item. Notably, however, the support for changing values and dealing with emotional problems was particularly pronounced. Thus, 93 percent of the respondents strongly agreed with this statement. This finding suggests that the public believes that rehabilitating youthful offenders involves more than equipping them with job and educational skills and must also seek to change the values they hold and to help them with the emotional struggles they experience.

Belief in Child Saving

Finally, the survey contained data that have implications for the degree to which the respondents embraced the goal of saving children from a life in crime. First, we asked the sample members whether the main priority in the time ahead should be to build more prisons and youth facilities to lock up as many juvenile offenders as possible or to invest in ways to prevent kids from

Table 4	Respondents' Perceptions on the Best Way to Rehabilitate Juvenile Offenders (in percentages)		
Method of Intervention		Agree[a]	Disagree[b]
Values-problems			
The best way to rehabilitate juvenile offenders is to try to help these offenders change their values and to help them with the emotional problems that caused them to break the law.		92.9	10.7
Job skills			
The best way to rehabilitate juvenile offenders is to teach them a skill that they can use to get a job when they are released from prison.		89.3	10.7
Good education			
The best way to rehabilitate a juvenile is to give them a good education.		76.5	23.5

a. Agree combines the responses of those who said they strongly agreed, agreed, and slightly agreed.

b. Disagree includes those who strongly disagreed, disagreed, and slightly disagreed.

committing crimes and ending up in gangs or prisons. Most significant, Tennessee citizens not only favored the prevention option over the imprisonment option but also did so by a wide margin: 93.5 percent chose prevention—a figure that is almost 14 times higher than the number who favored building more prisons.

Second, we asked the respondents if they thought there is an age at which it is too late to help a young person who has gotten involved in violence and crime. Again, the faith in the ability to turn around the lives of wayward youths was high. Three-fourths of the sample answered no to this question. Even among those who answered yes, most of them believed that it became too late to help a youthful offender only at age 16.

✉ Policy Implications

The data presented here do not mean that most Americans oppose punishing youthful offenders. As the attitudes of Tennessee citizens revealed, punishment and societal protection were seen as important goals of the correctional process. Furthermore, we should note that when questioned elsewhere on the survey as to whether the courts were dealing harshly enough with juvenile offenders, more than 70 percent of our sample chose the option of "not harshly enough." It is likely as well that if asked to sentence juveniles who had committed particularly egregious crimes (e.g., murder, forcible rape, or a shooting) our respondents might well have tempered their enthusiasm for treatment and recommended transferring these violent juveniles to adult court where lengthy prison terms could be imposed. In this regard, although not uniformly supporting the transfer policy, previous research suggests that, under certain circumstances, the public will accept the waiver of violent offenders to adult court (Sprott 1998). In studies of public preferences for sentencing, moreover, youthfulness has been found to mitigate the severity of the sentences that respondents choose; however, this effect is limited and does not prevent respondents from prescribing prison terms to juveniles (Applegate et al. 1997; Jacoby and Cullen 1998).

Although it would be inadvisable to underestimate the pool of punitive sentiment that exists toward offenders of any age, it would be equally misguided to assume that juvenile rehabilitation is dead. The results from our survey show clearly that the public does not simply wish to warehouse juvenile offenders and throw away the keys. Consistent with previous research, the respondents were not convinced that sending youths to jail would stop their offending. Nearly two in five citizens also felt that juvenile institution were schools of crime. Even home confinement was viewed skeptically by the sample members. In contrast, the Tennessee public displayed a strong preference that rehabilitation should be the purpose of juvenile institutions.

By substantial majorities, they also endorsed the rehabilitation of juveniles in the community and embraced attempting to treat even those who were repeat offenders. Although under court supervision in the community, the public supported—often fully—a multimodal approach to intervention that included counseling, drug treatment, skill building, restoration of harm done to the community, and some degree of monitoring. Finally, given the choice between spending money to build prisons or to fund prevention-oriented programs, more than 9 in 10 respondents chose prevention. Again, this finding is consistent with existing research (Cullen, Wright, Brown, Moon, Blankenship, and Applegate 1998; Fairbank et al. 1998).

Taken together, these findings lend support to the broad policy implication that the public wants the legal system to intervene in ways that save children from a life in crime.[4] Previous research has shown that, in general, citizens favor retaining rehabilitation as a goal of the adult criminal justice system, but that this preference may be particularly pronounced for the juvenile system (Applegate et al. 1997; Sundt et al. 1998). Although we do not have comparative data on adults, the absolute level of support for juvenile treatment in our study reinforces this view. Furthermore, nearly three-fourths of the sample stated that it was never too late to attempt to help a young person turn away from crime. This perspective likely is based on subsidiary assumptions about youths: they are malleable, are not fully responsible for their decisions, and have enough of their life ahead of them that not to save them would be morally wrong. In any case, residents from Tennessee—hardly a bellwether state known for its liberal approach to social issues—are firm in their belief that criminal justice officials should make a concerted effort to reform wayward adolescents.

This finding in turn has three specific policy implications. First it should give pause to commentators who are now arguing in favor not only of the abolition of the juvenile court but also of processing youths according to guidelines based on principles of just deserts and societal protection (Feld 1998; cf. Zimring 1998). Much like the progressive founders of the juvenile court a century ago, respondents in our study believed that intervention with juveniles should do more than exact just deserts and impose punishment in hopes of preventing crime (Cullen and Gilbert 1982; Rothman 1980). Instead, they favored state interventions that seek to invest in, and positively influence the lives of, delinquents. They wanted these interventions not simply to do justice but also to do good.

Second, these public opinion results suggest that punitive thinking is not hegemonic. Although the penal harm movement—as Clear (1994) appropriately calls it—has dominated American corrections for nearly three decades, its influence is not complete. At times, the belief that the public is exclusively punitive has helped to construct a reality that is self-fulfilling: There is no use to proposing liberal policies because citizens, and thus policy makers, will not support them In contrast, our data indicated that policies that offer a balanced approach to dealing with juvenile offenders—that do not ignore just deserts and societal protection, but that do vigorously seek to rehabilitate youngsters—will not give rise to a hostile public reaction. Instead, it appears that the public will endorse an array of policies that are fairly progressive in orientation; given, it seems, that these initiatives do not irresponsibly endanger public safety.

The Reasoned and Equitable Community and Local Alternatives to the Incarceration of Minors (RECLAIM) Ohio initiative is one example of a juvenile justice initiative that seeks to balance public safety with the rehabilitation of offenders (Moon, Applegate, and Latessa 1997). This program distributes money to all counties based on the number of youths with felony adjudications. Counties can use these funds to pay to send any given youth to a state institution. However, to reduce institutional crowding and to encourage counties to send only serious offenders to state facilities, Ohio also allows counties that do not incarcerate youths to keep the funds so as to establish or contract for local community-based programs. In short, the state is giving counties an incentive not to send youthful offenders to prison but rather to treat them in the community. The collateral goal is to reduce the inmate population at state juvenile facilities. Imprisonment is to be used to incapacitate truly serious offenders and, at the same time, to provide these youths with special treatment services. It is noteworthy that this program was an initiative of a Republican governor.

Third the public opinion data suggest that the empirical inroads now being made in showing what works in rehabilitating offenders may potentially find a receptive audience in the public. In an important way, citizens appear to want the correctional system to intervene effectively with youthful offenders. As our data show, they are not always certain that rehabilitation is the main goal of the system, but they clearly believe that it should be. It is noteworthy, therefore, that there is increasing empirical evidence that punishment-oriented interventions have virtually no effect on recidivism, but that treatment-oriented interventions diminish criminal participation (Andrews, Zinger, Hoge, Bonta, Gendreau, and Cullen 1990; Gibbons 1999; Henggeler 1997; Lipsey 1992; Lipsey and Wilson 1998). These interventions, moreover, achieve substantial reductions in recidivism (25 percent or higher) when targeted on high-risk offenders and when employing cognitive-behavioral and skill-building treatment modalities. There is also a collateral literature outlining an array of early prevention programs that have proven effective in protecting children from staying on or entering a criminal life course (Farrington 1994; Loeber and Farrington 1998; Yoshikawa 1994). Contrary to outdated notions that nothing works, the empirical basis for building effective programming is growing markedly. Again, this message—that there are programs that work to save wayward children—is likely to be welcome news to most Tennesseans, if not to most of their fellow Americans.

Finally, we should take notice of the remarkable tenacity of the public's belief that rehabilitation should remain an integral goal of juvenile corrections. Although noteworthy exceptions exist (see, e.g, Currie 1998), many criminologists have argued that rehabilitation does not work, leads to net widening, fosters the exercise of discretion that is arbitrary, and ultimately is coercive. These efforts at delegitimizing treatment have reinforced the cry from conservative quarters that juvenile criminals are "super-predators" who may be beyond redemption. Despite this sustained attack on rehabilitation, the nation's citizens are not prepared to relinquish the hope that kids who get in trouble can be saved. To do so, perhaps, would be to accept a vision of our children and of our society that is inconsistent with what Bellah, Madsen, Sullivan, Swidler, and Tipton (1985, 1991) have called our habits of the heart and our vision of the good society. Anderson (1998) has captured this issue with words that are a fitting end to our work:

That suggests the ultimate reason for holding onto the rehabilitative ideal, and it is profoundly moral. America's founding fathers may have been naïve about the possibility of rehabilitating people in prison, but they were not naïve about the importance of rehabilitation. An ethical society can choose to use criminal justice for more than maintaining domestic peace and reinforcing values codified in law. It may also . . . use criminal justice to acknowledge a belief that good lurks in the hearts of people who act bad; that even the worst-seeming criminals have the capacity, in time and with help, to change for the better. The: process is as imperfect and unpredictable as humanity itself: some are helped by programs; some find salvation on their own; and some never find it at all. But it is unenlightened in the extreme to deny the capacity for change or prohibit the chance to exercise it. . . . [Rehabilitation programs] send a powerful positive message about a society's deepest values, to criminals and to everyone else. (Pp. 16–17)

Notes

1. During the remainder of the mailings, an additional 125 surveys were returned as undeliverable and were not replaced.

2. For the initial mailing, respondents were sent a second copy of the survey at three weeks and a third copy at seven and a half weeks. The replacement respondents were sent a second copy at three weeks and, due to time constraints, a third copy at five and a half weeks.

3. These statements were changed somewhat from the statements in the original survey conducted by Resources For Youth.

4. Notably, it appears that juvenile court judges and other juvenile justice personnel also continue to support the treatment of youthful offenders (see Bazemore and Feder 1997; Leiber, Roth, Streeter, and Federspeil 1997).

References

Anderson, David C. 1998. *Sensible Justice: Alternatives to Prison.* New York: The New Press.

Andrews, D. A., Ivan Zinger, Robert D. Hoge, James Bonta, Paul Gendreau, and Francis T. Cullen. 1990. "Does Correctional Treatment Work? A Clinically-Relevant and Psychologically Informed Meta-Analysis." *Criminology* 28:369–404.

Applegate, Brandon K. 1997. "Specifying Public Support for Rehabilitation: A Factorial Survey Approach." Ph.D. dissertation, Division of Criminal Justice, University of Cincinnati, Cincinnati, OH.

Applegate, Brandon K., Francis T. Cullen, and Bonnie S. Fisher. 1997. "Public Support for Correctional Treatment: The Continuing Appeal of the Rehabilitative Ideal." *The Prison Journal* 77:237–58.

Bellah, Robert N., Richard Madsen, William M. Sullivan, Ann Swidler, and Steven M. Tipton. 1985. *Habits of the Heart: Individualism and Commitment in American Life.* Berkeley: University of California Press.

——. 1991. *The Good Society.* New York: Knopf.

Bazemore, Gordon and Susan E. Day. 1996. "Restoring the Balance: Juvenile and Community Justice." *Juvenile Justice* 3:3–14.

Bazemore, Gordon and Lynette Feder. 1997. "Rehabilitation in the New Juvenile Court: Do Judges Support the Treatment Ethic?" *American Journal of Criminal Justice* 21:181–212.

Clear, Todd R. 1994. *Harm in American Penology: Offenders, Victims, and Their Communities.* Albany: State University of New York Press.

Cullen, Francis T. Gregory A. Clark, and John F. Wosniak. 1985. "Attribution, Salience, and Attitudes Toward Criminal Sanctioning." *Criminal Justice and Behavior* 12:305–31.

Cullen, Francis T. and Karen E. Gilbert. 1982. *Reaffirming Rehabilitation.* Cincinnati, OH: Anderson.

Cullen, Francis T., Kathryn M. Golden, and John B. Cullen. 1983. "Is Child Saving Dead? Attitudes Toward Juvenile Rehabilitation in Illinois." *Journal of Criminal Justice* 11:1–13.

Cullen, Francis T., Sandra Evans Skovron, Joseph E. Scott, and Velmer S. Burton. 1990. "Public Support for Correctional Treatment: The Tenacity of the Rehabilitative Ideal." *Criminal Justice and Behavior* 17: 6–18.

Cullen, Francis T., John Paul Wright, Shayna Brown, Melissa M. Moon, Michael B. Blankenship, and Brandon K. Applegate. 1998. "Public Support for Early Intervention Programs: Implications for a Progressive Policy Agenda." *Crime & Delinquency* 44:187–204.

Currie, Elliott. 1998. *Crime and Punishment in America.* New York: Holt.

Dighton, John. 1999. "Balanced and Restorative Justice in Illinois." *The Compiler: Illinois Criminal Justice Information Authority* (Winter):4–5.

DiIulio, John J. Jr. 1995. "The Coming of the Super-Predators." *The Weekly Standard,* November 27, pp. 23–28.

Dillman, Don A. 1978. *Mail and Telephone Surveys: The Total Design Method.* New York: Wiley.

Doble Research Associates. 1995. *Crime and Corrections: The Views of the People of Oregon.* Englewood Cliffs, NJ: Doble Research Associates.

Fairbank, Maslin, Maullin, & Associates. 1998. *Mapping California's Opinion.* San Rafael, CA: Resources for Youth.

Farrington, David P. 1994. "Early Developmental Prevention of Juvenile Delinquency." *Criminal Behaviour and Mental Health* 4:209–27.

Feld, Barry C. 1993. "Criminalizing the American Juvenile Court." Pp. 197–208 in *Crime and Justice: A Review of Research,* Vol. 17, edited by M. Tonry. Chicago: University of Chicago Press.

——. 1998. "Juvenile and Criminal Justice Systems' Responses to Youth Violence." Pp. 189–261 in *Youth Violence—Crime and Justice: A Review of Research,* Vol. 24, edited by M. Tonry and M. H. Moore. Chicago: University of Chicago Press.

Gerber, Jurg and Simone Engelhardt-Greer. 1996. "Just and Painful: Attitudes Toward Sentencing Criminals." Pp. 62–74 in *Americans View Crime and Justice: A National Public Opinion Surrey,* edited by T. Flanagan and D. R. Longmire. Thousand Oaks, CA: Sage.

Gibbons, Don C. 1999. "Review Essay: Changing Lawbreakers—What Have We Learned Since the 1950s?" *Crime & Delinquency* 45:272–93.

Gonzalez, John W. 1998. "Many in Poll Want Stiffer Laws on Juvenile Criminals: Support Growing to Punish Parents." *Houston Chronicle,* June 21, p. 1.

Gottfredson, Stephen D. and Ralph B. Taylor. 1984. "Public Policy and Prison Populations: Measuring Options About Reform." *Judicature* 68:190–201.

Gottfredson, Stephen D., Barbara D. Warner, and Ralph B. Taylor, 1988. "Conflict and Consensus About Criminal Justice in Maryland." Pp. 16–55 in *Public Attitudes to Sentencing: Surveys From Five Countries,* edited by N. Walker and M. Hough. Brookfleld, VT: Gower.

Harris, Louis. 1968. "Changing Public Attitudes Toward Crime and Corrections." *Federal Probation* 32:9–16.

Henggeler, Scott W. 1997. *Treating Serious Anti-Social Behavior in Youth: The MST Approach.* Washington, DC: Department of Justice, Office of Juvenile Justice and Delinquency Prevention.

Jacoby, Joseph E. and Francis T. Cullen. 1998. "The Structure of Punishment Norms: Applying the Rossi-Berk Model." *Journal of Criminal Law and Criminology* 89:245–312.

Leiber, Michael J., Kurt Roth, Heide Streeter, and Shannon Federspeil. 1997. "Findings from a Survey of Juvenile Justice Personnel in Two States Concerning Correctional Responses and Services for Serious Violent Youth." Presented at the annual meeting of the Midwestern Criminal Justice Association, Indianapolis, IN.

Lipsey, Mark W. 1992. "Juvenile Delinquency Treatment: A Meta-Analytic Inquiry Into the Variability of Effects." Pp. 83–127 in *Meta-Analysis for Explanation: A Casebook,* edited by T. D. Cook, H. Cooper, D. S. Cordray, H. Hartman, L. V. Hedges, R. J. Light, T. A. Lewis, and F. Mosteller. New York: Russell Sage.

Lipsey, Mark W. and David B. Wilson. 1998. "Effective Interventions for Serious Juvenile Offenders: A Synthesis of Research." Pp. 313–66 in *Serious and Violent Juvenile Offenders: Risk Factors and Successful Interventions,* edited by R. Loeber and D. P. Farrington. Thousand Oaks, CA: Sage.

Loeber, Rolf and David P. Farrington, eds. 1998. *Serious and Violent Juvenile Offenders: Risk Factors and Successful Interventions.* Thousand Oaks, CA: Sage.

Makeig, John. 1994. "Most in Poll Favor Rehabilitation for Youthful Offenders." *Houston Chronicle,* February 19, p. 30A.

Moon, Melissa M., Brandon K. Applegate, and Edward J. Latessa. 1997. "RECLAIM Ohio: A Politically Viable Alternative to Treating Youthful Felony Offenders." *Crime & Delinquency* 43:438–56.

Moore, David W. 1994. "Majority Advocate Death Penalty for Teenage Killers." *Gallup Poll Monthly,* September, pp. 2–6.

Moore, Teresa. 1996. "S.F. Favors Help Over Jail for Youth, Poll Says." *San Francisco Chronicle,* October 2, pp. 11A and 17A.

Pettinico, George. 1994. "Crime and Punishment: America Changes Its Mind." *The Public Perspective* 5:29–32.

Platt, Anthony M. 1969. *The Child Savers: The Invention of Delinquency.* Chicago: University of Chicago Press.

Roberts, Julian V. and Loretta J. Stalans. 1997. *Public Opinion, Crime, and Criminal Justice.* Boulder, CO: Westview.

Rothman, David J. 1980. *Conscience and Convenience: The Asylum and Its Alternatives in Progressive America.* Boston: Little, Brown.

Schwartz, Ira M., John Johnson Kerbs, Danielle M. Hogston, and Cindy L. Guillean. 1992. *Combating Juvenile Crime: What the Public Really Wants.* Ann Arbor, MI: Center for the Study of Youth Policy.

Sickmund, Melissa, Howard N. Snyder, and Eileen Poe-Yamagata. 1997. *Juvenile Offenders and Victims:*

1997 Update on Violence. Washington, DC: Office of Juvenile Justice and Delinquency Prevention.

Sickmund, Melissa, Anne L. Stahl, Terrence A. Finnegan, Howard N. Snyder, Rowen S. Poole, and Jeffrey A. Butts. 1998. *Juvenile Court Statistics, 1995.* Washington, DC: Office of Juvenile Justice and Delinquency Prevention.

Snyder, Howard N. 1998a. "Juvenile Arrests 1997." *Juvenile Justice Bulletin.* Washington, DC: Department of Justice.

——, 1998b. "Serious, Violent and Chronic Juvenile Offenders: An Assessment of the Extent of and Trends in Officially Recognized Serious Criminal Behavior in a Delinquent Population." Pp. 428–444 in *Serious and Violent Juvenile Offenders: Risk Factors and Successful Intervention,* edited by R. Loeber and D. Farrington. Thousand Oaks, CA: Sage.

Sprott, Jane B. "Understanding Public Opposition to a Separate Youth Justice System." *Crime & Delinquency* 44:399–411.

Steinhart, David. 1988. *California Opinion Poll: Public Attitudes on Youth Crime.* San Francisco: National Council on Crime and Delinquency.

Sundt, Jody L., Francis T. Cullen, Brandon K. Applegate, and Michael G. Turner. 1998. "The Tenacity of the Rehabilitative Ideal Revisited: Have Attitudes Toward Offender Treatment Changed?" *Criminal Justice and Behavior* 25:426–42.

The Public Perspective: A Roper Center Review of Public Opinion and Polling. 1997. Storrs, CT: The Roper Center.

Torbet, Patricia and Linda Szymanski. 1998. *State Legislative Responses to Violent Juvenile Crime: 1996–97 Update.* Juvenile Justice Bulletin. Washington, DC: Department of Justice.

Triplett, Ruth. 1996. "The Growing Threat: Gangs and Juvenile Offenders." Pp. 137–50 in *Americans View Crime and Justice: A National Public Opinion Survey,* edited by T. Flanagan and D. R. Longmire. Thousand Oaks, CA: Sage.

Yoshikawa, Hirokazu. 1994. "Prevention as Cumulative Protection: Effects of Early Family Support and Education on Chronic Delinquency and Its Risks." *Psychological Bulletin* 115:28–54.

Zimring, Franklin E. 1998. "Toward a Jurisprudence of Youth Violence." Pp. 477–501 in *Youth Violence—Crime and Justice: A Review of Research,* Vol. 24, edited by M. Tonry and M. H. Moore. Chicago: University of Chicago Press.

DISCUSSION QUESTIONS

1. What are some reasons why juvenile rehabilitation was attacked and criticized by a variety of groups? Give examples of persons or groups you have known, who have voiced some criticisms.

2. Give examples from your experience or observations of support for rehabilitation such as the authors give from previous research.

3. How would you respond to the questions reported in Table 2? Give some reasons to support your answers.

4. Considering the various community corrections options, what do you think are the most and the least important options? Explain why.

5. Suggest one or two correctional programs that would address juvenile offenders' values and problems, job skills, and educational needs.

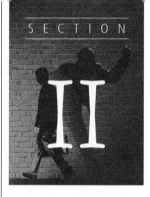

SECTION

II

POLICE AND JUVENILE OFFENDERS

The first contact that a young juvenile offender has with the juvenile justice system is with a police officer. The nature and circumstances of this police contact are likely to be significant and have a lasting impression on a young person. In Section II we examine police roles and responsibilities in general, and the unique roles that police have when dealing with juvenile offenders. Children and juveniles are involved in a variety of law violations ranging from status offenses to more serious offending, and present special challenges for the policing function. We will discuss alternatives to traditional law enforcement strategies such as community- or problem-oriented policing; curfew enforcement; gang suppression strategies; preventive efforts such as D.A.R.E. and School Resource Officers; police procedures for taking juvenile offenders into custody; legal guidelines for interrogation and gathering evidence; and use of discretion or referral to juvenile court.

The Police and Juvenile Crime

For juveniles, the police role is considered especially important because young persons' views and attitudes toward law enforcement are shaped by their first encounter with a police officer. Juvenile offenders are involved in a disproportionately large number of crimes relative to their percentage of the population, so they present a special challenge for law enforcement. In 2005, law enforcement agencies in the United States made an estimated 2.1 million arrests of persons under age 18. Juveniles accounted for about 16% of all violent crime arrests and 26% of all property crime arrests in 2005 (Snyder, 2007, p. 1).

The police role with juveniles is expanded because they handle many noncriminal matters referred to as *status offenses,* including running away, curfew violations, and truancy as well as nondelinquent juvenile matters such as neglect, abuse, and missing persons reports. Most urban police departments have special police units or juvenile bureaus for handling the increasing number of juvenile cases. Duties of special juvenile officers include taking missing children reports; examining runaway cases; investigating juvenile crimes; contacting and interviewing juveniles, their parents, school officials, and complainants regarding the circumstances of an offense; maintaining juvenile records; and appearing in juvenile court.

Juveniles are less predictable than adults and often exhibit less respect for the authority of officers. The immaturity of many children and youth means that they are more vulnerable to the dares of other youth, and they often engage in deviant behavior when in the company of their peers. Many youth view the police officer on patrol not as a deterrent to delinquent behavior, but as a challenge to avoiding detection and confrontation while loitering at night or engaging in behaviors ranging from petty mischief, to property damage and vandalism, to more serious crimes of theft and assaults. The immaturity of youth, coupled with limited parental supervision and negative peer influence, presents special problems for police, who frequently encounter juveniles with little respect for law and authority. Juveniles also present a special problem for police because they are less cognizant of the consequences of their actions and the effects of their delinquent behavior on their victims, their parents and families, their peers, and themselves. Before discussing police roles with juvenile offenders, we provide an overview of police roles in general.

Police Roles and Responsibilities

Police officers are the most visible officials in the criminal justice system. They introduce citizens to the justice process. That introduction ranges from taking a report from a victim or witness to a crime, to issuing a traffic citation, to questioning or taking into custody a suspect in a misdemeanor or felony offense. Police are charged with preventing crime and enforcing the law. They are given the authority to make arrests, to use reasonable physical force when necessary, and to take persons charged with crimes into custody. Society entrusts a great deal of authority to police, but also expects a lot from them. Police are expected to provide public order and safety; to prevent crimes from occurring, and find and apprehend offenders when crimes occur; and to perform a variety of law enforcement functions without violating constitutional rights. In reality, traditional police patrol does little to prevent crime. Police in most cases react to crime after it has already happened, responding to citizen calls, reporting to crime scenes, conducting investigations, and tracking and apprehending offenders. The fact that police are called upon for many services besides law enforcement makes their job even more difficult.

Police officers actually perform three roles in fulfilling their law enforcement responsibilities: law enforcement, order maintenance, and service (Wilson, 1968). The public and the police themselves have viewed the law enforcement function as the primary and most important task, and little attention was given to the others, which were considered less important and not "real law enforcement."

Law Enforcement

The traditional law enforcement role of police is to detect and investigate crimes and to apprehend those responsible for committing crimes. Police attempt to detect crimes through regular police patrols and by responding to complaints of victims and statements of witnesses. The traditional law enforcement role gives police visibility to the public as they "protect and serve." There are some additional challenges in policing crimes such as drug dealing, gambling, and prostitution, where there are no witnesses or clearly identified victims. To enforce laws against the so-called victimless crimes (or more appropriately termed "consensual" crimes, because persons involved are willing participants), police work as undercover officers to detect the crimes and make arrests. The law enforcement role includes enforcement of traffic laws and parking violations, and it is here that officers have the most interaction with the general public as law enforcers. To finalize their law enforcement role and ensure that suspects are brought to trial, police engage in interrogation of suspects, collection of physical evidence at a crime scene, and presentation of the evidence in court.

Order Maintenance

The order maintenance function of police involves crowd control during events such as parades, large public gatherings, music concerts, and sports competitions in indoor and outdoor stadiums; and patrolling on foot, on bicycle, on horseback, or in vehicles and on streets, sidewalks, and in public parks. The order maintenance function parallels the law enforcement role when officers intervene to control disorderly behavior. The order maintenance role is less clear (both to the public and to many police) than the law enforcement role, mainly because the behaviors being controlled are less clearly defined. "Disorderly behavior," for example, generally refers to behavior that disturbs the public peace, but the exact definition and an officer's determination whether the behavior warrants official intervention depend on the neighborhood location and the time during which the disturbance occurs. The officer's role may be that of telling participants of a loud party to quiet down or dispersing a group of juveniles who are loitering on a street corner or in front of a business establishment.

Service Function

The third role of police is that of providing services to the public. This may include providing aid or assistance to persons in need, such as calling a tow truck for a stranded motorist;

▲ **Photo II-1**   A juvenile offender suspect awaits verification of juvenile status and questioning by police.
(© CORBIS)

transporting abandoned or neglected children to a hospital or shelter facility; delivering a baby whose mother did not make it to the hospital on time. The service function often results in a combination of functions, such as when one officer transports abandoned children to a shelter, and another officer locates the parent(s) and initiates a child abuse investigation (a law enforcement function). The service function more recently has come to include an educational component, such as when police are assigned to schools to assist in the education of children and youth on the dangers of drugs and how to avoid drug abuse.

The three primary roles of police are very different on a number of dimensions: criminal versus noncriminal, urgent versus routine, and dangerous versus relatively safe (Dorne & Gewerth, 1995). Police officers generally view the law enforcement function as the primary role, while order maintenance and service tasks have been typically regarded with mixed feelings, ranging from ambivalence to disdain (Moore, 1992). Police officers hold varying opinions of the importance of each of the roles, and they do not undertake these three functions with equal degrees of enthusiasm. They are given considerable autonomy and independence in carrying out their law enforcement roles and are allowed to place greater or lesser importance on a given role depending on their assigned patrol area and individual circumstances. In a reading in this section, Susan Guarino-Ghezzi recommends that police reexamine the order maintenance and law enforcement roles as they pertain to juvenile offenders and victims.

✉ Police–Juvenile Relations

Police officers encounter a wide variety of deviant and delinquent behavior among children and youth, ranging from minor status offenses to serious crimes. The majority of police encounters with juveniles are in response to minor offenses that involve an order maintenance function of law enforcement (Friedman, Lurigio, Greenleaf, & Albertson, 2004). Regardless of the seriousness of the behavior, however, the nature of the police–juvenile encounter can make a significant difference on police–juvenile relations. Sherman (1997) noted that police themselves often create a risk factor for crime by using "bad manners." Research evidence indicates that when police are less respectful toward suspects and citizens in general, then citizens also tend to have less respect for police officers and for the law (Sherman, 1997, pp. 8–58). Juveniles are critical of police practices such as stopping and questioning them, asking them to "move on" and not loiter on street corners, parking lots, or in front of stores. African American and Hispanic youth, and those living in urban areas, are more critical of police than white students or those living in suburban or rural areas (Taylor, Turner, Esbensen, & Winfree, 2001). Students often have ambivalent or mixed feelings about police. Taylor et al. (2001) found that a majority of students in their study believed that police are friendly and hard working, but they also believed that officers are racially prejudiced and dishonest. They did *not* believe that police officers contribute directly to the negative feelings, however. The reasons for juveniles' negative attitudes toward police are likely the inevitable result of police officers' fair but unpopular restrictions on young peoples' behaviors (Taylor et al., 2001). Lieber, Nalla, and Farnsworth (1998) suggested that community policing practices and problem-oriented policing can positively influence youths' perceptions of police, but Hurst and Frank (2000) have noted that attempting to involve youths in community-oriented policing is a challenge because of their negative views and disapproval of many police functions. Friedman and his associates (2004) have noted that both police and youth's demeanors affect the perceived nature and outcomes of their encounters, so there is reason to believe that juveniles' negativity toward the police might have triggered officer disrespect, which in turn feeds juveniles' negative attitudes. In short, they believe that police–juvenile interactions are a two-way street. Young people react to how police officers treat them, and officers often respond in kind to juveniles' disrespectful behavior. Working with juveniles is a challenge, and police departments do well to provide officers with cultural awareness training to enhance their skills in working and interacting with juveniles (Friedman et al., 2004). Schools can also educate students about police responsibilities and procedures, and the appropriate responses when interacting with police. D.A.R.E. and School Resource Officers have an opportunity to improve juvenile and police relations through better understanding of police roles and functions. A description and evaluation of a D.A.R.E. program by Dennis Rosenbaum and his associates is included as a reading in this section.

The service functions of policing take on a special emphasis in relation to juveniles. Police are expected to *protect children* and to *prevent delinquency* (Sanborn & Salerno, 2005). Child protection may involve intervening in suspected cases of child neglect (being left at home alone, or left inside a vehicle in cold or hot weather conditions); of endangering a child's safety (failure to use a car seat or seat belts); or of child abuse such as physical punishment that may involve serious injury or even death. Child neglect and abuse have been shown to have a relationship with status offenses such as running away, which in turn often lead to more serious delinquency. The primary reason for the inclusion of status offenses in all juvenile statutes in fact is for child protection and delinquency prevention. Laws giving police the authority to intervene in noncriminal behaviors such as running away, truancy, and curfew violations are intended to protect juveniles and prevent worse delinquent behavior.

Many cities have implemented curfew laws in an effort to get children and youth off the streets at night, reduce their opportunities to get into trouble, and therefore prevent delinquency.

Curfew laws generally apply only to youth under the age of 16, and the hours during which youth are required to be off the streets may vary according to the age of the youth (the limit may be 10:00 p.m. for those under 14, and 11:00 or midnight for youth aged 15 or 16, for example). Violation of curfew laws is a status offense, illegal only for those of juvenile age, and not punishable by referral to juvenile court. Police responses to curfew violations vary, but may include a warning to get home, telephoning the parents, delivering the youths to their homes in a patrol car, or bringing them to a shelter where parents are asked to come to pick them up. Evidence of the effectiveness of curfew laws varies, with some researchers claiming that juvenile crime is reduced (McDowell, Loftin, & Wiersema, 2000), while others found no evidence of crime reduction that could be explained by the curfew (Reynolds, Seydlitz, Jenkins, 2000). Curfew laws may have little effect on juvenile crime because there is evidence that a significant proportion of juvenile crimes occur immediately after school hours (3:00 p.m.) and before 6:00 p.m. (Sickmund, Snyder, & Poe-Yamagata, 1997). Some cities have therefore attempted to enforce daytime, after-school curfews, but these present countless problems in affecting youth who are not engaging or would not engage in criminal activity (Bannister, Carter, & Shafer, 2001).

The child protection and delinquency prevention roles are service and order maintenance functions of police but are essential in supporting law enforcement with juveniles, particularly in a community policing context. We have included readings at the end of this section that address the special roles of police and curfew laws, truancy, gang suppression, and firearm possession and violations. These problems present police officers with demanding challenges when it comes to combining their order maintenance and law enforcement roles on a regular basis in cities throughout the country.

⬚ Police Roles and Discretion

Police are permitted to exercise a great deal of discretion in their duties. That is, they have the ability to choose between different courses of action, depending on their particular assignment. Individual autonomy and discretion are not unique to the police role, but tend to get more attention than in other professions. Employees in many organizations are given some discretionary authority and flexibility in carrying out job functions. In most organizations, however, discretion among personnel at the lower levels is very limited, and flexibility in decision making expands as one moves farther up organization levels. In police organizations the opposite is true. Discretionary authority among police is greater at the lowest levels of the organization, giving the line-level officer on patrol a considerable amount of discretion in carrying out and discharging his or her duties (Goldstein, 1977). In other organizations, the actions of line-level personnel are under close scrutiny. In police organizations, officers on patrol are out of sight of their superiors, and the low visibility means they are frequently beyond the commanding officers' control. Because of the considerable amount of discretion, much research and writing has been devoted to studying and understanding police discretion.

The nature of police discretion varies with the different police roles. In law enforcement situations, police must resolve whether a crime occurred: whether there is sufficient evidence to justify stopping a suspect for questioning, taking into custody, or making an arrest. Officers receive extensive training in the *law enforcement* function, including thorough education on the legal statutes and the appropriate legal interventions they are authorized to make for law violations. *Order maintenance* situations leave more room for police discretion, as "public order" and "disorderly conduct" are not so clearly defined. It is difficult or even impossible to determine, for example, whether a loud exchange of words on the street, in a public gathering, or in a home amounts to a violation of the "public order." It may depend on the context and circumstances of the verbal exchange. Police decisions and discretion in the *service function* are equally difficult. The police role in service situations has generally not been discussed in police training manuals or in books and research articles on policing (Moore, 1992). Many police regard calls for service, such as rendering first aid or helping a stranded motorist, as a waste of time and an interference with the real job of policing. Some police would maintain that calls for service can be better handled by other agencies and individuals.

A number of arguments have been made for reevaluating the negative attitude toward the service function of police: (1) police response to requests for service might result in more effective law enforcement; (2) response to such calls may prevent a crime later; (3) response to service calls helps establish a positive community presence; and (4) response to service helps enhance the flow of information from community sources and aids in crime detection and prevention (Moore, 1992). The emergence of community policing has diminished to a great extent some of the earlier sense of frustration and resistance of police officers in fulfilling service functions. Community policing includes emphases on police–community relations, citizen input, team policing, crime problem solving, and crime prevention (Cordner, 2005). With the emergence of community policing, officers have more readily come to accept that order maintenance and service functions are important functions of law enforcement. Police agencies that have adopted a community policing perspective accept and recognize that all three functions are equally important in carrying out effective police operations.

▨ Juvenile Offending and Police Discretion

Police have considerable discretionary power in handling juvenile matters, ranging from reprimand and release, to transporting a juvenile to detention and referral to juvenile court. Discretion is important in police work, for the officer's decision to intervene in any suspected law violation is the first stage in the juvenile justice process. Officers use their discretion in deciding whether or not to take official actions with offending juveniles or simply order them to "move on," "break it up," or "get on home." Most police contact with juveniles is nonofficial, and police make an arrest and take juveniles into custody in only a small percentage of cases. In a study of police responses with juveniles in two cities, Myers (2002) found that police took juveniles into custody in only 13% of their encounters with juveniles. Most of the police–juvenile encounters involved noncriminal matters, such as public disorder (22%), traffic offenses (14%), nonviolent conflicts (9%), and suspicious situations (7%); and about one fourth (27%) involved violent or nonviolent crimes (Myers, 2002, p. 123). In 2003, 20% of juvenile arrests were handled within law enforcement agencies, 71% were referred to juvenile court, and 7% were referred directly to criminal court. The remaining 2% were referred to a welfare agency or to another police agency. The proportion of arrests referred to juvenile court increased from 1980 to 2003, from 58% to 71% (Snyder & Sickmund, 2006, p. 152).

Police discretion has been criticized because some believe that police abuse their broad discretionary powers, and that they base their decisions on extralegal factors other than the offense. Extralegal factors such as sex, race, socioeconomic status, and individual characteristics of the offender have been shown to make a difference in police officers' decisions of whether or not to take official actions. Girls are less likely than boys to be arrested and referred to juvenile court, but they are often referred more than boys for status offenses such as running away or disobeying parents (Armstrong, 1977; Chesney-Lind, 1977). Researchers have reported differing results on the importance of race in police discretion. Some studies report few differences when controlling for offense seriousness and prior record. African American and other minority youths seem to be involved in more frequent and serious offenses than whites, so it is difficult to determine whether they are singled out more by police for official action. There is some evidence of racial bias, however, as minority youths have often been targeted more by police for official intervention (Wolfgang, Figlio, & Sellin, 1972, p. 252). Some critics of police discretion also contend that lower-class youths are processed into the justice system for the same offenses for which middle- or upper-class juveniles are simply reprimanded and released to their parents. Police and juvenile officers justify this use of discretion on the basis that middle- and upper-class youth are more likely to be corrected without referral to the justice system because their parents have the resources to provide their children with the necessary supervision and corrective services. Merry Morash (1984) found that an older juvenile with a prior record and who fits the image of a serious delinquent is more likely to be referred by police to the juvenile court. A juvenile's demeanor and attitude make a difference in a police officer's use of discretion. A youth who is polite and respectful is more likely to get off with a reprimand, while a negative and hostile attitude is likely to result in a court referral (Lundman, Sykes, & Clark, 1990; Piliavin & Briar, 1964).

⬚ Race as a Factor in Juvenile Arrests

The issue of race is a major concern in the criminal and juvenile justice systems. It is an undisputed fact that racial and ethnic minorities (especially African Americans) are disproportionately represented at each stage of the system: in police arrests, in jails and detention centers, in courts, and in correctional facilities. Research studies are mixed, however, as to whether that disproportionate representation is a result of racial bias in police arrest, prosecutors' decisions, and judicial sentencing (Conley, 1994; Wordes, Bynum, & Corley, 1994). African American youth are overrepresented in juvenile arrests when compared to their proportion of the population. Black youth, who accounted for 17% of the juvenile population in 2005, were involved in a disproportionate number of juvenile arrests for robbery (68%), murder (54%), motor vehicle theft (43%), and aggravated assault (42%) (Snyder, 2007, p. 9).

The question is whether the overrepresentation of black juveniles in police arrest rates is due to racial bias, or to the greater involvement of black youth in violent crimes. Violent crimes are more likely to be reported, detected, and result in a police arrest. To answer this question, Pope and Snyder (2003) analyzed National Incident-Based Reporting System (NIBRS) data from law enforcement agencies in 17 states, with a large sample of 102,905 juvenile offenders. They found no significant effects of race in police arrest decisions, and they were able to identify some characteristics that differentiated the crimes of white and nonwhite juvenile offenders. Compared to nonwhites, white juvenile offenders were:

- Less likely to have multiple victims
- More likely to act alone
- More likely to commit crimes indoors
- Less likely to possess a nonpersonal weapon (firearm, knife, or club)
- Less likely to offend against adults

▲ **Photo II-2** Police arrest a suspected juvenile offender for drug dealing. (© CORBIS)

- Less likely to offend against members of another race
- More likely to commit crimes against family members; equally likely to commit crimes against acquaintances; but less likely to commit crimes against strangers (Pope & Snyder, 2003, p. 4).

The findings revealed that the crime incident characteristics that increased the odds of arrest for violent crimes were largely the same for white and nonwhite offenders, with one important exception: Victim's race was correlated with arrest probability for nonwhite juvenile offenders, but *not* for white offenders. A nonwhite juvenile offender therefore was more likely to be arrested if the victim was white than if the victim was nonwhite. More research must be conducted on police arrest patterns, using larger samples that are more representative of the nation. Arrest patterns may differ among states and within regions of states and of the nation.

Race and ethnic background may be a factor in police decisions to arrest juvenile offenders, but based on research evidence it is clear that several other factors influence officers' decisions. In summary, the factors that may affect police officers' decisions to arrest a juvenile or to take less formal actions without court referral include factors relating to the:

- Offense (seriousness, type, time of day, gang related, use of weapon)
- Youth's record or status (prior police contact or arrest, school record, probation status)
- Offender (age, gender, race, social class, demeanor)
- Complainant (present at the scene, desire to prosecute, age, gender, and race)
- Location of the offense (type of neighborhood, low- or high-crime area)

- Parents (attitude, present at the scene or at home, concern, and ability to supervise)
- Officer (training and experience, view of justice system and diversion, workload)
- Police department (enforcement policies, community policing, or problem-solving emphasis) (Sanborn & Salerno, 2005, pp. 137–139).

Police discretion is necessary, and the juvenile justice system could not function without some use of discretion. Juvenile courts in urban areas have a backlog of cases, probation officers' caseloads are too high for them to provide adequate supervision, and correctional facilities are becoming overcrowded. The system must concentrate on those juvenile offenders who pose the greatest risk and need official intervention to prevent further offending.

◼ Alternatives to Police Arrest and Custody

A police officer may refer a minor offender to a youth services bureau, a community agency such as a Big Brother Big Sister program, or a similar delinquency prevention program. In the majority of cases where police have reason to believe that a juvenile has committed an offense, the youth will be taken to the police department juvenile bureau for questioning, may be fingerprinted and photographed, and then will be taken to the intake unit of the juvenile probation department where a decision will be made to detain the youth or release to the parents.

- *Questioning, warning, and release in the community.* The least severe sanction is when an officer questions a youth for a possible minor offense, and gives a warning and reprimand on the street without taking formal actions.

- *Station adjustment.* Police may take a youth into custody and to the station, record the alleged minor offense and actions taken, give the youth an official reprimand, and release the youth to the parents. The parents are generally contacted first and may be present when the youth is reprimanded. In smaller cities the youth may be placed under police supervision for a short period of time.

- *Referral to a diversion agency.* Police may release and refer a juvenile to a youth service bureau (YSB), Big Brother Big Sister program, runaway center, or a mental health agency. Diverting minor offenders from the juvenile justice system to a YSB that provides counseling and social services is considered preferable for many first-time offenders and troubled youth.

- *Issuing a citation and referring to juvenile court.* The police officer can issue a citation and refer the youth to juvenile court. The intake probation officer accepts the referral, contacts the parents if the police have not already done so, and releases the youth to the parents on the condition that they will report to the court when ordered to do so. The intake officer then determines whether a formal delinquency petition should be filed. In some states the decision is made by the prosecuting attorney assigned to the juvenile court.

- *Taking to a detention center or shelter home.* The police officer can issue a citation, refer the youth to the juvenile court, and take him or her to a detention center. The intake officer at the detention center then decides whether to hold the juvenile or release him or her to the parents. Juveniles are detained when they are considered dangerous, when there is a lack of parental supervision, or when there is a high probability that they will not report to the court when ordered to do so. If a detention center is felt to be too restrictive, and an appropriate parent or foster home is not available, the youth may be placed in a shelter care facility that might be either a private home or a group home. Most states now provide for a detention hearing within a day after the youth's referral in which a judge or referee must determine whether there is sufficient reason to continue to detain the juvenile. In cities without a separate juvenile detention center, juveniles who cannot be released to their parents are confined in a separate section of the county jail, or may be transported to a juvenile facility in another county. There has been a national effort to remove juveniles from adult jails. Removing juveniles from their homes and detaining them in juvenile centers is considered a last resort.

SUMMARY

- The police role with juvenile offenders is especially important because young persons' views and attitudes toward law enforcement are shaped by their first encounter with a police officer.
- Police face special challenges when dealing with juvenile offenders, because they must enforce noncriminal (status) offenses in addition to criminal violations; because of youths' immaturity; and because of youths' vulnerability to group influence.
- Police officers actually perform three roles in fulfilling their law enforcement responsibilities: law enforcement, order maintenance, and service functions.
- Police agencies attempt to improve relations with juveniles through cultural awareness training to enhance their skills in working and interacting with juveniles, and programs such as D.A.R.E. and School Resource Officers.
- Police discretion is a normal and necessary part of the law enforcement decision-making process that sometimes appears to be influenced by extralegal factors and that results in disproportionate processing of racial and ethnic minorities.
- Research findings on police discretion show mixed results as to whether disproportionate representation of minorities is due to racial discrimination in decision making, or to the greater involvement of minorities in offenses that are more likely to result in court processing and sentencing.
- Police officers have a number of alternatives to arrest and custody of offenders, and using these alternatives appropriately benefits the offender, the community, and the justice system.

KEY TERMS

Law enforcement role
Order maintenance
Police discretion
Police roles

Service function
Status offenses
Racial disparity

DISCUSSION QUESTIONS

1. Can you think of any experiences as a teenager when you or any of your friends had any encounters with a police officer that were negative and/or created poor relations with the police? Give an example.

2. Do you think police should spend much of their time responding to status offenses of juveniles? Explain why or why not. Do you think there is any relationship between status offenses and more serious juvenile crime?

3. Can you think of any examples when you, your friends or family, or any neighbors were affected or benefited by the police roles of order maintenance and service functions? Give an example.

4. Have you had a personal experience with a D.A.R.E. program or with a School Resource Officer? Explain the effects of that program from your perspective.

5. Have you or an acquaintance ever experienced police discretion, such as getting a warning rather than a citation or arrest; or getting a citation or arrest when you believe a warning was more appropriate?

WEB RESOURCES

The following Web sites provide information and discussion on the role of police in the juvenile justice system:

Juvenile Offenders and Victims: 2006 National Report: http://ojjdp.ncjrs.gov/ojstatbb/nr2006/downloads/NR2006.pdf

Community-oriented policing: http://www.cops.usdoj.gov/

D.A.R.E. Web site: http://www.dare.com/home/default.asp

READING

Cops In the Classroom

A Longitudinal Evaluation of Drug Abuse Resistance Education (DARE)

**Dennis P. Rosenbaum, Robert L. Flewelling,
Susan L. Bailey, Chris L. Ringwalt, Deanna L. Wilkinson**

National public opinion surveys in the late 1980s consistently identified drugs as "the most important problem facing this country today" (Bezilla and Gallup 1990). Despite recent changes in public opinion and debates about the nature and magnitude of the drug problem in the United States, a substantial "drug war" continues to be waged on a variety of fronts. In communities and cities across the nation, residents have fought back and demanded more government action against drug users and dealers (Davis, Lurigio, and Rosenbaum 1993). Hundreds of communitywide, multiagency partnerships have formed to develop new antidrug strategies, including a wide range of enforcement, education, and treatment initiatives (Cook and Roehl 1993).

Although a variety of solutions have been proposed to the drug problem, the primary

SOURCE: *Journal of Research in Crime and Delinquency, (31)*1, 3–31, February 1994. © 1994 Sage Publications, Inc.

thrust of local, state, and federal policy has been to promote aggressive enforcement programs designed to eradicate illegal drug activity. Drug laws have been created or strengthened to "get tough" on drug offenders, thousands of law enforcement agents have been hired at various levels to enforce these laws, and the criminal justice system has been primed to give priority attention to the prosecution of drug cases. As a result, drug enforcement statistics (such as arrests, asset seizures, prosecutions, convictions, and incarcerations) have risen dramatically in recent years (Timrots, Byrne, and Finn 1991).

The cost-effectiveness of these antidrug policies has been the subject of considerable debate. The available evidence suggests that enforcement programs have been oversold (Moore 1988; Weisheit 1990). Research documenting the effectiveness of police crackdowns, sweeps, and related enforcement programs at the neighborhood level is quite limited and shows mixed results (see Hayeslip 1989; Kleiman, Barnett, Bouza, and Burke 1988; Sherman 1990). Meanwhile, U.S. prisons and jails are grossly overcrowded and courts are severely backlogged with drug cases. In addition, the cost of these aggressive tactics to civil liberties and police-community relations can be substantial (see Rosenbaum 1993).

Recognizing the limits of this approach, pressure has continued to mount on the federal government to shift additional resources to drug education and treatment (Treaster 1992; White House 1992). In theory, the most cost-effective strategy to reduce future demand for drugs is primary prevention. If youths can be prevented from using drugs, the long-term savings to society should be substantial. One of the easiest ways to reach most youths is through school-based education programs.

⬚ School-Based Drug Education Programs

Cognizant of the importance of primary prevention, governments at all levels are now promoting and even requiring school-based drug education.

In 1986, the U.S. Congress passed the Drug-Free Schools and Communities Act to promote drug abuse education and prevention programs across the country. The federal contribution to drug prevention at the state and local level has grown precipitously from $189 million in fiscal year 1987 to $463 million in fiscal year 1990. In addition, state and local contributions to drug education have been significant, creating a substantial combined effort to prevent drug abuse among America's youth. In many states, schools are required by law to have drug education programs in place, and educational institutions that receive funds from the federal government must first show evidence that they have implemented a comprehensive drug prevention program.

In the face of this rapidly growing support for school-based drug education, the question remains as to whether existing programs, as currently delivered, are changing attitudes, beliefs, and behaviors with respect to the use of tobacco, alcohol, and other drugs. Given the massive onslaught of drug education programs in recent years, as well as the expansion of aggressive local enforcement programs, one would hypothesize that overall levels of drug use would decline. Indeed, recent trends are consistent with this prediction. The National Household Survey on Drug Abuse, for example, showed a 46% drop between 1985 and 1991 in the number of Americans over age 26 who reported using any illicit drug in the past month (National Institute on Drug Abuse [NIDA] 1993). Similarly, the use of drugs and alcohol among our nation's youth has declined over the past decade. The High School Senior Survey indicates that use of marijuana, alcohol, crack, and cocaine continues to decline. In 1992, 29% of all high school seniors reported they had used at least one illicit drug during the past year, compared to a peak of 54% in 1979 (Johnston, Bachman, and O'Malley 1992).[1]

The factors contributing to these national trends are difficult to isolate. Enforcement efforts have been strong in recent years, but American youth still perceive many drugs as widely available. Johnston and his colleagues who direct the High School Senior Survey argue that a reduction in demand among youth rather than a reduction in supply offers the most compelling explanation of these trends (Institute for Social Research [ISR] 1991). This position is based on the observation that the supply of drugs to American youth has remained fairly constant despite intensive law enforcement programs, while educational antidrug messages have never been more wide-spread. Also, recent data from the National Household Survey on Drug Abuse show that rates of current drug use have declined more sharply among adolescents than adults (Substance Abuse and Mental Health Services Administration [SAMHSA] 1993). In spite of these encouraging trends, explanations that favor antidrug educa-tion remain speculative in the absence of con-trolled experimentation.

If school-based drug prevention has played an important role in the decline of drug abuse, the nature and extent of this impact is important to document. Knowing the effectiveness of spe-cific educational interventions would help local, state, and federal government to move beyond the current shotgun approach to drug education and commit resources to programs that have known effects on students' attitudes, beliefs, and behaviors. However, because controlled longitu-dinal evaluations of school-based drug education are extremely rare, our knowledge of what works under what conditions is quite limited.

Seeing encouraging trends in drug use is a far cry from claiming that the drug problem has been solved in the United States. Current rates of drug use among U.S. youth are very high in compari-son to other industrialized nations (Johnston, O'Malley, and Bachman 1988). Alcohol and tobacco remain the most prevalent and costly problems for American youth. Although recent (30-day) use of alcohol among persons under 21 years of age has dropped from 72% in 1980 to 57% in 1990 (Johnston, O'Malley, and Bachman 1991), this figure still constitutes a majority of American youth. Most importantly, the conse-quences of drinking and driving are well-docu-mented in traffic fatality statistics (see Donelson 1988 for a review).

Data on cigarette smoking among youth reveal the most troubling drug trend. Although smoking rates have continued to decline in the general population over the past decade, the smoking rate among youth has failed to show a corresponding decrease (Johnston et al. 1991). From 1981 to 1990, the percentage of high school seniors who reported smoking in the past month was unchanged (29% at both points), and the rate of daily smoking dropped only 1% during this period (from 20% to 19%). Given the lethal consequences of cigarette smoking (i.e., hun-dreds of thousands of preventable deaths each year), the reduction of tobacco use among youth remains an important objective of many drug education initiatives.

The DARE program. DARE is the most widely disseminated school-based drug prevention program in the United States. It represents a cooperative venture between education and law enforcement and involves the use of trained, uni-formed police officers in the classroom to teach a highly structured drug prevention curriculum. Created in 1983 by the Los Angeles Police Department in collaboration with the Los Angeles Unified School District, DARE has spread to all 50 states and six foreign countries. The primary DARE curriculum targets youth in their last year of elementary school (usually the fifth or sixth grade) and is based on the assump-tion that children at this age are the most recep-tive to antidrug messages and are entering the drug experimentation phase where intervention could have maximum benefit.

Unlike most school-based drug education programs, DARE is highly structured and uni-formly administered across sites. Typically, DARE officers are given 80 hours of instructor training in classroom management, teaching strategies, communication skills, adolescent development, drug information, and instruction of the DARE lessons. The performance of DARE officers in the classroom is monitored closely by each classroom teacher and by visits from an experienced DARE officer to ensure the integrity and consistency of program delivery. The police agency responsible for the program provides all instructional materials, student workbooks, visual aids, and graduation certificates. Thus, law enforcement agencies pay the officer's salary and provide the materials, whereas schools provide the classroom time to present the DARE curriculum.

Police officers teach the DARE curriculum in hourly sessions over the course of 17 weeks, using a variety of techniques including lectures, workbook exercises, question and answer sessions, audiovisual materials, and role-playing sessions. The primary objective of the DARE curriculum is to teach peer resistance skills by offering students a variety of strategies to say "no" to drugs. However, DARE is clearly a comprehensive program in that it includes a number of other curriculum objectives, as summarized in Table 1. The DARE curriculum includes elements of several major drug prevention approaches, namely cognitive, affective, and social skills, with the greatest emphasis placed on the latter.

⧉ Theory and Evaluation of School-Based Drug Prevention

Several literature reviews and meta-analyses have been conducted to assess the theoretical underpinnings and behavioral impact of school-based drug prevention programs (see Botvin 1990; Hansen 1990; Bangert-Drowns 1988; Bruvold and Rundall 1987; Tobler 1986; Battjes 1985). Although each of these reviews provides a somewhat different scheme for classifying programs, prevention curricula generally fall into one of four major categories:

- *Cognitive strategies:* Designed to increase knowledge about the nature and effects of alcohol, tobacco, and other drugs.
- *Affective or intrapersonal strategies:* Designed to enhance personal growth through improved self-esteem, self-awareness, and/or values clarification without reference to drugs.

- *Social skills and influence strategies:* Designed to strengthen interpersonal skills and equip youth with the behavioral strategies needed to resist peer pressure to use drugs.
- *Comprehensive programs:* Designed to enhance cognitive, affective, and social skills through the provision of a comprehensive curriculum.

Beginning in the 1970s, school-based programs emphasized cognitive and information strategies—approaches that have since been largely discredited in the evaluation literature. The evidence suggests that although such programs tend to increase students' knowledge of drugs, they are unlikely to engender positive changes in attitudes or behaviors. In fact, researchers have found that these approaches, by themselves, can lead to undesirable changes in attitudes (Bruvold and Rundall 1988) and even increased drug use (Howard et al. 1988), which may indicate that students become more sophisticated consumers as a result of these information-focused curricula.

Even the affective strategies have not performed well in previous evaluations. Hansen, Johnson, Flay, Graham, and Sobel (1988) found that students who received an affective education program reported significantly more drug use than students in the control group, and these differences increased over time. Although psychological factors may contribute to drug abuse (Shedler and Block 1990), the affective interventions to correct these psychological states have not fared well (Tobler 1986).

What currently is considered to be the most promising approach is based on the social skills/social influence model. Programs designed to help youth recognize and respond appropriately to peer pressures have shown some positive effects for preventing drug abuse (Botvin 1990; Clayton, Cattarello, Day, and Walden 1991; Flay 1985; Tobler 1986). Based on the notion that youth use drugs for social reasons, these programs are derived from interventions targeting

Table 1	DARE Curriculum	
Session	Topic	Description
1	First Visit/Personal Safety	Introduction of DARE and law enforcement officer safety practices; discussion of personal rights
2	Drug Use and Misuse	Harmful effects from misuse of drugs
3	Consequences	Consequences of using and choosing not to use alcohol, marijuana, and other drugs
4	Resisting Pressures	Sources of pressure, types of pressure to use drugs
5	Resistance Techniques	Refusal strategies for different types of peer pressure
6	Building Self-Esteem	Identifying positive qualities in oneself; giving/receiving compliments, importance of self-image
7	Assertiveness	Personal rights/responsibilities discussion; situations calling for assertiveness skills
8	Managing Stress Without Drugs	Identification of sources of stress; when stress can be helpful or harmful; ways to manage stress; deep breathing exercise
9	Media Influences	Media influences on behavior; advertising techniques
10	Decision Making and Risk Taking	Risk-taking behaviors; reasonable and harmful risks; consequences of various choices; influences on decisions
11	Drug Use Alternatives	Reasons for using drugs; alternative activities
12	Role Modeling	Meet older student leaders/role models who do not use drugs
13	Forming Support Systems	Types of support groups; barriers to friendships; suggestions for barriers to forming friendships
14	Ways to Deal with Gang Pressures	Types of gang pressure; how gangs differ from groups; consequences of gang activity
15	DARE Summary	DARE review
16	Taking a Stand	Taking appropriate stand when pressured to use drugs
17	DARE Culmination	Award assembly: recognition of participants

cigarette smoking (Flay, D'Avernas, Best, Kersall, and Ryan 1983) and give special attention to the recognition of social norms and the development of social skills (Hansen 1990). The use of role playing to model social skills, especially resistance to peer pressure, is based on Bandura's (1977a, 1977b) social learning theory. Students are taught to recognize peer pressure, to resist it, and to gain confidence from knowing that others have been successful in using these skills.

As Botvin (1990) notes, a variety of strategies can be characterized as part of this psychosocial approach, but they generally fall into three categories: psychological inoculation, resistance skills training, and personal and social skills training. DARE is often considered a psychosocial approach because of its emphasis on resistance skills, but it also includes a cognitive component (e.g., information on drug use, misuse, and consequences; media influences, drug use alternatives) and an affective or intrapersonal component (e.g., self-esteem building, managing stress, decision making, and role modeling). Thus, the DARE curriculum can be distinguished from many drug education programs because of its comprehensive nature.

Previous evaluations have documented the positive effects of programs that emphasize social skills and behavioral strategies for coping with peer pressure. Hansen and his colleagues (1988) report significant delays in the onset of tobacco, alcohol, and marijuana use among students exposed to Project SMART, and Ellickson and Bell (1990) report reductions in the use of cigarettes and marijuana among students exposed to Project ALERT. However, in the latter case, the program had a boomerang effect on confirmed cigarette smokers and gains in alcohol use disappeared within 12 months. Despite a few examples of success, doubts remain about the strength and duration of these effects and about whether refusal skills are the key to drug prevention (cf. Moskowitz 1989).

In sum, although positive findings have been reported in some evaluations, taken as a whole, the literature leaves considerable doubt regarding the effectiveness of school-based drug prevention initiatives. Many researchers have expressed skepticism about program effectiveness, arguing that long-term reductions in drug use have yet to be demonstrated (e.g., Botvin 1986; Bruvold and Rundall 1988; Howard et al. 1988; Moskowitz 1989).

Prior DARE evaluations. There have been several evaluations of the DARE program, and the scientific rigor of these assessments varies considerably. The most widely publicized evaluation has yielded the most favorable results (DeJong 1987). The findings suggest that DARE in Los Angeles produced significant short-term reductions in

students' use of alcohol, cigarettes, and other drugs, despite having no effects on their knowledge or attitudes about drugs. The methodological shortcomings of this evaluation, however, were substantial and included the absence of a pretest and nonrandom assignment to experimental conditions.

This problem underscores the difficulty of reviewing the literature on DARE evaluations. The sizable variation in methodological rigor, if not recognized, can lead to false conclusions about the effectiveness of this drug education program. A number of evaluations have sought to estimate the impact of DARE on fifth- and sixth-grade students (e.g. Agopian and Becker 1990; Aniskiewicz and Wysong 1987; Clayton, Cattarello, Day, and Walden 1991; DeJong 1987; Evaluation and Training Institute 1990; Faine and Bohlander 1988, 1989; Manos, Kameoka, and Tanji 1986; Nyre 1985, 1986; Ringwalt, Ennett, and Holt 1991; Walker 1990). Generally speaking, the methodological weaknesses have been substantial and include the use of nonrandomized designs, the absence of pretest measurement, small sample sizes, unreliable measurement, and a lack of statistical controls in the analysis (for a discussion of these problems in drug education research, see Ellickson and Bell 1992 and Moskowitz 1989). Only two previous DARE evaluations have addressed the most common and critical threats to validity (cf. Cook and Campbell 1979), and this has been achieved primarily through the use of randomized experimental designs. The results of these studies are summarized below.

Ringwalt et al. (1991) conducted a randomized experiment in 20 schools in North Carolina and found that DARE had significant effects in the desired direction on general attitudes toward drugs, attitudes toward specific drugs, awareness of media influences regarding drug use, assertiveness, perceptions of peer attitudes about using drugs, and the perceived costs of drug use. DARE had no significant impact, however, on drug use, intentions to use drugs, perceived benefits of drug use, or self-esteem. In this study, measurement was taken immediately after students completed the 17-week DARE program, and hence, the persistence of these observed effects beyond this time period is unknown.

Clayton, Catterello, and Walden (1991) employed a randomized experiment in 31 schools to initiate a 5-year longitudinal evaluation of DARE in Lexington, Kentucky. Results from the immediate posttest showed desirable effects on general drug attitudes, attitudes toward specific drugs, and perceived popularity. No significant differences were found for drug use, resistance to peer pressure, and self-esteem. A follow-up was conducted after 1 and 2 years (Clayton, Catterello, and Walden 1991). After 1 year, students exposed to DARE reported significantly less use of marijuana than the control group, but this effect disappeared by the second year. Also, the initial attitudinal effects were apparently lost after 1 year because they were not reported. Some of these null results may be due to the fact that the control group was exposed to a standard health curriculum that included a unit on drug use.

To summarize, there have been few rigorous evaluations of DARE, and the best studies have left important questions unanswered. The consistent findings suggest that DARE has an immediate impact in the expected direction on general and specific attitudes toward drugs, but beyond this, the short-term results are inconsistent. Furthermore, program effects that extend beyond the immediate postintervention measurement period remain uncertain. In the one longitudinal study that employed random assignment to experimental conditions, the control group was contaminated to some degree by a standardized drug education program in the second year.

The present DARE evaluation. The present evaluation was designed to overcome some of the main shortcomings of previous evaluations of school-based drug education programs in general and DARE in particular. To accomplish this, the evaluation used a randomized longitudinal design for most of the sample, measures having known psychometric properties, and procedures that would ensure a high retention rate and high-quality data in the second year.

The selection of the knowledge, attitudinal, and behavioral outcome measures for this impact evaluation was derived from the general objectives of the DARE program and prior theories of drug prevention. Through the use of cognitive, affective, and social skills strategies, DARE was hypothesized to increase students' awareness of influence attempts by peers and the media, correct misperceptions about drug use norms, increase awareness of the adverse consequences of drug use, strengthen negative attitudes about drug use, build students' self-esteem, improve their decision making and assertiveness in social settings, and strengthen their ability to resist peer pressure to use drugs, alcohol, and cigarettes. By influencing these intervening variables, the assumption is that the use of alcohol, tobacco, and other drugs will be, in turn, prevented or reduced. Thus, by testing the impact of DARE on these mediating variables, this research offers some feedback about the efficacy of this highly standardized intervention for affecting key psychological and social processes considered theoretically important for the prevention of drug use. As a secondary objective, DARE was expected to produce more positive attitudes about police officers among fifth and sixth graders—a consequence that may have larger benefits for police-community relations in the future.

By evaluating the effects of DARE, this research also represents a test of the comprehensive model of drug prevention as articulated by Hansen (1990) and Botvin (1990). These authors suggest that a combination of approaches to drug education is often more effective than any individual approach. As noted earlier, the DARE curriculum is an excellent example of the comprehensive model and is based on the multifaceted theory-based SMART curriculum (see DeJong 1987). DARE would seem to be a good opportunity to test this model because of the breadth of the curriculum and the integrity of its implementation. Unlike most other drug prevention programs, instructors receive a highly standardized training program, the DARE curriculum is believed to be administered in a highly consistent manner across sites, and the performance of DARE instructors is monitored and evaluated.

However, testing a comprehensive program is problematical for evaluation research and theory assessment. When effects are observed, they suggest support for the overall model, but researchers are hard-pressed to isolate specific causal factors involved because of "multiple treatment interference" (Cook and Campbell 1979). Greater theoretical precision is often desirable. Although the various components of the DARE curriculum are based in theory, the objective of this study is not to test specific theories regarding the causes and prevention of adolescent substance use. Rather, this study evaluates the impact of a standardized and widely disseminated application of several theoretical perspectives. Because measures were employed that tap constructs specific to certain theoretical positions, the study does provide a means of assessing discrete components of the DARE program. For example, assertiveness and the ability to resist peer pressure are measurable objectives of the social skills component, enhanced self-esteem is a goal of the affective education component, and knowledge regarding the consequences of drug use is an important aim of the cognitive skills component. To the extent that change is registered on any one of these variables, it suggests that the corresponding curriculum lessons may have been responsible for this effect, and it provides the opportunity to determine whether drug use is consequently reduced in connection with this change.

▧ Methodology

Research Design

This DARE evaluation was designed as a randomized field experiment with one pretest and multiple planned posttests. Eighteen pairs of elementary schools were identified that were representative of urban, suburban, and rural areas in the northern half of the state of Illinois. Schools were matched in each pair by school type, ethnic composition, number of students with limited English proficiency, and the percent of students in that school from low income families.[2] None of the selected schools had previously received DARE. Twelve pairs of schools (six urban and six suburban) that matched exceptionally well were selected from a larger group of schools that had expressed a willingness to participate in the trial. For each of these 12 pairs, one school was randomly assigned to receive DARE in the spring of 1990 while the other served as a control.[3] In each of the remaining six pairs, all of which serve rural communities, a nonrandom assignment process was required because of substantial travel times in the very large geographic areas served by the DARE officers. Schools were selected from areas in which DARE officers were assigned, and comparison schools were then selected from nearby counties. Comparison schools were selected if they were a good match to DARE schools on ethnic composition, percent of students with limited English, and percent of students from low income families.

Recruitment of Schools and Students

Thirty-six schools were recruited for participation in the DARE evaluation in the fall of 1990. Schools in the experimental condition were offered the DARE program, whereas control schools were offered a financial incentive to participate. In each school, eligible students were those in their final year of elementary school (either fifth or sixth grade), and all classrooms at that level were included. Passive consent forms were mailed to parents requesting their child's participation. The letter informed parents of the purpose and content of the project, stressed the confidentiality of the information to be collected,[4] and invited parents to return the form in a stamped envelope if they did not wish their child to participate. Parents declined such permission in 2.7% of the cases.

In the second year, when students had left these elementary schools and entered approximately 150 middle schools, the recruitment process was repeated in order to track participating students. Cooperation was obtained through letters and telephone calls to all school superintendents and principals. Financial inducement to participate in the evaluation was offered to middle schools with a substantial number of students from the study.

Data Collection

The initial student questionnaire was administered to intact classrooms during the month of February 1991, immediately prior to DARE's implementation. The evaluation staff instructed students to write their name and address on the cover sheet of the questionnaire. Questionnaires were precoded with identification numbers and student names so that each student's pretest and posttest responses could be matched. Staff were careful to inform students that answers would be kept confidential and would never be shown to then-teachers, parents, police, or anyone else. Students were instructed to detach the cover sheet and pass it to the front of the room where project staff sealed them in an envelope, thus providing additional visual assurances to students of the confidentiality of their responses. The only remaining identifying information on the body of the instrument was the same precoded identification number as that which appeared on the cover sheet.

The research staff attended a training session to ensure that the data collection procedures remained consistent over time and across surveyors. The instrument was self-administered and took approximately 35 minutes to complete. Staff remained at the front of the room to avoid influencing student responses to sensitive questions.

Questionnaires for students who were absent were given to school counselors with the request to administer the survey within the next several days.

Extensive procedures were employed to protect the confidentiality of data received from these absentee respondents. For those missing, letters were sent to transfer schools asking administrators to verify enrollment of the students in question. Additional tracking methods included contact with a wide variety of persons and agencies, such as truant officers, school counselors, former classroom teachers, and postal inspectors. The tracking efforts generated an additional 226 surveys.

Characteristics of the Sample and Attrition Analysis

The analysis sample consisted of students surveyed both at the pretest and again during the following school year. The characteristics of this longitudinal sample are presented in Table 2. Pretest differences between the DARE and control students on background sociodemographic characteristics were small and in most cases not significant. Furthermore, there were no significant pretest differences between the DARE and control students on any of the drug use measures.

Of the 1,800 students surveyed at the pretest, 1,584 (88%) were surveyed again in the second year; the study thus experienced only 12% attrition between the two waves. Most of the attrition in the second year was due to three factors: students transferring to unknown locations outside the state, chronic absenteeism, and (to a lesser extent) refusals to participate.

To assess the impact of attrition on the results presented in this article, variables used in subsequent analyses were used to predict attrition in logistic regression models. Students who were lost to the study were coded one (1) on the dependent measure of attrition. Results of the regression reported in Table 3 show that only metropolitan status had a statistically significant effect on study attrition. More specifically, urban students were about three times more likely than rural students to be lost to the study. However, any bias in the estimates of DARE effects due to this condition are likely to be slight because of the relatively low levels of attrition even among urban students and the fact that attrition was not significantly different between the two experimental conditions.

Table 2	Characteristics of the Longitudinal Sample ($N = 1,584$)			
Characteristics	*Percentage*	*Characteristics*		*Percentage*
Sex		*Population Density*		
Male	50.3	Urban		39.1
Female	49.7	Suburban		35.8
		Rural		25.1
Race/Ethnicity				
White	49.9	*Exposure to DARE*		
African American	24.7	DARE		54.2
Hispanic	8.9	No DARE		45.8
Other[a]	16.5			
		Lifetime Alcohol Use at Wave 1		
Grade at Wave 1		Used		55.1
Fifth	33.5	Never used		44.9
Sixth	66.5			
		Lifetime Cigarette Use at Wave 1		
Family Composition		Used		20.2
Both parents	64.7	Never used		79.8
Other	35.3			

a. This category includes a significant number of African American students who were self-defined as "other."

Furthermore, any program effects that vary across metropolitan status will be reported separately for each category.

Description of Student Instrument

The impact of DARE was assessed using multiple outcome measures. Whenever possible, the reliability and validity of measurement was enhanced by using standardized scales and indices from previous research. The following constructs were measured.

Use of substances. Students were asked two sets of questions about their use of various drugs, including tobacco, alcohol, and other substances. The format for these questions was originally devised by Moskowitz, Schaeffer, Condon, Schaps, and Malvin (1981) for their Drug and Alcohol Survey. Students indicated whether they had used these substances in "their whole life" and "during the last month (30 days)." Summary

measures were constructed by combining responses to items regarding beer, wine, wine coolers, and hard liquor. These measures were used to calculate three dependent variables measuring changes in use status between waves for both alcohol and cigarette use. The three types of changes in drug use are (1) initiation, (2) increase in use, and (3) cessation (see Analysis Strategy for computations).

School performance. Measures of school performance and behavior included self-reported grades, number of time students reported being in trouble at school, and the number of times they reported skipping class. Self-reported grades ranged from 1 (less than Ds) to 8 (mostly As). Earlier analyses of these data indicated that the self-reported measure is acceptably valid (i.e., the correlation coefficient between self-reported grades and official grades abstracted from school records was 0.60). The number of times in trouble and the number of times skipped classes were skewed; therefore, the

| Table 3 | Logistic Regression Model Predicting Study Attrition |

Predictor Variables[a]	Odds Ratio Predicting Attrition
Sex	
Female	1.00
Male	1.33
Race/Ethnicity	
White	1.00
African American	1.26
Hispanic	0.81
Other	0.82
Grade at Wave 1	
Fifth	1.00
Sixth	0.79
Family Composition	
Both parents	1.00
Other	1.08
Metropolitan Status	
Urban	1.00
Suburban	0.86
Rural	0.32***
Exposure to DARE	
No DARE	1.00
DARE	0.93
Lifetime Alcohol Use at Wave 1	
Never used	1.00
Used	1.02
Lifetime Cigarette Use at Wave 1	
Never used	1.00
Used	1.19
(*N*)	(1,698)

a. For each predictor, the first subgroup is the reference group to which the other subgroups are compared.

***$p < .001$

natural log transformations of these variables were used for statistical analysis.

General attitudes toward drugs. Students indicated their level of agreement with five statements concerning drug use, which Moskowitz and associates (1981) originally developed for the Drug and Alcohol Survey. After reversing the scores of positively worded items, a five-item scale was computed by summing student responses (Alpha = .87).

Attitudes toward the use of specific drugs. These questions, also extracted from the Drug and Alcohol Survey, assess attitudes toward specific types of alcohol that youth are most likely to use. As with the index of 30-day alcohol use, responses to questions concerning their attitudes toward beer, wine coolers, and wine were summed (Alpha = .85).

Perceived benefits and costs of using drugs. Students were asked questions about the perceived benefits as well as the perceived costs of smoking cigarettes and drinking beer and wine coolers (Moskowitz et al. 1981). By adding student responses, four indices were created to assess the perceived costs and benefits of using cigarettes and alcohol (Alpha = .86, .92, .90, .92).

Perceived peer attitudes toward and use of substances. Answering questions derived from the Drug and Alcohol Survey (Moskowitz et al. 1981), students reported their perceptions concerning what most students in their class thought about using a variety of substances. Students' beliefs concerning their peers' use of cigarettes, alcohol (i.e., beer, wine, and wine coolers), and marijuana were measured with questions adapted from the University of Southern California Student Survey (Graham et al. 1984). Responses were then summed to create a three-item perceived peer attitudes index (Alpha = .82).

Perceptions of the media's influences on smoking and beer drinking. Two measures were employed to assess whether students recognized commercial media attempts to make beer drinking and cigarette smoking look attractive (Bauman 1985). Students reported what they thought the media made beer drinking and cigarette smoking "look like"—a "good" thing to do, a "bad" thing to do, both, or neither (Alphas = .67 and .73).

Self-esteem. This construct was measured by combining seven items extracted from Rosenberg's (1965) Self-Esteem scale, which was developed for use with adolescents. Questions were modified slightly to make the language more appropriate for contemporary sixth and seventh graders. (Alpha = .78).

Assertiveness. Students responded to an abbreviated four-item version of the Children's Assertive Behavior Scale (Michelson and Wood 1982), which was developed for use with children in the fourth through sixth grades. Response options vary with each question and reflect varying levels of assertiveness. A total assertiveness index was calculated following the authors' scoring instructions (Alpha = .78).

Attitudes toward police. Students rated nine items extracted from the Attitudes Toward Police scale developed by Faine and Bohlander (1989). The items were then summed (Alpha = .82).

Peer resistance skills. Students responded to four hypothetical situations in which either their best friend or an acquaintance offered them either cigarettes or alcohol (Hansen 1990). They then rated their ability to "say no" on a 4-point scale ranging from "not sure at all" to "very sure." The four items were summed (Alpha =.87).

Analysis Strategy

The assessment of DARE's impact on drug use was limited to alcohol and cigarettes because the prevalence of use for other substances was too low (1–3% lifetime use) to support definitive analysis. The outcome measures for alcohol and cigarette use were indicators of initiation, increased use, and quitting between the pretest and the follow-up. Students who had *initiated use* were those who reported no lifetime use at the pretest but did report lifetime use during the second year; they were compared to students who reported no lifetime use at both waves. Students were considered to have *increased their use* of alcohol and cigarettes if they reported no current use (i.e., use in the past 30 days) at the pretest but did report such use during the second year; they were compared to students who reported no current use at both waves. Students who *ceased or quit their use* of alcohol and cigarettes were those who reported current use at the pretest and no current use during the second year; they were compared to students who reported current use at both waves. The measures for initiation, increased use, and quitting were constructed as dummy-coded variables. Thus, initiation was coded 1, and continued abstinence was coded 0; increased use was coded 1, and continued nonuse on a current basis was coded 0; and quitting use since the pretest was coded 1, and continued use from the pretest to the second year was coded 0. Note that the samples for the analyses of increased use and quitting were mutually exclusive. The sample for the initiation analyses was a subset of the sample used to assess increased use.

The first set of analyses examined the main effect of DARE on each of the six dependent variables defined above. Because the research design did not completely control for pretest differences at the individual level, a multiple regression approach was employed to control for possible differences on the following antecedent covariates: race/ethnicity, sex, year in school, family structure, and metropolitan status (urban, suburban, or rural). These variables were selected either because of their established link to drug use in prior research or because of their importance to the sampling design.

Multiple logistic regression analysis was used to assess the effect of DARE exposure on the initiation, increased use, and cessation of alcohol and cigarettes. The effects of DARE on the drug use measures are expressed in terms of adjusted odds ratios, which reflect the likelihood of a given behavior among students exposed to DARE relative to that for the nonexposed students, controlling for the other variables in the model. Thus, for models predicting initiation or continued use, odds ratios of less than 1.0 represent a beneficial program effect whereas odds greater than 1.0 represent a detrimental effect. For measures predicting cessation, a beneficial effect is indicated by an odds ratio greater than 1.0. Odds ratios for specific subgroups of students are interpreted in an identical manner.

The same analytic approach was also used to assess DARE impacts on hypothesized intervening variables and on school performance. However, because these measures were continuous rather than dichotomous, ordinary least squares regression was employed. DARE effects are expressed as unstandardized regression coefficients, which represent the mean difference in the values of the dependent measure between the DARE group and the control group, adjusted for other variables in the model. Attitude and belief measures were recoded as necessary so that higher values indicate more desirable outcomes.

Additional post hoc analyses went beyond the question of whether DARE had a main effect on measured outcomes and focused instead on whether DARE might have different effects across sociodemographic subgroups. For each dependent variable an expanded model was assessed that included interaction terms for DARE by a dichotomous indicator of each sociodemographic control variable. Because nonsignificant interaction terms unduly complicate the interpretation of the models and may be due to chance rather than true subgroup variations in DARE effects, they were subjected to a backwards selection procedure. Thus, only interaction terms that were significant at the $p < .05$ level were retained in each model. Significant interaction terms indicate that DARE had differential impacts on outcome measures with respect to the categories of the interacting variables.

Most published evaluations of school-based programs use the individual as the unit of analysis and treat exposure/nonexposure to the program as the key independent variable of interest. Typically, however, schools rather than individuals are assigned to the experimental conditions. Failure to account for the nesting of individuals within experimental units will generally lead to an overestimation of the statistical significance of treatment effects. Methodologists now argue that the proper strategy for assessing treatment effects in this type of design is a nested (or hierarchical) analysis procedure that adjusts for the intraclass correlations within schools. (Murray and Hannon 1990; Hedeker and Gibbons forthcoming; Hedeker, Gibbons, and Davis 1991). Analyses for both logistic and linear regression models were conducted using SUDAAN (Survey Data Analysis software [Shah, Barnwell, Hunt, and Lavange 1992]), which was specifically developed to accommodate designs with nested error structures.

▧ Results

Effects of DARE on Alcohol and Cigarette Use

Odds ratios showing the effects of DARE on alcohol and cigarette use measures are presented in Table 4. Results of the logistic regression models show that DARE exposure had no statistically significant main effects on the initiation of alcohol or cigarettes, increased use of the substances, or quitting behavior. All odds ratios were relatively close to 1. However, it is noteworthy that

five of the six effects were in the direction favorable to DARE. The only outcome measure not suggestive of a favorable DARE effect was increased use of alcohol.

Effects of DARE on Attitudes and Beliefs

To determine the effects of DARE on attitudes and beliefs, linear regression models—incorporating a nested design structure—were analyzed using the second-year scale measures as dependent variables. Results of the regression analyses are presented in Table 5. The findings indicate that the only statistically significant main effect of DARE was on perceived media influences regarding the portrayal of beer drinking. That is, students exposed to DARE were significantly more likely than students in the control group to recognize the media's portrayal of beer drinking as desirable. Although no other effects were statistically significant, the differences were in the direction favorable to DARE for 10 of the 13 measures examined.

Effects of DARE on School Performance and Behavior

To determine the effects of DARE on school performance and behavior, linear regression models were tested in which school grades, number of times in trouble at school, and number of times skipped class were dependent variables. As the

Table 4 Logistic Regression Models Testing the Effects of DARE on Alcohol and Cigarette Use		
Outcome Measures	Odds Ratio[a]	(n)
Alcohol initiation	.93	673
Cigarette initiation	.89	1,181
Alcohol increase	1.27	1,092
Cigarette increase	.93	1,331
Alcohol quitting	1.13	372
Cigarette quitting	1.33	117

a. All main effects of DARE were nonsignificant at the $p < .05$ level.

Table 5	Linear Regression Models Testing the Effects of DARE on Attitudes and Beliefs	
Outcome Measures	*Coefficients*	*(n)*
General attitudes toward drugs	.01	1,521
Attitudes toward alcohol	.03	1,521
Perceived benefits of using alcohol	.01	1,524
Perceived benefits of using cigarettes	−.01	1,519
Perceived costs of using alcohol	−.01	1,525
Perceived costs of using cigarettes	.02	1,517
Perceived peer attitudes toward alcohol	.04	1,500
Perceived media influence (beer)	.05*	1,513
Perceived media influence (cigarettes)	.03	1,515
Self-esteem	.03	1,518
Assertiveness	−.01	1,502
Resistance to peer pressure	.03	1,509
Attitudes toward police	.01	1,519

*$p < .05$

results in Table 6 indicate, DARE had no statistically significant main effects on any of the school performance and behavior measures.

Subgroup Effects of DARE

Post hoc analyses revealed several significant interactions between DARE and various sociodemographic characteristics. These interactions suggested a positive impact of DARE for some subgroups and a negative impact for others. Consequently, the overall or average effect of DARE across subgroups where significant interactions occurred was typically small and nonsignificant. Results of the subgroup analyses, based on the regression models that included interaction terms for DARE by background characteristics, are presented in Table 7. Only interaction effects that were statistically significant at the .05 level are reported in the table.

One noteworthy finding is that DARE appears to have different effects on the cessation of alcohol for different gender groups. Specifically, females exposed to DARE were twice as likely as females without DARE to cease their use of alcohol. Males exposed to DARE, however,

Table 6	Linear Regression Models Testing the Effects of DARE on School Performance and Behavior	
Outcome Measures	*Coefficients[a]*	*(n)*
Grades	−.08	1,468
Number of times in trouble at school	.03	1,393
Number of times skipped school	.01	1,477

a. All main effects of DARE were nonsignificant at the $p < .05$ level.

| | Table 7   Subgroup Analyses of DARE Effects | | |

Outcome Measures	Subgroup	Parameter Estimates[a]
Alcohol quitting	Males	.69
	Females	2.10
Perceived benefits of using cigarettes	Hispanic	.16
	Non-Hispanic	−.03
Perceived costs of using alcohol	"Other" race	−.18
	White/African American/Hispanic	.02
Perceived peer attitudes toward alcohol	Intact family	.11
	Non-intact family	−.08
Perceived media influence (beer)	Urban	.13
	Rural/suburban	.01
Perceived media influence (cigarettes)	Urban	.11
	Rural/suburban	−.02
Self-esteem	Intact family	−.01
	Non-intact family	.11

NOTE: Only statistically significant ($p < .05$) interactions are reported. Variables considered for the subgroup analyses were race/ethnicity, gender, year in school, family structure, and metropolitan status.

a. Indicates adjusted odds ratios for alcohol quitting measure and multiple regression coefficients for all other outcome measures.

were less likely than males without DARE to quit using alcohol. Thus, relative to the control condition, DARE appears to encourage females to quit using alcohol but to have the opposite effect for males. DARE also appears to have been more successful with urban (than rural or suburban) students in terms of increasing their understanding of media influences regarding beer and cigarettes. The program also appears to have had a more favorable impact on Hispanics with regard to perceiving fewer benefits of smoking than other racial/ethnic groups.

⊠ Discussion

Contrary to popular belief and theory-based prediction, the DARE program had no statistically significant overall impacts on students' use of alcohol or cigarettes by the spring of the following school year (i.e., approximately 1 year after the completion of the DARE program). Furthermore, only 1 of the 13 intervening attitudinal/cognitive variables showed a significant program effect.

Several competing explanations may be offered for the failure of this evaluation to generate firm support for the DARE program or the comprehensive model of drug education. One concern commonly voiced relates to the potential inadequacy of measures used to assess study constructs. In this study we employed established measures with documented reliability and internal consistency. Although construct validity is more difficult to demonstrate (see Nunnally 1978), the items used to assess behavioral outcomes measures were similar in content and format to those used in the major national surveys on youth substance abuse (SAMHSA 1993; Johnston et al. 1991). Youth self-reports of alcohol and drug use have generally been shown to have high levels of reliability and validity (Barnea, Rahav, and Teichman 1987; Martin and Newman 1988; Nurco 1985), but the possibility of biased or inaccurate self-reporting should not be entirely discounted (Bailey, Flewelling, and Rachal 1992; Mensch and Kandel 1988) and could be, in part, responsible for biasing the results in favor of the null hypothesis. Unfortunately, biochemical measurement or validation of self-report measures is rarely a viable option for school-based prevention programs.

A second putative reason for the failure of this evaluation to yield significant positive results may be a function of insufficient power to detect small differences. Although the number of youths participating in the evaluation is substantial, the behaviors measured are relatively rare, and thus the opportunity to detect a statistically significant impact of DARE is less than if the behavioral outcomes were more prevalent. The rationale for administering DARE in the final grade of elementary school is that youth at that age have not yet begun to experiment with drugs, so that strategic preventive measures will have the greatest impact. Following this logic, the effects of DARE should become more detectable over time as the prevalence of drug use increases.

Empirical evidence, however, suggests that just the opposite is true; any immediate positive impacts of drug prevention education tend to become less discernible over time (Battjes 1985). Based on our prior analysis of immediate follow-up data, this appears to be true for the DARE program as well, as several immediate effects on attitudes and perceptions were observed (Ringwalt, Curtin, and Rosenbaum 1990). This effect may be due in part to the prevalence of other drug education programs to which youth are exposed. This evaluation faced the difficulty of detecting and measuring the effects of one of many complementary signals. Fortunately, the DARE curriculum is delivered in a unique fashion, and our survey data from school teachers

suggest that it is considerably more intensive than most other school-based programs. Nevertheless, it is possible that chances for observable programmatic impacts of DARE could be enhanced if the program was extended to include middle school grades. Other studies have supported the potential efficacy of booster sessions in years following the initial program (Ellickson and Bell 1990). DARE booster curricula have been implemented in some middle schools and high schools (none in the current study), but their impact has yet to be formally assessed.

Although the results do not demonstrate the superiority of DARE over other drug education programs already in place at the control schools, five of the six behavioral outcome measures were indicative of a positive impact of DARE, despite being nonsignificant. Similarly, the direction of the effect of DARE was positive for 10 of the 13 intervening variables examined. In an era of many both complementary and competing messages about drug use prevention, it is possible that no single prevention program will produce dramatic effects on preventing or reducing drug use.

Aside from methodological considerations, a third potential explanation of the null findings focuses on the nature of the comprehensive model and its ability to withstand empirical scrutiny. Although researchers and policymakers have encouraged this approach with the argument that it will maximize the chances of program impact (despite the difficulties that it creates for theory testing), DARE may be an example of how this approach can undermine itself. Almost by definition, a comprehensive curriculum focuses on breadth of coverage rather than depth. By giving limited attention to any one theoretical perspective, this curriculum may have lowered the chances that any one component will be strong enough to change students' attitudes or behavior. The social skills model received the most attention in the program (and showed no effects on skills-related outcomes), but even here, only a few lesson plans were devoted to this approach. The fundamental assumption of the comprehensive model is that the different approaches somehow work together, in a synergistic manner, to strengthen program impact. This assumption is certainly challenged by the present findings.

Although several significant interactions were identified between exposure to DARE and various social and demographic characteristics, it is prudent to exercise caution in interpreting such results. Given the number of statistical tests performed, the subgroup differences reported here should be considered exploratory and the programmatic implications of such effects should await confirmation by future research (cf. Friedman, Furberg, and DeMets 1985). Nevertheless, the gender difference in cigarette cessation may indicate that girls are more receptive to DARE than boys, but more research in this area is needed. A few positive gains for urban and Hispanic students, although limited, are encouraging. Evaluations of community-based prevention programs typically show the least success in reaching inner-city populations (Skogan 1990), who are at highest risk of arrest for drug offenses and other crimes (Reuter, MacCoun, and Murphy 1990; Sullivan 1990). In any event, previous evaluations have tended to report that drug education programs either work or don't work and pay little attention to the conditions under which these programs yield positive or negative results (MacKinnon, Weber, and Pentz 1989). This concern may be especially relevant to DARE because of its highly standardized curricula and the uniform manner in which the program is presented.

Conclusion and Recommendations

The results of this study suggest both a number of topics for future research and implications for the DARE program. First, the study provides relatively little empirical support for the comprehensive model of school-based drug education, of which DARE is a prime exemplar. This broad-based smorgasbord approach may water down rather than enhance alternative influence strategies. In particular, previous studies and reviews suggest that social skills approaches have exhibited the greatest potential for preventing adolescent drug use. Although the DARE curriculum emphasizes the acquisition of both general and specific skills required to resist inducements to use drugs, the efficacy of this strategy within the context of a comprehensive curriculum such as DARE remains to be demonstrated.

Second, the results of this study serve as a reminder to researchers and program advocates alike that positive outcomes are not guaranteed simply because a program is prosocial in nature and widely supported. In the case of DARE, the goal of preventing drug and alcohol use is highly laudable, the program itself is distinctive, and the investment of resources comes from the good intentions of so many individuals. Nevertheless, the present evaluation reminds us that measurable impacts of even very popular programs are sometimes difficult to attain and may vary across subgroups of the target population.

Third, the results of this evaluation, taken in conjunction with others relating both to DARE and other drug education programs, clearly suggest the need to review the various lessons that constitute the DARE curriculum. Although the curriculum does address some important causal or protective factors with regard to drug use, such as peer influence, resistance skills, and personal control, considerable time is spent on other issues that are not directly related to preventing substance use.[5] We recognize that some of these may represent important educational objectives by themselves (e.g., self-esteem building). On the other hand, we believe that it would be productive to give more attention to factors known to be powerful in predicting drug use. For example, attention should be given to changing what are often students' inaccurate perceptions concerning the extent to which drugs are both used and sanctioned by peers. This normative approach has been suggested by drug prevention researchers (Hansen et al. 1988; Moskowitz 1989). Generally speaking, if drug prevention programs (and school policies) would devote more resources to other known protective factors evident from current theory and research on delinquency and drug use (see Hawkins, Catalano, and Miller 1992), this should increase the probability of program impact. Concentrating on a few protective factors may yield greater benefits than giving insufficient attention to a wide range of factors, unless theory can provide guidance regarding interactive effects in the latter case.

At this stage, there is a need for more research on the processes involved in the delivery of school-based drug education programs. In addition to the messages that are being communicated, little is known about the impact of differences in teacher characteristics, teaching style, characteristics of the student population, or the educational environment. There is some debate, for example, about whether DARE is sufficiently interactive and involves peers enough in the curriculum compared to other social influence programs. In any event, most teachers would agree that the method of teaching is often as important as the content.

The inability to demonstrate significant impacts of school-based drug prevention programs on drug use behaviors has been the rule, rather than the exception, among carefully controlled evaluation studies (Bangert-Drowns 1988). The lack of demonstrable results for specific school-based programs contrasts with the dramatic declines over the past 13 years in the overall prevalence of drug use, especially illicit drugs, among the school-age population. Thus, we are faced with the question of whether factors other than school-based education are primarily responsible for the observed trend, or if our evaluations of school-based programs are simply not sensitive enough to detect the relative effectiveness of individual programs.

Although comparative reviews of school-based drug education programs suggest that programs based on the psychosocial model and which focus on social skills have shown some positive results, it seems unlikely that this select and relatively new subset of programs could be largely responsible for the recent declines in adolescent drug use. If Johnston et al. (1991) are correct in arguing that these declines are a result of greater awareness of the health risks of drug use, less social acceptance of drug use, and the greater credibility with which such messages are presented, then the overall lack of demonstrable impacts for specific programs relative to standard comparisons may not be so surprising. Most drug education programs present information on the health risks of drug use (Tobler 1986). These messages are amplified through many additional sources, including the media, parents, family members, and peers, and indeed seem to reflect a general societal change not limited to youth alone (SAMHSA 1993). Apparently we, as a society, are doing something right in preventing drug abuse among youth, but the specific impact of school-based drug education is not clearly discernible.

Notes

1. Although no change was detected in use of illicit drugs by adults between 1990 and 1991, the downward trend among youth has continued.

2. Aggregate family income was estimated by the percent of students at that school who were eligible for the free or reduced price lunch program of the U.S. Department of Agriculture.

3. Without the full cooperation of the Illinois State Police who run the program, this evaluation would not have been possible.

4. We have received a Confidentiality Certificate from the National Institute on Drug Abuse (NIDA), which provides broad legal protections against efforts to breach the confidentiality of our records.

5. The DARE curriculum has recently undergone a major review and revision in response to feedback from practitioners and evaluators. This new program will soon be implemented.

References

Agopian, M. W. and H. K. Becker. 1990. *Evaluation of Drug Abuse Resistance Education (DARE) in the Long Beach Unified School District: Final Report.* Long Beach: California State University, Criminal Justice Department.

Aniskiewicz, R. E. and E. E. Wysong. 1987. *Project D.A.R.E. Evaluation Report: Kokomo Schools.* Kokomo: Indiana University at Kokomo, Department of Sociology.

Bailey, S. L., R. L. Flewelling, and J. V. Rachal. 1992. "The Characterization of Inconsistencies in

Self-Reports of Alcohol and Marijuana Use in a Longitudinal Study of Adolescents." *Journal of Studies on Alcohol* 53:636–47.

Bandura, A. 1977a. *Social Learning Theory.* Englewood Cliffs, NJ: Prentice Hall.

———. 1977b. "Self-Efficacy: Toward a Unifying Theory of Behavioral Change." *Psychological Review* 84:191–215.

Bangert-Drowns, R. L. 1988. "The Effects of School-Based Substance Abuse Education—A Meta-analysis." *Journal of Drug Education* 18:243–65.

Barnea, Z., G. Rahav, and M. Teichman. 1987. "The Reliability and Consistency of Self-Reports on Substance Use in a Longitudinal Study." *British Journal of Addiction* 82:891–98.

Battjes, R. J. 1985. "Prevention of Adolescent Drug Abuse." *International Journal of the Addictions* 20:1113–24.

Bauman, K. 1985. "A Study of Cigarette Smoking Behavior Among Youth: Adolescent Questionnaire." Chapel Hill: Department of Maternal and Child Health, School of Public Health, University of North Carolina.

Bezilla, R. and G. Gallup. 1990. "How Drugs Became the Public's Most Important Problem Facing the Country." Paper presented at the American Association for the Public Opinion Research, Lancaster, PA.

Botvin, G. J. 1986. "Substance Abuse Prevention Research: Recent Developments and Future Directions." *Journal of School Health* 56:369–74.

———. 1990. "Substance Abuse Prevention: Theory, Practice, and Effectiveness." In *Drugs and Crime,* edited by M. Tonry and J. Q. Wilson. Chicago: University of Chicago Press.

Bruvold, W. H. and T. G. Rundall. 1988. "A Meta-analysis and Theoretical Review of School-Based Tobacco and Alcohol Intervention Programs." *Psychology and Health* 2:53–78.

Clayton, R. R., A. Cattarello, L. E. Day, and K. P. Walden. 1991. "Persuasive Communication and Drug Abuse Prevention: An Evaluation of the D.A.R.E. Program." Pp. 295–313 in *Persuasive Communication and Drug Abuse Prevention,* edited by L. Donohew, H. Sypher, and W. Bukoski.

Clayton, R. R., A. Cattarello, and K. P. Walden. 1991. "Sensation Seeking as a Potential Mediating Variable for School-Based Prevention Interventions: A Two-Year Follow-Up of DARE." *Journal of Health Communications* 3:229–39.

Cook, R. F. and J. A. Roehl. 1993. "National Evaluation of the Community Partnership Program: Preliminary Findings." In *Drugs and the Community,* edited by R. Davis, A. J. Lurigio, and D. P. Rosenbaum. Springfield, IL: Charles C Thomas.

Cook, T. D. and D. T. Campbell. 1979. *Quasi-Experimentation: Design and Analysis Issues for Field Settings.* Chicago: Rand McNally.

Davis, R., A. J. Lurigio, and D. P. Rosenbaum, eds. 1993. *Drugs and the Community,* Springfield, IL: Charles C Thomas.

DeJong, W. 1987. "A Short-Term Evaluation of D.A.R.E.: Preliminary Indications of Effectiveness." *Journal of Drug Education* 17:279–94.

Donelson, A. C. 1988. "The Alcohol-Crash Problem." In *Social Control of the Drinking Driver,* edited by M. D. Laurence, J. R. Snortum, and F. E. Zimring. Chicago: University of Chicago Press.

Ellickson, P. L. and R. M. Bell. 1990. "Drug Prevention in Junior High: A Multi-Site Longitudinal Test." *Science* 247:1299–1305.

———. 1992. "Challenges to Social Experiments: A Drug Prevention Example." *Journal of Research in Crime and Delinquency* 29:72–101.

Evaluation and Training Institute. 1990. *D.A.R.E. Evaluation Report for 1985–1989.* Los Angeles, CA: Author.

Faine, J. R. and E. Bohlander. 1988. *Drug Abuse Resistance Education: An Assessment of the 1987–1988 Kentucky State Police D.A.R.E. Program.* Bowling Green: The Social Research Laboratory, Western Kentucky University.

———. 1989. *D.A.R.E. in Kentucky Schools 1988–1989: An Evaluation of the Drug Abuse Resistance Education Program.* Bowling Green: The Social Research Laboratory, Western Kentucky University.

Flay, B. R. 1985. "Psychosocial Approaches to Smoking Prevention: A Review of Findings." *Health Psychology* 4:449–88.

Flay, B. R., J. R. D'Avernas, J. A. Best, M. W. Kersall, and K. B. Ryan. 1983. "Cigarette Smoking: Why Young People Do It and Ways of Preventing It." In *Pediatric and Adolescent Behavioral Medicine,* edited by P. McGrath and P. Firestone. New York: Springer-Verlag.

Friedman, L. M., C. D. Furberg, and D. L. DeMets. 1985. *Fundamentals of Clinical Trials,* 2nd ed. Littleton, MA: PSG.

Graham, J. W., B. R. Flay, C. A. Johnson, W. B. Hansen, L. Grossman, and J. L. Sobel. 1984. "Reliability of

Self-Report Measures of Drug Use in Prevention Research: Evaluation of the Project Smart Questionnaire via the Pretest-Posttest Reliability Matrix." *Journal of Drug Education* 14:175–93.

Hansen, W. B. 1990. *School-Based Substance Abuse Prevention: A Review of the State of the Art in Curriculum, 1980–1990.* Report submitted to the National Institute of Drug Abuse. Winston-Salem, NC: Bowman-Gray School of Medicine, Department of Public Health Sciences.

Hansen, W. B., C. A. Johnson, B. R. Flay, J. W. Graham, and J. L. Sobel. 1988. "Affective and Social Influences Approaches to the Prevention of Multiple Substance Abuse Among Seventh Grade Students; Results from Project SMART." *Preventive Medicine* 17:135–54.

Hayeslip, D. W. 1989. "Local-Level Drug Enforcement: New Strategies." *NIJ Reports* No. 213 (March/April).

Hawkins, J. D., R. F. Catalano, and J. Y. Miller. 1992. "Risk and Protective Factors for Early Alcohol and Other Drug Problems in Adolescence and Early Adulthood: Implications for Substance Abuse Prevention." *Psychological Bulletin* 112:64–105.

Hedeker, D., and R. D. Gibbons. Forthcoming. "A Random-Effects Ordinal Regression Model for Multilevel Analysis." *Biometrics.*

Hedeker, D., R. D. Gibbons, and J. M. Davis. 1991. "Random Regression Models for Multicenter Clinical Trials Data." *Psychopharmacology Bulletin* 27:73–77.

Hirschi, T. 1969. *Causes of Delinquency.* Berkeley: University of California Press.

Howard, J., J. Taylor, M. Ganikos, H. D. Holder, D. F. Godwin, and E. D. Taylor. 1988. "An Overview of Prevention Research: Issues, Answers, and New Agendas." *Public Health Reports* 103:674–83.

Institute for Social Research. 1991. "Drug Awareness Rises." *ISR Newsletter* 17:3–4.

Johnston, L. D., J. G. Bachman, and P. M. O'Malley. 1992. Press Release. Ann Arbor: University of Michigan.

Johnston, L. D., P. M. O'Malley, and J. G. Bachman. 1988. *Illicit Drug Use, Smoking, and Drinking by America's High School Students, College Students, and Young Adults* (DHHS Publication No. ADM 89–1602). Rockville, MD: National Institute of Drug Abuse.

——. 1991. *Drug Use Among American High School Seniors, College Students, and Young Adults, 1975–1990,* Vol. 1, High School Seniors (DHHS Publication No. ADM 91–1813). Rockville, MD: National Institute of Drug Abuse.

Kleiman, M., A. Barnett, A. Bouza, and K. Burke. 1988. *Street-Level Drug Enforcement: Examining the Issues.* Washington, DC: National Institute of Justice.

MacKinnon, D. P., M. D. Weber, and M. Pentz. 1989. "How Do School-Based Drug Prevention Programs Work and For Whom?" *Drugs and Society* 3:125–43.

Manos, M. J., C. F. Kameoka, and J. H. Tanji. 1986. *Evaluation of Honolulu Police Department's Drug Abuse Resistance Education Project.* Manoa, Hawaii: The Youth Development and Research Center, School of Social Work, University of Hawaii, Manoa.

Martin, G. L. and I. M. Newman. 1988. "Assessing the Validity of Self-Reported Adolescent Cigarette Smoking." *Journal of Drug Education* 18:275–84.

Mensch, B. S. and D. B. Kandel. 1988. "Underreporting of Substance Use in a National Longitudinal Youth Cohort." *Public Opinion Quarterly* 52:100–24.

Michelson, L. and R. Wood. 1982. "Development and Psychometric Properties of the Children's Assertive Behavior Scale." *Journal of Behavioral Assessment* 4:3–13.

Moore, M. 1988. "Drug Trafficking." In *Crime File Study Guide.* Washington, DC: National Institute of Justice.

Moskowitz, J. M. 1989. "The Primary Prevention of Alcohol Problems: A Critical Review of the Research Literature." *Journal of Studies on Alcohol* 50:54–88.

Moskowitz, J. M., G. A. Schaeffer, J. W Condon, E. Schaps, and J. Malvin. 1981. *Psychometric Properties of the "Drug and Alcohol Survey."* Washington, DC: NIDA.

Murray, D. M. and P. J. Hannon. 1990. "Planning for the Appropriate Analysis in School-Based Drug Prevention Studies." *Journal of Consulting and Clinical Psychology* 58:458–68.

National Institute on Drug Abuse. 1993. *National Household Survey on Drug Abuse: Highlights* (DHHS Publication No. SMA 93–1979). Rockville, MD: U.S. Department of Health and Human Services.

Nunnally, J. C. 1978. *Psychometric Theory.* New York: McGraw-Hill.

Nurco, D. N. 1985. "A Discussion of Validity." In *Self-Reported Methods of Estimating Drug Use: Meeting Current Challenges to Validity,* edited by B. A. Rouse, N. J. Kozel, and L. G. Richards. NIDA Research Monograph No. 57 (DHHS Publication

No. ADM 85–1402). Washington, DC: U.S. Government Printing Office.

Nyre, G. F. 1985. *Final Evaluation Report, 1984–1985: Project DARE (Drug Abuse Resistance Education)*. Los Angeles: Evaluation Training Institute.

Nyre, G. F. 1986. *Final Evaluation Report, 1985–1986: Project DARE (Drug Abuse Resistance Education)*. Los Angeles: Evaluation Training Institute.

Reuter, P., R. MacCoun, and P. Murphy. 1990. *Money from Crime: A Study of the Economics of Drug Dealing in Washington D. C.* Santa Monica, CA: RAND.

Ringwalt, C. L., T. R. Curtin, and D. P. Rosenbaum. 1990. A *First-Year Evaluation of D.A.R.E. in Illinois.* Report to the Illinois State Police.

Ringwalt, C. L., S. T. Ennett, and K. D. Holt. 1991. "An Outcome Evaluation of Project D.A.R.E." *Health Education Research: Theory and Practice* 6:327–37.

Rosenbaum, D. 1993. "Civil Liberties and Aggressive Enforcement: Balancing the Rights of Individuals and Society in the Drug War." In *Drugs and the Community,* edited by R. Davis, A. Lurigio, and D. Rosenbaum. Springfield, IL: Charles C Thomas.

Rosenberg, M. 1965. *Society and Adolescent Self-image.* Princeton, NJ: Princeton University Press.

Shah, B. V., B. G. Bamwell, P. N. Hunt, and L. M. Lavange. 1992. *SUDAAN Users Manual: Release 6.2.* Research Triangle Park, NC: Research Triangle Institute.

Shedler, J., and J. Block. 1990. "Adolescent Drug Use and Psychological Health: A Longitudinal Inquiry." *American Psychologist* 45:612–30.

Sherman, L. 1990. "Police Crackdown: Initial and Residual Deterrence." In *Crime and Justice,* Vol. 12, edited by M. Tonry and N. Morris. Chicago: University of Chicago Press.

Skogan, W. 1990. *Disorder and Decline: Crime and the Spiral of Decay in American Cities.* New York: Free Press.

Substance Abuse and Mental Health Services Administration. 1993. *National Household Survey on Drug Abuse: Main Findings 1991* (DHHS Publication No. SMA93–1980). Rockville, MD: Author.

Timrots, A., C. Byrne, and C. Finn. 1991. *Fact Sheet: Drug Data Summary.* Washington, DC: U.S. Department of Justice.

Tobler, N. 1986. "Meta-analysis of 143 Adolescent Drug Prevention Programs: Quantitative Outcome Results of Program Participants Compared to a Control or Comparison Group." *Journal of Drug Issues* 16:537–67.

Treaster, J. B. 1992. "Some Think the 'War on Drugs' Is Being Waged on Wrong Front." *New York Times,* July 28, Sec. 1, p. 1.

Walker, S. G. 1990. *The Victoria Police Department Drug Abuse Resistance Education Programme (D.A.R.E)* (Programme Evaluation Report No. 2). Victoria, British Columbia.

Weisheit, R., ed. 1990. *Drugs, Crime, and the Criminal Justice System.* Cincinnati, OH: Anderson.

White House. 1992. *National Drug Control Strategy: A Nation Responds to Drug Use.* Washington, DC: Office of National Drug Control Policy.

DISCUSSION QUESTIONS

1. What actions have been taken by the U.S. Congress that may explain the increase in school-based drug education programs?

2. What is the D.A.R.E. program, and what is the primary objective?

3. Based on the research design of this study, would you say that the results may be quite reliable, valid, and generalizable beyond the original study sample? Explain why or why not.

4. According to this study, is D.A.R.E. effective in students' use of alcohol, cigarettes, or other substances? Does D.A.R.E. have any positive effects on student behavior? If so, explain.

5. What is your personal reaction to the authors' findings and conclusions? Can you compare any personal experiences with D.A.R.E. or similar drug education?

READING

The author of this article addresses the issue of police control of disorder and crime in inner-city neighborhoods. Current police tactics are often ineffective, they fail to protect inner-city youths, and police fail to take advantage of helpful interagency relationships with juvenile corrections agencies. The author proposes a model called reintegrative surveillance, which is an integration of community-based corrections and community policing. Neither community-based corrections nor community policing is designed to handle serious, repeat offenders who are returning to high-crime neighborhoods. Guarino-Ghezzi believes that police need to reexamine their roles to ensure that (a) policies of maintaining order and consequences of disorder are not ambiguous or misleading to youths, and (b) order maintenance and law enforcement practices do not interfere with police ability to protect youths as victims of crime. Both tendencies are clearly widespread problems, and neither will be addressed as long as the "worst" neighborhoods and youths are considered beyond salvation. Correctional programs need to reevaluate police as a pivotal community resource. Reintegrative surveillance must include a gradational, consistent criminal justice response, protection, vigilance, interagency goal setting, and agency coordination.

Reintegrative Police Surveillance of Juvenile Offenders

Forging an Urban Model

Susan Guarino-Ghezzi

This policy essay examines how police should alter their procedures for dealing with juvenile offenders in inner-city neighborhoods. The recommendations are based on extensive literature about police work as well as a recent study of communication patterns between Boston police officers and juvenile offenders (Guarino-Ghezzi 1993). The Boston study specifically explored the intended and unintended messages that police communicate to youths through their words, actions, and inactions.[1] The article develops a model for policing juveniles that follows both from community policing and correctional philosophies.

The topics reviewed in this article are organized into the following segments. The first section examines the implications of police policies of controlling disorder among inner-city youths. Section 2 considers the lack of protection that police provide to inner-city youths. The third component focuses on the service gap for youths in transition from correctional programs to the community. The final segment considers how the police role needs to be reexamined to reduce the communication of messages that are inconsistent and self-defeating.

Order and Disorder Among Inner-City Youths

The control of disorder is a goal of policing that is believed by certain key experts (Skogan 1990; Wilson and Kelling 1982), but not all (Taylor and

Gottfredson 1986), to be directly linked to the control of crime. Loitering, public drunkenness, trespassing, vagrancy, prostitution, malicious destruction of property, graffiti, and even littering are believed to create neighborhood vulnerabilities that increase disorder and eventually lead to more serious crime. However, for several reasons, procedures used by police to respond to disorder are often ineffective. One reason is the ambiguity of disorderly conduct rules. That ambiguity unintentionally reinforces the very behavior those rules proscribe (Skolnick 1966).

Skogan (1990) summarized the particular ambiguities linked to the formal control of disorderly conduct: statutes are vaguely worded, and they may proscribe conduct that is constitutionally protected. In addition, the context in which behavior occurs is critical in evaluating its "disorderly" characteristics, including the location and circumstances of the activity, the person's intent, and how others react to it. Some evidence shows that police, responding to the lack of clarity in disorderly conduct laws, rely on factors unrelated to the legal elements of the offense, including cues from fellow officers, perceptions of how others view disorderly behaviors, and past experience (Brown 1993). Legal and normative subtleties can create myths of conduct rules among youths who congregate in public places, corresponding to the police rituals that have become familiar to them. For example, youths in the Boston study (Guarino-Ghezzi 1993) believed that an obviously visible no trespassing sign was a necessary precondition to being arrested for trespassing on private property and were surprised to learn otherwise.

A second problem of controlling disorder is that aggressive police tactics, such as saturation patrol and suspicion stops, may actually increase disorder. Skogan (1990) warned that without a problem-solving model for low-resource inner-city neighborhoods, police inevitably err on the side of mechanistic coercion rather than negotiation with community residents, fueling long-term resentment and frustration. Skolnick (1966) observed that the use of law enforcement to

achieve order subordinates the ideal of conformity to the ideal of legality, highlighting the gap between normative and legal boundaries. Interviews with Boston youths suggested that "stop and frisk" policies used by police in high-crime neighborhoods to confiscate weapons did not produce organized rebellion, but did increase defiance and frustration, weakening police-youth relations (Guarino-Ghezzi 1993).

Perhaps because of the difficulties of enforcing disorderly conduct laws through arrest, the use of formal authority by police in disorderly conduct cases has declined in large cities (see Figure 1).[2] However, the informal handling of disorder—police procedures that do not lead to arrest—makes it difficult to monitor harassment and encourages police to operate outside the law to punish people they dislike or to settle past accounts (Skogan 1990; Wolff 1993). In Boston, despite internal shielding of police for misconduct charges, the number of citizen complaints nearly tripled between 1981 and 1990, and the most common complaints were of physical abuse of citizens filed by Black residents of inner-city neighborhoods (Boston Police Department Management Review Committee 1992).

The effect of order maintenance on juveniles is an area of particular concern because of the frequency of order-maintenance contacts with inner-city juveniles, as well as issues raised by their age. Lundman, Sykes, and Clark's (1978) replication of Black and Reiss's (1970) study of police encounters supported the findings that police contacts with juveniles usually resulted from matters of minor legal significance initiated by citizens, they generally were handled informally, and sanctioning decisions strongly reflected the preferences of citizen complainants. Similarly, Muir (1977) found that police felt uncomfortable enforcing "nuisance" laws unless they were goaded by a citizen, and even then they felt resentment toward the citizen complainant. The probability that order-maintenance contacts are citizen initiated and are dealt with informally has been strengthened by organizational and legal trends, including radio dispatch, reduction of foot patrol, cars responding based on proximity, personnel rotation, large new districts, removal of vague disorder statutes, and the termination of "sweep" arrest policies, which were declared unconstitutional by the mid-1970s (Skogan 1990).

Reactive-only responses, which are usually prompted by citizen-initiated complaints, create haphazard patterns of control from the point of view of street youths. In the Boston study (Guarino-Ghezzi 1993), youths were surprised to learn that police interruption of their public "hanging-out" time was based on citizen-initiated complaints. Youths had interpreted the erratic nature of police reaction—chasing them off the steps of a building one day, ignoring them the next—as harassment, designed to inflate the egos of particular police officers by waging a war of unpredictability against them.

In the youths' view, police behavior was out of their control because it was independent of their actions. The youths' inability to link behavior to official consequences resulted from the self-imposed limitation of police, who generally interacted with youths only in narrow, selective contexts. Unfortunately, citizen-initiated order maintenance, which is particularly ineffective in connecting behavior to consequences, has been the most frequent context in which police interact with juvenile offenders on the streets. Matza's (1964) early work on delinquency and "drift" is particularly relevant in understanding that the weakness of law in controlling street crime and disorder is reinforced to youths through their everyday observations in high-disorder and/or high-crime neighborhoods.

Oddly, little concern has been expressed about the effect on juveniles of inconsistent

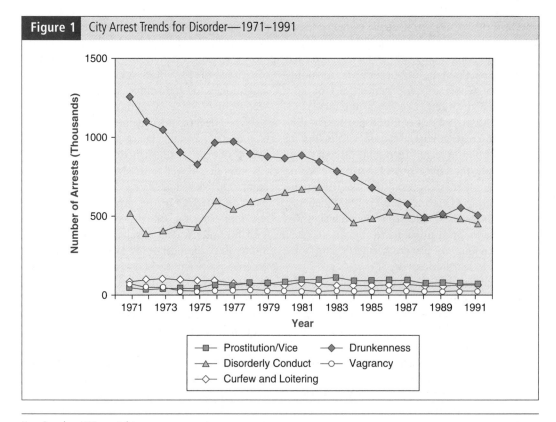

Figure 1   City Arrest Trends for Disorder—1971–1991

Number of Arrests (Thousands) — Year

Legend:
- Prostitution/Vice
- Disorderly Conduct
- Curfew and Loitering
- Drunkenness
- Vagrancy

NOTE: Based on UCR arrest data.

official reactions to public behavior, although studies have demonstrated that certainty of official response is more influential than severity in dealing with adolescents (Paternoster 1989; Schneider and Ervin 1990). Cognitive development factors also tend to be overlooked or crudely interpreted by police, particularly when compared to their importance in juvenile courts and corrections. The lack of police attention to developmental differences between juveniles and adults may have resulted, in part, from recent trends, including Supreme Court rulings in the 1960s and 1970s that granted adult protections to juveniles,[3] as well as the increased seriousness of offenses that juveniles commit (Kelling 1987). Moreover, police organizations do not need to subscribe to a separate model for juveniles as a legitimizing philosophy, as do juvenile courts and youth service agencies.

Current police practices with juveniles stand in stark contrast to August Vollmer's 1930s vision of police work, which included an expansive philosophy based on the goal of providing moral education (Kelling 1987). Instead, a variety of narrowly specialized units have proliferated in police departments, some of which relate to juveniles but with far less penetrating goals than Vollmer conceived. For instance, Needle and Stapleton (1983) observed that a prominent feature of gang control programming in the United States was its similarity to general police programming. Gang units consisted of recreation programs, preventive patrol, and other traditional suppression activities, school-based crime prevention programs, and street work oriented to suppression and prevention of gang activity. Standard patrol, investigation, and dispositional procedures were used to apprehend and process gang members in most cities. In some cities, special "gang-breaking" strategies were implemented, which targeted gang leaders for arrest, prosecution, and incarceration, based on the assumption that removing leaders weakens gangs for at least some period of time. It appeared that cities that employed gang-breaking strategies used a youth services model with younger adolescents, and a more aggressive gang-breaking approach with older teenagers. This suggests that services were used as the "carrot" for compliance with one population and gang breaking as the "stick" of control with the other However, dividing strategies in that way has received neither empirical support (Spergel 1990) nor the endorsement of the National Youth Gang Suppression and Intervention Program, which recommends a combination of surveillance and services (Spergel et al. 1993).

As juvenile correctional practitioners are well aware, juvenile offenders with service needs should not be expected to embrace services without a measure of control, nor should services be omitted from control strategies. For example, in well-run correctional programs, services, controls, and surveillance augment one another (Gendreau and Ross 1991; Guarino-Ghezzi and Byrne 1989; U.S. Department of Justice 1993). Moreover, the impersonality of police encounters, caused in part by centralized, reactive management, has placed practical limits on the perceived legitimacy of police authority (see Hummel 1977; Lipsky 1980).

In part as a result of the failures of overcentralized, reactive police management, many jurisdictions have been rapidly implementing community policing or problem-oriented policing models. Among the theoretical advantages of community policing is that police goals incorporate the values and needs of community residents. As a means to control inner-city youths, however, this advantage is equivocal. Heterogeneous, fragmented areas, as Skogan (1990) points out, defy consensus and result in conflicting definitions of conduct. Dominant definitions emerge, based on the social, political, and demographic advantages of certain groups within communities, that result in the alienation of other groups.

If, instead of trying to find common interests in this diversity, the police deal mainly with elements of their own choosing, they will appear to be taking sides. The police will get along best with those who share their outlook, and the "local values" they represent will be those of some in the community, but not all (Skogan 1990, p. 167).

The experience of police-citizen contacts demonstrates how those contacts are susceptible to demographic influences. Although the general citizenry has positive feelings toward police, members of racial minority groups tend to have more negative opinions (Jamieson and Flanagan 1987; McGarrell and Flanagan 1985). That is not surprising, given the evidence of differential treatment depending on the race of the officer, complainant, and victim that disfavors Black suspects, particularly when the complainant and officer are both White (Black 1980), and the routine questioning and detention to which teenagers, African Americans, and lower-income persons are subjected (Boston Police Department Management Review Committee 1992; Wilson 1975). A number of studies have documented inner-city Blacks' hostility toward the police and the police's negative attitude toward Black inner-city dwellers (e.g., Reuss-Ianni 1984).

Age seems to aggravate already strained relationships between police and inner-city residents. Bynum, Cordner, and Greene (1982) studied the hierarchy of victim status according to age of the victim, and they found that the probability of police follow-up investigation of a reported crime is lower for victims under age 21. An additional problem for improving policies for inner-city youths is that police seem to hold a one-dimensional, negative perception of youth gangs (Hagedorn 1988), which impedes their communication with youths, despite numerous studies identifying the varied social, psychological, and economic functions of gangs (Cohen 1955; Jankowski 1991; Miller 1976; Moore 1978; Thrasher [1927] 1963). One critic of the police has charged that the criminal image of Chicano gangs was exaggerated mainly to justify applications for federal grants to support specialized gang units in police departments (Zatz 1987).

Ironically, the reputations of inner-city youths and inner-city police are not dissimilar. Miller's (1958) description of lower-class focal concerns, which he applied to youth gangs (trouble, toughness, smartness, excitement, fate, and autonomy) is at least partially applicable to police, suggesting a mutual pattern of escalating hostilities. Trouble equals fighting; evidence of police causing trouble comes from police informants, citizen complaints, and encoded rap messages. Toughness equals fearlessness, which is the classic heroic facade of police. Smartness is the ability to con people to get them to do what you want; the Charles Stuart investigation in Boston produced allegations about strong-arm and coercive techniques used to pressure residents into cooperating in the search for the phantom Black killer (Murphy and Ellement 1992). Excitement is defined as fun and thrills; Price (1992) suggests that making arrests gives police an emotional "high"; the Rodney King incident can be described as an example of "police wilding." Fate means having no control over one's life or destiny; police are often described as cynical and fatalistic, believing that nothing will change the status quo (Wilson 1968). Autonomy means freedom from responsibility; the neglect to properly handle citizen complaints and police resistance to change reveal their autonomy from external forces. Stereotypical images of lower-class youths may have helped justify police in targeting them as a threat (Cashmore and McLaughlin 1991). Similarly, stereotypes of police have rapidly spread through the influential medium of rap music.

In Boston, numerous wedges have been driven between the Boston Police Department and inner-city youths. Philosophically, the Boston Police Department has used a reactive model for which it was lambasted recently by a mayoral committee known as the "St. Clair Commission" (Boston Police Department Management Review Committee 1992). Among the problems cited by the commission was the immobilizing fear of residents of the most crime-ridden communities to report crimes to the police. Also cited was a pattern in which a small number of officers with a long record of alleged misconduct, including physical abuse of citizens, remained on the force largely unidentified and unsupervised. The commission called for an overhaul of the Internal

Affairs complaint review process, including the creation of a community appeals board.

Adolescents' fears of police retaliation are of central importance. Inner-city youths in the Boston study reported being beaten by police, citing housing police in particular for their aggressive behavior (Guarino-Ghezzi 1993). A local rap song, "One in the Chamba," by the Almighty RSO, describes an incident in which James ("Sonny") Hall, a Boston police officer outside of his patrol area but within his own neighborhood, shot a male youth who was hiding under a car, and then began to leave the scene. Two years later Hall was convicted of manslaughter, but by then he had been dismissed from the force for an unrelated incident. The Boston Police Patrolman's Association is suing the Almighty RSO for recording a song about cop killing because the refrain advises listeners to keep one bullet in the chamber for corrupt cops like James Hall (Grant 1992).

It has been widely observed (Cohen 1955; Cohen and Short 1958) that many young offenders have difficulty showing deference to authority figures. It appears also that police are likely to react formally, with an arrest, if youths demonstrate either too little or too much deference to police, as both responses are viewed by police as abnormal and hence arouse their suspicions (Lundman, Sykes, and Clark 1978). Yet, for reasons in part relating to their methods of distancing themselves from juveniles, police lack consistency as a means for controlling the perceived legitimacy of their authority, unlike their counterparts in residential correctional facilities. Part of youths' defiance may well be rooted not merely in the impersonal control of police, but in its inconsistency. In addition, part of it stems from the lack of protection that police provide to youths when matters indeed become serious.

▧ Lack of Protection of Inner-City Youths

The current reactive model of police protection, which is generally considered to be a failed model

by experts in policing, is particularly unresponsive to the needs of young people of color. There is a growing sentiment that high-crime communities are beyond the point where they can benefit from police investment (Wilson and Kelling 1982). In Bynum, Cordner, and Greene's (1982) study of a medium-sized Midwestern city, 82% of reported serious crimes that were brought to detectives' attention actually received little or no investigative effort. Indeed, the rate of homicide cases resulting in arrest in large cities has fallen considerably over the past two decades. Clearance rates for murders and nonnegligent manslaughters in the nation's largest cities, in which approximately half of all such crimes occur, are shown in Figure 2. The clearance rate for murders and nonnegligent manslaughters in cities with populations of 250,000 and over declined by nearly one fourth between 1971 and 1991, from 82% to 63% (U.S. Department of Justice 1972–1992a). The clearance rates for such crimes in smaller cities and rural areas declined by only a few percentage points, indicating that large city murders have become increasingly difficult to solve due to factors present in major urban areas.[4] The mayor of Washington, D.C., believes that violent crime levels have surpassed the authority of police and that responsibility for controlling violent crime may be escalated to the National Guard (Berke 1993).

A dangerous adaptive style of retaliation against acquaintance aggressors, rather than cooperation with police, has emerged among inner-city youths (Garbarino, Dubrow, Kostelny, and Pardo 1992). Prison researchers have studied a similar relationship between victimization and offending within institutional walls, where inmates are in fear of one another due to reactive intervention (or no intervention) by correctional officers. Lockwood (1991) coined the term *target aggression* to explain how inmates who sense they are probable future victims of sexual assault learn to initiate physical aggression against others as a form of defense. Like prison inmates, inner-city children and adolescents learn to adapt to patterns of unprotected victimization by defining themselves not as victims, but as aggressors (Bell 1991;

Bandura 1973). This may be, in part, a result of youths' perceptions that police are indifferent to the chronic danger of their environments.

A related possibility contributing to violence in communities is the growing number of ex-prison inmates in crime-prone neighborhoods, brought about by the explosion of adult offenders sentenced to prison (see Spergel 1990, pp. 246–47). In the mid-1980s, 33 state prison systems reported the presence of gangs, but in only 21 states did prison gangs originate in the cities within the same states (Camp and Camp 1985), which implies that gangs spread through prisons faster than they do through cities. Prison subcultures have grown increasingly violent in the last two decades (Braswell, Dillingham, and Montgomery 1985; Irwin 1980), and ever larger

segments of inner-city communities are spending ever more time than before incarcerated in violent settings. The learned aggressiveness in such settings may well be following these offenders when they return to their communities, feeding already violence-prone subcultures. Thus the prison system may not only import the values and culture of incoming inmates, as many sociologists of the prison have observed, but may also export a more severely retaliatory and aggressive adaptation to violence back into the community. These possibilities give urgent new meaning to Palmer's (1984) call for "socially-centered treatment" in correctional facilities.

Virtually no comparative research exists on police handling of crime victims when they are also known or suspected offenders. However, a

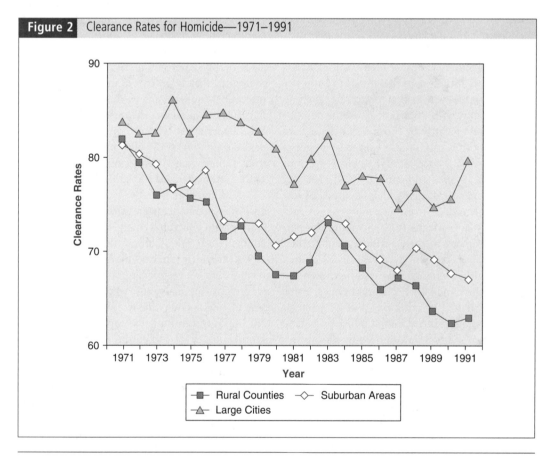

Figure 2 Clearance Rates for Homicide—1971–1991

Note: Based on UCR arrest data.

large literature suggests that police portray themselves as the "thin blue line" that separates the "good people" (nonoffenders, who are crime victims or potential victims) from the "public enemies" (offenders, delinquents, and suspected predelinquents), much as Whyte (1943) observed in his now classic study of "Eastern City" versus "Cornerville." However, communities more accurately contain a third category of residents who are "dual status" (i.e., current victims but prior offenders), and who may well comprise a substantial segment of high-crime communities. For example, an important study demonstrates a strong overlap of adolescent offenders and victims, such that previous victimization is a predictor of subsequent offending and previous offending is a predictor of subsequently being victimized (Lauritsen, Sampson, and Laub 1991).

The symbolic distinction between public enemies and victims superficially serves police (and other criminal justice agencies) in critical ways. The blue-line metaphor seems, at first, to validate police in their law enforcement role by implying that law violators are diligently controlled by police. In addition, the blue line serves a boundary maintenance function which, in theory, may appear to deter illegal behavior. Yet, as observers of the police have found (Skolnick 1966; Whyte 1943), instead of a strict law enforcement model operating, most offenses are handled informally, without sanctions, unless they arouse the concern of the good people in the community. Stated somewhat differently, as more and more residents of a community involve themselves in some type of illegal activity, the line must become ever more inclusive of illegality and hence ever less controlling. In high-crime areas, the gap between the law and its enforcement undoubtedly sends a message that certain crimes are tolerated. It is troubling when certain characteristics of victims (e.g., victims who are young, African American, dual status, or all three) create a predisposition against official intervention. The variability of police tolerance of crime creates ambiguity for juvenile offenders, who may then formulate attitudes that police are incompetent, uncaring, or both (Matza 1964).

Youthful offenders in the Boston study (Guarino-Ghezzi 1993), all of whom occupied the netherworld of dual status, believed that police were often incapable of performing what they perceived as a fundamental task of policing—distinguishing law-abiding from illegal behavior. That belief was expressed in three ways. Youths were angry at having been "harassed" by police while obeying the law, typically while walking, standing on the street, or waiting at a bus stop. Indeed, the primary way that youths saw themselves as crime victims was as victims of police harassment. On the flip side, youths also relished their belief that they could outsmart police by concealing illegal behaviors, disguising them within normal, routine activities. The youths seemed to be challenged by the "game" of outmaneuvering police. Finally, residents of juvenile correctional facilities were concerned about police overreacting to their behavior, resulting in unwarranted rearrests following their return to the community.

The apparent frequency of dual-status victims, particularly among adolescents, raises questions about whether the lifestyle of the juvenile offender denies him or her the right to be treated in the same way as law-abiding victims. In general, criminal justice agencies grew more attentive to the rights and needs of victims during the 1980s, which restored at least some credibility to processes that were constantly charged with insensitivity to victims of crime (Karmen 1990). However, chronically delinquent youths who become victims of crime are unlikely to reap the advantages of the victims' rights movement due to police failure to acknowledge their victim status. Indeed, a variety of victims' groups in the United States discovered that considerable organizational clout is a necessary ingredient for recognition. Groups like Mothers Against Drunk Driving, along with rape victims' advocates, have achieved favorable changes in police procedures, but only after lengthy political battles (Lawrence, Snortum, and Zimring 1988; Karmen 1990).

Adolescent offenders, when they are victimized, are likely to remain at or near the bottom of the victims' social hierarchy unless broad-based changes are forced onto police. Pressure for police to acknowledge these dual-status victims as victims is unlikely to come from the youths themselves, particularly after they become proficient at "self-help" retaliatory behaviors. Youths in the Boston study did not trust the criminal justice system to protect them from crime, choosing to leave town if their lives were in danger rather than contact police (Guarino-Ghezzi 1993). However, until youths feel that the legal establishment adequately protects them from the dangers of their communities, they have no interest in validating criminal justice agencies by reporting crimes, testifying in court, and so on.

✉ The Missing Link Between Corrections and Police

Results from the Office of Juvenile Justice and Delinquency Prevention's (OJJDP) controlled study of treatment and reintegration of violent juvenile offenders concluded that recidivism was primarily a function of weak reintegration and transition strategies (Fagan 1990). Similarly, Altschuler and Armstrong (1991) noted that the central—and unmet—challenge for juvenile correctional programs is to forge mutually beneficial partnerships with community social institutions.

Examining the role of police in offender reintegration is critical for fully understanding the gaps in surveillance and services. The link between reintegration and police is particularly important when considering repeat offenders because selective incapacitation theory not only instructs police to focus their investigative efforts on repeat offenders, but has led to the development of Repeat Offender Projects (ROPs) in many police jurisdictions (Gay and Bowers 1985; Martin and Sherman 1986; Moore, Estrich, McGillis, and Spelman 1984). However, in selectively targeting repeat offenders, police may be working at cross-purposes with juvenile corrections agencies, which are most likely attempting to maximize the rehabilitative potential of the correctional experience and to minimize the labeling effect on the offender once he or she has been discharged. In particular,

the independent effect of police labeling on future offending has been underscored by labeling theorists and empirical research (see, for example, Hagan and Palloni 1990).

Further justification for an interagency approach to crime control comes from the ineffectiveness of classic bureaucratic turf lines, which have divided police from corrections. Police finger pointing at correctional release decisions is common.[5] Related to the turf obstacle is the tendency that police are offended by special work models that threaten their ongoing objectification of inner-city youths. Early demonstration projects that united social work and policing models into teams (e.g., Treger 1975) were extremely promising, but generally have been resisted by police. Police rarely take advantage of the correctional setting as a more comprehensive source of knowledge about offenders' motivations compared to the volatile and desperate setting of the street, where police ordinarily draw their conclusions about human behavior.

The importance of coordinating the goals of correctional agencies and police was demonstrated in a Madison, Wisconsin, study of repeat sexual offenders (Goldstein and Susmilch 1982). The study found that there was little trust or communication between Madison police and the probation and parole officers employed by the Wisconsin Division of Corrections. The void in communication produced negative stereotypes by members of both the police and correctional agencies. However, those stereotypes dissolved after the agencies agreed to conduct joint supervision of repeat sexual offenders, who indeed had caused similar behavioral management problems for both agencies. Strategies for serious offenders advanced by the U.S. Department of Justice's (1993) OJJDP include the creation of neighborhood resource teams, composed of community police officers, social workers, health care workers, housing experts, and school personnel. In high-crime communities, it would be logical to add a youth correctional representative to the team as well.

Despite obvious differences in setting, it is quite likely that police can learn a great deal from observing correctional staff whose behavioral control techniques are tailored to youthful offenders. According to Altschuler and Armstrong (1991), a key component of juvenile offender reintegration is providing "consistent, clear, swift and graduated sanctions for misconduct" (p. 69), along with developing new resources and supports, working with existing supports, providing opportunities for youths to achieve, and preparing youths for gradually increased responsibility and freedom in the community. Similarly, Gendreau and Ross (1991) identified "authority— where rules and or formal legal sanctions are clearly spelled out" (p. 319) as a central component of community corrections, along with anti-criminal modeling and reinforcement, problem solving, use of community resources, and quality of interpersonal relationships. OJJDP recommendations for serious offenders (U.S. Department of Justice 1993, pp. 18–19) emphasized the importance of an immediate response to misbehavior, gradational sanctions, and coordination among police, courts, and corrections.

However, political support for reintegrative correctional programs is difficult to achieve and maintain, despite evidence of increased public safety (LeClair and Guarino-Ghezzi 1991). Precisely for that reason, the trend toward community policing may provide opportunities for correctional systems to reexamine their own reintegrative models and consider ways in which police knowledge of offenders in inner-city communities could provide needed support. Additional opportunities for developing a reintegrative role for police may come from a variety of states that are expanding their correctional mandate for community-based settings for juvenile offenders. For example, Alabama, Oregon, Delaware, New Hampshire, Maryland, Virginia, North Dakota, and potentially Georgia and Arizona are reducing their reliance on institutions and increasing the number of youths in non-secure community-based programs overseen by youth correctional agencies. Those changes are occurring primarily because of actual or threatened lawsuits that allege that the

institutional model has failed to provide adequate protection and services for youths (Guarino-Ghezzi and Loughran 1993).

▧ Developing A Model of Reintegrative Surveillance

Police need to examine how their actions are interpreted, or misinterpreted, by the individuals whom they seek to control. In particular, police are insensitive to the irrational appearance of intermittent control of disorder. In addition, youths perceive that police authority to enforce laws is unjustified when police are unable to protect or defend them. Police in Boston reported that sessions with incarcerated juvenile offenders helped them to identify communication problems and they strongly recommended that all officers have regular contact with juvenile correctional programs as part of their regular duty (Guarino-Ghezzi 1993). Potentially, further interaction with juvenile correctional programs could lead to sharing of effective mechanisms to control behavior. Rule enforcement within correctional programs (the analog to order maintenance on the street) is improved considerably with graduated, predictable sanctions (loss of privileges) for violators, staff training, and close supervision of staff and youths. Teaching residents that behavior has consequences has become a centerpiece for many correctional programs, and considerable time and effort is devoted to that simple lesson— in part because staff must undo the messages learned from parents, schools, and perhaps police that consequences following misbehavior are unpredictable and often avoidable.

A model for moral education is embedded in Braithwaite's (1989) theory of "reintegrative shaming," which has as its objective the reduction of recidivism. Braithwaite argues that the unintended consequence of attaching stigma to punishment—as is common in Western societies—is the increased attractiveness of criminal subcultures after the punishment has been imposed. This assumption is consistent with an established body of research (e.g., Schwartz and Skolnick 1962) on the long-term adverse effects of stigma on ex-offenders, and with labeling theory in general. In Braithwaite's model of crime control, a period of punishment is followed not by stigma, but by reintegrative shaming. When offenders are both shamed and reintegrated, their family and community express strong disapproval of the criminal act, pressuring genuine remorse, but at the same time agreeing to accept the offender back into the community. The ex-offender label is therefore not a "master status" that perpetuates criminality. The offender's expectation of the community response is essential to his or her decision to either reform or rebel once released to the community.

Several aspects of the theory of reintegrative shaming are applicable to the relationship between police and corrections and underscore the need for frequent interpersonal contact between police and juvenile offenders. First, the greater the social distance between the ex-offender and other individuals, including police, the higher the probability of a stigmatic reaction impeding reform (see Erickson 1977). Second, evidence suggests that when police know and can communicate with neighborhood residents, they are more effective in defusing violent confrontations (Fridell and Binder 1992). Third, in theory, police have a vested interest (albeit generally unacknowledged) in assisting with the moral education of youths. The most important consequences of successfully communicating law-abiding values to adolescents would be enhanced police authority, a less dangerous work environment, and gratification in accomplishing societal goals of crime reduction. As Garbarino et al. (1992) observe in their comparison of children in actual war zones (Mozambique, Cambodia, and the Middle East) with children in inner cities in the United States:

One of the most important domains of concern we have discovered is the domain of moral development, particularly as it is played out in alternative conceptions of revenge. All too often, this is a neglected dimension in efforts to understand and ameliorate the problem of community violence. In war zones around the world, we have seen children helped to find a way through the moral minefield of negative revenge to a positive moral consciousness in which being a good person becomes a child's revenge. We see precious little of this in the urban war zone. (p. 226)

To initiate the process of positive moral development, professionals who deal with children and adolescents must first establish trust, which requires continued personal interactions in which people are viewed as people, rather than "cases" (Hummel 1977; Polier 1989). Personal interaction is not easily accomplished because bureaucratic agencies place strong, "rationalizing" (Weber 1946) pressure on workers to fragment people into problems and characteristics, which maximizes the energy invested in bureaucratic procedures but minimizes attention to the outcome (success or failure) of their efforts. It follows that in police work, successful personal relationships between police and residents must be grounded in personalized community service rather than law enforcement (Morrison 1992) to counteract the bureaucratic tendency to dehumanize clientele. Research on the Community Organizing Response Team (CORT) in Houston, that city's version of storefront policing, suggested that even though storefronts increased the frequency of informal contacts with residents, they were not as effective as more aggressive door-to-door contacts (Skogan 1990). Just as important, service to low-resource communities is crucial to managing the disorder that perpetuates fear and crime (Wilson and Kelling 1982). It is now recognized that police services improve law enforcement, not the other way around (Sparrow, Moore, and Kennedy 1990). Bureaucratic distance among police, courts, corrections, and communities may be rooted in the interpretation of police roles as servicing short-term organizational rather than long-term societal needs.

Specific recommendations for police and inner-city youths may be drawn from pockets of innovation that involve aggressive outreach efforts by police. Several model programs for juveniles were reviewed and described by the United Conference of Mayors (U.S. Department of Justice 1992b). For example, in Aurora, Colorado, a community-based gang-prevention effort includes a victim/witness program established to support victims and witnesses of gang-related crimes and train police officers in assisting them. Gang intervention unit police officers wear modified uniforms so that they are not perceived as traditional police officers. They generally contact between 10 and 30 gang members on a daily patrol (from 4 P.M. to 2 A.M., 7 days a week). The unit attempts to give the gangs the impression that the police are constantly watching them. Indeed, the gang members and intervention unit members have gotten to know each other on a first-name basis, and reportedly, gang members have developed into information sources about rival gangs.

Another police program in Carlsbad, California, administers punishment to juveniles who have committed misdemeanors, on the theory that youths often learned it was "acceptable" to commit a minor crime because they received a "slap on the wrist" penalty. Youths often lost respect for society's institutions and the personnel who served the community, such as court and police officials. Also, victims of crime felt frustrated that the courts and police department did not adequately punish or prevent youths from committing such crimes. First-time offenders were slipping through the courts, with no certainty of punishment. The new program oversees a tribunal composed of community members to determine guilt or innocence and assign from 8 to 40 hours of community service and/or counseling (U.S. Department of Justice 1992b).

The innovative School Resource Officer (SRO) Program in St. Petersburg, Florida, is also being implemented in over 40 of Florida's 67 school districts and in many cities in the United States. Police officers in uniform (with a firearm) are stationed in secondary schools, where they serve as law enforcers, counselors, and instructors. In addition to helping maintain a safe school environment, the SRO program is designed to promote a positive relationship between students and police officers and to provide 200 hours per year of classroom instruction in law-related topics. Officers also counsel students who seek assistance, who are referred by teachers, and who are involved in the juvenile justice system. Officers may call on parents or make referrals to other school or community resources. Strategically, SROs figure prominently in city-sponsored youth activities. For example, they help organize "pool parties," which are particularly popular among youths and therefore provide the kind of reward for involvement with police that is often missing in communities. The (free) admission tickets are in demand, but only SROs and other uniformed police officers can distribute them, so young people who want to attend need to interact with the officers to obtain the tickets (U.S. Department of Justice 1992b).

The Police Citizens Youth Clubs in New South Wales, Australia, evolved in the late 1980s as a crime prevention program. The clubs arrange dozens of sports activities, music classes, and other lessons for youths, and they also work with police in several ways. Police conduct lectures on law and police roles during "law week," they offer crime prevention workshops, they provide transportation to youths under court order to attend substance abuse counseling, and they supervise court-referred youths who perform community service work at the youth clubs. Court-involved youths become familiar with youth club activities and learn from the positive involvement of other youths (Carter 1989). This model seems to be a significant improvement over other community-service sentencing programs supervised by police, such as the Newark program, which was lacking in positive alternative activities for youths or provision of role models (for a description of the program, see Skolnick and Bayley 1986).

The City of Boston's police department has recently begun to design a community-policing approach and has appointed a new chief of police. Among the department's pilot programs that are being replicated city wide is a witness-to-violence program, which brings psychiatrists in to counsel young children who have experienced or witnessed violent crime in their communities.

Another program to enhance community relations is the Neighborhood Information Post, a mobile trailer stationed in an accessible location within each neighborhood to provide support and retrieve information when critical incidents occur. However, an impediment to implementing inter-agency models between police and juvenile corrections is the absence of a juvenile unit in the Boston Police Department, despite the presence of such units in 89% of large U.S. cities (Reaves 1992). It should be noted, however, that specialized units can pose different obstacles at later stages of policy development by insulating regular patrol officers from procedural changes.

Although those programs represent advances in police-community relations and may have some positive impact on relationships with youths, they have several drawbacks: They are single-unit, as opposed to departmentally oriented; few of the programs focus on the marginal youths who can be reached only in the streets, and who need the most highly structured attention; and virtually no police programs are tied into correctional programs. For "marginal status" youths, the most frequent contact is with regular patrol officers, who are also the most likely to encounter ex-offenders returning to the community. Therefore, attention must be paid to patrol officers' approaches for handling juveniles so that an increasingly punitive system of alternatives to arrest is available, as well as rewards for interacting with police in some regular way. Youths returning from correctional programs must be reintegrated with familiar and personal encounters, and surveillance must be reinforced with certainty of response.

A comprehensive model for gang control that contains many of those principles, the Community-Based Youth Authority (CBYA) approach proposed by the National Youth Gang Information Center, would provide specialized training to CBYA staff, community residents, and representatives of schools and justice system agencies. The model would increase the frequency and quality of contacts between gang members, "wannabes," and trained workers. The CBYA mission would consist of six objectives: (a) socialization, (b) education, (c) family support, (d) training and employment, (e) social control, and (f) community mobilization and agency coordination. CBYA staff, based in communities, would perform both a case management and a surveillance function, and they would be responsible for consistent rule enforcement, as well as for the protection of youths, to demonstrate their authority as legitimate. CBYA workers would also serve as intermediaries between criminal justice agencies, schools, and neighborhood groups (Spergel et al. 1993).

At the same time, specially trained police officers would be required to cooperate with probation and parole regulations by reporting technical violations, and they would develop close liaisons with schools and service agencies (Ehrensaft and Spergel 1993). The primary strength of the model is the unification of diverse agencies under a common philosophy. The model limits police involvement to particular officers, a condition that may enhance interagency cooperation in the initial phases. Specialized training and supervision are provided only to the gang unit or detail. However, by excusing the majority of patrol officers from participating under its philosophy, the model does not anticipate long-term conflict between the trained and untrained officers that would produce contradictions in police handling of youths.

In reality, retraining field patrol officers requires, at a minimum, an understanding of how to apply gradational sanctions to minor offenses, the provision of adequate resources to devise such responses, the elimination of unnecessary harassment, and close monitoring of police by trained supervisors. One subject of a case study by Muir (1977) of a moderate-sized urban police force seemed to embody a long-term, humanizing approach to juveniles at a teenage hangout where juveniles played pinball instead of going to school. Officer Douglas devised his own gradational approach, which reflected the kind of consistency, predictability, and continual surveillance that, combined with his caring that youths go to school and his provision of an alternative activity, resembled the approach used in successful correctional settings:

In each encounter with juveniles Douglas anticipated miscalculation on their part and made allowance for it, giving them psychological room to readjust their initial estimates of matters. When Douglas walked into Caesar's, he allowed for the probability that they would misjudge him. He also concentrated on purposefully using time to dispel any irrationality. "So the next few days I walk into Caesar's, and I get myself about fifty names, and I tell each one, 'You do not play the machines. You go to school, and if you don't, I'll run you in.' So the first time down goes their name in my book. The second time I catch them, I make a little check right beside their name, just as big a gesture as I can. And the third time, I tell them 'they go to jail.' Well, I only locked up one. And I had no more trouble." (Muir 1977, p. 131)

In short, the police role needs to be reexamined as an important resource for juvenile offender reintegration and crime prevention, particularly in high-crime neighborhoods where other vital supports are lacking and disorder is prevalent. Systematically structuring the control of disorder will force police to orchestrate encounters with juveniles in a variety of contexts. Equally important are policies specific to inner-city youths that increase their protection from victimization. Present policies are dumbfounding to youths, as would be any administration of authority that appears haphazard and ineffective in performing fundamental objectives. Innovative police programs that combine reintegration with surveillance, along with training not only to increase communication with youths but to avoid the communication of unintended messages through the exercise of routine police work, are vital components for improving police effectiveness with juveniles.

Notes

1. Adolescents were all adjudicated for "street crimes"—drug dealing and property offenses—and were residents of the Judge Connelly Secure Treatment Program in the Massachusetts Department of Youth Services. Details of the study are available from the author.

2. The average annual rate of change based on least squares analysis of UCR arrest data for crimes involving disorder for 1971–1991 was –4.1% for drunkenness, –3.2% for vagrancy, –2.5% for curfew/loitering, +0.3% for disorderly conduct, and +3.7% for prostitution. For 1982–1991, all such crimes reflected rates of decrease: –5.9% for drunkenness, –0.3% for vagrancy and curfew/loitering, –2.4% for disorderly conduct, and –4.1% for prostitution.

3. For example, although the findings of *In re Gault* (387 U.S. 1, 1967) did not specifically address police investigative procedures, in making the privilege against self-incrimination applicable to juvenile court proceedings, the Supreme Court also made the procedural safeguards developed in *Miranda v. Arizona* (384 U.S. 436, 1966) applicable to juveniles. Following the Gault decision, virtually all of the courts that have considered the applicability of the *Miranda* requirements for juveniles have concluded that the requirements do indeed apply (Davis 1991).

4. The average annual rate of change based on least squares analysis of UCR clearance rates by type of jurisdiction for 1971–1991 was –1.1% for large cities, –0.9% for suburban areas, and –0.6% for rural counties. A slightly greater rate of decrease for 1982–1991 occurred in large cities: –1.5% for large cities compared to –0.9% for suburban areas and –0.5% for rural counties.

5. Ineffective communication and lack of problem-oriented teamwork across public service agencies are universal problems of bureaucratic myopia (Hummel 1977). However, criminal justice organizations may be successful in outwardly portraying a unified image by use of the metaphor "criminal justice system" (Kelling 1991). The term *system* implies interaction, interdependence, and the performance of vital functions; the various organizations comprising this self-proclaimed system are in fact rarely held to such standards.

References

Altschuler, David M. and Troy L. Armstrong. 1991. "Intensive Aftercare for the High-Risk Juvenile Parolee: Issues and Approaches in Reintegration and Community Supervision." Pp. 45–84 in *Intensive Interventions With High-Risk Youths: Promising Approaches in Juvenile Probation and*

Parole, edited by T. Armstrong. Monsey, NY: Criminal Justice Press.

Bandura, Albert. 1973. *Aggression: A Social Learning Analysis.* Englewood Cliffs, NJ: Prentice Hall.

Bell, Carl. 1991. "Traumatic Stress and Children in Danger." *Journal of Health Care for the Poor and Underserved* 2:175–88.

Berke, Richard L. 1993. "Politicians Feel a Crime-Induced Chill in the Air." *The New York Times Week in Review,* October 24, p. 1.

Black, Donald J. 1980. *The Manners and Customs of Police.* New York: Academic Press.

Black, Donald J. and Albert J. Reiss, Jr. 1970. "Police Control of Juveniles." *American Sociological Review* 35:63–77.

Boston Police Department Management Review Committee. 1992. *Report of the Boston Police Department Management Review Committee.* Boston, MA: City of Boston.

Braithwaite, John. 1989. *Crime, Shame and Reintegration.* Cambridge: Cambridge University Press.

Braswell, Michael, Steven Dillingham, and Reid Montgomery, Jr. 1985. *Prison Violence in America.* Cincinnati: Anderson.

Brown, David. 1993. "Dealing With Public Disorder: Enforcement of New Police Powers in England and Wales." Presented at the annual meeting of the American Society of Criminology, Phoenix, AZ.

Bynum, Tim S., Gary Cordner, and Jack Greene. 1982. "Victim and Offense Characteristics." *Criminology* 30:301–18.

Camp, George M. and Camille Graham Camp. 1985. *Prison Gangs: Their Extent, Nature and Impact on Prisons.* Washington, DC: U.S. Government Printing Office.

Carter, Percy. 1989. "The New-Look Police Club." Pp. 45–58 in *Preventing Juvenile Crime,* edited by J. Vernon and S. McKillop. Canberra: Australian Institute of Criminology.

Cashmore, Ellis and Eugene McLaughlin. 1991. "Out of Order?" Pp. 10–41 in *Out of Order,* edited by E. Cashmore and E. McLaughlin. London: Routledge, Chapman and Hall.

Cohen, Albert. 1955. *Delinquent Boys.* Glencoe, IL: Free Press.

Cohen, Albert and James F. Short, Jr. 1958. "Research on Delinquent Subcultures." *Journal of Social Issues* 14:20–35.

Davis, Samuel M. 1991. *Rights of Juveniles.* New York: Clark Boardman.

Ehrensaft, Kenneth and Irving Spergel. 1993. *Police Model.* Arlington, VA: National Youth Gang Information Center.

Erickson, Richard V. 1977. "Social Distance and Reaction to Criminality." *British Journal of Criminology* 17:16–29.

Fagan, Jeffrey A. 1990. "Treatment and Reintegration of Violent Juvenile Offenders: Experimental Results." *Justice Quarterly* 7:233–63.

Fridell, Lorie A. and Arnold Binder. 1992. "Police Officer Decision Making in Potentially Violent Confrontations." *Journal of Criminal Justice* 20:385–99.

Garbarino, James, Nancy Dubrow, Kathleen Kostelny, and Carole Pardo. 1992. *Children in Danger: Coping With the Consequences of Community Violence.* San Francisco: Jossey-Bass.

In re Gault, 387 U.S. 1 (1967): 1431–2.

Gay, William G. and Robert A. Bowers. 1985. *Targeting Law Enforcement Resources: The Career Criminal Focus.* Washington, DC: U.S. Department of Justice, National Institute of Justice.

Gendreau, Paul and Robert R. Ross. 1991. "Correctional Treatment: Some Recommendations for Effective Intervention." Pp. 316–29 in *The Dilemmas of Corrections,* 2d ed., edited by K. Haas and G. Alpert. Prospect Heights, IL: Waveland.

Goldstein, Herman and Charles E. Susmilch. 1982. "The Repeat Sexual Offender in Madison: A Memorandum on the Problem and the Community's Response." Vol. 3 of the Project on Development of a Problem-Oriented Approach to Improving Police Service. Madison: University of Wisconsin Law School.

Grant, Traci. 1992. "Police Plan to Sue Boston Rappers." *Boston Globe,* August 5, p. 43.

Guarino-Ghezzi, Susan. 1993. *Project Reinforcement: Program Description and Findings.* Boston, MA. Mimeo.

Guarino-Ghezzi, Susan and James Byrne. 1989. "Developing a Model of Structured Decision Making in Juvenile Corrections: The Massachusetts Experience." *Crime & Delinquency* 35:270–302.

Guarino-Ghezzi, Susan and Edward J. Loughran. 1993. *Juvenile Justice in a Web of Change.* Boston, MA. (mimeo)

Hagan, John and Alberto Palloni. 1990. "The Social Reproduction of a Criminal Class in Working-Class London, Circa 1950–1980." *American Journal of Sociology* 96:265–99.

Hagedorn, John M. 1988. *People and Folks.* Chicago: Lake View Press.

Hummel, Ralph. 1977. *The Bureaucratic Experience.* New York: St. Martin.

Irwin, John. 1980. *Prisons in Turmoil.* Boston: Little, Brown.

Jamieson, Katherine M. and Timothy Flanagan, eds. 1987. *Sourcebook of Criminal Justice Statistics—1986.* Washington, DC: U.S. Department of Justice.

Jankowski, Martin Sanchez. 1991. *Islands in the Street.* Berkeley: University of California Press.

Karmen, Andrew. 1990. *Crime Victims.* Belmont, CA: Wadsworth.

Kelling, George L. 1987. "Juveniles and Police: The End of the Nightstick." Pp. 203–18 in *From Children to Citizens, Volume II, The Role of the Juvenile Court,* edited by F. Hartmann. New York: Springer-Verlag.

——. 1991. "Crime and Metaphor: Toward a New Conception of Policing." *NY The City Journal,* Autumn, pp. 65–72.

Lauritsen, Janet L., Robert J. Sampson, and John H. Laub. 1991. "The Link Between Offending and Victimization Among Adolescents." *Criminology* 29:265–92.

Lawrence, Michael D., John R. Snortum, and Franklin E. Zimring. 1988. *Social Control of the Drinking Driver.* Chicago: University of Chicago Press.

LeClair, Daniel P. and Susan Guarino-Ghezzi. 1991. "Does Incapacitation Guarantee Public Safety? Lessons From the Massachusetts Furlough and Prerelease Programs." *Justice Quarterly* 8:8–36.

Lipsky, Michael. 1980. *Street-Level Bureaucracy.* New York: Russell Sage.

Lockwood, Daniel. 1991. "Target Violence." Pp. 87–104 in *The Dilemmas of Corrections,* edited by K. Haas and G. Alpert. Prospect Heights, IL: Waveland.

Lundman, Richard J., Richard E. Sykes, and John P. Clark. 1978. "Police Control of Juveniles: A Replication." Pp. 158–68 in *Juveniles in Justice: A Book of Readings,* edited by T. Rubin. Beverly Hills, CA: Sage.

Martin, Susan E. and Lawrence K. Sherman. 1986. *Catching Career Criminals: The Washington, D.C., Repeat Offender Project.* Washington, DC: Police Foundation.

Matza, David. 1964; *Delinquency and Drift.* New York: Wiley.

McGarrell, Edmund F. and Timothy J. Flanagan, eds. 1985. *Sourcebook of Criminal Justice Statistics-1984.* Washington, DC: U.S. Department of Justice.

Miller, Walter. 1958. "Lower Class Culture as a Generating Milieu of Gang Delinquency." *Journal of Social Issues* 14:5–19.

——. 1976. "Youth Gangs in the Urban Crisis Era." Pp. 91–122 in *Delinquency, Crime and Society,* edited by J. F. Short. Chicago: University of Chicago Press.

Miranda v. Arizona, 384 U.S. 436 (1966).

Moore, Joan. 1978. *Homeboys.* Philadelphia: Temple University Press.

Moore, Mark H., Susan R. Estrich, Daniel McGillis, and William Spelman. 1984. *Dangerous Offenders: The Elusive Target of Justice.* Cambridge, MA: Harvard University Press.

Morrison, Micah. 1992. "Cops Get Up-Close and Personal." *Insight,* August, p. 7.

Muir, William K. 1977. *Police: Street Corner Politicians.* Chicago: University of Chicago Press.

Murphy, Sean P. and John Ellement. 1992. "Internal Police Probe Discounts Most Allegations of Misconduct." *Boston Globe,* August 20, p. 1.

Needle, Jerome A. and William Vaughan Stapleton. 1983. *Police Handling of Youth Gangs.* Washington, DC: U.S. Department of Justice, Office of Juvenile Justice and Delinquency Prevention.

Palmer, Ted. 1984. "Treatment and the Role of Classification: A Review of the Basics." *Crime & Delinquency* 30:245–68.

Paternoster, Raymond. 1989. "Decisions to Participate in and Desist From Four Types of Common Delinquency: Deterrence and the Rational Choice Perspective." *Law and Society Review* 23:7–40.

Polier, Justine Wise. 1989. *Juvenile Justice in Double Jeopardy: The Distanced Community and Vengeful Retribution.* Hillsdale, NJ: Lawrence Erlbaum.

Price, Richard. 1992. *Clockers.* Boston: Houghton Mifflin.

Reaves, Brian A. 1992. *State and Local Police Departments 1990.* Washington, DC: U.S. Department of Justice, Bureau of Justice Statistics.

Reuss-Ianni, Elizabeth. 1984. *Two Cultures of Policing: Street Cops and Management.* New Brunswick, NJ: Transaction Books.

Schneider, Anne and Laurie Ervin. 1990. "Specific Deterrence, Rational Choice, and Decision Heuristics: Applications in Juvenile Justice." *Social Science Quarterly* 71:585–601.

Schwartz, Richard D. and Jerome H. Skolnick. 1962. "Two Studies of Legal Stigma." *Social Problems* 10:133–42.

Skogan, Wesley. 1990. *Disorder and Decline: Crime and the Spiral of Decay in American Neighborhoods.* New York: Free Press.

Skolnick, Jerome H. 1966. *Justice Without Trial.* New York: Wiley.

Skolnick, Jerome H. and David H. Bayley. 1986. *The New Blue Line.* New York: Free Press.

Sparrow, Malcolm, Mark Moore, and David Kennedy. 1990. *Beyond 911: A New Era for Policing.* New York: Basic Books.

Spergel, Irving. 1990. "Youth Gangs: Continuity and Change." Pp. 171–276 in *Crime and Justice: A Review of Research,* vol. 12, edited by M. Tonry and N. Morris. Chicago: University of Chicago Press.

Spergel, Irving, Ron Chance, Kenneth Ehrensaft, Thomas Regulus, Candice Kane, Robert Laseter, Alba Alexander, and Sandra Oh. 1993. *National Youth Gang Suppression and Intervention Program—Program Models.* Arlington, VA: National Youth Gang Information Center.

Taylor, Ralph B. and Stephen Gottfredson. 1986. "Environmental Design, Crime and Prevention." Pp. 387–416 in *Communities and Crime,* edited by A. J. Reiss and M. Tonry, Chicago: University of Chicago Press.

Thrasher, Frederick. [1927] 1963. *The Gang.* Abridged ed. Chicago: University of Chicago Press.

Treger, Harvey. 1975. *The Police-Social Worker Team.* Springfield, IL: Charles C Thomas.

U.S. Department of Justice, Federal Bureau of Investigation. 1972–1992a. *Uniform Crime Reports for the United States.* Washington, DC: U.S. Department of Justice.

U.S. Department of Justice. 1992b. *On the Front Lines: Case Studies of Policing in America's Cities.* Washington, DC: National Institute of Justice, The United States Conference of Mayors.

———. 1993. *A Comprehensive Strategy for Serious, Violent and Chronic Juvenile Offenders.* Washington, DC: U.S. Department of Justice, Office of Juvenile Justice and Delinquency Prevention.

Weber, Max. 1946. "Bureaucracy." Pp. 196–244 in *From Max Weber: Essays in Sociology,* edited by H. H. Gerth and C. W. Mills. New York: Oxford University Press.

Whyte, William F. 1943. *Street Corner Society.* Chicago: University of Chicago Press.

Wilson, James Q. 1968. *Varieties of Police Behavior: The Management of Law and Order in Eight Communities.* Cambridge, MA: Harvard University Press.

———. 1975. *Thinking About Crime.* New York: Basic Books.

Wilson, James Q. and George L. Kelling. 1982. "The Police and Neighborhood Safety." *The Atlantic,* March, pp. 29–38.

Wolff, Craig. 1993. "Tales of Police Corruption Not Surprising, 46th Precinct Residents Say." *The New York Times,* October 10, p. 35.

Zatz, Marjorie S. 1987. "Chicano Youth Gangs and Crime: The Creation of a Moral Panic." *Contemporary Crises* 11:129–58.

DISCUSSION QUESTIONS

1. According to the author's findings, what are some reasons police are not effective in controlling crime and disorder in inner-city neighborhoods?

2. Explain what the author means by the police failure to protect inner-city youths. Give an example from your own city or one near you, based on your observation or from a newspaper or television report.

3. Explain the "missing link" between corrections and the police, and give an example of how corrections agents and police could work together to reduce crime in your community.

4. Explain what the author means by "reintegrative surveillance" and give an example of how that approach might work in your city.

READING

Throughout history, during periods of disorder and criminal activity, or when any groups of people are perceived to be out of control and inclined toward criminal behavior, curfews have been used as a means of social control. Most recently in many cities, juveniles have been the subject of curfew ordinances. The authors of this article examine the constitutional ramifications and current status of curfew laws in the United States; they discuss the appropriate standard of constitutional review for cases involving curfews and examine the major state and federal cases addressing the constitutionality of juvenile curfew laws and their legal implications.

Juvenile Curfews and the Courts

Judicial Response to a Not-So-New Crime Control Strategy

Craig Hemmens, Katherine Bennett

A perception that juvenile crime is out of control is shared by the public, legislatures, and many criminal justice policy makers. Although the empirical evidence indicates that this perception is incorrect (Howell 1997), it has led to the adoption of a get tough approach to juvenile offenders. Legislatures and other government agencies are implementing a number of measures intended to reduce juvenile crime, including more liberal provisions for waiver to adult court (Fritsch and Hemmens 1995), increased use of incarceration as a sanction for serious juvenile offenders (Jeffs and Smith 1996), and modification of the goals of the juvenile justice system to align it more closely with the criminal justice system (Hemmens, Fritsch, and Caeti 1997).

Juvenile curfews are another currently popular approach to the problem of juvenile crime and delinquency. Although it is unclear whether they are effective in reducing crime, it is clear that they are being embraced by communities across the country (Conference of Mayors 1997). This article examines the constitutional ramifications and current status of juvenile curfew laws in the United States. The history, purpose, and form of juvenile curfews are first presented, followed by a discussion of the appropriate standard of constitutional review for cases involving curfews. Finally, the major state and federal cases addressing juvenile curfew constitutionality are examined and categorized.

A Brief History of Juvenile Curfews

Curfews, or laws requiring people to vacate public areas and streets, have existed for centuries. Early curfews were aimed at all inhabitants of a town, not just juveniles, and were used as a means of social control of the citizenry (Hall 1957; Ward 1956). In this country, curfews were used in the antebellum South to control when slaves and free Blacks could be on the streets (Federle 1995). Curfews have also been used during times of local or national emergency, such as

SOURCE: *Crime & Delinquency,* 45(1), 99–121, January 1999. © 1999 Sage Publications, Inc.

during World War II (Freitas 1996). Curfews have occasionally been used to proscribe a particular activity during certain time periods. For instance, at least 18 states have a night-driving curfew for young drivers and permit holders (Williams and Lund 1986).

Juveniles have been the most common curfew target in this country. Juvenile curfews began to gain popularity during the latter part of the nineteenth century. The first juvenile curfew ordinance was enacted in Omaha, Nebraska, in 1880 (Schwartz 1985). In 1884, juvenile curfews were endorsed as a panacea by President Harrison (Note 1958). By 1900, there were more than 3,000 juvenile curfew ordinances in this country (Mooney 1977). Progressive era reformers, largely responsible for the creation of a separate juvenile justice system, saw curfews as a means to control as well as to protect unsupervised and neglected children, an increasingly common phenomena in the new urbanized, industrial society (Platt 1969).

Although many cities have had curfew ordinances on the books for the better part of a century, enforcement has been sporadic. Police departments have frequently asserted that they were too busy investigating "serious" crimes to be bothered with enforcing a curfew or that they lacked the resources to enforce the curfew (Scherf 1992). Enforcement of juvenile curfews increased in this country during World War II, when juvenile delinquency again became a national concern. After the war, America experienced a population boom, leading to a tremendous increase in the number of teenagers by the late 1950s. Cities responded by enacting juvenile curfews. As of 1957, a little more than half of the 109 cities with populations in excess of 100,000 had juvenile curfew ordinances (Note 1958).

The 1970s saw the discarding of the rehabilitative ideal and adoption of the "justice" or "just deserts" model in criminal justice. Juvenile crime was perceived as spiraling out of control. One result was the get tough on juvenile crime movement and increased sanctions for youthful offenders (Boland and Wilson 1978; Fritsch,

Caeti, and Hemmens 1998; Fritsch and Hemmens 1995). These sanctions include juvenile curfews, which seem to some practitioners and legislators to be an ideal means of dealing with new problems such as juvenile street gangs and violent juvenile crime. Indeed, some commentators assert that the recent spate of curfew adoptions is directly attributable to gun violence committed by (and on) urban juveniles (Ruefle and Reynolds 1995).

A recent study reveals that 59 of the 77 (77 percent) American cities with a population in excess of 200,000 have juvenile curfew ordinances (Ruefle and Reynolds 1995). It has been estimated that approximately 1,000 local juvenile curfew ordinances have been adopted since 1990 (Sheperd 1996). President Clinton has endorsed juvenile curfews, and the 1996 Anti-Gang and Youth Violence Act provides $75 million for support of local initiatives such as curfews and antitruancy ordinances (Department of Justice 1996). Cities with curfew ordinances already on the books are suddenly enforcing them, while other cities are enacting curfew laws (Feldmann 1996; Sharp 1996; Smith 1994).

✎ Purpose, Form, Effectiveness, and Opinion of Juvenile Curfews

Proponents of juvenile curfews provide four major justifications for such ordinances: protecting juveniles from crime, reducing juvenile crime, protecting society, and reinforcing parental authority (Carmen, Parker, and Reddington 1997). Curfew laws are a manifestation of the twin goals of the juvenile justice system of the Progressive era—seeing to the best interests of the child while, at the same time, imposing stricter social controls on unruly youth (Platt 1969; Rothman 1980).

The vast majority of juvenile curfews are acts of local municipal legislation. Municipalities are free to enact regulatory ordinances in the exercise of their police powers as long as those ordinances do not unduly restrict or impair a constitutional right. The terms of juvenile curfews vary by city (see, e.g., Bilchik 1996). Many ordinances require that juveniles be off of the streets late at night, whereas others focus on preventing truancy by limiting their access to the streets or certain businesses during school hours. Most curfews are set at later hours on weekends and during the summer. Most of them also provide a number of exceptions to the general rule, allowing juveniles out past curfew for emergencies or to go to work or to a legitimate social function.

Different police responses to curfew violators are also permitted: Some cities require police officers to arrest juvenile curfew violators and bring them to a detention center; others permit them to take the child home; still others allow them to simply issue a ticket to the juvenile. Sanctions also vary by city. For example, many cities divert first offenders, whereas others permit the imposition on them of fines and/or community service (Bilchik 1996). Parents may also be held responsible in more egregious cases (Kalvig 1996).

There is strong support for juvenile curfews. Law enforcement and city officials applaud them as an effective tool for crime prevention (Conference of Mayors 1997; Trollinger 1996). A number of city residents also favor curfews. For example, a 1994 survey found that 92 percent of Cincinnati residents supported that city's curfew, whereas a survey of juveniles in the District of Columbia found that 77 percent of them supported the citywide curfew enacted in 1995 (Crowell 1996).

Although curfew opponents sometimes raise the specter of racist motivation for such laws, support for curfews is not limited to White citizens. Of Black residents living in Mobile, Alabama, 75 percent who were surveyed in 1994 supported a proposed curfew ordinance (Crowell 1996). Blacks comprise a majority of the District of Columbia city council, which enacted a juvenile curfew in 1995. The New Orleans juvenile curfew was proposed by a Black mayor, enacted by a majority Black city council, and enforced by a police department headed by a Black chief (Ruefle and Reynolds 1996).

From the beginning, there has been opposition to curfews. An 1896 critic voiced concerns echoed today: Juvenile crime occurs mainly during the day rather than at night when the curfew is in force, and there are a number of legitimate reasons for juveniles to be afoot at odd hours (Buck 1896). Other critics have argued that curfews do not foster family harmony and parental authority; rather, they damage family relations by interposing the authority of the state between parent and child (Chen 1997).

Another criticism is that law enforcement does not always enforce the curfew equitably (National Council on Crime and Delinquency 1972; Ruefle and Reynolds 1995). A belief held by some is that police officers target minority youth and use the curfew as an excuse to harass those youth. In jurisdictions in which juvenile curfews were enforced in the past, citizen complaints and claims of arbitrary and discriminatory enforcement were not uncommon.

There is remarkably little empirical research on the impact of curfews on either juvenile crime or the overall crime rate; thus, it is unclear how effective they are at reducing crime. Several cities that have begun vigorously enforcing curfew ordinances insist that doing so has resulted in a marked reduction in juvenile crime; juvenile victimization; and, in some instances, the overall crime rate (Bilchik 1996; Sharp 1996). Although these studies are incomplete, it is apparent that vigorous curfew enforcement has certainly had an impact on the lives of juveniles—almost 6,000 children have been arrested in New Orleans since the city began enforcing a curfew ordinance in June 1994 (Sheperd 1996).

Other studies suggest that curfews may simply cause temporal or geographic crime displacement. A study of the effects of a juvenile curfew that was adopted by Detroit in 1976 in response to a rash of crimes involving juveniles found that although juvenile crime dropped 6 percent during curfew hours, it actually increased by 13 percent in the curfews and antitruancy ordinances mid-afternoon hours (Hunt and Weiner 1977). Nationally, violent crimes committed by juveniles are most frequent between the hours of 3 P.M. and 4 P.M., and approximately 33 percent of all juvenile violent crime takes place between 3 P.M. and 7 P.M. Less than 20 percent of violent juvenile crime occurs during normal curfew hours (Snyder, Sickmund, and Poe-Yamagatta 1996). Although most juvenile curfews proscribe the presence of juveniles in public areas during the late night and early morning hours, less than 8 percent of all violent juvenile crime occurs between 11 P.M. and 1 A.M. (Fox and Newman 1997). These statistics suggest that reliance on curfews to substantially reduce juvenile crime may be misplaced, at best.

⊠ Constitutional Rights and Judicial Standards of Review

Juvenile curfews have been challenged as violating several different provisions of the constitution, including the First and Fourteenth Amendments. First Amendment freedoms restricted by juvenile curfews include those of association and assembly. Fourteenth Amendment rights affected by juvenile curfews include equal protection and due process. Claims involving violations of enumerated constitutional rights are often coupled with challenges based on overbreadth or vagueness (Toth 1995).

Although most challenges to juvenile curfews have centered on impairment of the rights of juveniles, from the beginning there have been challenges based on the infringement of the parents' rights to raise their children. The Supreme Court has historically accorded parents the authority to raise their children as they see fit, without state interference. In addition, most states have statutes expressly holding parents responsible for their children.

The Supreme Court has repeatedly asserted that the constitution and the protections found in the Bill of Rights apply to juveniles. It has also held on numerous occasions that states and municipalities may place restrictions on the constitutional rights of juveniles, which would be per se unconstitutional if applied to adults. This section discusses the differing standards of constitutional review that are applied to juvenile curfews.

Judicial Standards of Review

Often in constitutional law, the outcome of a case is determined as much by the standard of review that the court employs as by the facts of the case. Not all of the individual protections set forth in the Bill of Rights are accorded the same respect—rather, there is a hierarchy of rights. The court employs either strict scrutiny or rational basis review, depending on whether a fundamental right is implicated or a suspect classification is affected (Tribe 1988).

Fundamental rights are those freedoms that are essential to the concept of ordered liberty; they are rights without which neither liberty nor justice would exist. Examples include virtually all of the various provisions of the Bill of Rights. Fourteenth Amendment guarantees of due process and equal protection are also included in the list of fundamental rights. Such rights are fundamental for adults, but juveniles have traditionally been accorded fewer rights based on their youthful status; therefore, rights deemed fundamental for adults may not be seen as fundamental for juveniles.

To date, the Supreme Court has held that only race and religion are suspect classifications in all circumstances, although gender, illegitimacy, and poverty have occasionally been treated as suspect classifications by the high court (Tribe 1988). Although discrimination on the basis of a suspect classification is considered presumptively irrational and constitutionally invalid, age is not a suspect classification (Chen 1997). The Equal Protection Clause of the Fourteenth Amendment prohibits states from treating citizens in an arbitrary and discriminatory manner, but this does not mean that all disparate treatment is unconstitutional, only that the state may not treat people differently without a valid reason.

Strict Scrutiny Review

Under strict scrutiny review, the state may not enact legislation that abridges a fundamental right unless (1) it has a compelling interest that justifies restricting a fundamental right and (2) the legislation is narrowly tailored so that the fundamental right is not abridged any more than absolutely necessary to effectuate the state's compelling interest. In addition, the Supreme Court requires that for legislation to be narrowly tailored, there must exist a sufficient nexus between the legislative body's stated interest and either the classification drawn or the means chosen to advance the state's compelling interest. This standard of review is referred to as the strict scrutiny test because the court looks closely at the purpose and the effect of the legislation rather than merely accepting the claims of the legislature that the legislation is needed or accepting the legislation as presumptively valid. The reason for employing a higher standard of review when legislation affects a fundamental right or suspect classification is that closer analysis is required when individual liberties are threatened.

Rational Basis Review

If neither a fundamental right nor a suspect classification is implicated, a state may enact legislation abridging that right or affecting that class so long as there is a rational basis for the legislation. This standard of review is generally referred to as the rational basis test because under it, the court will not strike down legislation that appears to have some rational basis. The court does not look closely at the effects of the legislation, unlike the strict scrutiny test. Under this standard of review, state actions are presumptively valid (Tribe 1988). This standard of review is obviously a much easier one to pass. The legislature need not choose the best possible means; it must merely appear that it has chosen means that are not wholly unrelated to achievement of the legislative purpose.

The determination of whether a right is fundamental is the key to the outcome of many cases. The question for juvenile curfews, then, is do curfews impinge on any fundamental rights? If so, courts must apply strict scrutiny review and the curfew ordinance is likely to be invalidated. If, on

the other hand, courts determine that juvenile curfews do not abridge any fundamental rights, the ordinance need pass only rational basis review and, consequently, it is likely to be upheld.

 ## Supreme Court Cases Affecting the Constitutional Rights of Juveniles

Early Supreme Court cases involving regulation of juveniles treated the issue as a conflict between the interests of the state and the authority of the parents rather than as a conflict between the child and the state. In 1923, the court struck down a state law that prohibited the use of any language other than English in schools; in so doing, the court held that such a law infringed on the parents' "right of control" over their children by limiting who they could hire as a teacher (*Meyer v. Nebraska* 1923). Two years later, in *Pierce v. Society of Sisters* (1925), the court struck down an Oregon state law requiring children younger than age 17 to attend public, rather than private, schools. The court determined that such a law constituted an unreasonable interference with the authority of parents to determine the path of their child's education. The language of these cases suggested that children did not possess rights independent of their parents.

The Supreme Court continued to follow the approaches of *Meyer v. Nebraska* (1923) and *Pierce v. Society of Sisters* (1925) to juvenile rights for several decades. In *Wisconsin v. Yoder*, decided in 1972, the court struck down a state compulsory education statute as applied to members of the Amish religious order. The court focused not on how the law restricted children's religious freedoms but rather on how it limited parents' First Amendment rights.

The idea that juveniles were second-class citizens, subordinate to their parents, began to lose favor, however, during the 1960s. In *Tinker v. Des Moines Independent Community School District* (1969), the court determined that a school policy banning the wearing of black armbands to protest the Vietnam conflict violated the minor's fundamental right to freedom of speech. In doing so, it made no distinction between the rights of children (students) and adults (teachers and/or parents).

During the 1960s, the Supreme Court decided on a series of cases extending specific due process rights to juveniles involved in juvenile court proceedings. These rights included the right to counsel at a juvenile hearing, the right to notice of the charges, the privilege against self-incrimination, the right to a waiver hearing, and the requirement that guilt be proved beyond a reasonable doubt (Manfredi 1998). Although the court's extension of a number of rights is notable, also notable is its refusal to treat juveniles the same as adults. The Supreme Court has long recognized that the state has greater authority over children than it has over adults. In *Ginsberg v. New York* (1968), the Supreme Court held that juveniles do not have the same First Amendment rights as do adults; thus, the state could prohibit the sale of sexually explicit magazines to juveniles. In *McKeiver v. Pennsylvania* (1971), the Supreme Court declined to provide the right to a jury trial in juvenile proceedings. The rights accorded to juveniles by the court during this period were largely procedural in nature— states were required to process juveniles in the juvenile justice system in much the same manner as they processed adults in the criminal justice system. However, these decisions did not prevent states from enforcing laws that affected juveniles differently than they affected adults.

The Bellotti v. Baird *Test*

In *Bellotti v. Baird* (1979), the Supreme Court clearly illuminated its rationale for denying juveniles the protection of some fundamental rights while extending the protection of others to the same degree as enjoyed by adults. In striking down a Massachusetts statute requiring pregnant women younger than age 18 to obtain the consent of both parents before undergoing an abortion, the Supreme Court first noted that children are not without some constitutional protections. The court also acknowledged that children are different than adults and that the state has a special

duty to protect children. Consequently, although juveniles generally possess the same constitutional rights as do adults, the state may adjust its legal system to take into account the special vulnerability of children. From this, the court enunciated three considerations that provided states with the authority to infringe on the rights of a juvenile to a greater degree than on an adult's rights: (1) the "peculiar vulnerability of children"; (2) the inability of children to make important decisions in a mature, intelligent manner; and (3) the importance of the parent in child rearing.

This three-part test has been applied by federal and state courts to determine when the state may restrict fundamental rights of juveniles in contexts other than the decision whether to have an abortion. A number of courts faced with challenges to juvenile curfew ordinances have used the *Bellotti* test to determine the validity of the curfew, although the Supreme Court has yet to rule on the applicability of the *Bellotti* test to such curfews. Commentators have suggested that reliance on *Bellotti* by the lower courts is misplaced because that case dealt with the extremely sensitive and complex issue of abortion and the concerns expressed in that case may not extend to curfews (Toth 1995).

⊠ Cases Involving Juvenile Curfews

Although juvenile curfews have existed since the latter part of the nineteenth century, there are relatively few cases involving challenges to these ordinances. All of the early cases are state court decisions because no federal court considered a juvenile curfew case until 1975. This section reviews the leading state and federal cases dealing with juvenile curfews.

Early Juvenile Curfew Cases

Courts deciding early challenges to juvenile curfews did not look to the Fourteenth Amendment or the provisions of the Bill of Rights for guidance because the Supreme Court had not yet begun the process of incorporating the Bill of Rights into the Fourteenth Amendment's guarantee of due process. Instead, courts relied on general legal principles, such as vagueness and overbreadth.

The first case involving a juvenile curfew was decided in 1898. In *Ex parte McCarver* (1898), a Texas state court held unconstitutional a curfew ordinance that prohibited persons younger than the age of 21 from being on the public streets after 9 P.M. unless accompanied by a parent or seeking medical attention. The court criticized the curfew as "paternalistic," "an invasion of the personal liberty of the citizen," and an "attempt to usurp the parental functions."

In *Baker v. Borough of Steelton* (1912), a Pennsylvania court upheld as a lawful exercise of police power a municipal ordinance prohibiting those persons younger than age 16 from being on the streets after 9 P.M. unless accompanied by a parent or guardian or unless in possession of a note indicating that there was an emergency. The court noted that the city had a legitimate interest in protecting children from possible harm, determining that the curfew was related to this legitimate end and employing what is today referred to as the rational basis test.

In *People v. Walton* (1945), a California appellate court upheld a Los Angeles curfew prohibiting juveniles younger than age 16 from "remaining" or "loitering" on the street after 9 P.M. unless approval was obtained from the police. The court distinguished *McCarver* by noting that the Texas ordinance prohibited being on the streets altogether, whereas the Los Angeles ordinance prohibited the more narrow activities of "remaining" and "loitering." The court went on to say that juveniles are not accorded the same rights as adults, precisely because of their status as juveniles. As in *Baker,* the court used a rational basis standard of review.

Recent Juvenile Curfew Cases

Although the Supreme Court has not dealt directly with the issue of juvenile curfews, an increasing number of lower federal courts and state courts have done so in recent years. These courts have focused on the constitutionality of juvenile curfews and whether a fundamental right is implicated or a suspect classification exists. The crucial factor in these recent cases is whether the court applies rational basis or strict scrutiny review.

Many courts apply the rational basis standard of review. They do this (1) because they believe that the state has a heightened interest in the regulation of children's behavior, (2) because they believe that children possess lesser rights than adults and that no fundamental right is implicated, or (3) because children may be treated differently and are not a suspect classification.

Other courts have applied strict scrutiny analysis. Those doing so have generally found that the higher level of review is required because curfews implicate rights of minors similar to those of adults and, hence, are fundamental. Although strict scrutiny analysis often results in state legislation being invalidated, such is not always the case. Courts applying strict scrutiny analysis to juvenile curfews have struck down some curfews while upholding others. Courts striking down the curfews have done so because the state failed to establish a compelling state interest or because the means of achieving the state interest were not sufficiently narrowly tailored. Courts upholding juvenile curfews while applying strict scrutiny analysis have done so because the state established both a compelling state interest and the curfew ordinance appears to be sufficiently narrowly tailored.

State cases involving juvenile curfews. There have been a number of recent state court decisions involving juvenile curfews. These are presented in Table 1 and discussed below.

Several state courts have upheld juvenile curfews. In *People v. Chambers* (1976), the Illinois statewide curfew law was upheld by the state supreme court. The curfew was unusual in that it was enacted by the state legislature and covered the entire state, including rural and urban areas. The bulk of curfew laws are enacted at the local level in response to local problems. In upholding the law, the court acknowledged both the state's legitimate interest in reducing juvenile crime, which was increasing at the time, and the state's traditional authority to protect children. These interests permitted the state to infringe on the juvenile's rights. The fact that the law extended statewide was not a problem but rather a benefit because it indicated that the law did not discriminate in its application, at least in regard to geography.

In *In re J. M.* (1989), the Colorado Supreme Court upheld a local ordinance that made it unlawful for a person younger than age 18 to loiter in any public or private area between the hours of 10 P.M. and 6 A.M. unless accompanied by an adult. The court determined that the ordinance was a legitimate means by which the state could reinforce parental authority and that the curfew actually encouraged parents to take an active role in supervising their children. The court saw curfews as a necessary support mechanism for parents who were unable to adequately supervise and to be responsible for their children. In addition, the court determined that the city ordinance was narrowly drawn, thus achieving its goals without unduly infringing on the liberty interests of juveniles.

In *Panora v. Simmons* (1989), the Iowa Supreme Court upheld a juvenile curfew ordinance that prohibited juveniles younger than age 18 from being in a public place between the hours of 10 P.M. and 5 A.M. The state court determined that no fundamental rights or suspect classifications were implicated by the ordinance and therefore applied a rational basis standard of review. Under this level of analysis, the city met its burden of demonstrating that the juvenile curfew ordinance was rationally related to the legitimate state interest in protecting society.

The Arizona Court of Appeals, in *In re Maricopa County* (1994), upheld a 10 P.M. juvenile curfew enacted in 1993 by the city of Phoenix. The curfew provided an exception for juveniles "on reasonable, legitimate and specific business or activity directed or permitted by his parent." The court held that the juvenile curfew was a valid means by which the state could support parents and aid in supervising children in the "many cases [where] the traditional family unit . . . has dissolved." Using the three part *Bellotti* test in its analysis, the court determined that the peculiar circumstances of childhood dictated a heightened interest held by the state in

Table 1	Significant State Cases Challenging Juvenile Curfews		
Case	*Alleged Violation*	*Basis for Review*	*Violation Found*
People v. Chambers, 360 N.E.2d 55 (Illinois, 1976)	First, Fourteenth Amendments	Real and substantial relation to government interests	No
In re J. M., 768 P.2d 219 (Colorado, 1989)	Freedom of movement, overbroad	Rational basis	No
Panora v. Simmons, 445 N.W.2d 363 (Iowa, 1989)	Vagueness, right to travel	Rational basis	No
City of Maquoketa v. Russell, 484 N.W.2d 179 (Iowa, 1992)	First Amendment, overbroad	Strict scrutiny	Yes, not narrowly tailored to achieve state interests
In re Mariciopa County, 887 P.2d 599 (Arizona, 1994)	First Amendment	Rational basis	No

protecting children, thus justifying the limitation on a fundamental right.

Few state courts have struck down juvenile curfews. Just three years after the decision in *Panora v. Simmons* (1989) to uphold a curfew, the Iowa Supreme Court in *City of Maquoketa v. Russell* (1992) struck down an ordinance modeled after the one upheld in *Panora*. The city ordinance prohibited juveniles from being outside after 10 P.M., unless accompanied by a parent or going directly to or from work or a "parentally approved supervised activity." Justice Lavorato, who dissented in *Panora*, wrote the majority opinion. He asserted that juvenile curfew laws implicated fundamental rights of juveniles, including First Amendment freedoms of religion, speech, and association. Therefore, strict scrutiny, rather than rational basis, was the proper standard of review. Under this level of analysis, the juvenile curfew fell for not being narrowly tailored to achieve the state interests.

Federal cases involving juvenile curfews. Prior to 1975, no federal court had decided a case involving a juvenile curfew ordinance. Since the first decision in *Bykofsky v. Borough of Middletown* (1975), at least six cases have been decided in federal courts. These are presented in Table 2.

Several federal courts have upheld juvenile curfews, either under rational basis review or strict scrutiny. The juvenile curfew ordinance at issue in *Bykofsky v. Borough of Middletown* (1975) prohibited minors younger than age 18 from being on the street between the hours of 10 P.M. (younger than age 12), 10:30 P.M. (age 12 or 13), or 11 P.M. (age 14 to 17) and 6 A.M. unless one or more of several stated exceptions applied. Exceptions included being accompanied by a parent, in the case of an emergency, or if returning home from a legitimate social activity such as a school or church event.

The ordinance was challenged by the plaintiff mother on behalf of her 12-year-old son. No curfew violation had occurred; rather, the plaintiff sought an injunction and declaratory relief.

The plaintiff contended that phrases in the ordinance were impermissibly vague, violated First Amendment rights of minors, violated minors' right to travel, infringed on parents' right to control the upbringing of their children, and denied minors equal protection.

The district court determined that portions of the ordinance that gave virtually unfettered discretion to the mayor were too vague, but the court held that with the deletions of the impermissibly vague words and phrases, the ordinance as an entity was not unconstitutionally vague. The court also held that juveniles' constitutional rights may be regulated to a greater extent than adults without violating the Constitution. The court determined that although the curfew restricted freedom of movement, such freedom was personal rather than absolute and was subject to "reasonable regulations." The court thus ruled that freedom of movement was neither a fundamental right nor a First Amendment right. The court further concluded that there was a rational relationship between the ordinance and the interests of the city. Governmental interests in advancing and protecting the general community's welfare and safety outweighed the minor's freedom of movement interest.

The court did agree with plaintiffs that the minor's First Amendment right to freedom of association for social purposes was infringed. It held, however, that this right was outweighed by legitimate government interests furthered by the ordinance. The First Amendment right to free speech was not violated at all because the ordinance did not regulate speech, only "noncommunicative conduct."

Courts and commentators have argued that the *Bykofsky* court misapplied the process by which it is determined whether a fundamental right is implicated (Chen 1997; Tribe 1988). The proper method is to first determine the nature of the right that was restricted and then to select the appropriate standard of review. The *Bykofsky* court, however, reversed the process, first determining that the state had a heightened interest in the welfare of children and then concluding that

Table 2	Significant Federal Cases Challenging Juvenile Curfews		
Case	*Alleged Violation*	*Basis for Review*	*Violation Found*
Bykofsky v. Borough of Middletown, 401 F. Supp. 1242 (1975)	First, Fourteenth Amendments, right to travel, parental rights of child rearing, vagueness	Rational basis	Yes to vagueness; no to all other allegations
Naprstek v. City of Norwich, 545 F.2d 815 (Second Circuit, 1976)	First, Fourteenth Amendments, vagueness	Rational basis	Yes, voided curfew for vagueness
Johnson v. City of Opelousas, 658 F.2d 1065 (Fifth Circuit, 1981)	First, Fourteenth Amendments, right to travel, vagueness, overbroad	Strict scrutiny	Yes, unconstitutionally overbroad
McCollester v. City of Keene, 586 F. Supp. 1381 (D.N.H., 1984)	First, Fourteenth Amendments, overbroad	Strict scrutiny	Yes, facially overbroad
Waters v. Barry, 711 F. Supp. 1125 (D.D.C., 1989)	First, Fourth, Fifth Amendments, overbroad	Strict scrutiny	Yes to First, Fifth Amendments and overbreadth
Qutb v. Strauss, 11 F.3d 488 (Fifth Circuit, 1993)	First, Fifth, Fourteenth Amendments, vagueness, overbroad	Strict scrutiny	No
Hutchins v. District of Columbia, 942 F. Supp. 665 (D.D.C., 1996)	First, Fourth, Fifth Amendments, vagueness, overbroad	Strict scrutiny	Yes to Fifth Amendment violation of equal protection and due process
Nunez v. City of San Diego, 1997 WL304747 (Ninth Circuit, 1997)	First Amendment, vagueness, parental rights of child rearing	Strict scrutiny	Yes to vagueness, First Amendment, and parental rights

minors' freedom of movement was not a fundamental right.

In 1994, a court for the first time upheld a juvenile curfew while applying strict scrutiny review. In *Qutb v. Strauss* (1993), the Fifth Circuit Court of Appeals upheld a Dallas curfew that prohibited persons younger than age 17 "from remaining in a public place or establishment from 11 P.M. until 6 A.M. on week nights and from 12 midnight until 6 A.M. on weekends." The curfew provided several exceptions, including being accompanied by a parent or guardian; running an errand for a parent or guardian or an emergency errand; traveling in a motor vehicle to or from work; being involved in employment-related activities; or engaging in interstate travel. Minors affected by the curfew could still "attend school, religious, or civic organization functions, or generally exercise First Amendment speech and association rights." The curfew also permitted minors to remain on sidewalks in front of their homes or in front of neighbors' homes.

The Fifth Circuit noted that because the ordinance differentiated classes of individuals based on age, the curfew must be analyzed under the equal protection clause. The plaintiffs charged that the curfew impinged on the fundamental right "to move about freely in public." Assuming that the right to move about freely is a fundamental right and that it is impinged on by the curfew ordinance, the court accordingly subjected the ordinance to strict scrutiny review and asked whether it was sufficiently narrowly drawn to accomplish the state's compelling interest.

Dallas presented statistical data establishing the amount of juvenile crime and the time of day that violent crime was likely to occur. Even though the city could not provide data regarding juvenile crime committed during curfew hours or juvenile victimization occurring during those hours, the circuit court held that the city did provide adequate data to establish that the age classification of the curfew fit the state's compelling interest. The court further stated that the ordinance, particularly in light of the numerous exceptions, employed the least restrictive means of accomplishing its stated goals. The Fifth Circuit was unimpressed with the district court's examples of activities that would be curtailed by the curfew, such as "concerts, movies, plays, study groups, or church activities that may extend past curfew hours" or even "an innocent stroll or gazing at stars from a public park." The court noted that minors could engage in those activities if accompanied by a parent or guardian. The court then stated that "innocent strolls" could still be taken until 11 P.M. on weeknights and 12 A.M. on weekends; "indeed, a juvenile may stare at the stars all night long from the front sidewalk of his or her home or the home of a neighbor."

Several federal courts have struck down juvenile curfews, generally after employing a strict scrutiny analysis. In 1976, the Second Circuit in *Naprstek v. City of Norwich* invalidated a curfew ordinance, ruling it void for vagueness. The curfew had been in existence for 56 years. Constitutional issues raised by the plaintiffs were similar to those raised in *Bykofsky,* including violations of freedom of speech, assembly, association, and parents' rights to due process and

family privacy. The appellate court ruled that by failing to provide a termination time for the curfew, the ordinance was "void for vagueness" and unconstitutional in its application. *In Johnson v. City of Opelousas* (1981), the Fifth Circuit found the Opelousas ordinance to be unconstitutionally vague and facially overbroad, in violation of the First and Fourteenth Amendments, and in violation of the minor's right of interstate and intrastate travel. The curfew in Opelousas prohibited minors younger than age 17 from being on the street or in a public place between 11 P.M. and 4 A.M. between Sunday and Thursday and 1 A.M. and 4 A.M. on Friday and Saturday, unless accompanied by an adult or in response to an emergency. The Fifth Circuit recognized that restrictions on minors that would be unconstitutionally invalid if applied to adults may be justified, but only if they serve significant state interests. The court then held that the curfew was unconstitutionally overbroad because it unnecessarily prohibited minors from engaging in First Amendment activities, such as association and interstate travel. By including innocent activities in its list of prohibited activities, the curfew was not sufficiently narrowly drawn. The fault with the curfew in this case was that it allowed too few exceptions. The court decided that the nighttime activities prohibited by the curfew, such as religious or school meetings, burdened minors' fundamental rights. The ordinance at issue prevented minors from engaging in legitimate employment, being on the sidewalk in front of their own houses, and interstate travel.

In 1984, a federal district court struck down a New Hampshire city curfew ordinance in *McCollester v. City of Keene* (1984). The curfew applied to juveniles younger than age 16 and was in effect from 10 P.M. until 5 A.M. The ordinance contained several exceptions, including minors who were passengers in a motor vehicle and minors traveling before midnight to or from participation in a public assembly. The plaintiffs contended that the ordinance was still overly broad and violated due process guarantees against unreasonable governmental interference with citizens' liberty and privacy rights. The defendants claimed that the ordinance was narrowly drawn, given the exceptions provided for legitimate activity. Furthermore, the city argued that restrictions on the minors' or the minors' parents' liberty and privacy interests were justified by the "significant and legitimate public purposes" that were served by the ordinance.

The district court sided with the plaintiffs and found the ordinance to be overbroad and to impermissibly curtail liberty and privacy rights of both juveniles and their parents; the court also found it in violation of the three-pronged *Bellotti* test. The city's interests in suppression of crime, promotion of juvenile morality, and support of parental authority did not justify infringing on individual rights of travel and privacy. The court acknowledged that the state had a great interest in regulating the activities of children and a legitimate interest in controlling crime and promoting public welfare. Regardless, the court found the curfew to be too broad and in violation of the due process clause of the Fourteenth Amendment. The state's objectives were not sufficient enough to justify the juvenile curfew. The curfew provided no exemption for emergencies and the existing exceptions were limited to employment travel or being with a chaperone approved by the ordinance.

In *Waters v. Barry* (1989), the district court for the District of Columbia struck down a curfew ordinance that prohibited juveniles from being on the street or in public places between the hours of 11 P.M. and 6 A.M. Exceptions included minors traveling with their parents in a car, those returning from a job, and those on an emergency errand. The District of Columbia patterned its curfew exceptions after Middletown's curfew exemptions, which had withstood constitutional challenge. The District of Columbia district court held, however, that the District of Columbia's ordinance was more limiting than the Middletown ordinance. It also noted that it could not agree with the *Bykofsky* court that the constitutional rights of minors are less deserving of protection than are those of adults.

In reaching this decision, the district court applied the three *Bellotti* criteria in an in-depth analysis. Addressing the first criterion, the court noted that the District of Columbia posed just as much danger to adults as to children; therefore, there was no reason to place a "peculiar burden" on juveniles' constitutional rights. The second criterion, "juveniles' inability to make critical decisions in an informed mature manner," was not supported by the ordinance because a minor's "decision to either stay inside or roam at night does not present the type of profound decision which *Bellotti* would leave to the state." Likewise, the court viewed the ordinance as impermissibly encroaching on the third criterion: the importance of the parents' role in directing the upbringing of their children.

Thus, the court found no justification for according juveniles lesser rights. Because the curfew affected rights that the court determined fundamental and because there was no *Bellotti* justification for treating juveniles differently in this instance, the court applied strict scrutiny analysis. The court then determined that although the statute's purpose, to protect juveniles from harm, was legitimate and indeed a compelling state interest, the curfew ordinance was not narrowly tailored to effectuate that purpose. The court noted that the curfew was enacted without credible statistical evidence that juveniles either commit more crimes or are more frequently victims of crime during the hours of the curfew. Although violence was widespread, there was no evidence that juveniles were more likely to be involved in it than adults.

After the curfew ordinance was invalidated in *Waters,* the District of Columbia enacted a new ordinance. The curfew affected persons younger than age 17 and contained eight exceptions, which were copied verbatim after Dallas' juvenile curfew upheld in *Qutb.* In 1996, the district court addressed the constitutionality of this curfew in *Hutchins v. District of Columbia* (1996). Acknowledging that minors' fundamental rights may not always be treated in the same fashion as adults' fundamental rights, the court applied the three *Bellotti* factors to determine whether legitimate grounds existed for treating minors' right to free movement differently from adults' right to free movement. The court followed *Waters* in applying the first two factors. It noted an absence of necessary evidence showing that most parents in the District of Columbia were unable to control or protect their children to circumvent the third *Bellotti* factor, the importance of parental control in child rearing. The court concluded that there were no legitimate grounds for treating the minors' fundamental rights differently from adults; thus, the curfew was subject to strict scrutiny analysis.

The District of Columbia offered statistical information to substantiate its compelling state interest in reducing juvenile crime and victimization. Furthermore, it pointed to the exceptions as establishing that the curfew was narrowly drawn and the least intrusive means necessary to achieve its stated goals, but it failed to convince the court. The court was particularly unmoved by the statistical information and described the information as a "hodge-podge of national, as opposed to local, statistics, other cities' statistics, unverifiable charts, and statistics for people over the age of seventeen." Juvenile crime data included all persons younger than age 18; the curfew, however, targeted minors younger than age 17. Therefore, the statistics were overinclusive and, hence, unreliable. Furthermore, other crime statistics were not broken down by the time of day or night when the incident occurred or by the ages of perpetrators and victims. The court observed that the District of Columbia ignored "available statistics that show that more than ninety percent of all juveniles committed no crimes at all and were not arrested at night or any other time."

The District of Columbia acknowledged that it had adopted the Dallas juvenile ordinance that withstood strict scrutiny analysis in *Qutb*. The *Hutchins* court noted, however, that the District of Columbia "did not—and could not—also adopt wholesale the evidentiary statistics that allowed the Dallas ordinance in *Qutb* to withstand constitutional scrutiny." The court also stated that many of the exceptions were "vague and undefined." The district court held that the ordinance was not narrowly tailored to further the compelling interests of the District of Columbia and declared it unconstitutional.

San Diego enacted a juvenile curfew ordinance in 1947 and began enforcing it in 1993. Applying strict scrutiny analysis in *Nunez v. City of San Diego* (1997), the Ninth Circuit struck down the ordinance. The Ninth Circuit rejected the curfew for three reasons. First, it determined that the language in the ordinance was too vague. Juveniles could not be expected to be able to discern what kind of behavior was illegal. In addition, the loose language afforded law enforcement too much discretion in deciding how to enforce the ordinance. Second, the court held that the curfew unfairly limited juveniles' First Amendment rights of free speech, religion, and travel. Third, it found that the curfew unconstitutionally burdened parents, usurping their rights as guardians. The court said that the "ordinance [is] an exercise in sweeping state control irrespective of parents' wishes. Without proper justification, it violated the fundamental right to rear children without undue interference." The court did go on to make clear that a less restrictive curfew ordinance might withstand constitutional scrutiny. The 1947 statute contained dated language and requirements that were rarely found in newer ordinances.

⊠ Conclusion

Juvenile curfews are the latest fad in juvenile justice, a field strewn with the remnants of quick fixes to a serious problem (see, e.g., Bernard 1992; Hemmens et al. 1997). There is little evidence that curfews work, yet they have been adopted wholesale—the public wants action of some kind, any kind—a "just do something" mentality. This demand is related to feelings of loss of control over our youth, a feeling that appears periodically in American culture (Bernard 1992). Juvenile curfews are an attempt both to protect children and to prevent juvenile crime, thereby protecting society. Although these are laudable goals, it is less clear whether a curfew is the most appropriate means of achieving these ends.

Curfews are not going away—less than two weeks after the San Diego curfew ordinance was struck down in *Nunez,* the San Diego City Council approved a new ordinance modeled after the Dallas ordinance upheld in *Qutb* (Jones 1996). A recent study by the United States Conference of Mayors indicates that more than three quarters of American cities have some form of nighttime curfew, and more than 90 percent of these cities believe nighttime curfews are useful tools for law enforcement (Conference of Mayors 1997). These figures suggest that curfews are widely viewed as appropriate.

The question that enactment and enforcement of juvenile curfews begs is whether these laws are constitutional. The answer, according to the courts, is mixed. The Supreme Court has acknowledged that children are different and that the law must somehow reflect this fact. Yet, the Supreme Court has failed to establish a structured framework for minors' rights. The *Bellotti* test may not apply outside of the abortion context because the greater need to protect children considering an abortion may justify state action in instances in which it would otherwise be impermissible. Other cases involving juvenile rights are split. Whether juveniles have the same rights as adults is still in question until the Supreme Court issues a definitive pronouncement.

The consequence of an absence of a definitive pronouncement by the Supreme Court is confusion among the lower courts. There is disagreement about whether juveniles possess the same fundamental rights as adults. If not, then rational basis review applies and the curfew is likely to stand. If so, then strict scrutiny review applies and the curfew is likely to fall. Courts that uphold curfews while purporting to apply strict scrutiny have done so only by either misapplying the test or by accepting at face value crime statistics. This is not true strict scrutiny review. The Supreme Court should address the constitutionality of juvenile curfews and, in doing so, set forth a clear framework for consideration of the

(sometimes) competing interests of the child, parent, and state. Until the high court provides clear guidance, lower federal courts and state courts are likely to continue to issue conflicting rulings. The curfew ordinance upheld in *Qutb* and struck down in *Hutchins* is a prime example of the differing results that lower courts may reach when they work without sufficient guidance from the Supreme Court.

Curfews clearly threaten the exercise of a number of rights. The district court in *Waters v. Barry* (1989) likened the District of Columbia's curfew to "a bull in a china shop of constitutional values." Historically, juveniles have been treated as second-class citizens under the rationale that they needed more protection than adults. The question that blanket juvenile curfews raise is, When does protection become impairment?

The current trend is for courts to uphold juvenile curfews so long as the ordinance provides exceptions for legitimate activities and the city is able to make a showing of a serious juvenile crime problem. Lack of empirical evidence on curfew effectiveness works in a city's favor in two ways—it is easy to convince a court in these times that there is a juvenile crime problem and, without statistics, it is difficult to determine whether a curfew actually has any effect on juvenile crime. Courts are often reluctant to disagree with the conclusions of the elected representatives without explicit empirical evidence to the contrary.

"History teaches that grave threats to liberty often come in times of urgency, when constitutional rights seem too extravagant to ignore" (Justice Marshall dissenting *in Skinner v. Railway Labor Executives Association* [1989]). The recent surge in the popularity of curfew enactment and enforcement and the urgency with which some cities have turned to them, almost as a panacea, suggest that juvenile curfews are a sign of public hysteria rather than a reasoned response to juvenile crime and delinquency. Surely, criminalizing another activity instead of addressing the underlying social problems is unwise, unproductive, and doomed for failure.

✄ References

Baker v. Borough of Steelton, 17 Dauphin 17 (Pennsylvania, 1912).

Bellotti v. Baird, 443 U.S. 622 (1979).

Bernard, Thomas J. 1992. *The Cycle of Juvenile Justice.* New York: Oxford University Press.

Bilchik, Shay. 1996. "Curfew: An Answer to Juvenile Delinquency and Victimization?" *Juvenile Justice Bulletin* (April):1–11.

Boland, Barbara and James Q. Wilson. 1978. "Age, Crime, and Punishment." *The Public Interest* 51:22–34.

Buck, Winifred. 1896. "Objections to a Children's Curfew." *North American Review* 164:381–4.

Bykofsky v. Borough of Middletown, 401 F. Supp. 1242 (1975).

Carmen, Rolando V., del, Mary Parker, and Francis Reddington. 1997. *Briefs of Leading Cases in Juvenile Justice.* Cincinnati, OH: Anderson.

Chen, Gregory Z. 1997. "Youth Curfews and the Trilogy of Parent, Child, and State Relations." *New York University Law Review* 72:131–74.

City of Maquoketa v. Russell, 484 N.W.2d 179 (Iowa, 1992).

Conference of Mayors. 1997. *A Status Report on Youth Curfews in America's Cities.* Washington, DC: United States Conference of Mayors.

Crowell, Anthony. 1996. "Minor Restrictions: The Challenge of Juvenile Curfews." *Public Management* (August):4–12.

Department of Justice. 1996. *Anti-Gang and Youth Violence Act.* Washington, DC: Department of Justice.

Ex parte McCarver, 46 S.W. 936 (Texas, 1898).

Federle, Katherine H. 1995. "Children, Curfews, and the Constitution." *Washington University Law Quarterly* 73:1315–68.

Feldmann, Linda. 1996. "Cities Adopt Curfews, But Impact on Crime is Debated." *Christian Science Monitor,* January 4, p. A1.

Fox, James A. and Sanford A. Newman. 1997. "Juvenile Crime Rate Spikes When School Lets Out, Study Indicates." *Criminal Justice Newsletter* 28:5–6.

Freitas, Susan L. 1996. "After Midnight: The Constitutional Status of Juvenile Ordinances in California." *Hastings Constitutional Law Quarterly* 24:219–46.

Fritsch, Eric J., Tory J. Caeti, and Craig Hemmens. Forthcoming. "Juvenile Justice in Texas: An Analysis of Changing Policy Assumptions." *Law and Policy.*

Fritsch, Eric J. and Craig Hemmens. 1995. "Juvenile Waiver in the United States 1977–1995: A Comparison and Analysis of Waiver Statutes." *Juvenile and Family Court Journal* 46:17–35.

Ginsberg v. New York, 390 U.S. 629 (1968).

Hall, Donald M. 1957. "Note: Locomotion Ordinances as Abridgment of Personal Liberty." *Tulane Law Review* 32(1): 117–9.

Hemmens, Craig, Eric J. Fritsch, and Tory J. Caeti. 1997. "Juvenile Justice Code Purpose Clauses: The Power of Words." *Criminal Justice Policy Review* 8:221–46.

Howell, James C. 1997. *Juvenile Justice and Youth Violence.* Thousand Oaks, CA: Sage.

Hunt, A. Lee and Ken Weiner. 1977. "The Impact of a Juvenile Curfew: Suppression and Displacement Patterns of Juvenile Offenses." *Journal of Police Science and Administration* 5:407–12.

Hutchins v. District of Columbia, 942 F. Supp. 665 (D.D.C., 1996).

In re J. M., 768 P.2d 219 (Colorado, 1989).

In re Maricopa County, 887 P.2d 599 (Arizona, 1994).

Jeffs, Tony and Mark K. Smith. 1996. "Getting the Dirtbags Off the Streets: Curfews and Other Solutions to Juvenile Crime." *Youth and Policy* 53:1–14.

Johnson v. City of Opelousas, 358 F.2d 1065 (Fifth Circuit, 1981).

Jones, Charisse. 1996. "Cities Give Curfew Laws a Closer Look." *USA Today,* June 21, p. A1.

Kalvig, Kenneth A. 1996. "Oregon's New Parental Responsibility Acts: Should Other States Follow Oregon's Trail?" *Oregon Law Review* 75:829–901.

Manfredi, Christopher P. 1998. *The Supreme Court and Juvenile Justice.* Lawrence: University of Kansas Press.

McCollester v. City of Keene, 586 F. Supp. 1381 (D.N.H., 1984).

McKeiver v. Pennsylvania, 403 U.S. 528 (1971).

Meyer v. Nebraska, 262 U.S. 390 (1923).

Mooney, Martin E. 1977. "Note: Assessing the Constitutional Validity of Juvenile Curfew Statutes." *Notre Dame Lawyer* 52:858–81.

Naprstek v. City of Norwich, 545 F.2d 815 (Second Circuit, 1976).

National Council on Crime and Delinquency. 1972. "Juvenile Curfews: A Policy Statement." *Crime & Delinquency* 18:132–3.

Note. 1958. "Curfew Ordinances and the Control of Nocturnal Juvenile Crime." *University of Pennsylvania Law Review* 107:66–101.

Nunez v. City of San Diego, 1997 WL 304747 (Ninth Circuit, 1997).

Panora v. Simmons, 445 N.W.2d 363 (Iowa, 1989).

People v. Chambers, 360 N.E.2d 55 (Illinois, 1976).

People v. Walton, 161 P.2d 498 (California, 1945).

Pierce v. Society of Sisters, 268 U.S. 510 (1925).

Platt, Anthony. 1969. *The Childsavers.* Chicago: University of Chicago Press.

Qutb v. Strauss, 11 F.3d 488 (Fifth Circuit, 1993).

Rothman, David J. 1980. *Conscience and Convenience.* New York: HarperCollins.

Ruefle, William and Kenneth M. Reynolds. 1995. "Curfew and Delinquency in Major American Cities." *Crime & Delinquency* 41:347–63.

——. 1996. "Keep Them at Home: Juvenile Curfew Ordinances in 200 American Cities." *American Journal of Police* 15:63–84.

Scherr, Peter L. 1992. "The Juvenile Curfew. Ordinance: In Search of A New Standard of Review." *Washington University Journal of Urban And Contemporary Law* 41:163–92.

Schwartz, Robert. 1985. "Rights Issue Teen-Age Curfews—A Revival." *The Los Angeles Times,* August 10, p. D1.

Sharp, Deborah. 1996. "New Orleans Puts Its Curfew in Good Light." *USA Today,* October 4, p. A4.

Sheperd, Robert E. 1996. 'The Proliferation of Juvenile Curfews." *American Bar Association Criminal Justice Section Newsletter* (September):1–3.

Skinner v. Railway Labor Executives Association, 489 U.S. 602 (1989).

Smith, Wesley R. 1994. "Don't Stand So Close to Me." *Policy Review* (Fall):48–54.

Snyder, Howard, Melissa Sickmund, and Eileen Poe-Yamagatta. 1996. *Juvenile Offenders and Victims: 1996 Update on Violence.* Washington, DC: Department of Justice.

Tinker v. Des Moines Independent School District, 393 U.S. 503 (1969).

Toth, Jeremy. 1995. "Juvenile Curfew: Legal Perspectives and Beyond." *In the Public Interest* 14:39–82.

Tribe, Laurence H. 1988. *American Constitutional Law.* Minneapolis, MN: West.

Trollinger, Tona. 1996. "The Juvenile Curfew: Unconstitutional Imprisonment." *William and Mary Bill of Rights Journal* 4:949–1003.

Ward, Regina M. 1956. "Comment: Constitutional Law—Police Power—Municipal Ordinances—Philadelphia Curfew Law." *Villanova Law Review* 1:51–63.

Waters v. Barry, 711 F. Supp. 1125 (D.D.C., 1989).

Williams, Allan F. and Adrian K. Lund. 1986. "Adults' Views of Laws That Limit Teenagers' Driving and Access to Alcohol." *Journal of Public Health Policy* 7:190–7.

Wisconsin v. Yoder, 406 U.S. 205 (1972).

DISCUSSION QUESTIONS

1. Explain the purposes of curfew laws, and state whether you do or do not support those purposes.

2. What groups of persons, other than juveniles, have been the subject of curfew laws over the years?

3. Have the courts struck down or upheld curfew laws? Cite some example cases. In cases where a curfew was struck down, what was the courts' reasoning?

4. What does research show about the effectiveness of curfew laws, and whether they work? Are they, or could they be, effective in your city?

5. Based on the research and examples in other cities, do you believe curfew laws will be expanded or eliminated?

READING

The increase in gang membership and gang activities has elicited a number of police tactics to reduce the problem. Gang suppression is the primary strategy used by police, but some researchers believe it is the least effective strategy. The authors of this article report on the results of an anti-gang initiative of the Dallas Police Department. Strategies included saturation patrol and aggressive curfew and truancy enforcement. Control areas were selected, and preintervention and postintervention measures of gang violence and offenses that were reported to the police were analyzed. The findings indicated that aggressive curfew and truancy enforcement led to significant reductions in gang violence, whereas simple saturation patrol did not. In addition, there were no significant reductions in offenses reported to the police. The significance of these findings and policy implications are discussed.

Gang Suppression Through Saturation Patrol, Aggressive Curfew, and Truancy Enforcement

A Quasi-Experimental Test of the Dallas Anti-Gang Initiative (1999)

Eric J. Fritsch, Tory J. Caeti, Robert W. Taylor

For years, police agencies have pursued tactics designed to deal with the proliferation of gangs and gang violence. According to the National Youth Gang Survey, the primary strategy in many jurisdictions is suppression (Spergel and Curry 1990). Suppression tactics include tactical patrols by law enforcement, vertical prosecution by district attorneys, and intensive supervision by probation departments. Generally, suppression involves the arrest, prosecution, and incarceration of gang members. Although suppression is the primary strategy in many jurisdictions, it is also frequently viewed as the least effective (Spergel and Curry 1990).

In 1996, the Dallas Police Department received an anti-gang initiative grant from the Office of Community Oriented Policing Services to combat violent gang activity. The grant period lasted from June 1, 1996, through May 31, 1997. In 1996, the city of Dallas had 79 gangs with 6,145 documented gang members. In addition, there were 1,332 gang-related incidents recorded in 1996. The Dallas Police Department targeted five areas, made up of a varying number of patrol beats, which were home to seven of the most violent gangs in Dallas. In the year preceding the grant, the targeted gangs accounted for 18 percent of the known gang members in Dallas and were responsible for approximately 35 percent of the gang-related violent crimes.

The primary objective of the grant was to fund overtime enforcement in the five targeted

Source: *Crime & Delinquency, (45)*1, 122–139, January 1999. © 1999 Sage Publications, Inc.

areas in hopes of significantly decreasing violent gang activity through suppression. Gang Unit officers teamed with Interactive Community Policing (ICP) officers to develop innovative enforcement strategies for each of the targeted areas. Subsequently, teams of six to eight officers were assembled and received overtime pay to implement the developed strategy. These officers were freed from calls for service and instead spent their time implementing and carrying out the particular enforcement strategy. Although tactics such as "buy-bust" operations and warrant service were employed during the grant period, the vast majority of overtime funds were spent on three suppression tactics: aggressive curfew enforcement—juvenile curfew ordinances were strictly enforced whenever suspected gang members were encountered;[1] aggressive truancy enforcement—officers worked closely with local school districts in enforcing truancy laws;[2] and saturation patrol—officers conducted high-visibility patrols in target areas, stopping and frisking suspected gang members or other suspicious persons that they observed and making arrests when appropriate. The research reported in this article assessed the effectiveness of these strategies in reducing gang-related violence and gang-related offenses reported to the police.

Literature Review

The Police Role in Dealing With Gangs

Several authors, while noting that gangs per se probably cannot be eradicated, believe that the police can manage and, in effect, suppress the more negative aspects of gang activity (Huff and McBride 1993; Owens and Wells 1993; Rush 1996). The various strategies adopted by law enforcement to deal with gangs have been well documented (Dart 1992; Huff and McBride 1993; Jackson and McBride 1996; Johnson, Webster, Connors, and Saenz 1995; Klein 1993, 1995; Knox 1994; Spergel 1995; Weston 1993). Some have advocated the use of specialized patrols, especially foot patrol (Wilson and

Kelling 1989); others have embraced a philosophy best represented by the GREAT program, which integrates schools and law enforcement and teaches resistance (Howell 1996); and still others have advocated traditional and non-traditional law enforcement suppression techniques (Houston 1996; Johnson et al. 1995; Needle and Stapleton 1983; Rush 1996). However, empirical evaluations of the prescribed strategies have been few in number.

Gang suppression by law enforcement has also often included a broad range of tactics that frequently have taken the form of crackdowns. Crackdowns typically have involved "a sharp increase in law enforcement resources applied to the previously under-enforced laws, with a clear goal of enhancing general deterrence of the misconduct" (Sherman 1990b, p. 2). Most often, crackdowns have been effective initially, have had a short residual deterrent effect, and have been followed by an eventual return to preintervention levels of crime (Sherman 1990b). Generally, greater successes have been found in strategies focusing on specific offenses, offenders, and places than by simply increasing presence (Sherman 1990b). Although Sherman (1990b) has provided an extensive review of police crackdowns, including those emphasizing suppression of drug sales, drunk driving, prostitution, subway crime, and various other serious and nonserious crimes, no gang-specific crackdowns were examined or discussed in his review.

Gang crackdowns have not been evaluated systematically (Klein 1995). Some authors have dismissed the use of the crackdown entirely. "In the case of youth gang interdiction, this tactic is analogous to an attempt to put out a forest fire with a water bucket" (Shelden, Tracy, and Brown 1997, p. 212). However, a crackdown can be, and often is, a coordinated effort by a law enforcement agency to stop a certain type of crime or an offender using more than simple police presence. Indeed, the role of crime analysis in directing and supporting police crackdowns is growing; however, to date, very little empirical research examining well-coordinated crackdowns directed by crime analysis has been conducted. The studies that have been done have shown dramatic results, as was the case in the Minneapolis "hot-spots" research (Sherman 1990b) and the Kansas City Gun Experiment (Sherman, Shaw, and Rogan 1995).

Gang problems and behaviors vary widely from city to city as well as within cities (Weisel and Painter 1997). In accordance, it is doubtful that one strategy will be effective across and within all jurisdictions. Some law enforcement agencies have adopted a philosophy of total suppression, in which any gang member or wanna-be has been targeted, such as in the Los Angeles Police Department's (LAPD) Community Resources Against Street Hoodlums (CRASH) (Freed 1986; Klein 1993). Others, such as the Los Angeles Sheriff's Operation Safe Streets (OSS), have adopted a philosophy of target suppression, in which the police have only targeted hard-core gang members (Freed 1986; Klein 1993). Still others, such as the Oxnard, California, Police Department's Gang-Oriented Comprehensive Action Program (GOCAP) and the Westminster, California, Tri-Agency Resource Gang Enforcement Team (TARGET), have focused on information sharing and intelligence gathering to identify, arrest, and successfully prosecute gang members (Kent and Smith 1994; Owens and Wells 1993).

Most of the current prescriptive literature has focused on community-oriented tactics. Some have recommended that the police stop trying to eradicate gangs and that they communicate with gang youths in such a way as to demonstrate respect, acceptance, and concern for gang youths (Spergel 1995). The literature has also concluded that law enforcement alone cannot solve the gang problem—in fact, the typical police organization is ill-equipped and poorly structured to deal with gangs (Rush 1996). Dealing with gangs requires a comprehensive approach that involves all members of the criminal justice community, schools, community leaders, and the like (Owens and Wells 1993; Rush 1996). A fundamental problem with all of the aforementioned strategies, but especially the latter, has been the lack of reliable, well-documented,

well-designed, empirical evaluations of the strategies and tactics employed (Klein 1993, 1995; Knox 1994; Spergel 1995).[3] In fact, some of the evaluations of the tactics have been gleaned from newspapers (Freed 1986).

A recent review of several gang efforts has questioned the efficacy of police responses in dealing with the problem (Weisel and Painter 1997). In describing the gang enforcement tactics in five major cities in the United States, Weisel and Painter (1997) noted that "none of the agencies engaged in any identifiable long-term planning process or conducted research to monitor the changing nature of the problem. None . . . engaged in meaningful evaluations of effectiveness of specialized or other departmental efforts related exclusively to gang enforcement" (p. 83). In fact, some evaluative statements have been based on hunches because of the lack of empirical data. For example, Klein (1993) has said, "My informed hunch is that suppression programs, left to their own devices, may deter a few members but also increase the internal cohesiveness of the group" (p. 312). Indeed, much of the current literature has concluded that traditional law enforcement tactics alone will have little effect on reducing, managing, or suppressing gangs (Huff and McBride 1993; Rush 1996; Shelden et al. 1997; Spergel 1995).

Empirical Evaluations of the Effect of Police on Gang Activity

Spergel (1995) has concluded that the strategy of targeting gangs and gang members only for suppression purposes is flawed. However, in evaluating the effectiveness of suppression, Spergel also noted that "we have no systematic or reliable assessments of the effectiveness of a gang suppression strategy by criminal justice agencies, particularly law enforcement" (p. 198). Indeed, his analysis of the literature assessing the effectiveness of gang suppression by law enforcement consisted of a series of anecdotal comments from newspaper articles—hardly a scientific source. Klein (1995) reviewed several sweep programs that were undertaken in California. Operation Hammer, which was conducted by the LAPD, was a preannounced, media-covered gang sweep of Los Angeles that resulted in 1,453 juveniles being arrested; however, 1,350 were released without formal charges being filed. In the end, the operation was characterized by Klein and some LAPD officials as "all show" that was only for public relations. However, Klein also reported that when he rode along with Los Angeles County Sheriff's officials on a gang sweep that was not announced, not covered, and that was coordinated among several different targeted areas, the results were much different. Whereas Operation Hammer provided serious gang members with good laughing material, the Sheriff's sweep produced no humor among the arrestees that night.

Evaluations of community-based gang prevention programs are increasing. However, many of these have been qualitative and did not measure the impact of the program on crime in general or even on gang-related crime. For example, Thurman, Giacomazzi, Reisig, and Mueller (1996) evaluated a community-based gang prevention program implemented in Mountlake Terrace, Washington. Their evaluation included direct observation, focus group interviews, and official crime statistics. The program purported to provide an alternative outlet in which youths at risk or already involved in a gang could spend their time (Thurman et al. 1996). The official crime statistics used in the study were general calls for service to the police, with no breakdown given between gang-related calls for service and regular calls for service. Although Thurman et al. concluded that the intervention "appears to be a cost-effective gang prevention and intervention program" (p. 292), no data on crime; effect on the number of gang members, gang-related crimes, or gang-related calls for service; or other statistical evidence were offered to support this conclusion. Furthermore, the extent and scope of the gang problem in the area, the demographic characteristics of the community, and the crime statistics for the community were not discussed. The authors concluded that the program "offers

an effective alternative to traditional law enforcement approaches which typically rely on police crackdowns and curfews to regulate gang activity" (Thurman et al. 1996, p. 279), yet no evidence was offered to show that these latter techniques were ineffective or have not been effective in the past—either nationally or in Mountlake Terrace.

Palumbo, Eskay, and Hallett (1992) evaluated three gang prevention programs, including Arizona New Turf, GREAT, and Community Reliance Resource Effort (CARE). They found that although all of the programs were well implemented, there was no effect on the gang problem, even though police officers, students, and members of the community felt positively about the programs. Indeed, the majority of the community-based programs may fall victim to a common criticism—they sound good, feel good, look good, but do not work good. Many of the evaluations of these community programs have relied on qualitative data that typically show that everyone surveyed or interviewed thought the program was effective and useful, but no quantitative empirical support has been offered to indicate the impact on the gang problem, gang-related crime, or the gang members served by the program.

Much of the current literature has been dismissive, perhaps prematurely, of the ability of the police to suppress gang activity in that there are virtually no empirical studies that support such a claim. As Klein (1993) noted,

> The message is not so much that suppression does or does not "work": evidence one way of the other is sorely lacking. There are logical, as well as experiential, reasons to believe that suppression programs can have deterrent effects and thus, by our reasoning, can contribute substantially to gang and drug activity prevention. (P. 308; emphasis in original)

Curfew and Truancy Enforcement

The literature assessing curfew and truancy enforcement is still in its infancy; most existing studies have focused on tactics, descriptions of programs, and legal issues (Friend 1994; Garrett and Brewster 1994; "Juvenile Curfews" 1994; Ruefle and Reynolds 1995; Watzman 1994). Curfews have received attention recently because of their perceived effectiveness in reducing juvenile crime and juvenile victimization. Much anecdotal reference about their effectiveness has appeared in the popular media (LeBoeuf 1996; Ruefle and Reynolds 1995), but the existing academic literature on curfew and truancy enforcement has been limited to a few articles on the number of arrests and the various types of ordinances that have been enacted.

Hunt and Weiner (1977) studied a Detroit curfew that was specifically designed to reduce criminal gang activity by youths. They used before and after comparisons of crime rates and criminal temporal activity and concluded that the curfew enforcement seemed to effectively reduce or suppress the relative level of crime during curfew hours, although they also found evidence of temporal displacement (i.e., gang-related crime increased during noncurfew hours). Ruefle and Reynolds (1995) surveyed metropolitan police departments serving populations of more than 200,000 and found that curfews in one form or another existed in 59 (77 percent) of the 77 largest American cities. The Dallas Police Department's internal analysis revealed that following adoption of its aggressive curfew enforcement program, juvenile victimization during curfew hours dropped 17.7 percent and juvenile arrests dropped 14.6 percent from the previous year (Click 1994). Statistics from Phoenix, Arizona, revealed that 21 percent of all curfew violators were gang members. Furthermore, a 10 percent decrease in juvenile arrests for violent crimes occurred following implementation of an aggressive curfew program (LeBoeuf 1996). Decreases in various other juvenile crimes occurred in several other metropolitan areas (Chicago, Denver, Jacksonville, New Orleans, North Little Rock) that employed curfew programs (LeBoeuf 1996).

Truancy has been linked to a variety of negative consequences for youths (e.g., drug use, delinquency, unemployment) and for society (i.e., daytime crime, auto theft, vandalism) (Garry 1996; J. R. Martin, Schulze, and Valdez 1988; Rohrman 1993). However, the impact of aggressive truancy enforcement on crime rates remains essentially unevaluated. One evaluated program used a small squad of officers to enforce truancy laws; although numerous arrests were made, the impact on felonies and misdemeanors in the area was nominal (J. R. Martin et al. 1988). However, the study did not control for whether the crimes under study were committed by adults or by juveniles.

▨ Methodology

A quasi-experimental design was used for the evaluation reported in this article. The main objective of the initiative was to decrease gang-related violence in the five targeted areas. The five areas were composed of patrol beats and were selected on the basis of two criteria.[4] First, the areas had experienced a large amount of gang violence in the preceding year. Second, they overlapped some of the defined Enterprise Zones and Renaissance Areas in Dallas. Enterprise Zones are designated by the city to encourage economic development in an area, and businesses receive tax breaks for locating in the Zones. A Renaissance Zone is an area in which neighborhood organizations use federal funds to design and implement programs to reduce crime and disorder.

To estimate the impact of the enforcement strategies on crime, it was important to select control areas for comparison purposes. Four control areas were selected based on a two-stage selection process. First, the number of violent gang-related offenses from June 1, 1995, through May 31, 1996, for each patrol beat in the same patrol division as the corresponding target area was determined from data provided by the Dallas Police Department Gang Unit. Second, the beats with the largest number of violent gang-related offenses during the time period were matched with a corresponding target area and served as control areas.[5] The target and control areas were sufficiently similar to allow comparison and estimation of the efficacy of the gang suppression effort.

Two data sets were used to measure the anti-gang initiative's impact on crime. First, offenses reported to the police from June 1, 1995, through May 31, 1997, were obtained from the Crime Analysis Unit of the police department. Murder, rape, robbery, aggravated assault, burglary, auto theft, theft, arson, other assault, criminal mischief, drug offenses, and weapon offenses were analyzed. The last two offenses were measured by number of arrests rather than reported offenses. Second, data from the Gang Unit on all of the gang-related offenses reported to the police from June 1, 1995, through May 31, 1997, were collected. Several offenses were aggregated into the category of violent gang-related offenses.[6]

Because of the small sample size, gang-related property crimes were not analyzed. Final determination of whether an offense was gang related was made by Gang Unit detectives after a follow-up investigation based on police department criteria for gang-related crime.[7] Report formats clearly indicated that the offense was gang related by both a checked box and a narrative. Annual precomparisons and postcomparisons of crime in general and gang-related violence in particular were analyzed for each target and control area to determine the anti-gang initiative's impact on crime. For each comparison, a paired samples t test was computed to determine statistically significant differences between the mean values over two time periods. In instances in which statistically significant differences existed, efforts were made to determine the particular strategy employed during the time period (curfew enforcement, truancy enforcement, or saturation patrol).

Limitations

Determining the generalizability of any evaluation of a gang suppression strategy is at best difficult; at worst, it is impossible. One specific problem with gang intervention strategy evaluation is the fact that police, prosecutor, and legislative definitions of gangs, gang-related crime, and gang members differ widely (Caeti, Fritsch, and Hemmens 1995; Curry, Ball, and Decker 1996). A second problem occurs when there is wholesale adoption of any gang intervention strategy without looking carefully at evaluations of the strategy and its assumptions, especially suppression strategies. This practice is ill-advised and could in fact be destructive (Klein 1995). Therefore, results must be interpreted with caution and replicated across and within several jurisdictions before broad and definitive conclusions can be drawn about the overall usefulness of a particular strategy. The fact that definitions of gang-related crime vary makes this caution all the more salient.

Findings

Gang Violence

Table 1 compares the mean number of violent gang-related offenses in the five target areas per month with those in the four control areas. Overall, there was a statistically significant decrease (57 percent) in gang-related violence in the target areas during the grant period. Statistically significant decreases in gang violence were observed during the anti-gang initiative in the control areas as well, but the overall decrease was less substantial than in the target areas—37 percent in the control areas in comparison to 57 percent in the target areas.

Compared with the year prior to the anti-gang initiative (June 1, 1995, through May 31, 1996), there were statistically significant reductions in violent gang-related offenses in Target Areas 1, 4, and 5 during the grant period (June 1, 1996, through May 31, 1997). There was approximately a 73 percent reduction in violent gang-related activity in Target Areas 1 and 4 and a 64 percent reduction in Target Area 5. Little change in gang violence occurred in the control areas for these beats; indeed, Control Areas 4 and 5 experienced a 22 percent increase in gang violence during the grant year.

This increase in Control Areas 4 and 5 could be due to displacement of gang activity by the initiative. That is, increased police activity in a targeted area may have forced gang members into areas of the city with a lesser law enforcement

Table 1	Mean Number of Violent Gang-Related Offenses per Month by Area					
	Target Area			*Control Area*		
Area	*Time 1*	*Time 2*	*t Test*	*Time 1*	*Time 2*	*t Test*
Area 1	6.8	1.8	3.69*	2.9	2.6	0.46
Area 2	5.1	3.8	1.03	10.2	5.7	2.31*
Area 3	2.0	1.0	1.65	7.6	3.8	3.06*
Area 4	3.5	1.0	4.33*	1.9	2.3	−0.53
Area 5	3.5	1.3	3.04*	1.9	2.3	−0.53
All areas combined	20.9	8.9	7.21*	22.6	14.3	3.76*

NOTE: Time 1 = Year 1 (June 1995 through May 1996); Time 2 = Year 2 (June 1996 through May 1997).

$*p < .05.$

presence. Gang violence may have moved to another area instead of being eradicated. To investigate the possibility of displacement, the number of violent gang-related offenses for the 33 nontarget beats, contiguous to target beats, was determined and comparisons were examined. The sample size for each beat was small, which precluded the use of a paired samples *t* test; therefore, the raw frequencies were analyzed. Of the 33 beats contiguous to target beats, 15 experienced a decrease in gang violence during the grant period, whereas 10 experienced an increase and 8 experienced no change. Although the anti-gang initiative may have displaced some gang violence to other beats, the extent of displacement appears to have been minimal.

Further analysis was conducted to identify the strategies employed in Target Areas 1, 4, and 5 to determine which of them might be responsible for the significant decrease in gang violence. The strategies were obtained from weekly and monthly reports written by the sergeants responsible for a target area; they documented the overtime-funded enforcement strategies that were employed in the area during the study period. Of the strategies used in each area, the vast majority of overtime hours were spent on curfew enforcement in Target Area 1 (80 percent of overtime hours) and truancy enforcement in Target Areas

4 and 5 (89 percent of overtime hours). Therefore, concentrated efforts to enforce truancy and curfew laws had a positive impact on reducing gang violence.

In addition, there was also a 46 percent reduction in gang violence in Target Area 3 during the grant period and a 25 percent reduction in Target Area 2, but these reductions were not statistically significant. Differently, there were statistically significant decreases in gang violence in Control Areas 2 and 3, even though these areas did not receive overtime-funded enforcement strategies. There was a 44 percent reduction in violence in Control Area 2 and a 50 percent reduction in Control Area 3. However, these control areas may have received extra attention from the Gang Unit during on-duty hours. Because enforcement strategies in the five target areas were overtime funded, more on-duty time may have been spent in the control areas that did not have any overtime funds. Unfortunately, quantitative data to support this statement were unavailable.

It is important to recognize that the main strategies employed in Target Areas 2 and 3 differed from those in the other areas. Of the documented strategies in each area, the vast majority of overtime hours was spent on undirected saturation patrol. Officers in Target Areas 2 and 3 also employed other suppression strategies, such as truancy and curfew enforcement, but to a much lesser degree than did officers in Target Areas 1, 4, and 5. Therefore, saturation patrol to increase police presence alone was not effective in decreasing the level of gang violence in these areas.

Offenses Reported to the Police

Data were collected on index violent and property crimes reported to the police. In addition, data were obtained on other assaults, criminal mischief, drug offenses, and weapon offenses. The following two hypotheses were tested:

Hypothesis 1: Increased officer presence led to decreases in reported offenses, especially for suppressible crimes such as robbery, auto theft, burglary, and criminal mischief.

Hypothesis 2: Freedom from responding to calls for service led to greater officer-initiated activity, which resulted in more arrests for drug and weapon offenses.

Table 2 compares the mean number of offenses reported to the Dallas Police Department per month during the grant year with the number of offenses reported per month during the prior year. As shown in Table 2, there were statistically significant increases in reported robberies (23.8 percent increase) and auto thefts (15.4 percent increase) in the target areas during the grant period. In addition, there were statistically significant decreases in reports of criminal mischief (15 percent decrease) and arrests for weapons violations (30 percent decrease) in the target areas. The

Table 2	Mean Number of Offenses Reported to Dallas Police Department per Month					
	Target Area			Control Area		
Offense	Time 1	Time 2	t Test	Time 1	Time 2	t Test
Index violent						
Aggravated assault	92.3	90.4	0.30	65.6	74.9	−0.99
Murder	3.7	2.6	1.26	2.8	1.3	2.16
Rape	5.5	5.3	0.16	6.3	7.0	−0.60
Robbery	61.0	75.5	−2.42*	47.1	44.5	1.15
Index property						
Arson	2.3	2.3	0.00	3.4	3.6	−0.24
Auto theft	142.6	164.6	−2.66*	160.4	174.3	−1.34
Burglary	129.3	141.5	−1.76	154.1	168.5	−1.40
Theft	349.8	366.9	−1.69	348.6	388.2	−2.73*
Part II offenses						
Assault	181.6	239.3	−1.55	148.3	211.1	−1.81
Criminal mischief	181.9	154.7	2.56*	208.3	181.7	3.19*
Drug offense[a]	86.4	107.1	−1.84	53.1	57.5	−0.62
Weapon offense[a]	19.5	13.8	3.25*	10.7	10.3	0.21

NOTE: Time 1 = Year 1 (June 1995 through May 1996); Time 2 = Year 2 (June 1996 through May 1997).

a. Based on the number of arrests.

*$p < .05$.

statistically significant decrease in criminal mischief was also observed in the control areas during the grant period, despite the lack of overtime-funded enforcement strategies; thus, the decrease cannot be attributed to activities generated by the overtime funding in the target areas.

Neither of the two hypotheses was supported by the data. In fact, the direct opposite effect was noted in a few instances. For example, statistically significant increases in robbery and auto theft were observed in the target areas, perhaps because increased police presence encouraged the reporting of offenses due to the increased availability and presence of officers, but no data relevant to this explanation were available. Also, there was a statistically significant decrease, rather than the hypothesized increase, in arrests for weapons violations, which may be due to the deterrent effect of the increased presence of officers in these areas. Indeed, it is plausible that the strategies deterred gang members from visible criminal mischief and from carrying weapons once the word got out that the police were being more active. However, data were not available to support or refute this explanation.

⊠ Discussion and Conclusion

This study found that, consistent with previous research, undirected saturation patrol has little effect on reducing crime (Sherman 1990b). In short, simply adding more police officers, without direction, was not effective. Unfortunately, this conclusion has been overgeneralized to mean that policing and patrol does not work. Fortunately, other research has shown that directed patrol (whether directed toward offenders, places, victims, or offenses) was effective in varying degrees (Abrahamse, Ebener, Greenwood, Fitzgerald, and Kosin 1991; S. E. Martin 1986; S. E. Martin and Sherman 1986; Sherman, 1990a, 1990b, 1992; Sherman et al. 1995). The research reported in this article provides support for the latter statement because the aggressive enforcement of truancy and curfew laws was effective in reducing gang-related violence in target areas. This finding needs replication, particularly in a true experimental design.

Enforcement of curfew and truancy is frequently a low-priority task of officers, but it can have an impact on gang violence and may potentially have an even greater impact on juvenile victimization. For example, the number of homicides in Dallas (citywide) that involved a juvenile victim (excluding child abuse deaths) dropped from 18 during the year prior to the anti-gang initiative to 7 during the initiative. Furthermore, the number of gang-related juvenile homicide victims dropped from 6 during the first time period to 2 during the second (Caeti 1997).

We also found little effect on the number of offenses reported to the police. Increased officer presence did not lead to a decrease in offenses reported to the police. Sherman (1990b, 1992) reported that both increases and decreases in calls for service have been noted as the result of a crackdown. Thus, the validity of using calls for service as a measure of effectiveness must be questioned. In addition, freeing officers from responding to calls for service did not lead to greater officer-initiated activity, such as drug and weapons arrests. The question "What do officers do with their time?" needs greater empirical attention. Furthermore, suppressible crime was not affected greatly by the initiative overall. Perhaps this was because the enforcement activities that relied on curfew and truancy enforcement only had appreciable effects on the crimes that juvenile offenders commit. Indeed, criminal mischief and weapons offenses decreased dramatically in the targeted areas. Individuals who commit robberies and other serious felonies may be unaffected by curfew or truancy enforcement because they may be adults and/or not in the school system.

Many police scholars have concluded that traditional police activities and goals (preventive patrol, rapid response, investigations, etc.) have failed to achieve crime reduction and have increased problems of police-citizen alienation

(Kelling 1978). However, more recently, Kelling (1996), in discussing how to define the bottom line in policing, noted the following:

> A basic purpose of police is crime prevention. The idea that police cannot do anything about crime and that they stand helpless in the face of demographics, drugs, gangs, or whatever is unacceptable—often . . . a "cop-out" that covers lack of strategic commitment and absence of planning and implementation. (P. 31)

Police gang suppression activity may not affect gang membership or the conditions that create gangs. However, it is possible that those activities affect the nefarious effects of gangs—crime and violence.

Would we really care if kids joined gangs if gangs did not engage in criminal activity? Probably not; in fact, some positive gang values (group cohesiveness, loyalty, respect, discipline, etc.) are encouraged to a large extent in legitimate activities, such as youth sports, clubs, and various other groups. In any case, the gang suppression activities of law enforcement probably cannot and perhaps should not be concerned with the "whys" of gangs. As Spergel (1995) noted,

> The police cannot be held responsible for basic failures of youth socialization; lack of social and economic achievement by families, deficiencies of schools, decreased employment opportunities for African-American youth, the extensive street presence and accessibility of sophisticated weaponry, and the extensive racism and social isolation that appear to be highly correlated with the gang problem in some low-income minority communities. (P. 191)

The police should, however, concern themselves with a narrower mission of developing effective strategies to address the crime problems that gangs create. The idea that the police can change the underlying socioeconomic conditions that give rise to gangs or to the infinite reasons why kids join gangs is naive and unrealistic. This is not to say that other community agencies should not focus on such endeavors. The simple fact of the matter is that the police are designed, organized, staffed, and trained to deal with crime, not social services.

Although strategies that use offender-, place-, and crime-specific techniques are in their infancy and require greater empirical attention, much of the recent literature that has evaluated such strategies is promising (Sherman 1990b, 1992). For example, when overtime-funded officers were freed from calls for service in Houston, substantial reductions in suppressible crimes soon followed (Hoover and Caeti 1994). The philosophy is that police agencies can impact the level of crime and disorder in a community. The police *do* make a difference. Saying that crime and disorder are a product of social and economic forces the police cannot and should not affect is rejected (Hoover and Caeti 1994, p. 1).

The police should coordinate with other public agencies in their efforts to deal with gangs; and these efforts should be focused on the criminal problems that gangs create. Interagency cooperation and information-sharing models provide promise as well, especially the ability to successfully prosecute serious and habitual offenders (Owens and Wells 1993). Recent technological advances in the areas of computer mapping, object-oriented databases, management information systems, and offender identification and tracking all bode well for the ability of the police to increase their effectiveness in managing crime, particularly gang crime. More empirical evaluation research is needed concerning which law enforcement strategies can lead to reductions in gang violence and victimization through gang violence.

⊠ Notes

1. Dallas has a nocturnal curfew ordinance that requires individuals (not accompanied by their parent or guardian) younger than age 17 to be in their residence between the hours of 11 P.M. and 6 A.M. on weeknights (Sunday through Thursday) and between

the hours of 12 A.M. and 6 A.M. on weekends (Friday and Saturday).

2. The State of Texas truancy law requires juveniles between the ages of 7 and 16 to be enrolled in and attending school. Enforcement activity was conducted between the hours of 10 A.M. and 3 P.M. weekdays, concentrating on the gang-ridden target areas.

3. The Office of Juvenile Justice and Delinquency Prevention (OJJDP) has developed a comprehensive gang suppression and intervention strategy based on community models (Spergel, Curry, Chance, Kane, Ross, Alexander, Simmons, and Oh 1994). The Bureau of Justice Assistance (BJA) (1997) has also published a monograph on *Urban Street Gang Enforcement,* which is a comprehensive overview of the various tactics employed by all agencies that come into contact with gangs. These works are very extensive, yet they are completely prescriptive—there is little mention or review of any empirical studies that evaluate the police role in dealing with gangs.

4. The target areas were composed of the following patrol beats: Target Area 1—Beats 513, 514, and 515; Target Area 2—Beats 412, 413, 414, 415, 416, 417, and 419; Target Area 3—Beats 311, 312, 314, and 316; Target Area 4—Beats 112, 113, 115, 154, and 156; and Target Area 5—Beats 141, 143, 144, 145, 146, and 152.

5. The following beats comprise the control areas, which did not receive the overtime-funded enforcement strategies under the anti-gang initiative: Control Area 1—Beats 552, 553, and 555;. Control Area 2—Beats 423, 425, 426, 427, 445, 448, and 456; Control Area 3—Beats 325, 326, 327, and 328; Control Areas 4 and 5—Beats 114, 116, 131, 134, and 135. Because Target Areas 4 and 5 were in the same patrol division, the same control area was used for both.

6. Capital murder ($n = 2$); murder ($n = 19$); attempted murder ($n = 5$); aggravated assault ($n = 415$); misdemeanor assault ($n = 167$); sexual assault ($n = 1$); deadly conduct ($n = 64$); aggravated robbery ($n = 56$); robbery ($n = 46$); injury to a child ($n = 5$); terrorist threats ($n = 16$); retaliation ($n = 4$); and cruelty to animals ($n = 1$).

7. According to Dallas Police Department policy, an incident should be considered gang-related activity when participants, acting individually or collectively, are known to be gang members or gang associates and the criminal activity engaged in is aggravated assault, assault, robbery, homicide, possession for sale of narcotics, shooting at house and/or car, arson, retaliation/witness tampering, auto theft, criminal mischief (graffiti), sexual assault, kidnapping, or burglary.

Officers may also consider an incident as street gang activity when (1) the participants are identified as gang members or associates who are acting individually or collectively to further any criminal purpose of the gang; (2) a reliable informant identifies an incident as gang activity or a participant as a gang member, (3) an informant of previously untested reliability identifies an incident as a gang activity and it is corroborated by other existing circumstances or independent information; (4) there are strong indications that an incident is gang related, such as the nature of the offense (i.e., drive-by shooting) or the fact that the participants were wearing/using common identifying signs, symbols, or colors; or (5) gang members or associates are identified through existing police gang intelligence files.

✉ References

Abrahamse, Allan F., Patricia A. Ebener, Peter W. Greenwood, Nora Fitzgerald, and Thomas E. Kosin. 1991. "An Experimental Evaluation of the Phoenix Repeat Offender Program." *Justice Quarterly* 8:141–72.

Bureau of Justice Assistance. 1997. *Urban Street Gang Enforcement.* Washington, DC: National Institute of Justice.

Caeti, Tory J. 1997. "Who's Killing Our Kids? An Analysis of Juvenile Homicide Victims in Dallas 1993–1997." Research Initiation Grant Project, University of North Texas, Denton.

Caeti, Tory J., Eric J. Fritsch, and Craig Hemmens. 1995. "Bangin' in the Legislature: A Comparison of State Statutory Responses to Gangs." Presented at the annual meeting of the American Society of Criminology, Boston.

Click, Benjamin R. 1994. "Statistics in Dallas Encouraging." *Police Chief* 61 (12):33–6.

Curry, G. David, Richard A. Ball, and Scott H. Decker. 1996. "Estimating the National Scope of Gang Crime From Law Enforcement Data." *National Institute of Justice: Research in Brief.*

Dart, Robert W. 1992. "Chicago's 'Flying Squad' Tackles Street Gangs." *Police Chief* 59:96–8.

Freed, David. 1986. "Policing Gangs: Case of Contrasting Styles." Pp. 288–91 in *The Modern Gang Reader,* edited by M. W. Klein, C. L. Maxson, and J. Miller. Los Angeles: Roxbury.

Friend, Charles E. 1994. "Juvenile Curfew." *Policy Review* 6:1–4.

Garrett, Dennis A. and David Brewster. 1994. "Curfew: A New Look at an Old Tool." *Police Chief* (December):29–61.

Garry, Eileen M. 1996. "Truancy: First Step to a Lifetime of Problems." *Juvenile Justice Bulletin* (October).

Hoover, Larry T. and Tory J. Caeti. 1994, "Crime-Specific Policing in Houston." *Texas Law Enforcement Management and Administrative Statistics Program Bulletin* 1 (9).

Houston, James. 1996. "What Works: The Search for Excellence in Gang Intervention Programs." *Journal of Gang Research* 3:1–16.

Howell, James C. 1996. *Youth Gang Violence Prevention and Intervention: What Works.* Washington, DC: National Institute of Justice.

Huff, C. Ronald and Wesley D. McBride. 1993. "Gangs and the Police." Pp. 401–16 in *The Gang Intervention Handbook,* edited by A. P. Goldstein and C. R. Huff. Champaign, IL: Research Press.

Hunt, A. Lee and Ken Weiner. 1977. "The Impact of a Juvenile Curfew: Suppression and Displacement in Patterns of Juvenile Offenses." *Journal of Police Science and Administration* 5:407–12.

Jackson, Robert K. and Wesley D. McBride. 1996. *Understanding Street Gangs.* Incline Village, NV: Copperhouse.

Johnson, Claire M., Barbara A. Webster, Edward F. Connors, and Diana J. Saenz. 1995. "Gang Enforcement Problems and Strategies: National Survey Findings." *Journal of Gang Research* 3:1–18.

"Juvenile Curfews and Gang Violence: Exiled on Main Street." 1994. *Harvard Law Review* 107 (7):1693–710.

Kelling, George L. 1978. "Police Field Services and Crime: The Presumed Effects of a Capacity." *Crime & Delinquency* 24:173–84.

———. 1996. "Defining the Bottom Line in Policing: Organizational Philosophy and Accountability." Pp. 23–36 in *Quantifying Quality in Policing,* edited by L. T. Hoover. Washington, DC: Police Executive Research Forum.

Kent, Douglas R. and Peggy Smith. 1994. "The Tri-Agency Resource Gang Enforcement Team: A Selective Approach to Reduce Gang Crime." Pp. 292–96 in *The Modern Gang Reader,* edited by M. W. Klein, C. L. Maxson, and J. Miller. Los Angeles: Roxbury.

Klein, Malcolm W. 1993. "Attempting Gang Control by Suppression: The Misuse of Deterrence Principles." Pp. 304–13 in *The Modern Gang Reader,* edited by M. W. Klein, C. L. Maxson, and J. Miller. Los Angeles: Roxbury.

———. 1995. *The American Street Gang: Its Nature, Prevalence, and Control.* New York: Oxford University Press.

Knox, George W. 1994. *An Introduction to Gangs.* Bristol, IN: Wyndham Hall.

LeBoeuf, Donni. 1996. *Curfew: An Answer to Juvenile Delinquency and Victimization?* Washington, DC: Office of Juvenile Justice and Delinquency Prevention.

Martin, Joe R., Arnie D. Schulze, and Mike Valdez. 1988. "Taking Aim at Truancy." *FBI Law Enforcement Bulletin* 51:8–12.

Martin, Susan E. 1986. "Policing Career Criminals: An Examination of an Innovative Crime Control Program." *Journal of Criminal Law and Criminology* 77:1159–82.

Martin, Susan E. and Lawrence W. Sherman. 1986. "Catching Career Criminals: Proactive Policing and Selective Apprehension." *Justice Quarterly* 3:171–92.

Needle, Jerome A. and W. V. Stapleton. 1983. *Police Handling of Youth Gangs.* Washington, DC: American Justice Institute, National Juvenile Justice System Assessment Center.

Owens, Robert P. and Donna K. Wells. 1993. "One City's Response to Gangs." *Police Chief* 58:25–7.

Palumbo, Dennis J., R. Eskay, and Michael A. Hallett. 1992. *Do Gang Prevention Strategies Actually Reduce Grime?* Washington, DC: National Institute of Justice.

Rohrman, Doug. 1993. *Combating Truancy in Our Schools: A Community Effort.* Washington, DC: National Institute of Justice.

Ruefle, William and Kenneth Mike Reynolds. 1995. "Curfews and Delinquency in Major American Cities." *Crime & Delinquency* 41:347–63.

Rush, Jeffrey P. 1996. "The Police Role in Dealing With Gangs." Pp. 85–92 in *Gangs: A Criminal Justice Approach,* edited by J. M. Miller and J. P. Rush. Cincinnati, OH: Anderson.

Shelden, Randall G., Sharon K. Tracy, and William B. Brown. 1997. *Youth Gangs in American Society.* Belmont, CA: Wadsworth.

Sherman, Lawrence W. 1990a. "Police Crackdowns." *National Institute of Justice Reports* (March/April).

———. 1990b. "Police Crackdowns: Initial and Residual Deterrence." *Crime and Justice: A Review of Research* 12:1–48.

———. 1992. "Attacking Crime: Police and Crime Control." Pp. 159–230 in *Crime and Justice: A Review of Research,* vol. 14, edited by M. Tonry and N. Morris. Chicago: University of Chicago Press.

Sherman, Lawrence W., James W. Shaw, and Dennis P. Rogan. 1995. "The Kansas City Gun Experiment." *National Institute of Justice: Research in Brief.*

Spergel, Irving A. 1995. *The Youth Gang Problem.* New York: Oxford University Press.

Spergel, Irving A. and G. David Curry. 1990. "Strategies and Perceived Agency Effectiveness in Dealing With the Youth Gang Problem." Pp. 288–309 in *Gangs in America,* edited by C. R. Huff. Newbury Park, CA: Sage.

Spergel, Irving A., David Curry, Ron Chance, Candice Kane, Ruth Ross, Alba Alexander, Edwina Simmons, and Sandra Oh. 1994. *Gang Suppression and Intervention: Problem and Response.* Washington, DC: Office of Juvenile Justice and Delinquency Prevention.

Thurman, Quint C. Andrew L. Giacomazzi, Michael D. Reisig, and David G. Mueller. 1996. "Community-Based Gang Prevention and Intervention: An Evaluation of the Neutral Zone." *Crime & Delinquency* 42:279–95.

Watzman, Nancy. 1994. "Curfew Revival Gains Momentum." *Governing* 7:20–1.

Weisel, Deborah L. and Ellen Painter. 1997. *The Police Response to Gangs: Case Studies of Five Cities.* Washington, DC: Police Executive Research Forum.

Weston, Jim. 1993. "Community Policing: An Approach to Youth Gangs in a Medium-Sized City." *Police Chief 60* (August):80–4.

Wilson, James Q. and George L. Kelling. 1989. "Making Neighborhoods Safe." *Atlantic Monthly* (February):46–52.

DISCUSSION QUESTIONS

1. According to the authors, what are "police suppression tactics"? Give examples of how these tactics might be applied in cities.

2. Based on the research evidence, do police suppression tactics work, or are the results mixed? Explain.

3. Was there a reduction in gang violence in the Dallas study? What about offenses reported to police? Could this work in your city?

4. What do the authors conclude that police can and should do about gang activities?

❖

READING

Adult homicide rates in the United States declined in the 1980s and 1990s, but youth homicide rates have increased dramatically. Homicides committed by juvenile offenders with handguns accounted for more than 100% increases from the mid-1980s to mid-1990s. Police departments throughout the United States turned to "community-" and "problem-oriented" policing to deal with this increase in violent crimes by juvenile offenders. This article describes the results of a National Institute of Justice-funded evaluation of Boston's youth homicide reduction initiative. Operation Ceasefire was a problem-oriented policing intervention aimed at reducing youth homicide and youth firearms violence in Boston. It represented an innovative partnership between researchers and practitioners to assess the city's youth homicide problem and implement an intervention designed to have a substantial near-term impact on the problem. Operation Ceasefire was based on the "pulling levers" deterrence strategy that focused criminal justice attention on a small number of chronically offending gang-involved youth responsible for much of Boston's youth homicide problem. The evaluation suggests that the Ceasefire intervention was associated with significant reductions in youth homicide victimization, shots-fired calls for service, and gun assault incidents in Boston. A comparative analysis of youth homicide trends in Boston relative to youth homicide trends in other major U.S. and New England cities also supports a unique program effect associated with the Ceasefire intervention.

Problem-Oriented Policing, Deterrence, and Youth Violence

An Evaluation of Boston's Operation Ceasefire (2001)

Anthony A. Braga, David M. Kennedy, Elin J. Waring, Anne Morrison Piehl

Operation Ceasefire is a problem-oriented policing intervention aimed at reducing youth homicide and youth firearms violence in Boston. It represented an innovative partnership between researchers and practitioners to assess the city's youth homicide problem and implement an intervention designed to have a substantial near-term impact on the problem. Operation Ceasefire was based on the "pulling levers" deterrence strategy that focused criminal justice attention on a small number of chronically offending gang-involved youth responsible for much of Boston's youth homicide problem. Our impact evaluation suggests that the Ceasefire intervention was associated with significant reductions in youth homicide victimization, shots-fired calls for service, and gun assault incidents in Boston. A comparative analysis of youth homicide trends in Boston relative to youth homicide trends in other major U.S. and New England cities also supports a unique program effect associated with the Ceasefire intervention.

Although overall homicide rates in the United States declined between the 1980s and 1990s, youth homicide rates, particularly incidents involving firearms, increased dramatically. Between 1984 and 1994, juvenile (younger than 18) homicide victimizations committed with handguns increased by 418 percent, and juvenile homicide victimizations committed with other guns increased 125 percent (Fox 1996). During this time period, adolescents (ages 14 to 17) as a group had the largest proportional increase in homicide commission and victimization, but young adults (ages 18 to 24) had the largest absolute increase in numbers, and there was a good deal of crossfire between the two age groups (Cook and Laub 1998). All of the increase in youth homicide was in gun homicides (Cook and Laub 1998). For many cities, the bulk of this dramatic increase in youth homicide occurred in the late 1980s and early 1990s. In Boston, youth homicide (ages 24 and younger) increased more than threefold—from 22 victims in 1987 to 73 victims in 1990. Youth homicide remained high even after the peak of the epidemic; Boston averaged about 44 youth homicides per year between 1991 and 1995.

At the same time that the United States was experiencing this sudden increase in youth violence, the capacity of police departments to design and implement creative new operational strategies also increased through the advent of "community" and "problem-oriented" policing (Goldstein 1990; Sparrow, Moore, and Kennedy 1990). In Boston, an interagency problem-solving intervention, based in part on a tight link

SOURCE: *Journal of Research in Crime and Delinquency, (38)3*, 195–225, August 2001. © 2001 Sage Publications, Inc.

between research, the design of interventions, and operations, has shown much promise in reducing youth homicide (Kennedy, Braga, and Piehl 1997; Kennedy, Piehl, and Braga 1996). Nationally, without the support of a formal evaluation, the Boston program has been hailed as an unprecedented success (see, e.g., Butterfield 1996; Witkin 1997). This article describes the results of a National Institute of Justice-funded evaluation of Boston's youth homicide reduction initiative. Our analyses of Boston's youth homicide prevention program suggests that it was a very effective intervention; not only was the intervention associated with a significant reduction in youth homicide victimization, it also was associated with significant reductions in shots-fired calls for service and gun assault incidents.

⊠ The Boston Gun Project and the Operation Ceasefire Intervention

Problem-oriented policing holds great promise for creating a strong local response to youth homicide problems. Problem-oriented policing works to identify why things are going wrong and to frame responses using a wide variety of often untraditional approaches (Goldstein 1979). Using a basic iterative approach of problem identification, analysis, response, evaluation, and adjustment of the response, problem-oriented policing has been effective against a wide variety of crime, fear, and order concerns (Braga, Weisburd et al. 1999; Eck and Spelman 1987; Goldstein 1990). This adaptable and dynamic analytic approach provides an appropriate framework to uncover the complex mechanisms at play in youth homicide and develop tailor-made interventions to reduce youth homicide victimization.

The Boston Gun Project is a problem-oriented policing initiative aimed at reducing homicide victimization among young people in Boston. *Youth* was initially defined as "age 21 and under" and, as the project developed, "age 24 and

under."[1] Sponsored by the National Institute of Justice, the project was designed to proceed by (1) assembling an interagency working group of largely line-level criminal justice and other practitioners; (2) applying quantitative and qualitative research techniques to create an assessment of the nature of, and dynamics driving, youth violence in Boston; (3) developing an intervention designed to have a substantial, near-term impact on youth homicide; (4) implementing and adapting the intervention; and (5) evaluating the intervention's impact. The project began in early 1995 and implemented what is now known as the Operation Ceasefire intervention beginning in the late spring of 1996.

Core participating agencies, as defined by regular participation in the Boston Gun Project Working Group over the duration of the project, included the Boston Police Department; the Massachusetts departments of probation and parole; the office of the Suffolk County District Attorney; the office of the U.S. Attorney; the Bureau of Alcohol, Tobacco, and Firearms; the Massachusetts Department of Youth Services (juvenile corrections); Boston School Police; and gang outreach and prevention "streetworkers" attached to the Boston Community Centers program. Other important participants, either as regular partners later in the process or episodically, have included the Ten Point Coalition of activist Black clergy, the Drug Enforcement Administration, the Massachusetts State Police, and the office of the Massachusetts Attorney General.

Project research showed that firearms associated with youth, especially with gang youth, tended to be semiautomatic pistols, often ones that were quite new and apparently recently diverted from retail (Kennedy et al. 1996; Kennedy et al. 1997). Many of these guns were first sold at retail in Massachusetts, and others were smuggled in from out of state. Project research also showed that the problem of youth homicide was concentrated among a small number of chronically offending gang-involved youth.[2] Only about 1,300 gang members—less that 1 percent of their age group citywide—in about 61 gangs were responsible for at least 60 percent of all youth homicides in the city. These gangs were well known to the authorities and streetworkers; gang members were also often well known and tended to have extensive criminal records (Kennedy et al. 1996). Chronic disputes, or "beefs," among gangs appeared to be the most significant driver of gang violence (Braga, Piehl, and Kennedy 1999).

The research findings were discussed and analyzed within the working-group problem-solving process and were instrumental in the development of an operational strategy. The research findings and the working-group process thus led to the Operation Ceasefire intervention (for a complete discussion of the program development and implementation process, see Kennedy, Braga, and Piehl 1999). Operation Ceasefire included two main elements: (1) a direct law-enforcement attack on illicit firearms traffickers supplying youth with guns and (2) an attempt to generate a strong deterrent to gang violence. The working group framed a set of activities intended to systematically address the patterns of firearms trafficking identified by the research. These included the following:

- Expanding the focus of local, state, and federal authorities to include *intrastate* trafficking in Massachusetts-sourced guns, in addition to interstate trafficking.
- Focusing enforcement attention on traffickers of those makes and calibers of guns most used by gang members.
- Focusing enforcement attention on traffickers of those guns showing short time to crime and thus most likely to have been trafficked. The Boston Field Division of ATF set up an in-house tracking system that flagged guns whose traces showed an 18-month or shorter time to crime.
- Focusing enforcement attention on traffickers of guns used by the city's most violent gangs.

- Attempting restoration of obliterated serial numbers and subsequent trafficking investigations based on those restorations.
- Supporting these enforcement priorities through analysis of crime gun traces generated by the Boston Police Department's comprehensive tracing of crime guns and by developing leads through systematic debriefing of, especially, arrestees involved with gangs and/or involved in violent crime.

The "pulling levers" strategy, as the second element came to be known by working-group members, involved deterring violent behavior by chronic gang offenders by reaching out directly to gangs, saying explicitly that violence would no longer be tolerated, and backing that message by "pulling every lever" legally available when violence occurred (Kennedy 1997, 1998). Simultaneously, streetworkers, probation and parole officers, and later churches and other community groups offered gang members services and other kinds of help. The Ceasefire working group delivered this message in formal meetings with gang members, through individual police and probation contacts with gang members, through meetings with inmates of secure juvenile facilities in the city, and through gang outreach workers. The deterrence message was not a deal with gang members to stop violence. Rather, it was a promise to gang members that violent behavior would evoke an immediate and intense response. If gangs committed other crimes but refrained from violence, the normal workings of police, prosecutors, and the rest of the criminal justice system dealt with these matters. But if gang members hurt people, the working group focused its enforcement actions on them.

When gang violence occurred, the Ceasefire agencies addressed the violent group or groups involved, drawing from a menu of all possible legal levers. The chronic involvement of gang members in a wide variety of offenses made them, and the gangs they formed, vulnerable to a coordinated criminal justice response. The authorities could disrupt street drug activity, focus police attention on low-level street crimes such as trespassing and public drinking, serve outstanding warrants, cultivate confidential informants for medium- and long-term investigations of gang activities, deliver strict probation and parole enforcement, seize drug proceeds and other assets, ensure stiffer plea bargains and sterner prosecutorial attention, request stronger bail terms (and enforce them), and focus potentially severe federal investigative and prosecutorial attention on, for example, gang-related drug activity. The multitude of agencies involved in the working group assessed each gang that behaved violently and subjected them to such crackdowns. These operations were customized to the particular individuals and characteristics of the gang in question and could range from probation curfew checks to DEA investigations.[3]

The Ceasefire crackdowns were not designed to eliminate gangs or stop every aspect of gang activity but to control and deter serious violence. To do this, the working group explained its actions against targeted gangs to other gangs, as in "this gang did violence, we responded with the following actions, and here is how to prevent anything similar from happening to you." The ongoing working-group process regularly watched the city for outbreaks of gang violence and framed any necessary responses in accord with the Ceasefire strategy. As the strategy unfolded, the working group continued communication with gangs and gang members to convey its determination to stop violence, explain its actions to the target population, and maximize both voluntary compliance and the strategy's deterrent power.

A central hypothesis within the working group was the idea that a meaningful period of substantially reduced youth violence might serve as a "firebreak" and result in a relatively long-lasting reduction in future youth violence (Kennedy et al. 1996). The idea was that youth violence in Boston had become a self-sustaining cycle among a relatively small number of youth, with objectively high levels of risk leading to

nominally self-protective behavior such as gun acquisition and use, gang formation, tough street behavior, and the like: behavior that then became an additional input into the cycle of violence (Kennedy et al. 1996). If this cycle could be interrupted, a new equilibrium at a lower level of risk and violence might be established, perhaps without the need for continued high levels of either deterrent or facilitative intervention.

⊠ Deterrence and Crime Prevention

The Operation Ceasefire intervention is, in its broadest sense, a deterrence strategy. Deterrence theory posits that crimes can be prevented when the costs of committing the crime are perceived by the offender to outweigh the benefits of committing the crime (Gibbs 1975; Zimring and Hawkins 1973). Most discussions of the deterrence mechanism distinguish between "general" and "special" deterrence (Cook 1980). General deterrence is the idea that the general population is dissuaded from committing crime when it sees that punishment necessarily follows the commission of a crime. Special deterrence involves punishment administered to criminals with the intent to discourage them from committing crimes in the future. Much of the literature evaluating deterrence focuses on the effect of changing certainty, swiftness, and severity of punishment associated with certain acts on the prevalence of those crimes (Blumstein, Cohen, and Nagin 1978; Cameron 1988; Cook 1977, 1980; Paternoster 1987; Sherman 1990; Sherman and Berk 1984; Weisburd, Waring, and Chayet 1995). In addition to any increases in certainty, severity, and swiftness of sanctions associated with youth violence, the Operation Ceasefire strategy sought to gain deterrence through the advertising of the law enforcement strategy and the personalized nature of its application. It was crucial that gang youth understood the new regime that the city was imposing.

The pulling-levers approach attempted to prevent gang violence by making gang members

believe that consequences would follow on violence and gun use and choose to change their
behavior. A key element of the strategy was the
delivery of a direct and explicit "retail deterrence"
message to a relatively small target audience
regarding what kind of behavior would provoke a
special response and what that response would
be. Law enforcement agencies in Boston increased
the cost of gang-related violence. The deterrence
principles applied in the Operation Ceasefire intervention could be regarded as a "meso-deterrence"
strategy. Beyond the particular gangs subjected to
the intervention, the deterrence message was
applied to a relatively small audience (all gang-
involved youth in Boston) rather than a general
audience (all youth in Boston) and operated by
making explicit cause-and-effect connections
between the behavior of the target population
and the behavior of the authorities. Knowledge of
what happened to others in the target population
was intended to prevent further acts of violence
by gangs in Boston.

The effective operation of general deterrence
is dependent on the communication of punishment threats to the public. As Zimring and
Hawkins (1973) observe, "the deterrence threat
may best be viewed as a form of advertising"
(p. 142). One noteworthy example of this principle is an evaluation of Massachusetts' 1975
Bartley-Fox amendment, which introduced a
mandatory minimum one-year prison sentence
for the illegal carrying of firearms. The high
degree of publicity attendant on the amendment's passage, some of which was inaccurate,
was found to increase citizen compliance with
existing legal stipulations surrounding firearm
acquisition and possession, some of which were
not in fact addressed by the amendment (see
Beha 1977). Zimring and Hawkins further
observe that "if the first task of the threatening
agency is the communication of information, its
second task is persuasion" (p. 149). In his article
on the misapplication of deterrence principles in
gang suppression programs, Malcolm Klein
(1993) suggests that law enforcement agencies do
not generally have the capacity to "eliminate" all
gangs in a gang-troubled jurisdiction, nor do

they have the capacity to respond in a powerful
way to all gang-offending in such jurisdictions.
Pledges to do so, though common, are simply not
credible. The Operation Ceasefire working group
recognized that, for the strategy to be successful, it
was crucial to deliver a credible deterrence message to Boston gangs. Therefore, the Ceasefire
intervention targeted those gangs that were
engaged in violent behavior rather than expend-
ing resources on those who were not.

⊠ Impact Evaluation

Like most evaluations of crime prevention
programs (Ekblom and Pease 1995), our evaluation design departs from the desirable randomized
controlled experimental approach. The Operation
Ceasefire strategy was aimed at all areas of the city
with a serious youth violence problem. There were
no control areas (or control gangs) set aside within
the city because of the following: (1) The aim was
to do something about serious youth violence
wherever it presented itself in the city, (2) the target of the intervention was defined as the self-
sustaining cycle of violence in which all gangs were
caught up and to which all gangs contributed, and
(3) the communications strategy was explicitly
intended to affect the behavior of gangs and individuals not directly subjected to enforcement
attention (Kennedy et al. 1996). Therefore, it was
not possible to compare areas and groups affected
by the strategy to similar areas and groups not
affected. Our analysis of impacts within Boston
associated with the Ceasefire intervention follows a
basic one-group time-series design (Campbell and
Stanley 1966; Cook and Campbell 1979); we also
use a nonrandomized quasi-experiment to compare youth homicide trends in Boston to youth
homicide trends in other large U.S. cities (Cook
and Campbell 1979; Rossi and Freeman 1993).

Within-Boston Outcome Measures:
Homicide and Gun Violence

The key outcome variable in our assessment
of the impact of the Ceasefire intervention was

the monthly number of homicide victims ages 24 and younger. The Ceasefire intervention mostly targets violence arising from gang dynamics; our earlier research suggests that most gang members in Boston are ages 24 and younger (Kennedy et al. 1996; Kennedy et al. 1997). Therefore, our impact evaluation focuses on the number of youthful homicide victims in this age group. The homicide data used in these analyses were provided by the Boston Police Department's Office of Research and Analysis. The youth homicide impact evaluation examined the monthly counts of youth homicides in Boston between January 1, 1991, and May 31, 1998; the preintervention period included the relatively stable but still historically high postepidemic years of 1991 to 1995 (see Figure 1).

Beyond preventing youth homicides, the Ceasefire intervention was also designed to reduce other forms of nonfatal serious violence. As such, our evaluation also examines monthly counts of citywide shots-fired citizen calls for service data and citywide official gun assault incident report data. These data are available for a slightly shorter time period than our homicide data set due to lags in the Boston Police Department's data collection and preparation procedures. These data are examined for the January 1, 1991, through December 31, 1997, time period. The computerized Boston Police Department incident data have what is, for our purposes, an important shortcoming—the records do not capture the age of the victim (this is, of course, also true for shots-fired calls for service). To assess the effects of the intervention on gun assaults in specific age groups, we collected information on the age of the victim from hard copies of gun assault incident reports for the study time period. Because the collection and coding of this information was a time-consuming task, we chose to collect these data for one high-activity police district. District B-2 covers most of Boston's Roxbury neighborhood and has a very dense concentration of gangs; 29 of 61 identified gangs (47.5 percent) had turf in B-2 (Kennedy et al. 1997). Furthermore, there were 217 homicide victims ages 24 and younger in Boston between

1991 and 1995; a third of these victims were killed in B-2 (71 of 217, 32.7 percent).

Simple Pre/Post Comparisons

In these analyses, we selected May 15, 1996, the date of the first direct communications with Boston gangs, as the date Ceasefire was implemented because all elements of the strategy—the focus on gun trafficking, a special interagency response to gang violence, and the communications campaign with gangs—were in place as of that date. No other rival programs were implemented in Boston even roughly close to this time period (Piehl, Kennedy, and Braga 2000). The well-known large reduction in yearly Boston youth homicide numbers certainly suggests that something noteworthy happened after Operation Ceasefire was implemented in mid-1996. As discussed earlier, Boston averaged 44 youth homicides per year between 1991 and 1995. In 1996, the number of Boston youth homicides decreased to 26 and then further decreased to 15 youth homicides in 1997. It is noteworthy that the yearly total of youth homicides in 1997—the first full calendar year of data after the implementation of Operation Ceasefire—represents the smallest number of youth homicides in Boston since 1976. This suggests that it was unlikely that the youth homicide reduction was due to a regression to the mean number of yearly youth homicides of the pre-youth homicide epidemic years. This suggests that Operation Ceasefire was associated with a large reduction in youth homicides in Boston (see also Piehl et al. 2000).

Table 1 presents the results of the Poisson regressions controlling for trend and seasonal effects. The Ceasefire intervention was associated with a statistically significant decrease in the monthly number of youth homicides; according to the incidence rate ratio, the Ceasefire intervention was associated with a 63 percent decrease in the monthly number of youth homicides. The Ceasefire intervention was also associated with statistically significant decreases in the monthly numbers of citywide gun assault incidents, citywide shots-fired calls for service, and youth gun assault incidents in district B-2. According to the incidence rate ratios, the Ceasefire intervention was also associated with a 25 percent decrease in the monthly number of citywide gun assault incidents, a 32 percent decrease in the monthly number of citywide shots-fired calls for service, and a 44 percent decrease in the monthly number of youth gun assaults in district B-2. The likelihood ratio test result was also significant, confirming that the intervention variables significantly improved the fit of the models to the data. The deviance divided by degrees of freedom results were only slightly higher than 1.0; this suggests that the Poisson distribution was appropriate for the youth homicide, city gun assault incidents, and B-2 youth gun assault incidents models (see SAS Institute 1997:285). The results for the shots-fired calls for service model, however, suggested that these data were over dispersed. The significant reduction in shots-fired calls for service associated with the Ceasefire intervention remained after the model was run with a correction for overdispersion.

The youth homicide and gun violence reductions associated with the Ceasefire intervention could have been caused or meaningfully influenced by other causal factors (see Piehl et al. 2000). We therefore controlled for changes in Boston's employment rate as measured by the Massachusetts Department of Employment and Training, changes in Boston's youth population ages 5 to 24 as measured by the U.S. Bureau of the Census, changes in citywide trends in violence as measured by the robbery data reported in the Federal Bureau of Investigation Uniform Crime Reports, changes in homicide victimization among older victims (ages 25 and older), and changes in youth involvement in street-level drug market activity as measured by Boston Police Department arrest data. Admittedly, these controls are far from ideal. For example, measuring changes in Boston's citywide youth population does not directly measure population changes among our target audience—gang-involved youth offenders. However, these variables represent the best available information on

these alternate endogenous explanations for Boston's decrease in youth homicide. When these control variables were added to our models, our findings did not substantively change. The significant reductions in youth homicide, shots-fired calls for service, gun assault incidents, and youth gun assault incidents in B-2 associated with Operation Ceasefire remained when the control variables were added to our Poisson regression models.

Youth Homicide Trends in Boston Relative to Youth Homicide Trends in Other Cities

Although the within-Boston analyses support that a large reduction in youth homicide and gun violence was associated with the Ceasefire intervention, it is necessary to distinguish youth homicide trends in Boston from national trends in youth homicide. Many major cities in the United States have enjoyed noteworthy reductions in homicide and nonfatal serious violence (see, e.g., Blumstein and Rosenfeld 1998); the reductions in other cities could be associated with a number of complex and tightly interwoven endogenous or exogenous factors such as positive changes in the national economy, shifts in the age distribution of offending populations, or the stabilization of urban drug markets. Moreover, many cities, most notably New York (Kelling and Bratton 1998), have implemented crime prevention interventions that have been credited with substantial reductions in violence. The following analyses provide insight on whether Boston's reduction in youth homicide was part of national youth homicide trends and whether the program impact associated with the Ceasefire intervention was distinct in magnitude from other youth homicide reductions occurring at the same time as the Ceasefire intervention. Furthermore, because other cities were also taking intervention action to reduce youth homicide, these analyses will suggest whether any program impact in Boston was larger than, or distinct from, any other deliberate interventions implemented during the same time period. A priori, we predicted

Table 1	Results of the Poisson Regressions Controlling for Trend and Seasonal Effects			
	Youth Homicides	Gun Assaults	Shots Fired	B-2 Youth Gun Assaults
Incidence rate ratio	0.37	0.75	0.68	0.56
Parameter estimate	−0.9948	−0.2886	−0.3854	−0.5814
Standard error	0.2501	0.0514	0.0271	0.1339
Chi-square	15.8217	31.5819	202.6158	18.8439
Probability > chi-square	0.0001*	0.0001*	0.0001*	0.0001*
Likelihood ratio test chi-square	16.6259	31.9418	206.8892	19.6072
Probability > likelihood ratio test chi-square	0.0001*	0.0001*	0.0001*	0.0001*
Trend	−0.0014	−0.0093*	−0.0119*	−0.0093*
January	−0.0213	−0.0108	−0.0008	−0.0442
February	2.8335*	2.8736*	2.8356*	3.1343*
March	−0.0185	0.0508	−0.0111	0.0382
April	0.3767	1.0479*	1.0473*	0.9969*
May	0.1890	0.1048	0.3272*	0.1842
June	1.1827*	1.1471*	1.5021*	1.1553*
July	0.3444	0.2728*	0.4407*	0.4252*
August	0.1410	0.3388*	0.4416*	0.1975
September	1.3472*	1.1825*	1.2423*	1.2634*
October	0.3486	0.1141	0.2507*	0.1807
November	0.6932*	0.9248*	1.0636*	0.7601*
Log likelihood	47.5647	19680.27	111620.60	1535.6891
Deviance/*df*	1.12	1.65	9.18	1.47

Note: December was the reference category for the month dummy variables.
*$p < .05$.

that Boston would experience a significant reduction in monthly youth homicide counts associated with the timing of the Ceasefire intervention.

To compare youth homicide trends in Boston to national youth homicide trends, we analyzed youth homicide data for the largest cities in the United States. By rank ordering U.S. Census population data in 1990 and 1996, we selected 41 of the most populous cities in the US.[8] Boston was ranked 20th in population size among these cities in both

1990 and 1996 with an average population of about 565,000. We then obtained monthly counts of the number of homicide victims ages 24 and younger for the 41 comparison cities from Supplementary Homicide Report (SHR) data for the time period of January 1991 through December 1997. After a close examination of these data, 2 cities (Washington, D.C. and New Orleans) were excluded due to extensive missing data. This left us with 39 major U.S. cities in the comparison group.

Examination of the trends in youth homicides in the other cities with significant intervention coefficients also supports the distinctiveness of the Boston case. Although based on exploratory analysis, the presence of these differences undermines the argument that the changes in Boston reflect trends in other major U.S. cities.

The Role of Preventing Illegal Firearms Trafficking

Finally, there is the question of what degree, if any, of violence reduction in Boston should be attributed to the prevention of illegal firearms trafficking. Trafficking was, of course, one of the principal original foci of the Gun Project and attention to trafficking one of Operation Ceasefire's two fundamental planks. Evaluating the particular contribution of supply-side interventions in Boston is, we believe, essentially impossible. Antitrafficking efforts were implemented at the same time as violence deterrence efforts, and both might be expected to influence, for example, gun carrying, gun use, and the mix of illegal guns found on the street. A stand-alone trafficking prevention intervention would not face these difficulties and could lead to definitive answers on the impact of supply-side interventions. Operation Ceasefire, however, was not a stand-alone trafficking prevention intervention.

Here, as well, the distinctive characteristics of the decline in homicide and shootings in Boston offer the best insight into what might have happened. Two things are certain. First, supply-side efforts cannot be responsible for the abrupt reductions in gun-related violence over the summer of 1996. Boston trafficking cases follow that reduction rather than anticipate it. Second, antitrafficking efforts in Boston did nothing to reduce the existing stockpile of illegally acquired and possessed firearms in Boston. Those guns held by gang members in Boston in May of 1996 were, for the most part, still held by them several months later when the violence reached its new, lower equilibrium. The change that had occurred was not in the extent of gun

ownership but in gun *use*. The principal impact therefore was nearly certainly a demand-side, deterrence-based effect rather than a supply-side effect. It may well be that antitrafficking efforts strengthened and prolonged that impact. Whether any such effects were large or small cannot be independently established in this case.

✉ Conclusion

The Boston Gun Project was an attempt to bring problem-oriented policing to bear on one important problem, youth violence, in one city, Boston. The project assembled a working group with members from a wide variety of agencies and representing a wide variety of law enforcement, social service, and other operational capacities (Kennedy et al. 1996). It went through a variety of shifts typical of problem-solving operations: shifts in the problem definition, in the shape of the intervention, and in the management and membership of the core operational partnership Its core operational intervention, Operation Ceasefire, was designed to operate anywhere in the city where youth violence was a serious problem and was intended to interrupt the self-sustaining cycle the Gun Project hypothesized to be driving youth violence in the city (Kennedy et al. 1996). The pulling-levers deterrence strategy at the heart of Operation Ceasefire was designed to influence the behavior, and the environment, of the core population of chronic-offender gang-involved youth Gun Project research found to be at the heart of the city's youth violence problem (Kennedy 1997).

As we have noted, these interests and diagnoses—the desire to operate wherever youth violence presented itself and the belief that there was essentially one dynamic, which had to be addressed, driving violent behavior by various groups in various places within the city—made a classic experimental evaluation design impossible. It was appropriate neither from the viewpoint of participating agencies nor from the perspective of the forces believed to be driving youth violence to set aside particular areas, groups, or individuals as controls. There are thus irreducible limits to attributing any violence reduction in Boston to any particular operational intervention.

This article makes a weaker but still meaningful case: that there was an innovative intervention implemented, there were subsequent substantial reductions in youth violence in Boston, the timing of those reductions is consistent with the intervention having impact, those reductions were robust relative to proxy measures of rival causal factors in the city, the reductions in Boston were significantly larger than those in most other American cities at the time, and the large and abrupt changes that characterized the reduction in Boston differed from those of other American cities. There seems, then, to be reason to believe that something distinct happened in Boston and that its impact was both larger and of a different character than either secular trends or deliberate interventions then operating in other cities.

The results of the impact evaluation support the growing body of research that asserts that problem-oriented policing can be used to good effect in controlling crime and disorder problems (Braga, Piehl, et al. 1999; Clarke 1992; Eck and Spelman 1987; Goldstein 1990). In particular, the Ceasefire intervention suggests a new approach to controlling violent offenders from a more focused application of deterrence principles. In contrast to broad-based "zero tolerance" policing initiatives that attempt to prevent serious offending by indiscriminately cracking down on minor crimes committed by all offenders, the pulling-levers deterrence strategy controlled violence by focusing on particular groups that were behaving violently, subjecting them to a range of discretionary criminal justice system action, and directly communicating cause and effect to a very specific audience. Unfortunately, we were not able to collect the necessary pretest and posttest data to shed light on any shifts in street-level dynamics that could be associated with the pulling-levers deterrence strategy. Our research efforts during the pretest phase were focused on

problem analysis and program development. A priori, we did not know what form the intervention would take and who our target audience would be. In this regard, our assessment is very much a "black box" evaluation. Additional research on the deterrence mechanisms of the pulling-levers approach to controlling offenders is necessary.

We believe that the research presented here shows that the Boston Gun Project was a meaningful problem-oriented policing effort, bringing practitioners and researchers together in new ways, leading to a fresh assessment of the youth violence problem in Boston, and leading to operational activities that were a substantial departure from previous practice. The principal intervention, Operation Ceasefire, was likely responsible for a substantial reduction in youth homicide and youth gun violence in the city. At first blush, the effectiveness of the Operation Ceasefire intervention in preventing violence may seem unique to Boston. Operation Ceasefire was constructed largely from the assets and capacities available in Boston at the time and deliberately tailored to the city's particular violence problem. Operational capacities of criminal justice agencies in other cities will be different, and youth violence problems in other cities will have important distinguishing characteristics. However, we believe that the working-group problem-solving process and the pulling-levers approach to deterring chronic offenders are transferable to other jurisdictions. A number of cities have begun to experiment with these frameworks and have experienced some encouraging preliminary results (see, e.g., Coleman et al. 1999; Kennedy and Braga 1998). These cities include Minneapolis, Minnesota; Baltimore; Indianapolis, Indiana; Stockton, California; Lowell, Massachusetts; Los Angeles; Bronx, New York; High Point, North Carolina; Winston-Salem, North Carolina; Memphis, Tennessee; New Haven, Connecticut; and Portland, Oregon.

The Boston Gun Project applied the basic principles of problem-oriented policing to a substantial public safety problem. Addressing this problem required the involvement of multiple agencies and the community as well as substantial investments in analysis, coordination, and implementation. The experience of the Gun Project suggests that deploying criminal justice capacities to prevent crime can yield substantial benefits. The problem-solving orientation of the project means that the problem definition, the core participants, and the particulars of the intervention evolved over the course of the collaboration. Operation Ceasefire itself was highly customized to the goals of the collaboration, the particular nature of the youth violence problem in Boston, and the particular capacities available in Boston for incorporation into a strategic intervention. Therefore, Operation Ceasefire as such is unlikely to be a highly specifiable, transportable "technology." However, certain process elements of the Boston Gun Project, such as the central role of the line-level working group and the use of both qualitative and quantitative research to "unpack" chosen problems, should be generally applicable to other problem-solving efforts. Using the working-group problem-solving approach, criminal justice practitioners in other jurisdictions will develop a set of intervention strategies that fits both the nuances of their youth violence problem and their operational capacities. Although the resulting package of interventions may not closely resemble the tactics used in Operation Ceasefire, the frameworks will be similar.

within and across cities (Curry, Ball, and Fox 1994). The members of the working group used a definition that could be reduced to a self-identified group of kids who act corporately (at least sometimes) and violently (at least sometimes) (see Kennedy et al. 1997).

3. There were, in fact, only two major Ceasefire crackdowns. In May 1996, the Vamp Hill Kings were subjected to a multiagency operation that included street drug enforcement and drug market suppression, warrant service, stepped-up street enforcement by the Boston Police Department (10 arrests), Operation Night Light probation visits to suspected gang members (38 home visits, 10 probation surrenders), parole visits, 4 Department of Youth Services surrenders, seizure of pit bull dogs by animal control, special bail conditions established for cases presented to Massachusetts district courts, and 4 cases accepted for prosecution by the U.S. Attorney (3 pled guilty, 1 was deported). In August 1996, the Intervale Street Posse was subjected to a similar multiagency operation that included 15 federal arrests on drugs and homicide conspiracy charges (those federally charged were held out of state on pretrial detention) and 8 state drug arrests prosecuted by Suffolk Country District Attorney.

4. We ranked the top 40 cities according to U.S. Census population estimates in 1990 and 1996. In this procedure, we observed that Fresno, California, and Tulsa, Oklahoma, were not in the top 40 in 1990 but were in the top 40 in 1996. St. Louis, Missouri, and Oakland, California, were in the top 40 in 1990 but not in the top 40 in 1996. Rather than exclude either pair of cities, we decided to keep both pairs in the sample. After Boston was removed from this group of populous cities, we were left with 41 cities.

⊠ Notes

1. We expanded our study to include youth ages 24 and younger when Boston Gun Project research revealed that street gangs were an important driver in youth gun violence. Most Boston gang members were between the ages of 14 and 24 (see Kennedy, Braga, and Piehl 1997).

2. During the problem analysis phase of the project, the authors did not provide or press a definition of *gang* on the members of the working group. Defining gang is a core problem in analyzing and understanding gang- and group-related youth crime and violence (Ball and Curry 1995). The character of criminal and disorderly juvenile gangs and groups varies widely both

⊠ References

Aldrich, John and Forrest Nelson. 1984. *Linear Probability, Logit, and Probit Models.* Paper Series on Quantitative Applications in the Social Sciences. Beverly Hills, CA: Sage.

Ball, Richard and G. David Curry. 1995. "The Logic of Definition in Criminology, Purposes and Methods for Defining 'Gangs.'" *Criminology* 33:225–46.

Beha, James A. 1977. " 'And Nobody Can Get You Out': The Impact of a Mandatory Prison Sentence for the Illegal Carrying of a Firearm on the Use of Firearms and on the Administration of Criminal Justice in Boston-Part I." *Boston University Law Review* 57:96–146.

Blumstein, Alfred, Jacqueline Cohen, and Daniel Nagin, eds. 1978. *Deterrence and Incapacitation: Estimating the Effects of Criminal Sanctions on Crime Rates.* Washington, DC: National Academy of Sciences.

Blumstein, Alfred and Richard Rosenfeld. 1998. "Explaining Recent Trends in U.S. Homicide Rates." *Journal of Criminal Law and Criminology* 88:1175–216.

Braga, Anthony A., Anne M. Piehl, and David M. Kennedy. 1999. "Youth Homicide in Boston: An Assessment of Supplementary Homicide Report Data." *Homicide Studies* 3:277–99.

Braga, Anthony A., David L. Weisburd, Elin J. Waring, Lorraine Green Mazerolle, William Spelman, and Francis Gajewski. 1999. "Problem-Oriented Policing in Violent Crime Places: A Randomized Controlled Experiment." *Criminology* 37:541–80.

Butterfield, Fox. 1996. "In Boston, Nothing Is Something." *New York Times,* November 21, p. A20.

Cameron, Samuel. 1988. 'The Economics of Crime Deterrence: A Survey of Theory and Evidence." *Kyklos* 41:301–23.

Campbell, Donald T. and Julian Stanley. 1966. *Experimental and Quasi-Experimental Designs for Research:* Chicago: Rand McNally.

Clarke, Ronald V., ed. 1992. *Situational Crime Prevention: Successful Case Studies.* New York: Harrow and Heston.

Coleman, Veronica, Walter C. Holton, Kristine Olson, Stephen Robinson, and Judith Stewart. 1999. "Using Knowledge and Teamwork to Reduce Crime." *National Institute of Justice Journal,* October: 16–23.

Cook, Philip J. 1977. "Punishment and Crime: A Critique of Current Findings Concerning the Preventive Effects of Punishment." *Law and Contemporary Problems* 41:164–204.

———. 1980. "Research in Criminal Deterrence: Laying the Groundwork for the Second Decade." Pp. 211–68 in *Crime and Justice: An Annual Review of Research,* Vol. 2, edited by Norval Morris and Michael Tonry. Chicago: University of Chicago Press.

Cook, Philip J. and John H. Laub. 1998. "The Unprecedented Epidemic in Youth Violence." Pp. 27–64 in *Youth Violence,* edited by Michael Tonry and Mark H. Moore. Chicago: University of Chicago Press.

Cook, Thomas and Donald Campbell. 1979. *Quasi-Experimentation: Design and Analysis Issues for Field Settings.* Boston: Houghton Mifflin.

Curry, G. David, Richard Ball, and Richard Fox. 1994. *Gang Crime and Law Enforcement Record Keeping* (NCJ 148345). Washington, DC: National Institute of Justice.

Dobson, Annette. 1990. *An Introduction to Generalized Linear Models.* New York: Chapman and Hall.

Eck, John E. and William Spelman. 1987. *Problem-Solving: Problem-Oriented Policing in Newport News.* Washington, DC: National Institute of Justice.

Ekblom, Paul and Ken Pease. 1995, "Evaluating Crime Prevention." Pp. 585–662 in *Building a Safer Society: Crime and Justice,* Vol. 19, edited by Michael Tonry and David Farrington. Chicago: University of Chicago Press.

Fox, James Alan. 1996. *Trends in Juvenile Violence.* Washington, DC: U.S. Department of Justice, Bureau of Justice Statistics.

Gibbs, Jack P. 1975. *Crime, Punishment, and Deterrence.* New York: Elsevier.

Goldstein, Herman. 1979. "Improving Policing: A Problem-Oriented Approach." *Crime & Delinquency* 25:236–58.

———. 1990. *Problem-Oriented Policing.* Philadelphia: Temple University Press

Kelling, George L. and William J. Bratton. 1998. "Declining Crime Rates: Insiders' Views of the New York City Story." *Journal of Criminal Law and Criminology* 88:1217–32.

Kennedy, David M. 1997. "Pulling Levers: Chronic Offenders, High-Crime Settings, and a Theory of Prevention." *Valparaiso University Law Review* 31:449–84.

———. 1998. "Pulling Levers: Getting Deterrence Right." *National Institute of Justice Journal,* July:2–8.

Kennedy, David M. and Anthony A. Braga. 1998. "Homicide in Minneapolis: Research for Problem Solving." *Homicide Studies* 2 (3): 263–90.

Kennedy, David M., Anthony A. Braga, and Anne M. Piehl. 1997. "The (Un)Known Universe: Mapping Gangs and Gang Violence in Boston." Pp. 219–62 in *Crime Mapping and Crime Prevention,* edited by David Weisburd and J. Thomas McEwen. New York: Criminal Justice Press.

———. 1999. "Operation Ceasefire: Problem Solving and Youth Violence in Boston." Unpublished report submitted to the National Institute of Justice. Available on request from authors.

Kennedy, David M., Anne M. Piehl, and Anthony A. Braga. 1996. "Youth Violence in Boston: Gun Markets, Serious Youth Offenders, and a

Use-Reduction Strategy." *Law and Contemporary Problems* 59:147–96.

Kleck, Gary. 1995. *Targeting Guns: Firearms and Their Control.* New York: Aldine de Gruyter.

Klein, Malcolm. 1993. "Attempting Gang Control by Suppression: The Misuse of Deterrence Principles." *Studies on Crime and Crime Prevention* 2:88–111.

Littell, Ramon C, George A. Milliken, Walter W. Stroup, and Russell D. Wolfinger. 1996. *SAS System for Mixed Models.* Cary, NC: SAS Institute, Inc.

McCullagh, Peter and John Nelder. 1989. *Generalized Linear Models.* 2nd ed. New York: Chapman and Hall.

McDowall, David, Richard McCleary, Errol Meidinger, and Richard Hay. 1980. *Interrupted-Time Series Analysis.* Sage University Series on Quantitative Applications in the Social Sciences. Newbury Park, CA: Sage.

Paternoster, Raymond. 1987. "The Deterrent Effect of the Perceived Certainty and Severity of Punishment: A Review of the Evidence and Issues." *Justice Quarterly* 4:173–217.

Piehl, Anne M., Suzanne J. Cooper, Anthony A. Braga, and David M. Kennedy. 1999. "Testing for Structural Breaks in the Evaluation of Programs." NBER working paper no. 7226, National Bureau of Economic Research, Cambridge, MA.

Piehl, Anne M., David M. Kennedy, and Anthony A. Braga. 2000. "Problem Solving and Youth Violence: An Evaluation of the Boston Gun Project." *American Law and Economics Review* 2:58–106.

Rossi, Peter H. and Howard E. Freeman. 1993. *Evaluation: A Systematic Approach.* 5th ed. Newbury Park, CA: Sage.

SAS Institute. 1993. *SAS/STAT Software: The GEN-MOD Procedure.* Release 6.09, technical report P-243. Cary, NC: SAS Institute, Inc.

———. 1997. *SAS/STAT Software: Changes and Enhancements through Release 6.12.* Cary, NC: SAS Institute, Inc.

———. 1998. "V6 SAS Note: PROC MIXED Can Return Incorrect DF with DDFM=SATTERTH and REPEATED." February 18 (http://www.sas.com/service/techsup/unotes/V6/E/E660.html).

Sherman, Lawrence. 1990. "Police Crackdowns: Initial and Residual Deterrence." Pp. 1–48 in *Crime and Justice: A Review of Research,* Vol. 12, edited by Michael Tonry and Norval Morris. Chicago: University of Chicago Press.

Sherman, Lawrence and Richard Berk. 1984. "The Specific Deterrent Effects of Arrest for Domestic Assault." *American Sociological Review* 49:261–72.

Sparrow, Malcolm, Mark H. Moore, and David M. Kennedy. 1990. *Beyond 911: A New Era for Policing.* New York: Basic Books.

Weisburd, David, Elin J. Waring, and Ellen F. Chayet. 1995. "Specific Deterrence in a Sample of Offenders Convicted of White Collar Crimes." *Criminology* 33:587–607.

Witkin, Gordon. 1997. "Sixteen Silver Bullets: Smart Ideas to Fix the World." *U.S. News and World Report,* December 29, p. 67.

Zimring, Franklin and Gordon Hawkins. 1973. *Deterrence: The Legal Threat in Crime Control.* Chicago: University of Chicago Press.

DISCUSSION QUESTIONS

1. What is meant by the "pulling levers" strategy? Give an example of the strategy, and how the "pulling levers" strategy might serve as a deterrent to criminal activity.

2. Did Operation Ceasefire reduce gun ownership among Boston youth? If not, what was reduced?

3. Was the Boston program a broad-based "zero-tolerance" strategy, or did the police target certain crimes? Explain.

4. Based on the authors' recommendations, how do you think the Operation Ceasefire strategy might be applied to your city, or other cities?

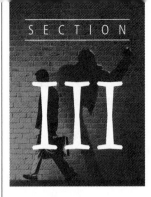
JUVENILE DETENTION AND COURT INTAKE

SECTION HIGHLIGHTS

- Juvenile Court Intake

- Juvenile Detention

- Trends and Variations in Detention

- Conditions of Confinement in Detention

- Consequences of Being Detained

- Preventive Detention and Predicting Dangerousness

- Assessment of Juvenile Risks and Needs

- Diversion and Alternatives to Juvenile Court Referral

- Prosecutor Role in Intake and Court Referral

In this section we provide an introduction to the postarrest process for juvenile offenders, the detention decision for youth who pose a risk to the community, assessment of youth risks and needs, and the prosecutor's role in the intake decision that may result in diversion, informal adjustment, or a petition for adjudication in juvenile court.

⬚ Juvenile Court Intake

Intake is the next major step in juvenile justice processing for youth arrested by police. The intake probation officer accepts referrals from police and is charged with decision-making authority involving screening cases, detention, diversion, or referral for court processing. The intake officer must verify that the court has jurisdiction in each case. This involves determining from the police report that the youth is allegedly in violation of a provision in the state juvenile code. The range of forbidden juvenile behavior is quite broad, ranging from status offenses to felony offenses. The intake officer must also verify the juvenile's date of birth, to ascertain that the department has jurisdiction. State juvenile codes vary, but most legal definitions of a juvenile are youth between the ages of 10 and 17. The intake officer must immediately inform the parents of the referral and decide whether to turn the youth over to the parents pending further action or to temporarily detain the child. Available options other than juvenile court referral include a "reprimand and release," diversion and referral to a community agency for informal supervision and intervention, or informal supervision by the probation agency without being adjudicated delinquent and placed on official probation. Various terms are used to describe youth recommended for informal supervision, such as a "child in need of supervision" (CINS) or "child in need of protective services" (CHIPS). These referrals are informal and voluntary, but they require admission of delinquent involvement and may be accompanied by the threat of more formal action if the youth is not cooperative. Under the "least restrictive" philosophy of the juvenile justice system, the goal of probation agencies is to divert minor juvenile offenders from being processed through the juvenile court, and to refer them to other agencies for short-term intervention and guidance. Diversion is considered most appropriate for status offenders and youth who have allegedly committed minor property crimes.

The intake officer serves a screening function, separating those cases that seem appropriate for diversion from cases that should be petitioned to juvenile court. The intake probation officer has considerable discretionary authority in this decision-making process. The decision of whether to file a petition for adjudication is made in consultation with the prosecuting attorney. Juvenile justice reforms in many states are placing the legal decisions solely in the office of the prosecuting attorney (discussed in more detail at the end of this section). Legal factors (current charge and previous record) are foremost in the decision of whether to release the youth to parents rather than detain, and whether to divert the youth to informal supervision or refer for juvenile court adjudication. Extralegal factors also play an important role in this decision-making process, however, and extensive research has been done on the effect that variables such as race, ethnicity, gender, socioeconomic level, and family history have on intake and detention decisions. We will discuss those research findings following an overview of juvenile detention.

⬚ Juvenile Detention

Juvenile detention centers were established to serve as an alternative to placing juveniles in adult jails. City, county, or state governments administer detention centers, though most are run by the county in conjunction with the juvenile court and the probation department. Detention centers serve as a temporary holding facility for juveniles who need to be held for their own safety or that of the community. They may be held temporarily after arrest and referral to the probation intake unit pending release to their parents. Juveniles are usually detained for a week or less, with exceptional cases being held up to 3 to 4 weeks or longer while awaiting their court hearing. The National Juvenile Detention Association (NJDA) adopted this definition:

> Juvenile detention is the temporary and safe custody of juveniles who are accused of conduct subject to the jurisdiction of the court who require a restricted environment for their own or the community's protection while pending legal action. . . . [J]uvenile detention provides a wide range of helpful services that support the juvenile's physical, emotional, and social development. Helpful services . . . include education, visitation, communication, counseling, continuous supervision, medical and health care services, nutrition, recreation, and reading. Juvenile detention includes or provides for a system of clinical observation and assessment that complements the helpful services and reports findings. (Roush, 2004, p. 219)

All states have a provision in the juvenile statutes requiring that a detention hearing be held within a day or two to determine whether a juvenile may be held longer or must be released. In the detention hearing a judge reviews the decision to detain a youth, the reasons for detention, and either orders the youth released or continues the detention. As a case is processed through the justice system, a juvenile may be detained and released more than once between referral and disposition. Juveniles who are on probation supervision and who commit another crime or violate probation conditions may be detained pending further court actions. Juveniles who have been committed to a correctional facility will also be detained while they are awaiting transportation.

▲ **Photo III-1**   A juvenile in custody awaiting further processing by an intake officer. (© Robert Essel NYC/CORBIS)

⊠ Trends and Variations in Detention

The number of delinquency cases involving detention was 329,800 in 2002, an increase of 42% since 1985 when 234,000 cases were detained (Snyder & Sickmund, 2006, p. 168). Property offense cases made up the largest percentage of detained cases (32%); person offenses accounted for 29%; public order cases 27%; and drug offense cases made up the smallest proportion of detained cases at 11% (Snyder & Sickmund, 2006, p. 168).

The use of detention varies by not only offense type, but also by gender, race, and age. The percentage of males charged with delinquency who were detained was 22%, compared to 17% of females. Youth age 16 or older involved in delinquency cases were more likely to be detained than were youth age 15 or younger. The greatest variation among cases detained was for race. In 2002, the black proportion of detained delinquency cases (36%) was much greater than the black proportion of the juvenile population (16%), and greater than the black proportion of delinquency cases handled during the year (29%). The overrepresentation of black juveniles in detention (compared to their proportion, 16%, in the general population) was even greater (41%) for person offenses, compared with 56% for white juveniles charged with a person offense who were detained (Snyder & Sickmund, 2006, p. 170). Black juveniles were detained at a disproportionately higher rate for property, drug, and public order offenses also, but the rate was not as extreme as that for personal offenses. Detention decisions are generally based on a judge's determination of whether a youth presents a risk of committing another offense, of not appearing for the court hearing, or presents a risk to self or others if not detained. Previous arrests would therefore be a logical factor in detention decisions. Studies have found, however, that after controlling for present offense and prior arrests, a juvenile's race is a significant factor in detention decisions (Feld, 1999, p. 148). In fact, a youth's race affects both police referral and detention, even after controlling for weapons use, victim injury, and socioeconomic and family structure (Wordes, Bynum, & Corley, 1994).

⊠ Conditions of Confinement in Detention

More juveniles were confined in correctional facilities in 2003 (65,636) than in detention centers (25,019), but between 1991 and 2003 the detained population increased more (38%) than the 28% increase in correctional facilities (Snyder & Sickmund, 2006, p. 200). Nearly half (48%) of detained juveniles were in large urban detention facilities that held more than 200 residents. The number of delinquency cases involving detention increased 42% between 1985 and 2002, although the proportion of cases (20%) detained was the same in 2002 as in 1985 (Snyder & Sickmund, 2006, p. 168). Cities and counties in the United States have been struggling to keep up with the growth of detention cases. Overcrowding affects a substantial proportion of juveniles in detention centers. According to the Juvenile Residential Facility Census in 2002, 34% of juveniles were held in facilities operating at or above their standard bed capacity, and detention centers were more likely than other types of juvenile corrections facilities to be at or above their rated capacity (Snyder & Sickmund, 2006, p. 223).

The physical structure of most metropolitan juvenile detention centers resembles adult jails. They are generally of concrete and steel construction with small individual cells or rooms containing a bed, toilet, and sink. If the cell has a window, it is only a small opening that allows some natural light into the tiny room. Detention centers are built and programmed almost entirely around custody and security concerns. Educational, recreational, and treatment programs are secondary. The emphasis on security over correctional programming is justified by the short-term nature of detention, of preventing additional crimes or harm to the individual juvenile and others before the court appearance, and to ensure presence in juvenile court on the assigned date.

Modern detention facilities are now built in a modular or "podular" architectural design that features a more open environment, with small rooms surrounding a day room. Residents are generally segregated by age and physical size, with just 10–15 rooms in each "pod." This design enables better supervision and control in a more relaxed setting that is less institutional in appearance, with space designed for educational, recreational, and treatment programs. Most new detention centers being constructed throughout the United States now incorporate this new design. Unfortunately, allocation of funds for building new juvenile detention centers is not a top priority among cities and counties. They are very expensive to build and operate, and county government officials are unable to allocate funds for better detention facilities in the face of competing budgetary demands. Many cities are therefore detaining children in facilities that are overcrowded and in worse condition than many adult jails. Juvenile courts in many nonurban settings often lack detention facilities and either detain juveniles in a section of the adult jail or transport youth more than an hour's drive away to the next available county detention center or regional facility. In addition to the travel costs, this practice presents clear disadvantages for family members wishing to visit, and probation officers are unable to make regular visits for gathering information relating to intake decisions and preparing predisposition reports. It is ironic that less attention is given to the conditions of confinement in detention than to training schools and juvenile correctional facilities, especially considering that detention centers house children as young as 10 or 12 years of age, those who have been arrested and incarcerated for the first time, and youth who have not yet been adjudicated delinquent.

▧ Consequences of Being Detained

The detention experience has lasting effects on children and youth, and may have a number of negative consequences. Despite the intended purpose of detention—for the protection of the charged youth and the community, to prevent additional crimes, and to ensure the youth's appearance in court—detention itself may have a number of unintended consequences. Detention centers, much like juvenile correctional facilities, may promote rather than prevent delinquency by bringing offenders together and isolating them from the community (Elliott, Huizinga, & Ageton, 1985). Detention adversely affects juveniles' school attendance and educational progress, current employment and future job prospects, and separates youths from their families (Fagan & Guggenheim, 1996). There is research evidence that detention increases the likelihood of a juvenile being adjudicated and committed to a training school. McCarthy (1987) found that even after controlling for crime severity and prior records, juvenile courts processed more detained youth further into the justice system, adjudicated them delinquent more frequently, and sentenced them more severely than youths who were not detained prior to the court hearing. Being detained appears to exert a greater influence on court decisions than other legal or social factors, acting in a manner that McCarthy (1987) referred to as a self-fulfilling prophecy. Once a juvenile is identified in a detention hearing as one who is predicted to pose a greater risk of danger and future delinquent involvement, that preliminary decision appears to have an influence on the adjudication and disposition decisions that in turn have greater and long-lasting consequences for the youth. The fact that judges disproportionately detain more minority youths means that the consequences of detention affect them even more. The negative effects of detention and the influence of detention on judges' court decisions are matters of concern for juvenile justice experts and child advocates. The practice of preventive detention also involves a prediction that a juvenile poses a risk and danger if not detained while awaiting court action.

Preventive Detention and Predicting Dangerousness

The pretrial detention of youths who have been arrested and charged with a crime but not yet found guilty and adjudicated has met with legal challenges. In *Schall v. Martin* (467 U.S. 283[1984]) the U.S. Supreme Court upheld the constitutionality of the preventive detention of juveniles. The Court ruled that a juvenile may be held in preventive detention if there is sufficient reason to believe the juvenile may commit additional crimes while the case is pending court action. The Court also ruled that the juvenile has the right to a hearing on the detention decision and a statement of the reasons on which the detention decision is based. The dissenting opinion of Justices Marshall, Brennan, and Stevens is especially noteworthy in this case, as they questioned the ability to predict dangerousness or to identify which juveniles will engage in serious violent crime while awaiting court action. The dissenting justices argued that because preventive detention infringed youths' "fundamental" liberty interests, the State must demonstrate a "compelling" interest to justify restrictions and provide more adequate procedural safeguards. They argued that judges could not accurately predict dangerousness and therefore the use of preventive detention could not significantly reduce crime. The majority ruling in *Schall* had rejected the lower court's findings that judges lacked the ability to accurately predict future criminal conduct, asserting that juvenile and criminal court judges could and did predict "dangerousness" regularly. The majority opinion relied on past and current judicial practices to uphold the argument. The dissenting opinion, on the other hand, relied on criminological, clinical, and legal studies that have concluded that there are no risk assessment instruments currently available that enable even the best experts to reliably predict which juveniles will engage in violent crime. Dissenting Justices noted that the decision to detain is made by a family court judge in a brief 5- to 15-minute hearing, with very limited information on which to base the detention decision. Feld (1999) has noted that the statutes relating to preventive detention in most states lack objective standards and clear criteria and allow judges broad discretion in detention hearings. The result is the detention of many juveniles who pose no threat to themselves or to others.

In contrast to the broad and nonspecific statutory limits on juvenile detention, the statutory criteria and limits on adult preventive detention are very clear and specific. Federal statute 18 U.S.C. § 3142(f) [1984], for example, authorized courts to detain only those defendants charged with crimes of violence, crimes punishable by death or life imprisonment, major drug offenses, or a felony committed by a defendant with two prior convictions of certain listed offenses. The prosecutor is expected to support the need for preventive detention "by clear and convincing evidence" that the defendant will flee and present a "demonstrable danger to the community" (see Feld, 1999, p. 138). The Court in *Schall v. Martin* (467 U.S. 255), in contrast, authorized a juvenile court judge to preventively detain a juvenile if it found a "serious risk" that the child "may . . . commit an act which if committed by an adult would constitute a crime." The Court did not specify the nature of the alleged offense, burden of proof, specific criteria, the probability of occurrence of future crime, or the type of evidence that the judge should consider when predicting that a youth posed a "serious risk" to commit a new crime.

Judicial and corrections officials make predictions of dangerousness every day, so researchers in criminal justice and criminology have conducted extensive research in an attempt to identify characteristics that may differentiate dangerous offenders from those who pose no serious risk of violent crime. Research findings do not support the view that judges can predict dangerousness from a legal point of view with an acceptable level of accuracy and reliability. Psychologists, psychiatrists, criminologists, and lawyers criticize the assumption that judges or mental health professionals can make valid and accurate predictions about future dangerousness (Monahan, 1981). Auerhahn (2006) asserts that our ability to predict violent behavior is severely limited. In contrast to "true positives" (accurately predicting who will commit another serious crime), "false positives" (wrongly predicting as dangerous offenders those who if released would not commit another dangerous crime) occur at an unacceptably high level. Research shows that when judges attempt to predict dangerousness they will make mistakes. False positive errors of 50% or more of offenders are common in prediction decisions (Auerhahn, 2006), resulting in the preventive detention and incarceration of numerous offenders who pose no risk to society, and a significant impact in cost and allocation of resources for the justice process. When youths are wrongly identified to be in need of preventive detention, they are deprived of liberty because they have some characteristics of potentially dangerous youths. The detention of youths who are incorrectly predicted to pose a risk to public safety results in the unnecessary incarceration of innocent youths (Feld, 1999, p. 142).

In addition to the inherent inaccuracy of predictions, judges tend to overpredict offenders believed to pose a risk to public safety. Errors will inevitably be made when predicting dangerousness, and the justice process prefers to err on the side of caution and in favor of the community over the loss of individual liberty. The judicial tendency to overpredict dangerousness nevertheless raises legal, moral, and policy questions. Feld poses an important question:

> How many false positives . . . can a morally defensible legal system incarcerate for no benefit in order to confine those fewer but unidentifiable individuals who actually will reoffend? Should judges speculate about a "serious risk" of future crime . . . if doing so means that they erroneously will preventively detain larger numbers of presumptively innocent false positives? How can a society balance predictive marginal crime reduction versus actual loss of individual liberty? (Feld, 1999, p. 142)

The available research on predicting dangerousness through clinical methods and using assessment tools does not show a high degree of accuracy and reliability. Auerhahn (2006) adds a cautionary note in support of Monahan (1981), Feld (1999), and others, concluding that the practice of depriving offenders of liberty based on questionable predictions is at the least ethically questionable and is potentially detrimental to the administration of justice. Ongoing research on violence risk screening (e.g., Davies & Dedel, 2006) shows promise of improving the reliability of predicting dangerousness, and more court services and community corrections agencies are utilizing instruments for risk assessment. Critics remain concerned, however, about the unacceptably high rate of false positives that result in the unnecessary incarceration of hundreds of individuals. We turn next to a discussion of risk assessment instruments.

⊠ Assessment of Juvenile Risks and Needs

Assessment is a term that has appeared in juvenile justice literature only in the past couple of decades, but it is actually based on one of the original concepts of probation. In order for probation to be a viable alternative to incarceration, probation officers have always had to identify those offenders who posed a lower risk of reoffending, could be safely supervised in the community, and who were considered amenable to treatment. A fundamental concept of juvenile justice has always been an emphasis on individualized treatment as opposed to court sanctions and punishment. The emphasis on individual offender treatment requires identification of the specific treatment needs of each juvenile. Gathering information for and writing a predisposition report has been a central responsibility of juvenile probation officers. The reports have traditionally been very comprehensive, including information on the juvenile's childhood and family background, educational progress, and prior arrest and court records. A psychological evaluation to assess intelligence and personality factors might be requested (depending on available resources) in serious cases involving violence, when the case may be waived and transferred to adult court. Predisposition reports nevertheless involve subjective judgments of probation officers. Individual officer judgments vary considerably, so that similar cases by different officers are likely to receive different recommendations. It has been readily apparent for decades that there was a need for more objective assessment instruments that would provide more accurate, consistent, and standardized results on offenders' risk level and treatment needs. It is generally accepted that when offender needs are clearly identified, the probation client can be provided with or referred to the appropriate rehabilitation programs, resulting in more efficient and effective probation outcomes.

A variety of assessment and classification systems have been developed and tested with juvenile and adult offenders. A nationwide survey found that corrections agencies in most states have some form of juvenile needs assessment (Towberman, 1992). The most common juvenile needs and risks that were assessed included substance abuse by juveniles or family members, mental and emotional health of the juvenile or family members, sexual or physical abuse in the family, education achievement and intellectual ability of the youth, vocational training needs of the youth; peer relationships, family dysfunction, medical or physical problems, and self-reported delinquency including violent behavior (Towberman, 1992, p. 232). In a study of juvenile justice practitioners in Texas, Mears and Kelly (1999) found that there is considerable variation among probation officers as to the need for and the goals of assessment in the intake process. They recommended that greater attention should be given to clarifying the purposes and goals of assessment. Young, Moline, Farrell, and Bierie (2006) have reported on the lessons learned from developing and implementing assessment tools in the Maryland juvenile justice system. They noted the importance of involving staff, supervisors, and judicial personnel in the process of developing and implementing assessment tools. These two studies (Mears & Kelly, 1999; Young et al., 2006) are included in our readings in this section.

⊠ Diversion and Alternatives to Juvenile Court Referral

Diversion programs have been promoted as a way to reduce the number of minor offenders processed through the juvenile justice system, while still providing supervision or services on an informal basis. Criminologists argued that processing minor offenders through the justice system had a stigmatizing effect that was likely to perpetuate rather than reduce the chance of further delinquent behavior. Proponents of diversion argued that court referrals should be restricted to juvenile offenses that would be crimes if committed by adults. Status offenders should be diverted to agencies outside the formal justice process, which would provide needed supervision and services, but should not be adjudicated delinquent or placed on official probation. Diversion was a recommendation of the 1967 President's Commission on Law Enforcement and Administration of Justice (1967b), and the Juvenile Justice and Delinquency Prevention (JJDP) Act of 1974 promoted diversion of minor juvenile offenders to community treatment programs in lieu of formal juvenile justice processing. Youth Service Bureaus (YSBs) were among the diversion agencies that were developed through federal funding to provide an alternative source of referrals by police and probation intake officers. The YSBs and similar diversion agencies provide services such as counseling, educational assistance, job training, and recreational opportunities as a means of preventing further delinquent involvement among minor and first-time young offenders. Diversion programs provide more flexible and efficient services than formal juvenile court processing and offer an alternative for youth in need of some supervision.

Deinstitutionalization of status offenders (DSO) was a major provision of the JJDP Act. The Act required states to provide that juveniles who were charged with offenses that would not be criminal if committed by an adult not be placed in juvenile detention or correctional facilities, but rather in shelter facilities. Amendments to the original act (in 1977, 1980, and 1992) required that states receiving JJDP Act grant funds provide assurance that they were taking action to remove status offenders and non-offenders from detention and correctional facilities and were not detaining juveniles in adult jails (Holden & Kapler, 1995). A comprehensive national evaluation of DSO programs found that they were successful in significantly reducing the number of status offenders in detention and institutions (Schneider, 1985b). Other studies have found mixed results, however. Kobrin and Klein (1982) conducted a national evaluation of DSO programs and found problems in the definition of status offenders. They found that "pure" status offenders were relatively rare; most status offenders had prior delinquent experiences. Some jurisdictions limited their programs to pure status offenders, so many otherwise eligible youth were not served by the programs. In other areas the number of juveniles referred to court intake actually increased, and many youngsters whose behavior did not justify police intervention were referred to diversion programs. This tendency led to a problem referred to as "net widening." Many status offenders who would previously have been handled by police or intake probation officers through a "reprimand and release" were drawn into diversion or DSO programs. Diversion programs have therefore been criticized because they have received referrals of youth who would not have been referred to probation intake or court (Decker, 1985). Recent juvenile justice reforms in many states have limited the discretionary decisions of intake probation officers and shifted most of those decisions to the responsibility of the prosecutor.

⊠ Prosecutor Role in Intake and Court Referral

The prosecutor is primarily responsible for the decision whether to file a petition for adjudication in most jurisdictions today. Under the traditional rehabilitative or "medical model" of juvenile justice, the intake probation officer had a considerable amount of discretion in deciding whether to handle the case informally or refer the case to juvenile court. Police referred a juvenile to the intake officer, who reviewed the charges, checked for previous arrest records, and interviewed the juvenile and the parents. Based on the information, the intake officer then made the decision either to divert the case, handle it on informal adjustment, or refer the case to the prosecutor with a recommendation to file a petition for court adjudication. The traditional intake model has given way to a more formal process with the prosecutor as the central figure responsible for the decision whether to file a petition. A prosecuting attorney is the more appropriate court official to make a determination whether to petition a case based on the evidence and the factors necessary for court jurisdiction (Whitehead & Lab, 2006). An example of the current trend is the state of Washington, which now gives sole responsibility of the intake decision to the prosecutor. Juvenile justice reform legislation in that state includes intake and sentencing guidelines based on seriousness of the offense, prior offenses, and age of the youth. The practice of informally adjusting cases at intake was completely eliminated (Schneider & Schram, 1986). The intent of the legislative reform was to hold juveniles accountable for their crimes and to hold the system accountable for what it does to juveniles. The traditional rehabilitation philosophy was replaced by a "justice" or "just deserts" model that emphasizes fairness, uniformity, and proportionality in the court's response to juvenile offenses. In support of this emphasis, status offenses were removed entirely from court jurisdiction (Schneider & Schram, 1986, p. 211). The current trend is for more states to move toward this more formal legal approach in the intake process. The intake decision now is based not on the "need for treatment," but on legal criteria and holding juveniles accountable for their crimes.

SUMMARY

- The intake probation officer accepts referrals from police and with the prosecutor decides whether to divert youth for informal adjustment or refer to court for adjudication.
- Detention centers serve as a temporary holding facility for juveniles who need to be held for their own safety or that of the community.
- A juvenile's race is a significant factor in detention decisions, and African American juveniles are detained at disproportionately higher rates.
- The number of delinquency cases involving detention increased dramatically in the past 20 years, and overcrowding affects a significant number of juveniles in detention centers.
- Being detained has a number of adverse consequences on juveniles, including the increased likelihood of being adjudicated and committed to a training school.
- Despite research evidence that questions the ability of a judge to reliably predict dangerousness, the U.S. Supreme Court has upheld the constitutionality of preventive detention for juveniles.
- Assessment tools have been developed to assist in juvenile court decision making, including intake, detention, and disposition alternatives.

- Diversion programs were developed to reduce the number of minor first-time offenders referred to juvenile court, while still providing supervision and services on an informal basis.
- Juvenile justice reforms in many states have reduced the discretionary authority of the intake probation officer, giving the prosecutor primary responsibility for case processing.

KEY TERMS

Assessment   Diversion
Dangerousness   Intake
Deinstitutionalization   Preventive detention
Detention   *Schall v. Martin*

DISCUSSION QUESTIONS

1. If intake and detention decisions are to be fair and just, is it appropriate that detention involves a disproportionate number of racial and ethnic minorities? What changes or reforms would you suggest?

2. Explain the difference between "false positives" and "false negatives" in predicting dangerousness and identifying offenders likely to pose a risk to public safety. Is it acceptable to have a "false positive" error rate of up to 50% if that means reducing the "false negative" rate to less than 5%? Explain and justify your response.

3. Based on the available research evidence, does it seem likely that risk and needs assessment instruments may reduce disparities due to extralegal factors used in juvenile court decision making? Explain.

4. Is there research support for the practice of giving intake officers some discretionary authority to divert or refer minor first-time offenders for informal adjustment? Explain, and cite the research evidence.

5. The current trend is moving away from the rehabilitative "medical model" and toward the "justice model," giving the prosecutor primary authority for decisions at the intake stage. What are some arguments for each model and which seems to be the most convincing argument, based on the research evidence?

WEB RESOURCES

The following Web sites provide information and discussion on the detention and intake procedures of the juvenile justice system:

National Juvenile Detention Association: http://www.njda.com/

Annie E. Casey Foundation, on detention reform: http://www.aecf.org

Juvenile Offenders and Victims: 2006 National Report: http://ojjdp.ncjrs.gov/ojstatbb/nr2006/downloads/NR2006.pdf

Youth Law Center, on juvenile confinement: http://www.buildingblocksforyouth.org/issues/

READING

An increasingly disproportionate number of minority youth are confined in secure detention facilities. This has led to a search for a better understanding of the reasons behind disproportionate minority confinement. The explanations of the problem vary, but generally focus on either differential rates of offending among minorities compared to white youth or selection bias within the juvenile justice system. The authors of this study examine the extent to which both may explain decision making by assessing the effect of race on detention and the degree that race and detention influence further court processing in one juvenile court jurisdiction in the state of Iowa. Multivariate analyses using juvenile court data show that although legal factors account for some of the decision making and minority overrepresentation, so too does race. Evidence is presented that, through detention, race has direct, interaction, and indirect effects that often work to the disadvantage of African American youth relative to white youth. Implications for future research and policy are discussed in the article.

Race and the Impact of Detention ——————— on Juvenile Justice Decision Making ———————

Michael J. Leiber, Kristan C. Fox

In 1997, 19% of all juvenile delinquent referrals resulted in detention, with African American youth comprising 47% of those detained (Hoytt, Schiraldi, Smith, & Ziedenberg, 2002). Furthermore, between 1983 and 1997, the overall youth detention population increased by 47%, and although the detained White youth population increased by 21%, the detained minority youth population grew by 76% (Justice Policy Institute, 2002, p. 2). This means that four out of five new youths detained during this 15-year period were youth of color (Justice Policy Institute, 2002). These numbers and racial differences as well as the overrepresentation of minority youth throughout the juvenile justice system, especially for secure corrections, are a concern for academics (e.g., Hawkins & Kempf-Leonard, in press), policy

makers, including the federal government (e.g., Hsia, Bridges, & McHale, 2004), and those concerned with justice in general (e.g., Hoytt et al., 2002). This concern, in part, has led to a search for the causes of the overrepresentation of minorities in the juvenile justice system (e.g., Leiber, 2002).

In the present research, we attempt to address how minority overrepresentation comes about by examining the effects of race and detention on juvenile justice decision making in one juvenile court jurisdiction in the state of Iowa.[1] More specific, we assess a sample of juvenile court records to ascertain the predictors of detention use and the effect of race and detention on five decision-making stages. Interpretations of the symbolic threat thesis and the consensus theory guide the study.

SOURCE: *Crime & Delinquency, (51)*4, 470–497, October 2005. DOI: 10.1177/0011128705275976. © 2005 Sage Publications, Inc.

⬚ Theoretical Background

The symbolic threat thesis is a perspective that attempts to identify the contingencies or the contexts of juvenile justice decision making by focusing on the characteristics of youth, especially minorities, and the social psychological emotions of juvenile court officers. These emotions have included identification (or the lack of identification) with the youth and his or her behavior and fear and jealousy of the youth. Emotions such as these are thought to manifest in beliefs that minority youth pose symbolic threats to middle-class standards and public safety. The symbolic threat is believed to be fostered by negative perceptions of African Americans and the corresponding stereotypes made by decision makers (Tittle & Curran, 1988).

The reliance on racial stereotypes by decision makers and how these subjective assessments of youth shaped case outcomes is highlighted in the research by Bridges and Steen (1998). Probation officers were found to use different causal attributions to assess the delinquent behavior of African Americans and Whites. African American youth involvement in delinquency was viewed as related to internal or dispositional attributions (i.e., lack of individual responsibility), whereas delinquency among White youth was attributed to external causes (i.e., impoverished conditions). Because internal attributions resulted in perceptions that the youths were at a higher risk for reoffending, decision makers recommended longer sentences for African Americans than for Whites. By exploring the subjective qualities that influenced the construction of a case, Bridges and Steen (1998) were able to determine how the values and beliefs of decision makers created a legally recognizable but racially stereotypic image of an offender that affected the decision-making process.

Leiber (2003) incorporated the emphasis on the subjective social psychological processes of decision makers and the factors that influence those processes in his study of four relatively homogenous juvenile courts in Iowa. More specifically, Leiber focused on the relationships among adherence to correctional orientations (such as retribution and rehabilitation) and decision makers' views concerning race, crime, family, and respect for authority with regard to case processing and case outcomes for youth. Quantitative and qualitative methodologies were used to determine the extent to which correctional ideologies and decision makers' stereotyping of minorities were fueled by a wide range of contingencies (e.g., community, organizational, and individual), by impact decisions, and by how the stereotyping varies by jurisdiction.

For example, in one jurisdiction, an ideology of holding offenders accountable combined with the racial stereotyping of African American youth as being more delinquent and in need of intervention resulted in African Americans being subjected to different case processing and case outcomes than were similarly situated Whites. In another juvenile court, a strong emphasis on *parens patriae* coupled with multiple minority groups moving into the area and perceptions that these groups of people do not abide to middle-class standards of dress, demeanor, marriage, and respect for authority led minority youth to be responded to differently than were White youth (Leiber, 2003).

A common theme running through these theoretical revisions and studies is the identification of the variable effects of race on decision making and the factors that foster these effects. Although the source of the contextual effects may vary, one emphasis is the racial stereotyping by decision makers of African American youth. These stereotypes include African Americans as undisciplined, as living in dysfunctional families that are primarily headed by young mothers, and as sexually promiscuous, dangerous, delinquent, and prone to drug offenses (Feld, 1999). These perceptions work to the disadvantage of African Americans relative to Whites and may account for the overrepresentation of minorities in detention and other stages in the juvenile justice system.

Consensus theory provides an alternative perspective for understanding the effects of race on detention and other decision-making stages (e.g., Engen, Steen, & Bridges, 2002). According to the Durkhemian perspective, state intervention into people's lives and the incarceration of individuals stems primarily from criminal and delinquent behavior and its severity. In the case of the juvenile justice system, extralegal factors, such as age and assessments about the family to supervise youth, can also be relied upon and are seen as legitimate criteria because of the historical underpinnings of this court to act in the best interests of youth (e.g., Feld, 1999). Racial bias or discrimination is seen as random and isolated. Differences between Whites and minorities in case processing and case outcomes are attributed mostly to differential involvement in crime (e.g., crime severity) and possibly family issues (e.g., unable to contact parent; Tracy, 2002).

Prior Research

Over the years, there have been numerous studies that have examined the extent to which race, legal criteria, and extralegal factors influence case processing and case outcomes in the juvenile justice system. Some research has shown that legal factors rather than race predict decision making and lend support for a consensus interpretation for minority overrepresentation in the juvenile justice system (e.g., Hindelang, 1978; Tracy, 2002). Five recent comprehensive reviews of this literature, however, demonstrate that legal and extralegal factors alone are unable to account for race differences in involvement in the juvenile justice system (Bishop, in press; Engen et al., 2002; Leiber, 2002; Pope & Feyerherm, 1992; Pope, Lovell, & Hsia, 2002). Although an in-depth discussion of these findings is beyond the scope of this article, race was found to have either a direct relationship with decision making and/or an interaction or combination effects with legal variables (e.g., crime type, prior record, etc.) and/or extralegal factors (e.g., age, family status, etc.).

For example, Sampson and Laub (1993) found that African Americans charged with drug offenses were more likely to receive detention and out-of-home placements in counties exhibiting racial inequality and impoverishment than in counties where these conditions did not exist. Sampson and Laub (1993) refined the symbolic threat thesis by emphasizing the interaction between structural inequality and racial stereotyping and the "get tough" movement and the war on drugs with juvenile court processing. African Americans were assumed to be seen by decision makers as dangerous and prone to drug offenses.

Race has also been discovered to have indirect effects on decision making. Paralleling research that revealed that dispositions imposed for prior offenses affected dispositions for current offenses (e.g., Henretta, Frazier, & Bishop, 1986), studies have found that decisions made at earlier stages such as detention affect outcomes at later stages and in particular judicial disposition (e.g., Engen et al., 2002; Frazier & Bishop, 1985; Frazier & Cochran, 1986). That is, being detained strongly predicts more severe treatment at judicial disposition. Although African American youth and White youth who have been detained may be treated similarly, because the former group is more likely to be detained they receive more severe dispositions than do their White counterparts (e.g., Bortner & Reed, 1985; Frazier & Bishop, 1995; McCarthy & Smith, 1986). Thus, if racial bias occurs early in the proceedings (at detention), it may reappear indirectly at later stages (at judicial disposition). Consequently, race may not directly influence judicial disposition, but its effects may be masked, operating through a racially tainted but legitimate criterion of detention.

Implications for the Present Research

Although the individual, joint, and indirect effects of race and detention on decision making have been studied extensively and although the results, for the most part, show an effect, much of the extant literature has limitations that the present study attempts to overcome. At the heart of the need for further research is that previous research is often devoid of a theoretical perspective. In addition, the studies themselves are old and/or rely on data from the late 1970s and mid 1980s. Also, only one to two stages are examined or many measures of the social situation of the youth (e.g., family structure, school situation) or the presence of legal counsel are not considered (e.g., Frazier & Bishop, 1985; McCarthy & Smith, 1986; Wordes, Bynum, & Corley, 1994). Furthermore, the race-detention association has not been studied in the juvenile court jurisdiction examined in the present research. Thus, the objective of the present study is to address these limitations to enhance our understanding of the interplay among race, detention, and decision making.

More specific, we examine decision making in one juvenile court jurisdiction to assess the effect of race on detention and the degree race and detention influence further court proceedings. The present study will be guided by hypotheses stemming from the symbolic threat thesis and the various refinements that focus on the racial stereotyping of African Americans and the consensus perspective emphasis on differential offending.

The first hypothesis guiding the study is:

Hypothesis 1 (H1): Controlling for legal criteria and extralegal factors will not eliminate the effects of race on detention.

H1 is based on the assumptions of the symbolic threat thesis and prior research that African American youth will be perceived by decision makers as dangerous, delinquent, or prone to drug offenses and in need of secure confinement (e.g., Sampson & Laub, 1993). Nonsupport for H1 lends validity to a counter hypothesis based on consensus theory that any observed race differences in detention will be accounted for by differences in crime and/or extralegal factors (e.g., Tracy, 2002).[2]

A second hypothesis to be studied emerges from the differential treatment perspective and prior research (e.g., Frazier & Bishop, 1995):

Hypothesis 2 (H2): Controlling for legal and extralegal criteria, race will have indirect effects through detention on other decision-making stages.

It is important to note that finding support for either of these two hypotheses does not assume that legal and extralegal factors will not be statistically significant predictors or the strongest predictors of decision making.

▧ The Present Research

Site

The regional detention facility opened in late March of 1989 and is governed by a 20-county membership commission that includes a detention supervisor who handles both preadjudicated and adjudicated youth from member and nonmember counties. The detention supervisor has been overseeing the facility since its inception. Originally built with 15 beds, the facility expanded to 31 beds in 1996 (North East Iowa Juvenile Detention Center, 2004). The regional detention facility is located in the largest of the 20 member counties. This county has a population of 130,224 people, with persons age 17 and younger constituting 24% of the population (Bureau of the Census, 2000). African Americans comprise the largest group of minority youth (11%-13%). In the largest city within this county, African American youth make up about 19% of all youth (Bureau of the Census, 2000). The present research focuses on youth handled within the juvenile court within this county.[3]

Data and Method

Because of the relatively small number of minority youth in Iowa, cases for the study were selected from juvenile court referrals over a 21-year period, 1980 through 2000, from one juvenile court involving youth accused of delinquent behavior. The court cases for the present research consisted of a random sample of referrals identified as White individuals ($n = 3,888$) and a disproportionate random sampling identified as African American individuals ($n = 1,666$). The weighted sample size used in the present research was 5,554.

Variables

Table 1 presents the variables, the coding scheme, and the distributions of the dependent and independent variables used in the study. The operationalization and inclusion of the variables is based on theory and prior research (e.g., Bishop & Frazier, 1988; Leiber, 1994; Leiber & Jamieson, 1995).

Table 1	Values and Frequency Distributions of Variables		
Variables	*Value*	n	%
Dependent			
Initial detention	0 = *no*	5,249	94
	1 = *yes*	305	6
Intake 1	0 = *release or diversion*	3,593	64
	1 = *refer to court*	1,961	36
Intake 2	0 = *refer to court or diversion*	4,180	75
	1 = *release*	1,374	25
Petition	0 = *no*	85	5
	1 = *yes*	1,876	95
Initial appearance[a]	0 = *consent decree*	362	27
	1 = *no consent decree*	957	73
Adjudication	0 = *no*	182	19
	1 = *yes*	775	81
Judicial disposition	0 = *community*	389	33
	1 = *noncommunity*	780	67
Independent			
Detention (at any point)	0 = *no*	5,193	93
	1 = *yes*	361	7
Race	0 = *White*	3,888	70
	1 = *African American*	1,666	30
Gender	0 = *male*	4,078	73
	1 = *female*	1,476	27
Age	$M = 15.48$		
	$SD = 1.92$		
	Range = 6–18		
Family status	0 = *married*	2,884	52
	1 = *one member*	2,670	48

Variables	Value	n	%
Attending school but problems[b]	0 = no	4,693	84
	1 = yes	861	16
School dropout[b]	0 = no	5,096	92
	1 = yes	458	8
No. of prior referrals	M = 1.79		
	SD = 2.54		
	Range = 0–10		
Court authority	0 = no	4,297	77
	1 = yes	1,257	23
Severity of prior referral	0 = no prior referral	3,587	65
	1 = less than adjudication	1,452	26
	2 = adjudication or placement	515	9
No. of charges	M = 1.32		
	SD = .81		
	Range = 1–7		
Crime severity	0 = misdemeanor	4,697	85
	1 = felony	857	15
Crime type[c]			
Property crime	0 = no	2,609	47
	1 = yes	2,945	53
Person crime	0 = no	4,777	86
	1 = yes	777	14
Drugs crime	0 = no	4,776	86
	1 = yes	778	14
Weapon	0 = no	5,315	96
	1 = yes	239	4
Counsel	0 = yes	1,348	24
	1 = no	4,216	76

NOTE: $N = 5,554$.

a. The difference between petition and initial appearance is due to referral to adult court ($n = 394$) and missing cases ($n = 163$).

b. These are dummy variables; the reference category is attending school with no problems.

c. This is a dummy variable; the reference category is other (e.g., disorderly conduct, etc.).

Dependent Variables

Following the suggestions of Pope and Feyerherm (1992), decision making in the juvenile justice system was viewed as a process consisting of many successive stages rather than as simply one or two discrete decisions. Each of the six stages examined constitute a dependent variable with the most severe decision outcome representing the reference category for analysis purposes.

Detention will first be treated as a dependent variable and will later be treated as an independent variable to capture possible indirect effects. As a dependent variable, initial detention consists of a youth being detained prior to the intake stage. Overall, a small percentage of youth (6%) have been held in detention at this point.[4]

To overcome the shortcoming of past conceptualizations of decision making at intake (Leiber & Stairs, 1999), this stage in the process was measured in two ways: Intake I was release or diversion versus further court processing, and intake 2 was release versus diversion or further court processing.[5] The most common outcome at intake was diversion (40%), followed by referral to court (35%) and release (25%). In Iowa, juvenile court officers make the decision to release, to offer an informal adjustment in the form of diversion, or to recommend further court processing at intake. State statute requires an admission of guilt as a prerequisite for diversion or an informal adjustment (see Iowa Juvenile Code Statute 232.29).

The decision to seek further formal court proceedings is made by the prosecutor and occurs at the stage of petition. A significant majority of the juveniles (95%) were petitioned.

The next stage in the proceedings is initial appearance, and analogous to the use of diversion or the informal adjustment at intake, 27% of the youth at this stage accept a consent decree, whereas the rest go on to the adjudication stage. As with the intake stage, these youth must admit guilt to participate in the diversionary option.

The adjudication stage is operationalized as dismissed and as the adjudication of delinquency. Overall, 81% of the cases reaching this stage were adjudicated delinquent.

Next to the death penalty, transfer to adult jurisdiction can be the most severe sanction given to a youth and disproportionately involves African Americans relative to Whites (Stahl, 1999). In the present research, youth transferred to adult court were included within the definition of judicial disposition (see also Bishop & Frazier, 1988). Judicial disposition was defined as an outcome that resulted in a change of placement (e.g., training school, residential facility, group home) or transfer to adult court versus probation and/or treatment within the community. Of the youth at this stage, 67% received

a disposition involving a change of placement or transfer to adult court.[6]

Independent Variables

In addition to being treated as a dependent variable, detention is also included as an independent variable. Youth detained at any point prior to or at the particular stage examined make up the detention variable. Only a small number of youth were detained following initial detention (306 at initial detention compared to 361; an increase of 56). Overall, 7% of the sample experienced detention when defined in this manner.

A significant majority of the respondents were White (70%), male (73%), and 15 years of age. Family living status was defined as a two-parent household versus a one-parent household. Of the sample, 48% resided in households with one parent present.

School status was measured by two dummy variables: attending but problems and not attending. The reference category was attending school.

Three measures of the juvenile's previous legal history included the number of prior contacts with the juvenile justice system (interval), whether the youth was under court authority at the time of the current referral (0 = no; 1 = yes), and the severity of the prior referral (0 = no prior referral; 2 = adjudication or placement). Characteristics of the current offense were the number of charges against the youth (interval), the seriousness of the offense (0 = misdemeanor; 1 = felony), the type of delinquency, and whether a weapon was involved (0 = no; 1 = yes). Because of the theoretical importance of offense type in juvenile justice decision making (e.g., Sampson & Laub, 1993), dummy variables were created to distinguish among property, person, and drug offenses.[7] Referrals consisting of disorderly conduct, resisting arrest, and so on comprised the reference category. Most cases were classified as misdemeanors (85%) and involved property crimes (51%). Only 14% of the sample was charged with a person offense or drug offense. Offenses of this sample of juveniles reflected national aggregate arrest statistics (Snyder & Sickmund, 1999) and were somewhat limited in severity.

The last independent variable is legal counsel. Although limited research exists on the topic, it has been found that most youth in the juvenile justice system are not represented by legal counsel and that when representation is present, the majority of youth have a public defender or a court-appointed attorney (e.g., Feld, 1988). Research has also shown that irrespective of the severity of the offense, youth with counsel receive more severe sanctions than do those without an attorney (e.g., Feld, 1988, 1989; Guevara, Spohn, & Herz, 2004). Because of the lack of research in this area and the possibility that legal representation may influence case processing and outcomes, it is included in the analysis (0 = *court-appointed or privately retained attorney*; 1 = *no counsel*). Similar to past research, a small percentage had counsel (24%).

◣ Results

Decision Making at Detention and Intake

Overall and as predicted by consensus theory, we can see that a number of the legal and extralegal variables predict detention and intake decision making (e.g., number of prior referrals, severity of prior disposition, crime severity, age) as does the procedural variable counsel. We also find support for H1 and H2. Race, directly in interaction with other independent variables and indirectly through detention, affects decision making. For the purpose of clarity, the discussion will be limited to the effects of detention and race on the decision-making stages.

. . . Race has an additive and interaction effect on detention. Compared to White youth, being African American increases the likelihood of being detained by 5%. Estimations for race interaction effects with each independent variable also produced a statistically significant relationship between race and drugs. Differentiating the race-drug interaction effect on detention by Whites and African Americans reveals in greater detail this association.

For Whites, participation in drugs has an inverse and nonstatistical significant effect on detention. For African Americans, involvement

with drugs has a positive and statistically significant effect on the dependent variable and increases the probability of being detained by 10%. This finding supports the symbolic threat thesis and previous research that African Americans are viewed by decision makers as drug offenders and as more problematic than similarly situated Whites (e.g., Chambliss, 1995; Sampson & Laub, 1993).

Next, we examined the predictors of intake decision making. . . . Although race is not a statistically significant determinant of the decision to refer youth for further court proceedings at intake, detention is. Being detained increases the likelihood of receiving the more severe outcome at intake by 19%. Thus, African American youth are more likely than are White youth to be referred for further court proceedings at intake because they were more likely to be detained.

Distinguishing between diversion or further court proceedings and release shows that detention has an inverse effect with intake decision making, whereas race has a positive effect. Being African American increases the chances of being released at intake by 26%. Thus, African Americans are both more likely to be referred at intake through detention as well as to be released, relative to Whites. What this also means is that, consistent with prior research (e.g., Leiber & Stairs, 1999), African Americans are less likely to participate in diversion than are Whites.

There is also evidence of race interaction relationships with family status, involvement in person offenses, and, once again, drug offenses and the decision to release. These relationships are made clearer when estimating separate models for Whites and African Americans.

Family status has a statistically significant effect for both Whites and African Americans on intake decision making. The effect of being from a single-parent household, however, varies by the racial group. For Whites, being from a single-parent household increases the chances of being released by 6%, whereas for African Americans in the same family situation, the chances of being released decrease by 6%. The varying effect of family status on decision making, especially at intake, for Whites and African Americans is consistent with not only previous study (e.g., DeJong & Jackson, 1998) but also the symbolic threat thesis and the premise that African Americans from single-parent households are perceived as problematic (Leiber & Mack, 2003).

Also consistent with interpretations of the symbolic threat thesis is the notion that African Americans are perceived by decision makers as prone to drug offenses, threatening, and potentially dangerous (e.g., Sampson & Laub, 1993). In line with this contention is the presence of the inverse effects that exist between being African American and involvement with either a person offense or a drug offense. Being African American and involved with a person offense decreases the likelihood of receiving a release at intake by 18%, and being involved with a drug offense decreases the likelihood by 16%. Neither person offenses nor drug offenses are statistically significant predictors of the decision to release for Whites.

Although there is no evidence of a race interaction effect with detention on the decision to release, the weight of detention operates differently for Whites relative to African Americans. For Whites, being detained decreases the probability of being released by 6%. For African Americans, being detained decreases the probability of receiving the more lenient outcome by 14%. The finding of detention status having a varying effect on decision making by race parallels the results of prior research (e.g., Kempf-Leonard & Sontheimer, 1995).

Up to this point in the analysis, we find strong support for the two hypotheses guiding the research. Race directly influences detention decisions and, in combination with participation with drugs, affects not only detention but also the decision to be released at intake even after controlling for relevant legal and extralegal factors. Race, in interaction with family status and person offenses, also influences intake decision making. These results support H1. Although race is not a predictor of the decision to recommend further court proceedings at intake, it indirectly affects this decision through detention status. This finding is consistent with H2.

Decision Making at Other Stages

. . . Results are presented for the next stages in the proceedings: petition, initial appearance, adjudication, and judicial disposition. For the purpose of clarity, once again the discussion will be limited to the effects of detention and race on each decision-making stage.

Although complex and not as consistent, the findings for the most part support those evident at detention and intake. Both detention and race individually, indirectly, and in interaction with one another and other independent variables influence case proceedings and case outcomes.

For petition, an examination of the results shows that neither detention nor race affect decision making at petition. However, estimations of race interaction effects produced a positive statistically significant relationship between race and the severity of the prior referral.

For Whites, a nonstatistically significant inverse effect is evident between severity of the prior referral with decision making at petition. For African Americans, a positive statistically significant association exists between the independent and the dependent variable. Being African American and having a more severe prior referral increases the likelihood of being petitioned by 3% relative to all other youth. This finding confirms previous research that the severity of a prior disposition may affect current decision making and disadvantage minorities more so than Whites (see Henretta et al., 1986; Thornberry & Christenson, 1984).

At the next stage of the proceedings, detention and race in combination with counsel predict decision making at initial appearance. The chances of moving on from this stage to adjudication increase by 18% if the youth is or has been detained. Counsel is not predictive of decision making for Whites but is for African Americans. The probability of receiving the more severe outcome at initial appearance is increased by 17% for African American youth who have no legal representation.

Although neither detention nor race have statistically significant additive effects on the adjudication process, the two act in combination to affect decision making. Interestingly and in contrast to expectations, Whites, if detained, are placed at a greater disadvantage than are African Americans who are or have been detained. Detention is statistically significant determinant of adjudication for Whites, whereas detention has no effect on the dependent variable for African Americans. For Whites held in detention, the chances of being adjudicated increase by 13%. However, once again corrections for sample bias indicate the factors that predict decision making at initial appearance increase the probability of being adjudicated for African Americans by 19%.

The final stage of decision making reveals that detention has a positive statistically significant effect on judicial disposition, whereas race has an inverse effect. Detention increases the likelihood of receiving an outcome involving a change of placement at judicial disposition by 16%. Being African American decreases the probability of receiving the more severe outcome by 18%. The hazard rate once again suggests sampling bias, and corrections for this indicate that the factors that predict decision making at the previous stage of adjudication predict outcomes at judicial disposition in an inverse manner by a staggering 68%.

▧ Summary and Disscussion

Interpretations of consensus theory indicate that minority youth differences in involvement in the juvenile justice system are the result of differences in legal and extra legal factors or differential involvement in crime (e.g., African Americans commit more crime and more serious crime). Methodologically, controlling for these factors should result in the disappearance of race effects. Versions of conflict theory and in particular the symbolic threat thesis argue that race differences in case processing and case out-comes, in part, can be attributed to racial stereotyping of African Americans as delinquent, prone to drug offenses, dangerous, and unsuitable for treatment. According to the differential selection argument, methodologically race effects will still be present even after controlling for legal and extralegal considerations. Prior research has also shown that detention itself may affect decision making at other stages and that race may indirectly influence decisions through detention. An examination of case processing and case outcomes in one juvenile court jurisdiction, for the most part, yields support for the hypotheses guiding the study and, in particular, the symbolic threat thesis and beliefs that detention works to the disadvantage of African Americans relative to Whites.

Results reveal that differential involvement in crime explains some of the overrepresentation in detention and the further contact with the juvenile justice system overall. Consistent with our hypotheses, however, race affects case processing and outcomes directly, in combination with other factors, and indirectly through detention.

African American youth were more likely than were Whites to receive the more severe outcome at detention, initial appearance, and adjudication even after controlling for relevant legal and extralegal criteria and legal representation. Most of the relationships involved interaction effects among being African American and factors such as committing a drug offense, being from a single-parent household, committing crimes against persons, not having counsel, and the severity of the outcome for a prior referral. African Americans also moved further through the system because of the effect of detention on decision making at intake, initial appearance, and judicial disposition. Thus, the presence of African Americans in the juvenile justice system including detention can be attributed to differential involvement in delinquency, differential selection, and detention, which to some degree is racially tainted.

The finding of differential selection or treatment is consistent with the symbolic threat thesis and the emphasis on the racial stereotyping of African Americans by decision makers. This is made even more evident by case outcomes influenced by the interaction relationships among being African American and committing drug offenses, residing in single-parent homes, and committing crimes against persons (e.g., Feld, 1999; Leiber,

2003; Sampson & Laub, 1993). Although the quantitative results infer support for this premise, future research that directly examines the interrelationships among racial stereotyping, decision making, and case outcomes is needed.

There may be some questions concerning the extent to which racial stereotyping underlies the observed race differences in case proceedings, but there is no denying that race and detention influence decision making. The results show a number of complex relationships, such as the association between being White and detention at adjudication, that sometimes affect Whites in a more severe manner. Also, African American youth who were not detained at some point during the proceedings were more likely than were White youth to receive the more lenient outcome at judicial disposition. In short, the findings lend further credence to the effect that earlier decisions may have on current or future outcomes (e.g., Henretta et al., 1986; Thornberry & Christenson, 1984) especially in terms of detention and greater penetration into the juvenile justice system for African Americans.

The results from the present study also add further support to the contention that decision making, especially in the juvenile justice system, needs to be viewed as a process. As many stages as possible should be included in researching the factors that affect case outcomes. The omission of any one of the six stages in Iowa's juvenile justice system may have resulted in the inability to capture both the direct and indirect effects of race and detention on decision making.

An additional implication for future research is the need to further explore the kinds of things or factors that influence case outcomes but that were not included in the present research. The significance of the statistical technique to correct for selection bias or the hazard rate, for example, highlights this point. Furthermore, although crime type was controlled in the analysis, what constituted the reason for the detention referral and if the behavior or non-behavior varies by race were not addressed. As discussed by Steinhart (2001), violation of probation as a justification for detention is increasing, has race implications,

and has been relatively neglected. Because of the significance of race at detention, there is cause to examine this issue in greater detail.

Another direction for future research is the role that legal representation has in juvenile proceedings. In the present study, counsel had effects on decision making at almost every stage and in one instance interacted with race at the adjudicatory hearing (African Americans with no legal representation had greater chances of being adjudicated delinquent). Most often, having no legal counsel resulted in receiving a more lenient outcome. Although this may not make intuitive sense, this finding is consistent with the limited research that exists. That is, youth with counsel generally receive more severe sanctions than do those without an attorney (e.g., Feld, 1988, 1989; Guevara et al., 2004). Further research that employs both quantitative and qualitative assessments into the dynamic between counsel and decision making is needed. In particular, future research could assess not only the type of legal counsel involved but the place in the proceedings where counsel comes into play, the quality of the legal representation, and the ways in which decision makers perceive and respond to the presence of counsel.

Despite the need for further research in this area, the present study makes a contribution to the existing literature by placing the race-detention issue within a theoretical context, by using relatively recent data in a jurisdiction where detention had not been previously assessed, by focusing on six stages, and by considering a wide array of measures that represent the social situation of youth and the presence of legal representation. Furthermore, although the results in general confirm those from prior research (e.g., Frazier & Bishop, 1995), the findings not only further illustrate the complexities of the race-detention relationship but also show that this effect was found to exist in a relatively small, homogenous Midwestern county. Not only did race and detention influence decision making, but the size of the effects, to varying degrees, are larger than those reported by studies that have focused on courts in more urban and diversified settings (e.g., Frazier

& Bishop, 1985; Wordes et al., 1994). Further research is needed to address why the effects are larger. Theory, however, provides us with several possible explanations.

For example, interpretations of traditional conflict theory suggest that a lower proportion of minorities in the population allows this relatively powerless group to be subjected to greater social control (e.g., Quinney, 1970). Alternatively, Weber's (1969) perspective on urbanization and formal and substantive rationality contends that because rural courts are not as bureaucratic as urban courts, informal criteria and legally irrelevant factors (i.e., substantive rationality) inform decision making. Thus, bias will be more evident in rural courts, and African Americans in rural courts will evidence higher rates of intervention compared to urban courts (cf. Zatz, 1987). Or, contextually, it may be that the historical, structural, and organizational factors associated with this particular community and court creates an environment among decision makers where race and racial stereotyping take on significant importance relative to other jurisdictions. Although there is a need for further research to address this issue, the results pave the way for policy reform.

The implications for policy center on the need to reform detention admission practices and the criteria used to make admissions. Until this is done, equitable treatment for all youth will not be attained. Suggestions for policy reform should involve the structuring of decision making, especially at detention and intake. One way to do this is to adopt detention and intake, risk-assessment instruments (Justice Policy Institute, 2002) and to be sure that these instruments are race neutral (Pope, 1995). In addition, the police, detention personnel, juvenile court decision makers, and community in general need to collaborate on devising a strategy to see detention in terms of a continuum of services (e.g., youth shelters, foster parents, etc.) rather than solely in terms of the most secure form of detention. Likewise, interested parties need to be made aware that the development and utilization of less secure alternatives to secure detention does

not necessarily mean increased threats to public safety or the implementation of race quotas (e.g., Hoytt et al., 2002; Justice Policy Institute, 2002). In fact, the issue is fairness across the board, and within this context the presence of African American youth in secure detention should decrease because they as a group are overrepresented in secure detention.

Last, detention reform is just one method to reduce overreliance on secure detention and minority overrepresentation. Other efforts are needed to eliminate or at least minimize minority overrepresentation in the system and racial bias. These efforts include programs aimed at delinquency prevention, cultural sensitivity training for decision makers, and building collaboration to address the issue among politicians, law enforcement, the juvenile court, local providers, and citizens.[8]

▨ Notes

1. In the early 1990s, minority youth and adults were overrepresented in both the juvenile and adult systems in Iowa and still are today (Division of Criminal and Juvenile Justice Planning and Statistical Analysis, 2004). For example, about 32% of the youth in the Boys State Training School are minority, with 20% of those African American. Minority youth comprise about 5% of the total population of Iowa and up to 10% or more in some cities (Bureau of the Census, 2000). For adults, at least 1 in 12 African American Iowans is in prison, on parole, or on probation, whereas the similar ratio for Whites is 1 in 110. The incarceration rate for African Americans in Iowa tops the national average ("A Generation," 2000).

2. A third position contends that race differences in case processing and case outcomes may disappear once legal and extralegal criteria are considered but that the criteria used to inform decision making, although legitimate, may also be racially tainted. For example, for a variety of reasons, African American youth may have lengthier and more problematic prior records than do Whites and/or may reside with families that are less able to provide proper supervision. Although legitimate criteria, these effects often

work to the disadvantage of minority youth (e.g., Frazier & Bishop, 1995; Pope & Feyerherm, 1992). Although there is validity to this position, for the purpose of theory competition, the present research relies on the competing premises of the consensus and interpretations of the conflict approaches to guide the study.

3. Relative to other counties in the state of Iowa, this county has been characterized as high on economic and racial inequality in terms of the percent of persons in poverty, the unwed teenage pregnancy rates, and criminal justice expenditures (Leiber, 2003). In addition, the organizational philosophy of the juvenile court has been one of accountability and intervention with an emphasis on the social control of youth (Leiber, 2003). A study of criminal justice sentencing in the state of Iowa echoes these sentiments as this county was found to send minor felons to prison more than most areas and for drug offenses nearly twice as often as the state average (Eby, 2001).

4. Similar to detention criteria across the country (Hoytt, Schiraldi, Smith, & Ziedenberg, 2002), state statute lacks specificity and provides a great deal of discretion to the police, juvenile court officers, and judges to determine whether detention is necessary (Iowa Code 2001, section 232.22, 232.52). Admission to the detention facility is controlled by the juvenile court specifically through individual juvenile court officers and a judge. Police officers that have a child in custody call a juvenile court officer and the juvenile court officer calls a judge prior to placing a youth into detention. Juvenile court officers may or may not have a recommendation for detention when contacting the judge. Recommendations and decisions to detain are based on an array of factors considered by the juvenile court officer and the judge. There is no written detention survey instrument to assist in detention decisions at this facility. Although a verbal court order can initiate placement, a written court order must be issued within 12 hours of detention. Detention can be used to minimize risk of reoffending while the current delinquent charge is determined and the case is settled, to prevent flight, and to protect the alleged offender from imminent bodily harm. Detention can also be used as a sanction for violation of court orders or probation rules or as a 48-hour or two-day dispositional placement (Iowa Code 2001, section 232.22; 232.52). A violation of probation does not entail a new crime and is generally viewed as a technical violation such as

failure to obey curfew or some other condition established by the court. The 48-hour dispositional hold was passed as a judicial sentencing option in 1996.

5. The intake variable may be viewed as ordinal. An examination of the proportional odds results, however, indicated that the variable's effects on the odds of a response equal to or above category k is not the same for all k when k is the cut point parameter of the model (Agresti, 1989). The violation of the proportional odds assumption necessitates the estimate of two equations (one using the lower cut point as the reference point release and another using the upper cut point referral for further court proceedings).

6. Detention as part of the two-day dispositional sanction was included as part of the change of placement outcome at the stage of judicial disposition. The small number of youth ($n = 76$; 1%) precluded treatment as a distinct dependent variable.

7. We were unable to differentiate the type of drug offense that youth were referred to court for. Although this is a shortcoming and a need for future research, differences in the type of drug offense can be captured to some degree by the measure of crime severity.

8. It is important to note that the county under study has made the problem of race and detention a targeted area for reform. For example, a local disproportionate minority contact task force that includes many of the key stakeholders (e.g., juvenile court, detention personnel, police) has been formed and meets at least once a month. Other strategies that are being used in this county include the development and use of programs to divert youth away from detention, the hiring of a coordinator to educate the community on this specific issue and on disproportionate minority contact in general, and the development of a data management system for the purpose of determining who is going into detention, for what reasons, and for how long. The task force is also currently working on a detention-screening instrument to aid in the decision-making process. Greater discussion on programs and initiatives such as these and others that focus on differential offending and differential selection can be found in the *Disproportionate Minority Confinement Technical Assistance Manual* (U.S. Department Of Justice, Office of Juvenile Justice and Delinquency Prevention, 2000) and elsewhere (Bridges, Hsia, & McHale, 2004; Feyerherm, 2000; Hsia & Hamparian, 1998; Mihalic, Irwin, Fagan, Ballard, & Elliott, 2004; Pope & Leiber, in press).

📖 References

Agresti, A. (1989). Tutorial on modeling ordered categorical response data. *Psychologist Bulletin, 105,* 290–301.

Belsley, D., Kuhn, E., & Welsh, R. (1980). *Regression diagnostics identifying influential data and source of collinearity.* New York: John Wiley.

Berk, R. A. (1983). An introduction to sample selection bias in sociological data. *American Sociological Review, 48,* 386–398.

Bishop, D. (in press). The role of race and ethnicity in juvenile justice processing. In D. Hawkins & K. Kempf-Leonard (Eds.), *Our children, their children: Confronting racial and ethnic differences in American juvenile justice.* Chicago: University of Chicago Press.

Bishop, D., & Frazier, C. (1988). The influence of race in juvenile justice processing. *Journal of Research in Crime and Delinquency, 22,* 309–328.

Bortner, M., & Reed, W. (1985). Race and the impact of juvenile deinstitutionalization. *Crime & Delinquency, 31,* 35–46.

Bridges, G., Hsia, H., & McHale, R. (2004). *Disproportionate confinement—2002 update.* Washington, DC: Office of Juvenile Justice and Delinquency Prevention.

Bridges, G., & Steen, S. (1998). Racial disparities in official assessments of juvenile offenders: Attributional stereotypes as mediating mechanisms. *American Sociological Review, 63,* 554–570.

Bureau of the Census. (2000). *2000 census of population: General population characteristics.* Washington, DC: Author.

Chambliss, W. (1995). Crime control and ethnic minorities: Legitimizing racial oppression by creating moral panics. In D. Hawkins (Ed.), *Ethnicity, race, and crime: Perspectives across time and place* (pp. 235–258). Albany, NY: State University of New York Press.

DeJong, C., & Jackson, K. (1998). Putting race into context: Race, juvenile justice processing, and urbanization. *Justice Quarterly, 15,* 487–504.

Division of Criminal and Juvenile Planning and Statistical Analysis. (2004). *Youth development approach for Iowa's children and families.* Des Moines, IA: Author.

Eby, C. (2001, February 25). Black Hawk sentences among the state's toughest. *Waterloo Courier,* pp. A1, A7.

Engen, R., Steen, S., & Bridges, G. (2002). Racial disparities in the punishment of youth: A theoretical and empirical assessment of the literature. *Social Problems, 49,* 194–220.

Feld, B. (1988). In Re Gault revisited: A cross-state comparison of the right to counsel in juvenile court. *Crime & Delinquency, 34,* 393–424.

Feld, B. (1999). *Bad kids: Race and the transformation of the juvenile court.* New York: Oxford University Press.

Feyerherm, W. (2000). Detention reform and overrepresentation: A successful synergy. *Corrections Management Quarterly, 4*(1): 44–51.

Frazier, C., & Bishop, D. (1985). The pretrial detention of juveniles and its impact on case dispositions. *The Journal of Criminal Law & Criminology, 76,* 1132–1152.

Frazier, C., & Bishop, D. M. (1995). Reflections on race effects in juvenile justice. In K. Kempf-Leonard, C. E. Pope, & W. Feyerherm (Eds.), *Minorities in juvenile justice* (pp. 16–46). Thousand Oaks, CA: Sage.

Frazier, C., & Cochran, J. (1986). Detention of juveniles its effects on subsequent juvenile court proceedings. *Youth and Society, 17,* 286–305.

A generation in prison editorial. (2000, December 30). *Des Moines Register,* p. 19.

Guevara, L., Spohn, C., & Herz, D. (2004). Race, legal representation, and juvenile justice: Issues and concerns. *Crime & Delinquency, 50,* 344–371.

Hawkins, D., & Kempf-Leonard, K. (Eds.). (in press). *Our children, their children: Confronting racial and ethnic differences in American juvenile justice.* Chicago: University of Chicago Press.

Heckman, J. (1974). Shadow prices, market wages, and labor supply. *Econometrica, 42,* 679–694.

Henretta, J., Frazier, C., & Bishop, D. (1986). The effect of prior case outcomes on juvenile justice decision making. *Social Forces, 65,* 555–562.

Hindelang, M. (1978). Race and involvement in common law personal crimes. *American Sociological Review, 43,* 93–109.

Hsia, H., Bridges, G., & McHale, R. (2004). *Disproportionate confinement—2002 update.* Washington, DC: Office of Juvenile Justice and Delinquency Prevention.

Hsia, H., & Hamparian, D. (1998). *Disproportionate minority confinement: 1997 update.* Washington, DC: Office of Juvenile Justice and Delinquency Prevention.

Hoytt, E., Schiraldi, V., Smith, B., & Ziedenberg, J. (2002). *Reducing racial disparities in juvenile detention: Pathways to juvenile detention reform.* Baltimore, MD: The Annie E. Casey Foundation.

Justice Policy Institute. (2002). *Reducing disproportionate minority confinement: The Multnomah County, Oregon success story and its implications.* Washington, DC: Justice Policy Institute.

Kempf-Leonard, K., & Sontheimer, H. (1995). The role of race in juvenile justice in Pennsylvania. In K. Kempf-Leonard, C. E. Pope, & W. Feyerherm (Eds.), *Minorities in juvenile justice* (pp. 98–127). Thousand Oaks, CA: Sage.

Leiber, M. (1994). A comparison of juvenile court outcomes for Native Americans, African Americans, and Whites. *Justice Quarterly, 11,* 257–279.

Leiber, M. (2002). Disproportionate minority youth confinement (DMC): An analysis of the mandate and state responses. *Crime and Delinquency, 48*(1), 3–45.

Leiber, M. (2003). *The contexts of juvenile justice decision making: When race matters.* Albany, NY: State University of New York Press.

Leiber, M., and Jamieson, K. (1995). Race, decision making and the implications of context in juvenile justice proceedings. *Journal of Quantitative Criminology, 11*(4), 363–388.

Leiber, M., & Mack, K. (2003). The individual and joint effects of race, gender, and family status on juvenile justice decision-making. *Journal of Research in Crime & Delinquency, 40*(1), 34–70.

Leiber, M., & Stairs, J. (1999). Race, contexts, and the use of intake diversion. *Journal of Research in Crime and Delinquency, 36,* 56–86.

McCarthy, B., & Smith, B. (1986).The conceptualization of discrimination in the juvenile justice process: The impact of administrative factors and screening decisions of juvenile court decisions. *Criminology, 24,* 41–64.

Mihalic, S., Irwin, K., Fagan, A., Ballard, D., & Elliott, D. (2004). *Successful program implementation: Lessons from blueprints.* Washington, DC: U.S. Department of Justice, Office of Juvenile Justice and Delinquency Prevention.

North East Iowa Juvenile Detention Center. (2004). *Annual report.* Black Hawk County, IA: Author.

Peterson, T. (1985). A comment on presenting results from logit and probit models. *American Sociological Review, 50,* 130–131.

Pope, C. E. (1995). Equity within the juvenile justice system: Directions for the future. In K. Kempf-Leonard, C. E. Pope, & W. Feyerherm (Eds.), *Minorities in juvenile justice* (pp. 201–216). Thousand Oaks, CA: Sage.

Pope, C. E., & Feyerherm, W. (1992). *Minorities and the juvenile justice system: Full report.* Rockville, MD: U.S. Department of Justice, Office of Juvenile Justice and Delinquency Prevention, Juvenile Justice Clearing House.

Pope, C. E., & Leiber, M. (in press). Disproportionate minority contact (DMC): The federal initiative. In D. Hawkins & K. Kempf-Leonard (Eds.), *Our children, their children: Confronting racial and ethnic differences in American juvenile justice.* Chicago: University of Chicago Press.

Pope, C. E., Lovell, R., & Hsia, H. M. (2002). *Synthesis of disproportionate minority confinement (DMC) research literature (1989–1999).* Washington, DC: U.S. Department of Justice, Office of Juvenile Justice and Delinquency Prevention.

Quinney, R. (1970). *The social reality of crime.* Boston: Little, Brown.

Sampson, R., & Laub, J. (1993). Structural variations in juvenile court processings: Inequality, the underclass, and social control. *Law & Society Review, 27,* 285–311.

Snyder, H., & Sickmund, M. (1999). *Juvenile offenders and victims: A national report.* Washington, DC: Office of Juvenile Justice and Delinquency Prevention.

Stahl, A. (1999). *Delinquency cases waived to criminal court, 1987–1996* (Fact Sheet No. 99). Washington, DC: Office of Juvenile Justice and Delinquency Prevention.

Steinhart, D. (2001). *Special detention cases: Strategies for handling difficult populations pathways to juvenile detention reform.* Baltimore, MD: Annie E. Casey Foundation.

Thornberry, T., & Christenson, R. L. (1984). Juvenile justice decision making as a longitudinal process. *Social Forces, 63,* 433–444.

Tittle, C., & Curran, D. (1988). Contingencies for dispositional disparities in juvenile justice. *Social Forces, 67,* 23–58.

Tracy, P. E. (2002). *Decision making and juvenile justice: An analysis of bias in case processing.* Westport, CT: Praeger.

U.S. Department Of Justice, Office of Juvenile Justice and Delinquency Prevention. (2000). *Disproportionate minority confinement technical assistance manual.* Washington, DC: Author.

Weber, M. (1969). *Max Weber on law in economy and society* (M. Rheinstein, Trans.). Cambridge, MA: Harvard University Press.

Wordes, M., Bynum, T., & Corley. C. (1994). Locking up youth: The impact of race on detention decisions. *Journal of Research in Crime and Delinquency, 31*(2), 149–165.

Zatz, M. (1987). The changing forms of racial/ethnic biases in sentencing. *Journal of Research in Crime and Delinquency, 24,* 69–92.

DISCUSSION QUESTIONS

1. What is the "symbolic threat" theory, and how does it explain the higher detention rate of minority youth?

2. Is it possible that minority youth are detained at higher rates because of legal factors? Explain.

3. Several studies find that legal and extralegal factors alone cannot account for the race differences in juvenile justice system involvement. Explain how race may have "indirect effects" on decision making.

4. According to the results of this study, does race affect the likelihood of being detained? How does participation in drug offenses affect decision making? Does being detained influence further court proceedings and decisions?

5. How do the findings explain the race differences in detention and case processing? Does racial stereotyping affect decision making in the juvenile justice system? Explain.

6. What do the authors suggest for future research and policy changes?

❖

READING

Recent reforms have increased the possibilities for gathering and sharing information during juvenile justice processing. Juvenile justice experts have called for more comprehensive assessments of all juvenile referrals. Little attention has been given, however, to questions concerning the timing, goals, or uses of assessments, the structure and goals of intake, or the role of assessments at intake. These questions deserve closer investigation because variation in assessment or intake goals and practices will limit the efficiency or efficacy of juvenile processing. The authors of this study used interview and survey data from a study of county-level intake processes in Texas. Based on the findings, they offer several policy recommendations that can improve on the effectiveness and efficiency of assessments in juvenile justice processing.

Assessments and Intake
Processes in Juvenile Justice Processing

Emerging Policy Considerations

Daniel P. Mears, William R. Kelly

The importance of juvenile screening, assessment, and referral has been strongly emphasized in the past few years (Beyer, Grisso, and Young 1997; Dembo and Brown 1994; Rivers, Dembo, and Anwyl 1998; Schwartz and Barton 1994), particularly in relation to mental health and substance abuse problems among juvenile offenders (Bilchik 1998). However, as one recent review found, "Quality screening and in-depth assessment of youths entering the juvenile justice system remains the exception rather than the rule" (Dembo and Brown 1994, p. 29). Similarly, in a 1988 national survey of juvenile-needs assessment practices, Towberman (1992) found that the "quality and point of initiation of needs assessment varied greatly" (p. 231), that in many states "juveniles do not receive an assessment of their needs until after commitment to the youth correctional system," and that only one-third of the states reported the use of any kind of formal needs assessment instruments (p. 233). Towberman's research led her to conclude that "juvenile justice officials need to clarify the purpose and philosophy of juvenile needs assessment" (p. 236).

Clarification of the purposes of assessments takes on added significance when we consider that there is a growing emphasis on conducting formal risk and needs assessments at the earliest stages of juvenile justice processing (Champion 1998, p. 470; Dembo and Brown 1994); that the vast majority of informally and formally processed juveniles ultimately have their cases dismissed, are diverted from the juvenile justice system, or receive probation (Sickmund, Stahl, Finnegan, Snyder, Poole, and Butts 1998, p. 9);

and that recent juvenile justice reforms have greatly expanded information gathering and sharing among various local and state agencies (National Criminal Justice Association 1997, pp. 36–40; Torbet, Gable, Hurst, Montgomery, Szymanski, and Thomas 1996, chap. 5; Torbet and Szymanski 1998, pp. 12–4). These developments, along with the trend since the 1960s toward criminalizing the juvenile court (Feld 1998, 1999), give rise to increasingly important questions. For example, what are the purposes of assessments and intake? What factors, such as the structure and goals of intake, affect the use and effectiveness of assessments and, ultimately, the efficiency and effectiveness of juvenile justice processing? Although diversion of certain delinquency cases from formal processing "can be cost-effective in terms of both public accountability and offender rehabilitation" (Snyder and Sickmund 1996, p. 131), few studies have examined systematically the diversion process, including the information and criteria that are used to identify juveniles who are appropriate for dismissal, counsel and release, or diversion.

This article examines these questions by using survey and interview data from a study of county-level juvenile intake processes in Texas. First, a brief overview of juvenile justice processing is provided to highlight the significance of intake processes and the potential role of assessments at intake. Second, after reviewing the data, findings are presented concerning the timing, goals, and uses of risk and needs assessments among Texas counties. Third, findings are presented concerning the structure and goals of intake, information collected at intake, and obstacles to efficient and effective intake processes. Finally, we conclude with a discussion of the policy considerations of our analyses and recent trends in juvenile justice.

Juvenile Justice Processing

An Overview of Juvenile Justice Processing

There are a number of stages in the processing of juvenile offenders: prearrest (e.g., when the police stop juveniles and determine whether to take official action), arrest, intake, detention, adjudication, and disposition (Champion 1998, chap. 3). However, the vast majority of juveniles are not detained, adjudicated, or given a disposition. Most juveniles have their cases dismissed or receive an informal sanction agreed upon through plea negotiations between defense attorneys and prosecutors, usually with recommendations from probation (Champion 1998; Feld 1998; Sickmund 1997; Sickmund et al. 1998).

Consider the 1995 national statistics on juvenile court processing of all delinquency cases. Table 1 shows that close to half of those were informally processed (45 percent), and, of all informally and formally processed cases, large proportions were dismissed (37 percent), given probation, a lesser sanction, or referred for services (53 percent), whereas a relatively small proportion was placed in a residential facility or committed to an institution (10 percent) or waived (less than 1 percent) (Sickmund et al. 1998, p. 9).[1] Although considerable variation exists nationally in the extent to which cases are processed informally or formally, it is noteworthy that relatively large percentages of both types of cases result in dismissal (47 percent and 28 percent, respectively) and that the majority of formally processed cases result in probation, a lesser sanction, or referral for services (54 percent; Sickmund et al. 1998, p. 9).

To set the context for the subsequent analyses, consider that, in 1995, only two other states (California and Florida) had more delinquency cases than Texas, which had 44,263 petitioned and 62,396 nonpetitioned cases (Sickmund et al. 1998, p. 83). The large volume of cases notwithstanding, processing of juveniles in Texas reflects national patterns: In 1997, 22 percent (24,311) of juvenile referrals resulted in dismissal, 51 percent (56,480) resulted in an informal disposition, and 27 percent (29,245) resulted in a formal disposition (Texas Criminal Justice Policy Council 1998, p. 10; see also Texas Criminal Justice Policy Council 1999a, p. 11).

Several additional facts about juvenile processing, nationally and in Texas, merit further consideration. First, in recent years, the percentage of referrals resulting in a formal disposition has slowly but steadily increased (Sickmund et al. 1998, p. 15; Texas Criminal Justice Policy Council 1999a, p. 7), but most cases still are informally processed. Second, there is considerable within-state and across-state variation in juvenile processing (Feld 1999, p. 113). For example, consider the outcomes of referrals across six of the largest counties in Texas in 1997: from 11 to 35 percent were dismissed, .1 to 51 percent received supervisory cautions, 14 to 42 percent received deferred prosecution, 21 to 32 percent received probation, 2 to 5 percent were committed to the Texas Youth Commission, and .1 to 1.1 percent were waived to adult court (Texas Criminal Justice Policy Council 1999a, p. 13). Third, most juveniles who enter the juvenile justice system have only one referral (Snyder and Sickmund 1996, p. 158; Texas Criminal Justice Policy Council 1999a, p. 3); thus rendering diversion or probation as arguably one of the most reasonable and potentially beneficial option for many youths (Greenwood 1996, p. 82).

Intake as a Critical Juncture in Juvenile Justice Processing

Youths who enter the juvenile justice system are initially processed through intake. Although 80 to 90 percent of all referrals come from law enforcement agencies, a relatively small percentage comes from other sources, including schools and parents (Sickmund et al. 1998, p. 7). After the completion of an initial screening, intake can result in dismissal, diversion

Table 1	Juvenile Court Processing of Delinquency Cases Nationally, 1995 (in percentages; $n = 1,714,300$)				
	Dismissed	*Probation*	*Other*	*Placement*	*Total*
Informally processed (45 percent of all delinquency cases)	47	31	21	1	100
Formally processed: nonadjudicated (23 percent of all delinquency cases)	60	22	16	3	100
Formally processed: adjudicated (31 percent of all delinquency cases)	5	53	14	28	100
Formally processed: waived (1 percent of all delinquency cases)	—	—	—	—	100

SOURCE: Sickmund, Stahl, Finnegan, Snyder, Poole, and Butts (1998, p. 9).

NOTE: Precise estimates of the outcomes associated with transfers to adult courts are currently lacking. However, research suggests that few waived youths have their cases dismissed and that roughly equal percentages of the remaining (nondismissed) youths receive either probation (or some other alternative to incarceration) or an incarcerative sanction (see Snyder and Sickmund 1996, p. 155).

to a social service agency, informal probation, payment of fines, community service or some type of restitution, or a petition for formal processing (Champion 1998, chap. 3; Sickmund et al. 1998, p. 2).[2] Cases may be dismissed for a variety of reasons: insufficient legal evidence, the offense is a relatively minor one, the offense is relatively minor and the juvenile is or appears to be a first-time offender, the juvenile or his or her family has compensated the victim, the family background is strong and the juvenile seems amenable to parental supervision, or formal processing is deemed unnecessary (U.S. General Accounting Office [GAO] 1995b, p. 4). In contrast to more serious sanctions, such as incarceration, probation and diversion are typically used to screen first-time or less serious cases from formal adjudicatory and dispositional processing. The idea is that offenders in such cases are inappropriate for formal processing but nonetheless require and may be amenable to

treatment through community-based programs and services (GAO 1995b, p. 4).

Intake frequently is structured differently across jurisdictions (Dedel 1998; GAO 1995a; Sickmund et al. 1998, p. 1) and intake officers frequently can exercise considerable discretion in how cases are processed (Champion 1998, p. 150). Consider Butts and Harrell's (1998) description of intake:

Usually managed by the court but sometimes by other agencies, intake is a sequence of screening and referral decisions designed to ensure that each offender receives the most appropriate response from the court. Intake workers sift a court's caseload into various classifications. Some are diverted or simply dismissed. Some are handled informally if the youth agrees to participate in counseling, job training, etc. Others are formally charged and scheduled for adjudication. Rather than making these decisions based only on the formal charges contained in a police report, the intake process depends on multiple indicators of each youth's individual situation (p. 13).

The variation in intake and the discretion afforded to intake officers is consonant with the *parens patriae* spirit of the original juvenile court, including the emphasis on nonadversarial proceedings and flexible decision making (Feld 1999). However, despite the importance of intake to decision making about juveniles, most research has focused on post-intake processing, especially detention and formal processing, even though most juveniles are never detained, formally processed, or waived to adult court (see Feld 1999). Given the potential for intake to influence all subsequent processing, it constitutes one of the most critical points in the entire juvenile justice process for applying prevention or early intervention strategies or both; yet, to date, it remains a largely underresearched aspect of juvenile processing.

Juvenile Justice Reforms: Increasing Emphasis on Information-Gathering and Sharing

Recent juvenile justice reforms have increased the potential for gathering and sharing information on juveniles who are referred to the juvenile court. These reforms have included decreasing the confidentiality of court proceedings and records, increasing the access to and sharing of information about juveniles among various local and state agencies, creating centralized repositories of juvenile records, enabling law enforcement agencies to fingerprint and photograph juvenile arrestees, and restricting or eliminating the conditions under which juvenile records can be sealed or expunged (National Criminal Justice Association 1997, pp. 36–40; Torbet et al. 1996, chap. 5; Torbet and Szymanski 1998, pp. 12–14). Torbet and colleagues (1996) have stated that "the rationale for sharing information among system actors with a 'need to know' is a better coordinated and more efficient

service delivery system that avoids duplication of services and better utilizes shrinking resources" (p. 35). Although such a goal is both reasonable and justified, it also raises issues about the precise goals of various system actors and the specific uses to which they put information. Rubin (1996), for example, has indicated that there frequently are "tensions between the court and the child welfare agency" (p. 50). Similarly, Feld (1999) has emphasized that the historical foundation of the juvenile court—locating social control and social welfare efforts in one agency—constitutes the "essential premise and the fundamental flaw of the juvenile court" (p. 332), which suggests that the juvenile court is divided as to the purposes to which it should put the information gathered about juveniles (see also Guarino-Ghezzi and Loughran 1996).

Increasing Calls for Early Assessment of Juvenile Referrals

In a get tough era of juvenile justice reform, in which expanded information collection and sharing have increasingly been promoted, there also has been a call for prevention efforts, including calls for early identification and treatment of juveniles (see Coordinating Council on Juvenile Justice and Delinquency Prevention 1996; Edwards 1996; Howell 1995; Sherman, Gottfredson, MacKenzie, Eck, Reuter, and Bushway 1997). For example, Dembo and Brown (1994) have argued that "resources should be placed in assessing and providing needed services to youths and their families at the earliest (ideally the first) point of contact with the juvenile justice system, rather than targeted primarily to youths with repeated contact with the juvenile courts" (pp. 29–30). Indeed, in recent years, greater numbers of local and state jurisdictions have been using assessments at increasingly earlier stages of juvenile justice processing, including prior to adjudication or disposition (Guarino-Ghezzi and Loughran 1996, pp. 128–32), detention (Schwartz and Barton 1994), and informal and formal processing in general (National Criminal Justice Association 1997, p. 28; Rivers et al. 1998).

To date, however, relatively little attention has focused on the precise timing or uses of assessments, particularly of less serious offenders and of juveniles not yet incarcerated (Champion 1998, pp. 302–3). Instead, emphasis has focused on the validity and predictive utility of risk assessments (Champion 1998, p. 297; Gottfredson 1987). Although such an emphasis is consonant with the view of the juvenile court as an agency of social control, it neglects the idea that the court, at least in part, is a social welfare agency guided by the doctrine *of parens patriae* (Feld 1999). From this latter perspective, it indeed is surprising that few researchers have focused on risk and needs assessment processes and outcomes (Towberman 1992); the screening and assessment of mental health and substance abuse treatment needs of juvenile offenders (Bilchik 1998; Rivers et al. 1998); or related issues, such as the efficacy of informal referral practices or due process rights at first contact with the juvenile justice system (Beyer et al. 1997; Dodge 1997; Puritz, Burrell, Schwartz, Soler, and Warboys 1995; Puritz and Shang 1998). Although one obvious goal of intake assessments is to promote early intervention with juveniles who are on track to becoming more serious offenders and to divert juveniles in need of particular services to appropriate programs (see Rivers et al. 1998, p. 441), clearly, there are other possible goals of intake assessments (e.g., to assist with detention decisions, adjudication, dispositional recommendations, and case management).

In short, despite their potential importance, there has been little research regarding the goals or uses of assessments, intake processes, or the role of assessments at intake. These aspects of juvenile processing will likely assume an even greater importance for the efficiency and effectiveness of juvenile justice as courts become increasingly formalized and criminalized (Feld 1998; Singer 1996), and as intake units are increasingly called on to route juvenile offenders to the most appropriate services or agencies (Butts and Harrell 1998, p. 13).

⊠ Data and Methods

This study examined the timing, goals, and uses of assessments; the structure and goals of intake; and the role of assessments at intake. Two sources of data were used: (a) in-depth, open-ended, in-person, and telephone interviews, conducted in fall 1998 and spring 1999 by one of the authors, with 20 Texas juvenile justice practitioners (probation officers, prosecutors, judges, and mental health and substance abuse program staff) from eight rural, suburban, and urban counties, and with state agency staff; and (b) a survey administered in spring 1999 to chief probation officers in all 162 juvenile court jurisdictions, representing 254 counties in Texas (66 percent response rate; $n = 107$).[3] The interviewees were selected through a process of purposive sampling (Babbie 1995). The interview protocol was designed to address respondent perceptions about the overall process of assessing and referring juvenile offenders, specific goals associated with assessments and intake, and issues affecting the efficiency and effectiveness of both assessments and intake. The survey, which was based on information from previous research and interviews, was designed to assess practitioners' views concerning specific aspects of the assessment and intake process, both to identify specific issues and to obtain a more generalizable picture of assessment and intake practices statewide.

The selection of Texas was justified for several reasons. First, juvenile justice reforms in this state have paralleled those nationally (Torbet et al. 1996); thus, knowledge of juvenile processing in Texas under the new reforms should be of direct relevance to other states. Second, evidence on assessment and intake processes in Texas should contribute directly to the understanding of juvenile processing nationally, given both the sheer magnitude of cases the state processes annually (Sickmund et al. 1998, p. 83) and the similarity to other states of patterns of informal and formal processing (Sickmund et al. 1998, p. 15; Texas Criminal Justice Policy Council 1999a, p. 7). Third, and perhaps most importantly, Texas recently enacted legislation mandating risk and needs assessments of all juveniles who are to receive informal or formal dispositions. Passage of this legislation provided a unique opportunity to examine the differential impact of such a policy on various jurisdictions, and to highlight key issues concerning the goals of assessments and intake.

⚅ Risk and Needs Assessments

Timing and Goals

In 1997, the Texas Legislature, through House Bill 2073, enacted section 141.042(e) of the Human Resources Code (HRC), which requires that probation departments complete a standard assessment tool (SAT), or its equivalent, for the initial assessment of juvenile referrals. The precise timing and goals of the assessment were left unclear. The SAT is to "facilitate assessment of a child's mental health, family background, and level of education" and "assist juvenile probation departments in determining when a child in the department's jurisdiction is in need of comprehensive psychological or other evaluation."[4] By contrast, the language in the relevant sections of the Texas Administrative Code (TAC), which operationalizes legislative mandates created in the HRC, indicates, on one hand, that assessments are to be completed at a "formal intake interview" (section 346.1 [4]) for all juveniles who receive informal or formal dispositions (section 346.2[a]) and, on the other hand, that the assessments are "to assist the supervising juvenile probation field officer in developing and implementing an effective case plan, appropriate level of supervision, and utilization of appropriate resources" (section 346.1[1]). That is, the stipulated goals range from facilitating assessment to assisting with case management of juveniles. Not surprisingly, interviews with practitioners revealed considerable variation in the interpretation of the HRC and TAC statutes. At the time of this writing, this variation was in the process of being addressed by staff from the Texas Juvenile

Probation Commission (TJPC), the agency responsible for enacting and enforcing those parts of the TAC applicable to juvenile probation.

Interviews with practitioners and agency staff suggested that one of the central causes of variation in the interpretation of HRC and TAC statutes stems from differing intake practices. For example, many jurisdictions distinguish between detention intake and formal intake, with the former focused solely on determining whether to detain a youth and the latter focused on collecting information about only those youths for whom informal or formal processing will occur. Thus, the actual timing and goals of the SAT can vary depending on a probation department's understanding of the HRC and TAC statutes, and of what constitutes intake. Another cause of variation in perceptions of the timing and goals of the SAT is that probation departments are required to complete a Strategies in Juvenile Supervision (SJS) plan for all juveniles who receive a disposition (TAC section 346.2[b]). For example, many probation officers expressed confusion about what appears to be overlapping goals of the SAT and SJS (e.g., assisting with case management). In jurisdictions where the SAT was viewed as assisting with earlier stages of juvenile processing (e.g., detention decisions), less confusion was expressed regarding this particular issue.

Results from the survey revealed that there has been considerable variation across jurisdictions in the timing of the SAT and in the use, in general, of comprehensive risk and needs assessments at initial intake (defined here as the first point of contact between juvenile referrals and probation). For example, virtually all jurisdictions reported using the SAT (93 percent) or its functional and approved equivalent (7 percent). However, only 68 percent reported administering any type of comprehensive risk and needs assessment during the initial intake, with urban jurisdictions more likely than rural or suburban jurisdictions to use supplementary or alternative assessment instruments.

Among jurisdictions not conducting a risk and needs assessment at initial intake, there was considerable variation in the timing of assessments, with some jurisdictions conducting them relatively early and others conducting them much later. Some of the differing stages identified by respondents included the following:

- prior to releasing juveniles on conditions of release or prior to making detention decisions
- after the initial intake meeting
- at a formal intake, which, depending on the jurisdiction and the definition of formal intake, may occur within minutes or days of the initial intake
- after a probable cause hearing or after a juvenile is placed on deferred prosecution
- after a petition is filed and prior to adjudication (among jurisdictions, this appears to be the most prevalent timing of assessments, when it is not conducted at the initial intake)
- after a social history report is completed
- after adjudication and prior to disposition
- immediately after the juvenile is placed on supervision by probation or by the court
- within a month after the juvenile has been placed on probation

Although not directly addressed in this study, it appears likely that this variation is due not only to differences among jurisdictions in interpreting the HRC and TAC statutes, but also to differences in the needs and capabilities of various jurisdictions. For example, in jurisdictions without access to drug and alcohol programs, it may be perceived as inefficient and unnecessary to expend resources providing comprehensive assessments that cannot be readily acted upon.

Uses

In both the interviews and the surveys, respondents were asked to identify advantages and disadvantages of a standardized risk and assessment tool. The most common advantage identified was quite general: The SAT is a relatively simple, straightforward instrument for quickly identifying a juvenile's history, needs, and potential problem areas. Some other prominent and more specific advantages of the SAT reported by respondents included the following:

- if given at the initial intake, it enables a juvenile's needs to be identified and addressed sooner and more efficaciously
- it assists with release and detain decisions
- it is useful in identifying the need for further psychological evaluation, especially regarding any potential risk for suicidal or homicidal behavior
- it is useful in identifying what programs or services a juvenile may need
- it assists in systematically identifying and organizing information about a juvenile's family, educational, health, drug use, and social and delinquent history, which assists with the creation of social history reports
- it is useful as a case management tool during supervision
- it assists in providing for consistent data collection and for consistent use of information regarding the processing of juveniles

By contrast, respondents identified the following prominent disadvantages of the SAT:

- it is redundant and thus unnecessary and a source of inefficiency
- it serves no clear purpose
- the usefulness of the information is limited compared to what can be obtained from schools, families, or general knowledge about youths (a view articulated most forcefully by rural jurisdictions)
- it is time consuming, and it detracts from a broader focus on the youth and his or her particular social or cultural context and needs
- much of the information required to complete the SAT cannot be obtained during an initial intake; instead, it requires considerable time and investigation

• the validity of the information obtained using the SAT is frequently suspect, given that it is based largely on self-reported information from youths or parents or on incomplete or inaccurate information from schools and other agencies

Although not systematically addressed by our study, it is notable that few jurisdictions reported having or using trained or certified clinicians to administer or interpret assessments. In addition, practitioners in rural, suburban, and urban jurisdictions reported discomfort with administering or interpreting assessments that they or others in their jurisdiction were unqualified to use.

In addition to questions about how risk and needs assessments are used, respondents were asked about the person who routinely receives information from initial intake assessments. Although virtually all jurisdictions reported that probation officers receive this information, far fewer jurisdictions reported that prosecutors (61 percent), judges (47 percent), residential or program staff (37 percent), defense attorneys (35 percent), detention workers (28 percent), or others (e.g., parents, schools, child welfare agencies, or doctors or psychologists; 11 percent) receive this information. Some variation across types of jurisdictions was identified. Suburban jurisdictions were more likely than rural or urban ones to provide program staff with information from intake; suburban and urban jurisdictions were more likely than rural ones to provide judges, defense attorneys, or detention workers with information from intake.

Apart from such county-level variation, the most striking item about these findings is the limited extent to which information, including results of risk and needs assessments, is shared with various practitioners who work with juveniles. Consider, for example, that detention officers routinely operate with little knowledge about a juvenile's background save for the understanding that he or she is a risk to self or others and thus is deemed appropriate for detention. Clearly, greater attention must be paid to factors that affect why some jurisdictions are more likely

than others to share information among practitioners, and how such factors may affect reforms aimed at facilitating increased collection and sharing of information among agencies.

Intake

Structure and Goals of Intake

Intake processes vary considerably within and across states (Dedel 1998; GAO 1995a; Sickmund et al. 1998, p. 1). As noted earlier, many jurisdictions in Texas distinguish between detention intake and formal intake, a distinction that directly affects the perceived goals of intake. Furthermore, the organizational structure of intake can affect how juveniles are processed. For example, more than 10 percent of jurisdictions reported that the initial intake process is supervised or administered by detention units or staff. This arrangement can influence detention patterns because the decision to detain may be motivated primarily by the referral caseload and whether there is sufficient available bed space to detain a juvenile (see Feld 1991, 1999; Snyder and Sickmund 1996, p. 136).

In addition to the type or structure of intake, there can be considerable variation in the goals or the prioritization of various goals that different jurisdictions associate with intake. In this study, survey respondents were asked to rank several possible goals of intake (1 = *most important*, 2 = *second most important*, etc.). Table 2 reveals the relative ranking that respondents gave to each goal (e.g., what percentage viewed the first listed goal as most important, second most important, etc.). However, because some respondents ranked fewer than the total number of listed goals, this table reveals only the approximate within-category support for each goal (e.g., what percentage of respondents view the first listed goal as the most important, the second listed goal as the most important, etc.).

Not surprisingly, a majority of respondents (59 percent) viewed identifying whether a juvenile is a risk to self or others as the most important goal of intake. However, it is noteworthy that some respondents ranked it as less important

Table 2	Probation Officer Rankings of the Relative Importance of the Goals of Juvenile Justice Intake Among Jurisdictions in Texas, 1999 (in percentages)								
	1	2	3	4	5	6	7	8	n
Identify whether a juvenile is a risk to self or others	58.5	24.5	16.0	.9	—	—	—	—	106
Determine whether a juvenile should be placed in detention	25.7	31.7	24.8	11.9	5.0	1.0	—	—	101
Determine if there is probable cause for referral to prosecutor	23.2	9.5	23.2	21.1	15.8	5.3	2.1	—	95
Identify juveniles who should be released with no conditions	9.5	23.2	23.2	29.5	7.4	6.3	1.1	—	95
Provide risk and needs assessments (regardless of whether mandated)	2.2	13.2	6.6	8.8	28.6	30.8	8.8	1.1	91
Identify issues that merit further investigation	—	5.5	7.7	18.7	28.6	34.1	5.5	—	91
Manage detention overcrowding	—	8.2	4.9	1.6	4.9	9.8	63.9	6.6	61

NOTE: Row percentages do not always equal 100 because of rounding. Percentages for within-category rankings (e.g., 1 = most important) do not add to 100 because some respondents ranked fewer than the total number of listed goals.

than other goals. For example, many respondents viewed determinations about detention or probable cause to be the most important goal of intake (26 percent and 23 percent, respectively). Nonetheless, all three of these goals were clearly viewed as more important than other goals, such as providing a comprehensive assessment or identifying issues that merit further investigation. Notably, however, many respondents reported managing detention overcrowding as a primary goal of intake (see Schwartz and Barton 1994). These rankings were largely consistent across jurisdictions. However, respondents in rural jurisdictions were more likely than those in suburban and urban ones to rank identifying whether a juvenile is a risk to self or others as the most important goal of intake. They were also more likely to view identifying issues that should be investigated at a later stage of processing as more important than other goals of intake. Other goals volunteered by respondents included assessing issues that lead to a juvenile's arrest, determining the need for further psychological testing, and identifying medical needs that require immediate attention.

Information Collected at Intake

Despite the fact that only 68 percent of respondents reported administering the SAT at the initial intake, almost all respondents routinely collect a wide range of risk and needs information at this stage of processing. Close to 90 percent of respondents reported that their jurisdiction collected information on most items, which range from peer problems (78 percent) to offense history (99 percent). Only the two items that are not included in the SAT—amenability to treatment and vocational deficits—were less consistently collected across jurisdictions at initial intake (53 percent and 48 percent, respectively). Interestingly, and perhaps because of insufficient local rehabilitative resources, rural jurisdictions were less likely than suburban or urban ones to collect information on amenability to treatment. Other types of information collected at the initial intake in various jurisdictions included the juvenile's family background, the financial status of the family and whether they had insurance, gang affiliation, and any history of referrals to other local or state agencies. It is important to emphasize that many respondents, in interviews and on surveys, indicated that much of the information collected with the SAT is already collected by their jurisdictions using other instruments or forms during other stages of processing.

Obstacles to Efficient and Effective Intake Processes

In an attempt to identify some of the central factors affecting the efficiency and effectiveness of intake processes, respondents were asked to identify whether certain factors served as significant obstacles or barriers. State-required paperwork and the need to obtain parental cooperation with juvenile releases were the most frequently cited obstacles (35 percent and 33 percent, respectively). Many respondents reported other obstacles, which range from staff turnover (13 percent) to excessive numbers of intake referrals (22 percent). Among respondents in different types of jurisdictions, the only statistically discernible difference that emerged was that those in rural jurisdictions were less likely than those in suburban and urban ones to report excessive numbers of intake referrals as a key obstacle.

The most prominent obstacles identified by interviewees include insufficient local resources to address juvenile needs, especially substance use/abuse and mental health needs; and, ironically, lack of communication, cooperation, or collaboration among juvenile court practitioners and child welfare agencies. Other obstacles identified by interviewees included the lack of monitoring for appropriateness of intermediate sanctions or referrals for services, incomplete arrest information, inadequate or inaccurate documentation from various agencies, linguistic barriers in bilingual communities, inappropriate use of detention by judges, and insufficient detention facilities (particularly among urban jurisdictions). Given the broad discretion historically enjoyed by intake

officers and the greater formalization of intake in recent years (Champion 1998, pp. 150–8), it is important to emphasize that many intake officers reported a considerable loss of discretion during the 1990s due to increasingly explicit criteria regarding the collection of information and to statutory changes that have resulted in certain types of cases (e.g., all felonies and any misdemeanors involving a weapon or serious injury to a victim) being forwarded to prosecutors.

Respondents were asked to identify ways in which intake processes have been working well in their jurisdiction. The most common observations listed in the surveys and identified in interviews included having police and probation officers who understand their respective roles at intake; having one probation officer follow a case from intake to disposition (which can potentially result in increased collection and use of information throughout juvenile processing); having experienced intake staff; affording intake officers more time to develop rapport with youths; having the ability to identify the needs of juveniles; having access to 48-hour holding facilities; and having good communication, cooperation, and collaboration among all practitioners and agencies.

⊠ Conclusions and Recommendations

There are logical and compelling arguments for conducting comprehensive risk and needs assessments of juveniles referred to the juvenile justice system and for increased collection and sharing of information among local and state agencies. Not the least of these arguments is that certain problems can be identified before they become worse or before they lead to increased criminal activity. The more general argument is that prevention and early intervention constitute the most efficient and effective means of addressing juvenile needs and offending (Feld 1999; Guarino-Ghezzi and Loughran 1996; Sherman et al. 1997; Snyder and Sickmund 1996, p. 160; Torbet et al. 1996). This study has focused primarily upon assessments, but many of the observations apply to attempts to collect or share other information among local and state agencies.

A central finding of this study is that there is considerable variation across jurisdictions in the timing and goals of assessments and the usage of assessment data; the variation can potentially undermine the success of attempts to implement assessments of all juvenile referrals. Similarly, variation in the structure and goals of intake will likely undermine attempts to implement early assessment of juveniles, particularly if the role of assessments at intake is not explicitly addressed. For example, one consistent finding was the confusion expressed by probation officers concerning the need for comprehensive assessments at initial intake; many emphasized that, in their view, assessment of all juveniles, a large proportion of whom will be counseled and released, is unnecessary and costly. Finally, this study identified a wide range of obstacles to having efficient and effective intake processes, many of which will likely confound attempts to implement or to make appropriate use of comprehensive assessments for all intake referrals.

These findings raise several policy considerations that merit closer attention. First, given the potential importance of early treatment and intervention with at-risk juveniles and the considerable costs associated with juvenile and criminal processing, greater attention needs to be given to understanding the extent to which assessments are associated with more efficient and effective processing of juveniles. That is, is the marginal return of assessments worth the cost? The question is not simply one of determining if assessments can lead to improved decision making; rather, it is one of determining if the associated cost is acceptable. For example, many respondents in this study reported that, even with a wealth of comprehensive and accurate information about juvenile needs, there were too few resources available locally for this information to be of any direct use. Other respondents emphasized, however, that such information could be used to identify the need for more resources (e.g., drug and mental health treatment programs). Ultimately, cost-benefit

determinations involve political decisions, but research could greatly inform such decisions, particularly in assisting states to develop priorities for allocating scarce resources for various prevention and early intervention efforts.

Second, although it is theoretically possible for assessments to result in more consistent and appropriate processing of juveniles, it is also possible that factors affecting the validity or use of assessments can result in more inconsistent and inappropriate processing. It is possible that different jurisdictions may differentially emphasize specific information (e.g., school reports) not obtained directly from risk and needs assessments, which can result in improved decision making but can also contribute to inconsistency across jurisdictions in the processing of juveniles. Such possibilities are likely to be greater in the absence of mechanisms for ongoing monitoring and evaluating of assessment and referral processes and of various informal and formal interventions (Edwards 1996, p. 137). Similarly, although there is justifiable concern about the considerable discretion that intake officers possess, especially in diverting youths from formal processing (Ainsworth 1996, p. 70), it does not necessarily follow that eliminating this discretion will improve the fairness and appropriateness of juvenile processing. Undoubtedly, clear criteria for rendering decisions about both informal and formal processing can likely be beneficial, but understanding the factors that affect how these criteria are applied and their purpose would increase the probability of any benefit being realized.

Third, greater attention to clarifying the goals of assessments and how these can vary depending on a given jurisdiction or stage within the juvenile justice process is needed. Without clear statements about the goals of assessment of merits or of any juvenile justice policy, it is impossible to render fair or appropriate evaluations of their effect (Mears 1998; Rossi, Freeman, and Lipsey 1999). For example, assessments can be used to assist with intake and detention decisions, dispositional recommendations, and case management, but it is unlikely that one instrument can be designed for all these purposes.

Fourth, for whom are assessments to be conducted? This study found considerable variation across jurisdictions in who was provided information from assessments. If risk and needs assessments are conducted at intake, clearly their usefulness hinges upon appropriate parties receiving any resulting information. Given recent concerns about access to counsel and quality of representation (Feld 1999; Puritz et al. 1995; Puritz and Shang 1998), particular attention should be given to the extent to which defense attorneys are provided access to juvenile assessments and the extent to which juveniles who are assessed are apprised of a right to counsel.

Fifth, additional research is needed on the informal processing of juveniles. To date, most research has focused on formal processing, which has meant neglect of the potential importance that informal processing can have for juveniles, particularly in fulfilling the *parens patriae* dictate of addressing the best interests of youths (e.g., identifying whether there is a need for rehabilitation). Of particular importance in this regard is research on the extent to which juveniles' substance abuse and mental health problems are being addressed (Bilchik 1998).

The points raised above suggest two broad-based policy recommendations for local jurisdictions and especially states. First, considerably more attention should be given (1) to clarifying the exact goals of assessments at all stages of juvenile processing, (2) to ensuring that all relevant court actors, including defense attorneys, have access to information obtained from assessments, and (3) to developing programs for ensuring that all jurisdictions understand the goals of assessments and that they can, and consistently are, appropriately conducting and using assessments. Such programs will need to address obstacles to jurisdictions and court actors in their willingness and capacity to implement and use assessments. Second, although assessments can be time-consuming and costly, especially if administered for all referrals, it is possible that the resulting information can greatly assist in identifying the need within and across jurisdictions for more and specific types of resources (e.g., substance abuse

and mental health interventions) and, in turn, for developing priorities about which needs should or can be effectively addressed. Thus, not only the juvenile justice system, but child and social welfare systems generally, stand to benefit greatly from increased use of assessments at the earliest stages of juvenile processing. This is not a recommendation for standardized assessments as a substitute for the exercise of discretion among jurisdictions or practitioners but rather as a potentially, and perhaps even critically, useful supplement, especially if all jurisdictions consistently interpret and accurately complete them.

To reiterate, the benefits of improved screening processes at the front-end of the juvenile justice system through efficient and appropriate use of risk and needs assessments are significant, particularly if we take a long-term view of the consequences of failing to intervene effectively and early. As Snyder and Sickmund (1996) have emphasized, "a small improvement in the effectiveness of juvenile justice interventions could have a substantial impact on State budgets if the savings amassed by the criminal justice system are taken into account" (p. 160). However, for such efforts to be successful, considerably more attention must be focused on the precise goals of assessments, their role in intake processes, and especially on factors that affect their use or that constrain the extent to which they can improve the efficiency and efficacy of the juvenile justice process.

⊠ Notes

1. Waiver does not always or even most of the time result in an incarcerative sentence (Howell 1996). The same pattern holds true in Texas. A recent study of juvenile waivers in twelve large counties in Texas reported that although the vast majority of waivers were for serious, violent offenses, only 5 to 8 percent of waived youths were sentenced to prison, with the remaining youths either placed on probation (27 percent) or processed in some other manner (e.g., sentenced to county or state jails, dismissed, not found guilty, or no-billed by a grand jury) (Texas Criminal Justice Policy Council 1999b, p. 20).

2. Juvenile offenders are not "charged," as adults are, with crimes. Rather, petitions are submitted to the juvenile court to establish either the issues upon which the juvenile will be "adjudicated" (as opposed to "convicted") or the justification for seeking transfer to adult court. If the proceedings result in an adjudication, which establishes that the juvenile committed the alleged offense and is "delinquent" (as opposed to "guilty"), then he or she is subject to a "disposition" (as opposed to a "sentence") (see Champion 1998, chap. 3).

3. In Texas, jurisdictions comprised of multiple counties are called "judicial districts."

4. The SAT includes four components: (1) risk (prior referrals, commitment or out-of-home placement for more than thirty days, age at time of assessment, drug/chemical use, alcohol abuse, parental control/influence, school discipline/employment problems, learning/academic performance problems, runaway/escape behavior, negative peer influence); (2) mental health needs (appearance of youth, violent behavior, behavioral history, peer relationships, disposition/self-image, identity problems, substance abuse, history of abuse, developmental history); (3) educational needs (education status, attendance history, school behavior, academic difficulties); and (4) family status needs (relationships, parental supervision, parental/family problems).

✑ References

Ainsworth, Janet E. 1996. "The Court's Effectiveness in Protecting the Rights of Juveniles in Delinquency Cases." *The Future of Children* 6:64–74.

Babbie, Earl R. 1995. *The Practice of Social Research.* 7th ed. Belmont, CA: Wadsworth.

Beyer, Marty, Thomas Grisso, and Malcolm Young. 1997. *More Than Meets the Eye: Rethinking Assessment, Competency and Sentencing for a Harsher Era of Juvenile Justice.* Washington, DC: American Bar Association Juvenile Justice Center.

Bilchik, Shay. 1998. *Mental Health Disorders and Substance Abuse Problems Among Juveniles.* Washington, DC: Department of Justice, Office of Juvenile Justice and Delinquency Prevention.

Butts, Jeffrey A. and Adele V. Harrell. 1998. *Delinquents or Criminals: Policy Options for Young Offenders.* Washington, DC: The Urban Institute.

Champion, Dean J. 1998. *The Juvenile Justice System: Delinquency, Processing, and the Law.* 2d ed. Upper Saddle River, NJ: Prentice Hall.

Coordinating Council on Juvenile Justice and Delinquency Prevention. 1996. *Combating Violence and Delinquency: The National Juvenile Justice Action Plan.* Washington, DC: Coordinating Council on Juvenile Justice and Delinquency Prevention.

Dedel, Kelly. 1998. "National Profile of the Organization of State Juvenile Corrections Systems." *Crime & Delinquency* 44:507–25.

Dembo, Richard and Richard Brown. 1994. "The Hillsborough County Juvenile Assessment Center." *Journal of Child and Adolescent Substance Abuse* 3:25–43.

Dodge, Douglas C. 1997. *Due Process Advocacy.* Washington, DC: Department of Justice, Office of Juvenile Justice and Delinquency Prevention.

Edwards, Leonard P. 1996. "The Future of the Juvenile Court: Promising New Directions." *The Future of Children* 6:131–9.

Feld, Barry C. 1991. "Justice By Geography: Urban, Suburban, and Rural Variations in Juvenile Justice Administration." *Journal of Criminal Law and Criminology* 82:156–210.

———. 1998. "The Juvenile Court." Pp. 509–41 in *The Handbook of Crime and Punishment,* edited by M. Tonry. New York: Oxford University Press.

———. 1999. *Bad Kids: Race and the Transformation of the Juvenile Court.* New York: Oxford University Press.

General Accounting Office (GAO). 1995a. *Juvenile Justice: Minimal Gender Bias Occurred in Processing Noncriminal Juveniles.* Washington, DC: General Accounting Office.

———. 1995b. *Representation Rates Varied as Did Counsel's Impact on Court Outcomes.* Washington, DC: General Accounting Office.

Gottfredson, Don C. 1987. "Prediction and Classification in Criminal Justice Decision Making." Pp. 1–51 in *Crime and Justice: An Annual Review of Research,* edited by M. Tonry. Chicago, IL: University of Chicago Press.

Greenwood, Peter W. 1996. "Responding to Juvenile Crime: Lessons Learned." *The Future of Children* 6:75–85.

Guarino-Ghezzi, Susan and Edward J. Loughran. 1996. *Balancing Juvenile Justice.* New Brunswick, NJ: Transaction.

Howell, James C., ed. 1995. *Guide for Implementing the Comprehensive Strategy for Serious, Violent, and Chronic Juvenile Offenders.* Washington, DC: Department of Justice, Office of Juvenile Justice and Delinquency Prevention.

———. 1996. "Juvenile Transfers to the Criminal Justice System: State of the Art," *Law and Policy* 18:17–60.

Mears, Daniel P. 1998. "Evaluation Issues Confronting Juvenile Justice Sentencing Reforms: A Case Study of Texas." *Crime & Delinquency* 44:443–63.

National Criminal Justice Association. 1997. *Juvenile Justice Reform Initiatives in the States: 1994–1996.* Washington, DC: Department of Justice, Office of Juvenile Justice and Delinquency Prevention.

Puritz, Patricia, Sue Burrell, Robert Schwartz, Mark Soler, and Loren Warboys. 1995. *A Call for Justice: An Assessment of Access to Counsel and Quality of Representation in Delinquency Proceedings.* Washington, DC: American Bar Association, Juvenile Justice Center.

Puntz, Patricia and Wendy Wan Long Shang. 1998. *Innovative Approaches to Juvenile Indigent Defense.* Washington, DC. Department of Justice, Office of Juvenile Justice and Delinquency Prevention.

Rivers, James E., Richard Dembo, and Robert S. Anwyl. 1998. "The Hillsborough County, Florida, Juvenile Assessment Center: A Prototype." *The Prison Journal* 78: 439–50.

Rossi, Peter H., Howard E. Freeman, and Mark W. Lipsey. 1999. *Evaluation: A Systematic Approach.* 6th ed. Newbury Park, CA: Sage.

Rubin, Ted H. 1996. "The Nature of the Court Today." *The Future of Children* 6:40–52.

Schwartz, Ira M. and William H. Barton, eds. 1994. *Reforming Juvenile Detention: No More Hidden Closets.* Columbus: Ohio State University Press.

Sherman, Lawrence W., Denise C. Gottfredson, Doris MacKenzie, John Eck, Peter Reuter, and Shawn Bushway, eds. 1997. *Preventing Crime: What Works, What Doesn't, What's Promising.* Washington, DC. Department of Justice, National Institute of Justice.

Sickmund, Melissa. 1997. *The Juvenile Delinquency Probation Caseload, 1985–1994.* Washington, DC:

Department of Justice, Office of Juvenile Justice and Delinquency Prevention.

Sickmund, Melissa, Anne L. Stahl, Terrence A. Finnegan, Howard N. Snyder, Rowen S. Poole, and Jeffrey A. Butts. 1998. *Juvenile Court Statistics 1995.* Washington, DC: Department of Justice, Office of Juvenile Justice and Delinquency Prevention.

Singer, Simon I. 1996. "Merging and Emerging Systems of Juvenile and Criminal Justice." *Law and Policy* 18:1–15.

Snyder, Howard N. and Melissa Sickmund. 1996. *Juvenile Offenders and Victims: A National Report.* Washington, DC: Department of Justice, Office of Juvenile Justice and Delinquency Prevention.

Texas Criminal Justice Policy Council. 1998. *An Overview of Texas Juvenile Justice Population Trends and Dynamics.* Austin: State of Texas.

———. 1999a. *A Look at Referrals to Selected Juvenile Probation Departments in Texas.* Austin: State of Texas.

———. 1999b. *An Overview of Juvenile Certification in Texas.* Austin: State of Texas.

Torbet, Patricia M., Richard Gable, Hunter Hurst IV, Imogene Montgomery, Linda Szymanski, and Douglas Thomas. 1996. *State Responses to Serious and Violent Juvenile Crime.* Washington, DC: Department of Justice, Office of Juvenile Justice and Delinquency Prevention.

Torbet, Patricia M. and Linda Szymanski. 1998. *State Legislative Responses to Violent Juvenile Crime: 1996–1997 Update.* Washington, DC: Department of Justice, Office of Juvenile Justice and Delinquency Prevention.

Towberman, Donna B. 1992. "National Survey of Juvenile Needs Assessment." *Crime & Delinquency* 38:230–8.

DISCUSSION QUESTIONS

1. Identify the stages in the processing of juvenile offenders. Approximately what percentage of offenders was processed at each stage after arrest?

2. For what reasons may juvenile cases be dismissed?

3. According to the survey results, what are some advantages of early assessment?

4. What do the survey respondents believe are the goals of juvenile justice intake?

5. What are the authors' recommendations based on the findings of this survey research study?

❖

READING

A great deal of attention has been given in recent years to advances in assessment technologies designed to aid decision making in the juvenile justice system. Adoption and implementation of these assessment tools, however, have progressed more slowly and hesitatingly than their development. Assessment in juvenile justice exemplifies the "science–practice gap" that has spurred a growing national interest in technology transfer. The authors of this article describe and assess efforts in one jurisdiction to develop and implement assessment tools and to introduce field supervisors and staff to advantages of using assessment technologies. The authors examine the capacity of the supervisors and staff to accept change and to engage in participative decision making and staff training, and the ability to integrate the technology with existing, related practices. The authors present and discuss their use of various data-driven monitoring reports designed to improve case monitoring, service delivery, and client change. They recommend ways to deal with resistance to the use of assessment tools for identifying dynamic need factors, and the process for eliciting staff support in ongoing program and policy developments.

Best Implementation Practices

Disseminating New Assessment Technologies in a Juvenile Justice Agency

Douglas Young, Karl Moline, Jill Farrell, David Bierie

The gap between science and practice has been well documented (Backer, 2000; Institute of Medicine, 1998). A growing literature has offered explanations for the lag between the development and implementation of new technologies in the behavioral sciences, and strategies for closing the gap (Brown & Flynn, 2002; Roman & Johnson, 2002; Simpson, 2002). Although the most extensive literature in this regard concerns mental health and substance abuse treatment, there have been discussions about similar problems in the adult and juvenile justice systems for at least the past decade (Bonta, Bogue, Crowley, & Mottuk, 2001; Gambrill & Shlonsky, 2000; Mears & Kelly, 1999). As in other, related fields, the ubiquitous call for

programs and systems to adopt best practices has emerged as the prevalent strategy for addressing the science-practice gap in criminal justice.

The call to apply research-based knowledge has been made perhaps most persistently in the area of assessment. Technologies for measuring and applying risk and needs assessment have developed demonstrably in the past two decades, while staff, particularly in juvenile justice systems, often continue to rely on "clinical intuition" in making decisions that can have life-changing consequences for individuals who are accused or adjudicated (Bonta et al., 2001; Maupin, 1993; Sarri et al., 2001). The need to address this problem is evident in the increasingly

SOURCE: *Crime & Delinquency* (52)1, 135–158, January 2006. DOI: 0.1177/0011128705281752. © 2006 Sage Publications, Inc.

detailed and pragmatic accounts of best practices provided by sources ranging from academic assessment experts to federal juvenile justice and technical assistance agencies (Bonta, 2002; Ferguson, 2002; Wiebush, Baird, Krisberg, & Onek, 1995).

In contrast to this prescriptive literature, however, there have been few published accounts documenting system-wide efforts to improve assessment technologies in specific jurisdictions. Our purpose in this is to advance discussion beyond best-practice descriptions and manuals to describe and assess our "real-world" efforts to develop and implement an integrated assessment system in one state. Following a more detailed review of relevant literature, we describe a progressive series of research-based strategies that were employed over the past several years in the Maryland juvenile justice system. Conclusions and lessons learned from these efforts to move the science of assessment to everyday practice are discussed in the article's final section.

⬛ Background

Increasingly, state juvenile justice systems are adopting assessment systems to assist with important case-processing decisions when handling youth referrals. Besides bringing fairness and consistency to decision-making processes, the popularity of assessment systems has been driven largely by the surge in juvenile crime in the 1980s and 1990s and the resulting rise in the population of youth served by juvenile justice systems. A closer look at this population has revealed that the majority fit into one of three groups—youth who commit trivial juvenile offenses, youth who have multiple co-occurring behavioral and situational problems related to their offending behavior, or serious and habitual offenders (Dembo & Walters, 2003). Even though the first group may not exhibit need for further juvenile justice or social service involvement, the latter groups raise greater concern for youth agencies in terms of prevention and intervention efforts.

Criminological and assessment researchers have identified characteristics common to these youth who are high risk and high needs and developed assessment systems to assist juvenile justice systems in how to identify and handle them.

In their efforts to capture the steady progression of juvenile assessment technologies over the past several decades, analysts have come to describe assessment tools in generational terms (Bonta, 1996; Ferguson, 2002). The first generation of assessment instruments involving delinquents and adult offenders was based on the professional judgment and intuition of the individual conducting the assessment. Second-generation tools involve more standardized assessments that make use of actuarial methods over subjective judgment. Typically, these tools focus on static risk factors, such as age at first arrest and age of first alcohol or drug use. The next generation incorporates static and dynamic risk and need factors in more comprehensive tools that can help guide various decisions, including placements in different levels of security, and type and levels of services. The fourth generation involves a series of specialized instruments for particular needs in such areas as education, family and peer relationships, mental and physical health, and substance abuse (Ferguson, 2002).

A number of reviews have documented the drawbacks of the early-stage assessment tools, particularly the kind of second-generation tools that remain in wide use in juvenile justice systems. Limited to static history items, second-generation tools are much less accurate in predicting recidivism than those that also incorporate dynamic criminogenic need factors such as substance abuse and mental health problems, and school attendance and performance (Andrews & Bonta, 1995; Hoge & Andrews, 1996; Lowenkamp, Holsinger, & Latessa, 2001). Second-generation measures are generally useless in making service referrals and devising and managing treatment plans to address these problems. Knowing this intuitively, juvenile case managers provided with an instrument that is limited to delinquency history will make their own inquiries about dynamic need factors.

However, research repeatedly shows that this exercise of discretion encourages the use of inconsistent assessment procedures and variability in the application of decision rules. This, in turn, tends to produce inconsistent decisions about clients and, thereby, contributes to inequalities in the processing of juvenile and adult offenders. These judgments have been labeled "irrational" by researchers (Doob & Beaulieu, 1993; Gottfredson & Gottfredson, 1988; Grisso & Conlin, 1984).

A consensus of support for the use of comprehensive, standardized assessment tools has been apparent in the literature for a decade or more. Standardized instruments lead to more effective treatment and custody decisions (Funk, 1999; Hoge, 1999) and can improve the management of youth within juvenile justice system settings (Hoge & Andrews, 1996). Assessment scores can predict recidivism and institutional adjustment, can measure rehabilitative progress and progress in treatment, and can assist with supervision and placement decisions (Barnoski, 1998; Bonta, 2002). Use of these tools increases staff accountability and can improve consistency in the treatment of youth and reduce disparity in decisions (Hoge, 2002; Jones, Harris, Fader, & Grubstein, 2001; Wiebush et al., 1995). Furthermore, needs assessments can provide agencies with important information about the levels and types of service demand.

Despite this preponderance of evidence and advocacy in support of third-generation and fourth-generation tools, juvenile justice systems have found it difficult to keep up with these changes in assessment technologies. Some combination of first-generation and second-generation assessment tools is the present, imperfect reality in most juvenile justice systems; this gap between the development and implementation of new assessment instruments has been endemic to justice systems for some time now. More than a decade ago, Maupin (1993) reported that practitioners frequently did not use risk and/or needs assessments to inform their decision making, even when required by law or administrative guidelines. Despite involving juvenile

parole officers in the design and implementation of a decision-making instrument for parole decisions, officers resented what they viewed as attempts to limit their discretion, especially at the expense of their time and effort. Maupin recommended that future efforts to implement these instruments should account for organizational and structural constraints faced by juvenile justice workers.

As in many other service and justice areas, efforts to close the science-practice gap in offender assessment include calls for best practices. Researchers are beginning to provide more detailed "how-to" reports and articles that discuss assessment systems and issues related to their implementation (Bonta et al. 2001; Ferguson, 2002; Grisso & Underwood, 2004; Hoge & Andrews, 1996; Wiebush et al., 1995). Bonta and colleagues have authored a series of articles that describe assessment tool options for both adult and juvenile populations. In multiple articles, Dembo and colleagues (Dembo et al., 1996; Dembo & Walters, 2003; Dembo, Walters, & Meyers, 2003) have discussed innovative strategies to restructure organizations to better accommodate assessment processes through the use of juvenile assessment centers. A key message in much of this literature is the need to replace old ways of assessment with valid, standardized tools. In a rush to implement the new methods, however, agencies often take tools "off the shelf and impose them in their jurisdictions without attention to the need for acceptance and assimilation by staff, and problems with nontransferability of validity result (Bonta et al., 2001; Jones et al., 2001).

These and other organizational and research challenges threaten the successful adoption and implementation of assessment reform efforts. Based on her experience attempting to implement a new system in an adult probation system in California, Ferguson (2002) described numerous such challenges, including the perceived loss of discretion by line staff, difficulty in obtaining quality information, resource limitations, time-consuming workloads, and staff resistance to change. Prescriptive strategies she offered for addressing these challenges include obtaining commitment from the highest levels of the agency, securing resources needed for implementing and sustaining the initiative, high-quality training, acknowledging and addressing staff concerns and resistance to change, and anticipating and responding quickly to barriers. In addition to recommending similar organizational-oriented strategies, Bonta et al. (2001) stressed the importance of utilizing research to help select and develop an appropriate assessment system, to monitor the integrity of the system over time, and to make improvements to the system as it becomes part of the organization's daily routine. This literature is important and useful for juvenile justice practitioners and researchers because it addresses some of the realities of implementation, beyond simply advocating for their adoption. The following account of our experience in Maryland seeks to build on these discussions of best implementation practices.

⬚ Building an Integrated Assessment System in Maryland

Maryland's Department of Juvenile Services (DJS) has widely encompassing statewide responsibilities that extend from the point of referral to the system (usually in the form of a police arrest) through community supervision, residential placement, and aftercare. DJS staff play a central role in making three key decisions where offender risk is an important consideration: (a) to detain or release a youth pending his or her first court appearance; (b) to forward the juvenile case to the state's attorney for prosecution, or to close or divert the case at intake; and (c) to determine the level of placement for a youth who is adjudicated.

When this project began in 2001, these decisions derived from a mix of local precedents, practices, and policies, few of which involved a systematic assessment of risk and/or need factors. The detention decision was the only one of the three that was made with some consistency across the state, following a simple, policy-based

protocol that specified certain arrest charge criteria. Policies on intake case forwarding were also charge based and left much room for discretion by intake staff. A systematic risk assessment protocol for postadjudication placement decisions had been developed and was in use in a small number of jurisdictions statewide; however, some administrators raised questions about the accuracy of this tool. Researchers from the Bureau of Governmental Research (BGR) at the University of Maryland were asked to review the instrument and other DJS assessment procedures. A retrospective validity study involving 694 DJS case files showed that several of the items used in the placement tool were not predictive of recidivism at 15 months follow-up (Pfeiffer, Young, Bouffard, & Taxman, 2001). Findings from this research also pointed to possible improvements to the instrument (through replacing items and changing the weights of others); however, it became evident in conducting this study that the data routinely recorded in paper and electronic files by DJS staff were insufficient for developing valid risk assessments at any of these three decision points. New methods of systematic data collection were needed for this purpose.

DJS administrators were quickly convinced that decision making at each of these three points should be recast to be more systematic, consistent, and valid. Planning and implementing an integrated system that achieves this goal has been a much more arduous, evolving process that is still under development. A few core principles drawn from contemporary research and descriptive literature helped guide the planning process: establish a foundation on research-based, actuarial approaches; consider dynamic, criminogenic needs items, and related protective factors in addition to static risk factors; seek to develop and employ instruments that are locally validated; and emphasize implementation fidelity and quality assurance.

An initial, threshold consideration concerned whether to use existing assessment instruments or to develop tools within the department. For several reasons, the decision was made to build instruments tailored for and by DJS. First, validated extant instruments are usually proprietary and can be costly if employed on an ongoing basis in large, statewide systems. Second, studies have shown that risk items, weights, scoring, and classification protocols that are valid in one jurisdiction do not generalize readily to another, and tools should be developed using samples drawn from the local population (Jones et al., 2001; Wright, Clear, & Dickson, 1984). Third, developing risk tools internally would provide opportunities for involving end users and their supervisors, lending credibility and a sense of ownership in the process of implementing a new technology. An added benefit of this approach was the opportunity to integrate aspects of assessments across the multiple decision points that required attention. Ferguson (2002) reported a similar rationale behind the decision by the adult probation agency in Maricopa County to develop an assessment instrument internally.

Drawing from the principles noted above, the development of each assessment has followed a two-phase process. The first phase involves creating an evidence-based version of the assessment tool that is grounded in reviews of research and instruments developed in other jurisdictions, available DJS data, and input from DJS and other juvenile justice stakeholders in the state. In Phase 1, the instrument was developed and initially implemented in a limited number of jurisdictions on a test basis. During this initial implementation the assessment instrument was refined, and forms and decision guideline protocols were finalized before expanding to statewide implementation. Efforts to engage staff and supervisors in the adoption of the new assessment process and to improve and ensure implementation fidelity were critical components of this phase at pilot and statewide implementation stage.

Data on risk factors that were collected during this first phase, combined with outcome data collected during a specified follow-up period, provided the basis for the analyses that drove the development of a locally validated, empirically based assessment instrument in Phase 2.

Consistent with recommendations made by Wiebush et al. (1995), validation methods were tailored to the purpose of each assessment. Follow-up periods ranged from relatively short for the Risk Assessment Instrument (RAI), which is concerned with offender behavior between release and the first court appearance, to 18 months and more for the assessment at disposition, where post-placement outcomes were considered. Furthermore, the outcome measures themselves can vary. Appearance in court is a critical outcome in validation of the detention instrument, for example, but not of great concern in developing the case-forwarding and placement tools. This is not to suggest, however, that the final assessment was strictly the product of statistical analysis. Input from stakeholders inside and outside the juvenile justice agency, discussed in depth below, was critical to understanding how other factors have to be incorporated. In the end, the assessment instrument was a melding of research and real-world considerations.

Three Assessment Tools

As noted previously, the three assessment tools that are the subject of this article are the Detention Risk Assessment Instrument (D-RAI), the intake screen for case forwarding, and the placement assessment at disposition (PAD) for youth who were adjudicated. In each case, evidence-based instruments have been developed and are now implemented in some or all of the state; construction of valid, empirically based versions is under way on two of the tools. In this section, we briefly summarize each instrument and their current stage of development. A discussion of efforts made in this first phase of development to address concerns about implementation fidelity follows in the next section.

Intake D-RAI

Development of an evidence-based D-RAI began in 2003 with two longstanding work groups—one a statewide group of DJS intake staff and supervisors, and the other a committee of Baltimore City-based stakeholders that met regularly on local juvenile case-processing issues. The two groups worked on parallel tracks for several months before coming together to reach agreement on a framework that was then assessed prospectively by simulating its use for 2 months in Baltimore City. This simulation, or pilot test, involved having DJS staff complete data collection forms that included the proposed D-RAI items but that did not include any scores. Following extensive analysis and review by BGR researchers and the stakeholder group in Baltimore, results from this initial pilot test were used to select items and develop a D-RAI scoring protocol that minimized changes to the overall numbers of youth assigned to detention and to programs designed as alternatives to detention (ATD). Implemented in Baltimore in early 2004 on a test basis, this instrument is composed of an 11-item measure and scoring system that yields a recommendation to detain, refer the youth to an ATD, or not detain. In addition to the scored items, there is a set of "mandatory override" items, in which intake officers' discretion is extremely limited. Discretionary overrides, where staff make and document a detention decision that differs from that recommended by the guidelines, are also permitted on the D-RAI.

Plans for use of a D-RAI tool statewide are currently the subject of additional research and considerable debate within the state. Many outside stakeholders and some DJS staff working in field offices outside Baltimore argued that juveniles referred to the department differ depending on the part of the state they are from, and that local concerns and tolerances for delinquent behavior vary, as do police practices. A number of other juvenile justice policy makers underscored the importance of equal justice and the need to treat all youth who come under the department's jurisdiction similarly. Decisions about constructing and employing one or more D-RAI variations are awaiting the results of a simulated application of the tool, which is currently under way in all regions of the state outside of Baltimore City.

Intake Screen for Risk and Needs

In addition to making emergency detention decisions, DJS intake staff is responsible for deciding whether to forward the case for prosecution. Intake to the system also presents an opportunity to assess DJS-referred youth for service needs, and efforts to develop and employ systematic, actuarial-based risk assessment for case forwarding merged early on with the efforts of researchers from Johns Hopkins University School of Public Health to develop an intake screen for substance abuse, mental health, and other treatment needs for DJS youth. An evidence-based version of the intake risk and needs screen was implemented statewide in Maryland in 2002, following an extensive development and refinement period that included pilot tests in Baltimore City, suburban Baltimore, and one rural jurisdiction. As with the D-RAI, the statewide intake screen reflects an iterative process founded in knowledge about current related research and experiences in juvenile justice systems outside Maryland, and informed by local pilot test findings and simulated applications of the risk and/or case-forwarding component, and the input of a workgroup of DJS field staff and managers responsible for intake throughout the system. Discussed further below, pilot tests of the intake tool revealed a number of lapses and potential barriers to implementing the screen that bespoke the importance of attention to dynamic need factors, staff training, accountability and supervision, and ongoing, systemic monitoring.

The current intake screen consists of three main components. The risk-based case-forwarding guidelines, now fully automated, generate a recommendation to resolve the case at intake, place the youth on informal precourt supervision for 90 days, or formally refer the case to the state's attorney, based on the nature of the current offense and the youth's delinquency history. The two service needs components of the screen include a voluntary interview that is designed to be conducted with the youth and parent or guardian and a service referral form, where staff record referrals in up to four service domains that are made as a result of the interview. A validated version of the case-forwarding assessment is currently under development. Ultimately, the validation results will lead to a refinement in the delinquency history score (e.g., by adding, replacing, or weighting certain items), and the inclusion of dynamic, criminogenic risk factors that are collected in the intake interview.

Placement Assessment at Disposition for Youth Who Are Adjudicated

Developed after the intake screen for risk and needs, the PAD is used to recommend supervision and custody "levels of care" to the court at disposition, after youth are adjudicated. The current evidence-based version of the PAD was developed primarily from a simulated administration of the tool conducted over 2 years in three diverse DJS jurisdictions. Data on risk items considered for inclusion in the PAD, along with actual probation and placement recommendations, were collected on about 1,200 youth. In addition to recording information on the adjudication charge and delinquency history, staff assessed youth at the time of disposition on criminogenic risk factors in such areas as school, peer relations, substance abuse, and family history. A small workgroup of DJS administrators, line managers, and BGR researchers met regularly over several months to discuss study findings, instrument items, scoring options, and implementation considerations. Results from different classification and scoring schemes were compared with actual staff recommendations. With youth assigned to probation, these included a recommendation to one of four levels of supervision; for youth with secure placements, DJS staff make a recommendation to one of three security-based levels of care that, in the department's designation, ranges from "secure confinement facilities" (large, prison-like institutions) to smaller, less secure "community-based residential" programs.[1]

The goal of this process was to develop scoring guidelines that yielded outcomes similar to the current pattern of recommendations—that is, under the new guidelines, the proportions of youth recommended for each of the levels of probation and placement levels of care would be similar to current figures—while ensuring that these recommendations were based on proven risk factors, assessed in a more consistent, uniform manner across the state. The workgroup reached consensus on a PAD instrument and scoring protocol that, based on pilot study data, would yield results that mirrored the current proportions of youth assigned to probation and secure placements, while slightly decreasing the numbers of youth who would be recommended for the large secure confinement facilities and increase placements in community-based residential programs. Using a matrix-type scoring system, the recommendation was based on the severity of the adjudication charge, a delinquency history score, and a summated risk score composed of static and dynamic items (including protective factors which can lower the score). Items addressing dynamic factors such as school attendance, associations with delinquent peers, and substance abuse are weighed equally but currently carry less weight than current charge and history factors. Scoring of all of these items will be modified on completion of a validation study that is now under way. Analyses will assess the predictive strength of risk factors assessed at disposition on pilot sample recidivism over a minimum 18-month follow-up period.

⬛ Implementation Strategies

In discussing the process of transferring new technologies within organizations, researchers and theorists described sequential stages involving adoption, implementation, and routine practice (Rogers, 1995; Simpson, 2002). DJS management fairly readily committed to adopting the new risk assessment technologies. Achieving change throughout the organization, however, has demanded much more effort. In this section, we describe a number of strategies that were developed and employed to facilitate the adoption and particularly the implementation of these assessment tools at the field level within DJS.

Early Involvement of Field Staff, Managers, and Stakeholders

Many staff members who had been at DJS for several years initially expressed skepticism about the new assessment technologies, having seen a number of different protocols come and go. The PAD for youth who were adjudicated replaced an assessment tool that had been developed and adopted in some jurisdictions under a prior DJS administration, and the new detention and case-forwarding protocols were replacing familiar, policy-based protocols that showed much variation in practice across regions and offices. At one level, addressing this resistance meant providing a strong rationale to field supervisors and staff for making the change to actuarial-based tools and scoring protocols. Trainings and manuals on the new assessment technologies now begin with discussions of the empirical basis of the approach, and their long-term value to the department. Sustained, vocal support by DJS leadership was also important in addressing resistance at this level. Potential barriers to adoption of the D-RAI in Baltimore City were resolved through the direct involvement of DJS' chief executive. Full-scale implementation of the intake risk and needs screen, on the other hand, appears to have lagged somewhat as administrators' attention to the screen, and monitoring and adherence efforts (see below), have diminished over time.

At another deeper level, resistance to the assessment technologies appears to reflect an organizational culture in field offices that is jaded about any new, "top-down" initiatives introduced by department headquarters. Likely typical of many juvenile justice systems, DJS has experienced relatively frequent turnover in executive staff, each bent on reform, often through the imposition of new initiatives. This cultural resistance was thus expressed in predictably dubious views, including that the originators of the initiative were inexperienced and did not "really know or understand the system," that a variation of the new initiative has been tried before and failed or morphed into some extant practice, and that there will be inadequate resources and follow-through when an initial, high-profile honeymoon period is over.

A principle strategy employed to counter this resistance was to involve field supervisors and staff as early and as much as possible in the planning and implementation process. Efforts to engage staff in each of the assessment tools have developed and improved, in part by lessons learned in the early implementation of the intake screen. In forming the planning group for the PAD, a field manager was given a central role, and DJS' intake workgroup developed the RAI framework in conjunction with BGR researchers and headquarters personnel. The same workgroup is reviewing the current evidence-based case-forwarding protocol, and when findings from the validation study are complete, they will help refine the protocol based on these results. Overcoming embedded cultural resistance—earning staff credibility and a sense of ownership—requires empowering field planners to make decisions that would directly affect the instruments they would ultimately be responsible for using.

Although most planning and implementation efforts have focused on DJS staff, gaining support from external stakeholders has also been critical to successful implementation. A series of stakeholder meetings were held across the state in the summer of 2004. Judges, juvenile court masters, prosecutors, defense attorneys, and law enforcement representatives were invited to participate in each meeting. The DJS secretary and/or deputy secretary led most of the meetings, with BGR researchers presenting the D-RAI and the PAD in detail, discussing the development and implementation plans for the assessments, and soliciting input and feedback.

Field Staff Training

Training on the assessment tools has also been a learning process that has evolved in response to earlier inexperience and oversights. The first set of trainings in this area, done on the intake screen, were fairly conventional, relying largely on DJS' departmental training unit and a manual with background information, "how to" material, and a handful of sample cases that were scored and discussed in the training session. Over time, peer training and a "training of the trainers" strategy were adopted, with an emphasis on developing expertise among one or two field staff or supervisors in each office. These staff (many of whom were also involved in the development process) were given in-depth training by BGR researchers and central office managers, and effectively turned into in-house experts on the assessments and on the training protocol. They then returned to their offices and trained the remaining staff members, with research and central office support as needed. In addition to providing training to the other staff, having experts in each office allows them to provide technical support to their offices, minimizing the need for the researchers or headquarters personnel to answer routine questions from the field.

Integration With Other DJS Activities

Skeptical of the single, new initiative *du jour*, staff was more accepting of the new assessments when they understood the linkages between each of them and with current DJS practices. Although not yet fully integrated, the three assessments were designed to build on each other, and in-depth clinical assessments, where appropriate. The D-RAI is generally the first assessment that was conducted when DJS received a police request for detention, followed by the intake screen for risk and needs, which is conducted during the intake interview. The PAD is designed to be used later in case processing and to follow extensive prior assessment and in many cases supervision experience, meaning that much of the PAD can be completed based on existing information. While instructing staff how to obtain current, updated information, the training manual for the PAD also shows how its items map to earlier screens, assessments, and other tools used by department staff. Integration of the PAD into DJS business practices also led to the

creation of a 90-day reassessment form and protocols for assessing youth who are rearrested while under DJS supervision. These tools help inform decisions about modifications to the type and level of supervision over time.

Employing Data to Foster Change

Use of feedback from monitoring results and other data has been a central strategy employed throughout the implementation process. At the most basic level, monitoring was used with field staff and supervisors to assess their understanding and adherence to new protocols. Employed early on in the statewide implementation of the intake screen, monitoring reports signaled to staff that DJS central office and field managers were serious about follow-through on the new assessments. For the first time, local area reports were generated that allowed field managers to identify problems down to the level of the individual intake officer. Staff-level and case-level feedback were used to identify and address variations in intake procedures that led to improved rates of completion (and more tailored monitoring reports) over time.

Similar reports were also used to provide feedback to staff about the use of needs data in the intake screen. As discussed further below, intake staff had no previous experience using structured needs items at this initial stage of case processing, and many had to be convinced of their utility. Messages from central office administrators and in trainings emphasized the potential value of identifying and responding to needs early on; an immediate referral, followed by voluntary participation in services or return to school, might reduce the chances of a punitive sanction at later stages of processing. At the same time, staff was reminded not to mandate service participation to avoid net widening at this stage in case processing.

Data are also used to address staff and management concerns about specific content in the assessments, beyond the generalized staff resistance discussed earlier. The most common content-specific objections raised in planning discussions and training on the assessments concerned the use of dynamic need factors, particularly as part of traditionally risk-based assessments done to inform intake case-forwarding and placement security levels at disposition. These objections took multiple, related forms, some of which echoed Ferguson's (2002) experience in attempting assessment reforms in Arizona. The most common of these was concern that youth "should not be penalized" by something they were not responsible for, such as parental substance abuse or involvement in crime, or child abuse or neglect. Some DJS practitioners were against the use of any factors that are "treatable," such as substance abuse or failure in school, arguing that service needs of any kind should never "drive the youth deeper into the system." Other objections to dynamic criminogenic factors stemmed from concerns that they were subjective. In planning the PAD, field-experienced managers were resistant to including items on youth beliefs and attitudes (e.g., toward crime, victims, and the need for rehabilitation) or prior behavior on supervision because they thought that even with training on use of the instrument, staff judgment would be too variable from day to day, or from one individual to the next.

Although the planning groups agreed to include nearly all these items in the intake screen and PAD assessments, to be responsive to field concerns, some were excluded from the additive scores in the initial evidence-based version of the case-forwarding and PAD protocols. Thus, while data on these items were being collected and included in validity analyses, some were not currently counted in reaching guidelines recommendations. We expected that validity findings showing the predictive power of these dynamic, criminogenic items will be very useful in addressing these concerns (besides being used to construct weighted scores for these items in the empirically based version of the instruments). In the meantime, we have developed another data-driven report that compares their impact on placement recommendations under the new assessment protocol with actual placements made by staff prior to implementation of the guidelines. The report used data collected during a preimplementation pilot phase, where staff conducted their standard psychosocial interview and recorded their placement recommendations with 1,243 youth adjudicated in Maryland between 2001 and 2003. At the same time, staff recorded data for these youth on all items under consideration for the PAD. These data were then applied in the subsequently constructed PAD instrument for analysis purposes.

The report shows that all but two of the items were given more weight by DJS staff under their standard procedures than they are in the PAD protocol. Despite DJS practitioners' voiced concerns about the use of these dynamic factors in making placement decisions, the data make clear that in the absence of a structured scoring protocol, staff routinely incorporate and in some cases heavily weight these factors in making recommendations to the court. We expect this report will be helpful in demonstrating that inclusion of these items in the new assessment is consistent with staffs' natural inclination to employ these items in decision making, whereas the PAD protocol can actually moderate the impact of staff's potentially subjective use of these factors. Implementation of the guidelines protocol ensures that dynamic factors are considered in a comparatively uniform, consistent, objective fashion in placement decisions.

Data-driven monitoring reports are also valuable for immediate and long-term planning purposes. In the short run, tracking and reporting decisions and outcomes are imperative for identifying any unexpected consequences of changes to assessment policy and practice. Observance of any unanticipated changes in the numbers or types of formalized cases or certain placements, for example, would likely necessitate prompt midcourse corrections in a new assessment protocol. Reports generated during the implementation of the new DJS assessment tools are also being used to inform future practice and policy.

Automation Development

Although monitoring results proved valuable, the simple database systems initially developed for recording and reporting on these data led to delays that reduced their effectiveness. Full automation of the new assessment protocols was an important implementation strategy for several reasons, including affording near real-time monitoring, and identification and correction of problems soon after they develop. Automation of assessment tools is valuable beyond facilitating the monitoring function, including speeding the process of conducting assessments, improving the validity of recorded and scored data, and enabling refinements to scoring protocols (e.g., changes in item's weights) to occur "behind the screen," thus avoiding the need for retraining and distribution of new paper forms.

Achieving automation of the assessments has involved a mixture of enhancements to the department's current management information system (MIS) and the adoption and development of another, linked information technology that is used in Maryland's adult corrections and treatment system. Through extensive discussions and demonstrations of this technology, DJS information technology (IT) managers came to acknowledge that the comparative time and costs required to build all the assessments in their existing system were prohibitive. The D-RAI and PAD have now been programmed into the new system, where they can look and "feel" like the paper versions, while eliminating hand scoring, providing internal value checks that improve data validity, and displaying guideline recommendations without staff having to employ a complex classification matrix. To facilitate adoption of this new technology, we are employing some of the same techniques learned in working with staff on the assessments, including peer and train-the-trainers approaches, and content that stresses the potential reductions in staff burden and gains in efficiency, accuracy, and accountability.

◪ Summary and Conclusions

On countless occasions we have been reminded of the accuracy of conclusions drawn from studies

of juvenile assessment that "it is far easier to develop a valid instrument than it is to implement its appropriate and effective use" (Sarri et al., 2001, p. 179; see also Gambrill & Shlonsky, 2000). Throughout the process of developing and implementing these assessment tools in Maryland's juvenile justice system, we have learned a number of lessons that are reflected in the discussion above.

First, decisions about whether to develop new assessments or employ or adapt off-the-shelf assessments must be made early on and supported consistently by agency administrators and researchers. To address resistance from staff and the questions of stakeholders outside the agency, it was important that senior DJS staff could commit to and articulate the rationale for these decisions. Similarly, we learned firsthand why it is necessary for internal and external stakeholders to be involved early and continuously in the process. Internal stakeholders (from field staff through senior managers) must be fully engaged in every aspect of the process, as they collectively determine whether the implementation of the assessments is successful. Although assessments and case management decisions are technically the sole purview of the juvenile justice agency in Maryland, we also found that external stakeholders can play a significant role in internal DJS decision making. This often differs considerably by jurisdiction, requiring tailored efforts to involve and engage these individuals. Local precedents and history, and the individual work styles and role perceptions of judges, prosecutors, defense attorneys, and even the local police affect the amount and type of influence stakeholders have on juvenile justice agency decisions and their outcomes. Gaining their support for the rationale of new assessment protocols, their confidence in the agency's ability to carry out them out, and keeping them informed and engaged through monitoring reports that address their interests and concerns are central to long-term success.

Strategies involving field staff and immediate supervisors are perhaps most critical to advancing implementation. Researchers must first identify and assess existing practices by working with all levels of the organization, not just administrators. In public organizations as large and dispersed as most juvenile justice agencies, there are often significant discrepancies between directions and policies promulgated by administrators and practices in the field. These discrepancies range from relatively small differences in the interpretation of policies to the wholesale disregard (or lack of knowledge) of policies by some field staff. Implementation planners must spend time in the field, observing and talking with field staff in the absence of managers to gain an accurate understanding of the work environment and the context of implementation from the bottom up.

Plans for development and implementation must take current practices and local work culture and climate into account. The early inclusion of field staff in the planning process provided important insights into the staff's ability to accommodate changes to existing practices. At DJS, staff and supervisor capacities dictated that the department not introduce technology that was highly discrepant with current practice and address resistance to including dynamic need factors as assessment items. This resulted in the two-phase development process and an implementation process that focused on measured and controlled change from existing practices and extensive feedback through various types of data-driven monitoring reports. Similarly, this strategic priority on staff engagement, combined with recognition of the limits of any institutional training capacity within DJS, led over time to much greater use of peer training and a training-of-the-trainers approach to disseminating new assessment technologies.

Documentation and close monitoring of implementation serve multiple purposes. In addition to improving data validity and tracking the outcomes of changes to assessment practices, monitoring provides tangible evidence of follow-through by management and reinforces accountability among both staff and supervisors. Monitoring data provide researchers with a powerful tool for identifying and correcting fidelity issues. Many DJS staff reacted initially with surprise and then were generally responsive to receiving detailed feedback in their adherence to new protocols. Data can also be targeted and packaged to help convince staff of the need for change, or how the outcomes of a proposed change compare favorably with current practice and policy. Finally, the utility of assessment data extends beyond implementation monitoring to include service planning and development.

Automation provides the only practical means of ongoing monitoring, while spurring implementation progress and the chances of success. Delays in the decision to develop automated versions of the new DJS assessments impeded the feedback process and initially reduced its impact, affirming the need to employ automation in concert with any new assessments. This lesson, like many others learned over the course of implementing the integrated assessment initiative in Maryland, underscores the need for flexibility, a sharp learning curve (often in response to inevitable missteps), and attention to past efforts to advance new technology and change in juvenile justice policy and practice.

≋ Note

1. In a separate planning process, Department of Juvenile Services' medical unit assumed the task of developing plans for needs assessments which would inform recommendations to more specific placements (e.g., to programs specializing in substance abuse or mental health services) within these security classes.

≋ References

Andrews, D. A., & Bonta, J. (1995). *The Level of Service Inventory-Revised*. Toronto, Canada: Multi-Health Systems.

Backer, T. E. (2000). The failure of success: Challenges of disseminating effective substance abuse prevention programs. *Journal of Community Psychology, 28*, 363–373.

Barnoski, R. (1998). *Juvenile Rehabilitation Administration assessments: Validity review and recommendations.* Olympia: Washington State Institute for Public Policy.

Bonta, J. (1996). Risk-needs assessment and treatment. In A. Harland (Ed.), *Choosing correctional options that work: Defining the demand and evaluating the supply* (pp. 18–32). Thousand Oaks, CA: Sage.

Bonta, J. (2002). Offender risk assessment: Guidelines for selection and use. *Criminal Justice and Behavior, 29*(4), 355–379.

Bonta, J., Bogue, B., Crowley, M., & Mottuk, L. (2001). Implementing offender classification systems: Lessons learned. In G. A. Bernfeld, D. P. Farrington, & A. Leschied (Eds.), *Offender rehabilitation in practice* (pp. 227–245). Chichester, UK: Wiley.

Brown, B. S., & Flynn, P. M. (2002). The federal role in drug abuse technology transfer: A history and perspective. *Journal of Substance Abuse Treatment, 22,* 245–257.

Dembo, R., Turner, G., Schmeidler, J. Chin Sue, C. Borden, P., & Manning, D. (1996). Development and evaluation of a classification of high risk youths entering a juvenile assessment center. *International Journal of the Addictions, 31,* 303–322.

Dembo, R., & Walters, W. (2003). Innovative approaches to identifying and responding to the needs of high risk youth. *Substance Use and Misuse, 38,* 1713–1738.

Dembo, R., Walters, W., & Meyers, K. (2003, April). *A practice/research collaborative: An innovative approach to identifying and responding to psychosocial functioning problems and recidivism risk among juvenile arrestees* [U.S. Department of Justice Community Oriented Policing Services Contract #2000-CKW0092]. Miami, FL: Miami-Dade Police Department Juvenile Assessment Center.

Doob, A. N., & Beaulieu, L. A. (1993). Variation in the exercise of judicial discretion with young offenders. In T. O'Reilly-Fleming & B. Clark (Eds.), *Youth injustice: Canadian perspectives* (pp. 231–248). Toronto: Canadian Scholars Press.

Ferguson, J. L. (2002). Putting the "what works" research into practice: An organizational perspective. *Criminal Justice and Behavior, 29*(4), 472–492.

Funk, S. J. (1999). Risk assessment for juveniles on probation: A focus on gender. *Criminal Justice and Behavior, 26*(1), 44–68.

Gambrill, E., & Shlonsky, A. (2000). Risk assessment in context. *Children and Youth Services Review, 22,* 813–839.

Gottfredson, M. R., & Gottfredson, D. M. (1988). *Decision making in criminal justice: Toward a rational exercise of discretion.* New York: Plenum.

Grisso, T., & Conlin, M. (1984). Procedural issues in the juvenile justice system. In N. Repucci, L. Weithorn, E. Mulvey, & J. Monohan (Eds.), *Children, mental health, and the law* (pp. 171–193). Beverly Hills, CA: Sage.

Grisso, T., & Underwood, L. (2004). *Screening and assessing mental health and substance use disorders among youth in the juvenile justice system: A resource guide for practitioners* (Doc. No. 204956). Washington, DC: Office of Juvenile Justice and Delinquency Prevention.

Hoge, R. D. (1999). An expanded role for psychological assessments in juvenile justice systems. *Criminal Justice and Behavior, 26*(2), 251–266.

Hoge, R,D. (2002). Standardized instruments for assessing risk and need in youthful offenders. *Criminal Justice and Behavior, 29*(4), 380–396.

Hoge, R. D., & Andrews, D. A. (1996). *Assessing the youthful offender: Issues and techniques.* New York: Plenum.

Institute of Medicine. (1998). *Bridging the gap between practice and research: Forging partnerships with community-based drug and alcohol treatment.* Washington, DC: National Academy Press.

Jones, P. R., Harris, P. W., Fader, J., & Grubstein, L. (2001). Identifying chronic juvenile offenders. *Justice Quarterly, 18*(3), 479–507.

Lowenkamp, C. T., Holsinger, A. M., & Latessa, E. J. (2001). Risk/need assessment, offender classification, and the role of childhood abuse. *Criminal Justice and Behavior, 28*(5), 543–563.

Maupin, J. R. (1993). Risk classification systems and the provision of juvenile aftercare. *Crime & Delinquency, 39*(1), 90–107.

Mears, D. P., & Kelly, W. R. (1999). Assessments and intake processes in juvenile justice processing: Emerging policy considerations. *Crime & Delinquency, 45*(4), 508–529.

Pfeifer, H. L., Young, D., Bouffard, J., & Taxman, F. (2001). *Department of Juvenile Justice Risk Screening Project. Report to the Maryland Department of Juvenile Justice.* College Park, MD: Bureau of Governmental Research.

Rogers, E, M. (1995). *Diffusion of innovations.* New York: Free Press.

Roman, P. M., & Johnson, J. A. (2002). Adoption and implementation of new technologies in substance abuse treatment. *Journal of Substance Abuse Treatment, 22,* 211–218.

Sarri, R., Shook, J. J., Ward, G., Creekmore, M., Albertson, C., Goodkind, S., & Chih Soh, J. (2001). *Decision making in the juvenile justice system: A comparative study of four states. Final report to the National Institute of Justice.* Ann Arbor, MI: Institute for Social Research.

Simpson, D. D. (2002). A conceptual framework for transferring research to practice. *Journal of Substance Abuse Treatment, 22,* 171–182.

Wiebush, R. G., Baird, C., Krisberg, B., & Onek, D. (1995). Risk assessment and classification for serious, violent, and chronic juvenile offenders. In J. C. Howell, B. Krisberg, J. D. Hawkins, & J. J. Wilson (Eds.), *A sourcebook: Serious, violent, and chronic juvenile offenders* (pp. 171–212). Thousand Oaks, CA: Sage.

Wright, K. W., Clear, T. R., & Dickson, P. (1984). A critique of the universal applicability of risk assessment instruments. *Criminology, 22*(1), 113–133.

DISCUSSION QUESTIONS

1. What are the three groups into which an increasing number of youth served by juvenile justice systems tend to fit? Can you give examples of the types of offenses or behavior problems common to each of those groups of youth?

2. Identify the four "generations" of juvenile assessment tools as they have developed in recent decades. In what ways are newer assessment tools better than older ones?

3. What are some of the purposes and advantages of assessment tools in juvenile justice decision making?

4. What are three key decisions juvenile justice officials make following referral and continuing to aftercare? What do you believe are the most difficult decisions?

5. What are some of the reasons for staff resistance to implementing assessment tools? What do the authors suggest for overcoming staff resistance and for implementing assessment technologies?

❖

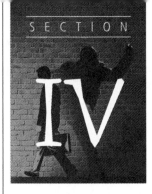

TRANSFER TO CRIMINAL COURT

⊠ Overview of Waiver and Transfer

Throughout the history of the juvenile court, all crimes involving juvenile-age offenders have first been filed in the juvenile court, regardless of the seriousness of the charge. All states and the District of Columbia, however, have laws that provide for criminal court prosecution of juveniles under certain circumstances. Transferring juveniles to criminal court is not a new practice. Juvenile courts have always had the authority to waive jurisdiction and transfer a case to criminal court. The statutes and the terms describing the process for waiver of juvenile court jurisdiction and transfer to criminal court differ somewhat from state to state. Traditionally the decision has been left to the discretion of the judge, who could *waive* juvenile court jurisdiction, *certify* the juvenile as an adult, and *transfer* the case to criminal court. The waiver decision essentially is a choice between punishment in adult criminal court or rehabilitation in juvenile court (Podkopacz & Feld, 1996). The juvenile court must determine whether the seriousness of the present offense and the juvenile's prior record justify transferring the case to criminal court. This is still the case in most jurisdictions, but recent get-tough legislation has led to statutory or automatic transfer of chronic or violent juvenile offenders (Torbet et al., 1996).

Judicial waivers were exceptionally rare in juvenile court through the 1970s, when the focus of the court was on the needs and "best interests" of the child. The traditional juvenile justice philosophy began to change in the 1980s and 1990s to more of a focus on the criminal acts of juvenile offenders and a presumed need for more coercive intervention. The change in philosophy brought changes in waiver policies. The number of juvenile cases waived to criminal court has never been more than only 1% to 2% of the total number of juvenile court cases, but the rate of increase in the 1990s was dramatic. The number of delinquency cases waived to criminal court from 1985 to 1994 increased from about 7,200 to 13,200, an 83% increase. The number then began a steady decline, dropping to 6,300 in 2001, which was 1% below the number in 1985 and less than 1% (0.8%) of all petitioned delinquency cases (Snyder & Sickmund, 2006, p. 186). The most recent available figures indicate a total of 9,399 juvenile cases waived in 2004 (Stahl, Finnegan, & Kang, 2007). The number of delinquency cases and the demographic percentages of juveniles waived to criminal court in 1985, 1994, and 2004 are presented in Table IV-1.

Person offenses are the types of cases most likely to be waived to criminal court, with a smaller percentage being waived for property, drug, and public order offenses. The majority of juveniles waived to criminal court are males (94%) and juveniles aged 16 and over (89%). A slightly higher percentage of white juveniles are waived than are blacks and other races, but a disproportionate percentage of black youth are waived to criminal court in comparison to their proportion of the juvenile population (see Table IV-1 and Stahl et al., 2007). The number of juvenile cases waived by judges to the criminal court has decreased since the 1990s. This decrease in court waivers is because of legislative changes in many states that provide for

Table IV-1	Delinquency Cases Waived to Criminal Court by Demographic Characteristics		
Characteristic	1985	1994	2004
Total Cases	7,158	13,107	9,399
Gender			
Male	95%	95%	94%
Female	5%	5%	6%
Race			
White	58%	53%	56%
Black	41%	43%	42%
Other races	2%	4%	2%
Age			
15 & under	6%	12%	11%
16 & over	94%	88%	89%

Sources: Adapted from Snyder & Sickmund, 2006, p. 186; Stahl, Finnegan, & Kang, 2007.

prosecutorial discretion and *legislative exclusion* as additional mechanisms to try juveniles as adults (Griffin, Torbet, & Szymanski, 1998). Therefore, many more juveniles have been tried in criminal court following prosecutorial discretion or legislative exclusion than the 9,399 recorded cases of juveniles transferred to criminal court following juvenile court waiver in 2004. Howard Snyder of the National Center for Juvenile Justice (NCJJ) has estimated that there are well over 100,000 juveniles tried in criminal court each year, but those numbers are not reported to the NCJJ, the OJJDP, or to the Bureau of Justice Statistics (H. N. Snyder, personal communication, July 31, 2007).

Some states have now developed an alternative to juvenile transfer known as "extended juvenile jurisdiction prosecution" (or EJJP), also referred to as "blended sentencing" (Sanborn & Salerno, 2005; Snyder, Sickmund, & Poe-Yamagata, 2000), which will be discussed in Section V (The Juvenile Court Process). In this section we examine developments in waiver and transfer, legislative changes providing for prosecutorial discretion and statutory exclusion, legal factors and scientific evidence relating to transfer, and research evidence on the effects of transferring juvenile offenders to criminal courts and adult corrections.

▧ Judicial and Legislative Developments in Juvenile Transfer

There are basically three ways in which juveniles can be prosecuted in the adult criminal justice system. They differ according to the terms used to describe them and according to who makes the transfer decision. The three different processes are: judicial waiver, statutory exclusion, and concurrent jurisdiction (Griffin et al., 1998; Snyder et al., 2000).

Judicial Waiver. Under judicial waiver the juvenile court judge has the authority to waive juvenile court jurisdiction and transfer a case to the criminal court. A total of 46 states give juvenile court judges this authority (Griffin et al., 1998). Judicial waiver is usually requested by the prosecuting attorney and is granted by the court after a hearing. States vary in the degree of flexibility they allow the court in decision making, but waiver decisions must comply with guidelines spelled out in the U.S. Supreme Court case of *Kent v. United States* (383 U.S. 541 [1966]). In *Kent,* the Supreme Court reversed the conviction of a 16-year-old youth who had been tried as an adult. The waiver to adult court was ruled invalid because the juvenile was denied a hearing with assistance of legal counsel and no written statement was made giving reasons for the waiver to criminal court. The waiver hearing is to consider evidence that relates to the criteria for waiver. The evidence presented is *not* to determine guilt on the present charge. The U.S. Supreme Court ruled in the 1975 case of *Breed v. Jones* (421 U.S. 519) that it was in violation of the double jeopardy clause of the Fourteenth Amendment to prosecute a juvenile in criminal court following adjudicatory proceedings in juvenile court. The purpose of the waiver hearing is not to determine guilt or innocence, but to assess a juvenile's threat to public safety and amenability to treatment under the juvenile justice system. Under most waiver statutes, the juvenile court judge considers such factors as the circumstances and seriousness of the alleged offense, prior adjudications, and the age and maturity of the youth. Most states that specify factors to be considered in waiver hearings either list or paraphrase some of the factors in the U.S. Supreme Court decision in *Kent* (Griffin et al., 1998, p. 4). See Box 4-1 for a summary of the *Kent* case and the criteria for judicial waiver decisions.

Box 4-1   *Kent v. United States,* 383 U.S. 541 (1966)

THE CASE

In 1961, while on probation from an earlier case, 16-year-old Morris Kent was arrested and charged with breaking into a residence, rape, and robbery. Kent confessed to the charges and offered information on other similar incidents. Kent's attorney anticipated that the District of Columbia Juvenile Court would consider waiver and transfer to the criminal court, so he filed motions requesting a hearing on the issue of jurisdiction. The juvenile court judge did not rule on this motion. Instead, he entered an order stating that the juvenile court was waiving jurisdiction over Kent after making a "full investigation." The judge did not describe the investigation or the grounds for the waiver.

When Kent was indicted in criminal court, his lawyer moved to dismiss the criminal indictment, arguing that the juvenile court's waiver had been invalid. The motion was overruled. Kent was subsequently tried in criminal court, found guilty on six counts of housebreaking and robbery, and sentenced to 30 to 90 years in prison.

On appeal, Kent's attorney again challenged the validity of the waiver. Appellate courts rejected the appeal, refused to examine the juvenile court judge's "investigation," and accepted the waiver as valid. On appeal to the U.S. Supreme Court, Kent's attorney argued that the judge had not made a complete investigation and that Kent had been denied his constitutional rights simply because he was a minor.

The Court Decision

The U.S. Supreme Court ruled the juvenile court order waiving jurisdiction invalid, holding that Kent's counsel should have had access to all records involved in the waiver decision and that the judge should have provided a written statement of the reasons for waiver. The Court also held that waiver hearings do not need to conform to all the formal requirements of a criminal trial, but that they must measure up to "the essentials of due process and fair treatment." In particular, the Court held that juveniles facing waiver are entitled to:

- Representation by counsel.
- Access to social services records.
- A written statement of the reasons for waiver.

Waiver Criteria

In an appendix to the decision, the Court provided detailed criteria and principles for juvenile court judges to follow in making a waiver decision:

An offense falling within the statutory limitations . . . will be waived if it has prosecutive merit and if it is heinous or of an aggravated character, or—even though less serious—if it represents a pattern of repeated offenses, which indicate that the juvenile may be beyond rehabilitation under Juvenile Court procedures, or if the public needs the protection afforded by such action.

The determinative factors which will be considered by the Judge in deciding whether the Juvenile Court's jurisdiction over such offenses will be waived are the following:

1. The seriousness of the alleged offense to the community and whether the protection of the community requires waiver.

2. Whether the alleged offense was committed in an aggressive, violent, premeditated or willful manner.

3. Whether the alledged offense was against persons or against property, greater weight being given to offenses against persons especially if personal injury resulted.

4. The prosecutive merit of the complaint, i.e., whether there is evidence upon which a Grand Jury may be expected to return an indictment. . . .

5. The desirability of trial and disposition of the entire offense in one court when the juvenile's associates in the alleged offense are adults who will be charged with a crime in [criminal court].

6. The sophistication and maturity of the juvenile as determined by consideration of his home, environmental situation, emotional attitude, and pattern of living.

7. The record and previous history of the juvenile, including previous contacts with [social service agencies], other law enforcement agencies, juvenile courts and other jurisdictions, prior periods of probation . . . or prior commitments to juvenile institutions.

8. The prospects for adequate protection of the public and the likelihood of reasonable rehabilitation of the juvenile . . . by the use of procedures, services and facilities currently available to the Juvenile Court. (as cited in Snyder et al., 2000, pp. 2–3)

Two variations of judicial waiver that exist in several states are mandatory waiver and presumptive waiver. *Mandatory waiver* (in the statutes of 14 states) makes waiver mandatory in cases that meet certain age, offense, or other criteria (Griffin et al., 1998, p. 4). Proceedings are initiated in the juvenile court, but the court has no role other than to confirm that the statutory requirements for mandatory waiver are met. The juvenile court must then transfer the case to criminal court. Mandatory waiver is different from statutory exclusion because the case originates in the juvenile court. Under statutory exclusion (discussed below) a case that meets statutory criteria originates in criminal court. The juvenile court's involvement under mandatory waiver is minimal, but it does initiate proceedings, conduct a preliminary hearing to confirm that the case meets the criteria for mandatory waiver, and issue a transfer order and other orders that may include appointment of counsel and pretrial detention (Griffin et al., 1998, p. 4).

Presumptive waiver (in the statutes of 15 states) designates a category of cases for which waiver to criminal court is presumed to be appropriate (Griffin et al., 1998, p. 6). In such cases the juvenile rather than the State has the burden of proof in the waiver hearing. If a juvenile who meets the age, offense seriousness, prior offense history, or other statutory criteria prompting the presumptive waiver fails to make a convincing argument against transfer, the juvenile court must send the case to criminal court.

Prosecutorial Discretion

The provision for *prosecutorial discretion* allows prosecutors to file certain juvenile cases in either juvenile or criminal court (Torbet et al., 1996). The statute, also referred to as *direct file* or *concurrent jurisdiction,* has been adopted by 15 states (Griffin et al., 1998, p. 7). These direct file provisions give both juvenile and adult criminal courts the power to hear cases that have been specified in the statute according to seriousness of offense and age of offender. Prosecutorial transfer, unlike judicial waiver, is not subject to judicial review and is not required to meet the due process requirements established in *Kent* (Snyder et al., 2000, p. 4). It is left up to the prosecutor's discretion whether to file the case in juvenile or criminal court. Prosecutors have broad discretionary authority under this provision, especially given the concurrent jurisdiction of either juvenile or criminal court for the stated offenses and age criteria in the statute. The direct file or concurrent jurisdiction process represents a dramatic departure from the waiver procedures specified in *Kent,* in which juvenile court judges were to determine through a preliminary hearing whether a youth was "amenable to treatment" in the juvenile justice system, or whether a combination of age, maturity, offense, and prior record constituted a risk to public safety. The waiver hearing generally has included social background information compiled by a probation officer, and often a psychological assessment. States also vary widely regarding the applicable offense categories and other criteria. For example, Arkansas authorizes direct file for soliciting a minor to join a street gang, and Florida allows even misdemeanors to be prosecuted in criminal court if the juvenile is 16 and has a prior serious record (Griffin et al., 1998, p. 8). Because prosecutor discretion does not involve a juvenile court hearing and transfer, no national data exist on the number or characteristics of the cases that prosecutors exclude from juvenile court jurisdiction (Snyder et al., 2000).

Critics of prosecutorial waiver have expressed concerns about giving exclusive authority to prosecutors and removing the judge from the transfer decision-making process. The practice runs contrary to the traditional principles of juvenile justice whereby judicial decisions were made based on not only the offense but also on the sophistication, culpability, maturity, and amenability to treatment of the offender. Feld (2004) has expressed concern over the practice of allowing elected prosecutors, who are subject to political pressure and are not likely to rely on any social background information, to make the important decision of jurisdictional waiver: "The shift of sentencing discretion from the judicial branch to the executive branch via direct file legislation raises a host of sentencing policy questions about institutional competencies and justice administration" (Feld, 2004, p. 600). He suggests that prosecutors are not likely to make better informed and appropriate transfer decisions than would judges in an adversarial waiver hearing in which they are assisted in the decision with clinical and social background evidence and guided by specific waiver criteria. A study of prosecutors' direct certification and waiver in Virginia found that only a small percentage of eligible offenders were actually transferred, suggesting that factors other than seriousness of offense may have been considered (Sridharan, Greenfield, & Blakley, 2004). Certifications varied across localities in the state, however, and the authors acknowledged the mixed findings and generally critical assessments of prosecutorial waiver. Critics of direct prosecutorial waiver have vehemently questioned the practice of allowing waiver decisions based on a punitive orientation without the balanced due process safeguards of a judicial hearing to consider relevant evidence and without a requirement to consider specific criteria for waiver, as specified by the U.S. Supreme Court in *Kent* (Bishop, 2004; Feld, 2000; Kupchik, 2004).

Statutory Exclusion

A total of 28 states have statutes that remove certain offenses or age and offense categories from juvenile court jurisdiction (Griffin et al., 1998, pp. 8–9). Most of these apply to cases of murder by juveniles 16 or older, but some states include juveniles 14 or older who commit person offenses. In practice, the laws simply exclude anyone fitting the criteria from being defined as a "child" for purposes of juvenile court jurisdiction. A juvenile charged with an excluded offense is therefore treated as an adult from the beginning of the judicial process. The prosecutor does not have discretion regarding the court in which the case is filed. Once the decision is made to charge the juvenile with an excluded offense, the case must be filed in criminal court. Statutory exclusion is part of the same trend toward get-tough legislation that has shifted decision making from judges to legislators and prosecutors (Feld, 2000). As with prosecutorial discretion discussed above, legislators have removed the judge from the decision-making process with statutory exclusion. The evidentiary hearing process mandated by the U.S. Supreme Court in *Kent* is circumvented by statutory exclusion in the same way as it is with prosecutorial discretion. Statutory exclusion provisions also circumvent most current state laws for transfer of juveniles to criminal court. Juvenile transfer laws in 46 states today explicitly direct the judge to consider the age, mental maturity, and capacity of the juvenile (Sanborn & Salerno, 2005).

Additional Transfer Laws

Reverse Waiver. Lawmakers in 23 states have added a provision referred to as *reverse waiver* whereby a juvenile who is being prosecuted as an adult in criminal court may petition to have the case transferred to juvenile court for adjudication or disposition (Griffin et al., 1998, p. 910). This statute basically authorizes the adult criminal court to consider the appropriateness of a juvenile case for criminal prosecution, regardless of whether the juvenile case is there due to waiver, transfer, or exclusion. The reverse waiver provision is an attempt to provide some balance to the broad discretion given to prosecutors under direct file statutes. In considering a juvenile's petition for juvenile court jurisdiction, the criminal court must consider the same criteria that are used by juvenile courts in transferring juveniles to criminal court (Griffin et al., 1998, p. 10).

"Once an Adult, Always an Adult." Laws have been passed in 31 states that apply to juveniles who have been prosecuted and convicted as adults and are subsequently accused of new offenses. Most of the states with "once an adult, always an adult" provisions require criminal prosecution for all subsequent offenses committed by the juvenile (Griffin et al., 1998, p. 10). Others exclude or require waiver of juveniles of a certain age or for sufficiently serious subsequent offenses.

⬛ The Law, Science, and Juvenile Transfer

A basic principle underlying the separate system of justice for juveniles is that they are different from adults. This principle is not disputed for most juvenile offenses and offenders. The difference between adult and juvenile offenders becomes blurred in cases of older juveniles who commit serious crimes (Zimring, 1998). Regardless of the age of the offender, however,

▲ **Photo IV-1**   Lee Malvo leaves court following his transfer from juvenile court and conviction as an adult for sniper killings in the Washington, DC, area. (© BRENDAN MCDERMID/Reuters/Corbis)

a fundamental legal premise in the justice system requires that a crime must include both an act and an intent to commit the act (or the *actus reus* and *mens rea*). The offender must be shown to have caused harm and be culpable for the offense. The principle of fundamental fairness was demonstrated in a recent U.S. Supreme Court ruling that banned the execution of mentally retarded persons who had committed murder. In support of the reduced culpability of mentally retarded defendants, the Court held that

> [They] frequently know the difference between right and wrong and are competent to stand trial. Because of their impairments, however, by definition they have diminished capacities to understand and process mistakes and learn from experience, to engage in logical reasoning, to control impulses, and to understand the reactions of others. . . . Their deficiencies do not warrant an exemption from criminal sanctions, but they do diminish their personal culpability. (*Atkins v. Virginia* [536 U.S. 304, 318 (2002)])

The Court's reasoning in relation to the mentally retarded is similar to reasons given for the reduced culpability of young people. All Western nations, including the United States, have separate systems of justice for juveniles based on the understanding that juveniles are less mature than adults and therefore are less culpable (Zimring, 2000).

Research findings in developmental psychology show that there is ample evidence and support for the reduced culpability of juveniles based on their lower level of maturity. Youth deserve to be treated as less culpable for a number of reasons (see Bishop, 2004, pp. 635–636; Feld, 1999, pp. 306–313; Zimring, 1998, 2000): (1) the lower cognitive development of youth means they do not process information and consider alternatives as well as adults; (2) adolescent judgment and emotional and social maturity are not as well developed as adults'; (3) youth are less aware of risks, and are more likely to take risks that may harm themselves and others; (4) youth have a different perspective of time than adults, and think more in terms of short-term rather than long-term consequences; (5) juveniles are more vulnerable to peer pressure than adults; (6) youth make poorer judgments because they have less experience in decision making; and (7) recent research in neuroscience indicates that portions of the brain responsible for impulse control and decision making are underdeveloped compared to adults.

The American Bar Association (ABA; 2004) has recognized the reduced culpability of youth based on differences in brain development between adults and juveniles. Based on neuroscientific studies of brain development of adolescents, the ABA supports the assertion that adolescents are less morally culpable for their actions than competent adults, and are more capable of change and rehabilitation. The ideal of not holding violent juveniles accountable and blameworthy the same as adults is difficult for many to accept. This is especially true for juveniles who are physically as big and strong as adults. Appearance and physical size may be deceiving, however. The appearance of physical maturity does not mean an adolescent has the same reasoning capacity as an adult. Research reported by the ABA (2004) indicates that because of slower development of parts of the brain that support clear reasoning and decision making, youth often rely on emotional parts of the brain. Another misconception is that commission of a serious crime is a sign of maturity. Some children and adolescents do tragically commit serious crimes and cause serious harm. Murder and violent crimes are not strictly "adult" activities, however, and it is illogical to reason that a youth who kills is more mature than a youth who steals (Bishop, 2004). It is understandable that the crime of murder triggers a desire for punishment, retribution, and vengeance. It is no more appropriate to hold an adolescent accountable the same as an adult, however, than it is to hold a mentally retarded offender accountable the same as a person of normal, average intelligence. The fact that adolescents are less mature than adults does not excuse them from punishment for violent crimes. It does, however, lessen their culpability and therefore the level of punishment. For this reason it is important to have a fair and just process of determining through a hearing whether a juvenile offender is "amenable to treatment" in the juvenile system, or may be held accountable for a crime the same as an adult. The American Bar Association (2004) reminds us that the concept of adolescents being less mature and less culpable is not new. We refer to those under 18 as "minors" and "juveniles" for a reason: They are less than adult.

▧ Research on the Effects of Transfer

The laws designed to send more juvenile offenders to criminal court and punish them as adult offenders are based on lawmakers' belief that serious juvenile crime is increasing, and the reason for the perceived increase is due to a lenient and ineffective juvenile justice system.

Violent juvenile crime has in fact been dropping for years (Snyder & Sickmund, 2006), and the assumption of a lenient, ineffective system is disputed by numerous juvenile justice experts (Bernard, 1992; Feld, 1988; Zimring, 1998). The stated purposes of most juvenile waiver and transfer laws nevertheless focus on public safety, reduction of serious crimes by juveniles, and punishing young offenders who are believed to be not amenable to treatment in the juvenile justice system. Rising juvenile crime rates in the 1970s led many to assume that the juvenile system had failed, that it was too lenient and was ineffective in deterring juvenile crime. It is generally taken for granted by politicians and the public that getting tougher with harsher punishment is an effective response to crime. Media accounts of violent juvenile offenders tend to portray them as incorrigible young criminals who view juvenile laws, the court, and the corrections system as "soft" on crime. Based on limited empirical evidence of what works in juvenile justice, state legislatures have revised juvenile codes with an emphasis on offender accountability, punishment, and public safety. Most states have revised their juvenile codes to make it easier to transfer young offenders to the criminal courts (Feld, 1995; Torbet et al., 1996). Does the transfer of juveniles to criminal court make a difference? Several studies have examined the types of cases that have been waived to criminal court and the question of whether transfers do in fact make a difference. Mears (2003) examined the leading intended and unintended effects of waiver and is included as one of the readings in this section.

Types of Juvenile Cases Transferred. There is evidence that many juveniles waived to adult court are *not* the most dangerous or serious offenders. Bortner (1986) examined 214 remanded juveniles and found that they were not more dangerous or intractable than nonremanded juveniles. Her analysis suggested that their remand did not enhance public safety, and she concluded that political and organizational factors accounted for the increased number of remands. There is evidence that criminal courts have given less severe sentences to waived juveniles than if those young offenders had been tried in juvenile court. Donna Hamparian and her associates (1982) found that most of the juveniles transferred to adult court in 1978 received sentences of fines, probation, or other alternatives to incarceration. and the small number who were incarcerated received sentences of 1 year or less. Donna Bishop and her associates (Bishop, Frazier, & Henretta, 1989) examined the practice of prosecutorial waiver in Florida and found that few of the juveniles transferred were dangerous or repeat offenders for whom the waiver would be justified. They found that a lack of statutory guidelines and the ease of prosecutorial waiver without judicial oversight accounted for many inappropriate cases being transferred to criminal court (Bishop et al., 1989, p. 198).

Crime Reduction Through Transfer. Research on the effects of the harsher juvenile code revisions indicates that the effects have not been in the intended direction. Bishop and her associates (Bishop, Frazier, Lanza-Kaduce, & Winner, 1996) compared matched samples of juveniles, some of whom were transferred and others who were not transferred, and found that transfer actually resulted in increased short-term recidivism rates. Despite being incarcerated for longer periods of time, the transferred youths committed more offenses. Even when controlling for time at risk, the rate of reoffending in the transfer group was significantly higher, and they were more likely to commit a subsequent felony offense. More of the matched sample of nontransferred youths improved their behavior over time, leading the authors to suggest that the stigmatizing effect of criminal court conviction and adult sentencing contributes to greater recidivism rather than reducing criminal behavior. The authors concluded that juvenile transfer did not have a deterrent effect, and removal from the streets through incapacitation did not result in improved public safety (Bishop et al., 1996).

Other research has indicated that juveniles waived to criminal court have received more severe sentences than if they had been retained in juvenile court, but there are significant disparities in the sentences for property and personal offenses and between adult and juvenile courts (Rudman, Hartstone, Fagan, & Moore, 1986; Podkopacz & Feld, 1996). In a study of criminal court data from the Pennsylvania Commission on Sentencing, Kurlychek and Johnson (2004) found that juvenile offenders transferred to adult court were sentenced more severely than their young adult counterparts. Their juvenile status did not act as a mitigating factor, but rather seemed to aggravate the sentence. Because prosecutorial decisions to transfer do not include an assessment of maturity or culpability, one might expect that criminal courts would at least take those factors into account when sentencing young offenders (Bishop, 2004). Contrary to youthfulness being a mitigating factor, the transferred juveniles received what the authors referred to as a "violent juvenile penalty" (Kurlychek & Johnson, 2004, p. 506). The findings contrast sharply with those of a 1978 survey of transferred juveniles receiving lighter sentences than adults (Hamparian et al., 1982). The study by Kurlychek and Johnson did not account for different types of transfer (judicial waiver, exclusion, or prosecutor direct file), so further research is needed to examine whether the mode of transfer makes a difference. The finding of transferred juveniles being sentenced in criminal court more severely than similar adult offenders raises serious questions of the effects of transfer policies, especially considering that transferred juveniles often have higher recidivism rates than those retained in the juvenile system (see Bishop et al., 1996).

Racial Disparity in Transfer. Juvenile arrests disproportionately involve minorities, and transfer policies have disproportionately affected black youth. Black youth accounted for 16% of the juvenile population in 2003, but were involved in a disproportionate number of juvenile arrests for robbery (63%), murder (48%), auto theft (40%), and aggravated assault (38%) in 2003 (Snyder & Sickmund, 2006, p. 125). Black youth are transferred to criminal court more than white youth. From 1985 to 2002, the likelihood of waiver was greater for black youth than for white youth regardless of offense category. Racial differences in case waivers were greatest for person offenses and especially for drug offenses, for which nearly twice as many black youths were waived to criminal court than were white youth (1.2% and 0.7%, respectively; Snyder & Sickmund, 2006, p. 187).

Despite the fact that white youth account for more than half of the violent crime arrests, violent crime has become associated more with black youth. Feld (2003) maintains that media reports and conservative political reactions have resulted in associating crime with racial minorities, specifically young black males. Media reports tend to focus on crimes that are considered more "newsworthy," resulting in disproportionate coverage of urban street crime. The news media exaggerate the true extent of violent crime, present a distorted picture of criminals (Surette, 1998), and news media coverage overreports and overemphasizes the role of minority youth in violent crime (Dorfman & Schiraldi, 2001). Crime policies are a central political agenda, and the public and political perceptions of race and youth crime were inevitably part of the incentive behind the get-tough reforms of juvenile statutes (Zimring, 1998). Feld (2003) has argued that media coverage, racial factors, and a conservative political agenda played a major role in punitive changes in juvenile justice laws and practices that have had a disproportionate impact on racial minorities.

Transfer: Solid Policy or Symbolic? Research evidence suggests that judicial waiver may have little more than symbolic value (Kupchik, 2004), relaying a message to the public that something is being done about violent juvenile crime, and "creating sentencing systems that bark much louder than they bite" (Zimring, 2005, p. 148). Legislative reforms that include get-tough provisions for juvenile offenders seem to have been driven more by political rhetoric than sound research. Slogans such as "if you're old enough to do the crime, you're old enough to do the time" resonate strongly with voters. Juvenile waiver and transfer, however, may not accomplish much in terms of reducing the growing number of serious and violent juvenile offenders. They do remove more serious offenders from the juvenile system, but there are questions whether the adult system is equipped to handle a growing number of youthful offenders. Rudman and his associates (1986) believe that waiver creates new problems for adult corrections and that it may be counterproductive to send juvenile offenders for several years of punishment with adult offenders rather than a few years of treatment in the juvenile system. According to Rudman et al. (1986), the effectiveness of juvenile justice system responses to violent youth will be improved not by removing them but rather by developing appropriate dispositional alternatives for the juvenile court. These might include increasing the age for juvenile corrections jurisdiction and improving the quality of services in secure juvenile corrections institutions. These alternatives would have more immediate impact on violent juvenile crime than simply transferring the problem to already overburdened criminal courts and correctional facilities. Zimring (1998) contends that transfer of juvenile homicide cases to criminal court simply relocates these difficult problems. It does not solve them.

Lesson Learned. Torbet and her associates (Torbet, Griffin, Hurst, & MacKenzie, 2000) have summarized a number of lessons learned based on case studies and research on juvenile transfer and waiver practices. Those lessons are highlighted below. Readers are encouraged to review the government document by Torbet et al. (2000), which is available online and listed in the Web Resources at the end of this section. More research is needed regarding the effects of juvenile transfer. The research findings currently available are important for lawmakers and justice officials who are considering additional sentencing reforms or applying those currently on the books.

- A disconnect exists between the legislative intent and the actual implementation of new laws.
- Blended sentencing laws encourage plea bargaining.
- Blended sentencing provisions expand judicial and prosecutorial discretion.
- Local application of new sentencing laws varies widely.
- New sentencing laws have a disproportionate impact on minorities.
- Expanded sentencing laws require new resources and interventions.
- More data collection and systematic follow-up are needed to judge the impact of reforms (Torbet et al., 2000, pp. 43–45).

The experiences, observations, and personal assessments of youths who have been transferred can also reveal much about the consequences and effectiveness of the policy. The third reading in this section is a report of a study by Jodi Lane and her associates in which they interviewed groups of juvenile offenders, half of whom had been transferred to the adult system and half of whom were retained in the juvenile system. The results are mixed, and depend upon the particular backgrounds and prior records of the juveniles.

⬚ Future Trends in Juvenile Transfer

There is some evidence that juvenile transfers may be waning in popularity. The number of juvenile transfers in the United States has declined steadily in the past decade, as noted in our introductory section above, and in Table IV-1 (Snyder & Sickmund, 2006). Donna Bishop (2004) cites several reasons for the reduction in juvenile transfers to criminal court: (1) there is less public support for simplistic, punitive responses to youth crime, particularly as we become aware of the monetary costs and ineffectiveness of transfers; (2) some state legislatures have actually reduced the number of crimes that are subject to prosecutorial transfer decisions; and (3) professionals in the juvenile justice system have responded to evaluation research and begun to develop new and more effective juvenile corrections programs and intervention strategies (Bishop, 2004, p. 641). Exclusion of some juvenile offenders from juvenile court will persist in most jurisdictions, however. In our final reading in this section, Joseph Sanborn, Jr., discusses the strengths and weaknesses of exclusion and concludes that exclusion policies should be selectively applied in cases of appropriate serious and chronic juvenile offenders. As with all justice policies and practices, juvenile transfer is an issue that demands further evaluative research to determine its appropriateness in responding to juvenile crime. It is important for legislators to consider policies for responding to juvenile crime that are most effective in producing long-term benefits for the protection of the community and change for juvenile offenders.

SUMMARY

- Transferring juveniles to criminal court is not a new practice. Juvenile courts have always had the authority to waive jurisdiction and transfer cases to criminal court.
- Three different transfer processes include judicial waiver, statutory exclusion, and concurrent jurisdiction (also called direct file or prosecutorial discretion).
- Several states have developed "blended sentencing" reforms as alternatives to waiver and transfer of juveniles. "Extended juvenile jurisdiction" (EJJ) is an example of blended sentencing.
- Legal principles and scientific research on mental maturity and culpability of youth raise questions regarding the fundamental fairness of processing juvenile offenders the same as adult offenders, regardless of the offense.
- Research on the effects of juvenile transfer indicate that it may not reduce serious juvenile crime but may in fact have the opposite effect; that its application varies widely between jurisdictions; that it has a disproportionate effect on minorities; and that it places additional demands on the adult corrections system, requiring additional resources and interventions.

KEY TERMS

Blended sentencing

Certification

Concurrent jurisdiction

Direct file

Extended juvenile jurisdiction

Mandatory waiver

Presumptive waiver

Prosecutorial discretion

Prosecutorial waiver

Remand

Reverse waiver

Statutory exclusion

Statutory or legislative exclusion

Transfer

Waiver

DISCUSSION QUESTIONS

1. Based on the U.S. Supreme Court ruling in *Kent v. United States,* what do you believe is the most appropriate, legally defensible method of transfer of juveniles to criminal court? Explain your reason and legal arguments.

2. Explain how "blended sentencing" is a blend between juvenile and criminal court, and what advantages it seems to have over other transfer processes.

3. Based on legal principles and scientific evidence of youths' level of maturity and understanding, do you believe it is legally justifiable to hold juveniles accountable for crimes in the same way as adults? Explain your answer.

4. What research findings on the effects of transfer do you believe offer the strongest support for or against increased use of transfer for juvenile offenders?

WEB RESOURCES

The following Web sites provide information and discussion on waiver and transfer of juveniles:

Griffin, P., Torbet, P., & Szymanski, L. (1998). *Trying Juveniles as Adults in Criminal Court: An Analysis of State Transfer Provisions:* http://www.ncjrs.gov/pdffiles/172836.pdf

Torbet, P., Griffin, P., Hurst, H., IV, & MacKenzie, L. R. (2000). *Juveniles Facing Criminal Sanctions: Three States That Changed the Rules:* http://www.ncjrs.gov/pdffiles1/ojjdp/181203.pdf

For a listing of each state's transfer provisions, see: http://www.ojjdp.ncjrs.gov/pubs/tryingjuvasadult/table1.html

Snyder, H. N., & Sickmund, M. (2006). *Juvenile Offenders and Victims: 2006 National Report.* Chapter 4 (Juvenile Justice System Structure and Process) describes juvenile transfers and how they apply to each state in relation to crime, age, and other matters. http://ojjdp.ncjrs.gov/ojstatbb/nr2006/downloads/NR2006.pdf

National Overview: *Trying Juveniles as Adults:* http://www.ncmm.org/stateprofiles/overviews/overviewtransfer.asp

For current statistics on waived cases, see the OJJDP Statistical Briefing site: http://ojjdp.ncjrs.org/ojstatbb/court/qa06502.asp?qaDate=2004

Youth Law Center, information on waiver and transfer: http://www.buildingblocksforyouth.org/issues/

READING

The authors of this article report on a long-term recidivism study that was conducted in Florida. The study compared differences in recidivism between matched pairs of juveniles, where one subject in each pair had been transferred to the adult system in 1987 and the other had been retained in the juvenile system. Rearrest information on the pairs from their release from sanctions through November 1994 was used to determine the probabilities of rearrest and the times to rearrest of transfers and nontransfers, adjusting for time at risk. They found that transfer diminished the rearrest chances for property felons, an advantage that was offset by an enhanced probability of rearrest among transfers for other offense categories. Survival analysis showed that transfers were rearrested more quickly and were rearrested more times on average. The findings of the study suggest that transfer of juveniles to adult jurisdiction is no panacea to crime prevention, and that transfer of juveniles to adult court may in fact be counterproductive.

_____ The Transfer of Juveniles to Criminal Court _____

Reexamining Recidivism Over the Long Term

Lawrence Winner, Lonn Lanza-Kaduce, Donna M. Bishop, Charles E. Frazier

▨ Introduction

Juvenile offenders have become increasingly subject to adult standards of culpability and punishment (see Feld 1987, 1988; Szymanski 1991; Torbet, Gable, Hurst, Montgomery, Szymanski, and Thomas 1996). In recent years, 40 states have adopted or modified laws to make it easier to prosecute juveniles in criminal courts (Torbet et al. 1996). Hundreds of thousands more juveniles will be dealt with as adults as a result of these changes (see Snyder and Sickmund 1995; Torbet et al. 1996). Initial research, however, has indicated that the "reforms" may be counterproductive, at least in regard to recidivism.

Fagan (1995) conducted a cross-jurisdictional analysis of the recidivism of robbery and burglary offenders over an eight-year period. He compared 15-and 16-year-old offenders from 1981–82, who were dealt with in the juvenile courts in two northern New Jersey counties, to their counterparts in two neighboring and similar New York counties. The New York youths were tried as adults. The New Jersey "juvenile" robbers reoffended less often and more slowly than did the New York "adult" robbers. No difference in recidivism between New Jersey and New York youths was found for burglary offenders.

Bishop, Frazier, Lanza-Kaduce, and Winner (1996) reported short-term recidivism rates for the population of juvenile offenders transferred to criminal court in Florida in 1987 for a broad range of offenses and for a matched group of offenders retained in juvenile court. In a short-term analysis of rearrest (through December 1988), they reported that youths who were transferred to

Source: *Crime & Delinquency, (43)*4, 548–563, October 1997. © 1997 Sage Publications, Inc.

criminal court were more likely to reoffend than were their matches who were processed as juveniles. This pattern was observed across seven offense categories ranging from personal felonies to minor misdemeanors. Bishop et al. also found that the transfers who reoffended were arrested more quickly and at a higher frequency (adjusted for time at risk) than were the nontransfers.

The analysis in this article extended the follow-up period for the cases studied by Bishop et al. (1996) through November 15, 1994, to determine whether the short-term differences in recidivism between transferred and nontransferred youths persisted over time for all types of offenders. The nearly six additional years of tracking provided insight into the long-term impact of differential processing on criminal careers. The research was focused narrowly on how the transfer decision affected recidivism over the long term. It did not address whether transferring juveniles to adult court altered the duration of criminal careers, affected crime specialization, or changed the age pattern of desistance.

Methodology

Case information was obtained through the Florida Department of Health and Rehabilitative Services' Client Information System (CIS). CIS contains case information on all referrals to the juvenile justice system from initial intake through final disposition. This study used data from the CIS system for all delinquency cases entering the state juvenile justice system from January 1, 1987 through December 30, 1987.

All juvenile cases that were transferred to the criminal court in 1987 ($N = 3,142$) were identified. Individual case histories were constructed from information contained on prior referrals in the CIS data. For the long-term analyses, matches for 2,700 of the transferred cases were obtained from cases disposed of in the juvenile justice system.[1]

The matching of nontransfer cases with transfer cases was done on each of the following variables:

1. the most serious offense for which the transfer was made using the 45 offense categories included in the CIS data (for subsequent statistical analyses, these 45 categories were grouped into the 7 offense classes listed in Table 1);

2. the number of counts included in the bill of information (coded 1, 2–3, or 4 or more);

3. the number of prior referrals to the juvenile system (coded 0, 1–2, or 3 or more);

4. the most serious prior offense (coded 1 = no prior referral, 2 = prior status offense, 3 = less serious misdemeanors not categorized as personal, property, or substance use offenses, 4 = middle-range misdemeanors including those involving drug/alcohol use, 5 = most serious misdemeanors including those involving property and personal offenses, 6 = felonies not categorized as involving drug, property, or personal crimes, 7 = drug felonies, 8 = property felonies, or 9 = personal felonies);

5. age (coded in years);

6. gender (coded male or female); and

7. race (coded White or non-White).

Matches were obtained through a sequential method in which each matching variable was added in the order just listed. Matches were successful for the first six variables. Race was the last variable in the matching sequence and the hardest one on which to match. Only two thirds of White transfers could be matched with White nontransfers, and only about half of non-White transfers could be matched with non-White nontransfers. When the race criterion was relaxed, 92% of the cases were matched.

The analysis focused on several aspects of recidivism, the first of which was the probability of any rearrest during the follow-up period (an indicator of the prevalence of recidivism). The second focus was on the time (in days) to first rearrest, which we treated as a failure time in statistical survival analysis (Kalbfleisch and Prentice 1980). Then, for the recidivists, the time to rearrest was reexamined and the incidence or frequency of rearrest was analyzed. Rearrest records were obtained from Florida Department of Law Enforcement data on arrests through November 15, 1994.[2]

Time-at-risk adjustments were made for time served in state adult and juvenile correctional facilities. Data were obtained from the Florida Department of Corrections (DOC) that indicated entry and release dates for transferred youths who spent time in state adult facilities. Data obtained from the DOC came in two disjointed segments, one with entry dates on or before December 31, 1988 and the other with entry dates on or after January 1, 1989. Information on release dates for those serving time on December 31, 1988 was not included, so 24 of the pairs with a subject in prison on that date were dropped from the analysis.

Information on county jail time served by transferred youths was unavailable. (Juveniles who were retained in the juvenile system could not be sentenced to jails.) For purposes of analyzing time at risk, we assumed that any youth not sentenced to a state facility was at risk immediately on disposition, which no doubt overestimated the actual time at risk for some transfers. That is, the average time to rearrest might have been shorter among transferred youths if information on jail time had been available. Thus, transfers were advantaged in time-to-rearrest comparisons to nontransfers.

It also was important to adjust for time at risk among nontransfers. The CIS data contained information on whether juveniles were sentenced to residential or institutional programs, but the CIS data did not include dates of entry or release, nor did they indicate the specific facilities or programs to which each youth was committed. Therefore, the average time served across all facilities was used to adjust for time at risk. Based on information supplied by Florida's Department of

Juvenile Justice, the estimated average time was set at three months.

Results

Probability of Rearrest

Among the 2,700 transfers in 1987, 1,128 (42%) were rearrested before November 15, 1994, whereas the number of matched nontransfers who were rearrested during that period was 1,163 (43%). This was a marked change from the 30% and 19% recidivism rates reported for the respective groups in the short-term analysis (Bishop et al. 1996). Over the long run, the probability of rearrest for the nontransferred juveniles caught up with (and very slightly surpassed) that for the transferred youths with which they were matched. According to McNemar's test (see Agresti 1990), however, the overall difference in probability of rearrest for the two study groups was not significant ($Z = .97$, $p = .332$). In other words, in the aggregate, transfers were as likely to be rearrested as were their matches who were not transferred.

When the probabilities of rearrest were broken down by broad felony versus misdemeanor offense classifications, some differences between the groups emerged. Some of the results parallel those of the earlier short-term analysis (see Bishop et al. 1996). The probability of rearrest remained greater over the long term for those transferred for misdemeanors in 1987 than for their nontransferred matches ($Z = -2.79$, $p = .005$), but the probability of rearrest for those transferred in 1987 for felony charges reversed direction. By 1994, the nontransfer matches were more likely to have been rearrested than were the transfers ($Z = 2.53$, $p = .011$).

The offense distinction was further broken down by degree of felony and misdemeanor (represented by seven offense classes). The enhanced probability of rearrest over the long term for nontransferred felons was due completely to cases in Class 2, those prosecuted for felony property offenses. This was the only offense class for which nontransfer matches were more likely than their transferred counterparts to be rearrested ($Z = 5.47, p < .001$). For Classes 3 to 7, the transfers were rearrested more often, a result consistent with the earlier short-term analysis. For Class 1, the personal felonies, there was no difference in the probability of rearrest between the transfer and nontransfer groups.

These results raised the possibility of an offense-specific difference in recidivism between transfers and nontransfers. Because of the imprecision in matching on race, we also examined whether racial differences between transfers and their matches complicated the analyses.

We conducted a multivariate analysis by estimating a logistic regression model in which rearrest was regressed simultaneously on the transfer/nontransfer status of the case and a series of dummy variables operationalizing the matching criteria. The coding categories were male versus female; White versus non-White; less than 14 years of age, 14–15 years of age, and 16 years versus 17 years of age; number of referrals prior to the 1987 offense (0 and 1–2) versus 3 or more referrals; the most severe charge level for prior referrals (see the nine categories in the matching procedure described previously); the number of charges involved in the 1987 case (1 and 2–3) versus 4 or more charges; and the most severe level of the 1987 charge from the seven offense classes described. Nontransfer status, females, non-Whites, 17–year-olds, a personal felony being the most severe prior offense, 4 or more counts in 1987, and Class 7 offense severity in 1987 (less severe misdemeanor) served as the reference categories. We constructed interaction terms between race and each of the 1987 charge levels and between transfer/nontransfer and the 1987 charge levels. These interaction terms also were included in the logistic regression model.

This multivariate approach had several advantages. First, it isolated the effects of transfer on recidivism while controlling for other variables. Second, it showed whether transfer interacted with specific offenses to predict recidivism. Third, it showed whether race interacted with specific offenses to predict recidivism, an issue that may be important because of the imprecision on race in our matching procedure. Finally, it indicated which of the matching variables had a direct effect on recidivism, something that we did not examine in the short-term analysis.

The effect of transfer status on the probability of rearrest was weak (Wald chi-square = 4.378, $p = .036$, standard estimate = .128) when other variables were controlled. Its direction indicated that the net effect of transfer was to increase recidivism in the long term, a finding that was consistent with the short-term analysis (Bishop et al. 1996).

This result seemed to contradict the absolute numbers, which showed that a few more nontransfer matches actually were rearrested than were transfers. The absolute numbers, however, were derived from an analysis that did not control for other influences on recidivism.

One of those other influences that was particularly strong had to do with Class 2 offenses (property felonies). The Class 2 offense category had two effects. Having committed a crime in this property felony class independently increased the rearrest probability (Wald chi-square = 16.533, $p < .001$, standard estimate = .258), and it interacted with transfer to reduce rearrest (Wald chi-square = 17.658, $p < .001$, standard estimate = –.210). In other words, property felons were more likely to be rearrested (a finding reported by others, for example, Gottfredson and Gottfredson 1988; Beck and Shipley 1989; Visher 1995) after controlling for other factors, but that tendency was counteracted when property felons were transferred to adult court (once again, after controlling for other factors). The class of felony property offenses was the only one that interacted with the transfer/nontransfer status of the case.

Belonging to two other offense classes, Class 3 (drug felonies) and Class 4 (felonies not classified as personal, property, or drug offenses), increased the probability of rearrest (standard estimates = .106 and .102, respectively).[3] However, neither interacted with transfer to predict recidivism.

The imprecision in matching on race did not affect our conclusions. The direct effect of race on the probability of rearrest was not significant (Wald chi-square = 1.342, p = .247) after controlling for other variables.[4] Podkopacz and Feld (1995) recently reported the same result in Minnesota over a two-year follow-up period. Moreover, race did not interact with property felonies, those Class 2 offenses for which transfer ameliorated rather than aggravated recidivism.

Race did interact with Class 3 offenses (drug felonies) to influence recidivism in 1987 (Wald chi-square = 5.398, p = .020), but the effect was weak (standard estimate = –0.065). White drug felons who were transferred were slightly *less* likely than White nontransferred youths to be rearrested, but non-White drug felons who were transferred were *more* likely to be rearrested than were their non-White counterparts who were not transferred.

The remaining significant effects from the logistic analysis did not address the differential impact of transfer on recidivism, but they did allay concerns about whether our study group was atypical. As expected, males were more likely to be rearrested than were females (odds ratio = 1.65), 16-year-olds were more likely to reoffend than were 17-year-olds (odds ratio = 1.38), and those with three or more priors were more likely to reoffend than were those with fewer prior referrals (odds ratio = 0.48 for no priors and 0.66 for 1 or 2 priors).

Time to Rearrest

We also obtained estimated survival functions of the time to rearrest for the transfers and nontransfers based on the Kaplan-Meier estimates (Kalbfleisch and Prentice 1980). The positive O-E value indicated that transfers tended to be rearrested more quickly than nontransfers. The survival functions based on the Kaplan-Meier estimates were plotted (see Figure 1). The function for the transfers descended more rapidly, but the nontransfer curve eventually caught up and intersected with the transfer function about 1,500 days into release. Transfers who reoffended did so quickly, whereas their matches were slower to reoffend.

The time-to-rearrest analysis also was broken out by type of offense charged in 1987. The two plotted survival functions were not significantly different (p = .481) for those charged with felonies. The rate of decline (the speed of rearrest) was sharp for the transfers until it began to level off about 500 days after release (or after the period covered by the short-term analysis in Bishop et al. [1996]). The decline for nontransfers was more gradual, but the plot intersected with that for the nontransfers about 1,250 days after release.

Among the subjects charged with misdemeanors, the two survival functions were significantly different (p = .002). The transferred subjects tended to be rearrested more quickly than the nontransferred subjects throughout the long follow-up period. The plotted function for the nontransfers never intersected with that for the transfers.

The log-rank tests of the more refined offense classes once again showed differences for those who committed Class 2 offenses (property felonies) in 1987. The negative O-E statistic indicated that transfers were rearrested *less* quickly only for this offense class (chi-square = 11.73, p = .001). For all other classes, transfers were rearrested more quickly over the entire follow-up period.[5] The negative O-E value for property felons probably reflected the fact that a larger percentage of them as compared to the nontransfers were not rearrested through November 1994, the end of the follow-up period.

Timing and Number of Rearrests Among Reoffenders

For the subset of subjects who were rearrested, we computed the means and standard deviations for the time (in days) to rearrest and the number of rearrests. We compared transfers to nontransfers for all cases and for cases broken out by the severity of their 1987 offenses.

When only the reoffenders were examined, the average number of rearrests was higher for transfers than for nontransfers, and the average time to rearrest was shorter. This pattern held for all offenses aggregated, for the breakdown between misdemeanors and felonies, and across all seven offense classes. These results paralleled those found in the short-term analysis (Bishop et al. 1996).

Discussion

This study compared the long-term recidivism of Florida juveniles who were transferred to adult court in 1987 to a matched sample of nontransferred delinquents. Consistent with results reported earlier for a one-year follow-up period (Bishop et al. 1996), transferred youths reoffended more quickly than did their nontransferred counterparts. However, by examining rearrest data through November 1994, the present analysis showed that the nontransfers eventually caught up with the transfers in terms of the prevalence of rearrest. Further analysis indicated that this was due to the impact of transfer on cases for one type of offense: property felonies. Transfer seemed to reduce recidivism for property felons; more transferred property felons avoided rearrest on release than was true for their nontransferred counterparts. Once the effect of offense type was controlled, the logistic regression analysis indicated that transfer led to more recidivism. Moreover, the transferred youths who subsequently reoffended were rearrested more times and more quickly than were the nontransferred youths who reoffended regardless of the offenses for which they were prosecuted in 1987. Although property felons who were transferred may have been less likely to reoffend, when they did reoffend they reoffended more often and more quickly.

The general conclusion drawn in the earlier short-term recidivism study was substantially confirmed over the long run: Transfer was more likely to aggravate recidivism than to stem it.

Several theoretical implications of this general conclusion were discussed previously (see Bishop et al. 1996) but bear repeating.

Although we would be the first to recommend replication of our research with better matches and controls and in other jurisdictions, . . . there may be no way to "explain away" the results. Transfer to criminal court may indeed increase the likelihood of recidivism. . . . Certainly, the original "Child Savers" would not be surprised by our results. Proponents of the labeling and social reaction perspectives have warned about the negative consequences of criminal sanctions for children. . . . Braithwaite's (1989) theory of reintegrative shaming cautions about the adverse impact of sanctions that reject and exclude, and the implications these have for future offending. . . . Lanza-Kaduce and Radosevich (1987), Tyler (1990), and Sherman (1993), in their discussions of procedural injustice and rule violations, suggest another possible interpretation for our findings. . . . An important question is whether transferred youths attribute procedural and substantive unfairness to criminal justice processing. If so, their higher rates of reoffending may be best understood in terms of anger and defiance (pp. 184–85).

The theoretical complication that was added by our long-term analyses concerns property felons. Why did transfer reduce the probability of rearrest only for them? Why did transfer not also reduce the number of times they reoffended? We know of no theory that would predict offense-specific effects for transfer or that would specify why only some of the impact was salutary. In fact, the label "property felon" is a loose one that provides few distinctions to help make theoretical sense of our findings.

Prior research does not shed light on the issue either. In general, juveniles are even less likely to specialize in a class of crimes than are adults, and the type of prior offense in the juvenile arrest record is not very helpful in predicting the next arrest charge (for a recent review, see Visher 1995). We note that Fagan (1995) found that transfer affected burglars differently than it did robbers (although he did not find it to have the salutary effect for burglars that we found for property felons). Our findings of a higher prevalence of recidivism for transfers except for those transferred for property offenses, of a quicker time to rearrest for transfers generally, and of a higher frequency of rearrest among those transfers who reoffended suggest avenues for future research. Formal interventions may have differential impacts on the patterns of offending during a criminal career, and these may vary by the type of offender and/or the type of intervention. Future research needs to examine whether and how the transfer decision alters escalation or specialization of offenses over criminal careers. Because of the debate over the invariance or mutability of the relationship between age and crime (cf. Blumstein, Cohen, and Farrington 1988; Gottfredson and Hirschi 1988), the impact of the timing of the intervention also is important to assess. For example, Smith and Gartin (1989) reported that the timing of juvenile arrests affects the likelihood of desistance. Perhaps the timing of transfer either alters the criminal career directly or interacts with offender or sanction differences to change patterns of offending.

While we try to reach a more complete understanding of how transfer affects offenders, the message to policy makers is clear: The transfer of juveniles to adult jurisdiction may be no panacea. The baffling long-term effects of transfer on property felons notwithstanding, our research suggests that efforts to expand transfer often will be counterproductive.

⊠ Notes

1. Matches were made for 92% of the cases. Matched pairs were lost for several reasons. No timely date of closure had been recorded for the transfer case or its match in 59 pairs. The records showed that in 87 of the pairs, either the nontransferred subject served

prison time before rearrest or the transferred subject had served two prison terms before rearrest; this indicated some problem in record keeping. Insufficient information was recorded about the 1987 offense for one of the subjects in 2 pairs. The length of the prison term for 24 transfers who were in prison as of December 31, 1988 could not be retrieved because of a break in the prison records. In addition, 15 pairs were eliminated when the transferred individual was cross-checked against identifiers that indicated he had been matched previously.

2. During much of this time, provisions of Florida law required fingerprinting for all juveniles who were taken into custody on probable cause that a law violation (including citations, misdemeanors, or felonies) had taken place.

3. The only prior offense code that predicted rearrest was drug felony. If a drug felony was the most serious prior offense, then rearrest was less likely (standard estimate = −.069).

4. The need for statistical controls became apparent in the course of exploring whether the mismatches on race created any problems. When the bivariate relationship between transfer status and recidivism was examined for only same-race pairs, it appeared that non-Whites in both transfer and nontransfer conditions were much more likely to reoffend than were Whites. Further elaborations suggested important differences between White pairs and non-White pairs. For example, among the pairs in the largest single offense category, those who in 1987 had committed Class 2 offenses (property felonies), more than 70% of the matched non-White pairs had three or more prior offenses, whereas more than 50% of the White pairs had fewer than three prior offenses. What appeared to be a race effect was driven by prior record. The multivariate logistic regression technique had the advantage of controlling for many predictors of recidivism simultaneously.

5. Because nearly 60% of the subjects in both the transfer and nontransfer groups were not rearrested, the survival functions were truncated for many pairs. To make sure that this truncation or censoring did not affect our conclusions, we reran the time-to-rearrest analyses on only those pairs in which both the transfer case and its match were rearrested before November 15,

1994. The log-rank tests for the analyses on this subset showed that transfers were arrested significantly more quickly than nontransfers overall for felonies, for misdemeanors, and for five of the seven offense classes. For two classes of misdemeanors (Classes 6 and 7), the differences between transfers and nontransfers in time to rearrest were not significant.

References

Agresti, Alan. 1990. *Categorical Data Analysis.* New York: John Wiley.

Beck, Allen and Bernard Shipley. 1989. *Recidivism of Prisoners Released in 1983.* Washington, DC: Bureau of Justice Statistics.

Bishop, Donna M., Charles E. Frazier, Lonn Lanza-Kaduce, and Lawrence Winner. 1996. "The Transfer of Juveniles to Criminal Court: Does It Make a Difference?" *Crime & Delinquency* 42:171–91.

Blumstein, Alfred, Jacqueline Cohen, and David P. Farrington. 1988. "Criminal Career Research: Its Value for Criminology." *Criminology* 26:1–35.

Braithwaite, John. 1989. *Crime, Shame and Reintegration,* Cambridge, UK: Cambridge University Press.

Fagan, Jeffrey. 1995. "Separating the Men From the Boys: The Comparative Advantage of Juvenile Versus Criminal Court Sanctions on Recidivism Among Adolescent Felony Offenders." Pp. 238–60 in *A Sourcebook: Serious, Violent, and Chronic Juvenile Offenders,* edited by J. C. Howell, B. Krisberg, J. D. Hawkins, and J. J. Wilson. Thousand Oaks, CA: Sage.

Feld, Barry C. 1987. "Juvenile Court Meets the Principle of Offense: Legislative Changes in Juvenile Waiver Statutes." *Journal of Criminal Law and Criminology* 78:471–533.

——. 1988. "Juvenile Court Meets the Principle of Offense: Punishment, Treatment, and the Difference It Makes." *Boston Law Review* 68:821–915.

Gottfredson, Michael R. and Don M. Gottfredson. 1988. *Decision Making in Criminal Justice: Toward the Rational Exercise of Discretion.* 2nd ed. New York: Plenum.

Gottfredson, Michael and Travis Hirschi. 1988. "Science, Public Policy, and the Career Paradigm." *Criminology* 26:37–55.

Kalbfleisch, John D. and Ross L. Prentice. 1980. *The Statistical Analysis of Failure Time Data.* New York: John Wiley.

Lanza-Kaduce, Lonn and Marcia J. Radosevich. 1987. "Negative Reactions to Processing and Substance Use Among Young Incarcerated Males." *Deviant Behavior* 8:187–48.

Podkopacz, Marcy R. and Barry C. Feld. 1995. "Judicial Waiver Policy and Practice: Persistence, Seriousness and Race." *Law & Inequality: A Journal of Theory and Practice* 14:73–178.

SAS Institute Inc. 1990. *SAS/STAT User's Guide, Version 6.* Vol. 2, 4th ed. Cary, NC: SAS Institute Inc.

——. 1992. "SAS Technical Report P-229." In *SAS/STAT Software Changes and Enhancements, Release 6.07.* Cary, NC: SAS Institute Inc.

Sherman, Lawrence W. 1993. "Defiance, Deterrence, and Irrelevance: A Theory of the Criminal Sanction." *Journal of Research in Crime and Delinquency* 30:445–73.

Smith, Douglas A. and Patrick A. Gartin. 1989. "Specifying Specific Deterrence: The Influence of Arrest on Future Criminal Activity." *American Sociological Review* 54:94–106.

Snyder, Howard N. and Melissa Sickmund. 1995. *Juvenile Offenders and Victims: A National Report.* Washington, DC: Office of Juvenile Justice and Delinquency Prevention.

Szymanski, Linda. 1991. *Juvenile Code Purpose Clauses.* Pittsburgh, PA: National Center for Juvenile Justice.

Torbet, Patricia, Richard Gable, Hunter Hurst IV, Imogene Montgomery, Linda Szymanski, and Douglas Thomas. 1996. *State Responses to Serious and Violent Juvenile Crime.* Washington, DC: Office of Juvenile Justice and Delinquency Prevention.

Tyler, Tom R. 1990. *Why People Obey the Law.* New Haven, CT: Yale University Press.

Visher, Christy A. 1995. "Career Offenders and Crime Control." Pp. 514–33 in *Criminology,* edited by J. F. Sheley. Belmont, CA: Wadsworth.

DISCUSSION QUESTIONS

1. Were there significant differences in the rearrest rates of the transferred youth compared with the nontransferred youth? Explain.

2. What were some "offense-specific" differences between the two groups?

3. Were there any differences between the two groups in length of time before rearrest? Any differences for number of rearrests?

4. What are the authors' overall conclusions?

5. What theories do the findings seem to support?

6. What do the findings suggest for juvenile justice policy makers?

READING

Waiver laws are among the most prominent of the numerous changes in juvenile justice in recent years. Waiver laws provide more options to transfer young offenders more easily to adult courts. The more frequent use of waiver laws has led some to question the need for a separate juvenile justice system. There has been relatively little systematic empirical research assessing the effectiveness of these laws, however. The author of this article attempts to develop a foundation for such an assessment. The author first discusses the context in which waiver laws became prominent among states; he describes different types of waiver and presents national statistics on the numbers of youth transferred to adult court. He then examines the intended and unintended impacts of waiver that have been identified by researchers and discusses critical research gaps that must be addressed if we are to develop a balanced and empirically informed assessment of the effectiveness of waiver.

_____ *A Critique of Waiver Research* _____

Critical Next Steps in Assessing the Impacts of Laws for Transferring Juveniles to the Criminal Justice System

Daniel P. Mears

 ## Introduction

The focus and administration of juvenile justice changed dramatically during the past decade.

Today, punishment and due process constitute central features of juvenile processing. Waiver of youth to the jurisdiction of adult court, sometimes referred to as the process of transferring or

SOURCE: *Youth Violence and Juvenile Justice, (1)2,* 156–172, April 2003. DOI: 10.1177/1541204002250876. © 2003 Sage Publications, Inc.

certifying cases to the criminal justice system, has emerged as a powerful symbol of the transformation of juvenile justice (Howell, 1996; Singer, 1996a).

The rapid proliferation of new laws has led to a dramatic increase in the study of waiver. This focus is understandable: Waiver provides an easily identifiable symbol for debates about the merits of maintaining two distinct juvenile and adult justice systems (Feld, 1999). Why have a separate juvenile justice system, for example, if we are going to send youth to adult courts?

Despite the wealth of research, the fact remains that we know relatively little about the true effects of waiver. Attention to this issue is important because a greater understanding about how exactly waiver laws are used and to what effect can teach us important lessons about juvenile justice. As Fagan and Zimring (2000) emphasized, by examining waiver we can explore the "content and coherence of a theory of juvenile justice" (p. 3). Just as important, we can learn whether this popular justice policy merits further support or whether it is time to invest in other, more effective responses to juvenile crime.

Taking these observations as a point of departure, this article critiques existing research with an eye toward identifying important issues that must be addressed to advance knowledge and practice. I begin by discussing the context in which waiver laws gained prominence and describe different types of waiver and national statistics on the numbers of youth transferred to adult court. I then summarize the results of waiver research and related studies relevant to assessing the likely effects of this policy. The main point will be to identify the range of effects relevant to providing a balanced assessment. Having established a foundation on which to place waiver laws and past research into context, I identify critical research gaps that must be addressed if we are to advance our knowledge of the effects and effectiveness of waiver. To this end, I conclude with suggestions for a research agenda to help achieve this goal.

⊠ Background

Concern About Rising Juvenile Crime

"Get-tough" approaches in juvenile justice emerged during the 1990s as a response to escalating violent juvenile crime, especially homicide (Torbet et al., 1996). Between 1984 and 1993, for example, the juvenile arrest rate for murder increased from 5 to 14 arrests per 100,000 juveniles (Butts & Travis, 2002). At the same time, reports about the rise of juvenile "super predators" and a coming demographic "time bomb" intimated that even greater levels of violence could be anticipated (Dilulio, 1995; Fox, 1996). No one at the time predicted that juvenile violent crime rates would drop almost as fast as they had risen (Butts & Travis, 2002; Snyder, 2001).

The passage of waiver laws, enacted by almost every state, represented the most striking of the get-tough reforms. Other reforms included sentencing guidelines and graduated sanctions models; greater information sharing within and among juvenile justice systems, law enforcement, schools, and child and social service agencies; and reduced confidentiality of court records (Torbet et al., 1996). To a greater extent than these, however, waiver symbolized the no-nonsense approach that policy makers took to address juvenile crime. Their goal was to promote greater accountability and punishment in juvenile justice (General Accounting Office, 1995). Indeed, in many states, punishment was either introduced into or made a higher priority in descriptions of the mission of the juvenile justice system (Feld, 1995; Mears, 1998a).

Types of Waiver

To expand the options for transferring youth to the adult system, legislatures created a diverse and sometimes bewildering array of waiver statutes (Griffin, Torbet, & Szymanski, 1998; Snyder & Sickmund, 1999). Broadly, these statutes fall into three categories: judicial waiver, prosecutorial discretion, and statutory exclusion.

Juvenile court judges historically have been allowed to waive—either at their own discretion or at the request of prosecutors—certain cases to the adult system. However, the opportunities for doing so have been greatly expanded by allowing judicial waiver to be applied to younger juveniles charged with less serious offenses. Three types of judicial waiver can be distinguished. The first, discretionary judicial waiver, gives judges the authority to determine whether a given case should be transferred to the adult justice system. By contrast, mandatory judicial waiver requires the transfer of certain cases assuming certain conditions are met. Presumptive judicial waiver anticipates that cases will be judicially waived unless a compelling argument can be presented why they should not.

Prosecutorial discretion describes approaches, such as direct file, that give prosecutors the authority to determine whether a youth will be tried in juvenile or adult court. Under direct file provisions, prosecutors can choose the jurisdiction they believe will be most responsive to their handling of a particular case.

Statutory exclusion provisions require that entire categories of offenses be tried in adult court, thus removing the waiver decision from judges and prosecutors. However, as some researchers have argued, prosecutors determine what charges are officially filed and thus determine whether a case in fact is excludable (Sanborn, 1994). As Feld (2000) wrote:

> Because offense categories are necessarily crude and imprecise indicators of the "real" seriousness of any particular offense, prosecutors inevitably exercise enormous sentencing-discretion when they decide whether to change a youth with an excluded offense rather than a lesser included offense, or to select the forum in a direct-file jurisdiction. (pp. 117–118)

Many states have also enacted reverse waiver and "once an adult, always an adult" provisions. Under reverse waiver, an offense begins in adult court, but specific mechanisms allow the case to be transferred back to the juvenile justice system. Once an adult, always an adult provisions apply to juveniles already tried or convicted as adults and involve the permanent termination of juvenile court jurisdiction.

A range of factors can determine when and how each of these waiver provisions is implemented, including the type of offense, a youth's prior record, and minimum age criteria. In general, most states allow for at least one or more of these different waiver options. As of 1997, for example, 46 states had discretionary judicial waiver, 14 had mandatory judicial waiver, 15 had presumptive judicial waiver, 15 allowed for prosecutorial direct file, 28 had statutory exclusion, 23 had reverse waiver, and 31 had once an adult, always an adult provisions (Griffin et al., 1998).

The Prevalence of Waiver

On the face of it, concern about waiver may seem to be misplaced: Annually, only about 1% of all formally processed delinquency cases are judicially waived (Snyder & Sickmund, 1999). In 1999, the most recent year for which national data are available, juvenile courts waived fewer than half of 1% (7,528) of the close to 1.7 million delinquency cases referred to juvenile courts that year (Stahl, Finnegan, & Kang, 2002).

But these cases only represent judicial waivers. We have no national data that capture the numbers of youth waived to adult court through prosecutorial discretion and legislative exclusion (Sickmund, 2000). Some evidence suggests that at least as many if not more youth are sent into the criminal justice system via these nonjudicial mechanisms. For example, Florida waived close to 7,000 cases to adult courts in 1995; the bulk of these cases were transferred via prosecutorial direct file (Bilchik, 1999; Butts & Harrell, 1998). In that same year, 9,700 delinquency cases were judicially waived nationally (Sickmund et al., 1998). Florida's nonjudicial waivers alone thus almost matched the nation's total number of judicial waivers.

Some evidence suggests that increases in the use of nonjudicial waiver mechanisms can be offset by declines in the use of judicial waiver (Snyder, Sickmund, & Poe-Yamagata, 2000). Yet the likely aggregate effect of the full set of different waiver options might reasonably be anticipated to double or more the total number of judicial waivers, if only because the many different options through which waiver now can be initiated. In 1999, that would have meant the transfer of approximately 15,000 youth to the criminal justice system.

Of course, not all transferred youth will be incarcerated. Data from the Bureau of Justice Statistics suggest that the number of juveniles age 17 and younger in state and federal prisons recently decreased. From 1990 to 1995, the number increased from 3,600 to 5,309 but then declined to 3,147 in 2001 (Beck, Karberg, & Harrison, 2002). These data do not, however, distinguish youth who were transferred to adult court from those who were incarcerated as adults—in some states, for example, youth who are age 17 are adults by statute.

Incarceration is, of course, but one possible outcome of waiver. Yet we also lack national statistics on the number of transferred juveniles who are placed on probation or intensive supervision or are diverted to alternative, nonincarcerative settings. We do not know how many youth begin their sentences in the juvenile justice system and under "blended sentencing" statutes complete them in the adult justice system (Torbet et al., 1996). Finally, we do not know how many youth are placed in juvenile residential facilities or probation as a result of prosecutors using the threat of waiver to plea bargain "down" to these lesser dispositions.

Criminologists sometimes refer to the "dark figure of crime" to refer to those offenses that official statistics fail to capture. Similarly, official statistics on the use of waiver fail to document all instances in which waiver or the threat of waiver is used. It is therefore appropriate to say that the "dark figure of waiver" not only exists but may be quite large.

Even were one to assume that self-adjusting mechanisms keep constant the small percentage of delinquency cases waived to adult court, it bears emphasizing that fewer than 10% of all delinquency cases in a given year result in residential placement, which can include training schools, camps, ranches, drug treatment or private placement facilities, or group homes (Sickmund, 2000). In 1999, for example, 163,708 of the 1,673,042 delinquency cases referred to juvenile courts led to placements in residential settings (Stahl et al., 2002). Thus, although 1% may seem relatively small, it represents a nontrivial number of cases compared with delinquency cases that result in residential placement. More important, this figure largely ignores the broader effect that waiver almost certainly has.

✂ The Effects of Waiver

In evaluating waiver policies, we want ideally to take account of both their intended and unintended effects. We otherwise risk giving undue weight to one outcome to the exclusion of others, or we fail to recognize that achievement of a particular intended goal may be offset by unintended effects. In a context where little guidance exists about which effects should be weighted the most, a systematic approach to identifying all potential effects, whether measured or not, becomes especially important (Mears, 2000). For policy makers, this information can yield insight into the long-term feasibility and effectiveness of waiver. For researchers, it can facilitate a more balanced approach to empirical evaluations of waiver policies.

In the following, I identify the intended and unintended effects of waiver as suggested by recent research and reviews of the literature. Much of this research documents different facts about the processing, conviction, sentencing, and recidivism rates associated with particular types of waiver and includes related analyses of the correlates associated with these different dimensions. A comprehensive listing of these disparate findings is neither possible nor relevant here (see, however, Butts & Mitchell, 2000; Fagan & Zimring, 2000; Feld, 1999; Howell, 1996; Myers, 2001). Rather, what is relevant from a policy perspective are the overarching patterns. These patterns include the many critical facts that we do not know or have only suggestive knowledge about but that nonetheless may be critical for improving juvenile crime and justice policy.

Intended Effects

Conventional wisdom states that policy makers created different mechanisms for waiving juvenile offenders to adult court because they felt that waiver would result in more certain and severe sanctions (Butts & Mitchell, 2000). However, waiver historically has been used to target two groups: (a) youth who are "beyond rehabilitation" and whose presence in the juvenile justice system might undermine the system's integrity and (b) youth who have committed offenses so terrible as to require the greater punishment available in the criminal justice system (Sanborn, 1994). From this perspective, waiver is effective if it removes certain undesirable youth from the juvenile justice system irrespective of whether it results in greater punishment. At the same time, many states appear to have expected significant deterrent effects of waiver laws. Evidence concerning each of these effects is summarized in the following sections.

The use of waiver for serious and violent offenders. In contrast to the stipulated goals in many statutes, waiver frequently is used for less serious property and drug offenders (Butts & Mitchell, 2000; Myers, 2001). However, Howell's (1996) review of judicial waiver studies found that "on average, 42 percent of waived juveniles were serious property offenders and 47 percent were violent offenders" (p. 21). These findings suggest that judicial waiver generally is reserved for serious offenses, including both property and violent crimes, and thus for youth who may be viewed as being beyond rehabilitation. Howell's review also

found that these percentages varied greatly across jurisdictions. In some, waiver cases consisted primarily of serious and violent offenders, whereas in others they consisted primarily of less serious offenders. Few studies have systematically examined nonjudicial waivers; among those that have, similar patterns and variation have been identified (e.g., Bishop, Frazier, & Henretta, 1989; Singer, 1996b).

Greater punishment. Despite the stated goal of many waiver policies to increase punishment, studies of waiver show that transfer to adult court can result in less tough punishments, including dismissals, than would have occurred in juvenile court (Butts & Mitchell, 2000; Myers, 2001). Howell's (1996) review documented, however, that "virtually every study has found that serious and violent juvenile offenders receive longer sentences in criminal court than in juvenile court" (p. 49). Explanations for the lesser punishment vary. Criminal courts may view youthful offenders as less culpable than adult offenders, whereas juvenile courts may view these same offenders as young adults. Regardless of the reason, existing research suggests that waiver may be effective in producing greater punishment than would occur in juvenile court but only for the most serious juvenile offenders and may yield less severe punishment for less serious offenders.

Preservation of the juvenile justice system and its capacity to rehabilitate youth. Whether waiver works effectively to preserve the juvenile justice system remains an open question (Sanborn, 1994). The recent debates about abolishing juvenile justice suggest some warrant to believe that waiver policies have been effective as no states to date have eliminated their juvenile justice systems. In the absence of these policies, it is possible that many state legislatures might have felt compelled to merge their juvenile and criminal justice systems, with emphasis given to the largely punishment and nonrehabilitative orientations of the latter (Hirschi & Gottfredson, 1993). Few studies have systematically examined this possibility or shown whether the removal of certain youth who are putatively beyond rehabilitation preserves the ability of the juvenile justice system to better provide treatment to youth under its jurisdiction (Sanborn, 1994).

Reduced recidivism (specific deterrence). Implicit in most waiver laws that emphasize punishment is the notion that waiver will deter sanctioned youth from future crime. On this score, existing research is decidedly mixed: Some studies identify lower recidivism rates, some higher, and some no difference (Butts & Mitchell, 2000; Howell, 1996; Myers, 2001). The idea that waiver can actually result in greater rates of recidivism constitutes a particular concern because such an outcome clearly suggests a problem with waiver. Few researchers have identified why recidivism may be higher, but some studies provide suggestive evidence. For example, Bishop and Frazier (2000) documented that youth processed in the adult system view the waiver experience as punitive, uncaring, and unfair, whereas youth processed in the juvenile justice system typically feel that various court actors care about and are fair in their treatment of them. These perceptions of unfairness might potentially contribute to increased recidivism (Sherman, 1993). It also is possible that experiences in adult prisons, including poorer adjustment and a greater risk of victimization than would occur in juvenile facilities, may affect subsequent criminal behavior (Maitland & Sluder, 1998; McShane & Williams, 1989).

Reduced delinquency (general deterrence). The few studies of the general deterrent effects of waiver suggest that at an ecological level (e.g., city or state) there is little if any effect (Butts & Mitchell, 2000; Howell, 1996). These studies examine the effects of waiver on juvenile crime rates before and after enactment of waiver legislation using other states or jurisdictions as a point of comparison (see, e.g., Jensen & Metsger, 1994; Singer & McDowall, 1988).

On logical grounds, it is difficult to imagine that waiver could reasonably be expected to result in general deterrence. How many youth in the general population are aware of what the juvenile and criminal justice systems do? We know that waiver policies are used in different ways in different counties, which presumably would dilute any potential general deterrent effect, at least at a state level. Moreover, any youthful offender experienced in the actual operations of these systems might well view waiver as a means by which to obtain lesser sanctions (Mears, 1998b). In turn, their contact with other youthful offenders might result in reduced, not greater, general deterrence. How? If these youth teach their peers that waiver actually provides an escape hatch through which lesser sanctions can be obtained, the peers may be more likely to engage in criminal behavior than they would have engaged in if waiver laws did not exist.

Unintended Effects

When a policy results in unintended effects, these can be important if they offset the achievement of intended effects. This issue is doubly relevant in the context of waiver. First, waiver has not been shown to achieve many of the goals for which it was designed, and in some cases the opposite has occurred (e.g., lesser punishment and greater recidivism). Second, it appears to have generated many negative unintended effects. Next, I focus on the latter, identifying unintended effects that have been documented or suggested by existing research and that are relevant to providing a more complete assessment of the full effects of waiver laws. Included in this discussion are several critical issues, such as the inconsistent meaning and use of waiver. These might be termed *implementation issues* (Mears, 1998a), but I refer to them here as effects because they directly affect the ability of waiver policies to achieve intended outcomes.

The inconsistent meaning and use of waiver. Research shows that the meaning and use of waiver can vary dramatically among jurisdictions (Brother, 1986; Feld, 1999; Howell, 1996; Singer,

1996a). This variation in turn most likely undermines the ability of waiver to achieve any particular effects (e.g., greater punishment). Sanborn (1994), for example, documented that in the three court settings he studied, waiver was viewed by court actors in quite different ways. In the rural and suburban court settings, probation officers played a more prominent role in the waiver process. There also was greater agreement among court actors about the appropriate use of waiver (e.g., belief that waiver was appropriate to remove youth who were beyond rehabilitation and "threatened to contaminate others' chances of rehabilitation"). By contrast, court actors in the urban setting viewed the use of waiver differently from one another, and there was much less trust among them, creating power struggles over how cases were handled.

The results of such differences, also documented for blended sentencing laws (e.g., Mears, 1998b) and the implementation of juvenile justice reforms in general (e.g., Bazemore, Dicker, & Nyhan, 1994), may likely account for the variation researchers have observed across jurisdictions in the composition and processing of waiver cases. Such variation may dilute the chances that the intended effects of waiver can be achieved. As important, it largely undermines the legitimacy of waiver by creating a form of "justice by geography" (Feld, 1991), where waiver to adult court depends almost entirely on where a youth commits an offense.

Plea bargaining to more serious outcomes ("unofficial" use of waiver). Plea bargaining constitutes the primary mechanism through which most cases in juvenile or adult court are handled (Champion, 1996; Dougherty, 1988; Sanborn, 1993). Yet few studies of waiver, especially of prosecutorial direct file and legislative exclusion, examine this issue that might be called the unofficial use of waiver. Those that do, typically focus on cases actually waived or "official" waivers (Fagan & Zimring, 2000; Howell, 1996). As studies of blended sentencing laws show (Mears, 2000), however, plea bargaining may result in

stipulations to juvenile court sanctions even if no waiver officially occurs or therefore is recorded. For example, the threat of waiver by prosecutors may be sufficient to motivate youth to accept a plea to a juvenile court sanction.

Given both the widespread practice of plea bargaining and the potential for waiver to result in tougher sanctions, it would be surprising if plea-bargained juvenile court sanctions were not the primary effect of waiver. Indeed, the fact that official waiver frequently is used for less serious property and drug offenders suggests that unofficial waiver is also used with these and similar types of offenders. The actual effect of waiver thus may extend far beyond the cases officially recorded in administrative databases. Whether the effects result in less or more severe punishments remains unknown.

Net widening. As with plea bargaining, few researchers have examined the extent to which net widening results from waiver laws. Because waiver typically is contemplated for the more serious, chronic, and violent offenders, the issue may seem moot—if not waived to adult court, then surely these youth would likely be sanctioned in the juvenile justice system. However, many waiver statutes specify general categories of offenses that are "necessarily crude and imprecise indicators of the 'real' seriousness of any particular offense" (Feld, 2000, p. 117). Zimring (1998) emphasized, for example, that "[assaults and robberies] account for 94 percent of all youth violence arrests" (p. 494). Many of these cases may be eligible for waiver even though their seriousness might not warrant more than a counsel-and-release sanction from juvenile court.

Applied such cases, net widening becomes a very real possibility. Mears and Field (2000), for example, described a policy in one large urban jurisdiction in which prosecutors automatically sought judicial waiver to adult court in all cases that were eligible. Such a policy creates considerable room for net widening, if only through plea bargains to lesser sanctions. Consequently, one of the primary effects of waiver may lie less with actual cases sent to adult court than with the sanctioning of cases that in the past might have resulted in dismissal.

Limited competency and unfair or harmful sanctions. Not all states require clinical evaluations concerning the legal criteria for seeking waiver to adult court. In those that do, evaluations serve to determine if a particular youth is a "danger to others" and to assess his or her "amenability to treatment" (Grisso, 2000, p. 325). In the latter instance, the standard involves assessing not only the youth's amenability but also whether his or her conduct can be "modified within the resources available to the juvenile court" (p. 326).

Given the centrality of these two dimensions to decisions to seek waiver or to file charges that would allow waiver to occur, it is remarkable that according to one recent review, "no studies have examined the nature and quality of waiver evaluations as they are performed in everyday practice" (Grisso, 2000, p. 331). We thus know little about who conducts waiver evaluations or how the evaluations are conducted. Moreover, until recently there were no clear standards for such evaluations. The lack of research in this area becomes more remarkable when we consider that a considerable body of literature has developed that documents the limited competency of many, although certainly not all, youthful offenders referred to the juvenile and criminal justice system (Bonnie & Grisso, 2000; Steinberg & Cauffman, 2000).

Limited competency need not vitiate the legitimacy of waiver. However, when waiver occurs in cases where youth have a limited ability to understand or appreciate the consequences of their decisions and the proceedings in which they are a part, unfair sanctions may result. These in turn may prove harmful to the youth, especially if an undetected mental disorder, which can affect competency, goes untreated by the criminal justice system.

Disparity in the use of waiver. Disparity can be defined in many ways (Pope & Feyerherm, 1995),

but a conventional view is that it occurs when similar cases are treated differently. Disparity is present when, for example, Black youth are waived more frequently to adult court than White youth who have committed similar offenses and have similar prior records. The problems with disparity may seem obvious but bear emphasizing. Disparity can indicate bias or discrimination, both of which are illegal. As important, when people come to view the justice system as unfairly targeting some groups more than others, it reduces the perceived legitimacy of the system.

Howell's (1996) review of waiver research documented that minority youth are "often disproportionately selected for transfer, conviction, and incarceration in adult prisons" (p. 51). In many studies, the effect of race/ethnicity drops out after factors such as offense severity are controlled for statistically. But recent assessments of this issue suggest that such snapshot approaches are methodologically limited in their ability to capture racial/ethnic differences in processing, including waiver (Feld, 1999; Podkopacz & Feld, 1995; Pope & Feyerherm, 1995). For example, there may be biases that are not readily apparent at any one stage of processing but that accumulate into larger differences at later stages. There also may be indirect effects of race/ethnicity as well as interactions between race/ethnicity and certain legal factors, such as prior record, that contribute to a disproportionate use of waiver among minorities (Bortner, Zatz, & Hawkins, 2000). Few site-specific studies systematically assess these different possibilities, but they nonetheless are critical to assessing the extent to which waiver policies disproportionately affect certain populations.

Lengthy pretrial detention, often in adult jail facilities. Waiver potentially entails a greater amount of processing than traditional juvenile court proceedings because of due process requirements and the likelihood of additional proceedings subsequent to the waiver decision. In addition, youth awaiting waiver proceedings may be held in pretrial detention facilities along with adults even though their case ultimately may not be transferred to the criminal justice system. As a result, they face a greater risk of victimization, especially if they are held in adult jails (Howell, 1996; Smith, 1998).

Both the extent to which waived youth remain in pretrial detention for longer periods of time than their counterparts in the juvenile justice system and the extent to which they are more frequently held in adult jails and victimized as a result of waiver remain largely unknown. For example, waived youth may be more likely to post bail, jurisdictions may rely on adult jail facilities even in the absence of waiver, and youth in juvenile facilities may also be victimized. Nonetheless, the potential for lengthier confinement and greater rates of victimization clearly exists and suggests the need for any balanced assessment of the effects of waiver to examine these dimensions.

Increased likelihood of victimization among youth incarcerated in adult prisons. Although policy makers contemplated that waiver laws would result in tougher punishment, few presumably anticipated that the punishment would include increased victimization. Nonetheless, studies show that youth in adult prisons are more likely to be victimized and to experience more difficult transitions to incarceration (Howell, 1996; Maitland & Sluder, 1998; McShane & Williams, 1989). The greater victimization itself is an undesirable outcome. At the same time, its potentially negative effect on prison control and successful transitions back into society represent additional concerns that have been largely unaddressed by waiver research.

Perceptions and experiences of unfair processing: Effects on longer-term outcomes. A small handful of studies have examined the perceptions and experiences of youth waived to adult court jurisdiction. They suggest that youth transferred to adult court have quite different views and experiences. Youth in adult prisons typically view the experience of criminal justice processing as

confusing, adversarial, and seemingly unconcerned about their best interests. By contrast, youth eligible for waiver but processed in the juvenile justice system typically view court processing as understandable, fair, and focused on their best interests (Bishop & Frazier, 2000; see also Forst, Fagan, & Vivona, 1989). This issue is critical because as noted earlier, if the process of sanctioning, including both the waiver process and adult processing, is perceived to be procedurally or substantively unfair, the likelihood increases that it will cause an increase in future offending and other negative outcomes, such as mental illness and unemployment (Sherman, 1993).

✂ Critical Knowledge Gaps: Next Steps in Creating Policy-Relevant Information

Increased and Better Information of Intended and Unintended Effects

As the previous discussion reveals, there are many dimensions of waiver that require much greater assessment if we are to determine the full effects of this crime and justice policy. To summarize, we need greater understanding and assessment of intended effects, including:

- targeting of serious and violent offenders,
- greater punishment,
- preservation of the juvenile justice system and its capacity to rehabilitate youth,
- reduced recidivism (specific deterrence),
- reduced delinquency (general deterrence).

We also need more in-depth, systematic accounts of the unintended effects of waiver, including but not restricted to:

- the inconsistent meaning and use of waiver across jurisdictions,
- plea bargaining to juvenile sanctions through the unofficial use of waiver,
- net widening through plea bargaining and sanctioning of lesser offenders,

- limited competency of juvenile defendants and thus unfair or harmful sanctions,
- disparity in the use of waiver,
- lengthy pretrial detention and victimization in adult jail facilities,
- increased likelihood of victimization among youth incarcerated in adult prisons,
- perceptions and experiences of unfair processing and negative effects on recidivism.

New research studies and evaluations are unlikely to yield additional knowledge over and above the current body of largely descriptive studies unless they are more closely coupled with information about the full range of possible effects. Without this information, they also are unlikely to produce knowledge about how to improve the design and implementation of waiver to achieve intended effects and minimize unintended ones. In addition, there are several other issues, discussed next, that both policy makers and researchers must address if they are to help waiver laws to become consistent and effective.

A Coherent Rationale for Waiver

Judicial waiver was until recently the primary mechanism through which certain young offenders could be processed in the criminal justice system (Dawson, 2000). Politically, waiver served as a "safety valve for the juvenile courts, a way to provide for punitive treatment of adolescents but still preserve the programs and policies of the juvenile court" (Fagan & Zimring, 2000, p. 2).

The emergence of different waiver options has created, however, a great deal of confusion about what exactly waiver is supposed to do and how it is supposed to do it. One recent review of research identified, for example, few instances of "a coherent legal rationale underlying waiver processes in any particular court" (Harris, Welsh, & Butler, 2000, p. 405). A review of court appeals of juvenile waivers reinforces this view (Clausel & Bonnie, 2000). Not only are waiver statutes highly variable across states, but the use of waiver and the reasons for employing it are equally variable

(Feld, 1999; Hamparian et al., 1982; Sanborn, 1994). In practice, for example, waiver appears to be differentially employed across racial/ethnic groups, males and females, and serious and less serious offenses, depending on the jurisdiction (Bortner et al., 2000; Harris et al., 2000).

Critical questions about the rationale for waiver remain largely unanswered (Sanborn, 1994). Is waiver needed because it helps remove youth who are beyond rehabilitation to avoid unnecessarily drawing resources away from youth who would benefit from available rehabilitative programming? If this is the justification, is it based on empirical information about the extent to which specific youth are beyond rehabilitation or the resources available in the juvenile justice system? What foundation is there for consistently identifying whether a youth is amenable to treatment (Grisso, 2000)? If greater punishment is the underlying rationale, can waiver reasonably be expected to achieve this outcome? If not, why not employ blended sentencing approaches (Dawson, 2000)? Is waiver needed primarily because even if rehabilitation or greater punishment is available in the juvenile justice system the retention of certain youthful offenders there may undermine its political viability?

Answers to each question suggest quite different standards for waiver (e.g., the availability of punishment and resources in the juvenile justice system, an offender's amenability to treatment, and the political effect of retaining certain youth in the juvenile justice system). These standards in turn suggest radically different criteria for assessing the effectiveness of waiver. Did a particular waiver law, for example, result in greater punishment or general deterrence, or did it help preserve the juvenile justice system?

Policy makers and practitioners need to develop a clearly articulated, logical, and theoretically grounded rationale for waiver as well as a process for ensuring that this rationale is consistently expressed in practice. Otherwise, we will continue to expend considerable legislative and courtroom activity on an effort that may be far more inefficient and ineffective than doing nothing or on an effort that with marginal tinkering could be considerably more efficient and effective than doing business as usual.

Systems-Level Responses to Waiver

Dawson (2000) recently observed that the abundance of diverse waiver options "makes it difficult to assess the relative importance of judicial waiver today as a mechanism for sorting criminal from juvenile cases" (p. 79). He might well have noted that these options make it difficult to assess any of the types of waiver, whether judicial or nonjudicial. The specific challenge raised by the many options lies in the fact that court sanctions occur within the context of a broader system, one that can be self-correcting, with changes in one part offset by changes in another. Moreover, the effects of waiver laws may be enhanced or inhibited by the near simultaneous enactment in many jurisdictions of blended sentencing laws and other juvenile justice reforms (Mears, 1998b).

The question thus arises: What is the true effect of waiver laws on overall processing? Not much, according to Snyder et al. (2000). They studied Pennsylvania's transition in 1996 from employing judicial waiver to relying on legislative exclusion of youth age 15 and older charged with certain offenses or previously adjudicated for an excluded offense. The researchers found that many cases were transferred back to juvenile court through a decertification process or that in many instances prosecutors decided not to prosecute. Under the new law, the numbers, types, and outcomes of juvenile cases retained in adult court greatly resembled those under the previous system of judicial waiver. The difference was that a large number of younger offenders were initially processed through the adult system and the process for achieving the same outcomes became considerably more complicated.

Similar patterns quite likely could be documented in almost all states that have enacted new waiver policies. Most in-depth studies of juvenile courts and systems document the integrated and interdependent nature of how cases are handled (e.g., Bortner, 1986). Yet, we know little about the precise ways in which juvenile justice systems have responded to waiver laws. Consider Florida, which witnessed a tremendous spike in waivers to adult court in the early 1990s and was a subject of considerable study. In recent years, the use of prosecutorial direct files there has dropped precipitously, declining from 6,643 to 2,617 between 1996 and 2001, a more than 60% drop in a 5-year period (Florida Department of Juvenile Justice, 2002). The lack of studies on systems-level responses to sentencing policies means that we have little foundation to understand or anticipate such changes.

The Utility of Waiver as a Symbol of Juvenile Justice Trends

One of the primary reasons that waiver has garnered considerable policy and research attention appears to be because it symbolizes debates about abolishing the juvenile court and more generally, trends in juvenile justice. But to what extent does the study of waiver teach us anything about these debates or trends?

Scholars such as Barry Feld (2000) argued convincingly that enactment of new and different waiver laws indicates a shift in juvenile justice from "individualized justice to just deserts, from offender to offense, from amenability to treatment to public safety, and from immature delinquent to responsible criminal" (pp. 128–129). The broader cultural and legal shift is one of no longer seeing youth as "innocent, immature, and dependent children" but instead viewing them as "responsible, autonomous, and mature offenders" (Feld, 2000, p. 129). Even a cursory review of many reforms in juvenile justice, such as offense-based sentencing guidelines and the reduced confidentiality of juvenile records, appears to support this view.

Yet, the passage of waiver laws can also symbolize an endorsement of the juvenile justice system rather than support for its abolishment. It can, for example, signify a belief in the need to retain the integrity of this system by ensuring that the small number of extremely serious, violent, and unrehabilitatable youth (if such can be determined) are removed. Critics argue that transfer of youth to adult court necessarily undermines the integrity of the juvenile justice system. Others counter that it does not. Sanborn (1994), for example, noted that such "challenges are unfair because they hold juvenile court accountable for the failures of criminal court and society" (p. 267). Each view can be supported anecdotally or on logical or theoretical grounds, but empirical studies documenting which view has more support remain few and far between.

At the same time, there have been many changes in juvenile justice that run counter to the get-tough trend suggested by an analysis of waiver laws (Butts & Mears, 2001; Mears, 2002). Two of the most prominent examples are the development of graduated sanctions models that explicitly argue for balancing punishment and rehabilitation and the emergence of specialized juvenile court models (e.g., drug, gun, mental health, and teen courts) (Butts & Harrell, 1998; Guarino-Ghezzi & Loughran, 1996). How exactly does waiver symbolize these trends? It might be argued that graduated sanctions models and specialized court models serve primarily to appear child friendly while in reality emphasizing punishment. But such determinations should be made empirically, not rhetorically (Zimring & Fagan, 2000).

In short, many recent reforms, such as waiver, reduced confidentiality of court records, and greater information sharing among court and noncourt systems, suggest a trend toward greater punitiveness. But whether that actually has resulted remains largely unknown, and there are many other reforms, such as those cited earlier, that suggest different, more child-focused trends.

⬛ Conclusion

During the past decade, almost every state enacted new waiver policies enhancing the options for transferring juvenile offenders to the criminal justice system. These policies represent a dramatic departure from the previous practice of giving judges the sole discretion to determine whether a youth should be waived to the jurisdiction of the adult court. As a result of these changes, many researchers conducted studies of waiver, the bulk of which examined the composition of waiver cases in specific jurisdictions. Their results suggest several broad patterns that should concern policy makers: Waiver laws frequently are not used as designed, they have not on the whole achieved their intended effects, and they have been documented to result in many negative unintended effects.

Unfortunately, without systematic information about the full range of effects, researchers are not well positioned to provide general assessments about the effectiveness of waiver policies. The risk at present is that anyone can select a particular effect and use it to support his or her view. Clearly, the broad-based assessment points to a policy that appears to serve primarily as a political symbol of getting tough on juvenile crime. In some jurisdictions, intended effects, such as greater punishment and reduced recidivism, may have been achieved. Yet, even in such cases, policy makers might well be concerned about potentially offsetting unintended effects, such as net widening and disparity in how waiver is applied to certain groups, such as racial/ethnic minorities. They also might be concerned that the primary use of waiver may be to plea bargain cases to juvenile court sanctions. This unofficial use of waiver is not reflected in the vast majority of studies that examine cases transferred to adult court. At the same time, it is important to emphasize that waiver may be quite effective in certain jurisdictions, depending on what effects are most relevant in specific court and justice systems.

In addition to more systematically assessing the intended and unintended effects of waiver policies, two critical challenges confront those who wish to place waiver policies on a more solid foundation. The first consists of developing a more coherent rationale for waiver and then ensuring that this rationale is implemented consistently. The second consists of developing a greater understanding about how exactly systems-level responses and adjustments may affect the implementation and effects of waiver. For researchers, there is an additional challenge: If we are to provide a balanced and empirically informed assessment of juvenile justice trends, it is critical to establish rather than assume that waiver policies accurately reflect these trends. To date, many scholarly reviews treat this relationship as a given. Although it may be true, many recent initiatives in juvenile justice, such as specialized courts, suggest otherwise.

⬚ References

Bazemore, G. S., Dicker, T. J., & Nyhan, R. (1994). Juvenile justice reform and the difference it makes: An exploratory study of the impact of policy change on detention worker attitudes. *Crime and Delinquency, 40,* 37–53.

Beck, A. J., Karberg, J. C, & Harrison, P. M. (2002). *Prison and jail inmates at midyear 2001.* Washington, DC: Bureau of Justice Statistics.

Bilchik, S. (1999). *A study of juvenile transfers to criminal court in Florida.* Washington, DC: Office of Juvenile Justice and Delinquency Prevention.

Bishop, D. M., & Frazier, C. E. (2000). Consequences of transfer. In J. Fagan & F. E. Zimring (Eds.), *The changing boundaries of juvenile justice: Transfer of adolescents to the criminal court* (pp. 227–276). Chicago: University of Chicago Press.

Bishop, D. M., Frazier, C. E., & Henretta, J. C. (1989). Prosecutorial waiver: Case study of a questionable reform. *Crime and Delinquency, 35,* 179–209.

Bonnie, R. J., & Grisso, T. (2000). Adjudicative competence and youthful offenders. In T. Grisso & R. G. Schwartz (Eds.), *Youth on trial* (pp. 73–103). Chicago: University of Chicago Press.

Bortner, M. A. (1986). Traditional rhetoric, organizational realities: Remand of juveniles to adult court. *Crime and Delinquency, 32,* 53–73.

Bortner, M. A., Zatz, M. S., & Hawkins, D. F. (2000). Race and transfer: Empirical research and social context. In J. Fagan & F. E. Zimring (Eds.), *The changing borders of juvenile justice: Waiver of juveniles to the criminal court* (pp. 277–320). Chicago: University of Chicago Press.

Butts, J. A., & Harrell, A. (1998). *Delinquents or criminals: Policy options for young offenders.* Washington, DC: Urban Institute.

Butts, J. A., & Mears, D. P. (2001). Reviving juvenile justice in a get-tough era. *Youth and Society, 33,* 169–198.

Butts, J. A., & Mitchell, O. (2000). Brick by brick: Dismantling the border between juvenile and adult justice. In C. M. Friel (Ed.), *Criminal justice 2000, Vol. 2. Boundary changes in criminal justice organizations* (pp. 167–213). Washington, DC: National Institute of Justice.

Butts, J., & Travis, J. (2002). *The rise and fall of American youth violence: 1980 to 2000.* Washington, DC: Urban Institute.

Champion, D. J. (1996). *Probation, parole, and community corrections.* Englewood Cliffs, NJ: Prentice Hall.

Clausel, L. E. F., & Bonnie, R. J. (2000). Juvenile justice on appeal. In J. Fagan & F. E. Zimring (Eds.), *The changing borders of juvenile justice: Waiver of juveniles to the criminal court* (pp. 181–206). Chicago: University of Chicago Press.

Dawson, R. O. (2000). Judicial waiver in theory and practice. In J. Fagan & F. E. Zimring (Eds.), *The changing borders of juvenile justice: Waiver of juveniles to the criminal court* (pp. 45–81). Chicago: University of Chicago Press.

DiIulio, J. J., Jr. (1995, December 15). Moral poverty. *Chicago Tribune,* p. A31.

Dougherty, J. (1988). Negotiating justice in the juvenile justice system: A comparison of adult plea bargaining and juvenile intake. *Federal Probation, 52,* 72–80.

Fagan, J., & Zimring, F. E. (Eds.). (2000). *The changing borders of juvenile justice: Waiver of juveniles to the criminal court.* Chicago: University of Chicago Press.

Feld, B. C. (1991). Justice by geography: Urban, suburban, and rural variations in juvenile justice administration. *Journal of Criminal Law and Criminology, 82,* 156–210.

Feld, B. C. (1995). Violent youth and public policy: A case study of juvenile justice law reform. *Minnesota Law Review, 79,* 965–1128.

Feld, B. C. (1999). *Bad kids: Race and the transformation of the juvenile court.* New York: Oxford University Press.

Feld, B. C. (2000). Legislative exclusion of offenses. In J. Fagan & F. E. Zimring (Eds.), *The changing borders of juvenile justice: Waiver of juveniles to the criminal court* (pp. 83–144). Chicago: University of Chicago Press.

Florida Department of Juvenile Justice. (2002). *2000–01 profile of delinquency cases and youths referred.* Tallahassee: Florida Department of Juvenile Justice, Bureau of Data and Research.

Forst, M. L., Fagan, J., & Vivona, T. S. (1989). Youth in prisons and state training schools: Perceptions and consequences of the treatment-custody dichotomy. *Juvenile and Family Court Journal, 40,* 1–14.

Fox, J. A. (1996). *Trends in juvenile violence: A report to the United States Attorney General on current and future rates of juvenile offending.* Washington, DC: Bureau of Justice Statistics.

General Accounting Office. (1995). *Juvenile justice: Juveniles processed in criminal court and case dispositions.* Washington, DC: Author.

Griffin, P., Torbet, P., & Szymanski, L. (1998). *Trying juveniles as adults in criminal court: An analysis of state transfer provisions.* Washington, DC: Office of Juvenile Justice and Delinquency Prevention.

Grisso, T. (2000). Forensic clinical evaluations related to waiver of jurisdiction. In J. Fagan & F. E. Zimring (Eds.), *The changing borders of juvenile justice: Waiver of juveniles to the criminal court* (pp. 321–352). Chicago: University of Chicago Press.

Guarino-Ghezzi, S., & Loughran, E. J. (1996). *Balancing juvenile justice.* New Brunswick, NJ: Transaction Books.

Hamparian, D., Estep, L., Muntean, S., Priestino, R., Swisher, R., Wallace, P., et al. (1982). *Youth in adult courts: Between two worlds.* Washington, DC: Office of Juvenile Justice and Delinquency Prevention.

Harris, P. W., Welsh, W. N., & Butler, F. (2000). A century of juvenile justice. In G. LaFree (Ed.), *Criminal justice 2000, Vol. 1. The nature of crime: Continuity and change* (pp. 359–425). Washington, DC: National Institute of Justice.

Hirschi, T., & Gottfredson, M. R. (1993). Rethinking the juvenile justice system. *Crime and Delinquency, 39,* 262–271.

Howell, J. C. (1996). Juvenile transfers to the criminal justice system: State of the art. *Law and Policy, 18,* 17–60.

Jensen, E. L., & Metsger, L. K. (1994). A test of the deterrent effect of legislative waiver on violent juvenile crime. *Crime and Delinquency, 40,* 96–104.

Maitland, A. S., & Sluder, R. D. (1998). Victimization and youthful prison offenders: An empirical analysis. *Prison Journal, 78,* 55–73.

McShane, M. D., & Williams, F. P., III. (1989). The prison adjustment of juvenile offenders. *Crime and Delinquency, 35,* 254–269.

Mears, D. P. (1998a). Evaluation issues confronting juvenile justice sentencing reforms: A case study of Texas. *Crime and Delinquency, 44,* 443–463.

Mears, D. P. (1998b). The sociology of sentencing: Reconceptualizing decision-making processes and outcomes. *Law and Society Review, 32,* 667–724.

Mears, D. P. (2000). Assessing the effectiveness of juvenile justice reforms: A closer look at the criteria and the impacts on diverse stakeholders. *Law and Policy, 22,* 175–202.

Mears, D. P. (2002). Sentencing guidelines and the transformation of juvenile justice in the twenty-first century. *Journal of Contemporary Criminal Justice, 18,* 6–19.

Mears, D. P., & Field, S. H. (2000). Theorizing sanctioning in a criminalized juvenile court. *Criminology, 38,* 983–1020.

Myers, D. L. (2001). *Excluding violent youths from juvenile court: The effectiveness of legislative waiver.* New York: LFB Scholarly.

Podkopacz, M., & Feld, B. C. (1995). Judicial waiver policy and practice: Persistence, seriousness, and race. *Law and Inequality Journal, 14,* 73–178.

Pope, C. E., & Feyerherm, W. (1995). *Minorities and the juvenile justice system.* Washington, DC: Office of Juvenile Justice and Delinquency Prevention.

Sanborn, J. B., Jr. (1993). Philosophical, legal and systemic aspects of juvenile court plea bargaining. *Crime and Delinquency, 39,* 509–527.

Sanborn, J. B., Jr. (1994). Certification to criminal court: The important policy questions of how, when, and why. *Crime and Delinquency, 40,* 262–281.

Sherman, L. W, (1993). Defiance, deterrence, and irrelevance: A theory of the criminal sanction. *Journal of Research in Crime and Delinquency, 30,* 445–473.

Sickmund, M. (2000). *Offenders in juvenile court, 1997.* Washington, DC: Office of Juvenile Justice and Delinquency Prevention.

Sickmund, M., Stahl, A. L., Finnegan, T. A., Snyder, H. N., Poole, R. S., & Butts, J. A. (1998). *Juvenile court statistics, 1995.* Washington, DC: Office of Juvenile Justice and Delinquency Prevention.

Singer, S. I. (1996a). Merging and emerging systems of juvenile and criminal justice. *Law and Policy, 18,* 1–15.

Singer, S. I. (1996b). *Recriminalizing delinquency: Violent juvenile crime and juvenile justice.* New York: Cambridge University Press.

Singer, S. I., & McDowall, D. (1988). Criminalizing delinquency: The deterrent effects of the New York juvenile offender law. *Law and Society Review, 22,* 521–535.

Smith, B. (1998). Children in custody: 20-year trends in juvenile detention, correctional, and shelter facilities. *Crime and Delinquency, 44,* 526–543.

Snyder, H. N. (2001). *Law enforcement and juvenile crime.* Washington, DC: Office of Juvenile Justice and Delinquency Prevention.

Snyder, H. N., & Sickmund, M. (1999). *Juvenile offenders and victims: 1999 national report.* Washington, DC: Office of Juvenile Justice and Delinquency Prevention.

Snyder, H. N., Sickmund, M., & Poe-Yamagata, E. (2000). *Juvenile transfers to criminal court in the 1990s: Lessons learned from four studies.* Washington, DC: Office of Juvenile Justice and Delinquency Prevention.

Stahl, A. L., Finnegan, T. A., & Kang, W. (2002). *Easy access to juvenile court statistics: 1990–1999.* Retrieved January 23, 2003, from http://ojjdp .ncjrs.org/ojstatbb/ezajcs/

Steinberg, L., & Cauffman, E. (2000). A developmental perspective on jurisdictional boundary. In J. Fagan & F. E. Zimring (Eds.), *The changing borders of juvenile justice: Waiver of juveniles to the criminal court* (pp. 379–406). Chicago: University of Chicago Press.

Torbet, P., Gable, R., Hurst, H., IV, Montgomery, I., Szymanski, L., & Thomas, D. (1996). *State responses to serious and violent juvenile crime.* Washington, DC: Office of Juvenile Justice and Delinquency Prevention.

Zimring, F. E. (1998). Toward a jurisprudence of youth violence. In M. H. Tonry & M. H. Moore (Eds.), *Youth violence* (pp. 477–501). Chicago: University of Chicago Press.

Zimring, F. E., & Fagan, J. (2000). Transfer policy and law reform. In J. Fagan & F. E. Zimring (Eds.), *The changing borders of juvenile justice: Waiver of juveniles to the criminal court* (pp. 407–424). Chicago: University of Chicago Press.

DISCUSSION QUESTIONS

1. What are the get-tough approaches in juvenile justice that are a response to violent juvenile crime?

2. What are the three types of judicial waiver? What other provisions allow for juvenile waiver and transfer?

3. What are the intended and the unintended effects of waiver?

4. How do waiver laws change our image of youth and the purpose of juvenile justice?

5. What are two critical challenges for waiver policies? Based on research and experts' opinions, how do you believe we might meet those challenges?

READING

When describing and assessing criminal justice programs and policies we regularly ask judges, prosecutors, and juvenile justice and law enforcement officials for their perspectives and viewpoints. Juvenile offenders and correctional residents, however, are rarely asked for their perspectives and viewpoints. The authors of this article report the findings from an exploratory study in Florida that involved interviews with youthful offenders, half of whom had been transferred to the adult system and half of whom were retained in the juvenile system. The study focused on the youths' assessments of the impact of their correctional experience in relation to subsequent offending, and whether it had a beneficial or negative impact on them. For youths who had multiple correctional dispositions, the researchers compared the relative impact of low-end versus deep-end juvenile commitments, and juvenile versus adult sanctions. The youths believed deep-end juvenile placements were most beneficial. Those programs were viewed as having provided education or life skills. When youths viewed adult sanctions as being beneficial, the benefit was linked to the time and pain of prison confinement. Those youths who attributed positive impact to prison had "skipped" deep-end juvenile placements.

Adult Versus Juvenile Sanctions

Voices of Incarcerated Youths

Jodi Lane, Lonn Lanza-Kaduce, Charles E. Frazier, Donna M. Bishop

We do not hesitate to ask what researchers, judges, prosecutors, law enforcement officers, juvenile advocates, and others involved with young offenders think about the relative value of juvenile and criminal sanctions. However, we rarely ask what those who experience the respective sanctions think. We know little about how different sanctions are viewed by youthful offenders or how they think their behaviors will be affected. In perhaps no other area of human endeavor would we so consistently and so confidently ignore the opinions of those on the receiving end of social action.

We probably should not be surprised that offenders' perceptions are largely disregarded. Offenders are, after all, unlike customers of commercial enterprises or students in educational institutions. Customers or students are easily seen as being "worthy and deserving" of the right to evaluate the services they receive. Offenders, by contrast, are unworthy. They have violated societal norms, broken trusts, and threatened our communities. So ignoring them might be natural, and it might even be justified were it not also the case that our official reactions are intended to make a difference.

In this article we report findings from an exploratory study in Florida involving face-to-face interviews with youthful offenders. The interviews focused on their experiences in the juvenile and/or adult justice systems and their perceptions of the effects of the respective

SOURCE: *Crime & Delinquency, (48)*3, 431–455, July 2002. © 2002 Sage Publications, Inc.

systems. These offenders, not unlike the "clients" of business or education, hold important information about the "services" delivered.

Florida began transferring large numbers of juveniles to the adult criminal justice system more than 20 years ago when it enacted prosecutorial waiver provisions. The history of Florida's transfer reforms has been documented (White, Frazier, Lanza-Kaduce, & Bishop, 1999). It shows input from all the official stakeholders and various public interest groups but nothing from juvenile offenders. This pattern is not unique to Florida (see Mays & Gregware, 1996).

Torbet et al. (1996) documented the extent to which almost all U.S. jurisdictions have expanded transfer or changed other provisions to make it easier to bring juveniles into the adult system. The expansion of transfer authority continues as illustrated by California's recently passed Proposition 21, which provides for prosecutorial waiver (Sanchez & Booth, 2000). These "get-tough" policies, in Florida and elsewhere, are based on the assumed deterrent and/or incapacitation benefits of the adult system's harsher penalties (Bishop & Frazier, 2000; Fagan, 1995). To date, research has not supported these assumptions (Bishop, Frazier, Lanza-Kaduce, & Winner, 1996; Fagan, 1991, 1995, 1996; Frazier, Bishop, & Lanza-Kaduce, 1999; Jensen & Metsger, 1994; Singer, 1996; Singer & McDowell, 1988; Winner, Lanza-Kaduce, Bishop, & Frazier, 1997). The Bishop et al. (1996) and Winner et al. (1997) research was done on Florida youths and indicates that exposure to adult sanctions is more likely than juvenile sanctions to produce rather than reduce recidivism. The next logical question is "why?" One source of relevant information comes from the youthful offenders themselves.

Only a few studies have collected survey data from transferred youths about the effects of juvenile or criminal justice practices (Bishop, Frazier, Lanza-Kaduce, & White, 1998; Forst, Fagan, & Vivona, 1989; Singer, 1996). These focus primarily on the important experiences the youths have *in* the institutions themselves. For example, they examine issues relevant to institutional setting,

institutionalization, disciplinary problems (including violence), and victimization (Bishop et al., 1998; Forst et al., 1989; Singer, 1996). The research reported below shifts the focus to the perceptions among serious young offenders of the impacts of juvenile versus adult dispositions on their subsequent criminal attitudes and behavior.

⬚ Sample and Method

In 1998 and 1999, the researchers conducted interviews with 144 males between the ages of 17 and 20 incarcerated in the Florida juvenile and adult correctional systems for crimes they committed while under the age of 18. These youth were serious offenders. More than 90% of them had multiple prior arrests—almost half (49.3%) had five or more priors. Moreover, many of these youth were very young when they began offending—about 25% were younger than 12 when they started. At the time of the interviews, half were retained in the juvenile system and the other half were in the adult correctional system. The subjects were sampled from four deep-end juvenile institutions and eight adult institutions in north or central Florida. Using the institutions' population records of "youthful" offenders, the researchers chose youths at various stages of their sentence (i.e., recently institutionalized, mid-sentence, and near release). Six of the transferred youths were on adult probation at the time of the interview. This sampling strategy was designed to get information about attitudes and perspectives relevant to a broader range of institutional experiences.

A total of 72 of the interviewees reported experience with the juvenile justice system only. They were housed in one of four residential commitment facilities designated as deep-end juvenile programs (Levels 8 and 10). In Florida, programs are designated Level 2, 4, 6, 8, or 10. According to the state (see Juvenile Justice Advisory Board, 1998), Level 8 and 10 facilities target high- and medium-risk offenders. Level 8 incarceration lasts from 9 to 18 months while periods of incarceration in Level 10 facilities range from 18 through

36 months. Level 8 and 10 programs are the most restrictive and have more physical security, more supervision, and longer periods of stay than do other juvenile commitment levels. Level 6 programs are also residential programs but are less restrictive and generally involve stays of 4 to 18 months, depending upon the youth's progress in the program. Level 4 programs are the least restrictive residential programs and are designed to administer specialized services such as mental health and drug counseling within a short time—often about a month. Level 2 programs are non-residential and are designed to work with minimum to low-risk youth. Although all youth in this juvenile institution subsample were in deep-end programs at the time of interview, many reported experience with judicial warning, juvenile probation, or programs in Levels 2, 4, and 6.

A total of 71 youths had been transferred to the adult system and housed in one of the adult institutions ($n = 65$) or were on adult probation ($n = 6$) at the time of interview. Of these youths, 63 reported experience with both systems, and 8 reported exposure only to the adult system. Experience with adult sanctions ranged from probation to prison. The prisons where they were housed were typically Youthful Offender facilities, which primarily held young adults through age 24. All but four of the jail sentences were part of Duval County's special "blended" program ($n = 22$), which combines adult sanctions with treatment programs more often associated with the juvenile justice system.

Because the research was exploratory, we developed an unstructured interview schedule primarily consisting of open-ended questions. The interview began with personal background information (e.g., demographics, living arrangements, school experiences, and important people in the youth's life) but focused on the juvenile's offense history (e.g., prior arrests) and experiences at each stage of the juvenile and/or criminal justice system (with police, courts, and corrections). It next focused on the juvenile's thoughts and perceptions about how these experiences influenced his attitudes and behaviors. In particular, we directed our questions to how the juvenile experienced justice and what impact he thought those experiences had on him. For this article, we focus on the latter group of questions. For example, we asked the following: What is your outlook on life now? How do you see the future? Do these views of your future prospects in any way relate to your experiences in the justice system? Do you think these experiences have affected your beliefs about crime and conformity? Have these experiences in the justice system affected the way you behave? How? Do you believe your behavior is better or worse or unchanged as a result of your experiences in the juvenile and/or criminal justice systems? Which experiences with the justice system were most important? The interviews lasted between one and three hours, depending on the youth.

The youths' responses were used to derive two kinds of global assessments about the perceptions of the impacts of juvenile and adult sanctions. First, the researchers assessed each interviewee's perceptions of the overall impact of each disposition recalled in the interview. For each disposition, a rating was assigned so that each disposition was characterized as having (a) an overall beneficial impact, (b) a mixed (some beneficial, some negative) impact, (c) no impact, or (d) an overall negative impact. These ratings measure the youths' description of the attitudinal and behavioral effects of each experience in the system. We assigned these ratings by examining the youth's "entire" description of the effects of the sanction throughout the interview (in response to different questions), rather than looking solely at one particular quotation. For example, a youth might say in response to one question that a certain program had no effect on him at all or that it made him worse but then later say that it did make him try to straighten up for a little while after release because he did not want to return. This response would have been coded as having a "mixed" impact. If all his descriptions of a program indicated that it helped him with his attitudes or behaviors, it was coded as an overall beneficial experience, and if all descriptions indicated negative effects, it was coded as having an overall negative impact. "No impact" indicates the youth felt there were generally no positive or negative effects on his attitudes and behaviors. Some responses were too incomplete to rate. The global ratings allowed us to look for patterns across the interviewees. Percentages are reported to indicate how often the offenders shared similar perceptions about the respective dispositions. Excerpts from the interviews are used to illustrate the patterns. The excerpts convey, using the youths' own words, the "reality" of the impact as they saw it.

Second, for youths who recalled more than one kind of disposition, global comparisons were made between the relative impacts of various dispositions. Researchers determined from the interview whether deep-end juvenile placements (Levels 8 and 10) were regarded as generally more beneficial than less secure short-term front-end juvenile interventions (Levels 2 through 6) and whether adult sanctions were thought to be more beneficial than juvenile ones. Again, percentages are used to establish patterns across cases about how they compare "deep-end" with other juvenile sanctions and how they compare adult dispositions with juvenile ones. Excerpts are also presented that illustrate the comparisons that the interviewees were making.

For both the ratings and the comparisons, the focus was on the projected outcome and not on the process. The impact may have been seen by the youth as beneficial (as making them less likely to reoffend or less likely to want to reoffend) because the process was one of treatment and help or because it was one of deprivation and punishment. We operationalize "impact" here as the effect a sanction had or was expected to have on the interviewee's attitudes about and participation in future criminal behavior.

▧ Results

Ratings of Juvenile Sanctions

The ratings reflected the respondents' views about the probable impact of a disposition on subsequent offending (or attitudes directly linked to reoffending). A total of 113 youths provided 221 ratings about the impact of low-end juvenile sanctions (judicial warnings, probation, and placements in programs at Levels 2, 4, or 6). A total of 86 youths provided 101 ratings about their perceptions of the impacts of deep-end (Levels 8 and 10) juvenile sanctions.

Low-End Sanctions

With regard to low-end sanctions (judicial warning, juvenile probation, and placements in programs at Levels 2, 4, and 6), very few of the youths believed their experiences had positive overall effects on their attitudes or behaviors. Little impact on these serious offenders is not surprising. As several youth indicated, they were already "beyond" what these low-end programs could offer when they were placed there. Nevertheless, as "serious" delinquents, the interviewees' beliefs about the impacts of their experiences may give insights to policymakers who wonder "why" youths continue to get in more trouble and eventually find themselves in institutions.

Many of the 135 youths who reported on juvenile dispositions had experience with more than one juvenile sanction. Of the 221 ratings of low-end juvenile dispositions, only 44 (or 20%) were characterized as beneficial. Of those ratings that indicated the offenders perceived the low-end disposition experience to be beneficial, almost three fourths ($n = 33$) were ratings of Level 6 programs—the most intensive low-end interventions. Generally, youths who thought the low-end programs were not effective in changing their delinquent attitudes and behaviors perceived these interventions to lack the intensity needed to address their problems or to give them the skills to do better.

Those who at some point received the lightest of the low-end sanctions—judicial warnings, probation, community service, or Level 2 day programs such as anger management or outpatient drug counseling—often saw these sanctions as inconsequential and believed that these programs did not affect their attitudes or behavior. For example, some mentioned that while on probation or attending a nonresidential program, they did not see a probation officer or complete their ordered community service; yet no one "seemed to notice." As one White respondent with four prior arrests who was now in a Level 8 program for a person offense said about juvenile probation, "I don't remember it much." A Black interviewee with four priors who was in a Level 10 for property offenses said, "I didn't do it [the requirements]. I really don't know what I was supposed to do, so I forgot all about it. They never called me." Some felt they were supervised (e.g., once a month or once a week) but that it did not help them change or keep them from committing more crime. As one Latino offender who was in a Level 10 for a person offense and had been arrested twice before said, "They didn't help me." Others liked their probation officers or felt the program sessions were helpful at some level (e.g., in helping with school) but said they did not prevent them from continuing their delinquency. As one Black interviewee with three prior arrests said, "Some of it helped, but then I back fell from hanging out in the street." Others participated in programming, such as drug counseling, and liked it, but "got locked back up" soon anyway—so obviously it did little to prevent subsequent criminal behavior.[1]

Youths who had been in the least restrictive, low-risk, residential programs (Level 4) also generally believed the sanctions had little effect and did not help them enough. One White offender in a Level 10 facility for a property offense but who remembered nine arrests before this one said that he felt none of the programs gave him "any treatment at all" (even though they had put him in groups) and they therefore had no effect on him. He believed he needed a job or job skills—something he could use to succeed outside. Another interviewee, who was Latino and was in a Level 10 for a person offense after five previous arrests, said

that he escaped from a Level 4 program because he did not like the rules, was not ready to change, and believed at the time that the staff were just interested in punishing rather than helping him. As he said, "I had a chance to straighten up, but I blew it."

Even when youths thought the programs helped, they recognized that they had little impact on their subsequent behavior. A White interviewee who was in a Level 8 for a drug offense and remembered 29 prior arrests said,

> It was a good program. Staff was fair and there to help us. They talked to us. When we did something wrong they talked to us instead of giving us extra days. But it didn't have an effect on me. I was too young.

The respondent liked the program, but he was unable to do well after release. In sum, even youths who felt good about these programs did not see them as having changed their attitudes and behaviors significantly.

Level 6 residential programs, which are designed for moderate-risk youths and have the most intensive treatment and skills training of the low-end programs, got somewhat better ratings. Although many of the youths thought these programs also had no overall impact on their behavior, some felt they were changed by their experiences there—either because they gained some life skills or because they left there motivated to do better. For example, a young Black respondent who was in a Level 8 for a person offense and who said he had about eight arrests prior to the current offense said,

> They put you [in] a lot of groups, feedback stuff, then they let you play sports and stuff; it was a good program. . . . It made me change a lot, give some respect for people and myself . . . [the Level 6] program helped me most, they taught me a lot. They taught me most about anger control, bein' respectful of peers and myself.

Many of our respondents said that they left these programs feeling very hopeful but that they had been unable to keep themselves from crime once they returned to their communities—either because they had trouble getting a job, because crime "was there" and available to them, or because they had relationship difficulties (e.g., family, girlfriend) that led them to stop trying. One of the Black interviewees who was in for a drug offense and had over 20 priors put it this way:

I stayed out only a short while and I was slingin' again, then I got the job on the side and my own place. I stopped selling drugs for a while but I felt like I just wasn't getting anywhere. My mom needed help, and I started slingin' again.

Another offender, who was White, had about 19 prior arrests, and was in a Level 10 for a person offense, related more serious complications on the outside.

After [the Level 6 placement] I got my life together a little bit. I was doing good, living on my own with my girlfriend. . . . Then we started having a lot of arguments and it was not good for the baby, and I lost my job and then she kicked me out. I was stressed out . . . I was awful. I started doin' drugs and feeling like I was going to explode. I imagined doing a robbery to make some money. I put on a ski mask and broke into a girl's house.

Deep-End Juvenile Sanctions

The majority of the ratings about deep-end juvenile sanctions (Levels 8 and 10) were positive overall. A total of 86 youths provided 101 ratings of deep-end juvenile sanctions. Of these, 58% ($n = 59$) indicated that the deep-end placements had a beneficial impact on their attitudes and behaviors. Only two (2%) of these 86 youths, both of whom were in more than one deep-end program, reported mixed impacts of these

sanctions. Of these youths, 84% ($n = 76$) were in deep-end facilities at the time of interview and were discussing the effects of the current program, so caution should be used in interpreting their responses. Some of these youths may have been parroting the official line advanced and reinforced by staff; others may have been trying to "work the system" by telling us what they thought the system wanted them to say. Nevertheless the youths could articulate reasons. Many believed they were being helped even if they had some doubts about what would happen when they were released.

Youths recognized that these longer more intensive programs provided the life skills and counseling that could affect their attitudes and behaviors the most, even though many of them realized that making it on the outside continued (or would continue) to be a struggle for them. The youths believed they were most influenced by educational and job skills in these deep-end programs. Specifically, they liked opportunities to get their high school education or General Equivalency Degree (GED) and the programs' reentry components, such as attempts to help them get into school (high school, college, or career training) and get jobs (reentry programs). As one young Black respondent who was in a Level 10 program for a drug offense and who had multiple priors (about 19 arrests) said,

This program alright because you can get your education . . . and they have community college people come teach here. They will help you get into college. That's what I'm planning on doin'. . . . I got to the 9th grade on the outside, then I dropped out. I made real progress since I been here. I'm up to 11th.

Another Black male who was in a Level 8 program for a drug offense but said he had about nine prior arrests echoed this belief about being in Level 8:

All along, this program helped me. For one, they give you more time to think about things, they give you chance to get your GED. I am on re-entry, so they help you with jobs. . . . This is the best program I been to.

Others believed some type of counseling was the most helpful to them—whether it was about "deal[ing] with people," controlling anger or impulses, being disciplined, or facing and working through their problems and emotions. Not all of the "counseling" they received was formal or by trained counselors. Some of them learned a lot by listening to officers who talked to them about their lives and how to improve themselves (e.g., how to walk away from confrontation or how to stay in school when they got out). As a White youth who had only one prior and was in a Level 8 program observed,

This is a good place. . . . They do treatment work. They help us deal with our issues, like mine are substance abuse and criminal mentality and impulse control. They try to make us better so when we get out we can be better. . . . I feel like this place has really made a difference for me. It made me look at what is important in life, like my family. . . . I hope I don't do drugs again. Here I learned that my peer group is important, and when I get out, I want new friends, not the ones I used to hang out with who all did drugs.

Another Latino youth who committed a person offense, had two priors, and was in a Level 10 program said,

This program is good. It makes you think. It helps with anger if you have that. . . . They put me in a drug rehabilitation program here that is also for other issues. I benefited from learning to speak out, to communicate my feelings. That helped me communicate better with my mother. . . . The future will be a lot better. . . . Hopefully I won't do crime no more. . . . The juvenile justice system should have more programs like this, programs that try to help.

Not all the benefits were linked to programs in these deep-end placements. Some offenders reckoned the longer sentences gave them more time to think about the future. For example, one Black youth who was in a Level 8 for a property offense but thought he had been arrested at least 60 times said, "It just the time. You need enough time to think about it and fix it." A couple of youths also indicated that they were worried about possible consequences if they continued (e.g., death on the streets, tougher punishments). They seemed to recognize their situation on the outside had been out of control and that the deep-end placement gave them time away from the many problems they faced so that they could think and have a chance to get their lives reoriented.

Comparing Deep-End and Low-End Juvenile Sanctions

The ratings of the low-end and deep-end placements suggest that deep-end programs may be more effective for these serious youthful offenders because they can provide more intensive interventions—especially in regard to skills and counseling. For offenders who had both deep-end and low-end exposure, the two experiences can be compared. A total of 73 juveniles who had experience at both ends of the juvenile continuum made comparisons about the relative impact of low-end versus deep-end juvenile sanctions. Of these comparisons, 40% ($n = 29$) indicated that deep-end commitments were or would be more beneficial in affecting subsequent criminal behaviors (or attitudes directly related to criminal behavior). Another 24% ($n = 17$) thought both low-end and deep-end programs had good effects. So, a majority of these youths believed that juvenile programs were helpful at some level. The remaining 32% ($n = 23$) indicated that both types of placements either had mixed, no, or negative effects on their attitudes and behaviors. Only three interviewees (5%) thought the low-end programs had more impact on them than did the more restrictive programs. For the serious offenders in this sample, the pattern was clear. They believed the more intensive, longer programs had more beneficial impacts than did the less-intensive, shorter programs.

The comparisons confirmed what the earlier discussion of ratings suggested. The longer length of time and greater intensity of the skills training and treatment in the deep-end programs were why youths believed deep-end programs were more beneficial. In the following excerpt, one White youth who had committed a person offense and had multiple priors discussed the differential impacts of probation (community control) and the level 10 program he was in at the time of interview:

> The [community control] system was soft. I didn't go in no programs. In one way it was good for me 'cuz I got to go home. In another way, it wasn't good, because I was messin' my life up. . . . I didn't like the community control counselor. . . . I was trying to get over on the system. I needed somebody to stop me. I needed a program to teach me manners and stuff. . . . This place [Level 10] is good. They treat me right. They understand and talk to you when you're mad. They are helping to try to teach me to spell and read, and I am learnin'. Somebody needed to make me sit in my seat and do stuff. I didn't like it, but it was good for me. . . . I been here for 8 months, I've made lots of changes. They taught me respect, to say, "sir, yes sir"—if you have a problem to talk it out, not use violence. They need to make more Level 10s.

A Black respondent who had three priors and said he had been on probation (community control) and in two Level 6 programs without changing—even though he thought the staff were encouraging—believed the current Level 8 program was having a bigger impact:

> Now here, I'm learning. Been here 2 years, can't help but learn. I learned anger control and not to take things in my hands. There's

staff here who tell us how to do and enjoy life, not backslide. About 10 years from now, I'd like to have a business in Georgia. . . . I need to finish school first. Then, I'd like to work in building construction, doing shingles and drywall. . . . When I get out I got to go to school and get me a little job and keep off the streets. . . . Next time, it's to prison, and I don't wanna be there, no way.

So, for him, the deep-end program taught him anger control, helped him develop goals and hope for the future and gave him time to think about the possible consequences if he continued committing crime.

Many of those who perceived that the deep-end placements were relatively more beneficial maintained a realistic appreciation of what the outside world would be like. They recognized that they had had previous chances. Going back to the same family or neighborhood or facing the difficulty of getting jobs with a criminal record had kept them from succeeding in the past. They now worried about how these issues would affect their futures.

When Juvenile Sanctions Are Perceived to Be Unhelpful

Some youths who had experience with both types of juvenile sanctions (32% of the comparisons) believed that none of their experiences to date had given them the skills they needed to stop committing crime. When they thought a program did not help, it was often because the program was perceived as being too easy or too short. Some mentioned, for example, that it was easy to just "endure" the shorter programs, rather than put energy into improving themselves. Others felt the programs themselves were problematic—either the program was just about punishment, it was inconsistently applied, or the staff was inconsistent or unfair. For example, some mentioned that the staff were either "mean" or "just there for the paycheck." Still others, especially those who had been in many low-end programs and eventually found themselves in a deep-end one, said they just had not been ready to change at the time—they still wanted to maintain their criminal activity or their street reputation.

Ratings of Adult Sanctions

The ratings regarding adult sanctions were mixed. In our sample, 71 youths were transferred to adult court and had some experience with adult punishments; several had exposure to more than one adult sanction or facility. Only 34 of the 102 ratings of these adult dispositions (33%) were beneficial overall. This percentage was higher than the ratings given to low-end juvenile dispositions (20%), but lower than the ratings given for deep-end juvenile placements (58%).

The ratings, however, varied by type of adult disposition. For example, more ratings of the "blended" jail program in Duval County were beneficial (55%) versus prison (33%), probation (12%), or other jails (0%). The reasons given also varied. Often when adult sanctions were perceived as being beneficial, the benefit was NOT attributed to anything gained from the disposition. Rather, many youths indicated that they expected to remain "crime-free" because their experience in the adult system had been so horrible. Youths who believed the adult sanctions would keep them from committing crime primarily pointed to three reasons: pain and denigration, time, and fear of future consequences, especially tougher sentences. Paradoxically, most of those who said the adult experience was negative also mentioned pain, denigration, and/or anger, but they gave these as reasons why the adult dispositions had made matters worse. Others attributed a negative impact to adult sanctions because they learned more crime while there. The remainder of this section discusses ratings of each type of adult sanction and, as before, illustrates the youths' perceptions using their own words.

Probation

Few of the youths in the sample experienced adult probation; there were only 16 ratings of adult probation. Two (13%) of these ratings indicated a beneficial impact overall on attitudes and behaviors. The youths for these two ratings believed that their adult probation officers were strict enough to keep them under control or were helping them get jobs. Most of the ratings of the youths' experiences with adult probation were categorized as having no impact on them. Some youths had gotten in trouble again after being placed on adult probation. But for others, the circumstances of their lives made it difficult to succeed. As one Black youth who had at least two priors observed, "probation is all right . . . I'm having trouble getting a job now. People see on my application the charges, and they don't hire me. It's not fair." Our numbers are small, but on the whole, adult probation was not perceived by this sample of serious offenders to have a substantial impact.

Jail

A total of 26 ratings were derived from information the transferred youths provided about their experiences in jail (postconviction).[2] Of these ratings, 22 came from youths who were in a special "blended" program for youthful offenders in Duval County, which combines jail incarceration with treatment programs.

About half of the ratings in the Duval County program at the Jacksonville Jail (55%, $n = 12$) characterized the impact as helping the youths change so they would not get in trouble again when they were released. The remaining 10 ratings from the Duval program (and the 4 from youths who were in other jail programs) indicated that the jail experience was negative or had no impact.

The youths who saw the Jacksonville program as beneficial sometimes credited the programming but more often thought that the pain and fear of future consequences were having the most impact. The perception that the benefits stemmed from the mix of programming and deprivation in Jacksonville (but with deprivation being more critical) is illustrated in the following quotation from a Black youth who was locked up for a person offense but had no prior arrests:

Before I came in here I was lookin' for the easy way for everything, not working, not earning it. Now, I feel like I need to work for what I get. I didn't think of how people might feel if someone took something they earned. I didn't have any goals. Just whatever happens happens was my attitude. Now, I set goals for myself, to finish school, get education, and pursue my athletic abilities. Bein' in here caused me to realize that crime is not a way to live. You can't do anything locked up. Now, I think of how somebody would feel if they have their stuff taken. Big difference is I think of other people before I think of myself. Being locked up caused the thinking, but the program in here and the other people help you realize those things. Basically, taking away freedom starts the thinkin'.

Another Black youth with multiple priors who was in for a property offense indicated that the primary effect of jail was seeing what the future consequences for him could be, even though he, too, believed the programming was helpful:

Well, the purpose is they have groups here to help you out. I think it is really if you want to help yourself program. They give you the groups, you have to go, decide you want help. This place here, to me, this be my last step. I see guys here callin' 'em out going to prison 10 or 15 years—one guy, 40 years. There [in prison] you go to restroom in front of your roommate, you eat when they tell you to eat. . . . I say to these guys I say how long you got? They say 35 year. They had me in a cell with a guy who killed two people. It had an influence on me to see you can actually go to prison—[made me] not want to come back. I feel as though if you done went through this, I think you can do right without the programs. Because you know what you got to do to do right. I am not sayin' the programs don't help but I think you could do it yourself.

Not all youths in the Jacksonville Jail, however, believed that programming was even part of the impact. For example, one Black youth who committed a property offense but had four priors said he wanted to succeed on release because it was the "worst place" he had been in his life. He said "all you ever do is wake up, eat, go to school, sit, sit, sit, sit . . . they don't talk to you or nothin'." Others echoed his concerns.

Perceptions about the "blended" jail program were decidedly mixed. Only a little more than half the ratings indicated a beneficial impact. Among these, the reasons varied and often the programming features were not credited with much of the overall beneficial impact.[3]

Prison

Of the 71 youths, 44 (62%) with adult punishment experience talked about the effects of prison. Because some of them reported experiences in more than one facility, 60 different prison experiences received ratings. Most of these ratings were negative; only 20 (33%) were positive. When the ratings of prison experience were beneficial, imprisoned youths did not mention programming as the key. In fact, most said there was no programming available for them. Instead, they indicated that they did not want to commit more crime because they risked coming back to prison. For many, prison had given them the time to think about their futures and their lives, but for others prison was so full of pain that they did not want to face it again. When prison was seen as beneficial, most of the interviewees indicated the benefit was due to the time itself or the maturity that came with serving the time. One young White man was locked up for a person offense, had four prior arrests, and had been in prison twice. He was now on probation after having been released and talked about his second prison stint this way:

This time I didn't hang out with too many people, did my job, read books, did a lot of thinking and planning about goals I wanted to reach. I could see I was going down the wrong road again and [prison] gave me time to clear my head.

Another Black youth who had been arrested a couple of times before said that prison had made him think both because he had matured and because it was painful:

You have more time to think on how things should have been. It's filthier than the street, and everybody is crooked. It ain't no place for young people. . . . It's like evil on evil, like war, like battle between the races and the police—different races fighting each other, all races fighting the guards. . . . I think my life will be better than it was before. I am more mature. I know more than the other inmates who are 16. . . . And, when I get out . . . I will use it for self. Coming here when you're 15 or 16, it hurts, seriously. . . . The system is organized to screw people.

Still others focused primarily on the pain as the primary reason for a beneficial impact. Some believed the prison experience was so harsh and unsafe that it had forced them to become a "man" and made them realize that they had to change their behavior to prevent themselves from going to prison again. For example, a White youth who had one prior arrest but was locked up for a person offense said,

Now, I came to prison as a boy. I will leave as a man. I don't want to see this again. . . . Here, you picked on. Officers can beat you up when they want to. Somebody can put a shank. They plant it on your bunk. . . . Inmate can catch you asleep and hit you in the head with a "sock and a lock." . . . I will try to encourage anybody out there, this is not a place for you and my actions will have to prove it.

Still others felt prison would have an impact on them because they now knew they faced much tougher, longer sentences if they committed more crime on release. Often they learned a lot from fellow, older inmates. The following excerpt from a Black youth who had only one prior but was locked up for a person offense illustrates their experience:

This is like a graveyard. . . . I would recommend this to other people because the older inmates who have life will talk sense into you. They let you know this ain't no place for nobody. They want you to get out and be somebody. I feel now I can get out and do something with my life, be a truck driver or electrician. And, I can talk to the young brothers and let them know what I learned . . . here, where you see old people rooting, you see what's going to happen if you keep on . . .

They knew the laws were getting tougher. As one young Black man who had a drug offense but almost 30 priors said, "Old Jeb Bush, he ain't foolin' around . . . that 10–20—Life . . . I value my freedom more than all that."

But, the majority of ratings of prison (61%) indicated that it had made them worse or would have no positive impact on their attitudes and behaviors.[4] They felt staff took their hope from them and were generally too mean or apathetic, that the environment was always unsafe, and that they learned too much about how to be better criminals. The following quotation from a young Asian man who had committed a person offense sums up the majority of ratings about the effects of adult prison:

Prison makes people monsters. The staff is worse than we are. . . . My experiences in here—to me—have made me worse, but to their eyes it made me better . . . I don't have [a future]. I just live day by day. There is no future. . . . Every time I try to do right, they kick me to the curb, so I just say fuck it, I'm not going to try. You can only tolerate so much.

In essence, these respondents thought prison was much too harsh for teenagers. They believed their childhood and hope for a good future had been taken from them in prison. Life in prison became a simple struggle to stay alive. As one Black youth said, "If you don't have a strong mind, you aren't going to survive here." If they wanted to change their behavior, it was because they did not want to face the "pains of imprisonment" again.

In sum, across all adult sanctions (102 ratings), only 33% ($n = 34$) indicated a positive impact. Of all adult punishment experiences, the ratings were highest for the "blended" program in Duval County, in part because it blended adult time with programming more characteristic of the juvenile system. It is interesting that more ratings about adult punishments were positive (37% overall) than were ratings of low-end juvenile sanctions (19% overall). But, this should be expected given this sample is made up of serious offenders. However, in terms of percentages, deep-end juvenile commitments were more likely than the other two categories to be rated as having a beneficial effect on the youths' attitudes and behaviors (58% overall).

Comparisons of Juvenile and Adult Sanctions

Enough interviewees reported experience with both juvenile and adult sanctions to allow us to make 62 comparisons of the relative impacts of adult versus juvenile dispositions. Of these, 25 comparisons (40%) indicated that the adult sanctions were more likely to have an overall beneficial impact on their lives[5] (see bottom of Table 3). This may be a surprising finding given evidence presented earlier that most youths who experienced adult sanctions believed they had no effect or a negative effect. There are two important points that help explain this finding.

First, 9 of the 25 comparisons indicating that adult sanctions were more beneficial came from the Jacksonville "blended" program, which had adult incarceration but also used programming

more similar to the juvenile system. Indeed, although more than half of the comparisons from the Jacksonville Jail (9 of 16) attributed beneficial impacts to the adult rather than to juvenile sanctions, only 35% of those coming from other adult dispositions attributed more overall benefit to the adult sanction (16 of 46).

Second, and more important, 20 of these 25 comparisons (80%) that attributed more beneficial impacts to the adult disposition reported *no juvenile deep-end experience*. None of the nine youths in the Jacksonville Jail did. And, in only 4 of the 16 comparisons (25%) in which other adult facilities (e.g., prison) were perceived to be more beneficial than juvenile sanctions did the youths have deep-end, juvenile experience. In essence, the youths who believed the adult system had a better impact had "skipped" the juvenile deep-end programs. Recall that the deep-end programs were the ones that the ratings indicated were most often beneficial because they required more time *and* provided life skills and counseling.

One Black youth who thought both the time and the Jacksonville Jail program helped him more than the Level 6 programs he had been in makes the following point:

This right here had a better effect, because you take it for a joke if you go there [Level 6], but here, this right here it don't give you no slack, no half-steppin' here. This one have a better effect. It is both the jail and programs. . . . They talk to you, they still have hope for you, they say you still have little hope, you got to take advantage with life management skills, talkin' to you and stuff. The most important part of program that keep me from comin' back is the time, just the time. You ain't got no TV. Yeah, just the time, it be it. It ring the bell. . . . It hard. I goin' try. It be temptation that will get me 'cause you get tired [of trying to make it on the outside].

Those who felt prison had a stronger impact on them primarily cited time and pain and denigration as the primary factors leading them to want to change their lives. As one young Black respondent who had committed a person offense and had three prior arrests said,

> This place wants to make you go home and do good because you're not going to do this much time in any juvenile program. . . . I think it takes treating people badly for us to realize that we need to change, that this isn't for me, and I need to do what's right.

⊠ Discussion and Conclusions

Summarizing Our Findings

Generally, when the juvenile justice system had an effect, it was because the youths *gained* life skills, got counseling, and were given "hope" there. When the adult system had an effect, it was because the youths *lost* things—hope, safety, amenities, family, and people in their environments who treated them with respect.

Most of the youths who experienced adult sanctions thought they had negative or no impacts on their attitudes and behaviors. Those who were housed in a special adult program at the Jacksonville Jail, which retained some of the treatment components characteristic of the juvenile justice system, were most positive about the adult experience. Some liked the programs there, but many also mentioned "time" and "pain" as reasons for the jail's effects on them. With regard to prison, youths felt time, pain and denigration, and fear of future consequences if they reoffended on release had the strongest effects on them. Some believed it made them want to succeed on release, and some thought it made them worse. Clearly, these youths were aware of the get-tough movement and the potential effects it would have on their lives. Recall, one youth said, "Old Jeb Bush, he ain't foolin' around . . . that 10–20—life." When youths compared adult and juvenile sanctions, those who did not have deep-end juvenile experience were likely to report that the adult sanction was more beneficial—usually because of the

longer "time" associated with the adult experience or because they did not want to experience the pain of prison again (see Tunnell, 1990).

On the whole, the youths in this study believed that life skills (e.g., GED program, training in job skills, reentry programs) and counseling (help with problems and personal behavior management) were the program components that were most effective in helping them change their attitudes and behaviors. They reported that they were most likely to find this help in the deep-end juvenile programs—in part because the programs were designed more for this purpose and in part because the deep-end programs were longer and more intense than low-end programs. Deep-end programs received the most favorable ratings of the dispositions.

A Theoretical Note

The interviews indicate that these youths learned from sanctions, at least those of longer duration. One way to think about the impact is to consider how some sanctions helped youths to contemplate "the relative frequency, amount, and probability of past, present, and anticipated rewards and punishments" they perceive to be attached to criminal behaviors (Akers, 1998, p. 66). The lessons, however, were nuanced. As Akers (1998) observed, "Social behavior is seldom a series of isolated acts proximally followed by contingent rewards or punishers" (p. 69). Any differential reinforcement and punishment involves subtle variations and becomes especially complex when the range of conforming and criminal alternatives is wide. The immediate pain and/or loss experienced during incarceration, for example, is undoubtedly punishing and should help extinguish criminal behavior. The pain and loss, however, are also fraught with symbolic meaning, and sometimes the experience (especially of prison) only increased the resentment, the anger, and the hostility that serve as cue stimuli for acting out. Moreover, any punishing consequences must be balanced against other contingencies prior to prison, during prison, and upon release to understand the ultimate impact. Some youths openly discussed learning how to do crime during incarceration—something that seemed to be offset in various treatment programs but was more likely to go unchecked in adult facilities. When youths reported treatment gains in education and skills or improvements in behavior management (e.g., anger control), they would incorporate these factors into their expectations about impact. Some of them recognized, however, that their sanction experiences might be outweighed once they returned to the streets. They could articulate the problem of returning to the neighborhoods, conditions, and associations through which they had learned crime in the first place.

Policy Implications

Florida and other states continue to move toward harsher sanctions for juveniles (e.g., pushing more to adult court and punishment). However, our findings indicate that youth believe they experience the greatest attitudinal and behavioral change in intensive treatment programs within the juvenile system. For policymakers who purport to care most about public safety, these findings indicate juvenile treatment programs may be the best bet—even for serious offenders. Unless we want to give up on these youth completely and lock them up until they die—which is difficult given the financial cost of continually building and running new prisons—they will "all come back" to our neighborhoods (see Travis, 2000). Policymakers who find it politically difficult to fund treatment for the youths' "own good" may be able to do it for the protection of their communities. Even serious offenders who were institutionalized for person offenses or who had multiple priors indicated that they thought that at least some of the juvenile programming was helpful. Granted, many of these youth were in these programs when we talked to them and may simply be reiterating what they hear every day or may be telling us what they think we want to hear, but many of them talked about negative components of their

programs as well (e.g., staff that did not care or their belief that the counseling was not helpful) (see Tunnell, 1990). The youths who said their experiences were helpful may really believe it and may have found ways to cope with their emotional stress (e.g., through anger management) and have gained life skills that they believe will help them face the external pressures that remain in the communities to which they will return. One way to help them succeed is to ensure them good aftercare, so they can transition into regular life more easily in the face of these pressures (Altschuler, 1998).

Our findings call into question the practice of "skipping" the deep-end programs when sentencing youths for serious crimes. The majority of youths who said they thought the adult experience had a bigger impact on their attitudes and behaviors did not have any experience with the deep-end programs, which got the best ratings overall. Rather, they initially were in low-end programs (probation or short-term treatment) and then were sentenced to adult sanctions. This "skipping" may be due to statutory exclusion—because the youths committed crimes that were automatic transfers to adult court. However, our initial examination of the data indicates most of their offenses were not within that category. Further examination of the case files of youths who "skip" directly from light sanctions to adult court or interviews with prosecutors themselves may give us more insight into the logic of prosecutors' decisions in these types of cases.

Directions for Future Research

Most of the youths in this sample were interviewed while in an institution. Consequently, when talking about their current punishment, they really were discussing their *expectations* about the behavioral effects of the sanction. The real test will be whether their expectations hold true on release. Previous research with adult offenders indicates that when on the outside, they sometimes "forget" about the possible legal consequences of their actions and instead think primarily of the good things that will come from crime, therefore continuing their behavior (Tunnell, 1990). In the future, after the youth have had some time "on the street," we will examine their official recidivism to determine whether these youths become "temporary desisters" or are able to remain crime free (Tunnell, 1990, p. 685).

This is a purposive sample with serious delinquents in deep-end juvenile or adult sanctions. Because we did not systematically sample these youths, we do not feel comfortable making conclusions about how their demographic characteristics, prior offense histories, and seriousness of the most recent offense affect how their sanction experiences influence their attitudes about crime and conformity. Our study was exploratory and was designed to gain an understanding of the youths' perspectives about their experiences rather than to test hypotheses about the attitudinal and behavioral impacts of different sanctions. Future research that uses a larger systematic sample of youths who are or have been incarcerated in both juvenile and adult institutions might be able to determine whether what the youths said here hold for different samples of youths in different places. Some of the hypotheses suggested by our study could include (a) intensive, long-term juvenile treatment programs have a more positive attitudinal and behavioral impact on serious repeat offenders than do adult punishments; (b) attitudinal change from juvenile sanctions is a result of skills *gained* there, whereas in adult institutions, it is a result of something lost (e.g., safety, self-esteem, hope); and (c) juvenile programs reduce recidivism and slow reentry into the justice system for those who do reoffend.

For the serious offenders in our sample, Florida's recent move to shift more money to deep-end sanctions and away from some low-end programs may be a good step (Fisher, 2000). But, serious, chronic delinquents are a small proportion of all youths who commit crime or are arrested (Snyder & Sickmund, 1999). Because we only had a few first-time offenders in our sample ($n = 10$ or 7%), further research should examine the extent to which our findings hold for less serious or first-time offenders—for example, whether our findings about adult prison experiences affect them in the same ways. Most of our sample believed that the low-end sanctions were not adequate to address their needs and change their behaviors, but there are many youths who are given no or light sanctions yet do not reoffend. For them, there may be components of low-end sanctions that are adequate to affect their behaviors. We have no reason to believe that most first-time offenders need to be placed in tougher sanctions to deter them. Future studies of youths who experience only low-end punishments but desist may give us more answers about why some youths continue delinquency and some do not after getting the lightest sanctions in the juvenile system. And, this information may allow us to pinpoint better who needs more intense programs earlier thereby allowing the low-end programs to focus on those youths for whom they have the biggest impact. Clearly, we have more to learn before we can say what "punishment" works best for whom—or whether punishment is an answer at all.

✎ Notes

1. This quote is from a White youth in a Level 8 who had one prior arrest. The focus of this article is on behavioral impact. That probation and the less intense programs did not have a positive impact on behavior does not mean the youth saw no value in them. Some of them mentioned that while in these low-end programs, they learned that they could succeed—for example, in community service or a job. Although one youth thought completing the community service hours was difficult, he said, "I did the hours at the Urban League, and I liked it because I never had worked before." Other youths mentioned that their probation officers cared about them and that the officers tried to help but that they were not ready for it or that they were still trying to "beat the system."

2. Almost all of the transferred youths had been in jail awaiting trial for at least some time.

3. The probable reason for this is that the jail programs were largely a mixture of unrelated things with no central philosophical bent. There were education programs, Toastmasters aimed at public speaking, drug treatment, and so on, but no coherent central theme.

4. A few of the ratings (6%) indicated that the impact of prison would be mixed—some beneficial impact and some negative impact.

5. A total of 22% ($n = 12$) thought juvenile programs generally had a better impact on them than did the adult sanctions. A few also thought that both juvenile and adult sanctions had changed their lives (6%, $n = 3$). The remaining 26% ($n = 14$) reported mixed effects of both juvenile and adult sanctions, thought neither had any impact, or thought they both had negative impacts. As before, many of them felt "society" made it difficult for them to do well, leading them to give up hope of succeeding on the outside. Others just did not believe the sanctions gave them the skills they needed to change.

≋ References

Akers, R. L. (1998). Social learning and social structure: A general theory of crime and deviance. Boston: Northeastern University Press.

Altschuler, D. M. (1998). Intermediate sanctions and community treatment for serious and violent juvenile offenders. In R. Loeber & D. P. Farrington (Eds.), *Serious and violent juvenile offenders: Risk factors and successful interventions* (pp. 367–385). Thousand Oaks, CA: Sage.

Bishop, D. M., & Frazier, C. E. (2000). Consequences of waiver. In J. Fagan & F. E. Zimring (Eds.), *The changing borders of juvenile justice: Transfer of adolescents to the criminal court* (pp. 227–276). Chicago: University of Chicago Press.

Bishop, D. M., Frazier, C. E., Lanza-Kaduce, L., & White, H. G. (1998). *Juvenile transfers to criminal court study: Phase 1 final report.* Submitted for publication.

Bishop, D. M., Frazier, C. E., Lanza-Kaduce, L., & Winner, L. (1996). The transfer of juveniles to criminal court: Does it make a difference? *Crime & Delinquency, 42,* 171–191.

Fagan, J. (1991). *The comparative impacts of juvenile and criminal court sanctions on adolescent felony offenders.* Final report. Submitted for publication.

Fagan, J. (1995). Separating the men from the boys: The comparative advantage of juvenile versus criminal court sanctions on recidivism among adolescent felony offenders. In J. C. Howell, B. Krisberg. J. D. Hawkins, & J. J. Wilson (Eds.). *Serious, violent, and chronic juvenile offenders: A sourcebook* (pp. 238–260). Thousand Oaks, CA: Sage.

Fagan, J. (1996). The comparative advantage of juvenile versus criminal court sanctions on recidivism among adolescent felony offenders. *Law & Policy, 18,* 77–114.

Fisher, L. (2000, June 28). Cuts leave few options for judges. *The Gainesville Sun,* pp. 1A, 4A.

Forst, M., Fagan, J., & Vivona, S. (1989). Youth in prisons and training schools: Perceptions and consequences of the treatment custody dichotomy. *Juvenile and Family Court Journal, 39,* 1–14.

Frazier, C. E., Bishop, D. M, & Lanza-Kaduce, L. (1999). Get-tough juvenile justice reforms: The Florida experience. *ANNALS, 564,* 167–184.

Jensen, E. L., & Metsger, L. K. (1994). A test of the deterrent effect of legislative waiver on violent juvenile crime. *Crime & Delinquency, 40,* 96–104.

Juvenile Justice Advisory Board. (1998). *1998 outcome evaluation report* (Vol. 1, Document #98–001-OE). Tallahassee, FL: Juvenile Justice Advisory Board.

Mays, G. L., & Gregware, P. R. (1996). The children's code reform movement in New Mexico: The politics of expediency. *Law & Policy, 18,* 179–193.

Sanchez. R., & Booth, W. (2000, March 13). California toughens juvenile crime laws: Rules to treat young offenders more like adults. *Washington Post,* p. A03.

Singer, S. I. (1996). *Recriminalizing delinquency: Violent juvenile crime and juvenile justice reform.* New York: Cambridge University Press.

Singer, S. I., & McDowall, D. (1988). Criminalizing delinquency: The deterrent effects of the New York juvenile offender law. *Law & Society Review, 22,* 521–535.

Snyder, H. N., & Sickmund, M. (1999). *Juvenile offenders and victims: 1999 national report.* Washington,

DC: Office of Juvenile Justice and Delinquency Prevention.

Torbet, P., Gable, R., Hurst, H., IV, Montgomery, I., Szymanski, L., &, Thomas, D. (1996). *State responses to serious and violent juvenile crime.* Washington, DC: Office of Juvenile Justice and Delinquency Prevention.

Travis, J. (2000). *But they all come back: Rethinking prisoner reentry.* Washington, DC: National Institute of Justice.

Tunnell, K. D. (1990). Choosing crime: Close your eyes and take your chances. *Justice Quarterly, 7,* 673–690.

White, H. G., Frazier, C. E., Lanza-Kaduce, L., & Bishop, D. M. (1999). A socio-legal history of Florida's juvenile transfer reforms. University of Florida. *Journal of Law and Public Policy, 10,* 249–275.

Winner, L., Lanza-Kaduce, L., Bishop, D. M., & Frazier, C. E. (1997). The transfer of juveniles to criminal court: Reexamining recidivism over the long term. *Crime & Delinquency, 43,* 548–563.

DISCUSSION QUESTIONS

1. Based on the authors' descriptions of the programs, suggest reasons why very few of the youths in low-end programs such as probation believed those programs had positive effects. What changes in low-end programs might make them more effective?

2. Give some examples, from this study and others you have read, in which youth fail not because of faulty programs but other individual or social factors. What other factors affect juveniles' behavior after release from correctional programs?

3. What are some reasons given by the youth for the effectiveness of deep-end programs?

4. Based on the findings, what are the most important components of effective programs? What juvenile corrections policies and programs would you recommend to your state legislators, based on these findings?

READING

In this reading, the author examines the various ways in which youth who are charged with criminal behavior are excluded from the juvenile court process and are prosecuted instead in criminal court. Sanborn's first objective is to eliminate the confusion and misrepresentations concerning exclusion that have dominated the juvenile justice literature. He offers suggestions for how this material should be conceptualized and organized so as to avoid this confusion. The author's second objective is to develop a rationale for exclusion that can serve as a foundation from which to develop sound exclusion policy. The strengths and weaknesses of the potential policy positions on exclusion are examined, and the article concludes with an explanation of the desirability of the selective exclusion of serious and chronic offenders from juvenile court.

Hard Choices Or Obvious Ones

Developing Policy for Excluding Youth From Juvenile Court

Joseph B. Sanborn, Jr.

Perhaps the most intriguing and contentious topic pertaining to the juvenile justice system today is which, if any, juvenile offenders merit prosecution for criminal offenses in criminal court. Excluding youth from the juvenile court is an emotionally charged issue, due in no small measure to the severity of the stakes involved. Prosecution in criminal court exposes youth to the prospects of very lengthy sentences (perhaps even life without parole) and even to the death penalty for some juvenile murderers in some states. Despite these stakes, every jurisdiction in this country permits (sometimes very) young offenders to be excluded from juvenile court, and nowhere is this limited to just the most serious charges (i.e., murder). Despite the universal presence of exclusion, supporting the practice, at least in academic circles, tends to be considered the equivalent of either promoting child abuse or defending domestic violence. The time appears ripe as does the venue, here within the first volume of the first peer-reviewed academic journal dedicated to examining the operation of the juvenile justice system, to develop elements of a policy of exclusion that are both sound and reasonable.

◪ The Dynamics of Exclusion

To develop exclusion policy it is critical to understand first what exclusion entails. Unfortunately, many of the observers in this area have misrepresented the nature of exclusion, impeding an understanding of what can versus what must happen via the exclusion process. Probably the least understood and most misused term in the literature is the adjective *mandatory*. Although *mandatory* clearly connotes a situation that must exist or occur, we will see shortly how the word has been linked frequently and inappropriately with exclusion arrangements that are completely optional or discretionary and thus are in no way mandatory or necessary. Before addressing exclusion methods that are truly discretionary and that are best thought of as decisions to transfer (or to waive or to certify) a youth to adult court, the exclusion procedures that are actually mandatory should be identified.

There is only one way for exclusion to be mandatory or for there to be a categorical imperative that a youth must be prosecuted for any and all crimes in adult court. The youth has to have been classified as an adult before the current offense was committed. Any other arrangement, such as one that relies on the severity of the current offense (e.g., murder), requires someone (usually a prosecutor) to interpret that offense after it has been committed. Any interpretation or analysis that occurs after the event/crime will necessarily be discretionary; no one can force or require a particular interpretation, as we will see presently.

To date, there are three ways in which youth, or individuals that typically are considered juveniles (at least in most of the country), can be converted to adulthood, which will require their prosecution for crimes in adult court. Because adulthood in this country is commonly believed to begin at 18 years of age (for everything but certain vices such as smoking and drinking), a state's decision to define adults (at least for the purposes of prosecution for

SOURCE: *Youth Violence and Juvenile Justice*, (10)2, 198–214, April 2003. DOI: 10.1177/1541204002250879. © 2003 Sage Publications, Inc.

crime) as beginning at 15 or 16 years of age amounts to converting juveniles into adults (again, for this limited purpose). Thirteen states have deviated from the norm and have elected to end their juvenile court jurisdiction at the relatively young ages of 15 (CT, NY, and NC) or 16 (GA, IL, LA, MA, MI, MO, NH, SC, TX, and WI) years of age instead of the more common maximum age of 17.[1] Thus, 16- and 17-year-old youth in these locations (or otherwise juveniles) cannot be prosecuted for criminal behavior in juvenile court (which lacks jurisdiction over them due to their age) and must be prosecuted, if anywhere, in criminal court. Although this example of mandatory exclusion is practiced in only 13 states, it accounts for the greatest proportion of all "juveniles" who are prosecuted in criminal court due to the considerable extent of the exclusion; all crimes (even shoplifting) must go to the adult system for processing.

Another version of mandatory exclusion involves youth who are still within the juvenile court's age limit but who have been converted to adults by virtue of having a previous conviction in criminal court.[2] That means these juveniles had been transferred to and convicted in adult court for a prior offense, which meant from that time forward (and before the current offense) the juvenile was considered legally as an adult in terms of commission of crimes. Altogether, 30 jurisdictions (AL, AZ, CA, CT, DE, DC, FL, HI, ID, IN, KS, LA, ME, MI, MS, MO, NV, NH, ND, OH, OK, OR, PA, RI, SD, TN, UT, VA, WA, and WI) provide that once convicted in adult court, youth henceforth are always to be considered adults in this context of crime, usually regardless of the age at which they were convicted initially in criminal court.

Florida alone practices the third and final form of mandatory exclusion. In a design resembling a three strikes law, Florida holds that juveniles that have accumulated three separate felony adjudications coupled with three separate commitment or placement sentences have been converted to adulthood in relation to their criminal behavior.

The common thread throughout the mandatory exclusion area is that these youth already were categorized as adults due to having reached a certain age or to having amassed a particular record before they perpetrated the offense that now has them facing trial in adult court. A prosecutor does not have the discretion to prosecute these youth in juvenile court for crimes. Only a mistake such as an inaccurate/forged birth certificate or court record could account for their presence in juvenile court for committing a crime.

Although the discretionary brand of exclusion accounts for fewer youth that are prosecuted in adult court, it attracts more criticism from observers and more attention in research studies than its mandatory counterpart. To some extent, this is due to the high-profile, media-saturated murder cases involving rather young offenders who often end up being tried in criminal court. For this prosecution to occur in that forum, the offender, who was defined legally as a juvenile at the time of the homicide, must be transferred or certified to adult court by either a prosecutor or a judge; the transfer amounts to a conversion of the youth to adult legal status.

Two court officials, then, prosecutors and judges, are the ones who determine whether certain youth will remain in or will be excluded from juvenile court. The legislature in each jurisdiction in turn determines whether the judge, the prosecutor, or both individuals will be authorized to transfer youth and in which situations. Although legislatures are the ultimate source of all transfer power in that they establish the boundaries of juvenile and adult courts (and exclusion), they cannot by themselves transfer any particular youth to adult court. To accomplish this task they must pass a law in which they authorize a prosecutor and/or a judge to do so, a maneuver that has occurred in every jurisdiction in this country. In fact, most jurisdictions (40 states, District of Columbia, and federal jurisdiction) employ both forms of transfer; judicial transfer exists in all but 4 states (CT, MT, NE, and NY), whereas prosecutorial transfer is present in all but 6 states (HI, ME, MO, NH, SD, and TN). In jurisdictions where there are both types of transfer, the tendency has been for judges to have transfer power over younger juveniles whose crimes and records are not particularly serious, whereas prosecutors' authority in this area is restricted mostly to older and/or more serious/ chronic offenders.

Judicial transfer is the method that is the easier of the two to understand. Simply put, it involves the judge's authority to certify a youth (depending usually on age, offense, and delinquent record) after a hearing that has investigated both the evidence supporting the alleged offense and the youth's amenability to juvenile court treatment (or ability to be rehabilitated). Typically, the burden is on the prosecutor to prove the youth is not amenable to treatment and thereby deserves exclusion from juvenile court. Numerous jurisdictions, however, have recently adopted a measure that makes judicial transfer more likely or actually presumptive, usually in more serious cases and/or for older/chronic offenders. Presumptive judicial transfer usually shifts the burden to the youth to prove amenability to treatment or of being a worthy candidate to retain in juvenile court; eliminating the amenability burden altogether is another way to make judicial transfer presumptive.

Although judicial transfer can be made presumptive, it cannot be made mandatory. In judicial transfer situations, judges are authorized to determine when exclusion is appropriate; they cannot be commanded to exercise that authority any more than they can be commanded to convict. Nevertheless, the holding of a transfer hearing itself can be made mandatory, as has occurred in four states (DE, FL, MO, and WA). Even still, for this hearing to be mandatory the prosecutor must elect to charge certain crimes that trigger the mandatory provision. Obviously, then, the prosecutor's failure to charge the qualifying crimes (despite the fact that they actually may have occurred) means that no transfer hearing need be held.

Prosecutorial transfer is a bit more complex and not coincidentally is subject to serious misinterpretation in the literature. One of the two forms of prosecutorial transfer is pretty straightforward. It involves what is commonly known as *concurrent jurisdiction,* meaning both juvenile and adult courts are authorized to hear a case involving a particular youth and that the prosecutor must simply choose the appropriate court. Usually a minimum age and a particular level of offense and/or record are required before a juvenile offender is subject to prosecution in either court and for a prosecutor thus to enjoy this transfer power. Assuming the youth's case satisfies the criteria threshold, prosecutors then choose whether to transfer (or in some states it is known as a decision to direct file) the matter to criminal court.

The second form of prosecutorial transfer is best referred to as *offense exclusion.* It involves denying juvenile court jurisdiction over youth (depending perhaps on age and prior record) when certain crimes (or maybe a category of crimes, e.g., first-degree felonies) are charged by the prosecutor. The language of the statute typically will read that the charge/case must be prosecuted in adult court or that juvenile court must transfer the case (usually if probable cause for the offense has been found). Nevertheless, the transfer here is discretionary and not mandatory. Unfortunately, offense exclusion has been identified frequently as mandatory, automatic, and nondiscretionary (Allen, 2000; Dawson, 2000; Feld, 1987, 1989); it supposedly lacks flexibility and any choice by the prosecutor. It also does not help when commentators refer to offense exclusion as "legislative/statutory" exclusion (Bishop & Frazier, 2000; Dawson, 2000; Feld, 2000; Griffin, Torbet, & Syzmanski, 1998; Snyder & Sickmund, 1995; Torbet et al., 1996), suggesting that offense exclusion is not a second way in which prosecutors transfer but rather is a separate or third type of transfer. All exclusion from juvenile court stems from a legislative decision to enact a statute in which it is announced that certain youth are targeted for exclusion due to age, record, and/or offense. So, all exclusion is legislative/statutory in origin, and offense exclusion is no more legislative or statutory in nature than any other form of exclusion.

It is important to realize that offense exclusion is purely discretionary. It relies completely on prosecutorial charging, which is one of the most discretionary-oriented decisions made by any criminal justice official. Prosecutors cannot be mandated to charge any particular offense or offender. To be sure, murder may be removed or excluded from juvenile court jurisdiction, indicating that a juvenile cannot be prosecuted for that crime in that forum. But even when a human has been killed unlawfully by a culpable/ responsible juvenile who acted with sufficient intent (or *mens rea*), a murder does not exist (and juvenile court does not lose jurisdiction) unless and until a prosecutor charges murder. A decision to charge a less serious offense, such as manslaughter, is totally within the prosecutor's discretion and would mean in this context that transfer to adult court will not occur. Thus, although legislatures certainly can strip juvenile court of jurisdiction for certain offenses, they cannot require prosecutors to charge those certain offenses even when those offenses have indeed been committed (and arguably should be charged as such). This charging reality also demonstrates that offense exclusion is of the same nature of prosecutorial transfer, as is concurrent jurisdiction. In both situations, prosecutors are selecting not only the proper charges but also the proper forum in which to try the alleged behavior. In both situations, prosecutors are deciding whether to transfer the youth to criminal court. The only significant difference is that offense exclusion forces the prosecutor to be sensitive to the charge that is selected for prosecution because pursuing particular (excluded) offenses will automatically and simultaneously determine the court as well.

In the final analysis, transfer (waiver or certification) should be recognized as a discretionary decision having no connection to the exclusionary methods that are mandatory in nature. Transfer is purely and simply a situation in which youth could have (because they were defined legally as juveniles at the moment they committed their current crime) and would have been prosecuted in juvenile court but for the decision of a prosecutor or a judge to send them to criminal court for trial.

✄ Putting Exclusion Into Context

Amid all the emotion and high-stakes jockeying involved in excluding youth from juvenile court, the larger picture of what exclusion represents tends to get lost. Exclusion simply means that instead of being diverted from criminal court (or prosecuted in juvenile court), youth will face actual and legitimate criminal charges for having committed serious and/or many crimes. Juvenile court was created to serve a number of purposes, the primary of which was to grant youth immunity or absolute protection from criminal liability. In other words, young criminals were diverted from the criminal court into an alternative system (i.e., juvenile court) to be spared the harsh consequences (both in terms of sentencing and court record) of criminal prosecution. It was the youthfulness of the offenders rather than the nature of their behavior that triggered this display of tolerance. This diversion to juvenile court was never designed to be wholesale; the oldest, most serious, and chronic offenders were subject to mandatory and discretionary exclusion from juvenile court (or reunion with criminal court) from the first days of juvenile court (Tannenhaus, 2000). Nevertheless, diversion or prosecution in juvenile court was considered the norm.

Thus, the juvenile justice system was implemented as a huge diversionary effort, bolstered by beliefs in the effectiveness of the newly emerging discipline of psychology, in the susceptibility of most youth to change via treatment-oriented interventions, and in the desire to not obliterate or even seriously damage the life chances or future prospects of most young criminals. Instead of acknowledging the diversionary nature of prosecuting criminal offenders in juvenile court, observers today are prone to identify nondiversion or prosecution in criminal court as "criminalizing delinquency" (Fagan, 1995; Singer, 1996) or the "adultification of youth" (Sanborn, in press). Titles such as these suggest that either the behavior or the individual is being wrongly converted into something it was not meant to be. For example, *criminalizing delinquency* implies that exclusion transforms otherwise mere petty or obnoxious conduct (i.e., delinquency) into a much more serious infraction (i.e., crime). Of course, exclusion does nothing of the kind. Instead, exclusion merely and only means that rather than granting offenders immunity from criminal prosecution (via diversion to and prosecution in juvenile court), youth will have to stand trial in criminal court for crimes they allegedly have committed. In other words, the crime will be treated like the crime it truly is rather than being subject to immunity.

Today, observers vary from one end of the spectrum to the other as to the *level* of exclusion that should exist. The extremes are that exclusion should be either nonexistent or total; in between are those who believe exclusion should be selective or reserved for the more serious/chronic juvenile offenders. Those opposed to exclusion point to three problems that attend the prosecution of juveniles in criminal court. The first problem involves juveniles' lack of competency and maturity; in short, they do not serve well as criminal defendants. Arguably, juveniles cannot participate adequately in the trial proceeding, which includes understanding the proceedings, assisting defense counsel, and selecting the proper course of action (i.e., to plead guilty or go to trial) (Bonnie & Grisso, 2000; Steinberg & Schwartz, 2000). In addition, juveniles supposedly lack sufficient culpability to be held criminally responsible for their behavior due to their relative immaturity. This immaturity stems from three related deficiencies of youth: the inability to know and use legal rules, the inability to control impulses, and the inability to resist peer pressure (Steinberg & Schwartz, 2000; Zimring, 1998, 2000). The second problem relates to the potential disaster that can result from incarcerating some youth in adult facilities after conviction in criminal court (Bishop & Frazier, 2000). Third and finally, several research studies have compiled data that suggest that some youth who are prosecuted in criminal court will be arrested sooner and more often (and for more serious crimes) than will supposedly comparable youth

who are retained by the juvenile justice system (Bishop, Frazier, Lanza-Kaduce, & Winner, 1996; Fagan, 1991, 1995). Other studies similarly suggest high recidivist rates for many youth prosecuted in criminal court (Myers, 2001; Podkopacz & Feld, 1996).

At the other extreme are individuals who promote the total exclusion of youth or the prosecution of all criminal defendants in criminal court (Ainsworth, 1991; Federle, 1990; Feld, 1990, 1993). The primary motivation behind this advocacy is the relative lack of due process in juvenile court. Suffice it to say that there are potential situations in the adjudicatory hearings of many juvenile courts that make it difficult to receive a fair trial there (Sanborn, 1994b).

Zero and total exclusion are extreme policy statements that have not been endorsed by any legislative body in this country. Instead, whereas discretionary exclusion is possible in every jurisdiction, one or both of the major forms of mandatory exclusion exist in all but 14 states (AK, AR, CO, IA, KY, MD, MN, MT, NE, NJ, NM, VT, WV, and WY). Moreover, not only is discretionary exclusion present in every jurisdiction, but also 42 jurisdictions practice both judicial and prosecutorial transfer; only 10 states (CT, HI, ME, MO, MT, NE, NH, NY, SD, and TN) observe only one type of transfer. Although it is selective in nature, in that it applies typically only to the older, more serious, and/or more chronic juvenile offenders, the machinery of exclusion is vast.

A reasonable inference to draw from the juvenile justice literature, nevertheless, is that the entire country has it wrong. Defenses of the practice tend to be rare (McCarthy, 1994; Sanborn, 1994a, 1996) or only reluctantly offered (Zimring, 1998). Instead, the tone of the majority of the literature is that either the entire concept of exclusion is flawed or the way in which it is practiced leaves much to be desired (Fagan & Zimring, 2000; Grisso & Schwartz, 2000). The latter criticism usually is aimed at prosecutorial transfer and more often at offense exclusion. Opponents of transfer in general will aim their criticisms most frequently in the direction of prosecutorial transfer because prosecutors are much more inclined than judges to exercise their transfer power. After all, prosecutors are law enforcers who are charged with protecting the community rather than with promoting the best interests of juvenile offenders per se. Prosecutors are more inclined to conclude that criminal court serves the objective of protecting society (one of its mandates) better than juvenile court (where protecting the youth has much higher standing). Judges, on the other hand, are expected to do justice, which can include "doing the best thing for the defendant." That will often translate into judges' deciding not to transfer a youth to criminal court. That judges are more reluctant than prosecutors to transfer is certainly no secret (McCarthy, 1994; Sanborn, 1994a), and just as certainly it explains in large part the considerable recent expansion in the prosecutors' authority to certify youth to adult court as well as the increased adoption of presumptive judicial transfer (where judges face much greater pressure to transfer cases).

✉ Developing a Rationale for Exclusion

Assuming we want to preserve juvenile court and not adopt total exclusion, the bottom line of exclusion becomes rather clear. The choice is to keep all juvenile defendants within the juvenile system regardless of the number and severity of their crimes and the advanced status of their young adulthood (i.e., being 17 years of age) or to allow the prosecution of some of these individuals in criminal court. It would seem constructive, then, to consider the potential consequences of retaining all youth in the juvenile system. Perhaps the first casualty of total retention would be the traditional primary purpose of the juvenile justice system, rehabilitating young offenders. If all offenders must be retained in the system, even those who have demonstrated conclusively through past treatment efforts that they are not amenable to treatment, then

rehabilitation is not as critical a purpose as is shielding all young offenders from criminal liability. Keeping all youth regardless means valuable, limited treatment resources will be wasted and/or that warehousing (at least some) youth will be encouraged. Moreover, total retention of dangerous, intractable youthful criminals threatens not only the rehabilitation but also the physical welfare of youth who have a chance of being helped by the system. Again, rehabilitation cannot be the primary purpose under such a scheme. It is interesting how those who fear placing chronic/violent juvenile offenders with adults voice no corresponding concern for the plight of less violent and criminal juveniles who are forced to cohabitate with youth who arguably should have been excluded from juvenile court. Finally, in terms of the prospect of rehabilitation, total retention likely guarantees the poorest results possible for the success of treatment programs, which in turn threatens the credibility and survival of juvenile court. Research that has examined the recidivism rates of somewhat comparable serious young offenders prosecuted in juvenile and criminal courts has discovered very poor results in both systems (Bishop et al., 1996; Fagan, 1991; Winner, Lanza-Kaduce, Bishop, & Frazier, 1997). Not surprisingly, retaining the worst criminals in the juvenile system portends poor treatment outcomes, at least as measured by recidivism rates. Whereas the rehabilitative prowess of criminal court has never been the justification of its existence, the same cannot be said of juvenile court. Its separate existence relies largely, if not primarily, on its ability to successfully rehabilitate young criminals. Unlike criminal court, then, the more the juvenile system fails to stem the tide of juvenile crime, the more counterproductive and unreasonable it can seem to continue to divert offenders to it from criminal court.

On the other hand, total retention would serve another announced purpose of the juvenile system, pursuing the best interests of the child; in this context, *best interests* refers to legal rather than treatment interests. Beyond a doubt, complete criminal immunity would serve that purpose to an extreme. The problem here becomes expecting society to have none of its interests served or protected in juvenile court, which would be a result of total retention. Diverting every young criminal from criminal court asks society always to look the other way, again regardless of the circumstances. Although juvenile court originated under and purportedly followed a one-dimensional, juvenile-only-interests formula for several decades, the past few decades have been marked by what Feld (1990) coined the *criminalization* of juvenile court. *Criminalization* refers to the ways in which juvenile court has adopted policies and practices more characteristic of criminal court. One adoption that mirrors the adult system is the revision of juvenile court purpose clauses so as to include protecting the public and promoting society's interests. These purposes become more pivotal to juvenile court proceedings when violent/chronic offenders are processed there. These purposes do not appear to be served by total retention, and it does not seem reasonable or plausible to simply ignore or marginalize society's interests, especially when it comes to serious criminal behavior. It certainly does not seem unreasonable to question whether only the juvenile's best interests should be served when serious, chronic, or violent crimes are at hand and to doubt whether the juvenile system can maintain a one-dimensional, imbalanced purpose in this situation.

Finally, in this regard, it does not seem unreasonable for society to want to condemn violent/chronic criminality on the part of juveniles. Criminal court is the proper and better location for the condemnation of behavior. Total retention encourages condemnation to become a part of juvenile court processing, which in turn promotes more punishment and warehousing (and less treatment) of juvenile offenders and greater promise to protect society through juvenile court intervention. The physical presence of chronic/violent youth heretofore processed in criminal court but now located in juvenile institutions could also lead to the institutions becoming much more security oriented and much less treatment program oriented. Similarly, total retention creates added pressure to invite the victim to become a significant and perhaps determining voice in juvenile court proceedings, as has occurred in much juvenile justice legislation recently. This potentially hostile party can further undermine and derail the rehabilitative focus of juvenile court and can introduce a more punitive atmosphere and its attending consequences into the proceedings (Sanborn, 2001b).

Total retention virtually demands an extension of the juvenile court's dispositional power over youth. Traditionally, supervision over juveniles did not extend beyond the youth's 21st birthday. Typically, this age limit provided ample opportunity for juvenile court to attempt the rehabilitation of older delinquents retained in the system. Of course, the very violent youth, whether pretty young or very near the upper age limit of the court's jurisdiction, has long been a candidate for transfer to adult court, especially when juvenile court authorities believed they lacked sufficient time to work with the offender. The inability to send this offender to criminal court would exert pressure on legislatures to exceed 21 years of age as the upper retention limit of juvenile court jurisdiction. A number of states have done this recently, even with the availability of transfer to adult court. Some juvenile courts now have dispositional retention over youth until their 23rd or 25th birthdays. Being forced to prosecute 17-year-old murderers in juvenile court would induce many jurisdictions to follow this lead and to maintain sentencing authority over youth until well into their adulthood. The problem with this formula is fourfold. First, giving juvenile courts the power to sentence youth to institutionalization for up to 10 years or more (at least if they were 15 or younger at the time of disposition and 25 is the upper limit) smacks of punishment and not of rehabilitation. Second, such extended sentencing power raises serious questions as to why offenders should be diverted from criminal court and criminal liability when very lengthy state control (and punishment) is believed necessary to correct/prevent their misbehavior. Third, developing extended dispositional options invites their corruption by exposing some youth whose behavior was not especially chronic/violent to be sentenced to the same outcomes (Zimring, 1998).[3] Fourth, the vast majority of juvenile courts do not provide anywhere near adequate due process in order to sustain such a substantial exertion of state control and punishment.

Total retention also could wreak havoc with the internal dimensions of juvenile court sentencing. That is, prosecuting all juvenile offenders in juvenile court could encourage greater adoption of minimum, mandatory, and longer (but within the upper age limit) sentences, provisions that historically are more characteristic of criminal court.

Historically, juvenile courts have been able to maintain a mostly rehabilitative and mostly moderate dispositional scheme (together with a mostly best-interests-of-the-child focus) because the most problematic/violent youth have been subject to transfer to adult court.

The abolition of exclusion certainly could prompt legislatures to restructure juvenile court dispositions so as to resemble a mini criminal court. This increased criminalization development would appear to be unavoidable. As word would spread through the neighborhood that no youth will ever again be prosecuted in criminal court, chances are that some juveniles would perceive no disincentive (or at least much less of one) to committing crime. The likely reaction within the juvenile justice system would be to raise the ante for punishments a youth could receive in that forum.

Finally, total retention likely would expand the recent tendency to allow juvenile court adjudications to be factored into subsequent criminal court sentencing, following eventual conviction in that forum. Currently, many jurisdictions permit adult court judges to significantly enhance the sentence offenders will receive in criminal court due to their juvenile court records. In some situations, juveniles effectively can carry two strikes from juvenile court and "strike out" on their first "pitch" (or conviction) in criminal court (Sanborn, 1998, 2000). Removing transfer to adult court would create even greater pressure to not ignore the indiscretions of youth, marked by adjudications in juvenile court. The desire to "get even" with youth who continue to commit crime as adults after having been given repeated, considerable leniency (and complete immunity from criminal liability throughout their juvenile years) would seem to be irrepressible. Allowing a juvenile court record to have such an effect in criminal court when that record was secured without serious due process in that forum only serves to exacerbate the relatively weak foundation of justice in juvenile court. Of course, the challenges to due process that have been identified by individuals who endorse the total exclusion position could prompt legislatures to convert juvenile court into the functional equivalent of criminal court, complete with the procedural rights granted adult defendants. Of course, juvenile court also could adopt a sentencing response similar to adult court and completely abandon any pretense at rehabilitation, or legislatures could perceive this evolution of juvenile court as a signal of the time for its abolition. Arguably, a good deal of the recent criminalization of juvenile court can be explained by the retention of too many serious juvenile criminals.

Clearly, total retention raises many problems, some of which could prove fatal to juvenile court and to the welfare of the vast majority of juvenile offenders appropriately prosecuted there. The next question becomes whether exclusion from juvenile court is equally problematic, as is argued by the antiexclusionists. Assuming that exclusion nearly always should involve youth over the age of 10 years, only rarely should a juvenile fail to qualify as a competent defendant. The constitutional threshold for competency established by the U.S. Supreme Court is relatively nondemanding and should be satisfied by virtually any nonmentally impaired adolescent. Moreover, anyone truly interested in ensuring adequate defendant competency should welcome the measurement of that facet in criminal court, where failure would seem more obvious—in contrast to the competent adult defendant and where failure appropriately would prevent prosecution. It cannot be ruled out that juvenile court would consider incompetence as an independent reason and need for adjudication. To be sure, some youth are immature. It strains credulity, however, to think that adolescents are incapable of knowing and using basic legal rules, especially those who have frequented the juvenile system on a previous occasion. A question that appears to defy an answer, moreover, is whether (and why only) some youth are truly physically and mentally unable to control impulses and to resist peer pressure or whether these individuals simply elect not to do so. These characteristics are certainly not necessary to or universal in adolescence. Regardless, accepting the relative immaturity of youth converts at best to granting (only) qualifying youth what some have called "diminished" culpability (Zimring, 1998). Importantly, diminished culpability (or penal proportionality) does not convert into criminal immunity for all (even qualifying) youth. Although it may justify a reduction in the criminal court's response to the offender, it does not automatically and categorically justify the elimination of a response from this court altogether.

Antiexclusionists have a valid point in criticizing adult penal policy that does not prevent the harmful mixture of youth with adult criminals. Of course, this is a (typically ignored) two-way street. Age is only one criterion by which to gauge the "right fit" of incarceration. Some adults can be harmed by an inappropriate mixture with violent juveniles, just like youth retained by the juvenile system can be harmed by these same violent juveniles were they to be retained as well. In fact, some states provide for youth convicted in criminal court to serve any sentence of incarceration in a juvenile facility at least while they are still of a juvenile age (usually until 16 or 18 years of age).[4] The wisdom of this policy is not beyond scrutiny, albeit this is not an issue that has received much, if any, attention in the literature.

Although adult penal policy certainly should aim to protect the physical safety of excluded youth, lapses in this policy do not invalidate exclusion policy in general or the prosecution of any particular juvenile in criminal court. The same logic applies to victimized adult inmates and the validity of their prosecution in criminal court.

Finally, there is the antiexclusion claim of the lack of effectiveness in excluding youth from juvenile court. That is, criminal court does not appear to do a better job in preventing recidivism among excluded youth than juvenile court does with supposedly comparable youth retained there. Probably the most discouraging aspect of the research that has measured this phenomenon is that the recidivism rates of both populations have been very high (Bishop et al., 1996; Fagan, 1991; Winner et al., 1997). It seems neither system prevents or deters crime well. This should not come as a surprise to observers who realize that recidivist tendencies among offenders prosecuted in both courts always have been pronounced.

To be sure, there are some proexclusion advocates who will base the need for exclusion entirely on an alleged need to better protect society. Seemingly every prosecutor interviewed by the media cites this factor as *the* motivation behind prosecuting youth in criminal court. This may make for politically plausible sound bites via the media, but there is hardly a prosecutor with experience that does not realize there are at least two major problems with putting all the eggs of exclusion in this one basket. First, there is the problem in securing a conviction, particularly if the youth does not plead guilty and insists on a jury trial. The chances for jury nullification, partial if not total, are always present. To the extent that it is simply more difficult to secure a jury conviction compared to a judicial one means there should be a better chance for acquittal in the adult system. Not only do the vast majority of states deny defendants the right to jury trial in juvenile court, but also judges are notorious for lowering the standard of proof so as to adjudicate youth who appear to need the system's intervention

(Sanborn, 1994b, 2001a). Prosecutors also cannot afford to ignore the possibility of judicial nullification should the youth elect to have a bench trial in criminal court. Even if there is a guilt plea via a plea bargain in criminal court, prosecutors may be willing to sweeten the deal considerably by reducing charges significantly so as to avoid the uncertainties of a jury trial. This could lead to a sentence that would be both shorter and less intrusive than that which the offender would have received in juvenile court. Second, unless the conviction is linked with a mandatory sentence or the judge's discretion is seriously restricted, there is always a prospect that the judge will not believe the incarceration of a young offender is necessary or beneficial. Probably the only way to ensure an effective payback from exclusion (assuming there is a conviction to begin with) is to let the juvenile record influence the adult court sentence. This likely would lead to more sentences of (lengthier) incarceration for chronic offenders excluded from juvenile court. Otherwise, it is possible that the youth could benefit from a first appearance in criminal court and be granted a lenient sentence due to the lack of a "criminal" record. It would be interesting to research how many offenders with a juvenile court history continue to commit crime into adulthood due in part at least to criminal court's continuance of a policy of leniency that mirrored experiences in juvenile court. Complementing this would be to call for presumptive sentencing (and incarceration) for violent offenders that discouraged leniency despite the lack of a record. One research study that analyzed the fate of excluded youth found that sentences of incarceration of substantial length contributed to a decrease in the recidivism rate of this population (Myers, 2001). Finally, it is possible in some exclusion scenarios that prosecutors are not counting as much on better prevention (e.g., through a long sentence of incarceration) via a conviction on the current offense as they are on at least beginning to develop a criminal court record for the youth that ultimately would help secure a lengthy

sentence should the offender be convicted again in the future. Securing (another) juvenile court adjudication could be viewed as simply delaying the opportunity to amass a usable criminal record with a better/significant effect in future criminal court sentencing (Sanborn, 1994a).

Exclusion involves much more than a question of which system does a better job in preventing recidivism. Also at stake are issues such as the preservation of the juvenile court and its pursuit of the rehabilitation and best interests of youth, the extent of justice and punishment available to the juvenile court, the promotion of society's interests, and the condemnation of violence and chronic offending. The inability to exclude at least some juveniles from juvenile court simply asks too much of both the juvenile court and society.

⊠ Selecting the Proper Methods of Exclusion

Assuming a case has been made for the desirability if not the necessity of selective exclusion, the next matter to resolve is choosing the method(s) by which youth can be excluded from the juvenile system. The two major forms of mandatory exclusion easily could receive very different support. Although it certainly makes sense to permanently exclude youth who have been convicted previously in criminal court after having been transferred there, the wisdom and appropriateness of reducing the maximum juvenile court age might just be another matter.[5] Unless the residents of a state believe that adulthood truly begins at the ages of 16 or 17, which seems doubtful, it seems strange and unnecessary to insist that the prosecution of all youth of these ages must occur in criminal court regardless of the nature of the offense and prior record. This policy appears to suffer from overkill because transfer of the most serious/chronic offenders to adult court can accomplish the same result without also needlessly subjecting all other types of young offenders to this outcome. The benefits of prosecuting 16-year-old first-time shoplifters and auto thieves en masse in criminal court would appear to be minimal.

Both types of discretionary transfer warrant approval, although as previously discussed, the antiexclusion camp prefers judicial to prosecutorial waiver. Actually, the formula followed in many jurisdictions has serious merit; in other words, perhaps many legislatures got it right. This formula allocates control over the most serious and chronic offenders to the prosecutor, whereas judges have been granted transfer authority over less violent youth who are nevertheless not likely to be rehabilitated by the juvenile system. Although this arrangement certainly is not universal (10 states do not provide for prosecutorial transfer), it has become the dominant way in which transfer authority has been divided between prosecutors and judges in this country. There is abundant logic behind this division of power.

Although transfer has been likened to sentencing (Zimring, 2000), certification to adult court is primarily a charging decision. That is, the central and pivotal question in transfer is whether the youth should be diverted from criminal court via a referral to juvenile court or should be prosecuted in criminal court. This choice properly belongs to the prosecutor, especially when serious/violent offenses are involved and/or when the defendant's prior record is lengthy. It is appropriate for legislatures to identify a threshold associated with crimes that are too serious and/or too numerous to be diverted to juvenile court. This threshold simultaneously establishes the location at which society's interests are thought to take precedence over the youth's best interests. Both the concurrent jurisdiction and offense exclusion brands of prosecutorial transfer establish such a threshold, accompanied often with a minimum age level. Prosecutors are charged with representing society's interests, which is why they should control the determination of when youth have exceeded that threshold. Unlike judges, prosecutors are experienced in evaluating charges and

cases that should be filed (or diverted). In addition, judges do not have access to witnesses and arresting officers so as to be able to gauge the appropriate level of charge to file. Moreover, judges are known to be less likely than prosecutors to transfer youth (McCarthy, 1994; Sanborn, 1994a), and thus they would be more likely to undercharge offenders so as to keep youth in juvenile court. That is not the proper orientation with which to initiate charging decisions, particularly when serious and violent crimes or chronic offenders are at hand. Finally, it is inappropriate and arguably a violation of separation of powers to invest judges with the executive-branch-based authority of charging offenders.

Beyond these considerations there are two fundamental problems with employing judicial transfer for juvenile court's most serious offenders. The first concerns the fact that in judicial transfer, the youth's amenability to treatment is supposed to be the primary focus. This focus correctly posits that the youth's best interests should prevail, which should not occur when crimes/cases beyond the threshold are involved. The second problem is that in judicial transfer, probation officers and/or clinicians form the most critical appraisals of the youth's amenability to treatment and typically convince the judge as to the appropriateness of transfer. This relationship effectively transfers the transfer decision to court officials and private citizens who are neither elected by nor accountable to the public. This arrangement is inappropriate when society's interests should be vindicated.

Judicial transfer should be used for youth whose behavior has not been sufficiently serious or chronic so as to trigger society's concerns and interests but who still may not be amenable to juvenile court intervention. These situations are the ones in which transfer most closely and logically resembles sentencing because the juvenile court's dispositional options are properly the major substance of the inquiry. Assumedly, this allocation of authority also would involve minimum ages, offenses, and records, which is typical in the legislation of most states. The presumption in these cases is that the youth's best interests should dominate the decision making, which is why it is proper to entrust it to a judge. Nevertheless, the presumption is not absolute and can be overcome by the judge's decision to certify the youth to adult court due to the youth's lack of amenability.

Perhaps the only pressing question remaining is which type of prosecutorial transfer is more suitable in the serious/chronic offender scenario. Arguably, each of the targets of prosecutorial transfer merits a different version. Offense exclusion appears to be the more appropriate method for the very serious juvenile offenders. Crimes of a certain nature, such as murder or aggravated rape, or of a particular degree, such as first-degree felonies, are more suited to offense exclusion than concurrent jurisdiction because the former draws a clear line or boundary as to where criminal court jurisdiction legitimately begins and where diversion to juvenile court is not acceptable. For example, it seems to make sense to assert that murder (perhaps depending on age) simply should not be subject to juvenile court processing and should be excluded thereby. Here, offense exclusion makes an unequivocal statement that society's interests must prevail when prosecutors determine that a murder charge is the correct allegation. On the other hand, concurrent jurisdiction for the most serious charges can raise issues of ambiguity, equality, and legitimacy. That is, why is it acceptable to prosecute some 17-year-old murderers in juvenile court while other 17-year-old murderers can be prosecuted in criminal court? Less serious (or maybe younger serious) and chronic offenders, however, would appear to be the most suitable candidates for concurrent jurisdiction. These youth do not appear to be as far above the threshold that automatically triggers society's interests, as are youth who murder and rape. Although their fate belongs within a charging rather than a treatment amenability framework because they too are above the threshold, there is a logic to allowing the prosecutor to determine that some of these youth do not require criminal

court prosecution; diversion to juvenile court is still a prospect for some.

Many jurisdictions that have adopted both forms of prosecutorial transfer as well as judicial waiver have constructed precisely this arrangement, although typically without a rationale offered. To be sure, this is far from a universal formula as of now. Nor is it a necessary relationship. Some states still prefer to place all the discretionary transfer power in the hands of a judge. The most important and compelling fact, however, is that all jurisdictions in this country have extended transfer authority to one or both of these officials. This is an allocation of power that is destined to persist regardless of to whom it is given.

⊠ Implications for Developing Policy and Examining Exclusion From Juvenile Court

This article raises a number of implications when it comes to considering the topic of exclusion from juvenile court. The first concerns accurate definitions of the various methods of exclusion. The cause of policy development is not advanced when examples of mandatory exclusion are confused and mixed with instances of discretionary exclusion, when the misuse of the word *mandatory* distorts what is actually occurring via the exclusion method, or when offense exclusion is not recognized as a type of prosecutorial transfer that is completely discretionary.

Similarly, sound policy development also requires a complete and balanced picture of what a practice entails. Heretofore, exclusion has been presented consistently in the literature as a virtual attack on an unsuspecting, merely mistake-prone youth; accounts tend to portray exclusion as both ignoring the child in the offender and making more of the behavior than it deserves. It is time to recognize that exclusion means only that the crime is not being ignored and that criminal prosecution for the commission of a crime will occur in lieu of criminally immunizing the event via a diversion to juvenile court; the offense itself is neither inflated nor enhanced thereby. Moreover, transfer certainly should involve a scrutiny of both the offense and the offender. Even prosecutors must be sensitive to both elements if for no other reason than subjecting either the wrong crime or the wrong criminal to trial in adult court easily could result in acquittal or in judicial or jury nullification in that forum.

Another major implication concerns the purposes to be served by exclusion. Certain observers, research studies, and even defenders of the practice have identified exclusion as serving one objective only, greater prevention of crime through criminal court prosecution. If this were the one and only purpose of exclusion, then it would be time for serious reconsideration of the policy. Because there are numerous important goals served by exclusion, however, then both the policy debate surrounding exclusion and the focus of research studies need to be expanded so as to include these elements. To date, a number of items, such as the potential effect of total retention on juvenile court, have been ignored in both circles. In addition, research analyses of the phenomenon have been mostly unhelpful to the extent that the inquiries have been directed toward collecting aggregate data indicating the recidivist tendencies of groups of youth who commit certain crimes. What needs to be tracked more often and more carefully is a longitudinal examination of the criminal careers of youth, complete with the results of interventions by the juvenile and criminal courts. These examinations may disclose a need for better integration of the sentencing policies of the two systems and the undesirability of repeating leniency in criminal court to offenders who experienced the same previously in juvenile court. To date, research studies have documented that the transfer decision is a critical one, one that should be made carefully and with an understanding of the implications for society and for youth who are placed in the adult system. Research also has demonstrated the need for sound adult penal policy that can respond appropriately, effectively, and humanely to youth who are convicted in and incarcerated by criminal court. What these studies have not established is that the problems discovered via research can or should serve as a bar to exclusion from juvenile court.

Finally, the proper allocation of transfer power between judges and prosecutors must be reviewed. Certification to criminal court must be recognized primarily as a charging decision or stated another way, as a decision not to divert the youth to juvenile court. Acknowledgement of this reality makes the appropriateness of locating most of the responsibility for transfer in the hands of the prosecutor, especially for serious and chronic offenders, all the more clear.

✉ Notes

1. The data on exclusion and transfer provisions cited throughout this article are derived from a recent review conducted by the author of the juvenile court statutes from all the jurisdictions in the country (50 states, Washington, D.C., and the federal jurisdiction).

2. This article will not address the various requirements many states have adopted concerning the situations in which a criminal court conviction guarantees that the youth is permanently an adult henceforth.

3. Several states (AR, CT, IL, KS, MN, MT, OH, and RI) have gone so far as to create a second tier for their juvenile courts to which youth can be transferred without experiencing criminal court physically. Youth on this tier typically are provided a jury trial and if adjudicated usually are given both a juvenile and an adult sentence. The adult sentence is suspended while the court imposes the juvenile sentence. The juvenile court eventually conducts a review hearing to determine how the youth has fared. If the juvenile sentence is successfully completed, the adult sentence must be dismissed. Although this internal transfer proceeding might result in some youth not being transferred to criminal court, it cannot completely replace (and nowhere has replaced) transfer to criminal court. This internal transfer procedure merely has supplemented other methods of exclusion from juvenile court and is not designed for the most egregious juvenile offenders that would be considered ineligible for one last chance at a juvenile court disposition. To be transferred to the juvenile court's second tier in these states, the youth would have to be considered amenable to a juvenile

court disposition (because that is what actually is imposed), albeit with a criminal court sanction hanging in abeyance.

For example, California and North Dakota prohibit the adult incarceration of any youth convicted in criminal court until the age of 16.

4. The policy outlined here will not develop what, if any, situations attending a conviction in criminal court would warrant a youth's regaining juvenile status.

⧆ References

Ainsworth, J. (1991). Re-imagining childhood and reconstructing the legal order: The case for abolishing the juvenile court. *North Carolina Law Review, 69,* 1083–1133.

Allen, F. A. (2000). Foreword. In J. Fagan & F. E. Zimring (Eds.), *The changing borders of juvenile justice: Transfer of adolescents to the criminal court* (pp. ix–xvi). Chicago: University of Chicago Press.

Bishop, D. M., & Frazier, C. E. (2000). Consequences of transfer. In J. Fagan & F. E. Zimring (Eds.), *The changing borders of juvenile justice: Transfer of adolescents to criminal court* (pp. 227–276). Chicago: University of Chicago Press.

Bishop, D. M., Frazier, C. E., Lanza-Kaduce, L., & Winner, L. (1996). The transfer of juveniles to criminal court: Does it make a difference? *Crime and Delinquency, 42,* 171–191.

Bonnie, R. J., & Grisso, T. (2000). Adjudicative competence and youthful offenders. In T. Grisso & R. G. Schwartz (Eds.), *Youth on trial: A developmental perspective on juvenile justice* (pp. 73–103). Chicago: University of Chicago Press.

Dawson, R. O. (2000). Judicial waiver in theory and practice. In J. Fagan & F. E. Zimring (Eds.), *The changing borders of juvenile justice: Transfer of adolescents to the criminal court* (pp. 45–81). University of Chicago Press.

Fagan, J. (1991). *The comparative impacts of juvenile court and criminal court sanctions on adolescent felony offenders* (Final report to the National Institute of Justice). Washington, DC: U.S. Department of Justice.

Fagan, J. (1995). Separating the men from the boys: The comparative advantage of juvenile versus criminal court sanctions on recidivism among adolescent felony offenders. In J. C. Howell, B. Krisberg, J. D. Hawkins, & J. J. Wilson (Eds.), *Serious, violent, and chronic juvenile offenders: A sourcebook* (pp. 238–260). Thousand Oaks, CA: Sage.

Fagan, J., & Zimring, F. E. (Eds.). (2000). *The changing borders of juvenile justice: Transfer of adolescents to the criminal court.* Chicago: University of Chicago Press.

Federle, K. H. (1990). The abolition of the juvenile court: A proposal for the preservation of children's legal rights. *Journal of Contemporary Law, 16,* 23–51.

Feld, B. C. (1987). The juvenile court meets the principle of offense: Punishment, treatment, and the difference it makes. *Boston University Law, 68,* 821–915.

Feld, B. C. (1989). Bad law makes hard cases: Reflections of teen-aged axe-murderers, judicial activism, and legislative default. *Law and Inequality: A Journal of Theory and Practice, 8,* 1–101.

Feld, B. C. (1990). The punitive juvenile court and the quality of procedural justice: Disjunctions between rhetoric and reality. *Crime and Delinquency, 36,* 443–466.

Feld, B. C. (1993). Juvenile (in)justice and the criminal court alternative. *Crime and Delinquency, 39,* 403–424.

Feld, B. C. (2000). Legislative exclusion of offenses from juvenile court jurisdiction: A history and critique. In J. Fagan & F. E. Zimring (Eds.), *The changing borders of juvenile justice: Transfer of adolescents to the criminal court* (pp. 83–144). Chicago: University of Chicago Press.

Griffin, P., Torbet, P., & Syzmanski, L. (1998). *Trying juveniles in adult court: An analysis of state transfer provisions.* Washington, DC: Office of Juvenile Justice and Delinquency Prevention, Office of Justice Programs, U.S. Department of Justice.

Grisso, T., & Schwartz, R. G. (2000). *Youth on trial: A developmental perspective on juvenile justice.* Chicago: University of Chicago Press.

McCarthy, F. B. (1994). The serious offender and juvenile court reform: The case for prosecutorial waiver of juvenile court jurisdiction. *Saint Louis University Law Journal, 38,* 629–671

Myers, D. L. (2001). *Excluding violent youths from juvenile court: The effectiveness of legislative waiver.* New York: LFB Scholarly.

Podkopacz, M. R., & Feld, B. C. (1996). The end of the line: An empirical study of judicial waiver. *Journal of Criminal Law and Criminology, 86,* 449–492.

Sanborn, J. B., Jr. (1994a). Certification to criminal court: The important policy questions of how, when, and why. *Crime and Delinquency, 40,* 262–281.

Sanborn, J. B., Jr. (1994b). Remnants of *parens patriae* in the adjudicatory hearing: Is a fair trial possible in juvenile court? *Crime and Delinquency, 40,* 599–615.

Sanborn, J. B., Jr. (1996). Policies regarding the prosecution of juvenile murderers: Which system and who should decide? *Law and Policy, 18,* 151–178.

Sanborn, J. B., Jr. (1998). Second-class justice, first-class punishment: The use of juvenile records in sentencing adults. *Judicature, 81,* 206–213.

Sanborn, J. B., Jr. (2000). Striking out on the first pitch in criminal court. *Barry Law Review, 1,* 7–61.

Sanborn, J. B., Jr. (2001a). A *parens patriae* figure or impartial fact finder: Policy questions and conflicts for the juvenile court judge. *Criminal Justice Policy Review, 12,* 311–332.

Sanborn, J. B., Jr. (2001b). Victims' rights in juvenile court: Has the pendulum swung too far? *Judicature, 85,* 140–146.

Sanborn, J. B., Jr. (in press). The adultification of youth. In A. V. Merlo & P. J. Benekos (Eds.), *Controversies in juvenile justice and delinquency.* Cincinnati, OH: Anderson.

Singer, S. I. (1996). *Recriminalizing delinquency: Violent juvenile crimes and juvenile justice reform.* New York: Cambridge University Press.

Snyder, H. N., & Sickmund, M. (1995). *Juvenile offenders and victims: A national report.* Washington, DC: Office of Juvenile Justice and Delinquency Prevention.

Steinberg, L., & Schwartz, R. G. (2000). Developmental psychology goes to court. In T. Grisso & R. G. Schwartz (Eds.), *Youth on trial: A developmental perspective on juvenile justice* (pp. 7–31). Chicago: University of Chicago Press.

Tannenhaus, D. S. (2000). The evolution of transfer out of the juvenile court. In J. Fagan & F. E. Zimring (Eds.), *The changing borders of juvenile justice: Transfer of adolescents to the criminal court* (pp. 13–43). Chicago: University of Chicago Press.

Torbet, P., Gable, R., Hurst, H., IV, Montgomery, I., Szymanski, L., & Thomas, D. (1996). *State responses to serious and violent juvenile crime.* Washington, DC: Office of Juvenile Justice and Delinquency Prevention.

Winner, L., Lanza-Kaduce, L., Bishop, D. M., & Frazier, C. (1997). The transfer of juveniles to criminal court: Reexamining recidivism over the long term. *Crime and Delinquency, 43,* 548–563.

Zimring, F. E. (1998). *American youth violence.* New York: Oxford University Press.

Zimring, F. E. (2000). Penal proportionality for the young offender: Notes on immaturity, capacity, and diminished responsibility. In T. Grisso & R. G. Schwartz (Eds.), *Youth on trial: A developmental perspective on juvenile justice* (pp. 27–89). Chicago: University of Chicago Press.

DISCUSSION QUESTIONS

1. Define and briefly explain judicial transfer and prosecutorial transfer.

2. For what reasons are some juvenile justice advocates opposed to exclusion?

3. Is it possible that exclusion of some chronic and violent juvenile offenders may be a way to preserve the traditional juvenile court? Explain the arguments in favor of exclusion.

4. What are the problems, according to Sanborn, with judicial transfer as opposed to exclusion?

5. What does the author recommend for additional research and developing policy regarding exclusion from juvenile court?

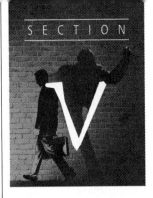

THE JUVENILE
COURT PROCESS

SECTION HIGHLIGHTS

- Juvenile Court Cases: Numbers and Trends

- Juvenile Court Officials and Their Roles

- The Juvenile Court Process

- "Blended Sentencing"

- Juvenile Court Trends and Reforms

The juvenile court process differs from the adult criminal court in several respects. We summarized the distinguishing characteristics of the two court systems in this book's Introduction. We reviewed the history and development of the juvenile court and the juvenile justice system in Section I. Readers will recall that the juvenile court in America was developed in the 19th century through the efforts of "child savers" and child advocates who recognized that children must be tried in separate courts with a different legal process than adult criminal offenders. The juvenile court was based upon the legal doctrines of *parens patriae* ("parent of the country") and *in loco parentis* ("in place of the parent"). The principle of *parens patriae* gives the court the authority over juveniles in need of guidance and protection, and the State may then act *in loco parentis* to provide guidance and make decisions concerning the best interests of the child, and to provide services in assistance to needy and wayward children who were deemed to be in need of care and supervision. It is important to have an understanding of the origins of the court and the foundations upon which it is based as we compare recent developments and trends in the juvenile court process. This section examines the changes in the juvenile court process and the developments that have brought juvenile offenders many of the same due process rights as adults in criminal court, the adjudication process, dispositional alternatives available to the juvenile court, and recent changes and trends toward a more punitive approach with juvenile offenders that is similar to policies and punishment in criminal court.

▧ Juvenile Court Cases: Numbers and Trends

In 2004, U.S. juvenile courts processed an estimated 1,660,700 delinquency cases that involved juveniles charged with criminal law violations (*OJJDP Statistical Briefing Book,* 2007). The delinquency court cases by offense types in 2004 are summarized in Table V-1. These estimates are based on data from more than 2,001 juvenile courts from 39 states, with jurisdiction over 77% of the U.S. juvenile population (*OJJDP Statistical Briefing Book,* 2007). The number of delinquency cases handled by juvenile courts increased 44% since 1985; but between 1995 and 2004 and 1999 and 2004, the nation's juvenile court delinquency caseload decreased 7% and 2%, respectively. The number of person offense cases increased dramatically (120%) since 1985, and saw modest increases (2% and 4%, respectively) since 1995 and 1999. Most property offense cases have decreased since 1985, drug law violation cases have increased, and public order offense cases have increased (*OJJDP Statistical Briefing Book,* 2007).

Gender. The vast majority of the delinquency cases handled by juvenile courts continued to involve males, but the female proportion of cases increased from 20% to 26% between 1993 and 2002. Females accounted for 28% (109,700) of person offense cases, 26% (164,500) of property offenses cases, 18% (35,100) of drug offense cases, and 28% (113,800) of public order offense cases (Stahl, 2006, p. 1).

Age. A total of 58% of the delinquency cases processed in 2002 involved a juvenile younger than 16 at referral, compared with 66% in 1990. In 2002, juveniles younger than 16 were responsible for 64% (249,800) of person offense cases, 60% (376,200) of property offense cases, 41% (80,100) of drug law violation cases, and 55% (224,300) of public order offense cases (Stahl, 2006, p. 1).

Race. In 2002, approximately 78% of the juvenile population in the United States was white and 16% was black. (Juveniles of Hispanic ethnicity are usually included in the white racial category.) White juveniles were involved in 67% (1,086,700) of the delinquency cases that juvenile courts handled, and black juveniles were involved in 29% (473,100). White juveniles were involved in 60% (233,700) of person offense cases, 68% (427,700) of property offense cases, 76% (146,300) of drug law violation cases, and 68% (279,100) of public order offense cases. Black juveniles were involved in 37% (141,900) of person offense cases, 28% (172,000) of property offense cases, 21% (41,400) of drug law violation cases, and 29% (117,800) of public order offense cases (Stahl, 2006, p. 2). The racial profile of delinquency cases overall was approximately the same in 1985 and 2002, although some of the general offense categories had noticeable changes. The proportion of black youth in juvenile court cases increased slightly from 23% in 1985 to 28% in 2002 for property offenses and from

| Table V-1 | Juvenile Court Cases by Offense Type, 2004* | | | |

		Percentage Change		
Most Serious Offense	Number of Cases	1985–2004	1995–2004	1999–2004
Total	**1,660,700**	**44%**	**−7%**	**−2%**
Total Person Offenses	**400,700**	**120**	**2**	**4**
Criminal homicide	1,700	42	−42	−16
Forcible rape	4,200	18	−27	6
Robbery	21,100	−15	−50	−18
Aggravated assault	44,600	35	−39	−10
Simple assault	284,300	181	23	11
Other violent sex offense	15,800	95	34	33
Other person offense	29,000	170	12	−17
Total Property Offenses	**603,200**	**−14**	**−33**	**−14**
Burglary	95,500	−33	−35	−16
Larceny-theft	278,300	−15	−34	−12
Motor vehicle theft	33,900	−12	−37	−12
Arson	8,500	20	−26	−7
Vandalism	96,300	13	−23	−9
Trespassing	5,700	−6	−25	−13
Stolen property offense	19,400	−29	−48	−27
Other property offense	20,700	17	−40	−31
Drug law violations	**193,700**	**159**	**19**	**4**
Public order offenses	**463,100**	**141**	**41**	**10**
Obstruction of justice	216,500	228	70	8
Disorderly conduct	121,600	174	35	30
Weapons offense	41,000	110	−12	2
Liquor law violations	29,000	53	78	22
Nonviolent sex offenses	13,800	11	48	14
Other public order offenses	41,000	33	5	−20

Sources: Adapted from Snyder & Sickmund, 2006, p. 157; and *OJJDP Statistical Briefing Book,* 2007.

*Estimated numbers and percentages. Details may not add to totals because of rounding. Percentage-change calculations are based on unrounded numbers.

21% to 29% for public order cases (Snyder & Sickmund, 2006, p. 163). Delinquency case-loads for black juveniles contained a greater proportion of person offenses than did case-loads for white juveniles and those of other races. In 2002, the delinquency case rate for blacks (94) was more than two times the rate for whites (44) and just over three times the rate for youth of other races (31) (Snyder & Sickmund, 2006, p. 163). The authors of the readings in this section address the factors that are believed to account for the disproportionate representation of black juveniles in the court process.

⊠ Juvenile Court Officials and Their Roles

The Juvenile Court Judge. The juvenile court was originally developed as an informal *quasi-judicial* process that incorporated more civil procedures than criminal court procedures. The judge was viewed as a "father figure" who presumably acted in "the best interests of the child." The first juvenile courts were private hearings not open to the public, informal, and nonadversarial. Julian W. Mack (1909), one of the nation's first juvenile court judges, emphasized the juvenile court judge's significant role in carrying out the court's benevolent, *parens patriae* philosophy. Ted Rubin, a former juvenile court judge, has noted that the ideal juvenile court judge would have

> a special interest in the legal and social problems of children and families, a special sensitivity toward minority groups, an appreciation of different life styles, an absence of rigid moral standards, a basic knowledge of the social sciences and the life experiences that confront court clients in their day to day living, and an ability to listen and to communicate with children and families. (Rubin, 1985, p. 366)

In reality, few juvenile court judges have all these qualities, but there is general agreement that judges should reflect the different purposes of juvenile court and the differences between juvenile and adult offenders.

Juvenile court judges were not originally required to have a law degree. After the U.S. Supreme Court in the 1960s and 1970s required due process procedures, the deficiencies of nonlawyer judges became readily apparent. Court rulings following the legal challenges in *Kent* and *Gault* brought an emphasis on legal formality and a more adversarial process. The changes in the adjudication process made it clear that judges must possess some legal training in order to perform their duties adequately. The National Advisory Committee on Criminal Justice Standards and Goals (1976) acknowledged that juvenile courts had relied on "quasi-judicial personnel" (referred to variably as "referees," "commissioners," or "masters") to assume much of the workload of juvenile court judges such as detention hearings and hearings resulting in community supervision. The Advisory Committee recommended that all juvenile court proceedings involving detention, shelter care, waiver, arraignment, adjudicatory, and dispositional hearings should be heard only by a judge. The Committee also recommended several qualifications of family court judges, including an interest in the problems of children and families; sensitivity to their respective legal rights; awareness of the fields of psychiatry, psychology, and social work; familiarity with local minority groups and the influence of cultural values on family behavior and child rearing; responsibility for leadership in developing services for children and families (1976, p. 284).

Juvenile Court Prosecutors

The original juvenile courts were informal and nonadversarial proceedings and therefore typically did not have prosecuting attorneys to present the evidence against the juvenile offender in court. Intake probation officers generally had the authority to determine whether to file a petition for delinquency. Police officers often performed the role equivalent to a prosecutor's, and some police departments had court officers who were assigned the role of presenting the charges and supporting evidence in the informal hearing process. The U.S. Supreme Court cases of *Kent* and *Gault* in the 1960s brought more formality to the juvenile court process, as the Court affirmed that a juvenile has the right to be represented by an attorney. Juvenile courts became more formal and adversarial in most jurisdictions after the demand for more due process rights, so defense counsel became a more common presence in juvenile court hearings. With the presence of defense counsel and a more formal hearing process came the recognition of the need to have prosecuting attorneys to represent the State in presenting evidence to support the petition for delinquency. The National Advisory Committee on Standards and Goals (1976) recommended that the prosecutor's office should have one or more attorneys devoted to representing the State in family court. Attorneys assigned to juvenile court from the prosecutor's office are generally the youngest attorneys with the least experience. Juvenile court prosecutors may then be reassigned to adult criminal court as they gain more experience. Juvenile court judges in fact tend to constrain overzealous prosecutors and defense attorneys from taking an adversarial approach similar to that in criminal courts.

Juvenile court prosecutors do have a great deal of discretionary authority in cases referred by the police department. We noted in the previous section on court intake and detention that the prosecutor has replaced the intake probation officer in deciding whether or not to file a petition for delinquency. The prosecutor, however, will consider the intake officer's recommendation of diversion or unofficial supervision for first-time offenders with no prior referrals who are involved in minor offenses. The decision whether or not to prosecute cases is determined by factors such as probable cause, the quality of evidence in the case, and due process issues. As we noted in the previous section on waiver and transfer, lawmakers have limited some prosecutorial discretion through legislative exclusion or mandatory waiver of cases involving serious and violent crimes.

Defense Attorneys. We have noted the relative absence of defense counsel for juveniles until the U.S. Supreme Court cases of *Kent* and *Gault.* Kent (charged with serious offenses of burglary and rape) was interrogated without being warned of his right to counsel and the right to remain silent, and he appeared before a juvenile court judge without legal representation. Justice Abe Fortas, in writing for the Court majority, emphasized that the status of being a boy did not justify what amounted to a "kangaroo court" (383 U.S. 541, 1966). The Court ordered that juveniles, like adults, had the right to be represented by counsel. In contrast to Morris Kent, Gerald Gault was charged with making an obscene phone call and, following a hearing without an attorney or testimony from the complainant, was sent to the Arizona Industrial School. The disposition greatly exceeded the maximum sentence he would have received as an adult: a fine of between $5 and $50, or a maximum of 2 months in jail. The Court majority in *Gault* held that juveniles must receive most of the same due process rights as adults, including notice of charges, right to counsel, and right to confront and cross-examine accusing witnesses (387 U.S. 41, 1967).

Defense counsel may be either private attorneys, court-appointed attorneys, or public defenders. Private attorneys may be retained personally by the family, or be court appointed and receive their fees from the county or state government. Public defenders are state employees who specialize in providing legal counsel for lower-income persons who qualify as indigents and unable to afford a private attorney. Most jurisdictions have either a court-appoint system or public defender office. Because of their experience in representing clients in juvenile and criminal court, public defenders are generally the most qualified to represent juveniles. Public defenders, however, usually have large caseloads that limit the amount of time for conferring with and advising clients before court hearings. Private attorneys, whether retained or court appointed, may specialize in areas of law other than criminal or juvenile court matters, and therefore may not provide the most qualified defense counsel.

Research on the right to counsel for juveniles has examined three important questions: First, whether most juveniles actually receive the assistance of legal counsel; second, whether juveniles can make a knowledgeable and informed waiver of their right to counsel; and third, whether representation by a defense attorney makes a difference in juvenile court. First, the constitutional right to counsel that the U.S. Supreme Court ordered for juveniles is *not* being applied in practice in many states and jurisdictions throughout the United States. Forty years after the U.S. Supreme Court cases of *Kent* and *Gault,* the presence of defense counsel in juvenile court varies greatly among states and among juvenile courts within the same state. In many states fewer than half of juveniles receive the assistance of legal counsel (Feld, 1999, p. 125). In Minnesota a majority of the juveniles in court appeared without counsel in the 1980s and 1990s (Feld, 1989, 1999). The American Bar Association (ABA; 1995) reported that many children throughout the United States go through the juvenile justice system without the benefit of legal counsel.

The second question relates to waiver of the right to counsel. A total of 25 jurisdictions require the presence of defense counsel for juveniles in certain circumstances, such as when institutional commitment is a possibility or there is an issue with the parents (Sanborn & Salerno, 2005, p. 319). Parental issues include cases of parental abuse, parents unwilling to retain counsel when they are financially able to do so, or similar adversarial relationships between parent and child. In such cases the judge is likely to appoint a *guardian ad litem* (an attorney appointed to advocate for and protect the child's best interests). Juveniles in nearly all (43) states are allowed to waive their right to counsel (Sanborn & Salerno, 2005, p. 320). The question is whether juveniles can make a knowledgeable, informed, and voluntary waiver of their right to counsel. Juvenile court procedures in several states work on the presumption that juveniles cannot intelligently waive their right to counsel. Judges are required to find, by clear and convincing evidence after questioning the youth, that the juvenile understands the right and the implications of waiver; that the waiver is made freely, voluntarily, and intelligently; and that the parent or guardian agrees with the juvenile's waiver (see Sanborn & Salerno, 2005, p. 320). Research has documented juveniles' limited understanding of their due process rights (Feld, 1999, p. 129). Grisso (1981) studied the legal and psychological competence of children and youth and questioned whether many of them have the maturity, knowledge, and understanding to waive their rights. He found that many juveniles had a poor knowledge and understanding of their legal rights, did not clearly understand the role of an attorney or the meaning of legal counsel and advice, and few understood that they had a right to an attorney before and during interrogation or during court hearings (Grisso, 1981). Lawrence (1983) replicated a part of Grisso's research in a metropolitan juvenile court and found that fewer than 20% of juveniles had a good understanding of their legal rights and the role of an attorney in providing legal counsel. The findings raise serious questions as to whether juveniles can make an informed and intelligent waiver of their rights to legal counsel. In a study of the right to counsel in juvenile court, Feld (1989) questioned whether the typical *Miranda* advisory and judges' acceptance of juveniles' waiver of rights under the "totality of circumstances" is sufficient to ensure a valid waiver of counsel.

The third question regarding defense attorneys in juvenile court is whether they make a difference. We noted above that juveniles may receive legal counsel and representation by either a private attorney, a court-appointed attorney, or a public defender. The quality of defense counsel is often compromised by attorneys' lack of training in juvenile law and the court process, by their lack of experience, or by the attorneys' caseload size and time available for each client. ABA (1995) reported that many juveniles who were represented by counsel had attorneys who were untrained in the complexities of juvenile court matters and failed to provide competent legal representation. The ABA surveyed public defender offices, court-appointed attorneys, and children's law centers and found the quality of legal counsel to be lacking. The caseloads of public defenders and the conditions under which they worked often greatly compromised the quality of legal counsel and representation they could provide their juvenile clients in court (ABA, 1995; see also Feld, 1999, pp. 131–134). The failure of most jurisdictions to comply with juveniles' constitutional right to counsel has not gone unnoticed. The American Bar Association Center on Children and the Law (2004) reported on developments among states in providing public defenders for juveniles in court. The ABA is particularly concerned that ethnic and racial minorities who tend to be disproportionately represented in juvenile court are also the least likely to have defense counsel.

Research on whether defense counsel makes a difference in the court disposition is contrary to expectations. The presence of counsel has been found to be associated with more severe dispositions. In an analysis of court data in six states, Feld (1988) found that juveniles with defense counsel were more likely to receive placement outside the home or secure confinement than juveniles without attorneys. Recent studies produced similar findings. Guevara, Spohn, and Herz (2004) found that the presence of a defense attorney (especially a private attorney) had a negative impact and resulted in more severe dispositions than youth without an attorney. Youth with a private attorney were the least likely to have the charges dismissed and the most likely to be committed to a secure facility. Guevara and her associates (2004) concluded that the findings of their study "provide evidence that calls into question the basic and fundamental right to counsel in juvenile court" (p. 366). The article by Guevara, Spohn, and Herz has been included as a reading in this section.

Juvenile Probation Officer. We have discussed in Section III (Juvenile Detention and Court Intake) the role of the intake probation officer in decisions regarding detention and alternatives to court referral, such as diversion or informal adjustment. Probation officers exercise what has been called a quasi-judicial role in the juvenile court process, including: (1) at court intake, (2) in recommending and enforcing conditions of probation, and (3) in reporting probation violations and initiating revocation procedures (Czajkoski, 1973). Juvenile probation officers, through their involvement with youth in the prejudicial process, often supplement the role of attorneys in providing information about legal rights and the court process (Lawrence, 1983). Their role as court officers has not always been well respected by judges and attorneys in some metropolitan jurisdictions, leading to the claim that probation officers were mere "judicial civil

▲ **Photo V-1**   Prosecuting and defense attorneys consult with the judge during a hearing in process. (© CORBIS)

servants" who lacked professional status in the court and whose role in the presentence decision was overrated (Blumberg, 1979). A study of probation officers in a southwestern state found that while they were not given equal status by judges and attorneys in the judicial process, the majority of probation officers did view themselves as professionals who provided important information in the sentencing process, and who had a positive and respected working relationship with judges and attorneys (Lawrence, 1984). Most research on probation officer roles has been on the supervision, surveillance, and treatment functions (Latessa & Allen, 2003), but the officers' role in the juvenile court process is important. Probation officers prepare a predisposition report (PDR, comparable to a PSI, or presentence investigation) to assist the judge in the predisposition decision following adjudication of a juvenile (discussed below). The juvenile probation officer may play a more critical role in the disposition than a probation officer in adult sentencing in criminal court because of the treatment orientation of the juvenile court (Sanborn & Salerno, 2005). Juvenile probation officers routinely spend from 1 to 3 hours or more in meetings with a juvenile and his or her parents prior to the court disposition hearing. They acquire a deeper level of knowledge and insight on the juvenile's background and problems related to the delinquent behavior than either the judge or attorneys involved in the case. Research on the roles of judges, prosecutors, defense attorneys, and probation officers, involving 100 court workers in urban, suburban, and rural courts, found that most probation officers conducted thorough investigations and presented comprehensive predisposition reports (Sanborn, 1996). Because the disposition decision relies on a multitude of factors ranging from prior legal history and severity of the crime, to individual and social extralegal factors including family background, attitude, school attendance, and behavior, Sanborn (1996) was unable to determine the actual factors that most influenced the disposition decision. It remains clear, however, that the probation officer's role in the courtroom is important, and that the judge's disposition is influenced by the probation officer assigned to the case and his or her orientation, experience, and the extent to which the investigation and predisposition report is complete and thorough (Sanborn & Salerno, 2005, p. 358). We have included the research report by Sanborn (1996) in the readings in this section.

⊠ The Juvenile Court Process

The juvenile court process consists of two separate parts and therefore is often referred to as a "bifurcated hearing." Juvenile court hearings are considered "quasi-civil" and not criminal proceedings. Juveniles found guilty are not convicted of a crime but are adjudicated delinquent. Since the U.S. Supreme Court decisions in *Gault* and *Winship,* juveniles are entitled to most of the same rights as adults in criminal court. Juvenile hearings are nevertheless more informal than criminal court and except for cases involving older, chronic, or serious juvenile offenders are generally closed to the public (see Sanborn & Salerno, 2005, p. 332). The *adjudication hearing* is the fact-finding part of the court process, comparable to the conviction phase of a criminal court hearing. Before hearing any evidence the judge will first determine if the juvenile understands his or her rights, and juveniles not represented by an attorney will be asked whether they understand that right and wish to waive the right to counsel. Procedures vary among jurisdictions, but the typical juvenile hearing is brief and quite perfunctory given the lengthy court dockets and limited time available. When the judge is satisfied that the juvenile understands the rights and is willing to waive a full hearing (presentation of evidence, testimony, confrontation, and cross-examination of witnesses), the charges and petition for delinquency are generally read by the prosecuting attorney. The judge asks the juvenile if he or she understands the charges and is willing to plead guilty and accept the adjudication of delinquency. Adjudication is based solely on the present charge, *not* on previous arrests, charges, adjudication, or any extralegal information.

Disposition Hearing. Once the juvenile has been adjudicated delinquent, the next stage in the court process is the disposition, comparable to the sentencing phase in adult criminal court. Disposition decisions are based on offense severity, prior offense history, and individual and social factors. The court relies on a juvenile probation officer's *predisposition report* (PDR, comparable to the presentence investigation or PSI in criminal court sentencing hearings). The probation officer's report is based on interviews with the child and the parents; it may include information from school officials, social service agencies, and mental health professionals. The report may include information on the child's family history and quality of parental supervision; peer relationships; attendance, grades, and behavior in school; participation in school and community activities; and previous court or police involvement. In contested hearings or cases that may result in institutional commitment, the disposition hearing may include testimony and cross-examination of the probation officer and any other persons who have provided information in the report. Juveniles may have legal counsel and may challenge the facts and information presented in the predisposition report. The most important factors in the disposition hearing are the seriousness of the offense and the juvenile's prior record. The social background information contained in the probation officer's report and the dispositional options available to the court are also important factors in the court disposition.

The *dispositional alternatives* available to juvenile courts vary considerably depending on the correctional services, resources, and residential placements that are available. The primary dispositional alternatives include the following:

1. *Dismissal.* Even though there may have been sufficient evidence to adjudicate a juvenile, a judge can dismiss the case if there is insufficient evidence that the child needs formal supervision by the court.

2. *Court Diversion Alternatives.* Many state juvenile codes include provisions that allow for suspension of the formal adjudication or disposition process, and the juvenile may be supervised under *informal adjustment* by a community agency (preadjudication) or by a probation officer (predispositional). The case may be terminated after 6 months or less of successful adjustment, or, otherwise, may be returned to court for adjudication and disposition. *Mediation* is an alternative for resolving conflicts and disputes outside the courtroom. Mediation can take place as an alternative to trial and adjudication, or after a finding of guilt to determine the disposition and often to establish restitution conditions. The Victim Offender Reconciliation Program is a form of mediation that operated in a number of courts (Coates, 1990). There is evidence that offenders involved in mediation are more likely to satisfactorily fulfill restitution conditions and are less likely to reoffend. Mediation and conflict resolution are examples of the "restorative justice" emphasis in juvenile justice (Bazemore & Umbreit, 1995).

3. *Probation.* The child may be released to the parents with orders to report to a probation officer and comply with specified conditions and rules of probation supervision. The juvenile may be ordered to pay restitution or complete community service restitution, or to participate in counseling or treatment programs for specific identified needs. We will discuss this in more detail in the next section.

4. *Placement in Community Residential Programs.* The court may order placement in a residential facility if there is evidence of inadequate parental supervision or poor parent–child relations. Such placements are short-term and in nonsecure residential programs. The court may also order short-term placement in a mental health facility or a residential drug and alcohol treatment facility.

5. *Institutional Commitment.* Juveniles who are considered a risk to public safety may be committed to more secure facilities, often called training schools or juvenile correctional facilities. These are generally administered and operated by the state, and range from minimum-security schools with open campuses and cottagelike settings to medium- or maximum-security correctional facilities for juveniles or young adults. We will discuss this dispositional option in more detail in Section VI.

⬚ "Blended Sentencing"

In Section IV we discussed waiver of juvenile court jurisdiction and transfer of juveniles to criminal court. The process of waiver and transfer is intended primarily for serious or chronic juvenile offenders for whom commitment to a juvenile facility does not provide adequate security or punishment. We noted the problems and consequences of waiver, particularly the committing of juvenile-age offenders to adult correctional institutions. Several states have developed sentencing reforms that are alternatives to waiver and transfer of juvenile offenders to adult criminal court. The most prominent is referred to as "blended sentencing." Under these laws serious juvenile offenders are sentenced to a juvenile or adult correctional facility after being adjudicated in juvenile court or convicted in criminal court (Torbet et al., 1996). The criteria for selection of cases appropriate for this option are generally the same as for transfer: offense seriousness, age, or a combination of both. Five models of blended sentencing have been developed in various states, and they differ primarily on whether the juvenile court or criminal court retains jurisdiction and responsibility for adjudicating the case (see Torbet et al., 1996, pp. 11–13). The most prominent example of blended sentencing is referred to as "extended juvenile jurisdiction" (EJJ) or "extended juvenile jurisdiction prosecution" (EJJP) (Sanborn & Salerno, 2005, p. 295). An EJJ proceeding is generally used for a serious or violent juvenile offender who would meet the criteria for transfer to criminal court. In processing a case as EJJ, a youth is given a hearing before a juvenile court judge to determine the appropriateness of transferring the case to criminal court. The disposition in an EJJ case is a combined or "blended" sentence. The youth is given both a juvenile court disposition and an adult sentence, but the adult sentence is stayed or suspended and the juvenile court disposition is implemented. If the juvenile complies with the requirements of the juvenile court disposition, the adult sentence is dismissed. If the juvenile violates those terms (through a new arrest or violation of probation or institutional rules), the adult sentence may be imposed following a hearing to document the failure (Sanborn & Salerno, 2005).

The state of Minnesota added an EJJ option as part of sentencing reforms in 1994. The legislative intent was to give juveniles who have committed serious or repeat offenses one last chance at success in the juvenile system, with the threat of criminal sanctions "hanging over their heads" if they reoffend (Torbet, Griffin, Hurst, & MacKenzie, 2000, p. xv). The Minnesota statute (Section 260B.130) provides for the adult criminal sentence to be stayed on the condition that the juvenile not violate the provisions of the disposition order and not commit a new offense. The juvenile disposition in most cases is commitment to a juvenile correctional facility or placement in a private residential treatment center, followed by a period of aftercare supervision until the young offender's 21st birthday. If the juvenile violates the conditions of the stayed sentence, typically by committing a new offense, the court may revoke the stay and require that the offender be taken into custody. The juvenile is then given written notice of the reasons for the revocation of the stayed sentence, and may have a hearing with representation of legal counsel if the revocation is challenged. If there are sufficient reasons to revoke the stay of the suspended adult sentence, then the court treats the offender as an adult and the adult sentence is implemented, with no credit given for the time served in juvenile facility custody (Minn. Stat. 260B.130, subd. 5). The extended juvenile jurisdiction alternative has a number of advantages over immediate transfer to criminal court (Lawrence, 2007, p. 233). First, the young offender is placed in a juvenile correctional facility rather than the "criminogenic" environment of adult correctional facilities. Second, the juvenile has the opportunity to receive educational and treatment services that are more available in juvenile corrections than in adult corrections. Third, the juvenile is given another chance to prove that he or she may be "amenable to treatment" in the juvenile system and not pose a risk to public safety.

Blended sentencing has been scrutinized by critics of juvenile sentencing reforms. Zimring (2005) has referred to the Minnesota blended sentencing statute as "one of the most dauntingly complicated in the history of criminal sentencing," and added that blended sentences may be "intentional efforts to design systems that sound much tougher just after conviction than they turn out to be in . . . time served in custody" (Zimring, 2005, p. 148). Research on the results of blended sentencing or EJJ is limited. Initial results indicate that the policies do provide an alternative to juvenile transfer to criminal court, but may not significantly reduce the number of youthful offenders who are incarcerated. Podkopacz and Feld (2001) found that nearly half (48%) of youth who received an EJJ sentence were revoked, and a majority of the revocations were not the result of new criminal charges. Judges sent nearly as many youths to jail or prison following EJJ revocations as they did directly through certification proceedings. Additional research is needed to evaluate the effects of extended juvenile jurisdiction prosecution and whether the results are significantly different from sentences resulting from juvenile transfer.

Juvenile Court Trends and Reforms

The juvenile court has come under criticism from two sides: those who want more control and punishment to hold juvenile offenders accountable, and those who point to social problems that contribute to delinquency. Those who advocate for more punishment contend that the court is "soft on crime" when it adopts the traditional goal of treating juvenile offenders rather than holding them accountable for their crimes. Crime control advocates believe that giving repeat offenders too many chances through diversion programs and community treatment alternatives sends a message to them and the community that we do not take juvenile crime seriously. Juvenile training schools, in their opinion, should be more like secure correctional facilities and more juveniles should be confined for longer sentences in a more punitive setting. Those who argue for harsher punishment generally believe that crime is a function of individual choice and poor moral character and that the answer to crime reduction lies primarily in deterrence through tougher sentences (Garland, 2001).

Criminologists, on the other hand, view juvenile delinquency as a function of individual and social variables that place many juveniles at risk of deviant and delinquent behavior (Gottfredson & Hirschi, 1990; Hirschi, 1969). Crime is a function of social and economic factors and not simply a matter of rational choice. Therefore, hoping to deter delinquency through tougher laws and threats of harsher punishment the same way as criminal justice policy is aimed at adult offenders is unlikely to be effective. Criminologists and juvenile justice advocates contend that delinquency prevention must address the social problems and lack of equal opportunities and resources for disadvantaged youth that place many children and youth at risk of involvement in gangs, drug use, and delinquency (Howell, 2003). Critics of the get-tough approach claim that tougher sentencing and transfers to criminal court often aggravate the problems and that institutional confinement in detention centers and training schools serves only to criminalize juveniles further (Garland, 2001). Judicial critics denounce the lack of procedural safeguards and uniformity in the informal juvenile court process, where many juveniles receive more punitive sanctions than adults for minor offenses that would result in no more than a fine in adult court.

Practitioners in the juvenile justice system also express dissatisfaction with current juvenile court policies and disagree among themselves. Police and prosecutors want tougher sanctions for juvenile offenders and fewer "second chances" through diversion programs and community alternatives. Probation officers contend that a large group of juvenile offenders have special needs that can be met through treatment and supervision in the community. Given their knowledge of the social and family background of referred juveniles, probation officers are reluctant to take a punitive approach except as a last resort after treatment alternatives have failed.

The criticisms leveled against the juvenile court from all sides stem in part from the judicial and legislative changes that have transformed the juvenile court from what was originally intended as a social rehabilitation welfare agency into what Feld (1999) has referred to as a "scaled-down, second-class criminal court for young people" (p. 286). The criticisms also underscore the reality that the juvenile court cannot be both a court of law and an agency for individual and social change. Probation officers, attorneys, and judges who see hundreds of young offenders pass through the courts each week readily acknowledge the numerous social problems that characterize the youth, none of which are their own fault. Most juvenile offenders and their families encounter lack of proper nutrition and health care, housing problems, lack of employment opportunities, and unequal access to quality schools. The sole reason juveniles appear before the court, however, is for the commission of a crime, so any compassion or mitigation of a disposition based on a youth's social disadvantages is secondary to their legal status as young law violators (see Feld, 1999, p. 295). The juvenile court's first responsibility is to impose legal sanctions and attempt to prevent further delinquent behavior, but it cannot fulfill the traditional promise of juvenile rehabilitation (Feld, 1999, p. 296; Grubb & Lazerson, 1982, p. 179). Changing many of the conditions that lead to juvenile delinquency is not the responsibility of the juvenile court, but lies with society, families, schools, other social institutions, and government social policies.

Juvenile Court Changes. The juvenile court has undergone significant changes and reforms. The reform movement began with U.S. Supreme Court decisions in *Kent, In re Gault,* and *In re Winship* in the 1960s, in which the Court required most of the same due process protections provided for adults in criminal courts. Juveniles were provided notice of the charges, right to counsel, and protection against self-incrimination and unlawful searches. Another step in juvenile court reform involved efforts to remove status offenders from formal adjudication and commitment to detention centers and juvenile institutions. Juvenile lockups and training schools housed many youths whose only "crime" was disobeying their parents, running away, or school truancy. Advocates of such practices argued that involvement in status offenses was the first step toward more serious delinquency, and thus early intervention might prevent serious delinquency. Opponents noted the unfairness of punishing youths for minor deviant behavior, and voiced concerns about the adverse effects on status offenders being housed with older, hardcore juvenile offenders. The President's Commission on Law Enforcement and Administration of Justice (1967b) recommended narrowing the range of offenses going before the juvenile court, and groups such as the American Bar Association–Institute of Judicial Administration (1982) called for an end to adjudicating and incarcerating status offenders in juvenile institutions.

Despite the changes that were implemented following *Gault* and *Kent,* children and youth appearing before juvenile court still do not have the same constitutional safeguards as adults in criminal court (Feld, 1999, p. 287; Sanborn & Salerno, 2005, p. 503). Juvenile laws still allow officials to intervene in noncriminal behavior, including incorrigibility, running away, and truancy. Parents may lose custody as their delinquent child is placed in state custody for placement in a juvenile facility. The juvenile justice system may retain control of children beyond their 18th birthday, when they become adults. Juvenile justice advocates would point to the positive side of the system, however. Juvenile justice interventions are justified based on multiple purposes that range from prevention, to treatment, to public safety. Preventing status offenders from becoming more serious delinquents is still considered a viable purpose of the court, since many believe that status offenses such as parental disobedience, leaving home without permission, and school truancy are precursors of delinquent behavior. Juvenile treatment programs that focus on substance abuse prevention, education, and skill development have been effective in reducing delinquency. Finally, the need for crime control and emphasis on public safety remains true for chronic and violent juvenile offenders.

Abolish or "Rehabilitate" the Juvenile Court? The current focus of discussion concerning juvenile court reform revolves around the very purpose of the juvenile court. The question at issue is whether the primary purpose of the juvenile court is for punishment or for treatment. Most U.S. states have revised their juvenile codes and redefined the purpose of the juvenile court, de-emphasizing rehabilitation and placing more importance on public protection and safety (Feld, 1995; Torbet et al., 1996). Barry Feld (1993) has argued that judicial and legislative changes have "criminalized" the juvenile court. The juvenile court reforms have altered the court's jurisdiction over status offenders, who are diverted from the system, and serious offenders, who are increasingly transferred to adult criminal court. He contends that there are fewer differences between the two courts. Following the tradition of criminal courts, juvenile courts now tend to punish youths for their offenses rather than treat them for their needs (Feld, 1993, p. 197). Beyond being punished for their crimes, however, Feld argues that the procedural safeguards that are standard in criminal courts would be beneficial to juveniles. Juvenile offenders receive an inferior quality of justice in juvenile courts, and this practice has been rationalized and justified because "they are only children" (1993, p. 267). Feld believes that a separate juvenile court must be based on more than simply a treatment-versus-punishment rationale, and he contends that "the current juvenile court provides neither therapy nor justice and cannot be rehabilitated" (Feld, 1999, p. 297).

Feld has therefore argued for abolition of the juvenile court as we know it. A more formal criminal court hearing would ensure that juvenile offenders receive the same due process safeguards and constitutional rights as adults in criminal court. Juveniles would be treated differently only at the sentencing phase, when they would receive a "youth discount" in consideration of their lower level of maturity and culpability (Feld, 1999, p. 317). The concept of a youth discount is not new or unique. Other juvenile justice policy groups, such as the American Bar Association–Institute of Judicial Administration (1980), have recommended a similar policy. The ABA–IJA noted that age is a relevant factor in determining the youth's level of responsibility for breaking the law, and in establishing an appropriate sentence or disposition in juvenile court (p. 35). In addition to a "youth discount" in sentencing, Feld (1999) recommended that youths who are sentenced to an institution be placed in separate correctional facilities for youthful offenders (p. 326). (We will discuss juvenile corrections in Section VI.)

Abolition of the juvenile court is unlikely in the near future, but juvenile justice experts welcome the ongoing reforms and agree that more changes are needed. Supporters of the current juvenile court acknowledge that juveniles receive "unequal" and "dual" processing in court: not the same quality of due process as adults, and for the purpose of both punishment and rehabilitation (Sanborn & Salerno, 2005). They also emphasize that not everything about juvenile justice is negative or unfair, especially when juvenile courts do pursue the "best interests" of the youthful offender and make positive efforts to provide beneficial interventions and programs aimed at offender change. The juvenile court in most cases does take into account the child's needs and risks, and aims to arrive at a disposition that will best facilitate offender change and public safety. Juvenile justice still does focus on both the youthful offender and the offense. "In short, juvenile justice is *still* largely about who the youth is (in addition to what the youth has done)" (Sanborn & Salerno, 2005, p. 503). The concept of individualized justice does risk differential treatment according to gender, race, and social class despite the intention of a court disposition based on perceived risks or needs of youthful offenders. Sanborn and Salerno (2005, p. 504) suggest that maintaining the rehabilitative purpose of juvenile court may require acceptance of some unequal processing in order to assist families who cannot or will not help resolve their child's problems. This is not to say that juvenile court dispositions based on race are acceptable, however, but that racial minorities and lower-class youth who come before the court often have problems for which resources and services available through the court may provide some relief.

The juvenile justice system must be vigilant in preventing the influence of racism in differential sentencing of juvenile offenders. The federal government, through the Office of Juvenile Justice and Delinquency Prevention, has made the elimination of disproportionate minority confinement a high priority. Feld (1999, 2003) has repeatedly emphasized the tendency of the individualized juvenile justice system to produce racial disparities in sentencing youthful offenders. Those who support the juvenile court believe that it can still provide a fair and just legal process and rehabilitative services better than would be available in the criminal court (Sanborn & Salerno, 2005). The majority of juvenile offenders—those who have not committed serious, violent crimes and who do not have lengthy records—will continue to benefit from the treatment-oriented juvenile court. For violent and chronic juvenile offenders, the options of transfer and blended sentencing are still available. Correctional and treatment services available as juvenile court dispositions are more properly tailored to meet the needs of most juvenile offenders. Professionals in the juvenile justice system have responded to evaluation research and have begun to develop new and more effective juvenile corrections programs and intervention strategies (Bishop, 2004, p. 641). The National Council of Juvenile and Family Court Judges (2005) has responded to the need to analyze the practices and results of the juvenile process and to identify areas for improvement. With support from the federal Office of Juvenile Justice and Delinquency Prevention (OJJDP), this national organization of juvenile and family court judges has developed resource guidelines that are directed at improving court practices in juvenile delinquency cases. The guidelines will assist juvenile courts in assessing current practices, identify areas in need of improvement, and help in planning and working toward positive change. The guidelines direct courts to a renewed focus on improving court handling of juvenile delinquency cases, innovative community-based collaborative responses to juvenile crime and delinquency, and expanding professional networks for improving government responses to at-risk youth (National Council of Juvenile and Family Court Judges, 2005, p. 11).

The public looks to the police and the courts to solve the nation's juvenile crime problem. As juvenile crime has become more rampant, and a disproportionate number of young people commit violent crimes, citizens have demanded tougher laws from their legislators. In an effort to show that "something is being done," legislators have enacted more severe punishment for juvenile offenders. It is well to remember, however, that there are "limits to the criminal sanction" (Packer, 1975). Police and the courts cannot prevent crime or the root causes of juvenile delinquency. They can only respond to criminal violations after they occur. Focusing all of our attention on laws and their enforcement is not an adequate approach to reducing the social and family problems that lead to juvenile delinquency (see Feld, 1995, pp. 980–982). As long as society relies solely on tougher laws and their enforcement to respond to juvenile crime, we are unlikely to see any changes in the current trends of increasing numbers of young people who are committing crimes. Juvenile courts and justice officials will continue to respond to the juvenile crime problem, but social institutions such as the family, schools, and community agencies are essential for reducing and preventing juvenile delinquency.

SUMMARY

- The number of delinquency cases in juvenile courts in the United States has increased more than 40% in the past 20 years, but decreased 11% from 1997 to 2002.
- Juvenile court judges have taken a more informal "parental" role compared with criminal court judges, and in addition to judicial qualifications are expected to have an understanding of the special needs of juvenile offenders.
- Prosecuting and defense attorneys take a less adversarial role in juvenile court than in criminal court, and are expected to consider the "best interests of the child" in court proceedings.
- Many juveniles appear without a defense attorney despite questions as to their ability to make a valid waiver of the right to counsel; research, however, indicates that defense attorneys may not be effective or helpful for juvenile clients.
- The juvenile court process consists of adjudication and disposition hearings that are more informal, "quasi-civil" proceedings compared to criminal court.
- "Blended sentencing" laws offer a dispositional alternative for serious or chronic juvenile offenders, providing for commitment to a juvenile facility followed by transfer to an adult facility if necessary.
- The juvenile court has seen a number of changes beginning with U.S. Supreme Court decisions in the 1960s and calls for more reforms to guarantee juveniles the same due process rights as adults in criminal court.

KEY TERMS

Adjudication hearing	Institutional commitment
"Best interests of the child"	Juvenile court judge
Bifurcated hearing	Juvenile court prosecutor
"Blended sentencing"	Mediation
Court-appointed attorney	Predisposition report
Court diversion	Probation
Defense attorney	Public defender
Dispositional alternatives	"Quasi-judicial" personnel
Disposition hearing	Residential placement
Guardian ad litem	Right to counsel
Informal adjustment	

DISCUSSION QUESTIONS

1. Based on your reading, what factors do you believe might explain the disproportionate representation of Black youth in U.S. juvenile courts? What juvenile justice policy changes or special programs would you recommend to address this issue?

2. What are some arguments for and against all juveniles having defense counsel in court? Should juveniles who are committed to a correctional institution be able to waive their right to counsel? Why, or why not?

3. Is it surprising that juveniles who are represented by a defense attorney often get harsher punishments than juveniles without an attorney? Based on the readings, what are some possible reasons for that research finding?

4. If a lawmaker in your state introduced legislation to abolish the juvenile court and try juveniles in adult court with a "youth discount" during sentencing, how would you argue for or against the proposal?

WEB RESOURCES

The following Web sites provide information and discussion on the juvenile court:

National Center for Juvenile Justice: http://www.ncjj.org/

National Council of Juvenile and Family Court Judges: http://www.ncjfcj.org/

"Best Practices": http://www.ncjfcj.org/content/view/411/411/

Juvenile Offenders and Victims: 2006 National Report: http://ojjdp.ncjrs.gov/ojstatbb/nr2006/downloads/NR2006.pdf

Current statistics on court cases from OJJDP Statistical Briefing site: http://ojjdp.ncjrs.org/ojstatbb/court/qa06201.asp?qaDate=2004

Youth Law Center, information on legal representation for juveniles in court: http://www.buildingblocksforyouth.org/issues/

READING

Critics of the juvenile court have claimed that its failure to make rehabilitative dispositions requires the court to extend to children the same constitutional safeguards accorded to adults accused of crimes. Supporters of the court argue that its exercise of the parental function of the state (*parens patriae*) generally works in the child's behalf and therefore reduces the need to define and protect the constitutional rights of juvenile delinquents. This debate has roots that originated before the advent of the juvenile court. Houses of refuge and reform schools that were established in America in the 19th century also attempted to give the State parental authority over destitute and delinquent children. Those institutions claimed that such control was necessary to protect children from parents whose indifference or bad example was the root cause of most delinquency. Courts supported the authority of the early institutions and reform schools, in part because of their exaggerated claims of reformation. After the Civil War, however, reform school life was increasingly characterized by the exploitation and brutality associated with the workshop system. The brutal conditions led to legal decisions that favored the rights of natural parents over those of the reform school, and that required courts to follow constitutional procedures when hearing cases involving children accused of crimes. In addition, the establishment of child-placing organizations and of early juvenile probation plans reflected a growing sentiment in favor of keeping children out of reform schools. In this context, the founding of juvenile courts may be seen as both the culmination of distrust in custodial institutions and an attempt to recast the parental authority of the State in a different mold. In this classic work on the development of the juvenile court, Mennel offers some observations on the origins of the *parens patriae* doctrine as applied to delinquent children and on the nature of efforts to prevent juvenile delinquency in the 19th century, in an attempt to provide a better understanding of what he believes are the exaggerated hopes of the "child savers."

Origins of the Juvenile Court

Changing Perspectives on the Legal Rights of Juvenile Delinquents

Robert M. Mennel

The widespread establishment of juvenile courts in the early years of this century represented one of the proudest achievements of progressive reformers. Grace Abbott, chief of the U.S. Children's Bureau, 1921–34, believed that these special tribunals had affected a historic breakthrough in public policy toward youthful crime. In her words, the child offender was no longer regarded "as a *criminal* but as a *delinquent*."[1] Jane Addams, equally enthusiastic, recalled:

> There was almost a change in *mores* when the Juvenile Court was established. The child was brought before the judge with no one to prosecute him and with no one to defend him—the judge and all concerned were merely trying to find out what could be done on his behalf. The element of conflict was absolutely eliminated and with it, all notions of punishment as such with its curiously belated connotation.[2]

Juvenile courts supposedly resembled the English High Court of Chancery which, under the principles of equity, exercised the Crown's prerogative to serve as *parens patriae* for children whose welfare was in jeopardy. Since the juvenile court purported to act in the best interest of the state's wards, it was exempt from the obligation to provide defendants with guarantees of due process which the Constitution ensured adult persons accused of crimes.

The juvenile court has always had its critics, but not until recent years have its theoretically benevolent purposes come under sustained attack. Recent decisions of the Supreme Court have questioned whether the court treats children humanely enough to justify its immunity from the safeguards of criminal law. Thus in the *Kent* case (1966), Justice Fortas, while praising the "laudable purposes" of the court, asked "whether actual performance measures well enough against theoretical purpose to make tolerable the immunity of the process from the reach of constitutional guarantees applicable to adults." He concluded, "There is evidence, in fact, that there may be grounds for concern that the child receives the worst of both worlds; that he gets neither the protection accorded to adults nor the solicitous care and regenerate treatment postulated for children."[3]

The *Kent* decision warned juvenile courts against "procedural arbitrariness." The following year the *Gault* decision went beyond *Kent* in guaranteeing juveniles such specific rights as notification, cross-examination of complainants and other witnesses, and warning of the privilege against self-incrimination. "Under our Constitution," said Justice Fortas, "the condition of being a boy does not justify a kangaroo court."[4]

Recent studies of the juvenile court have examined and questioned what Justice Fortas termed its "original laudable purposes." As early as 1923, Roscoe Pound pointed out that the juvenile court actually originated in criminal law rather than in chancery court proceedings, which traditionally considered cases involving neglected and dependent children.[5] In 1949 Paul Tappan characterized the *parens patriae* doctrine as an *ex post facto* justification for practices that in fact originated with the statutory creation of the juvenile court.[6] In *The Child Savers,* a study of the citizens who founded the original juvenile court in Illinois in 1899, Anthony Platt concludes that the reformers "implicitly assumed the 'natural' dependence of adolescents and created a special court to impose sanctions on premature independence and behavior unbecoming to youth." The juvenile court, according to Platt, did not herald a new system of justice but rather reinforced policies developed during the nineteenth century.[7]

Platt's work delineates the reform outlook toward juvenile delinquency in the late nineteenth century but does not probe the history underlying that outlook. A few observations, therefore, on the origins of the *parens patriae* doctrine as applied to delinquent children and on the nature of efforts to prevent juvenile delinquency in the nineteenth century may advance understanding of the exaggerated hopes of the "child savers."

⊠ Early Punishment

Before 1825, special institutions for delinquent children did not exist in the United States. Public authority sanctioned the power of parents and masters to punish youthful lawbreakers. Under the common law in England and America, the child under seven years of age was considered incapable of mischief, and the child between seven and fourteen was assumed to be incapable of felony but, according to Blackstone, "if it appear to the court and jury, that he could discern between good and evil, he may be convicted and suffer death."[8]

Both common law and customary practice assumed that children accused of misbehavior and crimes were guilty as charged. Possible innocence was not considered: the jury's responsibility was to determine whether children understood their offenses. Juries were reluctant to condemn children to jail and often acquitted them after a nominal trial, finding "lack of knowledge" the reason for the crime.[9]

By the early nineteenth century, this method of handling delinquent children had become unsatisfactory on two counts. First, it did not work all the time: despite courtroom partiality toward youths, increasing numbers were being convicted and sent to jails where, it was commonly believed, they were schooled by adult inmates for future crime. Second, and more important, some children gained acquittal by appealing to the jury's sympathy—an equally unsatisfactory disposition because it allowed them to escape the consequences of their actions.

These shortcomings in the criminal justice system prompted concerned citizens in New York, Boston, and Philadelphia to establish special institutions for delinquent children. The first was the New York House of Refuge, which was founded in 1824 by members of the Society for the Reformation of Juvenile Delinquents. In 1826, following the recommendation of Mayor Josiah Quincy, the Boston City Council founded the House of Reformation for juvenile offenders. At the same time, a group of prominent Philadelphians received a charter to form a House of Refuge, which they opened in 1828. The New

York and Philadelphia refuges were privately managed, though they received public sanction and aid; the Boston House of Reformation was a municipal institution. These three institutions were the only organized efforts to reform juvenile delinquents until 1847, when state institutions were opened in Massachusetts and New York.

Illustrative of the initial concern with juvenile delinquency is this comment by founders of the New York House of Refuge about the legal disposition of delinquent children in the early 1820's:

> If acquitted, they returned destitute, to the same haunts of vice from which they had been taken, more emboldened to the commission of crime by their escape from present punishment. If convicted, they were cast into a common prison with older culprits to mingle in conversation and intercourse with them, acquire their habits, and by their instruction to be made acquainted with the most artful methods of perpetrating crime.[10]

Although the task of the refuge was to prevent delinquent children from being punished cruelly, it was also to insure that they were punished correctly. The necessity of providing accused delinquents with the legal safeguards of due process was not an issue.

To implement their plan, founders of the New York Refuge drew upon an 1822 study of American penitentiaries conducted by the Society for the Prevention of Pauperism. This report called for "the erection of new prisons for juvenile offenders," concluding:

> These prisons should be rather schools for instruction, than places of punishment. . . . The youth confined there should be placed under a course of discipline, severe and unchanging, but alike calculated to subdue and conciliate. A system should be adopted that would prove a mental and moral regimen.[11]

Faithful to the words of the study, the managers of the New York Refuge—and the other refuge leaders too—established "a mental and moral regimen" to instill the habits of piety, honesty, sobriety, and hard work in their children. In 1835, a typical day in the New York Refuge featured two hours of school before breakfast, an eight-hour workday, and then 2½ more hours of school after which, the institution's journal informs us, "children are conducted to their dormitories . . . and are locked up for the night, when perfect silence reigns throughout the establishment."[12]

Under the terms of their incorporation, refuges received children who were destitute and orphaned as well as those who were actually convicted of felonies in state and local courts. Some of the "convicted" children were guilty of no greater crimes than vagrancy, idleness, or stubbornness—those familiar catchalls for mild youthful misbehavior. By training both destitute and delinquent children and by separating them from their natural parents and adult criminals, refuge managers believed that they were preventing poverty *and* crime.

⬚ The Refuge as Parent

Because these early child savers regarded convicted criminals and parents of delinquent children as one and the same, they sought to counter their influence by establishing the parental powers of the refuges. To do so, the institutions had to rebut claims that they were illegally depriving inmates of their liberty. In this instance, the significant legal challenge was *Ex parte Crouse*. In 1838, Mary Ann Crouse's father attempted to free her from the Philadelphia House of Refuge on a writ of habeas corpus. The Pennsylvania Supreme Court denied his claim, saying, "The right of parental control is a natural, but not an unalienable one"; and it continued:

> The object of the charity is reformation, by training its inmates to industry; by imbuing their minds with principles of morality and religion; by furnishing them with means to

earn a living; and, above all, by separating them from the corrupting influence of improper associates. To this end, may not the natural parents, when unequal to the task of education, or unworthy of it, be superseded by the *parens patriae,* or common guardian of the community? . . . The infant has been snatched from a course which must have ended in confirmed depravity; and, not only is the restraint of her person lawful, but it would be an act of extreme cruelty to release her from it.[13]

Alexis de Tocqueville and Gustave de Beaumont had reached a similar conclusion on the rights of refuge children during their tour of American penal institutions in 1831. "The children," they wrote, "were not the victims of persecution, but merely deprived of a fatal liberty."[14]

The New York legislature showed its sympathy for refuge aims by channeling revenue from several taxes to the institution. This money was derived in part—or, so it was thought—from the pernicious habits of the parents of refuge children. Stephen Allen, president of the Refuge corporation, lobbied successfully to gain a portion of the state's revenue from a tax on theater licenses. The legislature also taxed the taverns of New York City to support the refuge.[15]

The origins of these parents were as suspect as their habits. As early as 1801, Thomas Eddy, a founder of the New York Refuge, warned that West Indian and lower-class European immigration would result in an uncontrollable younger generation.[16] The New York legislature agreed by allotting part of the state's emigrant head tax to the refuge. By the mid-1830's, refuges were publishing the birthplaces of both inmates and their parents; the preponderance of Irish children reflected the beginning of the Irish migration to America.[17] Refuge managers did not view these poor peasants and their children sympathetically. Stephen Allen summarized the attitude when he said:

The tide of emigration . . . while it enriches our country, leaves much of its refuse in our city. Pauper families, and even felons, are not infrequently sent over to us as a cheap way of disposing of them . . . thus swelling the number of houseless, friendless and lawless youth, drifting loose upon society.[18]

The doctrine of *parens patriae* gave refuge managers the best of two worlds, familial and legal: it separated delinquent children from their natural parents, and it circumvented the rigor of criminal law by allowing courts to commit children, under loosely worded statutes, to specially created "schools" instead of jails. Once the child was received by the refuge, procedures of criminal law no longer applied.

The *parens patriae* argument provided criminal courts with a convenient rationale for disposing of dependent and delinquent children. It conferred parental powers upon institutions to prevent natural parents, who were usually impoverished or foreign or both, from gaining or regaining custody of their children. Refuges received state sanction to exercise parental power over inmates throughout the period of their minority, and thus these institutions could and did apprentice delinquents to whaling captains and farmers without informing the natural parents. In remote farming and nautical districts, the state's purposes were further promoted since the parent-child ties were often severed permanently.[19]

In this manner, houses of refuge gained a self-proclaimed "victory" over juvenile delinquency—one which depended on their control, though perhaps not their reform, of delinquent children. Annual reports of the institutions were notoriously self-promoting, reflecting until 1850 a serene pride in their accomplishments. Refuge managers boasted regularly that both juvenile crime in the city and juvenile incarceration in penitentiaries and jails had decreased dramatically as a result of refuge work. They claimed a high percentage of "saved" apprentices, citing as proof the number of favorable letters from farmers and the absence of detrimental reports.[20] Refractory inmates, though not yet considered a serious challenge to the institutions' authority or prestige, were severely handled. Although the punishment was usually corporal, some children were sent to the penitentiary. In the words of Nathaniel Hart, superintendent of the New York Refuge, "We will be fathers to them if they obey the rules."[21]

If imitation really is the sincerest form of flattery, by 1850 managers of the first refuges could brush aside criticism and reflect upon the exemplary nature of their institutions, because by this time a number of other municipal and state institutions either were in the planning stage or had been opened.[22] Invariably, inaugural ceremonies of the new reform schools were marked by tributes to the first institutions. Familiar sentiments were expressed—the need to remove children from jail and the even greater need to separate them from their parents or other adults in order to teach them values of thrift, honesty, and individual responsibility.[23]

⊠ The Failure of Refuges

Although early refuge leaders took pride in their creations, the very proliferation of reform schools bespoke not only their failure to put a stop to juvenile delinquency but also their inability to prevent its growth. The increasingly violent activities of street gangs in the larger municipal centers both during and after the Civil War are matters of common knowledge. The major point is not that reform schools, both old and new, were unable to hold all the youthful law violators (although, of course, they could not and many delinquents either were sent to jail or were simply left to roam). Rather, the notable characteristic of reform schools in the later nineteenth century was their inability to cope with the relatively few children who *did* come under their charge.

This failure resulted from the increasingly harsh nature of institutional life. Faced with large numbers of children and only limited public financial support, reform school managers were forced to rely upon the contract system. This system had been part of refuge life from the beginning, but it now assumed a more exploitative character. Clothing and shoe manufacturers, whose piecework was once welcomed because it was thought to encourage good habits, were

now viewed with greater skepticism because they often insisted upon replacing institution officials with company supervisors in order to squeeze maximum productivity out of the children's working hours. Officials at the Philadelphia Refuge complained of this practice in 1866:

> Those immediately entrusted with the government of the boys are generally but . . . qualified for so responsible a position. . . . If the work be well done and a responsible amount of it, they are satisfied. These seven and a half hours of labor are spent without one moral lesson taught the boys, at least so far as the workmen of the shops are concerned.[24]

In 1871, the New York Commission on Prison Labor, headed by Enoch Wines, investigated the contract system and uncovered many instances of exploitation and brutality. The commissioners received this picture of shop life from former New York Refuge employees Thomas Crowne and Valentine Feldman:

Q. Have you ever known instructors employed by the contractors to strike the boys?

A. (Crowne) I have seen them do it, though it is forbidden. I have also seen them, when a keeper was around, and they did not dare to strike, tread on the boys' bare toes . . . so as to cause them to squirm all around. . . .

Q. Have you ever seen any of the boys abused by the contractors' employees?

A. (Feldman) Often and often. They do not call it abusing a boy to give him a kick, or a blow on the head. . . .

Q. Please describe the way in which they are punished.

A. I have seen boys punished for not completing their tasks, so that blood ran down into their boots.[25]

The new cottage reform schools, founded in the 1850's and 1860's to discipline and care for children in small family units and to teach them the benefits of farm life, also fell victim to demands for economy. Rev. Marcus Ames, superintendent of the girls' cottage reformatory at Lancaster, Mass., resigned in 1874 rather than accept the installation of workshops.[26] At the New Jersey State Reform School at Jamesburg, farming and maintenance work gave way to shirt-making in 1875 and a factory appeared among the cottages. Legislative investigators found life in the institution "hard, routine and monotonous." James Leiby concludes in his comprehensive study of New Jersey institutions, "Jamesburg was not a family, nor a reformatory, but a boys' prison."[27]

Not surprisingly, incendiarism, rioting, and even murder marked the history of nearly every reform school. In 1859 Daniel Credan and five of his friends put the torch to the Massachusetts Reform School at Westborough.[28] On May 17, 1872, Justus Dunn stabbed to death Saul Calvert, an overseer in the North Shop of the New York Refuge.[29] Five years later, the superintendent of the Massachusetts girls' reformatory reported, "House No. 3, an old building . . . replete with interesting associations, was burned to the ground, having been set on fire by two of our inmates."[30]

These events posed serious questions for reformatory institutions whose custodial power depended upon the *parens patriae* doctrine. If reform schools did not improve—indeed, if they abused delinquent children—how could they then justify their parental role? How could they avoid being labeled prisons? How could they pretend that the scope of their custodial power extended to vagrant and semi-delinquent children, as well as to youths convicted of felonies?

◣ Changing Legal Decisions

Soon after the Civil War, legal decisions interpreting *parens patriae* began to reflect increasing distrust of the intentions and performance of reform schools and, conversely, new appreciation for natural parents. In 1870 the Illinois Supreme Court reversed the vagrancy sentence of Daniel O'Connell to the Chicago Reform School on the grounds that he had not committed a crime and

had been imprisoned without due process of law. "Why should minors be imprisoned for misfortune?" asked the court. "Destitution of proper parental care, ignorance, idleness and vice, are misfortunes, not crimes. . . . This boy is deprived of a father's care; bereft of home influences; has no freedom of action; is committed for an uncertain time; is branded as a prisoner; made subject to the will of others, and thus feels that he is a slave."[31] In 1897 an appellate court freed Jonie Becknell from the Whittier State School in California on the grounds that he had been committed solely on the basis of a grand jury hearing and "cannot be imprisoned as a criminal without a trial by jury."[32]

It is true, of course, that other decisions supported the state's traditional exercise of parental power. The case of a Chinese youth named Ah Peen, "minor child, of the age of sixteen, leading an idle and dissolute life," is representative. Ah Peen's commitment to an industrial school without a jury trial was a justifiable exercise of *parens patriae*, said the California Supreme Court, and therefore not subject to the safeguards of criminal law. The decision concluded, "The purpose in view is not punishment for offenses done, but reformation and training of the child to habits of industry, with a view to his future usefulness when he shall have been reclaimed to society."[33]

Nevertheless, the animus against reform schools was strong enough to find other means of expression. Beginning in the 1850's the New York Children's Aid Society shipped Manhattan Street urchins to western farms in wholesale lots to prevent philanthropists and local authorities from committing them to the Refuge. Charles Loring Brace, the society's founder, asked: "If enough families can be found to serve as reformatory institutions, is it not the best and most practical and economical method of reforming these children?"[34]

"Placing-out" remained a popular alternative to institutionalization, even after the demand for youthful workers subsided in the agrarian West. In 1890 the Children's Aid Society of Pennsylvania, with the cooperation of local courts, offered to place in foster homes delinquents who would otherwise be committed to reform schools. This probation experiment was not undertaken without misgiving.

"We have sometimes left our wards . . . and returned half expecting the next mail to announce their evildoing and disappearance," recalled Homer Folks, secretary of the Society. "But we have been happily surprised as weeks passed by and all the reports were hopeful."[35] The New York Society for the Prevention of Cruelty to Children established a similar program after influencing passage of state legislation which enabled it to receive children from the courts. Massachusetts continued to increase the size of its state visiting agency, which had been established in 1869 to serve as a probation and parole office for delinquents.

The idea of a juvenile court had, therefore, several roots. In many locales, children were still being detained in or sentenced to jail. Their plight was much lamented at philanthropic meetings and at state and national charity conferences. The creation of a probate tribunal, it was reasoned, would minimize and perhaps even eliminate this perennial problem. More important, however, in the origin of the juvenile court was the widespread belief that reform schools were no longer equal to the task of providing parental guidance for delinquent children. The reality of institutional life—the riots, the exploitation, the cruel punishments—mocked the ideal. In 1891, Homer Folks listed "the contaminating influence of association" and "the enduring stigma . . . of having been committed" as reasons to avoid sending children to reform school.[36]

The popularity of nineteenth-century probation plans—the forerunners of the juvenile court—can be traced directly to this distrust. The Illinois juvenile court act (1899) combined the Massachusetts and New York systems of probation with several New York laws providing delinquents with special court sessions and separate detention facilities.[37] Juvenile courts developed their own probation staffs, detention homes, and auxiliary services, thus relegating reform schools to places of "dernier resort," in the words of one superintendent.[38] By relieving institutions of their parental power, juvenile courts were declaring that their own exercise of parens patriae would seek, above all, to reform delinquents without institutionalizing them. In this context, it is easy to understand why Jane Addams believed

that the new tribunal "absolutely liminated . . . all notions of punishment."[39]

The Early Juvenile Court

The purpose of this paper is not to examine the many ways in which the juvenile court failed to live up to its promise. It is appropriate, however, to make observations about the court and the expectations with which it commenced. First, the brightness of the promise came in large measure from the preceding darkness: judges enhanced the reputation of their courts merely by refusing to send children to jail or commit them to reform school. Such dispositions made the juvenile court seem to be more of a miracle worker than it actually was. Second, and as a corollary, enthusiasm over the novelty of the institution encouraged its widespread adoption in one form or another throughout the United States. The sheer amount of organizational and promotional activity disguised for a long while the court's quite traditional attitudes and policies toward the legal rights of delinquent children and their parents. Far from limiting the parental power of the state, advocates of the juvenile court sought to increase it. A 1905 decision upholding the legality of a juvenile court in Pennsylvania is representative:

> To save a child from becoming a criminal, or from continuing in a career of crime, to end in maturer years in public punishment and disgrace, the legislatures surely may provide for the salvation of such a child, if its parents or guardians be unable or unwilling to do so, by bringing it into one of the courts of the state without any process at all, for the purpose of subjecting it to the state's guardianship and protection.[40]

Parents of delinquent children could not expect much sympathy from Ben Lindsey, the famous "children's judge," who regularly berated "the careless father, unworthy as a man, dangerous as a citizen."[41] On a more sophisticated level, psychologist Augusta Bronner urged that juvenile courts be allowed to remove children from "unworthy or stupid" parents who did not understand the principles of child psychology.[42] Homer Folks, without a trace of irony, concluded that the new court provided "a new kind of reformatory, without walls and without much coercion."[43]

The spirit of these comments would have seemed familiar to the father of Mary Ann Crouse. The juvenile court, like the early reform school, exercised parental power to punish parents for their children's delinquencies and to deny children legal rights on the pretext that they were being protected, not punished. In 1972 as in 1872, interest in providing delinquent children with legal safeguards is based upon belief that the state has not fulfilled its parental duties. Current legal interpretations protecting accused delinquents in the juvenile court resemble earlier decisions restricting the parental power of the reform school. The *Gault* case, like the *O'Connell* case nearly a century before, protects children against unfair loss of liberty; both of these decisions prefer the guardianship of natural parents to that of the state. Today, as then, we can no longer disqualify parents from caring for their children simply because they are poor or unfamiliar with the principles of child psychology. Parents may indeed abuse or fail to exercise their disciplinary authority. There is, however, little historical evidence to indicate that public authorities in the United States have provided viable and humane alternatives.

✑ Notes

1. Quoted in Sophonisba P. Breckinridge and Edith Abbott, *The Delinquent Child and the Home* (New York: Charities Publication Committee, 1912), p. 247.

2. Jane Addams, *My Friend Julia Lathrop* (New York: Macmillan, 1935), p. 137.

3. *Kent v. United States,* 383 U.S. 541, 545 (1966).

4. *In re Gault,* 387 U.S. 28 (1967).

5. Roscoe Pound, *Interpretations of Legal History* (New York: Macmillan, 1923), pp. 134–135.

6. Paul Tappan, *Juvenile Delinquency* (New York: McGraw-Hill, 1949), p. 169.

7. Anthony Platt, *The Child Savers* (Chicago: University of Chicago Press, 1969), p. 176.

8. William Blackstone, *Commentaries on the Laws of England* (London: A. Strahan and W. Woodfall, 1795), vol. 4, p. 23.

9. In a study of fourteen cases on the criminal responsibility of children, Platt concluded that guilty findings were seldom returned despite evidence indicating that the defendant understood that he had committed a crime. See Platt, *op. cit. supra* note 7, p. 202.

10. New York Society for the Reformation of Juvenile Delinquents, *Annual Report, 1826,* New York, 1827, pp. 3–4. (Herein-after cited as S.R.J.D.)

11. New York Society for the Prevention of Pauperism, *Report on the Penitentiary System in the United States,* New York, 1822, pp. 59–60.

12. S.R.J.D., *Annual Report, 1835,* pp. 6–7.

13. *Ex parte Crouse,* 4 Whart. 9 (Pa. 1838).

14. Gustave de Beaumont and Alexis de Tocqueville, *On the Penitentiary System in the United States,* Francis Lieber, transl. (Philadelphia: Carey, Lea and Blanchard, 1833), p. 115.

15. Stephen Allen to Walter Bowne, March 17, 1824, and Stephen Allen to John Morss, April 1, 1824. The Papers of Stephen Allen, New York Historical Society.

16. Thomas Eddy, *An Account of the State Prison or Penitentiary House in the City of New York* (New York: Isaac Collins, 1801).

17. S.R.J.D., *Annual Report, 1834,* p. 61; Philadelphia House of Refuge, *Tenth Annual Report, 1838,* p. 4; Boston Common Council, *City Doc.* 19 (1846), pp. 10–11.

18. S.R.J.D., *Annual Report, 1849,* p. 11.

19. See, for example, Philadelphia House of Refuge, *Third Annual Report, 1831,* pp. 5–6.

20. Boston Prison Discipline Society, *Second Annual Report.* This society, founded in 1826 by Louis Dwight, of Boston, collected annual reports from all types of penal institutions.

21. Quoted in Robert S. Pickett, *House of Refuge: Origins of Juvenile Reform in New York State, 1815–1857* (Syracuse: Syracuse University Press, 1969), p. 144. For an early criticism of the disciplinary methods of the New York House of Refuge see Elijah Devoe, *The Refuge System, or Prison Discipline Applied to Juvenile Delinquents* (New York: J. R. M'Gown, 1848).

22. The following reformatory and child-saving institutions were opened around mid-century: House of Refuge, New Orleans (1847); State Reform School (boys), Massachusetts (1847); Western House of Refuge, New York (1849); Colored House of Refuge, Philadelphia (1850); House of Refuge, Cincinnati (1850); New York Juvenile Asylum (1853); Children's

Aid Society, New York (1853); Western House of Refuge, Pittsburgh (1854); State Industrial School (girls), Massachusetts (1856); Ohio Reform School (1857).

23. See, for example, Michael Katz, *The Irony of Early School Reform: Educational Opinion in Mid-nineteenth Century Massachusetts* (Cambridge, Mass.: Harvard University Press, 1969), pp 167–70, an analysis of opinion favoring the establishment of a state reform school.

24. Enoch C. Wines and Theodore W. Dwight, *Report on the Prisons and Reformatories of the United States and Canada* (Albany, N.Y.: Van Benthuysen, 1867), p. 431.

25. New York State Assembly, *Documents, 1871*, IV, Doc. 18, "Report of the Commission on Prison Labor," Albany, 1871, pp. 164, 181.

26. Massachusetts, State Industrial School for Girls, *Annual Report, 1875*, Boston, 1875, pp. 8–9.

27. James Leiby, *Charities and Correction in New Jersey* (New Brunswick, N.J.: Rutgers University Press, 1967), p. 82.

28. Massachusetts, State Reform School at Westborough, *Thirteenth Annual Report, 1859*, Boston, 1959, pp. 3–4.

29. S.R.J.D., *Annual Report, 1872*, pp. 45–47.

30. Massachusetts, State Industrial School for Girls, *Annual Report, 1878*, Boston, 1878, p. 16.

31. *People v. Turner*, 55 Ill. 280 (1870).

32. *Ex parte Becknell*, 51 P. 692 (Calif. 1897).

33. *Ex parte Ah Peen*, 51 California 280 (1876).

34. Second Convention of Managers and Superintendents of Houses of Refuge and Schools of Reform, *Proceedings, 1859*, New York. 1860, p. 48.

35. Homer Folks, "The Care of Delinquent Children," *Proceedings*, National Conference of Charities and Corrections, 1891, pp. 137–39.

36. *Id.*, pp. 137–40.

37. For the New York laws, see "An Act for the Protection of Children, and to Prevent and Punish Certain Wrongs to Children," ch. 428, *Laws of the State of New York*, Albany, N.Y., 1877, p. 486, and "An Act . . . Relative to Criminal Charges against Children," ch. 217, *Laws of the State of New York, 1892*, Vol. I, Albany, N.Y., 1892, pp. 459–60.

38. H. W. Charles, "The Problem of the Reform School," *Proceedings*, Vol. II, Child Conference for Research and Welfare, 1910, p. 86.

39. Addams, *op. cit. supra* note 2, p. 137.

40. *Commonwealth v. Fisher*, 62 A. 198 (Pa. 1905); see also *Mill v. Brown*, 88 P. 609 (Utah 1905).

41. Benjamin B. Lindsey, "The Child, the Parent and the Law," *Juvenile Court Record*, May 1904, pp. 9–10.

42. Augusta F. Bronner, "The Contribution of Science to a Program for Treatment of Juvenile Delinquency," in Julia Lathrop *et al.*, *The Child, the Clinic and the Court* (New York: New Republic, 1925), p. 84.

43. Homer Folks, "Juvenile Probation," *Proceedings*, National Conference of Charities and Corrections, 1906, pp. 117–22.

DISCUSSION QUESTIONS

1. Compare and contrast the view of young offenders and how they were processed before the development of the juvenile court in the late 1800s with how they are viewed and processed in court today.

2. Early juvenile institutions were founded on work and economic production. Would that practice be accepted today? Why, or why not?

3. Is there a positive rehabilitative side to productive labor and corrections? What policies would you recommend to avoid the abuses of forced labor and corrections?

4. Mennel notes that early courts were critical of parents of delinquents, and exercised considerable power and authority in taking over the custody and discipline of children. Based on current laws and practices, should courts take a similar approach today? Is there evidence that the State can do a better job than parents of delinquents today?

❖

READING

The quality of procedural justice is especially relevant to recent changes in juvenile courts' sentencing policies. Juvenile court decisions have become increasingly punitive, as reflected in changes in juvenile code purpose clauses and court decisions supporting punishment; juvenile sentencing statutes and correctional guidelines that employ proportional, determinate, or mandatory sentences; and evaluations of dispositional decision making and conditions of institutional confinement. The shift from treatment to punishment raises basic issues of procedural justice, especially the delivery of legal services. In this article, Barry Feld notes that juvenile courts' sentencing practices increasingly resemble those of their criminal counterparts. He questions whether there is any reason to maintain a separate court for juveniles, especially when juvenile courts are characterized by more procedural deficiencies than the criminal courts.

The Punitive Juvenile Court and the Quality of Procedural Justice

Disjunctions Between Rhetoric and Reality

Barry C. Feld

The United States Supreme Court's decision *In re Gault* (1967) transformed the juvenile court into a very different institution than that envisioned by its progressive creators (Feld 1984; Rothman 1980; Ryerson 1978). Harmonizing juvenile justice administration with *Gault*'s constitutional mandate has modified the purposes, processes, and operations of contemporary juvenile courts (Feld 1984, 1988b). The Progressives envisioned a procedurally informal court with individualized, offender-oriented dispositional practices. The Supreme Court's due process decisions engrafted procedural formality at adjudication onto the traditional, individualized-treatment sentencing schema. As contemporary juvenile courts depart from their rehabilitative origins by endorsing punishment, they procedurally and substantively converge with criminal courts (Feld 1981a, 1988b).

The quality of procedural justice is especially relevant to recent changes in juvenile courts' sentencing policies and practices as "just deserts" (based on the offense), rather than "best interests" (based on an individualized evaluation of the offender), dominate dispositions. Legislative changes in juvenile code purpose clauses emphasize accountability for offenses rather than treatment of offenders; courts echo these punitive purposes. Sentencing statutes and correctional administrative guidelines that emphasize proportional and determinate sentences based on the offense and prior record further signal a retreat from a treatment model of justice. Empirical evaluations of dispositional decision making and conditions of juvenile correctional confinement also reflect the shift from treatment to punishment. Recognizing that punishment plays an increasing,

SOURCE: *Crime & Delinquency (36)*4, 443–466, October 1990. © 1990 Sage Publications, Inc.

if not dominant, role in juvenile court sentencing practices raises fundamental issues of procedural justice, especially the delivery of legal services. Finally, as juvenile courts resemble increasingly their criminal counterparts, does any reason remain to maintain a separate court whose sole distinguishing characteristic is its persisting procedural deficiencies?

⊠ Procedural Informality and Individualized, Offender-Oriented Dispositions in the Juvenile Court

Progressive criminal justice reforms in the early 20th century, including the juvenile court, reflected changes in ideological assumptions about crime and deviance. Whereas classical explanations attributed crime to free will choices, positivism focused on reforming offenders rather than punishing them for their offenses (Rothman 1980; Matza 1964; Allen 1964). The conjunction of positivistic criminology, medical analogies to treating offenders, and a growing class of social science professionals fostered the "rehabilitative ideal" (Allen 1978, 1981). Whether viewed as a humanitarian movement to "save" poor and immigrant children (Hagan and Leon 1977; Sutton 1988) or as an effort to expand social control over youths (Platt 1977; Fox 1970), juvenile courts were described as benign, nonpunitive, and therapeutic.

Juvenile courts used informal and flexible procedures to diagnose the causes of and prescribe the cures for delinquency. As a scientific and preventive alternative to punitive criminal law, rehabilitating deviants precluded uniform treatment or standardized criteria (Platt 1977; Ryerson 1978). Juvenile courts rejected the jurisprudence of criminal law and associated procedural safeguards such as juries and lawyers. Theoretically, dispositions reflected the child's best interests, background, and welfare rather than the crime committed. Because a youth's offense was only symptomatic of his or her "real needs," dispositions were

indeterminate, nonproportional, and continued for the duration of minority.

⊠ The Constitutional Domestication of the Juvenile Court-Procedural Formality and Individualized Offender-Oriented Dispositions

The Supreme Court's *Gault* decision mandated procedural safeguards and focused judicial attention initially on whether the child committed an offense as a prerequisite to sentencing (Feld 1984, 1988b). In shifting the formal focus of juvenile courts from real needs to legal guilt, the Court identified two crucial disjunctions between juvenile justice rhetoric and reality: (a) the theory versus practice of rehabilitation and (b) the procedural safeguards afforded adults versus those available to juveniles.

In both *In re Winship* (1970), which required delinquency to be proved by the criminal standard "beyond a reasonable doubt" rather than by lower civil standards of proof, and in *Breed v. Jones* (1975), which barred criminal prosecution of a youth after conviction in juvenile court, the Supreme Court posited a procedural and functional equivalence between criminal trials and delinquency proceedings.

In *McKeiver v. Pennsylvania* (1971), however, the Court denied juveniles the constitutional right to jury trials and halted the extension of full procedural parity with adult criminal prosecutions. The Court feared that jury trials would adversely affect traditional informality, render juvenile courts procedurally indistinguishable from criminal courts, and call into question the need for a separate juvenile court. In *McKeiver,* the Court justified the procedural differences between juvenile and criminal courts on the basis of the former's *treatment* rationale and the latter's *punitive* purposes, although it did not analyze the differences between treatment and punishment that warranted the differences in procedural safeguards.

☒ Punishment in Juvenile Courts—Offense-Based Sentencing Practices

Despite *McKeiver's* denial of procedural equality, contemporary juvenile courts increasingly pursue the substantive goals of the criminal law (Feld 1984, 1988b). Conceptually, punishment and treatment represent mutually exclusive penal goals (Feld 1984, 1987, 1988b). Criminal law punishes morally responsible actors for making blameworthy choices, whereas juvenile courts regard youths as less culpable or responsible for their criminal misdeeds. Punishment assumes that responsible actors make culpable choices and deserve to suffer prescribed consequences (Von Hirsch 1976; Hart 1968). By contrast, most rehabilitative efforts assume some degree of determinism. External, antecedent forces cause the individual's conduct and suggest forms of intervention that would modify or eliminate the effects of those forces (Gibbons 1965). Treatment focuses on the person's mental health, status, or future welfare rather than on the commission of a prohibited act (Allen 1964, 1981). A degree of determinism is one central tenet of the positivist criminology underlying rehabilitation in juvenile courts.

Punishment imposes unpleasant consequences because of *past offenses* whereas therapy seeks to improve the offender's *future welfare*. In analyzing juvenile court sentencing practices, it is useful to distinguish between sentences based on the past offense or the future welfare of the offender. When a sentence is based on past conduct—present offense and prior record—it is typically determinate and proportional with a goal of retribution or deterrence (Packer 1968; Twentieth Century Fund 1976; Von Hirsch 1976, 1986). When a sentence is focused on the offender, to rehabilitate or incapacitate, it is nonproportional and indeterminate. The open-ended nature of juvenile dispositions and a rejection of punishment for blameworthy choices provide the primary differences between juvenile and criminal court sanctions.

In the adult context, determinate sentences have increasingly superseded indeterminate sentences, as just deserts has displaced rehabilitation as the underlying sentencing rationale (American Friends Service Committee 1971; Von Hirsch 1976; Petersilia and Turner 1987). The Progressives' optimistic assumptions about human malleability have been challenged by empirical evaluations that question both the effectiveness of treatment programs that do not consistently rehabilitate and the "scientific" underpinnings of those who administer the enterprise (Martinson 1974; Sechrest et al. 1979; Greenberg 1977; Lab and Whitehead 1988). Proponents of just deserts reject rehabilitation as a justification for intervention for several reasons: (a) indeterminate sentencing vests too much discretionary power in presumed experts; (b) clinical experts are unable to justify their differential treatment of similarly situated offenders on the basis of validated classification schema, objective indicators, or improvements in outcomes; and, (c) as a consequence, gross inequalities, disparities, and injustices result from therapeutically individualized sentences (American Friends Service Committee 1971; Von Hirsch 1976, 1986; Feld 1988b). With its strong retributive foundation, just deserts sentencing punishes offenders equally, based on relatively objective, legally relevant factors such as offense or criminal history, rather than on who they are or who they may become.

Similar changes in sentencing philosophy are now appearing in the juvenile justice process (Feld 1987, 1988b). Some states have introduced just deserts principles because of the inability of juvenile courts to demonstrate the efficacy of treatment, because personal characteristics do not provide a principled basis for coercive intervention, or because discretionary sentences are perceived as overly lenient (Cohen 1978; Institute of Judicial Administration 1980). Several juvenile court sentencing policies and practices indicate whether a juvenile is being punished for past offenses or treated: (a) statutes for waiving a youth to criminal court for prosecution as an adult, (b) legislative purpose clauses in juvenile codes, (c) juvenile court sentencing statutes, (d) actual sentencing practices of juvenile courts, and (e) conditions of confinement in juvenile institutions (Feld 1987, 1988b). Examining these indicators reveals that juvenile court dispositional practices increasingly resemble those of punitive criminal courts. However, just deserts sentences for youths have important constitutional consequences because the Court in *McKeiver* posited a therapeutic, nonpunitive court as the basis for its procedural differences.

The Purpose of the Juvenile Court

Most state juvenile codes contain a *purpose clause* or preamble that provides a statutory rationale to aid courts in interpreting the legislation (Feld 1988b; Gardner 1982). Since the creation of the original juvenile court in Cook County, Illinois, in 1899, the historical purpose of juvenile court law has been

> to secure for each minor . . . such care and guidance . . . as will serve the moral, emotional, mental, and physical welfare of the minor and the best interests of the community; . . . removing him [sic] from the custody of his parents only when his welfare or safety or the protection of the public cannot be adequately safeguarded without removal. (Ill. 1972)

Many juvenile court preambles include the original statement of purpose (Iowa 1904; Ore. 1919; R.I. 1944; Utah 1931; Feld 1984; Walkover 1984), often with the additional goal of removing "the taint of criminality and the penal consequences of criminal behavior, by substituting therefore an individual program of counseling, supervision, treatment, and rehabilitation" (N.H. 1979; Ohio 1969; Tenn. 1970; Vt. 1967).

Although 42 state juvenile codes contain statements of legislative purpose (Feld 1988b, p. 842, n. 83), in the past decade, 10 states have redefined the purposes of their juvenile courts (Feld 1988b, p. 842, n. 84). These recent amendments de-emphasized the exclusive role of rehabilitation in the child's best interest and elevated the importance of public safety, punishment, and

individual and juvenile justice system accountability (Walkover 1984). For example, Washington adopted a *justice* model juvenile code that emphasized just deserts rather than individualized treatment (Feld 1981a; Walkover 1984). Although its purpose clause reflects these punitive goals, it still denies jury trials in juvenile proceedings (*Lawley* 1979; *Schaaf* 1987). Similarly, the purpose of Minnesota's juvenile courts is "to promote public safety and reduce juvenile delinquency by maintaining the integrity of the substantive law prohibiting certain behavior and by developing individual responsibility for lawful behavior" (Minn. 1980), although it too denies juveniles the right to a jury trial. In other states, the purposes of juvenile courts are to: "correct juveniles for their acts of delinquency" (Ark. 1979); "provide for the protection and safety of the public" (Cal. 1984; Private Sector 1987); "protect society . . . [while] recognizing that the application of sanctions which are consistent with the seriousness of the offense is appropriate in all cases" (Fla. 1978); "render appropriate punishment to offenders" (Hawaii 1976); "protect the public by enforcing the legal obligations children have to society" (Ind. 1980); "protect the welfare of the community and to control the commission of unlawful acts by children" (Tex. 1986); "protect the community against those acts of its citizens which are harmful to others and to reduce the incidence of delinquent behavior" (Va. 1982); and "reduce the rate of juvenile delinquency and provide a system for the rehabilitation or detention of juvenile delinquents and protect the welfare of the general public" (W. Va. 1978).

Courts recognize that changes in purpose clauses signal a basic philosophical reorientation, even as they endorse punishment as an acceptable juvenile court disposition (*D. D. H. v. Dostert* 1980; *In re D. F. B.* 1988). In *State v. Lawley* (1979), the Washington Supreme Court reasoned that "sometimes punishment is treatment" and upheld the legislature's conclusion that "accountability for criminal behavior, the prior criminal activity and punishment commensurate with age, crime and criminal history does as much to rehabilitate, correct and direct an errant youth as does the prior philosophy of focusing upon the particular characteristics of the individual juvenile" (p. 753). The Nevada Supreme Court in *In re Seven Minors* (1983) endorsed punishment as a purpose of juvenile courts: "By formally recognizing the legitimacy of punitive and deterrent sanctions for criminal offenses juvenile courts will be properly and somewhat belatedly expressing society's firm disapproval of juvenile crime and will be clearly issuing a threat of punishment for criminal acts to the juvenile population" (p. 950). Although punishing young offenders may be an appropriate strategy, these legislatures and courts fail to consider adequately whether a juvenile justice system can punish explicitly without providing routine criminal procedural safeguards such as a jury trial or the assistance of counsel.

Just Deserts Dispositions—Legislative and Administrative Changes in Juvenile Courts' Sentencing Framework[1]

For most of the 20th century, positivism and utilitarian or rehabilitative penal policies dominated sentencing practices. The precipitous decline of support for rehabilitation in the 1970s reawakened the quest for penal justice (Allen 1981; American Friends Service Committee 1971). Where systematic reform of offenders remains an elusive goal, the pursuit of equality, uniformity, and consistency in sentences acquires greater salience.

Juvenile court sentencing statutes provide another indicator of punitive or therapeutic purposes. Sentences based on the offense are usually determinate and proportional with a goal of retribution or deterrence, whereas sentences based on the offender are typically indeterminate with a goal of rehabilitation or incapacitation (Packer 1968; American Friends Service Committee 1971; Allen 1964). Historically, juvenile court sentences were indeterminate and nonproportional to achieve the offender's best interests. Most states' juvenile sentencing provisions continue to mirror their Progressive origins (Feld 1988b). Such statutes typically provide a range of alternatives—dismissal, probation, out-of-home placement, or institutional confinement—and give juvenile court judges broad discretion to impose any appropriate disposition (Fla. 1988; Hawaii 1987; Iowa 1985). Within these substantial ranges, the judge's authority is formally unrestricted and dispositions may range from one day up to the offender's age of majority or some other statutory termination (Feld 1988b). Some legislatures instruct the court to consider the "least restrictive alternative" from among its array of options (Ark. 1987; Iowa 1985).

Even states using indeterminate sentences recognize that the offense can provide a dispositional constraint. In North Carolina, for example, within the range of alternative sentences "the judge shall select the least restrictive disposition . . . that is appropriate to the seriousness of the offense, the degree of culpability indicated by the circumstances of the particular case and the age and prior record of the juvenile" (N.C. 1986). Iowa requires the judge to consider "the seriousness of the delinquent act, the child's culpability as indicated by the circumstances of the particular case, the age of the child and the child's prior record" (Iowa 1985).

Determinate Sentences in Juvenile Court

Despite the history of indeterminacy, about one third of the states now use either legislative or administrative offense criteria—determinate or mandatory minimum sentencing statutes or administrative sentencing guidelines—to regulate at least some juvenile court sentencing and institutional commitment and release decisions (Feld 1988b). Both determinate or mandatory minimum sentencing statutes and correctional release guidelines focus on the present offense and/or prior record.

The clearest departure from traditional juvenile court sentencing practices occurred in 1977 when Washington state enacted just deserts legislation that sought individual and system accountability, equality, and proportionality through presumptive sentences based on age, present offense, and prior record (Wash. 1984; Fisher et al. 1985; Schneider and Schram 1983).

Recent New Jersey legislation instructs juvenile court judges to consider the offense and criminal history when sentencing juveniles, enumerates "aggravating and mitigating" offense criteria to guide decisions, and provides enhanced sentences for serious or repeat offenders (N.J. 1987). In 1987, Texas adopted determinate sentencing legislation for juveniles charged with serious offenses and which provided special procedures including a jury trial (Tex. 1988).

Mandatory Minimum Terms of Confinement Based on Offense

In addition to determinate sentencing legislation, other states use offense criteria as sentencing guidelines (Colo. 1986) or impose mandatory minimum sentences for certain "designated felonies" (N.Y. 1987; Ohio 1987). Formally using offense criteria to mandate dispositions precludes individualized consideration of real needs.

Under some mandatory minimum sentencing statutes, the judge retains discretion whether or not to commit a juvenile to the state's department of corrections (Feld 1988b). If incarceration is ordered, the judge may prescribe the minimum length of sentence to be served for that offense (Ark. 1987; Colo. 1986). In some cases, a mandatory sentence is nondiscretionary, and the judge must commit the juvenile for the statutory minimum period (Del. 1986). Nondiscretionary mandatory minimum sentences are usually imposed on juveniles charged with a serious or violent present offense (N.Y. 1987) or who have prior delinquency convictions (Del. 1986). The minimum sentences may range from 12 to 18 months (Georgia Division of Youth Services 1985), to age 21 (Ill. 1988), or to the adult term for the same offense (Ky. 1988).

Colorado juvenile statutes include special provisions for sentencing "Violent and Repeat Juvenile Offenders," "Mandatory Sentence Offenders," and "Aggravated Juvenile Offenders" that include mandatory minimum out-of-home placements (Colo. 1986). "Serious Juvenile Offenders" in Connecticut receive offense-based sentences that include mandatory minimum out-of-home placement (Conn. 1986). "Designated felony" legislation in Georgia (1988) and New York (1987) prescribes the length of confinement and level of security for juveniles convicted of enumerated offenses and includes provisions for mandatory sentences. Other states, including Delaware (1986), Illinois (1988), Kentucky (1988), North Carolina (1987), Ohio (1987), Tennessee (1987), and Virginia (1988), provide mandatory minimum sentences for serious or repeat juvenile offenders.

Administrative Sentencing and Parole Release Guidelines

Another form of just deserts or offense-based sentencing occurs when a state's department of corrections administratively adopts institutional commitment and release guidelines that use offense criteria to structure confinement decisions. Although adult corrections and parole authorities have used such guidelines for decades, their use for juveniles is more recent.

Minnesota's Department of Corrections adopted determinate sentencing guidelines under which a juvenile's length of stay is based on the present offense and the weight of "risk of failure" factors (Minnesota Department of Corrections 1980). The juvenile risk factors include the same criteria as do Minnesota's Adult Sentencing Guidelines, which are explicitly designed to achieve just deserts (Feld 1988b). Arizona's Department of Corrections adopted "Length of Confinement Guidelines" that use five offense levels and specify proportional mandatory minimum terms to govern juvenile release decisions (Arizona Department of Corrections 1986). Georgia's Division of Youth Services uses an administrative determinate sentencing framework to supplement its designated felony statute and classifies juveniles into five risk levels based on the present offense and other "aggravating factors" (Forst et al. 1985). In California, if a juvenile court judge commits a youth to the Youth Authority, then the release decision is made by the Youthful Offender Parole Board, which establishes a parole consideration date based primarily on the seriousness of the offense.

Empirical Evaluations of Juvenile Court Sentencing Practices

Juvenile court judges decide what to do with a child, in part, by reference to statutory mandates. However, practical, bureaucratic considerations influence their discretionary decisions as well (Cicourel 1968; Emerson 1969; Bortner 1982). Because of the need to look beyond the present offense to best interests and due to paternalistic assumptions about the control of children, judges enjoy greater discretion than do their adult court counterparts.

The wide frame of relevance associated with individualized justice raises concerns about discretionary decision making and particularly its impact on lower class and non-White youths (Fagan et al. 1987; Krisberg et al. 1987; McCarthy and Smith 1986; Dannefer and Schutt 1982). When practitioners of individualized justice make discretionary judgments based on social characteristics or race rather than on legal variables, their decisions often result in differential processing and more severe sentencing of minority youths (Krisberg et al. 1987; Fagan et al. 1987; McCarthy and Smith, 1986). Or, despite the juvenile system's nominal commitment to individualized justice, sentences may be based on the offense, and the disproportionate overrepresentation of minority youths may result from real differences in their rates of delinquency (Wolfgang et al. 1972; Hindelang 1978; Huizinga and Elliott 1987).

To what extent do legal factors—present offense and prior record—or social characteristics—race, sex, or social class—influence judges' dispositional decision making? Although dispositional evaluation studies—conducted in different jurisdictions at different times and using different methodologies and theoretical perspectives—yield contradictory results (Fagan et al. 1987; McCarthy and Smith 1986), two general findings emerge from this research. First, most evaluations of dispositional practices indicate that offense considerations structure practical decision making, and present offense and prior record account for most of the explained sentencing variance (Horowitz and Wasserman 1980; McCarthy and Smith 1986; Clarke and Koch 1980; Feld 1989; Barton 1976; Phillips and Dinitz 1982)). Second, after controlling for offense variables, discretionary individualization is often synonymous with racial disparities in sentencing (Krisberg et al. 1987; Fagan et al. 1987; McCarthy and Smith 1986).

Practical administrative considerations provide an impetus for sentences based on offense. Bureaucratic desire to avoid scandal and unfavorable political and media attention constrain juvenile court dispositions and encourage more formal and restrictive responses to more serious juvenile deviance (Cicourel 1968; Emerson 1969; Bortner 1982; Matza 1964). People-processing organizations pursuing often contradictory, formal goals develop bureaucratic strategies to cope with the requirements of individualized assessments (Matza 1964; Marshall and Thomas 1983). Because juvenile courts routinely collect information about present offenses and prior records, they provide bases for decisions. Despite claims of individualization, juvenile and adult court sentencing practices are more similar than their statutory language suggests in their emphases on present offense and prior record (Greenwood et al. 1983).

Although offense variables exhibit a stronger relationship with dispositions than do social variables, most of the variance in the sentencing of juveniles remains unexplained (Clarke and Koch 1980; Thomas and Fitch 1975; Horowitz and Wasserman 1982). With only a weak relationship between offenses and sentences, recent statutory changes may reflect legislative disquiet with the underlying premises of individualized justice, the idiosyncratic exercises of discretion, and the inequalities that result (Feld 1987, 1988b).

Formal legislative and administrative sentencing guidelines and operational practices contradict the individualized, offender-oriented sentencing premises of juvenile courts. Evaluations of juvenile correctional facilities provide another indicator of whether juvenile court intervention constitutes punishment or treatment. The routinely deplorable institutional conditions reported in *Gault* (1967) motivated the Court to insist upon minimal procedural safeguards for juveniles. Although involuntary confinement per se does not necessarily constitute punishment, the Court in *Gault* correctly viewed incarceration as a severe penalty, a denial of autonomy, and a status degradation, all of which are elements of punishment.

The juvenile court's rhetorical commitment to rehabilitation has been contradicted since its inception by the reality of custodial institutional confinement. Rothman's (1980) study of early training schools described institutions that failed to rehabilitate and were scarcely distinguishable from their adult penal counterparts. Schlossman (1977) has provided an equally dismal account of Progressive juvenile correctional programs. The juvenile court's lineage of punitive confinement in the name of rehabilitation can be traced to its institutional precursor, the Houses of Refuge (Hawes 1971; Mennel 1973; Rothman 1971).

The inadequacy of juvenile correctional programs is not simply historical. Contemporary evaluations of juvenile correctional facilities reveal a continuing gap between the rhetoric of rehabilitation and its punitive reality (Bartollas, Miller, and Dinitz 1976; Feld 1977, 1981b; Lerner 1986). A study of juvenile institutions in Massachusetts described facilities in which staff physically abused inmates and were frequently powerless to prevent inmate abuse of other inmates (Feld 1977, 1981b). A study in an Ohio institution revealed a similarly violent and oppressive environment for rehabilitating young delinquents (Bartollas et al. 1976). Extensive scrutiny of Texas juvenile institutions during the 1970s revealed similar patterns of staff and inmate violence and degrading make-work tasks (Guggenheim 1978). A critical review of California Youth Authority institutions concluded that "a young man convicted of a crime cannot pay his debt to society safely. The hard truth is that the CYA staff cannot protect its inmates from being beaten or intimidated by other prisoners" (Lerner 1986, p. 12). Despite rehabilitative rhetoric, the daily reality of juveniles confined in many "treatment" facilities is one of staff and inmate violence, predatory behavior, and punitive, custodial incarceration.

Coinciding with these post-*Gault* evaluation studies, several lawsuits challenged conditions of confinement, alleged that the institutions violated inmates' "right to treatment" and inflicted "cruel and unusual punishment," and provided another outside view of juvenile correctional facilities (Feld 1984). In *Nelson v. Heyne* (1974), the court found that inmates were routinely beaten with a "fraternity paddle," injected with psychotropic drugs for social control purposes, and deprived of minimally adequate care and individualized treatment. In *Inmates of Boys' Training School v. Affleck* (1972), the court found youths confined in dark and cold dungeon-like cells in their underwear, routinely locked in "solitary confinement, and subjected to a variety of punitive practices." In *Morales v. Turman* (1976), the court found numerous instances of physical brutality and abuse, including hazing by staff and inmates, staff-administered beatings and tear gassings, homosexual assaults, extensive use of solitary confinement, repetitive and degrading make-work, and minimal clinical services. Unfortunately, these cases are not atypical, as the list of decisions documenting institutional abuses demonstrates (Krisberg et al. 1986). Rehabilitative euphemisms, such as "providing a structured environment," cannot disguise the punitive reality of juvenile institutional confinement. Although not as uniformly bad as adult prisons, juvenile correctional facilities are not so benign or therapeutic as to justify dispensing with procedural safeguards. Although the prospect of incarcerating juveniles in barbarous adult facilities is not appealing, the prevalence of violence, aggression, and homosexual rape in juvenile facilities is hardly consoling (Bartollas et al. 1976; Feld 1977). Evaluation research provides scant support for the effectiveness of such rehabilitative programs (Lab and Whitehead 1988).

Summary of Changes in Juvenile Court Sentencing Practices

The preceding analyses of de jure and de facto sentencing practices demonstrate a strong nationwide movement, both in theory and in practice, away from therapeutic, individualized dispositions toward punitive, offense-based sentences. When

McKeiver was decided in 1970, no states used determinate or mandatory minimum sentencing statutes or administrative sentencing guidelines. In 1976, New York and Kentucky adopted designated felony legislation. In 1977, Washington adopted determinate sentencing guidelines and Colorado passed its first juvenile offender sentencing law. In 1979, serious offender sentencing legislation was adopted in Connecticut, Illinois, and North Carolina. Since 1980, 11 more states—Arizona, Arkansas, California, Delaware, Georgia, Minnesota, New Jersey, Ohio, Tennessee, Texas and Virginia—have adopted mandatory minimum serious offender laws, determinate sentencing laws, or administrative guidelines (Feld 1988b). Currently, about one third of the states employ one or more of these sentencing strategies.

These legislative and administrative changes and operational practices have eliminated most of the significant differences between juvenile and adult sentencing practices. Determinate sentences based on present offense and prior record challenge any therapeutic purpose for juvenile dispositions. Mandatory minimum sentences based on the seriousness of the offense avoid any reference to a youth's real needs or best interest. Revisions in juvenile court purpose clauses that place greater emphasis on the goals of criminal law and protecting public safety, and similar decisions by courts, eliminate even rhetorical support for the traditional rehabilitative goals of juvenile justice. As a result, "the purposes of the juvenile process have become more punitive, its procedures formalistic, adversarial and public, and the consequences of conviction much more harsh" (*Javier A.* 1984, p. 964). These policy changes repudiate most of the basic assumptions of the original juvenile court: that juvenile offenders should be treated differently than adults, that juvenile courts operate in a youth's best interest, and that rehabilitation is an indeterminate process that cannot be limited by fixed-time punishment (Coates et al. 1985). These changes also challenge the premise of the Court in *McKeiver* that juvenile dispositions are exclusively rehabilitative and require fewer procedural safeguards.

▨ The Punitive Juvenile Court and the Quality of Procedural Justice

The shift in sentencing focus from the offender to the offense, and the elevation of punishment over treatment raises questions about the quality of procedural justice that *McKeiver* avoided. Since *Gault*, there has been substantial convergence between the formal procedural attributes of criminal courts and those of juvenile courts (Feld 1984). The emphasis on procedural formality reflects the shift from the traditional therapeutic missions of juvenile courts to their current social control functions.

Despite the criminalizing of juvenile court procedures, it remains nearly as true today as two decades ago that "the child receives the worst of both worlds: [the child] gets neither the protections accorded to adults nor the solicitous care and regenerative treatment postulated for children" (*Kent* 1966, p. 555). Even as states increasingly punish young offenders, most juvenile codes provide neither special procedural safeguards to protect juveniles from their own immaturity nor the full panoply of adult criminal procedural safeguards to protect them from punitive state intervention. Instead, juvenile courts employ procedures that assure that youths continue to "receive the worst of both worlds," treating juvenile offenders just like adult criminal defendants when formal equality redounds to their disadvantage while at the same time using less adequate juvenile court safeguards when those deficient procedures redound to the advantage of the state (Feld 1984).

Jury Trials in Juvenile Court

The right to a jury trial and the assistance of counsel are two critical procedural safeguards when sentences are based on the nature of the offense rather than on the needs of the offender. In denying juveniles a right to a jury trial, *McKeiver* posited virtual parity between the factual accuracy of juvenile and adult adjudications. However, juries serve special protective functions to assure factual accuracy and are more likely to acquit than are judges (Kalven and Zeisel 1966). Moreover, criminal guilt is not just "factual" guilt but an assessment of culpability; juries provide the nexus between statutory language and the community's sense of justice in applying the law to the particular case. By dispensing with juries, *McKeiver* rendered it easier to convict a youth appearing before a judge in juvenile court than to convict him or her, on the basis of the same evidence, before a jury of detached citizens in a criminal proceeding (Greenwood et al. 1983; Feld 1984).

Moreover, *McKeiver* ignored the additional function that procedural safeguards serve of preventing governmental oppression (Feld 1981a, 1984, 1988b). In *Duncan v. Louisiana* (1968), the Supreme Court held that fundamental fairness in adult criminal proceedings requires a jury to achieve both factual accuracy *and* protection against governmental oppression. The Court in *Duncan* (1968) noted several benefits that a jury trial provides: (a) protection from a weak or biased judge, (b) injection of the community's values into the process, and (c) visibility and accountability for justice administration. These arguments are equally applicable to juvenile proceedings.

The increased punitiveness of juvenile justice raises a dilemma of constitutional dimensions: "Is it fair, in the constitutional sense, to expose minors to adult sanctions for crimes, without granting them the same due process rights as adults?" (Private Sector 1987, p. 7). Few of the states that sentence juveniles on the basis of their offenses provide jury trials; several of those states have explicitly rejected constitutional challenges requesting jury trials.

For juvenile justice operatives, the jury trial has symbolic importance out of all proportion to its practical impact. Even in states where jury trials are available, they are seldom used (Feld 1988b). Providing a jury trial requires candor and honesty about the punitive reality of juvenile justice and the corresponding need to provide safeguards against even benevolently motivated governmental coercion. Assessing the need for jury trials in juvenile court requires recognizing what actually transpires in the name of rehabilitation.

Benevolence and rehabilitation are expansive concepts that may widen the net of social control and lead to great abuse through self-delusion (Allen 1964, 1981). Punishment, by contrast, frankly acknowledges the harmfulness of coercion and carries with it limits and proportionality (Cohen 1978).

If one does not accept uncritically self-serving claims of a benevolent, therapeutic purpose, is there anything about juveniles or justice that justifies denying jury trials in juvenile courts? Given the fundamental shift in underlying assumptions, proponents of the traditional juvenile court should demonstrate why juvenile procedures should not be structured just like those of other courts that impose punishment. Is there anything about a criminal justice system for youths that justifies or requires procedures different than those for adults? If there is, does the difference lie in the nature of juveniles or in the nature of the punishments imposed? The express punitiveness of juvenile courts shifts to its proponents the burden of proof to justify with evidence, and not just rhetoric, every procedural difference between juvenile and criminal courts.

The Right to Counsel in Juvenile Court

Procedural justice hinges on access to and the assistance of legal counsel. The Supreme Court held *In re Gault* (1967) that juvenile offenders were constitutionally entitled to counsel in juvenile delinquency proceedings. It also held that juveniles were entitled to the privilege against self-incrimination and the right to confront and cross-examine their accusers at a hearing. Without the assistance of counsel, these other rights could be negated.

In the decades since *Gault*, the promise of counsel remains unrealized. Although national statistics are not available, surveys of representation by counsel in several jurisdictions suggest that lawyers appear much less frequently than generally believed. The available data indicate that in many states less than half of all juveniles receive the assistance of counsel to which they are constitutionally entitled (Feld 1984, 1988a, 1989).

Prior to *Gault*, an attorney's appearance in delinquency proceedings was a rare event, occurring in perhaps 5% of cases. Despite formal legal changes, the actual delivery of legal services has lagged behind. Shortly after *Gault*, Lefstein et al. (1969) examined institutional compliance with the decision and found that juveniles were neither adequately advised of their right to counsel nor had counsel appointed for them. Ferster and Courtless (1972) found that 27% of juveniles had lawyers, and in most of the proceedings in which counsel were present, they did nothing.

Recent evaluations indicate that lawyers still appear less often than might be expected. Clarke and Koch (1980) found that only 22.3% and 45.8% of juveniles were represented in two sites in North Carolina. Aday (1986) found rates of representation of 26.2% and 38.7% in a southeastern state. Only 32% of juveniles in a large north central city were represented (Walter and Ostrander 1982). Bortner (1982) reported that only 41.8% of juveniles in a large, Midwestern county's juvenile court had an attorney. Most youths in Minnesota were unrepresented, with county-by-county variations in rates of representation ranging from a high of 100% to a low of less than 5% (Feld 1984, 1988a, 1989). A substantial minority of youths removed from their homes (30.7%) and those confined in state juvenile correctional institutions (26.5%) were unrepresented (Feld 1989). The most comprehensive study available reported that in half of the six states surveyed, only 37.5%, 47.7%, and 52.7% of delinquents had counsel (Feld 1988a). It appears that *Gault's* promise of counsel remains unkept for most juveniles in most states.

One common pattern is a direct relationship between the offense and rates of representation. Juveniles charged with serious offenses generally have higher rates of representation (Feld 1988a, 1989). In most jurisdictions, however, serious offenses are only a small part of juvenile court dockets and substantially larger proportions of youths charged with "kid stuff" lack counsel. It is these youths who are most likely to be incarcerated without representation (Feld 1988a, 1989).

There are a variety of possible explanations for why so many youths are unrepresented: (a) parental reluctance to retain an attorney; (b) inadequate public-defender legal services in nonurban areas; (c) judicial encouragement of and readiness to find waivers of the right to counsel to ease administrative burdens on the courts; (d) cursory and misleading judicial advisories of rights that convey inadequately the importance of the right to counsel and suggest that waiver is simply a meaningless technicality; (e) continuing judicial hostility to an advocacy role in a traditional, treatment-oriented court; or (f) judicial predetermination of dispositions and denial of counsel where probation is the anticipated outcome (Feld 1984, 1989; Bortner 1982; Lefstein et al. 1969; Stapleton and Teitelbaum 1972). Whatever the reasons, many juveniles who face potentially coercive state action never see a lawyer, waive their right to counsel without consulting with or appreciating the consequences of relinquishing counsel, and confront the power of the state alone and unaided.

The most common explanation is that juveniles waive their right to counsel. For juveniles to validly relinquish a constitutional right, most states requires a judge to determine whether there was a "knowing, intelligent, and voluntary waiver" under the "totality of the circumstances" (*Johnson* 1938; *Fare* 1979; Feld 1984, 1989). The Supreme Court held that an adult defendant has the right to waive counsel and appear *pro se* in state criminal trials so long as he or she is capable of self-representation and voluntarily and intelligently elects to do so (*Johnson* 1938; *Faretta* 1975).

The crucial issue for juveniles, as for adults, is whether a waiver can be "voluntary and intelligent," particularly if made without consulting with counsel. The problem is exacerbated when the judges giving the counsel advisories seek predetermined results, that is, waiver of counsel, which influences both the information they convey and their interpretation of the juvenile's response. The "totality" approach to waivers of rights by juveniles has been criticized extensively (Feld 1984; Grisso 1980). Despite judicial approval, juveniles simply are not as competent as adults to waive their constitutional rights in a knowing and intelligent manner (Grisso 1980, 1981). Several states recognize this developmental fact and prohibit either waivers of counsel or incarceration of unrepresented delinquents (Iowa 1985; Wisconsin 1983; Institute of Judicial Administration 1980), but most states allow juveniles to waive their right to counsel in delinquency proceedings unaided by counsel. The variations in rates of representation within a state and by types of offense suggest that the denial of counsel reflects deliberate judicial policies rather than differences in minors' competence to waive the assistance of lawyers.

Uncounselled Convictions and Enhanced Sentences

The questionable validity of many waivers of counsel by juveniles raises collateral legal issues as well. In *Scott v. Illinois* (1979). the Court held that even in misdemeanor proceedings, unless validly waived, counsel must be appointed as a prerequisite to any sentence of incarceration. The dubious validity of children's waivers of rights affects every disposition in which a juvenile is removed from home or confined. Moreover, using prior uncounselled convictions to enhance subsequent sentences is also invalid. In *Baldasar v. Illinois* (1980), the Court reaffirmed an earlier line of cases that held that uncounselled prior conviction could not be used to enhance later sentences (*Tucker* 1972; *Burgett* 1967), Courts have applied the principle that prior convictions should not be used to enhance subsequent sentences in several contexts involving prior juvenile convictions obtained without counsel (Feld 1989).

Although juvenile court judges in most states do not follow formal sentencing guidelines, they routinely rely upon prior uncounselled convictions when sentencing juveniles (Feld 1989). Many "guidelines" suggest that states consider the prior record when imposing mandatory minimum or enhancing sentences. Judges also consider prior uncounselled convictions when deciding whether or not to waive a juvenile for

adult prosecution, and many criminal courts consider juvenile prior convictions when sentencing young offenders as adults. Juvenile courts also use their criminal contempt power to "bootstrap" unrepresented status offenders who violate conditions of probation into delinquents who then may be incarcerated in detention facilities or secure institutions (*Walker* 1972).

⊠ The Punitive Juvenile Court and the Quality of Justice

The procedural deficiencies of juvenile courts are untenable in an institution that is increasingly and explicitly punitive. Recent changes in juvenile sentencing legislation and practices reflect a basic philosophical ambivalence about the continued role of the juvenile court. As juvenile courts converge with adult criminal courts both procedurally and substantively, is there any reason to maintain a separate juvenile criminal court whose sole distinction is inadequate procedures under which no adult would consent to be tried?

The juvenile court is at a philosophical crossroads that cannot be resolved by simplistic "treatment versus punishment" formulations. In reality, there are no practical or operational differences between the two—"sometimes punishment is treatment." Recognizing the punitive reality of juvenile court intervention, however, carries with it a concomitant obligation to provide appropriate procedural safeguards, because "the condition of being a [child] does not justify a kangaroo court" (*Gault* 1967, p. 28). The Supreme Court in *Gault* concluded that the appointment of counsel is the prerequisite to procedural justice in the juvenile court. As the likelihood of coercive action in juvenile courts increases, *Gault's* insistence on the right to counsel acquires even greater salience.

Although providing young offenders with full procedural parity may realize the Court's fear in *McKeiver* (1971) of sounding the death knell of the traditional juvenile court, to fail to do so perpetuates injustice. Moreover, abolishing the juvenile court may be desirable from the standpoint of both juveniles and society. The only remaining virtue of the punitive juvenile court is that juveniles convicted of serious offenses typically receive shorter sentences than do adults for similar offenses. If shorter sentences for reduced culpability is the principal justification for juvenile courts, then providing youths with fractional reductions of adult sentences could just as readily meet that goal. This could take the form of an explicit "youth discount" at sentencing (Feld 1988b). Some of the statutes surveyed in this article provide examples of sentences for youths that are considerably shorter than those imposed on adults. Sentencing "discounts" do not require incarcerating juveniles in adult prisons; existing juvenile institutions provide the option of age-segregated dispositional facilities.

Full procedural parity in criminal courts, coupled with alternative safeguards for children, can more adequately provide protections than does the current juvenile court. For more than 2 decades, juvenile courts have demonstrated a distressing capacity to deflect, co-opt, ignore, and absorb ameliorative procedural reform with minimal institutional change. For example, 20 years after *Gault* guaranteed the right to counsel, many unrepresented juveniles continue to appear in juvenile courts, including many who are subsequently sentenced to institutions. The overall quality of procedural justice routinely afforded to youths would be intolerable for adult defendants facing incarceration. With the explicit emergence of retribution in juvenile courts coupled with a continuing public and political unwillingness to commit scarce social resources to the welfare of children in general, much less to those who commit crimes, is there any remaining reason to believe that the juvenile court can be rehabilitated?

⊠ Note

1. A table summarizing juvenile court sentencing statutes and correctional guidelines is available on request from the author.

⊠ References

Aday, David P. Jr. 1986. "Court Structure, Defense Attorney Use, and Juvenile Court Decisions." *Sociological Quarterly* 27:107–19.

Allen, Francis A. 1964. "Legal Values and the Rehabilitative Ideal." Pp. 25–41 in *Borderland of the Criminal Law*. Chicago: University of Chicago Press.

——1978. "The Decline of the Rehabilitative Ideal in American Criminal Justice." *Cleveland State Law Review* 27:147–56.

——1981. *The Decline of the Rehabilitative Ideal: Penal Policy and Social Purpose*. New Haven: Yale University Press.

American Friends Service Committee. 1971. *Struggle for Justice*. New York: Hill & Wang.

Arizona Department of Corrections. 1986. *Length of Confinement Guidelines for Juveniles*. Tucson: Author.

Bartollas, Clemens, Stuart J. Miller, and Simon Dinitz. 1976. *Juvenile Victimization*. New York: Wiley.

Barton, William. 1976. "Discretionary Decision-Making in Juvenile Justice." *Crime and Delinquency* 22:470–80.

Bortner, M. A. 1982. *Inside a Juvenile Court*. New York: New York University Press.

Cicourel, Aaron V. 1968. *The Social Organization of Juvenile Justice*. New York: Wiley.

Clarke, Stevens H. and Gary G. Koch. 1980. "Juvenile Court: Therapy or Crime Control, and Do Lawyers Make a Difference?" *Law and Society Review* 14:263–308.

Coates, Robert, Martin Forsl, and Bruce Fisher. 1985. *Institutional Commitment and Release Decision-making for Juvenile Delinquents: An Assessment of Determinate and Indeterminate Approaches—A Cross-State Analysis*. San Francisco: URSA Institute.

Cohen, Fred. 1978. "Juvenile Offenders: Proportionality vs. Treatment." *Children's Rights Reporter* 8:1–16.

Dannefer, Dale and Russell Schutt. 1982. "Race and Juvenile Justice Processing in Court and Police Agencies." *American Journal of Sociology* 87:1113–32.

Emerson, Robert M. 1969. *Judging Delinquents*. Chicago: Aldine.

Fagan, Jeffrey, Ellen Slaughter, and Eliot Hartstone. 1987. "Blind Justice? The Impact of Race on the

Juvenile Justice Process." *Crime and Delinquency* 33:224–58.

Feld, Barry C. 1977. *Neutralizing Inmate Violence.* Cambridge, MA: Ballinger.

——1981a. "Juvenile Court Legislative Reform and the Serious Young Offender: Dismantling the 'Rehabilitative Ideal.'" *Minnesota Law Review* 69:141–242.

——1981b. "A Comparative Analysis of Organizational Structure and Inmate Subcultures in Institutions for Juvenile Offenders." *Crime and Delinquency* 27:336–63.

——1984. "Criminalizing Juvenile Justice: Rules of Procedure for Juvenile Court." *Minnesota Law Review* 69:141–276.

——1987. "Juvenile Court Meets the Principle of Offense: Legislative Changes in Juvenile Waiver Statutes." *Journal of Criminal Law and Criminology* 78:471–533.

——1988a. "*In re Gault* Revisited: A Cross-State Comparison of the Right to Counsel in Juvenile Court." *Crime and Delinquency* 34:393–424.

——1988b. "Juvenile Court Meets the Principle of Offense: Punishment, Treatment, and the Difference it Makes." *Boston University Law Review* 68:821–915.

——1989. "The Right to Counsel in Juvenile Court: An Empirical Study of When Lawyers Appear and the Difference They Make." *Journal of Criminal Law and Criminology* 79:1185–1346.

Ferster, Elyce Zenoff and Thomas F. Courtless. 1972. "Pre-dispositional Data, Role of Counsel and Decisions in a Juvenile Court." *Law and Society Review* 7:195–222.

Fisher, Bruce, Mark Fraser, and Martin Forst. 1985. *Institutional Commitment and Release Decision-Making for Juvenile Delinquents: An Assessment of Determinate and Indeterminate Approaches, Washington State—A Case Study.* San Francisco: URSA Institute.

Forst, Martin, Elizabeth Friedman, and Robert Coates. 1985. *Institutional Commitment and Release Decision-Making for Juvenile Delinquents: An Assessment of Determinate and Indeterminate Approaches, Georgia—A Case Study.* San Francisco, CA: URSA Institute.

Fox, Sanford J. 1970. "Juvenile Justice Reform: An Historical Perspective." *Stanford Law Review* 22:1187–1239.

Gardner, Martin. 1982. "Punishment and Juvenile Justice: A Conceptual Framework for Assessing Constitutional Rights of Youthful Offenders." *Vanderbilt Law Review* 35:791–847.

Georgia Division of Youth Services. 1985. *Policy and Procedure Manual.* Atlanta: Georgia Department of Human Resources.

Gibbons, Don C. 1965. *Changing the Lawbreaker.* Englewood Cliffs, NJ: Prentice Hall.

Greenberg, David, ed. 1977. *Corrections and Punishment.* Beverly Hills, CA: Sage.

Greenwood, Peter, A. Lipson, A. Abrahamse, and Frank Zimring. 1983. *Youth Crime and Juvenile Justice in California.* Santa Monica, CA: RAND.

Grisso, Thomas. 1980. "Juveniles' Capacities to Waive Miranda Rights: An Empirical Analysis." *California Law Review* 68:1134–1166.

——1981. *Juveniles' Waiver of Rights.* New York: Plenum.

Guggenheim, Martin. 1978. "A Call to Abolish the Juvenile Justice System." *Children's Rights Reporter* 2:7–19.

Hagan, John and Jeffrey Leon. 1977. "Rediscovering Delinquency: Social History, Political Ideology and the Sociology of Law." *American Sociological Review* 42:587–98.

Hart, H.L.A. 1968. *Punishment* and *Responsibility.* New York: Oxford University Press.

Hawes, Joseph. 1971. *Children in Urban Society.* New York: Oxford University Press.

Hindelang, Michael. 1978. "Race and Involvement in Common Law Personal Crimes." *American Sociological Review* 43:93–109.

Horowitz, Allan and Michael Wasserman. 1980. "Some Misleading Conceptions in Sentencing Research: An Example and Reformulation in the Juvenile Court." *Criminology* 18:411–24.

Huizinga, David and Delbert S. Elliott. 1987. "Juvenile Offenders: Prevalence, Offender Incidence, and Arrest Rates by Race." *Crime and Delinquency* 33:206–23.

Institute of Judicial Administration—American Bar Association. 1980. *Juvenile Justice Standards Relating to Juvenile Delinquency and Sanctions.* Cambridge, MA: Ballinger.

Kalven, Harry and Hans Zeisel. 1966. *The American Jury.* Chicago: University of Chicago Press.

Krisberg, Barry, Ira Schwartz, Gideon Fishman, Zvi Eisikovits, Edna Guttman, and Karen Joe. 1987. "The Incarceration of Minority Youth." *Crime and Delinquency* 33:173–205.

Krisberg, Barry, Ira Schwartz, Paul Lisky, and James Austin. 1986. "The Watershed of Juvenile Justice Reform." *Crime and Delinquency* 32:5–38.

Lab, Steven P. and John T. Whitehead. 1988. "An Analysis of Juvenile Correctional Treatment." *Crime and Delinquency* 34:60–83.

Lefstein, Norman, Vaughan Stapleton, and Lee Teitelbaum. 1969. "In Search of Juvenile Justice: *Gault* and Its Implementation." *Law and Society Review* 3:491–562.

Lerner, Steven. 1986. *Bodily Harm.* Bolinas, CA: Common Knowledge Press.

Marshall, Ineke H. and Charles W. Thomas. 1983. "Discretionary Decision-Making and the Juvenile Court." *Juvenile and Family Court Journal* 34:47–59.

Martinson, Robert. 1974. "What Works? Questions and Answers About Prison Reform." *The Public Interest* 35:22–54.

Matza, David. 1964. *Delinquency and Drift.* New York: Wiley.

McCarthy, Belinda and Brent L. Smith. 1986. "The Conceptualization of Discrimination in the Juvenile Justice Process: The Impact of Administrative Factors and Screening Decisions on Juvenile Court Dispositions." *Criminology* 24:41–64.

Mennel, Robert. 1973. *Thorns and Thistles.* Hanover, NH: University Press of New England.

Minnesota Department of Corrections. 1980. *Juvenile Release Guidelines.* St. Paul, MN: Minnesota Department of Corrections.

Packer, Herbert L. 1968. *The Limits of the Criminal Sanction.* Stanford, CA: Stanford University Press.

Petersilia, Joan and Susan Turner 1987. "Guideline-based Justice: Prediction and Racial Minorities." Pp. 151–218 in *Crime and Justice: An Annual Review,* Vol. 9, edited by Michael Tonry and Norval Morris. Chicago: University of Chicago Press.

Phillips, Charles D. and Simon Dinitz. 1982. "Labelling and Juvenile Court Dispositions: Official Responses to a Cohort of Violent Juveniles." *Sociological Quarterly* 23:267–78.

Platt, Anthony. 1977. *The Child Savers.* Chicago: University of Chicago Press.

Private Sector Task Force on Juvenile Justice. 1987. *Final Report.* San Francisco: National Council of Crime and Delinquency.

Rothman, David J. 1971. *The Discovery of the Asylum.* Boston: Little, Brown.

——1980. *Conscience and Convenience.* Boston: Little, Brown

Ryerson, Ellen. 1978. *The Best-laid Plans.* New York: Hill & Wang.

Schlossman, Steven. 1977. *Love and the American Delinquent.* Chicago: University of Chicago Press.

Schneider, Anne and Donna Schram. 1983. *A Justice Philosophy for the Juvenile Court.* Seattle, WA: Urban Policy Research.

Sechrest, Lee B., Susan O. White, and Elizabeth D. Brown, eds. 1979. *The Rehabilitation of Criminal Offenders.* Washington, DC: National Academy of Sciences.

Stapleton, W. Vaughan and Lee E. Teitelbaum. 1972. *In Defense of Youth.* New York: Russell Sage.

Sutton, John R. 1988. *Stubborn Children.* Berkeley: University of California Press.

Thomas, Charles W. and W. Anthony Fitch. 1975. "An Inquiry Into the Association Between Respondents' Personal Characteristics and Juvenile Court Dispositions." *William and Mary Law Review* 17:61–83.

Twentieth Century Fund Task Force. 1976. *Fair and Certain Punishment.* New York: McGraw-Hill.

Von Hirsch, Andrew. 1976. *Doing Justice.* New York: Hill & Wang.

——1986. *Past vs. Future Crimes.* New Brunswick, NJ: Rutgers University Press.

Walkover, Andrew. 1984. "The Infancy Defense in the New Juvenile Court." *University of California Los Angeles Law Review* 31:503–62.

Walter, James D. and Susan A. Ostrander. 1982. "An Observational Study of a Juvenile Court." *Juvenile and Family Court Journal* 33:53–69.

Wolfgang, Marvin, Robert Figlio, and Thorsten Sellin, 1972. *Delinquency in a Birth Cohort.* Chicago: University of Chicago Press.

✑ Cases

Baldasar v. Illinois, 446 U.S. 222 (1980).

Breed v. Jones, 421 U.S. 519 (1975).

Burgett v. Texas, 389 U.S. 109 (1967).

In re D.F.B., 430 N.W.2d 476 (1988)

D. D. H. v. Dostert, 269 S.E.2d 401 (1980).

Duncan v. Louisiana, 391 U.S. 145 (1968).

Inmates of Boys' Training School v. Affleck, 346 F. Supp. 1354 (1972).

Fare v. Michael C., 442 U.S. 707 (1979).

Faretta v. California, 422 U.S. 806 (1975).

In re Gault, 387 U.S. 1(1967).

In re Javier A., 159 Cal. App.3d 913, 206 Cal Rptr. 386 (1984).

Johnson v. Zerbst, 304 U.S. 458 (1938).

Kent v. United States, 383 U.S. 541 (1966).

State v. Lawley, 91 Wash.2d 654, 591 P.2d 772 (1979).

McKeiver v. Pennsylvania, 403 U.S. 528 (1971).

Morales v. Turman, 535 F.2d 864 (1976).

Nelson v. Heyne, 491 F.2D 352 (1974).

State v. Schaaf, 109 Wash.2d 1, 743 P.2d 240 (1987).

Scott v. Illinois, 440 U.S. 367 (1979).

In re Seven Minors, 99 Nev. 427, 664 P.2d 947 (1983).

United States v. Tucker, 404 U.S. 443 (1972).

In re Walker, 191 S.E.2d 702 (1972).

In re Winship, 397 U.S. 358 (1970).

✑ Statutes

Ark. Stat. Ann. § 45–402.1 (1979).

Ark. Stat. Ann. § 45–436 (3) (1987).

Cal. Welf. & Inst. Code § 202 (West 1984).

Colo. Rev. Stat. §§ 19–3–113, -113.1, -113.2 (1986).

Conn. Gen. Stat. § 46B-141(a) (1986).

Del. Code Ann. tit. 10, § 937 (1986).

Fla. Stat. Ann. § 39.001(2)(a) (1978).

Fla. Stat. Ann. § 39.11 (1988).

Ga. Code Ann. § 15–11–37 (1988).

Hawaii Rev. Stat. § 571–1 (1976).

Hawaii Rev. Stat. § 571–48 (1987).

Ill. Ann. Stat. ch. 37, § 701–2 (Smith-Hurd 1972).

Ill. Ann. Stat. § 705–12, 805–33 (1988).

Ind. Code Ann. § 31–6-1–1 (Burns 1980).

Iowa Code Ann. § 232.1 (1904).

Iowa Code Ann. § 232.52 (1985).

Ky. Rev. Slat. § 208.194 (1988).

Minn. Stat. § 260.011 (2) (1980).

N.H. Stat. Ann. § 169-B:1 II (1979).

N.J. Stat. Ann. §§ 2A:4A-43(a) (West Supp. 1987).

N.Y. Fam. Ct. Act §§ 301.2(8), (9), 352.2 353.5 (1987).

N.C. Gen. Stat. §7A-646 (1986).

N.C. Gen. Stat. § 7A-652(b)(2) (1987).

N.D. Cent. Code § 27–20–01 (1969).

Ohio Rev. Code Ann. § 2151.01 (1969).

Ohio Rev. Code Ann. § 2151.353, -.355 (1987).

Or. Rev. Stat. § 419.474 (2) (1919).

R.I. Gen. Laws § 14–1-2 (1944).

Tenn. Code Ann. § 37–1-101 (1970).

Tenn. Code Ann. §§37–1-131, -137 (1987).

Tex. Fam. Code Ann. § 51.01 (2) (1986).

Tex. Fam. Code §§ 53.045; 54.03(b) and (c); 54.04 (1988).

Utah Code Ann. § 78–3a-1 (1931).

Va. Code § 16.1–227 (1982).

Va. Code § 16.1–285.1 (1988).

Vt. Stat. Ann. tit. 33 § 631 (1967).

Wash. Rev. Code Ann. § 13.40.010(2) (Supp. 1984).

W.Va. Code, 49–1-1(a) (1978).

Wis. Stat. An. § 48.23 (1983).

DISCUSSION QUESTIONS

1. Many states have changed the purpose clause of their juvenile codes. Argue for or against this statement: "If the purposes of juvenile and criminal court are now similar and nearly identical, then the legal rights (to counsel, jury trial) should also be equal."

2. Suggest arguments for and against the use of both legal and social factors in sentencing juveniles. What recommendations would you make to your state lawmakers on guidelines for sentencing juveniles?

3. According to Feld and other experts, can juveniles make an intelligent, voluntary waiver of their right to counsel? Are there cases in which judges should not accept a waiver of the right to counsel?

4. Forty years have passed since *In re Gault* (1967). Do you believe the juvenile court has or has not met the standards given by the Supreme Court?

5. Explain why you agree or disagree with Feld's suggestion of a "youth discount" in sentencing juvenile offenders.

❖

READING

The dispositional stage is the most critical decision-making level that delinquents encounter in juvenile court. The factors that have been found to have an impact on juvenile court sentencing include legal, administrative, and social factors. Previous research has produced inconsistent results about what motivates juvenile court officials in making sentencing decisions, and there is little agreement among researchers as to which factors account for most juvenile court dispositions. In addressing this question, Sanborn did not examine the actual factors that influenced the disposition decision; instead, he examined juvenile court workers' perspectives on court decision making. In this article he reports on the results of interviews with judges, prosecutors, defense attorneys, and probation officers from three juvenile courts representing urban, suburban, and rural areas. The court workers were asked what factors should and did influence disposition decisions in juvenile court. Sanborn found considerable variation in their perspectives, and suggested that we may never be able to establish conclusively what factors most influence court decisions.

Factors Perceived to Affect Delinquent Dispositions in Juvenile Court

Putting the Sentencing Decision Into Context

Joseph B. Sanborn, Jr.

✉ The Problem of Studying Delinquent Dispositions in Juvenile Court

Disposition is widely recognized as the most important decision-making level in the juvenile court process (Lotz, Poole, and Regoli 1985; Siegel and Senna 1994). Not surprisingly, this court stage has been subjected to considerable empirical scrutiny and most of this research has focused on the factors which are believed to influence the dispositional decision. The factors which have been found to have an impact on juvenile court sentencing can be grouped into three areas: legal (e.g., severity of offense and previous record); administrative (e.g., the particular court and judge); and social (e.g., race, class, gender, and age). The data from these research efforts indicate there is little consensus and much confusion as to which factors are actually responsible for delinquent dispositions in juvenile court.

The problem in examining the disposition stage is methodological and concerns the accuracy and comprehensiveness of previous research. Virtually all of the empirical studies to date have addressed only a limited number of factors and have been based on data from official records, which rarely capture the dynamics of the disposition hearing and which frequently ignore, misrepresent, or both, a number of factors that are critical to it. Research that has analyzed sentencing in multiple juvenile courts is even more problematic in that important,

measurement-defying court characteristics generally have been overlooked.

✉ The Present Study

Research Design and Methodology

The study reported here examined the factors perceived by various juvenile court workers to affect the disposition decision. Interviewing was chosen as the method of data collection; an open-ended survey interview was used (Babbie 1992; Fitzgerald and Cox 1987). A uniform set of questions was posed to standardize the results and to ensure accurate recording. The interview was administered to 100 workers from three juvenile courts during the summer of 1992; it was designed to last approximately 40 minutes.

Research Sites

Three juvenile courts were selected so as to determine whether demographic composition or size of the court and its caseload had any bearing on the perceptions of the juvenile court workers (Ito 1982, 1984; Stapleton, Aday, and Ito 1982). The first court was located in a large urban center (Court A), the second was in a suburban setting (Court B), and the third was in rural surroundings (Court C). All three were situated in a northeastern state.

The county in which Court A sat consisted of one major city. In 1991, approximately 7,700 delinquency petitions were referred to Court A.

SOURCE: *Crime & Delinquency* (42)1, 99–113, January 1996. © 1996 Sage Publications, Inc.

There were six judges, 22 assistant district attorneys (including supervisors), and 17 assistant public defenders (including supervisors) assigned to full-time duty in the urban court; all participated in this study. Court-appointed and privately retained attorneys represented about 25% of the juvenile defendants. A sample of 10 of these lawyers was randomly selected from the court. Of the 130 probation officers in the urban court, 10 were randomly selected to be interviewed.

Court B was in a suburban county contiguous to the urban center. There were approximately 1,560 delinquency petitions filed in 1991. Two masters, four judges, two assistant district attorneys, and two assistant public defenders, who handled approximately 70% of the caseload, worked part-time in the court; all participated in this study. Five of the 35 probation officers who worked in Court B and five private attorneys were randomly selected for the interview.

Court C was situated in what was mostly a rural county with two major towns; it was contiguous to the suburban county. There were approximately 825 delinquency petitions filed in 1991. Two masters, one judge, one assistant district attorney, and one public defender, who handled approximately 80% of the caseload, were assigned to part-time duty in the rural court; all participated in this study. Five of the 25 probation officers who worked in Court C and five private attorneys were randomly selected for the interview.

⊠ Research Findings

Factors Related to the Disposition Decision

Members of the sample were first asked which factors should be considered at the disposition stage and whether these factors were actually considered in the sentencing of juvenile delinquents. The factor cited most frequently by workers in all three courts was the family. However, most respondents went on to emphasize that, by the family, they did not mean simply whether one or two parents were in the child's life (which is how most record data-oriented research has defined this variable), but rather whether or not the family was dysfunctional (i.e., was the family able to control/supervise the child and was the family able/willing to assist in the rehabilitative effort). Delinquent record was the second most frequently cited factor. Again, many workers noted that they had in mind not only how many felonies or misdemeanors were committed (the focus of most research), but also when the delinquent behavior had begun, the time interval between offenses, and whether there had been an escalation in or tempering of the severity of crimes in the youth's history (see Table 1).

Similarly, the current offense, school record, and previous dispositions were mentioned by a majority of the sample, but not in the terms in which most research has examined them. Workers claimed that the severity of the crime (usually the only aspect of offense that research has addressed) had to be considered in its broader context, including where the crime occurred (child's neighborhood versus school, downtown, etc.); with whom the crime was committed (alone or delinquent peers); when the crime took place (during school or curfew hours); who was victimized by the offense (especially if the victim was very young, very old, a stranger, a teacher, a parent, or a police officer) and the impact of the crime on the victim; and the level of the youth's participation/sophistication in the criminal act. Consequently, not all felonies or misdemeanors that are legally equivalent were regarded as equally severe by the workers. School record was not considered complete by many workers unless it included grade performance, absenteeism and disciplinary infractions (the only criteria research has included in this variable), and an evaluation of the child's mental condition and capabilities (i.e., was there a reason to try to force better performance from the child in this capacity) as well. Finally, previous dispositions were interpreted by most workers to mean more than a simple accounting of probationary versus institutional dispositions (the way research has identified this factor). The quality of the juvenile's performance and response to previous rehabilitative efforts, together with time intervals between dispositions and any escape

| Table 1 | Percentage of Court Workers Citing Factors That Should Be Related to Delinquent Dispositions* |

Factors	Court			Total
	A	B	C	
Family	80.0	80.0	86.7	81
Delinquent record	70.8	65.0	73.3	70
Crime	63.1	70.0	53.3	63
School record	61.5	35.0	60.0	56
Previous dispositions	52.3	50.0	53.3	52
Child's character	38.5	40.0	40.0	39
Treatment needs	21.5	45.0	66.7	33
Parents' character	24.6	35.0	33.3	28
Mental condition	29.2	15.0	6.7	23
Age	24.6	20.0	13.3	22
System resources	13.8	35.0	6.7	17
Drug/alcohol abuse	7.7	20.0	26.7	13
Community resources	9.2	10.0	20.0	11

NOTE: *Includes factors cited by at least 10% of the sample.

history, also were declared to be critical dimensions (see Table 1).

Nearly two fifths of the respondents observed that the juvenile's character, that is, his or her potential for successful rehabilitation (willingness to change behavior), attitude about the crime (sense of guilt/remorse), and respect for the court and authority, should be taken into account in the disposition decision. Official records are not likely to fully reveal these aspects of the youth's personality, especially to the extent that the latter are considered during the disposition hearing itself, although not officially made part of the court record. The same can be said of the parents' character (i.e., their abuse/neglect of the child and their willingness to accept juvenile court intervention), which was also cited by many workers as properly influencing dispositions (see Table 1).

The child's treatment needs, mental condition/illness, age, and history of drug/alcohol abuse have been investigated in previous research and, as here, have been perceived as affecting the dispositional outcome. Several respondents noted, however, that the very young (i.e., 10 to 12 years old) or very old (i.e., 17 or 18 years old) delinquent could be statutorily or practically (i.e., resources would not be wasted on older youths) prevented from being placed, and thus age should influence dispositions in opposite directions. Finally, although research has generally ignored both the system's and the community's resources, several respondents maintained that these matters should be considered in delinquent dispositions (see Table 1).

More than three fourths of the respondents (76%) insisted that juvenile court considered most or all of these factors in making disposition decisions. Nevertheless, more workers in Court B (95%) and Court C (86.7%) than in Court A (67.7%) were convinced that the system actually took all these factors into account. The urban court workers complained that the youth's treatment needs, the family, or the victim were most likely to be ignored in juvenile court dispositions.

Table 2	Priority Ranking of Factors That Should Be and Are Considered in Delinquent Disposition Decisions					
	Should Be Considered in Court			Are Considered in Court		
Factors	A	B	C	A	B	C
Crime	1	1	3	1	1	1
Delinquent record	2	2	1	2	2	2
Treatment needs	3	4	2	10	4	3
Previous dispositions	4	3	4	5	3	4
Family	5	5	5	11	6	5
School record	6	6	6	7	9	7
Age/character	7	8	9	6	10	9
Work record	11	7	7	14	13	10
Parents' character	8	11	8	13	11	8
System resources	9	9	10	4	5	6
Adjudication method	10	12	11	8	12	11
Child in detention	12	10	12	15	7	12
Court official	14	13	13	3	8	13
Complainant	13	14	14	9	15	14
Race/sex/class	15	15	15	12	14	15

Each participant was then given a list of 15 factors which could affect the disposition decision. The respondents were asked for a priority ranking of the factors that should and do influence juvenile court sentencing. Interestingly, the workers in all three courts ranked the "should be" factors similarly; they all listed the same top four factors, albeit in different order. There were also numerous similarities registered as to how factors are considered. The crime and delinquent record were ranked first and second, respectively; previous dispositions and resources were placed high on the lists; school record enjoyed a medium position; and work record and race/sex/class received low rankings in all three courts. Moreover, school record was deemed to be relatively unimportant whereas resources were given a high priority in all three courts (see Table 2).

Perhaps the most striking differences in the ranking of the "are considered" factors involved the relatively low placement of the family and the child's treatment needs in Court A compared to the relatively high location of these factors in Court B and Court C. Similarly, who the complainant was, the child's character, and the method of adjudication (i.e., guilty plea or trial) were perceived as having more influence in the urban court than in the suburban and rural courts. The court officials making the disposition decision were placed high on the list in Court A, in the middle in Court B, and at the bottom in Court C. The parents' character was seen as having relatively high impact only in the rural court, while detention appeared to matter most to individuals in the suburban court, Finally, whereas race and sex were acknowledged as having some effect in Court A, class was more likely to be noted as influencing some dispositions in Court B and Court C.

The respondents were then given an opportunity to comment on the priority ranking; many elaborated on the nature and positioning of some of the factors. For example, in the urban court, where court officials were described as competing for domination of sentencing, many workers observed that the personalities and perspectives of their judges varied markedly; that prosecutors generally exhibited an oppressive, "hang 'em all" mentality, although a few of them were truly concerned about the welfare of the juvenile; that defense attorneys varied from aggressive advocates who wanted to minimize the juvenile court's intervention, to concerned guardians who wanted to ensure that the youth was channeled into the proper rehabilitation program, to incompetent bystanders who did not have a clue or a care about what transpired at sentencing. Also, whereas some probation officers were thorough in their analyses of children's treatment needs, a majority were viewed as lazy, overworked, and seeking the path of least resistance when making the dispositional recommendation. Consequently, the court official was viewed as exercising a significant influence in Court A's disposition stage.

In Court B and Court C, however, the probation departments still controlled court operations, court officials were not seen as vying for power, and greater supervision of the probation officers was believed to have resulted in more consistency in dispositional recommendations. Thus the court official was perceived as a less influential factor in these courts than in the urban court. Nevertheless, differences between the two prosecutors and among the several judges who worked in Court B accounted for the court official's receiving a moderate ranking in that court. Workers from all three courts claimed that judges gave preferential treatment to cases represented by privately retained counsel; this was often explained as the judges' feeling that the family had already been penalized sufficiently by having to pay for a lawyer's services.

The method of adjudication achieved a higher standing in the urban court compared to the suburban and rural courts primarily because the latter two permitted only charge bargaining (which did not limit the judges' and probation officers' sentencing authority), whereas the urban court allowed sentence bargaining that largely eliminated input from these two court officials. The charge bargaining-only policy also was believed to result in less discrepancy in the dispositions extended to guilty plea vis-à-vis trial adjudications. Nevertheless, respondents from all three courts noted that dispositions were adversely influenced when a defendant had taken the stand, lied, showed no remorse, or when a victim had testified as to the horrors of the offense; none of these events was believed likely to accompany a guilty plea.

The juvenile's character was perceived to be critical, especially in Court A, at two stages: (a) during the presentence investigation and (b) at the disposition hearing. The youth's personality also was perceived as important inasmuch as some juveniles had been talked into tendering guilty pleas and thus possibly had avoided harsher consequences. Similarly, some juveniles had been encouraged to dress well, to appear cooperative, and to show remorse to the court and the victim. Judges also pointed out that the child's demeanor was significant in that "bad actors" received harsh sentences.

System resources were regarded as important in all three courts for at least three reasons. First, finances have been limited, especially in the urban court; many Court A workers ranked treatment costs as the No. 1 factor that was actually considered at sentencing. Second, females were described as getting a "big break" because there were no facilities to which to commit these delinquents. Finally, private institutions in the juvenile justice network have had the ability to reject youths who have been regarded as not fitting into their programs. Thus juvenile court sentencing has often been at the mercy of decisions made by the staff of these private facilities.

One of the most disturbing findings was the frequent assertion that in some cases particular factors have assumed atypical, disproportionate

Table 3	Percentage of Court Workers Citing Factors/Characteristics Associated With Harsh Dispositions*			

	Court			
Factors/Characteristics	A	B	C	Total
Bad record	60.0	70.0	53.3	61
Serious/violent offense	56.9	65.0	46.7	57
Bad/no school	44.6	20.0	13.3	35
Failed treatment	24.6	45.0	46.7	32
Bad character	23.1	30.0	60.0	30
Bad family	24.6	40.0	33.3	29
Black	30.8	30.0	13.3	28
Older	32.3	20.0	6.7	26
Previous placement	20.0	15.0	20.0	19
1 or no parent	18.5	15.0	13.3	17
Male	21.5	10.0	0.0	16
Low income	15.4	10.0	6.7	13
Inarticulate/bad appearance	15.4	5.0	6.7	12
No remorse	12.3	15.0	6.7	12
Drug crime	10.8	20.0	0.0	11
Bad neighborhood	15.4	0.0	0.0	10

NOTE: *Includes factors cited by at least 10% of the sample.

influence which positively or adversely affected disposition. For example, some young juveniles without lengthy records who committed nonserious offenses nevertheless have been severely sentenced when any one of the following was involved: a significant treatment problem, a very dysfunctional family, a prominent complainant, a lack of community or system resources (or a rejection by a private institution), a particularly ugly outburst in court by the youth or the parent, or a failure in a previous treatment effort. At the other extreme, the crimes of older juveniles with lengthy, negative delinquent and treatment histories have been virtually ignored if their offenses were not serious enough to warrant the attention of criminal court and they were not perceived as likely to benefit from intensive juvenile court intervention.

The workers were then asked if a composite picture could be drawn of a juvenile who was likely to get "slammed" or to receive a harsh delinquency disposition. Only five individuals claimed that no such composite figure could be sketched. The six most frequently cited factors/characteristics were not surprising: bad record; serious/violent offense; bad/no school; failed treatment history; bad character; and bad family (see Table 3). Seven other factors, which were mentioned by at least 10% of the respondents, were also relatively noncontroversial: older; previously placed; one or no parent with the youth in court; inarticulate; no remorse; drug crime; and a juvenile from a bad neighborhood. Nevertheless, nearly one third of the respondents (32%) cited one or more characteristics that are considered inappropriate: race, sex, or class. However, only two workers (a prosecutor and a probation officer from the urban court) listed these factors alone. The other 30 respondents associated at least one of the top six, unsurprising characteristics with the inappropriate ones (one half of them mentioned three or more), and, in addition, most of these people cited one or more of the seven other factors that were identified as part of the composite figure.

A follow-up question asked whether juvenile court discriminated for or against any particular youth in the sentencing decision. Only 13 workers answered negatively. Juveniles were perceived as receiving breaks from the court when they came from strong families, were female, had good school records, were young, White, from the middle/upper classes, or had hired private counsel. Virtually everyone who mentioned race or class in this context tied these factors to a strong family, a good school record, or to a family's having access to resources that provided an alternative to juvenile court intervention; two urban prosecutors maintained that a White defendant who victimized another White person would be treated more leniently than if the crime were interracial (see Table 4).

Conversely, juvenile court dispositions were perceived as being discriminatory against youths who came from dysfunctional families, were Black males, from the lower class, with bad school records and character, and from a bad neighborhood. Everyone who mentioned race or class in this context linked them with one of the other attributes that was identified as being subject to discriminatory sentencing in juvenile court (see Table 4).

Court Characteristics Related to the Delinquent Disposition Decision

The second phase of the study addressed characteristics of the juvenile court that could be associated with the delinquent disposition decision.

The members of the sample were asked to give a priority ranking of their juvenile courts' dispositional goals.[2] Although workers from all three courts ranked rehabilitation and treatment first, there was little agreement as to how the other goals actually entered into juvenile court dispositions (see Table 5). For example, in support of their contention that the crime problem had become particularly severe in their jurisdiction, urban court respondents positioned incapacitation and punishment at higher levels than the staff from the suburban and rural courts. In addition, Court A individuals commented that preserving the family, although statutorily mandated, was a low priority in their jurisdiction because usually there was no family to preserve, which probably explains why the family received a low ranking in the factors that were considered in sentencing in the urban court.

To ascertain if and how the method of adjudication was perceived as influencing sentencing, the workers were asked if there would likely be differences in the dispositions handed to two delinquents who were similar in every way save for the way in which the case was resolved. There were 15 individuals, mostly from the suburban and rural courts where there was no sentence bargaining, who believed the dispositions would be the same, regardless of a trial adjudication or guilty plea. Besides allowing only charge bargaining, Court B and Court C operated with probation officers conducting plans and evaluations of all defendants; Court A probation officers did not typically develop plans for most first offenders nor for some petty offenders who were already on probation. Thus, if a case was resolved during the early stages of the urban court process, probation officers were not likely to have been involved in the disposition. Probation officers (and judges for that matter) were not typically excluded from the disposition of any case in the suburban and rural courts.

Nevertheless, a majority of respondents (85%) believed that the dispositions of the two cases would differ and that the trial would probably produce the harsher disposition. More than

| Table 4 | Percentage of Court Workers Citing Factors Associated With Discriminatory Dispositions* |

A. Factors Juvenile Court Discriminated for Court

Factors	A	B	C	Total
Strong family	23.1	35.0	20.0	25
White male	16.9	10.0	13.3	15
Upper class	21.5	20.0	33.3	14
Girl	16.9	15.0	0.0	14
Good school	13.8	5.0	0.0	10
Private counsel	7.7	15.0	6.7	9
Young	4.6	5.0	6.7	5

B. Factors Juvenile Court Discriminated Against Court

Factors	A	B	C	Total
Bad family	30.8	15.0	13.3	25
Black male	16.9	10.0	0.0	13
Lower class	15.4	0.0	0.0	10
Bad school	12.3	0.0	0.0	8
Bad character	6.2	5.0	6.7	6
Bad neighborhood	7.7	0.0	0.0	5

NOTE: *Includes factors cited by at least 5% of the sample.

one third (37%) of the workers, especially from Court A (46.2%), explained that plea bargaining allowed for manipulation and rewards of leniency (especially sentence bargaining). Almost as many persons (34%), again especially from Court A (40%), argued that trials provide victims a real and possibly dramatic input into the proceedings and youths an opportunity to lie or appear badly when testifying. Slightly more than one fourth of them (27%) claimed that trials meant both that more information would come to light as more time went on and as more people looked into the situation (especially in Court A, 33.8%), and that there was no leniency and perhaps even a penalty. Almost one fifth of the workers (19%) contended

that admissions (i.e., the guilty plea) were seen as the first step along the path of rehabilitation (especially as opposed to a denial being seen as an obstacle to treatment). Finally, 10 urban court individuals maintained that different dispositions could occur because personnel with different philosophies had worked at the earlier versus the later stages of the court process.

The respondents next commented on the disposition ladder and how it operated in their courts. The ladder represents increasing levels of severity in the state's intervention into the delinquent's life. The comments provided by the workers are critical to understanding how dispositions can vary among juvenile courts. First,

	Court		
Table 5 — Priority Ranking of Dispositional Goals as They Influence Juvenile Court Dispositions			
Goals	A	B	C
Rehabilitation/treatment	1	1	1
Deterrence	3	2	3
Incapacitation/protect society	2	3	5
Accountability	5	5	2
Preserve family	7	4	4
Punishment	4	6	6
Vindicate victim	6	7	7

although most first offenders in all three courts were headed to probation, the urban court had three sanction levels which preceded probation, and thus probation officers in that court, unlike those in Court B and Court C, saw some offenders for the first time after the latter had been adjudicated for a second offense.[3] Second, there were numerous variants of both probationary and institutional dispositions. Thus not all probation sentences were equal, and the same held for incarceration as well. Third, although there were numerous similarities, different courts used different numbers of rungs of the ladder and different definitions, making cross-court comparisons difficult. For example, the three courts varied as to where Vision Quest, a national juvenile treatment program for serious offenders, fit precisely into the dispositional scheme, whereas the second level of intensive probation in the suburban court actually involved a 30-day placement. There was no uniformity among the three courts as to what the different levels of court intervention entailed nor how they were used.[4]

The workers next addressed the roles of each of the participants in the disposition hearing; the defense attorney was considered first. Whereas the public defenders were regarded mostly as advocates in the urban court (81.5%), they were perceived mostly as guardians or a mixture of advocate and guardian in the suburban (80%) and rural (100%) courts. Privately retained counsel, on the other hand, were more consistently categorized in all three courts as either advocates or a mixture of the two types (primarily because these lawyers were accused of simply following the wishes of the parents). Assigned or appointed counsel appeared regularly only in the urban court; the Court A respondents divided fairly closely in describing these lawyers as: advocates (32.3%), a mixture (26.2%), guardians (23.1%), and incompetent (18.5%). As the workers observed, these numbers suggest that variations among the lawyers affiliated with cases could affect dispositions due to the attorneys' competency level. Several Court A members noted that public defenders provided better representation at disposition because their office employed a group of full-time social workers who aided in the formation of disposition plans, whereas many private counsel were seen as not being familiar enough with juvenile court sentences to meaningfully participate at the disposition level.

Although it was agreed by all that judges were supposed to listen to all the parties and reach a disposition accordingly, more of the urban court workers (47.7%) than their counterparts from the suburban (25%) or rural (0%) courts complained that judges failed at this task more often than they succeeded.[5] Whereas more than three fourths of the respondents (78.5%) in Court A characterized prosecutors as simply seeking the most restrictive disposition, prosecutors in Court B (80%) and Court C (60%) were portrayed mostly as either having no role or balancing society's and the child's interests at sentencing. To an even greater degree, the workers in the suburban (90%) and rural (86.7%) courts were more convinced than those in the urban court (30.8%) that probation officers thoroughly investigated the youth's situation and devised treatment plans that were appropriate. Although the probation officers' failures in Court A and Court B were described as involving laziness/overwork and not doing a complete investigation, their failures in Court C were attributed to their prosecutorial perspectives.

The respondents' views on the roles of the nonsystem participants at the disposition hearing also varied considerably by court. Most workers wanted parents to cooperate with the court at the sentencing stage by providing information about the youth.[6] Although most workers in the suburban (75%) and rural (80%) courts viewed parents as fulfilling their role, only about one third of the workers (35.4%) in the urban court thought that most parents were cooperative at disposition. Some parents, particularly in Court A, were thought to have wanted to rid themselves of responsibility for their children and to have requested juvenile court intervention; these parents often made placement a necessity because they refused to take the youths home. More workers in Court B (45%) and Court C (66.7%) than in Court A (9.2%) described defendants as likely to speak at sentencing and to express remorse.[7] Finally, more respondents in the suburban (25%) and rural courts (33.3%) than in the urban court (9.2%) thought victims had some input into the disposition decision.

The final structural characteristic of the court examined in this study was that of the court official who was perceived as most influential in making the disposition decision. More than four fifths of the workers (81%) identified either the judge or the probation officer; the remainder mentioned a combination of these two officials or the defense attorney. However, whereas the judge was most often perceived as the most influential person in Court A (50.8%), the probation officer was most often awarded that honor in Court B (70%) and Court C (53.3%).

⊠ Discussion

This research did not examine the actual factors that influenced the disposition decision. Rather, it examined the perspectives on decision making of the juvenile court workers. The data lead to concern regarding the accuracy and comprehensiveness of previous research efforts in two respects. The first involves an understanding of disposition-related factors. The workers identified a number of factors which they believed to be critical to disposition that have been measured either incompletely or inappropriately in previous studies. The respondents also identified several important factors that research has mostly ignored, while numerous factors mentioned by the workers as potentially critical to disposition defy measurement either because they can work in opposite directions at one and the same time or because they are too complex to isolate.

The second problem involves an understanding of juvenile court. There was considerable variation in the dispositional structure and operation among the three juvenile courts; many of these facets defy measurement. Thus, even assuming that the factors affecting dispositions can be adequately identified and measured, accurate cross-court comparisons remain a formidable, if not insurmountable, task.

In short, disposition may simply involve too many factors, with interactions too subtle and complex and varying too much among courts, to be subjected to the scrutiny of sound research; we may never be able to derive a completely accurate picture of the factors affecting juvenile court sentencing.

⊠ Notes

1. The list in Table 2 was developed in collaboration with several workers representing different occupations in all three juvenile courts. The list was likely not exhaustive, but at least should have covered

most of the major factors that affected juvenile court dispositions. Each participant was asked to rank the factors as to the first most important, second most important, and so on. The respondents were advised that they could give more than one factor the same rank and that they could give a zero ranking if a factor should not or did not affect dispositions in juvenile court. I then scored the rankings like a track meet. The factor listed first was given 15 points, the second 14 points, and so on.

2. The list in Table 5 was developed and scored in the same manner as with the list in Table 2.

3. All three courts used consent decrees as a nondelinquent sanction. Interestingly, the rural court allowed for two levels of consent decree probation.

4. There would very likely be little agreement as well among workers in the three courts as to how quickly each youth should progress up the dispositional ladder, whether a successive delinquency always means a youth must climb *up* the ladder; and precisely when the youth has reached the very top of the ladder, which indicates that the youth has exhausted the resources of the juvenile justice system and has warranted transfer to adult court.

5. The urban court judges were often accused of deferring to the probation officer, rendering a decision too quickly, following their own agenda, pursuing the least expensive remedy, and giving the child too many breaks.

6. Several defense attorneys in all three courts maintained that parents should convince the court that they can resolve the child's problems at home.

7. Some defendants, particularly in the urban court, were described as actually seeking incarceration, at least in some of the private residential facilities.

References

Babbie, Earl. 1992. *The Practice of Social Research*, 6th ed. Belmont, CA: Wadsworth.

Fitzgerald, Jack D. and Steven M. Cox. 1987. *Research Methods in Criminal Justice: An Introduction.* Chicago: Nelson-Hall.

Ito, Jeanne A. 1982. "Inside Metropolitan Juvenile Courts: How Their Structure Affects the Outcome of Cases." *State Court Journal* 6:16–22.

——. 1984. *Measuring the Difference for Different Types of Juvenile Courts.* Williamsburg, VA: National Center for the Study of State Courts.

Lotz, Roy, Eric D. Poole, and Robert M. Regoli. 1985. *Juvenile Delinquency and Juvenile Justice.* New York: Random House.

Siegel, Larry J. and Joseph T. Senna. 1994. *Juvenile Delinquency: Theory, Practice, and Law,* 5th ed. St. Paul: West.

Stapleton, W. Vaughan, David Aday, and Jeanne A. Ito. 1982. "An Empirical Typology of American Metropolitan Juvenile Courts." *American Sociological Review* 88:549–61.

DISCUSSION QUESTIONS

1. The factor cited most frequently as important in the disposition was the family. What would due process advocates say about the fundamental fairness of the importance of this extralegal factor in disposition? How might court officials justify its importance?

2. What other factors (legal and social) are related to the disposition decision? How do you believe court officials might argue in support of those factors?

3. Suggest arguments for and against whether a juvenile's character, demeanor, or dress and appearance are legitimate and accurate predictors of future behavior.

4. Sanborn comments on a "most disturbing finding" of some extralegal factors in dispositions. Identify those and explain your agreement or disagreement with the author.

READING

The U.S. Supreme Court in *Gault* held that juveniles have due process rights in adjudication hearings if the court disposition may result in institutional commitment. Previous research has indicated that juveniles appearing with legal counsel often receive a harsher court disposition than those who appear without an attorney. The objective of this study by Guevara and her associates was to examine the influence of type of counsel across race on juvenile court outcomes. They used data from a sample of juvenile court referrals from two Midwestern juvenile courts to examine the interaction of race and type of counsel on disposition outcome. The results indicated that youth without an attorney were the most likely to have the charges dismissed, and this effect was more pronounced for nonwhite youth. In addition, nonwhite youth represented by a private attorney were significantly more likely than similar white youth to receive a secure confinement disposition. The findings of this study suggest that there are differences in the influence of legal counsel for white and nonwhite juveniles, and they raise serious questions about the basic right to counsel in juvenile court and the effects of legal representation.

Race, Legal Representation, and Juvenile Justice

Issues and Concerns

Lori Guevara, Cassia Spohn, Denise Herz

The *In re Gault* decision in 1967 established that a child had procedural due process rights in delinquency adjudication proceedings where the consequences were that the child could be committed to a state institution. The holding of *Gault* was narrow in two respects. First, the Court held that juveniles were entitled to only four specific elements of due process: right to notice of charges, right to counsel, privilege against self-incrimination, and the right to confront and cross-examine witnesses (*In re Gault,* 1967). Second, *Gault* was limited because it dealt solely with the adjudicatory stage of the juvenile proceeding, where facts are presented and the juvenile is declared delinquent (Nesburg, 1971). The

Court held that a state could no longer successfully argue that a juvenile proceeding was "civil" when, in reality, the commitment of adults and juveniles was indistinguishable in terms of loss of liberty (Neigher, 1967; Winslade, 1974).

The *Gault* decision indicates that for fairness and due process to occur in juvenile court hearings, all youth must be given the opportunity to consult with legal counsel. However, previous research indicates that not all juveniles are represented by counsel. For example, studies have revealed that anywhere from 15% to 95% of juveniles were assisted by an attorney (Aday, 1986; Clarke & Koch, 1980; Feld, 1988, 1991, 1993b; Langley, 1972; Reasons, 1970). Therefore, the individual

SOURCE: *Crime & Delinquency (50)*3, 344–371, July 2004. DOI: 10. 1177/0011128704264514. © 2004 Sage Publications, Inc.

right to counsel as set forth in *Gault* has not been fully implemented. Moreover, research indicates that presence/absence of counsel and type of counsel may affect juvenile court outcomes. Specifically, these studies have revealed that youth appearing with counsel received a harsher disposition than those who appeared without an attorney (Feld, 1988, 1991, 1993a). In addition, juveniles represented by private attorneys received better outcomes than youth represented by public defenders (Carrington & Moyer, 1990; Clarke & Koch, 1980; Duffee & Siegel, 1971; Erickson, 1975; Lefstein, Stapleton, & Teitelbaum, 1969; Reasons, 1970; Stapleton & Teitelbaum, 1972). Furthermore, there is some evidence that racial minorities are either less likely than Whites to be represented by counsel or are more likely than Whites to be represented by a public defender than a private attorney (Feld, 1988, 1991, 1993b).

In addition to evidence of difference in type of legal representation by race, there is also some evidence that White and minority youth appearing in the juvenile court receive different treatment. African Americans represent 15% of all juveniles younger than age 18 in the United States but represent 32% of adjudicated delinquency cases and 40% of juveniles in residential placement (U.S. Department of Justice, Office of Justice Programs [OJJDP], 1999). African American males are also confined at a rate 7 to 9 times that of White males (Hawkins & Jones, 1989). Moreover, previous research has indicated that non-White juveniles received more severe outcomes than Whites (Bishop & Frazier, 1996; Frazier & Bishop, 1995; Frazier, Bishop, & Henretta, 1992). In addition, studies have revealed that minority youth were discriminated against at all stages of the juvenile justice system (Bishop & Frazier, 1988; DeJong & Jackson, 1998; Fagan, Slaughter, & Hartstone, 1987; Kempf-Leonard & Sontheimer, 1995). Finally, some studies have indicated that when controlling for seriousness of current offense and prior record, White and minority youth received similar outcomes (Frazier & Bishop, 1985; Henretta, Frazier, & Bishop, 1986; Marshall & Thomas, 1983).

In summary, the Supreme Court expanded the due process rights of youth in juvenile court through the *Gault* decision. This decision applied requirements that are essential to due process and fair treatment but do not supplant the "unique benefits" derived from the juvenile proceeding (Melton, 1989; Nesburg, 1971). As part of protecting the interests of children, the juvenile court is challenged with ensuring fair and equitable treatment in its proceedings through due process guarantees. Focusing on outcomes in the juvenile court raises questions regarding the equity and influence of legal representation across race in the juvenile court. Certain outcomes based on race and type of legal counsel would be expected within a conflict theory approach about the way juvenile justice operates. According to conflict theory, racial minorities receive harsher dispositions because they lack the power and resources to ensure equal treatment. Historically, detention centers and secure confinement facilities have been disproportionately populated by poor, racial minority youth (Platt, 1969; Schlossman, 1977). A conflict theory approach would propose that material resources determine relationships to the legal system. Therefore, youth who were able to retain private legal counsel would be expected to receive more lenient outcomes. In addition, Hawkins's (1987) revision of conflict theory proposes that minorities receive harsher punishments when their power threatens the dominant group. Therefore, minority youth who have the power to retain private legal counsel would be expected to receive the most severe outcomes. The current study explores these issues and attempts to ascertain how race and type of counsel affect juvenile court outcomes.

⬛ Research on Juvenile Court Outcomes

Previous research assessing juvenile court outcomes has examined various stages in the process. Some studies analyzed the police decision to arrest or release the youth (Black & Reiss, 1970; Piliavin

& Briar, 1964; Wordes & Bynum, 1995). Other studies focused on the intake decision. At this stage, the juvenile has been arrested and the intake officer must decide if the youth should be released, sent to diversion, or petitioned to juvenile court (Bell & Lang, 1985; Thomas & Sieverdes, 1975). Still other studies examined the decision to detain a youth after arrest as well as the subsequent disposition decision (Bailey, 1981; L. Cohen & Klugel, 1979a; Frazier & Cochran, 1987; Marshall & Thomas, 1983; Thornberry & Christensen, 1984; Wordes, Bynum, & Corley, 1994). Some studies have taken a more comprehensive approach, examining several juvenile justice processing stages, including detention, referral, adjudication, and disposition decisions (Bishop & Frazier, 1988, 1996; DeJong & Jackson, 1998; Johnson & Secret, 1990; Leiber, 1994; McCarthy & Smith, 1986). The current study focuses specifically on the effect of two independent variables—presence/type of counsel and offender race—on juvenile court outcomes. Therefore the findings relevant to these two variables are discussed in detail.

Influence of Counsel

Research that has focused on the effect of Presence/Type of Counsel on juvenile court outcomes indicates that type of counsel does have an effect; however, the direction of the effect is not consistent. Most of the research addressing the performance of juvenile defense counsel has focused on comparing juvenile court outcomes for those youths represented by an attorney to those for youths without counsel. Some research indicates that juveniles appearing in court with counsel were actually at a disadvantage. Duffee and Siegel (1971) found that the presence of counsel in juvenile court significantly increased the likelihood of incarceration and decreased the likelihood of dismissal. Langley (1972) looked at two groups of delinquents: those who received probation as their disposition and those who were securely confined. The results indicated that youth who appeared without an attorney received probation at a higher rate than those

who appeared with legal counsel. In addition, Burruss and Kempf-Leonard (2002) found that an out-of-home placement was more likely in cases where legal counsel was present.

Feld's (1988, 1991, 1993b) research similarly reveals that the presence of an attorney is an aggravating legal factor in the juvenile court. He found that youths represented by counsel were 3 times more likely than those without counsel to receive a severe disposition. Specifically, when the seriousness of the offense and prior record were controlled, youths appearing with an attorney were more likely to receive an out-of-home placement and secure confinement.

In contrast to the results discussed above, Ferster, Courtless, and Snethen (1971) and Ferster and Courtless (1972) found that although only a small percentage (27%) of juveniles were represented by counsel, these youth had better outcomes than youth who appeared without counsel. Specifically, juveniles with legal representation were more likely to have their case dismissed and, if formally processed, were less likely to receive a secure confinement disposition than juveniles without representation.

Research has also revealed that type of attorney has an effect on juvenile court outcomes. Dootjes, Erickson, and Fox (1972) and Erickson (1975) interviewed public and private defense attorneys in juvenile court. This research revealed that juveniles did not expect the public defender to be an adversary for them. On the other hand, the private attorney was expected to spend a long time with the juvenile and was expected to "get the child off." Consistent with this, some studies reveal that private attorneys in juvenile court obtain better outcomes than public defenders. Carrington and Moyer (1990) found that youth represented by a private attorney were less likely to be adjudicated and more likely to have the charges dismissed. In addition, Feld's research (1993b) also revealed that youths with private counsel had the lowest rates of out-of-home placement and secure confinement. Finally, Clarke and Koch (1980) examined what effect the presence and type of counsel had on dispositions.

They found that youth who were either unrepresented or represented by private counsel had high rates of dismissal and low rates of confinement.

In summary, studies focusing on juvenile court outcomes generally find that youth represented by private attorneys are more likely than those represented by public defenders to have their cases dismissed and are less likely to be placed in secure confinement following adjudication. Research focusing on juvenile court outcomes also reveals, however, that youth appearing with counsel receive more severe outcomes than those appearing without counsel.

Influence of Race

The findings of studies examining the effect of race can first be assessed by looking at Pope and Feyerherm's (1990) review of 46 studies assessing the influence of race on juvenile court outcomes. Their review revealed that research examining juvenile justice processing indicates that, in some cases, race and other extralegal factors make a difference in outcome decisions while in others they do not. They also concluded that "race effects may be accounted for by the informal nature of the juvenile justice system which may then lead to differences in outcome between minority and White youth" (Pope & Feyerherm, 1990, p. 330). Four general themes emerge from this research. First, the findings suggest direct and indirect race effects or a mixed pattern being present at some stages but not at others. Second, when selection bias did exist, it occurred at all stages of juvenile processing. Third, small racial differences may accumulate and become more pronounced as minority youth are processed further into the juvenile justice system. Fourth, studies that concluded there were mixed race effects achieved that result by utilizing control variables in a multivariate analysis. In summary, the authors concluded from their examination of previous research that there is "substantial support for the statement that there are race effects in operation within the juvenile justice system, both direct and indirect in nature" (Pope & Feyerherm, 1990, p. 335).

Overall, research examining the influence of race on juvenile court outcomes indicates different race effects at different stages of processing with some of it occurring at the initial stages. Several studies have revealed that minority youth were more likely to be taken into custody by the police (Black & Reiss, 1970; Conley, 1994; Dannefer & Schutt, 1982; Piliavin & Briar, 1964; Thornberry, 1973; Wordes & Bynum, 1995). In addition, research has indicated that minority youth were more likely to be detained following arrest and formally petitioned to juvenile court (Bortner, Sunderland, & Winn, 1985; DeJong & Jackson, 1998; Frazier & Bishop, 1995; Johnson & Secret, 1990; Kempf-Leonard & Sontheimer, 1995; McGarrell, 1993; Thomas & Sieverdes, 1975; Wordes et al., 1994). Finally, several studies have revealed a cumulative effect of racial bias at the early processing decisions (detention and petition) on later court decisions (disposition). Specifically, youth who were predetained were more likely to receive a harsh disposition, and minority youth were the most likely to be predetained (Bishop & Frazier, 1996; Bortner & Reed, 1985; Feld, 1993a; Frazier & Cochran, 1987; McCarthy & Smith, 1986; Poole & Regoli, 1980). This cumulative effect of racial bias results in a compound risk of harsher outcomes for minority youth. At almost every stage in the juvenile justice process, racial bias may be present but may not be extreme. However, "because the system operates cumulatively, the risk is compounded and the end result is that Black juveniles are three times as likely as White juveniles to end up in residential placement" (McCord, Spatz-Widom, & Crowell, 2002, p. 257).

Previous research assessing either the influence of Type of Counsel or Race on juvenile court outcomes has limitations in design and measurement.

A majority of the research in the two areas of interest has examined only two options at the disposition stage (left in the home vs. removed from the home). This research design may be missing the various options available in the juvenile court; there are several possible outcomes a juvenile could receive at a disposition hearing ranging from dismissal of charges to secure confinement. In addition, previous research has examined either the influence of legal counsel or the influence of race on juvenile court outcomes. What is lacking in prior studies is an assessment of the interaction of these two variables. Failure to examine the interaction of legal counsel and race can result in misleading findings. For example, main effects of race may not be found, however, the effects of other factors (such as type/presence of counsel) may vary depending on the race of the juvenile. The current study is the first to specifically explore the interaction of race and presence/type of counsel on juvenile court outcomes using a multicategory dependent variable.

Interaction Between Counsel and Race

The current study examined the interaction of Race and Presence/Type of Counsel on juvenile court outcomes. An interaction effect occurs when the effect of one variable is not the same at all levels of the other variable. Therefore, the influence of either the presence or type of legal counsel could vary depending on the race of the juvenile. Previous research has indicated that Race interacts with other variables to influence outcomes. For example, DeJong and Jackson (1998) examined the interaction of Race with Living Arrangement and found that living with both parents protected White youth against secure confinement. However, minority youth were treated the same way regardless of whether they lived with both parents or with their mother only. Bishop and Frazier (1996) looked at the interaction of Race with Status Offenses. Their results indicated that for these offenses, White youth were more likely than minority youth to move further into the system, and they also received harsher dispositions. Finally, Leiber (1994) focused on the interaction of Race and Type of Offense on juvenile court outcomes. He found that Native American youth who were charged with a drug offense were more likely to receive diversion than similarly charged White and African American youth. Therefore, there is some evidence that the influence of Race may be conditioned by other variables.

▧ Research Design

Data Sources

The data used for the current study were collected from case files in two Midwestern juvenile courts for the years 1990 through 1994 as part of a larger study to examine disproportionate minority confinement. The two counties used in the current study include the two largest counties in a Midwestern state. County A is the largest and includes a large metropolitan area. This county has a total population of 416,444 with minorities 16% of the population (U.S. Bureau of the Census, 1990). Approximately 23% of the total population is between the ages of 7 to 17 years. Of the juvenile population in County A, 79% is White, African American and Latino youth are 15% each, and Native American and Asian American youth are 1%. County B is the second largest and includes a moderately sized metropolitan area. This county has a total population of 203,013 with minorities 5% of the total (U.S. Bureau of the Census, 1990). Approximately 25% of the total population is juveniles younger than the age of 19. Of this juvenile population, White youths are 92%, African American youth are 3%, Latino youth are 2%, Native American youth are 1%, and Asian American youth are 2%.

The sampling procedures used in the two counties resulted in an undersampling of White youth and an oversampling of non-White youth relative to their percentages in the total referral population. Therefore, the data were weighted to reflect each racial category's representation in the total referral population.[1]

Dependent Variable

One dependent variable is analyzed in this study. Type of Disposition is a categorical variable that measures the final outcome after the juvenile has been adjudicated a delinquent. Therefore, this dependent variable is measuring sentence severity. These outcomes are coded as 0 for dismissal of the charges, 1 for probation, 2 for residential placement in a group or foster home, or 3 for confinement in a secure facility. For the analyses, the final category (secure confinement) is the reference category.

Previous research on juvenile justice processing indicates that a multistage approach is the preferred method. For example, examining the predetention, petition, arraignment, adjudication, and disposition decisions would constitute a comprehensive study. However, according to the *Gault* decision, a juvenile is entitled to legal representation only in adjudicatory hearings that could result in confinement to a state institution. Therefore, the stage that would best examine the influence of legal representation in the juvenile court is the disposition hearing.

Independent Variables

The independent variables in the analyses reflect offender characteristics, legal characteristics, and case characteristics. Because of the small number of Latinos, Native Americans, and Asian Americans in the sample, these cases are combined with those involving African Americans into a non-White category.[2] Race is thus a dichotomous variable with White coded 1 and non-White coded 0. Gender is a dichotomous variable (male = 0, female = 1) and age is a ratio-level variable. Prior Record reflects the juvenile's number of prior court referrals and is coded 0 for no priors, 1 for one prior referral, 2 for two previous referrals, 3 for three prior referrals, and 4 for more than three previous court referrals.

Previous research has identified seriousness of the current offense and several case characteristics as predictors of juvenile court outcomes. Therefore, these are controlled for in the analyses. Instant Offense refers to the most serious charge in a referral. This variable is coded as a dummy variable that differentiates between felonies and misdemeanors with misdemeanor offense as the reference category.[3] Pretrial Detention is a dichotomous variable that indicates whether the juvenile was in custody (coded 1) or released (coded 0) after arrest. This measure was included based on previous research indicating that predetention status may influence disposition outcome (Bailey, 1981;

L. Cohen & Klugel, 1979b; Frazier & Cochran, 1987; Marshall & Thomas, 1983; Thornberry & Christensen, 1984; Wordes et al., 1994).

Type of Counsel is measured by three dummy variables: no attorney, public defender, or private attorney with no attorney as the reference category. The final variable controls for the county in which the case was adjudicated (County A = 1, County B = 0). In a study examining the influence of Type of Counsel on court outcomes, an ideal control variable would be socioeconomic status as this may indirectly affect what type of attorney represents the juvenile. However, for this data set, socioeconomic status of the juvenile or the juvenile's family was not available.

☒ Method

Data analyses were conducted on one sample that combines the referrals from both counties with a control for county included. Combining the data from the two counties allowed the proposed statistical procedure to be done. These two juvenile courts operate similarly in a conservative Midwestern state with similar organizational structure and procedures. However, combining the two jurisdictions may obscure some differences in the counties—namely the difference in the overrepresentation of minority youth in juvenile court referrals relevant to the total juvenile population. In County A, minority youth are 21% of the juvenile population but 42% of the referrals. In County B, minority youth are 8% of the juvenile population but 24% of the referrals.

The hypotheses were tested using multinomial logistic regression. The dependent variable in this study (Disposition Outcome) is a categorical variable with four outcomes measured. The most appropriate statistical technique for a dependent variable with several categories is multinomial logistic regression.[4] This technique estimates the effects of explanatory variables on a dependent variable with unordered response categories (Liao, 1994). In multinomial logistic regression, one value of the dependent variable is designated as the reference category. The probability of membership in other categories is compared with the probability of membership in the reference category (Aldrich & Nelson, 1984; Menard, 1995). For the current study, probabilities of membership in three categories of the dependent variable (dismissed, probation, residential placement) were compared with the probability of membership in the reference category (secure confinement).

The current study examined the interaction of Race and Type of Counsel and the resulting influence on Disposition Outcome. An interaction effect occurs when the effect of one factor is not the same at all levels of the other factor (Aiken & West, 1991; J. Cohen & Cohen, 1983). In other words, the effect of Type of Counsel may vary by race of the juvenile. This approach essentially tests the hypothesis that Whites obtain more "benefit" than non-Whites from legal representation or from representation by a particular type of attorney.

Hypotheses

Based on previous research regarding the influence of Race and Counsel on juvenile court outcomes and a conflict theory approach, the current study proposes the following hypotheses to examine the interaction of Race and Counsel on Disposition Outcome. For each hypothesis, seriousness of the current offense, prior offenses, predetention status, and age will be controlled.

Hypothesis 1: Race/ethnicity will affect juvenile court outcomes: non-White youth will receive more severe outcomes than White youth.

Hypothesis 2: Representation by counsel will affect juvenile court outcomes.

Hypothesis 2a: Juveniles represented by counsel will receive more severe dispositions than juveniles not represented by counsel.

Hypothesis 2b: Juveniles represented by private attorneys will receive less severe outcomes than juveniles represented by public defenders.

Hypothesis 3: Race/ethnicity will interact with type of counsel to produce differential outcomes for White and non-White youth:

non-White youth represented by a private attorney will receive the most severe outcome.

[Editors' Note: The Results section is not reprinted here. Interested readers are encouraged to see the original document.]

⌦ Discussion

This research sought to examine whether the effect of legal counsel on juvenile court outcomes varied by race. The results suggested that a youth's race interacted with type of legal representation to influence juvenile court dispositions. Representation by an attorney disadvantaged White and non-White youth, and it hurt them in different ways. The relationships among type of counsel, race, and disposition outcome, however, were not simple or straightforward. These relationships are discussed in the following sections.

Influence of Presence/Type of Counsel on Juvenile Court Outcomes

The results of the current study indicated that presence or type of counsel affected some disposition outcomes but not others. The dismissal, residential placement, and secure confinement decisions were affected most by presence/type of legal counsel. Presence/Type of Legal Counsel influenced disposition outcomes in that youth appearing without an attorney were the most likely to have charges dismissed and the least likely to receive secure confinement. Representation by a private attorney reduced the chance of charge dismissal and increased the likelihood of secure confinement. In addition, representation by a public defender versus a private attorney increased the likelihood of dismissal and residential placement while reducing the likelihood of secure confinement. This outcome contradicted the conflict theory perspective. Youth represented by private counsel should have had more material resources that should have resulted in more lenient dispositions. Finally, Presence/Type of Counsel did not influence the probation decision.

The differential outcomes based on Presence/Type of Legal Counsel may be due to several factors. First, appearing without an attorney may send the message that the youth is "throwing himself or herself on the mercy of the court" and relying on the informal nature of the juvenile court resulting in dismissal of charges. Research suggests that in the absence of legal counsel, the courtroom team falls into a "paternalistic approach" and reverts to the original philosophy of the juvenile court. In this situation, the judge acts as a father figure and determines what would be in the "best interest of the child" (Bishop & Frazier, 1996; Feld, 1988, 1993a, 1993b). In addition, the *Gault* decision provided procedural justice and legitimized punitiveness in juvenile courts. When the court "adheres to due process (right to counsel), the judge feels less vulnerable to having their decisions overturned by appellate courts and more secure in imposing more severe sanctions" (Feld, 1999, p. 195). Second, private attorneys may be more likely to appear if the juvenile is charged with a serious offense. It is possible that the public defender versus private attorney differences may reflect selection effects and not attorney effects per se. Therefore, type of representation may indirectly affect the disposition outcome with private representation yielding a more severe disposition (Feld, 1988, 1993b).

Third, appearing with a private attorney may send the opposite message; the juvenile court is a formal proceeding. The disadvantage that youth with a private attorney experience is also consistent with the influence of the courtroom workgroup and research in the adult court. The courtroom workgroup (Eisenstein & Jacob, 1977) includes all the regular participants in the day-to-day activities of a particular courtroom; judge, prosecutor, and defense attorney interact on the basis of shared norms. Public defenders are typically regular members of the workgroup whereas private attorneys are seen as "outsiders." Prior research has indicated that those who were on good terms with other members of the courtroom workgroup were better able to predict the actions of the court, which ultimately benefited their clients (Mather, 1974; Neubauer, 1974). Therefore, youth represented by a private attorney did not always "get what they paid for;" in fact, they were actually at a disadvantage in juvenile court.

Fourth, appearing with a public defender may be seen as "expected." Although judges/court officials may be inclined toward leniency for youth appearing without counsel, they also may accept the fact that defense attorneys are part of the juvenile court. The most accepted type of legal representation may be a public defender because this individual is a member of the courtroom workgroup. Because this type of defense attorney may be seen as "usual" by judges/court officials, any differences in the likelihood of the outcomes may be because of other mitigating or aggravating influences.

Influence of Race on Juvenile Court Outcomes

Due to the informal nature of the juvenile justice system, there are fewer constraints on decision making than in the adult criminal justice system, which may lead to differences in outcomes for White and non-White youth. The results of the current study indicated that race of the juvenile had an effect on the disposition outcome. After controlling for offense type and prior record, White youth were more likely than non-White youth to receive probation or residential placement and were thus less likely than non-White youth to receive a secure confinement. This outcome was consistent with the conflict theory perspective that minority youth receive harsher dispositions because of lack of power and resources. In addition, race of the youth did not influence dismissal of charges.

The differential outcomes based on race of the juvenile may be because of subtle rather than overt discrimination. For example, White youth may be more likely to receive probation or residential placement because they are easier to place in these situations than are non-White youth. Non-White youth may be less likely than White youth to receive these dispositions because services such as mental health or counseling typically require insurance coverage that may not be available to non-White youth. Therefore, access to these services for non-White youth may only be available through a secure confinement. In addition, the race differences in disposition may, in part, be a result of agency policies and practices that focus on family support and cooperation as considerations for disposition decisions (Bishop & Frazier, 1996). Non-White youth may be more likely to have a single parent who is unemployed or underemployed and may lack access to transportation or other services that would make a less restrictive disposition more problematic. Finally, the pretrial screening of non-White youth may be less rigorous than of White youth; that is, more non-White youth pass the preliminary "gate-keepers," and weaker cases are formally processed into the juvenile justice system and arrive at the disposition hearing. This explanation is consistent with previous research indicating that the greatest racial disparities in juvenile justice processing occur at the entry points to the system.

Interaction of Legal Counsel and Race on Juvenile Court Outcomes

The results of the current study indicated that the effect of type/presence of counsel varied by race of the juvenile. Several key findings emerged from the interaction results. First, White and non-White youth with a private attorney were less likely to have the charges dismissed or receive a residential placement and thus more likely to be securely confined with the effect more pronounced for non-White youth. Second, the influence of counsel across race on the probation decision was significant and somewhat contradictory. Specifically, White youth represented by counsel (public or private) were less likely than Whites without counsel to receive probation and more likely to receive a secure confinement. Conversely, non-White youth with legal representation (public or private) were more likely to receive probation and thus less likely to be securely confined. The probation decision may be influenced by extralegal factors. In this situation, the influence may be type of counsel. Presence of legal counsel may be seen as an aggravating legal factor for White youth and a mitigating legal factor for non-White youth.

Third, the influence of the public defender versus the private attorney was significant across race for only the residential placement decision. Specifically, White and non-White youth with a public defender were more likely than White and non-White youth with a private attorney to receive a residential placement and less likely to be securely confined with the influence stronger for White youth. This finding may be a double advantage for White youth represented by a public defender. Specifically, White youth overall were more likely than non-White youth to receive a residential placement, and youth with a public defender were more likely than those otherwise represented to receive a residential placement. Finally, non-White youth with a private attorney were the most likely to receive a secure confinement disposition. This outcome was consistent with Hawkins's (1987) revised conflict theory. Racial minorities who use their power to threaten the dominant class receive harsher punishments.

◪ Conclusion

The juvenile court was created based on the established doctrine of *parens patriae*, which holds that the state has a right and a duty to care for children who are neglected, delinquent, or in some other way disadvantaged. The strength and nature of the *parens patriae* doctrine was drawn from a number of legal challenges in the 19th century. Legal challenges to *parens patriae* in the 1960s and 1970s significantly affected the juvenile justice system. In particular, the *Gault* decision in 1967 guaranteed due process safeguards to all juveniles in adjudicatory hearings in which the child could be committed to a state institution. In this case, the Supreme Court ruled that the basic philosophy of the juvenile court (*parens patriae*) and due process rights could coexist and noted that both were intended to protect the interests of children. As a result of the *Gault* decision, all youth are afforded the right to legal counsel, and the Supreme Court stated that this particular right is fundamental to the administration of justice in the juvenile court. The current study sought to examine the influence of this fundamental right on juvenile court outcomes.

Similar to previous research, the results of the current study indicated that the presence of an attorney (especially a private attorney) was an aggravating factor. Specifically, youth who appeared with a private attorney were the least likely to have the charges dismissed and the most likely to be securely confined. Although legal factors (seriousness of current offense and prior offense history) influenced the disposition outcome, race and type of legal representation influenced disposition outcome separately as well as in interaction with one another. The results indicating differences in outcome based on type of attorney could also be because of the relative lack of prestige or legal training accorded to juvenile law. Most experienced juvenile attorneys focus on custody and child welfare cases that differ considerably from delinquency proceedings. Improving the pool of legal counsel for juveniles may influence these findings in the future. In addition, these results could be because of the capacity of youth to understand the legal arena. Juveniles are hindered by cognitive and psychological immaturity that renders them less competent than adults to assist counsel in making important legal decisions (Scott & Grisso, 1998).

The results of the current study provide evidence that calls into question the basic and fundamental right to counsel in the juvenile court. The juvenile court was established as a benevolent and regenerative institution that was less concerned with punishing a particular act than with providing the appropriate intervention to respond to the juvenile's needs. Over the years, the juvenile court has been transformed into an institution incorporating the principles of *parens patriae* and procedural safeguards. As the court has changed, questions have been raised about the differential treatment of White and non-White youth. In addition, allegations that procedural safeguards, including the right to counsel, are differentially applied have arisen. The current study addressed these issues.

The findings of the current study suggest that there are differences in the influence of legal counsel across race. Non-White youth were at a disadvantage from representation by a private attorney. On the other hand, White youth at times benefited from representation by a public defender but at other times were at a disadvantage as a result of this type of legal representation. In summary, the current study reveals some interesting observations regarding juvenile justice processing in two Midwestern juvenile courts. The results of the current study indicate that White and non-White youth received different disposition outcomes. As found in the current study, the effect of race may result in more severe dispositions but could also result in a lenient outcome. In addition, youth of each racial category received different outcomes based on type of legal representation. Public defenders are accepted as part of the juvenile court workgroup in many jurisdictions, however in many others they remain absent; private attorneys may or may not be present; and no legal representation may be perceived as reliance on the juvenile court to determine the best outcome.

The finding of an interaction effect of Race and Type of Counsel may reflect individualized justice—one goal of the juvenile court. However if the findings point to individual justice, it points to a strange variety of it. The severity or leniency of the disposition was determined by race, by type of counsel, and by an interaction of the two. The complexity of the juvenile justice system and the myriad factors that affect decision making seem daunting. The analyses and interpretations presented in the current study do not point to simple conclusions but do provide an assessment of how race and type of legal counsel affect juvenile court outcomes in two Midwestern juvenile courts.

✍ Notes

1. In County A, White male referrals were given a weight of 20, White female referrals given a weight of 12.50, African American male referrals given a weight

of 14.29, African American female referrals given a weight of 7.14, Native American and Asian American referrals given a weight of 4. In County B, no-action White referrals were given a weight of 20, no-action non-White referrals given a weight of 3.60, petitioned White referrals given a weight of 7.69, and petitioned non-White referrals given a weight of 1.39.

2. To determine if there was a statistically significant difference between outcomes for African American, Latino, and Native American youth, t tests were conducted. Results indicated no significant differences so the above racial categories were combined into a non-White category.

3. Initially, this variable was coded with nine categories ranging from a traffic offense to a felony against a person with the majority of cases either property felonies or property misdemeanors. Because of wide dispersion in each of the categories, the variable was recoded to felony/misdemeanor. This was necessary to complete the statistical analysis and may not adequately depict differences in offense seriousness of those who are and are not represented by counsel.

4. Ordered logit was attempted, however because the analysis failed the score test, this type of analysis could not be used.

⋙ References

Aday, D., Jr. (1986). Court structure, defense attorney use, and juvenile court decisions. *Sociological Quarterly, 27,* 107–119.

Aiken, L., & West, S. (1991). *Multiple regression: Testing and interpreting interactions.* Newbury Park, CA: Sage.

Albonetti, C. (1997). Sentencing under the federal sentencing guidelines: Effects of defendant characteristics, guilty pleas and departures on sentence outcomes for drug offenses, 1991–1992. *Law and Society Review, 31,* 278–322.

Aldrich, J., & Nelson, F. (1984). *Linear probability, logit and probit models.* Beverly Hills, CA: Sage.

Bailey, W. (1981). Preadjudicatory detention in a large metropolitan juvenile court. *Law and Human Behavior, 5,* 19–43.

Bell, D., Jr., & Lang, K. (1985). The intake dispositions of juvenile offenders. *Journal of Research in Crime and Delinquency, 22,* 309–328.

Bishop, D., & Frazier, C. (1988). The influence of race in juvenile justice processing. *Journal of Research in Crime and Delinquency, 25,* 242–263.

Bishop, D., & Frazier, C. (1996). Race effects in juvenile justice decision-making: Findings of a statewide analysis. *Journal of Criminal Law and Criminology, 86,* 392–414.

Black, D., & Reiss, A., Jr. (1970). Police control of juveniles. *American Sociological Review, 35,* 63–77.

Bortner, M., & Reed, W. (1985). The pre-eminence of process: An example of refocused justice research. *Social Science Quarterly, 66,* 413–425.

Bortner, M., Sunderland, M., & Winn, R. (1985). Race and the impact of juvenile deinstitutionalization. *Crime & Delinquency, 31,* 35–46.

Burruss, G., & Kempf-Leonard, K. (2002). The questionable advantage of defense counsel in juvenile court. *Justice Quarterly, 19,* 37–67.

Carrington, P., & Moyer, S. (1990). The effect of defense counsel and outcome in juvenile court. *Canadian Journal of Criminology, 32,* 621–637.

Clarke, S., & Koch, G. (1980). Juvenile court: Therapy or crime control, and do lawyers make a difference? *Law and Society Review, 14,* 263–308.

Cohen, J. (1992). Quantitative methods in psychology. *Psychology Bulletin, 112,* 155–159.

Cohen, J., & Cohen, P. (1983). *Applied multiple regression/correlation analysis for the behavioral sciences.* Hillsdale, NJ: Lawrence Erlbaum.

Cohen, L., & Klugel, J. (1979a). The detention decision: A study of the impact of social characteristics and legal factors in two metropolitan juvenile courts. *Social Forces, 58,* 146–161.

Cohen, L., & Klugel, J. (1979b). Selecting delinquents for adjudication: An analysis of intake screening decisions in two metropolitan courts. *Journal of Research in Crime and Delinquency, 16,* 143–163.

Conley, D. (1994). Adding color to a Black and White picture: Using qualitative data to explain racial disproportionality in the juvenile justice system. *Journal of Research in Crime and Delinquency, 31,* 135–148.

Dannefer, D., & Schutt, R. (1982). Race and juvenile justice processing in court and police agencies. *American Journal of Sociology, 87,* 1113–1132.

DeJong, C., & Jackson, K. (1998). Putting race into context: Race, juvenile justice processing and urbanization. *Justice Quarterly, 15,* 487–504.

Dootjes, I., Erickson, P., & Fox, R. (1972). Defense counsel in juvenile court: A variety of roles. *Canadian Journal of Criminology, 14,* 132–149.

Duffee, D., & Siegel, L. (1971). The organization man: Legal counsel in the juvenile court. *Criminal Law Bulletin, 7,* 544–553.

Eisenstein, J., & Jacob. H. (1977). *Felony justice: An organizational analysis of criminal courts.* Boston: Little, Brown.

Erickson, P. (1975). Legalistic and traditional role expectations for defense counsel in juvenile court. *Canadian Journal of Criminology, 17,* 78–93.

Fagan, J., Slaughter, E., & Hartstone, E. (1987). Blind justice? The impact of race on the juvenile justice process. *Crime & Delinquency, 33,* 224–258.

Feld, B. (1988). In re Gault: A cross-state comparison of the right to counsel in juvenile court. *Crime & Delinquency, 34,* 393–424.

Feld, B. (1991). Justice by geography: Urban, suburban and rural variations in juvenile justice administration. *Journal of Criminal Law and Criminology, 82,* 156–210.

Feld, B. (1993a). Criminalizing the American juvenile court. In M. Tonry (Ed.) *Crime and justice: A review of research* (Vol. 17, pp. 197–280). Chicago: University of Chicago Press.

Feld, B. (1993b). *Justice for children: The right to counsel and the juvenile courts.* Boston: Northeastern University Press.

Feld, B. (1999). A funny thing happened on the way to the centenary. *Punishment and Society, 1,* 187–214.

Ferster, E., & Courtless, T. (1972). Pre-dispositional data, role of counsel, and decisions in a juvenile court. *Law and Society Review, 7,* 195–222.

Ferster, E., Courtless, T., & Snethen, E. (1971). The juvenile justice system: In search of the role of counsel. *Fordham Law Review, 39,* 375–412.

Frazier, C., & Bishop, D. (1985). The pretrial detention of juveniles and its impact on case dispositions. *Journal of Criminal Law and Criminology, 76,* 1132–1152.

Frazier, C., & Bishop, D. (1995). Reflections on race effects in juvenile justice. In K. Kempf-Leonard, C. Pope, & W. Feyerherm (Eds.), *Minorities in juvenile justice* (pp. 16–46). Thousand Oaks, CA: Sage.

Frazier, C., Bishop, D., & Henretta, J. C. (1992). The social context of race differentials in juvenile justice dispositions. *Sociological Quarterly, 33,* 447–458.

Frazier, C., & Cochran, J. (1987). Detention of juveniles: Its effect on subsequent juvenile court processing decisions. *Youth & Society, 17,* 286–305.

Hawkins, D. (1987). Beyond anomalies: Rethinking the conflict perspective on race and criminal punishment. *Social Forces, 65,* 719–745.

Hawkins, D., & Jones, H. (1989). Black adolescents and the criminal justice system. In R. Jones (Ed.), *Black adolescents* (pp. 403–425). Berkeley, CA: Lobbard Henry.

Henretta, J., Frazier, C., & Bishop, D. (1986). The effect of prior case outcomes on juvenile justice decision-making. *Social Forces, 65,* 554–562.

In re Gault, 387 U.S. 1 (1967).

Johnson, J., & Secret, P. (1990). Race and juvenile court decision making revisited. *Criminal Justice Policy Review, 4,* 159–187.

Kempf-Leonard, K., & Sontheimer, L. (1995). The role of race in juvenile justice processing in Pennsylvania. In K. Kempf Leonard, C. Pope, & W. Feyerherm, (Eds.), *Minorities in juvenile justice* (pp. 98–127). Thousand Oaks, CA: Sage.

Langley, M. (1972). The juvenile court: The making of a delinquent. *Law and Society Review, 7,* 273–298.

Lefstein, N., Stapleton, V., & Teitelbaum, L. (1969). In search of juvenile justice: Gault and its implementation. *Law and Society Review, 3,* 491–563.

Leiber, M. (1994). A comparison of juvenile court outcomes for Native Americans, African Americans, and Whites. *Justice Quarterly, 11,* 257–278.

Liao, T. (1994). *Interpreting probability models: Logit, probit, and other generalized linear models.* Thousand Oaks, CA: Sage.

Long, J. (1997). *Regression models for categorical and limited dependent variables.* Thousand Oaks, CA: Sage.

Marshall, I., & Thomas, C. (1983). Discretionary decision-making and the juvenile court. *Juvenile and Family Court Journal, 34,* 47–59.

Mather, L. (1974). The outsider in the courtroom: An alternative role for the defense. In H. Jacob (Ed.), *The potential for reform of criminal justice* (pp. 263–290). Beverly Hills, CA: Sage.

McCarthy, B., & Smith, B. (1986). The conceptualization of discrimination in the juvenile justice process: The impact of administrative factors and screening decisions on juvenile court dispositions. *Criminology, 24,* 41–64.

McCord, J., Spatz-Widom, C., & Crowell, C. (2002). *Juvenile crime, juvenile justice.* Washington, DC: National Academy Press.

McGarrell, E. (1993). Trends in racial disproportionality in juvenile court processing: 1985–1989. *Crime & Delinquency, 39,* 29–48.

Melton, G. (1989). Taking Gault seriously: Toward a new juvenile court. *Nebraska Law Review, 68,* 146–181.

Menard, S. (1995). *Applied logistic regression analysis.* Thousand Oaks, CA: Sage.

Myers, S., Jr. (1985). Statistical tests of discrimination in punishment. *Journal of Quantitative Criminology, 1,* 191–218.

Neigher, A. (1967). The Gault decision: Due process and the juvenile courts. *Federal Probation, 31,* 8–18.

Nesburg, A. (1971). Juvenile due process in the lower courts. *Journal of Criminal Law, Criminology, and Police Science, 62,* 335–349.

Neubauer, D. (1974). *Criminal justice in middle America.* Morristown, NJ: General Learning Press.

Paternoster, R., Brame, R., Mazerolle, P., & Piquero, A. (1998). Using the correct statistical test for the equality of regression coefficients. *Criminology, 36,* 859–866.

Piliavin, I., & Briar, S. (1964). Police encounters with juveniles. *American Sociological Review, 51,* 91–119.

Platt, A. (1969). *The child savers.* Chicago: Chicago University Press.

Poole, E., & Regoli, R. (1980). An analysis of juvenile court dispositions. *Juvenile and Family Court Journal, 31,* 23–32.

Pope, C., & Feyerherm, W. (1990). Minority status and juvenile justice processing: An assessment of the research literature (parts I and II). *Criminal Justice Abstracts,* (June and September), 327–335; 527–542.

Reasons, C. (1970). Gault: Procedural change and substantive effect. *Crime & Delinquency, 16,* 163–171.

Schlossman, S. (1977). *Love and the American delinquent: The theory and practice of "progressive" juvenile justice, 1825–1920.* Chicago: University of Chicago Press.

Scott, E., & Grisso, T. (1998). The evolution of adolescence: A developmental perspective on juvenile justice reform. *Journal of Criminal Law and Criminology, 88,* 137–193.

Stapleton, V., & Teitelbaum, L. (1972). *In defense of youth: A study of the role of counsel in American juvenile courts.* New York: Russell Sage Foundation.

Thomas, C., & Sieverdes, C. (1975). Juvenile court intake: An analysis of discretionary decision-making. *Criminology 12,* 413–432.

Thornberry, T. (1973). Race, socioeconomic status and sentencing in the juvenile justice system. *Journal of Criminal Law and Criminology, 64,* 90–98.

Thornberry, T., & Christensen, R. (1984). Juvenile justice decision-making as a longitudinal process. *Social Forces, 63,* 433–444.

U.S. Bureau of the Census. (1990). *Census of Population and Housing.* Washington, DC: U.S. Government Printing Office.

U.S. Department of Justice, Office of Justice Programs. (1999). *Juvenile offenders and victims: 1999 national report.* Pittsburgh, PA: National Center for Juvenile Justice.

Winslade, W. (1974). The juvenile court: From idealism to hypocrisy. *Social Theory and Practice, 3,* 181–199.

Wordes, M., & Bynum, T. (1995). Policing juveniles: Is there bias against youths of color? In K. Kempf-Leonard, C. Pope, & W. Feyerherm (Eds.), *Minorities in juvenile justice* (pp. 47–65). Thousand Oaks, CA: Sage.

Wordes, M., Bynum, T., & Corley, C. (1994). Locking up youth: The impact of race on detention decisions. *Journal of Research in Crime and Delinquency, 31,* 149–165.

Zatz, M. (1987). The changing forms of racial/ethnic bias in sentencing. *Journal of Research in Crime and Delinquency, 24,* 69–92.

DISCUSSION QUESTIONS

1. Are the findings of previous research on the influence of counsel in accord with public expectations of the advocate role of defense counsel? Explain, and suggest reasons for the findings.

2. The authors suggest the findings may be partly explained by differences in how private attorneys and public defenders are perceived by judges. Should the "courtroom work group" be influential in sentencing decisions?

3. This study produced contradictory findings about the effects of race and presence of legal counsel in juvenile court. If you were asked to write policy guidelines to supplement your state's legal code regarding juvenile court process, what would you write?

❖

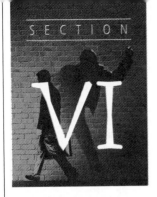

JUVENILE CORRECTIONS

SECTION HIGHLIGHTS

- History and Development of Juvenile Corrections
- Institutional and Residential Programs
- Juvenile Probation and Community Corrections
- Intermediate Sanctions
- Aftercare or Parole Supervision
- Effectiveness of Juvenile Corrections
- Current Issues and Future Trends in Juvenile Corrections

The field of corrections is the third major component of the juvenile justice system and administers the disposition (sentence) of the juvenile court. The juvenile court disposition options discussed in the previous section vary according to the risk level and correctional service needs of the juvenile offender. Corrections programs accordingly range from probation supervision in the community to secure institutional programs. Correctional programs and facilities for juvenile offenders have historically emphasized a treatment objective rather than the goal of punishment that is common for adult corrections. Juvenile institutions often resemble adult prisons, however, marked by abusive and oppressive conditions and with few rehabilitative programs. This section examines the history and development of institutional and community corrections for juveniles, the development of intermediate sanctions, disproportionate minority confinement, research on the effectiveness of correctional programs, and future trends in juvenile corrections.

The juvenile justice system recognizes the differences and unique needs of youthful offenders. The guiding principles have been to make judicial decisions that are "in the best interests of the child," and to use the "least restrictive" dispositional alternatives that fulfill the goals of correctional treatment and public safety. *Community corrections* refers to supervision in the community on *juvenile probation,* and may be combined with other alternatives to incarceration such as fines, restitution, and community service. The choice of available alternatives and programs varies in different jurisdictions, but the majority of juvenile offenders are placed on juvenile probation. *Institutional corrections* refers to placement in secure or semi-secure institutional and residential facilities, including temporary detention centers or juvenile shelters, state training schools, public or private residential facilities, group homes, and wilderness camps.

History and Development of Juvenile Corrections

Juvenile corrections has a long history in America, beginning with the development of Houses of Refuge and probation in the 19th century (discussed in Section I). Juveniles are confined in separate correctional facilities from adults, but many state training schools differ very little from prisons for adult criminals. Juvenile training schools came under criticism in the 1960s and 1970s as reformers highlighted the inhumane conditions in them, claiming that housing minor juvenile offenders with more serious and violent offenders made the facilities nothing more than "schools for crime." Jerome Miller received national attention in the early 1970s when, as director of the Massachusetts juvenile corrections agency, he closed all the training schools. Juveniles were placed in alternative public and private residential programs. Research evaluating the effects of closing the state schools indicated that the reform did not result in an increase in delinquency in the state (Coates, Miller, & Ohlin, 1978). Barry Krisberg and James Austin (1993) reported that a cost analysis of the Massachusetts system compared with other state juvenile corrections systems indicated that the Massachusetts system was cost-effective while providing public safety and offender rehabilitation (p. 163). The Massachusetts experience has been closely followed and many other states have considered reforms similar to those initiated by Jerome Miller.

Incarceration of juvenile offenders is very costly and does little to reduce juvenile crime. The increase in the number of offenders who are being sentenced to correctional institutions has placed enormous demands on state and federal budgets. The cost of building and operating correctional institutions has required states to cut back on other expenditures. From 1960 to 1985, state and local spending per capita increased 218% for corrections, significantly more than the increase for hospitals and health care (119%), police (73%) or education (56%; Bureau of Justice Statistics, 1988, p. 120). The proportion of taxpayer dollars that go to corrections has increased at a higher rate than the proportion allocated for education. We are in effect taking dollars from school classrooms to pay for more prison cells (Lawrence, 1995). A better use of taxpayer dollars is to invest in educational programs that have been shown to be effective in reducing delinquency, and to concentrate correctional spending on community-based programs that are more cost-effective than incarceration, while still providing for public safety. Krisberg and Austin (1993) suggested that a better use of tax dollars might be neighborhood-based crime prevention efforts that are directed at reducing child abuse, school dropout rates, youth unemployment, and drug dealing. The correctional reform movement of the 1970s was unfortunately replaced by a get-tough approach in the 1990s in response to what some believed to be a youth crime plague.

▨ Institutional and Residential Programs

According to the Juvenile Residential Facility Census (JRFC) in 2002, a total of 102,388 juveniles were held in 2,964 facilities (Sickmund, 2006). Some of the characteristics of the juveniles and the residential facilities in which they were held include the following:

- There were more private facilities (1,773) than public facilities (1,182), but more juveniles (70,243 or 69%) were held in public facilities than in private ones (31,992 or 31%).
- The number of delinquent offenders in residential facilities decreased 7% from 2000 to 2002.
- The national U.S. rate of custody for juvenile offenders was 326 per 100,000 juveniles in the population.
- The rate of custody among the states varied widely, from 85 to 688 per 100,000 juveniles in the state populations.
- Crowding is a problem in many facilities, with a total of 1,069 (36%) of facilities (mostly public) reporting being at or over capacity, affecting 39,200 (34%) of the residents in 2002 (Sickmund, 2006, pp. 2–9).

A study of trends of children in custody found that the average length of stay for juveniles in a residential facility is about 4 months, the average yearly cost for custody in a public facility was more than $32,000 in 1998, and private facilities increased in average annual costs to more than $45,000 in 1995 (Smith, 1998, p. 537). Placement in a residential facility is generally used for the most serious or chronic juvenile offenders who require secure confinement and treatment. As many as one fifth (25,000 or 19%) of confined youth in 1999, however, were not charged or adjudicated for an offense (Sickmund, 2004). Residential placement is very costly compared with community corrections, and there are questions whether the education, training, and treatment received in juvenile institutions are effective in reducing delinquent behavior.

In 2002, residential placement was ordered in 23% of cases in which youth were adjudicated delinquent. A total of 144,000 (23%) were ordered to placement, and 385,400 (62%) were ordered to probation supervision in the community. From 1985 to 2002, both residential and probation cases had increased proportions of person, drug, and public order offenses. Cases ordered to residential placement in 2002 had a greater share of personal and public order cases and a smaller share of drug cases than cases ordered to formal probation (Snyder & Sickmund, 2006, p. 174). Table VI-1 summarizes the proportion of delinquency cases ordered to residential placement and to probation.

Table VI-1	Probation and Residential Placement of Delinquency Cases, 2002	
Offense	*1985*	*2002*
Residential Placement	**100%**	**100%**
Person	18	26
Property	56	37
Drugs	5	10
Public order	22	28
Formal probation	**100%**	**100%**
Person	16	24
Property	61	38
Drugs	7	13
Public order	16	25

SOURCE: Snyder & Sickmund, 2006, p. 174.

Juvenile Training Schools. The physical structure of juvenile training schools varies from cottage settings to open dormitories, and maximum security facilities may house residents in individual cells. The secure training schools have an institutional appearance inside and out, with high fences surrounding them, locked doors, and screens or bars on windows. Residents' movements throughout the facility are restricted and closely supervised by the staff. The living quarters of the medium security cottage and dormitory-style facilities are more homelike, but they offer little privacy for residents. Medium security training schools often are surrounded by fences and therefore resemble maximum security juvenile facilities. Few juvenile training schools are minimum security, because most juveniles are sent to a training school because they need restricted confinement.

Juvenile training schools represent the most punitive sanction available in the juvenile justice system. Removing youth from their families, communities, and public schools is a significant punishment for many of them. They live under close 24-hour supervision with strict rules and discipline. Serious rule violations such as fighting and assaults result in short-term commitment to disciplinary segregation, which is a secure detention setting within the training school. Staff members maintain discipline among the residents by withholding privileges or extending the length of stay for those who violate any rules.

Many training schools do have some good programs, including medical and dental care, an accredited school, vocational training, recreation, and treatment programs. Rehabilitation is still the primary purpose of juvenile training schools. The treatment methods that are used most widely are behavior modification, guided group interaction, transactional analysis, reality therapy, and positive peer culture. Efforts are made to prepare the juveniles for return to their families and communities. Juveniles who have made satisfactory adjustment and are within a few weeks of their release may be allowed to make home visits or take part in work-release programs in the community.

The goal of rehabilitation has seldom been achieved in most juvenile training schools. Studies indicate that few of the programs being used in training schools are effective in preventing future delinquency, although there is some evidence that institutional treatment may work with some youth. Carol Garrett (1985) reviewed more than 100 studies conducted between 1960 and 1983 on juvenile corrections treatment programs such as counseling, behavior modification, and life-skill improvement. Garrett found no single treatment strategy that was most effective, but she concluded that the majority of interventions did show change in a positive direction. On the other hand, Steven Lab and John Whitehead (1988) analyzed juvenile correctional research done from 1975 to 1984 and concluded that treatment has little impact on recidivism. One problem seems to be that the programs themselves are not being used effectively (Whitehead & Lab, 1989). The youth workers and counselors of juvenile training schools face the dilemma of trying to adapt programs to a diverse and varied juvenile offender population. The institutional setting in which the primary concern is control of some of the most serious delinquents presents a challenge for the correctional staff in fulfilling educational and treatment goals.

Despite the goals of treatment, juvenile training schools remain institutional settings marked by oppressiveness and fear. As states confine dangerous juvenile offenders together with younger, smaller, or less serious offenders in the same institution, even the closest supervision and the best programs have little positive effects. Training school staff members are often powerless to prevent incidents of inmate abuse by other inmates (Feld, 1977). Bartollas, Miller, and Dinitz (1976) examined victimization in a maximum security juvenile institution in Columbus, Ohio, and found that 90% of the residents were either perpetrators or victims of abuse. Juveniles who are confined in training schools find the institutional environment oppressive and stressful. Despite any good intentions of treatment or "training," staff must first be concerned with maintaining security and close supervision among the residents. Wooden (1976) documented multiple examples of abuse of juvenile inmates by oppressive correctional workers in state training schools. In such an oppressive and abuse environment adaptation to the institutional setting becomes a higher priority for the juvenile residents than treatment.

In summary, there is little that can be positively stated about juvenile training schools. Despite goals of education, training, and treatment, the first priority of training school staff is to maintain close supervision and security. In correctional institutions, treatment programs and correctional services are secondary to the primary goal of maintaining order and control. Residential facilities that house juvenile offenders who do not pose a public safety or security risk are able to place more emphasis on rehabilitation programs.

Other Residential Programs. The main types of community-based residential programs are group homes, foster care, and day treatment programs. *Group homes* are small residential facilities in the community that are designed to house about 10 to 15 youths. Group homes serve as an alternative to incarceration; they are a short-term community placement for youth on probation or aftercare supervision, and they serve as a "halfway house" for youth needing semi-secure placement but less than that of a training school. *Foster care programs* offer temporary placement for juveniles who must be removed from their own homes. Foster parents provide a temporary home for neglected, abused, or delinquent children and receive a subsidy from local or state governments to cover their expenses. Foster parents are able to provide more consistent and firm supervision than troubled juveniles may have been receiving in their own homes. Short-term placement with foster parents gives more time for probation officers to seek other placement alternatives. It is difficult to get enough persons who are willing to serve as foster parents, especially for delinquent youth. Foster care places considerable stresses on a home because many delinquent youth have experienced abusive parental relationships and are therefore distrustful and often rebellious toward foster parents. *Day treatment*

▲ **Photo VI-1** A secure juvenile corrections facility. (© CORBIS)

programs are nonresidential programs that offer delinquent youth a variety of educational, counseling, recreational, and training activities. They are less expensive to operate because they are nonresidential and require fewer staff members.

Boot Camps. Boot camps were developed as part of the trend toward harsher treatment for juvenile offenders. Boot camps are alternatives to correctional facilities; they house youths for periods of 3 to 6 months in facilities that resemble military training camps. Officers resembling a "drill instructor" supervise the residents and begin each day with calisthenics, running, and conditioning exercises. Proponents of boot camps believe that the focus on military-type discipline and physical training will be effective in changing the attitudes and bad habits of many chronic juvenile offenders. Boot camps have also been promoted as a way to reduce crowding in correctional facilities and to reduce costs. Research results on the effectiveness of boot camps are mixed. Some residents have responded well to the discipline and training, but MacKenzie (1994) found that any positive results that come from boot camps are not from the military atmosphere but from educational and rehabilitative programming. In a study included as one of the readings in this section, MacKenzie, Wilson, Armstrong, and Gover (2001) examined the impact of boot camps and traditional institutions on juvenile residents' perceptions, adjustment, and change. They found some benefits in both types of placements, and concluded that youths' background and histories made a difference in their adjustment, perceptions, and change. Overall, boot camps have not been found to be more effective than traditional juvenile training schools.

Wilderness Camps. Outdoor education and training programs—the most widely known is "Outward Bound"—have developed as effective institutional alternatives for juvenile offenders.

The goals of Outward Bound and similar wilderness programs are to help youth gain self-confidence and self-reliance by placing them in outdoor settings and challenging them with new physical tasks that appear seemingly impossible, especially for most metropolitan juvenile offenders who are unfamiliar with wilderness settings (Greenwood & Zimring, 1985). Wilderness programs attempt to accomplish the goals through backpacking in wilderness areas, high-altitude camping, mountain hiking, rock climbing, and rappelling from platforms, trees, or cliffs. Participants first receive training in basic skills, then participate in an expedition, and are eventually tested in a solo experience. The wilderness experience lasts from 3 to 4 weeks.

VisionQuest is a survival program based in Tucson, Arizona. The program contracts with juvenile courts and takes juveniles who are committed to the program from California, Pennsylvania, and several other states. VisionQuest programs, lasting from 12 to 18 months, include wilderness camps, cross-country travel on a wagon train, or a voyage on a large sailboat. The youth are closely supervised and rigorously challenged emotionally, intellectually, and physically. VisionQuest has drawn some controversy for its confrontational style with juveniles who do not perform up to expectations, slack off, or act out (Greenwood & Zimring, 1985).

Several states have developed wilderness camps as alternatives to placement in a correctional facility. The state of Minnesota operates a camp for offenders who have failed to comply with probation conditions but who do not need secure training school placement. Thistledew Camp, located between two lakes in a remote forest area of northern Minnesota, features a unique educational facility intended to serve delinquent youth who have experienced failure in the home, school, and community. Education is provided for youths at all levels, and all classroom teachers are certified in Learning Disabilities (LD) or Emotional/Behavioral Disorders (EBD) to provide optimum services for students with special needs. About a third of the time at Thistledew Camp is devoted to Challenge, an outdoor wilderness survival program similar to Outward Bound. Challenge is a high-adventure wilderness experience designed to build individual self-confidence, develop leadership abilities, and teach the importance of group effort. Residents receive training and instruction in the use of equipment and in basic wilderness techniques. Expeditions are conducted throughout the year and geared to the seasons. Treks include canoeing, backpacking, rock climbing, cross-country skiing, and traveling by snowshoe. Expeditions are planned to be rugged and difficult in order to build self-confidence and to teach the importance of teamwork. "Solo camping" is a final phase of Challenge. Camping alone in an isolated area for 3 days and nights, residents experience loneliness, hunger, and cold, and they learn how to handle those situations in a self-reliant manner (Minnesota Department of Corrections, 2007).

Wilderness programs are also used in conjunction with probation supervision. Staffed by probation officers and lay volunteers, wilderness probation involves juveniles in outdoor expeditions to give them a sense of confidence and purpose (Callahan, 1985). Counseling and group therapy are combined with day hikes and a wilderness experience. The programs provide an opportunity for juveniles on probation to confront difficulties in their lives and to attain some personal satisfaction. Wilderness programs have been effective in producing some positive changes in juvenile offenders, but research shows mixed results as to their effectiveness in reducing recidivism. Lipsey, Wilson, and Cothern (2000) found that wilderness and challenge programs were not effective in reducing recidivism among serious juvenile offenders. Programs that combine education, skills development, and counseling show more positive results (Lipsey et al., 2000).

▲ **Photo VI-2**   Juveniles in the cafeteria line in a secure juvenile corrections facility. (© Bill Gentile/CORBIS)

Juvenile Probation and Community Corrections

The concept of probation was originally developed through the efforts of John Augustus, a Boston boot maker who persuaded a judge in 1841 to release an offender to him for supervision in the community rather than sentence him to prison. Augustus worked with hundreds of offenders and set the stage for probation as we know it today. As the first probation officer, John Augustus developed many of the probation strategies that continue to be used in probation today: investigation and screening, supervision, educational and employment services, and providing guidance and assistance. Probation has been called "the workhorse of the juvenile justice system" (Torbet, 1996) and is the most common juvenile court disposition and the predominant form of community supervision and treatment in the juvenile justice system. Today virtually all counties in the nation have juvenile probation services. In 2002, adjudicated delinquents ordered to probation (385,400 cases) accounted for 62% of all delinquency cases placed on probation. The number of adjudicated cases that resulted in court-ordered probation rose 103% between 1985 and 2002 (from 189,600 to 385,400) (Livsey, 2006, p. 1). The offense profiles of cases placed on probation and ordered to residential placement for the years 1985 and 2002 are presented in Table VI-1.

Probation Goals and Objectives. Four components of juvenile probation have been identified: (1) As a *legal disposition:* juveniles are under court supervision with conditions and rules with which they must comply before being released. (2) As an *alternative to incarceration,* probation is a nonpunitive disposition that emphasizes correctional treatment and reintegration of juvenile offenders. (3) Probation is a *subsystem* of the juvenile justice system. (4) As a *court service agency,* probation officers conduct investigations for the court, supervise juveniles, and provide services that are helpful to youth, their families, and the community (National Advisory Commission on Criminal Justice Standards and Goals, 1973, p. 312). Probation is the most common disposition used by juvenile court judges, but probation is a privilege and not a right (del Carmen, 1985). Juveniles are placed on probation supervision in the community on the condition that they will follow specified court orders. Failure to comply with probation conditions may result in revocation of probation and placement in a residential or institutional facility.

Juvenile probation is administered either by the juvenile court or a group of courts in the jurisdiction, or by a state or local department of youth services, a department of social services, or some combination of these (Torbet, 1996). In either organizational context, the juvenile court judge and the probation staff have a close working relationship. Larger metropolitan juvenile probation departments are administered by a chief probation officer, with one or more assistants overseeing specialized units within the department. Larger departments may have units specializing in intake services, investigation and court report writing, a field supervision unit, and detention services.

Probation has been criticized as a lenient sentence that provides little supervision or close monitoring of offenders. Community corrections experts have countered such criticism and noted the multiple advantages of probation: (1) reintegration of offenders in the community while under court orders and supervision; (2) furthering the goals of justice and protecting the community from further delinquent behavior; (3) monitoring probation conditions and providing services to help change offenders and meet probation objectives; (4) retaining young offenders in the community, with their families, in public or alternative schools, and thus avoiding the difficulties of reintegration; and (5) avoiding the fiscal costs and the negative influence and stigma of commitment to a correctional facility (Latessa & Allen, 2003, pp. 101–102).

The Practice of Probation. In practice, probation is basically an agreement between the juvenile court and the young offender. The adjudicated delinquent agrees to comply with the court orders and probation conditions and is released to his or her parents. In cases where the probation officer's investigation has indicated that parental supervision is lacking, the youth may be placed with a legal guardian, foster parents, or in a group home. In either case, the placement is less punitive than commitment to a juvenile institution. The time period for probation supervision is generally for an indefinite period of time, but it usually does not exceed 2 years. Each probation case is usually reviewed periodically to ensure that some progress is being made, treatment goals are being met, and to ensure that the juvenile is not kept on probation unnecessarily. If a juvenile is not complying with probation conditions, then the probation officer is expected to take the case before the judge, who may choose to revise the probation conditions, or order the youth referred to a different placement, including commitment to a more secure setting if he or she seems to present a danger to him- or herself or the community.

Probation Officer Responsibilities. Probation officers have three primary responsibilities: intake, investigation, and supervision. The first two functions were discussed in Section III (Juvenile Detention and Intake) and Section V (The Juvenile Court Process). The third major function of a probation officer is to provide *supervision of offenders* in the community and to monitor the court-ordered probation conditions. Following the judge's probation order, the probation officer meets with the youth and parents to explain the rules and conditions of probation, answer any questions about the term of probation and the court's expectations, and to ensure that they understand the importance of complying with the probation conditions. Special probation conditions require additional explanation, especially if the court has included an order to make restitution payments to victims or community service restitution, to avoid drinking or drug use, or to participate in drug-treatment programs. Juvenile probation officers face a special challenge in supervising delinquents because they often receive little assistance and support from the parents. Many juvenile offenders have a poor relationship with their parents and show little respect for their parents' authority. Families of delinquents are often characterized by parental negligence or abuse, inconsistent discipline, poor communication, and poor parenting skills. Probation supervision is more difficult without solid parental and family support. Under those rare but ideal conditions, parents can play an important role in helping a youth comply with probation conditions, in closely supervising their child, and by communicating regularly with the probation officer. Parental support is especially important in closely monitoring the child's school attendance and behavior, peer associations, and in complying with curfew requirements. Probation officers must perform a dual role of encouraging, helping, and assisting the young offender to make a positive adjustment; but also act as an authority figure who will report probation violations to the court.

Probation Officer Roles. In carrying out the supervision responsibility, probation officers fulfill three major roles and functions: casework management, treatment, and surveillance. *Casework management* involves maintaining current files on each juvenile in a caseload averaging 40 or more cases (Torbet, 1996). In addition to the police offense reports and social history report, the case file includes periodic contact reports of every personal visit and telephone call regarding the juvenile. Contacts are made with each juvenile varying from once a week to once a month or less, depending upon the intensity level of supervision needed. Documentation in the juvenile's file is important. Cases are often managed by more than one caseworker or may be transferred to another officer who is less familiar with the case. If the probation officer files a court petition for revocation of probation, he or she may be called to testify as to the violations of probation conditions, including the exact dates, circumstances, and details of the violations. Paperwork and file management are sources of frustration and complaints among probation officers, but are an important part of the job responsibilities (Lawrence, 1984).

The *treatment* function of juvenile probation officers focuses on their role as caseworkers or counselors. One of the most difficult challenges faced by probation officers is the large number of juveniles from dysfunctional families. Parents have lost both control and the respect of their child. The parent–child relationship has deteriorated to the point that the youth has become incorrigible, refusing to comply with the parents' demands. Many of the parents have never learned to use effective communication and management strategies. Because a poor parent–child relationship is one of the major problems faced by probation officers in working with delinquents, some educational background in family counseling, social work, or general counseling skills has traditionally been one of the job requirements for juvenile probation. Training seminars in family intervention and guidance are often provided for juvenile probation officers, and probation conferences often include at least one session on the subject. Since the minimum educational requirement for probation officers is a 4-year college degree, they are not expected to provide professional counseling services, nor are they qualified to do so. One of their responsibilities is to identify problems that require more professional treatment and then refer the child and family to mental health services for family counseling and guidance. The National Advisory Commission on Criminal Justice Standards and Goals (1973) recommended that probation agencies should "redefine the role of probation officer from caseworker to community resource manager" (p. 320). As a *resource manager* the officer's responsibility is to assess the juvenile's needs and then make appropriate referrals to other social agencies that can best provide the needed services. Implementation of the resource manager model of probation depends, however, on the available resources and agencies to assist in the treatment function. Probation clients in jurisdictions with fewer available resources receive only the extent of counseling and guidance that the probation officers themselves are able to provide.

The *surveillance* function requires the probation officer to monitor juveniles closely to make certain that they are complying with the probation conditions. This may be accomplished through questions directed at the juvenile during office visits, through telephone calls, or through personal visits to the juvenile's home or school. Probation agencies may require drug testing for juveniles suspected of illegal drug use. The surveillance function is much like that of a police officer, and probation officers have the authority to take probationers into custody for violating conditions of probation. Juvenile probation officers work closely with police and depend on police officers to arrest and take into custody any juveniles on probation who commit a new crime. Violation of probation conditions is considered a "technical violation," and probation officers have more latitude in whether to file for revocation of probation than when a youth is rearrested by police for a new crime. In either case, probation revocation is not automatic. The juvenile is entitled to a probation revocation hearing under due process guidelines established by the U.S. Supreme Court in the 1972 case of *Morrissey v. Brewer* (408 U.S. 471, 92 S.Ct. 2593). If the judge finds that there is sufficient evidence that probation conditions have been violated, he or she may revoke probation and commit the juvenile to a state training school, or may choose a range of less punitive alternatives, including more intensive probation supervision with more restrictive conditions, or temporary placement in a semi-secure group home placement.

Probation Officer Role Conflict. Probation officers are charged with helping offenders to change, but as officers of the court they are also expected to monitor compliance with court orders. The two roles represent treatment versus surveillance: acting as a counselor or social worker one moment, and a law enforcement officer the next. Probation officers experience "role conflict" in attempting to fulfill both functions at the same time (Latessa & Allen, 2003; Lawrence, 1984). The opposing roles of treatment versus surveillance present probation officers with a dilemma: attempting to be a counselor or advocate for a juvenile while simultaneously enforcing probation rules and threatening revocation as a consequence for violations. The officer cannot choose one role over the other. Attention to both responsibilities is necessary. The objectives of probation are to help probationers adjust to problems at home, school, and in the community, but officers are also responsible for monitoring probationers' compliance with probation rules and reporting probation violations to the court. Considerable research has been conducted on the dilemmas and difficulties presented by probation officer role conflict (Latessa & Allen, 2003, pp. 258–263). The nature of the job requirements means that some role conflict will always be present, but education and training can minimize the adverse effects of role conflict on probation officers and other community corrections personnel.

⊠ **Intermediate Sanctions**

The juvenile court judge traditionally was limited to the sentencing options of either probation or residential placement. Many offenders require more supervision than regular probation, but do not require 24-hour care and supervision for several months in a residential placement or secure correctional facility. The concept of "intermediate sanctions" was developed to provide supervision and correctional services that are literally "between prison and probation" (Morris & Tonry, 1990). A variety of "intermediate sanctions" have been developed to provide more public safety than regular probation, while being less intrusive and expensive than residential placements. These alternatives to incarceration include intensive probation supervision, day reporting centers, electronic monitoring, and restitution programs. They are commonly used by probation agencies as a part of and in addition to probation supervision. There is evidence that intermediate sanctions are more successful than regular probation supervision, and have advantages over institutional commitment in that they are less expensive and avoid severing ties between the juvenile's family and the community (Latessa & Allen, 2003).

Intensive Probation Supervision. Probation has been criticized for being too lenient and for providing only minimal supervision. There is no question that many juveniles need more supervision than is possible for a probation officer with a large caseload to provide. Intensive supervision programs have been adopted by many probation agencies as an alternative to sending high-risk juveniles to a correctional institution (Byrne, 1986). A small number of cases (about 15 to 25) are assigned to a probation officer, who is expected to make daily contacts and to closely monitor juveniles' daily activities. The recidivism rates of juveniles on intensive probation supervision are often higher than those on regular probation, due in part to the higher-risk juveniles in the programs and the officer's close surveillance detecting probation violations that may go unnoticed on regular probation supervision. Even if intensive supervision is no more effective in reducing recidivism of high-risk juvenile offenders, the cost benefits (about one third that of confinement) make it a desirable alternative over incarceration (Latessa, 1986).

Day Reporting Centers. Day reporting centers have been implemented as an alternative means of assisting probation officers to keep up with the task of monitoring probation clients through personal visits. It is not possible for most probation officers to personally see each of their clients with a caseload of 40 or more cases. Day reporting centers were developed to monitor a larger number of probationers with a smaller number of officers. Offenders in the program are court ordered to report in person to a reporting center, to provide a schedule of planned activities, and to participate in designated activities. Offenders must also call the centers by phone throughout the day, and can also expect random phone calls from the center staff during the day and at home following curfew (Gowdy, 1993). In addition to monitoring probationers' activities, day reporting centers offer a variety of services, including job skills training and placement, drug abuse education, and counseling. Research evidence indicates that day reporting centers have been effective in providing closer monitoring of probation clients without significantly increasing the cost of probation services (Latessa & Allen, 2003, pp. 339–343).

Electronic Monitoring and House Arrest. Juveniles may be placed on probation under special conditions requiring that they remain in their home at all times except for school, employment, or medical reasons. House arrest may be coupled with frequent random phone calls or personal visits, or electronic monitoring. In this technological innovation, probationers are fitted with a nonremovable monitoring device attached to their ankle that signals a probation department computerized monitoring station if the offender leaves the house (Charles, 1986). The monitoring device is connected to the telephone in the house and makes random phone calls to verify the probationer's presence. Electronic monitoring has the advantage of operating as an effective alternative to incarceration in a detention center at less than half the cost. Joseph Vaughn (1989) conducted a survey of eight juvenile electronic monitoring programs and found that most were successful in reducing the number of days that juveniles spent in detention; furthermore, the youth were able to participate in school and work activities during the time they were not confined to their homes. Recent evaluations of electronic monitoring, however, have found little evidence that it has a positive impact on offender recidivism (Latessa & Allen, 2003, p. 351).

Restitution Programs. One of the goals of community corrections is to have offenders accept responsibility and to have them be accountable for the harm they have done. Restitution programs represent a way for juvenile offenders to literally "pay for" their crimes while on probation. Four goals of restitution programs have been identified: (1) holding juveniles accountable, (2) providing reparation to victims, (3) treating and rehabilitating juveniles, and (4) punishing juveniles (Schneider, 1985a). Restitution can be in the form of either monetary or service restitution to either the victim or to the community. Under monetary restitution the probationer may be ordered to reimburse the victim of the crime for property damages or the medical costs of personal injury. Under the second form, a juvenile may be required to provide some service directly to the victim or to the community. Victim restitution is done with the consent of the victim, and service restitution is usually done under the supervision of a probation officer. Juvenile restitution programs existed in more than 400 jurisdictions throughout the nation, and by 1985 most states had legislation authorizing such programs as part of probation (Schneider & Warner, 1989). Restitution directs attention to the forgotten persons in the justice process, the victims; it provides monetary compensation or service to them. It is rehabilitative in that the juvenile has an opportunity to compensate the victim for injury or damages, and encourages him or her to be accountable for wrongful actions and become a productive member of society. Evaluations of restitution programs indicate that they are quite effective as a treatment alternative. Schneider (1986) evaluated programs in four states and found that program participants had lower recidivism rates than control groups of youths placed on regular probation. The differences were not dramatic (a difference of only 10% in recidivism rates in some comparisons), but the restitution programs did seem to result in more positive attitudes among many juveniles (Schneider, 1986). Restitution programs have been recognized as one of the programs that represent the best practices for juvenile court and probation, as they focus on offender accountability and offer an opportunity for juvenile offenders to make reparations to the victim and the community (Kurlychek, Torbet, & Bozynski, 1999).

⊠ Aftercare or Parole Supervision

Supervision of juveniles in the community following release from an institutional facility is referred to as "aftercare" (comparable to "parole supervision" in some jurisdictions). Intensive aftercare programs provide social control and treatment services for juveniles returning to the community from out-of-home placements and are important for making the transition from the institution to the community. Aftercare can serve to protect public safety by monitoring

▲ **Photo VI-3**   A juvenile meeting with his counselor. (© CORBIS)

the juvenile's reintegration into the community. Aftercare services help the juvenile to over-come negative influences and risk factors by enhancing the skills needed to become a produc-tive and law-abiding member of society. Successful aftercare programs begin developing an offender's aftercare plan early in the residential placement, create links to the youth's family and school throughout treatment, and provide high levels of both social control and treat-ment services (Gies, 2003).

The Office of Juvenile Justice and Delinquency Prevention (OJJDP) initiated an Intensive Community-Based Aftercare Program (IAP) in 1987 that had three emphases:

- Prerelease and preparatory planning during incarceration
- Structured transition that required the participation of institutional and aftercare staff prior to and following community reentry
- Long-term, reintegrative activities that ensure adequate service delivery and the neces-sary level of social control (Altschuler & Armstrong, 1996)

Research on the IAP model has indicated that when aftercare supervision is predominantly or exclusively surveillance and social control (e.g., drug testing and electronic monitoring) and treatment services are lacking or inadequate, then neither a reduction in recidivism nor an improvement in social, cognitive, or behavioral functioning are likely to occur (Altschuler, Armstrong, & MacKenzie, 1999). Development of successful aftercare programs faces a number of challenges, including not enough qualified staff; cost sharing and contracting between public and private agencies; developing organizational capacity to deliver consistent and compatible services between the institution and the community; and applying those services to problems in the family, peer group, school, work, and drug involvement (Altschuler et al., 1999, p. 4). A review of the research of aftercare programs indicates that they show promise of assisting with successful reentry and reintegration of juvenile offenders returning from institutions to community programs, and can combine interventions for individual behavior change with surveillance methods to protect the community (Gies, 2003). A reading in this section by Altschuler and Brash (2004) examines the connection between young offenders' transition into adulthood and reentry into their communities. The authors discuss the mission and purpose of institutional and community corrections, the process of reentry within a broader "reintegration" paradigm, and the essential elements of successful reentry and aftercare.

✎ Effectiveness of Juvenile Corrections

There is no unanimous agreement on how to assess correctional outcome. Recidivism has been the traditional measure of effectiveness in corrections. Recidivism may refer to a new arrest, a new conviction, or return to prison, however, so evaluative research must clearly specify the exact criteria being used to measure success or failure. Violations of probation conditions ("technical violations") are also indicators of failure, but are less likely to result in revocation of probation. The practice of assessing effectiveness of corrections based on arrests or other measures of recidivism has clear limitations (Latessa & Allen, 2003, p. 471). Corrections researchers believe that success or failure should be viewed on a continuum using multiple indicators rather than as a dichotomous win–lose criterion. Petersilia (1993) has recommended that community corrections should be assessed according to several performance indicators that are based on clearly stated goals, methods, and activities. Five goals of community corrections that should be included in an assessment of outcome are the quality and extent to which the probation agency and officer have been able to: (1) assess the offender's suitability for placement, (2) enforce court-ordered sanctions, (3) protect the community, (4) assist offenders to change, and (5) restore crime victims for harm done to them (Petersilia, 1993, pp. 78–79). Evaluating the effectiveness of community corrections according to these five goals takes into account the multiple roles and responsibilities of probation officers, including investigation, supervision, and monitoring of court orders, including restitution payments to victims. Multiple performance indicators are included to assess the performance of corrections professionals and the responses of offenders to correctional services and supervision. Number of days employed, vocational education, school attendance, and the number of drug- and alcohol-free days are included as performance indicators in addition to the number of arrests and technical violations (Petersilia, 1993, pp. 78–79).

Measures of the effectiveness of juvenile corrections should also assess the quality of programs, including those conducted in institutions, in public and private residential facilities, and those providing supervision and treatment in the community (Latessa & Allen, 2003).

While assessment of program effectiveness is important, corrections researchers acknowledge that recidivism remains the most common measure of the effectiveness of corrections programs. A meta-analysis of studies of institutional and community corrections interventions for serious juvenile offenders concluded that the most effective types of treatment were interpersonal skills training, individual counseling, and behavioral programs (Lipsey et al., 2000; Cothern, 2000). Lipsey and colleagues found that community-based programs showed greater reductions in recidivism than institutional programs. Offenders in nonsecure community supervision programs do commit some new crimes, but the fact that they do as well or better than youths sent to training schools and released to aftercare supervision suggests that community supervision presents no more risk to public safety and recidivism than incarceration. Research on get-tough measures such as Scared Straight programs, boot camps, and intensive supervision has indicated that harsher measures, without additional educational or skills training components, do not reduce recidivism (Whitehead & Lab, 2006).

Cullen, Eck, and Lowenkamp (2002) have proposed a new paradigm for effective probation and parole supervision called "environmental corrections," based on environmental criminology, a theory that links crime causation and crime reduction to the presence or absence of opportunities to commit crime. Cullen and his associates believe that probation and parole officers would be more effective if they worked closely with offenders, the family, community members, and the police in order to reduce offenders' opportunities and temptations to commit crime. In addition to maintaining the usual responsibilities of assessment and investigation, probation and parole officers would use a problem-solving approach in supervising offenders to help them avoid the opportunities and temptations that lead to offending. Cullen and his associates (2002) acknowledge that considerable efforts will be required to put it into practice. A new problem-solving approach for probation and parole officers engaged in "environmental corrections" will add to their responsibilities, but may improve community supervision and be more cost-effective.

⬚ Current Issues and Future Trends in Juvenile Corrections

Disproportionate Minority Confinement

Minority youth accounted for 7 in 10 (65%) of juveniles held in custody for a violent offense in 1999 (Sickmund, 2004). Blacks (39%) and Hispanics (18%) outnumbered white youth (38%) among the juvenile offenders held in residential placement in 1999. The percentage of minority youth committed to public facilities nationwide (66%) was nearly twice their proportion of the juvenile population (34%). In six states and the District of Columbia, the minority proportion of the total population of juvenile offenders in residential placement was greater than 75%. Custody rates present a dramatic picture of disproportionate minority confinement. For every 100,000 black juveniles in the United States, 1,004 were in a residential placement in 1999, compared with 485 Hispanics and 212 white youth per 100,000 in the general population (Sickmund, 2004, p. 10).

Disproportionate minority confinement (DMC) may be explained by three factors: (1) overrepresentation, (2) disparity, and (3) discrimination (Sickmund, 2004). *Overrepresentation* means that a larger proportion of a group is in the justice system than the proportion in the general population. *Disparity* means that the chance of being arrested, detained, or adjudicated differs for different groups of youth. *Discrimination* means that justice officials treat one group of juveniles differently because of their gender, race, or ethnicity. If racial and ethnic discrimination exists, then minorities are more likely to be arrested by police, referred to court intake, petitioned for formal processing, adjudicated delinquent, and placed in a residential facility. Differential decision making throughout the juvenile justice system by police, probation, and court officials may account for minority overrepresentation. Disparity and overrepresentation may on the other hand be the result of minority youth committing disproportionately more crimes than white youth, or being involved in more serious crimes that come to the attention of police and are more likely to be processed through the justice system. Thus, minority overrepresentation in the justice system and in confinement may be explained by behavioral and legal factors, rather than by discrimination (Sickmund, 2004).

Minority youths are disproportionately represented at every stage of the juvenile justice process (Pope & Feyerherm, 1995). Police arrests involve a disproportionate number of minority youth, especially for more serious violent crimes (Snyder, 2004), and a disproportionate number of minority youth are represented in juvenile court cases (Puzzanchera, Stahl, Finnegan, Tierney, & Snyder, 2003). Results of self-report measures show that delinquent behavior is spread equally among youth of all social classes and racial/ethnic groups, and white middle-class youth in fact report more drug violations than lower-class and minority youths (Elliott, Huizinga, & Ageton, 1985). Data from victimization surveys have indicated, however, that the violent offending rate for black juveniles was four times higher than for white juveniles during the years 1992–1998 (Lynch, 2002; Sickmund, 2004), but there is evidence that victims report a higher rate of violent offenses committed by African Americans compared to white and Hispanic youth (Rubin, 2001).

Research evidence confirms that minority youths receive more severe juvenile court dispositions than do white youths, even after controlling for legal variables. In California, African American youth comprise 8.7% of the youth population but 37% of youths in confinement. Police arrest black youths at 2.2 times greater than their share of the population, and judges sentence them to juvenile institutions at rates 4.6 times greater than white youths (Krisberg & Austin, 1993, pp. 123–125). Among youths referred for violent crimes, California juvenile courts detained almost two thirds (64.7%) of black youth compared with fewer than half (47.1%) of white juveniles; and sentenced to juvenile institutions 11.4% of black youths compared with 9.4% of Latino youth and only 3.4% of white youths (Krisberg & Austin, 1993, p. 125). Race clearly seems to play at least an indirect role in juvenile court decision making, and African Americans are disproportionately represented throughout the system, particularly in detention centers and state training schools. Analyses of juvenile court dispositions in Florida showed a consistent pattern of unequal treatment. Bishop (1996) found that nonwhite youths were more likely than comparable white youths to be recommended for petition to court, to be held in detention prior to the court hearing, to be formally processed in juvenile court, and to receive the most restrictive court dispositions. More recent studies have found mixed results for differential treatment of minority youths in the juvenile justice system. In a study of the arrests of juveniles for violent crimes, Pope and Snyder (2003) found no differences in the overall likelihood of arrest of white and nonwhite juveniles after controlling for legal factors and the specific crime, such as characteristics of the victim and extent of injury.

Racially disproportionate rates of arrest and confinement may not be simply a benign result of juvenile justice officials' decision making based on youths who presumably need more intervention and social control. Barry Feld (1999) has argued that the juvenile court was designed and intended to discriminate between white middle-class children and the children of poor and immigrant parents, and it should come as no surprise that arrests and confinement are racially disproportionate.

> If young people's real needs differ because of social circumstances, such as poverty or a single-parent household that correlate strongly with race, then the ideology of "individualized treatment" necessarily will have a racially disparate impact. Racial disproportionality in a system designed to differentiate on the basis of social structural, economic, or personal circumstances should come as no surprise. But in a society formally committed to racial equality, punitive sentences based on social and personal attributes that produce a disparate racial impact implicate the legitimacy, fairness, and justice of the process. (Feld, 1999, p. 265)

David Cole (1999) has argued that while our criminal justice system is based theoretically on equality before the law, the practices and administration of justice are in fact "predicated on the exploitation of inequality." He contends that we have not simply ignored the effects of inequality in the justice process or tried but failed to achieve equality in administering justice. Rather, he contends that

> *our criminal justice system affirmatively depends on inequality.* Absent race and class disparities, the privileged among us could not enjoy as much constitutional protection of our liberties as we do; and without those disparities, we could not afford the policy of mass incarceration that we have pursued over the past two decades. (Cole, 1999, p. 5; italics in original)

Cole cites the example of how the "war on drugs" shifted attention from the users of drugs to the dealers and sellers. In the 1960s, the use of marijuana spread from being a ghetto problem where it was used by the lower class, to widespread use on college campuses. Laws and practices then changed to focus more on the dealers and sellers than on users. The same might be said for the spread of cocaine use since the 1990s, in which many users are middle- and upper-class persons, but a significant number of dealers and sellers are lower-class minorities. Cole (1999) noted that police and prosecutors began to leave users alone, and instead targeted dealers and sellers. He contends that when the criminal law begins to affect the children of the white majority, our response is not to get tough, but rather to get lenient. Americans maintain a harsh tough-on-crime attitude as long as the burden of punishment falls disproportionately on minority populations. "The white majority could not possibly maintain its current attitude toward crime and punishment were the burden of punishment felt by the same white majority that prescribes it" (Cole, 1999, p. 153).

Drug abuse is a problem that has serious consequences including health problems, school failure and dropout, unemployment, family problems, and criminal sanctions. The question is not whether the "war on drugs" was the most effective approach for control and prevention of drugs. The issue is the unfair and unequal application of the laws regarding the possession, use, and selling of illegal drugs. The enforcement of drug laws by police and the courts has contributed to the disproportionate confinement of minority offenders.

Changes and Future Trends. Dramatic changes have taken place in juvenile corrections in the past few decades. Juvenile corrections policies have changed from an emphasis on deinstitutionalization and "least restrictive" alternatives, to a get-tough approach that emphasizes accountability and social control. Juvenile justice officials recognized three decades ago that committing delinquents together in isolated training schools away from the community was not an effective long-range answer to juvenile crime. Thus began a trend toward deinstitutionalization and greater use of community alternatives. That trend was reversed in the 1990s and continues today in the new century. Policy makers have been pressured by public demands to "do something" about youth involvement in drugs, gangs, and violent crime. The usual response has been to "get tough" on crime and criminals, which usually means a return to incarceration of offenders. Statistics indicate that after a decade of deinstitutionalization efforts, the number of juveniles being incarcerated has increased. From 1985 to 1989 the average daily population and total census count of juveniles in public facilities increased 14%, and the juvenile custody rate per 100,000 increased 19% during that period (Allen-Hagen, 1991, p. 2). According to the Census of Juveniles in Residential Placement (CJRP) in 1999, a total of 134,011 juveniles were held in 2,939 facilities, and the number of delinquent offenders in residential facilities increased 5% between 1997 and 1999 and 50% between 1991 and 1999 (Sickmund, 2004). The increasing number of adjudicated youths sent to juvenile corrections facilities does not even include the increasing number who are waived to criminal court, tried as adults, and often sent to adult institutions. Juvenile corrections policies in the 1990s and beyond 2000 are being dominated by a more conservative, control-oriented philosophy.

The commitment to rehabilitation of offenders began to shift by the 1970s, in part due to a widely publicized report by Robert Martinson (1974; see also Lipton, Martinson, & Wilks, 1975) claiming that rehabilitation programs had not had an effect on recidivism. Martinson's conclusions that "nothing works" in corrections had a great national impact, despite the fact that Ted Palmer (1975) wrote a detailed rebuttal questioning Martinson's findings, and Martinson (1979) himself retracted some of his earlier premature and exaggerated conclusions. The demise of the rehabilitative ideal actually had less to do with whether correctional programs were effective in changing offenders, and more to do with a shift in the viewpoints of the public and politicians regarding crime and criminals. Cullen and Gilbert (1982) suggested that crime control policies reflect lawmakers' ideological assumptions about the causes of crime and the most effective strategies to reduce crime. Garland (2001) has contended that cultural patterns structure how the public and politicians feel about offenders. The politics of the 1980s produced a greater division between the jobless and those employed, between blacks and whites, and between the affluent suburbs and the struggling inner cities, and social problems such as violence, street crime, and drug abuse became worse. Accompanying these political and social changes was the view that punishing individuals for criminal and delinquent behavior was more appropriate than rehabilitation and change strategies. Contrary to the views of positivist criminologists, that crime was caused by individual and social problems over which an individual had little control, law violators were now seen as evil individuals who deserved to be punished. Crime was seen not as a sign of need or deprivation, but was viewed as a rational choice by persons who lacked discipline and self-control, who needed to be deterred and deserved to be punished harshly (Garland, 2001, p. 102). Intolerance of crime and criminals has pervaded society and legislative chambers and the proposed solutions are harsh discipline and punishment.

There are signs that rehabilitation is making a comeback (Cullen, 2005). Reasons for a return to the rehabilitative ideal (Allen, 1981) are not necessarily due to a softening of attitudes toward crime and criminals, but to a realization that attempting to control crime through incarceration is costly and produces no significant reduction in crime rates. Although there is considerable disagreement as to whether training schools and prisons are effective deterrents to crime, many criminal justice experts point to research evidence that greater use of incarceration may increase rather than decrease crime rates (Garland, 2001). Cullen and his associates have conducted studies on public opinions about rehabilitation and have found that Americans still strongly support the view that efforts should be made to rehabilitate offenders (Cullen, 2005; Cullen, Fisher, & Applegate, 2000). The field of juvenile corrections may well see a resurgence of rehabilitative strategies in this new century, particularly with new developments based on best practices and what works. We examine some of the future trends in juvenile justice in the next and final section.

SUMMARY

- The field of juvenile corrections has a long history in America, beginning with the Houses of Refuge and probation in the 19th century, continuing with correctional reforms in the 1970s, to growing support for institutionalization and formal control of juvenile offenders today.
- In 2002, a total of 102,388 juveniles were held in 2,964 facilities, with most juveniles (70,243 or 69%) being held in public facilities; more than one third (1,069 or 36%) of the facilities (mostly public) were at or over capacity.
- In 2002, adjudicated delinquents ordered to probation (385,400 cases) accounted for 62% of all delinquency cases placed on probation. The number of adjudicated cases that resulted in court-ordered probation rose 103% between 1985 and 2002 (from 189,600 to 385,400).
- Probation officers' responsibilities include both control and rehabilitation, resulting in "role conflict" for many officers.
- "Intermediate sanctions" such as intensive probation supervision, day reporting centers, electronic monitoring, and restitution programs provide more control than regular probation, but are less intrusive and expensive than residential placements.
- Aftercare or parole supervision is essential for successful reentry of juveniles returning from institutional commitment back to the community.
- Evaluating the effectiveness of corrections by recidivism alone has limitations. Performance assessment based on the quality and extent to which probation officers and agencies are able to accomplish five goals of community corrections offers a more complete outcome assessment.
- Minority youth are disproportionately represented in juvenile corrections programs, and federal legislation and mandates have been directed toward examining the sources and reducing disproportionate minority confinement.
- The emphasis in juvenile corrections the past two decades has been on individual accountability and punishment, but there are signs that rehabilitation is making a comeback.

KEY TERMS

Aftercare

Boot camps

Casework management

Community corrections

Day reporting centers

Day treatment

Discrimination

Disparity

Disproportionate minority
confinement (DMC)

Electronic monitoring

Foster care

Group homes

Institutional corrections

Intensive probation supervision

Intermediate sanctions

Juvenile training schools

Probation

Probation effectiveness

Probation officer roles

Residential programs

Resource manager

Restitution

Role conflict

Surveillance

Treatment

Wilderness camps

DISCUSSION QUESTIONS

1. Based on the available research, what do you see as the strengths and limitations of juvenile institutions and residential placement? What types of juvenile offenders are most appropriate for those facilities and placements?

2. As a new probation officer, you are assigned a beginning caseload of 30 juvenile offenders, ranging from first-time offenders with single occurrences of property offenses or drug violations, to second- and third-time offenders with several prior arrests and some history of probation violations. What probation officer roles are you likely to use with various types of offenders?

3. Imagine you have been appointed to your State Youth Commission, and the governor has asked for recommendations for the "best practices" that have shown effectiveness in juvenile corrections. List the five most important points you would offer.

WEB RESOURCES

Juvenile Offenders and Victims: 2006 National Report: http://ojjdp.ncjrs.gov/ojstatbb/nr2006/downloads/NR2006.pdf

Juvenile Probation: "Workhorse of the Juvenile Justice System": http://www.ncjrs.gov/pdffiles/workhors.pdf

Census of Juveniles in Residential Placement Databook: http://www.ncjrs.gov/pdffiles1/ojjdp/fs200008.pdf

"Innovative Information on Juvenile Residential Facilities": http://www.ncjrs.gov/pdffiles1/ojjdp/fs200011.pdf

Juvenile Residential Facility Census, 2002: http://www.ncjrs.gov/pdffiles1/ojjdp/211080.pdf

Overview of aftercare services: http://www.ncjrs.gov/pdffiles1/ojjdp/201800.pdf

READING

Community corrections have experienced several changes in the past 20 years. The purpose of this article is to examine some of those changes in terms of the emphases and roles of community corrections agents. Historically, community corrections was based on models of diversion, advocacy, and reintegration. Increases in crime and more high-risk offenders being sentenced to probation led to changes in emphases on control and surveillance. The original models were replaced by emphases on just deserts, adversary, and restitution models. The author of the article argues for strategies of internalization, reintegrative shaming, and victim–offender reconciliation for a comprehensive community corrections model promoting change in the offender, the correctional process, and the community.

Reexamining Community Corrections Models

Richard Lawrence

Community corrections have undergone significant changes in the past 2 decades. The emphasis through the 1960s and 1970s was on rehabilitation focused on offenders' needs and problems, along with justice and fairness in the supervision process. The probation officer was seen as a caseworker or counselor whose primary responsibility was to help and change the client through rehabilitative means, even though he or she was given the authority to use coercive means when necessary to involve the offender in rehabilitative programs. Efforts were made to provide resources, programs and services within the agency and the community so as to facilitate the change process.

In the caseworker model, presentence investigations identified causes of the offender's behavior and recommended interventions necessary to deal with those causes. This rehabilitative approach assumed that most clients could be changed into well-adjusted, law-abiding citizens. Although control and surveillance were not primary emphases, probation, parole and community correctional programs *did* involve compliance with rules and conditions. Even so, surveillance and control were viewed as more appropriate for

law enforcement, jails, and prisons than for community corrections. The three primary community corrections models of the past 2 decades, diversion, advocacy and reintegration, focused on services and assistance *for* the offender. Punishment and community protection were not viewed as primary roles.

Do the dominant community corrections emphases of the 1960s and 1970s have any relevance today? Is community corrections headed in the right direction? Many current programs are centered around a "just deserts" philosophy and sentencing has taken a more retributive direction. Offenders are expected to pay for their crimes, both figuratively and literally. Courts are ordering restitution payments to the victim, community service work, and fees to court and correctional agencies (Galaway and Hudson 1990). Probation and parole officers are adopting a control and surveillance role, focusing on community protection more than offender rehabilitation (McAnany, Thomson, and Fogel 1984). Some evidence suggests that the shift in emphasis is a necessary response to larger caseloads and more serious offenders who require more control

SOURCE: *Crime & Delinquency, (37)*4, 449–464, October 1991. © 1991 Sage Publications, Inc.

(cf. Petersilia, Turner, Kahan, and Peterson 1985). Are the current emphases more appropriate for long-term crime reduction than were the emphases of the past 2 decades? Is there still a role for the older community corrections models of diversion, advocacy, and reintegration? This article examines those questions.

⬚ Three Models of Community Corrections

Community corrections was founded on three models which distinguished it from institutional corrections: diversion, advocacy, and reintegration (see e.g., Symkla 1981, pp. 14–16). Community corrections agents have worked with offenders diverted by police and the courts, often acting in the interests of the offenders as advocates. The reintegration of offenders into society after prison or jail incarceration has been a major role of community corrections.

Diversion. The 1960s and 1970s were characterized by increasing disillusionment with the formal criminal justice system. Many questioned whether it was capable of producing positive changes in offenders. Many observers argued that formal processing through the system often had a labeling effect whereby many offenders became worse rather than better (Lemert 1972; Becker 1963; Schur 1965). They suggested that the judicial process often had a stigmatizing effect. Incarcerating minor offenders with more serious ones in correctional institutions often made them worse, so it was said. Although the labeling hypothesis was often overstated and has been questioned by some criminologists, the recommendation of diverting less serious offenders from the formal criminal or juvenile justice process won wide support.

Diversion generally has meant the use of alternative community programs in place of formal processing by law enforcement, courts and corrections (National Advisory Commission on Criminal Justice Standards and Goals 1973). It has been based on the assumption that deserving offenders would voluntarily become involved in rehabilitative and educational programs in return for being shunted out of the formal judicial process. (Diversion also sometimes was done without service provision, in which case the offender was expected to avoid any further criminal or delinquent behavior and was under threat of having the case reactivated.) Appropriate cases were those that posed little risk to the community and required only minimal supervision. Diversion used the threat of conviction to encourage the accused to voluntarily participate in the program, thus some critics argued that many offenders were coerced into treatment programs in violation of due process. Another criticism of diversion was that it often "widened the net," filling programs with minor offenders whose offense would not have resulted in a conviction or formal sanction in the absence of diversion programs (Austin and Krisberg 1981; Duffee and McGarrell 1990). When used appropriately, however, it probably benefited both the offender and the community. Many offenders received helpful intervention without the stigma and adverse effects of more punitive sanctions and the community may have achieved crime reduction at considerably less cost.

Advocacy. The advocacy model in community corrections originally involved two emphases. First, the offender often needed an advocate to balance the broad authority of the police and judiciary in applying the criminal sanction. Second, the client needed an advocate for referral and acceptance to community resources, programs, housing, and employment opportunities. Advocacy stressed the need for changes in the community and the criminal justice system as well as the offender, and was intended to curb arbitrary decision making by judicial and correctional personnel (Symkla 1981, p. 16). Proponents of advocacy asserted that it is not enough to simply sentence offenders to traditional probation and rely on existing programs and resources. More community programs must be made available to juvenile and adult lawbreakers if they truly are to be corrected. Offenders also need advocates to help them overcome public intolerance which impedes the rehabilitation process.

Reintegration. A third community corrections model was reintegration (e.g., O'Leary and Duffee 1971), which focused both on the offender and the community in order to reduce crime and delinquency. Proponents note that most offenders are persons who are alienated from mainstream society and its institutions. Delinquents are often school dropouts or are "pushed out" because of misbehavior and poor performance, and many adult offenders lack education, job skills and labor market credentials. This model attempted to involve community resources such as alternative schools, vocational counseling and employment to help the offender establish a legitimate role in the community. Community-based reintegration programs have included halfway houses, work-release programs, study-release programs, group homes, and prerelease centers (Smykla 1981, p. 16).

Demise of the Community Corrections Models

A number of developments contributed to the demise of the diversion, advocacy, and reintegration models. For one, studies of the effectiveness of correctional rehabilitation raised serious questions about whether correctional programs result in reduced crime for program participants (Lipton, Martinson, and Wilks 1975).[1] However, it should be noted that the "nothing works" view was not unanimously held, for a number of persons have continued to detect some signs in the evidence that some intervention programs do make a difference. Nevertheless, although some programs have shown positive results, the role of rehabilitation in community corrections has been questioned and acceptance of the rehabilitative ideal has declined (Allen 1981).

The "justice model" of corrections (Fogel 1975) emerged about the same time that the rehabilitation model was being questioned. The latter involved considerable discretion and authority,

and often resulted in longer periods of control and supervision than when sentences were based on the crime alone, which is generally the case under determinate sentencing procedures. Fogel and a number of others argued for a greater emphasis on justice and fairness. They placed greater stress on the justice of administration than simply the administration of justice (Fogel 1975). The justice model *was* a step toward questioning the role of rehabilitation in general, and parole in particular.

The concept of "just deserts" (von Hirsch 1976) involved some of the concerns of the justice model, focusing on the crime more than the criminal. In it, emphasis was placed on the criminal sanction and on determining the appropriate sentence for the severity of the crime. A common theme in the deserts model is the concern with reducing sentencing disparity, that is, the wide range of sentences that specific offenders have received for a particular crime, even when their criminal histories have been similar. This new emphasis has led many states to abolish parole (von Hirsch and Hanrahan 1978) and to develop determinate sentencing guidelines (see e.g. Knapp 1982; Parent 1988).

The community corrections models of advocacy, diversion and reintegration have also been affected by other developments. America has witnessed a growing conservatism over the past 2 decades. Politicians have rushed to embrace punishment rather than rehabilitation. "Getting tough on crime" has been seen as a sure way to gain voter approval. Probation and parole, prison furloughs, and various alternatives to incarceration have become identified as too lenient and "soft on crime." The readiness of politicians to increase prison sentences but not allocate sufficient funds either to persons or community corrections programs, has resulted in overcrowded prisons and overflowing probation caseloads that render meaningful supervision impossible. The media magnify the hard line on crime, highlighting crimes of offenders on probation, parole, or prison furlough. A growing intolerance of crime, coupled with a belief that community corrections cannot control crime, has resulted in demands for greater use of jails and prisons.

The conservative trend has been initiated more by policymakers than by the public. Gottfredson and Taylor (1984) found public attitudes about correctional goals to be liberal, non-punitive, and reform oriented. Apparently, policymakers act out of serious misperceptions of the public's correctional views. Professionals in corrections do not subscribe to singular punitive correctional goals. Studies indicate that correctional officers (Jacobs 1978; Cullen, Lutze, Link, and Wolfe 1989) and probation officers (Lawrence and Johnson, 1990) still rank rehabilitation as a major goal of corrections.

Restitution programs have been instituted in many states. Proponents have argued for the rehabilitative and reintegrative effects of restitution. But many states and jurisdictions with relatively little previous commitment to community corrections have turned to restitution programs mainly as a method of reducing prison commitments. Legislators reluctant to support community corrections programs can sell these prison alternatives to the public without appearing "soft on crime," for the offender "pays for crime" through restitution. Texas—with one of the largest prison populations and highest incarceration rates—now diverts more than 800 offenders from prison each year, and collects more than $2 million from them annually to cover costs of the program and to compensate victims (Lawrence 1990). Although the program has been successful in diverting many offenders from prison, the primary motive is to relieve prison overcrowding. The emphasis is on controlling the offender more than on reintegrating him or her into the community.

▧ "New" Models: Just Deserts, Adversary, Restitution

Recent emphases on offender control and punishment have brought marked changes in community corrections. Delivering the court sanction, or "just deserts," is more important than is diversion and probation officers now often view themselves more as adversaries of the offender. Offender restitution has replaced offender reintegration.

Probation and parole as "control." Probation and parole officers have been criticized for being too lenient and for providing less supervision than most felony offenders need (Petersilia et al. 1985; Morris and Tonry 1990). It seems likely that the public often views a probation sentence as "getting off," thus it is not seen as a sanction in its own right. And the fact is that increasingly large caseloads have made probation supervision meaningless. It is impossible for officers to adequately monitor their cases, or offer any helpful services. Some have suggested that probation must emphasize control (Barkdull 1976), and others have advocated specialization whereby some probation officers would carry out a control and policing function, whereas probation counselors would provide rehabilitative services, or act as brokers, referring clients to needed programs and services (Conrad 1984; McAnany et al. 1984).

One recent trend has been toward intensive supervised probation (ISP; Byrne 1986; Latessa 1986; Lurigio 1990).[2] The emphasis is not on service provision, counseling, education or training, however; rather, it is on control. ISP officers act basically as police officers with a small probation caseload. Their primary role is monitoring, surveillance, and enforcing probation conditions. Most programs do report success in reducing recidivism (Byrne 1986; Erwin and Bennett 1987).

Client advocacy is no longer emphasized by probation/parole officers, many of whom have adopted an adversarial role in relation to the client, viewing themselves as advocates for the court, criminal justice system, and community protection. Although probation officers say rehabilitation is important, most (77%) of a sample of Texas probation officers disagreed that their role was as an advocate for the probationer; and most (78%) stated their primary allegiance was to the agency and/or the court—findings indicative of "role conflict" (Lawrence 1984).

Demands for victims' rights contributed in part to this change. The older versions of community corrections focused on offenders' problems and needs. This emphasis on programs and services for the offender has drawn dual criticisms: (1) in addition to their lack of proven effectiveness, these programs appear to reward rather than punish the offender; and (2) victims are virtually ignored in the judicial and correctional process. Many sentences now include orders for victim restitution payments, community service, and payment of court and probation fees. Probation officers in some states and the federal courts are required to include a "victim impact statement" with the presentence investigation report. Judges often seek input from the victim before sentencing. Some victim compensation programs reimburse victims for property loss and damage and for medical expenses from personal injury resulting from the crime. Probation officers seem to believe that advocacy for victims and for probation clients are mutually exclusive—one must be either "for" the offender *or* the victim.

Harris (1987) has discussed the shift away from the advocate role, noting how probation/parole personnel have become the avowed enemies of their charges, operating . . . to incarcerate and, as . . . urine takers, money collectors, compliance monitors, electronic surveillance gadget readers, and law enforcers (1987, p. 21).

In my view, a strategy of crime control through compliance is impossible to carry out effectively because it requires constant monitoring and surveillance (O'Leary and Duffee 1971). The probation officer who believes that a strategy of tough compliance through control and surveillance can effectively change offenders makes a mockery of the justice system. We too often threaten what we cannot deliver. We cannot adequately monitor probation rules for all persons in impossibly large caseloads nor can we provide the community protection which is implicitly promised. Our clients have long known that these are empty threats. The public has become more aware that some probationers continue to commit crimes, and have begun demanding tougher sanctions than probation.

Control is a necessary part of probation, but not the sole one. Probation officers can emphasize compliance with court orders and can help clients comply with them without taking on an adversarial posture. Further, adopting an advocate role need not imply being "soft" on enforcement. Indeed, most probation officer job descriptions emphasize the helping role as much as the officer role.

More offenders with extensive criminal histories are now being sentenced to probation, so probation officers have had to adopt more of a control function. A study of probation in California led the researchers to conclude that we should rethink probation and its role in punishing and supervising convicted felons, because probation was originally conceived and structured for offenders who present little threat to society (Petersilia et al. 1985). Petersilia and her associates stated that "it is our opinion that routine probation, by definition, is inappropriate for most felons" (1985, p. 64). Granting probation to felony offenders who pose a public risk will require more intensive supervision than regular probation. The implementation of intensive supervision programs and similar "intermediate sanctions" is a response to this need (McCarthy 1987; Morris and Tonry 1990; Lurigio 1990).

Under the old model, community corrections personnel were advocates for the offender, providing alternatives for their release from prisons and jails. By contrast, community corrections in the form of intermediate sanctions represent the "new" jail in the community. The old model emphasized reintegration into the community, but in the new model, prisons and jails are replaced by house arrest, electronic surveillance, and intensive supervision probation. The thrust of intermediate sanctions is control and close monitoring and they reflect a concern with limiting government spending on correcting offenders. Reintegration into the community and establishing meaningful ties are no longer the primary objectives.

The entire movement toward ISPs is economically driven. It is commonly acknowledged that if prison crowding disappeared tomorrow, thereby eliminating the need to create less expensive sanctions, so would the incentive to develop ISPs (Petersilia 1990, p. 133).

⊠ Integrating Old and New Community Corrections Models

Integrating the two models is difficult, but not impossible. I argue that such a merger can and must be done. We must develop strategies for crime control which focus on offender change as well as on control and punishment. The current emphasis on the latter represents a reactive correctional response. McShane and Williams (1989) have criticized the current correctional agenda for lacking clear, shared goals—and any creativity. Crime increases and the growing disillusionment with the ability to effectively deter or rehabilitate criminals have led to demands for greater punishment and control. Punishment and control are seen as a panacea by many policymakers (Dean-Myrda and Cullen 1985). Even so, I argue that punishment and control are at best short-term strategies. Clear and O'Leary (1983) have argued that the most effective method of crime control is treatment. Factors most related to probationer recidivism include problems with employment, education, and substance abuse (see e.g. Allen, Eskridge, Latessa, and Vito 1985, p. 263). Providing help for offenders in these areas is a more meaningful form of "crime control."

Diversion and deserts. Diversion is still an appropriate community corrections model, providing that it is *true diversion* from prison and jail, and avoids net widening. However, diversion should include offender services, and not focus solely on punishment and control as with most intermediate sanctions.

The emphasis of just deserts is appropriate for its focus on crime-specific factors in sentencing. Social factors and offender needs are relevant in making a treatment plan following sentencing,

but have been used unfairly under indeterminate sentencing structures. The Minnesota Sentencing Guidelines (based on the just-deserts model) specifically prohibit demographic and social variables as aggravating or mitigating factors in sentencing (Minnesota Sentencing Guidelines Commission 1989, p. 18). The deserts model has not been shown to be effective, however, when applied solely from a retributive, "paying for crime" perspective.

Advocacy versus adversary. It is short-sighted to believe one is either for the offender or the victim. Some mistakenly believe that it is impossible to be an advocate for the victim *and* the offender—or that community protection necessarily implies offender isolation and punishment. Probation and parole officers can firmly and fairly monitor probation/parole rules and conditions without taking an adversarial role.

Advocacy is still a necessary and viable model for community corrections. The offender needs an advocate as long as there are barriers in the community standing in the way of rehabilitation and reintegration. Probation and parole officers need to be advocates for equal access of their clients to housing, jobs, social services and treatment programs. Byrne (1989) and Currie (1985) emphasize the importance of advocacy in community corrections. Byrne (1989) notes the importance of probation and parole officers as "resource advocates" where there are limited resources for substance abuse treatment and employment training; and he emphasizes that advocacy should include the needs of victims (1989, p. 492). The probation officer role of resource broker is consistent with the advocacy role, and considered essential for effective service delivery in community corrections (Allen et al. 1985, p. 181; Dell'Apa, Adams, Jorgenson, and Sigurdson 1976).

Reintegration and restitution. The key element in community corrections emphasizes reintegration—the transition process from correctional institutions back into the community. Reintegration includes the need for both the offender and the community to change (O'Leary and Duffee 1971). Byrne (1989) emphasizes the importance of community structure in effective community-based corrections strategies. He invokes Reiss (1986) in noting that *offender-based* community control strategies are incomplete, since they take a "closed system" view of correctional interventions: *change the offender and not the community* (Byrne 1989, p. 487; emphasis in original).

It is unrealistic to expect offenders to solve their problems with substance abuse, employment, and education absent some community changes in reducing the source of the problems, and unless community services and resources are also provided. True reintegration involves the offender and the community.

The concept of restitution is not inconsistent with reintegration if the restitution program is aimed at helping the offender establish meaningful ties with the community. On the other hand, if it is primarily a court sanction emphasizing "paying for" the crime, it does little more than gain public support for community corrections as punishment and control. Restitution programs which provide services for offenders and which require community service and monetary restitution to victims accomplish the objectives of community corrections. Changes occur in offenders and the community.

The Case for Correctional Reintegration

I argue that control and reintegration are both necessary ingredients of effective community corrections. Intensive supervision is necessary for those higher-risk offenders with extensive criminal histories who need closer supervision due to family or personal problems, unemployment, or substance abuse. We must develop intermediate sanctions which offer the necessary degree of control but we must also give equal importance to reintegrating the offender in the community. We need programs which aim to

"maximize the protection of the general public and . . . maximize the chances of offenders being able to untangle themselves from lawbreaking conduct" (Gibbons 1987, p. 19).

Emphasis on Community and Offender

Correctional policies have often focused solely on either the offender or on protecting the community. At one extreme are rehabilitation programs that focused on the offender with little regard for community protection, to the opposite extreme of isolating offenders from the community via prison or jail sentences, with few if any rehabilitative or reintegrative emphases. A more rational correctional policy is one directed at both community protection and offender change, involving both the offender and the community in the correctional process.

Correctional policies have been categorized as placing emphasis on either the community or the offender (O'Leary and Duffee 1971). The original theoretical base for the O'Leary-Duffee model was Herbert Kelman's (1958) theory of behavior change strategies. Kelman categorized all efforts at changing human behavior as compliance, identification, or internalization (1958, p. 53). Efforts to "reform" offenders depend on compliance, forcing them to change by threats of punishment. The emphasis is on control, enforcing community standards by authoritarian means, and offenders' attitudes or needs are irrelevant. A reform policy requires maintaining constant surveillance, and places severe demands on correctional agents (O'Leary and Duffee 1971, p. 376). Most correctional programs use a reform policy: offenders modify their behavior, but only to the extent that they perceive a high probability of being detected and sanctioned. They may comply with the law but have not internalized community standards and values. In a correctional policy based on compliance, the legal and correctional systems focus more on the process than on confronting offenders with their need to change. The few minutes in court with procedures and terms which few offenders even understand makes little impression on them (Rosett and Cressey 1976). Probation officers often concentrate more on managing their cases than on confronting their clients with the responsibility for their crime and dealing with related problems.

Internalization, shame, and reintegration. Community corrections must adopt strategies whereby offenders are confronted with the wrongfulness of crime and its consequences to victims and the community. Emphasis must be placed on making the formal judicial and correctional processes more meaningful and consequential. Studies of the effectiveness of community corrections show mixed results (see Albanese, Fiore, Powell, and Storti 1981; Allen et al. 1985; and Lurigio 1990) and raise questions about the ability of the current judicial and probation process—even intensive supervision—to change offenders and protect the community. Large caseload sizes and more high-risk offenders present a dilemma: how to maintain control and surveillance and facilitate offender reintegration into the community. I argue for a community corrections model that incorporates internalization, shaming, and reintegration.

Internalization is the strategy of behavior change on which a reintegration correctional policy is based (Kelman 1958). Unlike the reform model, the offender is not merely told what to do, but has a variety of alternatives from which to choose. The reintegration model "attempts to reduce the stigma attached to criminality, a block to entrance to the community" (O'Leary and Duffee 1971, p. 382). Reintegration focuses on both the offender and the community, but it means more than just conforming to community standards. In addition to offender change, reintegration pushes for changes in community institutions to provide opportunities for offenders, reducing alienation and discrimination, with the goal of involving them in community life and work. Under a policy of correctional reintegration, probation and parole officers would be located in the neighborhoods where their clients live and work, intervening in the community as well as in clients' lives. The agents would be involved with community institutions such as businesses, churches and schools. O'Leary and Duffee emphasized the agent's advocate role as well as that of counselor and mediator (1971, p. 382). Community protection and monitoring of probation rules must not be overlooked, however. A successful reintegration policy today requires probation agents to monitor behavior and facilitate offender change.

Braithwaite (1989) argues that crime is punished in one of two ways, either by reintegrative shaming or by stigmatization. *Reintegrative shaming* means that "expressions of community disapproval, which may range from mild rebuke to degradation ceremonies, are followed by gestures of reacceptance into the community of law-abiding citizens" (Braithwaite 1989, p. 55). Unlike shaming, stigmatization involves labeling the person because of his/her lawbreaking, and the person rather than the behavior is rejected. By stigmatizing law violators, we treat them as criminal outcasts which may result in high crime rates. Reintegrative shaming is based on the "family model" in which punishment is administered by supportive family members. Braithwaite argues that his theory explains crime variations better than other major theories, and suggests it explains the lower crime rates in countries like Japan that emphasize public shaming and acknowledgement of responsibility followed by reacceptance of the wrongdoers. There is evidence that countries with lower crime rates less frequently use stigmatization, such as prison sentences, than do the United States and other countries with high crime rates (Braithwaite 1989, pp. 84–97, 164–5). Granted, there are problems with America adopting the Japanese model of crime control. Braithwaite himself admits he would not want to live in Japan because he "would find the informal pressures to conformity oppressive" and he notes that "while Japanese culture emphasizes duties (including . . . the law), it deemphasizes rights" (1989, p. 158).

There are dangers with advocating a shaming strategy for corrections in America, for it may be wrongly interpreted as a revival of old colonial sanctions such as the ducking stool, the scarlet letter, and the stocks and pillory. A number of persons today support public shaming practices as effective deterrents, but they omit the reintegrative element of acceptance and support by the community. For example, ordering persons convicted of driving while intoxicated to display bumper stickers announcing their conviction may be intended to "shame them into compliance," but it carries a stigma and is not followed with community reacceptance. Requiring violators to make public apologies in the newspaper more closely resembles *reintegrative* shaming, but the sanction must be accompanied by actions geared to community forgiveness and reacceptance. The American judicial and correctional systems, along with news media and the community, have become fairly adept at labeling and stigmatizing law violators (especially certain classes of offenders and offenses) but few serious efforts are made toward reintegrating offenders as part of the correctional process.

⊠ Reintegrative Shaming in Community Corrections

Reintegrative shaming seeks to encourage offenders to accept responsibility, to internalize laws and community expectations, and then works toward acceptance and support of them. According to Braithwaite, shame first "deters criminal behavior because social approval of significant others is something we do not like to lose. Second . . . both shaming and repentance build consciences which internally deter criminal behavior" (p. 75).

Probation officer responsibilities under a policy of reintegrative shaming might include bringing in representatives of the offender's school, employer, and similar groups to attend the court hearing and offer opinions of how they might be able to contribute to monitoring the offender's behavior and assist in his/her rehabilitation (Braithwaite 1989, p. 173). The objectives of such practices would be to increase the degree of informal social control and achieve reintegration from those same groups.

Restitution in community corrections (as discussed above) is effective when it goes beyond simply "paying for crime" and is applied as more than simply a cost-effective alternative to prison. Galaway and Hudson (1990) believe that restitution is now moving beyond the idea of offenders repaying victims, and a theory of "restorative justice" is emerging from the practice (1990, p. 1). Victim-Offender Reconciliation Programs (VORPs) have also emerged from the concept of restitution and both reflect traditional justice principles that when a person wrongs another, he or she has a responsibility to make amends to the victim and to society. VORP extends this principle by actually bringing the victim and the offender together in a face-to-face meeting. The goals of VORP include humanizing the criminal justice process through face-to-face mediation, increasing offenders' personal accountability, providing restitution for victims, enhancing community understanding of crime and justice, and providing an alternative to incarceration (Coates 1990, p. 126). Community service, restitution, and victim-offender reconciliation are meaningful sanctions that avoid stigmatization, giving the offender an opportunity to "pay his debt" and be reintegrated with the community (Braithwaite 1989, p. 179).

In conclusion, elements of old and new community corrections models are appropriate—if they include the *community* as well as the offender as targets of change. Intermediate sanctions have emerged as alternatives to incarceration for the increasing numbers of high-risk offenders who need closer supervision and monitoring than regular probation. We have replaced the old models of advocacy, diversion and reintegration with new models which are adversarial, with sanctions based on retribution and just deserts. I argue that throwing out the advocacy and reintegrative roles is a short-sighted approach to crime control, and suggest strategies of internalization, reintegrative shaming, and victim-offender reconciliation. A truly comprehensive community corrections model is one which facilitates change in the offender, the criminal justice process, and the community. Until community corrections professions and policymakers approach the crime problem from this broader perspective, our crime control efforts will continue to be short-term, futile—and will inevitably fail.

⊠ Notes

1. This study has often been referred to as the "Martinson report," because he published a shorter version of the study (Martinson 1974). The findings, summarized as "nothing works," actually concluded: "With few and isolated exceptions, the rehabilitative efforts that have been reported so far have had no appreciable effect on recidivism" (Martinson 1974, p. 25).

2. For some of the latest and most thorough research and analyses of intensive probation supervision programs, see the entire issue of *Crime & Delinquency*, Vol. 36 (January 1990).

3. The crime increase is not because of a failure of the old model with its emphasis on offender treatment, and there is little evidence that more crime control and punitive sanctions reduce the severity or frequency of crime (Gibbons 1988).

⊠ References

Albanese, Jay S., Bernadette A. Fiore, Jerie H. Powell, and Janet R. Storti. 1981. *Is Probation Working?* Washington, DC: University Press of America.

Allen, Francis A. 1981. *The Decline of the Rehabilitative Ideal.* New Haven: Yale University Press.

Allen, Harry E., Chris W. Eskridge, Edward J. Latessa, and Gennaro F. Vito. 1985. *Probation and Parole in America.* New York: Free Press.

Austin, James and Barry Krisberg. 1981. "Wider, Stronger and Different Nets: The Dialectics of Criminal Justice Reform." *Journal of Research on Crime and Delinquency* 18: 165–196.

Barkdall, Walter, 1976. "Probation: Call It Control—and Mean It!" *Federal Probation* 40: 3–8.

Becker, Howard S. 1963. *Outsiders.* New York: Free Press.

Braithwaite, John. 1989. *Crime, Shame and Reintegration.* Cambridge, NY: Cambridge University Press.

Byrne, James. 1986. "The Control Controversy: A Preliminary Examination of Intensive Probation Supervision in the United States," *Federal Probation* 50: 4–16.

——. 1989. "Reintegrating the Concept of *Community* into Community-Based Corrections." *Crime & Delinquency* 35: 471–499.

Clear, Todd R. and Vincent O'Leary. 1983. *Controlling the Offender in the Community.* Lexington, MA: Lexington Books.

Coates, Robert B. 1990. "Victim-Offender Reconciliation Programs in North America: An Assessment." Pp. 125–134 in *Criminal Justice, Restitution and Reconciliation,* edited by B. Galaway and J. Hudson Monsey, NY: Criminal Justice Press.

Conrad, John. 1984. "The Redefinition of Probation Drastic Proposals to Solve an Urgent Problem." Pp. 251–273 in *Probation and Justice Reconsideration of Mission,* edited by P. McAnany, D. Thomson, and D. Fogel. Cambridge, MA: Oelgeschlager, Gunn, & Hain.

Cullen, Francis T., Faith E. Lutze, Bruce G. Link, and Nancy Travis Wolfe. 1989. "The Correctional Orientation of Prison Guards: Do Officers Support Rehabilitation?" *Federal Probation* 53: 33–42.

Currie, Elliott. 1985. *Confronting Crime.* New York: Pantheon.

Dean-Myrda, Mark and Francis T Cullen. 1985. "The Panacea Pendulum: An Account of Community as a Response to Crime. "Pp. 9–29 in *Probation, Parole, and Community Corrections,* edited by L. F. Travis III. Prospect Heights, IL: Waveland Press.

Dell'Apa, Frank, Tom W. Adams, James D. Jorgenson, and Herbert R. Sigurdson. 1976. "Advocacy, Brokerage, Community: The ABC's of Probation and Parole." *Federal Probation* 40: 37–44.

Duffee, David E. and Edmund F. McGarrell. 1990. *Community Corrections.* Cincinnati, OH: Anderson.

Erwin, Billie S. and Lawrence A. Bennett. 1987. "New Dimensions in Probation: Georgia's Experience with Intensive Probation Supervision (IPS)." Washington, DC: National Institute of Justice.

Fogel, David. 1975. *We Are the Living Proof—The Justice Model of Corrections.* Cincinnati, OH: Anderson.

Galaway, Burt and Joe Hudson, eds. 1990. *Criminal Justice, Restitution, and Reconciliation.* Monsey, NY: Criminal Justice Press.

Gibbons, Don C. 1988. *The Limits of Punishment as Social Policy.* San Francisco, CA: National Council on Crime and Delinquency.

Gottfredson, Stephen and Ralph Taylor. 1984. "Public Policy and Prison Populations Measuring Opinions about Reform." *Judicature* 68:190–201.

Harris, M. Kay. 1987. "Observations of a 'Friend of the Court' on the Future of Probation and Parole." *Federal Probation* 51:12–21.

Jacobs, James B. 1978. "What Prison Guards Think: A Profile of the Illinois Force." *Crime & Delinquency* 24:185–96.

Knapp, Kay A. 1982. "Impact of the Minnesota Sentencing Guidelines on Sentencing Practices." *Hamline Law Review* 5:237–56.

Kelman, Herbert. 1958. "Compliance, Identification, and Internalization: Three Processes of Attitude Change." *Journal of Conflict Resolution* 2:51–60.

Latessa, Edward. 1986. "The Cost Effectiveness of Intensive Supervision." *Federal Probation* 50:70–74.

Lawrence, Richard. 1984. "Professionals or Judicial Civil Servants? An Examination of the Probation Officer's Role." *Federal Probation* 48:14–21.

Lawrence, Richard. 1990. "Restitution as a Cost-Effective Alternative to Incarceration." Pp. 207–16 in *Criminal Justice, Restitution, and Reconciliation,* edited by B. Galaway and J. Hudson. Monsey, NY: Criminal Justice Press.

Lawrence, Richard and Shelva Johnson. 1990. "Effects of the Minnesota Sentencing Guidelines on Probation Agents." *Journal of Crime and Justice* 13:77–104.

Lemert, Edwin M. 1972. *Human Deviance, Social Problems and Social Control,* 2nd ed. Englewood Cliffs, NJ: Prentice Hall.

Lipton, Douglas, Robert Martinson, and Judith Wilks. 1975. *The Effectiveness of Correctional Treatment: A Survey of Treatment Evaluation Studies.* New York: Praeger.

Lurigio, Arthur J. 1990. "Introduction" (to Special Issue: "Intensive Probation Supervision: An Alternative to Prison in the 1980s"). *Crime & Delinquency* 36:3–5.

Martinson, Robert. 1974. "What Works?—Questions and Answers about Prison Reform." *The Public Interest* 35:22–54.

McAnany, Patrick, Doug Thomson, and David Fogel, eds. 1984. *Probation and Justice: Reconsideration of Mission.* Cambridge, MA: Oelgeschlager, Gunn, & Hain.

McCarthy, Belinda, ed. 1987. *Intermediate Punishments: Intensive Supervision, Home Confinement and Electronic Surveillance.* Monsey, NY: Willow Tree Press.

McShane, Marilyn D. and Frank P. Williams III. 1989. "Running on Empty: Creativity and the Correctional Agenda." *Crime & Delinquency* 35:562–76.

Minnesota Sentencing Guidelines Commission. 1989. *Minnesota Sentencing Guidelines and Commentary.* St. Paul: Author.

Morris, Norval and Michael Tonry. 1990. *Between Prison and Probation: Intermediate Punishments in a Rational Sentencing System.* New York: Oxford University Press.

National Advisory Commission on Criminal Justice Standards and Goals. 1973. *Corrections.* Washington, DC: U.S. Department of Justice.

O'Leary, Vincent and David Duffee. 1971. "Correctional Policy Models: A Classification of Goals Designed for Change." *Crime & Delinquency* 17:373–86.

Parent, Dale G. 1988. *Structuring Criminal Sentences: The Evolution of Minnesota's Sentencing Guidelines.* Stoneham, MA: Butterworth Legal Publishers.

Petersilia, Joan. 1990. "Conditions That Permit Intensive Supervision Programs to Survive." *Crime & Delinquency* 36:126–45.

Petersilia, Joan, Susan Turner, James Kahan, and Joyce Peterson. 1985. *Granting Felons Probation: Public Risks and Alternatives.* Santa Monica, CA: RAND.

Reiss, Albert J., Jr. 1986. "Why Are Communities Important in Understanding Crime?" Pp. 1–33 in *Communities and Crime,* edited by A. J. Reiss and M. Tonry. Chicago: University of Chicago Press.

Rosett, Arthur and Donald R. Cressey. 1976. *Justice by Consent.* Philadelphia, PA: Lippincott.

Schur, Edwin M. 1965. *Crimes Without Victims.* Englewood Cliffs, NJ: Prentice Hall.

Symkla, John. 1981. *Community-Based Corrections: Principles and Practices.* New York: Macmillan.

von Hirsch, Andrew. 1976. *Doing Justice.* New York: Hill & Wang.

von Hirsch, Andrew and Kathleen Hanrahan. 1978. *Abolish Parole?* Washington, DC: National Institution of Law Enforcement and Criminal Justice.

DISCUSSION QUESTIONS

1. Give an example of how a probation officer or similar community corrections agent would implement each of the strategies of diversion, advocacy, and reintegration.

2. Give an example of how a probation officer or similar community corrections agent would implement each of the strategies of just deserts, adversary, and restitution.

3. Based on the sources and arguments provided in the article, what are the strengths and limitations of each of the models of community corrections?

4. Given what you have learned from the community corrections experts and research findings in this article, what models of community corrections would you be most likely to use when working with various types of community corrections clients?

❖

READING

"Boot camps" have been popular correctional alternatives, particularly among legislators and the public, and have been the subject of news media coverage. Despite their popularity, boot camps for juvenile offenders are controversial and there have been mixed research results as to their effectiveness when compared with traditional correctional alternatives. The authors of this article examined the experiences of juveniles in boot camps and compared them to the experiences of juveniles in traditional correctional facilities. There were no reported differences between juveniles' anxiety and depression in the two types of facilities during their first month of confinement. Overall, juveniles in boot camps perceived their environment to be more positive and therapeutic, less hostile and dangerous, and as providing more structure with less freedom than juveniles in traditional facilities. Compared with others in the same facility, youth who viewed their facility negatively experienced more stress, anxiety, and depression. Measures of changes over time found that youth in boot camps became less antisocial and less depressed than youth in traditional facilities. Analyses suggested, however, that it was not the facility type but positive perceptions of the environment that determined these changes. Finally, youth with histories of abuse reported higher levels of stress and exhibited less improvement overall, faring better in traditional facilities than in boot camps.

The Impact of Boot Camps and Traditional
Institutions on Juvenile Residents

Perceptions, Adjustment, and Change

Doris Layton MacKenzie, David B. Wilson, Gaylene Styve Armstrong, Angela R. Gover

Despite their continuing popularity, correctional boot camps for juveniles remain controversial. The debate involves questions about the impact of the camps on the adjustment and behavior of juveniles while they are in residence and after they are released. According to advocates, the atmosphere of the camps is conducive to positive growth and change (Clark and Aziz 1996; MacKenzie and Hebert 1996). In contrast, critics argue that many of the components of the camps are in direct opposition to the type of relationships and supportive conditions that are needed for quality therapeutic programming (Andrews, Zinger et al. 1990; Gendreau, Little, and Groggin 1996; Morash and Rucker 1990; Sechrest 1989). Research on the recidivism of releasees from correctional boot camps has not been particularly helpful in settling the controversy over the camps. Neither adult nor juvenile boot camps appear to be effective in reducing recidivism. In general, no differences are found in recidivism when boot camp releasees are compared to comparison samples who served other sentences or who had been confined in another type of juvenile facility (MacKenzie 1997; MacKenzie et al. 1995).

This research examines the experiences of 2,668 juveniles confined in 26 boot camps and compares these experiences to those of 1,848 juveniles residing in 22 traditional facilities. We examine whether juveniles in the boot camps experience more anxiety and depression in comparison to those in traditional facilities and whether these experiences are related to perceptions of the environment. In addition, we compare the changes juveniles make during residency in the facilities. Specifically, we were interested

in changes in stress (anxiety, depression) and impulsivity, social bonds, and antisocial attitudes. The latter characteristics have been found to be associated with criminal activity and are, therefore, reasonable targets for intermediate change during the time juveniles reside in the facilities. We also measured juveniles' perceptions of the environment to examine whether they perceived the environments of the two types of facilities differently and, if so, whether these perceptions were related to the type of changes they made while in the facilities.

Critics of boot camps propose that some juveniles will experience more difficulties than others in the boot camps due to the confrontational nature of the interactions between the juveniles and the staff (Morash and Rucker 1990). In particular, boot camps are proposed to be particularly stressful for girls and for juveniles who have experienced a past history of family violence. To examine this proposal, we compared whether there were differences in the impact of the boot camps on those who had experienced family violence.

For a subset of respondents, data were collected at two points in time, enabling us to examine change in anxiety and depression as well as social bonds, impulsivity, and social attitudes during the time juveniles were in the two different types of facilities. These characteristics are theoretically associated with criminal behavior. Increased social bonds and positive social attitudes and, conversely, decreased impulsivity are anticipated to be associated with reductions in later criminal activity. Thus, facilities that have an impact on these characteristics of juveniles may be successful in reducing recidivism.

SOURCE: *Journal of Research in Crime and Delinquency* (38)3, 279–313, August 2001. © 2001 Sage Publications, Inc.

We begin by reviewing the research literature to establish the importance of understanding the environments of facilities and the effects of different environments on the residents. Following this, we review the literature on juveniles' adjustment in facilities, the changes juveniles are hypothesized to make during their time in residential facilities, and the association of these changes with future criminal activities.

The Perceived Environment

The impact of the prison environment on inmates' adjustment and behavior both while they are in the facility and when they are released has been well established in the research literature (Ajdukovic 1990; Goffman 1961; Johnson and Toch 1982; Moos 1968; Wright 1985, 1991; Wright and Goodstein 1989; Zamble and Porporino 1988). Facilities possess unique characteristics that "impinge upon and shape individual behavior" (Wright and Goodstein 1989:266).

Few people who have visited correctional boot camps doubt that the environments of these facilities are radically different from the environment of traditional facilities (Lutze 1998; MacKenzie and Hebert 1996; MacKenzie and Parent 1992; Styve, MacKenzie, Gover, and Mitchell 2000). Juveniles in these facilities are awakened early each day to follow a rigorous daily schedule of physical training, drill and ceremony, and school. They are required to follow the orders of the correctional staff. Orders are often presented in a confrontational manner, modeled after basic training in the military. Summary punishments such as push-ups are frequently used to sanction misbehavior. In comparison to traditional juvenile facilities, boot camps appear to be more physically and emotionally demanding for the residents. In fact, research on adult boot camps suggests that inmates in the boot camps will voluntarily drop out even if this means they will have to serve a longer term in the prison than they would if they completed the boot camp (MacKenzie and Souryal 1995).

Perceptions of inmates in the different types of facilities would be expected to reflect the differences in environments. Continuing controversy exists about the appropriateness of the camps for managing and treating juvenile delinquents. Advocates of the boot camps argue that the focus on strict control and military structure provides a safer environment conducive to positive change (Steinhart 1993; Zachariah 1996). From their perspective, the intense physical activity and healthy atmosphere of the camps provides an advantageous backdrop for treatment and education (Clark and Aziz 1996; Cowles and Castellano 1996).

Critics disagree with this perspective (Morash and Rucker 1990) and claim that the confrontational nature of the camps is diametrically opposed to the constructive, interpersonally supportive environment necessary for positive change to occur (Andrews, Zinger et al. 1990). According to critics, juveniles in the boot camps, when compared to youth in traditional facilities, will perceive their facilities as less caring and less therapeutic and, in general, will be less prepared for reentry into the community. Furthermore, juveniles may be worried about their safety while they are in a boot camp facility. Given the hypothesized negative environmental characteristics, youth in boot camps would be expected to experience much more stress than youth in traditional facilities.

Morash and Rucker (1990) are particularly concerned that the boot camps will have a detrimental impact on girls and on both girls and boys who have experienced abuse. The confrontational nature of the interactions between staff and inmates is expected to be particularly problematic for these youth. For those who have a history of abuse and for girls who have dependency issues, these interactions will be reminiscent of the difficulties they faced in an abusive relationship; as a result, the environment will be particularly stressful and countertherapeutic for them.

The environments of the facilities would also be expected to have an impact on the types of changes inmates make during their time in the different facilities. For example, research demonstrates that treatment programs with particular characteristics are effective in changing antisocial attitudes. An environment that emphasizes therapeutic programming instead of physical activity would be expected to have a greater impact on such attitudes (Andrews and Bonta 1998; Goodstein and Wright 1989).

In summary, we propose that juveniles in the boot camps and the traditional facilities will perceive the environment of their institutions differently and that the characteristics of the environments will have an impact on the level of stress experienced by the residents and on the changes they make in social bonds, antisocial attitudes, and impulsivity.

Stress

One concern regarding the boot camps is whether the environment creates dysfunctional stress for the participants. Some levels of stress may actually be beneficial. For example, critical life events may create stress, and this stress may result in changing the trajectories of the lives of those involved in criminal activities (Sampson and Laub 1993). Instead of continuing in the previous path (e.g., criminal), youth may change and make a commitment to family, school, or employment. The stress created by the critical life event in such cases has a functional and beneficial impact. In contrast, some stress is so severe that an individual's level of functioning is compromised. In such cases, the stress is considered dysfunctional.

The adjustment of inmates to the environments of correctional facilities has been the topic of numerous research studies (e.g., Goodstein and Wright 1989). A concern has been that institutions such as prisons create a total environment that may severely limit inmates' development and create dysfunctional stress, particularly in youth (Goffman 1961; Johnson and Toch 1982; Moos 1968; Wright 1991). Critics of boot camps fear that the demanding nature of the boot camp environment will be beyond the coping ability of youth and, as a result, will be detrimental to them.

In contrast, advocates argue that it is a healthy environment that creates the type of stress that will lead youth to reevaluate their lives

and make changes. Some level of stress may be effective in bringing about change. For example, Zamble and Porporino (1988) found that adult inmates experienced stress when they first entered prison. This was also the time inmates were most willing to enter programs designed to help them make changes in their lives. Zamble and Porporino propose that the stress associated with entry to prison might be instrumental in getting inmates to reevaluate their lives and take steps toward positive change. This proposal is similar to the type of critical life event Sampson and Laub (1993) consider conducive to bringing about changes in life trajectories. That is, entering a new situation like a residential facility may be the type of life event that leads to changes in the trajectory of the lives of some juveniles. As a result of this event, juveniles may become more prosocial and begin to build ties and bonds with conventional social institutions.

Frequently, boot camp staff refer to the early period in boot camps as a period when they "break down" youth before they begin the "build-up period." The question is whether the breakdown period creates functional or dysfunctional stress. That is, do the youth in the boot camp experience the type of anxiety that will result in a reevaluation of their lives and a decision to make changes, or is the stress so severe that they become depressed, anxious, and unable to adequately function in the new environment? Critics would suggest that the stress in boot camps is so severe as to be dysfunctional; advocates of the camps argue that it creates the type of stress that leads to positive changes.

Changing Youth

If institutional programs are going to have an impact on the future criminal activities and adjustment of youth, the programs must change the youth in some way. These intermediate changes can be thought to be signals of the impacts the facilities will have on the future criminal activities of the youth. This research examines adjustment and short-term change in boot camp facilities and compares these to the changes juveniles in traditional facilities make. Three correlates of criminal activity are social bonds, impulsivity, and antisocial attitudes. These characteristics are theoretically and empirically associated with criminal activity and other antisocial behavior. We begin by reviewing evidence that these characteristics are associated with criminal behavior and that changes in the characteristics are associated with changes in criminal activity.

Increasing social bonds. Evidence exists that increases in social bonds are associated with declines in criminal activity. According to Sampson and Laub (1993), informal social controls form a structure of interpersonal bonds linking individuals to social institutions such as work, family, and school. These ties or bonds are important in that they create obligations and restraints that impose significant costs for translating criminal propensities into action. Although Sampson and Laub acknowledge that there is continuity in individual antisocial behavior, they argue, unlike the continuity theorists (e.g., Gottfredson and Hirschi 1990), that such continuity does not preclude large changes in individuals' offending patterns. In a reanalysis of the Glueck and Glueck (1950) data, Sampson and Laub found support for the proposal that childhood antisocial behavior and deviance can be modified over the life course by adult social bonds. Job stability and marital attachment were significant predictors of adult crime even when childhood delinquency and crime in young adulthood were statistically controlled.

Further evidence that criminal propensity can be modified comes from research by Horney, Osgood, and Marshall (1995) that examined the self-reported criminal activities of offenders. They found that life circumstances indicative of changes in social bonds and commitment to conformity influenced offending behavior even over relatively short time periods.

Similar to the findings from research with adults, increased social bonds have been found to be associated with declines in the criminal activities of juveniles (Jang 1999; Simons et al. 1998). For example, Simons et al. (1998) found that stronger ties to family and school and decreased affiliation with deviant peers lowered the probability that youth who had behavior problems during childhood would graduate to delinquency during adolescence.

In summary, the research on social bonds demonstrates that increased social bonds are associated with decreased criminal activity. The research does not demonstrate how or why bonds change. Sampson and Laub (1993) propose that bonds may change as a function of critical life events that lead individuals to reevaluate their lives and begin to make positive changes. Theoretically, such a critical life event could occur for juveniles who enter a residential facility. If the experience of being in the facility or the programs provided in the facility increases the attitudes of commitment to conformity or ties the juveniles have to social institutions like family, work, and school, then theoretically the future criminal activities of these youth may decrease. The major characteristics of boot camps do not suggest that these programs will incorporate elements that would increase ties or commitments to conventional activities outside the facility. Restrictions on visitation may limit contact with the outside, and the environment of the camps is very different from the environment of work or school outside the camps. The traditional facilities may be much more likely to strengthen these ties or attitudes. Theoretically, a critical life event such as entering an institution could initiate changes in ties or attitudes. If either type of facility did have an impact on attitudes or ties, we would anticipate that this would be a hopeful sign that such changes would be associated with reduction in future criminal activities for the participants.

Impulsivity and control. The connection between impulsivity and criminal activities is well established. According to Gottfredson and Hirschi's (1990) *A General Theory of Crime*, antisocial acts are committed by people with low self-control. Impulsivity is one of the major characteristics of such individuals. Theorists interested in individual differences in temperament and personalities have also emphasized the need to consider differences in impulsivity. For example, in her psychosocial control theory, Mak (1990, 1991) emphasizes the importance for understanding criminal activity and delinquency of individual differences in thinking through consequences, a preference for immediate gratification, poor planning, and a lack of patience. These impulsive characteristics are similar to the temperament and personality characteristics Glueck and Glueck (1950) linked to persistent and serious delinquent behavior.

Numerous key criminological studies have shown that impulsivity is a strong correlate of delinquent and criminal behavior (Caspi et al. 1994; Farrington 1998; Glueck and Glueck 1950; Loeber et al. 1998; White et al. 1994). In comparison to nondelinquents, delinquents show markedly higher levels of impulsivity. These results held despite differences in whether impulsivity was measured by self-reports, teachers, independent raters, staff psychologists, or parents. Stronger impulsivity was related to increases in official measures of offending and delinquency, self-reported criminal activities, and childhood behavior problems as reported by teachers, mothers, and peers. The association between impulsivity and crime is stronger than those of intelligence or socioeconomic status (White et al. 1994).

Controversy exists regarding whether an individual's impulsivity can be changed during the life course. Gottfredson and Hirschi (1990) assert that "people who lack self-control will tend to be impulsive" (p. 90) and that variation in self-control is a latent trait that provides the primary explanation for individual differences in involvement in antisocial behavior throughout the life course (Hirschi and Gottfredson 1994). In contrast, others believe that individuals can change during their life course. For example, the life-course perspective views life-course trajectories as a sequence of events and transitions that either accentuate or redirect behavioral tendencies

(Elder 1992; Simons et al. 1998). From this perspective, characteristics such as antisocial behavior and impulsivity are associated with criminal activity, but a trajectory may change as a result of life circumstances or critical life events. In their study, Simons et al. (1998) found evidence that the correlation between childhood and adolescent deviant behavior reflects a developmental process as proposed by those with a life-course perspective rather than the latent antisocial trait proposed by Gottfredson and Hirschi.

A critical life event that may change a juvenile's life trajectory is institutionalization in a juvenile facility. Impulsivity is a particular target for change in boot camps. The rigorous structure in the camps and the strict requirements for military bearing are designed, in part, to get youth to think before they act. We anticipate that this is one characteristic of juveniles that would change as a result of the boot camp experience. The traditional facilities are not expected to impact a youth's impulsivity.

Antisocial attitudes. According to correctional theorists, treatment programs that are effective in reducing recidivism have certain clearly defined characteristics (Andrews, Bonta, and Hoge 1990; Andrews and Kiessling 1980; Gendreau and Ross 1979, 1987; Glaser 1974; Palmer 1974). These authors argue that "appropriate" treatment delivers services to higher risk cases, uses styles and modes of treatment that are capable of influencing criminogenic "needs," and is matched to the learning styles of offenders. Criminogenic needs are defined as those that are dynamic or changeable as opposed to static (not changeable) and directly related to the criminal behavior of the offender. Meta-analyses examining the effectiveness of treatment programs have supported the proposed importance of these appropriate treatment characteristics (Andrews, Zinger et al. 1990; Lipsey 1992). Procriminal or antisocial attitudes have consistently shown significant associations with criminal behavior for adults (Andrews and Bonta 1998, Bonta 1990) and youthful offenders (Shields and Ball 1990; Shields and Whitehall 1994). The evidence showing the association between procriminal or antisocial attitudes and criminal behavior makes these prime criminogenic needs and, therefore, targets for change in correctional treatment.

Summary

In summary, there is strong empirical evidence that social bonds, antisocial attitudes, and impulsivity are associated with criminal activity. Recent research supports the proposal that these characteristics do change during the life course. The question is how this change can be initiated. Life-course theorists propose that critical life events may bring about change in adolescence or adulthood. One such critical life event, at least for some adolescents, may be incarceration in a juvenile correctional facility. Differences in the environments and programming in correctional boot camps and traditional facilities lead us to predict that the impacts of these facilities on the youth who spend time there will be different. Given the environment and programming in the boot camps, we anticipate that the camps may reduce the impulsivity of the youth who reside there. On the other hand, we anticipate that the traditional facilities may be more apt to change the social bonds and antisocial attitudes of the youth who reside there. For correctional facilities to have an impact on the future offending behavior of youth, these are the changes we would hope to observe during residency in a juvenile facility.

✎ Method

Site Identification

In April of 1997, all juvenile boot camps in operation in the United States, excluding Hawaii and Alaska, were identified for inclusion in this study. At that time, 50 privately and publicly funded secure residential boot camps were

identified. All facilities were contacted and asked to participate, and 27 agreed. The 23 programs that did not participate did so for various reasons, including parental consent issues, staffing and resource limitations, and impending program closure. Thus, the 27 boot camps agreeing to participate in this project represented 54 percent (27 out of 50) of the residential juvenile boot camps operating in 1997 and unfortunately cannot be considered a random sample of the population of facilities.[1]

For each boot camp agreeing to participate, a comparison facility was sought to allow the contrast of youth's experiences in a boot camp with youth's experiences in traditional juvenile correctional facilities. Comparison facilities were selected by identifying those secure residential facilities in which the juveniles would have been confined if the boot camp programs were not in operation. This method of selection ensured that the residents at the comparison facilities were as similar as possible to the boot camp residents. With this definition of a comparison facility in mind, the facility administrator at each boot camp or an individual from within the state's juvenile justice department recommended the most appropriate comparison facility. Comparison facilities were then contacted and asked to join the research project. All comparison facilities identified agreed to participate in the research project. Although there were 26 boot camp facilities included in the study, there were only 22 comparison facilities. There were two reasons for this discrepancy. First, two boot camps did not have a viable comparison facility within the state. Second, in two states, the same non-boot camp facility was identified as the most appropriate comparison for two different boot camps. In these instances, one facility served as the comparison for each of the two boot camps.

Participants

A full census of all juveniles at each facility on two occasions was sought. A total of 4,516 juveniles were surveyed: 2,668 from the boot camp facilities and 1,848 from the traditional facilities. The overall response rate for this survey was high and represented 85 percent of the juvenile population at the surveyed facilities. A common reason for nonparticipation was a juvenile's overriding need to be somewhere else at time of survey administration, such as a court hearing or medical visit outside of the facility. A small number of youths started the survey but chose to not complete it. A total of 2,473 were surveyed at the Time 1 administration and 2,030 at the Time 2 administration. The first administration of the survey was designed to include juveniles shortly after their entry into the boot camp program. The second administration of the survey was designed to include juveniles just prior to release from the boot camp. The time interval between the two survey administrations in the comparison facilities was matched to the time interval between administrations for the corresponding boot camp. The interval between Time 1 and Time 2 administrations ranged from three months to eight months with a median of four months. The Time 2 administration included 530 juveniles, 264 in boot camps and 266 in traditional facilities, who also were surveyed at Time 1. This subsample of the data is the major focus of this article.

Juvenile Survey

The survey questionnaire for the youths included 266 questions. Thirteen questions were open ended (primarily demographic items) with the remaining questions based either on a four- or five-point Likert-type response scale or a yes-no dichotomous response format. Overall, there was a high completion rate of more than 85 percent of the population. Surveys were administered to groups of 15 to 20 youths in classroom-type settings in accordance with prevailing ethical principles. A videotaped presentation of the survey was shown on a large television providing instructions and the survey questions to ensure uniform administration and provide assistance to juveniles with reading difficulties.[2]

Administrator Interview and Institutional Records

A structured interview was conducted with the facility administrators to obtain information about the facilities where the juveniles resided. Some items in the interview survey required information from institutional records (e.g., hours of treatment per week) that was obtained by the administrator after the completion of the interview. Researchers placed follow-up telephone calls within two weeks of the site visit to obtain outstanding information.

The interview included 264 items and provided information on a variety of factors including the size of the facility (the average number of juveniles who usually reside in the facility), how selective the facility could be about who enters the facility (selectivity index), the seriousness of the delinquency history of the juveniles who were admitted to the facility (seriousness index), the number of hours the juveniles participated in treatment in a one-week period, the contact juveniles had with the outside (contact with outside index), the staff-to-juvenile inmate ratio, the juveniles' average length of stay, and whether someone at the facility collected or obtained information on the juveniles who were released—including rearrest for delinquent or criminal activities, return to school, residence with family, and reinstitutionalization.[3]

[Note: The editors have omitted detailed discussion of the measures and presentation of statistical analysis. Readers are encouraged to see the original document.]

The goal of this study was to assess the impact of the facility environment on the changes juveniles made while in the facilities using the five indicator variables (depression, anxiety, dysfunctional impulsivity, social attitudes, commitment to conventional behavior) discussed . . . , not the impact of an individual's perception of the environment on his change while residing in the facility. Thus, we averaged the perception of the environment measures across individuals to create a facility-level rating on each of the three dimensions using the three-factor solution for the environmental measures.

⋈ Results

Juvenile Characteristics

The demographic characteristics between boot camps and traditional facilities were comparable. The boot camps tended to have a higher percentage of girls, although boys dominated both facility types. The traditional facilities had a population that was more criminally involved, on average, than the boot camps, with a substantially higher mean number of prior nonviolent and violent arrests. Furthermore, at the time of the survey, the typical youth in the traditional facility had resided in the facility roughly twice as long as the typical boot camp youth. This reflects the generally longer lengths of stay in these facilities relative to the boot camps and the method of determining when to conduct the surveys at each facility.

The two samples were highly similar on the psychosocial indices. A statistically significant but small difference was observed in the history of family violence, with higher levels of previous violence reported by the youths in the traditional facilities. A small difference was also observed on the commitment to conventional behavior index, with higher levels reported by the youth in the boot camps. Although the traditional facilities were selected because they were facilities to which the boot camp youths would have been sent in the absence of the boot camp, the general impression from these data is that the traditional facilities also serve youth who are more seriously delinquent, on average, than the youth admitted to the boot camps. It appears that whereas all of the boot camp youth may have been appropriate for the comparison facility, not all of the youth at the comparison facility may have been appropriate for the boot camp facilities.

Juveniles' Perception of the Facility Environment

The juveniles' perception of the environment differed between the two facility types. Surprisingly, the boot camps were perceived, on average, as more therapeutic and less hostile than the traditional facilities. Consistent with expectation, the youths perceived the boot camps as more restrictive of personal freedom and choice than the traditional facilities. These findings are consistent with the qualitative observations made within the facilities by the research staff. Within the typical juvenile boot camp, the increased structure does not appear to be associated with an increase in hostility or perceived danger from staff (an element of this factor). The greater selectivity of the boot camps in admissions criteria (see below) may also contribute to a safer overall environment if the more troubled and potentially violent youth are not allowed admission. These differences remained after statistically adjusting for measured characteristics of the youth. Thus, the evidence suggests that the observed differences represent actual differences in the environments and not just differential perceptions of comparable environments. We cannot determine from this data, however, whether the differences are produced by the structural, organizational, programmatic, and staffing aspects of a facility or by the juveniles themselves. That is, a facility with a higher proportion of violent offenders may genuinely be more dangerous, despite staffing and organization aspects. It is likely that both the characteristics of a program and the juveniles served contribute to the environmental conditions.

Facility Characteristics

On average, the boot camps were smaller and more selective about the entrants than the traditional facilities. Traditional facilities permitted juveniles with more serious criminal histories to enter the program and were generally less selective about whom they admitted. The typical length of stay in the traditional facilities was nearly double that of the boot camps. Only 46 percent of the boot camps and 32 percent of the traditional facilities had any follow-up information on the releasees, including whether the youth were returned to the same facility sometime after being released (Gover, MacKenzie and Styve 2000).

Initial Levels of Anxiety and Depression

The first hypothesis addressed was whether boot camp youths had higher initial levels of depression and anxiety. Although some individuals are generally more anxious or depressed than other individuals, depression and anxiety are not static, and an individual's level of each will rise and fall depending on life stressors and environmental circumstances. The transition into an institutional setting, whether it is a traditional juvenile delinquency facility or a boot camp, is stressful and may lead to increased depression and anxiety for some youths. The boot camp, with its highly structured militaristic style and reputation, may be a more stressful environment, at least initially, for juveniles.

A history of family violence is a risk factor for affective disorders, such as depression and anxiety. It was hypothesized that a history of family violence would be related not only to the initial level of anxiety and depression of the juveniles but also that it would interact with facility type. We presumed that the more aggressive "in-your-face" atmosphere of the boot camps would be more traumatic for juveniles with a history of family violence and would therefore lead to a higher level of anxiety and depression. We tested this hypothesis for both anxiety and depression using a random-effects regression model estimated via maximum likelihood. Two regression analyses were estimated, one for depression and one for anxiety, each regressed on both individual-level and facility-level variables. These analyses were restricted to boys because there were only four girls in traditional facilities for this subsample of the data set. Both analyses showed a statistically significant relationship between a history of family violence and level of anxiety and depression. Facilities that were perceived, on average, as more hostile had higher levels of anxiety but not depression. Contrary to expectation, however, the interactions of facility type and facility-level hostility with history of family violence were not statistically significant. Based on these data, a history of family violence does not appear to interact with the type of facility (boot camp or traditional) or

with the degree of perceived hostility. The regression analyses did show that youths perceiving the facility as more hostile and having less freedom and choice relative to their peers in the same facility were more likely to be anxious and depressed. It may well be that anxious and depressed youths are more likely to perceive their environment negatively.

Changes in Anxiety, Depression, Social Bonds, Dysfunctional Impulsivity, and Prosocial Attitudes

A main question of this article is whether the boot camp and traditional facilities produce positive changes in correlates of delinquency. That is, during youths' stay in a facility, do they become less impulsive, increase their bonds to conventional society, decrease their antisocial attitudes, and become less anxious and less depressed? To address this issue, we examined a sub-sample of the study that was measured on two occasions, ranging from one to six months between occasions, four months on average. For this sample (264 boot camp respondents and 266 traditional facility respondents), a maximum-likelihood estimated random-effects regression model (Bryk and Raudenbush 1992; StataCorp 1999) was used to examine change in the five outcome variables.

Facility type was statistically nonsignificant across all models with the full complement of covariates. For both change in depression and change in social attitudes (a predictor of delinquency), however, the overall rating of the facility environment was related to change in the desired direction. It appears that the boot camp versus traditional facilities distinction is far less relevant than how positively the youth perceive an environment to be. Recall that in these models, it is the facility means of the youths' perceptions that are used. Presumably, the composite of all of the youths' perceptions of the environment produced an index of the facility environment that is relatively independent of each individual youth's perceptions, although it might be affected by the composition of youths completing the survey.

A hypothesis of these analyses was that facility type would interact with history of family violence. As expected, youth with histories of family violence changed less in social attitudes, on average, than youth without histories of family violence. Also, as expected, this relationship interacted with facility type and was stronger for boot camp facilities. That is, there is only a slight relationship between history of family violence and change in social attitudes for the traditional facilities. The boot camp environment appears detrimental (or at least less therapeutic), based on these data, for youths with a history of family violence. This pattern of effect, albeit statistically nonsignificant, was consistent across all five regression models. Thus, youths with a history of family violence exhibit less positive change overall yet fare better relative to their peers in traditional facilities.

An unexpected finding was the relationship between race and change in social attitudes and the interaction of this effect with the overall rating of the facility environment. On average, African Americans exhibited less positive change in social attitudes. Furthermore, a plot of the regression function shows that the relationship between the overall rating of the facility environment and change in social attitudes is not evident for African Americans. The average amount of change in social attitudes is roughly equal across facilities rated differentially on overall rating. These two regression coefficients are statistically significant at the rather liberal level of $p < .10$ and were not hypothesized effects. Therefore, these findings need replication for any confidence to be placed in them.

A final finding in this regression model worth noting is the positive relationship between the time in facility at first measurement and the amount of positive change in social attitudes. This coefficient suggests that larger changes in social attitudes tend to occur in later periods of a youth's stay in these facilities.

The amount of reduction in depressed mood was related, as expected, to a history of family violence. The higher the level of prior family violence, the less decrease in depressed mood between administrations of the survey instrument. Also as expected, youth in environments judged positively were more likely to have decreased depression between survey administrations, as were youth in facilities that were highly selective of the youth admitted.

▧ Discussion

Boot camps for delinquent juveniles are a modern alternative to traditional detention and treatment facilities, although the notion that strict discipline and physical exercise will straighten out wayward youth has a long history. The debate surrounding boot camps has focused on the potential stressfulness of the environment and the plausibility that the confrontation and militaristic style will be harmful to the juveniles, particularly those with a history of abuse. This study contributes to the debate by examining the environment of boot camps relative to traditional facilities as perceived by the youths in the facilities, the initial stress levels of the youths in the two facilities types, and the intermediate changes of the youths on variables associated with future offending behavior.

Contrary to the expectation of the critics of boot camps, the juveniles perceived the boot camp environments more favorably relative to the traditional facilities. These differences in perceptions remained after accounting for measured differences in the characteristics of the youths across the two facility types. Not only did the youths in the boot camps generally feel safer, they also perceived the environment to be more therapeutic or helpful. Thus, the fears that the boot camps, in general, would be hostile, negative environments appear not to have been realized. Although the boot camps were more structured and placed more constraints on the freedom of the juveniles, the implementation of the boot camp model for juveniles does not appear to produce environments that are perceived by juveniles as negative relative to existing alternatives. Based on observational information gained through site visits to all of the surveyed facilities, it is our opinion that this finding reflects the positive atmosphere of many but not all of the boot camps. Most boot camps have strict rules and discipline for disobedience; however, despite this, or because of this, close and caring relationships seem to form between youth and staff.

A concern regarding boot camps is that the militaristic environment may contrast so sharply with the past home and community experiences of the juveniles that the camps will produce harmfully high levels of stress, resulting in high levels of depression and anxiety. It was not possible with the available data to determine if the observed levels of anxiety and depression among the youths in this study were at dysfunctional levels. A contrast between the initial levels of anxiety and depression between traditional and boot camp facilities, however, showed that youths in boot camps do not appear to have higher levels of anxiety and depression than comparable youths in traditional facilities. Considering the positive perception of the boot camp environment, this finding is not surprising, although it is counter to the expectation of many. Initial levels of depression and anxiety were related, however, to a history of family violence or abuse. Contrary to expectation, this relationship was not mediated by the facility type.

We hypothesized that the structured, disciplined nature of boot camps would increase the effectiveness of these facilities at reducing impulsivity among juveniles relative to traditional facilities. Furthermore, we anticipated that traditional facilities would be more effective at modifying a youth's social bonds and antisocial attitudes. These predictions were not confirmed. The raw differences in the mean change from pretest to posttest favored the boot camps for all three of these intermediate outcomes. These differences were substantially attenuated, and statistically nonsignificant, once the facility environment variable was included in the model, as well as characteristics of the individuals and other facility features. Thus, it appears that any

differences in the effects of boot camps relative to traditional facilities on these variables can be explained by how positive the youths perceived the environment.

There is concern that the boot camp environment may be detrimental to youth with abuse histories (e.g., Morash and Rucker 1990). This study provides some support for this view. For the antisocial attitude measure, youth with abuse histories exhibited substantially less change in the desired direction. Furthermore, this effect was twice as large for boot camps as for traditional facilities. That is, there was a statistically significant interaction between facility type and abuse history for antisocial attitudes, suggesting that boot camps may be ineffective and potentially detrimental to persons with a history of family violence.

An unexpected finding that deserves additional research was an interaction between the perceptions of the facility environment and race/ethnicity (African American versus other). For African Americans, there was virtually no relationship between the characteristics of the facility environment, as measured by our single factor, and change in social attitudes, whereas non-African Americans exhibited greater change in the desired direction as the environment became more positive. As the result of an exploratory analysis, the finding may represent sampling error. However, if it is confirmed by additional research, it points to the need to examine the effect of environmental conditions on juvenile adjustment and change separately for African Americans relative to Caucasians and other racial/ethnic groups.

Almost anyone who visits a juvenile correctional boot camp recognizes the large difference between the environment of the camps and the environment of more traditional juvenile facilities. The question is whether this is a positive atmosphere conducive to positive growth and change or whether it is detrimental to juveniles and is in opposition to a high-quality therapeutic environment. Our findings suggest that, at least from the perspective of the juveniles residing in the facilities, the boot camps are a more positive environment than traditional facilities. Boot camp residents perceive their environments as less hostile and more therapeutic than juveniles in traditional facilities. Furthermore, according to their self-reports, they are no more (or less) anxious or depressed even during the early period in boot camps when adjustment is hypothesized to be the most difficult. The boot camps also appear to have a more positive impact on the juveniles in regard to antisocial attitudes and depression; however, this effect appears to be related to the more positive atmosphere, not whether a facility is a boot camp or not. The only problematic impact of the boot camps was for juveniles with a history of abuse and family violence. These youth did not do as well in the boot camps as they did in the more traditional facilities.

Several selection bias effects are obvious in our data. First, juveniles sent to boot camps may differ from those sent to traditional facilities. Juveniles sent to boot camps may be those who would not otherwise be incarcerated, or they may be adjudicated for less serious crimes and sent to the boot camp because it requires a shorter period of confinement. When we compared the characteristics of the two samples given our knowledge of these facilities, it appears that the boot camp youth were appropriate for the traditional facilities, but not all those in the traditional facilities would be appropriate for the boot camps. To control for this in our multivariate analysis, we included measured characteristics of the youth. Our analyses are unlikely to completely control for all selection bias. Although we cannot rule out all selection bias, our examination of the data led us to believe this is not a major threat to our conclusions.

Prior research examining boot camp facilities has not demonstrated any differences in recidivism when those released from boot camps are compared to those released from traditional facilities (MacKenzie 1997). One possible reason

for this finding is that the two types of facilities being compared in the prior studies were similar in environmental characteristics. Our results suggest that whether a facility is called a boot camp or not is less important than the characteristics of the environment of the facilities. Facilities perceived as having more positive environments will be more apt to have an impact on social attitudes, and, in past research, these attitudes have been found to be associated with recidivism. Despite a generally more positive assessment of the boot camp environment by the youth, both boot camp and traditional facilities varied greatly on these measures.

Overall, we found only small changes during their time in the facilities in the characteristics of these juveniles that are related to delinquent behavior. This is disappointing. This finding may reflect deficiencies in the scales or the short period of time between the pre- and postmeasures of change. However, if this change truly reflects the very limited change these juveniles make during their time in the facilities, it is worrisome because the characteristics we measured have been linked to criminal behavior. This suggests to us that these facilities will have a very limited impact on the future delinquent and criminal activities of these youth. Disappointingly, few of these facilities had any information about the juveniles who left their care. Few even knew if the juveniles returned to the same facility, and fewer still had any information about whether the juveniles had recidivated, returned to a community school, or found employment. We wonder how staff and administrators who view their mission as the rehabilitation of juveniles can plan and improve programs if they do not know what happens to the youth once they leave the facility.

✎ Notes

1. Although 27 boot camps agreed to participate, one of the sites was very distinct from all other programs due to its three-year length and transitory nature

from a boot camp into a detention program. As a result of these anomalies, this program was excluded from analyses herein.

2. A copy of this survey is available from the first author.

3. A copy of this survey is available from the first author.

4. We label this scale social attitude because a high score on the scale reflects more positive social attitudes, or conversely less antisocial attitudes.

≥ References

Ajdukovic, D. 1990. "Psychosocial Climate in Correctional Institutions: Which Attributes Describe It?" *Environment and Behavior* 22:420–32.

Andrews, D. A. and J. Bonta. 1998. *The Psychology of Criminal Conduct.* Cincinnati, OH: Anderson.

Andrews, D. A., J. Bonta, and R. D. Hoge. 1990. "Classification for Effective Rehabilitation: Rediscovering Psychology." *Criminal Justice and Behavior* 17:19–52.

Andrews, D. A. and J. J. Kiessling. 1980. "Program Structure and Effective Correctional Practices: A Summary of the CaVIC Research." Pp. 439–63 in *Effective Correctional Treatment,* edited by R. R. Ross and P. Gendreau. Toronto, Canada: Butterworth.

Andrews, D. A., I. Zinger, R. D. Hoge, J. Bonta, P. Gendreau, and F. T. Cullen. 1990. "Does Correctional Treatment Work? A Clinically Relevant and Psychologically Informed Meta-Analysis." *Criminology* 28(3): 369–404.

Bonta, J. 1990. "Antisocial Attitudes and Recidivism." Presented at the annual convention of the Canadian Psychological Association, Ottawa, Ontario.

Bryk, A. S. and S. W. Raudenbush. 1992. *Hierarchical Linear Models: Applications and Data Analysis Methods.* Newbury Park, CA: Sage.

Campbell, D. T. and D. A. Kenny. 1999. *A Primer on Regression Artifacts.* New York: Guilford.

Caspi, A., T. E. Moffitt, P. A. Silav, M. Stouthamer-Loeber, R. F. Krueger, and P. S. Schmutte. 1994. "Are Some People Crime-Prone? Replications of the Personality-Crime Relationships across Countries, Genders, Races and Methods." *Criminology* 32:163–95.

Clark, Cheryl L. and David W. Aziz. 1996. "Shock Incarceration in New York State: Philosophy, Results, and Limitations." Pp. 39–68 in *Correctional Boot Camps: A Tough Intermediate Sanction,* edited by D. L. MacKenzie and E. E. Hebert. Washington, DC: National Institute of Justice, U.S. Department of Justice.

Cowles, E. L. and T. C. Castellano. 1996. "Substance Abuse Programming in Adult Correctional Boot Camps: A National Overview." Pp. 207–32 in *Correctional Boot Camps: A Tough Intermediate Sanction,* edited by D. L. MacKenzie and E. E. Hebert. Washington, DC: National Institute of Justice, U.S. Department of Justice.

Elder, G. H., Jr. 1992. "The Life Course." Pp. 1120–30 in *The Encyclopedia of Sociology,* edited by E. F. Borgatta and M. L. Borgatta. New York: Macmillan.

Farrington, D. P. 1998. "Individual Differences and Offending." Pp. 241–68 in *The Handbook of Crime and Punishment,* edited by M. Tonry. New York: Oxford University Press.

Gendreau, P., T. Little, and C. Groggin. 1996. "A Meta-Analysis of the Predictors of Adult Offender Recidivism: What Works!" *Criminology* 34:575–607.

Gendreau, P. and R. R. Ross. 1979. "Effective Correctional Treatment: Bibliotherapy for Cynics." *Crime and Delinquency* 25:463–89.

———.1987. "Revivication of Rehabilitation: Evidence from the 1980s." *Justice Quarterly* 4:349–408.

Glaser, D. 1974. "Remedies for the Key Deficiency in Criminal Justice Evaluation Research." *Journal of Research in Crime and Delinquency* 10:144–54.

Glueck, S. and E. T. Glueck. 1950. *Unraveling Juvenile Delinquency.* Cambridge, MA: Harvard University Press.

Goffman, E. 1961. *Asylums: Essays on the Social Situation of Mental Patients and Other Inmates.* Garden City, NY: Anchor.

Goodstein, L. and K. Wright. 1989. "Adjustment to Prison." Pp. 253–70 in *The American Prison,* edited by L. Goodstein and D. L. MacKenzie. New York: Plenum.

Gottfredson, M. R. and T. Hirschi. 1990. *A General Theory of Crime.* Stanford, CA: Stanford University Press.

Gover, A. R., D. L. MacKenzie, and G. J. Styve. 2000. "Boot Camps and Traditional Correctional Facilities for Juveniles: A Comparison of the Participants, Daily Activities, and Environments." *Journal of Criminal Justice* 28(1):53–68.

Hirschi, T. and M. R. Gottfredson. 1994. "The Generality of Deviance." In *The Generality of Deviance,* edited by Travis Hirschi and Michael R. Gottfredson. New Brunswick, NJ: Transaction.

Horney, J. D., W. Osgood, and I. H. Marshall. 1995. "Criminal Careers in the Short-Term: Intra-Individual Variability in Crime and its Relationship to Local Life Circumstances." *American Sociological Review* 60:655–73.

Jang, S. J. 1999. "Age-Varying Effects of Family, School, and Peers on Delinquency: A Multilevel Modeling Test of Interactional Theory." *Criminology* 37(3): 643–86.

Jesness, C. F. 1962. *Jesness Inventory.* North Tonawanda, NY: MultiHealth Systems.

Johnson, R. and H. Toch, eds. 1982. *The Pains of Imprisonment.* Beverly Hills, CA: Sage.

Kirk, R. E. 1982. *Experimental Design.* 2nd ed. Belmont, CA: Wadsworth.

Lipsey, M. 1992. "Juvenile Delinquency Treatment: A Meta-Analytic Inquiry into the Variability of Effects." Pp. 83–127 in *Meta-Analysis for Explanation: A Casebook,* edited by T. Cook. New York: Russell Sage Foundation.

Loeber, R., Farrington, D. P., Stouthamer-Loeber, M., Moffitt, T. E., and Caspi, A. 1998. "The development of male offending: Key findings from the first decade of the Pittsburgh Youth Study." *Studies on Crime & Crime Prevention* 7:141–71.

Lutze, F. 1998. "Do Boot Camp Prisons Possess a More Rehabilitative Environment than Traditional Prison? A Survey of Inmates." *Justice Quarterly* 15:547–63.

MacKenzie, D. L. 1997. "Criminal Justice and Crime Prevention." Pp. 9.1–9.76 in *Preventing Crime: What Works, What Doesn't, What's Promising,* edited by L. W. Sherman, D. C. Gottfredson, D. MacKenzie, J. Eck, P. Reuter, and S. Bushway.

Washington, DC: Office of Juvenile Justice and Delinquency Prevention.

MacKenzie, D. L., R. Brame, D. McDowall, and C. Souryal. 1995. "Boot Camp Prisons and Recidivism in Eight States." *Criminology* 33 (3): 401–30.

MacKenzie, D. L. and E. E. Hebert, eds. 1996. *Correctional Boot Camps: A Tough Intermediate Sanction.* Washington, DC: National Institute of Justice, U.S. Department of Justice.

MacKenzie, D. L. and D. Parent. 1992. "Boot Camp Prisons for Young Offenders." Pp. 103–19 in *Smart Sentencing: The Emergence of Intermediate Sanctions,* edited by J. M. Byrne, A. J. Lurigio, and J. Petersilia. Newbury Park, CA: Sage.

MacKenzie, D. L. and C. Souryal. 1995. "Inmate Attitude Change during Incarceration: A Comparison of Boot Camp with Traditional Prison." *Justice Quarterly* 12 (2): 325–54.

MacKenzie, D. L., G. J. Styve, and A. R. Gover. 1998. "Performance-Based Standards for Juvenile Corrections." *Corrections Management Quarterly* 2:28–35.

Mak, A. S. 1990. "Testing a Psychological Control Theory of Delinquency." *Criminal Justice and Behavior* 17:215–30.

——. 1991. "Psychosocial Control Characteristics of Delinquents and Nondelinquents." *Criminal Justice and Behavior* 18:287–303.

Mitchell, O., A. R. Gover, G. J. Styve, and D. L. MacKenzie. (forthcoming). "Staff Perceptions of the Environment and Work Conditions in Juvenile Boot Camps and Traditional Facilities." *Justice Research and Policy* 1:1–22.

Moos, R. H. 1968. "The Assessment of the Social Climates of Correctional Institutions." *Journal of Research in Crime and Delinquency* 5:173–88.

Morash, Merry and Lila Rucker. 1990. "A Critical Look at the Idea of Boot Camp as a Correctional Reform." *Crime and Delinquency* 36:204–22.

Palmer, T. 1974. "The Youth Authority's Community Treatment Project." *Federal Probation* 30:3–14.

Sampson, R. J. and J. H. Laub. 1993. *Crime in the Making.* Cambridge, MA: Harvard University Press.

Sechrest, D. D. 1989. "Prison 'Boot Camps' Do Not Measure Up." *Federal Probation* 53:15–20.

Shields, I. W. and M. Ball. 1990. "Neutralization in a Population of Incarcerated Young Offenders." Presented at the annual meeting of the Canadian Psychological Association, Ottawa, Ontario.

Shields, I. W. and G. C. Whitehall. 1994. "Neutralizations and Delinquency among Teenagers." *Criminal Justice and Behavior* 21:223–35.

Simons, R. L., C. Johnson, R. D. Conger, and G. Elder, Jr. 1998. "A Test of Latent Trait versus Life-Course Perspectives on the Stability of Adolescent Antisocial Behavior." *Criminology* 36 (2): 217–44.

Spielberger, C. D., R. L. Gorsuch, and R. E. Lushene. 1970. *Manual for the State-Trait Anxiety Inventory.* Palo Alto, CA: Consulting Psychologists Press.

StataCorp. 1999. *Stata Statistical Software: Release 6.0.* College Station, TX: Stata Corporation.

Steinhart, D. 1993. "Juvenile Boot Camps: Clinton May Rev Up an Old Drill." *Youth Today,* January/February. 2:15–16.

Styve, G. J., D. L. MacKenzie, A. R. Gover, and O. Mitchell. 2000. "Perceived Conditions of Confinement: A National Evaluation of Juvenile Boot Camps and Traditional Facilities." *Law and Human Behavior* 24 (3): 297–308.

White, J. L., T. E. Moffitt, A. Caspi, D. J. Bartusch, D. J. Needles, and M. Stouthamer-Loeber. 1994. "Measuring Impulsivity and Examining Its Relationship to Delinquency." *Journal of Abnormal Psychology* 103:192–205.

Wright, K. N. 1985. "Developing the Prison Environment Inventory." *Journal of Research in Crime and Delinquency* 22:257–77.

——. 1991. "A Study of Individual, Environmental, and Interactive Effects in Explaining Adjustment to Prison." *Justice Quarterly* 8:217–42.

Wright, K. and L. Goodstein. 1989. "Correctional Environments." Pp. 253–70 in *The American Prison,* edited by L. Goodstein and D. L. MacKenzie. New York: Plenum.

Zachariah, J. K. 1996. "An Overview of Boot Camp Goals, Components, and Results." Pp. 17–38 in *Correctional Boot Camps: A Tough Intermediate Sanction,* edited by D. L. MacKenzie and E. E. Hebert. Washington, DC: National Institute of Justice, U.S. Department of Justice.

Zamble, E. and F. J. Porporino. 1988. *Coping, Behavior, and Adaptation in Prison Inmates.* New York: Springer-Verlag.

DISCUSSION QUESTIONS

1. Provide an argument for and against the use of stressful and anxiety-provoking activities to encourage change in residents of boot camps or other correctional programs or facilities.

2. Give examples of how a juvenile boot camp or a traditional juvenile facility may change youths' positive social bonds, impulsivity and control, and antisocial attitudes.

3. What were some surprising or unexpected findings in this study? Based on previous research and the authors' discussion of the findings in this study, what do you believe are some reasons for the findings of juveniles' different perceptions of boot camps and traditional institutions?

4. Imagine that a Special Legislative Committee on Corrections in your state has requested suggestions and recommendations for boot camp and traditional correctional institutions. Based on the findings of this study, what would you recommend?

READING

The number of incarcerated juveniles has not increased as dramatically as the adult prison population in the United States, but institutionalized juveniles who have committed violent offenses constitute the population most at risk of becoming the next generation of adult prisoners. The authors of this article selected a sample of youth incarcerated in state training schools of the Texas Youth Commission. They examined gender differences among numerous self-report measures, including violence, maltreatment, life stress, and depression. Statistical analyses revealed that age, minority status, substance dependency, life stress, and gang membership were significantly related to violent offending. Analyses also revealed that several variables were related to depression among incarcerated male and female delinquents. The article concludes with a discussion of policy implications for incarcerated delinquents.

_____ The Next Generation of Prisoners _____

Toward an Understanding of Violent Institutionalized Delinquents

Ashley G. Blackburn, Janet L. Mullings, James W. Marquart, Chad R. Trulson

On any given day in the United States, there are more than 90,000 juveniles confined in juvenile correctional institutions (Sickmund, Sladky, & Kang, 2005). Of these 90,000 institutionalized juveniles, 40% have been confined for committing a violent offense (Sickmund et al., 2005). Although policy makers and politicians tend to place a disproportionate focus on adult offenders, attention to institutionalized juvenile populations is justified on a number of fronts. One of the most significant concerns with the population of institutionalized juveniles is that they are most at risk of facing adult imprisonment once they exit the juvenile justice system and transition from adolescence to adulthood. In essence, previously institutionalized delinquents are most at risk of becoming the next generation of prisoners.

This concern is not without merit, for recidivism figures have estimated that, in some states, as many as 55% of institutionalized juveniles will recidivate back into the criminal justice system as adults, many for a violent offense (Snyder & Sickmund, 2006). Although not all repeat offenders will be institutionalized as adults, a significant portion will be, which makes a focus on institutionalized delinquents particularly important.

Perhaps more so than other institutionalized delinquents, incarcerated delinquents with violent tendencies often enter state institutions with multiple problems ranging from substance abuse, to mental illness, to stress brought on by traumatic life events. Many of these problems co-occur, making it increasingly difficult to treat and rehabilitate these multiple problem offenders.

SOURCE: *Youth Violence and Juvenile Justice* (5)1, 35–56, January 2007. DOI: 10.11/1541204006295156. © 2007 Sage Publications, Inc.

Juvenile correctional institutions are often faced with the responsibility of attending to these multiple problems while also ensuring that the juvenile is sufficiently punished for his or her acts. These sometimes-conflicting goals of rehabilitation and punishment often confound the process of juvenile corrections. Increased awareness concerning the special problems of the violent juvenile offender may decrease the chance that they will return to either the juvenile or adult correctional systems as violent adult offenders.

The route to violent offending by juveniles is long and influenced by many social and psychological factors. This article examines a group of juvenile offenders, many of whom are violent, housed in the Texas Youth Commission (TYC). This article first reviews the relevant literature concerning violent juvenile offending. It then examines gender differences in delinquent history and self-reported violent offending among this sample of institutionalized delinquents. It also examines gender differences on indicators such as maltreatment, life stress, mental health history, and depression. Multivariate analyses then examine the predictors of violent offending and depression among this sample of institutionalized offenders. This article concludes with a discussion of policy implications for institutionalized juveniles.

Violence Committed by Incarcerated Juveniles

An increase in juvenile arrests for Violent Crime Index offenses between the years 1988 and 1994 returned the national spotlight to violent juveniles. Awareness of increased violence among juvenile populations resulted in a media blitz on the issue as well as new policy initiatives focused on violent juvenile offenders, including more stringent arrest and court-based policies. After peaking in 1994, juvenile arrests for Violent Crime Index offenses declined steadily from 1995 to 1999 (Snyder, 2000). In 2003, the juvenile arrest rate for Violent Crime Index offenses

continued to decline for the ninth consecutive year, reaching its lowest level since at least 1980 and falling 48% from its highest peak in 1994 (Snyder, 2005).

Even with a decline in the juvenile crime rate, according to the Census of Juveniles in Residential Placement (CJRP), in 2003 there was a nationwide total of 96,655 delinquent juveniles housed in residential placement facilities: 878 for homicide offenses, 7,452 for sexual assault offenses, 7,495 for aggravated assault offenses, and 6,230 for robbery offenses, for a total of 22,055 Violent Crime Index offenders (Snyder & Sickmund, 2006). Between 1997 and 1999, the state of Texas witnessed a 10% increase in the incarcerated juvenile male population and a 16% increase in the incarcerated juvenile female population. Of that population, 29% were Violent Crime Index offenders (Sickmund, 2004). In 2003, 6,687 boys and 972 girls in the state of Texas were housed in residential placement, of which 2,049 (1,881 males and 168 females) were incarcerated for committing Violent Crime Index offenses (Sickmund et al., 2005). Although violent arrests have decreased in the past several years, there is clearly a need to continue to examine the experiences and outcomes of violent juvenile populations.

Factors Affecting the Onset and Continuance of Juvenile Violence

Violent behavior is thought to progress in one of two developmental trajectories: early and late-onset violent behaviors. Early onset groups include those children committing their first violent act before puberty. Late-onset groups include those youth who do not become violent until adolescence. Early onset individuals are projected to be more violent, with increased rates of offending and a greater persistence of violent offending between childhood and adulthood (Stattin & Magnusson, 1996). Although the majority of violent youths are late onset

Sameroff, 1985; Compas, 1987; Compas, Howell, Phares, Williams, & Giunta, 1989). Therefore, it is important that attention is focused on life events causing stress among juveniles, especially juveniles who react to such stress with violent behaviors or delinquency.

Inner-city youth living in impoverished neighborhoods feel stress because of their existence in an unpredictable and often unsafe environment (Warner & Weist, 1996). In their examination on the effects of socioeconomic status and maltreatment on delinquency, Leiter, Myers, and Zingraff (1994) found socioeconomic status to be a significant risk factor in delinquency for children living below the poverty line. McLoyd (1998) further described the negative impact of poverty on academic achievement, aggression, and overall socioemotional functioning. It is certainly true that not all individuals raised in poverty-stricken families turn to delinquency or violence. The increased stress and fear found among those living in impoverished environments, however, does raise the chance of youth turning to delinquency for economic gain or becoming part of a subculture, such as a gang, in which violence is used as a form of expression. Therefore, characteristics of these environments as well as the effects such an environment has on individual attitudes and behaviors should be further examined.

Parental incarceration has also been shown to be a life stressor for youth. Adolescents who lose one or both of their parents to incarceration are affected by not only the loss of their parent but also by the behavior of their parental role model. It has been noted in the literature that children raised in families in which a parent is incarcerated are negatively affected as pertains to their development into well-functioning adolescents and adults (Johnson, 1995). In her examination of 1,112 youth, of which 31% had a parental history of incarceration, Dannerbeck (2005) found that juveniles with such a history will often be negatively affected by ineffective parenting and therefore more likely to have more serious and longer lasting delinquent histories themselves. However, Dannerbeck did not find evidence that parental incarceration history predicts delinquency. It is evident that losing a parent, whether to an illness, death, or incarceration, can be an extremely stressful event in a child's life that often has long-lasting negative effects.

School failure or becoming a "dropout" may also serve as an increased stressor for youth. Such behavior is often related to issues such as poverty and school environment (Kozol, 1991). The stigma attached to academic failure can be difficult for an adolescent to overcome. However, studies examining the relationship between academic failure and violent delinquency have found that this relationship is not causal. For example, Snyder and Sickmund (1995) have argued that although academic failure may lead to achievement problems as an adult, such failure does not predict violence or other serious delinquency. Academic achievement or failure could, however, affect the self-esteem of an individual. Although causal links have not been found between school failure and violent delinquency, such failure could lead to other problems that follow adolescents throughout their life course and therefore should not be ignored.

Rates of depression and suicide among adolescents in the United States are among the highest as compared to other countries across the globe (Sheras, 2000). Increased rates of depression have also been found among incarcerated populations (Boothby & Durham, 1999; Eyestone & Howell, 1994). Messier and Ward (1998) found that 37% of their sample of incarcerated youth were at risk for clinical depression. Although the prevalence rate of major depression is estimated to be between 5% and 8% among the U.S. population (Shaffer et al., 1996; U.S. Department of Health and Human Services, 2000), Teplin, Abram, McClelland, Dulcan, and Mericle (2002), in their study of detained youth, found that 13.0% of boys and 21.6% of girls met the criteria for a major depressive episode in the past 6 months. Higher rates of depression among incarcerated juveniles pose a significant concern for juvenile justice officials in that the disorder must be recognized, diagnosed, and treated for each individual. This translates into a need for increased staff, training, and other resources, which may stretch an already tight budget.

There are various pathways leading to depression or depressive episodes among youth. Child maltreatment, especially sexual and physical abuse, has been found to severely increase the probability that a juvenile will become depressed (Cermak & Molidor, 1996; Kaufman, 1991). Depression has been found in higher rates among adolescents who were direct victims of abuse as compared to those adolescents who never suffered such victimizations (Allen & Tarnowski, 1989; Kaufman, 1991). Interestingly, Gover (2004), in her examination of sexually abused incarcerated youth, found gender differences to be invariant as pertains to depressive relationships. This implies that although the rates of depression are higher among incarcerated juvenile females, their male counterparts who have been sexually abused are also more likely to report depression.

Although maltreatment has been shown again and again to be related to depression in adolescents, there are other factors that may lead to depressed feelings among incarcerated youth. The life stressors discussed above may also enhance feelings of depression. Living in an impoverished, unsafe environment; losing a loved one, especially a parent, to death or incarceration; and/or academic failure and the resulting shame can each have a negative effect on a child's sense of self-worth and emotional stability. Confinement may also increase the appearance of depression in institutionalized youth samples. The mere loss of freedom and perhaps the realization of, and guilt concerning, their actions may increase the chance of depressive symptoms among this population.

Depression is found at alarming rates among the incarcerated juvenile population. Mental issues associated with depression have been found to be related to increased aggression among both juvenile males and females (Knox, Carey, & Kim, 2003). Conducting further research on this disorder and its related symptoms will determine whether there is a causal relationship between depression and violent juvenile offending. In the meantime, establishing prevention efforts and treatment paradigms for those incarcerated juveniles suffering from depression provides a way to confront the issue before it worsens.

Summary

Each of the factors discussed above has been shown to contribute to violent juvenile offending and will be examined further in the present study. Exposure to violence—whether through media, family, or peers, including fellow gang members—leaves youth, both male and female, prone to accept and participate in violent activities. Childhood maltreatment and other life stressors have also been shown to negatively affect a juvenile's ability to function normally in everyday life. Traumatized or overstressed children may turn to violence and delinquency for a number of reasons, including learning such behavior from a parent who is abusive or incarcerated. Furthermore, depression and substance abuse have been shown to increase the likelihood of aggression by afflicted individuals. If these issues are recognized and attended to by juvenile correctional officials as a cause of violent juvenile offending, perhaps it would lessen violent recidivism.

⊠ The Present Study

This study aims to add to the existing literature by offering a comparison of juvenile males to juvenile females incarcerated in TYC facilities. The goal is to ascertain whether there are significant differences concerning the above-mentioned issues between these populations. It is hoped that the findings and implications can be used to better understand gender differences in violence and mental health among violent incarcerated delinquents, leading to an increased awareness of this issue and to enhanced policy and treatment initiatives.

Previous research has identified numerous factors related to violent juvenile delinquency. Although in the past female juvenile delinquents were not thought to be violent offenders, the gender gap appears to be closing. The fact that more than 90,000 juveniles nationwide are currently incarcerated, many for violent offenses, poses a complex problem for the community at large and the justice system as a whole (Sickmund, Sladky, & Kang, 2005). Much of the research in this area examines individual issues as they relate to violent delinquency. Based on the research, our analyses examine whether there are gender differences in violent behavior and depression among a sample of newly incarcerated youth while considering the effects of maltreatment, poverty, life stress, gang membership, substance dependency, academic failure, and parental incarceration.

Specifically, we look to answer the following research questions: (a) Are there significant differences between male and female institutionalized delinquents in self-reported violent behavior? (b) Are there significant differences between male and female institutionalized delinquents in self-reported depression? and (c) Are intervening variables such as gang membership, life stress, child maltreatment, mental health, and substance abuse significant in predicting violent behavior and depression? Based on the literature, we hypothesize that there will be significant gender differences in both the self-reporting of violent behavior and depression. Furthermore, we hypothesize that gang membership, child maltreatment, mental health, substance abuse, and life stress will all be significant predictors of violent behavior and depression.

⚒ Data and Methods

Data Collection

Secondary data analysis will be employed to examine data originally collected for the Texas Commission on Alcohol and Drug Abuse (TCADA) by the Texas A&M University Public Policy Research Institute. Face-to-face interviews were conducted with newly admitted male and female delinquent youth to the TYC intake facility at Marlin, Texas between February 2000 and February 2001. Texas is home to the third-largest youth correctional system in the United States, which provides a unique opportunity for in-depth examination of a sizeable number of incarcerated youthful offenders ($N = 1,083$) who demographically mirror national level data (Snyder & Sickmund, 2006).

Youth were randomly selected from newly entering offender rosters and were asked to participate in the study. Few refusals produced a response rate of 98%. The face-to-face interviews took an average of 45 minutes to complete. The questionnaire consisted of six areas: prevalence of licit and illicit substance use, criminal history, physical and mental health, high-risk sexual behaviors, prior physical and sexual abuse, and demographics. Trained local public school teachers conducted the face-to-face interviews in private administrative offices located in the facility using laptops with Computer Assisted Personal Interviewing software.

Measures

Dependent Variables

The overall objective of this study is to examine differences in violent offending and depression between newly incarcerated male and female youth. The first dependent variable is violent offending and reflects recent (rather than lifetime) violent offending activity. To capture recent violent offending, subjects were asked how often they had engaged in the following behaviors during the 12 months prior to incarceration: (a) robbery with a gun, (b) robbery with a knife, (c) robbery without a weapon, (d) injured or killed someone, (e) threatened another with a gun, (f) threatened another with a knife, (g) shot a gun at someone, (h) cut someone with a knife, (i) sexually assaulted another, (j) beat up another person, and (k) participated in a drive-by shooting. These 11 items were summed together to create a violent behavior scale (range 0–10). This scale was dichotomized (0 = no, 1 = yes), representing what we termed "violent offender," which included those youth who reported currently serving a sentence for a violent crime and/or had committed at least one of the violent behaviors listed above in the past year ($n = 812$).

The second dependent variable of interest in this study was reported levels of depression between male and female youth. Using a shortened scale taken from the Center for Epidemiologic Studies Depression (CES-D) scale measure, we examined responses to five widely used items for depression. Subjects were asked how often during the same 12-month period, they had (a) a poor appetite, (b) felt depressed, (c) restless sleep, (d) felt sad, and/or (e) lost interest in usually enjoyable things. Reliability analysis revealed that these five items produced an alpha of .76. In addition, a confirmatory factor analysis indicated that all five items factored on one factor with all items loading at the .60 level or higher. This depression factor explained 50% of the variance among the items.

Demographic and Control Variables

Age was measured as a continuous metric variable in years. Race was dichotomized to represent 0 = nonminority, or White, and 1 = minority, or non-White. For gender, 0 = female and 1 = male. A proxy measure for "poverty" was measured by whether the subjects reported qualifying for free lunch programs at their school (0 = no, 1 = yes). The variable "drop out" represents youth who reported that they had dropped out of school prior to incarceration (0 = no, 1 = yes).

Stressful Life Events

Two single-item measures represent childhood abuse experiences of the subjects. Child sexual and child physical abuse were measured by two items asking: "About how many times while growing up were you: (a) beaten or seriously physically hurt by an adult? and (b) sexually mistreated, abused, or raped?" Youth who reported these experiences were classified as having been sexually and/or physically abused. Also, childhood neglect experiences were assessed by six items asking how often the youth (a) had no place to live, (b) did not have enough food to eat, (c) had inadequate clothing to wear, (d) was left alone when too young, (e) was not taken care of when sick or hurt, and (f) felt unsafe or in danger. These six items were summed together to represent childhood neglect. Reliability analysis produced an alpha of .75 for all six items. Confirmatory factor analysis revealed that all items factored on one factor with factor loadings of .63 and higher. This factor explained 48% of the variance among all six items.

To assess the impact of stressful life events as they differentiate violent offending and depression between boys and girls, a life stress scale was developed. Respondents were asked whether the following events had occurred during the past 2 years: (a) A parent or guardian lost his or her job, (b) parents or guardians divorced, (c) a new adult moved into their household, (d) they moved to a new place, (e) they changed schools, and/or (f) someone close to them had died. These six dichotomous items were summed to create the life stress scale.

Three additional single-item measures frequently associated with violent offending and depression among youth were also examined: (a) whether a parent had ever served time in jail or prison; (b) whether the youth had ever felt dependent on alcohol or drugs; and (c) whether the youth had ever been a gang member. All three dichotomous variables were measured as 0 = no and 1 = yes.

Analytic Strategy

Analysis for this study proceeds in three stages. First, we use descriptive bivariate statistics (i.e., chi-square and *t* tests) to examine differences in violent offending behavior, mental health histories, and depression scores between male and female offenders. In addition, bivariate correlation analysis is used to examine associations among all of the variables in the study. The second stage of analysis uses logistic regression to examine the effect of the predictor variables on violent offending. This analysis also allows us to determine whether gender is a significant predictor of violent offending after controlling for other demographic and independent variables. The final stage of the analysis uses OLS multiple regression to examine the effect of predictor variables when regressed on the depression scores. Again, we focus on the impact of gender on predicting differences in depression scores among the sample.

Sample

The average age of the subjects in this study ($N = 1,083$) was 15 years old. The majority was male (81%) and non-White (76%). Twenty percent reported that they had dropped out of school prior to incarceration, and the majority (58%) qualified for "free lunch" programs at their school. Regarding criminal histories, on average, the youth reported that they had been arrested six times ($M = 5.96$; $SD = 5.36$), served nearly five times ($M = 4.74$; $SD = 3.86$) in a juvenile detention facility, and had been placed on juvenile probation nearly two times ($M = 1.75$) in the past. For each measure of contact with the juvenile justice system, the average age for first contact was 13 years old. This sample generally parallels national data regarding background characteristics of incarcerated youth in general (Snyder & Sickmund, 2006).

Results

Table 1 presents demographic, criminal history, and violent offending behavior differences between males ($n = 874$) and females ($n = 208$) in the sample. Few significant differences for demographic and criminal history characteristics were noted between males and females. Males were significantly more likely to be older than females ($M = 15.4$ and $M = 15.3$, respectively). Males were also significantly more likely to be minorities than females (79% versus 64%).

Interestingly, females reported having been arrested more times than males ($M = 6.64$ and $M = 5.36$, respectively). Furthermore, female offenders were significantly more likely to have reported involvement in various violent offending behaviors during the prior year than male offenders (see Table 1). Specifically, girls were more likely to have threatened someone with a knife, cut someone with a knife, seriously injured or killed someone, or participated in a drive-by shooting and were more likely to be currently incarcerated for a violent offense than boys. Their increased violent involvement resulted in a higher mean on the summed violent behavior scale ($M = 2.60$; $SD = 2.40$) than the boys ($M = 2.17$; $SD = 2.21$). The dichotomized measure for any violent behavior revealed no significant gender differences, thus revealing that although males and females were equally as likely to report involvement in any violent activity in the past year, girls were more likely to engage in four of the specific offenses and to be incarcerated for a violent offense.

These findings are consistent with other research purporting the current trend of increased violent offending by female youth (Steffensmeier, Shwartz, Zhong, & Ackerman, 2005). Furthermore, the finding by Loper and

Table 1   Bivariate Differences in Demographic Characteristics and Offending Patterns

Variables Demographics	Total Sample (N = 1,083)		Males (n = 874)		Females (n = 208)	
	M	SD	M	SD	M	SD
Age (range 11–18)	15.4	1.12	15.4*	1.13	15.3	1.08
	No.	%	No.	%	No.	%
Minority	824	76	690***	79	134	64
School dropout	215	20	167	19	48	23
Qualify for free lunch	631	58	517	59	114	55
Criminal history	M	SD	M	SD	M	SD
No. times arrested	5.96	5.36	5.79	5.25	6.64*	5.72
Age at first arrest	13.02	1.71	13.02	1.73	13.02	1.59
No. times juvenile detention	4.74	3.86	4.65	3.86	5.09	3.84
Age at first detention	13.45	1.60	13.47	1.60	13.34	1.58
No. times juvenile probation	1.75	1.31	1.77	1.34	1.65	1.14
Age at first probation	13.39	1.56	13.41	1.57	13.29	1.45
This past year, have you engaged in:	No.	%	No.	%	No.	%
Robbery with no weapon	210	19	176	20	34	16
Robbery with gun	140	13	113	13	27	13
Robbery with knife	39	4	29	3	10	5
Beat someone up without weapons	600	56	473	54	127	61
Threaten with knife	193	18	133	15	60	29***
Threaten with gun	208	19	168	19	40	19
Cut someone with knife	111	10	66	8	45	22***
Shot someone with gun	211	20	183*	21	28	14
Seriously injured or killed someone	190	18	142	16	48	23*
Sexual assault or rape	77	7	67	8	10	5
Participate in drive-by	190	18	143	16	47	23*
Currently sentenced for violent offense	276	26	210	24	66	32*
	M	SD	M	SD	M	SD
Violent scale mean (range 0–10)	2.25	2.21	2.17	2.15	2.60*	2.40
	No.	%	No.	%	No.	%
Violent offender	812	75	650	74	162	78
Ever been a gang member	416	38	346	40	70	34
Parents ever serve time	325	30	253	29	72	35

*p < .05, ***p < .000.

Cornell (1996), that girls are more likely to use knives rather than firearms, is supported. The reported instances of violence also support the literature concerning girls' increased involvement in female gangs, as violent activities such as drive-by shootings and assaults are oftentimes common within the violent gang subculture (Prairie View Prevention Services, 2000). Taken as a whole, these findings support the current literature on violent delinquency committed by girls, both in frequency and type.

Of additional interest, no significant gender differences emerged for whether the youth had ever been a gang member, with 40% of the boys and 34% of the girls responding that they had been in a gang in the past. Also, both boys (29%) and girls (35%) were equally as likely to report having a parent who served time in jail or prison.

Table 2 presents the bivariate findings for gender differences in maltreatment and life stress among the sample. Child maltreatment experiences are prevalent for the total sample, with nearly one third of all of the youth offenders having experienced either sexual and/or physical abuse. Neglect experiences were also reported by many of the youth in the sample. When looking at gender differences in maltreatment experiences, it is clear that female offenders are significantly more likely than males to have experienced nearly all of the maltreatment items, a finding that supports past research (Wood et al., 2002). Specifically, more than half (54% compared to 24% of the boys) of the girls reported having experienced either sexual and/or physical abuse. Girls were also significantly more likely to have had no place to live (24% versus 15%), to have been left alone when they were too young (30% versus 19%), to have not been taken care of when sick or hurt (17% versus 10%), and to have felt unsafe or in danger while growing up (42% versus 28%). These combined neglect experiences resulted in higher mean scores on the neglect scale for girls ($M = 1.73$, $p < .01$) than for boys ($M = 1.02$).

Females were slightly more likely to report having experienced most of the stressful life events during the past 2 years. Females were significantly more likely (37%; $p < .000$) than boys (24%) to report having had a new adult move into their household. Girls also had a significantly higher mean score (2.65; $p < .05$) for the summed life stress items scale than boys (2.42).

Table 3 reveals that mental health issues and problems were most prevalent among the female offenders. Girls were significantly more likely to report having had contact with mental health systems. Specifically, girls reported being more likely to have seen a mental health professional in the past (53% versus 41%), more likely to have been subscribed prescription drags for mental health problems (50% versus 32%), and more likely to have been hospitalized in a mental health facility in the past (26% versus 11%). Moreover, girls reported greater suicide ideation ($M = .88$ versus .34 for males) and reported more mean attempts at suicide ($M = .66$ versus .21) than boys. Females were also more likely to report having felt dependent on drugs compared to males. The single item in Table 3 in which boys scored significantly higher than girls was the measure that asked them to rate their current mental health. Higher average scores for boys ($M = 3.13$) than girls ($M = 2.74$) indicates that male offenders rated their current mental health condition more favorably than did the females.

Similarly, female offenders scored higher on each depression measure than male offenders (see Table 3). Girls reported more frequently having a poor appetite ($M = 1.38$; $p < .000$; versus .73 for boys), feeling depressed ($M = 2.11$; $p < .000$; versus 1.41), having restless sleep ($M = 1.63$; $p < .000$; versus 1.27), feeling sad ($M = 2.08$, $p < .000$; versus 1.59), and losing interest in usually enjoyable things ($M = 1.73$; $p < .000$; versus 1.42). Higher levels of reporting for girls on the individual items resulted in a higher overall depression score ($M = 8.95$; $p < .000$) than boys ($M = 6.41$). These findings support past research finding that girls, more so than boys, will report symptoms of depression (Sheras, 2000; Teplin et al., 2002).

| Table 2 | Bivariate Differences in Maltreatment and Life Stress Scale Items |

Variables	Total Sample (N = 1,083)		Males (n = 874)		Females (n = 208)	
Maltreatment	No.	%	No.	%	No.	%
Abuse						
Physical	247	22.8	174	9.9	73	35.1**
Sexual	169	15.6	78	8.9	91	43.8**
Physical/sexual combined	326	30.1	213	24.4	113	54.3**
Neglect						
No place to live	181	16.7	132	15.1	49	23.6**
No food to eat	188	17.4	146	16.7	42	20.2
No clothes to wear	153	14.1	124	14.2	29	13.9
Left alone too young	226	20.9	163	18.6	63	30.3**
No care when sick/hurt	124	11.5	89	10.2	35	16.8**
Feel unsafe/in danger	329	30.4	242	27.7	87	41.8**
	M	SD	M	SD	M	SD
Neglect scale (range 0–6)	1.11	1.53	1.02	1.47	1.46**	1.73
Stress scale	No.	%	No.	%	No.	%
In the past 2 years, have/has:						
Your parent/s lost job?	352	33	283	33	69	33
Your parents divorced/separated?	262	24	208	24	54	26
You moved to new place?	547	51	443	51	104	50
A new adult moved into household?	285	26	209	24	76	37***
You changed schools?	606	56	479	55	127	61
Someone close to you died?	617	57	495	57	122	59
	M	SD	M	SD	M	SD
Stress scale (range 0–6)	2.46	1.45	2.42	1.42	2.65*	1.53

*$p < .05$, **$p < .01$, ***$p < .000$.

Table 4 presents correlations for the variables included in our multivariate analysis. The correlations show support for several hypotheses. In particular, having been physically abused, drug or alcohol dependent, having experienced more of the stressful life events, and having been a gang member are significantly associated with violent offending. Being a younger minority offender was also significantly associated with being a violent offender.

Table 3	Bivariate Differences in Mental Health Measures and Depression Scale Items					
Variables	Total Sample (N = 1,083)		Males (n = 874)		Females (n = 208)	
Mental health (MH)	No.	%	No.	%	No.	%
Have you ever:						
Seen an MH professional	467	43.2	357	40.8	110	52.9**
Taken MH prescription drugs	387	35.8	283	32.4	104	50.0***
Been hospitalized in a MH facility	151	14.0	96	11.0	55	26.4***
	M	SD	M	SD	M	SD
How often in the past year have you:[a]						
Had thoughts of suicide	0.45	0.87	0.34	0.76	0.88***	1.12
Attempted suicide	0.30	0.74	0.21	0.63	0.66***	1.00
How would you rate[b] your MH currently?	3.05	0.91	3.13***	0.88	2.74	0.96
	No.	%	No.	%	No.	%
Have you ever felt dependent on drugs?	302	27.9	230	26.3	72	34.6*
	M	SD	M	SD	M	SD
Depression scale						
How often in the past year have you:[a]						
Had a poor appetite	0.86	1.06	0.73	1.00	1.38***	1.15
Felt depressed	1.54	1.11	1.41	1.09	2.11***	0.98
Experienced restless sleep	1.34	1.17	1.27	1.17	1.63***	1.14
Felt sad	1.67	1.03	1.59	1.03	2.08***	0.93
Lost interest	1.48	1.13	1.42	1.12	1.73***	1.15
Depression scale (range 0–15)	6.90	3.90	6.41	3.79	8.95***	3.70
Alpha = .75						

a. Scale: 0 = never, 1 = rarely, 2 = sometimes, 3 = frequently.
b. Scale: 1 = poor, 2 = fair, 3 = good, 4 = excellent.

$*p < .05$, $**p < .01$, $***p < .000$.

Table 4 Correlations Among Study Variables

	1	2	3	4	5	6	7	8	9	10	11	12	13	14
1 Depression scale	1.00													
2 Violent juvenile	0.10**	1.00												
3 Age	−0.03	−0.07*	1.00											
4 Gender	−0.25**	−0.03	0.06*	1.00										
5 Minority	−0.15**	0.06*	0.01	0.13**	1.00									
6 School dropout	0.08**	0.05	0.10**	−0.03	0.05	1.00								
7 Qualify for free lunch	0.01	−0.01	−0.05	0.03	0.17**	0.02	1.00							
8 Physical abuse	0.23**	0.07*	0.01	−0.14**	−0.09**	0.00	0.06*	1.00						
9 Sexual abuse	0.27**	0.04	−0.02	−0.37**	−0.20**	−0.01	0.01	0.31**	1.00					
10 Neglect	0.30**	0.05	0.01	−0.13**	−0.16**	0.07*	0.11**	0.45**	0.35**	1.00				
11 Parents served time	0.01	0.05	−0.04	−0.04	0.10**	0.05	0.08**	0.05	0.02	0.08**	1.00			
12 Drug/alcohol dependent	0.26**	0.09**	0.09**	−0.07*	−0.13**	0.12**	−0.05	0.09**	0.08**	0.25**	0.08**	1.00		
13 Stress scale	0.14**	0.09**	−0.05	−0.06*	−0.04	−0.02	0.03	0.15**	0.07**	0.19**	0.14**	0.07*	1.00	
14 Gang member	0.03	0.20**	−0.05	0.04	0.16**	0.09**	0.04	0.00	−0.03	0.04	0.06*	0.16**	0.18	1.00

*p < .05, **p < .01.

Table 5	Logistic Regression of Effects of Variables on Violent Offending			
Variables	*B*	*SE*	*Wald*	*Exp. (B)*
Age	−0.16*	0.06	5.80	0.85
Gender	−0.06	0.20	0.10	0.93
Minority	0.35*	0.17	4.00	1.42
School dropout	0.25	0.19	1.68	1.29
Qualify for free lunch	−0.19	0.15	1.58	0.82
Any physical abuse	0.35	0.21	2.83	1.42
Any sexual abuse	0.27	0.24	1.25	1.31
Neglect	−0.01	0.06	0.05	0.98
Parents served time	0.07	0.16	0.18	1.07
Drug/alcohol dependent	0.35*	0.18	3.36	1.42
Stress scale	0.12*	0.05	5.76	1.13
Gang member	0.94***	0.17	31.14	2.59
Constant	2.64	1.06	6.20	14.08
X^2/df	76.27/12			
P	<.000			
Nagelkerke R^2	0.10			
Cox & Snell R^2	0.07			

*p < .05, **p < .01, ***p < .000.

The correlations also reveal important associations among many of the variables and depression scores. Specifically, being a violent offender; dropping out of school; having been physically or sexually abused, neglected, and drug or alcohol dependent; and having experienced more life-stress events are significantly associated with higher depression scores. Females and White, nonminority offenders also had higher depression scores.

Multivariate Analysis

The bivariate findings offer partial support for our hypotheses. Research examining violent offending and depression among male and female delinquents has identified many of these factors as important predictors of violence and depression. No studies, however, have examined all factors simultaneously with a large sample of incarcerated youth. To address this gap, we used logistic regression and OLS multiple regression to examine which variables predict (a) violent offenders and (b) depression scores among our sample of incarcerated youth.

Table 5 provides the results of the logistic regression model assessing the impact of control and predictor variables on violent offending. Three variables significantly predicted violent offending among the total sample. Specifically, we found that violent offenders in our sample were younger and of minority racial/ethnic classification. Our model reveals that younger offenders were 15% (odds ratio .85) more likely to be classified as a violent offender. Minority offenders were 42% (odds ratio 1.42) as likely to

| Table 6 | Multiple Regression Results for Study Variables Predicting Depression Score |

	Total			Males			Females		
Variables	b	SE	Beta	b	SE	Beta	b	SE	Beta
Age	−0.14	0.09	−0.04	−0.10	0.10	−0.03	−0.17	0.22	−0.05
Gender	−1.55***	0.29	−0.15						
Minority	−0.53*	0.26	−0.05	−0.63*	0.31	−0.06	−0.10	0.51	−0.01
School dropout	0.49	0.27	0.05	0.49	0.31	0.05	0.79	0.56	0.09
Qualify for free lunch	0.16	0.22	0.02	0.19	0.25	0.02	−0.30	0.47	−0.04
Physical abuse	0.71*	0.29	0.07	0.88**	0.33	0.09	0.31	0.56	0.04
Sexual abuse	1.20***	0.34	0.11	1.42**	0.44	0.10	1.16*	0.54	0.15
Parents served time	−0.31	0.23	−0.03	−0.11	0.27	−0.01	−0.94	0.48	−0.12
Neglect	0.34***	0.08	0.13	0.40***	0.09	0.15	2.55	0.17	0.01
Drug/alcohol dependent	1.64***	0.25	0.18	1.46***	0.29	0.17	2.38***	0.53	0.30
Stress scale	0.18*	0.07	0.06	9.98	0.08	0.03	0.51**	0.15	0.21
Violent juvenile	0.55*	0.25	0.06	0.49	0.28	0.05	0.88	0.57	0.09
Gang member	−4.45	0.23	−0.06	−0.15	0.25	−0.02	0.56	0.52	0.07
Constant	8.60***	1.54		6.67***	1.71		8.33*	3.55	
R^2	0.21			0.15			0.27		

*$p < .05$. **$p < .01$. ***$p < .000$.

report violent behavior as were White, nonminority youth. Furthermore, substance dependence, life stress, and gang membership were all significant predictors of violent offending. Our model reveals that substance-dependent juveniles were 42% (odds ratio 1.42) as likely to report violent behavior as non-substance-dependent juveniles. Juveniles experiencing high life stress during the past 2 years were 13% (odds ratio 1.13) more likely to be violent offenders. In addition, juveniles who reported membership in a gang were 2.5 times (odds ratio 2.59) more likely to be violent offenders. This indicates that gang membership is an exceptional predictor as to whether juveniles engage in violent activity. Most

important for the purposes of this study, gender did not significantly predict violent offending in our sample while controlling for other variables that have been identified as important factors in explaining gender differences in violent offending.

Depression Among Male and Female Offenders

When examining gender differences in self-reported depression among the sample, we were interested in exploring how many of the same variables used to predict violent offending might also explain higher levels of self-reported depression. In addition, we examined whether being a violent offender would result in higher levels of depression. Table 6 presents the results for three OLS regression models for the total sample, for males only, and for females only. Results for the total model reveal significant gender differences in levels of depression, with females having significantly higher scores on the depression scale. Gender accounts for the second most variance (Beta = −.15) in the depression scale, following drug or alcohol dependence (Beta = .18). Childhood maltreatment experiences emerged as significant for the total sample with physical abuse, sexual abuse, and neglect all predicting higher depression scores, a finding supported by past research (Briere, 1989; Finkelhor, 1990; Ratican, 1992). Those offenders who reported having experienced stressful life events in the past 2 years and those classified as violent offenders also significantly predicted higher depression scores. The total sample model predicted 21% of the variance in the depression scale ($R^2 = .21$).

To examine which factors might explain gender differences in depression scores, two separate models were developed by gender. Table 6 reveals several differences in predictors of depression between males and females. The regression model for males revealed that nonminority boys had higher depression scores. Furthermore, males who reported physical abuse, sexual abuse, or neglect also scored higher on the depression scale. Finally, males who were drug or alcohol dependent had higher depression scores. The model for males explained less variance than the model for the total sample ($R^2 = .15$).

The final model presented in Table 6 provides the coefficients for the female sample. Fewer factors emerged as significant predictors for female depression scores. Girls who reported sexual abuse, dependency on drugs or alcohol, and those experiencing life-stress events in the past 2 years had higher depression scores. However, these fewer factors explain the greatest variance in depression scores among the three models ($R^2 = .27$) and account for more than one quarter of the variance in the scores.

Limitations of This Study

The data used in this study are cross-sectional. Thus, the results reveal associations among the variables in this analysis. We cannot make causal statements about the findings because we do not know which variables precede others in time. The self-reporting nature of our data also presents limitations. Participants, if asked to report for a certain time period, may telescope events, including these in their responses. Furthermore, subjects can be untruthful in their answers, leading to over- or underestimation of occurrence. Finally, given the sensitive nature of some of the questions and the issue of social desirability, whereby answers thought to be expected were given rather than the truthful answers, may have confounded the findings. Although these limitations exist, our results do give insight into the lives of a large sample of newly incarcerated juvenile delinquents.

✎ Discussion

National statistics report that thousands of juveniles are committed annually to institutions for violent offenses. Although the rate of juvenile crime has slowed, institutional commitment levels remain high. The more than 90,000 juveniles currently incarcerated nationwide represent a significant treatment and managerial dilemma for the administrators of youth facilities. What makes their job increasingly difficult is that the public's focus has been—and probably will continue to be so for some time—on adult crime and adult corrections. Violent juveniles therefore represent a form of compound interest that clearly needs our focused attention.

The findings reported in this article paint a disturbing picture of violent delinquent offenders committed to Texas institutions. Girls, although they represent a clear minority of commitments, reported to have perpetrated more violent offenses than their male counterparts. Girls also reported higher levels of maltreatment and depression than did the male delinquents. The analysis of the incarcerated Texas delinquents also showed that physical abuse, drug or alcohol dependence, stressful life events, and gang membership were significantly related to violent offending. The data also clearly demonstrated that many violent juvenile offenders, both male and female, enter institutions with significant mental health issues. How these youth cope with and adjust to institutional life and then deal with their own personal issues and maladies, although beyond the scope of this article, represents a serious challenge for policy makers and the public alike.

On a larger level, mental health issues pose significant problems for juvenile justice administrators too. With so many violent juvenile delinquents under their care it is imperative that administrators develop policies and procedures conducive to both the treatment of mental illness, especially depression, and the securing of violent juveniles. Increased resources are needed to provide counseling, behavioral reconditioning, medications, and security for incarcerated juveniles suffering from mental illnesses. Resources are scarce however. For example, the Pennsylvania Department of Corrections estimates that the cost of incarceration for an average offender is $80 per day, whereas the cost of incarceration for a seriously mentally ill offender is $140 per day (American Psychiatric Association, 2004) Although this example uses incarcerated adult populations, it is estimated that the cost differentials are similar to those of incarcerated juvenile populations. In a study of a national sample of juvenile detention centers conducted by the Bazelon Center for Mental Health Law and the Special Investigations Division for the Democratic Staff of the U. S. House of Representatives, it was discovered that 347 of 500 facilities across the United States were currently housing youth awaiting treatment for mental illness (Santini, 2005).

Violent, mentally ill offenders are also more likely to reoffend and return to juvenile or adult institutions, especially if they are not diagnosed and treated. This only increases the need for early recognition and treatment of mentally ill populations coming to the attention of the juvenile justice system. Scarcity of resources is not just a juvenile justice problem. There is often a lack of community resources to treat mentally ill, violent juveniles as well. A lack of resources and treatment increases the likelihood that more violent juveniles will enter the juvenile justice system because they have not received the care, attention, education and treatment needed to control their feelings of anger and aggression.

It must be said that institutionalization of these offenders represents the easy way out, a convenient solution to a nagging social problem. However, our conscience tells us that we as a society cannot afford to "throw away" anyone. This is the dilemma that confronts our society when dealing with the thousands of violent youthful offenders who flow into state institutions annually. We realize that violent juvenile delinquents represent a hard-core group of offenders. Although these offenders are in the minority, they represent the "fodder" for adult institutions. Given the constellation of issues these offenders bring to an institution, single-treatment regimens, such as substance abuse treatment, may not be enough to keep these offenders from returning.

Overall there needs to be increased research, training, and services provided to incarcerated juveniles, especially violent girls and boys. Policy makers and funding organizations need to be aware of this critical issue that affects both the juvenile justice system and the communities to which these juveniles will one day return. Screening and assessment is imperative to identify those violent juveniles suffering from mental illnesses. If these youth are not identified, they will not receive the treatment needed to understand their disorder and overcome the violent tendencies often initiated by symptoms of mental illness. Treatment through the juvenile justice system should be integrated as well as gender-sensitive and gender-specific, recognizing that boys and girls suffer from different issues and their needs are diverse. Finally, re-entry programs will only serve to enhance the treatment obtained in the juvenile justice system and further increase juvenile delinquents' chances for success once they return to their families and communities. All of these issues need to be considered by juvenile justice system officials when creating and implementing new policies and programs directed at violent juvenile delinquents.

References

Allen, D., & Tarnowski, K. (1989). Depressive characteristics of physically abused children. *Journal of Abnormal Child Psychology, 17*, 1–11.

American Psychiatric Association (APA). (2004). *Mental illness and the criminal justice system: Redirecting resources toward treatment, not containment.* Retrieved on February 15, 2006, from the APA Web site: http://www.psych.org/downloads/MentalIllness.pdf

Barocas, R., Seifer, R., & Sameroff, A. J. (1985). Defining environmental risk: Multiple dimensions of psychological vulnerability. *American Journal of Community Psychology, 13*, 433–447.

Boothby, J. L., & Durham, T. W. (1999). Screening for depression in prisoners using the Beck Depression Inventory. *Criminal Justice and Behavior, 26*, 107–124.

Briere, J. (1989). *Therapy for adults molested as children.* New York: Springer.

Cermak, P., & Molidor, C. (1996). Male victims of child sexual abuse. *Child and Adolescent Social Work Journal, 13*, 385–398.

Compas, B. E. (1987). Stress and life events during childhood and adolescence. *Child Psychology Review, 7*, 275–302.

Compas, B. E., Howell, D. C., Phares, V., Williams, R. A., & Giunta, C. T. (1989). Risk factors for emotional/behavioral problems in young adolescents: A prospective analysis of adolescent and parental stress and symptoms. *Journal of Consulting and Clinical Psychology, 57*, 732–740.

Dannerbeck, A. (2005). Differences in parenting attributes, experiences, and behaviors of delinquent youth with and without a parental history of incarceration. *Youth Violence and Juvenile Justice, 3*(3), 199–213.

D'Unger, A. V., Land, K. C., McCall, P. L., & Nagan, D. S. (1998). How many latent classes of delinquent/criminal careers? Results from mixed Poisson regression analysis. *American Journal of Sociology, 103*, 1593–1620.

Eyestone, L. L., & Howell, R. J. (1994). An epidemiological study of attention-deficit hyperactivity disorder and major depression in a male prison population. *Bulletin of the American Academy of Psychiatry and the Law, 22*, 181–193.

Finkelhor, D. (1990). Early and long-term effects of child sexual abuse: An update. *Professional Psychology: Research and Practice, 21*, 325–330.

Gover, A. R. (2002). The effects of child maltreatment on violent offending among institutionalized youth. *Violence and Victims, 17*, 655–668.

Gover, A. R. (2004). Childhood sexual abuse, gender, and depression among incarcerated youth. *International Journal of Offender Therapy and Comparative Criminology, 48*(6), 683–696.

Gover, A. R., & MacKenzie, D. (2003). Child maltreatment and adjustment to juvenile correctional institutions. *Criminal Justice and Behavior, 30*(3), 374–396.

Huff, C. R. (1998). *Criminal behavior of gang members and at-risk youths* (NCJ Publication No. 164725). Washington, DC: U.S. Department of Justice (USDOJ), Office of Justice Programs, Office of Juvenile Justice and Delinquency Prevention (OJJDP).

Huizinga, D., Loeber, R., & Thornberry, T. P. (1995). *Recent findings from the program of research on the causes and correlates of delinquency* (NCJ 159042). Washington, DC: USDOJ, Office of Justice Programs, OJJDP.

Joe, K. A., & Chesney-Lind, M. (1995). "Just every mother's angel": An analysis of gender and ethnic variations in youth gang membership. *Gender and Society, 9*, 408–431.

Johnson, D. (1995). Effects of parental incarceration. In K. Gabel & D. Johnston (Eds.), *Children of incarcerated parents* (pp. 59–88). New York: Lexington Books.

Kaufman, J. (1991). Depressive disorders in maltreated children. *Journal of the American Academy of Child Adolescent Psychiatry, 30*, 257–265.

Knox, M., Carey, M., & Kim, W. J. (2003). Aggression in inpatient adolescents: The effects of gender and depression. *Youth and Society, 35*(2), 226–242.

Kozol, J. (1991). *Savage inequalities.* New York: Harper Perennial.

Leiter, J., Myers, K., & Zingraff, M. (1994). Substantiated and unsubstantiated cases of child maltreatment: Do their consequences differ? *Social Work Research, 18*(2), 67–82.

Levinthal, C. (2006). *Drugs, society, and criminal justice.* New York: Pearson Education.

Lexcen, F., & Redding, R. (2000). *Mental health needs of juvenile offenders. Juvenile justice fact sheet.* Charlottesville: University of Virginia Institute of Law, Psychiatry, and Public Policy.

Loeber, R., Farrington, D. P., & Waschbusch, D. A. (1998). Serious and violent juvenile offenders. In R. Loeber & D. P. Farrington (Eds.), *Serious and violent juvenile offenders: Risk factors and successful interventions* (pp. 13–29). Thousand Oaks, CA: Sage.

Loper, A. B., & Cornell, D. G. (1996). Homicide by juvenile girls. *Journal of Child and Family Studies, 5,* 323–336.

McLoyd, V. C. (1998). Socioeconomic disadvantage and child development. *American Psychologist, 53,* 185–204.

Messier, L. P., & Ward, T. J. (1998). The coincidence of depression and high ability in delinquent youth. *Journal of Child and Family Studies, 7,* 97–105.

Miller, W. B. (2001). *The growth of youth gang problems in the United States: 1970–98.* Washington, DC: USDOJ, Office of Justice Programs, OJJDP.

Nagin, D., & Tremblay, R. E. (1999). Trajectories of boys' physical aggression, opposition, and hyperactivity on the path to physically violent and nonviolent juvenile delinquency. *Child Development, 70,* 1181–1196.

Osgood, D. W. (1995). *Drugs, alcohol, and adolescent violence.* Boulder, CO: Center for the Study of the Prevention of Violence, Institute of Behavioral Sciences.

Palmer, C. T., & Tilley, C. F. (1995). Sexual access to females as a motivation for joining gangs: An evolutionary approach. *Journal of Sexual Research, 32,* 213–217.

Prairie View Prevention Services. (2000). *Gangs: What every adult needs to know.* Retrieved on March 20, 2006, from: http://www.prairieview.net/Gangs%201.htm

Ratican, K. L. (1992). Sexual abuse survivors: Identifying symptoms and special treatment considerations. *Journal of Counseling and Development, 77,* 33–38.

Reese, L., Vera, E., Thompson, K., & Reyes, R. (2001). A qualitative investigation of perceptions of violence risk factors in low-income African American children. *Journal of Clinical Child Psychology, 30*(2), 161–171.

Santini, J. (2005). *More mentally ill teens landing in justice system.* Retrieved February 10, 2006, from the National Alliance for the Mentally Ill—Santa Cruz County Web site: http://www.namiscc.org/News/2005/Winter/TeensNeedMentalHealthServices.htm

Shaffer, D., Gould, M. S., Fisher, P., Trautment, P., Moreau, D., Kleinman, M., et al. (1996). Psychiatric diagnosis in child and adolescent suicide. *Archives of General Psychiatry, 53,* 339–348.

Sheras, P. L. (2000). *Depression and suicide in juvenile offenders, Juvenile justice fact sheet.* Charlottesville: University of Virginia, Institute of Law, Psychiatry and Public Policy.

Sickmund, M. (2004). *Juveniles in corrections.* Juvenile Offenders and Victims Bulletin. Washington, DC: USDOJ, Office of Justice Programs, OJJDP.

Sickmund, M., Sladky, T. J., & Kang, W. (2005). *Census of juveniles in residential placement databook.* Retrieved March 16, 2006, from http://www.ojjdp.ncjrs.org/ojsatbb/cjrp

Simkin, S., & Katz, S. (2002). Criminalizing abused girls. *Violence against Women, 8*(2), 1474–1499.

Snyder, H. (2000). Juvenile arrests 1999. *Juvenile Justice Bulletin.* Washington, DC: USDOJ, Office of Justice Programs, OJJDP.

Snyder, H. (2005). Juvenile arrests 2003. *Juvenile Justice Bulletin.* Washington, DC: USDOJ, Office of Justice Programs, OJJDP.

Snyder, H., & Sickmund, M. (1995). *Juvenile offenders and victims: A national report.* Washington, DC: USDOJ, Office of Justice Programs, OJJDP.

Snyder, H., & Sickmund, M. (2006). *Juvenile offenders and victims: 2006 national report.* Washington, DC: USDOJ, Office of Justice Programs, OJJDP, National Center for Juvenile Justice.

Stattin, H., & Magnusson, D. (1996). Antisocial development: A holistic approach. *Development and Psychopathology, 8,* 617–645.

Steffensmeier, D., Shwartz, J., Zhong, H., & Ackerman, J. (2005). An assessment of recent trends in girls' violence using diverse longitudinal sources: Is the gender gap closing? *Criminology, 43*(2), 355–406.

Steiner, H., Garcia, I. G., & Matthews, Z. (1997). Posttraumatic stress disorder in incarcerated juvenile delinquents. *Journal of the American Academy of Child and Adolescent Psychiatry, 36*, 357–365.

Teplin, L. A., Abram, K. M., McClelland, G. M., Dulcan, M. K., & Mericle, A. A. (2002). Psychiatric disorders in youth in juvenile detention. *Archives of General Psychiatry, 59*, 1133–1143.

Thornberry, T. P., & Burch, J. H. (1997). *Gang members and delinquent behavior* (NCJ Publication No. 165154). Washington, DC: USDOJ, Office of Justice Programs, OJJDP.

Tolan, P. H., & Gorman-Smith, D. (1998). Development of serious and violent offending careers. In R. Loeber & D. P. Farrington (Eds.), *Serious and violent juvenile offenders: Risk factors and successful interventions* (pp. 68–85). Thousand Oaks, CA: Sage.

U.S. Department of Health and Human Services. (2000). *Mental health: A report of the Surgeon General.* Rockville, MD: Author.

Warner, B. S., & Weist, M. D. (1996). Urban youth as witnesses to violence: Beginning assessment and treatment efforts. *Journal of Youth and Adolescence, 25*, 361–377.

Watters, J. K., Reinarman, C., & Fagan, J. (1985). Causality, context, and contingency: Relationships between drug abuse and delinquency. *Contemporary Drug Problems, 12*, 351–373.

Weist, M., Acosta, O., & Youngstrom, E. (2001). Predictors of violence exposure among inner-city youth. *Journal of Clinical Child Psychology, 30*(2), 187–198.

Wood, J., Foy, D., Layne, C., Pynoos, R., & James, C. B. (2002). An examination of the relationships between violence exposure, posttraumatic stress symptomatology and delinquent activity: An "eco-pathological" model of delinquent behavior among incarcerated adolescents. *Journal of Aggression, Maltreatment and Trauma, 6*(1), 127–147.

DISCUSSION QUESTIONS

1. Based on your understanding of previous research cited in the reading, what are some of the factors related to juveniles' involvement in violent behavior?

2. Based on the findings presented in Table 2, are there gender differences, and is there a relationship between maltreatment, abuse, and juvenile offending? Based on your understanding of crime causation, do you believe that is a causal relationship? Explain your reasons.

3. Based on the findings in Table 3, do mental health and depression seem to have a relationship with juvenile offending, and are there gender differences?

4. Based on the multivariate analyses, which variables seem to be most significant in explaining violent juvenile offending? Can you offer some possible explanations for those findings?

5. Despite some limitations to this study noted by the authors, what policies or prevention and treatment programs for at-risk youth seem to be appropriate as a means of reducing juvenile violent offending?

READING

One of the most critical challenges for juvenile corrections is the transition when juveniles reenter the community from correctional facilities. The authors of this article examine the connection between young offenders' transition into adulthood and reentry into their communities. In the article they discuss (a) reentry within a broader "reintegration" paradigm; (b) the mission and purpose of institutional and community corrections, as well as the tensions between them; (c) the intersection of chronological age and legal status; (d) the intersection of chronological age and stages of development; (e) risk and protective factors; and (f) the seven specific domains of reentry: family and living arrangement, peer groups, mental and physical health, education, vocational training and employment, substance abuse, and leisure and avocational interests. Particular attention is given to the need for reentry policies to be developmentally appropriate and age specific. The authors conclude with a discussion of the implications for reentry policy.

Adolescent and Teenage Offenders Confronting the Challenges and Opportunities of Reentry

David M. Altschuler, Rachel Brash

In the past several years, interest in offender reentry has grown. The reentry of offenders from correctional facilities back into community settings takes on a whole new meaning when the offenders are adolescents and teenagers. During the adolescent and teenage years, young people are in the midst of a developmental transition from childhood to adulthood, which spans physical, cognitive, emotional, and social conditions. Experimentation, rebellion, impulsiveness, insecurity, and moodiness frequently characterize this critical time period. In addition to facing this developmental transition, adolescent and teenage offenders must contend with a transition when reentering the community from correctional facilities. The challenges that arise from this dual transition are multifaceted and formidable.

The purpose of the article is to examine the connection between the transitions young offenders go through as they develop into adulthood and the transitions they face when reentering their communities. The article will also examine the various challenges and opportunities they face regardless of developmental phase. Understanding the double transition and how it affects young offenders across domains such as family, peer groups, and education is key to developing correctional programs and policies

SOURCE: *Youth Violence and Juvenile Justice,* (2)1, 72–87, January 2004. DOI: 10.1177/1541204003260048. © 2004 Sage Publications, Inc.

that ease young offenders' reentry to their communities and improve their likelihood of success.

Reentry should include both preparation for release (i.e., prerelease planning) and what happens following release from confinement (i.e., postrelease supervision and services in the community), although in practice reentry programs often address only the latter. In juvenile corrections, the term *aftercare* is frequently used to describe the postrelease community corrections period. The term *reintegration* conveys a much broader meaning than the terms *aftercare* and *reentry* (Altschuler & Armstrong, 2001). Reintegration focuses on offenders and their ability to function within society, as well as offenders' effect on their families, victims, the community at large, public safety, and the corrections system itself (e.g., prisons, parole, and contracted services). It addresses what occurs both while offenders are incarcerated and when they are back in the community.

The Reintegration Paradigm

Reintegration recognizes that the vast majority of offenders will eventually return to the community from confinement and that in the interest of both public safety and offender reformation, it makes sense to address the various risk and protective factors associated with offending behavior. We view reintegration as encompassing what occurs during and after confinement. Regardless of the level or type of reintegration, all programs based on a reintegration model do the following: (a) prepare offenders for reentry into the specific communities to which they will return, (b) establish the necessary arrangements and linkages with the full range of public and private sector organizations and individuals in the community that can address known risk and protective factors, and (c) ensure the delivery of prescribed services and supervision in the community. But this view of reintegration stands in marked contrast to routinely practiced reentry and aftercare programs, which focus primarily, if not exclusively, on supervision after community reentry and largely

ignore what takes place during confinement. In addition, community aftercare all too often falls far short on services and treatment, relying mostly on surveillance and monitoring.

Reentering the community from a correctional facility can be difficult even without the added challenge of handling the transition from childhood to adulthood (Travis, Solomon, & Waul, 2001). Most released offenders have difficulty simply managing the transition from the world of a correctional facility, where rigid, institutional culture predominates, to community corrections, which is characterized by much less regimentation and guidance. Release from a correctional facility is commonly followed by a period of time under community corrections authority, which may be termed *aftercare, postrelease supervision,* or *parole.* Institutional and community corrections, even when they are part of the same agency, have historically not coordinated their respective operations very well (Altschuler & Armstrong, 1995). Regardless of the specifics of the problems faced by youth, the reintegration paradigm helps show more clearly the range of challenges youth confront as they transition into society.

Mission and Purpose

Corrections policies, and the tensions within them, make up a central challenge to successful reentry. Institutional and community corrections differ by the very nature of their settings; the former involves residential facilities, whereas the latter does not. But the differences extend further. Institutional corrections typically focus principally on the offender. It ordinarily involves little to no direct involvement with the offender's social network (e.g., family, friends, and other peers) and other potential community-based resources and supports. Despite its proposed goal of offender change, an institutional correction often does not provide the means for such change. In some facilities, treatment for mental health problems and substance abuse as well as education, vocational training, and work experience are nonexistent, in short supply, of questionable quality, or inappropriate.

Community corrections is intended to focus on the offender's ecology, which refers to the environment an offender is returning to and all the complex elements that make up that environment, such as family, schooling, employment, and peer groups. It is widely acknowledged, however, that it often fails to do so. Upon an offender's reentry to the community, if not shortly beforehand, aftercare or parole staff assumes responsibility for the case. An offender may find the change in setting anxiety-producing, exhilarating, or both. At this point, an offender's social network, community resources and opportunities, and a host of temptations, influences, and realities come into play. Both the offender and the community corrections worker may find the many forces and influences hard to juggle. The qualifications and abilities of the corrections worker, the specific nature of the job responsibilities, caseload size, extent and nature of identified offender need and risk, overall workload, and the capacity of the community to join forces with corrections (e.g., ability and willingness to collaborate) are among the factors that will influence how the case gets handled.

Reintegration is the means by which institutional and community corrections can be bridged, for it takes into account both what happens when an offender is incarcerated and afterward. It also involves both offender change and offender ecology. The concept of reintegration rests on the premise that public safety is ultimately accomplished by offender reformation and opportunity. Accordingly, reintegration programs aim to develop offender competencies through various types of services and to guide offenders to crime-free lifestyles in the community. The central tenets or balanced and restorative justice (competency, public safety, and accountability) are compatible with reintegration (Bazemore & Umbreit, 1995). The same is not true for the more common deterrence model, the goal of which is not rehabilitation but punishment. Supporters of deterrence and zero tolerance approaches often view "doing time" or being appropriately punished as justice precisely because the sanction is demanding, depriving, and properly retributive. They view purposes such as restoration or rehabilitation as undermining the intent of the punishment. Supporters of deterrence may even regard such efforts as coddling offenders, despite evidence that offenders can emerge from deterrence-based programs embittered, disadvantaged, or vengeful (National Research Council, 1993; National Research Council & Institute of Medicine, 2001).

As a result of both changes in law and funding at the federal, state, and local levels, corrections has experienced a shift of support away from such areas as drug treatment, education, vocational training, job placement, housing assistance, and mental health services ("From Prison to Society," 2001; "Rethinking Prisoner Reentry," 2001). Family involvement (e.g., parents, children, and siblings of those incarcerated) and attention to living arrangements following release have long been an Achilles heel of corrections, where efforts and expertise have paled in comparison to the demonstrated need.

As part of "get tough" changes that flourished in the 1980s and 1990s, many states have made their juvenile laws more punitive (Guarino-Ghezzi & Loughran, 1996). These legal changes include greater use of incarceration, longer terms of imprisonment and correctional supervision, handling more juveniles in the criminal justice (i.e., courts and corrections) system, and modifying the juvenile justice system such that it mimics the more punitive, deterrence-oriented criminal justice system.

As long as institutional or community corrections reflect a predominantly deterrence or zero tolerance orientation, reintegration will be impossible to implement. After all, it is upon reentry into the community when offenders are likely to face difficulty remaining crime-free and functioning productively. When the underlying factors that predispose or propel them toward offending behavior are not addressed during incarceration and afterward, the likelihood is great that young offenders will reoffend upon release. If being literate, holding a legitimate job, and maintaining stable and positive personal relationships are key to making successful transitions both to adulthood and law abidance in the community, then lacking such attributes—as is the case presently with many young offenders—would logically make it much more difficult to succeed.

✄ Chronological Age and Legal Status

One effect of the various "get tough" changes is that the traditionally straightforward relationship between chronological age and legal status has eroded. Children and teenagers are increasingly being transferred into the adult correctional system, creating potentially even greater challenges for their postincarceration transitions. Children as young as 13 can be judicially waived from the juvenile court to criminal court in a handful of states, whereas in many more states, youth can be waived to criminal court at age 14 (Snyder, Sickmund, & Poe-Yamagata, 2000). Between 1992 and 1997, most states made it easier to transfer juveniles. In addition to lowering the minimum age at which a juvenile can be transferred by various means, states have added statutory exclusions and expanded the list of offenses eligible for transfer. When a child is transferred to criminal court or, for that matter, when they are handled by adult corrections, they are in effect no longer considered juveniles for legal purposes. Researchers have found that transferred youth are more likely to be incarcerated for longer periods of time and that they are more likely to be rearrested (Bishop, Frazier, Lanza-Kaduce, & Wiener, 1996). Regardless of length of stay, youth may be adversely affected by exposure to more serious adult offenders. Requiring youth to abide by adult norms can create "hybrid inmates" with more social, emotional, and interpersonal problems (Glick, 1998). Furthermore, transferred youth carry with them an adult record upon release.

Although juvenile justice has historically had its own problems with correctional facilities that have not provided the expected treatment or care, it has generally been more rehabilitation-oriented than adult corrections. This orientation has been steadily losing favor, and the juvenile system has increasingly come to resemble the more deterrence- and punishment-based adult corrections system, which is reflected in the changes summarized above. As already noted, in many states even the juvenile justice system has adopted numerous criminal justice practices, such as fingerprinting, expanding public access to hearings, and maintaining juvenile records.

Although chronological age was in the past largely the basis for determining whether an individual would be handled by the juvenile or criminal justice system, that is clearly no longer the case. Except for juvenile court judges who traditionally had the sole authority to make transfer decisions, the process was otherwise clear-cut; the juvenile justice system handled youngsters up to a certain age, after which they were considered adults in judicial proceedings. Now, a majority of the states statutorily mandate that certain categories of juveniles will be handled by criminal courts, and in 15 states the prosecutors decide. Chronological age is no longer the assurance it once was to channeling an adolescent offender through the juvenile justice system.

✄ Chronological Age and Adolescent Development

There is little argument with the general notion that adolescence is a time of enormous transition characterized by (a) exploration and discovery, (b) distinctive developmental stages during which identity, values, psychosocial maturity, skill building, self-control, and independence are progressively fostered and developed, and (c) change (Glick & Sturgeon, 1998). Glick and Sturgeon point out that, historically, children assumed adult roles earlier in their chronological development than they do today. At the same time, adolescence begins at an earlier age than it used to (age 10 or whenever pubescence begins) and extends later, to age 23 or 24.

Whatever age range is used, however, it seems clear that, in general, adolescent and teenage offenders are behind their nondelinquent peers in terms of development (Chung, Little, & Steinberg, forthcoming). Although there is debate on the extent to which "arrested" adolescent development predates entry into the justice system, as opposed to being a consequence of corrections, broad agreement exists that young people reentering the community from correctional facilities are often behind developmentally and face an uphill battle.

The battle can be conceived as a set of challenges linked both to the chronological age and corresponding developmental stage in which adolescents find themselves. The challenges can be quite formidable, partly because the customary correspondence between chronological age and developmental stage is interrupted for many youthful offenders. As a result, what signifies "normal" developmental mastery for someone in middle adolescence, for example, may not be applicable to a juvenile offender within this age range. If a 17-year-old juvenile offender possesses the values, psychosocial maturity, and self-control of a typical 14-year-old nondelinquent, he or she will undoubtedly face greater challenges returning to school, finding employment, or building positive relationships, among other difficulties.

Developmental psychologists tend to divide adolescent development into three age groupings— early (approximately ages 11–14), middle (15–17), and late (18–early 20s)—during which young people develop physically (P), cognitively (C), emotionally (E), and socially (S) (see, for example, Glick & Sturgeon, 1998). During each of the three developmental stages, particular characteristic behaviors and problems are more pronounced than in the other stages. Consequently, certain challenges will be more imposing depending on a youth's developmental stage and his or her PCES state at the time of release.

For example, early adolescents are predominantly influenced by their parents. Thus, early adolescents may face a greater challenge when returning to the community if they are returning to an unstable family setting or living arrangement. On the other hand, middle adolescents place a great amount of importance on peer relations and acceptance and may have trouble adjusting after the restrictiveness and regimentation commonly experienced in correctional facilities, which prevents normal socialization among peers (Chung et al., forthcoming). During late adolescence, youths develop a strong sense of independence and more mature relationships— based on empathy, trust, self-disclosure, and loyalty—with peers, family, and adults (Glick & Sturgeon, 1998). Young offenders reentering society at this stage may face particular frustration establishing any measure of independence because of poor educational achievement or inadequate work preparation.

In short, the combination of arrested development that may place adolescent offenders at a developmental stage out of sync with their chronological age and the fact that each developmental stage is associated with the mastery of certain tasks and functions not easily accomplished in correctional facilities represents an especially "tall order" for the reintegration of younger offenders. This is likely an even greater challenge when an adult corrections system, not juvenile corrections, is handling the younger adolescent offender (Altschuler, 1999).

Risk and Protective Factors

It is not surprising that research suggests that risk and protective factors affecting recidivism vary depending on the age and developmental stage of young people (see, for example, Hawkins et al., 1998; Lipsey & Derzon, 1998; Rutter, Giller, & Hagell, 1998). This is consistent with the notion that certain capabilities and vulnerabilities are more pronounced depending on which developmental stage young offenders find themselves. For example, the peer group as a dominant source of influence, positive or negative, is generally recognized as secondary to parental and family factors the younger the adolescent. Stable and positive intimate relationships and gainful employment are associated with positive outcomes, circumstances that are more applicable to older adolescents.

It is clear that identifying the array of risk and potential protective factors associated with each youthful offender is a necessary first step toward developing a bona fide reintegration plan. Risk and protective factors can be found within individual offenders, families, social networks (e.g., peers and friends), schools, neighborhoods, and public and private sector agencies and groups (e.g., faith-based organizations, governmental authorities). Risk and protective factors may also be affected by racial, ethnic, and gender differences, as well as sexual orientation. A reintegration plan needs to be developed at admission to a correctional facility or shortly thereafter. If reintegration plans are developed just prior to or upon community reentry, there is little reason to expect that the offenders, their social network, or the community will be prepared for reentry in any meaningful way.

A number of reintegration programs across the country are attempting to match the level and type of reintegration services provided with the potential for recidivism of each youthful offender (Altschuler, Armstrong, & MacKenzie, 1999). Such matching is based on the premise that lower risk offenders are likely best handled in a more routine, less intensive fashion with more attention and resources devoted to offenders deemed at greater risk. The age and developmental stage of an offender both at the time of admission to a correctional facility and at reentry into the community, as well as the projected length of stay at the facility and duration of community correctional supervision, are critical considerations. All of this requires a standardized assessment and classification capability that cuts across correctional units not normally accustomed to cooperation. In general, continuity and consistency rarely exist in either the juvenile or adult correctional systems. Nevertheless, inroads have been

made and efforts continue. The current priority being placed on reintegration is likely to keep the pressure on the need to restructure and reform current policies and practices that are at odds with the basic requirements of reintegration.

As risk and protective factors cut across parochial organizational boundaries, levels of government and multiple domains so too must reintegration. We point to seven domains known to play a role in the adjustment process that young people encounter as they reenter the community from correctional facilities: family and living arrangement, peer groups, mental and physical health, education, vocational training and employment, substance abuse, and leisure and vocational interests (see Table 1). The discussions of the seven domains are not intended to be exhaustive; they are illustrative of the kinds of challenges and opportunities each domain may present. As noted above, both age and developmental stage will influence and be shaped by what has been confronted in each domain and what will be confronted at the time of community reentry. Each domain potentially presents challenges as well as opportunities, which means that active engagement across the reintegration continuum is necessary if challenges are to be confronted head-on and opportunities both created and seized.

✉ Family and Living Arrangements

Family problems and conflicts, along with decisions on where juvenile offenders reentering the community will reside, make up one major domain (Perkins-Dock, 2001). Age and developmental stage are crucial determinants for how and in what ways such issues can be addressed. Older adolescents may be suitable for independent living programs, if they exist. This option is not available to younger adolescents who potentially can be returned home or placed in some other alternative living situation, perhaps with extended family or another responsible adult who might assume guardianship. Prior victimization in the form of child abuse and neglect is

Table 1	Service Options by Developmental Stage and Domain	
Domain	Early Adolescence	Late Adolescence
Family and living arrangements	Family management, parent effectiveness training	Independent living
Employment	Preemployment skills, aptitude and career exploration	Work experience and placement
Peer groups	Linkages to positive peer groups	→
Substance abuse	Age-specific and developmentally appropriate drug treatment	→
Mental, behavioral, and physical health	Continuity in range of services and content	→
Education and schooling	Individualized and competency-based schooling	Linkages to vocational training and employment
Leisure time and recreation	Activities matched to interests and abilities, teamwork ethic	→

not uncommon and cannot be ignored. Older adolescents may have an ongoing intimate relationship with another person, and there may be children to consider. A return to the former neighborhood or relocation to a disadvantaged neighborhood presents further challenges. The main issue from a reintegration perspective is that the assessment of the entire situation, the charted course of action, and the delivery of the services and supervision requires continuity and consistency from admissions to a correctional facility until release from community aftercare.

Peer Group and Friends

The influence of peers and friends tends to overshadow that of family once middle adolescence has begun. Kazdin (2000) discusses the reciprocal nature of the influence of problem behavior on interactions with deviant peers: Youth at risk for problem behaviors tend to seek out deviant peers, and over time such peer groups reinforce deviancy. Meanwhile, association with deviant peers can disrupt parent-child interaction, contribute to poor bonding with family, and prompt the rejection of prosocial peers. If there is a pre-existing problem with family and prosocial peers in the home community, a youth returning to the same community likely will have a more difficult time handling the temptations and pressures created by the situation. A youth may develop resiliency if a connection can be made with an attentive, nurturing adult, even if that adult is not a parent or caretaker (Burns, 1996). Encouraging such a relationship, however, is likely to require the effort of staff to locate prospects and assist in getting the connection started. It may involve nothing more than identifying who among the network of people already involved with the youngster may be willing and able to become such a person. Regardless, it will likely require the involvement of staff who understand through training and job requirements what they will need to do to foster this type of relationship (Altschuler & Armstrong, 2001).

Another factor that may complicate a youth's reentry is the use of group counseling, either while the child is in custody or after reentry. Research has shown that high-risk youth tend to support and reinforce one another's antisocial or delinquent behavior when they are grouped together for intervention (National Research Council & Institute or Medicine, 2001). This phenomenon appears to be especially evident in early adolescence and less so during late adolescence. Regardless of developmental stage, there is research suggesting that placing one or two high-risk juveniles in groups with prosocial youth is more likely to reduce antisocial behavior (Feldman, 1992).

✎ Mental, Behavioral, and Physical Health

The high prevalence of mental disorders among adolescent and teenage offenders is yet another potential barrier to a smooth reintegration process. Prevalence rates among juvenile offenders for less serious mental disorders, such as conduct disorder, attention-deficit disorder, and mood and anxiety disorders, are estimated at about 80% (Cocozza & Skowyra, 2000; Mears, 2001). Even conservative estimates show the prevalence of mental disorders among delinquent youth as four times greater than among the general youth population (Kazdin, 2000). Serious disorders, such as schizophrenia, major depression, and bipolar disorder, have been found to have a combined prevalence among youthful offenders of 20%, compared to 9% to 13% in the general youth population (Mears, 2001).

It is well known that several disorders, including mood, eating, and conduct disorders, as well as substance abuse and schizophrenia, increase markedly at the onset of pubescence, which of course is exactly when early adolescence begins. If untreated or ineffectively treated during incarceration, these disorders can especially confound early adolescents' reentry. Not only will they be facing other barriers, but they may be struggling with the symptoms of the newly developed disorder.

Although researchers have studied the effect that mental disorders have on the ability of young offenders to make decisions, they have been unable to draw any firm conclusions (Kazdin, 2000). Still, researchers agree that the core symptoms of mental and behavioral disorders in many cases would likely impair a youth's ability to make decisions. If such disorders have not been identified or treated while the child is in custody, he or she could clearly suffer upon reentry from continued poor decision making.

It is quite likely that youth with mental health disorders who come in contact with the justice system will not receive adequate treatment during their commitment. According to Mears (2001), a 1990 national study of needs assessment instruments found that many states did not administer needs assessments until after a youth was committed, that only one third of states used a formal needs assessment instrument, that only one half of states assessed emotional and psychological needs, and that the quality of the assessment varied dramatically across the country. Mears points out that although it is likely that the use and quality of needs assessment tools may have increased since the study, only very significant increases would begin to meet the mental health needs of committed young people. Another complicating factor for proper mental health treatment is that treatment approaches are often unidimensional, that is, they focus just on mental health, chemical dependency, or parental abuse, rather than use an integrated approach. Given the high prevalence of co-occurring disorders (about half the population of youth receiving mental health services suffer from multiple problems, and the prevalence is considerably higher among delinquent youth), treatment modalities that address only one problem at a time are likely to prove ineffective (GAINS Center, 1997).

In any case, youth may receive mental health treatment—as well as substance abuse treatment and certain physical health care—for the first time while incarcerated. This care will likely be of little use if it is not maintained upon the youth's community reentry and afterward. Failure to continue with medications after release is a common problem for treatment of young offenders with mental health or physical conditions. If medications prescribed and taken while a young person is incarcerated are not continued upon release, the condition will most likely return and may even worsen. Continuity of treatment does not simply mean providing any form of intervention but rather using at least a similar approach. Many believe that reinforcing what offenders have accomplished in placement—and employing the same approach—after they are released increases their likelihood of success in the community (Altschuler, 1984; Coates, Miller, & Ohlin, 1978; Empey & Lubeck, 1971; Haley, 1980; Whittaker, 1979; Wolfensberger, 1972). Triggers, negative influences, and temptations can be readily found in community settings, and it is there that the lasting power of what was accomplished in placement is truly tested. Most experts do not regard reentry into the community as the time to dramatically change course or withhold treatment.

Substance Abuse

Usage of alcohol and illicit drugs is very common among adolescent and teenage offenders, but the increasing scarcity of drug treatment both in correctional institutions and in the community surely complicates reentry for youth (Muck et al., 2001). In a 1997 survey of short- and long-term juvenile corrections facilities, SAMSHA found that 36% offered various types of substance abuse treatment (Reclaiming Futures, 2003), which indicates that the great majority of facilities offer no treatment whatsoever.

This is clearly problematic, given the prevalence of substance abuse among teenage and youthful offenders: A 1998 study by the Arrestee Drug Abuse Monitoring Program found illegal substances in urine samples of 40% to 60% of male juvenile arrestees (National Research Council & Institute of Medicine, 2001). Other researchers have found that 9% of institutionalized offenders younger than 18 reported having committed the offense leading to their commitment

under the influence of alcohol, 15% reported having been under the influence of illicit drugs, and 23% reported having been under the influence of both drugs and alcohol (Kazdin, 2000). Altogether, more than half had been under the influence of alcohol or illicit drugs when they committed their offense. This does not count the number that may have committed the crime to get money to buy drugs.

Adolescent and teenage offenders with substance abuse problems are likely to continue to struggle with their abuse of alcohol and drugs, or resume it, if they start treatment while in a facility but do not continue to receive it upon community reentry. Just as there is a shortage of slots for treatment in correctional facilities, so there is a shortage in the community. The Reclaiming Futures project (2003) estimates that there are only 140,000 publicly funded treatment slots for juveniles in the United States, less than one sixth the number needed to provide treatment to juvenile arrestees in need of drug or alcohol treatment.

Another significant problem with the substance abuse treatment adolescent offenders end up receiving is that the treatment models used in correctional institutions, as well as in the community, are often based on adult substance abuse treatment programs. Research has shown, however, that because of the developmental differences between adolescents and adults, these adult treatment models are not appropriate for adolescents and, as a result, are often not effective (Muck et al., 2001; Stevens & Morral, 2003; Wagner, Brown, Monti, Myers, & Waldron, 1999).

Education and Schooling

Education and schooling present another hurdle for youthful offenders reentering the community. To begin with, one quarter of delinquent adolescents have diagnosable learning disorders that set them behind their peers in school (Chung et al., forthcoming). In many instances, incarceration only exacerbates the effect of the learning disorders. Even for those without learning disabilities, returning to school can be frustrating. Delinquency is associated with poor school performance, truancy, and leaving school at an early age (National Research Council & Institute of Medicine, 2001). Low intelligence, poor academic achievement, limited vocabulary, and poor verbal reasoning are also associated with delinquency. Parent et al. (1994) received reports from teachers in juvenile facilities that 32% of the juveniles read at or below a fourth-grade level, 27% at a fifth- to sixth-grade level, 20% at a seventh- to eighth-grade level, and 21% at or above a ninth-grade level. Other research has found that because of poor schooling within the juvenile justice system, 75% of students in custody advance less than one full grade level per year while in custody (Dedel, 1997).

Faced with these limitations, delinquent youth are likely to have great difficulty returning to school unless they receive special interventions, and these are in short supply. Because many delinquent youth come from inner-city schools already strapped for resources and because the schools face many other problems, school systems have often not been receptive to enrolling juvenile offenders. Also contributing to the problem with schools are zero-tolerance policies that make it difficult, if not impossible, to admit or readmit juvenile offenders.

✑ Vocational Training and Employment

Poor and disrupted education makes it more difficult for young offenders to find meaningful employment upon release. In addition, in states with so-called blended sentencing, where juveniles are transferred to the criminal justice system when they reach the upper limit of juvenile jurisdiction, youths carry a criminal record with them upon release, which may exclude them from certain jobs and will generally disadvantage them in the search for employment. Increasingly, states are even making juvenile records public, which can also be detrimental in the search for employment.

By the time adolescents and teenagers enter the corrections system, they may have already reduced their chances of obtaining legitimate employment, damage that youth may find exceedingly difficult to overcome upon their release. As Hagan (1993) points out, delinquent behavior isolates youth from conventional job networks, whereas court appearances and incarceration remove youth from whatever job referral networks that school and the community might provide. In an effort to counter these ill effects and to prepare youthful offenders for employment, some facilities provide vocational training and work experience. The research evidence concerning the effect of employment and vocational programs on recidivism is quite mixed (see, for example, Lipsey, 1992, 2003a; Lipsey & Wilson, 1998; Redondo, Sanchez-Meca, & Garrido, 1999). Lipsey has evidence suggesting that the reason for the mixed results may be, at least in part, that employment programs including actual placement in work are frequently combined with employment programs that include job training but no actual work experience. A meta-analysis by Lipsey (2003b) suggests it is only the programs that provide actual work experience that reduce recidivism.

It is also recognized that a variety of other factors are likely critical to increase the likelihood of success in the labor market, including the involvement of employers early on in the lives of offenders, placement in a paid position as soon as possible, and a recognition of age-specific, developmentally appropriate strategies (Sherman et al., 1997; Task Force on Employment and Training, 2000; Walker, 1997).

One avenue through which juvenile offenders could be connected more directly to the workforce development system is the Workforce Investment Act's One-Stop delivery system. The Workforce Investment Act, which was enacted in August 1998 and succeeded the Job Training Partnership Act, called for the establishment of One-Stop Centers that were to serve as a single point of entry for young people seeking employment. Some jurisdictions have even established

One-Stop Centers focused exclusively on youth, as distinct from adults. But not all One-Stops have been youth-friendly or accepting, and even fewer can be expected to warmly welcome explicitly labeled offenders (Task Force on Employment and Training, 2000).

Another complicating factor in the pursuit of employment for youths returning home is their attachment to illegitimate sources of income. Youthful offenders earning income from crime tend to begin working before their nondelinquent peers enter the legitimate workforce (Chung et al., forthcoming). The income generated through an early introduction to the world of work in a criminal enterprise and even the thrill seeking encountered in the effort may outweigh any benefits associated with a legitimate workplace.

Leisure Time, Recreation, and Avocational Interests

Last, youths reentering the community often face difficulty both in finding and partaking in leisure time activities. Young offenders recovering from drug or alcohol abuse often have not had experience filling their time with anything but consuming drugs and being high. In some instances, being high may have been connected to particular leisure time activities. In either event, a whole new behavior pattern may have to be developed. Confinement often may not help in a young person's development in this area. This is because of the structured nature of some correctional facilities—and the confinement experience itself—which can limit a youth's time for, and access to, recreational opportunities.

Implications and Conclusion

Adolescent and teenage offenders who are placed into juvenile or adult correctional facilities and then released back into the community face an uphill battle. Young incarcerated offenders confront not one but two transitional challenges: the transition from childhood to adulthood (the developmental transition) and the transition from life in a correctional facility to community living (the correctional transition). Each of these two transitions is difficult in its own right. When combined, the two transitions are probably greater than the sum of their parts.

Understanding the connection between the two interrelated transitions clarifies not just specific challenges but, just as important, possible solutions. Efforts focused on educational, social, and work opportunities, which are central to a reintegration paradigm, facilitate both the developmental and correctional transitions. Efforts that involve family management and parent effectiveness training can be particularly beneficial for younger adolescents. They can also benefit from educational programming that is individualized and competency-based, whereas older adolescents can benefit more from education that is linked to vocational training. Programs for younger and older adolescents that provide linkages to positive peer groups or age-specific and developmentally appropriate substance abuse treatment also show promise.

The challenges young offenders face transitioning after incarceration are intensified by the unwillingness or inability of institutional and community corrections personnel to pay attention to lessons offered by other related fields, such as developmental psychology. Developmental theorists and psychologists routinely focus on the unique physical (P), cognitive (C), emotional (E), and social (S) conditions of young people in the throes of adolescence and on how the seven domains both affect and are affected by the four PCES conditions (Glick, 1998). Discussions about correctional transition revolve around the very same seven domains, but in practice it is rare to see institutional or community corrections discussing PCES conditions. It is even rarer to see them working collaboratively on how PCES conditions can be incorporated into each of the seven domains.

As noted, part of the problem is that institutional and community corrections tend to operate independently of one another and pursue a distinctly different focus and mission. Moreover, corrections overall has increasingly assumed a deterrent, zero-tolerance orientation, which runs directly counter to creating opportunities and addressing both risk and protective factors in a developmentally appropriate, age-specific context. Correction policies and programs intended largely to deter potential offenders and ex-offenders from committing crime by punishment, irrevocable consequences, and surveillance make it more difficult, if not impossible, for offenders to assume a productive, crime-free way of life.

It is in the public interest to keep young offenders returning to the community crime-free. But overly harsh correctional policies and ones that are not age-specific or developmentally appropriate may hinder the reintegration of adolescent and teenage offenders. These young people are in the midst of a developmental transition and their development may be arrested by their contact with the juvenile justice system. Attention to the developmental needs of these young people is imperative. Adolescents and teenagers require and deserve specialized staff, facilities, and resources. Such programs—with explicitly designed facility and community phases—can be demanding, provide accountability, and address both risk and protective factors. Get-tough, zero-tolerance policies that actually impede the ability of such programs to accomplish reintegration objectives and make it more difficult for youth to remain crime-free must be rescinded.

⊠ References

Altschuler, D. M. (1984). Community reintegration in juvenile offender programming. In R. Mathias, P. DeMuro, & R. Allinson (Eds.), *Violent juvenile offenders: An anthology* (pp. 365–376). San Francisco: National Council on Crime and Delinquency.

Altschuler, D. M. (1999). Trends and issues in the adultification of juvenile justice. In P. M. Harris (Ed.), *Research to results: Effective community corrections* (pp. 233–271). Lanham, MD: American Correctional Association.

Altschuler, D. M., & Armstrong, T. L. (1995). Managing aftercare services for delinquents. In B. Glick & A. P. Goldstein (Eds.), *Managing delinquency programs that work* (pp. 137–170). Lanham, MD: American Correctional Association.

Altschuler, D. M., & Armstrong, T. L. (2001). Reintegrating high-risk juvenile offenders into communities: Experiences and prospects. *Corrections Management Quarterly, 5,* 72–88.

Altschuler, D. M., Armstrong, T. L., & MacKenzie, D. L. (1999). *Reintegration, supervised release, and intensive aftercare* [Juvenile Justice Bulletin]. Washington, DC: Office of Juvenile Justice and Delinquency Prevention, Office of Justice Programs, U.S. Department of Justice.

Bazemore, G., & Umbreit, M. (1995). Rethinking the sanctioning function in juvenile court: Retributive or restorative responses to youth crime. *Crime & Delinquency, 41,* 296–316.

Bishop, D. M., Frazier, C. E., Lanza-Kaduce, L., & Wiener, L. (1996). The transfer of juveniles to criminal court: Does it make a difference? *Crime & Delinquency, 42,* 171–191.

Burns, E. (1996). *From risk to resilience: A journey with heart for our children, our future.* Dallas, TX: Marco Polo Publishers.

Chung, H. L., Little, M., & Steinberg, L. (in press). The transition to adulthood for adolescents in the juvenile justice system: A case of "arrested" development. In W. Osgood, M. Foster, & C. Flanagan (Eds.), *On your own without a net: The transition to adulthood for vulnerable populations.* Chicago: MacArthur Research Network on Transitions to Adulthood.

Coates, R. B., Miller, A. D., & Ohlin, L. E. (1978). *Diversity in a youth correctional system: Handling delinquents in Massachusetts.* Cambridge, MA: Ballinger.

Cocozza, J. J., & Skowyra, K. (2000). Youth with mental health disorders: Issues and emerging responses. *Juvenile Justice, 7,* 3–13.

Dedel, K. (1997). *Assessing the education of incarcerated youth.* San Francisco, CA: National Council on Crime and Delinquency.

Empey, L. T., & Lubeck, S. G. (1971). *The Silverlake experiment: Testing delinquency theory and community intervention.* Chicago: Aldine.

Feldman, R. A. (1992). The St. Louis experiment: Effective treatment of antisocial youths in prosocial peer groups. In J. McCord & R. E. Tremblay (Eds.), *Preventing antisocial behavior: Interventions from birth through adolescence* (pp. 233–252). New York: Guilford Press.

From prison to society: Managing the challenges of prisoner reentry [Special issue]. (2001). *Crime & Delinquency, 47*(3).

GAINS Center. (1997). *Screening and assessment of co-occurring disorders in the justice system.* Delmar, NY: Author.

Glick, B. (1998, August). Kids in adult correctional systems: An understanding of adolescent development can aid staff in managing youthful offender populations. *Corrections Today,* pp. 96–99.

Glick, B., & Sturgeon, W. (1998). *No time to play: Youthful offenders in adult correctional systems.* Lanham, MD: American Correctional Association.

Guarino-Ghezzi, S., & Loughran, E. J. (1996). *Balancing juvenile justice.* New Brunswick, NJ: Transaction.

Hagan, J. (1993). The social embeddedness of crime and unemployment. *Criminology, 31*(4), 465–490.

Haley, J. (1980). *Leaving home: The therapy of disturbed young people.* New York: McGraw-Hill.

Hawkins, J. D., Herrenkohl, T., Farrington, D. P., Brewer, D., Catalano, R. F., & Harachi, T. W. (1998). A review of predictors of youth violence. In R. Loeber & D. P. Farrington (Eds.), *Serious and violent juvenile offenders: Risk factors and successful interventions* (pp. 106–146). Thousand Oaks, CA: Sage.

Kazdin, A. (2000). Adolescent development, mental disorders, and decision making in delinquent youth. In T. Grisso & R. Schwartz (Eds.), *Youth on trial* (pp. 33–65). Chicago: University of Chicago Press.

Lipsey, M. W. (1992). Juvenile delinquency treatment: A meta-analytic inquiry into the variability of effects. In T. D. Cook, H. Cooper, D. S. Cordray, H. Hartmann, L. V. Hedges, R. J. Light, T. A. Louis, & F. Mosteller (Eds.), *Meta-analysis for explanation: A casebook* (pp. 83–127). New York: Russell Sage Foundation.

Lipsey, M. W. (2003a, January). Effective correctional treatment enhances public safety. *The ICCA Journal on Community Corrections.*

Lipsey, M. W. (2003b, February). *Prevention and treatment for juvenile delinquents: Results from meta-analysis.* Lecture, Johns Hopkins University Institute for Policy Studies.

Lipsey, M. W., & Derzon, J. H. (1998). Predictors of violent or serious delinquency in adolescence and early adulthood: A synthesis of longitudinal research. In R. Loeber & D. P. Farrington (Eds.), *Serious and violent juvenile offenders: Risk factors and successful interventions* (pp. 86–105). Thousand Oaks, CA: Sage.

Lipsey, M. W., & Wilson, D. B. (1998). Effective intervention for serious juvenile offenders: A synthesis of research. In R. Loeber & D. Farrington (Eds.), *Serious and violent juvenile offenders: Risk factors and successful interventions* (pp. 313–345). Thousand Oaks, CA: Sage.

Mears, D. (2001). Critical challenges in addressing the mental health needs of juvenile offenders. *Justice Policy Journal, 7,* 41–61.

Muck, R., Zempolich, K. A., Titus, J. C., Fishman, M., Godley, M. D., & Schwebel, R. (2001). An overview of the effectiveness of adolescent substance abuse treatment models. *Youth and Society, 33*(2), 143–167.

National Research Council. (1993). *Losing generations: Adolescents in high risk settings.* Panel on High Risk Youth, Commission on Behavioral and Social Sciences and Education. Washington, DC: National Academy Press.

National Research Council & Institute of Medicine. (2001). *Juvenile crime, juvenile justice.* Washington, DC: National Academy Press.

Parent, D. G., Lieter, V., Kennedy, S., Livens, L., Wentworth, D., & Wilcox, S. (1994). *Conditions of confinement: Juvenile detention and correctional facilities.* Washington, DC: Office of Juvenile Justice and Delinquency Prevention, Office of Justice Programs, U.S. Department of Justice.

Perkins-Dock, R. E. (2001). Family interventions with incarcerated youth: A review of the literature. *International Journal of Offender Therapy and Comparative Criminology, 45*(5), 606–625.

Reclaiming Futures. (2003). *Kids, drugs, and crime: Quick facts* [Online]. Portland, OR: Reclaiming Futures National Program Office, School of Social

Work, Portland State University. Available: www.reclaimingfutures.org

Redondo, S., Sanchez-Meca, J., & Garrido, V. (1999). The influence of treatment programmes on the recidivism of juvenile & adult offenders: A European meta-analytic review. *Psychology, Crime & Law, 5*, 251–278.

Rethinking prisoner reentry: Implications for corrections. (2001). *Corrections Management Quarterly, 5*(3).

Rutter, M., Giller, H., & Hagell, A. (1998). *Antisocial behavior by young people.* New York: Cambridge University Press.

Sherman, L. W., Gottfredson, D., MacKenzie, D. L., Eck, J., Reuter, P., & Bushway, S. (1997). *Preventing crime: What works, what doesn't, what's promising.* Washington, DC: National Institute of Justice, U.S. Department of Justice.

Snyder, H. N., Sickmund, M., & Poe-Yamagata, E. (2000). *Juvenile transfers to criminal court in the 1990s: Lessons learned from four studies.* Washington, DC: Office of Juvenile Justice and Delinquency Prevention, U.S. Department of Justice.

Stevens, S. J., & Morral, A. R. (Eds.). (2003). *Adolescent substance abuse treatment in the United States: Exemplary models from a national evaluation study.* New York: The Haworth Press.

Task Force on Employment and Training for Court-Involved Youth. (2000). *Employment and training for court-involved youth.* Washington, DC: Office of Juvenile Justice & Delinquency Prevention, U.S. Department of Justice.

Travis, J., Solomon, A. L., & Waul, M. (2001). *From prison to home: The dimensions and consequences of prisoner reentry.* Washington, DC: The Urban Institute.

Wagner, E. F., Brown, S. A., Monti, P. M., Myers, M. G., & Waldron, H. B. (1999). Innovations in adolescent substance abuse intervention. *Alcoholism: Clinical and Experimental Research, 23,* 236–249.

Walker, G. (1997). Out of school and unemployed: Principles for more effective policy and programs. In *A generation of challenge: Pathways to success for urban youth* (pp. 73–86). Baltimore: Sar Levitan Youth Policy Network.

Whittaker, J. K. (1979). *Caring for troubled children: Residential treatment in a community-based context.* San Francisco: Jossey-Bass.

Wolfensberger, W. (1972). *Normalization.* New York: National Institute on Mental Retardation.

DISCUSSION QUESTIONS

1. Summarize the similarities and differences between community corrections and institutional corrections. What is the role of "reintegration" and "balanced and restorative justice" in each type of corrections?

2. Imagine that you are a juvenile counselor in a reentry program. Develop interview questions that would assess each of the following challenges faced by youth: (a) family and living arrangements; (b) employment; (c) peer groups; (d) substance abuse; (e) mental, behavioral, and physical health; (f) education and schooling; and (g) leisure time and recreation.

3. Considering the dual challenges that youthful offenders face—from childhood to adulthood, and from institutional life to community living—suggest some major components and emphases of a juvenile reentry program that you might develop in your region or state.

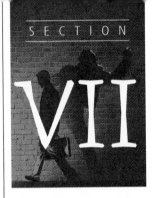

VII

THE FUTURE OF JUVENILE JUSTICE

J uvenile justice has changed dramatically over the past century, from a "child-saving" movement, to a treatment-oriented system, and more recently to a get-tough emphasis that aims to hold juvenile offenders more accountable, like adult criminals. This concluding section of the book begins with a summary of developments and policy changes in juvenile justice over the past 40 years that are likely to shape the future. We examine social, cultural, and political factors affecting the future of juvenile justice, issues that must be addressed in the future, and areas that are likely to see more change, and we conclude with a discussion of broader strategies and a comprehensive framework for delinquency prevention and juvenile justice in the 21st century.

▧ The Past as Prologue to the Future

Juvenile crime is a local community problem, but the federal government has played an important role in crime control and delinquency prevention the past several decades. It became increasingly apparent that many local communities lacked the resources to deal adequately with the challenges of juvenile crime. The federal government has in the past 40 years provided funding for research, technical assistance, policy recommendations, and resources for implementing delinquency prevention strategies.

The Federal Government and Juvenile Justice. One of the first major federal government initiatives in juvenile delinquency assessment and prevention was the President's Commission on Law Enforcement and Administration of Justice (1967b), which produced a series of reports, including the *Task Force Report: Juvenile Delinquency and Youth Crime.* The report contributed to our understanding of delinquency, informed legislators and government officials of the nature and sources of juvenile crime, recommended a number of legislative and statutory changes to juvenile court processes, and urged policy makers to allocate funding and resources for delinquency prevention programs. The major recommendations of the task force were:

- Decriminalization of status offenses
- Diversion of youth from court procedures into public and private treatment programs
- Due process rights for juveniles
- Deinstitutionalization of youth from large training schools to group homes or non-residential treatment programs
- Diversification of services
- Decentralization of control agencies and services (President's Commission on Law Enforcement and Administration of Justice, 1967a, 1967b; see also Ohlin, 1998, p. 145).

The second major presidential crime commission, the National Advisory Commission on Criminal Justice Standards and Goals (1976), supported the recommendations of the 1967 President's Commission, and spelled them out in more detail with a series of specific standards and goals relating to juvenile justice and delinquency prevention. The recommendations of these two presidential commissions received broad support among juvenile justice experts, practitioners, and researchers. Most states and larger jurisdictions have made progress in responding to the recommendations with legislative and policy changes, and have implemented programs and agency practices reflecting the goals and standards. Implementation of the recommendations has not been uniform or universal throughout the United States, however, and the results have been difficult to evaluate (Krisberg, 2005; Ohlin, 1998).

The Federal Juvenile Justice and Delinquency Prevention Act of 1974 (JJDPA) increased efforts to *decriminalize* status offenders, and the results have been a significant reduction of juveniles being held in adult jails (Krisberg, 2005; Snyder & Sickmund, 2006, p. 236). *Diversion* programs were implemented in cities throughout the United States, and the result has been that many youth who would have been processed through the formal court system have been referred to alternative community programs. The *due process* emphasis has been supported through a number of U.S. Supreme Court decisions and continues to be a major emphasis of juvenile justice advocates who are calling for equal justice for juvenile offenders comparable to those in the criminal court (Feld, 1999). Efforts to *deinstitutionalize* produced mixed results, the most dramatic being Massachusetts's closing of most of the state juvenile training schools in the early 1970s (cf. Krisberg, 2005). Other states have attempted to follow that example and have worked to reduce the number of juvenile commitments to training schools, recognizing that institutions are an expensive and ineffective alternative (Snyder & Sickmund,

2006, p. 198). Referrals and purchase of services from the private sector have increased *diversification* and *decentralization* of services in many states. Private juvenile treatment programs often provide better services in residential settings that are more humane and less institutional. They represent a significant portion of the annual budgets of county and state juvenile corrections programs, however, and many private programs refuse to accept the more serious and chronic juvenile offenders (Ohlin, 1998). Despite some questions and hesitation to fully implement early federal commission recommendations, we believe that those policies and practices will continue to play a role in the future of juvenile justice.

The Shift to "Law-and-Order" and "Get-Tough" Policies. In the 1980s and 1990s we saw a dramatic shift away from many of the policies advocated by the national crime commissions. A number of factors accounted for the shift in juvenile justice policies. First, from 1984 to 1994 the United States experienced an increase in juvenile delinquency that many referred to as a "juvenile crime wave." Some criminologists predicted an ongoing trend of serious and violent juvenile crime, spurred by a group of "super-predators" (Fox, 1996; DiIulio, 1996). Increased news media coverage on serious and violent juvenile crime focused more attention on these youth and gave the impression that they were more numerous than at any time in U.S. history. The increase in juvenile crime and the perception that traditional juvenile justice policies were not working led to law-and-order, get-tough policies. Statutory revisions to state juvenile codes included reducing the maximum juvenile court age, expanding the number of youths eligible for transfer to adult court, shifting transfer power from the judge to the prosecutor, increasing the number of serious offenses subject to mandatory sentences of incarceration, and opening juvenile court records for use in criminal court sentencing (Sanborn & Salerno, 2005, p. 506). Given the public intolerance for juvenile violence, lawmakers are likely to continue the trend of a tough response to serious and chronic offending.

A second reason for the shift in juvenile justice policy was in part due to a widely publicized report by Robert Martinson (1974; Lipton, Martinson, & Wilks, 1975) in which he argued that rehabilitation programs have not had an effect on recidivism. Martinson's conclusions that "nothing works" in corrections had a great national impact, despite the fact that Ted Palmer (1975) wrote a detailed rebuttal questioning Martinson's findings, and Martinson (1979) himself retracted some of his earlier premature and exaggerated conclusions. The disproportionate national attention questioning correctional rehabilitation nevertheless had a significant and lasting impact on lawmakers, who were also finding that more public support and votes rested on a law-and-order position on crime, while there was less support for a rehabilitation emphasis.

There are signs that rehabilitation is making a comeback (Cullen, 2005). Reasons for a return to the rehabilitative ideal (see Allen, 1981) are not necessarily due to a softening of attitudes toward crime and criminals, but to a realization that attempting to control crime through incarceration is costly and produces no significant reduction in crime rates. Although there is considerable disagreement as to whether training schools and prisons are effective deterrents to crime, many criminal justice experts point to research evidence that greater use of incarceration may increase rather than decrease crime rates (Garland, 2001). Cullen and his associates have conducted studies on public opinions about rehabilitation and have found that Americans still strongly support the view that efforts should be made to rehabilitate offenders (Cullen, 2005; Cullen, Fisher, & Applegate, 2000). There is evidence of significant public and legislative support for rehabilitation of juvenile offenders, who are still generally seen as more amenable to treatment than adult offenders. The exceptions are the serious and chronic juvenile

▲ **Photo VII-1**   Gangs and gun violence are a challenge for juvenile justice and delinquency prevention.
(Getty Images)

offenders who are likely to face waiver to criminal court or extended juvenile jurisdiction prosecution (as discussed in Section VI). The majority of juvenile offenders may receive some rehabilitative interventions on juvenile probation and community supervision.

A third reason for the shift in juvenile justice policy is a change in how we view those who violate the law as well as the reasons for criminal and delinquent behavior. The demise of the rehabilitative ideal actually had less to do with whether correctional programs were effective in changing offenders and more to do with a shift in the viewpoints of the public and politicians regarding crime and criminals. Cullen and Gilbert (1982) suggested that crime control policies reflect lawmakers' ideological assumptions about the causes of crime and the most effective strategies to reduce crime. Garland (2001) has contended that cultural patterns structure how the public and politicians feel about offenders. We noted in Section IV how the public and politicians feel about offenders. The politics of the 1980s produced a greater division between the jobless and those employed, between blacks and whites, and between the affluent suburbs and the struggling inner cities; social problems such as violence, street crime, and drug abuse became worse. Accompanying these political and social changes was the view that punishing individuals for criminal and delinquent behavior was more appropriate than rehabilitation and change strategies. Contrary to the views of positivist criminologists, that crime was caused by individual and social problems over which an individual had little control, law violators were now seen as bad individuals who deserved to be punished. Crime was seen not as a sign of need or deprivation, but was viewed as a rational choice by persons who lacked discipline and self-control, who needed to be deterred and deserved to be punished harshly (Garland, 2001, p. 102). Garland (2001) noted that the term that best describes this new conservative crime control policy is "zero tolerance." Intolerance of crime and criminals has pervaded society and legislative chambers, communities and school hallways, and the proposed solutions are harsh discipline and punishment.

Lawmakers are constantly faced with difficult choices of trying to improve public education, social and medical services, law enforcement, and public safety with limited resources and revenues and without raising taxes. In the age of what Garland (2001) refers to as the "culture of control," crime is viewed as a product of bad choices by bad individuals and not a result of unequal educational and employment opportunities for low-income persons who are disproportionately ethnic and racial minorities. Faced with increasing public demands to "do something" about youth involvement in drugs, gangs, and violent crime, the usual response of policy makers has been to "get tough" on crime and criminals. Getting tough usually means a return to incarceration of offenders. Statistics indicate that after a decade of deinstitutionalization efforts, the number of juveniles being incarcerated has increased. From 1985 to 1989 the average daily population and total census count of juveniles in public facilities increased 14%; the juvenile custody rate per 100,000 increased 19% during that period (Allen-Hagen, 1991, p. 2). According to the Census of Juveniles in Residential Placement (CJRP) in 1999, a total of 134,011 juveniles were held in 2,939 facilities, and the number of delinquent offenders in residential facilities increased 5% from 1997 to 1999 and 50% from 1991 to 1999 (Sickmund, 2004). The increasing number of adjudicated youths sent to juvenile corrections facilities does not even include the increasing number who are waived to criminal court, tried as adults, and often sent to adult institutions. Juvenile corrections policies in the 1990s were dominated by a more conservative, control-oriented philosophy.

⊠ Factors Affecting the Future of Juvenile Justice

Throughout its history and development, the juvenile court has been shaped by numerous social and political factors. Most of those same factors will continue to have a significant impact on the future of the juvenile justice system. An overview of the social, cultural, and political factors that will continue to affect the court and the juvenile justice system will aid our vision of the future. The juvenile court was developed in the context of social science and the social welfare responses to individual, family, and social problems. Criminological explanations and theories of juvenile delinquency were based primarily on positivism and the recognition that most delinquency originated from structural, social, and individual factors that were beyond the control of the juvenile. The positivist model of delinquency promoted juvenile court responses based on the "rehabilitative ideal." The primary educational qualifications for juvenile probation officers and caseworkers in metropolitan juvenile courts throughout the United States were college degrees in psychology, sociology, and social work. Social histories and background information included in predisposition reports emphasized juveniles' family circumstances and child development, socioeconomic factors, school background, and social environment. Legislative and political changes in the past 20 years now emphasize personal accountability and punishment of juvenile offenders, based on a rational choice model. This trend reflects a general "culture of control" in the United States that has increased punitive responses to both juvenile and adult offenders in recent decades (Garland, 2001).

Social Factors Versus Individual Responsibility. Research evidence based on a wealth of excellent criminological research shows that the causes and explanations of delinquent behavior remain virtually unchanged in the past 50 years. The social and economic causes of delinquency have *not* changed; the responses to delinquency have changed. The majority of juvenile offenders today are characterized by the same social conditions as those in the past century, including poverty; unemployment; unequal opportunities for quality education; and different treatment based on race, ethnicity, and social class. Today legislators, prosecutors, and judges portray youthful offenders as responsible and autonomous individuals, rather than as dependent and vulnerable children, and view their behavior as deliberate rather than as determined. The portrayal of children and youth as mature and responsible when they commit crimes is used by many lawmakers to justify holding them accountable as adults for offenses committed and punishing them as criminals.

Neither the rehabilitative ideal nor the social control approach has been effective in significantly reducing juvenile crime in America, but for different reasons. First, the juvenile court ideal of attempting to combine social control and social welfare in one single institution has proven to be an impossible goal (Feld, 1999). The juvenile court over the past 100 years has been able to adjudicate and order graduated sanctions for juvenile offenders within the limited probation and community resources available. The juvenile court, however, can accomplish few if any changes in parents, families, schools, social service agencies, and the political and social structure that includes poverty, unemployment, and inequalities that limit young people's chances for growth and development. Second, justice policies based on social control too often perpetuate the inequalities already present in society that disproportionately affect racial minorities and lower social class youth and families.

Poverty and Juvenile Crime. Poverty is the biggest single risk factor for the welfare of young people. Children represent a disproportionate share of the poor in the United States. In 2004, a total of 13 million children (17.8%) were poor. They are 25% of the total population but 35% of the poor population (U.S. Bureau of the Census, 2004, pp. 52–57). The poverty rate for children also varies substantially by race and Hispanic origin. Compared with the 10.5% of white children living in poverty, 33.2% of black children and 28.9%. Hispanic children were living in poverty (U.S. Bureau of the Census, 2004, pp. 52–57). According to the National Center for Children in Poverty at Columbia University (Cauthen & Fass, 2007), of the total of 73 million children in the United States, 28.4 million (39%) live in low-income families, and 12.8 million (18%) live in poor families. The rate of child poverty in the United States (20.4%) is more than double that of Canada (9.3%) and 4 to 8 times that of Western European industrial democracies (Feld, 1999, p. 334).

Wheeler (1971) studied the relationship of child neglect and delinquency to poverty, and noted that a majority of neglect and delinquency cases can be attributed to economic stress. Sociological research has generally treated poverty as a dependent variable or a secondary influence on family social functioning. Wheeler argued that we must treat poverty as an independent variable or determinant factor in other social problems, including child neglect, abuse, and delinquency. Loeber and Farrington (2001) maintain that risk factors such as family problems and poverty predict greater involvement in delinquency. Findings from studies of childhood exposure to family poverty have been very consistent. Children raised in poor, disadvantaged families are at greater risk for offending than children who are raised in relatively affluent families. In a critical analysis of poverty in America, Gans (1995) suggested that affluent people stereotype the poor as undeserving. In describing American policy as a "war against the poor," Gans contended that the poor are labeled and stigmatized as persons with questionable morals and values. His thesis is that the terms and labels that designate poor people as undeserving may be obstacles preventing their escape from poverty. Cultural and political views of poverty in America are intertwined with racial and social justice. Politicians and the public tend to view youth crime, violence, and child poverty in the same context as race and social class (Feld, 1999; Gans, 1995). Both crime and poverty are characterized as the *private* problems of minority families and children, rather than as matters of *public* concern for the entire community (Feld, 1999, p. 336). Because poverty is a major factor in the quality of child development and is an important risk factor in delinquency, any public policies directed at reducing youth crime must consider ways to enhance the economic status of families with children (Feld, 1999; National Commission on Children, 1991).

Because poverty is the biggest single risk factor for youth development, Feld has contended that public policies must address child poverty (Feld, 1999, p. 334). Juvenile court and justice policies have developed with a focus on children and families at risk, but the court faces increasingly greater challenges as the social conditions of young people continue to deteriorate. Poverty poses overwhelming challenges and adversely affects children's health, development, educational attainment, and socioeconomic potential. These social and economic factors become more evident as children reach adolescence (Feld, 1999; National Research Council, 1993).

Social Factors and the Future of Juvenile Justice. Poverty, social class, and racial biases shape public attitudes and juvenile justice policies. We have noted previously the disproportionate confinement of ethnic and racial minorities in juvenile corrections. Although research has not established a pattern of intentional bias against minority youth, the fact remains that minority youth are more likely to be arrested, taken into custody, processed in juvenile court, and committed to correctional facilities than are white youth. Children of families in poverty, living in high-crime neighborhoods, and struggling to overcome the challenges of lower socioeconomic conditions are at greater risk of delinquency and involvement with the juvenile justice system. The juvenile court has come to be viewed as the court for primarily lower-class children from poor families with parents who are unable to control and properly supervise their children. The public and policy makers tend to view juvenile crime as a problem of poor judgment and irresponsibility, rather than as a product of social and economic factors. Social class and racial biases are illustrated by the tendency of Americans to distinguish between their own children and "other people's children" (Feld, 1999, p. 337; Grubb & Lazerson, 1982, p. 85). Viewing poverty, low educational attainment, and unemployment as personal failures and individual irresponsibility explains the change in policy toward punishment and social control. How we view crime determines how we choose to prevent crime. Fear of crime and public perceptions of young criminals presented by sensational media depictions have a great influence on juvenile justice policies (Ohlin, 1998). For some people, poverty, lower school achievement, and youth crime demonstrate the need to improve the conditions for minority children and to pursue social justice. For others, these recurring social problems demonstrate that government efforts to reduce poverty and improve education just do not work for all people, but provide evidence with which to "blame the victims" and confirm why government should initiate no further social action (Feld, 1999, p. 337; Ohlin, 1998).

⊠ Policy Issues for Juvenile Justice in the 21st Century

The juvenile justice system must face a number of issues and questions, including the future of the juvenile court, the jurisdictional definition of a "juvenile" and the age of responsibility, the role and responsibilities of juvenile justice personnel, greater demands on correctional workers in an age of limited resources, the use of technology in monitoring offenders, and community and public support for crime prevention strategies.

The Future of Juvenile Court. Most states have revised their juvenile codes and redefined the purpose of the juvenile court, de-emphasizing rehabilitation and placing more importance on public protection and safety (Torbet et al., 1996). Feld (1999) has argued that judicial and legislative changes have "criminalized" the juvenile court. There are now fewer differences between the two courts, and he contends that the current juvenile court provides neither therapy nor justice and cannot be rehabilitated (Feld, 1999). Feld has therefore argued for abolition of the juvenile court as we know it. A more formal criminal court hearing would ensure that juvenile offenders receive the same due process safeguards and constitutional rights as adults in criminal court. Juveniles would be treated differently only at the sentencing phase, when they would receive a "youth discount" in consideration of their lower level of maturity and culpability (Feld, 1999, p. 317). In addition to a youth discount in sentencing, Feld recommends that youths who are sentenced to an institution be placed in separate correctional facilities for youthful offenders (p. 326).

Abolition of the juvenile court is unlikely in the near future, but juvenile justice experts welcome the ongoing reforms and agree that more changes are needed. Supporters of the current juvenile court acknowledge that juveniles receive "unequal" and "dual" processing in court: not the same quality of due process as adults, and for the purpose of both punishment and rehabilitation (Sanborn & Salerno, 2005). Supporters emphasize that not everything about juvenile justice is negative or unfair, especially when juvenile courts do pursue the "best interests" of the youthful offender and make positive efforts to provide beneficial interventions and programs aimed at offender change. The juvenile court in most cases does take into account the child's needs and risks, and aims to arrive at a disposition that will best facilitate offender change and public safety. Juvenile justice still does focus on both the youthful offender and the offense (Sanborn & Salerno, 2005).

The National Council of Juvenile & Family Court Judges (2005) has responded to the need to analyze the practices and results of the juvenile process and to identify areas for improvement (discussed previously in Section V). With support from the federal Office of Juvenile Justice and Delinquency Prevention (OJJDP), this national organization of juvenile and family court judges has developed resource guidelines that are directed at improving court practices in juvenile delinquency cases. The guidelines are intended to assist juvenile courts in assessing current practices, to identify areas in need of improvement, and to help in planning and working toward positive change. Assessment of juvenile court initiatives toward these goals may help determine the extent to which the courts are able to improve on the handling of juvenile delinquency cases, and improve on public and private agency responses to at-risk youth.

Juveniles and the Age of Responsibility. States vary in statutory definitions of the ages for juvenile court jurisdiction (Snyder & Sickmund, 2006, p. 103), ranging from a minimum age of 10 to a maximum age of 16 or 17. Recent trends are for treating younger offenders as adults in cases of serious offenses. The inconsistencies in laws defining juvenile jurisdiction reflect different assumptions about adolescent maturity and the age of responsibility as well as sentencing policies of deterrence and punishment rather than rehabilitation. The juvenile age inconsistency question goes beyond juvenile court jurisdiction. Minors can be executed at age 18 for murder, 3 years before they can legally purchase and use tobacco products, alcohol, or acquire handguns (Zimring, 2005, p. 64). Juveniles aged 15 and 16 who commit serious crimes may be held accountable and tried in criminal court with adults. Criminal behavior is supposedly a sign of maturity and therefore legal culpability. The age question poses an interesting paradox in the United States: Violent criminal behavior brings adult consequences, but the same juvenile under 18 years of age is presumed to be immature and irresponsible in other matters so is not allowed to sign contracts, enlist in the military, or legally purchase tobacco and alcohol products (Zimring, 2005, p. 64).

The 2005 U.S. Supreme Court case of *Roper v. Simmons* (U.S. 125 S.Ct. 1183) took a step toward defining the age of responsibility when a majority of the Court limited the sentence of death to convicted murderers 18 years of age and older. As we noted in Section I on the history and development of juvenile justice, this recent Supreme Court case will have some impact on juvenile justice trends in sentencing juveniles. The majority opinion cited scientific findings on brain research and differences in maturity between adolescents and adults. The close 5–4 decision was not without controversy and is unlikely to put to rest the differences of opinion on the age of responsibility and culpability of juveniles aged 16 or 17 who commit violent crimes. The Supreme Court decision in *Roper* is nevertheless one indication that states can and must address the age inconsistency question. The growing body of scientific research and knowledge about adolescent brain structure and chemistry compared with adults supports the need to address the question (American Bar Association, 2004). Scientific evidence can help temper the current wave of demands for accountability for violent juvenile offenders and may reduce the tendencies toward retributive justice based on strong emotions that are evoked by violent victimization. Research results from the field of developmental psychology show that there is ample evidence and support for reduced culpability of juveniles based on their lower level of maturity (Bishop, 2004; see also discussion in Section V of this volume). It is appropriate to continue to treat youth under 18 as too immature and irresponsible to purchase alcohol or tobacco products, to serve in the military or sign contracts. It is inconsistent to treat them as mature and responsible adults for commission of violent crimes. Murder and violent crimes are not exclusively adult activities, and therefore it is illogical to reason that a youth who kills is more mature than a youth who steals (Bishop, 2004). Persons who are under 18 years of age are referred to as minors and juveniles for a reason: They are less than adult. A challenge for lawmakers in the 21st century is to acknowledge and address the inconsistency in laws and policies for dealing with juvenile offenders.

The Role of Juvenile Justice Personnel. The 21st century will bring greater demands on juvenile court officers and correctional workers in an age of limited resources. Juvenile corrections officers are confronted with a number of challenges that will require changes in qualifications and training, and we are likely to see changes in the juvenile offender population, crowding, litigation, and greater use of technology (Mays & Winfree, 2000). These challenges will require a reexamination of the *probation and correctional officer training and qualifications*. Changes in legislation and juvenile statutes require regular ongoing or periodic training for juvenile court workers. Federal legislation has mandated the deinstitutionalization of status offenders, but intake probation officers in most jurisdictions continue to receive referrals of status offenders for curfew violations, school truancy, and running away. These "children in need of protective services or supervision" ("CHINS" or "CHIPS") must be processed for some form of informal adjustment or supervision. Adding to the diversity and complexity of the juvenile probation population are the chronic, habitual, and serious juvenile offenders, many of whom are "state-raised youths" (Mays & Winfree, 2000). *Changes in the juvenile offender population* are being addressed with demands for more "evidence-based practices" such as tools for risk and needs assessment of offenders. More objective and reliable classification of offenders provides more accurate recommendations for court dispositions and better management of juvenile clients on probation supervision and in correctional facilities. Administration and analyses of risk–need assessments require regular and ongoing education and training.

The problem of *crowding* affects workers in both community corrections and residential facilities. Probation officers are seeing more court cases requiring extensive time for investigation and report writing. Metropolitan juvenile court offices have specialized intake, investigative, and supervision units, but they have growing caseload sizes as probation agencies are faced with limited resources for hiring additional personnel. Smaller jurisdictions are experiencing the same problems, and juvenile court workers are responsible for the entire process from intake to supervision. Caseload sizes will increase for most juvenile court officers, exceeding 100 cases, with larger metro courts seeing caseloads of 200 or more (Mays & Winfree, 2000). One exception to the growing caseload sizes is for officers assigned to intensive supervision probation (ISP) for violent juveniles, drug offenders, the mentally ill, and sex offenders (Clear, Cole, & Reisig, 2006; Mays & Winfree, 2000). Residential and correctional facilities are experiencing the stresses of too many inmates in too little space. Added to the problem of crowding is the diversity of juvenile residents, ranging in ages and in the levels of risks and needs. Corrections workers must maintain appropriate separation of residents for safety and security, and must provide some types of meaningful programming.

The problem of *litigation* is likely to increase in the future as correctional facilities face population increases, crowding, and poor conditions. Federal courts began to target state departments of corrections more than 20 years ago for crowded and inhumane conditions that constituted a violation of the Eighth Amendment against cruel and unusual punishment (Clear, Cole, & Reisig, 2006). Litigation involving juvenile inmates has also addressed the conditions of confinement, and courts have ruled that the conditions in some juvenile facilities do constitute cruel and unusual punishment. A second legal issue is the question of protecting children from harm and maintaining safe conditions while in the state's care and custody. Federal courts have ruled that states do have an obligation to take reasonable steps to protect children in their care from assaults by other inmates, and are liable for nonaccidental injuries sustained as a result of inattention and inaction (del Carmen, Parker, & Reddington, 1998). States are faced with the dilemma of immense costs associated with litigation, and the growing cost of building and operating correctional facilities. Litigation is directly linked to crowded facilities that increase the stress levels of residents and workers who are struggling to maintain control of a growing and diverse population of offenders. Trying to maintain adequate staffing levels and reduce personnel costs often results in underqualified and undertrained workers who may increase the risk of abusive behavior toward a diverse and growing institutional population.

The *use of technology* in monitoring offenders will continue to expand and develop in the future, as the helping philosophy may grow dimmer or disappear entirely (Mays & Winfree, 2000). Over the past couple of decades we have seen a change from the rehabilitative ideal in corrections to a control emphasis whereby probation officers focus on accountability and monitoring offender behavior (Lawrence, 1991). Probation officers are routinely involved in administering urinalyses to probation clients with a history of substance abuse. Electronic surveillance has become a common form of technology for most community corrections agencies as an aid to control and monitor offenders. The use of technology has changed the roles and responsibilities of officers and can be expected to grow more abundant in the future. Developments in the use of global positioning satellites may well be applied to monitoring offenders in the future (Mays & Winfree, 2000). Advances in technology offer advantages in offender supervision and will enable probation officers to monitor and track more offenders more efficiently (Scott, 1996). Using portable laptop computers in their offices and in their automobiles would enable officers to gain access to offender case files and to record chronological and contact reports as they are completed. Greater use of technology also raises questions about the direction of juvenile corrections. Technology aids in monitoring offenders and enhances the control or punishment function of probation. It will not eliminate the challenges of changing offender behavior, and may actually reduce the amount of personal contact and interpersonal communication between workers and clients that is considered essential for long-term offender change.

Responding to More Demands With Fewer Resources. Juvenile court and corrections workers will have to find ways to meet the growing demands with fewer resources in the future. There is likely to be a growing tendency for the juvenile justice system to develop and implement policy responses based on the worst crimes and on the most publicized cases that are in fact "behavioral anomalies" (Mays & Winfree, 2000, p. 363). School shootings involving multiple fatalities are a case in point. Although victims of school shooting incidents involve no more than 1% of juvenile homicide cases per year, the media attention focused on the judicial process in these few cases puts the court under public scrutiny (Lawrence & Mueller, 2003). The media, however, do reflect a public concern with serious and violent juvenile offenders. From a practical standpoint, it makes sense for the juvenile justice process to focus on the most serious and violent crimes. In the face of limited resources, it is necessary to identify this small group from among all the other serious offenders (Walker, 1998, p. 70). A policy of directing limited resources to maximize benefits is supported by research and practice in Orange County, California, where juvenile probation administrators found that a majority of crimes were committed by only a small percentage (8%) of the most chronic, habitual offenders (Schumacher & Kurz, 1999). They documented the characteristics of this small group of chronic juvenile offenders and found that they could be reliably identified after the first contact with the juvenile justice system. An evaluation of the probation department's "8% solution" has shown that the number of chronic juvenile recidivists can be reduced through a coordinated program of early intervention and treatment of high-risk youth and families (Office of Juvenile Justice and Delinquency Prevention, 2001). ▪

▲ **Photo VII-2**   Involving youth in prosocial activities is important for delinquency prevention, such as these youth painting a wall mural over gang graffiti. (Photo by Taro Yamasaki/Time Life Pictures/Getty Images)

⊠ Delinquency Prevention and Juvenile Justice for the 21st Century

Juvenile justice has a long history during which a variety of correctional interventions have been tried, ranging from punishment to different methods of treatment interventions. Considerable debate has ensued around the question of whether correctional programs have been effective in changing offenders (Martinson, 1974). Murray and Cox (1979) argued that juvenile institutions have a "suppression effect" and have been a more effective deterrent to delinquency than community-based corrections programs. Others have raised questions about that conclusion, however, with evidence indicating that community-based treatment is as effective as juvenile residential programs, without the detrimental effects of institutionalization (Lundman, 1986; Whitehead & Lab, 2006). The juvenile justice process has several limitations as a primary source of delinquency prevention for a number of reasons: (1) The justice system is always a "reactive" response, not "proactive" or preventive. The juvenile court can intervene only after a juvenile's delinquent involvement is serious or persistent enough to warrant police arrest and referral. Delinquency prevention is more effective at an early age, before the onset of more serious behavior (Hawkins & Lishner, 1987). (2) Correctional agencies may actually promote rather than prevent delinquency, by bringing offenders together and isolating them from the community. Juvenile correctional institutions have been called "schools for crime," where young offenders' delinquent tendencies often became worse (Tannenbaum, 1938). Criminologists have suggested that group interventions such as Positive Peer Culture and Guided Group Interaction used in juvenile institutions may actually maintain and enhance delinquent behavior of the youth (Elliott, Huizinga, & Ageton, 1985, p. 149; Gottfredson, 1987, p. 710). The factors that generate and influence delinquent behavior usually lie within the community, the family, and the school—factors that are for the most part beyond the power of correctional agencies to change. Delinquency prevention requires a coordinated and consolidated effort of the entire community (Sherman, Snyder, & Poe-Yamagata, 1997). A proactive approach to delinquency prevention must include communitywide efforts to address unequal educational opportunities, unemployment, poverty, and racism. This requires the combined efforts of lawmakers with the support of citizens. Delinquency prevention requires long-range, comprehensive programs that combine the coordinated efforts of multiple agencies. Such programs will be expensive and require financial commitments that many voters and legislators will be reluctant to accept. The threat of punitive sanctions has little deterrent effect on desperate youth who foresee little future for themselves. A comprehensive strategy of delinquency prevention must offer more opportunities for at-risk youth to experience positive alternatives and to succeed in productive social and economic roles.

A Public Health Approach to Delinquency Prevention. Despite the fact that there are many serious mental and physical health consequences of crime and violence, crime has been addressed solely by the criminal justice system and not as a concern for the public health system. The juvenile justice system, through law enforcement, the courts, and corrections agencies, responds to crime after it has occurred, but it cannot stem the increase in violence by and against youth. Former U.S. Surgeon General Koop and his colleague Lundberg (1992) argued that a public health approach could be effective for preventing youth violence. The public health approach addresses critical health concerns by placing emphasis on primary prevention; that is, prevention taking place before the onset of disease or injury. The main features of the public health model are: (1) community-based methods for problem identification; (2) data collection to track incidents, trends, and relevant risk factors; (3) intervention design and evaluation; and (4) outreach, education, and information dissemination (Hamburg, 1998, p. 40). The public health approach differs from a law-and-order approach in that it views violence as a threat to community health rather than community order, and follows scientific principles in primary prevention strategies as opposed to a reactive approach to the problem (Welsh, 2005). We have included a reading on the public health approach to juvenile violence prevention. Welsh (2005) emphasizes that this relatively new approach should be seen not as a challenge to law and order, but rather as a complementary effort to create a more balanced and comprehensive strategy for preventing and reducing juvenile crime and violence.

Redefining Juvenile Justice Objectives. Juvenile justice administrators and agencies have called for a revitalized juvenile justice system as we move into the 21st century. With a focus on chronic and serious juvenile offenders, there has been a call to make it clear to young people that they will be held accountable if they break the law. It is clear that a system of graduated sanctions must be developed so that agencies can make immediate responses to juvenile crime with appropriate sanctions. Recognizing that much delinquent behavior is associated with problems in families, schools, and the community, effective interventions and treatment programs must be developed. The balanced and restorative justice model provides the framework for redefining juvenile justice objectives (Bazemore & Umbreit, 1995). The model is being adopted in juvenile justice agencies throughout the United States as a means for balancing the needs of victims, the community, and the juvenile. An effective juvenile justice system must meet three objectives: (1) hold the juvenile offender accountable; (2) enable the juvenile to become a capable, productive, and responsible citizen; and (3) ensure the safety of the community (Bilchik, 1998, p. 90). In order to meet these objectives, the juvenile justice system must have the support and cooperation of community agencies, including health and mental health, schools, and social services, working together with law enforcement and the juvenile court (Bilchik, 1998). This interagency cooperation must include more frequent and open communication and information sharing. To develop a more effective juvenile justice system, it is essential to place equal emphasis on the goals of victim assistance, offender accountability, and public safety.

A Comprehensive Approach to Juvenile Justice. A comprehensive strategy to help communities prevent delinquency and establish a more effective juvenile justice system was developed by two administrators of the Office of Juvenile Justice and Delinquency Prevention (OJJDP; Howell, 2003; Wilson & Howell, 1993). They summarized the available research and received

▲ **Photo VII-3** A comprehensive strategy for delinquency prevention emphasizes a cooperative effort of parents, schools, counselors, and community agencies working with the juvenile justice system. (© CORBIS)

input from researchers and practitioners on the policies and practices that appear to be most effective in reducing and preventing juvenile offending. Because the Comprehensive Strategy for Serious, Violent and Chronic Juvenile Offenders was based on research on the causes and correlates of delinquent behavior, it focused more on prevention than on law-and-order responses. Social institutions such as schools and youth-serving organizations, faith-based groups, recreational services, and cultural organizations in the community were important components of effective prevention strategies (Howell, 2003; Krisberg, 2005). Research has indicated that there is a relatively small number of chronic, serious, and violent juvenile offenders. The Comprehensive Strategy is to identify these offenders through assessment; use graduated sanctions to control them; and provide a range of services for early intervention, prevention, and treatment programming with juvenile justice responses (Bilchik, 1998; Howell, 2003; Krisberg, 2005). Implementing the Comprehensive Strategy for an effective juvenile justice system will require statutory changes to include prevention, intervention, and treatment in the purpose clauses of state juvenile codes. Effective implementation of the Strategy will require coordination and oversight by a state-level agency that focuses on juvenile justice matters, local and regional advisory boards and offices to develop and manage service-delivery programs, and funding mechanisms by which the state gives financial incentives to local juvenile justice programs to reduce the number of commitments to state juvenile facilities (Bilchik, 1998; Howell, 2003). The Comprehensive Strategy was for a time the official policy view of the U.S. Department of Justice, and was implemented in nearly 50 communities (Krisberg, 2005). Although the Strategy has not been a focal point for the OJJDP in the past decade, if properly implemented and adequately funded, expected benefits include (1) increased juvenile justice system responsiveness, (2) increased juvenile accountability, (3) decreased costs of juvenile corrections, and (4) increased program effectiveness (Bilchik, 1998, pp. 96–97). We believe that a comprehensive strategy is essential, and is the only approach that shows promise for effectively preventing and reducing juvenile crime while reducing the growing costs of controlling and punishing juvenile offenders. There are no easy or simple answers for preventing and responding to the complexities and problems posed by juvenile crime and violence. The question is not whether we have the knowledge and ability to respond to the problem, but whether we have the will and determination to commit adequate funds and resources to implement the best evidence-based practices. We have included some of the best available readings on the future of juvenile justice, including readings on the public health model and the comprehensive strategy.

SUMMARY

- The historical foundation of juvenile justice and developments through the past 100 years will continue to have an influence on juvenile justice policies in the future.
- Social factors including poverty, racial and ethnic biases, and a "culture of control" will affect the future of juvenile justice.
- Policies and strategies for juvenile justice in the 21st century must address poverty and the sense of hopelessness among many youth, and must limit the easy access to handguns among youth.
- The public health model and the comprehensive approach to delinquency prevention represent promising strategies for the future of juvenile justice.

KEY TERMS

Comprehensive approach

Correctional crowding

Correctional demands

Correctional litigation

Correctional resources

Correctional technology

Decentralization of services

Decriminalization of status offenders

Deinstitutionalization

Delinquency prevention

Diversification of services

Diversion

Due process rights

"Get-tough"

Individual responsibility

"Law and order"

Officer qualifications

Poverty and crime

Public health approach

Social factors

DISCUSSION QUESTIONS

1. Based on your understanding of the history and past developments in juvenile justice, list and briefly explain five issues that are likely to be important for the future of juvenile justice.

2. Persons have different views and opinions about the social, cultural, and political factors affecting juvenile crime. Based on what you have read, what factors do you believe will continue to have the greatest impact, and what policies would you recommend for dealing with those social factors?

3. The question of whether to punish juveniles who commit violent crime draws a variety of strong opinions from most Americans. Based on your reading of the inconsistencies in juvenile age and responsibilities, U.S. Supreme Court arguments, and scientific evidence on brain development of juveniles, how is this inconsistency likely to be resolved in the 21st century?

4. Based on the proposed changes that are likely to face juvenile justice workers in the future, what do you believe are some of the qualifications and skills that will be most important for successfully working in this field in the future?

5. What do you believe are three advantages of the public health model or the comprehensive strategy for meeting the challenges of juvenile crime and violence in the future?

WEB RESOURCES

Office of Juvenile Justice & Delinquency Prevention (OJJDP), for funding, technical assistance, research and training, e-news, and publications on juvenile justice and delinquency prevention programs and initiatives: http://ojjdp.ncjrs.org/

Guide for Implementing the Comprehensive Strategy, OJJDP: http://www.ncjrs.gov/pdffiles/guide.pdf

National Juvenile Justice Action Plan, OJJDP: http://www.ncjrs.gov/pdffiles/165925.pdf

Public health strategy to reduce gun violence, OJJDP: http://www.ncjrs.gov/pdffiles1/yfs9903.pdf

READING

In this article Brandon Welsh takes the position that the juvenile justice system in the United States, as it presently functions, represents an unsustainable approach to the prevention of juvenile violence and juvenile crime in general. He suggests that it is government's reliance on a law-and-order approach and an increasingly punitive nature in recent years in dealing with juvenile violence that are at the heart of the problem. A public health approach to addressing juvenile violence represents an important alternative to a law-and-order response, and deserves further exploration. A public health approach emphasizes primary prevention, views violence as a threat to community health rather than community order, and adheres to scientific principles. Welsh emphasizes, however, that this approach should be viewed not as a challenge to law and order, but rather as a complement to it, and as part of an effort to create a more balanced, comprehensive, and sustainable strategy for preventing and reducing juvenile violence.

Public Health and the Prevention
of Juvenile Criminal Violence

Brandon C. Welsh

Faced with any type of social ill, society often has numerous approaches at its disposal to try to ameliorate or eliminate the problem at hand. Aside from doing nothing, which is hardly a viable alternative, approaches can range from the humane to the draconian. However, not all approaches can be considered sustainable: producing desirable results today, but not at the expense of burdening society in future years. The world is rife with examples of unsustainable approaches to social, economic, health, and other problems that have, in many cases, exacerbated the very problems that they were set out to remedy (see e.g., Forrant, Pyle, Lazonick, & Levenstein, 2001). In the case of criminal violence perpetrated by young people—a serious problem that faces all societies (Krug, Dahlberg, Mercy, Zwi, & Lozano, 2002) and one that presents an immediate and long-lasting threat to the sustainability of cities and communities (through the victimization, fear, urban decay, and other negative impacts that it engenders)—the approach that is taken has important implications for a sustainable society.

A society that relies solely on punishing—in the form of incarceration—its young people who have come in conflict with the law cannot be said to be contributing to a sustainable future for its young people or the population at large. If, on the other hand, punishment resulted in lower reoffending rates, did not cause some juvenile offenders to become more violent, did not exacerbate emotional trauma (e.g., depression from past abuse) often suffered by juvenile offenders, among other iatrogenic results that punishment can produce, then there may be fewer objections to expanding its already widespread use. However, this is not the case at all. Studies abound on the iatrogenic effects of incarceration (see MacKenzie, 2002; McCord,

SOURCE: *Youth Violence and Juvenile Justice*, (3)1, 23–40, January 2005. DOI: 10.1177/1541204004270911. © 2005 Sage Publications Inc.

Widom, & Crowell, 2001; Spohn & Holleran, 2002), and there is little empirical evidence or professional consensus on the ability of prisons to substantially reduce recidivism rates and improve public safety over the long term (see MacKenzie, 2002; Petersilia, 2003; Zimring & Hawkins, 1995). In the U.S. juvenile justice system, these circumstances are magnified because secure confinement is to be a measure of last resort. All other available measures, such as probation, house arrest, or residential community treatment (e.g., group homes) are to be exhausted prior to consideration of a sentence of secure confinement. Yet juvenile incarceration rates in the United States tell a very different story (see below).

It is the position of this article that the juvenile justice system in the United States, as it presently functions, represents an unsustainable approach in the prevention of juvenile violence (and juvenile crime in general). This is not to suggest that the juvenile justice system is wholly ineffective and is a complete waste of taxpayer dollars and thus should be disbanded. Rather, it is government's reliance on a law-and-order approach, and its increasingly punitive nature in recent years, in dealing with juvenile violence that are at the heart of the problem. Public health represents an important alternative to a law-and-order response to juvenile violence and is deserving of further exploration.

The public health approach to addressing juvenile violence has garnered much attention and support during the past 3 decades, mostly in the United States. It is seen not so much as a challenge to law and order but rather as a complement to it (Moore, 1995)—part of an effort to create a more balanced and comprehensive strategy in reducing juvenile violence. Public health brings a focus on primary prevention; that is, prevention in the first instance, well before a young person has committed a violent act. According to the International Centre for Sustainable Cities (1994), it is this focus on prevention that is the foundation of a more sustainable approach to crime and violence:

A sustainable approach to the control of crime in urban places must reorient governmental policies to focus on crime prevention. This must include reallocation of resources and shifting decision making closer to the community. It must also involve a reorientation of traditional criminal justice agencies to enable them, in concert with other social and governmental organizations, to focus on crime prevention. While the traditional criminal justice system will continue to be needed to incapacitate violent and incorrigible offenders, commitment of resources beyond certain levels to reactive justice is not cost-effective. A wholly reactionary criminal justice system is unsustainable. (p. 12)

This article has two main aims: first, to review the role that public health currently plays in preventing juvenile criminal violence, with a major emphasis on the U.S. experience, and, second, to explore how the law-and-order approach—the dominant response to juvenile criminal violence—can benefit from the involvement of the health community. It begins with a look at the nature and extent of juvenile criminal violence in the United States and discusses how juvenile violence represents a threat to the sustainability of cities, towns, and communities. In the next part, the U.S. juvenile justice system is profiled in the context of how it contributes to the prevention of juvenile violence. The next two parts of the article describe the public health approach to the prevention of violence and the present status of this approach to preventing juvenile violence cross-nationally, with a particular focus on the United States. The final part of the article presents a discussion and some concluding comments.

◪ Young People, Criminal Violence, and Threats to Sustainability

This article is concerned with criminal violence perpetrated by young people. It adopts the definition of criminal violence of the National Research Council's Panel on the Understanding and Control of Violent Behavior: "*behaviors by individuals that intentionally threaten, attempt, or inflict physical harm on others*" (Reiss & Roth, 1993, p. 2). In this definition, violence is interpersonal in nature and includes the Federal Bureau of Investigation's (FBI) Part I or index offenses of murder and non-negligent manslaughter, forcible rape, robbery, and aggravated assault, as well as some Part II offenses, such as school fights and gang activity. Political or terrorist violence is not addressed here. Suicide, a form of intrapersonal violence, is also not addressed. For the current purposes, young people or juveniles are those younger than age 18 years, which typically means between the ages of 10 and 17 years (Snyder, 2002).

The consequences of juvenile violence can be destructive and wide reaching, affecting individual victims, their families, and society as a whole. Death, physical injury, psychological trauma, and reduced quality of life are some of the very real impacts that can be caused by juvenile violence (Miller, Fisher, & Cohen, 2001). One study estimated that violent crime by juveniles costs the United States $158 billion each year (Children's Safety Network Economics and Insurance Resource Center, 2000). Not included in this total are the costs of society's response to juvenile violence, which include early prevention programs, services for juveniles, and the juvenile justice system. These costs are unknown.

Young people are disproportionately involved in criminal activity. In 2000, young people younger than age 18 years made up about 8% of the U.S. population; yet they were responsible for about 16% of the violent crime arrests and about one third (32%) of the property crime arrests (Federal Bureau of Investigation [FBI], 2001). Juveniles accounted for 9% of all murder arrests, 16% of all arrests for rape, 25% of all robbery arrests, and 14% of all aggravated assault arrests (FBI, 2001).

Longitudinal studies carried out in Western industrialized countries that follow samples of,

typically, boys from their early childhood experiences to the peak of their involvement in criminal activity and beyond consistently show that the frequency of offending reaches a peak in the teenage years and then declines in the 20s (Farrington, 1998). Violent crime arrests peak at around age 18, and property crime arrests peak at around age 16 (FBI, 2001). Age-level crime rates decline substantially after these years, and by the mid-20s violent crime arrests are about two thirds and property crime arrests are about one third of what they were at their peak (FBI, 2001).

Although juvenile violence and juvenile crime, in general, remain a pressing problem in the United States, juvenile crime rates have decreased substantially in recent years. This has corresponded with substantial declines in total crime rates (juvenile and adult combined; see Blumstein & Wallman, 2000). The juvenile violent crime arrest rate in 2000 was 41% lower than its peak in 1994, dropping from 527 to 309 arrests for every 100,000 persons age 10 to 17 years. From 1993 (the peak year) to 2000, the juvenile homicide arrest rate dropped by 74%, from 14.4 to 3.8 (Snyder, 2002). Juvenile violence was not alone in its substantial decline. The juvenile property crime arrest rate in 2000 also showed a substantial reduction (37%) from its highest point in 1994, dropping from 2,546 to 1,615 arrests for every 100,000 persons age 10 to 17 years (Snyder, 2002).

Despite these recent declines, juvenile criminal violence continues to present a very real threat to the sustainability of cities, towns, and communities. The impact of violence on sustainability has many sources. According to the International Centre for Sustainable Cities (1994), violence (and crime in general) undermines the sustainability of cities,

because it may discourage investment, employment and financial activity. Abandonment of cities because of fear of crime can result in physical deterioration of neighborhoods and loss of employment to groups which may be most vulnerable precisely because they are least equipped to follow changing job opportunities. There may then appear a tendency toward concentration of social problems including mental disorder, suicide, prostitution, and drug and alcohol addiction which underlie some criminal behaviour. (p. 11)

One study estimated the financial loss to American cities because of property and violent crime at $50 billion per year (Mandel, Magnusson, Ellis, DeGeorge, & Alexander, 1993). Lost jobs, store closings, fewer people on the streets at night, a declining tax base because of urban flight—residents moving to the suburbs—all contribute to what can be described as urban decay. Juvenile violent crime may account for as much as $7.5 billion of this total.[1]

✉ Juvenile Justice and Violence Prevention

The juvenile justice system provides young people with a further set of legal and social protections that are not available in the adult justice system, such as not being allowed to be identified in the press and a higher level of parental involvement throughout the proceedings. At the heart of these extra safeguards is the belief that the primary purpose of the juvenile system is protection and treatment, whereas in the adult system it is punishment of the guilty.

The prevention of criminal violence by young people is one of the chief concerns of the juvenile system. From a public health perspective, a justice system response is considered largely a form of tertiary prevention. This response is not about preventing violence in the first instance (before the onset of violent offending), for example, through early childhood programs (primary prevention). Nor is this response about intervening with young people who are at higher levels of risk for involvement in violence because of, for example, their association with antisocial peers or the use of illicit substances (secondary prevention). Rather, a justice response

to violence involves dealing with the young person after the fact, that is, when an offense has been committed, when someone has been victimized. One exception to the justice system being solely a form of tertiary prevention is when the police intervene with high-risk young people by way of giving them a warning or participating in various violence prevention programs in schools, public housing communities, and other settings (see Rosenfeld & Decker, 1993, for a discussion of law enforcement and public health). However, when violent offending is the subject a justice response has come to be known as interventions on the part of courts and corrections: interventions of last resort.

A More Punitive System

The juvenile justice system has become increasingly punitive, especially toward violent juvenile offenders (McCord et al., 2001). This has involved juvenile courts delivering harsher sentences, more juvenile offenders being transferred to adult court, a greater reliance on the use of confinement than rehabilitation (Howell, 1997), and a growing number of juvenile offenders serving time in prison. According to the Office of Juvenile Justice and Delinquency Prevention's Census of Juveniles in Residential Placement, the juvenile incarceration rate for violent offenses grew by 5% between 1997 and 1999, from 123 to 129 per 100,000 juveniles (Sickmund & Wan, 2001). This increased punitiveness has lead many scholars to argue that the treatment and protection aims of the juvenile system have become more a matter of the abstract than of reality. According to Feld (1998):

Evaluations of juvenile court sentencing practices, treatment effectiveness, and conditions of confinement reveal increasingly punitive juvenile court and corrections systems. These various indicators strongly suggest that despite juvenile courts' persisting rehabilitative rhetoric, the reality of *treating* juveniles closely resembles *punishing* adult criminals. (p. 222)

Focusing just on violent juvenile offenders, Hagan and Foster (2001) added: "American public policy is increasingly focused on restricting or eliminating protections based on adolescent status. Thus, a growing policy of 'recriminalization' is reducing the ages at which youth charged with violent acts are waived or transferred to adult courts" (p. 874).

In addition to being the target of increasingly punitive policies, juvenile offenders, especially those sentenced to correctional facilities, must often endure harsh conditions, In their assessment of the conditions of juvenile facilities and their effects on juvenile offenders, the National Research Council Panel on Juvenile Crime (McCord et al., 2001) concluded:

> Detained and incarcerated juveniles have higher rates of physical injury, mental health problems, and suicide attempts and have poorer educational outcomes than do their counterparts who are treated in the community. Detention and incarceration also cause severe and long-term problems with future employment, leaving ex-offenders with few economic alternatives to crime. (p. 223)

To many, this increased punitiveness in dealing with juvenile offenders, whether they be violent, and the many problems experienced by incarcerated juveniles, makes the juvenile justice system seem less appealing as a vehicle for preventing crime. On the other hand, critics of this position charge that if a more punitive approach works, and especially for violent juveniles, there may be a great deal of merit in continuing it (see Gest, 2001, pp. 83–108, for a recent history of the federal government's responses to juvenile violence). So what does the research evidence have to say?

Punishment and Juvenile Violence

In a study on recidivism of incarcerated offenders (adults and juveniles) in 15 states, it was found that, of 816 juveniles (age 14 to 17 years at release), 82% or 669 offenders were rearrested within 3 years (Langan & Levin, 2002). In the same 3-year period, 56% were reconvicted, 39% were returned to prison with a new prison sentence, and 57% were returned to prison with or without a new prison sentence (includes technical violations; Langan & Levin, 2002). This age group, the youngest in the study, had the highest rate of recidivism for all four measures (Langan & Levin, 2002). Among the juvenile offenders serving time for a violent offense (n = 188; 23% of 816 juveniles), 62% or 117 offenders were rearrested within 3 years after release. The rearrest rates for juvenile property and drug offenders were slightly higher at 74% and 67%, respectively.[2]

Few studies have investigated the effects of criminal sanctions on juvenile violent crime rates. A study evaluated the effects of a 1997 law in Washington State that granted judges more discretion to sentence juvenile offenders to confinement (Aos, 2002). According to Aos (2002), the law resulted in a small reduction in recidivism: "a 10 percent increase in the detention admission rate (the number of admissions per 1,000 juveniles 10 to 17 years old) leads to about a 2 to 4 percent reduction in juvenile violent and property arrest rates" (p. 4).

Some smaller-scale, experimental studies designed to test the efficacy of juvenile correctional treatment programs in prisons compared to usual services provided to juveniles in these settings (e.g., drug counseling) demonstrate that a focus on treatment can produce modest to substantial reductions in recidivism rates. In a meta-analysis involving 83 evaluation studies of these types of programs and focused on serious and violent juvenile offenders, it was found that treatment for institutionalized juveniles, compared to the usual services, reduced recidivism rates by about 9% (Lipsey & Wilson, 1998). The most effective of treatment programs for institutionalized juveniles, compared to the usual services, reduced recidivism rates by as much as 40% (Lipsey & Wilson, 1998).

Just locking up violent juvenile offenders seemingly pays few dividends to society. When incarceration is required, treatment programs, some types more than others, can improve the life chances of juveniles on return to the community. Correctional facilities with a special focus on treatment may also be creating a safer and healthier environment for juvenile offenders. Still, however, incarceration is an after-the-fact response, the last resort to dealing with juvenile violence. Is there a more effective, humane, and sustainable approach? In the next two sections, the role of public health in preventing juvenile criminal violence is explored.

⊠ Public Health and Violence Prevention: Part 1

Public health can mean many different things to many different people. As Krug et al. (2002) noted, by addressing diseases and conditions and problems affecting health, public health's focus is not on individual patients per se but rather on entire populations, with the aim "to provide the maximum benefit for the largest number of people" (p. 3).[3] The public health approach to criminal violence has some of the following characteristics:

- Criminal violence is viewed as a threat to community health rather than community order (Moore, 1995). "Violent crimes are viewed as intentional injuries within the wider context of health problems such as illnesses and accidental injuries. What all of these problems share is that they contribute to the morbidity and mortality of the population" (Gabor, Welsh, & Antonowicz, 1996, p. 324).
- The foundation of the public health model is primary prevention: the prevention of violence before it occurs. This involves targeting risk factors associated with becoming involved in violent behavior or being a victim. Some of the key risk factors for involvement in delinquency and later violent offending

include childhood disruptive behavior (e.g., opposition, aggression), poor child-rearing methods, parental discord, and growing up in poor, disorganized neighborhoods (Tremblay & Craig, 1995).

- Criminal violence "is seen as resulting from a complex system of causes: It cannot be understood from offender motivation alone. These factors can be structural (e.g., economic inequality), situational (arising from disputes), and pertain to commodities such as guns or alcohol. Attention is also paid to the role of the media and other social institutions in cultivating a culture of violence" (Gabor et al., 1996, p. 324).
- "Public health problems are tackled through a systematic approach involving health event surveillance, epidemiological analysis, intervention design, and evaluation focused on a single, unambiguous outcome—the prevention of a particular illness or injury" (Gabor et al., 1996, p. 324).
- Public health acknowledges that it alone cannot solve the violence problem: "Solving the problem of violence will require an interdisciplinary approach. Professionals from sociology, criminology, economics, law, public policy, psychology, anthropology, and public health must work together to understand the causes and develop the solutions" (Rosenberg & Mercy, 1991, p. 11).

An Interest in Juvenile Criminal Violence

Why has the health community shown an interest in juvenile criminal violence? One of the first reasons for this interest is that public health perceives juvenile criminal violence as more of a social rather than juvenile justice problem. In part, this is because the majority of juvenile-perpetrated criminal violence and resulting deaths and injuries occurs among family members and acquaintances (Bureau of Justice Statistics, 2003). Intentional criminal violence on the part of juveniles is also seen by public health as more of a social problem because of the social circumstances in which some of this violence takes place (e.g., dating violence, fights at school; Elliott, Hamburg, & Williams, 1998; Silverman, Raj, Mucci, & Hathaway, 2001). These are problems that are, in many ways, beyond the reach of the juvenile justice system working alone (Galant, 2003; Rosenberg, O'Carroll, & Powell, 1992).

Another reason for public health's interest in juvenile criminal violence is that, as noted above, young people are heavily overrepresented as offenders (and as victims). This is the case not just in the United States but in other countries as well. According to the World Health Organization's (WHO) first *World Report on Violence and Health* (Krug et al., 2002), in 2000, there were about 200,000 youth-perpetrated homicides across the world, for a global rate of 9.2 per 100,000 young people. (The WHO report defines young people as being between age 10 and 29 years.) This translates into a daily average of 565 deaths of children, adolescents, and young adults. Victims of criminal violence are also relevant here, because in the United States the majority of victims of juvenile criminal violence are young people (Bureau of Justice Statistics, 2003). The WHO report also estimated that for each youth-perpetrated homicide, there are about 20 to 40 victims of nonfatal youth violence that receive hospital treatment.

In the United States, where the interest of public health in criminal violence in general has been the strongest (see below for a comparison with other industrialized countries), public health's interest in juvenile violence has also been marked by homicide becoming a leading cause of death among young people in the past 2 decades. In 1999, homicide was the second leading cause of death among young people between age 15 and 24 years; for African Americans in this group and in the age 25-to-34-years group, homicide was the leading cause of death (Centers for Disease Control and Prevention, 2002a, 2002b).

Medical expenditures relating to juvenile criminal violence have also been a cause for concern. One study estimated that direct medical expenditures (e.g., payments for hospital and physician care, emergency medical transport) from treating victims of violent crime perpetrated by juveniles cost the United States $5.9 billion each year (Children's Safety Network Economics and Insurance Resource Center, 2000). In another study that measured the costs of juvenile violence in the Commonwealth of Pennsylvania in 1993, medical care costs for victims of juvenile criminal violence were estimated at $95 million (Miller, Fisher, et al., 2001).

⬙ Public Health and Violence Prevention: Part 2

Before examining how public health's interest in juvenile criminal violence has been translated into action, it is useful to first take stock of how this interest stands today in the United States and in other parts of the world. During the years, international and regional health organizations, notably WHO and the Pan American Health Organization (PAHO), have led the charge in raising awareness of the impact of juvenile violence on public health as well as the role that public health providers can play in its prevention. With a full chapter devoted to youth violence and its prevention (Mercy, Butchart, Farrington, & Cerda, 2002), WHO's *World Report on Violence and Health* (Krug et al., 2002) has garnered much attention and has made some progress in increasing awareness of juvenile criminal violence as a global public health problem (see World Health Organization, 2003). Although it is too early to say whether the report and its associated regional campaigns to spread its message will lead to concrete action, particularly at the local level, it marks an important first step. This is best reflected in the words of WHO's former director general, Dr. Gro Harlem Brundtland (2002):

> The Report is not an end in itself. It changes our way of thinking about how violence permeates our societies and how it can be

prevented. It helps us recognise the scale of this problem, and encourages us to respond and offers practical means to do so. (p. 2)

In the Americas, PAHO's efforts on this front date back to 1994 with its sponsorship of the Inter-American Conference on Society, Violence, and Health, convened in Washington, D.C. The conference's Declaration called for greater national, regional, and international commitment to the prevention of juvenile criminal violence and violence generally (Pan American Health Organization [PAHO], 1994). PAHO (2000) published an important report, titled *Juvenile Violence in the Americas: Innovative Studies in Research, Diagnosis, and Prevention.*

At a country level, the United States is by far the most advanced in its recognition of juvenile criminal violence as a public health problem and in its mobilization of public health resources to address this problem. This is evident on a number of fronts. Since 1983, a permanent branch has existed at the Centers for Disease Control and Prevention (CDC) to carry out research and fund programs to prevent intentional violence, including juvenile criminal violence. At present, juvenile violence is the mandate of the Division of Violence Prevention under the National Center for Injury Prevention and Control. Recent activities of this division have included basic research on the reduction of injuries from firearms and school violence, and evaluation research of school- and community-based youth violence prevention programs (Potter & Saltzman, 2000).

In 2001, the former U.S. surgeon general, Dr. David Satcher, released the first-ever report on youth violence from this office: *Youth Violence: A Report of the Surgeon General* (U.S. Department of Health and Human Services [USDHHS], 2001). The report brings together leading research on the magnitude, causes, and prevention of juvenile violence and sets out a course of action for policy makers, researchers, service and treatment providers, juvenile justice personnel, and citizens. Some of the recommendations

include the following: improving understanding of the decision making of youths to use firearms in violent encounters; providing more intervention opportunities for young people in conflict with the law instead of relying on punitive approaches; and improving training for intervention personnel (USDHHS, 2001).

In the two other countries examined for the current research (Canada and the United Kingdom), public health seemingly plays a comparatively small role as part of government policy on the prevention of juvenile criminal violence. In Canada, emergency physicians and other health-care providers are engaged in research and various other capacities to reduce the criminal use of firearms by young people (Canadian Public Health Association, 1994); however, unlike the United States, there is no government infrastructure that supports or advocates for public health's involvement in addressing this problem. The same can be said about the United Kingdom. A similar search of the relevant central government departments that are involved in addressing juvenile criminal violence (e.g., Home Office, Department of Health) did not reveal any infrastructure or policy that embraced public health providers let alone the public health approach.

One other piece of evidence that points to the scant attention that has been accorded so far in Canada and the United Kingdom to the potential contribution of the health community in addressing juvenile criminal violence is the limited input by academia, as measured by publishing in medical journals. In a 15-year review (1987 to 2001) of the flagship journals of the Canadian Medical Association (*Canadian Medical Association Journal [CMAJ]*), British Medical Association (*British Medical Journal [BMJ]*), and the American Medical Association (*Journal of the American Medical Association [JAMA]*), the average number of published articles on interpersonal violence in *BMJ* was lower than *JAMA* and *CMAJ* was substantially lower than *JAMA*.[4] The difference was even more pronounced for published articles focused only on juvenile criminal violence, with many of these articles in *JAMA* being on school violence, dating violence, and firearms.

From Interest to Action

In an article titled "Murder and Medicine," Harris, Thomas, Fisher, and Hirsch (2002) found that advances in emergency medical technology and care (e.g., development of 911 call systems and trauma units at hospitals, improved training for medical technicians) during the past 4 decades in the United States have played an important role in increasing the chances that a victim of a violent criminal assault will not end up dying. They estimated that the lethality of violent assaults (i.e., assaults resulting in homicides) decreased over this time period by 2.5% to 4.5% per year (Harris et al., 2002). This is just one example of the many contributions that the health community has made to a safer, more sustainable society. What follows are a number of primary and secondary prevention measures that public health providers are engaged in to specifically reduce juvenile criminal violence.

Primary prevention. This involves efforts to prevent violent behavior before it occurs; that is, before any signs of it become evident. It aims positively to influence the early risk factors or root causes for delinquency or violent behavior. Some of the major risk factors that health-care providers can help to address include early childhood behavior problems (e.g., aggressiveness toward parents, acting out in school), poor child-rearing methods (e.g., poor parental supervision, harsh or inconsistent discipline), low socioeconomic status, and poor school performance or school failure (Rivara & Farrington, 1995). Pediatricians, family physicians, and health nurses are among the many health-care providers that are involved in primary prevention.

According to Rivara and Farrington (1995), pediatricians can play a particularly important role in primary prevention approaches, because they

are likely to be the professionals who have the most contact with the greatest number of young children and their families. Few children and their parents at that stage have contact with helpful social service agencies and many of those at greatest risk have few effective advocates other than their physician. (p. 422)

Much of the pediatrician's role in helping to address some of the above risk factors involves (a) gauging the level of risk through a detailed family history and regular screening for specific problems and (b) providing advice and educational information, such as parenting tips and links to community resources.

Slaby and Stringham (1994) acknowledged the importance of these roles in the lives of at-risk children and families but also emphasized the need for pediatricians to provide "follow-up support for the changes they make" and "engag[e] in community outreach activities designed to change community norms about violence" (p. 614). This latter role can involve public information campaigns to address misconceptions about juvenile violence and effective responses and promoting prosocial alternatives to violence (Wilson-Brewer & Spivak, 1994). This role also stresses a key element of the public health approach to prevent juvenile violence: the need to collaborate with other professionals.

Health nurses can also play a key role in primary prevention approaches. One way is through the provision of family support for new mothers and their children in the form of home visits. The only home visitation program with a long-term follow-up of juvenile criminal violence is the Prenatal/Early Infancy Project (PEIP), which was started in Elmira, N.Y., in the early 1980s. The program targeted first-time mothers-to-be who had at least one of the following high-risk characteristics prone to health and developmental problems in infancy: younger than age 19 years, unmarried, or low socioeconomic status. One of the aims of the program was to prevent child abuse and neglect. Based on past research (e.g., Widom, 1989), the PEIP researchers speculated that preventing child abuse and neglect by the mothers would translate into less involvement in violent criminal activity on the part of the children when they reached adolescence. In all, 400 women were enrolled in the program. The mothers-to-be received home visits from health nurses during pregnancy and during the first 2 years of the child's life. Each home visit lasted about 1¼ hours, and the mothers were visited on average every 2 weeks. The nurses gave advice to the mothers about care of the child, infant development, and the importance of proper nutrition and avoiding smoking and drinking during pregnancy.

A randomized experimental design was used to evaluate the program's impact on a number of outcomes. At the completion of the program, a substantial reduction in child abuse and neglect was found for high-risk program mothers compared to their control counterparts (4% vs. 19%; see Olds, Henderson, Chamberlin, & Tatelbaum, 1986). Thirteen years after the completion of the program, fewer experimental compared to control mothers in the total sample were identified as perpetrators of child abuse and neglect (29% vs. 54%; Olds, Eckenrode, et al., 1997). At the age of 15, children of the mothers (in the total sample) who received the program committed fewer violent and other major delinquent acts than their control counterparts (a mean of 3.02 compared to 3.57).[5] It was also found that the experimental children, compared to the controls, had fewer convictions and violations of probation, were less likely to run away from home, and were less likely to drink alcohol (Olds, Henderson, Cole, et al., 1998). A cost-benefit analysis of the program found it to have been a worthwhile use of taxpayer dollars (Greenwood et al., 2001; see also Welsh & Farrington, 2000).

Secondary prevention. This level of prevention is distinguished from primary prevention by its targeted interventions at older children and adolescents who show signs of involvement in antisocial behavior or possess related risk factors

(e.g., using illicit substances, carrying firearms, associating with delinquent peers). The above example of advances in emergency medical care that helped to improve the life chances of victims of violent assaults is a form of secondary prevention. As noted by Prothrow-Stith (1992), "Emergency room workers must resort to secondary intervention strategies because they are faced with a person at considerable risk for future morbidity or mortality resulting from violence" (p. 202). However, this is not limited to dealing with the physical and emotional trauma suffered by victims of violence. According to Prothrow-Stith (1992), medical professionals also need to work with victims of violence to prevent an escalation of violence:

> Instead of merely stitching up the victims and discharging them—which only leads to retaliation and additional bloodshed— hospital emergency departments should attempt to evaluate the circumstances leading up to the injury-related incident. Diagnostic and service intervention protocols should automatically be instituted for victims of street and family violence, just as they are for victims of other forms of intentional injury such as child abuse, sexual assault, or attempted suicide. (p. 202)

Preventing firearm injuries is one of the most important elements of the public health approach to preventing juvenile criminal violence. The contribution of public health on this front has been largely "to advance the scientific understanding of ways in which firearm injuries can be prevented" (Mercy, Rosenberg, Powell, Broome, & Roper, 1993, p. 17). This contribution has paid dividends. As noted by Gabor et al. (1996), "Some of the best and most influential research bearing on the firearms/public safety issue over the last ten years has been conducted by specialists in emergency medicine, epidemiology, pediatrics, and psychiatry" (p. 319). This has involved research showing a strong link between firearm availability and homicide in the home

(Sloan et al., 1988), the risk that firearm ownership presents to firearm-related deaths and injuries in the home (Kellermann et al., 1993), and underlying patterns of firearm-related violence, including the distribution of gun violence being highly concentrated in space, subgroups of the population are at higher risk of firearm violence, a subset of firearms is disproportionately involved, and a small, concentrated group of individuals perpetrate criminal violence involving firearms (Wintemute, 2000; see also Braga, Cook, Kennedy, & Moore, 2002).

This epidemiological knowledge is being acted on to reduce juvenile gun violence in the United States. The Boston Gun Project (also known as Operation Ceasefire) is one example. The program included a direct law enforcement focus on illicit firearms traffickers who supply youth with guns and a strong deterrent threat to gang violence by youths (Braga, Kennedy, Waring, & Piehl, 2001). A wide range of measures were used to reduce the flow of guns to young people, including pooling the resources of local, state, and federal justice authorities to track and seize illegal guns, and targeting traffickers of guns most used by gang members. The response to youth gang violence was to pull every deterrence lever available, including shutting down drug markets, serving warrants, enforcing probation restrictions, and making disorder arrests (Kennedy, 1997). A before-and-after evaluation of the program showed a 63% reduction in the mean monthly number of youth homicide victims across the city. In a comparison with the 39 largest cities in the United States (the majority of which also experienced a reduction in youth homicide rates over the same period) and 29 large New England cities, it was found that the significant reduction in youth homicides in Boston was associated with the program (Braga, Kennedy, et al., 2001). Of great interest is the replication of this program in an area of Los Angeles that suffers from high rates of juvenile violence, with results of an impact evaluation expected in the near future (Tita, Riley, & Greenwood, 2003).

Another example of the utilization of research by public-health professionals to reduce youth gun violence is the Office of Juvenile Justice and Delinquency Prevention's Partnerships to Reduce Juvenile Gun Violence Program. Implemented in the highest gun-crime areas of three cities across the country (Baton Rouge, LA; Oakland, CA; and Syracuse, NY), the program involves suppression (e.g., targeted gun sweeps by police, tracing of illegal guns), intervention (e.g., conflict resolution training, job training and placement), and prevention (e.g., gun violence education programs in schools, mentoring) components (Sheppard, Grant, Rowe, & Jacobs, 2000). An evaluation of the effectiveness of the program in reducing juvenile gun violence is under way (Lizotte & Sheppard, 2001).

Schools are a particularly important setting in which health-care providers are often directly involved in secondary prevention efforts to reduce juvenile criminal violence. These efforts almost always involve collaborations with teachers or school counselors and focus on, but are not limited to, students who have been involved in fights or bullying at school or suspended from school. Some schools employ mental health clinicians to help students who exhibit symptoms of post-traumatic stress disorder (PTSD) from having personally witnessed or directly experienced interpersonal violence. In a randomized controlled experiment to test the efficacy of one such program with sixth-grade students in Los Angeles, which used a short-term cognitive-behavioral therapy intervention, it was found that after 3 months the intervention group compared with a no-intervention control group had significantly lower scores on symptoms of PTSD, depression, and psychosocial dysfunction (Stein et al., 2003).

Violence prevention curricula as part of health education classes are one type of program that has received much attention in the United States. However, very few rigorous evaluations of these programs or other instructional-based violence prevention programs in schools have assessed effects on violent behavior

(Gottfredson, Wilson, & Najaka, 2002). One of these evaluations of a violence prevention curriculum introduced in health education classes showed a "marginally significant main effect of treatment for fighting in the past week" among the young people who attended the sessions compared to a control group that did not receive the curriculum (Wilson-Brewer, Cohen, O'Donnell, & Goodman, 1991, p. 48). This program was implemented in a number of urban high schools across the country. The curriculum was designed to do five main things over the course of 10 sessions: (a) provide statistical information on adolescent violence and homicide; (b) present anger as a normal, potentially constructive emotion; (c) create a need in the students for alternatives to fighting by discussing the potential gains and losses from fighting; (d) have students analyze the precursors to a fight and practice avoiding fights using role-play and videotape; and (e) create a classroom ethos that is nonviolent and values violence prevention behavior (Larson, 1994). More evaluations of violence prevention programs in schools are needed.

✉ Discussion and Conclusion

This article had two main aims: (a) to review the role that public health currently plays in preventing juvenile criminal violence, with a major emphasis on the U.S. experience and (b) to explore how the law-and-order approach—the dominant response to juvenile criminal violence—can benefit from the involvement of the health community.

Despite public health's emphasis on prevention and the many benefits this has to offer, not to mention the limitations of punitive measures, the public health approach should be seen neither as a replacement to the law-and-order approach nor as a panacea to dealing with juvenile criminal violence. On the former, Prothrow-Stith (1992) reminded us that the

public health approach to the prevention of adolescent violence complements the existing criminal justice approach. Whereas the latter concentrates on incarceration or other punishment for crimes already committed against society, the former seeks to avert those crimes by changing the perception of violence as glamorous and successful and by applying behavior modification techniques to children and teenagers exhibiting high-risk behavior. (p. 207)

Each approach surely has its own strengths and limitations. Recognizing this and drawing on the experience of the other is important. In doing so, and by emphasizing to a much greater degree a public health approach, the makings of a more effective and sustainable approach to preventing juvenile criminal violence can be realized. However, even so, similar to the law-and-order approach, the public health model is ill equipped to ameliorate the social conditions, such as poverty, joblessness, and racism, that are at the root of violent criminal behavior. Ruttenberg (1994) contended that "the public health model promises to be much more effective in *reducing the lethality* of violent behavior (by addressing the lethality of firearms) than in *preventing* that behavior" (p. 1888).

Public health is very clear on these points. It is not a panacea to the problem of juvenile criminal violence. It recognizes the complex causes of violence. It emphasizes preventive interventions in collaboration with other key stakeholders to tackle proximal and distal causes of juvenile violence. It is very much about working to change behavior to prevent juvenile violence, either directly through violence prevention curricula in high schools or community outreach activities, or indirectly through home visitation services for new mothers or by providing families with advice and information on effective child-rearing methods. Public health goes a long way toward improving society's response to preventing and reducing juvenile criminal violence.

⬚ Notes

1. This is based on a rough calculation that includes the finding that the cost of violent crime (not including drunk driving) accounts for 94% of total costs of property and violent crime (Miller, Cohen, & Wiersema, 1996) and that juveniles account for 16% of all violent crime arrests (FBI, 2001): $50 billion x .94 x .16 = $7.5 billion.

2. These figures were not reported by Langan and Levin (2002) but were derived from extrapolations from the full sample of offenders in the study ($N = 272,111$). It is possible that the rearrest rates for these juvenile offenders may be slightly higher or lower than for the full sample, which is largely made up of adult offenders.

3. In contrast, it is the medical model that is concerned with the "diagnosis, treatment, and mechanisms of specific illnesses in individual patients" (U.S. Department of Health and Human Services, 2001, p. 4).

4. This takes into account that *JAMA* is published twice as often (weekly) as *BMJ* and *CMAJ* (both biweekly). Over this 15-year period, the average number of published articles per year on interpersonal violence were: for *JAMA*, 3.7; for *BMJ*, 3.1; and for *CMAJ*, 1.7.

5. The major delinquent acts were the following: hurt someone who needed bandages, stole something worth more than $50, stole something worth less than $50, trespassed, damaged property on purpose, hit someone because did not like what he or she said, carried a weapon, set fire on purpose, and been in fight with gang members (Olds, Henderson, Cole, et al., 1998, p. 1242, Table 4).

⬚ References

Aos, S. (2002). *The 1997 revisions to Washington's juvenile offender sentencing laws: An evaluation of the effect of local detention on crime rates.* Olympia: Washington State Institute for Public Policy.

Blumstein, A., & Wallman, J. (Eds.). (2000). *The crime drop in America.* New York: Cambridge University Press.

Braga, A. A., Cook, P. J., Kennedy, D. M., & Moore, M. H. (2002). The illegal supply of firearms. In M. Tonry (Ed.), *Crime and justice: A review of research, 29,* 319–352. Chicago: University of Chicago Press.

Braga, A. A., Kennedy, D. M., Waring, E. J., & Piehl, A. M. (2001). Problem-oriented policing, deterrence, and youth violence: An evaluation of Boston's Operation Ceasefire. *Journal of Research in Crime and Delinquency, 38,* 195–225.

Brundtland, G. H. (2002). Statement by the Director General for the global launch of the *World report on violence and health* on October 3 in Brussels, Belgium. Retrieved October 4, 2002, from www5.who.mt/violence_injury_prevention/mam.cim

Bureau of Justice Statistics. (2003). *Criminal victimization in the United States, 2001: Statistical tables.* Washington, DC: U.S. Department of Justice, Bureau of Justice Statistics.

Canadian Public Health Association. (1994). *Violence in society: A public health perspective.* Ottawa: Canadian Public Health Association.

Centers for Disease Control and Prevention. (2002a). *10 leading causes of death, United States, 1999, all races, both sexes.* Atlanta, GA: Centers for Disease Control and Prevention, National Center for Injury Prevention and Control, Office of Statistics and Programming. Retrieved October 20, 2002, from http://webapp.cdc.gov/cgi-bin/broker.exe

Centers for Disease Control and Prevention. (2002b). *10 leading causes of death, United States, 1999, Blacks, both sexes.* Atlanta, GA: Centers for Disease Control and Prevention, National Center for Injury Prevention and Control, Office of Statistics and Programming. Retrieved October 20, 2002, from http://webapp.cdc.gov/cgi-bin/broker.exe

Children's Safety Network Economics and Insurance Resource Center. (2000). *State costs of violence perpetrated by youth* (Updated on July 12, 2000). Retrieved August 30, 2002, from www. csneirc.org/pubs/tables/youth-viol.htm

Elliott, D. S., Hamburg, B. A., & Williams, K. R. (1998). Violence in American schools: An overview. In D. S. Elliott, B. A. Hamburg, & K. R. Williams (Eds.), *Violence in American schools: A new perspective* (pp. 3–28). New York: Cambridge University Press.

Farrington, D. P. (1998). Predictors, causes, and correlates of male youth violence. In M. Tonry &

M. H. Moore (Eds.), *Youth violence: Crime and justice: A review of research* (Vol. 24, pp. 421–475). Chicago: University of Chicago Press.

Federal Bureau of Investigation. (2001). *Crime in the United States, 2000.* Washington, DC: U.S. Government Printing Office.

Feld, B. C. (1998). Juvenile and criminal justice systems' responses to youth violence. In M. Tonry & M. H. Moore (Eds.), *Youth violence: Crime and justice: A review of research* (Vol. 24, pp. 189–261). Chicago: University of Chicago Press.

Forrant, R., Pyle, J. L., Lazonick, W., & Levenstein, C. (Eds.). (2001). *Approaches to sustainable development: The public university in the regional economy.* Amherst: University of Massachusetts Press.

Gabor, T., Welsh, B. C., & Antonowicz, D. H. (1996). The role of the health community in the prevention of criminal violence. *Canadian Journal of Criminology, 38,* 317–333.

Galant, D. (2003). Violence offers its own lessons. (2003, June 15). *The New York Times.* Available at www.nytimes.com

Gest, T. (2001). *Crime and politics: Big government's erratic campaign for law and order.* New York: Oxford University Press.

Gottfredson, D. C., Wilson, D. B., & Najaka, S. S. (2002). School-based crime prevention. In L. W. Sherman, D. P. Farrington, B. C. Welsh, & D. L. MacKenzie (Eds.), *Evidence-based crime prevention* (pp. 56–164). New York: Routledge.

Greenwood, P. W., Karoly, L. A., Everingham, S. S., Houbé, J., Kilburn, M. R., Rydell, C. P., et al. (2001). Estimating the costs and benefits of early childhood interventions: Nurse home visits and the Perry preschool. In B. C. Welsh, D. P. Farrington, & L. W. Sherman (Eds.), *Costs and benefits of preventing crime* (pp. 123–148). Boulder, CO: Westview.

Hagan, J., & Foster, H. (2001). Youth violence and the end of adolescence. *American Sociological Review, 66,* 874–899.

Harris, A. R., Thomas, S. H., Fisher, G. A., & Hirsch, D. J. (2002). Murder and medicine: The lethality of criminal assault 1960–1999. *Homicide Studies, 6,* 128–166.

Howell, J. C. (1997). *Juvenile justice and youth violence.* Thousand Oaks, CA: Sage.

International Centre for Sustainable Cities. (1994). *Urban security and sustainable development in the 21st century* (Report of the expert group meeting on urban security, Vancouver, British Columbia, Canada, July 11–14, 1994). Vancouver, Canada: Author.

Kellermann, A. L., Rivara, F. P., Ruthforth, N. B., Banton, J. B., Reay, D. T., Francisco, J. T., et al. (1993). Gun ownership as a risk factor for homicide in the home. *New England Journal of Medicine, 329,* 1084–1091.

Kennedy, D. M. (1997). Pulling levers: Chronic offenders, high-crime settings, and a theory of prevention. *Valparaiso University Law Review, 31,* 449–484.

Krug, E. G., Dahlberg, L. L., Mercy, J. A., Zwi, A. B., & Lozano, R. (Eds.). (2002). *World report on violence and health.* Geneva, Switzerland: World Health Organization.

Langan, P. A., & Levin, D. J. (2002). *Recidivism of prisoners released in 1994* (Special report). Washington, DC: U.S. Department of Justice, Bureau of Justice Statistics.

Larson, J. (1994). Violence prevention in the schools: A review of selected programs and procedures. *Psychology Review, 23,* 151–164.

Lipsey, M. W., & Wilson, D. B. (1998). Effective intervention for serious juvenile offenders: A synthesis of research. In R. Loeber & D. P. Farrington (Eds.), *Serious and violent juvenile offenders: Risk factors and successful interventions* (pp. 313–345). Thousand Oaks, CA: Sage.

Lizotte, A., & Sheppard, D. (2001). *Gun use by male juveniles: Research and prevention* (Juvenile Justice Bulletin). Washington, DC: U.S. Department of Justice, Office of Juvenile Justice and Delinquency Prevention.

MacKenzie, D. L. (2002). Reducing the criminal activities of known offenders and delinquents: Crime prevention in the courts and corrections. In L. W. Sherman, D. P. Farrington, B. C. Welsh, & D. L. MacKenzie (Eds.), *Evidence-based crime prevention* (pp. 330–404). New York: Routledge.

Mandel, M. J., Magnusson, P., Ellis, J. E., DeGeorge, G., & Alexander, K. L. (1993, December 13). The economics of crime. *Business Week,* 72–75, 78–81.

McCord, J., Widom, C. S., & Crowell, N. A. (Eds.). (2001). *Juvenile crime, juvenile justice* (Panel on Juvenile Crime: Prevention, Treatment, and Control). Washington, DC: National Academy Press.

Mercy, J. A., Butchart, A., Farrington, D. P., & Cerdá, M. (2002). Youth violence. In E. G. Krug, L. L. Dahlberg, J. A. Mercy, A. B. Zwi, & R. Lozano (Eds.), *World report on violence and health* (pp. 23–56). Geneva, Switzerland: World Health Organization.

Mercy, J. A., Rosenberg, M. L., Powell, K. E., Broome, C. V., & Roper, W. L. (1993). Public health policy for preventing violence. *Health Affairs, 12,* 7–29.

Miller, T. R., Cohen, M. A., & Wiersema, B. (1996). *Victim costs and consequences: A new look.* Washington, DC: U.S. Department of Justice, National Institute of Justice.

Miller, T. R., Fisher, D. A., & Cohen, M. A. (2001). Costs of juvenile violence: Policy implications. *Pediatrics, 107*(1). Available from www.pediatrics .org/cgi/content/full/107/l/e3

Moore, M. H. (1995). Public health and criminal justice approaches to prevention. In M. Tonry & D. P. Farrington (Eds.), *Building a safer society: Strategic approaches to crime prevention: Crime and justice: A review of research* (Vol. 19, pp. 237–262). Chicago: University of Chicago Press.

Olds, D. L., Eckenrode, J., Henderson, C. R., Kitzman, H., Powers, J., Cole, R., et al. (1997). Long-term effects of home visitation on maternal life course and child abuse and neglect: Fifteen-year follow-up of a randomized trial. *Journal of the American Medical Association, 278,* 637–643.

Olds, D. L., Henderson, C. R., Chamberlin, R., & Tatlebaum, R. (1986). Preventing child abuse and neglect: A randomized trial of nurse home visitation. *Pediatrics, 78,* 65–78.

Olds, D. L., Henderson, C. R., Cole, R., Eckenrode, J., Kitzman, H., Luckey, D., et al. (1998). Long-term effects of nurse home visitation on children's criminal and antisocial behavior: 15-year follow-up of a randomized controlled trial. *Journal of the American Medical Association, 280,* 1238–1244.

Pan American Health Organization. (1994, November 16–17). *Declaration.* Presented at the Inter-American Conference on Society, Violence, and Health, Washington, DC.

Pan American Health Organization. (2000). *Juvenile violence in the Americas: Innovative studies in research, diagnosis, and prevention.* Washington, DC: Author.

Petersilia, J. (2003). *When prisoners come home: Parole and prisoner reentry.* New York: Oxford University Press.

Potter, R. H., & Saltzman, L. E. (2000). Violence prevention and corrections-related activities of the Centers for Disease Control and Prevention. *Criminologist, 25*(2), 1, 4–6.

Prothrow-Stith, D. (1992). Can physicians help curb adolescent violence? *Hospital Practice, 27,* 193–196, 199, 202, 205–207.

Reiss, A. J., Jr., & Roth, J. A. (Eds.). (1993). *Understanding and preventing violence* (Panel on the Understanding and Control of Violent Behavior). Washington, DC: National Academy Press.

Rivara, F. P., & Farrington, D. P. (1995). Prevention of violence: Role of the pediatrician. *Archives of Pediatric and Adolescent Medicine, 149,* 421–429.

Rosenberg, M. L., & Mercy, J. A. (1991). Introduction. In M. L. Rosenberg & M. A. Fenley (Eds.), *Violence in America: A public health approach* (pp. 1–12). New York: Oxford University Press.

Rosenberg, M. L., O'Carroll, P. W., & Powell, K. E. (1992). Let's be clear: Violence is a public health problem. *Journal of the American Medical Association, 267,* 3071–3072.

Rosenfeld, R., & Decker, S. H. (1993). Where public health and law enforcement meet: Monitoring and preventing youth violence. *American Journal of Police, 12,* 11–57.

Ruttenberg, H. (1994). The limited promise of public health methodologies to prevent youth violence. *Yale Law Journal, 103,* 1885–1912.

Sheppard, D., Grant, H., Rowe, W., & Jacobs, N. (2000). *Fighting juvenile gun violence* (Juvenile Justice Bulletin). Washington, DC: U.S. Department of Justice, Office of Juvenile Justice and Delinquency Prevention.

Sickmund, M., & Wan, Y.-C. (2001). *Census of juveniles in residential placement databook.* Retrieved October 13, 2002, from www.ojjdp.ncjrs.org/ ojstatbb/cjrp

Silverman, J. G., Raj, A., Mucci, L. A., & Hathaway, J. E. (2001). Dating violence against adolescent girls and associated substance use, unhealthy weight control, sexual risk behavior, pregnancy, and suicidality. *Journal of the American Medical Association, 286,* 572–579.

Slaby, R. G., & Stringham, P. (1994). Prevention of peer and community violence: The pediatrician's role. *Pediatrics, 94*(4), S608–S616.

Sloan, J. H., Kellermann, A. L., Reay, D. T., Ferris, J. A., Koepsell, T., Rivara, F. P., et al. (1988). Handgun regulations, crime, assaults, and homicide: A tale of two cities. *New England Journal of Medicine, 319,* 1256–1262.

Snyder, H. S. (2002). *Juvenile arrests 2000* (Juvenile Justice Bulletin). Washington, DC: U.S. Department of Justice, Office of Juvenile Justice and Delinquency Prevention.

Spohn, C., & Holleran, D. (2002). The effect of imprisonment on recidivism rates of felony offenders: A focus on drug offenders. *Criminology, 40,* 329–358.

Stein, B. D., Jaycox, L. H., Kataoka, S. H., Wong, M., Tu, W., Elliott, M. N., et al. (2003). A mental health intervention for schoolchildren exposed to violence: A randomized controlled trial. *Journal of the American Medical Association, 290,* 603–611.

Tita, G. K., Riley, J., & Greenwood, P. W. (2003). From Boston to Boyle Heights: The process and prospects of a "pulling levers" strategy in a Los Angeles barrio. In S. H. Decker (Ed.), *Policing gangs and youth violence* (pp. 102–130). Belmont, CA: Wadsworth.

Tremblay, R. E., & Craig, W. M. (1995). Developmental crime prevention. In M. Tonry & D. P. Farrington (Eds.), Building a safer society: Strategic approaches to crime prevention. *Crime and justice: A review of research* (Vol. 19, pp. 151–236). Chicago: University of Chicago Press.

U.S. Department of Health and Human Services. (2001). *Youth violence: A report of the surgeon general.* Rockville, MD: Author.

Welsh, B. C., & Farrington, D. P. (2000). Monetary costs and benefits of crime prevention programs. In M. Tonry (Ed.), *Crime and justice: A review of research* (Vol. 27, pp. 305–361). Chicago: University of Chicago Press.

Widom, C. S. (1989). The cycle of violence. *Science, 244,* 160–166.

Wilson-Brewer, R., Cohen, S., O'Donnell, L., & Goodman, I. F. (1991). *Violence prevention for young adolescents: A survey of the state of the art.* New York: Carnegie Corporation.

Wilson-Brewer, R., & Spivak, H. (1994). Violence prevention in schools and other community settings: The pediatrician as initiator, educator, collaborator, and advocate. *Pediatrics, 94*(4), S623–S630.

Wintemute, G. (2000). Guns and gun violence. In A. Blumstein & J. Wallman (Eds.), *The crime drop in America* (pp. 45–96). New York: Cambridge University Press.

World Health Organization. (2003, April). Opening piece. *Global Campaign for Violence Prevention Newsletter.* Geneva, Switzerland: Author.

Zimring, F. E., & Hawkins, G. (1995). *Incapacitation: Penal confinement and the restraint of crime.* New York: Oxford University Press.

DISCUSSION QUESTIONS

1. Based on the research findings and conclusions of studies on punishment and juvenile violence, do longer sentences of incarceration and institutionalization of juvenile offenders result in a reduction of recidivism and less juvenile violence?

2. Based on your reading, how would you summarize the major distinguishing characteristics of the public health approach to violence prevention?

3. Where does the United States stand in general in its implementation of a public health approach to criminal violence? Give some examples of applications of a public health approach to violence prevention.

4. Explain how a public health approach is considered a preventive rather than a reactive approach to crime as practiced by the criminal and juvenile justice process. Give examples of primary and secondary prevention practices.

5. The state legislator in your district has convened a Special Commission on Crime Prevention and has invited your participation and input as a Criminal Justice student concerned about the future of criminal justice and crime prevention. Write a summary statement outlining the advantages of a public health approach to crime prevention, its advantages, and how it could work with the present justice system.

❖

READING

State and local jurisdictions throughout the United States enacted a wide array of new juvenile justice policies in recent years. Many of these policies were intended to make the juvenile justice system tougher, but others improved prevention, increased rehabilitation, and enhanced the restorative features of the juvenile justice system. The authors of this article describe the most prominent new ideas in juvenile justice and address a question usually asked by policy makers: What works? They conclude that recent get-tough policies weakened the integrity of the juvenile justice system, but they note that there is growing evidence about the effectiveness of new ideas in prevention and rehabilitation, and they suggest that a new generation of innovative programs might revive the spirit of American juvenile justice.

Reviving Juvenile Justice in a Get-Tough Era

Jeffrey A. Butts, Daniel P. Mears

In response to widespread concern about juvenile crime during the 1980s and 1990s, state and local jurisdictions throughout the United States implemented numerous changes in their juvenile justice systems. Many of these changes were designed to increase the ability of juvenile courts to punish youthful offenders. Nearly all states, for example, increased the number of juveniles eligible for transfer to adult court. Yet even while policy makers were passing new policies to "get tough," other parts of the juvenile justice system were being reinvented, and researchers were finding support for the effectiveness of preventive and rehabilitative programs. Numerous innovations were implemented to improve the quality of treatment programs and to ensure early intervention before young juveniles become further involved in crime. Other changes focused on the organization and methods of juvenile justice itself, such as the growth of new specialized courts, the increasing application of restorative justice principles, and enhanced coordination and collaboration among juvenile justice and social service agencies.

SOURCE: *Youth & Society*, (33)2, 169–198, December, 2001. © 2001 Sage Publications, Inc.

The broad scope of these recent changes raises important questions. What do we want the juvenile justice system to be? Are we sure we still want to have a juvenile justice system? It is important to remember that dividing the justice system into two parts—one for juveniles and one for adults—was an explicit policy choice made a little more than a century ago. State laws refer to young people who break the law before reaching legal adulthood as *juveniles* to indicate that they are under the jurisdiction of the juvenile court rather than the criminal (or adult) court. Technically, juveniles are not even arrested for committing crimes. The criminal code does not apply to people younger than a certain age, usually 17 or 18 years. Instead, juveniles are charged with *acts of delinquency*. A 20-year-old who breaks into a neighbor's house is arrested for the crime of burglary. By contrast, a 15-year-old who does the same thing is taken into custody for an act of delinquency that would be burglary if the youth were an adult.

In recent years, support for this traditional view of juvenile delinquency seemed to decline. The distinction between juvenile delinquency and adult crime appeared to trouble many people, especially elected officials. Defining juvenile law-breaking as delinquency rather than crime, in their view, diminishes the consequences of illegal behavior by juveniles. This underlying skepticism was aggravated further when violent juvenile crime arrests jumped between 1984 and 1994. The focus of juvenile crime policy shifted perceptibly toward incarceration, and state and federal lawmakers stepped up efforts to make the juvenile justice system more like the adult justice system. States across the country enacted sweeping policy changes to make the juvenile system tougher.

In this article, we review the most prominent new developments in juvenile justice. We find that juvenile justice is alive and well, adhering in many respects to the principles envisioned by the juvenile court's founders but in a more politicized environment that adds conflict to the formulation of policies and programs. We place these recent changes in historical context, exploring the underlying motivations that established the juvenile justice system. Next, we examine the most visible policy change in juvenile justice—the get-tough movement of the 1980s and 1990s. Then we focus on some of the more promising ideas in rehabilitation, prevention, and early intervention as well as transformations in the administration and organization of juvenile justice. We conclude that recent get-tough policies weakened the integrity of the juvenile justice system, but growing evidence about the effectiveness of new ideas in prevention and rehabilitation may save the system yet.

⊠ The Origins of Juvenile Justice

Contemporary observers must understand the heritage of American juvenile justice to appreciate the relevance of recent policy changes. The juvenile justice system in the United States is a broad network of juvenile and family courts, state and local youth services agencies, juvenile correctional institutions and detention centers, private social service organizations, and other private youth and family programs. Added to this mix are organizations such as school systems and law enforcement agencies that work hand in hand with the juvenile justice system but that are technically not part of it.

All of these organizations existed in one form or another for most of America's history, but they came together in a brand new way in the early 1900s to form a separate and distinct system of justice for juveniles. The official start of juvenile justice occurred in Chicago in 1899 with the founding of the first separate juvenile court. Within 20 years, juvenile courts were established throughout the United States, and the modern juvenile justice system began to take shape (Bernard, 1992; Watkins, 1998).

Separate juvenile courts emerged during the early 1900s for a number of reasons, including those most often cited by the popular press (e.g., efforts to increase the rehabilitative potential of the courts, protect vulnerable children from adult prisoners, and save young people from the stigma of criminal conviction). However, there was another, less publicized reason for the founding of juvenile courts. Much of the early pressure for separate juvenile courts came from judges, law enforcement agencies, and prosecutors. These groups favored juvenile courts for their crime control potential (Platt, 1977; Schlossman, 1977).

During the 19th century, city and state officials had been frustrated by the criminal court system's inability to deal with young offenders. It was clear to most Americans at the time that children and youth became involved in criminal behavior because of urban disorder, chronic poverty, poor parenting and inadequate supervision of children, rampant alcoholism, and family violence. Then, as now, children growing up in deprived and stressful conditions were more likely to become criminals or at least more likely to become involved with the justice system as a result of illegal behavior.

The problem in the 1800s was that American communities lacked an adequate intervention method to detect and intervene with youth at risk. Police, courts, and prisons were traditionally responsible for dealing with crime, but they could not intervene until an offender had actually committed a crime and been convicted, something judges and juries were reluctant to do when faced with inexperienced and obviously disadvantaged young people. As a result, politicians, social reformers, and justice system officials called for a completely separate system of courts and agencies that could intervene to prevent youth crime and take charge of young offenders whether or not they had been convicted of criminal offenses.

The Birth of the Juvenile Court

Inspiration for a new approach came from the poorhouses and reformatories established throughout Europe and America during the 1800s. Courts allowed state and local officials to place people in these institutions against their will based only on a legal finding that they were in danger of becoming paupers and that institutionalization was in their own best interests. American reformers in search of a new way to deal with young offenders seized this idea. They argued that courts should be able to take charge of minor children as well even if they had not been convicted of a crime and based solely on the grounds that they were in danger of becoming criminals in the future (Bernard, 1992; Rothman, 1980). The trick was to create a new type of court that would have the power to intervene but would not have to abide by the restrictions of criminal procedure and due-process rights.

As the idea spread, state officials began to enact such provisions into law. Illinois was the first state to do so, establishing its juvenile court in 1899. These new state laws, or *juvenile codes,* were distinct from the criminal code. They created a separate classification of illegal behavior called *delinquency,* and they authorized local courts to take custody of young offenders without the need to obtain a criminal conviction. Juvenile courts were empowered to intervene with young offenders free of the bureaucratic and legal restrictions placed on criminal courts. Essentially, America's juvenile justice system was invented to loosen the reins on police, prosecutors, and judges. Under juvenile law, the courts could take charge of young offenders and even incarcerate them long before there was sufficient legal evidence to warrant a criminal conviction (Butts & Mitchell, 2000).

In return for the broad discretion they received under juvenile law, the nation's juvenile courts accepted a different mandate from that of criminal courts. Rather than simply punish young offenders with sentences proportionate to their offenses, juvenile courts were to employ an individualized approach that would provide each youth with a program of services and sanctions designed to prevent future offending and return him or her to the law-abiding community.

As the juvenile justice system assumed its modern form during the 20th century, the twin goals of crime control and youth services were combined in unique ways. Juvenile courts became more responsive than adult courts to the social and developmental characteristics of children and youth. The services and sanctions imposed by juvenile courts were designed to address the particular causes of each individual youth's misbehavior to restore the youth to full and responsible membership in his or her family as well as the larger community. In some cases, the juvenile court's intervention strategy may have included a period of incarceration, but the intent of confinement was never supposed to be simple punishment. It was to ensure the delivery of needed services and to correct behavior.

The End of Traditional Juvenile Justice

From the very beginning of the juvenile court movement, some critics doubted whether the expansive mission of the juvenile justice system could be achieved or was even desirable (Feld, 1999). By the 1960s, the legal foundations of the traditional model of juvenile justice began to unravel completely. The informality and individualization that was so highly valued by social reformers and youth advocates in the early 1900s made the juvenile court vulnerable from a due-process perspective. Legal activists began to challenge the sweeping discretion given to juvenile court judges. An influential law review article in 1960 charged juvenile courts with violating important principles of equal protection and argued that "rehabilitation may be substituted for punishment, but a Star Chamber cannot be substituted for a trial" (Beemsterboer as cited in Manfredi, 1998, p. 39). While public criticism of the juvenile court intensified, juvenile courts began to exhibit the worst features of criminal courts. Caseloads grew and began to overwhelm staff workers. Courtrooms fell into disrepair. The professional status of a juvenile court appointment dipped among judges, and policy makers became less enthusiastic about the viability of the juvenile justice ideal.

Eventually, the U.S. Supreme Court intervened and imposed new constitutional protections for juveniles, thereby ending the traditional

juvenile court as conceptualized at the beginning of the century. In a series of important cases beginning in 1966, the court raised the standard of evidence used in juvenile courts, protected juveniles from the risks of double jeopardy, and ruled that any youth facing possible confinement as a result of juvenile court adjudication was entitled to an attorney, the right to confront and cross-examine witnesses, the right to formal notice of charges, and the protection against self-incrimination (see reviews in Bernard, 1992; Manfredi, 1998; Watkins, 1998). By the 1980s, America's juvenile courts had been largely "constitutionally domesticated" as they were forced to follow similar procedures and establish evidentiary standards similar to those of the criminal courts (Feld, 1999, p. 79).

The imposition of greater due-process rights for juveniles necessarily limited the discretion of juvenile court judges. This made the juvenile justice process more bureaucratic and formalized. It also helped to limit the juvenile court's jurisdiction over many categories of young offenders, especially those charged with minor infractions of the law such as truancy and curfew violations. Finally, and ironically, the well-intentioned efforts of youth advocates to enhance procedural protections for juveniles paved the way for the next large-scale policy reform in juvenile justice, the get-tough movement of the 1980s and 1990s.

▧ The New Focus on Punishment

The direction taken by juvenile justice policy during the closing decades of the 20th century was a clear, although perhaps unexpected, consequence of bringing due process to the juvenile court. Lawmakers began to infuse the juvenile court with the values and philosophical orientation of the criminal court. Most states altered their laws to reduce the confidentiality of juvenile court proceedings and juvenile court records (Torbet & Szymanski, 1998). Most states also increased legal formalities in the juvenile court, shifted the focus of the juvenile justice process away from individualized intervention, and made the juvenile justice process more responsive to offense severity, adding concepts such as sentencing guidelines to juvenile justice decision making (Butts & Mitchell, 2000). The juvenile justice process began to focus on public safety, offender accountability, and imposing appropriate measures of punishment based on the severity of each juvenile's offenses. During the 1980s and 1990s, the juvenile court system became so much like the criminal court system that some observers began to wonder whether it was necessary to maintain a separate juvenile justice system at all (Feld, 1999).

Transfer to Criminal Court

The most visible plank in the get-tough movement—and the issue that has had the greatest effect on public understanding of juvenile justice in recent years—is the transfer of juveniles to criminal court. Juveniles transferred to adult court lose their status as minor children and become legally culpable for their behavior. State and federal lawmakers expended considerable time and energy during the 1980s and 1990s debating which juveniles should be transferred to adult court and which agencies and individuals should do the transferring. The outcome of these debates had a profound effect on the juvenile justice system.

State laws provide several mechanisms for moving juveniles into criminal court (see Snyder & Sickmund, 1999). Most states place the responsibility for at least some transfer decisions within the juvenile court itself. Juvenile court judges review the unique circumstances of every juvenile offender and then decide on a case-by-case basis whether to retain jurisdiction over each case or to waive jurisdiction and allow the matter to be handled in adult court. Until the 1980s, judicial waiver was the most common method used by states to transfer juveniles to criminal court. Nationwide, juvenile court judges usually waive 8,000 to 12,000 cases per year to the criminal court (Puzzanchera et al., 2000).

Since the 1980s, lawmakers in every state have enacted new transfer laws. Many of these new laws altered the decision-making authority for transfer, taking responsibility away from judges and giving it to prosecutors and legislators. Nonjudicial mechanisms now account for the vast majority of juvenile transfers nationwide. Some states allow prosecutors to file charges against juveniles in either juvenile or adult court (known as *concurrent jurisdiction* or *prosecutor direct file*). A growing number of states move juveniles into criminal court without the involvement of either judges or prosecutors by using *automatic transfer* or *mandatory waiver* laws. These laws place some juveniles immediately under the jurisdiction of the adult court whenever certain conditions are met, such as when a juvenile of a certain age commits a violent felony or when a youth with a lengthy record of prior offenses is charged with another serious crime.

There are no sources of national data about nonjudicial transfers, but the number of youth affected is likely to outweigh those judicially waived by a substantial margin. Prosecutor transfer laws, for example, greatly increased nationwide in recent years. In 1960, just 2 states (Florida and Georgia) permitted prosecutor transfers (Feld, 1987). Eight states had such provisions by 1982, whereas 14 states and the District of Columbia allowed prosecutor transfers by 1997 (Griffin, Torbet, & Szymanski, 1998; Torbet & Szymanski, 1998; Torbet et al., 1996). Thus, it is likely that prosecutor transfers now greatly outnumber judicial waivers. Florida prosecutors alone sent approximately 6,000 juvenile cases to adult court each year during the 1990s, nearly as many as juvenile court judges nationwide (Butts & Mitchell, 2000).

The popularity of legislative or automatic transfer also increased significantly in recent decades. In 1960, just 3 states had enacted legislation to transfer certain types of juveniles automatically to adult court (Feld, 1987). By 1997, 28 states had passed such laws. Furthermore, during the 1990s, nearly every state with these laws already on the books either expanded the offense criteria for automatic transfer, lowered the minimum age at which offenders could be transferred, or both (Torbet & Szymanski, 1998).

During the 1990s, many states passed laws to transfer a wider range of juvenile matters to criminal court. Transfer was traditionally used for juveniles charged with serious and violent offenses, but many of the youthful offenders transferred to adult court today have committed lesser offenses, such as property charges and drug law violations. About a third of all juveniles tried for felonies in adult courts, for example, are charged with property offenses, drug violations, or other nonviolent charges (Snyder & Sickmund, 1999). In one recent survey, more than 4 in 10 state prison inmates younger than 18 had been imprisoned for nonviolent offenses, including property crimes (21%), drug crimes (10%), and even alcohol-related charges (3%) (Austin, Johnson, & Gregoriou, 2000).

The Ineffectiveness of Criminal Court Transfer

Policy makers and the public generally assume that juvenile offenders are sent to criminal court to receive more certain and more severe punishments. State officials enact transfer provisions based on this assumption, but until recently, it was not tested by research. Until the 1980s, very few studies existed on the effect of transfer, but more research began to appear during the subsequent 20 years. The consensus of these studies was that the expansion of criminal court transfer had little effect on public safety (Table 1).

Transfer does appear to increase the certainty and severity of legal sanctions but only for the most serious juvenile cases, perhaps a third of all transferred juveniles. In about half of all transfers, offenders receive sentences comparable to what they might have received in juvenile court. Some (perhaps one fifth) actually receive more lenient treatment in criminal court, often because the charges against them are reduced or dismissed due to the greater evidentiary scrutiny in criminal court.

Taken together, studies of transfer outcomes indicate that conviction rates for transferred youth vary from 60% to 90%, with 30% to 60% of convictions resulting in incarceration. The most recent research suggests that incarceration among transferred youth is contingent on offenses. Youth convicted of violent offenses are more likely to be incarcerated if they are handled in criminal court. Youth charged with property and drug offenses, on the other hand, tend to receive sentences in criminal court that are no more (and sometimes less) severe than the dispositions usually imposed by juvenile court. The bottom line seems to be that criminal court transfer does not ensure incarceration, and it does not always increase sentence lengths even in cases that do result in incarceration. It is perhaps because of this fact that researchers have not been able to find evidence that juvenile crime and violence overall is affected by the scope and severity of transfer policies (Jensen & Metsger, 1994; Risler, Sweatman, & Nackerud, 1998; Singer, 1996; Singer & McDowall, 1988).

There are many reasons for the apparent ineffectiveness of transfer laws. One of the simplest reasons may be that the juvenile justice system is in fact a system. Policies designed to expand the use of transfer are never implemented exactly as legislators hope. Justice policies are implemented by a complex network of individual decision makers that may respond in ways not anticipated by lawmakers. Singer (1996) argued that the juvenile justice system is "loosely coupled," meaning there are so many areas of discretion in the juvenile justice system that the decisions of any individual or group are at best an imperfect reflection of the decisions and priorities of others. Police do not refer every arrested youth for prosecution, prosecutors do not charge every youth referred by police, and judges do not adjudicate every youth charged by prosecutors. Loose coupling creates a system in which case-processing decisions are structured by interorganizational negotiations, reducing the chances that any single policy initiative can have a consistent effect on crime.

Table 1	Research Findings on the Effects of Criminal Court Transfer for Juvenile Offenders

Court outcomes

- Criminal court conviction rates (including guilty pleas) for transferred youth vary from 60% to 90%, and chances of incarceration for those convicted range from 30% to 60%. Thus, the odds of incarceration may be as low as 20% or as high as 50% to 60% for transferred cases.
- Youth convicted of violent offenses are somewhat more likely to be incarcerated when they are handled in criminal court rather than in juvenile court.
- Youth charged with property and drug offenses tend to receive sentences in criminal court that are no more severe (and sometimes less severe) than dispositions typically imposed by juvenile courts in such cases.
- When criteria for automatic transfer are expanded to include younger juveniles and those charged with less serious offenses, transferred youth are particularly unlikely to be convicted and incarcerated in adult court.

Key studies: Bortner (1986); Fagan (1995, 1996); Greenwood, Lipson, Abrahamse, and Zimring (1983); Hamparian et al. (1982); McNulty (1996); Podkopacz and Feld (1996); Snyder, Sickmund, and Poe-Yamagata (2000)

Individual youth behavior

- Youth handled in adult court are no more or less likely to recidivate than similar youth handled in juvenile court for similar offenses.
- Among youth that recidivate after court sanctioning, transferred youth may reoffend more quickly.
- The prevalence of recidivism among youth handled in juvenile court may eventually catch up to recidivism levels among transferred youth, but transferred youth tend to reoffend more often during follow-up periods.

Key studies: Bishop, Frazier, Lanza-Kaduce, and Winner (1996); Fagan (1995, 1996); Podkopacz and Feld (1996); Winner, Lanza-Kaduce, Bishop, and Frazier (1997)

Aggregate juvenile crime

- There is no clear association between the use of criminal court transfer and juvenile crime levels.
- Expansions of juvenile transfer are not followed by significant changes in juvenile crime.
- Juvenile crime rates do not vary systematically between jurisdictions according to the availability and use of transfer provisions.

Key studies: Jensen and Metsger (1994); Risler, Sweatman, and Nackerud (1998); Singer (1996); Singer and McDowall (1988)

The most recent studies on the effects of transfer support this explanation (Snyder & Sickmund, 1999; Snyder, Sickmund, & Poe-Yamagata, 2000). Researchers in Pennsylvania studied nearly 500 court cases that were excluded from juvenile court by a 1996 law that automatically transferred youth age 15 and older if they were charged with certain violent offenses and had committed the offense with a weapon or were previously adjudicated for an excluded crime. Prior to 1996, Pennsylvania had relied largely on judicial

waiver to send youth to criminal court. The new law automatically transferred many of the same types of juveniles who were routinely waived by judges, but it also targeted youth who would have been unlikely candidates for waiver prior to 1996 (i.e., younger offenders, females, and those with limited arrest records).

The Pennsylvania researchers found that half of the cases targeted by the new law were either sent back to juvenile court by decertification, or criminal court prosecutors declined to proceed for various reasons (e.g., lack of evidence). Even when cases were approved for criminal prosecution, more than half ended in dismissal, probation, or some other sanction that did not involve incarceration. Of all youth that were automatically excluded by the new law, just 19% were incarcerated. Moreover, the offenders that actually ended up in jail or prison were basically the same type of youth that were waived by judges before 1996. They tended to be older, to have used weapons, and to have more extensive prior offense histories. Thus, in the end, Pennsylvania's new law seemed to achieve very little beyond complicating and most likely delaying the decision-making process for juvenile offenders.

Pennsylvania's experience underscores the realities of criminal court transfer. Lawmakers across the country tried to get tough in recent years by expanding the use of adult court transfer for juvenile offenders, but in doing so, they swept younger and less serious offenders into the criminal court process. Not only are these offenders unlikely to receive serious sanctions from the adult court system, but the amount of crime hypothetically averted by transfer necessarily falls as the criminal severity and age of transferred juveniles declines. As a crime control policy, therefore, criminal court transfer appears to be merely a symbol of toughness.

In combination with other recent policy changes in juvenile courts—reduced confidentiality, increased formality, and greater due process—the increasing use of criminal court transfer reflects a declining faith in juvenile justice among policy makers, but the get-tough movement has not been the only story. The past decade has also seen the emergence of a wide range of new ideas in rehabilitation, prevention, and early intervention as well as new ways of administering and organizing juvenile justice. The critical question for policy makers and the public is "Where should we invest our crime-fighting dollars?" The remaining sections of this discussion address this question by reviewing the research evidence for other new ideas.

◪ Rehabilitation

In 1974, Robert Martinson's influential report on the effectiveness of rehabilitative programming led to the widely held view that "nothing works." Recent research suggests that this view is incorrect (Aos, Barnoski, & Lieb, 1998; Coordinating Council on Juvenile Justice and Delinquency Prevention, 1996; Cullen & Gendreau, 2000; Durlak & Wells, 1997; Howell, 1995; Howell & Hawkins, 1998; Lipsey, 1999a, 1999b; Lipsey & Derzon, 1998; Lipsey & Wilson, 1998; Lipsey, Wilson, & Cothern, 2000; Mackenzie, 2000; Mendel, 2000). Treatment programs can reduce recidivism, often by at least 10%, with much larger effects for well-designed and effectively implemented programs (Cullen & Gendreau, 2000; Lipsey, 1999b; McGuire, 1995). The critical task is to identify which approaches work, for whom, and under what conditions. As Lipsey (1999b) stated, "Rehabilitative programs of a practical 'real world' sort clearly can be effective; the challenge is to design and implement them so that they, in fact, are effective" (p. 641).

Concern about the costs and social consequences of America's swelling prison population helped to generate renewed interest in rehabilitation during the 1990s. Policy makers and justice practitioners called for proven program ideas that could have a substantial effect on offender behavior and perhaps avoid some of the costs of incarceration. Fortunately, research began to generate some useful answers. In recent years, a consensus emerged among researchers that treatment programs will have the most effect when they are grounded in established principles of effective intervention (see e.g., Andrews & Bonta, 1998; Cullen & Gendreau, 2000; Lipsey, 1999a, 1999b). Research suggests that the most effective juvenile justice programs incorporate accurate risk assessments and dynamic/criminogenic needs assessments, focus services on the criminogenic needs of high-risk offenders, rely on a cognitive-behavioral orientation, design customized intervention strategies that focus on the particular needs of each offender, use local and community-based services whenever possible, and provide comprehensive aftercare services for youth after their release from placement or supervision (Table 2).

Accurate assessment is essential for ensuring that an appropriate and effective response is developed for each individual youth. High-risk offenders clearly represent more of a danger to society, and programs will naturally focus a great deal of resources on them, but other youth may respond well to early intervention that could substantially reduce their likelihood of recidivism. Identifying these various subpopulations among juvenile offenders requires accurate assessment. Unfortunately, many jurisdictions rely on informal risk assessment although actuarial-based instruments, such as the Level of Supervision Inventory, are considerably better at identifying high-risk and high-needs offenders (Cullen & Gendreau, 2000; Harland, 1996).

A second principle of effective intervention involves targeting criminogenic needs, or factors that predict recidivism and are amenable to change (e.g., attitudes and behaviors) (Cullen & Gendreau, 2000), as well as factors that may discourage criminal behavior (Howell & Hawkins, 1998). Examples include drug use; education; vocational training; antisocial attitudes, values, and beliefs; association with criminals; and low self-control and impulsiveness (Andrews & Bonta, 1998). High-risk offenders should be targeted for services because they are the most likely to recidivate and are amenable to treatment (Cullen & Gendreau, 2000; Lipsey et al., 2000).

A third cornerstone of effective intervention is a reliance on *general responsivity,* or the use of programming grounded in cognitive-behavioral treatment modalities that address the particular needs and abilities of specific youth. Cognitive-behavioral approaches, which focus on individual counseling and interpersonal skill development, are well suited to addressing antisocial attitudes, behaviors, and personality characteristics and have been shown to be particularly effective in reducing recidivism among certain populations of offenders (Andrews & Bonta, 1998; Lipsey et al., 2000). However, programs must focus on *specific responsivity,* which means that treatment accommodates the particular strengths and limitations of each offender as well as individual learning styles (Andrews & Bonta, 1998). The emphasis on general and specific responsivity recognizes that juvenile offender populations may differ considerably. For example, research increasingly suggests that adolescent girls may have needs that are distinct or potentially more pronounced than those of boys, including patterns of physical, sexual, and emotional abuse and victimization as well as self-abuse or criminal behavior (Prescott, 1998).

Finally, where possible, intervention programs should be located in the same communities where their clients reside to allow for greater community involvement and to assist offenders with transitioning back into social environments that might have contributed to their behavior (see, generally, Cullen & Gendreau, 2000). For youth with serious substance abuse problems or mental illness or histories of sex or violent offending, follow-up services must be provided after release from probation, incarceration, or any other form of supervision. As always, it is important that treatment programs be implemented as designed, that they be well staffed, and that treatment and service delivery be monitored and evaluated routinely.

Policy makers inevitably ask, "But is treatment and rehabilitation cost-effective?" The answer, almost invariably, is yes, assuming that treatment is based on principles of effective intervention and is implemented appropriately and consistently. Cost-benefit analyses have shown that effective rehabilitative programs, especially those targeting high-risk offenders, can provide substantial long-term savings (Cohen, 1998; Greenwood, Model, Rydell, & Chiesa, 1996). As Snyder and Sickmund (1999) noted, "Under almost any reasonable set of assumptions, intervention efforts that are narrowly focused on high-risk youth and that succeed at least some of the time are likely to pay for themselves many times over" (p. 83).

Table 2 Policy and Practice Principles for Reducing Juvenile Crime: Guidance From Research

Utilize different types of interventions

Hold youth accountable with a range of sanctions

- Implement graduated sanctions, including treatment and youth development services, to ensure appropriate, predictable, and proportionate responses whenever delinquent youth commit additional crimes or violate probation or parole.
- Ensure a balance of punishment with rehabilitative and restorative programming.
- Incapacitate and treat chronic, serious, and violent youthful offenders.
- Provide reentry assistance and aftercare during transitions back into communities.

Identify, treat, and rehabilitate offenders

- Use objective risk and needs assessment screening criteria to identify and intervene with youthful offenders who are at highest risk to reoffend or have special service needs.
- Provide immediate intervention and appropriate treatment for delinquent youth.
- Develop treatment programming based on the principles of effective intervention (risk/needs assessment, targeting of criminogenic needs and of high-risk offenders, use of cognitive-behavioral approaches responsive to the unique needs of particular youth, reliance on local, community-based services, and provision of aftercare services).

Intervene early and support prevention

- Support intensive early childhood intervention programs to promote the healthy development of infants and toddlers in high-risk families.
- Provide research-proven treatment and services for young children with behavioral problems and their families.
- Provide a network of programs designed to strengthen communities, families, and schools.
- Organize to reduce the victimization, abuse, and neglect of children and youth.
- Organize to reduce youth involvement with guns, drugs, and gangs.

Emphasize restorative justice

- Include victims, families, and communities in the sanctioning process.
- Facilitate offender reparations to individuals, families, and communities harmed by juvenile offenses.

Target different populations, areas, and organizations

- Coordinate and organize the efforts of all actors in the juvenile justice system (including child welfare, social service agencies, schools, etc.).
- Maintain an appropriate and continuous focus on victims and offenders, their families, schools, and communities.

Share responsibility for interventions

- Mobilize communities to plan and implement comprehensive youth crime prevention strategies that involve families, schools, and neighborhoods.
- Reinforce the idea that crime and crime prevention are as much community responsibilities as government responsibilities.
- Recruit local volunteers and engage community-based organizations to work directly with high-risk and delinquent youth.
- Involve the victims of juvenile crime in the sanctioning process.

Develop and use effective programming to target local needs

- Use broad range of diversion programs as alternatives to incarceration
  - Offer alternatives to detention for nondangerous juvenile offenders awaiting trial.
  - Provide alternatives and opportunities for children and youth.
  - Deliver community/family-based treatment for youth that pose minimal risk.

- Develop alternative programs such as drug courts, teen courts, mental health courts, family group conferencing, and victim-offender mediation to hold young offenders accountable while connecting them to positive resources in their communities.
- Coordinate services among agencies (juvenile justice, education, mental health, and child welfare) that share responsibility for troubled youth.
- Implement an aggressive public outreach campaign on effective strategies to combat juvenile crime.

Monitor and evaluate trends, policies, and programs

- Monitor and evaluate crime and capacity trends to assist with allocation of resources and assess previous decision making.
- Use management information and data systems to ensure youth are sanctioned appropriately and to focus incarceration resources on the most serious, violent, and high-risk offenders.
- Act to correct justice system biases that perpetuate unequal access to treatment and services as well as disproportionate confinement of minority youth.
- Support the development of high-quality, comprehensive databases and innovative approaches to research and evaluation even if immediate benefits appear to be minimal.

SOURCES: Coordinating Council on Juvenile Justice and Delinquency Prevention (1996); Cullen and Gendreau (2000); Guarino-Ghezzi and Loughran (1996); Howell (1995); Howell and Hawkins (1998); Lipsey (1999a, 1999b); Lipsey and Wilson (1998); Mendel (2000); Oldenettel and Wordes (2000); Sherman et al. (1997); Wilson and Howell (1993).

One of the most widely known and evaluated treatment programs that embodies many of the principles of effective intervention described earlier is multisystemic therapy (MST) (Henggeler, 1997, 1999). MST has been shown to reduce recidivism among high-risk, serious offenders and to be effective across many different places (Cullen & Gendreau, 2000). It is grounded in the notion that individuals are parts of interconnected family, school, peer, and neighborhood systems and that individual behavior can be influenced by any or all of these factors. Thus, MST focuses on systematically addressing each dimension (i.e., developing family strengths, disengaging youth from peer influences, etc.).

MST may be one of the more widely known programs for juvenile offenders, but it is not the only program with documented results. Researchers have evaluated a range of other programs that focus on individual, family, and community interventions, and these studies are available for review by policy makers and practitioners (e.g., American Youth Policy Forum, 1997; Coordinating Council on Juvenile Justice and Delinquency Prevention, 1996; Cullen & Gendreau, 2000; Elliott, 1998; Howell, 1995; Lipsey & Wilson, 1998; MacKenzie, 2000; McCord, Widom, & Crowell, 2001; McGuire, 1995; Mendel, 2000; Mrazek & Haggerty, 1994).

Of course, some interventions have been studied and found not to work, including boot camps, simple incarceration, and increased sentence lengths. Indeed, research suggests that these interventions may actually increase recidivism

(Cullen & Gendreau, 2000; MacKenzie, 2000). Unwanted effects are especially likely when programs fail to implement rehabilitative programming and aftercare services along with punitive sanctions (Cullen & Gendreau, 2000). Given the emphasis on get-tough reforms during the past decade, such findings assume particular importance because they suggest many states have focused their juvenile justice resources on the very interventions that are least likely to reduce juvenile crime. Although it may be an increasingly acceptable practice to impose sanctions on juveniles for purely retributive purposes, it is important for policy makers to realize that such measures are unlikely to have long-term benefits for the community as a whole.

✄ Prevention and Early Intervention

There has also been a renewed and growing interest in prevention and early intervention in recent years. Studies show that such efforts can significantly reduce both criminal behavior and other unhealthy or injurious social behaviors (see e.g., Coordinating Council on Juvenile Justice and Delinquency Prevention, 1996; Howell, 1995; Mrazek & Haggerty, 1994; Sherman et al., 1997). Yet, prevention and early intervention programs are difficult to sustain politically because their effects are often evident only in the long term. For policy makers who want to demonstrate a short-term effect on public safety, such policies may lack appeal. Effective prevention and early intervention programs, however, provide the greatest chance of achieving lasting benefits to individuals, communities, and society at large.

For example, programs that target young children with conduct disorders may reduce behavior problems in 70% to 90% of the children involved through the use of parent training and social competency development (Mendel, 2000). Indeed, researchers have found that prevention policies are cost-effective and that the earlier an

intervention occurs, the more likely it is to be cost-effective and to reduce negative outcomes such as criminal behavior (Aos et al., 1998; Cohen, 1998; Coordinating Council on Juvenile Justice and Delinquency Prevention, 1996; Crowe, 1998; Cullen & Gendreau, 2000; Durlak & Wells, 1997; McCord et al., 2001; Mendel, 2000; Mrazek & Haggerty, 1994).

There are many varieties of prevention and early intervention initiatives (see Mrazek & Haggerty, 1994). They can be classified according to the following two dimensions: the target of the intervention (specific individuals, groups, populations, social/geographic locations, etc.) and the timing of the intervention (prior to the development of a problem, as soon as certain risk/need markers emerge, immediately after a problem has emerged, only after a certain threshold of problem severity has arisen, etc.). Clearly, many juvenile justice interventions are aimed at individuals (i.e., youthful offenders) who have already shown evidence of a problem (i.e., delinquent behavior). One of the more important trends in recent years, however, is the recognition that crime problems may be most effectively prevented by targeting interventions on specific groups (e.g., at-risk youth) or on communities rather than individuals.

One prominent example is the Boston Gun Project (see Braga, Kennedy, Piehl, & Waring, 2000), which used a problem-oriented policing strategy to substantially reduce gun-related crime. The Boston Gun Project focused on a particular problem, high homicide victimization rates among youth, and selectively targeted the high-profile gangs that committed most of the homicides. The project's strategy emerged from discussions among researchers, police, juvenile and criminal justice practitioners, and local community organizations. They reviewed the findings of quantitative and qualitative research on the nature and causes of youth crime in Boston, and the intervention that emerged reflected an understanding of local problems coupled with systematic, coordinated action. The strategy involved not only the police but also the entire community (youth workers, probation and parole officers, churches and community groups, etc.). The success of the Boston Gun Project shows that targeted, problem-centered, collaborative interventions can work. Their success may stem from drawing on the strengths of many different groups, being selective about the problem being addressed and the strategy for changing it, and taking proactive steps to stop or reduce a problem rather than merely reacting to it.

Other types of prevention and early intervention initiatives have focused on specific factors linked to crime and on different groups or areas. In recent years, for example, researchers have found support for community-, school-, and family-oriented interventions designed to prevent crime and other problems or to reduce their prevalence (Sherman et al., 1997). Effective family-based interventions (e.g., functional family therapy) can focus on risk factors such as poor socialization practices, family conflict, low parental/child attachment, and lack of supervision and discipline (Alvarado & Kumpfer, 2000). School-based interventions, such as Families and Schools Together (McDonald & Frey, 1999), focus on early and persistent antisocial behavior, academic progress, and gun and drug availability within schools (Howell, 1995; Mrazek & Haggerty, 1994). At the community level, potential targets for effective intervention can include reducing drug and gun availability, enhancing neighborhood organization and integration, alleviating poverty, and reducing media portrayals of violence (Coordinating Council on Juvenile Justice and Delinquency Prevention, 1996). Without careful implementation, however, interventions targeting these factors are unlikely to have a substantial effect (Mendel, 2000). In each instance, research indicates that the most effective policies and programs are those that reduce or eliminate risk factors while enhancing protective factors that minimize the likelihood of crime occurrence (Coordinating Council on Juvenile Justice and Delinquency Prevention, 1996; Howell, 1995; Sherman et al., 1997; Wilson & Howell, 1993).

For youth entering the juvenile justice system, early assessment and intervention in cases of substance abuse, mental health, and co-occurring disorders may be one of the most prominent program strategies of the past decade (Cocozza & Skowyra, 2000; Crowe, 1998; Durlak & Wells, 1997; Mendel, 2000; Tonry & Wilson, 1990). Recent research suggests the importance of adopting several strategies for addressing the needs of youthful offenders, with early screening representing one of the most important tools for effective intervention:

All individuals entering the criminal justice system should be screened for mental health and substance use disorders. Universal screenings are warranted due to the high rates of co-occurring disorders among individuals in the criminal justice system and to the negative consequences for nondetection of these disorders. (Peters & Bartoi, 1997, p. 6; also see Howell, 1995; Morris, Steadman, & Veysey, 1997)

Additional strategies that can effectively address offender needs include screening and assessment throughout all stages of juvenile court processing, use of court liaisons to ensure that offender needs are addressed throughout processing, development of crisis intervention and short-term treatment programs, coordination and collaboration with local and state agencies, and implementation of discharge plans and assistance with transitioning offenders to specific services (Morris et al., 1997). Truly effective interventions are ultimately derived from empirical knowledge about crime problems and the risks and needs of youth in specific communities. As Howell and Hawkins (1998) emphasized,

To be effective, a change strategy must be grounded in research on the problems to be addressed. Communities are likely to have different profiles of risk and protection. The greatest effects will likely result from interventions that address those factors that put children in a particular community at most danger of developing criminal or violent behavior. (p. 301)

◪ Transforming Juvenile Justice

Public discussions about juvenile justice usually focus on the big issues, such as the legal ethics of criminal court transfer, the value of punishment versus rehabilitation, and the relative effectiveness of prevention. Although elected officials and the general public concentrated on these issues during recent decades, there was another, vitally important area of policy and program development undertaken by professionals inside the juvenile justice system. In many areas of the country, judges, attorneys, probation workers, and others were transforming the administration and organization of juvenile justice. These changes show great promise for creating more effective approaches to addressing juvenile crime.

For example, many parts of the juvenile justice system have begun to adopt the framework of *community justice* or *problem-solving justice*. Drawing on various program innovations, including community crime prevention, community policing, community prosecution, and community courts, the concept of community justice refocuses the nature of justice system intervention (see e.g., Connor, 2000; Karp & Clear, 2000; Rottman & Casey, 1999). Rather than simply identifying offenders, weighing the evidence against them, and imposing punishment, the community justice perspective calls on all actors in the justice system to use the processes of investigation, arrest, prosecution, and sentencing to solve problems in the community. Each incident of criminal behavior is viewed within the context of the community in which it occurs, and professionals within the justice system work to develop relationships with community leaders and other residents to understand why crime happens and to prevent future occurrences.

A community justice perspective shifts the focus of the justice system to the well-being of the entire community, and the community becomes the client for all crime-fighting agencies. Within juvenile justice, this shift in focus was suggested by the Office of Juvenile Justice and Delinquency Prevention's *Comprehensive Strategy for Serious, Violent, and Chronic Juvenile Offenders* (Wilson & Howell, 1993) and the Coordinating Council on Juvenile Justice and Delinquency Prevention's (1996) *National Juvenile Justice Action Plan,* both of which feature prominent emphases on community-based initiatives.

Another equally important shift in juvenile justice thinking is the growing emphasis on *restorative justice*. Restorative justice is an alternative framework for justice system intervention, replacing or at least counterbalancing retributive justice. Whereas retributive justice ensures that each offender suffers a punishment in proportion to the harm inflicted on the victim of the offense, restorative justice provides a means for each offender to restore that harm or at least to compensate the victim even if the victim is only the general community. There are several programs and interventions that could be called part of the restorative justice movement, but the most popular are victim-offender mediation and family group conferencing. The number of these programs increased sharply during the 1990s, and research suggests that they may offer an effective alternative to traditional court processing, especially for young offenders (Bazemore & Umbreit, 1995, 2001; McGarrell, Olivares, Crawford, & Kroovand, 2000).

Courts themselves are also being reinvented by the juvenile justice system. Many jurisdictions recently began to experiment with specialized courts for young offenders, especially teen courts and juvenile drug courts. The number of teen courts across the country increased from a few dozen programs in the 1970s to more than 600 by the end of the 1990s (Butts & Buck, 2000). In some jurisdictions, such as Anchorage, Alaska, teen courts are beginning to shoulder a majority of law enforcement referrals involving first-time delinquent offenders charged with relatively minor offenses, and early evaluations on these programs are beginning to show promise.

In addition to new program models, many states are implementing the graduated sanctioning approach (Howell, 1995; Torbet et al., 1996). Grounded in both research and common sense, graduated sanctioning ensures that there is at least some response to each instance of illegal behavior as juveniles begin to violate the law. In jurisdictions that embrace graduated sanctioning, there is a full continuum of sanctions available for responding to young offenders, including immediate sanctions for first-time offenders, intermediate and community-based sanctions for more serious offenders, and secure/residential placement for those youth who commit especially serious or violent offenses. Such approaches have the ability to introduce a greater degree of consistency in how youth within and across jurisdictions are sanctioned. More importantly, they can promote balanced and restorative sanctioning that includes victims, families, and communities; relies on the demonstrated effectiveness of rehabilitation and treatment; and emphasizes responsiveness, accountability, and responsibility as cornerstones of an effective juvenile justice system. (For more discussion of restorative justice concepts, see the articles by Bazemore, 2001 [this issue], Braithwaite, 2001 [this issue], and Karp & Breslin, 2001 [this issue].)

Many jurisdictions are also discovering the importance of providing better and earlier screening and assessment of youth to identify those with special needs and to provide appropriate and timely interventions (Cocozza & Skowyra, 2000; Crowe, 1998; Rivers & Anwyl, 2000). Juvenile Assessment Centers (JACs), for example, are an emerging approach. JACs provide centralized, systematic, and consistent assessment of youth referred to the juvenile justice system. The underlying goal of a JAC is to provide an empirical basis for decision making for young offenders (Rivers & Anwyl, 2000). Potential benefits of the JAC model include the ability to identify and eliminate gaps and redundancies in services, better integration of case management, improved communication among agencies, greater awareness of youth needs, more appropriate interventions, and ultimately, improved outcomes for youth (Oldenettel & Wordes, 2000).

The lack of coordination and collaboration among service agencies is one of the most potent barriers to effectively preventing and reducing juvenile crime (Cocozza & Skowyra, 2000; Howell, 1995; Lipsey, 1999a; Lipsey & Wilson, 1998; Rivers, Dembo, & Anwyl, 1998; Slayton, 2000). Traditionally, human services agencies were established to provide specific programs (substance use/abuse intervention, sex offender treatment, education, mental health, etc.), and each agency worked individually with its own particular client population. The result was often inefficient and ineffective interventions, and jurisdictions found it difficult to identify and work with youth who presented co-occurring disorders involving mental health problems, family problems, substance abuse, educational deficits, and other social problems (Peters & Bartoi, 1997; Peters & Hills, 1997). In response, many states have made intra- and interagency collaboration a priority in recent years (National Criminal Justice Association, 1997; Rivers & Anwyl, 2000).

Finally, in recent years, jurisdictions across the country began to recognize the need for greater investments in long-term planning as well as research and evaluation of their policies and programs (Danegger, Cohen, Hayes, & Holden, 1999). Research and evaluation in juvenile justice has been difficult in the past due to the lack of quality data. During the 1980s and 1990s, however, many states worked to enhance their data collection and analysis capacity as well as their ability to share information across agency boundaries (National Criminal Justice Association, 1997; Torbet et al., 1996). Confidentiality and privacy issues have required agencies to move carefully in this area, but the juvenile justice system has gained much from the increased availability of reliable and valid data for monitoring program operations and evaluating interventions. With sound, reliable data, agencies can assess whether a particular policy, such as a change in sentencing, has been implemented consistently (Mears, 1998). They are also more likely to identify any unintended consequences that could offset the potential benefits of a new policy (National Criminal Justice Association, 1997). With good information, agencies are beginning to finally be able to answer those all-important questions: "What works, when, and for whom?"

◪ Conclusion

Juvenile justice policy received much attention during the 1980s and 1990s. Policy makers implemented a range of new programs designed to make the system tougher. Even as the rate of juvenile violence dropped from 1994 through 2000, policy makers continued to demand that young offenders be transferred more often to adult courts and treated with more harshness by juvenile courts. Researchers investigated the effects of these changes but were unable to detect any clear benefits. The broader use of criminal court transfer, for example, did not appear to increase public safety significantly either in terms of individual behavior by affected juveniles or in the overall rate of juvenile crime.

While the critics of juvenile justice were focusing on criminal court transfer, professionals within the juvenile justice system continued working to develop new program models and intervention strategies. Juvenile justice practitioners improved the quality and scope of prevention, broadened the range of treatment techniques for juveniles, and enhanced the community orientation of the juvenile justice system. In the past 20 years, state and local agencies have produced a steady stream of new ideas in substance abuse treatment, family-focused interventions, and community-wide crime prevention. These lesser known innovations, supported by the findings of evaluative research, helped to revive the juvenile justice system in the face of withering attacks from the political arena.

For the juvenile system to survive another century, policy makers, practitioners, and researchers will need to work together to focus on what works and to avoid polarizing debates that result in symbolic and ineffective policies. It is tempting for each new generation of policy makers to look for a silver-bullet solution to juvenile crime, but it is highly unlikely that such a strategy will generate lasting rewards. The public will benefit far more from a juvenile justice system that focuses on broad prevention efforts, early intervention with young offenders, proven rehabilitation programs, and meticulous administration. An effective system would rely on community- and restorative-based models of justice as well as greater collaboration and communication among child welfare, social service, and justice agencies.

Effective juvenile justice policy will always include the use of incarceration, but lawmakers must realize that beyond the immediate benefits of incapacitation, getting tough on juvenile offenders has limited long-term value for crime prevention and public safety. Ultimately, responsible juvenile justice policy comes from being clear about who or what is the target of each intervention, focusing first on the conditions that are most susceptible to change and least costly to change, carefully implementing and monitoring interventions, and continually evaluating whether each intervention actually works. A juvenile justice system in this mold would be more efficient and effective. It would embody the principles envisioned by the founders of the juvenile court and be consistent with the theoretical foundations of community and restorative justice.

◪ References

Alvarado, R., & Kumpfer, K. (2000). Strengthening America's families. *Juvenile Justice, 7,* 8–18.

American Youth Policy Forum. (1997). *Some things do make a difference for youth: A compendium of evaluations of youth programs and practices.* Washington, DC: Author.

Andrews, D. A., & Bonta, J. (1998). *The psychology of criminal conduct* (2nd ed.). Cincinnati, OH: Anderson.

Aos, S., Barnoski, R., & Lieb, R. (1998). Preventive programs for young offenders effective and cost-effective. *Overcrowded Times, 9,* 1–11.

Austin, J., Johnson, K. D., & Gregoriou, M. (2000). *Juveniles in adult prisons and jails: A national assessment* (NCJ 182503). Washington, DC: Department of Justice, Bureau of Justice Assistance.

Bazemore, G. (2001). Young people, trouble, and crime: Restorative justice as a normative theory of informal social control and social support. *Youth & Society, 33,* 199–226.

Bazemore, G., & Umbreit, M. (1995). Rethinking the sanctioning function in juvenile court: Retributive or restorative responses to youth crime. *Crime and Delinquency, 41,* 296–316.

Bazemore, G., & Umbreit, M. (2001). *A comparison of four restorative conferencing models* (Juvenile Justice Bulletin NCJ 184738). Washington, DC: Department of Justice, Office of Juvenile Justice and Delinquency Prevention.

Bernard, T. J. (1992). *The cycle of juvenile justice.* New York: Oxford University Press.

Bishop, D. M., Frazier, C. E., Lanza-Kaduce, L., & Winner, L. (1996). The transfer of juveniles to criminal court: Does it make a difference? *Crime and Delinquency, 42,* 171–191.

Bortner, M. A. (1986). Traditional rhetoric, organization realities: Remand of juveniles to adult court. *Crime and Delinquency, 32,* 53–73.

Braga, A. A., Kennedy, D. M., Piehl, A. M., & Waring, E. J. (2000). *The Boston Gun Project: Impact evaluation findings* (Research report). Washington, DC: Department of Justice, National Institute of Justice.

Braithwaite, J. (2001). Restorative justice and a new criminal law of substance abuse. *Youth & Society, 33,* 227–248.

Butts, J. A., & Buck, J. (2000). *Teen courts: Focus on research* [Juvenile justice bulletin]. Washington, DC: Department of Justice, Office of Juvenile Justice and Delinquency Prevention.

Butts, J. A., & Mitchell, O. (2000). Brick by brick: Dismantling the border between juvenile and adult justice. In C. M. Friel (Ed.), *Criminal justice 2000, Vol. 2: Boundary changes in criminal justice organizations* (pp. 167–213). Washington, DC: Department of Justice, National Institute of Justice.

Cocozza, J. J., & Skowyra, K. (2000). Youth with mental health disorders: Issues and emerging responses. *Juvenile Justice, 7,* 3–13.

Cohen, M. A. (1998). The monetary value of saving a high-risk youth. *Journal of Quantitative Criminology, 14,* 5–32.

Connor, R. (2000, January). Community oriented lawyering: An emerging approach to legal practice. *National Institute of Justice Journal,* 26–33.

Coordinating Council on Juvenile Justice and Delinquency Prevention. (1996). *Combating violence and delinquency: The national juvenile justice action plan.* Washington, DC: Department of Justice, Office of Juvenile Justice and Delinquency Prevention.

Crowe, A. H. (1998). *Drug identification and testing in the juvenile justice system.* Washington, DC: Department of Justice, Office of Juvenile Justice and Delinquency Prevention.

Cullen, F. T., & Gendreau, P. (2000). Assessing correctional rehabilitation: Policy, practice, and prospects. In J. Horney (Ed.), *Criminal justice 2000, Vol. 3: Policies, processes, and decisions of the criminal justice system* (pp. 109–175). Washington, DC: Department of Justice, National Institute of Justice.

Danegger, A. E., Cohen, C. E., Hayes, C. D., & Holden, G. D. (1999). *Juvenile accountability incentive block grants: Strategic planning guide.* Washington, DC: Department of Justice, Office of Juvenile Justice and Delinquency Prevention.

Durlak, J. A., & Wells, A. M. (1997). Primary prevention mental health programs for children and adolescents: A meta-analytic review. *American Journal of Community Psychology, 25,* 115–152.

Elliott, D. (1998). *Blueprints for violence prevention.* Boulder, CO: Center for the Study and Prevention of Violence. Institute of Behavioral Science.

Fagan, J. (1995). Separating the men from the boys: The comparative advantage of juvenile versus criminal court sanctions on recidivism among adolescent felony offenders. In J. C. Howell, B. Krisberg, J. D. Hawkins, & J. J. Wilson (Eds.), *Sourcebook on serious, violent, and chronic juvenile offenders* (pp. 238–260). Thousand Oaks, CA: Sage.

Fagan, J. (1996). The comparative advantage of juvenile versus criminal court sanctions on recidivism among adolescent felony offenders. *Law and Policy, 18,* 77–113.

Feld, B. C. (1987). The juvenile court meets the principle of the offense: Legislative changes in juvenile waiver statutes. *Journal of Criminal Law and Criminology, 78,* 471–533.

Feld, B. C. (1999). *Bad kids—Race and the transformation of the juvenile court.* New York: Oxford University Press.

Greenwood, P. W., Lipson, A. J., Abrahamse, A., & Zimring, F. (1983). *Youth crime and juvenile justice in California: A report to the legislature* (R-3016-CSA). Santa Monica, CA: RAND.

Greenwood, P. W., Model, K.E.C., Rydell, P., & Chiesa, J. (1996). *Diverting children from a life in crime: Measuring costs and benefits.* Santa Monica, CA: RAND.

Griffin, P., Torbet, P., & Szymanski, L. (1998). *Trying juveniles as adults in criminal court: An analysis of state transfer provisions* (OJJDP Report NCJ 172836). Washington, DC: Department of Justice, Office of Juvenile Justice and Delinquency Prevention.

Guarino-Ghezzi, S., & Loughran, E. J. (1996). *Balancing juvenile justice.* New Brunswick, NJ: Transaction Books.

Hamparian, D., Estep, L., Muntean, S., Priestino, R., Swisher, R., Wallace, P., & White, J. (1982). *Youth in adult courts: Between two worlds.* Washington, DC: Department of Justice, Office of Juvenile Justice and Delinquency Prevention.

Harland, A. T. (Ed.). (1996). *Choosing correctional interventions that work: Defining the demand and evaluating the supply.* Thousand Oaks, CA: Sage.

Henggeler, S. W. (1997). *Treating serious anti-social behavior: The MST approach.* Washington, DC: Department of Justice, National Institute of Justice.

Henggeler, S. W. (1999). Multisystemic therapy: An overview of clinical procedures, outcomes, and policy implications. *Child Psychology and Psychiatry, 4,* 2–10.

Howell, J. C. (1995). *Guide for implementing the comprehensive strategy for serious, violent, and chronic juvenile offenders.* Washington, DC: Department of Justice, Office of Juvenile Justice and Delinquency Prevention.

Howell, J. C., & Hawkins, J. D. (1998). Prevention of youth violence. In M. H. Tonry & M. H. Moore (Eds.), *Youth violence* (pp. 263–315). Chicago: University of Chicago Press.

Jensen, E. L., & Metsger, L. K. (1994). A test of the deterrent effect of legislative waiver on violent juvenile crime. *Crime and Delinquency, 40,* 96–104.

Karp, D. R., & Breslin, B. (2001). Restorative justice in school communities. *Youth & Society, 33,* 249–272.

Karp, D. R., & Clear, T. R. (2000). Community justice: A conceptual framework. In C. M. Friel (Ed.), *Criminal justice 2000, Vol. 2: Boundary changes in criminal justice organizations* (pp. 323–368). Washington, DC: Department of Justice, National Institute of Justice.

Lipsey, M. W. (1999a). Can intervention rehabilitate serious delinquents? *Annals, 564,* 142–166.

Lipsey, M. W. (1999b). Can rehabilitative programs reduce the recidivism of juvenile offenders? An inquiry into the effectiveness of practical programs. *Virginia Journal of Social Policy and Law, 6,* 611–641.

Lipsey, M. W., & Derzon, J. H. (1998). Predictors of violent or serious delinquency in adolescence and early adulthood. In R. Loeber & D. P. Farrington (Eds.), *Serious and violent juvenile offenders: Risk factors and successful interventions* (pp. 86–105). Thousand Oaks, CA: Sage.

Lipsey, M. W., & Wilson. D. B. (1998). Effective interventions for serious juvenile offenders: A synthesis of research. In R. Loeber & D. P. Farrington (Eds.), *Serious and violent juvenile offenders: Risk factors and successful interventions* (pp. 313–345). Thousand Oaks, CA: Sage.

Lipsey, M. W., Wilson, D. B., & Cothern, L. (2000). *Effective intervention for serious juvenile offenders.* Washington, DC: Department of Justice, Office of Juvenile Justice and Delinquency Prevention.

MacKenzie, D. L. (2000). Evidence-based corrections: Identifying what works. *Crime and Delinquency, 46,* 457–471.

Manfredi, C. P. (1998). *The supreme court and juvenile justice.* Lawrence: University Press of Kansas.

Martinson, R. (1974). What works? Questions and answers about prison reform. *Public Interest, 35,* 22–54.

McCord, J., Widom, C. S., & Crowell, N. A. (Eds.). (2001). *Juvenile crime, juvenile justice.* Washington, DC: National Academy Press, National Research Council and Institute of Medicine.

McDonald, L., & Frey, H. M. (1999). *Families and Schools Together: Building relationships.* Washington, DC: Department of Justice, Office of Juvenile Justice and Delinquency Prevention.

McGarrell, E. F., Olivares, K., Crawford, K., & Kroovand, N. (2000). *Returning justice to the community: The Indianapolis juvenile restorative justice experiment.* Indianapolis, IN: Hudson Institute.

McGuire, J. (Ed.). (1995). *What works: Reducing offending.* Chichester, UK: Wiley.

McNulty, E. W. (1996). The transfer of juvenile offenders to adult court: Panacea or problem? *Law and Policy, 18,* 61–75.

Mears, D. P. (1998). Evaluation issues confronting juvenile justice sentencing reforms: A case study of Texas. *Crime and Delinquency, 44,* 443–463.

Mendel, R. A. (2000). *Less hype, more help: Reducing juvenile crime, what works—and what doesn't.* Washington, DC: American Youth Policy Forum.

Morris, S. M., Steadman, H. J., & Veysey, B. M. (1997). Mental health services in United States jails: A survey of innovative practices. *Criminal Justice and Behavior, 24,* 3–19.

Mrazek, P. J., & Haggerty, R. J. (Eds.). (1994). *Reducing risks for mental disorders: Frontiers for preventive intervention research.* Washington, DC: National Academy Press.

National Criminal Justice Association. (1997). *Juvenile justice reform initiatives in the states: 1994–1996.* Washington, DC: Department of Justice, Office of Juvenile Justice and Delinquency Prevention.

Oldenettel, D., & Wordes, M. (2000). *The community assessment center concept.* Washington, DC: Department of Justice, Office of Juvenile Justice and Delinquency Prevention.

Peters, R. H., & Bartoi, M. G. (1997). *Screening and assessment of co-occurring disorders in the justice system.* Delmar, NY: GAINS Center.

Peters, R. H., & Hills, H. A. (1997). *Intervention strategies for offenders with co-occurring disorders: What works?* Delmar, NY: GAINS Center.

Platt, A. M. (1977). *The child savers: The invention of delinquency.* Chicago: University of Chicago Press.

Podkopacz, M. R., & Feld, B. C. (1996). The end of the line: An empirical study of judicial waiver. *Journal of Criminal Law and Criminology, 86,* 449–492.

Prescott, L. (1998). *Improving policy and practice for adolescent girls with co-occurring disorders in the juvenile justice system.* Delmar, NY: GAINS Center.

Puzzanchera, C., Stahl, A., Finnegan, T., Snyder, H., Poole, R., & Tierney, N. (2000). *Juvenile court statistics 1997* (NCJ 180864). Washington, DC: Department of Justice, Office of Juvenile Justice and Delinquency Prevention.

Risler, E. A., Sweatman, T., & Nackerud, L. (1998). Evaluating the Georgia legislative waiver's effectiveness in deterring juvenile crime. *Research in Social Work Practice, 8,* 657–667.

Rivers, J. E., & Anwyl, R. S. (2000). Juvenile Assessment Centers: Strengths, weaknesses, and potential. *The Prison Journal, 80,* 96–113.

Rivers, J. E., Dembo, R., & Anwyl, R. S. (1998). The Hillsborough County, Florida, Juvenile Assessment Center. *The Prison Journal, 78,* 439–450.

Rothman, D. J. (1980). *Conscience and convenience: The asylum and its alternatives in progressive America.* Glenview, IL: Scott, Foresman.

Rottman, D., & Casey, P. (1999, July). Therapeutic jurisprudence and the emergence of problem-solving courts. *National Institute of Justice Journal,* 12–19.

Schlossman, S. L. (1977). *Love and the American delinquent.* Chicago: University of Chicago Press.

Sherman, L. W., Gottfredson, D., MacKenzie, D., Eck, J., Reuter, P., & Bushway, S. (Eds.). (1997). *Preventing crime: What works, what doesn't, what's promising.* Washington, DC: Department of Justice, National Institute of Justice.

Singer, S. I. (1996). *Recriminalizing delinquency: Violent juvenile crime and juvenile justice reform.* Cambridge, UK: Cambridge University Press.

Singer, S. I., & McDowall, D. (1988). Criminalizing delinquency: The deterrent effects of the New York juvenile offender law. *Law and Society Review, 22,* 521–535.

Slayton, J. (2000). *Establishing and maintaining intera-gency information sharing.* Washington, DC: Department of Justice, Office of Juvenile Justice and Delinquency Prevention.

Snyder, H. N., & Sickmund, M. (1999). *Juvenile offend-ers and victims: 1999 national report* (NCJ 178257). Washington, DC: Department of Justice, Office of Juvenile Justice and Delinquency Prevention.

Snyder, H. N., Sickmund, M., & Poe-Yamagata, E. (2000). *Juvenile transfers to criminal court in the 1990s: Lessons learned from four studies* (NCJ 181301). Washington, DC: Department of Justice, Office of Juvenile Justice and Delinquency Prevention.

Tonry, M. H., & Wilson, J. Q. (Eds.). (1990). *Drugs and crime.* Chicago: University of Chicago Press.

Torbet, P., Gable, R., Hurst, H. IV, Montgomery, I., Szymanski, L., & Thomas, D. (1996). *State*

responses to serious and violent juvenile crime. Washington, DC: Department of Justice, Office of Juvenile Justice and Delinquency Prevention.

Torbet, P., & Szymanski, L. (1998). *State legislative responses to violent juvenile crime: 1996–97 update* (Juvenile Justice Bulletin NCJ 172835). Washington, DC: Department of Justice, Office of Juvenile Justice and Delinquency Prevention.

Watkins, J. C., Jr. (1998). *The juvenile justice century.* Durham, NC: Carolina Academic Press.

Wilson, J. J., & Howell, J. C. (1993). *Comprehensive strategy for serious, violent, and chronic juvenile offenders: Program summary.* Washington, DC: Department of Justice, Office of Juvenile Justice and Delinquency Prevention.

Winner, L., Lanza-Kaduce, L., Bishop, D. M., & Frazier, C. E. (1997). The transfer of juveniles to criminal court: Reexamining recidivism over the long term. *Crime and Delinquency, 43,* 548–563.

DISCUSSION QUESTIONS

1. Based on the findings of the effects of laws and policies in the 1980s and 1990s, what does the future hold for juvenile justice? What laws and policies should we keep? What should we change?

2. Based on the authors' tabular presentation and discussion of policy and practice principles for reducing juvenile crime, what laws and policies would you recommend for your city, county, and state?

3. Based on your reading, which of the following examples of transforming the juvenile justice system may be feasible and appropriate for your county or state: (a) community justice or problem-solving justice; (b) restorative justice; (c) specialized courts such as teen courts; (d) a graduated sanctioning approach; (e) earlier screening and assessment of youth; (f) better coordination and collaboration among service agencies; and (g) more investment in long-term planning, research, and evaluation of policies and programs?

4. Draft a policy statement and recommendations for lawmakers and juvenile justice adminis-trators based on what you believe to be the most appropriate and feasible recommendations and conclusions of the authors of this article.

READING

Crime and public policy continue to be salient issues in the 21st century. The authors of this article review juvenile justice policy and examine initiatives that demonstrate positive directions for the future of the juvenile justice system. They summarize the history of juvenile justice and review recent developments that warrant further research to demonstrate rational, effective policies and strategies for responding to juvenile delinquency. The authors identify ideology, politics, and the media as major influences on public perceptions of juvenile crime and justice policy, and they consider future issues in juvenile justice and social policy.

Defining Juvenile Justice in the 21st Century

Alida V. Merlo, Peter J. Benekos

The brief but highly publicized increase in youth violence in the 1980s and early 1990s has ended, but its effects continue to erode the foundation and principles of the juvenile justice system. Arguably, the violence resulting from the nexus of guns, youth gangs, and drugs generated three forces that have presented new challenges to the basic justification for preserving a separate system of handling youth offenders.

First, the portrayal of youth violence fueled public fear of crime and contributed to emotional reactions that approached hysterical proportions. Media coverage reinforced themes of random violence by youth and victimization of innocent strangers. As a result, public perceptions of crime were distorted, and citizens developed an exaggerated sense of vulnerability (Kappeler, Blumberg, & Potter, 2000; Merlo & Benekos, 2000).

Second, attitudes toward youth that were based primarily on images of youth offenders shifted to more anger and resentment, and youth were demonized as representing a new and different breed of delinquent (Vogel, 1994). In this context, Triplett (2000) used Tannenbaum's concept of dramatization of evil to explain how

reactions to violent youth were generalized to all youth, especially inner-city male minorities. As a result, adolescent offenders were characterized as "super predators" who were both dangerous and unrepentant (Bazelon, 2000; Dilulio, 1995).

Finally, in a climate of hardening attitudes, the juvenile justice system was viewed as incapable of curbing youth crime and ineffective in controlling youth offenders. The efficacy of the system itself was challenged. As summarized by Austin, Johnson, and Gregoriou (2000) in their national assessment of juveniles in adult correctional facilities, "This concept of a distinct justice system for juveniles focused upon treatment has come under attack in recent years" (p. ix).

These factors—heightened fear of crime, demonization of youth, and perceived ineffectiveness of the juvenile justice system—were exploited in the political arena to advance get-tough legislation and public policies that adultified youth offenders and shifted discretion in determining transfer of cases to criminal court from judges to prosecutors. Essentially, individualized responses that considered the circumstances and nature of the adolescent were displaced by legislation prescribing decisions based on the

SOURCE: *Youth Violence and Juvenile Justice, (1)*3, 276–288, July 2003. DOI: 10.1177/1541204003254826. © 2003 Sage Publications, Inc.

category and nature of the offense. In addition, therapeutic goals of intervention were replaced with those of deterrence, incapacitation, and punishment. The resulting convergence of the juvenile and criminal justice systems led some to argue for the abolition of the juvenile justice system (Feld, 1993, 1999).

This article reviews some of the themes that characterize the state of juvenile justice and provides a context for assessing future initiatives for the juvenile justice system. The authors identify ideology, politics, and the media as salient influences on public perceptions and social policy.

⊠ Intention and Performance of Juvenile Justice

The orthodox view of the founding of the juvenile court is represented as a humanitarian initiative of child savers and do-gooders who were intent on helping wayward children by removing them from the harms of the criminal court and by providing them with therapeutic social services (Bortner, 1988; Platt, 1977). The specialty court established in 1899 for children was based on the assumptions that children were different from adults, that they were malleable and could be reformed, and that the benevolence of the state would be exercised by the judge who would be guided by the doctrine of *parens patriae,* which would ensure individualized care for child miscreants. As Albanese (1993) explained, "The juvenile court corresponded with the rise of positivism" (p. 9), which defined juvenile delinquency as the result of environmental influences rather than free will. This view justified removal of children from their homes and neighborhoods as an effort to correct negative influences and to direct children toward more socially productive behaviors (Albanese, 1993).

In addition to its therapeutic intention, the separate system was characterized by an informal, nonlegalistic forum where children's interests were protected by the court. Paternalism, rather than due process, and best interests, rather than

guilt, were established as the parameters for court procedures. In the context of substantive rationality, Ferdinand and McDermott (2002) discussed that youth receive different responses: "Under *parens patriae,* juveniles, for example, have a right to treatment for their offenses instead of full punishment" (p. 91).

The development of the juvenile court, however, was not without its critics (Bernard, 1992; Feld, 1999; Platt, 1977). Although the idea of helping dependent and neglected children fit "comfortably into the historic and philosophical context of the day," Bernard (1992) noted that "like the new idea of juvenile delinquency, the juvenile court was probably popular in part because it sounded new and different but it actually wasn't" (p. 101). New ideas and a new legal rationale were used to institutionalize and control children for their "own good," but at the same time served to "increase the power of the state" (Bernard, 1992, p. 106) over poor urban youth.

This benevolent social control eventually manifested abuses of informal authority, resulting in a series of Supreme Court decisions that began to transform the juvenile court. Feld (1993, 1999) has described the processes and consequences of this transformation as follows: The juvenile court shifted from informal to formal procedures, from a therapeutic to crime control jurisprudence, and from separate jurisdiction for children and youth to the diversion of status offenders and the transfer of serious adolescent offenders to criminal court. This juvenile-criminal court convergence of procedure, jurisprudence, and jurisdiction raised the question, "What was the justification for separate but parallel systems of justice?" For Feld, there was none, and he proposed to abolish the juvenile court in favor of a unified model (Feld, 1993, 1999).

Arguably, whereas the expressed intent of the specialty diversion court for dependent and neglected children may have been noble, the performance of protecting and caring for youth was challenged and discredited. As convergence blurred the distinction between juvenile and criminal courts, the confluence of factors summarized previously (fear of crime, demonization of youth, and dissatisfaction with the juvenile justice system) further diminished support for the juvenile justice system.

⬚ Deconstructing Juvenile Justice

In assessing the state of juvenile justice policy in the 1980s and 1990s, Merlo and Benekos (2000) identified the interaction of ideology, politics, and the media as the dynamic that both distorted the ideal of juvenile justice and deconstructed the juvenile justice system. During the wars on crime and drugs, get-tough attitudes replaced the rehabilitative ideals of post-World War II. Neo-classical assumptions of free will, rational choice, and deterrence replaced the positivist concepts of development, determinism, and treatment.

The youth crime spike of 1987 to 1994 occurred in the context of this prevailing conservative, neoclassical ideology. The get-tough reactions to adult offenders were easily transferred to youth who were vilified as "godless, fatherless, jobless" criminals who behaved like adult offenders (Dilulio, 1995). The public outcry to do something about adolescent offenders who were seen as "Public Enemy No. 1" (Magill, 1998) was channeled into the political response to treat "adult crime with adult time." "The demands of modern political campaigns require politicians to fit proposed solutions to complex problems into short, snappy soundbites" (Merlo, 2000, p. 652). The political lessons of Willie Horton underscored the effectiveness of simplifying the problem, invoking a punitive, moral position, and legislating tougher sanctions (Merlo & Benekos, 2000).

As a result, rational choice ideology and punitive politics generated legislation in several states that lowered the age that juveniles were presumptively treated as adults and prosecuted in criminal court (Sickmund, Snyder, & Poe-Yamagata, 1997). For example, a special legislative session on juvenile justice held in 1995 in Pennsylvania resulted in lowering the age to 14

for juveniles to be transferred to criminal court for offenses committed with a weapon (Juvenile Court Act, 1995; Torbet & Thomas, 1997). As a result of this type of legislative reform, by 1997, the nationwide adultification response resulted in the incarceration of 5,400 inmates younger than age 18 in state prisons and 9,100 in jails (Strom, 2000). From 1985 to 1997, the number of youth younger than age 18 sentenced to adult state prisons increased from 3,400 to 7,400, and the number held in state prisons increased from 2,300 to 5,400. As Strom (2000) concluded, "Relative to the number of arrests, the likelihood of incarceration in state prison increased for offenders under 18" (p. 1).

Because public perceptions of crime and victims are largely shaped by media reports and presentations, "the role of the media in informing public opinion and influencing citizen reaction to crime issues is central to understanding the framing of crime policy" (Merlo & Benekos, 2000, p. 4). Kappeler et al. (2000) also critiqued the role of the media and described the social construction of crime myths. Although the media industry has an "important role" in reporting crime, Kappeler et al. cautioned that "social policy should not be developed based on distortion, sensationalism, or a few newsworthy events" (p. 7).

Unfortunately, celebrated cases of youth violence, including school shootings, have been instrumental in developing such policies, some of which have underscored zero tolerance and expanded control over adolescents (Merlo & Benekos, 2000). For example, in his comments on the Supreme Court ruling that students can be subject to random drug testing, Schwartz (2002) concluded that the Court's decision and its rationale underscore that "the rights of young people are shredded when they walk through the schoolhouse gates" (p. 2). Although somewhat hyperbolic, Schwartz recognized that on one hand, youth who commit crimes can be held to the legal standards and consequences used for adults, and on the other hand, as students, they experience a "reduced expectation of privacy" (p. 2).

This suggests the ambivalence toward youth and reflects the cyclic nature of policy discussed by Ferdinand and McDermott (2002):

At first . . . children were treated like adults, using the same laws and courts and receiving the same punishments as adults. Then, from early in the 19th century to the mid-1960s, criminal justice officials recognized and accepted the social immaturity of adolescents and their easily manipulated, impulsive nature . . . In the third phase, we returned to treating youngsters like adults . . . culminating in the retributive policies that target serious juvenile offenders today . . . Treating youths as adults emphasizes punishment and accountability; treating them as adolescents emphasizes rehabilitation. We have swung between the two as first one paradigm and then the other gains prominence. (pp. 102–103)

The dynamic of neoclassical ideology, conservative politics, and media-influenced policies previously discussed has generated a shift in public policy that rejects the assumptions of adolescent development and tolerance for youthful indiscretions. In endorsing get-tough, quick-fix responses to youth crime, legislators appeal to the public, win support, but ignore evidence of effective strategies in preventing delinquency and treating youth offenders. The next section considers some of these strategies and the initiatives that warrant further study and evaluation.

⊠ Politics, Research, and Juvenile Justice

The 1990s witnessed political rhetoric regarding violent youth, extensive media coverage of youth crime, particularly school violence, and an ideology that was sometimes harsh and punitive toward youth. Simultaneously, the public's response to juvenile crime was alternately reactionary and preventive. In this section, some exemplary and promising programs for youth are examined and contrasted with some of the more political and reactive approaches. The policies and initiatives can be categorized as those that emphasize prevention, education, and treatment (PET); balanced and restorative justice (BARJ); or retribution, adultification, and punishment (RAP) (see Benekos & Merlo, 2002).

Beginning in the fall of 1997, the incidence of school violence began to be perceived by the public as one more manifestation that juveniles were becoming increasingly violent and homicidal. Through extensive media coverage and seven school shootings (from 1997 through 2001), parents, teachers, students, and the public became fearful of youth violence. For the most part, the school districts embraced an old strategy for addressing the problem: zero tolerance.

Zero-Tolerance Policies in Schools

Zero-tolerance initiatives were introduced in the 1980s to address drug enforcement policies by the federal and state governments (Skiba & Peterson, 1999). In the late 1980s, school districts in Orange County, California, and Louisville, Kentucky, embraced zero-tolerance policies, requiring expulsion for gang-related activity or drug possession. By 1993, school boards throughout the United States had adopted such policies for offenses ranging from tobacco violations to school disruptions (Skiba & Peterson, 1999). However, it was a congressional initiative that became the impetus for the "new" zero tolerance. The Gun-Free School Zones Act of 1994 required any school that received federal funding to expel for not less than 1 year "any student found with a weapon on school grounds" (Bogos, 1997, p. 374). Furthermore, the legislation empowered the Department of Education to stop providing federal funds to states that did not adopt equally stringent policies within 1 year (Bogos, 1997; Levick, 2000; Skiba, 2000). Cognizant of the effects of federal money being withdrawn or withheld, states swiftly enacted legislation that not only met the federal requirements, but even exceeded them.

These policies are collectively referred to as zero-tolerance laws or initiatives. Zero-tolerance legislation, mandates, and requirements are indicative of the panic surrounding the incidents and public pressure to do something to stop violence. They are emblematic of a political response to find the "quick fix" rather than a logical, rational approach to address a problem.

Embracing zero-tolerance initiatives as a panacea for school violence illustrates an ideology most closely associated with RAP. For the most part, the policies are punitive and intransigent. There appears to be little discretion in interpreting the policies, and school officials treat every incident the same, whether it is a 5-year-old kindergarten child or a 17-year-old high school senior. The students' motivations, degree of understanding, or actual behaviors do not seem to merit consideration (Bogos, 1997; Levick, 2000). There are numerous examples of how zero-tolerance policies have resulted in suspension or expulsion for students from elementary through high school for relatively minor behaviors, such as bringing a nail clipper to school (Benekos, Merlo, Cook, & Bagley, 2002). Behaviors that were once considered adolescent indiscretions were now criminalized.

School Bullying

Rather than focusing on zero-tolerance policies as the first line of defense against school violence, some school systems have begun to emphasize and implement antibullying strategies. Recent evidence suggests that bullying is related to school violence and other problem behaviors. In its report on school violence, the Secret Service found that a number of the school shooters "experienced bullying and harassment that were longstanding and severe" (Preventing School Shootings, 2002, p. 14). Interviewing youth who engaged in school violence, the Secret Service found that the bullying of the youth was close to torment (Preventing School Shootings, 2002). Bullying "involves a real or perceived imbalance of power, with the more powerful child or group attacking those who are less powerful" (Ericson, 2001, p. 1).

According to Ericson (2001), bullying is manifest in three ways: physical, which includes pushing, kicking, and hitting; verbal, which includes making threats and taunting; and psychological, which includes intimidation and social exclusion. The extent of bullying in schools is not entirely known, but the National Institute of Child Health and Human Development estimated that 1.6 million children in the 6th through 10th grades are the victims of bullying at least once per week, and 1.7 million children engage in the bullying of others just as frequently. Clearly, the effects of bullying are serious, but not only as they relate to school violence. Research indicates that those who are victimized, as well as those who are perpetrators, experience short- and long-term problems, including psychological and emotional dysfunction and criminal behavior (Ericson, 2001).

By involving parents, peers, and school personnel, successful antibullying measures (such as those developed by Olweus in Bergen, Norway) can have a positive effect on elementary, middle, and junior high school students (Olweus & Limber, as cited in Ericson, 2001). A number of school systems have emulated that program or incorporated some of its components. Antibullying programs foster an increased awareness about bullying, require more intervention to stop intimidation, stipulate the articulation of clear rules regarding inappropriate behavior, and provide victim support and protection (Ericson, 2001). Clearly, schools can prevent and reduce the incidence of bullying on school grounds and create a safer environment for children. In fact, the Bergen study demonstrated that incidents of bullying decreased by more than 50% in the 2 years that the program was used (Ericson, 2001).

The Secret Service report also indicates that prior to the shooting incidents, most of these youth engaged in some type of behavior that demonstrated their need for help. From attempted suicide to threats to commit suicide, as well as expository writing assignments that focused on homicide, suicide, and depression, there were manifestations that the youth were experiencing difficulties (Preventing School Shootings, 2002). These findings suggest a more active role for schools in the prevention of violence. Efforts to encourage greater communication among parents, students, and school personnel and the creation of an environment where youth are able to approach teachers and staff members with their concerns through extended before- and after-school programs can help prevent youth from engaging in violent behavior.

Youth Victimization and Prevention Initiatives

Beginning in 1992, official data indicate that violence in school has been decreasing. By contrast, schools have become safer places than they had been prior to 1992, and school-related violent deaths have decreased (Brooks, Schiraldi, & Zeidenberg, 2000; Justice Policy Institute, 1999; Powell, 1999; Repenning, Powell, Doane, & Dunkle, 2000). In fact, school is one of the safest places for children to be (Snyder & Hoffman, as cited in Preventing School Shootings, 2002). In 1998, "students were twice as likely to be victims of serious violent crime away from school than at school" (Girouard, 2001, p. 1).

Youth between the ages of 12 and 17 are much more likely to be the victims of crime than are youth ages 11 and younger. In analyzing the 1997 FBI data from 12 states, Finkelhor and Ormrod (2000) found that juveniles were more likely to be victimized by family members when they were younger than 5, but more likely to be victimized by peers as they move into adolescence. Although adolescents typically victimize peers, they also continue to be victimized by adults (Finkelhor & Ormrod, 2000).

Youth victimization is a serious problem, and its consequences are deleterious. Although earlier research has examined the effects of child maltreatment and later delinquency and criminal behavior, little research had been conducted on adolescent maltreatment as separate from child maltreatment

(Widom, 1995). Using data from the National Youth Survey, Menard (2002) found that violent victimization during adolescence increases the victim's likelihood of being a violent offender or victim in adulthood, increases the odds of property offending in adulthood, and "doubles the odds of problem drug use in adulthood" (p. 14).

Similarly, Ireland, Smith, and Thornberry (2002) highlighted the importance of understanding the long-term effects of substantiated maltreatment. With data from the Rochester Youth Development Study, Ireland et al. found maltreatment that occurred only in adolescence and persistent maltreatment that occurred in childhood and adolescence were related to both delinquency and drag use. Adolescents who were the victims of maltreatment were more likely to be arrested in their sample than youth who had not been victimized (Ireland et al., 2002).

The National Council of Juvenile and Family Court Judges has worked closely with an advisory committee to develop strategies for intervening in the lives of victims of domestic violence and child maltreatment (Kracke, 2001). The *Green Book* provides the guidelines for creating a collaborative approach to address both domestic violence and child maltreatment among child protective services, the juvenile and criminal courts, and community groups (Ireland et al., 2002; Kracke, 2001). With the goal of protecting and empowering the victims of abuse, it is currently being evaluated at six demonstration sites throughout the United States.

The Office of Juvenile Justice and Delinquency Prevention has also taken a proactive role in intervening in the lives of at-risk children and youth through its comprehensive strategy, which has two major components: reform of the juvenile justice system and prevention efforts (Wiebush, Freitag, & Baird, 2001). In examining the factors that are identified as precursors to delinquency and violence, the comprehensive strategy separates risk factors into four main areas: community, family, school, and individual and peer (Wiebush et al., 2001). In the area of maltreatment, efforts focus on the family.

To help child protective agencies deal with child maltreatment more successfully, the structured decision-making model has been implemented in a number of jurisdictions. It uses a risk-assessment tool that provides agencies and professionals with an equitable and effective method of dealing with victims of child maltreatment and also includes a research instrument that enables comprehensive assessment and planning (Wiebush et al., 2001). The structured decision-making model facilitates the delivery of services, the agencies' accountability, and the outcome evaluation process (Wiebush et al., 2001).

The Office of Juvenile Justice and Delinquency Prevention established the Child Protection Division in 2000 to deal with child protection issues (T. Cullen, 2001). One of the Child Protection Division's programs is the Safe Kids/Safe Streets project, which is currently operating at five demonstration sites. Its goal is to reduce childhood and adolescent victimization through a coordinated approach that involves strengthening the family, creating neighborhood programs, improving child protective agency services, establishing home visitation protocols, implementing court reforms, and enlisting child advocacy center teams that involve law enforcement, medical, court, and social service agency representatives who collaboratively investigate and intervene in the lives of child and adolescent victims (T. Cullen, 2001). Through these kinds of research initiatives, the federal government is taking steps to ameliorate the lives of children and adolescents who have been victimized and to prevent the possible victimization of children who may be at risk.

According to Widom and Maxfield (2001), the message is fairly straightforward. First, early intervention is critical. Community police officers, teachers, and health care workers must attempt to identify those children and youth who are victimized by abuse and neglect. Second, both abuse and neglect hinder the healthy development of children. Although neglect cases are more widely reported in the system, both kinds of victimization merit intervention efforts.

Third, agencies need to reexamine how they respond to abused and neglected children, particularly regarding out-of-home placements. They recommend that child protective service agencies review their policies and conduct research on the effects of out-of-home placements versus in-home supervision (Widom & Maxfield, 2001).

Early Intervention Programs for Children and Parents

Recent research and longitudinal studies have provided service providers with a much more detailed look at child abuse and neglect and its effects throughout the life course. In addition, research has supported the importance of early intervention and delinquency prevention programs (Merlo, 2000). Public support for early intervention has also been documented. In a survey of the public, F. Cullen et al. (1998) found that "a clear majority" of citizens still favor "governmental efforts designed to intervene with families and children" (p. 197). Using a sample of respondents in Tennessee, Moon, Sundt, Cullen, and Wright (2000) found that the public strongly supported allocating resources for prevention-oriented programs over the construction of new prisons.

Some of the more promising approaches to prevention of juvenile offending focus on intervening in a child's life long before delinquency occurs. For more than 40 years, the High/Scope Perry Preschool Project has been in the forefront as a successful early intervention effort. Initially, 123 high-risk African American children were invited in 1962 to participate in the research study. Children from the ages of 3 and 4 were randomly assigned to the control or experimental group. They were from low socioeconomic backgrounds, had low IQ scores, and were considered to be high risk in terms of school failure (Parks, 2000).

The High/Scope Perry Project is characterized by low staff-to-client ratios, an environment that involves active learning, and a home visitation program that encourages and enlists parents to become involved. Staff, programming, and families have all contributed to its success (Parks, 2000). Part of the project's strength is attributed to the fact that it combined early education with family support. According to Parks (2000), offering both of these kinds of services to preschool children was critical in preventing future delinquency and lowering welfare dependency while increasing academic achievement, employment, and prosocial behavior.

Another early intervention strategy, "The Incredible Years: Parents, Teachers, and Children Training Series," targets parents of children from ages 3 to 12. The 11-week program attempts to support and enhance parents' monitoring and disciplinary skills while simultaneously improving their confidence (Alvarado & Kumpfer, 2000). In addition to focusing on parental techniques for discipline, the program also introduces and encourages parents to become involved in their children's education. Research has indicated that this program effectively reduces children's problem behaviors and engages them academically (Alvarado & Kumpfer, 2000).

These kinds of strategies symbolize prevention, education, and treatment, and are considered to be far more beneficial in terms of cost-effectiveness and outcome measures than the reactive stance of the past (i.e., RAP). Research has enlightened the development of the curriculum and objectives of the programs and results demonstrate the need for collaboration and cooperation among parents, schools, communities, and social service and justice professionals.

Legislative Changes in Juvenile Justice

One manifestation of the RAP approach to youth can be discerned from the legislative changes that occurred in juvenile justice. By the mid-1990s, 45 states introduced and enacted legislation that facilitated the transfer of juveniles from the juvenile justice system to the adult court system (Snyder & Sickmund, 1999). An ideological shift

toward youth was occurring, and it was manifested in legislative provisions that made it easier to move juveniles into the adult system from the juvenile system. Coupled with the changes in the procedures for waiving juveniles into adult court, legislators in 47 states amended or revised statutes dealing with the confidentiality of juvenile records (Snyder & Sickmund, 1999).

Legislators not only altered the procedures for waiver and confidentiality, they also amended the statutory purpose clause of juvenile courts. According to Torbet and Szymanski (1998), by the end of 1997, 17 states redefined their juvenile court purpose clauses to emphasize public safety, punishment for youth, certain sanctions, and/or offender accountability. Although the earlier language had focused only on children's best interests, the new legislation emphasized the protection of the community, the need for accountability, and the importance of providing treatment, but with a balanced approach (see Bazemore & Day, 1996).

When Governor Tom Ridge signed Act 33 into law in Pennsylvania in 1995, the changes were dramatic. Rather than focusing singularly on the youth's needs as previously stipulated, the revised statute elevated the protection of the public interest and required that programs should address community protection, offender accountability, and competency development to assure that children would become responsible and productive members of the community (Juvenile Court Act, 1995; Torbet & Thomas, 1997). According to Pennsylvania's Juvenile Act, the victim, the community, and the offender are to receive "balanced attention," and the resources of the state through the juvenile justice system should be allocated to all three client groups to achieve these goals (Juvenile Court Judges' Commission, 1997). Bazemore and Umbreit's (1995) conceptualization of BARJ was consistent with the evolution of the Pennsylvania Juvenile Act.

To successfully implement the principles and objectives of the BARJ model, funding has been provided through the Pennsylvania Commission on Crime and Delinquency to train juvenile justice professionals; to coordinate the initiative with the juvenile court judges in the state; to provide victim services, including services for juvenile crime victims; and to assist in evaluating the initiative (see http://www.pccd.state.pa.us/JUVENILE/barjl.htm).

BARJ is popular with various constituencies. By incorporating elements of a punitive stance with those of a treatment stance, BARJ is widely acclaimed and endorsed because it satisfies the conservative political demands to be tough on juvenile offenders with its emphasis on accountability and community safety while simultaneously courting more liberal voters with its emphasis on competency development. The actual degree to which BARJ is implemented and supported differs from jurisdiction to jurisdiction. Most commonly, BARJ is applied to juveniles on probation or unofficial supervision. For example, requiring a youth to participate in community service satisfies the accountability requirement because the youth attempts to make amends to the community. Simultaneously, the youth who engages in community service is developing certain competencies, including work habits and skills due to the experience. Finally, the benefits for the community in terms of its need for safety and protection are fulfilled by the fact that the youth's time is structured, and the community is involved in the supervision (Ellis & Sowers, 2001).

BARJ emphasizes the importance of victim-offender mediation, community conferencing, and other initiatives designed to make juvenile offenders accountable and to recognize the harm done to victims and communities. It reflects a more equitable approach to juvenile offending, and it provides justice professionals with an opportunity to work with offenders and communities simultaneously. Continued evaluation will determine its effectiveness in reducing juvenile recidivism, providing greater responsiveness to victims, promoting the development of positive behaviors, and protecting the community.

⌗ Conclusion

Juvenile justice has undergone significant transformation in the past 103 years. Perceptions of youth have changed and now reflect a more punitive, reactionary stance. One of the characteristics of the political policy initiatives of the 1990s is the lack of research guiding decision-making processes. In their haste to enact new, tougher sanctions against juveniles, legislators rarely paused to ask, "Where are the data?" (Merlo, 2000). While official reports documented that juvenile crime was decreasing, legislators were amending transfer legislation, authorizing and funding the construction of new juvenile prisons, and implementing harsh sanctions. Although the long-term consequences of these kinds of legislative initiatives are not yet fully known, more youth have been sentenced to adult prisons; more school districts have expelled or suspended children and youth for minor misbehaviors; and adolescence, as a developmental stage, has been challenged.

Simultaneously, research-based initiatives are becoming increasingly prominent. Juvenile justice programs and strategies are responding to the demand for outcome assessments, accountability in programming, and classic experimental design. Programs that were once considered sacrosanct, such as DARE (Drug Abuse Resistance Education), are being reformulated after research demonstrated they were not effective in preventing youth from engaging in drug abuse. Rather than eschewing evaluation, programs are embracing it.

Early intervention, prevention, and parenting programs are becoming more widespread. There is evidence that the public supports these efforts and that they are successful. In addition, the government encourages and funds collaborations between justice agencies, social service agencies, schools, and the public. There is ample evidence of creative and highly motivated practitioners working in the system with coordinated responses between various agencies.

The current research has enlightened approaches and assisted efforts in preventing and controlling juvenile offending. Some of the greatest strides have been made in research on childhood neglect and abuse and the effects of childhood and adolescent maltreatment. The challenge will be to use the findings in developing and refining intervention strategies.

Ireland et al. (2002) noted that the emphasis on punishment toward juveniles and the accompanying movement to transfer juveniles to adult court to hold them accountable for their offending might result in fewer initiatives to identify and treat adolescents who may be victims of abuse or neglect. Although there have been some efforts to address the problem of childhood and adolescent victimization equitably, there is not much evidence to suggest a softening in the public's attitudes toward adolescents who have been victimized.

Whereas ambivalence toward youth persists, there is evidence of a retreat from the punitive, get-tough approaches emblematic of the 1990s. Highly publicized school shootings have not continued to occur, and the public is now more focused on the economy and terrorism. Bernard's (1992) conceptualization of the cycles of juvenile justice would appear to suggest that we are moving toward a more liberal treatment- and prevention-oriented approach toward youth (Merlo, 2000). These changes are not likely to occur immediately, but they do provide an opportunity to use a more research-based approach in dealing with the prevention and treatment of youth offenders.

⬚ References

Albanese, J. S. (1993). *Dealing with delinquency: The future of juvenile justice* (2nd ed.). Chicago: Nelson Hall.

Alvarado, R., & Kumpfer, K. (2000). Strengthening America's families. *Juvenile Justice, 7,* 8–18.

Austin, J., Johnson, K. D., & Gregoriou, M. (2000). *Juveniles in adult prisons and jails: A national assessment.* Washington, DC: Bureau of Justice Assistance.

Bazelon, L. A. (2000). Exploding the superpredator myth: Why infancy is the preadolescent's best defense in juvenile court. *New York University Law Review, 75,* 159–198.

Bazemore, G., & Day, S. E. (1996). Restoring the balance: Juvenile and community justice. *Juvenile Justice, 3,* 3–14.

Bazemore, G., & Umbreit, M. (1995). *Balanced and restorative justice for juveniles. A national strategy for juvenile justice in the 21st century. The balanced and restorative justice project.* Washington, DC: Office of Juvenile Justice and Delinquency Prevention.

Benekos, P. J., & Merlo, A. V. (2002) Reaffirming juvenile justice. In R. M. Muraskin & A. R. Roberts (Eds.), *Visions for change: Criminal justice in the 21st century* (3rd ed., pp. 265–286). Englewood Cliffs, NJ: Prentice Hall.

Benekos, P. J., Merlo, A. V., Cook, W. J., & Bagley, K. (2002). A preliminary study of student attitudes on juvenile justice policy. *Journal of Criminal Justice Education, 13,* 273–296.

Bernard, T. J. (1992). *The cycle of juvenile justice.* New York: Oxford University Press.

Bogos, P. M. (1997). "Expelled. No excuses. No exceptions."—Michigan's zero tolerance policy in response to school violence: M.C.L.A. Section 380.1311. *University of Detroit Mercy Law Review, 74d,* 357–387.

Bortner, M. A. (1988). *Delinquency and justice: An age of crisis.* New York: McGraw-Hill.

Brooks, K., Schiraldi, V., & Ziedenberg, J. (2000). *School house hype: Two years later.* Available from http://www.cjcj.org

Cullen, F. T., Wright, J. P., Brown, S., Moon, M., Blankenship, M. B., & Applegate, B. K. (1998). Public support for early intervention programs: Implications for a progressive policy agenda. *Crime & Delinquency, 44,* 187–204.

Cullen, T. (2001). Keeping children safe: OJJDP 's child protection division. *OJJDP Juvenile Justice Bulletin.* Washington, DC: U.S. Department of Justice.

Dilulio, J. J. (1995, November 27). The coming of the superpredators. *Weekly Standard,* p. 23.

Ellis, R. A., & Sowers, K. A. (2001). *Juvenile justice practice: A cross-disciplinary approach to intervention.* Belmont, CA: Wadsworth.

Ericson, N. (2001). *Addressing the problem of juvenile bullying* (OJJDP fact sheet). Washington, DC: Office of Juvenile Justice and Delinquency Prevention.

Feld, B. C. (1993). Juvenile (in)justice and the criminal court alternative. *Crime & Delinquency, 39,* 403–424.

Feld, B. C. (1999). *Bad kids: Race and the transformation of the juvenile court.* New York: Oxford University Press.

Ferdinand, T. N., & McDermott, M. J. (2002). Joining punishment and treatment in substantive equality. *Criminal Justice Policy Review, 13,* 87–116.

Finkelhor, D., & Ormrod, R. (2000). *Characteristics of crimes against juveniles* (OJJDP Juvenile Justice Bulletin). Washington, DC: Office of Juvenile Justice and Delinquency Prevention.

Girouard, C. (2001). *School resource officer training program* (OJJDP fact sheet). Washington, DC: Office of Juvenile Justice and Delinquency Prevention.

Ireland, T. O., Smith, C. A., & Thornberry, T. P. (2002). Developmental issues in the impact of child maltreatment on later delinquency and drug use. *Criminology, 40,* 359–400.

Justice Policy Institute. (1999). *New report shows no increase in school shooting deaths over six-year period.* Retrieved January 27, 1999, from http://www.cjcj.org/jpi/schoolhousepr.html

Juvenile Court Act, 42 PA. C.S.A., Sec. 6301 (1995).

Juvenile Court Judges' Commission. (1997). *Balanced and restorative justice in Pennsylvania: A new mission and changing roles within the juvenile justice system* (Pamphlet). Harrisburg, PA: Juvenile Court Judges Commission.

Kappeler, V. E., Blumberg, M., & Potter, G. W. (2000). *The mythology of crime and criminal justice* (3rd ed). Prospect Heights, IL: Waveland.

Kracke, K. (2001). *The "green book" demonstration* (OJJDP fact sheet). Washington, DC: Office of Juvenile Justice and Delinquency Prevention.

Levick, M. L. (2000). Zero tolerance: Mandatory sentencing meets the one room schoolhouse. *Kentucky Children's Rights Journal, 8,* 5–6.

Magill, S. (1998). Adolescents: Public enemy #1. *Crime & Delinquency, 44,* 121–126.

Menard, S. (2002). Short- and long-term consequences of adolescent victimization. *Youth Violence and Research Bulletin.* Washington, DC: Office of Juvenile Justice and Delinquency Prevention.

Merlo, A. V. (2000). Juvenile Justice at the Crossroads: Presidential Address to the Academy of Criminal Justice Sciences. *Justice Quarterly, 17,* 639–661.

Merlo, A. V., & Benekos, P. J. (2000). *What's wrong with the criminal justice system? Ideology, politics, and the media.* Cincinnati, OH: Anderson.

Moon, M. M., Sundt, J., Cullen, F. T., & Wright, J. P. (2000). Is child saving dead? Public support for juvenile rehabilitation. *Crime & Delinquency, 46,* 38–62.

Preventing school shootings: A summary of a U.S. Secret Service safe school initiative. (2002). *National Institute of Justice Journal, 248,* 10–15.

Parks, G. (2000). *The high/scope Perry preschool project.* OJJDP Juvenile Justice Bulletin. Washington, DC: Office of Juvenile Justice and Delinquency Prevention.

Platt, A. M. (1977). *The child savers: The invention of delinquency* (2nd ed.). Chicago: University of Chicago Press.

Powell, H. (1999). School violence: Statistics reveal school violence declining. *The Mentor, 1,* 4–6.

Repenning, K., Powell, H., Doane, A., & Dunkle, H. (2000, March). *Demystifying school violence: A national, state, and local perspective on the phenomenon of school violence.* Paper presented at the annual meeting of the Academy of Criminal Justice Sciences, New Orleans, Louisiana.

Schwartz, H. (2002, July 22). The court's terrible two. *The Nation.* Available from http://www.thenation.com

Sickmund, M., Snyder, H., & Poe-Yamagata, E. (1997). *Juvenile offenders and victims: 1997 update on violence.* Washington, DC: Office of Juvenile Justice and Delinquency Prevention.

Skiba, R. (2000, January 14). No to zero tolerance. *The Washington Post,* p. A27.

Skiba, R., & Peterson, R. (1999). The dark side of zero tolerance: Can punishment lead to safe schools? *Phi Delta Kappan, 80,* 372–376, 381–382.

Snyder, H. N., & Sickmund, M. (1999). *Juvenile offenders and victims: 1999 national report.* Washington,

DC: Office of Juvenile Justice and Delinquency Prevention.

Strom, K. J. (2000). *Profile of state prisoners under age 18, 1985–1997.* Washington, DC: Bureau of Justice Statistics.

Torbet, P., & Szymanski, L. (1998). *State legislative responses to violent juvenile crime: 1996–1997 update.* Washington, DC: Office of Juvenile Justice and Delinquency Prevention.

Torbet, P., & Thomas, D. (1997, October). Balanced and restorative justice: implementing the philosophy. *Pennsylvania Progress,* 4.

Triplett, R. (2000). The dramatization of evil: Reacting to juvenile delinquency during the 1990s. In S. S. Simpson (Ed.), *Of crime and criminality* (pp. 121–138). Thousand Oaks, CA: Pine Forge press.

Vogel, J. (1994, July/August). Throw away the key: Juvenile offenders are the Willie Hortons of the '90s. *UTNE Reader,* 56–60.

Widom, C. S. (1995). *Victims of childhood sexual abuse- later criminal consequences* (Research in brief). Washington, DC: U.S. Department of Justice, Office of Justice Programs.

Widom, C. S., & Maxfield, M. G. (2001). *An update on the "cycle of violence"* (National Institute of Justice, Research in Brief). Washington, DC: Office of Juvenile Justice and Delinquency Prevention.

Wiebush, R., Freitag, R., & Baird, C. (2001). *Preventing delinquency through improved child protection ser- vices* (OJJDP, Juvenile Justice Bulletin). Washington, DC: Office of Juvenile Justice and Delinquency Prevention.

DISCUSSION QUESTIONS

1. Assume that juveniles aged 14–17 are as mature as adults aged 18 and older, and that they make rational choices to commit crimes. Based on that assumption, summarize three policies, laws, and sanctions that you would recommend to lawmakers to reduce juvenile crime.

2. Based on this reading, cite evidence that indicates that prevention programs appear to be more effective than zero-tolerance and punishment policies to reduce juvenile crime in communities and in schools.

3. Based on the research cited in this reading, offer arguments to support a "balanced and restorative" (BARJ) approach in place of a "RAP" approach.

❖

READING

In this reading James Howell describes the structure and development of a comprehensive strategy to reduce serious, violent, and chronic juvenile delinquency. He discusses the general principles, theoretical foundations, and major components of the strategy, and reviews previous research and cites numerous references that support the comprehensive strategy. A major goal of the comprehensive strategy is juvenile justice system improvement, and this is accomplished by two processes. First, a community must conduct an assessment of the risk and protective factors for delinquency in that jurisdiction. Because each community is different, this is a critical component of the strategy. Second, juvenile justice agencies must assess the delinquent populations in their jurisdiction for risk and treatment needs in order to identify juvenile clients for appropriate graduated sanctions. The Comprehensive Strategy aims to maximize cost-effectiveness of juvenile justice systems in communities and states by promoting integrated, multidisciplinary, and multiagency service delivery systems for problem youth and juvenile offenders. The Comprehensive Strategy has been implemented in North Carolina and shows great potential for reducing juvenile delinquency at significant cost savings.

The Comprehensive Strategy Framework

James C. Howell

In this chapter, I describe the structure and operational tools of the Comprehensive Strategy for Serious, Violent, and Chronic Juvenile Offenders. In the pages that follow, I explain the general principles of the Comprehensive Strategy, its theoretical foundations, and tools that are used in its implementation. I use the case of North Carolina to illustrate how these tools can be used to build a comprehensive plan. In this chapter, I highlight juvenile justice system structures to clarify the key features of the Comprehensive Strategy framework.

⬚ General Principles of the Comprehensive Strategy

The Comprehensive Strategy calls for a proactive and balanced approach that integrates prevention and control. It is based on the following five general principles:

- We must strengthen the family in its primary responsibility to instill moral values and provide guidance and support to children. Where there is no functional family unit, we must establish a family surrogate and assist that entity to guide and nurture the child.
- We must support "core" social institutions such as schools, religious institutions, and

community organizations in their roles of developing capable, mature, and responsible youth. A goal of each of these societal institutions should be to ensure that children have the opportunity and support to mature into productive, law-abiding citizens. In a nurturing community environment, core social institutions are actively involved in the lives of youth.

- We must promote delinquency prevention as the most cost-effective approach to reducing juvenile delinquency. Families, schools, religious institutions, and community organizations, including citizen volunteers and the private sector, must be enlisted in the nation's delinquency prevention efforts. These core socializing institutions must be strengthened and assisted in their efforts to ensure that children have the opportunity to become capable and responsible citizens. When children engage in acting-out behavior, such as status offenses, the family and community, in concert with child welfare agencies, must respond with appropriate treatment and support services. Communities must take the lead in designing and building comprehensive prevention approaches that address known risk factors and target other youth at risk of delinquency.

SOURCE: Howell, James C. (2003). *Preventing and reducing delinquency: A comprehensive framework.* Thousand Oaks, CA: Sage Publications, Inc.

- We must intervene immediately and effectively when delinquent behavior occurs to prevent delinquent offenders from becoming chronic offenders or committing progressively more serious and violent crimes. Initial intervention efforts, under an umbrella of system authorities (police, intake, and probation), should be centered in the family and other core societal institutions. Juvenile justice system authorities should ensure that an appropriate response occurs and act quickly and firmly if the need for formal system adjudication and sanctions is demonstrated.

- We must identify and control the small group of serious, violent, and chronic juvenile offenders who have committed felony offenses or have failed to respond to intervention and nonsecure community-based treatment and rehabilitation services offered by the juvenile justice system. Measures to address delinquent offenders who are a threat to community safety may include placement in secure community-based facilities, training schools, and other secure juvenile facilities. Even the most violent or intractable juveniles should not be moved into the criminal justice system before they graduate from the jurisdiction of the juvenile justice system.

The Comprehensive Strategy is a two-tiered system for responding proactively to juvenile delinquency and crime. In the first tier, delinquency prevention and early intervention programs are relied upon to prevent and reduce the onset of delinquency. If these efforts fail, then the juvenile justice system, the second tier, needs to make proactive responses to juvenile delinquency by addressing the risk factors for recidivism and associated treatment needs of delinquents, particularly those with a high likelihood of becoming serious, violent, and chronic juvenile

offenders. To reduce this likelihood, a continuum of sanctions and services for juvenile offenders needs to be in place.

Thus the Comprehensive Strategy is based on two principal goals: (a) preventing youth from becoming delinquent by focusing prevention programs on at-risk youth, and (b) improving the juvenile justice system's response to delinquent offenders through a system of graduated sanctions and parallel programs. Both of these goals are addressed through an integrated or "seamless" continuum of prevention, early intervention, and treatment options linked with graduated sanctions.

The Comprehensive Strategy is research based, data driven, and outcome focused. It is a blueprint or framework that is based on the findings of a decade of reviews and syntheses of research and program evaluation results. It empowers communities to assess their own delinquency problems and needs, and guides them in how to use these data to design and develop their own comprehensive strategies, because local ownership of programs and strategies breeds success (Tolan, Perry, & Jones, 1987). Finally, the Comprehensive Strategy is outcome focused in that it guides communities in the development of action plans that specify measurable outcomes.

The Comprehensive Strategy is comprehensive in four respects:

1. It encompasses the entire juvenile justice enterprise—prevention, early intervention, and the juvenile justice system.

2. Although it specifically targets serious, violent, and chronic juvenile offenders, it provides a framework for dealing with all juvenile offenders as well as other problem children and adolescents.

3. It calls for an integrated multiagency response to childhood and adolescent problems, bringing the juvenile justice system together with the mental health, child welfare, education, and law enforcement

systems, and community organizations as well, to address multiple youth, family, and community problems.

4. It links the resources of all juvenile justice system components in an interactive manner. Comprehensive juvenile justice is not a zero-sum game. Resources are shared, and so are decisions as to the allocation of resources. An ideal mantra for participating agency officials is "Put your money on the table and take your hands away."

The Comprehensive Strategy guides jurisdictions in developing continuums of responses that parallel offender careers, beginning with early intervention and followed by prevention and graduated sanctions. By building such a continuum, a community can organize an array of programs that correspond with further development of offender careers. The collective effect of these programs is likely to be much greater than the impact of a single program, as illustrated in a RAND cost-benefit study of juvenile delinquency prevention and treatment programs (Greenwood, Model, Rydell, & Chiesa, 1996). The researchers found that, if implemented statewide, a combination of four delinquency prevention and treatment programs could achieve the same level of serious crime reduction as California's "three strikes" law, which mandated imprisonment for the third strike. The RAND researchers projected that the four juvenile delinquency prevention and treatment programs would cost less than $1 billion per year to implement throughout California, compared with about $5.5 billion per year for "three strikes." Thus, at less than one-fifth the cost, the state could fund the four programs and prevent more serious crimes rather than fund imprisonment. As the RAND researchers note, "Based on current best estimates of program costs and benefits, investments in some interventions for high-risk youth may be several times more cost-effective in reducing serious crime than

mandatory sentences for repeat offenders" (Greenwood et al., 1996, p. 40).

Offender careers develop over time, thus a continuum of programs aimed at different points along the life course have a much better chance of succeeding than a single intervention. As noted in Chapter 6, certain risk factors operate at particular times in individuals' lives. Early on, programs are needed that address family risk factors. A few years later, in childhood, preschool- and elementary school-focused programs are needed, along with family support programs. Then, in adolescence, peer influences are predominant, and programs are needed that buffer the effects of exposure to delinquent peer influences and the spread of delinquency and violence in adolescence. Interventions that counter individual (e.g., mental health problems) and community risk factors are needed all along the life course.

⊠ Target Populations

The initial target population for prevention programs is juveniles at risk of involvement in delinquent activity. Although primary delinquency prevention programs provide services to all youth wishing to participate, communities can achieve maximum impact on future delinquent conduct by seeking to identify and involve in prevention programs those youth at greatest risk of involvement in delinquent activity. This includes youth who exhibit known risk factors for future delinquency—in the family, school, peer group, individual, and community domains. It includes youth who have had contact with the juvenile justice system as nonoffenders (neglected, abused, and dependent), status offenders (runaways, truants, alcohol offenders, and incorrigibles), or minor delinquent offenders (e.g., child delinquents). Finally, it includes youth who have had contact with other social service systems—mental health, child welfare, social services, child protective services, and education—and evidence potential delinquency involvement.

Box 1   BENEFITS OF USING THE COMPREHENSIVE STRATEGY

- Increased prevention of delinquency (and thus fewer young people enter the juvenile justice systems)
- Enhanced responsiveness from the juvenile justice system
- Greater accountability on the part of youth
- Decreased costs of juvenile corrections
- A more responsible juvenile justice system
- More effective juvenile justice programs
- Less delinquency
- Fewer delinquents become serious, violent, and chronic offenders
- Fewer delinquents become adult offenders

SOURCE: Wilson and Howell (1993).

The next target population is youth, both male and female, who have committed delinquent (criminal) acts, including juvenile offenders who evidence a high likelihood of becoming, or who already are, serious, violent, and chronic offenders. Interventions should target the highest-risk offenders, in keeping with what Canadian/American criminologists call the risk principle. Lipsey and Wilson's (1998) meta-analysis has shown that treatment programs reduce recidivism most among serious and violent juvenile offenders. Perhaps this is because they possess the highest level of risks and needs, and also have the most room to improve their behavior. In any event, a key Comprehensive Strategy principle is that the most intensive services and sanctions should be used for the most serious, violent, and chronic offenders. Treatment is likely to be effective for them, recidivism is most likely to be reduced, and public safety is most likely to be enhanced when they are targeted.

Comprehensive Strategy Rationale

What can communities and the juvenile justice system do to prevent the development of and interrupt the progression of delinquent and criminal careers? Juvenile justice agencies and programs are one part of a larger picture that involves many other local agencies and programs that are responsible for working with at-risk youth and their families. It is important that juvenile delinquency prevention and intervention programs are integrated with graduated sanctions and a continuum of rehabilitation programs: All programs must reflect those problems and program priorities that the local community has determined to be most pressing.

Comprehensive approaches to delinquency prevention and intervention require the integration of efforts between the juvenile justice system and other service provision systems, including mental health, health, child welfare, and education. Developing mechanisms that effectively link these different service providers at the program level will strengthen treatment programs because of the multiple problems that serious and violent offenders exhibit.

Theoretical Foundations of the Comprehensive Strategy

Developmental criminology and the public health model are the two overarching theoretical models on which the Comprehensive Strategy is based. Developmental criminology organizes the research base with respect to identifying the risk and causal factors for development of delinquent behavior over the periods of childhood and adolescence (see, e.g., Le Blanc & Loeber, 1998; Loeber & Le Blanc, 1990). This theoretical framework also focuses attention on the development of offender careers—from childhood disorders to involvement in serious, violent, and chronic delinquency.

Application of the public health model in prevention programming involves preventing delinquency by reducing risk factors and increasing protective factors (Institute of Medicine, 1994). A focus on risk and protective factors in delinquency prevention is supported theoretically by the social development model (Catalano & Hawkins, 1996), a developmental theory that integrates learning theory (Akers, Krohn, Lanza-Kaduce, & Radosevich, 1979; Bandura, 1977) and control theory (Hirschi, 1969). The social development model hypothesizes that youths commit offenses across developmental periods because they encounter antisocial influences in the family, peer group, school, and community domains that reinforce (learning) offending (Bronfenbrenner, 1979). Conversely, they resist or desist from offending if they encounter prosocial influences that inhibit (control) offending. If risk and protective factors are addressed at or slightly before the developmental points at which they begin to predict later delinquency or violence, it is likely that risk reduction efforts will be effective (Hawkins, Catalano, & Brewer, 1995).

Both learning theories and control theories are reflected in the key principles of the Comprehensive Strategy, which advocates strengthening the family and other core social institutions—such as schools, religious institutions, and community organizations—in their roles of developing capable, mature, and responsible youth. In contrast, control theory is reflected in the emphasis on controlling serious, violent, and chronic juvenile offenders with graduated sanctions.

Like the prevention component, the graduated sanctions component of the Comprehensive Strategy is grounded in developmental theory (see Chapter 4). From its inception, the juvenile justice system has employed a developmental perspective in responding to child and adolescent delinquency (Krisberg & Austin, 1993). A central premise in juvenile court jurisprudence is that children are not developmentally mature, and hence should be treated differently from adults. Children often need protection from unhealthy situations. They should not be held as fully responsible for their acts as adults, because their behavior is shaped by risk factors that, for the most part, are beyond their control (Howell, 1997).

The concept of graduated sanctions also has a theoretical basis in learning theory (Bandura, 1973, 1986, 1999; Sutherland, 1973). As Bandura (1999) explains, individuals repeat reinforced behaviors, especially in situations akin to those in which the behaviors were previously reinforced. Conversely, individuals avoid behaviors that elicit negative reactions from others. Thus cognitive-behavioral treatment approaches should be effective in a graduated sanctions context.

The graduated sanctions component also integrates *positivist criminology* (use of rehabilitation) and *classical criminology* (use of sanctions) in a balanced approach to recidivism reduction. We did not use the word *punishment* in the original formulation of the Comprehensive Strategy (Wilson & Howell, 1993) because it is well established that punishment does not reduce recidivism. Instead, we chose the term *sanctions*. Although sanctions that restrict freedom may help bring antisocial behavior under control and may restrain offenders from committing delinquent acts in the short term, severe sanctions (punishment) may increase recidivism in the long term (Gendreau, 1996; Gendreau & Goggin, 1996). Hence sanctions should be viewed as providing only the setting for service delivery; it is the intervention within the setting that has the actual power to produce change in offenders (Andrews & Bonta, 1998; Bonta, 1996; Gendreau, Cullen, & Bonta, 1994). Sanctions themselves do not address the treatment needs of offenders.

⊠ Components of the Comprehensive Strategy

The Comprehensive Strategy for Serious, Violent, and Chronic Juvenile Offenders consists of two principal components:

- *Prevention and early intervention:* The Comprehensive Strategy empowers communities to prevent juvenile delinquency by conducting risk- and protection-focused prevention and selecting needed prevention and early intervention programs from a menu of effective program options.
- *A system of graduated sanctions and a parallel continuum of treatment alternatives:* The elements in this system include immediate intervention, intermediate sanctions, intensive supervision, community-based correctional programs, secure corrections, and aftercare.

The Prevention and Early Intervention Component

An understanding of the evidence on risk and protective factors for serious and violent delinquency suggests a set of principles that should guide prevention programming (Hawkins, Catalano, & Brewer, 1995, pp. 51–52):

- To be effective, prevention efforts must address known risk factors for delinquency, violence, and substance abuse.
- Prevention efforts must make clear connections between program activities and the goal of risk reduction. For example, family management problems have been identified as a risk factor for health and behavior problems in children. These problems may emerge from different sources. If it appears that family management problems are occurring in a particular community because parents who work need more effective ways to monitor

their children's behavior, child-care centers, schools, and latchkey programs could supervise children's daily behavior for parents, to assist them in monitoring their children's behavior when they are not present. Alternatively, if a community's family management problems arise from parents' lack of knowledge of effective discipline techniques, programs that provide parents with opportunities to learn and practice a variety of discipline techniques may be effective.

- The link between prevention activities and the risk reduction objective should be clearly specified.
- Prevention programs should seek to strengthen protective factors while reducing risk.
- Risk reduction activities should address risks at or before the time they become predictive of later problems. Intervening early to reduce risk is likely to minimize the effort needed and maximize the outcome. For example, interventions aimed at improving family management practices that are implemented very early (e.g., with expectant mothers and parents of infants) are likely to be more effective than interventions that are not initiated until after referrals for abuse and neglect.
- Interventions should target individuals and communities that are exposed to multiple risk factors. Given the evidence that those exposed to multiple risks are at elevated risk, efforts to prevent chronic and serious problems of crime, violence, and substance abuse are most likely to be effective if they are focused on these populations. Targeting high-risk communities is particularly advantageous in that it can prevent individual children in these communities from being labeled as potential problems at very early ages. Families at risk include those headed by single, poor, and/or

teenage mothers. Communities at risk include poor and disorganized neighborhoods with high levels of crime, violence, and substance abuse. A communitywide approach allows higher- and lower-risk families in a neighborhood to work and learn together, modeling, supporting, and reinforcing efforts to strengthen protective factors and processes.

- Because the presence of multiple risks in multiple domains is a predictor of serious crime, violence, and substance abuse, prevention approaches should be multifaceted, addressing the key risk factors affecting the neighborhood or community.

- Prevention programs must be designed and implemented so that they will reach and be acceptable to members of all the diverse racial, cultural, and socioeconomic groups to be included.

Recent advances in prevention science and health epidemiology have resulted in new tools that communities can use to plan and implement strategic, outcome-focused plans for reducing the prevalence of antisocial behavior among adolescents and young adults. Enormous progress has been made in the past 20 years in the development of the research base for prevention science (Hawkins, 1999). A fundamental principle of this research is that increased exposure to risk factors increases delinquency involvement and other problem behaviors, whereas an increase in protective factors decreases delinquency and associated problems (Durlak, 1998). Longitudinal studies under way in Europe, North America, and New Zealand have identified the major factors associated with communities, families, school experiences, peer groups, and individuals themselves that increase the probability of delinquency in adolescence and criminality in early adulthood. . . . Many of these factors have been found to increase the probability of substance abuse, teen pregnancy, and dropping out of school as well as delinquency and violence.

A second major breakthrough in prevention science is related to the remarkable advances that have been made in the past decade in the development and testing of effective prevention interventions (Hawkins, 1999). Numerous studies have shown that prevention actions that reduce risk and enhance protection can prevent later delinquency and violence. As Hawkins (1999) notes, "It is possible now to move to outcome focused prevention, that is, to design systems for risk reduction and protective factor enhancement to achieve specified prevention outcomes" (p. 449).

Adoption of the public health model in the delinquency prevention enterprise serves to provide a structured approach to prevention—using the tools of prevention science. . . . Most communities take a "hit or miss" approach to delinquency prevention. Use of the public health model to engage communities will help to align prevention programs with science-based risk and protective factors.

The approach most clearly proven to be effective for engaging entire communities in risk- and protection-focused prevention is the Communities That Care (CTC) operating system (Hawkins, 1999). It contains research-based tools to help communities, promote the positive development of children and adolescents, and prevent adolescent substance abuse, delinquency, teen pregnancy, school dropout, and violence.

The Graduated Sanctions Component

The juvenile justice system has always had a rudimentary system of graduated sanctions, ranging from police apprehension and arrest to informal handling at court intake, adjudication and probation, and secure confinement (Bernard, 1992). Figure 1 illustrates a continuum of graduated sanctions that cover the entire juvenile justice system. This model shows how offenders are stepped up and stepped down in a graduated sanctions system. Youth first enter the system with police contact, which in the first or second instance may result in their being counseled and released or their being arrested. The severest sanction (at the top of the figure) is confinement in a secure correctional institution. Although aftercare programs are less common today than in the past, the downward steps in the continuum of graduated sanctions ideally consist of decreasing restrictions and services.

To be most effective, the components in a graduated sanctions system need to match the developmental history of the delinquent career and the risk of recidivism. When offenders persist in serious and violent delinquency, their position in a graduated sanctions system should be advanced. As offenders progress in the graduated sanctions system, linked rehabilitation programs must become more structured and intensive, to deal effectively with the intractable problems that more difficult and dangerous offenders present, while reserving secure confinement for the much smaller number of serious, chronic, and violent juvenile offenders. To accomplish these twin goals, the graduated sanctions component of the Comprehensive Strategy framework consists of five levels of sanctions, moving from least to most restrictive.

1. Immediate intervention with first-time delinquent offenders (misdemeanors and nonviolent felonies) and nonserious repeat offenders

2. Intermediate sanctions for first-time serious or violent offenders, including intensive supervision for chronic and serious/violent offenders

3. Community confinement

4. Secure corrections for the most serious, violent, chronic offenders

5. Aftercare

These gradations—and the sublevels that can be created within them—form a continuum of intervention options that should be paralleled by a continuum of treatment options, which should include an array of referral and disposition resources for law enforcement, juvenile courts, and juvenile corrections officials. Intensive aftercare programs are critical to the success of juveniles once they complete treatment, for reinforcement, and when they return to their families, neighborhoods, and communities following confinement.

In many jurisdictions, juvenile justice systems need to be reformed so that system interventions parallel more exactly the progression in offenders' careers. The linking of graduated sanctions with a continuum of rehabilitation options is intended to interrupt offender career progression. Communities can greatly reduce their likelihood of implementing "hit or miss" rehabilitation practices by applying the current research-based knowledge of effective treatment programs, including effective practical, everyday rehabilitation programs. Below, I describe the tools that juvenile justice system agencies can use to align sanctions and treatment programs more closely with the stages in offenders' delinquent careers.

◼ Linchpins of the Comprehensive Strategy

The Comprehensive Strategy is activated by two processes that are considered linchpins in the process of developing comprehensive juvenile justice models. First, the community must conduct a comprehensive assessment of risk and protective factors for delinquency in that specific jurisdiction, instead of arbitrarily selecting prevention programs that may miss the mark. The best system for scientific yet community-controlled prevention is the Communities That Care process (Hawkins, Catalano, & Associates, 1992). Each community is different from all other communities, with its own combination of predominant risk factors, therefore this assessment process is critical to successful prevention programming (Catalano, Arthur, Hawkins, Berglund, & Olson, 1998; Catalano, Loeber, & McKinney, 1999; J. D. Hawkins, 1995, 1999). I will describe this process in more detail shortly.

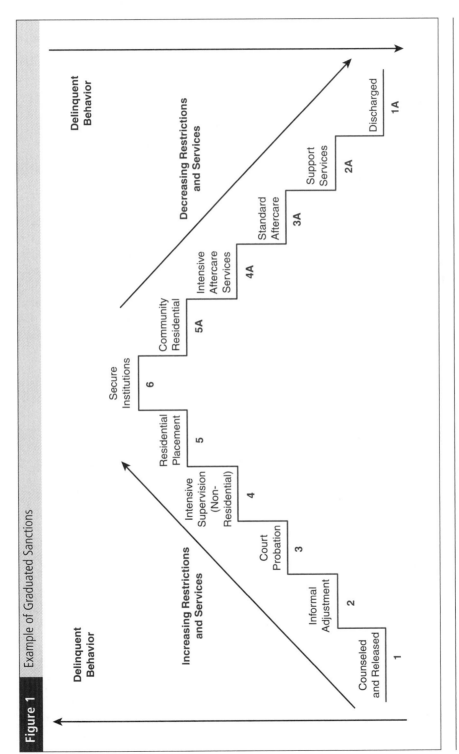

Figure 1   Example of Graduated Sanctions

Delinquent Behavior

Increasing Restrictions and Services

Decreasing Restrictions and Services

Delinquent Behavior

1   Counseled and Released
2   Informal Adjustment
3   Court Probation
4   Intensive Supervision (Non-Residential)
5   Residential Placement
6   Secure Institutions
5A   Community Residential
4A   Intensive Aftercare Services
3A   Standard Aftercare
2A   Support Services
1A   Discharged

Source: *Risk and Needs Assessment for Juvenile Justice*, by D. Wagner, 2001. © 2001 by National Council on Crime and Delinquency. Reprinted with permission.

Second, juvenile justice system agencies must assess the community's delinquent population for risk and treatment needs, to classify and position offenders within a structured system of graduated sanctions. To develop comprehensive juvenile justice systems, many communities need to change their thinking about how to manage the operations of these systems. Instead of relying on "magic bullets," juvenile justice systems need to make use of available tools to improve the management of juvenile delinquent populations in the various parts of the juvenile justice system. If communities make the management and control of serious, violent, and chronic offenders the top priority in their juvenile justice systems, then management of the remainder of the delinquent offender population will be easier and more cost-effective.

Three tools are used in this process; these tools make up what has been called a *structured decision-making model* (Wiebush, Baird, Krisberg, & Onek, 1995). First, juvenile justice officials use risk assessment to determine the level of sanctions needed to protect the public from a particular offender. They next use needs assessment to determine the offender's treatment needs. Then, to find the best match between offender and program, which is critical for effective rehabilitation (Bonta, 1996; Gendreau, 1996 Jones, 1996), they use the results of the offender's needs assessment in tandem with those of his or her risk assessment to place the offender in a particular supervision level and then in a program within that supervision level; to accomplish this step, they use a matrix that organizes sanctions and programs by risk level and offense severity. I present an example of this process in the next section.

⊠ How to Build a Comprehensive Juvenile Justice Plan

In this section, I describe the necessary tools for implementing the prevention component of the Comprehensive Strategy, and then use North Carolina's experience to illustrate the graduated sanctions component.

How to Build a Comprehensive Prevention Plan

The Communities That Care prevention planning system (Hawkins, 1999; Hawkins, Catalano, & Associates, 1992) effectively empowers communities to organize themselves to engage in outcome-focused prevention planning using the tools of prevention science. CTC must be implemented at the community level, because profiles of risk and protection vary from community to community (Hawkins, 1999, p. 450). The CTC prevention planning system is based on the theoretical framework of the social development model (Catalano & Hawkins, 1996). As noted above, this integrated theory combines control and social learning theories. The social development model has been demonstrated to be a valid theory for explaining adolescence drug use, delinquency, and violence.

The implementation of CTC involves five phases (Hawkins, 1999, pp. 451–455). In the first, called the Readiness Phase, key community stakeholders assess their community's readiness to engage in risk- and protection-focused prevention. In the second phase, key community stakeholders are educated about prevention science and involved in the CTC planning process. This necessitates the formation of a structure—a community planning board or coalition—to move the community toward its vision for the future of its children. This coalition or planning board of key leaders must have broad community representation. Community assessments are conducted in the third phase. Using CTC's validated archival indicators of risk and outcomes and CTC's Youth Survey, the coalition develops a profile of the community based on community-specific data on levels of risk factors, protective factors, delinquency, and crime in the community's neighborhoods. In the fourth phase, the coalition drafts the community's strategic youth development and prevention plan after using the results of the preceding assessments to arrive at a baseline assessment of risk and protective factors and a prioritized subset of two to five risk factors that are most prevalent. The strategic plan is based on an inventory of community resources that already address priority risk factors and are designed to enhance protective factors. It builds on existing community resources, avoids duplication of effort, and fills gaps in existing policies and programs. Coalition members select new programs from a menu of promising programs that have been tested and shown to be effective in changing selected risk and protective factors and preventing delinquency, violence, or other problem behaviors (Hawkins, 1999). In the fifth phase, the coalition implements and evaluates the strategic plan.

Box 2   Common Juvenile Justice System Conditions

- Unbalanced emphasis on prevention versus graduated sanctions
- Overreliance on detention, incarceration, and residential programs
- Poor targeting of serious, violent, and chronic juvenile offenders
- Poor matching of offenders with appropriate levels of supervision, sanctions, and programs
- Use of ineffective programs
- Poor program planning
- Lack of continuity between juvenile court and corrections system operations
- Underdeveloped parole supervision/aftercare and transitional services
- Ineffective allocation of court and correctional resources
- Lack of a clear focus on the use of and objectives for confinement resources (often demonstrated in poor classification systems and excessive numbers of lengthy placements)
- Inadequate data collection on offenders in the system, management information systems, and information sharing
- Lack of good policy guidance in the development of institutional classification, length of commitment, and release criteria
- Lack of good policy guidance for state executive, legislative, and judicial stakeholders in the development of legislation, standards, and other policy directives that create data-driven, outcome-based, and results-oriented juvenile justice policy reforms

---

During the fourth phase of the CTC process, CTC managers guide the community coalition members in the selection of promising and effective prevention programs, using the community's risk and protective factor profiles to develop clear, measurable outcomes. This involves reviewing programs and activities that have been tested and shown to be effective in reducing specific risk factors and enhancing protective factors, and selecting the approaches the coalition members wish to include in the community's continuum. The product is a written action plan for implementing new programs and strategies, enhancing/expanding existing resources, and planning for evaluation. Some 400 communities across the United States have implemented CTC, as have communities in the United Kingdom (Scotland, England, and Wales) and the Netherlands (Hawkins, 1999). CTC is now a commercial product of the Charming Bete Company, Inc.

It is possible, of course, for a community to organize and implement risk- and protection-focused prevention without using the CTC process. For a community to be successful in preventing delinquency, it must use a process that is research based, data driven, and outcome focused. In addition, to be effective, community-wide delinquency prevention needs to adhere to the risk- and protection-focused framework of the public health model (Institute of Medicine, 1994) and be grounded in developmental theory. In order to have the most comprehensive impact on child and adolescent problem behaviors, prevention programs and strategies must target the broad array of risk factors and protective factors that are linked to intersecting positive and negative outcomes for children and adolescents. For the largest impact on delinquency, it also is crucial that prevention strategies and programs be meshed with existing community resources and linked with the juvenile justice system and other child-serving/development agencies, as prescribed in the Comprehensive Strategy.

How to Build a Graduated Sanctions System

Because of the seventh moral panic over juvenile delinquency, some states have had difficulty maintaining a good balance between public safety considerations and rehabilitation. One of these goals need not be sacrificed for the other. North Carolina is a case in point. In the mid-1990s, the juvenile justice system in North Carolina was experiencing the consequences of "get tough" policies. Some of the state's juvenile reformatories—called Youth Development Centers (YDCs)—were overcrowded and overpopulated with minor offenders. Admissions were increasing at a rate of approximately 10% per year (Lubitz, 2001). In 1996, only one-fifth of the juveniles confined in YDCs were violent felony offenders; the majority (nearly 60%) were moderately serious offenders (Lubitz, 2001), and about one-fifth were misdemeanant offenders. The growth in admissions had been driven by the increased confinement of misdemeanant and moderately serious offenders, not by any increase in the numbers of violent offenders.

Influenced by the Comprehensive Strategy for Serious, Violent, and Chronic Juvenile Offenders (Wilson & Howell, 1993), North Carolina state officials and legislators saw a way to address two policy concerns. First, they wanted to increase public safety by targeting the most serious, violent, *and* chronic juvenile offenders for more restrictive sanctions, particularly confinement in the YDCs. Second, they wanted to preserve the futures of the state's young people by increasing early intervention efforts with community treatment programs.

North Carolina's 1998 Juvenile Justice Reform Act incorporated the Comprehensive Strategy framework and addressed both of these policy goals by incorporating the graduated sanctions scheme recommended in the Comprehensive Strategy. The act mandated the use of the structured decision-making model recommended in the *Guide for Implementing the Comprehensive Strategy* (Howell, 1995), consisting of risk and needs assessments and an offender classification matrix to place offenders along a continuum of programs and sanctions. The North Carolina classification matrix uses two factors to determine the placement of adjudicated juvenile offenders: current offense and risk level. A complex formula—factoring in chronic offending and whether or not the current offense was committed while the offender was on probation—guides determination of the risk level. The intersection of the risk level and current offense governs placement of an offender at Level 1, 2, or 3. For example, an offender with a serious and chronic offense history (i.e., high risk) who has been adjudicated for a violent offense would earn a Level 3 disposition, commitment to a Youth Development Center. Level 2 is an intermediate disposition, and Level 1 is a community disposition.

The continuum of sanctions and services, which the act mixed for each disposition level, is shown in Table 1. Only three of the possible Level 1 disposition alternatives require removal from the home: residential placement with a relative or in a group home, intermittent confinement, and placement in Eckerd Wilderness Camp. In contrast, several of the Level 2 disposition alternatives remove the child from the home, and only one disposition alternative is possible for Level 3, placement in a YDC. Note also that regular probation is a disposition option in Level I, and intensive supervision probation is prescribed in Level 2. Thus the disposition alternatives in the three levels clearly demonstrate the graduated sanctions concept. The legislature made an attempt to permit flexibility in the choice of sanctions and services by permitting use of Level 1 disposition alternatives for Level 2 cases.

Table 1	North Carolina Disposition Levels[a]	
Level 1 Community	*Level 2 Intermediate (may also include Level 1 dispositions)*	*Level 3 Commitment*
Community-based program	Eckerd Wilderness Camp	Commitment to training school
Victim-offender reconciliation program	Structured day program	
Community service (up to 100 hours)	Community service (up to 200 hours)	
Restitution (up to $500)	Restitution ($500 and over)	
Suspension of driver's license	Regimented training program	
Curfew	Intensive supervision probation	
Counseling, including intensive substance abuse treatment	House arrest with or without electronic monitoring	
Vocational or educational program	Multipurpose group home	
Regular probation	Residential placement in treatment facility or group home	
Residential placement with relative or group home	Placement in an intensive nonresidential treatment program or intensive substance abuse program	
Intermittent confinement (up to 5 days)	Short-term secure confinement (up to 14 days)	
Fine		
Eckerd Wilderness Camp		

SOURCE: *Fiscal Year 1999 Juvenile Justice Statistics for North Carolina: Juveniles Adjudicated Delinquent* (p. 4), by D. M. Dawes and P. Ross, 2000. Raleigh: North Carolina Sentencing and Policy Advisory Commission. Copyright © 2000 by North Carolina Sentencing and Policy Advisory Commission. Reprinted with permission.

a. See N.C.G.S. §§ 7B-2506, 7B-2508.

Where the matrix indicates alternative disposition options at a given risk level, court officials are expected to make the final determination using risk and needs assessment results. For example, if an offender's risk assessment score indicates that he or she does not warrant a higher-level disposition, and the needs assessment instrument indicates that the youth would benefit from a program that is available for lower-risk offenders, then the youth should be placed in the lower disposition level in order to access the needed service.

The North Carolina Department of Juvenile Justice and Delinquency Prevention (DJJDP) has blended these dispositions with early intervention, prevention, community-based intervention, residential, and secure residential programs to form a continuum of programs and sanctions. This continuum will be refined as the state learns more about program effectiveness from the North Carolina project, which I will describe shortly.

With the assistance of the National Council on Crime and Delinquency (NCCD), the DJJDP developed, by committee, an instrument to assess juveniles' risks of future offending as well as an instrument to assess juveniles' and families' strengths and treatment needs. The risk assessment instrument incorporates the major research-based predictors of juvenile offender recidivism. It is used to classify offenders as low, medium, or high risk, depending on how many points they accumulate.

The needs assessment instrument is more detailed than most such instruments, because it was designed to provide very explicit information on treatment needs for future development of comprehensive treatment plans. Unlike some needs assessment instruments, it assigns a "total needs score" that is useful for the immediate task at hand—assisting court officials in determining proper placement of the assessed offender in the disposition matrix. . . .

The North Carolina experience shows how a state or community can use risk assessment and classification instruments to improve the efficiency, consistency, and fairness of the juvenile justice system. In addition, it shows that the policy goal of reserving costly long-term confinement for the most dangerous offenders is achievable. In other words, these data demonstrate the reliability of the classification matrix and the risk and needs assessment instruments for placing offenders at the proper level of risk. It is apparent that the Comprehensive Strategy tools have helped ensure that North Carolina's juvenile reformatories are reserved for the most serious, violent, and chronic juvenile offenders. . . .

Early Intervention With Delinquent Children and Their Families

Social services, child protective services, the education system, child welfare agencies, and mental health agencies need to do a better job of addressing the risk factors and precursor behaviors that lead to delinquency. Many of the children who need effective services in these systems—particularly children with mental health problems—end up being dumped into the juvenile justice system (Teplin, 2001). This inappropriate response may further exacerbate the problems of these youngsters, because the juvenile justice system is not equipped to meet their mental health treatment needs.

Early intervention programs aim to ameliorate risky conditions and, simultaneously, build resilience to them in hopes of preventing progression of early problem behavior into full-blown delinquency. Juveniles who continue delinquency involvement move into the juvenile justice system, into graduated sanctions and treatment programs. Even earlier identification of potential serious, violent, and chronic juvenile offenders may be possible, at multiple points, using multiple informants, multiple variables, and multiple screening tools (Howell, 2001).

. . . Community assessment centers may constitute an effective early intervention mechanism for integrating service delivery for youths with multiple problems that cut across several social service agencies. Such centers can help to integrate the services of several agencies by conducting comprehensive assessments of at-risk youth and providing case management of comprehensive treatment plans. School-based centers are one viable option.

If risk and needs assessments cannot be made at a single physical point of entry, then all agencies and organizations evaluating youth should use uniform assessment procedures, tools, and training. In either event, a two-step assessment process should be employed. First, each youth should receive an initial broad-based screening to determine whether more in-depth assessments are needed. Then, if a problem is revealed, a more comprehensive assessment pertaining to that specific area should be conducted. Objective risk and needs assessments should be driven by public safety concerns and youths' needs, not by funding streams or the agendas of individual agencies.

Immediate Intervention

First-time delinquent offenders (misdemeanors and nonviolent felonies) and nonserious repeat offenders (generally misdemeanor repeat offenses) make up the appropriate target group for immediate intervention. The overwhelming majority of these offenders will not become serious, violent, and chronic juvenile offenders. For those in this group, nonintrusive sanctions are most appropriate.

However, there is a subgroup of offenders within this category who score high on risk assessment instruments, and these offenders must be provided more intensive services based on their multiple problem behaviors and high probability of becoming more serious, violent, and chronic in their delinquent activities (Wilson & Howell, 1993). Nonresidential community-based programs, including prevention programs for at-risk youth, may be appropriate for many of these offenders. Such programs are small and open, located in or near the juveniles' homes, and maintain community participation in program planning, operation, and evaluation. Other offenders may require sanctions tailored to their offenses and their needs to help control them so that they do not commit additional crimes and to provide the necessary program structure for treatment to work.

Early juvenile court intervention with these kinds of offenders can be very effective. Tracy and Kempf-Leonard (1996) found that use of court adjustment and probation early in the offender career, particularly in the case of the most chronic offenders, reduced subsequent offenses, including continuation into adulthood. The earlier in chronic offender careers that probation and informal court handling were applied, as opposed to police lecture and release, the lower the recidivism rates among serious offenders. Compared with delinquents who received late-career probation, delinquents who received informal court adjustment, early probation, or mid-career probation had significantly lower odds of continuing their recidivism

and becoming adult offenders. Tracy and Kempf-Leonard's analysis showed that as the frequency of delinquency increased, and probation occurred later in the delinquent career, the more likely the offender was to become an adult criminal. When probation was administered later and later, especially for high-rate delinquents, the probability of adult crime escalated dramatically.

Other studies have shown that early juvenile court intervention in offender career paths, especially combining treatment with probation, produces lower recidivism rates (Brown, Miller, & Jenkins, 1991; Land, McCall, & Williams, 1990; Smith, Aloisi, & Goldstein, 1996). One of the programs that has produced such findings is Orange County's 8% Early Intervention Program (Schumacher & Kurz, 2000). In a North Carolina study, Dean, Brame, and Piquero (1996) found lower recidivism rates among incarcerated juvenile offenders who had been adjudicated delinquent at an early age in juvenile court. In a 6-year follow up with more than 800 juveniles released from state training schools, the researchers found that an increased number of prior adjudications had a restraining effect on recidivism—measured by arrests following release—among those who were first adjudicated at very young ages. For those who experienced a later first adjudication, exactly the opposite result was found. Early intervention with juvenile court probation makes a big difference in the success of juvenile rehabilitation with chronic offenders.

Intermediate Sanctions

Intermediate sanctions programs are appropriate for first-time serious or violent offenders and for chronic offenders who have not yet committed serious or violent offenses. These generally are moderate risk offenders. Intermediate sanctions include programs such as probation, day reporting centers, and electronic monitoring. Intensive supervision is an appropriate level of sanction for such offenders who score at the upper extreme of the moderate-risk category.

However, these sanctions are more effective when they are coupled with treatment programs, such as the programs Lipsey has identified as falling within the highest effectiveness tier. Multisystemic therapy is an excellent intermediate sanction that serves as an alternative to incarceration. Alternatives to confinement can now safely be used far more widely than they have been used in the past. Alternatives to incarceration are more effective than confinement. Jurisdictions need a structured way of ensuring that intermediate sanctions are used for most juvenile offenders; placing them in training schools is both needlessly expensive and not particularly effective.

Only a small number of juvenile offenders require secure confinement. At the other end of the risk continuum, there is another relatively large group of offenders for whom secure confinement should never be used. For the large middle portion of the juvenile offender population, however, the decision as to whether to use confinement is not obvious. It is a complex, uncertain, and sometimes highly contentious process involving a wide assortment of policy makers, practitioners, and even members of the community (Butts & Adams, 2001).

At this stage, it would be appropriate to place many serious and violent offenders in intensive supervision programs as an alternative to secure incarceration. Lipsey's (1999) meta-analysis of "practical" juvenile justice programs has shown that intensive supervision programs (ISPs) nested in probation and parole/aftercare sanctions effectively reduce recidivism. . . .

Residential or Secure Corrections for Serious, Violent, and Chronic Offenders

The criminal behavior of many serious, violent, *and* chronic juvenile offenders requires the application of secure sanctions to ensure public safety and to provide a structured treatment environment. Large congregate-care juvenile facilities have not proven to be effective in rehabilitating juvenile offenders. In those cases

where secure confinement of juveniles is necessary to protect the public, small secure facilities work best. Small community-based facilities that provide intensive services in a secure environment offer the best hope for successful treatment. Secure sanctions are most effective in changing future conduct when they are coupled with comprehensive treatment and rehabilitation services. Two graduated sanctions strategies are proposed within the secure corrections option: community confinement and incarceration in secure correctional facilities.

Community Confinement

Offenders whose presenting offenses are sufficiently serious (such as violent felonies) or who fail to respond to intermediate sanctions, as evidenced by continued reoffending, may be appropriate for community confinement. Offenders at this level represent the more serious (such as repeat felony drug trafficking or property offenders) and violent offenders among the juvenile justice system correctional population. In addition to having been adjudicated for serious or violent offenses, candidates for community confinement should also have chronic offense histories.

Community confinement refers to secure confinement in small community-based facilities that offer intensive treatment and rehabilitation services. These services include individual and group counseling, educational programs, medical services, and intensive staff supervision. The proximity of such facilities to the offenders' community enables direct and regular family involvement with the treatment process as well as a phased reentry into the community that draws upon community resources and services.

Incarceration in Training Schools, Camps, and Ranches

The very few juveniles who cannot be confined safely in the community, who constitute an ongoing threat to community safety, or who have failed to respond to high-quality community-based correctional programs may require placement in training schools, camps, ranches, or other secure care options that are not community based. These facilities should offer comprehensive treatment programs for these youth, with a focus on interpersonal skills development, cognitive-behavioral treatment, education, and vocational or employment training. Juveniles convicted and sentenced in the criminal justice system should be provided rehabilitation services in these juvenile facilities until they reach the age at which they are no longer eligible to remain in the juvenile justice system.

Transfer to the Criminal Justice System

The original Comprehensive Strategy (Wilson & Howell, 1993) permitted transfer of the most violent or intractable juveniles to the criminal justice system. This is no longer recommended. . . . The criminal justice system has neither the capacity to handle juveniles in a fair and just manner that can ensure their health and safety nor the necessary programs to rehabilitate them. If punishment is the aim, juveniles can be confined more safely and humanely in the juvenile justice system. Moreover, the juvenile justice system is effective even with serious and violent juvenile offenders. Thus there is no longer any justification for transferring juveniles to the criminal justice system. In states that permit transfer, only judicial waiver, which requires constitutional safeguards, should be statutorily permitted.

Aftercare

Effective aftercare is an important component of residential programs for serious, violent, and chronic juvenile offenders. Standard parole practices, particularly those that have a primary focus on social control, have not been effective in normalizing the behavior of high-risk juvenile parolees over the long term. Consequently, there is growing interest in intensive aftercare programs that provide high levels of social control and treatment services. Aftercare program components must be highly structured, must begin prior to release, and must combine treatment programming with stepped-down controls as the offender is reintegrated into the community. Two models of aftercare programs have been developed that incorporate these principles: the intensive supervision program and the intensive aftercare program. Such programs can be implemented in any community.

Aftercare can be conceptualized in a number of ways. The term *aftercare* is generally used in reference to "reintegrative" services that aim to link newly released incarcerated youths with their communities, families, schools, and/or employment. However, the term also has a much broader application, including relapse prevention (booster training following participation in a treatment program) and the transitional services provided in the course of moving a client from one treatment program to another. Thus aftercare services need to be provided at every major transition throughout a graduated sanctions system. Aftercare also should be provided at any point in the juvenile justice system for youths returning to the community from any type of secure program or facility.

Aftercare programs are not likely to be very successful for offenders in the deep end of a juvenile correctional system that does not have a structure of graduated sanctions. In the absence of a well-structured system, it is unlikely that any treatment and rehabilitation programs preceding an inmate's release would have been effective, because there probably would have been a poor match between the offender's risks and needs and the sanctions and treatment the offender has received. A foundation needs to be laid for aftercare to build upon. Thus jurisdictions that implement the graduated sanctions component of the Comprehensive Strategy are in a much better position to implement effective aftercare programs than others that mismatch offenders with programs and sanctions. . . .

◪ Tools for Building a Comprehensive Juvenile Justice System

The Comprehensive Strategy guides jurisdictions in the development of integrated and coordinated systems that link prevention and early intervention programs with the juvenile justice system. By using the science-based framework of risk and protective factors found in the public health model, communities can structure the delinquency prevention enterprise. In the remainder of this chapter, I describe the tools that communities need to use to optimize the effectiveness of their juvenile justice systems.

Basic Comprehensive Strategy Tools

Over the past 20 years or so, many tools have been developed for building a comprehensive juvenile justice system. Below, I discuss a number of these tools in relation to the two main components of the Comprehensive Strategy: prevention and graduated sanctions linked with a program continuum.

Delinquency Prevention

Delinquency prevention is a haphazard enterprise in most communities. Despite the efforts of many researchers to disseminate information about science-based prevention practices and effective programs, many communities still use prevention approaches that show little or no evidence of effectiveness (Arthur, Glaser, & Hawkins, 2001). It is quite common for community leaders to design prevention strategies without first assessing the risk factors for delinquency that exist in their particular communities. . . . Then the leaders select their favorite programs—typically, these are the programs that the most powerful community leader(s) presume are most effective (leaders who presume drug use is the main cause of delinquency often select the ineffective D.A.R.E. program. This might be called the "shotgun" approach to delinquency

prevention planning. In addition, these problems—of community leaders not engaging in systematic problem assessment and not selecting effective programs—are often compounded by the ineffective implementation of the programs that are selected (Gottfredson & Gottfredson, 2002).

Delinquency prevention science incorporates the risk- and protection-focused prevention model that initially was pioneered in public health research. The public health model demonstrated that certain health conditions, such as cardiovascular disease, can be prevented through a reduction of the risk factors for those conditions and an increase of the protective factors that buffer or counter those risk factors (Institute of Medicine, 1994). Similarly, the aim of risk- and protection-focused prevention is to interrupt the causal processes that lead to problem behaviors.

Because several factors put children at risk of becoming juvenile offenders, multiple-component programs are needed, and priority should be given to preventive actions that reduce risk factors in multiple domains. This is important because, at this point, it is difficult to disentangle risk factors from correlates of serious and violent juvenile offending (Farrington, 2000, p. 7). Moreover, many of the risk factors that predict delinquency and violence also predict other adolescent problem behaviors, including substance abuse, school dropout, early sexual involvement, and teen pregnancy. Thus the community benefits of early intervention and prevention programs can be wide-ranging.

The public health approach can be effective with serious and violent juvenile offenders because preventive actions work best when they are implemented at the community level (Catalano et al., 1998). For example, school-based strategies are useful, especially those focused on school organization or classroom-based curricula emphasizing the reinforcement of prosocial and academic skills. The community can intervene by reducing the availability of firearms and drugs and by encouraging norms and laws favorable to prosocial behaviors. Fear of crime is likely to remain high in a community unless local crime conditions are directly addressed (Lane & Meeker, 2000). . . .

Juvenile Justice System

The juvenile justice system needs tools that help minimize the wasteful use of resources on low-risk offenders and maximize allocation of resources to high-risk offenders. This problem is particularly acute at the present time because of the overload of offenders, especially minor ones, in juvenile justice systems across the country. Police, juvenile courts, and correctional systems tend to ignore minor delinquent offenders several times and then crack down on them, pushing them deep into the system to no avail. Conversely, they often fail to recognize potentially serious, violent, and chronic delinquents, and these youths do not receive the necessary sanctions and services. The findings of three studies illustrate these system shortcomings.

In an Oklahoma offender classification study, Wiebush, Wagner, Prestine, and Van Gheem (1993) examined the relationship between the assigned level of supervision (determined informally by the probation officer and the supervisor) and the level of supervision indicated by the results of a structured risk assessment. They found that under current practices, only 2% of the community-supervised youth were assigned to the intensive supervision level; 73% were assigned to the low level of supervision. In contrast, the formal risk assessment results indicated that 27% of the youth were high risk (and therefore should have received intensive supervision) and just 29% were low risk. These extraordinary discrepancies between presumed levels of risk and the levels indicated by formal risk assessments clearly show that the use of informal methods resulted in a significant degree of underclassification. In turn, this finding raises important public safety issues, given that such a small proportion of high-risk offenders were actually receiving the highest level of supervision (Wiebush, 2000).

The second study involved an analysis of offense histories and risk characteristics of training school populations in 14 different states. In each state, Krisberg, Onek, Jones, and Schwartz (1993) applied a structured risk assessment tool to the current training school population to determine the proportion of incarcerated youth who, according to the risk assessment guidelines, required long-term placement in a secure facility, required only short-term secure care, or could be directly placed in a community-based setting. The researchers found that an average of one-third of the training school population in the 14 states scored at low or medium risk on the scales; that is, these youths did not require confinement. It is clear that states do not reserve the use of juvenile corrections facilities for the dangerous few; rather, many have sizable populations of relatively less serious juvenile offenders (Wiebush, 2000).

In the third study, Austin et al. (1994) examined the offenses for which youths were admitted to states' juvenile reformatories in 1993. About half (51%) of the juvenile offenders were not committed for serious or violent offenses, nor had they previously been confined. Only 14% of them were admitted for serious or violent offenses. . . .

A state or community cannot know for sure whether it is properly protecting the public from juvenile offenders and using its juvenile justice resources in the most cost-effective manner unless it performs formal risk assessments. In addition, without the information that such assessments provide, it has little chance of effectively targeting serious, violent, and chronic delinquents. Better screening of court-referred youth to identify those with multiple risk factors for recidivism can provide a basis for early intervention, which is likely to impede their progression to more serious and violent behavior. Multiple-problem youth—those experiencing a combination of mental health and school problems along with drug use and victimization—are at greatest risk for continued and escalating offending (Huizinga & Jakob-Chien, 1998; Huizinga, Loeber, Thomberry, & Cothern, 2000).

Organizational constraints limit how many juveniles a particular jurisdiction can screen to identify subsets of chronic offenders who can be targeted for special interventions, such as more intensive supervision and more intensive treatment (Smith & Aloisi, 1999). Each jurisdiction needs to set priorities with respect to which subgroups of offenders it wishes to address in a concerted manner, given limited resources. Many jurisdictions choose to assess correctional populations first, because of the high daily costs of confinement. Others choose to assess juvenile court populations first, in a strategy aimed at reducing correctional populations in the future. The next threshold issue is, Which juvenile court subpopulation should be screened? One option is to screen first-time court referrals and allocate additional resources to potential serious, violent, and chronic offenders. This would be an immediate intervention strategy. Another option is to screen repeat offenders and allocate additional resources to them, using intensive probation supervision in a delinquency reduction strategy. . . .

It should be noted that there are arguments both pro and con regarding the legal and moral fairness of graduated sanctions systems in which sanctions are based on risk assessments (Jones, 1996; Le Blanc, 1998; Smith & Aloisi, 1999; Taxman, Soule, & Gelb, 1999). The main issue is that the risk of harm to society must be balanced against the constraints on liberty associated with juvenile justice system intervention (Smith & Aloisi, 1999). Constraints on individual liberties are unfair when assessments result in "false positives" (that is, juveniles who are not high risk are classified as high risk) and sanctions are wrongly imposed. In addition, excessive punishment may increase recidivism. Conversely, there are higher costs to society when assessments result in "false negatives" (that is, juveniles who are high risk are misclassified as low risk); uncontrolled high-risk juveniles may pose a threat to public safety.

However, whether or not graduated sanctions and risk assessments are used, juvenile justice system staff routinely make judgment calls that result in intrusions in juvenile offenders' lives; for example, they often rely on official records of arrests, which may have little correspondence to the individuals' actual prior behavior (Elliott, 1995). Thus a risk-based classification process that is validated with recidivism data stands a very good chance of increasing the fairness of a system that in the past has often arrived at decisions based on subjective judgments (Wiebush, 2002). In addition, fairness is enhanced by increased consistency in the decisions made in similar cases.

Development of a Structured Decision-Making Model

To improve the administration of juvenile justice, many state and local juvenile justice systems need more structured decision-making systems, driven by risk and needs assessments, governed by individual case management principles, and supported by management information systems. Indeed, in a recent national survey of juvenile probation departments, Torbet (1999) found that this is the general area in which they most need technical assistance. More than one-third of the respondents said that they need help in developing and validating risk and needs assessment instruments, in developing or enhancing their automation capability, and in conducting systemwide assessments of offenders for classification.

These management tools permit juvenile justice system staff to classify offenders based on risk assessments and match offenders with appropriate treatment interventions based on needs assessments. Because all offenders are not the same, jurisdictions need to make concerted efforts to identify subgroups of like offenders who can be dealt with using a similar management approach, thus facilitating individualized treatment. Jurisdictions will not only be able to target serious, violent, and chronic juvenile offenders more effectively using these tools, their overall effectiveness will be improved by the allocation of scarce resources in the most cost-beneficial manner. However, in addition to being trained in the use of risk and needs assessment instruments, state and local professionals need to be educated concerning the value of using these assessments in a structured decision-making model. When such training is not provided, professionals are not apt to see the utility of these instruments; instead, they are likely to see the work of conducting assessments as burdensome and a waste of time and resources (Mears & Kelly, 1999). Local professionals also need training that addresses a number of legal and process issues (Mears & Kelly, 1999; see also Beyer, Grisso, & Young, 1997).

Objective classification systems are superior to informal, discretionary assessments in that they promote consistent decisions and improve the efficiency of court operations (Office of State Courts Administrator, 2002). A number of negative consequences may result when assessment and classification procedures consistently fail to link youth with the interventions designed for them (Wiebush, 2002).

The National Council on Crime and Delinquency has developed a structured decision-making model that includes risk assessment strengths and need assessment, offender classification, and other management functions. Needs assessments are used in tandem with risk assessments to place offenders in different supervision levels, and in programs within various supervision levels, using an offender classification matrix that is organized by risk level and offense severity. Strengths/needs assessments are then used to ensure the best matches between offenders' treatment needs and available programs. In the remainder of this section, I describe the three essential tools of a structured decision-making model: a risk assessment instrument, a needs assessment instrument, and an offender classification matrix.

Risk Assessment and Classification of Offenders

Risk assessment is a statistical procedure for estimating the likelihood that a "critical" event will occur at some time in the future (Wiebush, 2002). In the automobile insurance industry, for example, a critical event is an accident involving an insured driver. In the juvenile justice system, a critical event is generally a new offense committed by a juvenile offender who is on probation or parole. A critical event could also be a new adjudication (finding of guilt) for a new offense or a subsequent commitment (sentencing to placement) to a juvenile reformatory. . . .

Risk assessments serve to accomplish two important juvenile justice system objectives: the objective of predicting recidivism (a public safety consideration) and the objective of placing offenders in programs that will increase the likelihood of successful rehabilitation (thus serving probation and correctional rehabilitation goals). To fulfill the latter objective, jurisdictions must conduct needs assessments in conjunction with risk assessments in order to make the best matches between offender treatment needs and intervention options.

Risk assessment instruments are composed of predetermined sets of scale items that research has shown to be statistically related to recidivism. Offenders' scores on these instruments are used to sort them into groups with differing probabilities of reoffending. A set of core variables have been identified repeatedly as recidivism predictors for juvenile offenders. . . . Wiebush (2000) found that some items increase the classification power of the scales in some jurisdictions but not in others. This finding suggests that there are site-specific factors that influence either recidivism or the measurement of it. Therefore, it is essential that each jurisdiction validate its own risk assessment instrument. . . .

Canadian/American researchers are incorporating needs assessment items with risk factors in an attempt to strengthen the predictive power of assessment instruments. Their studies suggest that needs assessment also has predictive validity for recidivism (Andrews & Bonta, 1998; Bonta, 1996; Holsinger & Latessa, 1999). Thus treatment needs are viewed as a subset of risk factors in the Canadian/American prediction studies. . . .

Needs Assessments

Needs assessments are used to determine the specific program interventions to be delivered within the designated custody/supervision level (Wiebush et al., 1995, p. 181). A needs assessment is intended to do the following:

- Provide an overview of the level of seriousness of the juvenile offender's treatment needs
- Provide information that can assist professionals in developing a treatment plan to address the juvenile's needs
- Provide a baseline for monitoring the juvenile's progress
- Provide a basis for establishing workload priorities
- Aid agency administrators in evaluating resource availability throughout the jurisdiction and determining program gaps that need to be filled

The use of formal needs assessment instruments to identify critical treatment needs of offenders is rare (Latessa, Cullen, & Gendreau, 2002), but rapidly gaining in popularity. Unlike risk assessments, needs assessments do not predict future behavior, thus they are not developed through empirical research. Instead, jurisdictions employ a consensus approach to identify and set priorities for the most important service issues. Local professionals are responsible for selecting the items to include in the needs assessment instrument. They are guided in this effort by existing state and federal laws (e.g., laws addressing special education services), research identifying effective and promising programs, and local philosophies about effective rehabilitation services. In the structured decision-making model, needs assessment results are used to adjust the placement of offenders in various risk levels (as recommended by risk assessment results). For example, a juvenile offender who is determined to be at medium risk and has a very high treatment needs score might be placed in a program

for high-risk juveniles to take advantage of the relatively intensive treatment services offered by the program.

Needs assessment instruments typically include items concerning offender needs in areas that correspond with risk factors for delinquency, including family functioning or relationships, school attendance and behavior, peer relationships (e.g., negative peer associations and gang involvement), and individual problems (e.g., substance abuse and emotional stability) (Wiebush et al., 1995, p. 183). . . .

A structured needs assessment serves several purposes in addition to its usefulness for program selection and case planning. It ensures that all staff examines certain treatment issues consistently for all youth. It provides a simple, easy-to-use overview of an individual's problems for the case manager; program staff, and service providers. Needs assessment scores also provide additional measures that can be used in setting priorities; that is, more time can be devoted to cases with higher scores. Periodic reassessments of treatment needs also help case managers monitor client progress and can indicate when adjustments might be needed in individual treatment regimens. Finally, aggregated information derived from needs assessments provides a database for agency planning and evaluation, especially for determining whether there are sufficient treatment resources in the community to meet current client treatment needs.

A third type of assessment tool frequently used in the juvenile justice system is the *placement assessment* or *custody assessment* instrument (Wiebush et al., 1995, pp. 179–180). Although such instruments may include predictive items, they generally are driven by policy considerations (issues of public safety) rather than by recidivism results. They may be used in several different ways: as screening tools to determine whether youths should be placed in detention pending their adjudication hearings, as guides for corrections officials to use in determining youths' appropriate placement or level of security, or as methods for determining the custody needs of incarcerated youths (Roush, 1996). Because public safety is the main consideration in the use of these instruments, they typically include measures of current and prior offense severity. . . .

Information Systems

Jurisdictions need automated information systems to help them carry out the essential functions of a juvenile justice case management system. Missouri has developed the J-TRAC system, which is an ideal automated information system that is compatible with the state's Juvenile Offender Risk and Need Assessment and Classification System (Office of State Courts Administrator, 2002). J-TRAC allows users to complete risk and needs assessments, assign dispositions for delinquency cases, and collect case management information on juvenile offenders and victims of neglect and abuse online. As the acronym suggests, J-TRAC automates the four basic functions of the full classification strategy:

- *Tracking:* Information on juvenile offenders is stored in J-TRAC's central repository. This secure system is accessible to juvenile and family court professionals and fully documents official activities involving the offender.
- *Referral:* Demographic, offense, and disposition information is collected and warehoused in J-TRAC for use in future case management decision making and administrative planning.
- *Assessment:* J-TRAC provides for interactive, online risk and needs assessment of juvenile offenders.
- *Classification:* J-TRAC selects from the classification matrix a set of graduated sanctions for a given risk classification and offense severity level.

The Missouri Juvenile and Adult Court Programs Division is currently integrating the classification system (risk and needs) with sanctions and programs within the juvenile case management automated information system.

This will provide a full profile—across the state—of offender risk levels, sanctions that are used for them, treatment needs, and programs that are provided, by risk and treatment need levels. Juvenile justice staff will then be able to identify gaps in sanctions and services without any guesswork.

Detention Reform

Over the past decade, the numbers of youths who are being detained have grown, largely because of increases in the numbers of juvenile court cases. A majority of these youths are held in overcrowded facilities. Because of the overuse of detention and the unacceptable conditions in many detention centers (Burrell, 2000), in 1992 the Annie E. Casey Foundation launched the Juvenile Detention Alternatives Initiative (JADI), a multimillion-dollar 5-year, five-site experiment designed "to streamline and rationalize local juvenile detention systems" (Stanfield, 2000, p. 1). This very successful initiative provides a blueprint for detention reform that any jurisdiction experiencing common detention problems can follow.

Confining juvenile offenders in detention centers is very expensive. The cost of constructing a detention center averages $100,000 per bed, and operating costs hover around $100 per bed per day (Steinhart, 2000, p. 54). These combined costs amount to as much as a half million dollars for one bed over a 10-year period. Steinhart (2000) describes in detail the major milestones in a comprehensive juvenile detention planning strategy:

Stage 1: Document and describe the current juvenile detention system (Steinhart, 2000, pp. 20–36). . . .

Stage 2: Identify local juvenile detention goals, which constitute the essential framework for local detention policy (Steinhart, 2000, pp. 37–39). . . .

Stage 3: Define the reformed system. Key reform strategies should include (a) developing objective screening criteria and risk assessment instruments, (b) addressing unnecessary case processing delays, (c) developing alternatives to secure detention, (d) dealing with minors in postdisposition detention, (e) addressing conditions of confinement, (f) dealing with disproportionate minority and female confinement, and (g) deciding to build or not to build additional detention capacity (Steinhart, 2000, pp. 40–57).

Stage 4: Identify the cost of reforms, resources needed, and barriers to reform (Steinhart, 2000, pp. 58–62). These are important considerations in the development of a realistic plan.

Stage 5: Finalize and draft the action plan. (Steinhart, 2000 pp. 63–67). . . .

A similar prescriptive guide is needed for the reform of juvenile reformatories, but such reform is more difficult because rehabilitation programs are involved, whereas detention— because of the short stays—involves few treatment programs. In addition, detention facilities typically are locally controlled, whereas reformatories are usually state controlled. Nevertheless, the use of Comprehensive Strategy tools will take states a long way toward reforming juvenile corrections. For example, use of tools in the structured decision-making model will reduce reliance on long-term confinement, because few low- and medium-risk offenders will be placed in long-term facilities. This would be a major first step toward reform, but improvements in many other areas are also needed.

Observations on System Reform and Evaluation

Many states are not ready to undertake the kinds of broad-scale system reforms and attendance improvements that North Carolina and other states have achieved. Juvenile justice and youth service officials in many states are content with the status quo. Many allow egregious youth service and juvenile justice system problems,

such as misuse and overuse of detention, to go unattended. In many cases, they do so because they feel that the resources they would need to change the situation simply are not available. Reforming juvenile justice systems for the better currently is not a priority in most state legislatures. It is as difficult for many legislators to foresee the long-term benefits of system reform as it is for them to foresee the long-term negative consequences of punishment-oriented systems.

Other states and localities are enticed by piecemeal approaches, such as importing a single highly touted program that they are led to believe will magically improve their overall system. Simplistic solutions for oversimplified delinquency problems are very appealing. Boot camps are a current example. In an era almost, but not completely, gone by, Scared Straight programs represented a panacea. Jurisdictions that opt for risky, simplistic solutions can easily get "caught with [their] panacea down around [their] ankles" (Miller, 1996, p. 77). Several lawsuits have been filed to challenge the conditions of confinement in boot camps, and the deaths of several youngsters sentenced to boot camps have been reported (Blackwood, 2001; Krajicek, 2000).

States go through cycles in which attitudes shift from liberal to conservative or from rehabilitation to punishment in juvenile justice policies, just as the entire nation does (Bernard, 1992). States and localities that get a grip on the management of their juvenile justice systems by using a structured decision-making model driven by research and by formal risk and needs assessment and placement instruments are much more likely to sustain comprehensive system reforms. In contrast, states that do not systematically use these tools tend to drift back and forth between progressive and business-as-usual policies and practices.

Implementation of the Comprehensive Strategy is a long-term system reform process. Complete implementation of the prevention, early intervention, and graduated sanctions components may take as long as 4 or 5 years.

Approximately a year is required to complete the "linchpin" assessment in the prevention component. Development and implementation of the tools for the structured decision-making model (risk and needs assessment instruments and a classification matrix) and validation studies of the risk assessment instruments may take 3 to 4 years. Then, the development of a continuum of program responses takes time. For example, development of the graduated sanctions component of San Diego's Comprehensive Strategy—Breaking Cycles—took approximately 2 years from start-up to stabilization of services. Thus, as a first step in redesigning its juvenile justice system, a community needs to develop a 5-year strategic plan that lays out the multiple steps involved in establishing a comprehensive framework that integrates prevention, early intervention, and graduated sanctions components.

Thus the Comprehensive Strategy needs to be evaluated in a long-term context. Several process evaluations have been completed on pilot implementation sites (Coolbaugh & Hansel, 2000). Evaluation of the San Diego Breaking Cycles program has been completed. The other three pilot sites were not evaluated. Preliminary results are available from the Orange County, California, implementation. Another evaluation, in Richmond, Virginia, assessed the implementation of the city's graduated sanctions continuum (Virginia Department of Criminal Justice Services, 2000).

Some evaluation tools are built into the Comprehensive Strategy framework. A well-developed prevention plan is based on a baseline of risk and protective factors. Programs selected to address these factors are expected to change the baseline risk and protective factors. If they do not, they are not effective and should be either improved or discarded.

Similarly, a structured decision-making model that includes reassessments of risks and needs makes evaluation of a continuum of programs possible at two levels. Evaluation at the first level involves determining whether or not programs and services are successfully reducing

risks and meeting the treatment needs of offenders. An automated management information system that includes risk-needs assessments and reassessments will facilitate this level of program evaluation. Evaluation at the second level involves determining whether or not programs and services are reducing recidivism, which also can be tracked using the automated management information system. . . . Communities should arrange for periodic independent experimental evaluations of programs to verify whether or not the tracked outcomes are actually the result of programs in the graduated sanctions continuum.

If the Standardized Program Evaluation Protocol development work currently under way in North Carolina is successful, it may be feasible for researchers to develop a protocol of sufficient scope that it will have general applicability elsewhere. Such a protocol might enable the evaluation of the entire continuum of juvenile justice programs in a given jurisdiction and, collectively, statewide. Independent evaluation is needed to measure the extent to which risk and needs assessments, and the use of a structured decision-making model, produce better matches between offenders' risk and needs and particular sanctions and program interventions. This is a key principle of the Comprehensive Strategy. The extent to which the Comprehensive Strategy provides a context within which the wraparound process can be more effective also needs to be evaluated.

◼ Summary

In this chapter, I have described the Comprehensive Strategy for Serious, Violent, and Chronic Juvenile Offenders (Wilson & Howell, 1993). I have discussed the general principles of the Comprehensive Strategy framework, the strategy's theoretical foundations, and its major components. I have also cited some of the research supporting the Comprehensive Strategy. In addition, I have defined and explained the major tools that are used in the implementation of the Comprehensive Strategy.

A major goal of the Comprehensive Strategy is juvenile justice system improvement. This goal is activated by two processes that are considered to be linchpins in comprehensive juvenile justice strategy development. First, a community must conduct a comprehensive assessment of the risk and protective factors for delinquency in its specific jurisdiction, instead of arbitrarily selecting interventions that may miss the mark. Communities are different from one another. Because each has a distinct combination of predominant risk factors, this assessment process is critical to successful prevention programming.

Second, juvenile justice system agencies must assess the delinquent populations in their jurisdictions for risk and treatment needs, to classify and position offenders within a structured system of graduated sanctions. Comprehensive risk and needs assessments are needed to get the best matches between offenders and programs (Bonta, 1996; Gendreau, 1996; Jones, 1996). Good matches cannot be achieved until risk assessments are done to determine which offenders belong in various classification levels of the juvenile justice system. In the structured decision-making model developed by the National Council on Crime and Delinquency, juvenile justice officials use needs assessments in tandem with risk assessments to place offenders in different supervision levels, then in programs within various supervision levels, by consulting a matrix that organizes sanctions and programs by risk level and offense severity (Howell, 1995; Wiebush, 2002; Wiebush et al., 1995).

The overall goal of a graduated sanctions system is to achieve a good fit between the positions of delinquents in pathways toward serious, violent, and chronic careers and interventions that are graduated in concert with progression in delinquent pathways. Offenders can be stepped up through the levels of sanctions as they progress in delinquent careers and stepped down as they decelerate and desist from delinquent activity. Aftercare is a critical component of a comprehensive system, because it constitutes step-down interventions and continuous treatment.

The prevention and early intervention components of the Comprehensive Strategy uses a risk and protection assessment process that is grounded in the public health model. In this chapter, I have used the Communities That Care system to illustrate how communities can better focus prevention program on priority risk factors. I have also described a structured decision-making model that employs the tools of risk and needs assessment instruments and an offender classification matrix to place offenders along a continuum of graduated sanctions and programs. The structured decision-making model should be combined with other tools—especially an automated management information system—for cost-effective operation of the juvenile justice system.

To maximize the cost-effectiveness of their juvenile justice systems, communities and states need integrated, multidisciplinary, multiagency wraparound service delivery systems that can simultaneously address multiple child and adolescent problem behaviors and ensure public safety. Adoption of the framework for system reform will enable communities to address effectively most of the juvenile justice system problems outlined at the beginning of this chapter, particularly the following:

- Poor targeting of serious, violent, and chronic juvenile offenders
- Poor matching of offenders with appropriate levels of supervision, sanctions, and programs
- Overreliance on detention, incarceration, and residential programs
- Inadequate data collection on offenders in the system, management information systems, and information sharing
- Lack of good policy guidance for state executive, legislative, and judicial stakeholders in the development of legislation, standards and other policy directives that create data-driven, outcome-based, and results-oriented juvenile justice policy reforms

Because the Comprehensive Strategy is research-based, data-driven, and an outcome-focused process, participating communities use the data gathered in these initial steps to determine needed system reforms and improvements. In the North Carolina example, a sharp reduction in training school admissions was achieved using risk and needs assessments in a structured decision-making model. An $11 million reduction in training school costs was realized in just 3 years.

References

Akers, R. L., Krohn, M. D., Lanza-Kaduce, L., & Radosevich, M. (1979). Social learning and deviant behavior: A specific test of a general theory. *American Sociological Review, 44*, 636–655.

Andrews, D. A., & Bonta, J. (1998). *The psychology of criminal conduct* (2nd ed.). Cincinnati, OH: Anderson.

Arthur, M. W., Glaser, R. R., & Hawkins, J. D. (2001). *Community implementation of science-based prevention programming.* Seattle: University of Washington, Social Development Research Group.

Austin, J., Krisberg, B., DeComo, R., Del Rosario, D., Rudenstine, S., & Elms, W. (1994). *Juveniles Taken Into Custody research program: FY 1993 annual report.* Oakland, CA: National Council on Crime and Delinquency.

Bandura, A. (1973). *Aggression: A social learning analysis.* Englewood Cliffs, NJ: Prentice Hall.

Bandura, A. (1977). Self-efficacy: Toward a unifying theory of behavioral change. *Psychological Review, 84*, 191–215.

Bandura, A. (1986). Social foundations of thought and actions: A social cognitive theory. Englewood Cliffs, NJ: Prentice Hall.

Bandura, A. (1999). Social learning and aggression. In F. T. Cullen & R. Agnew (Eds.), *Criminological theory: Past to present* (pp. 21–32). Los Angeles: Roxbury.

Bernard, T. (1992). *The cycle of juvenile justice.* New York: Oxford University Press.

Beyer, M., Grisso, T., & Young, M. (1997). *More than meets the eye: Rethinking assessment, competency and sentencing for a harsher era of juvenile justice.* Washington, DC: American Bar Association, Juvenile Justice Center.

Blackwood, A. (2001, July 8). Boy's death puts spotlight on boot camps. *News and Observer* (Raleigh, NC), p. 15A.

Bonta, J. (1996). Risk-needs assessment and treatment. In A. T. Harland (Ed.), *Choosing correctional options that work* (pp. 18–32). Thousand Oaks, CA: Sage.

Bronfenbrenner, U. (1979). *The ecology of human development: Experiments by nature and design.* Cambridge, MA: Harvard University Press.

Brown, W. K., Miller, T. P., & Jenkins, R. L. (1991). The human costs of "giving the kid another chance." *International Journal of Offender Therapy and Comparative Criminology, 35*, 296–302.

Burrel, S. (2000). *Pathways to juvenile detention reform: Vol. 6. Improving conditions of confinement in secure detention facilities.* Baltimore: Annie E. Casey Foundation.

Butts, J. A., & Adams, W. (2001). *Anticipating space needs in juvenile detention and correctional facilities* (Juvenile Justice Bulletin). Washington, DC: Office of Juvenile Justice and Delinquency Prevention.

Catalano, R. F., Arthur, M. W., Hawkins, J. D., Berglund, L., & Olson, J. J. (1998). Comprehensive community- and school-based interventions to prevent antisocial behavior. In R. Loeber & D. P. Farrington (Eds.), *Serious and violent juvenile offenders: Risk factors and successful interventions* (pp. 248–283). Thousand Oaks, CA: Sage.

Catalano, R. F., & Hawkins, J. D. (1996). The social development model: A theory of anti-social behavior. In J. D. Hawkins (Ed.), *Delinquency and crime: Current theories* (pp. 149–197). New York: Cambridge University Press.

Catalano, R. F., Loeber, R., & McKinney, K. (1999). *School and community interventions to prevent serious and violent offending* (Juvenile Justice Bulletin). Washington, DC: Office of Juvenile Justice and Delinquency Prevention.

Coolbaugh, K., & Hansel, C. J. (2000). *The comprehensive strategy: Lessons learned from the pilot sites* (Juvenile Justice Bulletin). Washington, DC: Office of Juvenile Justice and Delinquency Prevention.

Dean, C. W., Brame, R., & Piquero, A. R. (1996). Criminal propensities, discrete groups of offenders, and persistency in crime. *Criminology, 34,* 547–574.

Durlak, J. A. (1998). Common risk and protective factors in successful prevention programs. *American Journal of Orthopsychiatry, 68,* 512–520.

Elliott, D. S. (1995, November). *Lies, damn lies and arrest statistics.* Paper presented at the annual meeting of the American Society of Criminology, Boston.

Farrington, D. P. (2000). Explaining and preventing crime: The globalization of knowledge. The American Society of Criminology 1999 Presidential Address. *Criminology, 26,* 1–24.

Gendreau, P. (1996). The principles of effective interventions with offenders. In A. T. Harland (Ed.), *Choosing correctional options that work* (pp. 117–130). Thousand Oaks, CA: Sage.

Gendreau, P., Cullen, F. T., & Bonta, J. (1994). Intensive rehabilitation supervision: The next generation in community corrections. *Federal Probation, 58*(1), 72–78.

Gendreau, P., & Goggin, C. (1996). Principles of effective correctional programming. *Forum on Correctional Research, 8,* 38–41.

Gottfredson, D. C., & Gottfredson, G. D. (2002). Quality of school-based prevention programs. *Journal of Research in Crime and Delinquency, 39,* 3–35.

Greenwood, P. W., Model, K. E., Rydell, C. P., & Chiesa, J. (1996). *Diverting children from a life of crime: Measuring costs and benefits.* Santa Monica, CA: RAND.

Hawkins, J. D. (1995, August). Controlling crime before it happens: Risk-focused prevention. *National Institute of Justice Journal, 229,* 10–12.

Hawkins, J. D. (1999). Preventing crime and violence through Communities That Care. *European Journal on Crime Policy and Research, 7,* 443–458.

Hawkins, J. D., Catalano, R. F., & Associates. (1992). *Communities That Care.* San Francisco: Jossey-Bass.

Hawkins, J. D., Catalona, R. F., & Brewer, D. D. (1995). Preventing serious, violent, and chronic juvenile offending: Effective strategies from conception to age 6. In J. C. Howell, B. Krisberg, J. D. Hawkins, & J. J. Wilson (Eds.), *Serious, violent, and chronic juvenile offenders: A sourcebook* (pp. 47–60). Thousand Oaks, CA: Sage.

Holsinger, A. M., & Latessa, E. J. (1999). An empirical evaluation of a sanction continuum: Pathways through the juvenile justice system. *Journal of Criminal Justice, 27,* 155–172.

Howell, J. C. (Ed.). (1995). *Guide for implementing the Comprehensive Strategy for Serious, Violent and Chronic Juvenile Offenders.* Washington, DC: Office of Juvenile Justice and Delinquency Prevention.

Howell, J. C. (1997). *Juvenile justice and youth violence.* Thousand Oaks, CA: Sage.

Howell, J. C. (2001). Juvenile justice programs and strategies. In R. Loeber & D. P. Farrington (Eds.), *Child delinquents: Development, intervention and service needs* (pp. 305–322). Thousand Oaks, CA: Sage.

Huizinga, D., & Jakob-Chien, C. (1998). The contemporaneous co-occurrence of serious violent offending and other problem behavior. In R. Loeber & D. P. Farrington (Eds.), *Serious and violent juvenile offenders: Risk factors and successful interventions* (pp. 46–67). Thousand Oaks, CA: Sage.

Huizinga, D., Loeber, R., Thornberry, T. P., & Cothern, L. (2000). *Co-occurrence of delinquency and other problem behaviors* (Juvenile Justice Bulletin). Washington, DC: Office of Juvenile Justice and Delinquency Prevention.

Institute of Medicine. (1994). *Reducing risks for mental disorders: Frontier for preventive intervention research.* Washington, DC: National Academy Press.

Jones, P. R. (1996). Risk prediction in criminal justice. In A. T. Harland (Ed.), *Choosing correctional options that work* (pp. 33–68). Thousand Oaks, CA: Sage.

Krajicek, D. J. (2000, February). Boot camps get a kick in the head. *Youth Today,* p. A2.

Krisberg, B., & Austin, J. (1993). *Reinventing juvenile justice.* Newbury Park, CA: Sage.

Krisberg, B., Onek, D., Jones, M., & Schwartz, I. (1993). *Juveniles in state custody: Prospects for community-based care of troubled adolescents.* San Francisco: National Council on Crime Delinquency.

Land, K. C., McCall, P. L., & Williams, J. R. (1990). Something that works in juvenile justice: An evaluation of the North Carolina Court Counselors' Intensive Protective Supervision randomized experimental project, 1987–1989. *Evaluation Review, 14,* 574–606.

Lane, J., & Meeker, J. W. (2000). Subcultural diversity and the fear of crime and gangs. *Crime & Delinquency, 46,* 497–521.

Latessa, E. J., Cullen, F. T., & Gendreau, P. (2002). Beyond correctional quackery: Professionalism and the possibility of effective treatment. *Federal Probation, 66*(2), 43–49.

Le Blanc, M. (1998). Serious, violent and chronic juvenile offenders: Identification, classification, and prediction. In R. Loeber & D. P. Farrington (Eds.), *Serious and violent juvenile offenders: Risk factors and successful interventions* (pp. 167–193). Thousand Oaks, CA: Sage.

Le Blanc, M., & Loeber, R. (1998). Developmental criminology updated. In M. Tonry (Ed.), *Crime and justice: An annual review of research* (Vol. 23, pp. 115–198). Chicago: University of Chicago Press.

Lipsey, M. W. (1999). Can rehabilitative programs reduce the recidivism of juvenile offenders? An inquiry into the effectiveness of practical programs. *Virginia Journal of Social Policy and the Law, 6,* 611–641.

Lipsey, M. W., & Wilson, D. B. (1998). Effective interventions with serious juvenile offenders: A synthesis of research. In R. Loeber & D. P. Farrington (Eds.), *Serious and violent juvenile offenders: Risk factors and successful interventions* (pp. 313–345). Thousand Oaks, CA: Sage.

Loeber, R., & Le Blanc, M. (1990). Toward a developmental criminology. In M. Tonry & N. Morris (Eds.), *Crime and justice: An annual review of research* (Vol. 12, pp. 375–473). Chicago: University of Chicago Press.

Mears, D. P., & Kelly, W. R. (1999). Assessments and intake processes in juvenile justice processing: Emerging policy considerations. *Crime & Delinquency, 45,* 508–529.

Miller, N. (1996). *Understanding juvenile waiver: The significance of system resources in case allocation between juvenile and criminal court.* Washington, DC: Institute for Law and Justice.

North Carolina Department of Juvenile Justice and Delinquency Prevention. (2002). *Calendar year 2001 annual report.* Raleigh, NC: Author.

Office of State Courts Administrator, Juvenile and Adult Court Programs Division. (2002). *Missouri's juvenile offender risk and needs assessment and classification system: User manual.* Jefferson City, MO: Author.

Roush, D. W. (1996). *Desktop guide to good juvenile detention practice.* Washington, DC: Office of Juvenile Justice and Delinquency Prevention.

Schumacher, M., & Kurz, G. (2000). *The 8% solution: Preventing serious, repeat juvenile crime.* Thousand Oaks, CA: Sage.

Smith, W. R., & Aloisi, M. F. (1999). Prediction of recidivism among "second timers" in the juvenile justice system: Efficiency in screening chronic offenders. *American Journal of Criminal Justice, 23,* 201–222.

Smith, W. R., Aloisi, M. F., & Goldstein, H. (1996). *Early court intervention: A research and demonstration project.* West Trenton, NJ: Juvenile Justice Commission.

Stanfield, R. (2000). *Pathways to juvenile detention reform: Overview. The JDAI story: Building a better detention system.* Baltimore: Annie E. Casey Foundation.

Steinhart, D. (2000). *Pathways to juvenile detention reform: Vol. 1. Planning for juvenile detention reforms.* Baltimore: Annie E. Casey Foundation.

Sutherland, E. H. (1973). Development of the theory. In K. Schuster (Ed.), *Edwin Sutherland on analyzing crime* (pp. 13–29). Chicago: University of Chicago Press.

Taxman, F. S., Soule, D., & Gelb, A. (1999). Graduated sanctions: Stepping into accountable systems and offenders. *Prison Journal, 79,* 182–204.

Teplin, L. A. (2001). *Addressing alcohol, drug, and mental disorders in juvenile detainees* (Fact Sheet No. 2001–02). Washington, DC: Office of Juvenile Justice and Delinquency Prevention.

Tolan, P. H., Perry, M. S., & Jones, T. (1987). Delinquency prevention: An example of consultation in rural community mental health. *American Journal of Community Psychology, 15,* 43–50.

Torbet, P. M. (1999). *Holding juvenile offenders accountable: Programming needs of juvenile probation departments.* Pittsburgh, PA: National Center for Juvenile Justice.

Tracy, P. E., & Kempf-Leonard, K. (1996). *Continuity and discontinuity in criminal careers.* New York: Plenum.

Virginia Department of Criminal Justice Services, Criminal Justice Research Center. (2000). *Evaluation of the Richmond City Continuum of Juvenile Justice Services Pilot Program.* Richmond, VA: Author.

Wagner, D. (2001, June 5). *Risk and needs assessment for juvenile justice.* Paper presented at the North Carolina Juvenile Justice Retreat, Burlington, NC.

Wiebush, R. G. (2000). *Risk assessment and classification for serious, violent, and chronic juvenile offenders.* Madison, WI: National Council on Crime and Delinquency.

Wiebush, R. G. (Ed.). (2002). *Graduated sanctions for juvenile offenders: A program model and planning guide.* Oakland, CA: National Council on Crime and Delinquency and National Council of Juvenile and Family Court Judges.

Wiebush, R. G., Baird, C., Krisberg, B., & Onek, D. (1995). Risk assessment and classification for serious, violent, and chronic juvenile offenders. In J. C. Howell, B. Krisberg, J. D. Hawkins, & J. J. Wilson (Eds.), *Serious, violent, and chronic juvenile offenders: A sourcebook* (pp. 171–212). Thousand Oaks, CA: Sage.

Wilson, J. J., & Howell, J. C. (1993). *A comprehensive strategy for serious, violent and chronic juvenile offenders.* Washington, DC: Office of Juvenile Justice and Delinquency Prevention.

DISCUSSION QUESTIONS

1. Identify three to five of the general principles or theoretical foundations of the Comprehensive Strategy that you believe to be most important for improving the juvenile justice system in your community or jurisdiction.

2. "Graduated sanctions" have always been a part of juvenile justice, but the Comprehensive Strategy presents clearer structure. Give examples of juvenile services for both "increasing" and "decreasing" restrictions, and explain how they may help prevent more delinquent behavior.

3. The Comprehensive Strategy calls for coordinated efforts of multiple agencies. Give an example of how police, probation, and the juvenile court can work together in your community with schools, churches, mental health agencies, and social organizations such as Big Brothers Big Sisters, to reduce juvenile delinquency.

References

Agnew, R. (1992). Foundation for a general strain theory of crime and delinquency. *Criminology, 30,* 47–87.

Allen, F. A. (1981). *The decline of the rehabilitative ideal.* New Haven, CT: Yale University Press.

Allen-Hagen, B. (1991). *Children in custody 1989.* Washington, DC: U.S. Department of Justice.

Altschuler, D., & Armstrong, T. (1996). Aftercare not afterthought: Testing the IAP model. *Juvenile Justice, 3*(1), 15–25.

Altschuler, D., Armstrong, T., & MacKenzie, D. L. (1999). Reintegration, supervised release, and intensive aftercare. *OJJDP Juvenile Justice Bulletin.* Washington, DC: U.S. Department of Justice.

Altschuler, D., & Brash, R. (2004). Adolescent and teenage offenders confronting the challenges and opportunities of reentry. *Youth Violence and Juvenile Justice, 2*(1), 72–87.

American Bar Association. (1995). *A call for justice: An assessment of access to counsel and quality of representation in delinquency proceedings.* Washington, DC: ABA Juvenile Justice Center.

American Bar Association. (2004). *Adolescence, brain development, and legal culpability.* Washington, DC: American Bar Association/Juvenile Justice Center. Retrieved May 19, 2007, from www.abanet.org/crimjust/juvjus/Adolescence.pdf

American Bar Association Center on Children and the Law. (2004). *National court improvement progress report.* Chicago: American Bar Association. Retrieved February 3, 2007, from http://www.abanet.org/abanet/child/home.cfm

American Bar Association–Institute of Judicial Administration. (1980). *Juvenile justice standards relating to dispositions.* Cambridge, MA: Ballinger.

American Bar Association–Institute of Judicial Administration. (1982). *Juvenile standards relating to non-criminal misbehavior.* Cambridge, MA: Ballinger.

Armstrong, G. (1977). Females under the law—protected but unequal. *Crime & Delinquency, 23,* 109–120.

Auerhahn, K. (2006). Conceptual and methodological issues in the prediction of dangerous behavior. *Crime and Public Policy, 5*(4), 771–778.

Bandura, A. (1977). *Social learning theory.* Englewood Cliffs, NJ: Prentice Hall.

Bannister, A. J., Carter, D. L., & Schafer, J. (2001). A national police survey on juvenile curfews. *Journal of Criminal Justice, 29,* 233–240.

Bartollas, C., Miller, S. J., & Dinitz, S. (1976). *Juvenile victimization: The institutional paradox.* Beverly Hills, CA: Sage.

Bazemore, G., & Umbreit, M. (1995). Rethinking the sanctioning function in juvenile court: Retributive or restorative responses to youth crime. *Crime & Delinquency, 41*(3), 296–316.

Becker, H. S. (1963). *Outsiders.* New York: Free Press.

Benekos, P. J., & Merlo, A. V. (2005). Juvenile offenders and the death penalty: How far have standards of decency evolved? *Youth Violence and Juvenile Justice, 3*(4), 316–333.

Bennett, W. J., DiIulio, J. J., & Walters, J. P. (1996). *Body count: Moral poverty . . . and how to win America's war against crime and drugs.* New York: Simon & Schuster.

Bernard, T. J. (1992). *The cycle of juvenile justice.* New York: Oxford University Press.

Bilchik, S. (1998). A juvenile justice system for the 21st century. *Crime & Delinquency, 44*(1), 89–101.

Bishop, D. M. (1996). Race effects in juvenile justice decision-making: Findings of a statewide analysis. *Journal of Criminal Law and Criminology, 86,* 392–413.

Bishop, D. M. (2004). Reaction essay: Injustice and irrationality in contemporary youth policy. *Criminology & Public Policy, 4*(3), 633–644.

Bishop, D. M., Frazier, C. E., & Henretta, J. C. (1989). Prosecutorial waiver: Case study of a questionable reform. *Crime & Delinquency, 35,* 179–201.

Bishop, D. M., Frazier, C. E., Lanza-Kaduce, L., & Winner, L. (1996). The transfer of juveniles to criminal court: Does it make a difference? *Crime & Delinquency, 42*(2), 171–191.

Blumberg, A. (1979). *Criminal justice: Issues and ironies* (2nd ed.). New York: New Viewpoints.

Bortner, M. (1986). Traditional rhetoric, organizational realities: Remand of juveniles to adult court. *Crime & Delinquency, 32*(1), 53–73.

Bureau of Justice Statistics. (1988). *Report to the nation on crime and justice* (2nd ed.). Washington, DC: U.S. Department of Justice.

Byrne, J. (1986). The control controversy: A preliminary examination of intensive probation supervision programs in the United States. *Federal Probation, 50,* 4–16.

Callahan, R. (1985). Wilderness probation: A decade later. *Juvenile & Family Court Journal, 36,* 31–35.

Cauthen, N. K., & Fass, S. National Center for Children in Poverty. (2007). *Measuring income and poverty in the United States.* New York: Columbia University, National Center for Children in Poverty. Retrieved May 5, 2007, from http://www.nccp.org/publications/pub_707.html

Charles, M. (1986). The development of a juvenile electronic monitoring program. *Federal Probation, 53,* 3–12.

Chesney-Lind, M. (1977). Judicial paternalism and the female status offender. *Crime & Delinquency, 23,* 121–130.

Clear, T. R., Cole, G. F., & Reisig, M. D. (2006). *American corrections* (7th ed.). Belmont, CA: Thomson Wadsworth.

Cloward, R., & Ohlin, L. (1960). *Delinquency and opportunity.* New York: Free Press.

Coates, R. B. (1990). Victim–offender reconciliation programs in North America: An assessment. In B. Galaway & J. Hudson (Eds.), *Criminal justice, restitution, and reconciliation* (pp. 125–134). Monsey, NY: Criminal Justice Press.

Coates, R. B., Miller, A. D., & Ohlin, L. E. (1978). *Diversity in a youth correctional system: Handling delinquents in Massachusetts.* Cambridge, MA: Ballinger.

Cohen, L., & Felson, M. (1979). Social change and crime rate trends: A routine activities approach. *American Sociological Review, 44,* 588–608.

Cole, D. (1999). *No equal justice: Race and class in the American criminal justice system.* New York: New Press.

Conley, D. J. (1994). Adding color to a black and white picture: Using qualitative data to explain disproportionality in the juvenile justice system. *Journal of Research in Crime and Delinquency, 31*(2), 135–148.

Cordner, G. W. (2005). Community policing: Elements and effects. In R. G. Dunham & G. P. Alpert (Eds.), *Critical issues in policing* (pp. 401–418). Long Grove, IL: Waveland.

Cothern, L. (2000). *Juveniles and the death penalty.* Washington, DC: Office of Juvenile Justice and Delinquency Prevention. Retrieved December 3, 2007, from www.ncjrs.org/html/ojjdp/coordcouncil/index.html

Cullen, F. T. (2005). The twelve people who saved rehabilitation: How the science of criminology made a difference. *Criminology, 43*(1), 1–42.

Cullen, F. T., Eck, J. E., & Lowenkamp, C. T. (2002). Environmental corrections—A new paradigm for effective probation and parole supervision. *Federal Probation, 66*(2), 28–37.

Cullen, F. T., Fisher, B. S., & Applegate, B. K. (2000). Public opinion about punishment and corrections. In M. Tonry (Ed.), *Crime and justice: A review of research* (Vol. 27, pp. 1–79). Chicago: University of Chicago Press.

Cullen, F. T., & Gilbert, K. (1982). *Reaffirming rehabilitation.* Cincinnati, OH: Anderson.

Czajkoski, E. (1973). Exposing the quasi-judicial role of the probation officer. *Federal Probation, 37*(2), 9–13.

Davies, G., & Dedel, K. (2006). Violence risk screening in community corrections. *Criminology & Public Policy, 5*(4), 743–769.

Davis, S. M. (1980). *Rights of juveniles: The juvenile justice system* (2nd ed.). New York: Clark Boardman.

Death Penalty Information Center. (2007). U.S. Supreme Court: Roper v. Simmons, No. 03-633. Retrieved August 9, 2007, from http://www.deathpenaltyinfo.org/article.php?scid=38&did=885

Decker, S. (1985). A systematic analysis of diversion: Net widening and beyond. *Journal of Criminal Justice, 13,* 206–216.

del Carmen, R. V. (1985). Legal issues and liabilities in community corrections. In L. F. Travis, III (Ed.), *Probation, parole, and community corrections: A reader* (pp. 47–70). Prospect Heights, IL: Waveland.

del Carmen, R. V., Parker, M., & Reddington, F. P. (1998). *Briefs of leading cases in juvenile justice.* Cincinnati, OH: Anderson.

DiIulio, J. D. (1996). How to stop the coming crime wave. *Manhattan Institute Civil Bulletin, 2,* 1–4.

Dorfman, L., & Schiraldi, V. (2001). *Off balance: Youth, race and crime in the news. Building blocks for youth.* Retrieved June 5, 2006, from http://www.buildingblocksforyouth.org

Dorne, C., & Gewerth, K. (1995). *American juvenile justice: Cases, legislation and comments.* Bethesda, MD: Austin & Winfield.

Elliott, D. S. (1994). Serious violent offenders: Onset, developmental course, and termination. *Criminology, 32*(1), 1–21.

Elliott, D. S., Huizinga, D., & Ageton, S. E. (1985). *Explaining delinquency and drug use.* Beverly Hills, CA: Sage.

Fagan, J., & Guggenheim, M. (1996). Preventive detention and the judicial prediction of dangerousness for juveniles: A natural experiment. *Journal of Criminal Law and Criminology, 86,* 415–488.

Faust, F. L., & Brantingham, P. J. (1979). *Juvenile justice philosophy: Readings, cases and comments* (2nd ed.). St. Paul, MN: West.

Federal Bureau of Investigation. (2006). *Crime in the United States, 2005.* Washington, DC: U.S. Department of Justice.

Feld, B. C. (1977). *Neutralizing inmate violence: The juvenile offender in institutions.* Cambridge, MA: Ballinger.

Feld, B. C. (1988). *In re Gault* revisited: A cross-state comparison of the right to counsel in juvenile court. *Crime & Delinquency, 34,* 393–424.

Feld, B. C. (1989). The right to counsel in juvenile court: An empirical study of when lawyers appear and the difference they make. *Journal of Criminal Law and Criminology, 79,* 1185–1346.

Feld, B. C. (1993). Criminalizing the American juvenile court. In M. Tonry (Ed.), *Crime & justice: An annual review of research* (Vol. 16, pp. 197–280). Chicago: University of Chicago Press.

Feld, B. C. (1995). Violent youth and public policy: A case study of juvenile justice law reform. *Minnesota Law Review, 79,* 965–1128.

Feld, B. C. (1999). *Bad kids: Race and the transformation of the juvenile court.* New York: Oxford University Press.

Feld, B. C. (2000). Legislative exclusion of offenses from juvenile court jurisdiction: A history and critique. In F. Fagan & F. E. Zimring (Eds.), *The changing borders of juvenile justice: Transfer of adolescents to the criminal court* (pp. 83–144). Chicago: University of Chicago Press.

Feld, B. C. (2003). The politics of race and juvenile justice: The "due process revolution" and the conservative reaction. *Justice Quarterly, 20,* 765–800.

Feld, B. C. (2004). Editorial introduction: Juvenile transfer. *Criminology & Public Policy, 4*(3), 599–603.

Ferdinand, T. N. (1991). History overtakes the juvenile justice system. *Crime & Delinquency, 37*(2), 204–224.

Fox, J. A. (1996). *Trends in juvenile violence: A report to the United States Attorney General on current and future rates of juvenile offending.* Washington, DC: Bureau of Justice Statistics.

Friedman, W., Lurigio, A. J., Greenleaf, R., & Albertson, S. (2004). Encounters between police officers and youths: The social costs of disrespect. *Journal of Crime & Justice, 27*(2), 1–25.

Gans, H. J. (1995). *The war against the poor: The underclass and antipoverty policy.* New York: Basic Books.

Garland, D. (2001). *The culture of control: Crime and social order in contemporary society.* Chicago: University of Chicago Press.

Garrett, C. (1985). Effects of residential treatment on adjudicated delinquents: A meta-analysis. *Journal of Research in Crime and Delinquency, 22,* 287–308.

Gies, S. V. (2003). Aftercare services. *OJJDP Juvenile Justice Bulletin.* Washington, DC: U.S. Department of Justice.

Goldstein, H. (1977). *Policing a free society.* Cambridge, MA: Ballinger.

Gordon, R. A. (1987). SES versus IQ in the race-IQ-delinquency model. *International Journal of Sociology and Social Policy, 7,* 30–96.

Gottfredson, G. D. (1987). Peer group intervention to reduce the risk of delinquent behavior: A selective review and a new evaluation. *Criminology, 25,* 671–714.

Gottfredson, M. R., & Hirschi, T. (1990). *A general theory of crime.* Stanford, CA: Stanford University Press.

Gowdy, V. B. (1993). *Intermediate sanctions.* Washington, DC: U.S. Department of Justice.

Greenwood, P., & Zimring, F. (1985). *One more chance: The pursuit of promising intervention strategies for chronic juvenile offenders.* Santa Monica, CA: RAND.

Griffin, P., Torbet, P., & Szymanski, L. (1998). *Trying juveniles as adults in criminal court: An analysis of state transfer provisions.* Washington, DC: U.S. Department of Justice.

Grisso, T. (1981). *Juveniles' waiver of rights: Legal and psychological competence.* New York: Plenum.

Grubb, W. N., & Lazerson, M. (1982). *Broken promises: How Americans fail their children.* New York: Basic Books.

Guevara, L., Spohn, C., & Herz, D. (2004). Race, legal representation, and juvenile justice: Issues and concerns. *Crime & Delinquency, 50*(2), 292–314.

Hamburg, M. A. (1998). Youth violence is a public health concern. In D. S. Elliott, B. A. Hamburg, & K. R. Williams (Eds.), *Violence in American schools* (pp. 31–54). Cambridge, UK: Cambridge University Press.

Hamparian, D. M., Estep, L., Muntean, S., Priestino, R., Swisher, R., Wallace, P., & White, J. (1982). *Major issues in juvenile justice information and training youth in adult courts—Between two worlds.* Washington, DC: U.S. Department of Justice.

Hamparian, D. M., Schuster, R., Dinitz, S., & Conrad, J. (1978). *The violent few: A study of dangerous juvenile offenders.* Lexington, MA: Lexington Books.

Hawkins, J. D., & Lishner, D. M. (1987). Schooling and delinquency. In E. H. Johnson (Ed.), *Handbook on crime and delinquency prevention* (pp. 179–221). New York: Greenwood.

Heron, M. P., & Smith, B. L. (2007). Deaths: Leading causes for 2003. *National Vital Statistics Reports, 44*(10), 17.

Hirschi, T. (1969). *Causes of delinquency.* Berkeley: University of California Press.

Hirschi, T., & Hindelang, M. (1977). Intelligence and delinquency: A revisionist review. *American Sociological Review, 42,* 471–486.

Holden, G. A., & Kapler, R. A. (1995). Deinstitutionalizing status offenders: A record of progress. *Juvenile Justice (OJJDP), 2,* 3–10.

Howell, J. C. (2003). *Preventing and reducing juvenile delinquency: A comprehensive framework.* Thousand Oaks, CA: Sage.

Hurst, Y. G., & Frank, J. (2000). How kids view cops: The nature of juvenile attitudes toward the police. *Journal of Criminal Justice, 28*(3), 189–202.

Johnston, L., O'Malley, P., Bachman, J., & Schulenberg, J. (2004). *Monitoring the future: National survey results on drug use, 1975–2003: Vol. I. Secondary school students.* Bethesda, MD: National Institute on Drug Abuse.

Kobrin, S., & Klein, M. W. (1982). *National evaluation of the deinstitutionalization of status offender programs: Executive summary.* Washington, DC: U.S. Department of Justice.

Kohlberg, L. (1969). *Stages in the development of moral thought and action.* New York: Holt, Rinehart & Winston.

Koop, C. E., & Lundberg, G. D. (1992). Violence in America: A public health emergency. *Journal of the American Medical Association, 267,* 3075–3076.

Krisberg, B. (2005). *Juvenile justice: Redeeming our children.* Thousand Oaks, CA: Sage.

Krisberg, B., & Austin, J. F. (1993). *Reinventing juvenile justice.* Newbury Park, CA: Sage.

Kupchik, A. (2004). Direct file of youth to criminal court: Understanding the practical and theoretical implications. *Criminology & Public Policy, 4*(3), 645–650.

Kurlychek, M. C., & Johnson, B. D. (2004). The juvenile penalty: A comparison of juvenile and young adult sentencing outcomes in criminal court. *Criminology, 42*(2), 485–515.

Kurlychek, M. C., Torbet, P., & Bozynski, M. (1999). Focus on accountability: Best practices for juvenile court and probation. *JAIBG Bulletin.* Washington, DC: U.S. Department of Justice.

Lab, S., & Whitehead, J. (1988). Analysis of juvenile correctional treatment. *Crime & Delinquency, 34,* 60–83.

Latessa, E. J. (1986). The cost effectiveness of intensive supervision. *Federal Probation, 50,* 70–74.

Latessa, E. J., & Allen, H. E. (2003). *Corrections in the community* (3rd ed.). Cincinnati, OH: Anderson.

Law Enforcement Assistance Administration. (1976). *Two hundred years of American criminal justice: An LEAA bicentennial study.* Washington, DC: U.S. Department of Justice.

Lawrence, R. (1983). The role of legal counsel in juveniles' understanding of their rights. *Juvenile & Family Court Journal, 34*(4), 49–58.

Lawrence, R. (1984). Professionals or judicial civil servants? An examination of the probation officer's role. *Federal Probation, 43*(4), 14–21.

Lawrence, R. (1991). Reexamining community corrections models. *Crime & Delinquency, 37*(3), 449–464.

Lawrence, R. (1995). Classrooms vs. prison cells: Funding policies for education and corrections. *Journal of Crime & Justice, 18,* 113–126.

Lawrence, R. (2007). *School crime and juvenile justice* (2nd ed.). New York: Oxford University Press.

Lawrence, R., & Mueller, D. (2003). School shootings and the man-bites-dog criterion of newsworthiness. *Youth Violence and Juvenile Justice, 1*(4), 330–345.

Lieber, M. J., Nalla, M. K., & Farnsworth, M. (1998). Explaining juveniles' attitudes toward the police. *Justice Quarterly, 15*(1), 151–174.

Lipsey, M. W., Wilson, D. B., & Cothern, L. (2000). Effective intervention for serious juvenile offenders. *OJJDP Juvenile Justice Bulletin*. Washington, DC: U.S. Department of Justice.

Lipton, D., Martinson, R., & Wilks, J. (1975). *The effectiveness of correctional treatment: A survey of treatment evaluation studies*. New York: Praeger.

Livsey, S. (2006). Juvenile delinquency probation caseload, 1985–2002. *OJJDP fact sheet*. Washington, DC: U.S. Department of Justice.

Loeber, R., & Farrington, D. P. (Eds.). (2001). *Child delinquents: Development, intervention, and service needs*. Thousand Oaks, CA: Sage.

Lundman, R. J. (1986). Beyond probation: Assessing the generalizability of the delinquency suppression effect measures reported by Murray and Cox. *Crime & Delinquency, 32*, 134–147.

Lundman, R. J., Sykes, R. F., & Clark, J. P. (1990). Police control of juveniles: A replication. In R. A. Weisheit & R. G. Culbertson (Eds.), *Juvenile delinquency: A justice perspective* (2nd ed., pp. 107–115). Prospect Heights, IL: Waveland.

Lynch, J. P. (2002). Trends in juvenile violent offending: An analysis of victim survey data. *OJJDP Juvenile Justice Bulletin*. Washington, DC: U.S. Department of Justice.

Mack, J. W. (1909). The juvenile court. *Harvard Law Review, 23*, 104–122.

MacKenzie, D. L. (1994). Results of a multisite study of boot camp prisons. *Federal Probation, 58*(2), 60–66.

MacKenzie, D. L., Wilson, D. B., Armstrong, G. S., & Gover, A. R. (2001). The impact of boot camps and traditional institutions on juvenile residents: Perceptions, adjustment and change. *Journal of Research in Crime and Delinquency, 38*(3), 279–313.

Malmgren, K., Abbott, R. D., & Hawkins, J. D. (1999). Learning disabilities and delinquency: Rethinking the link. *Journal of Learning Disabilities, 32*, 194–200.

Martinson, R. (1974). What works? Questions and answers about prison reform. *Public Interest, 35*, 22–54.

Martinson, R. (1979). New findings, new views: A note of caution regarding sentencing reform. *Hofstra Law Review, 7*, 243–258.

Mays, G. L., & Winfree, L. T. (2000). *Juvenile justice*. Boston: McGraw-Hill.

McCarthy, B. (1987). Preventive detention and pretrial custody in the juvenile court. *Journal of Criminal Justice, 15*, 185–200.

McDowell, E., Loftin, C., & Wiersema, B. (2000). The impact of youth curfew laws on juvenile crime rates. *Crime & Delinquency, 46*, 76–91.

Mears, D. P. (2003). A critique of waiver research: Critical next steps in assessing the impacts of laws for transferring juveniles to the criminal justice system. *Youth Violence and Juvenile Justice, 1*(2), 156–172.

Mears, D. P., & Kelly, W. R. (1999). Assessments and intake processes in juvenile justice processing: Emerging policy considerations. *Crime & Delinquency, 45*(4), 508–529.

Mennel, R. M. (1972). Origins of the juvenile court: Changing perspectives on the legal rights of juvenile delinquents. *Crime & Delinquency, 18*, 68–78.

Mennel, R. M. (1973). *Thorns and thistles*. Hanover, NH: University Press of New England.

Merton, R. K. (1957). *Social theory and social structure*. New York: Free Press.

Miller, W. (1958). Lower class culture as a generating milieu of gang delinquency. *Journal of Social Issues, 14*, 5–19.

Minnesota Department of Corrections. (2007). Facility information: MCF-Togo. St. Paul: Minnesota Department of Corrections. Retrieved December 3, 2007, from http://www.doc.state.mn.us/facilities/togo.htm

Moffitt, T. E. (1993). Adolescence-limited and life-course-persistent antisocial behavior: A developmental taxonomy. *Psychological Review, 100*(4), 674–701.

Moffitt, T. E., Gabrielli, W. F., Mednick, S. A., & Schulsinger, F. (1981). Socioeconomic status, IQ, and delinquency. *Journal of Abnormal Psychology, 90*(2), 152–156.

Monahan, J. (1981). *Predicting violent behavior: An assessment of clinical techniques*. Beverly Hills, CA: Sage.

Moon, M. M., Sundt, J. L., Cullen, F. T., & Wright, J. P. (2000). Is child saving dead? Public support for juvenile rehabilitation. *Crime & Delinquency, 46*(1), 38–60.

Moore, M. H. (1992). Problem-solving and community policing. In M. Tonry & N. Morris (Eds.), *Crime and justice: An annual review of research: Vol. 15. Modern policing* (pp. 99–158). Chicago: University of Chicago Press.

Morash, M. (1984). Establishment of a juvenile police record. *Criminology, 22,* 97–111.

Morris, N., & Tonry, M. (1990). *Between prison and probation.* New York: Oxford University Press.

Murray, C., & Cox, L. (1979). *Beyond probation.* Beverly Hills, CA: Sage.

Myers, S. M. (2002). *Police encounters with juvenile suspects: Explaining the use of authority and provision of support.* Washington, DC: National Institute of Justice.

National Advisory Commission on Criminal Justice Standards and Goals. (1973). *Corrections.* Washington, DC: U.S. Department of Justice.

National Advisory Commission on Criminal Justice Standards and Goals. (1976). *Report of the Task Force on Juvenile Justice and Delinquency Prevention.* Washington, DC: U.S. Department of Justice.

National Commission on Children. (1991). *Beyond rhetoric: A new American agenda for children and families.* Washington, DC: Government Printing Office.

National Council of Juvenile & Family Court Judges. (2005). *Juvenile delinquency guidelines: Improving court practice in juvenile delinquency cases.* Reno, NV: National Council of Juvenile & Family Court Judges.

National Research Council. (1993). *Losing generations: Adolescents in high-risk settings.* Washington, DC: National Academy Press.

Needleman, H., Riess, J., Tobin, M., Biesecker, G., & Greenhouse, J. (1996). Bone lead levels and delinquent behavior. *Journal of the American Medical Association, 275,* 363–369.

Needleman, H., Schell, A., Bellenger, D., Leviton, A., & Allred, E. (1990). The long-term effects of exposure to low doses of lead in children. *New England Journal of Medicine, 322,* 83–88.

Office of Juvenile Justice and Delinquency Prevention. (2001). The 8% solution. *OJJDP Fact Sheet.* Washington, DC: U.S. Department of Justice. Retrieved May 16, 2007, from http://www.ncjrs .gov/pdffiles1/ojjdp/fs200139.pdf

Office of the High Commissioner for Human Rights. (1989). *Convention on the rights of the child.* Retrieved August 9, 2007, from http://www.unhchr .ch/htmo/menu3/b/k2crc.htm

Ohlin, L. E. (1998). The future of juvenile justice policy and research. *Crime & Delinquency, 44*(1), 143–153.

OJJDP statistical briefing book. (2007). Washington, DC: U.S. Department of Justice. Retrieved July 30, 2007, from http://ojjdp.ncjrs.gov/ojstatbb/court/ qa06201.asp?qaDate=2004

Packer, H. L. (1975). *The limits of the criminal sanction.* Stanford, CA: Stanford University Press.

Palmer, T. (1975). Martinson revisited. *Journal of Research in Crime and Delinquency, 12,* 133–152.

Petersilia, J. (1993). Measuring the performance of community corrections. In BJS–Princeton Project (Ed.), *Performance measures for the criminal justice system* (pp. 61–84). Washington, DC: Bureau of Justice Statistics.

Piaget, J. (1932). *The moral judgement of the child.* London: Kegan Paul.

Piliavin, I., & Briar, S. (1964). Police encounters with juveniles. *American Journal of Sociology, 70,* 206–214.

Pisciotta, A. W. (1982). Saving the children: The promise and practice of *parens patriae,* 1838–98. *Crime & Delinquency, 28*(3), 410–425.

Platt, A. (1977). *The child savers: The invention of delinquency.* Chicago: University of Chicago Press.

Podkopacz, M. R., & Feld, B. C. (1996). The end of the line: An empirical study of judicial waiver. *Journal of Criminal Law and Criminology, 86,* 449–492.

Pope, C. E., & Feyerherm, W. (1995). *Minorities and the juvenile justice system: Research summary.* Washington, DC: U.S. Department of Justice.

Pope, C. E., & Snyder, H. N. (2003). Race as a factor in juvenile arrests. *OJJDP Juvenile Justice Bulletin.* Washington, DC: U.S. Department of Justice.

President's Commission on Law Enforcement and Administration of Justice. (1967a). *The challenge of crime in a free society.* Washington, DC: Government Printing Office.

President's Commission on Law Enforcement and Administration of Justice. (1967b). *Task force report: Juvenile delinquency and youth crime.* Washington, DC: Government Printing Office.

Puzzanchera, C. M., Stahl, A. L., Finnegan, T. A., Tierney, N., & Snyder, H. N. (2003). Juvenile court statistics 1998. Pittsburgh, PA: National Center for Juvenile Justice. Retrieved December 3, 2007, from http://www.ncjrs.gov/html/ojjdp/193696/ contents.html

Quinney, R. (1974). *Criminal justice in America: A critical understanding.* Boston: Little, Brown.

Reiman, J. (1990). *The rich get richer and the poor get prison: Ideology, class, and criminal justice* (3rd ed.). New York: Macmillan.

Reynolds, K. M., Seydlitz, R., & Jenkins, P. (2000). Do juvenile curfew laws work? A time-series analysis of the New Orleans law. *Justice Quarterly, 17,* 205–230.

Roush, David W. (2004). Juvenile detention: Issues for the 21st century. In A. R. Roberts (Ed.), *Juvenile justice sourcebook* (pp. 217–246). New York: Oxford University Press.

Rubin, H. T. (1985). *Juvenile justice: Policy, practice, and law* (2nd ed.). New York: Random House.

Rubin, H. T. (2001). A community imperative: Curbing minority overrepresentation in the juvenile justice system. *Juvenile Justice Update, 7*(2), 1–2, 14–16.

Rudman, C., Hartstone, E., Fagan, J., & Moore, M. (1986). Violent youth in adult court: Process and punishment. *Crime & Delinquency, 32*(1), 75–96.

Sampson, R. J., & Laub, J. H. (1993). *Crime in the making: Pathways and turning points through life.* Cambridge, MA: Harvard University Press.

Sanborn, J. B., Jr. (1996). Factors perceived to affect delinquent dispositions in juvenile court: Putting the sentencing decision into context. *Crime & Delinquency 42*(1), 99–113.

Sanborn, J. B., Jr., & Salerno, A. W. (2005). *The juvenile justice system: Law and process.* Los Angeles: Roxbury.

Schauss, A. (1981). *Diet, crime, and delinquency.* Berkeley, CA: Parker House.

Schneider, A. L. (1985a). *Guide to juvenile restitution.* Washington, DC: U.S. Department of Justice.

Schneider, A. L. (1985b). *The impact of deinstitutionalization on recidivism and secure confinement of status offenders.* Washington, DC: U.S. Department of Justice.

Schneider, A. L. (1986). Restitution and recidivism rates of juvenile offenders: Results from four experimental studies. *Criminology, 24,* 533–552.

Schneider, A. L., & Schram, D. D. (1986). The Washington state juvenile justice reform: A review of findings. *Criminal Justice Policy Review, 2,* 211–235.

Schneider, A. L., & Warner, J. (1989). *National trends in juvenile restitution programming.* Washington, DC: U.S. Department of Justice.

Schumacher, M., & Kurz, G. A. (1999). *The 8% solution: Preventing serious, repeat juvenile crime.* Thousand Oaks, CA: Sage.

Scott, L. (1996). Probation: Heading in new directions. In R. Muraskin & D. Sheppard (Eds.), *Visions for changes: Crime and justice in the twenty-first century* (pp. 172–183). Upper Saddle River, NJ: Prentice Hall.

Shaw, C. R., & McKay, H. D. (1942). *Juvenile delinquency and urban areas.* Chicago: University of Chicago Press.

Sherman, L. W. (1997). Policing for crime prevention. In L. W. Sherman, D. Gottfredson, D. MacKenzie, J. Eck, P. Reuter, & S. Bushway (Eds.), *Preventing crime: What works, what doesn't, what's promising* (pp. 8–58). Washington, DC: U.S. Department of Justice.

Sickmund, M. (2004). Juveniles in corrections. *Juvenile offenders and victims national report series bulletin.* Washington, DC: U.S. Department of Justice.

Sickmund, M. (2006). Juvenile residential facility census, 2002: Selected findings. *Juvenile offenders and victims national report series bulletin.* Washington, DC: U.S. Department of Justice. Retrieved December 3, 2007, from http://www.ncjrs.gov/pdffiles1/ojjdp/211080 .pdf

Sickmund, M., Snyder, H. N., & Poe-Yamagata, E. (1997). *Juvenile offenders and victims: 1997 update on violence.* Washington, DC: Office of Juvenile Justice and Delinquency Prevention.

Smith, B. (1998). Children in custody: 20-year trends in juvenile detention, correctional, and shelter facilities. *Crime & Delinquency, 44*(4), 526–543.

Snell, T. L. (2006). *Capital punishment, 2005* (Bureau of Justice Statistics bulletin). Washington, DC: U.S. Department of Justice.

Snyder, H. N. (2004). Juvenile arrests 2002. *OJJDP Juvenile Justice Bulletin.* Washington, DC: U.S. Department of Justice.

Snyder, H. N. (2007). Juvenile arrests 2005. *OJJDP Juvenile Justice Bulletin.* Washington, DC: U.S. Department of Justice.

Snyder, H. N., & Sickmund, M. (1999). *Juvenile offenders and victims: 1999 national report.* Washington, DC: U.S. Department of Justice.

Snyder, H. N., & Sickmund, M. (2006). *Juvenile offenders and victims: 2006 national report.* Washington, DC: Office of Juvenile Justice and Delinquency Prevention.

Snyder, H. N., Sickmund, M., & Poe-Yamagata, E. (2000). *Juvenile transfers to criminal court in the 1990's: Lessons learned from four studies.* Washington, DC: Office of Juvenile Justice and Delinquency Prevention.

Sridharan, S., Greenfield, L., & Blakley, B. (2004). A study of prosecutorial certification practice in Virginia. *Criminology and Public Policy, 4*(3), 605–632.

Stahl, A. L. (2006). Delinquency cases in juvenile court, 2002. *OJJDP Fact Sheet.* Washington, DC: U.S.

Department of Justice. Retrieved March 25, 2007, from http://www.ncjrs.gov/pdffiles1/ojjdp/fs 200602.pdf

Stahl, A. L., Finnegan, T., & Kang, W. (2007). *Easy access to juvenile court statistics: 1985–2004.* Pittsburgh, PA: National Center for Juvenile Justice. Retrieved July 30, 2007, from http://ojjdp .ncjrs.gov/ojstatbb/ezajcs/

Streib, V. L. (2005). *The juvenile death penalty today: Death sentences and executions for juvenile crimes, Jan. 1, 1973–Feb. 28, 2005.* Retrieved December 3, 2007, from http://www.law.onu.edu/faculty_staff/faculty_profiles/coursematerials/streib/juvdeath.pdf

Surette, R. (1998). *Media, crime, and criminal justice: Images and realities* (2nd ed.). Pacific Grove, CA: Brooks/Cole.

Sutherland, E. H., & Cressey, D. R. (1970). *Principles of criminology.* New York: J. B. Lippincott.

Tannenbaum, F. (1938). *Crime and the community.* New York: Columbia University Press.

Taylor, T. J., Turner, K. B., Esbensen, F., & Winfree, T. L. (2001). Coppin' an attitude: Attitudinal differences among juveniles toward police. *Journal of Criminal Justice, 29*(4), 295–305.

Tibbetts, S. G., & Hemmens, C. (in press). *Criminological theory.* Thousand Oaks, CA: Sage.

Torbet, P. (1996). Juvenile probation: The workhorse of the juvenile justice system. *OJJDP Juvenile Justice Bulletin.* Washington, DC: U.S. Department of Justice.

Torbet, P., Gable, R., Hurst, H., Montgomery, I., Szymanski, L., & Thomas, D. (1996). *State responses to serious and violent juvenile crime: Research report.* Washington, DC: Office of Juvenile Justice and Delinquency Prevention.

Torbet, P., Griffin, P., Hurst, H., IV, & MacKenzie, L. R. (2000). *Juveniles facing criminal sanctions: Three states that changed the rules.* Washington, DC: Office of Juvenile Justice and Delinquency Prevention.

Towberman, D. B. (1992). National survey of juvenile needs assessment. *Crime & Delinquency, 38*(2), 230–238.

U.S. Bureau of the Census. (2004). *Income, poverty, and health insurance coverage in the United States: 2004, Report P60.* Washington, DC: U.S. Bureau of the Census.

Vaughn, J. B. (1989). A survey of juvenile electronic monitoring and home confinement programs. *Juvenile and Family Court Journal, 40,* 1–36.

Walker, S. (1998). *Sense and nonsense about crime and drugs* (4th ed.). Belmont, CA: West/Wadsworth.

Walsh, A. (1987). Cognitive functioning and delinquency: Property versus violent offenses.

International Journal of Offender Therapy & Comparative Criminology, 31, 285–289.

Warr, M. (2000). Public perceptions of and reactions to crime. In J. Sheley (Ed.), *Criminology: A contemporary handbook* (3rd ed., pp. 13–31). Belmont, CA: Wadsworth.

Welsh, B. C. (2005). Public health and the prevention of juvenile criminal violence. *Youth Violence and Juvenile Justice, 3*(1), 23–40.

Wheeler, G. R. (1971). Children of the court: A profile of poverty. *Crime & Delinquency, 17*(2), 152–159.

Whitehead, J., & Lab, S. (1989). Meta-analysis of juvenile correctional treatment. *Journal of Research in Crime and Delinquency, 26,* 276–295.

Whitehead, J., & Lab, S. (2006). *Juvenile justice: An introduction.* Cincinnati, OH: Anderson/ LexisNexis.

Wilson, J. Q. (1968). *Varieties of police behavior.* Cambridge, MA: Harvard University Press.

Wilson, J. W., & Howell, J. C. (1993). *A comprehensive strategy for serious, violent, and chronic juvenile offenders.* Washington, DC: U.S. Department of Justice.

Wolfgang, M. F., Figlio, R. M., & Sellin, T. (1972). *Delinquency in a birth cohort.* Chicago: University of Chicago Press.

Wooden, K. (1976). *Weeping in the playtime of others: America's incarcerated children.* New York: McGraw-Hill.

Wordes, M., Bynum, T. C., & Corley, C. J. (1994). Locking up youth: The impact of race on detention decisions. *Journal of Research in Crime and Delinquency, 31*(2), 149–165.

Young, D., Moline, K., Farrell, J., & Bierie, D. (2006). Best implementation practices: Disseminating new assessment technologies in a juvenile justice agency. *Crime & Delinquency, 52*(1), 135–158.

Zimmerman, J., Rich, W., Keilitz, I., & Broder, P. (1981). Some observations on the link between learning disabilities and juvenile delinquency. *Journal of Criminal Justice, 9,* 9–17.

Zimring, F. E. (1998). *American youth violence.* New York: Oxford University Press.

Zimring, F. E. (2000). Penal proportionality for the young offender: Notes on immaturity, capacity, and diminished responsibility. In T. Grisso & R. G. Schwartz (Eds.), *Youth on trial: A developmental perspective on juvenile justice* (pp. 271–290). Chicago: University of Chicago Press.

Zimring, F. E. (2005). *American juvenile justice.* New York: Oxford University Press.

Index